www.wadsworth.com

wadsworth.com is the World Wide Web site for Wadsworth Publishing Company and is your direct source to dozens of online resources.

At *wadsworth.com* you can find out about supplements, demonstration software, and student resources. You can also send e-mail to many of our authors and preview new publications and exciting new technologies.

wadsworth.com
Changing the way the world learns®

AMERICAN
CONSTITUTIONAL
THIRD EDITION
LAW

OTIS H. STEPHENS, JR.
University of Tennessee, Knoxville

JOHN M. SCHEB II
University of Tennessee, Knoxville

THOMSON
WEST

Australia • Canada • Mexico • Singapore • Spain
United Kingdom • United States

THOMSON

WEST

Publisher, Political Science: Clark Baxter
Executive Editor: David Tatom
Assistant Editor: Julie Iannacchino
Editorial Assistant: Jonathan Katz
Marketing Manager: Caroline Croley
Marketing Assistant: Mary Ho
Advertising Project Manager: Brian Chafee
Project Manager, Editorial Production: Matt Ballantyne
Print/Media Buyer: Judy Inouye
Permissions Editor: Bob Kauser

Production Service: Hespenheide Design
Text Designer: Hespenheide Design
Photo Researcher: John Scheb
Copy Editor: Michele Gitlin
Proofreader: Bridget Neumayr
Cover Designer: Brian Salisbury
Cover Image: Copyright © Jeff Hunter/Getty Images
Compositor: Hespenheide Design
Text and Cover Printer: Phoenix Color Corp.

Wadsworth/Thomson Learning
10 Davis Drive
Belmont, CA 94002-3098
USA

Asia
Thomson Learning
5 Shenton Way #01-01
UIC Building
Singapore 068808

Australia
Nelson Thomson Learning
102 Dodds Street
South Melbourne, Victoria 3205
Australia

Canada
Nelson Thomson Learning
1120 Birchmount Road
Toronto, Ontario M1K 5G4
Canada

Europe/Middle East/Africa
Thomson Learning
High Holborn House
50/51 Bedford Row
London WC1R 4LR
United Kingdom

Latin America
Thomson Learning
Seneca, 53
Colonia Polanco
11560 Mexico D.F.
Mexico

Spain
Paraninfo Thomson Learning
Calle/Magallanes, 25
28015 Madrid, Spain

For more information about our products, contact us at:
Thomson Learning Academic Resource Center
1-800-423-0563
For permission to use material from this text, contact us by:
Phone: 1-800-730-2214 Fax: 1-800-730-2215
Web: http://www.thomsonrights.com

PHOTO CREDITS
1 National Archives; **15** Supreme Court Historical Society; **16** Historical Pictures/Stock Montage; **81** Library of Congress; **163** Library of Congress; **220** Supreme Court Collection; **264** Supreme Court Collection; **331** Library of Congress; **332** Historical Pictures/Stock Montage; **332** Supreme Court Historical Society; **375** Historical Pictures/Stock Montage; **427** Supreme Court Collection; **509** Library of Congress; **572** Historical Pictures/Stock Montage; **659** Historical Pictures/Stock Montage; **720** Historical Pictures/Stock Montage; **798** Supreme Court Collection

Library of Congress Control Number: 2002107283
ISBN 0-534-54570-X

About the Authors

Otis H. Stephens, Jr., is Alumni Distinguished Service Professor of Political Science and Resident Scholar of Constitutional Law in the College of Law at the University of Tennessee. He holds a Ph.D. in political science from Johns Hopkins University and a J.D. from the University of Tennessee. Professor Stephens is the author of *The Supreme Court and Confessions of Guilt* (1973); he is coauthor, with Gregory J. Rathjen, of *The Supreme Court and the Allocation of Constitutional Power* (1980) and, with John M. Scheb II, of *American Constitutional Law: Essays and Cases* (1988). He has contributed chapters to *Comparative Human Rights* (1976) and *The Reagan Administration and Human Rights* (1985). He has also authored or coauthored a number of articles in professional journals, including the *Georgetown Law Journal*, the *Journal of Public Law*, the *Tennessee Law Review*, the *Widener Journal of Public Law*, the *Southeastern Political Review*, and the *Criminal Law Bulletin*. Professor Stephens teaches courses in constitutional law, administrative law, Supreme Court decision making and jurisprudence in the UT College of Law. Dr. Stephens is also a member of the Tennessee Bar.

John M. Scheb II is Professor of Political Science at the University of Tennessee, where he teaches graduate and undergraduate courses in American government, constitutional law, civil rights and liberties, administrative law, criminal law and procedure, the judicial process, and law in American society. Professor Scheb received his Ph.D. from the University of Florida in 1982. He has authored or coauthored numerous articles in professional journals, including the *Journal of Politics, American Politics Quarterly, Political Research Quarterly, Law and Policy, Judicature, State and Local Government Review, Social Science Quarterly, Political Behavior, Southeastern Political Review,* and the *Tennessee Law Review*. Professor Scheb has also coauthored five other textbooks: *American Constitutional Law: Essays and Cases* (1988), with Otis H. Stephens, Jr.; *American Government: Politics and Political Culture* (1995), with William Lyons and Lilliard E. Richardson, Jr.; *An Introduction to the American Legal System* (2002), with Judge John M. Scheb; *Criminal Law and Procedure,* 4th edition (2002), also with Judge John M. Scheb; and *Government and Politics in Tennessee* (2002), with William Lyons and Billy Stair.

v

Dedicated with love
to Mary Stephens
and Sherilyn Scheb

CONTENTS

PREFACE

American constitutional law, to paraphrase Charles Evans Hughes, is what the Supreme Court says it is. But of course it is much more than that. Constitutional law is constantly influenced by numerous actors' understandings of the meaning of the U.S. Constitution. Lawyers, judges, politicians, academicians, and, of course, citizens all contribute to the dialogue that produces constitutional law. Consequently, the Constitution remains a vital part of American public life, continuously woven into the fabric of our history, politics, and culture. Our goal in writing this textbook is to illustrate this premise in the context of the most salient and important provisions of the Constitution.

This book contains thirteen chapters covering the entire range of topics in constitutional law. Each of the chapters includes an extended essay providing the legal, historical, political, and cultural context of Supreme Court jurisprudence in a particular area of constitutional interpretation. Each introductory essay is followed by a set of edited Supreme Court decisions focusing on salient constitutional issues. In selecting and editing these cases, we have emphasized recent trends in major areas of constitutional interpretation. At the same time, we have included many landmark decisions, some of which retain importance as precedents while others illustrate the transient nature of constitutional interpretation.

Although the Supreme Court plays a very important role in American politics, its function is limited to deciding cases that pose legal questions. Accordingly, its political decisions are rendered in legal terms. Because it is both a legal and a political institution, a complete understanding of the Court requires some knowledge of both law and politics. While political discourse is familiar to most college students, the legal world can seem rather bewildering. Terms such as *habeas corpus, ex parte, subpoena duces tecum,* and *certiorari* leave the impression that one must master an entirely new language just to know what is going on, much less achieve a sophisticated understanding. Although we do not believe that a complete mastery of legal terminology is necessary to glean the political from the legal, we recognize that understanding the work of the Supreme Court is a complex task. We have tried to minimize this complexity by deleting as much technical terminology as possible from the judicial opinions excerpted in this book without damaging the integrity of those opinions. Nevertheless, despite our attempts at editing out distracting citations, technical terms, and mere verbiage, the task of understanding Supreme Court decisions remains formidable. It is one that requires concentration, patience, and above all the determination to grasp what may at times seem hopelessly abstruse. We firmly believe that all students of American politics, indeed all citizens, should make the effort.

In preparing the third edition, we have endeavored to incorporate the significant developments that have taken place in American constitutional law during the four years since the second edition was completed. Chief among these is the Rehnquist Court's continuing commitment to redraw the boundaries between national and state power through its interpretation of the Commerce Clause and the Tenth and Eleventh Amendments. As to the most recent developments, we have given specific attention to the Supreme Court's dramatic and controversial decision in *Bush v. Gore* (2000) and to the constitutional questions raised by the "war on terrorism" following the catastrophic attacks of September 11, 2001.

In recent years state appellate courts have played an increasingly important role in American constitutional development by selectively extending state constitutional protections beyond those provided by the federal Constitution as interpreted by the U.S. Supreme Court. Throughout this book we acknowledge the importance of this "new judicial federalism." In this edition, we have taken the additional step of including two recent state supreme court decisions, *Powell v. State* (Ga. 1998) and *Baker v. State* (Vt. 1999), illustrating this important trend.

In completing this new edition, we have benefited from the encouragement and advice of our colleagues and students in the Department of Political Science and the College of Law at the University of Tennessee. In particular, we wish to thank John Barbrey, Keith Clement, Daniel Hull, and Melanie Morris, who assisted us during their tenure as graduate students in political science at the University of Tennessee. We also acknowledge the valuable assistance of University of Tennessee law students Kim Lane, Allison Major, Richard Major, Linda Noe, and Patricia Trentham.

We wish to express our gratitude to Clark Baxter, our editor at Wadsworth, for his support and encouragement throughout the project. Thanks are due as well to assistant editor Julie Iannacchino for her steadfast support and encouragement of this project throughout its completion.

We would also like to express our appreciation to the many scholars who reviewed this edition and its predecessors, a list of whom appears on the following page. Their comments, criticisms, and suggestions were extremely helpful.

Finally, we wish to acknowledge the support provided by our wives, Mary Stephens and Sherilyn Scheb. This book is dedicated to them.

Although many people contributed to the development and production of this book, we, of course, assume full responsibility for any errors that may appear herein.

Otis H. Stephens, Jr.
John M. Scheb II
Knoxville, Tennessee
May 10, 2002

REVIEWERS AND AFFILIATIONS

The authors and publisher wish to thank the following individuals who reviewed the manuscript of this or the previous editions:

Henry Abraham
University of Virginia

Ralph Baker
Ball State University

Paul R. Benson
The Citadel

Walter A. Boroweic
SUNY College at Brockport

Robert Bradley
Illinois State University

Saul Brenner
University of North
Carolina–Charlotte

Robert V. Burns
South Dakota State University

Angelo J. Corpora
Palomas College

Larry Elowitz
Georgia College

Philip Fishman
Augsburg College

Marilyn Glater
Tufts University

William Haltom
University of Puget Sound

Sharon Jennings
New Mexico State
University–Grants Campus

William E. Kelly
Auburn University

Kent A. Kirwan
University of Nebraska–Omaha

Mark Landis
Hofstra University

Timothy O. Lenz
Florida Atlantic University

Sarah H. Ludwig
Mary Baldwin College

Connie Mauney
Emporia State University

William P. McLauchlan
Purdue University

Nasser Momayezi
Texas A&M University

R. Christopher Perry
Indiana State University

E. C. Price
California State
University–Northridge

Donald I. Ranish
Antelope Valley College

Wilfred E. Rumble
Vassar College

Elliot E. Slotnick
Ohio State University

John R. Vile
Middle Tennessee State University

Diane E. Wall
Mississippi State University

John Winkle
University of Mississippi

AMERICAN
CONSTITUTIONAL
LAW

INTRODUCTION

"The Constitution . . . shall be the supreme Law of
the Land. . . ."

—Article VI, U.S. Constitution

WHAT IS CONSTITUTIONAL LAW?

American constitutional law refers to the principles of the U.S. Constitution as they relate to the organization, powers, and limits of government and to the relationship between government and the American people. American constitutional law has two basic components: the institutional dimension and the civil rights/civil liberties dimension. The former area embraces issues of presidential, congressional, and judicial power, as well as questions of state versus national authority and problems of interstate relations. The latter area involves claims of personal freedom and legal and political equality, usually asserted in opposition to exercises of governmental power. These components are equally important and are given more or less equal emphasis in this book.

The Constitution is not a self-executing document. It is only through **interpretation** in the context of live disputes over real-world issues that the Constitution takes on continuing meaning, force, and relevance. Interpretation is the process by which the abstract principles of the Constitution are given operational meaning. Most important are the interpretations rendered by the U.S. Supreme Court. Although Congress, the president, and lower courts participate in deciding what the Constitution means, the Supreme Court's interpretations of the nation's charter are the most authoritative. Thus, constitutional law consists primarily of the Supreme Court's decisions applying the Constitution to a broad range of social, economic, and political issues.

Why Study Constitutional Law?

Questions of constitutional law may seem abstract, remote, or even hopelessly esoteric to the average citizen. In reality, however, the Constitution touches the lives of ordinary Americans in countless ways, many of which are revealed in this book. In constitutional law one sees all of the theoretical and philosophical questions underlying our political system, as well as the great public issues of the day, acted out in a series of real-life dramas. Questions of constitutional law are therefore too important to be reserved exclusively to judges, lawyers, and scholars. Every citizen, and certainly every student of American government, ought to have at least a rudimentary understanding of constitutional law.

THE ADOPTION AND RATIFICATION OF THE CONSTITUTION

The study of constitutional law begins logically with the adoption and ratification of the Constitution itself. The Constitution was adopted in 1787 by a convention of delegates representing twelve of the thirteen states in the Union at that time. Fifty-five delegates convened at Independence Hall in Philadelphia during the hot summer of 1787 to devise a plan for a successful national government. The delegates went to Philadelphia because the existing arrangements had proved to be anything but successful.

The Articles of Confederation

Since the end of the American Revolution, the United States had been governed by a weak national authority consisting only of the Congress and a few administrators. This arrangement had been formalized under the **Articles of Confederation**, proposed in 1777 but not ratified until 1781. At this stage in its history, the United States was hardly a nation at all, but rather a mere collection of independent states, each jealous and suspicious of the others. Most ominous of all was the ever-present threat of the European colonial powers, which still had designs on the New World and were ready to intervene should the United States government collapse.

The Articles of Confederation were adopted to provide the basis for a "perpetual union" among the states, but the system of government established by the Articles proved to be dysfunctional. Congress, the sole organ of the government under the Articles, was a **unicameral** (one-house) **legislature** in which each state had one vote. A supermajority of nine states was required for Congress to adopt any significant measure, making it impossible for it to act decisively.

Under the Articles of Confederation, Congress had no power to tax and was reduced to requisitioning funds from the states, which were less than magnanimous. During the first two years under the Articles, Congress received less than $1.5 million of the more than $10 million it requested from the states. This was especially problematic as Congress tried to fund the Continental Army, which was still at war with the British until the Peace of Paris was signed in 1783. After the peace, Congress struggled to repay the massive war debt it had incurred; the states, for the most part, treated the national debt as somebody else's problem.

Perhaps most significantly, Congress lacked the power to regulate **interstate commerce.** It was therefore powerless to prevent the states from engaging in trade protectionism that prevented the emergence of an integrated national economy and exacerbated the depressed and unstable economy that existed in the wake of the Revolutionary War. Commercial regulations varied widely among the states. The states sought to protect their interests by instituting **protective tariffs** and fees. A tariff is a charge made on a product being brought into a country, or in this case, a state. The purpose of a tariff is to protect those in the state who wish to produce and sell that product. Of course, when one state instituted a tariff, it was predictable that other states would retaliate with tariffs of their own. As a result, farmers in New Jersey had to pay a fee to cross the Hudson River en route to sell their products in New York City. This frustrated the development of a national economy and depressed economic growth. Although Congress could coin money, the states were not prohibited from issuing their own currency, which further inhibited interstate economic activity.

Under the Articles, there was no presidency to provide leadership and speak for the new nation with a unified voice. This omission was, of course, deliberate, because many Americans feared a restoration of the monarchy. As a consequence, states began to develop their own foreign policies; some even entered into negotiations with other countries.

The Articles of Confederation provided for no national court system to settle disputes between states or parties residing in different states. The lack of predictable enforcement of contracts between parties in different states inhibited interstate economic activity. The fact that no one could look to any overarching authority to settle disputes or provide leadership contributed to the sense of disunity.

Finally, by their own terms, the Articles could not be amended except by unanimous consent of the states. Any state could veto a proposed change in the confederation. Under the Articles of Confederation, the national government was ineffectual. Meanwhile, much to the delight of the European colonial powers, the "perpetual union" was disintegrating.

Shays's Rebellion

By 1786 it was widely recognized that the Articles of Confederation were in serious need of repair, if not replacement. This recognition was reinforced by a seminal event that occurred in Massachusetts in the summer of 1786. Daniel Shays, a veteran of the Battle of Bunker Hill, led a ragtag army composed primarily of disgruntled farmers in a rebellion against state tax collectors and courts. The object of **Shays's rebellion** was to prevent foreclosure on numerous farms whose owners were bankrupt. Unable to put down the rebellion by itself, the Massachusetts state government requested assistance from the national confederation. Congress adopted a plan to raise an army, but most states were unwilling to provide the necessary funds. Shays's army succeeded in taking over a considerable area of western Massachusetts until it was defeated by a band of mercenaries hired by wealthy citizens who feared a popular uprising. The inability of the national government to respond effectively to Shays's rebellion was the single most important event in generating broad support for a constitutional convention.

The Annapolis Convention

In September 1786, shortly after Shays's rebellion, delegates from five states met in Annapolis, Maryland, to consider ways to resolve growing problems of interstate commerce. While the Annapolis Convention resolved nothing, two of the delegates, James Madison of Virginia and Alexander Hamilton of New York, took this opportunity to call for a national convention to consider general revision of the Articles of Confederation. Responding to this initiative, Congress, on February 21, 1787, issued the call for a federal convention to meet in Philadelphia "for the sole and express purpose of revising the Articles of Confederation." The several states were invited to send delegations, each of which would have an equal vote at the convention. The delegates were chosen by their respective state legislatures. Only Rhode Island refused to participate.

Delegates to the Philadelphia Convention

The fifty-five representatives of twelve states who gathered in Philadelphia were drawn, for the most part, from the nation's elite: landowners, lawyers, bankers, manufacturers, physicians, and businessmen. The delegates were, on the whole, highly educated men of wealth and influence. Some commentators, most notably Charles A. Beard, have suggested that the delegates to the **Constitutional Convention of 1787** were motivated primarily by their own upper-class economic interests, interests that would be threatened by political instability. In Beard's view, the overriding motivation of the delegates was the protection of private property rights against actions of the state legislatures.

Other commentators have argued that the delegates were first and foremost practical politicians who were concerned both about the economic interests of their respective states and about their common nationality. Certainly those who gathered in Philadelphia were aware that whatever document they produced would have to be approved by their respective states. Their goal was to design an effective system of national government that could win popular approval in a nation that had just fought a revolution and was still highly suspicious of centralized power.

Like most of their fellow citizens, the delegates to the Constitutional Convention were sensitive to the dangers of concentrated power and were thus committed to the Lockean notion of **limited government.** Although most of the Framers of the Constitution were not democrats in the modern sense, they did subscribe (at least in principle) to the idea of **popular sovereignty.** Thus they were also committed to the goal of **representative government.** But the Framers were equally mindful of the danger that unchecked representative government might degenerate into the **tyranny of the majority.** They certainly accorded great importance to the need to protect the liberty and property of the individual. Their goal was to design an effective national government that would not oppress the people nor threaten their liberties.

The Framers accepted the existence of the states as sovereign political entities, and indeed they drew from the recent experience of the states in adopting their own constitutions after independence from England was declared in 1776. There was no question of doing away with the states and creating a **unitary system** of government. Yet most of the delegates knew that without a strong national government, economic growth and political stability would be seriously undermined by interstate rivalries. Thus, the underlying theme of the Framers' thinking was the need for balance, moderation, and prudence. This levelheaded, pragmatic approach to the daunting task of designing a new system of government was largely responsible for the success of the Constitutional Convention.

The Constitutional Convention

After electing George Washington as the presiding officer and deciding to conduct their business in secret, the delegates chose to abandon the Articles of Confederation altogether and fashion a wholly new constitution. The decision to "start from scratch" was risky because, although there was broad consensus on the need for a new and improved governmental system, there were many issues that sharply divided the delegates. There was no guarantee that they would ever be able to agree on a substitute for the Articles of Confederation. While the delegates agreed on basic assumptions, goals, and organizing principles, they differed sharply over a number of important matters.

By far the two greatest sources of disagreement were (1) the conflict between the small and large states over representation in Congress and (2) the cleavage between northern and southern states over slavery. But there were a number of other divisive issues. Should there be one president or a multiple executive? How should the president be chosen? Should there be a national system of courts, or merely a national supreme court to review decisions of the existing state tribunals? What powers should the national government have over interstate and foreign commerce? Some of these disagreements were so serious as to cause a number of the delegates to pack their bags and leave Philadelphia, and for a time it appeared that the convention might fail.

Representation in Congress   As noted earlier, under the Articles of Confederation all states were equally represented in a unicameral Congress. Representatives of the larger states preferred that representation be proportional to state population. The **Virginia Plan,** conceived by James Madison and presented to the convention by Virginia Governor Edmund Randolph, called for a bicameral Congress in which representation in both houses would be based on state populations. Delegates from the smaller states, fearing that their states would be dominated by such an arrangement, countered with the **New Jersey Plan,** which called for preserving Congress as it was under the Articles. After a few days of intense debate described by Alexander Hamilton as a "struggle for power, not for liberty," Roger Sherman of Connecticut proposed a compromise. Congress would be comprised of two houses: a House of Representatives in which representation would be based on a state's population and a Senate in which all states would be equally represented.

Slavery   Although it was not fully apparent in 1787, the most fundamental conflict underlying the convention was the cleavage between North and South over the slavery question. It was a conflict about human rights, to be sure. But it was also a clash of different types of political economies and different political cultures. In the South there was a thriving plantation economy, where slave labor played an important part in generating wealth for the plantation owners. The political culture of the South was more aristocratic and traditional. By contrast, the North was on the verge of an industrial revolution. Agriculture in the North was based on family farms. The political culture was more democratic, and, from the southern point of view, considerably more moralistic. Southern delegates at the Constitutional Convention feared that the new national government would try to end the slave trade and possibly try to abolish slavery altogether. At the same time, southern delegations wanted slaves in their states to be counted as persons for the purpose of determining representation in the new House of Representatives. Northern delegates, realizing that the support of the South was crucial to the success of the new nation, finally agreed to two compromises over slavery. First, they agreed that Congress would not have the power to prohibit the importation of slaves into the United States until 1808. And then, for purposes of representation in Congress (and the apportionment of direct taxes), each slave would count as three-fifths of a person.

The Battle over Ratification

On September 17, 1787, thirty-nine delegates representing twelve states placed their signatures on what they hoped would become the nation's new fundamental law. They then adjourned to the City Tavern to celebrate their achievement and discuss a final challenge: The Constitution still had to be ratified, as provided in Article VII, before it could become the "supreme Law of the Land." Today we look to the Constitution as a statement of our national consensus-an expression of our shared political culture. But in 1787 the Constitution was a divisive political issue, and ratification was by no means a foregone conclusion. Interestingly, while the small states had been the obstacle at the Philadelphia Convention, it was in the largest states—Massachusetts, New York, and Virginia—that opposition to ratification was the most intense. But there was division within every state.

Unlike the Articles of Confederation, the Constitution of 1787 did not require unanimous consent of the states to be ratified. Rather, it called for the Constitution to take effect upon ratification by nine of the thirteen states. Instead of allowing the state legislatures to consider ratification, the Constitution called for a popular convention to be held in every state. And by rejecting a motion to hold another constitutional convention, the Framers presented the states with an all-or-nothing situation.

Federalists versus Anti-Federalists   Supporters of the Constitution called themselves Federalists; opponents were dubbed Anti-Federalists. Federalist sympathies were found mainly in the cities, among the artisans, shopkeepers, merchants, and, not insignificantly, the newspapers. Anti-Federalist sentiment was strongest in rural areas, especially among small farmers. The Anti-Federalists were poorly organized and, consequently, less effective than their Federalist opponents. Moreover, they were constantly on the defensive. Because they were opposing a major reform effort, they were seen as defending a status quo that was unacceptable to most Americans. Still, the Anti-Federalists had considerable support and succeeded in making ratification a close question in some states.

The most eloquent statement of the Anti-Federalist position was Richard Henry Lee's *Letters of the Federal Farmer,* published in the fall of 1787. Lee, a principal architect of the Articles of Confederation, thought that the newly proposed national government would threaten both the rights of the states and the liberties of the individual. Perhaps Lee's most trenchant criticism of the new Constitution was that it lacked a bill of rights. Lee pointed out that state constitutions, without exception, enumerated the rights of citizens that could not be denied by their state governments. The only conclusion Lee could draw was that the Philadelphia Convention and its handiwork, the Constitution, did not place a premium on liberty. However wrongheaded this criticism, it touched a nerve among the American people. Ultimately, the Federalists would secure ratification for the new Constitution only by promising to support a series of amendments that would become the **Bill of Rights.**

The Federalist Papers   Despite their popular appeal, *Letters of the Federal Farmer* and the other Anti-Federalist tracts were no match for the brilliant essays written by James Madison, Alexander Hamilton, and John Jay in defense of the new Constitution. ***The Federalist Papers*** were published serially in New York newspapers during the winter of 1788 and without question helped to secure ratification of the Constitution in that crucial state. Yet *The Federalist,* as the collected papers are generally known, was much more than a set of time-bound political tracts. *The Federalist* represented a clear statement of the theoretical underpinnings of the Constitution. It continues to be relied on, not only by scholars but by judges and legislators in addressing questions of constitutional interpretation.

The Ratifying Conventions   Delaware was the first state to ratify the Constitution, approximately three months after the close of the Philadelphia Convention. Within nine months after the convention, the necessary ninth state had signed on. But the two largest and most important states, Virginia and New York, became battlegrounds over ratification. Although the Constitution became the "supreme Law of the Land" when the ninth state, New Hampshire, approved it in June 1788, it was vital to the success of the new nation that Virginia and New York get on board.

At the Virginia ratifying convention, Patrick Henry, a leader of the Anti-Federalist cause, claimed that four-fifths of Virginians were opposed to ratification. But the oratory of Edmund Randolph, combined with the prestige of George Washington, finally carried the day. The Federalists won Virginia by a vote of 89 to 79. The news that Virginia had approved the new Constitution gave the Federalists considerable momentum. In July, New York followed Virginia's lead in approving the Constitution by three votes. The two holdouts, North Carolina and Rhode Island, not wanting to be excluded from the Union, followed suit in November 1789 and May 1790, respectively. The new Constitution was in effect and fully legitimized by "the consent of the governed."

THE UNDERLYING PRINCIPLES OF THE CONSTITUTION

The document the Framers produced has been characterized as "conservative," and when the Constitution is compared to the Declaration of Independence, the label is not altogether inappropriate. Whereas the Declaration of Independence sought to justify a revolution, the Framers of the Constitution were concerned with the inherently more conservative task of nation building. But in 1787, the political philosophy underlying the Constitution was fairly revolutionary. It fused classical republican ideas of the rule of law and limited government with eighteenth century liberal principles of individual liberty and popular sovereignty.

Equally radical in the late eighteenth century was the notion of a written constitution to which government would be forever subordinated. The English constitution, with which the Framers were well acquainted, consists of unwritten traditions and parliamentary enactments that are seen as fundamental but which may be altered through ordinary legislation. The Framers rejected the concept of legislative supremacy, opting instead for a government subordinated to a supreme written charter that could not be easily changed.

The framework of government delineated in the Constitution is built on five fundamental principles: (1) the **rule of law;** (2) **separation of powers** among the legislative, executive, and judicial branches of government; (3) a system of **checks and balances** among these branches; (4) a system of **federalism,** or division of power between the national government and the states; and (5) **individual rights.**

The Rule of Law

The Constitution is the embodiment of the founders' belief in the rule of law. The idea is that government and society can be regulated by law, not subjected to the whims of powerful but potentially capricious rulers. The Constitution rests on the belief that no one in power should be above the law. Even the legislature, the people's elected representatives, should be bound to respect the principles and limitations contained in the "supreme Law of the Land." The subordination of government to law was seen by the Framers as a means of protecting individual rights to life, liberty, and property.

It must be understood that the Constitution imposes limits on government action. Private actions are beyond the scope of constitutional law. Individuals are not constrained by the Constitution unless they are government officials or persons acting under the authority of government. Yet the actions of private individuals are subject to the constraints of the civil and criminal law. In addition to imposing constitutional limitations on government, the rule of law requires that citizens who are wronged by others have opportunities to seek justice through the courts. It also means that persons who offend society's rules are brought into court to answer for their crimes. Of course, the rule of law is a two-way street: Defendants in civil and criminal cases are entitled to procedural fairness.

Separation of Powers

The Framers of the Constitution had no interest in creating a **parliamentary system,** because they believed that parliaments could be manipulated by monarchs or captured by impassioned but short-lived majorities. Accordingly, parliaments provided insufficient security for liberty and property. The delegates believed that only by allocating the three basic functions of government (legislative, executive, and judicial) into three separate, coordinate branches could power be appropriately dispersed. As James Madison wrote in *The Federalist,* No .47, "the accumulation of all powers, legislative, executive, and judiciary, in the same hands . . . may justly be pronounced the very definition of tyranny." Thus the Constitution allocates the legislative, executive, and judicial powers of the national government across three separate, independent branches. The first three articles of the Constitution, known as the **distributive articles,** define the structure and powers of Congress (Article I), the executive (Article II), and the judiciary (Article III).

Separation of powers was not a totally original idea. James Madison and the other delegates were well aware of Montesquieu's arguments for separation of powers and the fact that the new state constitutions adopted during or after the Revolutionary War were based on separation of powers. Yet the Framers were equally aware that in most states the legislatures dominated the executive and judicial branches. The system of checks and balances created by the Framers ensures that Congress cannot dominate the executive and judicial branches of the national government.

Checks and Balances

At the urging of James Madison, the delegates became convinced that a system of checks and balances would be necessary if separate, coordinate branches of government were to be maintained. In Madison's view, power must be divided, checked, balanced, and limited. In *The Federalist*, No. 51, one of his greatest essays, Madison expounded on this theme:

> [T]he great security against a gradual concentration of the several powers [of the government] in the same department, consists in giving to those who administer each department, the necessary constitutional means, and personal motives, to resist encroachments of the others. The provision for defense must in this, as in all other cases, be made commensurate to the danger of attack. Ambition must be made to counteract ambition. . . . It may be a reflection on human nature, that such devices should be necessary to control the abuses of government. But what is government itself, but the greatest of all reflections on human nature? If men were angels, no government would be necessary. If angels were to govern men, neither internal nor external controls on government would be necessary. In framing a government which is to be administered by men over men, the great difficulty lies in this: You must first enable the government to control the governed; and in the next place, oblige it to control itself. A dependence on the people is, no doubt, the primary control on the government; but experience has taught mankind the necessity of auxiliary precautions.

The Constitution contains a number of "auxiliary precautions." The president is authorized to veto bills passed by Congress, but Congress can override the president's veto by a two-thirds majority in both houses. The president is given the power to appoint judges, ambassadors, and other high government officials, but the Senate must consent to these appointments. The president is commander in chief, but Congress has the authority to declare war, raise and support an army and a navy, and make rules governing the armed forces. The president is empowered to call Congress into special session, but is duty bound to appear "from time to time" to inform Congress as to the "State of the Union." These provisions were designed to create a perpetual competition between the Congress and the executive branch for control of the government, with the expectation that neither institution would permanently dominate the other. That is, in fact, how things have worked out.

As we have noted, the Framers were concerned not only with the possibility that one institution might dominate the government, but that a popular majority might gain control of both Congress and the presidency and thereby institute a tyranny of the majority. An important feature of the system of checks and balances is the different length of terms for the president, members of the House, and U.S. Senators. Representatives are elected every two years; Senators serve for six-year terms. Presidents, of course, hold office for four years. The staggered terms of the president and the Senate, in particular, are designed to make it difficult (although certainly not impossible) for a transitory popular majority to get and keep control of the government.

The Framers said much less about the judiciary, which Alexander Hamilton described in *The Federalist*, No. 78, as the "least dangerous branch" of the new national government. The president and the Senate are given the shared power to appoint federal judges, but these appointments are for life. Congress is authorized to establish lower federal courts and determine their jurisdiction; it may even regulate the appellate jurisdiction of the Supreme Court. But Congress is prohibited from reducing the salaries of sitting judges. The only means of removing members of the judiciary is through a cumbersome impeachment process, but this requires proof that the judge has committed "high crimes" or misdemeanors. Clearly, the Framers wanted to create an independent federal judiciary that would be insulated from partisan political pressures.

Judicial Review   The text of the Constitution is silent on the means by which the judiciary can check and balance the other branches. In *Marbury v. Madison* (1803), the single most important case in American constitutional history, the Supreme Court asserted the power to review acts of Congress and declare them null and void if they are found to be contrary to the Constitution. Seven years later, in *Fletcher v. Peck* (1810), the Court extended this power to encompass the validity of state laws under the federal Constitution. Commonly referred to as **judicial review**, the power of the federal courts to rule on the constitutionality of legislation is nowhere explicitly provided for in the Constitution. However, many of the Framers supported the concept of judicial review, and most probably expected the courts to exercise this power. In any event, the power of judicial review is now well established. By assuming this power, the federal judiciary greatly enhanced its role in the system of checks and balances. Moreover, the courts took on primary responsibility for interpreting and enforcing the Constitution.

Federalism

As noted previously, the states had well-established governments by the mid-1770s. It was simply inconceivable that the state governments would be abolished in favor of a unitary system—that is, one in which all political power rests in the central government. But the decision to retain the states as units of government was much more than a concession to political necessity. The Framers, who after all represented their respective states at the Constitutional Convention, believed in federalism as a means of dispersing power. After a revolutionary war fought against distant colonial rulers, the founders believed that government should be closer to the governed. Moreover, there were dramatic differences in political culture among the states; there was no way that a distant national government could command the loyalty and support of a diverse people. Finally, there were the practical problems of trying to administer a country spread out along a thousand-mile seaboard. The states were much better equipped to do this.

Individual Rights

There is no question but that the protection of the liberty and property of the individual was among the Framers' highest goals. Yet the original Constitution had little to say about individual rights. This is because the Framers assumed that the limited national government they were creating would not be a threat to individual liberty and property. Of course, not everyone shared this perspective. Thomas Jefferson, who has been described as the "missing giant" of the Constitutional Convention, was disappointed that the Framers failed to include a bill of rights in the document they adopted. Jefferson's concern was widely shared in his native state of Virginia, where ratification of the Constitution was a close question. Fortunately, a gentleman's agreement was worked out whereby ratification was obtained in Virginia and other key states on the condition that Congress would immediately take up the matter of creating a bill of rights. The first ten amendments to the Constitution, known collectively as the Bill of Rights, were adopted by the 1st Congress in 1789 and ratified by the requisite nine states in 1791. Today, issues arising under various provisions of the Bill of Rights (for example, abortion, the death penalty, and school prayer) are both important questions of constitutional law and salient issues of public policy.

THE LIVING CONSTITUTION

The Constitution has been amended seventeen times since the ratification of the Bill of Rights. Undoubtedly the most important of these amendments are the Thirteenth, Fourteenth, and Fifteenth, ratified in 1865, 1868, and 1870, respectively. The Thirteenth Amendment abolished slavery, or "involuntary servitude." The Fourteenth Amendment was designed primarily to prohibit states from denying equal protection and due process of law to the newly freed former slaves. The Fifteenth Amendment forbade the denial of voting rights on the basis of race. These so-called Civil War Amendments attempted to eradicate the institution of slavery and the inferior legal status of black Americans. Although the abstract promises of the Civil War Amendments went unfulfilled for many years (some would say they remain unfulfilled even today), they represented the beginning of a process of democratization that has fundamentally altered the character of the American political system. It is important to recognize that the Fourteenth Amendment in particular, with its broad requirements of equal protection and due process, has become a major source of legal protection for civil rights and liberties, extending far beyond issues of racial discrimination.

Constitutional Democracy

When the Framers met in Philadelphia in 1787, the right to vote was, for the most part, limited to white men of property. In fact, all fifty-five of the delegates to the Constitutional Convention were drawn from this segment of the population. Women were regarded as second-class citizens and most blacks, being slaves, held no legal rights. The Civil War, industrial and commercial expansion, and waves of immigration in the late nineteenth century, together with two world wars and the Great Depression in the twentieth century, produced fundamental changes in the nature of American society. Inevitably, social forces have produced dramatic changes in the legal and political systems. The basic thrust of these changes has been to render the polity more democratic-that is, more open to participation by those who were once excluded. Through constitutional amendment and changing interpretations of existing constitutional language, the **constitutional republic** designed by the Framers has become a **constitutional democracy**. This fundamental change in the character of the political system testifies to the remarkable adaptability of the Constitution itself.

Built-In Flexibility

Although the Constitution was intended to limit the power of government, it was not designed as a straitjacket. Through a number of general, open-ended provisions, the Constitution enables government to respond to changing social, political, and economic conditions. Obviously, America at the beginning of the twenty-first century is a radically different place from the America the founders knew. Yet the United States is governed essentially by the same set of institutions the Framers designed, and by the same Constitution (with twenty-six amendments) adopted in 1787. In fact, the U.S. Constitution is the oldest written constitution still in effect in the world.

The adaptability of the Constitution is fundamentally due to the open-ended nature of numerous key provisions of the document. This is particularly evident in the broad language outlining the legislative, executive, and judicial powers. Article I permits Congress to tax and spend to further the "general welfare," a term that has taken on new meaning in modern times. Article II gives the "executive Power" to the president but does not define the precise limits thereof. Article III likewise invests the Supreme Court with "judicial Power" without elaborating on the limits of that power. Such open-ended provisions endow the Constitution with a built-in flexibility that has enabled it to withstand the test of time.

Judicial Interpretation of the Constitution

The Constitution's remarkable adaptability is to a very considerable degree a function of the power of the courts, and especially the U.S. Supreme Court, to interpret authoritatively the provisions of the document. In *Marbury v. Madison* (1803), the Supreme Court asserted that "[i]t is, emphatically, the province and duty of the judicial department, to say what the law is." In *Marbury,* Chief Justice John Marshall was referring not only to the interpretation of ordinary legislation, but to the interpretation of the Constitution itself. While the courts do not have a monopoly on constitutional interpretation, ever since *Marbury v. Madison* it has been widely recognized and generally accepted that the interpretations rendered by the courts are authoritative.

Judges, lawyers, politicians, and scholars have long debated theories of how the eighteenth century Constitution should be understood and applied to the issues of the day. As the federal courts have assumed a more central role in the public policy making process, the debate over constitutional interpretation has become more heated and more public.

On one side of the debate are those who subscribe to the **doctrine of original intent**, which holds that in applying a provision of the Constitution to a contemporary question, judges should attempt to determine what the Framers intended the provision to mean. On the other side are those who champion the idea of a "living Constitution," the meaning of which must change to reflect the spirit of the age. This debate is often lurking behind disagreements over particular constitutional questions ranging from abortion to women's rights. It is being constantly reargued and rekindled by the decisions of the Supreme Court.

In some instances, the language of the Constitution leaves little room for varying judicial interpretation. For example, Article I, Section 3, provides unequivocally that "[t]he Senate of the United States shall be composed of two Senators from each State." But not all of the Constitution's provisions are as obvious in meaning. Perhaps the best example is the Necessary and Proper Clause of Article I, Section 8. It is through this clause that the Supreme Court, in what can certainly be considered the second most important case in American constitution law, *M'Culloch v. Maryland* (1819), endowed Congress with a deep reservoir of **implied powers.** Another example of broad language is Article I, Section 8, Clause 3, giving Congress the authority to "regulate Commerce . . . among the several States." Under this clause the Supreme Court has upheld sweeping congressional action in the fields of labor relations, antitrust policy, highway construction, airline safety, environmental protection, criminal justice, and civil rights, to name just a few of the more prominent examples.

The Constitution and Modern Government

The central tendency of modern constitutional interpretation has been to increase the power and scope of the national government. Some would say that this expansion has occurred at the expense of **states' rights** and individual freedom. There is no doubt that the modern Constitution, largely by necessity, allows for a far more extensive and powerful federal government than the Framers would have desired or could have imagined. Yet the Supreme Court has not lost sight of the Framers' ideal of limited government and has shown its willingness and ability to curtail the exercise of governmental power. In *United States v. Nixon* (1974), the Watergate tapes case, the Court refused to condone an assertion of presidential power that flatly contradicted the Framers' principle of the rule of law. More recently, in *City of Boerne v. Flores* (1997), the Court stood up to Congress, striking down a popular statute, the Religious Freedom Restoration Act. Irrespective of whether one approves of the decisions rendered in *Nixon* and *Boerne,* these rulings demonstrated that the Supreme Court takes the Constitution seriously, and that the Constitution still embodies the Framers' idea that the government may not always do what it pleases.

The Constitution in Times of Crisis

In the wake of the terrorist attacks on America on September 11, 2001, the government effectively declared a new war on terrorism. After obtaining congressional approval, President George W. Bush ordered military force to be used against Osama bin Laden's al-Qaeda forces in Afghanistan as well as the Taliban government that provided them sanctuary. Congress enacted new laws aimed at increasing security at the nation's borders and at airports and giving law enforcement authorities broader powers to investigate suspected terrorists. Federal agencies proposed new regulations to increase domestic security. In the face of the new war on terrorism, some wondered whether constitutional values of limited government, federalism, checks and balances, and especially civil rights and liberties might be cast aside. Would the government exceed constitutional restraints? Would courts stand up for civil rights and personal liberties in the face of overwhelming public sentiment to protect American security? Only time will tell. But it is worth noting that the Constitution has withstood many crises, including a civil war, two world wars, and a great depression. The Constitution endured the dramatic social, economic, and technological changes of the twentieth century. It survived the Cold War and the cultural revolution of the 1960s. Although the Constitution will be sorely tested by a potentially prolonged war on terrorism, history suggests that it will pass this test too.

KEY TERMS

interpretation	limited government	*The Federalist Papers*	judicial review
Articles of Confederation	popular sovereignty	rule of law	constitutional republic
unicameral legislature	representative government	separation of powers	constitutional democracy
interstate commerce	tyranny of the majority	checks and balances	doctrine of original intent
protective tariffs	unitary system	federalism	implied powers
Shays's rebellion	Virginia Plan	individual rights	states' rights
Constitutional Convention of 1787	New Jersey Plan	parliamentary system	
	Bill of Rights	distributive articles	

FOR FURTHER READING

Ackerman, Bruce. *We the People: Foundations*. Cambridge, Mass.: Harvard University Press, 1991.

Adler, Mortimer. *We Hold These Truths*. New York: Macmillan, 1987.

Beard, Charles A. *An Economic Interpretation of the Constitution of the United States*. New York: Macmillan, 1960.

Bowen, Catherine Drinker. *Miracle at Philadelphia*. New York: Little, Brown, 1986.

Bryce, James. *The American Commonwealth* (3rd ed.). New York: Macmillan, 1911.

Farrand, Max (ed.). *The Records of the Federal Convention of 1787*. New Haven, Conn.: Yale University Press, 1937.

Hamilton, Alexander, John Jay, and James Madison. *The Federalist Papers*. Clinton Rossiter (ed.). New York: Mentor Books, 1961.

Jensen, Merrill. *The Articles of Confederation*. Madison: University of Wisconsin Press, 1940.

Kammen, Michael. *A Machine That Would Go of Itself: The Constitution in American Culture*. New York: Vintage Books, 1987.

Kelly, Alfred H., Winfred A. Harbison, and Herman Belz. *The American Constitution: Its Origins and Development* (7th ed., 2 vols.). New York: Norton, 1991.

Kenyon, Cecilia (ed.). *The Antifederalists*. Indianapolis: Bobbs-Merrill, 1966.

McDonald, Forrest. *Novus Ordo Seclorum: The Intellectual Origins of the Constitution*. Lawrence: University Press of Kansas, 1985.

McDonald, Forrest. *We the People: The Economic Origins of the Constitution*. Chicago: University of Chicago Press, 1958.

Morris, Richard B. *The Forging of the Union, 1781–1789*. New York: Harper and Row, 1987.

Rakove, Jack N. *The Beginnings of National Politics: An Interpretive History of the Continental Congress*. New York: Knopf, 1979.

Rossiter, Clinton. *1787: The Grand Convention*. New York: Macmillan, 1966.

Storing, Herbert. *What the Anti-Federalists Were For*. Chicago: University of Chicago Press, 1981.

Swisher, Carl Brent. *American Constitutional Development* (2nd ed.). New York: Houghton-Mifflin, 1954.

Vose, Clement E. *Constitutional Change*. Lexington, Mass.: Lexington Books, 1972.

Warren, Charles. *The Making of the Constitution*. Boston: Little, Brown, 1928.

PART **1**

SOURCES OF POWER AND RESTRAINT

Sandra Day O'Connor: Associate Justice, 1981–

"Just as the separation and independence of the coordinate branches of the Federal Government serves to prevent the accumulation of excessive power in any one branch, a healthy balance of power between the States and the Federal Government will reduce the risk of tyranny and abuse from either front."

–JUSTICE SANDRA DAY O'CONNOR, WRITING FOR THE COURT IN *GREGORY V. ASHCROFT* (1991)

1

THE SUPREME COURT IN THE CONSTITUTIONAL SYSTEM

Chapter Outline

"It is emphatically the province and duty of the judicial department, to say what the law is."

–CHIEF JUSTICE JOHN MARSHALL, WRITING FOR THE COURT IN
MARBURY V. MADISON (1803)

John Marshall: Chief Justice, 1801–1835

INTRODUCTION

The U.S. Supreme Court is the leading actor on the stage of American constitutional law. While other courts (federal and state) have occasion to interpret the U.S. Constitution, they can be and often are overruled by the Supreme Court. Unlike the decisions of other courts, Supreme Court decisions have authoritative nationwide application. Accordingly, the Supreme Court occupies a position of preeminence in the American constitutional system.

The Supreme Court operates within an elaborate framework of legal principles, precedents, and procedures. However, because of its institutional status as an independent branch of government, and the fact that the legal questions it addresses often involve important issues of public policy, the Court is a political entity as well as a legal one. The Court's political role is highlighted every time the Court addresses a controversial public issue such as abortion, school prayer, gay rights, affirmative action, or the death penalty. On occasion the Court's decisions have immediate impacts on the political process itself. Such was the case in *Bush v. Gore* (2000), in which the Court effectively decided the outcome of a presidential election (for further discussion and an excerpt of the decision, see Chapter 13).

Because the Supreme Court is at once a legal and a political institution, an understanding of the Court and its most significant product, constitutional law, requires knowledge of both law and politics. In this book we attempt to enhance both. In this first chapter we examine the Supreme Court as an institution-its practices, powers, and procedures. We explain how constitutional cases reach the High Court and how they are decided once there. Most importantly, we describe the origin and development of **judicial review**, the crux of judicial power and the principal means by which constitutional law develops. We examine the exercise of judicial review and, just as important, the constraints on the exercise of this power. Finally, we examine the behavior of the Court from the standpoint of modern political science.

THE COURTS: CRUCIBLES OF CONSTITUTIONAL LAW

Constitutional law evolves through a process of judicial interpretation in the context of particular cases. These cases may arise in either state or federal courts. Each of the fifty states has its own court system, responsible for cases arising under the laws of that state. These laws include the state constitution, statutes enacted by the state legislature, orders issued by the governor, regulations promulgated by various state agencies, and ordinances (local laws) adopted by cities and counties. But state courts also have occasion to consider questions of federal law, including federal constitutional questions.

Although no two state court systems are identical, all of them contain trial and appellate courts (see Figure 1.1). **Trial courts** make factual determinations based on the presentation of evidence and apply established legal principles to resolve disputes. **Appellate courts**, on the other hand, exist to correct legal errors made by trial courts and to settle controversies about disputed legal principles. Both trial and appellate courts are called on from time to time to decide questions of constitutional law. Each state has a court of last resort, usually called the state supreme court, which speaks with finality on matters of state law.

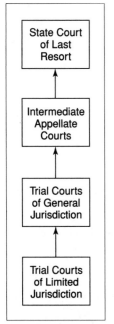

FIGURE 1.1
A Model State Court System

FIGURE 1.2

The Federal Court System

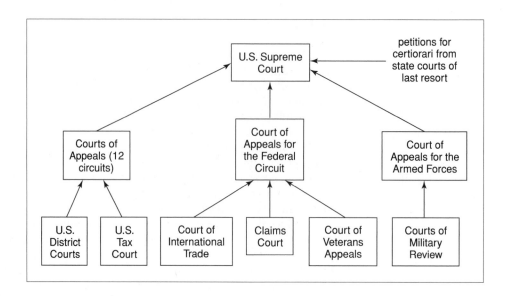

The Federal Court System

The national government operates its own system of **federal courts** with authority throughout the United States and its territories. Federal courts decide cases arising under the Constitution of the United States and statutes enacted by Congress. In addition, the **jurisdiction** of these courts extends to cases involving executive orders issued by the president, regulations established by various federal agencies, and treaties and other agreements between the United States and foreign countries.

The **court of last resort** in the federal judiciary is, of course, the U.S. Supreme Court. The Supreme Court sits atop a hierarchy of appellate and trial courts, as displayed in Figure 1.2. Article III of the Constitution provides that "[t]he judicial Power of the United States, shall be vested in one supreme Court, and in such inferior Courts as the Congress may from time to time ordain and establish." Beginning with the landmark Judiciary Act of 1789, Congress used this authority primarily to create and empower the federal court system. Over the years Congress has expanded and modified the system, giving us the three-tiered structure we have today.

The U.S. District Courts   The **U.S. District Courts** are the major trial courts in the federal system. These courts are granted authority to conduct trials and hearings in civil and criminal cases arising under federal law. Normally, one federal judge presides at such hearings and trials, although federal law permits certain exceptional cases to be decided by panels of three judges. In 2000, slightly more than 322,000 cases were filed in the federal district courts.

Section 2 of the Judiciary Act of 1789 created thirteen District Courts, one for each of the eleven states then in the Union and one each for the parts of Massachusetts and Virginia that were later to become the states of Maine and Kentucky, respectively. From the outset, then, the District Courts have been state contained, with Congress adding new districts as the nation has grown. Today, there are ninety-four federal judicial districts, each state being allocated at least one. Tennessee, for example, has three federal judicial districts corresponding to the traditional eastern, middle, and western "grand divisions" of the state. California, New York, and Texas are the only states with four federal judicial districts.

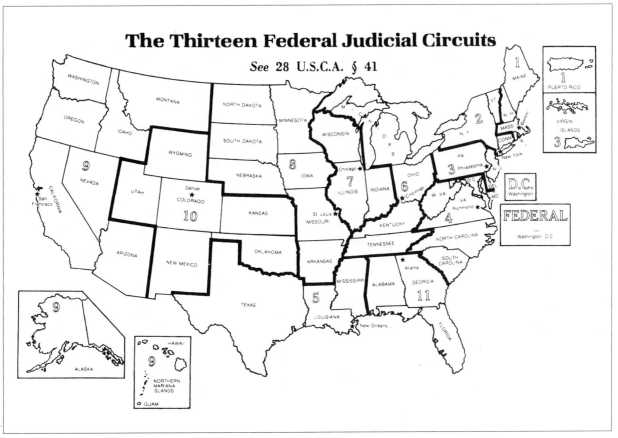

FIGURE 1.3
The Thirteen Federal Judicial Circuits
Source: See 28 U.S.C.A. § 41.

The U.S. Courts of Appeals   The intermediate appellate courts in the federal system are the **U.S. Courts of Appeals.** These courts did not exist until passage of the Judiciary Act of 1891. Prior to that time, appeals from the decisions of the District Courts were heard by the Supreme Court or by Circuit Courts that no longer exist. Today, the Courts of Appeals are commonly referred to as the "circuit courts," because each one of them presides over a geographical area known as a circuit (see Figure 1.3). The nation is divided into twelve circuits, each comprising one or more federal judicial districts, plus one "federal circuit" that is authorized to grant appeals from decisions of specialized federal courts. Typically, the circuit courts hear appeals from the federal districts within their circuits. For example, the U.S. Court of Appeals for the Eleventh Circuit, based in Atlanta, hears appeals from the District Courts located in Alabama, Georgia, and Florida. The Court of Appeals for the District of Columbia Circuit, based in Washington, D.C., has the very important additional function of hearing appeals from numerous quasi-judicial administrative agencies in the federal bureaucracy.

Appeals in the circuit courts are normally decided by rotating panels of three judges, although under exceptional circumstances these courts will decide cases en banc, meaning that all of the judges assigned to the court will participate in the decision. On average, twelve judges are assigned to each circuit, but the number varies according to caseload. In 2000, the caseload of the federal circuit courts was approximately 55,000 filings.

The U.S. Supreme Court   Although the **U.S. Supreme Court** is explicitly recognized in Article III of the Constitution, it was not formally established until passage of the **Judiciary Act of 1789.** The Judiciary Act provided for a Court composed of a chief justice and five associate justices. In 1807 the Court was expanded to include seven justices, and in 1837 Congress increased the number to nine. During the Civil War, the number of justices was briefly increased to ten. In 1869 Congress reestablished the number at nine, where it has remained to this day. Although Congress theoretically could expand or contract the membership of the Court, powerful tradition militates against doing so.

The Supreme Court's first session was held in February 1790. It had no cases on the docket and adjourned after ten days. During its first decade, 1790–1801, the Court met twice a year for brief terms beginning in February and August. Over the years, the Court's annual sessions have expanded along with its workload and its role in the political and legal system. As society has grown larger, more complex, and more litigious, the Supreme Court's agenda has swelled. The Court now receives more than 7,000 petitions each year from parties seeking review, and there is no indication that the Court's caseload will soon decline.

Since 1917, the Court's annual term has begun on the "first Monday of October." Until 1979, the Court adjourned its sessions for the summer, necessitating special sessions to handle urgent cases arising in July, August, or September. Since 1979, however, the Court has stayed in continuous session throughout the year, merely declaring a recess (typically near the end of June) for a summer vacation.

Federal Court Jurisdiction

The jurisdiction of the federal courts is determined both by the language of Article III of the Constitution and statutes enacted by Congress. The jurisdiction of the federal courts, while broad, is not unlimited. There are two basic categories of federal jurisdiction. First, and most important for students of constitutional law, is **federal question jurisdiction.** The essential requirement here is that a case must present a federal question—that is, a question arising under the U.S. Constitution, a federal statute, regulation, executive order, or treaty. Of course, given its expansive modern role, the federal government has produced a myriad of statutes, regulations, and executive orders. Consequently, most important questions of public policy can be framed as issues of federal law, thus permitting the federal courts to play a tremendous role in the policy making process.

The second broad category, **diversity of citizenship jurisdiction,** applies only to civil suits and is unrelated to the presence of a question of federal law. To qualify under federal diversity jurisdiction, a case must involve parties from different states and an amount in controversy that exceeds $75,000.

Although the issue of jurisdiction can be viewed as an external constraint on the courts, in that Congress actually writes the statutes that define jurisdiction, it functions as an internal constraint as well. This is especially true at the Supreme Court level, where the exercise of jurisdiction is subject to the discretion of the justices. In 1988 Congress made the appellate jurisdiction of the Supreme Court almost entirely discretionary by greatly limiting the so-called **appeals by right.** Rather, the Court's appellate jurisdiction is exercised almost exclusively through the **writ of certiorari,** which is issued at the Court's discretion. Federal law authorizes the Court to grant certiorari to review all cases, state or federal, that raise questions of federal law. This extremely wide discretion permits the Court to set its own agenda, facilitating its role as a policy maker, but allowing the Court to avoid certain issues that may carry undesirable institutional consequences. The Court may deflect, or at least postpone dealing with, issues that it considers "too hot to handle." This flexible jurisdiction, then, can be used as a means to expand or limit the Court's policy making role, depending on the issue at hand.

Article III of the Constitution declares that the Supreme Court shall have **original jurisdiction** "[i]n all Cases affecting Ambassadors, other public Ministers and Consuls, and those in which a State shall be Party" (modified by the Eleventh Amendment). Congress has enacted legislation giving the District Courts **concurrent jurisdiction** in cases dealing with "Ambassadors, other public Ministers and Consuls," as well as in cases between the United States government and one or more state governments. As a result, the Supreme Court has exclusive original jurisdiction only in suits between state governments, often involving boundary disputes. These cases, while important in themselves, represent a minute proportion of the Court's caseload.

The Supreme Court's **appellate jurisdiction** extends to all federal cases "with such Exceptions, and under such Regulations as the Congress shall make" (U.S. Constitution, Article III, Section 2). Appellate cases coming to the Supreme Court from the lower federal courts usually come from the thirteen Courts of Appeals, although they may come from the U.S. Court of Appeals for the Armed Forces, or, under special circumstances, directly from the District Courts. Appellate cases may also come from the state courts of last resort, usually, but not always, designated as state supreme courts.

Although Congress is authorized to regulate the appellate jurisdiction of the Supreme Court, it has rarely used this power to curtail the Court's authority. Rather, Congress has facilitated the institutional development of the Court by minimizing its mandatory appellate jurisdiction and thus giving it control over its own agenda. Likewise, Congress has delegated to the Court the authority to promulgate **rules of procedure** for itself and the lower federal courts. Consequently, the Supreme Court is nearly autonomous with respect to the determination of its decision making process.

TO SUMMARIZE:

- Constitutional law evolves through a process of judicial interpretation in the context of particular cases. These cases may arise in either state or federal courts.
- The most authoritative judicial interpretations of the Constitution are those rendered by the U.S. Supreme Court.
- Although the Supreme Court has both original and appellate jurisdiction, its appellate jurisdiction is far more important because the Court's principal function is to review lower federal court decisions and state court decisions involving federal questions. Federal law authorizes the Court to grant certiorari to review all cases, state or federal, that raise substantial federal questions. Because certiorari is granted at the Court's discretion, the Court has extensive control over its own agenda. This facilitates the Court's role as a policy making body.

CROSSING THE THRESHOLD: ACCESS TO JUDICIAL REVIEW

With few exceptions, American courts are not in the business of rendering advisory opinions (see *Hayburn's Case* [1792]). Rather, their decisions are limited to real controversies between adverse parties. These controversies take the form of cases. The court case is the basic building block of American law. Cases, including those presenting constitutional questions, begin in one of two ways: as **civil suits** or **criminal prosecutions**.

The Genesis of Constitutional Law Cases

A civil suit begins when one party, the **plaintiff**, files suit against another party, the **defendant**. Sometimes, a plaintiff files a **class action** on behalf of all "similarly situated" persons. In a constitutional case, the plaintiff accuses the defendant of violating his or her constitutional rights. Because constitutional rights are essentially limitations on the actions of government, the **respondent** in such a civil suit is generally a governmental official. Suits against government agencies *per se* are often, but not always, barred by the doctrine of **sovereign immunity**. Congress and every state legislature have passed laws waiving sovereign immunity with regard to certain types of claims.

Every civil suit seeks a remedy for an alleged wrong. The remedy may be monetary compensation for **actual damages or punitive damages**. It may be a court order requiring **specific performance** from or barring specified action by the defendant. It may be a simple **declaratory judgment**—a statement from the court declaring the rights of the litigants. Sometimes, a plaintiff will seek an **injunction** against a defendant to cause an ongoing injury to cease or to prevent an injury from occurring.

In a civil suit alleging the violation of a constitutional right, all of the aforementioned remedies are available to the plaintiff. However, because many government officials (judges, legislators, governors, and so forth) are immune from suits for monetary damages stemming from their official decisions or actions, suits against government officials tend to seek declaratory judgments and/or injunctions.

In certain instances individuals whose constitutional rights have been violated may recover monetary damages. The Civil Rights Act of 1866 (42 U.S.C. § 1983) permits courts to award monetary damages to plaintiffs whose constitutional rights are violated by persons acting under "color of law." A good example of this type of action is seen in the Rodney King case, in which the plaintiff recovered monetary damages in a Section 1983 lawsuit stemming from an incident of police brutality in Los Angeles that was witnessed on TV by the entire nation.

Criminal Prosecutions   Criminal prosecutions often raise constitutional issues. A person who is threatened with prosecution under an unconstitutional statute may seek an injunction against enforcement of the law by filing a civil suit against the prosecutor. *Roe v. Wade*, the landmark abortion decision, began when Jane Roe, an unmarried pregnant woman, brought suit against Henry Wade, the district attorney in Dallas, Texas, seeking to restrain Wade from enforcing the state's abortion law against her and other women "similarly situated" (see Chapter 11).

Once a prosecution is under way, the usual remedy is to challenge the statute in the trial court through a **demurrer** to an **indictment** or through the appropriate **pretrial motion**. If one is convicted under an arguably unconstitutional statute, the appropriate remedy is, of course, an appeal to a higher court. Most criminal convictions are challenged in this way. As an illustration, consider the case of *Texas v. Johnson* (1989), the landmark "flag burning" case. Gregory Johnson was convicted of violating the Texas law making it a crime to desecrate the American flag. He appealed his conviction to the Texas Court of Criminal Appeals, the state court of last resort in criminal cases, arguing that the conviction violated his constitutional rights. The Court of Criminal Appeals agreed, saying the state flag desecration law was unconstitutional. The state of Texas obtained review in the U.S. Supreme Court on a writ of certiorari, but to no avail. The Supreme Court, in a highly publicized and controversial decision, agreed with the Texas Court of Criminal Appeals: It was held unconstitutional to punish someone for the act of burning the American flag as a form of political protest (see Chapter 8).

Very often constitutional issues arise in criminal cases owing to the actions of the police or the prosecutor, or decisions made by the trial judge on the admission of evidence or various trial procedures. The federal Constitution provides a host of protections to persons accused of crimes; these protections are often invoked by persons challenging their convictions on appeal.

Habeas Corpus The Constitution explicitly recognizes the **writ of habeas corpus**, an ancient common law device that persons can use to challenge the legality of arrest or imprisonment. One who believes that he or she is being illegally detained, even if that person is in prison after being duly convicted and exhausting the ordinary appeals process, may seek a writ of habeas corpus in the appropriate court.

The federal habeas corpus statute affords opportunities to convicted criminals to obtain review of their convictions in federal courts, even if they received extensive appellate review in the state courts. Critics of federal habeas corpus have long called for its curtailment or outright abolition. The Supreme Court has restricted access to federal habeas corpus somewhat, and in 1996 Congress imposed further restrictions (see Chapter 10). At this time, however, it remains a fairly common means by which constitutional questions are raised in the federal courts.

Standing

After determining that a real case or controversy exists, a federal court must ascertain whether the parties to the litigation have **standing**. This is simply a determination of whether the parties in the lawsuit are the appropriate ones to litigate the legal questions in the case. The Supreme Court has developed an elaborate body of principles defining the nature and contours of standing. Essentially, to have standing a party must have a personal stake in the case. A plaintiff must have suffered some direct and substantial injury, or be likely to suffer such an injury if a particular legal wrong is not redressed. A defendant must be the party responsible for perpetrating the alleged legal wrong.

In most situations a taxpayer does not have standing to challenge policies or programs that he or she is forced to support. In *Frothingham v. Mellon* (1923), the Supreme Court held that one who invokes federal judicial power "must be able to show that he has sustained or is immediately in danger of sustaining some direct injury as the result of the statute's enforcement, and not merely that he suffers in some indefinite way common with people generally." In a modern application of the prohibition against **taxpayer suits** the Court denied standing to a group of taxpayers challenging a transfer of federal property to a private Christian college (see *Valley Forge College v. Americans United for Separation of Church and State, Inc.* [1982]). Writing for a sharply divided Court, Justice William H. Rehnquist said:

> We simply cannot see that respondents have alleged an *injury of any kind*, economic or otherwise, sufficient to confer standing. Respondents complain of a transfer of property located in Chester County, Pa. The named plaintiffs reside in Maryland and Virginia; their organizational headquarters are located in Washington, D.C. They learned of the transfer from a news release. Their claim that the Government has violated the Establishment Clause does not provide a special license to roam the country in search of wrongdoing and to reveal their discoveries in federal court. The federal courts were simply not constituted as ombudsmen of the general welfare.

In the 1997 case of *Raines v. Byrd* the Court denied standing to six members of Congress who sought to challenge the constitutionality of an act of Congress providing the president with line-item veto authority. Each of the plaintiffs had voted against the act, but the Court concluded that because the president had not yet exercised his line-item veto power, they could not show that they had been injured by the measure. By the end of 1997, President Bill Clinton had exercised the line-item veto a number of times, and several of these instances provoked affected parties to file suit. In 1998, the Court reached the merits of the dispute and declared the line-item veto law unconstitutional (see *Clinton v. City of New York*, an excerpt of which is reprinted in Chapter 3).

The issue of standing is far more than a mere technical aspect of the judicial process. The doctrine of standing determines who may challenge government policies and, to some extent, what types of policies may be challenged. Arguments over standing reflect different conceptions of the role of the federal courts in the political system. Dissenting in *Warth v. Seldin* (1975), Justice William O. Douglas observed that "standing has become a barrier to access to the federal courts." Douglas insisted that "the American dream teaches that if one reaches high enough and persists there is a forum where justice is dispensed." He concluded that the "technical barriers" should be lowered so that the courts could "serve that ancient need." A sharply contrasting position is offered by Justice Lewis Powell, concurring in *United States v. Richardson* (1975):

> Relaxation of standing requirements is directly related to the expansion of judicial power. It seems to me that allowing unrestricted . . . standing would significantly alter the allocation of power at the national level, with a shift away from a democratic form of government.

Mootness

A case is moot if the issues that gave rise to it have been resolved or have otherwise disappeared. Such a case is apt to be dismissed because a court decision would have no practical effect. An excellent example of a constitutional case being dismissed for **mootness** is *School District 241 v. Harris* (1995). In 1991, a group of students and parents, backed by the American Civil Liberties Union, filed suit to challenge two prayers and a hymn that were part of a graduation ceremony at an Idaho public high school. The federal district court in Idaho rejected the challenge, but the Ninth Circuit Court of Appeals declared the practice unconstitutional under the Establishment Clause of the First Amendment. The Supreme Court remanded the case, instructing the Court of Appeals to dismiss it as moot because the students who filed the suit had graduated. This illustrates how the Court can use the mootness doctrine to avoid consideration of a controversial constitutional question.

If the federal courts strictly adhered to the mootness rule, certain inherently time-bound questions would never be addressed. Such issues are, in the Supreme Court's words, "capable of repetition, yet evading review." *Roe v. Wade* (1973), the landmark abortion case, provides an excellent example. The gestation period of the human fetus is nine months; the gestation period for constitutional litigation tends to be much longer! Thus, by the time the *Roe* case reached the Supreme Court, Jane Roe had given birth to her child. Explaining the Court's refusal to dismiss the case as moot, Justice Harry R. Blackmun's majority opinion stated:

> The usual rule . . . is that an actual controversy must exist at stages of appellate or certiorari review, and not simply at the date the action is initiated. But when, as here, pregnancy is a significant fact in the litigation, the normal 266-day human gestation period

is so short that the pregnancy will come to term before the usual appellate process is complete. If that termination makes a case moot, pregnancy litigation will seldom survive much beyond the trial stage, and appellate review will be effectively denied. Our law should not be that rigid. Pregnancy often comes more than once to the same woman, and in the general population, if man is to survive, it will always be with us. Pregnancy provides a classic justification for a conclusion of nonmootness.

In *Roe*, the Court chose to relax the mootness rule to address an important issue. However, had the Court been disinclined to deal with the divisive abortion question, the mootness doctrine would have provided a convenient "out."

Ripeness

A case that comes to court too late, like *School District 241 v. Harris*, may be dismissed as moot; one that comes to court too soon may be dismissed as "not ripe for review." The purpose of the **ripeness doctrine** is to prevent the courts from getting prematurely involved in issues that may ultimately be resolved through other means. Like the doctrines of standing and mootness, the ripeness doctrine is not merely a means of conserving judicial power, but can be used flexibly as part of the judicial agenda-setting process.

A classic example of the use of the ripeness doctrine to avoid an important constitutional issue occurred in *Poe v. Ullman* (1961). In this case, the Supreme Court dismissed a challenge to a nineteenth century Connecticut law that prohibited practicing birth control through artificial means. The Court said that since the law had not yet been enforced against the plaintiffs, the case was not ripe for judicial review. Eventually, the Court reviewed and struck down the Connecticut statute, but only after an individual was convicted and fined for violating the law (see *Griswold v. Connecticut* [1965], discussed and reprinted in Chapter 11).

Exhaustion of Remedies

A close cousin of the ripeness doctrine is the **exhaustion of remedies** requirement. For a case to be ripe for judicial consideration, the parties must first have exhausted all nonjudicial remedies. This doctrine applies primarily to cases that involve decisions by administrative or regulatory agencies. Thus, for example, a corporation that has been denied a broadcasting license by the Federal Communications Commission must first exhaust all means of appeal within the FCC before taking the case to federal court. The exhaustion of remedies doctrine is designed to avoid unnecessary litigation and allows the courts to defer to agency "experts" in the resolution of what can be complex and technical issues.

In *Natural Gas Pipeline Company v. Slattery* (1937), the Supreme Court said that the exhaustion requirement had "especial force" when the case involved a state, as distinct from a federal, agency. In such cases the Court's customary deference to the executive branch is compounded with its traditional deference to state governments. Judicial intervention into state or federal agency decision making may be justified, however, in order to prevent "irreparable injury" from being inflicted on a citizen or company (see *Oklahoma Natural Gas Company v. Russell* [1923]).

The Doctrine of Abstention   Closely akin to exhaustion of remedies is the **doctrine of abstention**. Whereas the principal application of the exhaustion of remedies doctrine is to bureaucratic decision making, the primary application of abstention is to the state court systems. Essentially, the abstention doctrine prohibits the federal courts from intervening in state court proceedings until they have been finalized. Thus a person convicted of a crime in a state court normally must exhaust all means of appeal in the state judiciary before petitioning the U.S. Supreme Court for a writ of certiorari or a federal district court for a writ of habeas corpus.

Under the doctrine of abstention, federal judges normally abstain from issuing injunctions to prevent persons from being prosecuted under unconstitutional state statutes. For example, in *Younger v. Harris* (1971), the Supreme Court said it was improper for a federal court to enjoin a state prosecutor from trying a man under a state law virtually identical to one that had recently been declared unconstitutional. Writing for the Court, Justice Hugo Black stressed the notion of "comity," which entails mutual respect between the state and federal governments.

The Political Questions Doctrine

Even though a case may meet the formal prerequisites of jurisdiction, standing, ripeness, and exhaustion of remedies, the federal courts may still refuse to consider the merits of the dispute. Under the **political questions doctrine**, cases may be dismissed as nonjusticiable if the issues they present are regarded as extremely "political" and thus inappropriate for judicial resolution. Of course, in a broad sense, all constitutional cases that make their way into the federal courts are political in nature. The political questions doctrine really refers to those issues that are likely to draw the courts into a political battle with the executive or legislative branch, or that are simply more amenable to executive or legislative decision making.

The doctrine of political questions originated in *Luther v. Borden* (1849). In this case, the Supreme Court refused to take sides in a dispute between two rival governments in Rhode Island, one based on a popular referendum, the other based on an old royal charter. Writing for the Court, Chief Justice Roger B. Taney observed that the argument in the case "turned on political rights and political questions." Not insignificantly, President John Tyler had agreed to send in troops to support the charter government before the case ever went to the Supreme Court.

The best established application of the political questions doctrine is the federal courts' unwillingness to enter the fields of international relations, military affairs, and foreign policy making. This was demonstrated in *Massachusetts v. Laird* (1970), in which the Supreme Court dismissed a suit challenging the constitutionality of the Vietnam War. This position was reaffirmed in *Goldwater v. Carter* (1979), in which the Court refused to entertain a lawsuit brought by a United States senator challenging President Carter's unilateral termination of a defense treaty with Taiwan.

For many years, the federal courts used the political questions doctrine to stay out of controversies involving the apportionment of legislative districts. In *Colegrove v. Green* (1946), Justice Felix Frankfurter warned of the dangers of entering the "political thicket" of reapportionment. But in *Baker v. Carr* (1962), the Supreme Court held that legislative malapportionment (that is, gross disparities in population among districts) was a justiciable question in federal court. This decision signaled a veritable revolution, in which federal courts directed the reapportionment of legislative districts at all levels of government, from the House of Representatives to local school boards, on the basis of "one person, one vote."

In *Nixon v. United States* (1993) the Justices voted 9 to 0 to dismiss a suit challenging the Senate's current method for holding impeachment trials. Under this shortcut procedure, a committee of twelve senators hears testimony, reviews the evidence, and prepares a summary report to the full Senate. After hearing oral arguments from the accused and the "impeachment managers" from the House of Representatives, the full Senate votes on whether the accused should be removed from office. Former federal district judge Walter L. Nixon, who had been removed from office after being impeached, argued that the shortcut procedure violated Article I, Section 3, clause 6, which provides that the "Senate shall have the sole Power to try all Impeachments." The Supreme Court found the Senate's choice of the means for fulfilling its obligation under the Impeachment Trial Clause to be a nonjusticiable political question.

TO SUMMARIZE:

- Federal courts are not in the business of rendering advisory opinions on the meaning of the Constitution. Rather, their decisions are limited to real controversies between adverse parties.
- The Supreme Court has articulated several doctrines that limit access to judicial review. Chief among them are standing, ripeness, mootness, exhaustion of remedies, and the political questions doctrine.

THE SUPREME COURT'S DECISION MAKING PROCESS

The exclamation "I'll fight it all the way to the Supreme Court if I have to!" is a stock phrase in American political rhetoric. Yet it is extremely difficult to get one's case before the High Court. The Supreme Court uses its limited resources to address the most important questions in American law. The rectification of injustices in individual cases is usually accorded much lower priority.

There are three mechanisms by which the Supreme Court reviews lower court decisions. By far the rarest is **certification**, in which a federal appeals court formally asks the Supreme Court to certify or "make certain" a point of law. The second is on appeal by right in which, at least theoretically, the Court must rule on the merits of the appeal. As noted earlier, however, Congress has restricted such appeals to a few narrow categories of cases. By far the most common means by which the Court grants review is through the writ of certiorari.

One who loses an appeal in a state court of last resort or a federal court of appeals may file a petition for certiorari in the Supreme Court. The filing fee is currently $300, which may be waived for indigent litigants on the filing of a motion to proceed *in forma pauperis.* About two-thirds of the cert petitions the Supreme Court receives are filed *in forma pauperis;* most of these come from prisoners seeking further review of their convictions or sentences.

The chances of the Supreme Court granting review in a given case are very slim. The odds are somewhat improved if the case originated in a federal court. The odds are much better still if the petitioner is the federal government, the most frequent litigator in the federal courts. Of the more than 7,000 petitions for certiorari coming to it each year, the Court will normally grant review in only a few hundred, and even some of these cases will be dismissed later without a decision on the merits. Others will be disposed of through brief **memorandum decisions,** in which the Court does not provide its reasoning through the issuance of opinions. During the 1990s the Supreme Court averaged about 85 full opinion decisions annually, in contrast to a yearly average of about 150 in the early 1980s.

The process of case selection actually begins with the justices' **law clerks** (staff attorneys) reading the numerous petitions for certiorari and preparing summary memoranda. With the assistance of clerks, the chief justice, who bears primary responsibility for Court administration, prepares a **discuss list** of cases to be considered for certiorari. The associate justices may add cases to the list. Unless at least one justice indicates that a petition should be discussed, review is automatically denied, which disposes of more than 70 percent of the petitions for certiorari.

The Court considers petitions on the discuss list in private conferences. A conference, usually lasting the better part of a week, is held immediately before the commencement of the Court's term in October. This **preterm conference** is devoted entirely to consideration of cert petitions. Regular conferences are held throughout the term, both for the purpose of reviewing cert petitions and for discussing and deciding the cases in which the Court has granted review.

At least four justices must vote to grant certiorari in order for the Court to accept a case from the discuss list. The **rule of four** permits a minority of justices to set the Court's agenda. There is evidence that this happens fairly routinely. In such situations, it would be possible for the five justices who voted against cert to vote subsequently to dismiss the case without reaching the merits. Yet institutional norms militate against this strategy, suggesting the collegiality of the Court as a decision making body.

More than 95 percent of the petitions for certiorari coming to the Supreme Court are denied. A denial of certiorari, just like the dismissal of an appeal, has the effect of sustaining the lower court decision under challenge. An important distinction is made, however, between denials of certiorari and dismissals of appeal. According to the Supreme Court's decision in *Hopfman v. Connolly* (1985), a denial of cert carries no weight as **precedent**, whereas dismissal of an appeal "for want of a substantial federal question" has binding precedential effect on lower courts. The fact that the Court has decided not to review a lower court decision does not mean that the Court necessarily approves of the way it was decided. There is nothing to prevent the Court from reaching the same issue in a future case and deciding it differently. Denial of certiorari thus may be as much a function of scarce judicial resources as it is an expression of approval of the lower court decision. Because it entails the authoritative allocation of values by government, the Court's case selection process must be viewed as inescapably political.

Summary Decisions

As noted previously, not all cases accepted by the Supreme Court are afforded **plenary review,** or "full-dress treatment." Some cases are decided summarily—that is, quickly, without the benefit of full argumentation before the Court. These decisions are rendered in the form of a memorandum or *per curiam* (unsigned) opinion, usually with little discussion or justification. Although memorandum decisions are fully binding on the parties to the case, they are accorded little individual significance as precedents. The major function of **summary decisions** is **error correction;** they have little impact on constitutional lawmaking.

Submission of Briefs

In cases slated for plenary review, lawyers for both parties (the petitioner and the respondent; or the appellant and the appellee) are requested to submit **briefs.** Briefs are written documents containing legal arguments in support of a party's position. By Court rule, the parties' briefs are limited to fifty pages. In addition to the briefs submitted by the parties to the litigation, the Court may permit outside parties to file **amicus curiae** ("friend of the court") briefs. *Amicus* briefs are often filed on behalf of organized groups that have an interest in the outcome of a case. Examples of interest groups that routinely file *amicus* briefs in the Supreme Court include the American

Civil Liberties Union (ACLU), the National Association for the Advancement of Colored People (NAACP), and the National Rifle Association (NRA).

Oral Argument and Conference

After the briefs of parties and *amici* have been submitted, the case is scheduled for **oral argument**, a public hearing where lawyers for both sides appear before the Court to make verbal presentations and, more importantly, answer questions from the bench. The oral argument is the only occasion on which lawyers in a case have any direct contact with the justices.

Oral arguments are normally held on Mondays, Tuesdays, and Wednesdays beginning on the first Monday in October and ending in late April. Oral argument on a given case is usually limited to one hour. Four cases will be argued before the Court on any given oral argument day. "Court watchers" (including representatives of interest groups, the media, and academia) often attend oral argument hoping to learn something about the Court's predisposition with respect to the case under consideration or something about the general proclivities of the justices, especially the most recent appointees.

Within days after a case is orally argued, it is discussed in private **conference** among the justices. Conferences are usually held on Wednesdays, Thursdays, and Fridays. At conference, the chief justice opens the discussion by reviewing the essential facts of the case at hand, summarizing the history of the case in the lower courts, and stating his view as to the correct decision. This provides the chief with a chance to influence his colleagues, an opportunity that only a few occupants of the office have been able to exploit. It is well known, however, that Chief Justice Charles Evans Hughes was on occasion able to overwhelm other members of the Court by a photographic memory that gave him command of legal and factual details.

After the chief justice has presented the case, associate justices, speaking in order of seniority, present their views of the case and indicate their "votes" as to the proper judgment. This original vote on the merits is not binding, however, and justices have been known to change their votes prior to the announcement of the decision. The final vote is not recorded until the decision is formally announced.

Judgment and Opinion Assignment

In deciding a case that has been fully argued, the Court has several options. First, the Court may decide that it should not have granted review in the first place, whereupon the petition is dismissed as having been "improvidently granted." This occurs infrequently. Alternatively, the Court may instruct the parties to reargue the case, focusing on somewhat different issues. The case is then likely to be carried over to the Court's next term and not decided with finality until more than a year after the original argument. This is precisely what happened in two of the most significant cases of the twentieth century: *Brown v. Board of Education* (1954), the school desegregation case, and *Roe v. Wade* (1973), the abortion case. It is interesting to note that in the *Brown* case, the Court not only called for reargument of the issues, but, under the leadership of the newly appointed Chief Justice Earl Warren, delayed its decision until unanimity could be achieved.

If the Court decides to render judgment, it will either **affirm** (uphold) or **reverse** (overturn) the decision of the lower court. Alternatively, it may modify the lower court's decision in some respect. Reversal or modification of a lower court decision requires a majority vote, a quorum being six justices. A tie vote (in cases where one or more justices do not participate) always results in the affirmance of the decision under review.

Once a judgment has been reached, it remains for the decision to be explained and justified in one or more written opinions. In the early days of the Court, opinions were issued *seriatim*—that is, each justice would produce an opinion reflecting his views of the case. John Marshall, who became chief justice in 1801, instituted the practice of issuing an Opinion of the Court, which reflects the views of at least a majority of justices. The **Opinion of the Court**, referred to as the **majority opinion** when the Court is not unanimous, has the great advantage of providing a coherent statement of the Court's position to the parties, the lower courts, and the larger legal and political communities.

It must be understood, however, that even a unanimous vote in support of a particular judgment does not guarantee that there will be an Opinion of the Court. Justices can and do differ on the rationales they adopt for voting a particular way. Every justice retains the right to produce an opinion in every case, either for or against the judgment of the Court. A **concurring opinion** is one written in support of the Court's decision; a **dissenting opinion** is one that disagrees with the decision. An **opinion concurring in the judgment** is one that supports the Court's decision, but disagrees with the rationale expressed in the majority opinion.

Dissenting opinions, indicative of intellectual conflict on the Court, are very important in the development of American constitutional law. It is often said that "yesterday's dissent is tomorrow's majority opinion." Usually, the time lag is much longer, but there are a number of examples of dissents being vindicated by later Court decisions. Nevertheless, it is more frequently the case that a dissenting vote is merely a defense of a dying position.

Since the 1930s the number of concurring and dissenting opinions has dramatically increased, reflecting both the growing complexity of the law and the demise of consensual norms in the Court itself. The modern Court appears to be less collegial in its decision making and to operate more like "nine separate law firms."

When the Court fails to produce a majority opinion, at least one opinion will announce the judgment of the Court and state the views of those justices who endorse that opinion. This is referred to as the plurality opinion if it garners the most signatures among those justices who support the Court's decision. Note that, because it does not express the views of a majority of justices, the plurality opinion has no official weight as precedent.

Alternatively, the judgment of the Court may be expressed in a ***per curiam*** opinion, which is not attributed to any particular justice. Thus, the maximum number of opinions that may be produced in one decision is ten: one *per curiam* opinion announcing the decision of the Court followed by nine individual concurring or dissenting opinions. This occurred in the famous Pentagon papers case of 1971. The Court voted 6 to 3 to permit the *New York Times* and the *Washington Post* to publish the Pentagon papers despite an attempt by the Nixon administration to prevent the newspapers from doing so. The decision was announced in a three-paragraph *per curiam* opinion. Six justices (namely, Black, Douglas, Brennan, Stewart, Marshall, and White) authored concurring opinions. Three of their colleagues (Chief Justice Burger and Justices Blackmun and Harlan) wrote dissenting opinions (see *New York Times Company v. United States* [1971], discussed and reprinted in Chapter 8).

Persistent criticism of the Court's failure to produce majority opinions in a number of important constitutional cases, especially in the 1970s and 1980s, may have contributed to a moderate reversal of this trend in the 1990s. It is understandable that judicial scholars as well as lower court judges and others responsible for implementing Supreme Court decisions would attach great value to the Opinion of the Court. Of course, the agreement of at least five justices on a coherent rationale in support of virtually any constitutional decision is not easily achieved. It requires both a high degree of collegiality among the justices and leadership from the chief justice. The many complex issues coming before the Court allow for a wide range of responses from individual justices, compounding the difficulty of forging a majority opinion.

In an effort to obtain this level of agreement, the chief justice, assuming he is in the majority, will either prepare a draft opinion himself or assign the task to one of his colleagues in the majority. If the chief is in dissent, the responsibility of opinion assignment falls on the senior associate justice in the majority. Sometimes, in a 5-to-4 decision, a majority opinion may be "rescued" by assigning it to the swing voter—that is, the justice who was most likely to dissent. On the modern Court, the task of writing majority opinions is more or less evenly distributed among the nine justices. However, majority opinions in important decisions are more apt to be authored by the chief justice or a senior member of the Court.

After the opinion has been assigned to one of the justices, work begins on a rough draft. At this stage the law clerks play an important role by performing legal research and assisting the justice in the writing of the opinion. When a draft is ready, it is circulated among those justices in the majority for their suggestions and, ultimately, their signatures. A draft opinion that fails to receive the approval of a majority of justices participating in a given decision cannot be characterized as the Opinion of the Court. Accordingly, a draft may be subject to considerable revision before it attains the status of majority opinion.

The Supreme Court announces most of its plenary decisions in open court, often late in the term. A decision is announced by the author of the majority or plurality opinion, who may even read excerpts from that opinion. In important and controversial cases, concurring and dissenting justices will read excerpts from their opinions as well. When several decisions are to be announced, the justices making the announcements will speak in reverse order of their seniority on the Court. After decisions are announced, summaries are released to the media by the Court's public information office. Today, the nation is informed of an important Supreme Court decision within minutes of its being handed down.

Publication of Supreme Court Decisions

The decisions of the Supreme Court, indeed of all appellate courts in this country, are published in books known as **case reporters.** The official reporter, published by the U.S. Government Printing Office, is titled the *United States Reports* (abbreviated U.S. in legal citations). West Publishing Company publishes a commercial edition entitled *Supreme Court Reporter* (abbreviated S.Ct.). Finally, the Lawyers' Cooperative Publishing Company publishes the *United States Supreme Court Reports, Lawyers' Edition* (abbreviated L.Ed. or, for volumes since the mid-1950s, L.Ed. 2d). Lawyers, judges, academics, and students wishing to read the decisions of the Supreme Court may utilize any of these reporters, and references to the Court's decisions usually cite all three. For example, the Pentagon papers case, *New York Times v. United States*, is cited as 403 U.S. 713, 91 S.Ct. 2140, 29 L.Ed. 2d 822 (1971). This indicates that the case can be located in Volume 403 of the *United States Reports*, beginning on page 713, or Volume 91, page 2140, and Volume 29, page 822, of the *Supreme Court Reporter* and *Lawyers' Edition*, respectively.

In the last several years, the Court has made its decisions available to the public on the Internet, a boon to students and scholars. One of the easiest ways to access these decisions is to go to http://www.findlaw.com, which is a very comprehensive legal resources Web site.

TO SUMMARIZE:

- The Supreme Court hands down both plenary and summary decisions. Summary dispositions are made without the benefit of full argumentation before the Court. The major function of summary decisions is error correction, as opposed to legal policy making.
- Plenary decisions are characterized by the submission of briefs by the parties, oral argument, and the issuance of full opinions from the Court.
- The justices reach their decisions in private conferences in which votes are taken and opinion assignments are made.
- Decisions and their accompanying opinions are published in the *United States Reports*, the *Supreme Court Reporter*, and the *Lawyers' Edition*. The Court also makes electronic versions of its decisions available to the public via the Internet.

THE DEVELOPMENT OF JUDICIAL REVIEW

As we have noted, judicial review is the cornerstone of American constitutional law. In American constitutional law, judicial review denotes the power of a court of law to review a policy of government (usually a legislative act) and to invalidate that policy if it is found to be contrary to constitutional principles. In effect, a court of law has the power to nullify an action of the people's elected representatives, if what they have done is determined to be unconstitutional.

Judicial review is a uniquely American invention. Although **English common law** courts exercised the power to make law in some instances, no English court claimed the authority to nullify an act of Parliament. However, in *Dr. Bonham's Case* (1610), the great English jurist Sir Edward Coke recognized that parliamentary enactments were subordinate to the fundamental principles of the common law. Although this was not an outright endorsement of judicial review as we know it today, Coke's holding was important in recognizing that legislative acts must conform to some higher law.

While judicial review is normally associated with the U.S. Supreme Court, it is a power possessed by most courts of law in this country. In fact, a nascent form of judicial review had already been exercised by a few state courts prior to the adoption of the U.S. Constitution (see, for example, *Trevett v. Wheeden*, Rhode Island [1786]). The Framers of the Constitution, however, did not explicitly resolve the question of whether the newly created federal courts should have this power. Article III is silent on the subject. It remained for the Supreme Court, in a bold stroke of legal and political genius, to assert this power.

Marbury v. Madison

The Supreme Court assumed the power to review legislation as early as 1796, when it upheld a federal tax on carriages as a valid exercise of the congressional taxing power (see *Hylton v. United States*). Although this decision approving congressional action implied the power of judicial review, it did not establish it; to do that the Court would have to strike down an act of Congress. The opportunity to do so came in 1803. The decision in *Marbury v. Madison* would become the single most important ruling the Supreme Court would ever make.

The *Marbury* case arose out of what may be fairly described as a bizarre set of circumstances. After the national election of 1800, in which the Federalists lost the presidency and both houses of Congress to the Jeffersonian Republicans, the Federalists sought to preserve their influence within the national government by enlarging their control over the federal courts. The lame duck Congress, in which the Federalists held a majority, quickly passed the Judiciary Act of 1801, which was signed into law by the lame duck president, John Adams. The Judiciary Act created a number of additional federal judgeships, which under the Constitution President Adams would be able to fill with good Federalists, of course. Congress also adopted legislation creating a number of minor judgeships for the newly established District of Columbia. Here again, the power to fill these posts lay primarily with the president.

William Marbury was one of the many Federalist politicians appointed to judicial office in the waning days of the Adams administration. Marbury's commission as justice of the peace for the District of Columbia had been signed by the president following Senate confirmation on March 3, 1801, President Adams's last day in office. Everything was in order, and after Secretary of State John Marshall placed the seal of the United States on the letter of commission, it was ready to be delivered to Mr. Marbury. But for some reason, yet to be fully explained, the delivery, which was entrusted to John Marshall's brother James, never took place. Marbury's commission was returned to John Marshall's office on the evening of March 3 or the morning of March 4, along with several other justice of the peace commissions that James Marshall also failed to deliver. These commissions simply disappeared in the last-minute confusion of moving records and other papers from the office of the outgoing secretary of state, who was moving from the cabinet to his new post—chief justice of the United States.

Thomas Jefferson was sworn in as the nation's third president on March 4, 1801. The new secretary of state, James Madison, fully supported by the president, declined to deliver copies of the commissions to Marbury and the other Federalists who had failed to get their judgeships. After Marbury and others began to press the issue, Jefferson mounted an effort to repeal the Judiciary Act of 1801. A willing Congress, now dominated by Jeffersonian Republicans, was happy to oblige. Not only did Congress repeal the Judiciary Act, but it abolished the Supreme Court term of 1802! (Whether Congress could take such a bold step today is highly unlikely, since the annual Supreme Court term has become an institution in itself.)

Although having to wait until 1803 for a decision, Marbury and three other frustrated appointees filed suit against James Madison in the Supreme Court, invoking the Court's original jurisdiction. Marbury asked the Court to issue a writ of mandamus, an order directing Madison to deliver the disputed judicial commission to him. The stage was now set for a head-on collision between the Court, staffed entirely by Federalists, and the Jefferson administration.

It seems not to have occurred to the new chief justice that he should have recused himself (abstained) in the *Marbury* case. By today's standards of professional responsibility, Marshall's impartiality would have been doubted, to say the least. At the time of Marbury's appointment, John Marshall was a leader in the Federalist Party. He was central to the planning of the Judiciary Act of 1801 that had so enraged the Jeffersonians. Moreover, it was Marshall's failure as secretary of state to deliver Marbury's commission that necessitated the lawsuit!

John Marshall and his Federalist brethren on the Supreme Court found themselves in a dilemma. On the one hand they could issue the writ of mandamus and risk the very real possibility that the Jefferson administration would refuse to obey the Court, in which case the Court would suffer a serious blow to its prestige. To make matters worse, President Jefferson had strongly intimated that if the Court were to issue the mandamus, he would seek to have several members of the Court, including his distant cousin John Marshall, brought before Congress on articles of impeachment! On the other hand, if the Court were to deny Marbury his commission, it would have been widely perceived as an admission of weakness and would have damaged the prestige of the Court, not to mention that of the Federalist Party. While Chief Justice Marshall, a longtime opponent of Thomas Jefferson, did not back away from an opportunity to confront the new administration, neither of the aforementioned alternatives seemed palatable.

Marshall was an imposing figure—a man of great intellect and forceful personality who dominated the Court during his thirty-four-year tenure as chief justice. There is no doubt that Marshall arrived at the solution to the *Marbury* puzzle and persuaded his colleagues on the Court to embrace it. His solution, announced in an opinion he read from the bench on February 24, 1803, was as follows: William Marbury was held to have a legal right to his commission; by implication, the Jefferson administration was legally and morally wrong to deny it to him. However, the Court would not issue the writ of mandamus. The reason it would not do so, said John Marshall, was that the Court had no authority to issue the writ.

The Supreme Court's presumed authority to issue the writ of mandamus had been based on Section 13 of the Judiciary Act of 1789. Section 13 granted the Court the authority to "issue . . . writs of mandamus, in cases warranted by the principles and usages of law." According to John Marshall's opinion in *Marbury*, however, the Court could not issue the writ because the relevant provision of Section 13 was unconstitutional. It was invalid, according to Marshall, because it expanded the Court's original jurisdiction.

Article III, Section 2, of the Constitution expressly provides that Congress has authority to regulate the appellate jurisdiction of the Supreme Court. The implication is that Congress has no such authority with respect to the Court's original jurisdiction. In Marshall's view, Section 13 was invalid insofar as it permitted the Court to issue a writ of mandamus in a case under the Court's original jurisdiction. The Court had held for the first time that an act of Congress was null and void.

Many legal scholars have questioned John Marshall's reasoning. One can argue that all that Congress had done in crafting Section 13 of the Judiciary Act was to recognize the Court's power to issue certain kinds of writs in cases appropriately before it. In other words, Congress had not expanded the Court's jurisdiction at all, but merely recognized a legal remedy that the Court might have possessed even in the absence of the statute! At the time, however, Marshall's reasoning on this issue was not seriously challenged.

A much larger question is posed in *Marbury v. Madison* than the validity of Section 13 of the Judiciary Act of 1789. Even assuming the invalidity of the act, where does the Supreme Court get the power to strike down the law? After all, the Constitution does not explicitly recognize judicial review. In support of this assumption of power, John Marshall reasoned that, because the Constitution is the "supreme law of the land," and it is the duty of the judiciary to interpret the law, judicial review is both necessary and inevitable. Perhaps because the Supremacy Clause of Article VI focuses on the subordinate relationship of state to federal law, Marshall relied more heavily on Article III, which established and broadly defined federal judicial power. It was in this context that Marshall made his frequently quoted assertion that "[i]t is emphatically the province and duty of the judicial department, to say what the law is." In reaching this conclusion, Marshall stressed the fact that judges take an oath to support and defend the Constitution. Marshall ended his landmark opinion with the question: "Why does a judge swear to discharge the duties agreeable to the Constitution of the United States, if that constitution forms no rule for his government?"

Rejoinder to John Marshall

One of the most effective refutations of Marshall's position was offered by Justice John B. Gibson of the Pennsylvania Supreme Court. In a dissenting opinion in an otherwise unremarkable decision, *Eakin v. Raub* (1825), Gibson contended that the courts had no more authority to strike down legislative acts than the legislatures had to strike down judicial decisions. In Gibson's view, each branch of the government is ultimately responsible to the people for the constitutionality of its own acts. In support of this argument, Gibson noted that "[t]he oath to support the Constitution is not peculiar to the judges, but is taken indiscriminately by every officer of the government."

Although Justice Gibson's position might still have some appeal in theory, judicial review has long been accepted as an essential power of American courts and an important feature of the system of checks and balances. Indeed, one can argue that without judicial review the system of checks and balances is incomplete, since judicial review is the only significant check that the courts have on the actions of the legislative and executive branches.

Early Development of Judicial Review

The Supreme Court's assertion of judicial review in *Marbury v. Madison* went largely unchallenged for two reasons. First, although claiming the right to review legislation, the Court avoided a confrontation with the president and Congress. Second, the provision invalidated by the Court was not a major element of public policy. Rather it was a minor provision of a law dealing with the judicial process itself, an area in which the Supreme Court might be presumed to have greater expertise and hence a greater claim to exercise judicial review.

Marbury v. Madison was the only instance in which the Supreme Court under John Marshall struck down an act of Congress. The significance of *Marbury* as a precedent for the broad exercise of judicial review does not appear to have been fully recognized until roughly the end of the nineteenth century. The Marshall Court did, however, use its power of judicial review to strike down a number of state laws in some very important cases. The Court first exercised this power in 1810, in the highly politicized case of *Fletcher v. Peck*. In this case the Court struck down a Georgia law interfering with private property rights (see Chapter 7).

Perhaps the most important of these state cases was *M'Culloch v. Maryland* (1819), in which the Court invalidated an attempt by a state to tax a branch of the Bank of the United States (see Chapter 2). Nearly as important was *Gibbons v. Ogden* (1824), in which the Court invalidated a New York law granting a monopoly to a steamboat company in contravention of a federal law granting a license to another company (see Chapter 2). Not only were the decisions in *M'Culloch v. Maryland* and *Gibbons v. Ogden* important as assertions of power by the Supreme Court, they were instrumental in enlarging the powers of Congress vis-à-vis the states.

In addition to asserting the power to invalidate state laws, the Marshall Court established its authority to overrule decisions of the highest state appellate courts on questions of federal law, both constitutional and statutory. Article VI provides that the Constitution, laws, and treaties of the United States "shall be the supreme Law of the Land; and the Judges in every State shall be bound thereby, any Thing in the Constitution or Laws of any State to the Contrary notwithstanding." Section 25 of the

Judiciary Act of 1789 provided that appeals could be brought to the Supreme Court from certain decisions of the highest state courts. Against the strenuous objections of states' rights advocates, led by Judge Spencer Roane of Virginia, the Marshall Court successfully asserted federal judicial authority over the states with respect to the interpretation of federal law. Judge Roane conceded that state judges were bound by federal law, but asserted that state court decisions ought to be final in regard to the interpretation of federal law, including the U.S. Constitution.

When the Supreme Court invalidated Virginia's alien-inheritance and confiscation laws in 1813, the Virginia Supreme Court responded with an opinion by Chief Judge Roane declaring Section 25 of the Judiciary Act of 1789 unconstitutional. This action brought the case back to the U.S. Supreme Court. In a detailed opinion by Justice Joseph Story (John Marshall having recused himself due to earlier participation in this litigation, which had begun in the 1780s), the Supreme Court affirmed its power to review state court decisions on matters of federal law (*Martin v. Hunter's Lessee* [1816]).

States' rights advocates continued to assail Supreme Court authority to review the decisions of state courts on matters of federal law. The issue reached the Supreme Court once again in *Cohens v. Virginia* (1821). P. J. and M. J. Cohen had been convicted in a Virginia court of violating that state's law prohibiting the sale of lottery tickets. The Cohens had been selling tickets in Norfolk for the Washington, D.C., lottery, which had been authorized by Congress to finance civic improvements in the capital. The Cohens challenged their convictions in the Supreme Court, arguing that the federal law authorizing the lottery took precedence over the Virginia law criminalizing the sale of lottery tickets. On this point the Cohens ultimately lost, the Supreme Court concluding that Congress had not authorized the sale of lottery tickets outside the District of Columbia. From a technical standpoint this was a minor criminal case involving a fine of only $100. However, the competing forces of states' rights and national supremacy converted it into a major constitutional battle. Responding to Virginia's denial of the Supreme Court's authority to hear the Cohens' appeal, Chief Justice Marshall forcefully asserted the Supreme Court's jurisdiction over state court decisions "which may contravene the Constitution or the laws of the United States."

The *Dred Scott* Case

Although the Supreme Court under John Marshall succeeded in establishing and expanding the scope of judicial review, under Marshall's successor the Court damaged its credibility and prestige by an impolitic use of this power. The case was *Scott v. Sandford* (1857), the first Supreme Court decision after *Marbury v. Madison* to declare an act of Congress unconstitutional.

Slavery had been a divisive political issue as early as the Constitutional Convention of 1787. By the early nineteenth century it was clear that slavery threatened to disunite the United States. Congress responded by adopting a series of compromises on the issue. Perhaps the most important of these was the Missouri Compromise of 1820. Under this act of Congress, Missouri was admitted to the Union as a slave state—that is, one in which slavery would be legal. However, slavery would be prohibited in the remaining western territories north of 36 degrees 30 minutes latitude, a line corresponding to the southern boundary of Missouri.

The *Scott* case began when Dred Scott, a slave backed by Abolitionist forces, brought suit seeking emancipation from his owner, John Sandford. Scott was formerly owned by a Dr. Emerson, a surgeon in the U.S. Army. In 1834 Emerson had taken Scott from Missouri, where he had long resided, into the free state of Illinois and from there to Fort Snelling in the Wisconsin territory, which was also free under the Missouri Compromise. After several years Emerson and Dred Scott returned to Missouri.

Within a short time, Emerson died, and title to Scott ultimately passed to John Sandford, a New Yorker. In 1846 Scott brought suit against Sandford in the Missouri courts to obtain his freedom, arguing that his several-year residency on free soil had nullified his status as a slave.

After a favorable decision for Scott at the lower court level, the Missouri Supreme Court rejected his claim. Dred Scott then initiated a federal lawsuit on the jurisdictional ground that he and Sandford were citizens of different states. In response to Scott's claim, Sandford contended that since Scott was a Negro, he was not a citizen of Missouri and that, accordingly, the federal courts had no jurisdiction in his case. Scott filed a demurrer in answer to this plea, arguing that Sandford's contention had no legal effect. Although the federal trial court sustained Scott's demurrer, thus possibly conceding his citizenship, it ruled against Scott's claim that his residency in a free territory entitled him to freedom. Scott appealed to the Supreme Court, and the case soon became the focal point of the slavery controversy.

Both sides in the slavery controversy looked to the Court for a constitutional ruling vindicating their divergent views on the legal status of blacks and the power of Congress to regulate slavery in the territories. In 1857 five members of the Court, Chief Justice Roger B. Taney and four southern colleagues (Justices Campbell, Catron, Daniel, and Wayne) supported the institution of slavery without reservation. Two of the four northerners on the Court, Justices Nelson and Grier, if not supporters of slavery, were at least anti-Abolitionist in their sentiments. These seven justices comprised the majority in the *Dred Scott* decision. Justices Curtis and McLean wrote strong dissenting opinions.

The *Dred Scott* decision was rendered in an atmosphere of intense emotion and political partisanship. Chief Justice Taney's impassioned majority opinion went far beyond the jurisdictional question presented in the case. The opinion held that blacks, not just slaves but free blacks as well, were not citizens of the United States and could "therefore claim none of the rights and privileges which [the Constitution] provides." Indeed, in Taney's view, blacks "had no rights or privileges except such as those who held the power and the Government might choose to grant them." The Court further ruled that the Missouri Compromise was an arbitrary deprivation of the property rights of slaveholders and, as such, offended the provision of the Fifth Amendment that prohibits government from depriving persons of property without "due process of law."

The *Dred Scott* opinion embraces the doctrine of **substantive due process,** under which courts examine the *reasonableness* of governmental policies. The more conventional interpretation of the Due Process Clause is that government must follow certain procedures before taking a person's life, liberty, or property. In *Dred Scott* the Court used the Due Process Clause not to scrutinize government procedures, but to condemn the very substance of a government policy. This controversial doctrine would later be used by the Supreme Court in very different contexts from slavery.

The *Dred Scott* decision is also an extreme form of **judicial activism.** The decision was activist in the sense that the Court invalidated an act of Congress by invoking a novel, some would say dubious, constitutional doctrine. More fundamentally, it was activist in that the Court inserted itself into the slavery controversy, a deeply divisive issue that it could well have avoided. Far from resolving the slavery issue, the Court's decision greatly intensified the sectional conflict. A large and growing segment of the public simply rejected the legitimacy of the Court's constitutional theorizing on the slavery question. The *Dred Scott* decision and Chief Justice Taney soon became objects of ridicule in Abolitionist circles. The Court's intemperate decision thus not only hastened the arrival of the Civil War, but severely damaged the Court's prestige and credibility.

The *Dred Scott* decision itself was eventually nullified by the ratification of the Thirteenth Amendment, which outlawed slavery, and the Fourteenth Amendment, which provides that "[a]ll persons born or naturalized in the United States . . . are citizens of the United States and of the State wherein they reside."

Judicial Review in the Latter Part of the Nineteenth Century

In light of the furor produced by the *Dred Scott* decision, it is significant that the institution of judicial review survived the Civil War intact. While the Supreme Court conspicuously avoided conflict with Congress and the president during the Civil War era (see, in particular, the later discussion of *Ex parte McCardle*), the Court soon reasserted its authority to invalidate acts of Congress. In the decades to follow, it would exercise the power of judicial review much more frequently than it did in the early nineteenth century. Yet it managed to avoid the great issues of public debate, and, accordingly, avoided the conflict that had characterized the *Dred Scott* decision. The period from 1865 to 1890 was thus one in which the Court quietly went about the task of rebuilding its prestige and credibility.

Judicial review again became a subject of political controversy near the end of the nineteenth century as the Supreme Court exercised its power to limit government activity in the economic realm (see Chapter 2). A tendency to insulate *laissez-faire* capitalism from government intervention brought the Court, and its power of judicial review, under an increasing barrage of criticism from Populists and Progressives.

The Income Tax Case   In *Pollock v. Farmer's Loan and Trust Company* (1895), the Court invalidated a federal law that imposed a 2 percent tax on incomes of more than $4,000 a year. Fourteen years earlier, in *Springer v. United States* (1881), the Court had upheld an income tax measure adopted by Congress during the Civil War. Article I of the Constitution requires that "direct Taxes shall be apportioned among the several States . . . according to their respective Numbers." In *Springer*, the Court had concluded that the income tax was an indirect tax not subject to the apportionment requirement. But in *Pollock* the Court, by a 5-to-4 margin, changed direction. The Court held that the new income tax was a direct tax insofar as it was based on incomes derived from land and, as such, had to be apportioned among the states. Since the law did not provide for apportionment, it was unconstitutional.

The Supreme Court was influenced in *Pollock* by the imposing briefs and oral arguments of prominent attorneys including Joseph H. Choate, who, representing corporate interests, branded the income tax as a populist assault on the institutions of capitalism. Choate condemned the tax as part of the "Communist march," which if not blocked would lead to further incursions on private property, "the very keystone of the arch upon which all civilized government rests." The Court was heavily influenced by this point of view, as evidenced by the following passage from a concurring opinion by Justice Stephen J. Field:

> The present assault upon capital is but the beginning. It will be a stepping stone to others larger and more sweeping till our political contests will become a war of the poor against the rich, a war constantly growing in intensity and bitterness.

The *Pollock* decision was assailed by numerous critics as proof that the Court was aligning itself with business interests and in opposition to a moderate revenue measure broadly supported by the American people. The Court itself had exhibited deep internal division in reaching final disposition of the case. With Justice Howell Jackson not participating due to illness, the Court was evenly split when the case was first argued. Prior to reargument before a full Court later in the year, one of the justices changed his position, underscoring the shakiness of the majority. Consequently, *Pollock* was regarded as a dubious precedent.

Some observers believed that if Congress enacted another income tax measure, the Court would return to the *Springer* rationale and uphold the tax. This view was furthered by the replacement of several members of the *Pollock* majority in the late 1890s, Justice Field among them. In 1900 the Court upheld a graduated inheritance tax in *Knowlton v. Moore*. Then, in *Flint v. Stone Tracy Company* (1911), the Court sustained a tax levied on corporations as an excise tax on the privilege of doing business, even though the tax was measured by income. Before this ruling, however, Congress had proposed the Sixteenth Amendment, specifically authorizing taxation of income from any source without the requirement of apportionment among the states. By early 1913 the requisite three-fourths of the states had ratified the amendment, thus formally overruling the *Pollock* decision. As in the case of *Dred Scott v. Sandford*, a controversial Supreme Court decision had been nullified through constitutional amendment.

Judicial Review in the Twentieth Century

One of the most controversial decisions of the early twentieth century was *Lochner v. New York* (1905), in which the Supreme Court struck down a state law regulating working hours in bakeries. In the Court's view, the law was an unjustified interference with "the right to labor, and with the 'liberty of contract' on the part of the individual, either as employer or employee." In an oft-quoted dissent, Justice Oliver Wendell Holmes, Jr., argued for judicial restraint:

> This case is decided upon an economic theory which a large part of the country does not entertain. If it were a question of whether I agreed with that theory, I should desire to study it further and long before making up my mind. But I do not conceive that to be my duty, because I strongly believe that my agreement or disagreement has nothing to do with the right of a majority to embody their opinions in law.

In Justice Holmes's view, the Court in *Lochner* had transcended the proper judicial role and usurped the function of the legislature. *Lochner*, like *Dred Scott*, is an example of judicial activism in support of a politically conservative result. It is important to recognize that the term activism alone carries no ideological connotation. It may be applied to liberal and conservative decisions alike.

Throughout the early twentieth century the Supreme Court continued to use its power of judicial review to frustrate state and federal attempts at economic regulation. In *Hammer v. Dagenhart* (1918), for example, the Court struck down an act of Congress that sought to discourage the industrial exploitation of child labor. Relying on its earlier decision in *United States v. E. C. Knight* (1895), the Court found that the federal law went beyond the regulation of interstate commerce and invaded the legislative realm reserved to the states under the Tenth Amendment.

The Constitutional Battle over the New Deal   The age of laissez-faire activism entered its final phase in a constitutional showdown between the Supreme Court and President Franklin D. Roosevelt. In 1932, in the depths of the Great Depression, Roosevelt was elected in a landslide over the Republican incumbent, Herbert Hoover. FDR promised the American people a "New Deal." A bold departure from the traditional theory of *laissez-faire* capitalism, the New Deal greatly expanded the role of the federal government in the economic life of the nation. Inevitably, the New Deal would face a serious challenge in the Supreme Court, which in the 1930s was still dominated by justices with conservative views on economic matters.

The first New Deal program to be struck down was the National Recovery Administration (NRA). In *Schechter Poultry Corporation v. United States* (1935), the Supreme Court held that Congress had exceeded its authority under the Commerce Clause and had gone too far in delegating legislative power to the executive branch (see Chapter 4). In 1935 and 1936 a host of New Deal programs were declared unconstitutional by the Supreme Court (see Table 1.1).

President Roosevelt responded to the adverse judicial decisions by trying to enlarge the Court and change its direction through new appointments. Although the infamous Court-packing plan ultimately failed to win approval in Congress, the Supreme Court may have gotten the message. In an abrupt turnabout, the Court approved two key New Deal measures, the National Labor Relations Act and the Social Security Act, as well as a state minimum wage law (see Chapter 2).

The Constitutional Revolution of 1937   The Court's sudden turnabout signaled the beginning of a constitutional revolution. For decades to come, the Court would cease to interpret the Constitution as a barrier to social and economic legislation. After 1937 the Court consistently upheld even more sweeping federal legislation affecting labor relations, agricultural production, and social welfare. The Court exercised similar restraint with respect to state laws regulating economic activity.

The Supreme Court's post-1937 restraint in the area of economic regulation was counterbalanced by a heightened concern for civil rights and liberties. This concern was foreshadowed in a footnote in Justice Harlan Fiske Stone's majority opinion in *United States v. Carolene Products* (1938), upholding a federal regulation of the content of milk sold to the public. In footnote 4, Justice Stone maintained that "[t]here may be a narrower scope for the . . . presumption of constitutionality when legislation appears on its face to be within a specific prohibition of the Constitution, such as those of the first ten amendments." In essence, Justice Stone was suggesting that the traditional **presumption of validity** accorded to legislation ought to be reversed when that legislation touches on freedoms protected by the Bill of Rights. Stone's footnote also expressed the Court's willingness to be especially solicitous to the claims of minorities, saying that "prejudice against **discrete and insular minorities** [emphasis added] may be a special condition, which tends seriously to curtail the operation of those political processes ordinarily to be relied upon to protect minorities and . . . may call for a more searching judicial scrutiny."

The Impact of the Warren Court   Supreme Court activity in the modern era, at least up until the 1980s, tended to follow the philosophy stated in *Carolene Products*. This was especially the case under the leadership of Chief Justice Earl Warren from 1953 to 1969. The Warren Court had an enormous impact on civil rights and liberties. Its most notable decision was *Brown v. Board of Education* (1954), where the Court declared racially segregated public schools unconstitutional. In *Brown* and numerous other decisions, the Warren Court expressed its commitment to ending discrimination against African-Americans.

The Warren Court used its power of judicial review liberally to expand the rights not only of racial minorities but of persons accused of crimes, members of unpopular political groups, and the poor. Moreover, the Court revolutionized American politics by entering the "political thicket" of legislative reapportionment in *Baker v. Carr* (1962) and subsequent cases. Without question, the Warren era represents the most significant period of liberal judicial activism in Supreme Court history. The Warren Court was praised as heroic and idealistic; it was also denounced as lawless and accused of "moral imperialism."

TABLE 1.1 SUPREME COURT DECISIONS INVALIDATING NEW DEAL PROGRAMS		
Case	**Year**	**Law Invalidated**
Schechter Corp. v. United States	1935	National Industrial Recovery Act of 1933 (48 Stat. 195)
Hopkins Savings Assoc. v. Cleary	1935	Provision, Home Owners' Loan Act of 1933 (48 Stat. 646, Sec. 6)
Railroad Retirement Board v. Alton	1935	Railroad Retirement Act of 1934 (48 Stat. 1283)
Louisville Bank v. Radford	1935	Frazier-Lemke Act of 1934, Amending the Bankruptcy Act (48 Stat. 1289, Ch. 869)
United States v. Butler	1936	Agricultural Adjustment Act of 1933 (48 Stat. 31)
Rickert Rice Mills v. Fontenot	1936	1935 Amendments to the Agricultural Adjustment Act of 1933 (49 Stat. 750)
Carter v. Carter Coal Company	1936	Bituminous Coal Act of 1935 (49 Stat. 991)
Ashton v. Cameron County District	1936	Act of May 24, 1934, Amending Bankruptcy Act (48 Stat. 798)

Notes: 1. Other federal statutes were invalidated by the Court during the period 1935 to 1937, but these laws were enacted prior to the New Deal. 2. Stat. refers to United States Statutes-at-Large

The Burger and Rehnquist Courts   President Richard Nixon's appointment of Chief Justice Warren E. Burger and three associate justices (Harry Blackmun, Lewis Powell, and William Rehnquist) had the effect of tempering somewhat the liberal activism of the Warren Court. Yet it was the Burger Court that handed down the blockbuster decision in *Roe v. Wade* (1973), effectively legalizing abortion throughout the United States.

In the 1980s the Supreme Court became increasingly conservative as older members retired and were replaced with appointments made by Presidents Ronald Reagan and George H. W. Bush. In 1986, Associate Justice William Rehnquist was elevated to chief justice when Warren Burger resigned to work on the national celebration of the bicentennial of the Constitution. The Rehnquist Court continued the Burger Court's movement to the right, although it did not dismantle most of what was accomplished by the Warren Court in the realm of civil rights and liberties. Indeed, the Court's 5-to-4 decision in *Texas v. Johnson* (1989), invalidating a state law making it a crime to desecrate the American flag, was surprisingly reminiscent of the Warren Era.

Two of President Ronald Reagan's three Supreme Court appointees, Justices Sandra Day O'Connor and Anthony Kennedy, emerged as leading moderates on the Court of the 1990s. President George H. W. Bush's first Supreme Court appointee, David Souter, came to occupy a position slightly left of the Court's center, while Clarence Thomas, Bush's second appointee, joined Chief Justice Rehnquist and Reagan appointee Antonin Scalia to form the Court's conservative bloc. President Bill Clinton's appointments of Ruth Bader Ginsburg in 1993 and Stephen Breyer in 1994 had the general effect of preventing the conservative bloc from gaining a position of dominance. The votes of O'Connor and Kennedy came to be more critical in determining the Court's response to major constitutional questions in the 1990s. These two justices sided with the conservatives to place outer limits on the congressional power under the Commerce Clause (see *United States v. Lopez* [1995] and *United States v. Morrison* [2000]) and in striking down a provision of the Brady Gun Control Act in

1997 (see Chapter 2). The same five-member majority expanded the scope of state sovereign immunity under the Eleventh Amendment, striking down significant federal legislation including provisions of the Age Discrimination in Employment Act and the Americans with Disabilities Act (see *Kimel v. Florida* [2000] and *Board of Trustees of the University of Alabama v. Garrett* [2001], both of which are discussed in Chapter 5). On the other hand, Kennedy joined the more liberal justices, Stevens, Souter, Ginsburg, and Breyer, to block the effort to impose term limits on members of the U.S. House of Representatives (see *U.S. Term Limits, Inc. v. Thornton* [1995], discussed and reprinted in Chapter 2).

TO SUMMARIZE:

- Judicial review is the power of a court of law to invalidate governmental policies that are contrary to constitutional principles.
- The Framers of the Constitution did not explicitly provide for the power of judicial review. The Supreme Court asserted this authority in *Marbury v. Madison* (1803), although the full reach of the power of judicial review was not realized until the twentieth century.
- In *Scott v. Sandford* (1857), the Court damaged its credibility and prestige by invalidating a legislative compromise on the divisive issue of slavery.
- Judicial review again became a subject of political controversy in the late nineteenth and early twentieth centuries as the Supreme Court exercised its power to limit government activity in the economic realm. This age of laissez-faire activism entered its final phase in a showdown between the Supreme Court and President Franklin D. Roosevelt over the constitutionality of the New Deal.
- From 1937 until the mid-1990s, the Court consistently upheld sweeping federal legislation affecting commerce. The Court exercised similar restraint with respect to state laws regulating economic activity.
- The modern Court has shown heightened concern for civil rights and liberties. This concern was especially pronounced during the Warren era (1953–1969).
- The Burger Court (1969–1986) and the Rehnquist Court (1986–present) attenuated somewhat the scope of civil rights and liberties.

THE ART OF CONSTITUTIONAL INTERPRETATION

As the foregoing historical sketch indicates, the Supreme Court's power of judicial review may be used boldly or with caution. To some extent, the approach the Court adopts in a given case depends on the nature of the issue and the complexion of political forces surrounding the case. It also depends, however, on the philosophies of the justices who happen to be on the Court at a given time. The justices have varying views about the role of the Court in the political system and the conditions under which judicial review ought to be exercised. They also differ in their understandings of the Constitution and their theories as to how the Constitution should be interpreted.

Interpretivism and Originalism

The most orthodox judicial philosophy is known as **interpretivism,** so called because of its insistence that the proper judicial function is interpretation, as opposed to lawmaking. Interpretivism holds that judicial review is legitimate only insofar as judges base their decisions squarely on the Constitution. In interpreting the Constitution, judges must be guided by the plain meaning of the text when it is clear. In the absence of plain textual meaning, judges should attempt to determine the original intentions of the Framers. This element of the interpretivist perspective is often referred to as **originalism** or the **doctrine of original intent.**

The doctrine of original intent took on a distinctly political aspect during the 1980s. It was very much a part of the Reagan administration's judicial philosophy. Attorney General Edwin Meese made a series of public speeches in 1985 in which he castigated the modern Court for allegedly ignoring original intent. In a highly publicized speech at Georgetown University, Justice William Brennan rebutted Meese, saying, "It is arrogant to pretend that from our vantage point we can gauge accurately the intent of the Framers on application of principle to specific, contemporary questions." Brennan argued that judges must "read the Constitution the only way we can: as twentieth century Americans" (*Newsweek*, October 28, 1985, pp. 97–98).

The doctrine of original intent also played an important role in the Reagan administration's attempt to reshape the federal judiciary. It was in large measure due to his adherence to this doctrine that Robert Bork was nominated to the Supreme Court when Justice Powell retired in 1987. Bork's defense of strict originalism was one of several factors contributing to his rejection by the Senate following a heated confirmation battle.

In addition to its emphasis on original intent, interpretivism stresses the need for judges to respect history and tradition and, in particular, legal precedent. Essentially, interpretivism calls for judges to maintain as best they can the original Constitution, with a minimum of judicial modification.

Noninterpretivism

Many judges and constitutional scholars do not accept the interpretivist view. They raise serious questions about the practicability and desirability of interpretivism, especially on the issue of original intent. It is often argued that the "intent of the Framers" is impossible to discern on many issues. Many would argue that original intent, even if knowable, should not control contemporary constitutional decision making. These commentators tend to view the Constitution as a living document, the meaning of which evolves according to what Justice Oliver Wendell Holmes called the "felt necessities" of the times.

Numerous noninterpretive theories have been developed, drawing on a number of schools of legal thought. Some have suggested that the Court should strive to reflect societal consensus. Others have urged that the Court adopt an explicit position of moral leadership, striving to elevate and enlighten society rather than merely reflect prevailing norms. Noninterpretivists, whatever their particular philosophies, are united in their rejection of the idea that the meaning of the Constitution is rigid and static.

Natural Law

Another perspective, not easily identified with either interpretivism or noninterpretivism, is one that argues for judicial reliance on **natural law.** Natural law is a complex term with many connotations, but it generally refers to a set of principles transcending human authority that may be discovered through reason. Natural law is often associated with religion and, in particular, the moral and ethical values of the Judeo-Christian tradition. Although occasionally invoked by individual justices, the natural law perspective has, for the most part, been eschewed by the modern Supreme

Court. Students should recall, however, that natural law and the related concept of natural rights, with its emphasis on inalienable freedoms, contributed significantly to the intellectual foundations of the American republic.

An Ongoing Dialogue

The Supreme Court has never wed itself to any one judicial philosophy or theory of constitutional interpretation. Rather, the Court's numerous constitutional decisions reflect an ongoing philosophical and theoretical dialogue, both from within and without the Court. The Court's opinions are rife with arguments about fidelity to the "intent of the Framers" versus the need to keep the Constitution "in tune with the times." These debates are fundamentally about the proper role of a powerful, life-tenured, black-robed elite within a democratic polity, and about the duty of that elite to ensure that our eighteenth century Constitution is both meaningful and relevant in the twenty-first century.

TO SUMMARIZE:

- Interpretivism holds that in interpreting the Constitution, judges must be guided by the plain meaning of the text when it is clear. In the absence of plain textual meaning, judges should attempt to determine the original intentions of the Framers. Interpretivism also stresses history and tradition and, in particular, legal precedent. Essentially, interpretivism calls for judges to maintain as best they can the original Constitution, with a minimum of judicial modification.
- Noninterpretivists argue that original intent, even if knowable, should not control contemporary constitutional decision making. They view the Constitution as a living document, the meaning of which evolves according to what Justice Oliver Wendell Holmes called the "felt necessities" of the times.
- The Supreme Court has never adhered to any one judicial philosophy or theory of constitutional interpretation. Rather, the Court's numerous constitutional decisions reflect an ongoing philosophical and theoretical dialogue, both from within and without the Court.

JUDICIAL ACTIVISM AND RESTRAINT

Scholarly commentary on the Supreme Court often uses the terms activism and restraint—sometimes referred to as maximalism and minimalism—to describe particular decisions, doctrines, or justices' approaches. These terms denote opposing philosophies regarding the exercise of judicial power. Under the philosophy of **judicial restraint**, federal courts are viewed as performing a circumscribed role in the political system. They are not seen as Platonic Guardians or "philosopher kings." They are not the primary custodians of the general welfare, since that role belongs to Congress and the state legislatures. Doctrines like standing, mootness, ripeness, and the like are reflections of judicial restraint in that they serve to limit judicial inquiry into constitutional matters.

The countervailing philosophy to judicial restraint is judicial activism. Activist judges tend to see the courts as coequal participants, along with the legislative and executive branches, in the process of public policy making. Activists are thus impatient with self-imposed limitations on judicial review, and tend to brush aside doctrinal restraints. A jurist of activist views, Justice William O. Douglas once remarked that "[i]t is far more important to be respectful to the Constitution than to a coordinate branch of government" (*Massachusetts v. Laird* [1970], dissenting opinion). Dissenting in *Paul v. Davis* (1976), Justice Brennan expressed similar sentiments regarding the role of the Supreme Court:

> I had always thought that one of this court's most important roles was to provide a bulwark against governmental violation of the constitutional safeguards securing in our free society the legitimate expectations of every person to innate human dignity and a sense of worth.

One should remember that judicial power can be used for liberal or conservative policy goals. The debate over judicial activism is a long-standing one, and can be traced to decisions like *Scott v. Sandford* (1857), in which a conservative Supreme Court actively defended the institution of slavery on dubious constitutional grounds. Along the same lines, in *Lochner v. New York* (1905), a conservative Court used its power without restraint to frustrate the implementation of progressive economic legislation.

Much of American constitutional law can be seen as an ongoing debate between judicial activism and judicial restraint. In a system committed both to representative democracy and avoiding the tyranny of the majority, it is inevitable that the courts will wrestle with the problem of defining the proper judicial role. This dynamic tension is most visible in the Supreme Court's exercise of the power of judicial review.

Limiting Doctrines

The philosophy of judicial restraint counsels judges to avoid broad or dramatic constitutional pronouncements. Accordingly, various doctrines limit the exercise of judicial review, even after a federal court has reached the merits of a case. Some of these rules are codified in Justice Brandeis's oft-cited concurring opinion in *Ashwander v. Tennessee Valley Authority* (1936). In *Ashwander*, the Supreme Court upheld the federal government's program of building dams to generate electrical power in the Tennessee Valley region. Justice Brandeis's concurring opinion has become a classic statement of the principles of judicial restraint. The *Ashwander* rules, as they have come to be known, seek to protect judicial power not only by deflecting constitutional questions but by making narrow rulings when constitutional pronouncements cannot be avoided.

The Doctrine of Strict Necessity   Under the **doctrine of strict necessity,** federal courts will attempt to avoid a constitutional question if a case can be decided on nonconstitutional grounds. For example, in *Communist Party of the United States v. Subversive Activities Control Board* (1956), the Supreme Court remanded a case to a government agency for further proceedings rather than reach the sensitive political issue of whether the Communist Party enjoyed constitutional protection. Similarly, in *Hurd v. Hodge* (1948), the Court addressed the issue of "restrictive covenants," private agreements prohibiting the sale and rental of housing to blacks and other minorities. The Court held that enforcement of restrictive covenants by federal courts in the District of Columbia would violate national public policy, but it did not reach the question of whether such enforcement would violate the Constitution. The Court said: "It is a well settled principle that this court will not decide constitutional questions where other grounds are available and dispositive of the issues of the case." The Court chose not to avoid this constitutional issue in a similar case arising in a state court, however, ruling that state judicial enforcement violates the Equal Protection Clause of the Fourteenth Amendment (see *Shelley v. Kraemer* [1948], discussed in Chapter 12).

The *Ashwander* Rules: Principles of Judicial Restraint

- The court will not pass upon the constitutionality of legislation in a friendly, nonadversary proceeding, declining because to decide such questions is legitimate only in the last resort, and as a necessity in the determination of a real, earnest, and vital controversy between individuals.
- The Court will not anticipate a question of constitutional law in advance of the necessity of deciding it.
- It is not the habit of the Court to decide questions of a constitutional nature unless absolutely necessary to a decision of the case.
- The Court will not formulate a rule of constitutional law broader than is required by the precise facts to which it is to be applied.
- The Court will not pass upon a constitutional question although properly presented by the record, if there is also present some other ground upon which the case may be disposed of.
- The Court will not pass upon the validity of a statute upon complaint of one who fails to show that he is injured by its operation.
- The Court will not pass upon the constitutionality of a statute at the instance of one who has availed himself of its benefits.
- When the validity of an act of the Congress is drawn in question, and even if a serious doubt of constitutionality is raised, it is a cardinal principle that this Court will first ascertain whether a construction of the statute is fairly possible by which the question may be avoided.

Adapted from: *Ashwander v. Tennessee Valley Authority* (1936), Brandeis, J., concurring.

The Doctrine of Saving Construction   Before a court can determine the constitutionality of a statute, it must first determine its exact meaning. This is known as **statutory construction.** In construing statutes, courts often look beyond the language of the law to the intent of the legislature. Sometimes, the intent is clearly revealed in the legislative debate surrounding the adoption of the law. Often, however, legislative intent is not clear, and courts must exercise discretion in deciding what the law means.

Sometimes, the judicial interpretation of the statute may determine its constitutionality. Where a challenged law is subject to different interpretations, judicial restraint demands that a court choose an interpretation that preserves the constitutionality of the law. This is known as the **doctrine of saving construction.** In *National Labor Relations Board v. Jones & Laughlin Steel Corporation* (1937), the Supreme Court upheld the Wagner Act of 1935, a controversial federal statute regulating labor-management relations in major industries (see Chapter 2). The Jones & Laughlin Steel Corporation argued that the act was a thinly disguised attempt to regulate all industries, rather than merely those that affected interstate commerce. This point was crucial, because Congress's power in this field is limited to the regulation of interstate commerce. Given the choice between two interpretations of the act, the Court chose the narrower one, leading to a conclusion that the act was valid. Writing for the majority, Chief Justice Charles Evans Hughes observed:

> The cardinal principle of statutory construction is to save and not to destroy. We have repeatedly held that as between two possible interpretations of a statute, by one of which it would be unconstitutional and by the other valid, our plain duty is to adopt that which will save the act.

On April 24, 1996, President Clinton signed into law the Antiterrorism and Effective Death Penalty Act of 1996. One of the provisions of this statute curtails second habeas corpus petitions by state prisoners who have already filed such petitions in federal court. Under the new statute, any second or subsequent habeas petition must meet a particularly high standard and must pass through a gatekeeping function exercised by the U.S. Courts of Appeals. A circuit court must grant a motion giving the inmate permission to file the petition in a district court; denial of this motion is not appealable to the Supreme Court. A prisoner on death row in Georgia challenged the constitutionality of this provision, posing two constitutional objections: (1) that the new law amounted to an unconstitutional suspension of the writ of habeas corpus; and (2) that the prohibition against Supreme Court review of a circuit court's denial of permission to file a subsequent habeas petition is an unconstitutional interference with the Supreme Court's jurisdiction as defined in Article III of the Constitution. In *Felker v. Turpin* (1996), the Supreme Court unanimously rejected these challenges to the statute. In a saving construction, the Court interpreted the statute in such a way as to preserve the right of state prisoners to file habeas petitions directly in the Supreme Court. The Court stated, however, that it would exercise this jurisdiction only in "exceptional circumstances."

The Presumption of Constitutionality   Perhaps the most fundamental self-imposed limitation on the exercise of judicial review is the **presumption of constitutionality.** Under this doctrine, courts will presume a challenged statute is valid until it is demonstrated otherwise. In other words, the party attacking the validity of the law carries the burden of persuasion. This doctrine is based on an appreciation for the countermajoritarian character of judicial review and a fundamental respect for the legislative bodies in a democratic system.

The modern Supreme Court has modified the doctrine of presumptive constitutionality with respect to laws discriminating against citizens on grounds such as race, religion, and national origin. Such laws are now seen as inherently suspect and are subjected to **strict scrutiny.** Similarly, laws abridging **fundamental rights** are not afforded the traditional presumption of validity.

The Narrowness Doctrine   When a federal court invalidates a statute, it usually does so on fairly narrow grounds. The **narrowness doctrine** counsels courts to avoid broad pronouncements that might carry unforeseen implications for future cases. A narrowly grounded decision accomplishes the desired result, striking down an unconstitutional statute, while preserving future judicial and legislative options.

In *Bowsher v. Synar* (1986), the Supreme Court struck down a provision of the Gramm-Rudman-Hollings Act, a law designed to reduce the federal deficit through automatic spending cuts. The plaintiff, Congressman Mike Synar, asked the Court to invalidate the statute on the grounds that it delegated Congress's lawmaking power to the comptroller general, an appointed official. Instead, the Court held that Congress could not exercise removal powers over the comptroller general since he performed executive functions under the act. Thus the Court avoided the issue of congressional delegation of legislative power altogether. The delegation issue is potentially explosive because so many of the regulations promulgated by the federal bureaucracy are based on authority delegated by Congress to the executive branch (see Chapter 4).

Avoiding the Creation of New Principles   A variation on the narrowness doctrine is that courts should not create a new principle if a case may be decided on the basis of an existing one. Thus, in *Stanley v. Georgia* (1969), the Supreme Court struck down a state law making it a crime to possess obscene material in the home. Stretching the boundaries of the First Amendment, the Court held that this law was a violation of the freedom of expression. Alternatively, the Court could have created a right of privacy to engage in certain activities in the home that might be subject to arrest outside the home. This, however, would have required the Court to consider the constitutionality of numerous criminal prohibitions, including laws governing possession and use of "recreational" drugs.

The federal appellate courts are not bound to address constitutional issues precisely as they have been framed by the litigants. In its grant of certiorari, the Supreme Court may direct the parties to address certain issues, and then refuse to decide these issues. For example, in *Illinois v. Gates* (1983), the Supreme Court directed the parties to argue the so-called "good faith exception" to the Fourth Amendment exclusionary rule (see Chapter 10). In its final decision in Gates, the Court did not address the highly controversial good faith exception, but decided the case on other grounds, thus postponing for one year the creation of a new principle of constitutional law.

Stare Decisis   The term *stare decisis* ("stand by decided matters") refers to the doctrine of precedent. It is axiomatic that American courts of law should follow precedent whenever possible, thus maintaining stability and continuity in the law. As Justice Louis Brandeis once remarked, "*Stare decisis* is usually the wise policy, because in most matters it is more important that the applicable rule of law be settled than that it be settled right" (*Burnett v. Coronado Oil Company* [1932], dissenting opinion).

Devotion to precedent is considered a hallmark of judicial restraint. Obviously, following precedent limits a judge's ability to determine the outcome of a case in a way that he or she might choose if it were a matter of first impression. The decision in *Roe v. Wade* poses an interesting problem for new Supreme Court justices who believe the decision legalizing abortion was incorrect. Should a new justice who believes *Roe* was wrongly decided vote to overrule it, or should *stare decisis* be observed?

Although the doctrine of *stare decisis* applies to American constitutional law, it is not uncommon for the Court to depart from precedent. Perhaps the most famous reversal is *Brown v. Board of Education* (1954), in which the Supreme Court repudiated the separate but equal doctrine of *Plessy v. Ferguson* (1896). The separate but equal doctrine had legitimized racial segregation in this country for nearly six decades. Beginning with the *Brown* decision, official segregation was invalidated as a denial of the equal protection of the laws.

The Severability Doctrine   Under the doctrine of **severability**, federal courts will generally attempt to excise the unconstitutional elements of a statute while leaving the rest of the law intact. In *Champlin Refining Company v. Corporation Commission of Oklahoma* (1932), the Supreme Court said that invalid provisions of a law are to be severed "unless it is evident that the Legislature would not have enacted those provisions which are within its power, independently of that which is not." The severability doctrine is consistent with the philosophy of judicial restraint, in that judicial review is employed with a minimum of "damage" to the work of the legislature.

In *Immigration and Naturalization Service v. Chadha* (1983), for example, the Supreme Court invalidated Section 244(c)(2) of the Immigration and Nationality Act. This specific provision permitted one house of Congress to veto decisions of the executive branch regarding deportation of aliens. The Court found this "legislative veto" to be an unconstitutional exercise of power by Congress (see Chapter 4). The remainder of the Immigration and Nationality Act, a very important statute from the standpoint of immigration policy, was left intact.

Frequently Congress will attach a severability clause to a piece of legislation, indicating its desire that any unconstitutional provisions be severed from the rest of the statute. Absent a severability clause, federal courts may presume an enactment was intended to be judged as a whole.

Related to the concept of severability is the inclusion of a "saving" clause in many statutes. In attempting to keep pace with social change and current demands on government, Congress routinely enacts legislation repealing earlier statutes. Logically, a repeal would set aside or bring to an end all pending matters governed by the repealed statute. The saving clause simply indicates that repeal of the earlier statute is subject to certain exceptions. For example, in repealing criminal statutes, Congress often provides that prosecutions initiated prior to repeal may be pursued under repealed provisions. Although serious constitutional questions may be raised with respect to such clauses, the Supreme Court generally recognizes their validity.

The point is well illustrated by the decision in *Bradley v. United States* (1973). Bradley was convicted in 1971 of conspiring to sell cocaine in violation of a federal statute that imposed a mandatory five-year prison term on offenders. The statute under which he was prosecuted was repealed five days before his conviction and sentencing. The new law contained less punitive sentencing requirements. Nevertheless, Bradley was sentenced to the mandatory five-year term under the original statute. The Supreme Court affirmed his conviction and sentence, upholding the validity of the saving clause contained in the act of repeal.

Unconstitutional as Applied   The severability clause from the Immigration and Nationality Act just discussed distinguishes between judicial invalidation of a law as inherently unconstitutional and invalidation of a law as applied to particular persons or circumstances. The philosophy of judicial restraint suggests that, if possible, courts refrain from making declarations that a challenged statute is invalid "on its face." Whether a federal court will invalidate a statute on its face or as applied depends on the language of the law and the facts of the case in which the law is challenged.

By way of illustration, consider the Supreme Court's decision in *Cohen v. California* (1971). There, the Supreme Court held that a state "offensive conduct" law was **unconstitutional as applied** to a case where a man was prosecuted for wearing a jacket bearing the slogan "Fuck the Draft." The Court held that to punish Cohen's "immature antic" as offensive conduct would be to deny his right of free speech guaranteed by the First Amendment. On the other hand, in *Brandenburg v. Ohio* (1969), the Court struck down a state criminal syndicalism law as inherently unconstitutional under the First Amendment, because the law prohibited the "mere advocacy" of violence. (Both *Cohen* and *Brandenburg* are discussed in Chapter 8.)

It must be noted that all of the **limiting doctrines** are subject to a degree of manipulation to achieve desired outcomes. The doctrines are sufficiently complex and imprecise to permit two judges to reach opposite conclusions about their application to a given case. Nevertheless, the creation and continuance of these doctrines suggest sensitivity on the part of the federal judiciary to the inherent tensions surrounding the exercise of judicial review in a democratic polity.

TO SUMMARIZE:

- Constitutional lawmaking involves an ongoing debate between judicial activism and judicial restraint. Today, these perspectives are sometimes labeled *maximalism* and *minimalism*.
- Under the philosophy of judicial restraint, federal courts are viewed as performing a circumscribed role in the political system. Activist judges tend to see the courts as coequal participants, along with the legislative and executive branches, in the process of public policy making.

- The philosophy of judicial restraint counsels judges to avoid broad or dramatic constitutional pronouncements. Accordingly, various doctrines limit the exercise of judicial review, even after a federal court has reached the merits of a case. Some of these rules are codified in Justice Brandeis's concurring opinion in *Ashwander v. Tennessee Valley Authority* (1936).
- The most important principles of judicial restraint are the doctrine of strict necessity, the doctrine of saving construction, the narrowness doctrine, the presumption of constitutionality, the severability doctrine, and *stare decisis*.

EXTERNAL CONSTRAINTS ON JUDICIAL POWER

Although the federal courts, and the Supreme Court in particular, are often characterized as guardians of the Constitution, the judicial branch is by no means immune to the abuse of power. Accordingly, the federal judiciary is subject to constraints imposed by Congress and the president. In a constitutional system that seeks to prevent any agency of government from exercising unchecked power, even the Supreme Court is subject to checks and balances.

Judicial Dependency on Congress

Article III of the Constitution recognizes the judiciary as a separate branch of government, but it also requires the courts to depend on Congress in a number of ways. The federal courts, including the Supreme Court, depend on Congress for their budgets, although Congress is prohibited from reducing the salaries of federal judges. The organization and jurisdiction, indeed the very existence, of the lower federal courts are left entirely to Congress by Article III. It is quite conceivable that Congress might have chosen not to create a system of lower federal courts at all. It could have granted existing state tribunals original jurisdiction in federal cases, although it certainly would have been required to provide some degree of appellate review by the U.S. Supreme Court, the one federal tribunal recognized by the Constitution. Rather quickly, however, Congress passed the Judiciary Act of 1789, which provided the basis for the contemporary system of lower federal courts.

Restriction of the Supreme Court's Jurisdiction

The Supreme Court's original jurisdiction is fixed by Article III of the Constitution. *Marbury v. Madison* made clear that Congress may not alter the Court's original jurisdiction. Congress may, however, authorize lower federal courts to share this jurisdiction. The Supreme Court's appellate jurisdiction is another matter. Article III indicates that the Court "shall have appellate Jurisdiction, both as to Law and Fact, with such Exceptions, and under such Regulations as the Congress shall make."

On only one occasion since 1789 has Congress significantly limited the appellate jurisdiction of the Supreme Court. It happened during the turbulent Reconstruction period. After the Civil War, Congress passed the Reconstruction Acts, which, among other things, imposed military rule on most of the southern states formerly comprising the Confederacy. As part of this program, military tribunals were authorized to try civilians who interfered with Reconstruction. William H. McCardle, editor of the *Vicksburg Times*, published a series of editorials highly critical of Reconstruction. Consequently, he was arrested by the military and held for trial by a military tribunal.

McCardle sought release from custody through a petition for habeas corpus in federal court. Congress in 1867 had extended federal habeas corpus jurisdiction to cover state prisoners. Since McCardle was in the custody of the military government of Mississippi, the 1867 act applied to him. It also provided a right of appeal to the Supreme Court. Having lost his bid for relief in the lower court, McCardle exercised his right to appeal.

After *Ex parte McCardle* was argued in the Supreme Court, Congress enacted legislation, over President Andrew Johnson's veto, withdrawing the Supreme Court's appellate jurisdiction in habeas corpus cases. The legislation went so far as to deny the Court's authority to decide a case already argued. The obvious motive was to prevent the Court from ruling on the constitutionality of the Reconstruction Acts, which McCardle had challenged in his appeal. The Court could have invalidated this blatant attempt to prevent it from exercising its power of judicial review. But the Court chose to capitulate. By acquiescing in the withdrawal of its jurisdiction in *McCardle*, the Court avoided a direct confrontation with Congress at a time when that institution was dominant in the national government. Shortly before *McCardle* was decided, the House of Representatives had impeached President Andrew Johnson, and he escaped conviction in the Senate by only one vote. It is likely that the Court's decision to back down was somewhat influenced by the Johnson impeachment.

Does *Ex parte McCardle* imply that Congress could completely abolish the Court's appellate jurisdiction? Whatever the answer might have been at the time, the answer today would certainly be no. It is highly unlikely that Congress would ever undertake such a radical measure, but if it did the Supreme Court would almost certainly declare the act invalid. Since the Court's major decision making role is a function of its appellate jurisdiction, any serious curtailment of that jurisdiction would in effect deny the Court the ability to perform its essential function in the constitutional system.

There is even doubt that the *McCardle* decision would be reaffirmed if the contemporary Supreme Court were faced with a similar question. In *Glidden v. Zdanok* (1962), Justice William O. Douglas mused that "there is a serious question whether the *McCardle* case could command a majority today." One can argue that the Court would not, and should not, permit Congress to restrict its appellate jurisdiction if by so doing Congress would curtail the Court's ability to enforce constitutional principles or protect citizens' fundamental rights.

Congress has, on many occasions, debated limitations on the Supreme Court's appellate jurisdiction. In the late 1950s, there was a movement in Congress to deny the Supreme Court appellate jurisdiction in cases involving national security, a reaction to Warren Court decisions protecting the rights of suspected Communists. Although the major legislative proposals were narrowly defeated, the Court retreated from the most controversial decisions of 1956 and 1957. In this regard, it is instructive to compare *Pennsylvania v. Nelson* (1956) and *Watkins v. United States* (1957) with *Uphaus v. Wyman* (1959) and *Barenblatt v. United States* (1959).

In the early 1980s, a flurry of activity in Congress was aimed at restricting Supreme Court jurisdiction to hear appeals in cases dealing with abortion and school prayer. A number of proposals surfaced, but none was adopted. The constitutionality of such proposals is open to question, in that they might be construed as undermining the Court's ability to protect fundamental constitutional rights. The question remains academic, however, because Congress has not enacted such a restriction on the Court. Denial of jurisdiction as a limiting strategy depends greatly on the substantive issue area involved, what the Court has done in the area thus far, and what it is likely to do in the future. As retaliation against the Court for one controversial decision, the curtailment of appellate jurisdiction is not likely to be an effective strategy.

Can Congress Override a Constitutional Law Decision via Statute?

Although it is generally conceded that the Supreme Court has final authority to interpret the Constitution, Congress persists in occasionally attempting to substitute its own collective judgment on controversial questions for that of the justices. This legislative revision of judicial interpretation is well illustrated by Congress's passage of the Religious Freedom Restoration Act of 1993 (RFRA). This statute was enacted in direct response to the Supreme Court's 1990 decision in *Employment Division v. Smith*. In *Smith*, the Court upheld Oregon's prohibition on the use of peyote, even as applied to sacramental use by members of the Native American Church.

In determining that Oregon had not violated the Free Exercise Clause, the Court departed from precedent and refused to consider whether the challenged state policy "substantially burdened" religious practices and, if so, whether the burden could be justified by a "compelling governmental interest." Under *Smith*, no one can claim a religion-based exemption from a generally applicable criminal law.

Negative reaction to *Smith* convinced a majority in Congress to vote in favor of a law designed to reinstate the **compelling government interest** standard. In thus enacting RFRA, Congress challenged Justice Scalia's interpretation of constitutional history and of the requirements of the Free Exercise Clause of the First Amendment, as applied to the states by the Fourteenth Amendment.

In *City of Boerne v. Flores* (1997) (excerpted in Chapter 2), the Supreme Court, dividing 6 to 3, declared RFRA unconstitutional. While conceding that Congress has broad power to enforce the provisions of the Fourteenth Amendment, Justice Kennedy, writing for the majority, concluded that "RFRA contradicts vital principles necessary to maintain separation of powers and the federal balance." In this decision the Court stressed the primacy of its role as interpreter of the Constitution. It was firm and unequivocal in rejecting, on broad institutional grounds, a direct congressional challenge of final judicial authority on a question of constitutional interpretation.

Constitutional Amendment

Without question, the only conclusive means of overruling a Supreme Court or any federal court decision is through adoption of a constitutional amendment. If Congress disapproves of a particular judicial decision, it may be able to override that decision through a simple statute, but only if the decision was based on statutory interpretation. It is much more difficult to override a federal court decision that is based on the U.S. Constitution. Congress alone cannot do so. Our system of government concedes to the courts the power to interpret authoritatively the nation's charter. A Supreme Court decision interpreting the Constitution is therefore final unless and until one of two things occurs. First, the Court may overrule itself in a later case. This has happened numerous times historically. The only other way to overturn a constitutional decision of the Supreme Court is through constitutional amendment. This is not easily done, because Article V of the Constitution prescribes a two-thirds majority in both houses of Congress followed by ratification by three-fourths of the states. Yet on several occasions in our history, specific Supreme Court decisions have been overturned in this manner.

The Eleventh Amendment   The first ten amendments to the Constitution were proposed simultaneously in 1789 (ratified in 1791) and are known collectively as the Bill of Rights. These amendments were not responses to judicial decisions, but rather to a perception that the original Constitution was incomplete. The Eleventh Amendment, however, was added to the Constitution in the aftermath of the Supreme Court's first major decision—*Chisholm v. Georgia* (1793).

Alexander Chisholm brought suit against the state of Georgia in the Supreme Court to recover a sum of money owed to an estate of which he was executor. Chisholm was a citizen of South Carolina, and since he was suing the state of Georgia, he maintained that the Supreme Court had original jurisdiction under Article III of the Constitution. The state of Georgia denied that the Supreme Court had jurisdiction, claiming sovereign immunity. The state relied on statements made by James Madison, John Marshall, and Alexander Hamilton during the debates over ratification of the Constitution that states could not be made parties to federal cases against their consent. Indeed, Georgia failed to send a legal representative to defend its position when *Chisholm v. Georgia* came up for oral argument in the Supreme Court. Dividing 4 to 1, the Supreme Court decided that the state of Georgia was subject to the lawsuit, sovereign immunity notwithstanding. This decision precipitated considerable outrage in the state legislatures, which feared an explosion of federal litigation at their expense. One newspaper, the *Independent Chronicle*, predicted that "refugees, Tories, etc. . . . will introduce such a series of litigations as will throw every State in the Union into the greatest confusion." Five years later, in 1798, the Eleventh Amendment was ratified. It reads:

> The Judicial power of the United States shall not be construed to extend to any suit in law or equity, commenced or prosecuted against one of the United States by Citizens of another State, or by Citizens or Subjects of any Foreign States.

The adoption of the Eleventh Amendment assuaged widespread fears of the new national government, and of the federal courts in particular. The amendment also demonstrated that an unpopular Supreme Court decision was reversible, given sufficient political consensus. (For a discussion of the Eleventh Amendment, see Chapter 5.)

The Civil War Amendments   As previously noted, the *Dred Scott* decision was effectively overruled by adoption of the Thirteenth Amendment, abolishing slavery, and the Fourteenth Amendment, granting citizenship to all persons born or naturalized in the United States.

The Sixteenth Amendment   Recall also that the Sixteenth Amendment, granting Congress the power to "lay and collect" income taxes, overruled the *Pollock* decision of 1895 in which the Court had declared a federal income tax law unconstitutional.

The Twenty-sixth Amendment   In 1970 Congress enacted a statute lowering the voting age to 18 in both state and federal elections. The states of Oregon and Texas filed suit under the original jurisdiction of the Supreme Court seeking an injunction preventing the attorney general from enforcing the statute with respect to the states. In *Oregon v. Mitchell* (1970), the Supreme Court ruled that Congress had no power to regulate the voting age in state elections. The Twenty-sixth amendment, ratified in 1971, accomplished what Congress was not permitted to do through statute. The amendment provides:

> The right of citizens of the United States, who are eighteen years of age or older, to vote shall not be denied or abridged by the United States or by any State on account of age.

Other Proposed Constitutional Amendments   Over the years numerous unsuccessful attempts have been made to overrule Supreme Court decisions through constitutional amendments. In 1983, an amendment providing that "[t]he right to an abortion is not secured by this Constitution," obviously aimed at *Roe v. Wade*, failed to pass the Senate by only one vote. In November 1971, a proposal designed to overrule the Supreme Court's school prayer decisions (see, for example, *Abington Township v.*

Schempp [1963]) fell twenty-eight votes short of the necessary two-thirds majority in the House of Representatives. In his 1980 presidential campaign, Ronald Reagan called on Congress to resurrect the school prayer amendment, but Congress proved unwilling to give the measure serious consideration. In the mid-1960s, a widely publicized effort to overrule the Supreme Court's reapportionment decisions (for example, *Reynolds v. Sims*, 1964) was spearheaded by Senate minority leader Everett Dirksen (R–Ill.). Despite auspicious beginnings, the Dirksen amendment ultimately proved to be a flash in the pan.

The most recent example of a proposed constitutional amendment aimed at a Supreme Court decision dealt with the emotional public issue of flag burning. In *Texas v. Johnson* (1989), the Court held that burning the American flag as part of a public protest was a form of symbolic speech protected by the First Amendment. Many, including President Bush, called on Congress to overrule the Court. Congress considered an amendment that read: "The Congress and the States shall have power to prohibit the physical desecration of the flag of the United States." Votes were taken in both houses, but neither achieved the necessary two-thirds majority. In the wake of the failed constitutional amendment, Congress adopted a statute making flag desecration a federal offense. Like the state law struck down in *Texas v. Johnson*, this measure was declared unconstitutional by the Supreme Court (see *United States v. Eichman*, 1990). As recently as July 17, 2001, the U.S. House of Representatives passed another proposed constitutional amendment designed to overrule the Court's flag burning decisions. However, at this writing, the Senate has not acted on the measure.

The Appointment Power

All federal judges (including justices of the Supreme Court) are appointed by the president subject to the consent of the Senate. Normally, the Senate consents to presidential judicial appointments with a minimum of controversy. However, senatorial approval is by no means pro forma, especially when the opposing political party controls the Senate. In fact, historically the Senate has rejected about 20 percent of presidential nominations to the Supreme Court.

Article III, Section 1, of the Constitution states that "Judges, both of the supreme and inferior Courts, shall hold their Offices during good Behaviour." This grant of life tenure to federal judges was intended to make the federal courts independent of partisan forces and transitory public passions so that they could dispense justice impartially, according to the law. In *The Federalist*, No. 78, Alexander Hamilton argued that:

> The standard of good behavior for the continuance in office of the judicial magistracy is certainly one of the most valuable of the modern improvements in the practice of government. In a monarchy it is an excellent barrier to the despotism of the prince; in a republic it is a no less excellent barrier to the encroachments and oppressions of the representative body. And it is the best expedient which can be devised in any government to secure a steady, upright and impartial administration of the laws.

Hamilton's views on the need for a life-tenured, appointed federal judiciary were not universally accepted in 1788 nor are they today. In a democratic nation that extols the "will of the people," such sentiments are apt to be viewed as elitist, even aristocratic. While the states vary widely in their mechanisms for judicial selection, only in Rhode Island are judges given life tenure. From time to time proposals have surfaced to impose limitations on the terms of federal judges, but no such effort has ever gained serious political momentum. Life tenure for federal judges, like most of the elements of our eighteenth century Constitution, remains a firmly established principle of the political order.

The shared presidential–senatorial power of appointing federal judges is an important means of influencing the judiciary. For example, President Richard Nixon made a significant impact on the Supreme Court and on American constitutional law through his appointment of four justices. During the 1968 presidential campaign, Nixon criticized the Warren Court's decisions, especially in the criminal law area, and promised to appoint "strict constructionists" (widely interpreted to mean "conservatives") to the bench. President Nixon's first appointment came in 1969, when Warren Earl Burger was selected to succeed Earl Warren as chief justice. In 1970, after the abortive nominations of Clement Haynsworth and G. Harold Carswell, Harry Blackmun was appointed to succeed Justice Abe Fortas, who had resigned from the Court amid scandal in 1969. Then, in 1972, President Nixon appointed Lewis Powell to fill the vacancy left by Hugo Black's retirement and William Rehnquist to succeed John M. Harlan, who had also retired. The four Nixon appointments had a definite impact on the Supreme Court, although the resulting swing to the right was less dramatic than many observers had predicted.

FDR's Court-Packing Plan   Unquestionably, the most dramatic attempt by a president to control the Supreme Court through the appointment power was launched by Franklin D. Roosevelt in 1937. The Court, as previously mentioned, had invalidated a number of key elements of FDR's New Deal program, beginning in 1935 with the National Industrial Recovery Act. FDR criticized the Court for being out of touch with the realities of an industrialized economy and holding to a "horse-and-buggy definition of interstate commerce." Privately, FDR, who referred to the justices as the "nine old men," began to plan a strategy to curb the Court. His resolve was strengthened by his landslide reelection in 1936 and by the Court's continuing willingness to invalidate New Deal legislation. Finally, in early 1937 Roosevelt unveiled his court-packing plan, which called for Congress to increase the number of justices by allowing the president to nominate a new justice for each incumbent beyond the age of 70 who refused to retire. This would have given Roosevelt the opportunity to appoint as many as six additional justices, raising the membership of the Court to fifteen.

FDR initially attempted to sell his plan to Congress and the American people by portraying it merely as a measure to enhance the efficiency of the Supreme Court. He suggested that some of the incumbent justices were too old or infirm to stay abreast of their caseloads. Roosevelt soon admitted in one of his famous "fireside chats" that his motivation was to produce a Supreme Court that would "not undertake to override the judgment of Congress on legislative policy."

Responding to the president's assault on the Court, Chief Justice Charles Evans Hughes sent a carefully timed letter to Senator Burton K. Wheeler, chairman of the Senate Judiciary Committee, stating that the Court was fully abreast of its docket and implying that the court-packing plan might be unconstitutional. Senator Wheeler read this letter aloud at a session of the Judiciary Committee that was being broadcast by radio into millions of homes around the country.

FDR's court-packing plan was denounced by the Senate Judiciary Committee as "needless, futile and utterly dangerous." The plan failed to win approval by Congress. In the meantime, however, the Supreme Court manifested a dramatic about-face in the spring of 1937 when it upheld the National Labor Relations Act, another important element of New Deal policy (see *National Labor Relations Board v. Jones & Laughlin Steel Corporation*). The Court's famous "switch in time that saved nine" obviated the need for FDR to pack the Court. Within five years, seven of the "nine old men" had retired or died in office, and Roosevelt was able to "pack" the Court through normal procedures. The Roosevelt Court, as it came to be known, brought about a revolution in American constitutional law.

Without question, the shared presidential-senatorial power to appoint judges and justices is the most effective means of controlling the federal judiciary. Congress and the president may not be able to achieve immediate results using the appointment power, but they can bring about long-term changes in the Court's direction. The appointment power ensures that the Supreme Court and the other federal courts may not continue for very long to defy a clear national consensus.

Impeachment of Federal Judges

The only means of removing a federal judge or Supreme Court justice is through the **impeachment** process provided in the Constitution. First, the House of Representatives must approve one or more articles of impeachment by at least a majority vote. Then, a trial is held in the Senate. To be removed from office, a judge must be convicted by a vote of at least two-thirds of the Senate.

Since 1789 the House of Representatives has impeached fewer than twenty federal judges, and fewer than ten of these were convicted in the Senate. Only once has a Supreme Court Justice been impeached by the House. In 1804 Justice Samuel Chase fell victim to President Jefferson's attempt to control a federal judiciary largely comprised of Washington and Adams appointees. Justice Chase had irritated the Jeffersonians by his haughty and arrogant personality and his extreme partisanship. Nevertheless, there was no evidence that he was guilty of any crime. Consequently, Chase narrowly escaped conviction in the Senate.

The Chase affair set an important precedent: A federal judge may not be removed simply for reasons of partisanship, ideology, or personality. Thus, despite strong support in ultraconservative quarters for the impeachment of Chief Justice Earl Warren during the 1960s, there was never any real prospect of Warren's removal. Barring criminal conduct or serious breaches of judicial ethics, federal judges do not have to worry that their decisions might cost them their jobs.

Enforcement of the Court's Decisions

Courts generally have adequate means of enforcing their decisions on the parties directly involved in litigation. Any party who fails to comply with a court order, such as a **subpoena** or an injunction, may be held in **contempt.** The Supreme Court's decisions interpreting the federal Constitution are typically nationwide in scope. As such they automatically elicit the compliance of state and federal judges. Occasionally one hears of a recalcitrant judge who, for one reason or another, defies a Supreme Court decision, but this phenomenon, while not uncommon in the early days of the republic, is an eccentric curiosity today.

On the other hand, courts have greater difficulty enlisting the compliance of the general public, especially when they render unpopular decisions. Despite the Supreme Court's repeated rulings against officially sponsored prayer in the public schools, such activities continue at the present time in some parts of the country. The school prayer decisions, even after four decades, have failed to generate public acceptance (see Chapter 9). Without the assistance of local school officials, there is little the Court can do to effect compliance with its mandates regarding school prayer unless and until an unhappy parent files a lawsuit.

Sometimes the Supreme Court must depend on congressional and/or presidential cooperation to secure compliance with its decisions. This is particularly true when such decisions are actively resisted by state and local officials. For example, the efforts of Arkansas governor Orval Faubus to block the court-ordered desegregation of Central High School in Little Rock in 1957 resulted in President Dwight D. Eisenhower's commitment of federal troops to enforce the court order. A year later, in *Cooper v. Aaron* (1958), the Supreme Court issued a stern rebuke to Governor Faubus, reminding him of his duty to uphold the Constitution of the United States. Would the Court have been able to take the constitutional high ground if Eisenhower, who had reservations about court-ordered desegregation, had decided not to send the troops to Little Rock? In using military force to implement a Supreme Court decision about which he had doubts, Eisenhower was recognizing the authority of the Court to speak with finality on matters of constitutional interpretation. However, the ultimate decision to enforce the Court's authority belonged to the president. Accordingly, *Cooper v. Aaron* is more a testament to judicial dependency on the executive than an assertion of judicial power.

Unlike the president, Congress is seldom in a position to enforce a decision of the Supreme Court. On the other hand, Congress has often enacted legislation without which the broad objectives of the Court's decisions could not have been fully realized. This was certainly true during the 1960s in the field of civil rights. The Supreme Court in a series of decisions had stated the general policy objective of eradicating racial discrimination. It remained for Congress to adopt sweeping legislation in pursuit of this goal-namely, the Civil Rights Act of 1964, the Voting Rights Act of 1965, and the Fair Housing Act of 1968.

The Supreme Court often depends on the president to enforce and the Congress to "flesh out" its decisions. But the Court cannot force either of the coordinate branches of the national government to do anything. This limitation is perhaps best encapsulated in a famous comment attributed to President Andrew Jackson: "Well, John Marshall has made his decision. Now let him enforce it." In *Worcester v. Georgia* (1832), the Court had held that the state of Georgia's attempt to regulate the Cherokee Indian nation violated the Constitution and certain treaties. The decision required Georgia to release missionaries whom it had prosecuted for ministering to the Cherokees in violation of state law. Georgia's refusal to comply with the decision of the Supreme Court led to President Jackson's alleged remark.

The Supreme Court's lack of enforcement power is an inherent limitation on the power of the Court, but one that makes sense in terms of the principle of separation of powers. Law enforcement, after all, is an aspect of executive power. To permit a court of law to mobilize law enforcement authorities *without the consent of the chief executive* would be to concentrate governmental powers in a manner flatly inconsistent with the Framers' plan. As James Madison observed in *The Federalist*, No. 47, "[t]he accumulation of all powers, legislative, executive, and judiciary, in the same hands . . . may justly be pronounced the very definition of tyranny."

TO SUMMARIZE:

- Like the other branches, the judiciary is subject to checks and balances. The organization and jurisdiction of the lower federal courts are left entirely to Congress by Article III. Congress may regulate the appellate jurisdiction of the Supreme Court, but it is unclear how far Congress may go in this regard.
- Supreme Court decisions based on statutory interpretation may be overridden by Congress through the ordinary legislative process. Court decisions based on constitutional interpretation may be overridden only by the Court itself, or by constitutional amendment. Historically, at least four Supreme Court decisions have been overturned by constitutional amendments.
- Because impeachment of federal judges is limited to cases of criminal misconduct, the most significant control over the personnel on the Supreme Court is the

appointment power shared by the president and the Senate. Presidents have used the appointment power to change the direction of the Court.

- The Court often depends on the other branches of government to enforce and implement its decisions. Ultimately, the Court relies on the public's willingness to comply.

EXPLAINING THE COURT'S BEHAVIOR

Since *Marbury v. Madison* (1803), commentators have sought to explain and predict, as well as evaluate, Supreme Court decision making. Traditional legal commentary relied almost exclusively on legal factors—principles, provisions, procedures, and precedents. Modern analysis tends to look beyond the law to explain judicial decision making. Political scientists in particular are interested in the political factors that influence **judicial behavior.** Indeed, the study of judicial behavior is a subfield of the public law field of contemporary political science.

The law is complex, rich, and subtle. Judicial decision making, especially at the level of the Supreme Court, is hardly a mechanical process. Legal reasoning is certainly important, but it is inevitably colored by extralegal factors as well (see Figure 1.4). It is not unlikely that two judges, equally well trained and capable in legal research, will reach different conclusions about what the law requires in a given case. The fluidity of judicial choice is most apparent when the Supreme Court is called on to interpret the many open-ended clauses of the Constitution. Although the Court's constitutional decisions are rendered in a legal context, they cannot be fully explained by legalistic analysis. To believe otherwise is to subscribe to the **myth of legality**, the idea that judicial decisions are wholly a function of legal rules, procedures, and precedents.

Ideologies of the Justices

Political scientists who have studied Supreme Court decision making have amassed considerable evidence that the Court's decisions are influenced by the ideologies of the justices. This is inferred from regularities in the voting behavior of the justices, mainly the tendency of certain groups of justices to form **voting blocs.** In the 2000–2001 term, for example, Chief Justice Rehnquist and Justices Scalia and Thomas comprised a conservative bloc, often opposed by a liberal bloc consisting of Justices Stevens, Souter, Ginsburg, and Breyer. As the Court has become somewhat more conservative in the last decade or so, Justices O'Connor and Kennedy have come to occupy a commanding position in the middle, sometimes joining Rehnquist, Scalia, and Thomas to form a conservative majority, and sometimes, either individually or in tandem, joining the other four justices in support of a more liberal result.

Although many observers characterize Supreme Court decisions and voting patterns in simplistic liberal–conservative terms, judicial ideology may well include more than general political attitudes or views on specific issues of public policy (for example, school prayer or abortion). It may also embrace philosophies regarding the proper role of courts in a democratic society. There is reason to believe that, at least for some justices, considerations of judicial activism versus restraint ("maximalism" versus "minimalism") weigh as heavily as policy preferences in determining how the vote will be cast in a given case. Justices inclined toward activism, or maximalism, are more likely to support expansion of the Court's jurisdiction and powers and more likely to embrace innovative constitutional doctrines and policy choices. These justices are less likely than restraintists, or minimalists, to follow precedent or defer to the judgment of elected officials.

FIGURE 1.4
A Model of Supreme Court
Decision Making

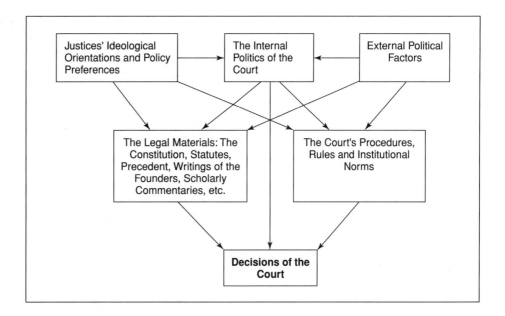

The Political Environment

In addition to the ideologies of the justices, research has pointed to a number of political factors that appear to influence Supreme Court decision making. While the Court is often characterized as a counter-majoritarian institution, there is reason to believe that public opinion does influence the Court. Extensive evidence indicates that the actions, or threatened actions, of Congress and the president can have an impact on its decisions. And in a constitutional system emphasizing checks and balances, one should not expect that it would be otherwise! The political environment, in short, strongly influences Supreme Court decision making.

The Internal Politics of the Court

Finally, the Court's decision making is intensely political in the sense that the internal dynamics of the Court are characterized by conflict, bargaining, and compromise—the very essence of politics. Such activities are difficult to observe because they occur behind the "purple curtain" that separates the Court from its attentive public. Conferences are held in private, votes on certiorari are not routinely made public, and the justices tend to be tight-lipped about what goes on behind the scenes in the "marble temple." Yet from time to time evidence of the Court's internal politics appears—in the form of memoirs, autobiographies, posthumously opened papers, and other writings of the justices, and in the occasional interviews the justices and their clerks give to journalists and academicians. Some may be offended at the attempt of journalists and scholars to penetrate the purple curtain, to examine the political realities lurking behind the veil of law and mythology in which the Supreme Court is shrouded. However, in a democratic society it is the right, and arguably the duty, of citizens to have a realistic understanding of the institutions of their government. Armed with such an understanding of the Supreme Court, one can begin to make reasonable judgments about its decisions. Realism does not lead inexorably to cynicism.

Some observers believe that the Supreme Court is nothing more than a miniature legislature and that the justices are nothing more than "politicians in black robes." The Court's enormously controversial decision in *Bush v. Gore* (2000) may be cited in support of this perspective. However, it is important to bear in mind that the Supreme Court is at once a legal and a political institution, which makes it unique in the scheme of American government. As a legal entity, the Court's decisions are usually characterized by reason and principle, characteristics not regarded as essential to the legislative process. This distinctive character may also account for the reverence with which the American people (even the most jaded political scientists) tend to regard the Court.

TO SUMMARIZE:

- The Supreme Court is at once a legal and a political institution. Therefore its decisions are affected both by legal and political factors.
- The political factors include the justices' own philosophical orientations and policy preferences, the internal politics of the Court, and the external political environment.
- The relative privacy in which the Court's key business is conducted makes it more difficult to observe the interplay of political factors.

CONCLUSION

The Supreme Court has evolved considerably over two centuries. It began as a vaguely conceived tribunal, with no cases to decide, and no permanent home. Over the years, the Court's caseload increased, as did its prominence in national affairs. The Court assumed increasing power and managed to hold its own against the legislative and executive branches of government. Eventually, the Court found a home in the Capitol, although its chambers were less than spectacular. In 1935 the Court moved into its own building. The majestic "marble temple" across the street from the Capitol houses not only a coequal branch of the national government, but the most powerful and prestigious judicial body in the world.

The tremendous growth in the power and prestige of the Supreme Court was the inevitable consequence of the constitutional design that created the judiciary as a separate branch of the federal government. It is also a function of the Court's institutional development, which was accomplished through numerous assertions of power and equally numerous instances of prudent self-restraint. Throughout American history, moreover, the elected branches of government have found it useful to permit the life-tenured Court to decide difficult and controversial issues. Perhaps most fundamentally, the growth in the Court's power and prestige can be attributed to the degree to which the American people and their elected representatives have accepted the political role that the Court has established for itself.

Students of American government must consider whether the power of judicial review is compatible, not only with the intentions of the Framers of the Constitution, but with our modern notions of democracy. Is judicial review an arrogation of power by the courts? Is it a vestige of aristocracy? Or is it a necessary and desirable element of constitutional democracy? Before reaching conclusions on these questions, one should examine the ways in which judicial review has been applied over the years since *Marbury v. Madison*. It is also important to take into account the constraints, both external and self-imposed, under which judicial review is exercised.

The concept of checks and balances is one of the fundamental principles of the American Constitution. Each branch of the national government is provided specific means of limiting the exercise of power by the other branches. For example, the president may veto acts of Congress, which will not become law unless the veto is overridden by a two-thirds vote in both Houses. Although the federal courts, and the Supreme Court in particular, are often characterized as guardians of the Constitution, the judicial branch is by no means immune to the abuse of power. Accordingly, the federal judiciary is subject to checks and balances imposed by Congress and the president. In a constitutional system that seeks to prevent any agency of government from exercising unchecked power, even the Supreme Court is subject to external limitations.

In *The Federalist*, No. 78, Alexander Hamilton sought to persuade his countrymen that the Supreme Court would be the "least dangerous" branch of the national government under the new Constitution, which had yet to be ratified. Hamilton observed that:

> [T]he judiciary . . . has no influence over either the sword or the purse; no direction of the strength or of the wealth of a society; and can take no active resolution whatever. It may be truly said to have neither force nor will, but merely judgment.

It is true that the Supreme Court's power of enforcement is limited; it is also true that the Court does not determine taxing and spending policies. Yet the almost hallowed character of the Court's "mere judgment" makes the Court as likely to secure compliance with its policy pronouncements as institutions having direct control over appropriations or law enforcement agencies. Clearly, the power of the federal courts, and of the Supreme Court in particular, to secure compliance goes far beyond the issuance of orders and decrees and the availability of a few federal marshals to enforce them.

The power and prestige of the Supreme Court, indeed of the entire federal judiciary, have grown tremendously during the past two centuries. Nevertheless, the Court works within a constitutional and political system that imposes significant constraints on its power.

The Supreme Court can, and occasionally does, speak with finality on important questions of constitutional law and public policy. But it must consider the probable responses of Congress, the president, and, ultimately, the American people. More than 200 years after the ratification of the Constitution, Alexander Hamilton's characterization of the federal judiciary as the "least dangerous" branch of the national government remains credible.

KEY TERMS

judicial review	appeals by right	actual damages	exhaustion of remedies
trial courts	writ of certiorari	punitive damages	doctrine of abstention
appellate courts	original jurisdiction	specific performance	political questions doctrine
federal courts	concurrent jurisdiction	declaratory judgment	certification
jurisdiction	appellate jurisdiction	injunction	*in forma pauperis*
court of last resort	rules of procedure	demurrer	memorandum decisions
U.S. District Courts	civil suits	indictment	law clerks
U.S. Courts of Appeals	criminal prosecutions	pretrial motion	discuss list
U.S. Supreme Court	plaintiff	writ of habeas corpus	preterm conference
Judiciary Act of 1789	defendant	standing	rule of four
federal question jurisdiction	class action	taxpayer suits	precedent
diversity of citizenship	respondent	mootness	plenary review
jurisdiction	sovereign immunity	ripeness doctrine	summary decisions

error correction	opinion concurring in the	doctrine of original intent	*stare decisis*
briefs	judgment	natural law	severability
amicus curiae	*per curiam*	judicial restraint	unconstitutional as applied
oral argument	case reporters	doctrine of strict necessity	limiting doctrines
conference	English common law	statutory construction	compelling government interest
affirm	substantive due process	doctrine of saving construction	impeachment
reverse	judicial activism	presumption of	subpoena
Opinion of the Court	presumption of validity	constitutionality	contempt
majority opinion	discrete and insular minorities	strict scrutiny	judicial behavior
concurring opinion	interpretivism	fundamental rights	myth of legality
dissenting opinion	originalism	narrowness doctrine	voting blocs

FOR FURTHER READING

Abraham, Henry J. *The Judiciary: The Supreme Court in the Governmental Process* (7th ed.). Boston: Allyn and Bacon, 1987.

Agresto, John. *The Supreme Court and Constitutional Democracy.* Ithaca, N.Y.: Cornell University Press, 1984.

Baum, Lawrence. *The Supreme Court* (7th ed.). Washington, D.C.: Congressional Quarterly Press, 2000.

Beveridge, Albert J. *The Life of John Marshall* (4 vols.). Boston: Houghton-Mifflin, 1916–1919.

Bickel, Alexander M. *The Least Dangerous Branch: The Supreme Court at the Bar of Politics.* Indianapolis: Bobbs-Merrill, 1962.

Black, Charles L., Jr., *A New Birth of Freedom: Human Rights Named and Unnamed.* New Haven, Conn.: Yale University Press, 1999.

Brigham, John. *The Cult of the Court.* Philadelphia: Temple University Press, 1987.

Clinton, Robert Lowry. *Marbury v. Madison and Judicial Review.* Lawrence: University Press of Kansas, 1989.

Epstein, Lee, and Jack Knight. *The Choices Justices Make.* Washington, D.C.: Congressional Quarterly Press, 1998.

Fehrenbacher, Don E., *The Dred Scott Case: Its Significance in American Law and Politics.* New York: Oxford University Press, 1978.

Garraty, John (ed.). *Quarrels That Have Shaped the Constitution* (rev. ed.). New York: Harper and Row, 1987.

Halpern, Stephen C., and Charles M. Lamb (eds.). *Supreme Court Activism and Restraint.* Lexington, Mass.: D. C. Heath, 1982.

Jackson, Robert H. *The Struggle for Judicial Supremacy.* New York: Knopf, 1941.

Lazarus, Edward. *Closed Chambers: The First Eyewitness Account of the Epic Struggles inside the Supreme Court.* New York: Times Books, 1998.

McCloskey, Robert G. *The American Supreme Court* (3rd ed.). Chicago: University of Chicago Press, 2000.

McPherson, James M. *Battle Cry of Freedom: The Civil War Era.* New York: Oxford University Press, 1988.

Melone, Albert P. *Researching Constitutional Law.* Glenview, Ill.: Scott, Foresman, 1990.

Murphy, Walter. *Elements of Judicial Strategy.* Chicago: University of Chicago Press, 1964.

O'Brien, David. *Storm Center: The Supreme Court in American Politics* (4th ed.). New York: Norton, 1996.

Pacelle, Richard L. *The Role of the Supreme Court in American Politics: The Least Dangerous Branch?* Boulder, Colo.: Westview Press, 2002.

Provine, Doris Marie. *Case Selection in the United States Supreme Court.* Chicago: University of Chicago Press, 1980.

Rosenberg, Gerald. *The Hollow Hope: Can Courts Bring about Social Change?* Chicago: University of Chicago Press, 1991.

Schwartz, Bernard, with Stephen Lesher. *Inside the Warren Court.* Garden City, N.Y.: Doubleday, 1983.

Smith, Jean Edward. *John Marshall: Definer of a Nation.* New York: Henry Holt, 1996.

Van Geel, T. R. *Understanding Supreme Court Opinions.* New York: Longman, 1991.

Wasby, Stephen. *The Supreme Court in the Federal Judicial System* (3rd ed.). Chicago: Nelson-Hall, 1988.

Westin, Alan F. (ed.). *An Autobiography of the Supreme Court: Off-the-Bench Commentary by the Justices.* New York: Macmillan, 1963.

Wolfe, Christopher. *The Rise of Modern Judicial Review: From Constitutional Interpretation to Judge-Made Law* (rev. ed.). Lanham, Md.: Littlefield Adams Quality Paperbacks, 1994.

Woodward, Bob, and Scott Armstrong. *The Brethren: Inside the Supreme Court.* New York: Simon and Schuster, 1979.

Yarbrough, Tinsley. *The Rehnquist Court and the Constitution.* New York: Oxford University Press, 2000.

INTERNET RESOURCES

Name of Resource	Description	URL
United States Supreme Court home page	The Supreme Court's own Web site	http://www.supremecourtus.gov
Federal courts home page (Administrative Office of the U.S. Courts)	A clearinghouse for information from and about the federal courts	http://www.uscourts.gov
FindLaw	A comprehensive legal Web site, including a database of Supreme Court decisions and various constitutional law materials	http://guide.lp.findlaw.com/casecode/supreme.html
Legal Information Institute (Cornell University)	A searchable database of Supreme Court opinions	http://supct.law.cornell.edu/supct
Federal Judicial Center	The federal courts' agency for research and continuing education	http://www.fjc.gov
The Oyez Project	A multimedia database about the U.S. Supreme Court	http://oyez.at.nwu.edu/oyez.html

A Note on Briefing Cases

Each chapter in this book includes a number of excerpts from Supreme Court decisions. These excerpts have been chosen to illustrate some of the important concepts and principles described in the chapters. Some instructors may wish to have their students "brief" some or all of these cases. Whether or not the instructor requires case briefs, students may find briefing cases useful for learning material and preparing for examinations.

A case brief is simply a summary of a court decision, usually in outline format. Typically, a case brief contains the following elements:

- The name of the case and the date of the decision
- The essential facts of the case
- The key issue(s) of law involved (or those applicable to a point of law being considered)
- The holding of the Court
- A brief summary of the Court's opinion, especially as it relates to the key issue(s) in the case
- Summaries of concurring and dissenting opinions, if any
- A statement commenting on the significance of the decision and/or stating the student's view as to the correctness of the decision.

Here is a sample case brief:

PLESSY V. FERGUSON (1896)

Issue: Is a state law requiring "equal but separate" facilities for whites and blacks a violation of the Thirteenth or Fourteenth Amendment?

Facts: Homer Plessy, who was seven-eighths white and one-eighth black, was arrested after refusing to vacate a seat in a railroad car reserved for whites. He was convicted under a Louisiana statute mandating "equal but separate" accommodations on railroads. After unsuccessfully attacking the statute in the Louisiana state courts, Plessy appealed to the U.S. Supreme Court.

Supreme Court Decision: Judgment of state court affirmed; conviction and statute upheld. Vote: 7–1 (Justice Brewer not participating).

Opinions:

Majority (Brown): Segregation is a reasonable exercise of the state's police power in that it is conducive to the maintenance of public order and peace. Segregation is not *per se* a "badge of slavery" and is therefore not a violation of the Thirteenth Amendment. The compulsory segregation of the races is permissible under the Equal Protection Clause of the Fourteenth Amendment as long as equal accommodations are provided. The Fourteenth Amendment was not intended to abolish all distinctions based on color, nor was it intended to enforce social as distinct from political equality.

Dissenting (Harlan): Compulsory segregation is an infringement on the personal liberties of persons of African descent. The Constitution is color-blind; therefore, government is prohibited from treating people differently merely on account of their race. Forcible segregation is a badge of inferiority, a vestige of slavery, and therefore a violation of the Thirteenth Amendment.

Comment:
The "separate but equal" doctrine propounded in *Plessy* provided a justification for the entire regime of Jim Crow laws enacted in the late nineteenth century. The Supreme Court eventually repudiated this doctrine, beginning with *Brown v. Board of Education* (1954).

Case

MARBURY V. MADISON

1 Cranch (5 U.S.) 137; 2 L.Ed. 60 (1803)
Vote: 4–0

In this, the most significant opinion in American constitutional law, Chief Justice John Marshall asserts the power of the federal judiciary to invalidate acts of Congress that are determined to be unconstitutional. The facts of the case are discussed in some detail on pages 33–34. It is interesting to note that, in order to accommodate Justice Samuel Chase, who was ill at the time, Chief Justice Marshall read the Opinion of the Court not in the Court's chamber located in the Capitol but before an attentive audience in the living room of Stelle's Hotel, located on the present site of the Library of Congress. For a fascinating account of the details surrounding Marbury v. Madison, *see Jean Edward Smith,* John Marshall: Definer of a Nation, *New York: Henry Holt, 1996, chapter 13.*

Mr. Chief Justice Marshall delivered the opinion of the Court.

It is . . . the opinion of the Court that by signing the commission of Mr. Marbury, the President . . . appointed him a justice of peace . . . in the District of Columbia; and that the seal of the United States, affixed thereto by the Secretary of State, is conclusive testimony of the verity of the signature, and of the completion of the appointment; and that the appointment conferred on him a legal right to the office for the space of five years.

. . . [H]aving this legal title to the office, [Marbury] has a consequent right to the commission; a refusal to deliver which is a plain violation of the right, for which the laws of his country afford him a remedy.

. . . It remains to be inquired whether, [Marbury] is entitled to the remedy for which he applies. This depends on 1st. The nature of the writ applied for; and, 2d. The power of this court.

[After a lengthy discussion of the nature of the writ of mandamus and its historical basis, Marshall continues:]

. . . The act [the Judiciary Act of 1789] to establish the judicial courts of the United States authorizes the Supreme Court, "to issue writs of mandamus, in cases warranted by the principles and usages of law, to any courts appointed or persons holding office, under the authority of the United States" [Section 13].

The Secretary of State, being a person holding an office under the authority of the United States, is precisely within the letter of this description; and if this court is not authorized to issue a writ of mandamus to such an officer, it must be because the law is unconstitutional and, therefore, absolutely incapable of conferring the authority, and assigning the duties which its words purport to confer and assign.

The Constitution vests the whole judicial power of the United States in one Supreme Court, and such inferior courts as Congress shall, from time to time, ordain and establish. This power is expressly extended to all cases arising under the laws of the United States; and consequently, in some form, may be exercised over the present case; because the right claimed is given by a law of the United States.

In the distribution of this power, it is declared, that "the Supreme Court shall have original jurisdiction, in all cases affecting ambassadors, other public ministers and consuls, and those in which a state shall be a party. In all other cases, the Supreme Court shall have appellate jurisdiction." . . .

To enable this Court, then, to issue a mandamus, it must be shown to be an exercise of appellate jurisdiction; or to be necessary to enable them to exercise appellate jurisdiction.

It has been stated at the bar, that the appellate jurisdiction may be exercised in a variety of forms, and that if it be the will of the legislature that a mandamus should be used for that purpose, that will must be obeyed. This is true, yet the jurisdiction must be appellate, not original.

It is the essential criterion of appellate jurisdiction, that it revises and corrects the proceedings in a cause already instituted, and does not create that cause. Although, therefore, a mandamus may be directed to courts, yet to issue such a writ to an officer, for the delivery of a paper, is, in effect, the same as to sustain an original action for that paper, and therefore, seems not to belong to appellate, but to original jurisdiction. Neither is it necessary in such a case as this, to enable the court to exercise its appellate jurisdiction.

The authority, therefore, given to the Supreme Court by the act establishing the judicial courts of the United States, to issue writs of mandamus to public officers, appears not to be warranted by the Constitution; and it becomes necessary to inquire, whether a jurisdiction so conferred can be exercised.

The question, whether an act, repugnant to the Constitution, can become the law of the land, is a question deeply interesting to the United States; but, happily, not of an intricacy proportioned to its interest. It seems only necessary to recognize certain principles, supposed to have been long and well established, to decide it.

That the people have an original right to establish, for their future government, such principles as, in their opinion, shall most conduce to their own happiness, is the basis on which the whole American fabric has been erected. The exercise of this original right is a very great exertion; nor can it, nor ought it, to be frequently repeated. The principles, therefore, so established, are deemed fundamental: and as the authority from which they proceed is supreme, and can seldom act, they are designed to be permanent.

This original and supreme will organizes the government, and assigns to different departments their respective powers. It may either stop here, or establish certain limits not to be transcended by those departments.

The government of the United States is of the latter description. The powers of the legislature are defined and limited; and that those limits may not be mistaken or forgotten, the Constitution is written. To what purpose are powers limited, and to what purpose is that limitation committed to writing, if these limits may, at any time, be passed by those intended to be restrained? The distinction between a government with limited and unlimited powers is abolished, if those limits do not confine the persons on whom they are imposed, and if acts prohibited and acts allowed, are of equal obligation. It is a proposition too plain to be contested, that the constitution controls any legislative act repugnant to it; or that the legislature may alter the Constitution by an ordinary act.

Between these alternatives, there is no middle ground. The Constitution is either a superior paramount law, unchangeable by ordinary means, or it is on a level with ordinary legislative acts, and, like other acts, is alterable when the legislature shall please to alter it.

If the former part of the alternative be true, then a legislative act, contrary to the Constitution, is not law; if the latter part be true, then written constitutions are absurd attempts, on the part of the people, to limit a power, in its own nature, illimitable.

Certainly, all those who have framed written constitutions contemplate them as forming the fundamental and paramount law of the nation, and consequently, the theory of every such government must be, that an act of the legislature, repugnant to the Constitution, is void.

This theory is essentially attached to a written constitution, and is, consequently, to be considered, by this Court, as one of the fundamental principles of our society. It is not, therefore, to be lost sight of, in the further consideration of this subject.

If an act of the legislature, repugnant to the Constitution, is void, does it notwithstanding its invalidity, bind the courts, and oblige them to give it effect? Or, in other words, though it be not law, does it constitute a rule as operative as if it was a law? This would be to overthrow, in fact, what was established in theory; and would seem, at first view, an absurdity too gross to be insisted on. It shall, however, receive a more attentive consideration.

It is, emphatically, the province and duty of the judicial department, to say what the law is. Those who apply the rule to particular cases, must of necessity expound and interpret that rule. If two laws conflict with each other, the courts must decide on the operation of each.

So, if a law be in opposition to the Constitution; if both the law and the Constitution apply to a particular case, so that the court must either decide that case, conformable to the law, disregarding the Constitution; or conformable to the Constitution, disregarding the law; the court must determine which of these conflicting rules governs the case: this is of the very essence of judicial duty.

If then, the courts are to regard the Constitution, and the constitution is superior to any ordinary act of the legislature, the Constitution, and not such ordinary act, must govern the case to which they both apply.

Those, then, who controvert the principle, that the Constitution is to be considered, in court, as a paramount law, are reduced to the necessity of maintaining that courts must close their eyes on the Constitution, and see only the law.

This doctrine would subvert the very foundation of all written constitutions. It would declare that an act which, according to the principles and theory of our government, is entirely void, is yet, in practice, completely obligatory. It would declare, that if the legislature shall do what is expressly forbidden, such act, notwithstanding the express prohibition, is in reality effectual. It would be given to the legislature a practical and real omnipotence, with the same breath which professes to restrict their powers within narrow limits. It is prescribing limits, and declaring that those limits may be passed at pleasure. . . .

The judicial power of the United States is extended to all cases arising under the Constitution. Could it be the intention of those who gave this power, to say, that in using it, the constitution should not be looked into? That a case arising under the Constitution should be decided, without examining the instrument under which it arises?

This is too extravagant to be maintained.

In some cases, then, the constitution must be looked into by the judges. And if they can open it at all, what part of it are they forbidden to read or to obey? . . .

. . . [I]t is apparent, that the framers of the Constitution contemplated that instrument as a rule for the government of courts, as well as the legislature.

Why otherwise does it direct the judges to take an oath to support it? This oath certainly applies in an especial manner, to their conduct in their official character. How immoral to impose it on them, if they were to be used as the instruments, and the knowing instruments, for violating what they swear to support!

. . .Why does a judge swear to discharge his duties agreeable to the Constitution of the United States, if that constitution forms no rule for his government? If it is closed upon him, and cannot be inspected by him?

If such be the real state of things, this is worse than solemn mockery. To prescribe, or to take this oath, becomes equally a crime.

It is also not entirely unworthy of observation, that in declaring what shall be the supreme law of the land, the Constitution itself is first mentioned; and not the laws of the United States, generally, but those only which shall be made in pursuance of the Constitution, have that rank.

Thus, the particular phraseology of the Constitution of the United States confirms and strengthens the principle, supposed to be essential to all written constitutions, that a law repugnant to the Constitution is void; and that courts, as well as other departments, are bound by that instrument.

The rule must be discharged.

[*Justice Cushing* and *Justice Moore* did not participate in this decision.]

Case

EAKIN V. RAUB

12 Sergeant & Rawle (Pennsylvania Supreme Court) 330 (1825)

Although the specific issue before the Pennsylvania Supreme Court is of little interest today, Justice Gibson's dissenting opinion is still considered to be the most effective rejoinder to Chief Justice Marshall's argument in support of judicial review.

Gibson, J. [dissenting].

. . . I am aware, that a right to declare all unconstitutional acts void . . . is generally held as a professional dogma; but, I apprehend rather as a matter of faith than of reason. I admit that I once embraced the same doctrine, but without examination, and I shall therefore state the arguments that impelled me to abandon it, with great respect for those by whom it is still maintained. . . .

. . .The Constitution and the right of the legislature to pass the act, may be in collision; but is that a legitimate subject for judicial determination? If it be, the judiciary must be a peculiar organ, to revise the proceedings of the legislature, and to correct its mistakes; and in what part of the Constitution are we to look for this proud preeminence? Viewing the matter in the opposite direction, what would be thought of an act of assembly in which it should be declared that the Supreme Court had, in a particular case, put a wrong construction on the Constitution of the United States, and that the judgment should therefore be reversed? It would doubtless be thought a usurpation of judicial power. But it is by no means clear, that to declare a law void which has been enacted according to the forms

prescribed in the Constitution, is not a usurpation of legislative power. . . .

. . . But it has been said to be emphatically the business of the judiciary, to ascertain and pronounce what the law is; and that this necessarily involves a consideration of the Constitution. It does so: but how far? If the judiciary will inquire into any thing beside the form of enactment, where shall it stop? There must be some point of limitation to such an inquiry; for no one will pretend that a judge would be justifiable in calling for the election returns, or scrutinizing the qualifications of those who composed the legislature. . . .

But the judges are sworn to support the Constitution, and are they not bound by it as the law of the land? In some respects they are. In the very few cases in which the judiciary, and not the legislature, is the immediate organ to execute its provisions, they are bound by it in preference to any act of assembly to the contrary. In such cases, the Constitution is a rule to the courts. But what I have in view in this inquiry, is the supposed right of the judiciary, to interfere, in cases where the Constitution is to be carried into effect through the instrumentality of the legislature, and where that organ must necessarily first decide on the constitutionality of its own act. The oath to support the Constitution is not peculiar to the judges, but is taken indiscriminately by every officer of the government, and is designed rather as a test of the political principles of the man, than to bind the officer in the discharge of his duty; otherwise it were difficult to determine what operation it is to have in the case of a recorder of deeds, for instance, who, in the execution of his office, has nothing to do with the Constitution. But granting it to relate to the official conduct of the judge, as well as every other officer, and not to his political principles, still it must be understood in reference to supporting the Constitution, only as far as that may be involved in his official duty; and consequently, if his official duty does not comprehend an inquiry into the authority of the legislature, neither does his oath. . . .

But do not the judges do a positive act in violation of the Constitution, when they give effect to an unconstitutional law? Not if the law has been passed according to the forms established in the Constitution. The fallacy of the question is in supposing that the judiciary adopts the acts of the legislature as its own; whereas the enactment of a law and the interpretation of it are not concurrent acts, and as the judiciary is not required to concur in the enactment, neither is it in the breach of the Constitution which may be the consequence of the enactment; the fault is imputable to the legislature, and on it the responsibility exclusively rests. In this respect, the judges are in the predicament of jurors who are bound to serve in capital cases, although unable, under any circumstance, to reconcile it to their duty to deprive a human being of life. To one of these, who applied to be discharged from the panel, I once heard it remarked, by an eminent and humane judge, "You do not deprive a prisoner of life by finding him guilty of a capital crime; you but pronounce his case to be within the law, and it is, therefore, those who declare the law, and not you, who deprive him of life."

. . . But it has been said that this construction would deprive the citizen of the advantages which are peculiar to written constitution, by at once declaring the power of the legislature, in practice, to be illimitable. I ask, what are those advantages? The principles of a written constitution are more fixed and certain, and more apparent to the apprehension of the people than principles which depend on tradition and the vague comprehension of the individuals who compose the nation, and who cannot all be expected to receive the same impressions or entertain the same notions on any given subject. But there is no magic or inherent power in parchment and ink, to command respect and protect principles from violation. In the business of government, a recurrence to first principles answers the end of an observation at sea with a view to correct the dead reckoning; and, for this purpose, a written constitution is an instrument of inestimable value. It is of inestimable value, also, in rendering its principles familiar to the mass of the people; for, after all, there is no effectual guard against legislative usurpation but public opinion, the force of which, in this country, is inconceiv-

ably great. Happily this is proved, by experience, to be a sufficient guard against palpable infractions. The Constitution of this state has withstood the shocks of strong party excitement for thirty years, during which no act of the legislature has been declared unconstitutional, although the judiciary has constantly asserted a right to do so in clear cases. But it would be absurd to say, that this remarkable observance of the Constitution has been produced, not by the responsibility of the legislature to the people, but by an apprehension of control by the judiciary. Once let public opinion be so corrupt as to sanction every misconstruction of the Constitution and abuse of power which the temptation of the moment may dictate, and the party which may happen to be predominant, will laugh at the puny effort of a dependent power to arrest it in its course.

For these reasons, I am of the opinion that it rests with the people, in whom full and absolute sovereign power resides to correct abuses in legislation, by instructing their representatives to repeal the obnoxious act. What is wanting to plenary power in the government, is reserved by the people for their own immediate use; and to redress an infringement of their rights in this respect, would seem to be an accessory of the power thus reserved. It might, perhaps, have been better to vest the power in the judiciary; as it might be expected that its habits of deliberation, and the aid derived from the arguments of counsel, would more frequently lead to accurate conclusions. On the other hand, the judiciary is not infallible; and an error by it would admit of no remedy but a more distinct expression of the public will, through the extraordinary medium of a convention; whereas, an error by the legislature admits of a remedy by an exertion of the same will, in the ordinary exercise of the right of suffrage—a mode better calculated to attain the end, without popular excitement. It may be said, the people would probably not notice an error of their representatives. But they would as probably do so, as notice an error of the judiciary; and, beside, it is a postulate in the theory of our government, and the very basis of the superstructure, that the people are wise, virtuous, and competent to manage their own affairs; and if they are not so, in fact, still every question of this sort must be determined according to the principles of the Constitution, as it came from the hands of its framers, and the existence of a defect which was not foreseen, would not justify those who administer the government, in applying a corrective in practice, which can be provided only by a convention. . . .

Case

SCOTT V. SANDFORD

19 Howard (60 U.S.) 393; 15 L.Ed. 691 (1857)
Vote: 7–2

Dred Scott was a slave belonging to a surgeon in the U.S. Army. He was taken by his master into territories in which slavery was forbidden by the Missouri Compromise of 1820. Several years after his return to Missouri, Dred Scott brought suit to obtain his freedom, arguing that his temporary residence in a "free" territory had abolished his servitude. After an adverse ruling in the U.S. Circuit Court, Scott took the case to the Supreme Court on a writ of error.

The U.S. Supreme Court first heard oral arguments in Scott v. Sandford in February 1856. By this time, the case had achieved notoriety in the stormy sectional controversy over slavery. Reluctant to announce its decision during what promised to be a bitterly fought presidential election campaign, the Court ordered that the case be reargued at the beginning of its next term, in December 1856. One of the most controversial questions addressed on reargument was whether Congress had acted constitutionally in passing the Missouri Compromise of 1820, thereby asserting the power to regulate slavery in the territories. President-Elect James Buchanan, whose position on the territorial issue had been equivocal, stated that the "great object" of his administration would be "to destroy the dangerous slavery agitation and thus restore peace to our distracted country." He ardently hoped that through its anticipated decision in the Dred Scott case, the Supreme Court would help him achieve this objective.

Acting on this hope, Buchanan wrote his old friend, Justice John Catron, on February 3, 1857, wanting to know whether the Court would deliver its decision before March 4, Inauguration Day, so that he could take it into account in preparing his inaugural address. In responding to this highly unusual inquiry, Catron said that the Court had not yet taken action on the case, but that he would try to obtain this information, since he believed Buchanan was entitled to it. Professor Don E. Fehrenbacher, in his authoritative study of the Dred Scott case (The Dred Scott Case: Its Significance in American Law and Politics), has argued convincingly that only a decision on the constitutionality of the Missouri Compromise would have been important to Buchanan in preparing his inauguration speech. On February 10, Catron wrote Buchanan, advising him that the case would be decided in conference on February 14 but that the justices probably would not rule on the power of Congress over slavery in the territories. This prediction seemed to be confirmed when the majority opinion was assigned to Justice Samuel Nelson, a northern centrist on the Taney Court. In his narrowly focused draft opinion, Nelson maintained that there was no need to consider the constitutionality of the Missouri Compromise's restriction on slavery in the territories. In a sudden about-face, a Court majority decided to take on the territorial issue as well as all other constitutional questions raised in the case. The formidable task of writing a new majority opinion was assigned to Chief Justice Taney. On February 19, Catron again wrote to Buchanan, informing him of the dramatic change in the Court's plans and suggesting that Buchanan's inaugural address might include a passage leaving the territorial matter with the "appropriate tribunal" and declining to "express any opinion on the subject." In the same letter, Catron urged Buchanan to help persuade his fellow Pennsylvanian, Justice Robert C. Grier, to support the broad approach taken by Taney and his four southern colleagues. Buchanan immediately wrote to Grier urging him to fall into line. Grier then conferred with Taney and wrote to Buchanan on February 23, indicating that he would support Taney's opinion, which would hold the Missouri Compromise "to be of non-effect." He and his colleague Justice James M. Wayne would try "to get Brothers Daniel and Campbell and Catron to do the same." After informing Buchanan that the decision would not be delivered before March 6, Grier concluded his lengthy letter with the following revealing comments: "We will not let any others of our brethren know anything about the cause of our anxiety to produce this result [a majority opinion supported by six or possibly seven justices], and though contrary to our usual practice, we have thought due to you to state to you in candor and confidence the real state of the matter." It is clear from this selective summary of events leading up to Buchanan's inauguration, that the president-elect was fully informed by two members of the Supreme Court—each initially unaware of the other's actions—of the substance of the forthcoming Dred Scott decision.

On March 4, 1857, Chief Justice Taney administered the oath of office to President-Elect Buchanan. During a pause in the ceremonies, the two men had a brief conversation, a fact accorded grave significance by some of Buchanan's critics as they listened to his inaugural address. He noted with approval that Congress, through the Kansas-Nebraska Act, had left the people free to deal with the institution of slavery as they saw fit, subject only to the Constitution. Admittedly, a minor problem remained unresolved: "A difference of opinion has arisen in regard to the point of time when the people of a territory shall decide this question for themselves. This is, happily, a matter *of but little practical importance. Besides, it is a judicial question which legitimately belongs to the Supreme Court of the United States, before whom it is now pending, and will, it is understood, be speedily and finally settled. To their decision, in common with all good citizens, I shall cheerfully submit, whatever this may be." A more disingenuous statement has seldom appeared in an inaugural address. Buchanan not only knew what the Court was about to decide in the Dred Scott case, but it is fair to say that he had a hand in forging the Court majority that endorsed that decision.*

Mr. Chief Justice Taney delivered the opinion of the Court.

. . . The question is simply this: Can a negro, whose ancestors were imported into this country, and sold as slaves, become a member of the political community formed and brought into existence by the Constitution of the United States, and as such become entitled to all the rights, and privileges, and immunities, guaranteed by that instrument to the citizen? One of which rights is the privilege of suing in a court of the United States in the cases specified in the Constitution. . . .

We think . . . [that Negroes] . . . are not included, and were not intended to be included, under the word "citizens" in the Constitution, and can therefore claim none of the rights and privileges which that instrument provides for and secures to citizens of the United States. On the contrary, they were at that time considered as a subordinate and inferior class of beings, who had been subjugated by the dominant race, and, whether emancipated or not, yet remained subject to their authority, and had no rights or privileges but such as those who held the power and the Government might choose to grant them.

It is not the province of the court to decide upon the justice or injustice, the policy or impolicy, of these laws. The decision of that question belonged to the political or law-making power; to those who formed the sovereignty and framed the Constitution. The duty of the court is, to interpret the instrument they have framed, with the best lights we can obtain on the subject, and to administer it as we find it, according to its true intent and meaning when it was adopted. . . .

The question then arises, whether the provisions of the Constitution, in relation to the personal rights and privileges to which the citizen of a State should be entitled, embraced the negro African race, at that time in this country, or who might afterwards be imported, who had then or should afterwards be made free in any State; and to put it in the power of a single State to make him a citizen of the United States, and endow him with the full rights of citizenship in every other State without their consent? Does the Constitution of the United States act upon him whenever he shall be made free under the laws of a State, and raised there to the rank of a citizen, and immediately clothe him with all the privileges of a citizen in every other State, and in its own courts?

The court thinks the affirmative of these propositions cannot be maintained. And if it cannot, the plaintiff in error could not be a citizen of the State of Missouri, within the meaning of the Constitution of the United States, and, consequently, was not entitled to sue in its courts. . . .

In the opinion of the court, the legislation and histories of the times, and the language used in the Declaration of Independence, show, that neither the class of persons who had been imported as slaves, nor their descendants, whether they had become free or not, were then acknowledged as a part of the people, nor intended to be included in the general words used in that memorable instrument. . . .

They had for more than a century before been regarded as beings of an inferior order, and altogether unfit to associate with the white race, either in social or political relations; and so far inferior, that they had no rights which the white man was bound to respect; and that the negro might justly and lawfully be reduced to slavery for his benefit. He was bought and sold, and treated as an ordinary article of merchandise and traffic, whenever a profit could be made by it. This opinion was at that time fixed and universal in the civilized portion of the white race. It was regarded as an axiom in morals as well as in politics, which no one thought of disputing, or supposed to be open to dispute; and men in every grade and position in society daily and habitually acted upon it in their private pursuits, as well as in matters of public concern, without doubting for a moment the correctness of this opinion. . . .

The only two provisions [of the Constitution] which point to them [slaves] and include them [Article I, Section 9, and Article IV, Section 2], treat them as property, and make it the duty of the Government to protect it; no other power, in relation to this race, is to be found in the Constitution; and as it is a Government of special, delegated, powers, no authority beyond these two provisions can be constitutionally exercised. The Government of the United States had no right to interfere for any other purpose but that of protecting the rights of the owner, leaving it altogether with the several States to deal with this race, whether emancipated or not, as each State may think justice, humanity, and the interests and safety of society, require. The States evidently intended to reserve this power exclusively to themselves.

No one, we presume, supposes that any change in public opinion or feeling, in relation to this unfortunate race, in the civilized nations of Europe or in this country, should induce the court to give to the words of the Constitution a more liberal construction in their favor than they were intended to bear when the instrument was framed and adopted. Such an argument would be altogether inadmissible in any tribunal called on to interpret it. If any of its provisions are deemed unjust, there is a mode prescribed in the instrument itself by which it may be amended; but while it remains unaltered, it must be construed now as it was understood at the time of its adoption. It is not only the same in words, but the same in meaning, and delegates the same powers to the Government, and reserves and secures the same rights and privileges to the citizen; and as long as it continues to exist in its present form, it speaks not only in the same words, but with the same meaning and intent with which it spoke when it came from the hands of its framers, and was voted on and adopted by the people of the United States. Any other rule of construction would abrogate the judicial character of this court, and make it the mere reflex of the popular opinion of the day. . . .

What the construction was at that time, we think can hardly admit of doubt. We have the language of the Declaration of Independence and of the Articles of Confederation, in addition to the plain words of the Constitution itself; we have the legislation of the different States, before, about the time, and since, the Constitution was adopted; we have the legislation of Congress, from the time of its adoption to a recent period; and we have the constant and uniform action of the Executive Department, all concurring together, and leading to the same result. And if anything in relation to the construction of the Constitution can be regarded as settled, it is that which we now give to the word "citizen" and the word "People." . . .

The act of Congress, upon which the plaintiff relies, declares that slavery and involuntary servitude, except as a punishment for crime, shall be forever prohibited in all that part of the territory ceded by France, under the name of Louisiana, which lies north of thirty-six degrees thirty minutes north latitude, and not included within the limits of Missouri. And the . . . inquiry is whether Congress was authorized to pass this law under any of the powers granted to it by the Constitution; for if the authority is not given by that instrument, it is the duty of this court to declare it void and inoperative, and incapable of conferring freedom upon any one who is held as a slave under the laws of any one of the States.

The counsel for the plaintiff has laid much stress upon that article in the Constitution which confers on Congress the power "to dispose of and make all needful rules and regulations respecting the territory or other property

belonging to the United States," but, in the judgment of the court, that provision has no bearing on the present controversy, and the power there given, whatever it may be, is confined, and was intended to be confined, to the territory which at that time belonged to, or was claimed by the United States, and was within their boundaries as settled by the treaty with Great Britain, and can have no influence upon a territory afterwards acquired from a foreign Government. It was a special provision for a known and particular territory, and to meet a present emergency, and nothing more.

. . . The powers of the Government and the rights and privileges of the citizen are regulated and plainly defined by the Constitution itself. And when the Territory becomes a part of the United States, the Federal Government enters into possession in the character impressed upon it by those who created it. It enters upon it with its powers over the citizen strictly defined, and limited by the Constitution, from which it derives its own existence, and by virtue of which alone it continues to exist and act as a Government and sovereignty. It has no power of any kind beyond it; and it cannot, when it enters a Territory of the United States, put off its character and assume discretionary or despotic powers which the Constitution has denied to it. It cannot create for itself a new character separated from the citizens of the United States, and the duties it owes them under the provisions of the Constitution. The Territory being a part of the United States, the Government and the citizen both enter it under the authority of the Constitution, with their respective rights defined and marked out; and the Federal Government can exercise no power over his person or property, beyond what that instrument confers, nor lawfully deny any right which it has reserved. . . .

. . . An Act of Congress which deprives a citizen of the United States of his liberty or property, merely because he came himself or brought his property into a particular Territory of the United States, and who had committed no offense against the laws, could hardly be dignified with the name of due process of law.

The powers over person and property of which we speak are not only not granted to Congress, but are in express terms denied, and they are forbidden to exercise them. And this prohibition is not confined to the States, but the words are general, and extend to the whole territory over which the Constitution gives it power to legislate, including those portions of it remaining under Territorial Government, as well as that covered by States. It is a total absence of power everywhere within the dominion of the United States, and places the citizens of a Territory, so far as these rights are concerned, on the same footing with citizens of the States and guards them as firmly and plainly against any inroads which the General Government might attempt, under the plea of implied or incidental powers. And if Congress itself cannot do this—if it is beyond the powers conferred on the Federal Government—it will be admitted, we presume, that it could not authorize a Territorial Government to exercise them. It would confer no power on any local Government, established by its authority, to violate provisions of the Constitution. . . .

Upon these considerations, it is the opinion of the court that the act of Congress which prohibited a citizen from holding and owning property of this kind in the territory of the United States north of the line therein mentioned, is not warranted by the Constitution, and is therefore void; and that neither Dred Scott himself, nor any of his family, were made free by being carried into this territory; even if they had been carried there by the owner, with the intention of becoming a permanent resident. . . .

Mr. Justice Curtis, joined by **Mr. Justice McLean,** dissenting.

I dissent from the opinion pronounced by the Chief Justice, and from the judgment which the majority of the court think it proper to render in this case. . . .

To determine whether any free persons, descended from Africans held in slavery, were citizens of the United States under the Confederation, and consequently at the time of the adoption of the Constitution of the United States, it is only necessary to know whether any such persons were citizens of either of the States under the Confederation, at the time of the adoption of the Constitution.

Of this there can be no doubt. At the time of the ratification of the Articles of Confederation, all free native-born inhabitants of the States of New Hampshire, Massachusetts, New York, New Jersey, and North Carolina, though descended from African slaves, were not only citizens of those States, but such of them as had the other necessary qualifications possessed the franchise of electors, on equal terms with other citizens. . . .

I dissent, therefore, from that part of the opinion of the majority of the court, in which it is held that a person of African descent cannot be a citizen of the United States; and I regret I must go further, and dissent both from what I deem their assumption of authority to examine the constitutionality of the act of Congress commonly called the Missouri Compromise act, and the grounds and conclusions announced in their opinion.

Having first decided that they were bound to consider the sufficiency of the plea to the jurisdiction of the Circuit Court, and having decided that this plea showed that the Circuit Court had no jurisdiction, and consequently that this is a case to which the judicial power of the United States does not extend, they have gone on to examine the merits of the case as they appear on the trial before the court and jury, on the issues joined on the pleas in bar, and so have reached the question of the power of Congress to pass the act of 1820. On so grave a subject as this, I feel obliged to say that, in my opinion, such an exertion of judicial power transcends the limits of the authority of the court. . . .

Case

Ex parte McCardle

7 Wall. (74 U.S.) 506; 19 L.Ed. 264 (1869)
Vote: 8–0

In the wake of the Civil War, Congress chose to rely on military rule as the most effective means to "reconstruct" the South. As part of this regime, the Reconstruction Acts authorized military commissions to try civilians who interfered with the program. William H. McCardle, editor of the Vicksburg Times, *published a series of editorials that was highly critical of Reconstruction and of the military government that ruled Mississippi. He was subsequently arrested and held for trial by a military commission on the charge of sedition. McCardle sought release* *by filing a habeas corpus petition in federal circuit court. Shortly before McCardle's case arose, the Congress had authorized the circuit courts to hear habeas corpus cases involving anyone held by state authorities in violation of the U.S. Constitution or federal statutes. The act included the right to appeal a circuit court denial of habeas corpus to the Supreme Court. McCardle lost his bid for release in the circuit court and exercised his option to appeal. After the case was argued in the Supreme Court, but before a decision on the constitutionality of the Reconstruction Acts was reached, the Congress amended the law to remove the Supreme Court's appellate jurisdiction in habeas corpus cases. Quite obviously, Congress was attempting to prevent the Supreme Court from ruling on the constitutionality of the Reconstruction Acts.*

Mr. Chief Justice Chase delivered the opinion of the Court.

This cause came here by appeal from the Circuit Court for the Southern District of Mississippi. A Petition for the writ of habeas corpus was preferred in that court by [McCardle], alleging unlawful restraint by military force. The writ was issued and a return was made by the military commander, admitting the restraint, but denying that it was unlawful.

It appeared that the petitioner was not in the military service of the United States, but was held in custody by military authority, for trial before a Military Commission, upon charges founded upon the publication of articles alleged to be incendiary and libelous, in a newspaper of which he was editor.

Upon the hearing, [McCardle] was remanded to military custody; but upon his prayer, an appeal was allowed him to this court, and upon filing the usual appeal bond for costs, he was admitted to bail. . . .

Subsequently, the case was argued very thoroughly and ably upon the merits, and was taken under advisement. While it was held, and before conference in regard to the decision proper to be made, an Act was passed by Congress, . . . returned, with objections by the President, and repassed by the constitutional majority, which, it is insisted, takes from this court jurisdiction of the appeal. The 2d section of this act was as follows:

> And be it further enacted, that so much of the Act approved February 5, 1867, . . . as authorized an appeal from the judgment of the circuit court to the Supreme Court of the United States, . . . is hereby repealed.

The attention of the court was directed to this statute at the last term, but counsel having expressed a desire to be heard in argument upon its effect, and the Chief Justice being detained from his place here by his duties in the Court of Impeachment, the cause was continued under advisement.

At this term we have heard arguments upon the effect of the repealing Act, and will now dispose of the case.

The first question necessarily is that of jurisdiction; for, if the Act . . . takes away the jurisdiction defined by the Act of February, 1867, it is useless, if not improper, to enter into any discussion of other questions.

It is quite true, as was argued by the counsel for [McCardle], that the appellate jurisdiction of this court is not derived from acts of Congress. It is, strictly speaking, conferred by the Constitution. But it is conferred "with such exceptions and under such regulations as Congress shall make.". . .

The exception to appellate jurisdiction in the case before us . . . is not an inference from the affirmation of other appellate jurisdiction. It is made in terms. The provision of the act of 1867, affirming the appellate jurisdiction of this court in cases of habeas corpus is expressly repealed. It is hardly possible to imagine a plainer instance of positive exception.

We are not at liberty to inquire into the motives of the legislature. We can only examine into its power under the Constitution; and the power to make exceptions to the appellate jurisdiction of this court is given by express words.

What, then, is the effect of the repealing act upon the case before us? We cannot doubt as to this. Without jurisdiction the court cannot proceed at all in any cause. Jurisdiction is power to declare the law, and when it ceases to exist, the only function remaining to the court is that of announcing the fact and dismissing the cause. And this is not less clear upon authority than upon principle.

Several cases were cited by the counsel for [McCardle] in support of the position that jurisdiction of this case is not affected by the repealing act. But none of them, in our judgment, afford any support to it. They are all cases of the exercise of judicial power by the legislature, or of legislative interference with courts in the exercising of continuing jurisdiction. . . .

On the other hand, the general rule, supported by the best elementary writers . . . is, that "when an act of the legislature is repealed, it must be considered, except as to transactions past and closed, as if it never existed." And the effect of repealing acts upon suits under acts repealed, has been determined by the adjudications of this court. . .

It is quite clear, therefore, that this court cannot proceed to pronounce judgment in this case, for it has no longer jurisdiction of the appeal; and judicial duty is not less fitly performed by declining ungranted jurisdiction than in exercising firmly that which the Constitution and the laws confer.

Counsel seem to have supposed, if effect be given to the repealing act in question, that the whole appellate power of the court, in cases of habeas corpus, is denied. But this is an error. The act of 1868 does not except from that jurisdiction any cases but appeals from Circuit Courts under the act of 1867. It does not affect the jurisdiction which was previously exercised. . . .

The appeal of [McCardle] must be dismissed for want of jurisdiction.

Case

COOPER V. AARON

358 U.S. 1; 78 S.Ct. 1401; 3 L.Ed. 2d 5 (1958)
Vote: 9–0

In this case the Supreme Court responds to the efforts of state officials to block the court-ordered desegregation of Central High School in Little Rock, Arkansas, in 1957.

Opinion of the Court by **The Chief Justice, Mr. Justice Black, Mr. Justice Frankfurter, Mr. Justice Douglas, Mr. Justice Burton, Mr. Justice Clark, Mr. Justice Harlan, Mr. Justice Brennan,** and **Mr. Justice Whittaker.**

As this case reaches us it raises questions of the highest importance to the maintenance of our federal system of government. It necessarily involves a claim by the Governor and Legislature of a State that there is no duty on state officials to obey federal court orders resting on this Court's considered interpretation of the United States Constitution. Specifically it involves actions by the Governor and Legislature of Arkansas upon the premise that they are not bound by our holding in *Brown v. Board of Education* [1954]. . . . That holding was that the Fourteenth Amendment forbids States to use their governmental powers to bar children on racial grounds from attending schools where there is state participation through any arrangement, management funds or property. We are urged to uphold a suspension of the Little Rock School Board's plan to do away with segregated public schools in Little Rock until state laws and efforts to upset and nullify our holding in *Brown v. Board of Education* have been further challenged and tested in the courts. We reject these contentions. . . .

While the School Board was . . . going forward with its preparation for desegregating the Little Rock school system, other state authorities, in contrast, were actively pursuing a program designed to perpetuate in Arkansas the system of racial segregation which this Court had held violated the Fourteenth Amendment. . . .

The School Board and the Superintendent of Schools nevertheless continued with preparations to carry out the first stage of the desegregation program. Nine Negro children were scheduled for admission in September 1957 to Central High School. . . .

On September 2, 1957, the day before these Negro students were to enter Central High, the school authorities were met with drastic opposing action on the part of the Governor of Arkansas who dispatched units of the Arkansas National Guard to the Central High school grounds and placed the school "off limits" to colored students. As found by the District Court in subsequent proceedings, the Governor's action had not been requested by the school authorities, and was entirely unheralded. . . .

The Governor's action caused the School Board to request the Negro students on September 2 not to attend the high school "until the legal dilemma was solved." The next day, September 3, 1957, the Board petitioned the District Court for instructions, and the court, after a hearing, found that the Board's request of the Negro students to stay away from the high school had been made because of the stationing of the military guards by the state authorities. The court determined that this was not a reason for departing from the approved plan, and ordered the School Board and Superintendent to proceed with it.

On the morning of the next day, September 4, 1957, the Negro children attempted to enter the high school but . . . [the] National Guard "acting pursuant to the Governor's order, stood shoulder to shoulder at the school grounds and thereby forcibly prevented the 9 Negro students . . . from entering," as they continued to do every school day during the following three weeks. . . .

. . . After hearings, . . . the District Court found that the School Board's plan had been obstructed by the Governor through the use of National Guard troops, and granted a preliminary injunction . . . enjoining the Governor and the officers of the Guard from preventing the attendance of Negro children at Central High School, and from otherwise obstructing or interfering with the orders of the court in connection with the plan. . . . The National Guard was then withdrawn from the school.

The next school day was Monday, September 23, 1957. The Negro children entered the high school that morning under the protection of the Little Rock Police Department and members of the Arkansas State Police. But the officers caused the children to be removed from the school during the morning because they had difficulty controlling a large and demonstrating crowd which had gathered at the high school. . . . On September 25, however, the President of the United States dispatched federal troops to Central High School and admission of the Negro students to the school was thereby effected. . . .

We come now to the aspect of the proceedings presently before us. . . . [T]he School Board and the Superintendent of Schools filed a petition in the District Court seeking a postponement of their program for desegregation. Their position in essence was that because of extreme public hostility, which they stated had been engendered largely by the official attitudes and actions of the Governor and the Legislature, the maintenance of a sound educational program at Central High School, with the Negro students in attendance, would be impossible. The Board therefore proposed that the Negro students already admitted to the school be withdrawn and sent to segregated schools, and that all further steps to carry out the Board's desegregation program be postponed for a period later suggested by the Board to be two and one-half years. . . .

One may well sympathize with the position of the Board in the face of the frustrating conditions which have confronted it, but, regardless of the Board's good faith, the actions of the other state agencies responsible for those conditions compel us to reject the Board's legal position. Had Central High School been under the direct management of the State itself, it could hardly be suggested that those immediately in charge of the school should be heard to assert their own good faith as a legal excuse for delay in implementing the constitutional rights of these respondents, when vindication of those rights were rendered difficult or impossible by the actions of other state officials. The situation here is in no different posture because the members of the School Board and the Superintendent of Schools are local officials; from the point of view of the Fourteenth Amendment, they stand in this litigation as the agents of the State.

The constitutional rights of respondents are not to be sacrificed or yielded to the violence and disorder which have followed upon the actions of the Governor and Legislature. . . . Thus law and order are not here to be preserved by depriving the Negro children of their constitutional rights. The record before us clearly established that the growth of the Board's difficulties to a magnitude beyond its unaided power to control is the product of state action. . . .

The controlling legal principles are plain. The command of the Fourteenth Amendment is that no "State" shall deny to any person within its jurisdiction the equal protection of the laws. . . . [T]he prohibitions of the Fourteenth Amendment extend to all actions of the State denying equal protection of the laws; whatever the agency of the State taking the action. . . . In short, the constitutional rights of children not to be discriminated against in school admission on grounds of race or color declared by this Court in the Brown case can neither be nullified openly and directly by state legislators or state executive or judicial officers, nor nullified indirectly by them through evasive schemes for segregation whether attempted "ingeniously or ingenuously." . . .

What has been said, in the light of the facts developed, is enough to dispose of the case. However, we should answer the premise of the actions of the Governor and Legislature that they are not bound by our holding in the Brown case. It is necessary only to recall some basic constitutional propositions which are settled doctrine.

Article 6 of the Constitution makes the Constitution the "supreme Law of the Land." . . . Chief Justice Marshall . . . declared in *Marbury v. Madison*: . . . "It is emphatically the province and duty of the judicial department to say what the law is." This decision declared the basic principle that the federal judiciary is supreme in the exposition of the law of the Constitution, and that principle has ever since been respected by this Court and the Country as a permanent and indispensable feature of our constitutional system. It follows that the interpretation of the Fourteenth Amendment enunciated by this Court in the Brown Case is the supreme law of the land, and Art 6 of the Constitution makes it of binding effect on the States "any Thing in the Constitution or Laws of any State to the Contrary notwithstanding." Every state legislator and executive and judicial officer is solemnly committed by oath taken pursuant to Art 6, cl 3, "to support this Constitution." . . .

No state legislator or executive or judicial officer can war against the Constitution without violating his undertaking to support it. Chief Justice Marshall spoke for a unanimous Court in saying that: "If the legislatures of the several states may, at will, annul the judgments of the courts of the United States, and destroy the rights acquired under those judgments, the Constitution itself becomes a solemn mockery. . . ." . . . A Governor who asserts a power to nullify a federal court order is similarly restrained. . . .

It is, of course, quite true that the responsibility for public education is primarily the concern of the States, but it is equally true that such responsibilities, like all other state activity, must be exercised consistently with federal constitutional requirements as they apply to state action. . . . State support of segregated schools through any arrangement, management, funds, or property cannot be squared with the Amendment's command that no State shall deny to any person within its jurisdiction the equal protection of the laws. . . . The basic decision in Brown was unanimously reached by this Court. . . . Since the first Brown opinion three new Justices have come to the Court. They are at one with the Justices still on the Court who participated in that basic decision as to its correctness, and that decision is now unanimously reaffirmed. The principles announced in that decision and the obedience of the States to them, according to the command of the Constitution, are indispensable for the protection of the freedoms guaranteed by our fundamental charter for all of us. Our constitutional ideal of equal justice under law is thus made a living truth.

Mr. Justice Frankfurter, concurring. . . .

Case

BAKER V. CARR

369 U.S. 186; 82 S.Ct. 691; 7 L.Ed. 2d 663 (1962)
Vote: 6–2

The term "apportionment" refers to the way in which legislative districts are drawn. Malapportionment exists to the extent that numbers of voters are unequal across legislative districts. In a malapportioned system, voters in the more populous districts are underrepresented, while voters in the less populous districts are overrepresented in the legislature (see Chapter 13 for a discussion of the apportionment issue). In the middle of the twentieth century, critics of malapportionment turned to the courts for relief. In Colegrove v. Green *(1946) the Supreme Court dismissed a lawsuit directed against the malapportionment of congressional districts in Illinois. In his plurality opinion, Justice Felix Frankfurter argued that "due regard for the Constitution as a viable system precludes judicial correction" of the problem. In Frankfurter's view, "[t]he remedy for unfairness in districting is to secure State legislatures that will apportion properly, or to invoke the ample powers of Congress." In what became the most frequently quoted language from the opinion, Frankfurter admonished courts not to enter the "political thicket" of reapportionment. Sixteen years after* Colegrove v. Green, *the Supreme Court reconsidered Justice Frankfurter's admonition in the landmark case of* Baker v. Carr. *The case began when voters residing in Chattanooga, Knoxville, Memphis, and Nashville brought a federal class action challenging the apportionment of the Tennessee General Assembly. The general assembly had not been reapportioned since 1901 and, as a result of population growth in the cities, had become badly malapportioned. Plaintiffs argued that they were being "denied the equal protection of the laws accorded them by the Fourteenth Amendment . . . by virtue of the debasement of their votes." As expected, the federal district court dismissed the case on the authority of* Colegrove v. Green. *The plaintiffs appealed.*

Mr. Justice Brennan delivered the opinion of the Court.

. . . [Baker et al.] seek relief in order to protect or vindicate an interest of their own, and of those similarly situated. Their constitutional claim is, in substance, that the 1901 [Tennessee apportionment] statute constitutes arbitrary and capricious state action, offensive to the Fourteenth Amendment in its irrational disregard of the standard of apportionment prescribed by the State's Constitution or of any standard, effecting a gross disproportion of representation to voting population. The injury which appellants assert is that this classification disfavors the voters in the counties in which they reside, placing them in a position of constitutionally unjustifiable inequality vis-à-vis voters in irrationally favored counties. . . .

In holding that the subject matter of this suit was not justiciable, the District Court relied on *Colegrove v. Green* . . . . We understand the District Court to have read the . . . case as compelling the conclusion that since [Baker] sought to have a legislative apportionment held unconstitutional, [his] suit presented a "political question" and was therefore nonjusticiable. We hold that this challenge to an apportionment presents no nonjusticiable "political question." . . .

We have said that "In determining whether a question falls within [the political question] category, the appropriateness under our system of government of attributing finality to the action of the political departments and also the lack of satisfactory criteria for a judicial determination are dominant considerations.". . . The nonjusticiability of a political question is primarily a function of the separation of powers. Much confusion results from the capacity of the "political question" label to obscure the need for case-by-case inquiry. Deciding whether a matter has in any measure been committed by the Constitution to another branch of government, or whether the action of that branch exceeds whatever authority has been committed, is itself a delicate exercise in constitutional interpretation, and is a responsibility of this Court as ultimate interpreter of the Constitution. To demonstrate this requires no less than to analyze representative cases and to infer from them the analytical threads that make up the political question doctrine. We shall then show that none of those threads catches this case.

[Justice Brennan discusses several categories of cases in which the Court has labeled particular controversies as "political." He concludes:]

It is apparent that several formulations which vary slightly according to the settings in which the questions arise may describe a political question, although each has one or more elements which identify it as essentially a function of the separation of powers. Prominent on the surface of any case held to involve a political question is found a textually demonstrable constitutional commitment of the issue to a coordinate political department; or a lack of judicially discoverable and manageable standards for resolving it; or the impossibility of deciding without an initial policy determination of a kind clearly for nonjudicial discretion; or the impossibility of a court's undertaking independent resolution without expressing lack of the respect due coordinate branches of government; or an unusual need for unquestioning adherence to a political decision already made; or the potentiality of embarrassment from multifarious pronouncements by various departments on one question.

Unless one of these formulations is inextricable from the case at bar there should be no dismissal for nonjusticiability on the ground of a political question's presence. The doctrine of which we treat is one of "political questions," not one of "political cases." The courts cannot reject as "no law suit" a bona fide controversy as to whether some action denominated "political" exceeds constitutional authority. The cases we have reviewed show the necessity for discriminating inquiry into the precise facts and posture of the particular case, and the impossibility of resolution by any semantic cataloguing. . . .

We come, finally, to the ultimate inquiry whether our precedents as to what constitutes a nonjusticiable "political question" bring the case before us under the umbrella of that doctrine. A natural beginning is to note whether any of the common characteristics which we have been able to identify and label descriptively are present. We find none: The question here is the consistency of state action with the Federal Constitution. We have no question decided, or to be decided, by a political branch of government coequal with this Court. Nor do we risk embarrassment of our government abroad, or grave disturbance at home if we take issue with Tennessee as to the constitutionality of her action here challenged. Nor need [Baker], in order to succeed in this action, ask the Court to enter upon policy determinations for which judicially manageable standards are lacking. Judicial standards under the Equal Protection Clause are well developed and familiar, and it has been open to courts since the enactment of the Fourteenth Amendment to determine, if on the particular facts they must, that a discrimination reflects no policy, but simply arbitrary and capricious action.

This case does, in one sense, involve the allocation of political power within a State, and [Baker] might conceivably have added a claim under the Guaranty Clause. Of course, as we have seen, any reliance on that clause would be futile. But because my reliance on the Guaranty Clause could not have succeeded it does not follow that [Baker] may not be heard on the equal protection claim which in fact [he tenders]. True, it must be clear that the Fourteenth Amendment claim is not so enmeshed with those political question elements which render Guaranty Clause claims nonjusticiable as actually to present a political question itself. But we have found that not to be the case here. . . .

. . . [I]n *Gomillion v. Lightfoot* [1960] . . . we applied the Fifteenth Amendment to strike down a redrafting of municipal boundaries which effected a discriminatory impairment of voting rights, in face of what a majority of the Court of Appeals thought to be a sweeping commitment to state legislatures of the power to draw and redraw such boundaries. . . .

. . . [To the argument] that *Colegrove v. Green* . . . was a barrier to hearing the merits of the case, the Court responded that *Gomillion* was lifted "out of the so-called 'political' arena and into the conventional sphere of constitutional litigation" because here was discriminatory treatment of a racial minority violating the Fifteenth Amendment. . . .

We conclude that the complaint's allegations of a denial of equal protection present a justiciable constitutional cause of action upon which [Baker is] entitled to a trial and a decision. The right asserted is within the reach of judicial protection under the Fourteenth Amendment.

The judgment of the District Court is reversed and the Cause is remanded for further proceedings consistent with this opinion.

Reversed and remanded.

Mr. Justice Whittaker did not participate in the decision of this case.

Mr. Justice Douglas, concurring. . . .

Mr. Justice Clark, concurring. . . .

Mr. Justice Stewart, concurring. . . .

Mr. Justice Frankfurter, whom ***Mr. Justice Harlan*** joins, dissenting.

The Court today reverses a uniform course of decision established by a dozen cases. . . . The impressive body of rulings thus cast aside reflected the equally uniform course of our political history regarding the relationship between population and legislative representation—a wholly different matter from denial of the franchise to individuals because of race, color, religion, or sex. Such a massive repudiation of the experience of our whole past in asserting destructively novel judicial power demands a detailed analysis of the role of this Court in our constitutional scheme. Disregard of inherent limits in the effective exercise of the Court's "judicial Power" not only presages the futility of judicial intervention in the essentially political conflict of forces by which the relation between population and representation has time out of mind been and now is determined. It may well impair the Court's position as the ultimate organ of "the supreme Law of the Land" in that vast range of legal problems, often strongly entangled in popular feeling, on which this Court must pronounce. The Court's authority—possessed of neither the purse nor the sword—ultimately rests on sustained public confidence in its moral sanction. Such feeling must be nourished by the Court's complete detachment, in fact and in appearance, from political entanglements and by abstention from injecting itself into the clash of political forces in political settlements. . . .

The *Colegrove* doctrine, in the form in which repeated decisions have settled it, was not an innovation. It represents long judicial thought and experience. From its earliest opinions this Court has consistently recognized a class of controversies which do not lend themselves to judicial standards and judicial remedies. To classify the various instances as "political questions" is rather a form of stating this conclusion than revealing of analysis. . . .

Dissenting opinion of **Mr. Justice Harlan,** whom **Mr. Justice Frankfurter** joins. . . .

Case

RAINES V. BYRD

521 U.S. 811;117 S.Ct. 2312; 138 L.Ed. 2d 849 (1997)
Vote: 7–2

In 1996 Congress adopted legislation giving the president of the United States line-item veto authority (see Chapter 3 for further discussion). Six members of Congress (four senators, two representatives) who voted against the bill brought suit to challenge its constitutionality. In April 1997, the U.S. District Court for the District of Columbia declared the Line-Item Veto Act unconstitutional. The Supreme Court took the case pursuant to a provision of the act allowing for expedited direct appeal.

Chief Justice Rehnquist delivered the Opinion of the Court.

. . . Under Article III, § 2 of the Constitution, the federal courts have jurisdiction over this dispute between appellants and appellees only if it is a "case" or "controversy." This is a "bedrock requirement." . . .

One element of the case or controversy requirement is that appellees, based on their complaint, must establish that they have standing to sue. . . . The standing inquiry focuses on whether the plaintiff is the proper party to bring this suit, . . . although that inquiry "often turns on the nature and source of the claim asserted." . . . To meet the standing requirements of Article III, "[a] plaintiff must allege personal injury fairly traceable to the defendant's allegedly unlawful conduct and likely to be redressed by the requested relief." . . . We have consistently stressed that a plaintiff's complaint must establish that he has a "personal stake" in the alleged dispute, and that the alleged injury suffered is particularized as to him. . . .

We have also stressed that the alleged injury must be legally and judicially cognizable. This requires, among other things, that the plaintiff have suffered "an invasion of a legally protected interest which is . . . concrete and particularized," . . . and that the dispute is "traditionally thought to be capable of resolution through the judicial process." . . .

We have always insisted on strict compliance with this jurisdictional standing requirement. . . . And our standing inquiry has been especially rigorous when reaching the merits of the dispute would force us to decide whether an action taken by one of the other two branches of the Federal Government was unconstitutional. . . . In the light of this overriding and time honored concern about keeping the Judiciary's power within its proper constitutional sphere, we must put aside the natural urge to proceed directly to the merits of this important dispute and to "settle" it for the sake of convenience and efficiency. Instead, we must carefully inquire as to whether appellees have met their burden of establishing that their claimed injury is personal, particularized, concrete, and otherwise judicially cognizable.

We have never had occasion to rule on the question of legislative standing presented here. In *Powell v. McCormack* . . . (1969), we held that a Member of Congress' constitutional challenge to his exclusion from the House of Representatives (and his consequent loss of salary) presented an Article III case or controversy. But *Powell* does not help appellees. First, appellees have not been singled out for specially unfavorable treatment as opposed to other Members of their respective bodies. Their claim is that the Act causes a type of institutional injury (the diminution of legislative power), which necessarily damages all Members of Congress and both Houses of Congress equally. . . . Second, appellees do not claim that they have been deprived of something to which they personally are entitled—such as their seats as Members of Congress after their constituents had elected them. Rather, appellees' claim of standing is based on a loss of political power, not loss of any private right, which would make the injury more concrete. . . .

The one case in which we have upheld standing for legislators (albeit state legislators) claiming an institutional injury is *Coleman v. Miller* . . . (1939). Appellees, relying heavily on this case, claim that they, like the state legislators in *Coleman*, "have a plain, direct and adequate interest in maintaining the effectiveness of their votes," . . . sufficient to establish standing. In *Coleman*, 20 of Kansas' 40 State Senators voted not to ratify the proposed "Child Labor Amendment" to the Federal Constitution. With the vote deadlocked 20–20, the amendment ordinarily would not have been ratified. However, the State's Lieutenant Governor, the presiding officer of the State Senate, cast a deciding vote in favor of the amendment, and it was deemed ratified (after the State House of Representatives voted to ratify it). The 20 State Senators who had voted against the amendment, joined by a 21st State Senator and three State House Members, filed an action in the Kansas Supreme Court seeking a writ of mandamus that would compel the appropriate state officials to recognize that the legislature had not in fact ratified the amendment. That court held that the members of the legislature had standing to bring their mandamus action, but ruled against them on the merits. . . .

This Court affirmed. By a vote of 5–4, we held that the members of the legislature had standing. In explaining our holding, we repeatedly emphasized that if these legislators (who were suing as a bloc) were correct on the merits, then their votes not to ratify the amendment were deprived of all validity. . . .

It is obvious, then, that our holding in *Coleman* stands . . . for the proposition that legislators whose votes would have been sufficient to defeat (or enact) a specific legislative act have standing to sue if that legislative action goes into effect (or does not go into effect), on the ground that their votes have been completely nullified.

It should be equally obvious that appellees' claim does not fall within our holding in *Coleman*, as thus understood. They have not alleged that they voted for a specific bill, that there were sufficient votes to pass the bill, and that the bill was nonetheless deemed defeated. In the vote on the Line Item Veto Act, their votes were given full effect. They simply lost that vote. Nor can they allege that the Act will nullify their votes in the future in the same way that the votes of the *Coleman* legislators had been nullified. In the future, a majority of Senators and Congressmen can pass or reject appropriations bills; the Act has no effect on this process. In addition, a majority of Senators and Congressmen can vote to repeal the Act, or to exempt a given appropriations bill (or a given provision in an appropriations bill) from the Act; again, the Act has no effect on this process. *Coleman* thus provides little meaningful precedent for appellees' argument. . . .

Not only do appellees lack support from precedent, but historical practice appears to cut against them as well. It is evident from several episodes in our history that in analogous confrontations between one or both Houses of Congress and the Executive Branch, no suit was brought on the basis of claimed injury to official authority or power. The Tenure of Office Act, passed by Congress over the veto of President Andrew Johnson in 1867, was a thorn in the side of succeeding Presidents until it was finally repealed at the behest of President Grover Cleveland in 1887. . . . It provided that an official whose appointment to an Executive Branch office required confirmation by the Senate could not be removed without the consent of the Senate. . . . In 1868, Johnson removed his Secretary of War, Edwin M. Stanton. Within a week, the House of Representatives impeached Johnson. . . . One of the principal charges against him was that his removal of Stanton violated the Tenure of Office Act. . . . At the conclusion of his trial before the Senate, Johnson was acquitted by one vote. . . . Surely Johnson had a stronger claim of diminution of his official power as a result of the Tenure of Office Act than do the appellees in the present case. Indeed, if their claim were sustained, it would appear that President Johnson would have had standing to challenge the Tenure of Office Act before he ever thought about firing a cabinet member, simply on the grounds that it altered the calculus by which he would nominate someone to his cabinet. Yet if the federal courts had entertained an action to adjudicate the constitutionality of the Tenure of Office Act immediately after its passage in 1867, they would have been improperly and unnecessarily plunged into the bitter political battle being waged between the President and Congress. . . .

In sum, appellees have alleged no injury to themselves as individuals . . . , the institutional injury they allege is wholly abstract and widely dispersed . . . , and their attempt to litigate this dispute at this time and in this form is contrary to historical experience. We attach some importance to the fact that appellees have not been authorized to represent their respective Houses of Congress in this action, and indeed both Houses actively oppose their suit. . . . We also note that our conclusion neither deprives Members of Congress of an adequate remedy (since they may repeal the Act or exempt appropriations bills from its reach), nor forecloses the Act from constitutional challenge (by someone who suffers judicially cognizable injury as a result of the Act). Whether the case would be different if any of these circumstances were different we need not now decide.

We therefore hold that these individual members of Congress do not have a sufficient "personal stake" in this dispute and have not alleged a sufficiently concrete injury to have established Article III standing. The judgment of the District Court is vacated, and the case is remanded with instructions to dismiss the complaint. . . .

Justice Souter, concurring in the judgment, with whom *Justice Ginsburg* joins, concurring. . . .

Justice Stevens, dissenting.

The Line Item Veto Act purports to establish a procedure for the creation of laws that are truncated versions of bills that have been passed by the Congress and presented to the President for signature. If the procedure were valid, it would deny every Senator and every Representative any opportunity to vote for or against the truncated measure that survives the exercise of the President's cancellation authority. Because the opportunity to cast such votes is a right guaranteed by the text of the Constitution, I think it clear that the persons who are deprived of that right by the Act have standing to challenge its constitutionality. Moreover, because the impairment of that constitutional right has an immediate impact on their official powers, in my judgment they need not wait until after the President has exercised his cancellation authority to bring suit. Finally, the same reason that the respondents have standing provides a sufficient basis for concluding that the statute is unconstitutional. . . .

. . . .[T]he appellees convincingly explain how the immediate, constant threat of the partial veto power has a palpable effect on their current legislative choices. . . . Because the Act has this immediate and important impact on the powers of Members of Congress, and on the manner in which they undertake their legislative responsibilities, they need not await an exercise of the President's cancellation authority to institute the litigation that the statute itself authorizes. . . .

Given the fact that the authority at stake is granted by the plain and unambiguous text of Article I, it is equally clear to me that the statutory attempt to eliminate it is invalid.

Accordingly, I would affirm the judgment of the District Court.

Justice Breyer, dissenting.

. . . In sum, I do not believe that the Court can find this case nonjusticiable without overruling *Coleman.* Since it does not do so, I need not decide whether the systematic nature, seriousness, and immediacy of the harm would make this dispute constitutionally justiciable even in *Coleman's* absence. Rather, I can and would find this case justiciable on *Coleman's* authority. I add that because the majority has decided that this dispute is not now justiciable and has expressed no view on the merits of the appeal, I shall not discuss the merits either, but reserve them for future argument.

2 CONGRESS AND THE DEVELOPMENT OF NATIONAL POWER

"In republican government, the legislative authority necessarily predominates. The remedy for this inconvenience is to divide the legislature into different branches; and to render them by different modes of election, and different principles of action, as little connected with each other, as the nature of their common functions, and their common dependence on the society will admit. It may even be necessary to guard against dangerous encroachments, by still further precautions."

—JAMES MADISON, *THE FEDERALIST*, No. 51

James Madison: The principal architect of the Constitution

INTRODUCTION

The first three articles of the Constitution are known as the **distributive articles**, because they deal with the three branches of the national government and distribute powers among them. It is no accident that the first article deals with Congress, because the legislature is the most basic institution of republican government. Under the Articles of Confederation, the national government consisted exclusively of the Congress and a few administrators. There was no executive branch and no system of federal courts. Thus it is not surprising that the Framers of the Constitution placed the legislative article before the articles dealing with the executive and judicial branches.

Over the years, as government at all levels has expanded in size and responsibility, the power of the executive and judicial branches has grown more dramatically than that of Congress. In attempting to address ever more complicated social and economic problems, Congress has created and delegated extensive authority to numerous administrative and regulatory agencies. As a result of this transformation of American government, Congress, once recognized as preeminent, now shares essentially coequal status with the presidency and the judiciary. Indeed, many observers would contend that today all three constitutional branches of the national government are overmatched by a mammoth bureaucracy that has emerged as a virtual fourth branch of government. (Constitutional issues relative to the bureaucracy are addressed in Chapter 4.) Nevertheless, Congress, through its vast legislative powers, has been dominant in establishing and defining the authority of executive departments, federal courts, and regulatory agencies. It also continues to play a key role in the formulation of public policy. Accordingly, the legislative branch merits primary attention in any study of constitutional law.

STRUCTURAL ASPECTS OF CONGRESS

Article I, Section 1, of the Constitution states: "All legislative Powers herein granted shall be vested in a Congress of the United States, which shall consist of a Senate and a House of Representatives." Article I delineates the composition of both houses of Congress, indicates minimal requirements for members, specifies how members are to be chosen, grants broad authority to each house to determine its own procedures, and extends certain privileges to members of Congress. Article I also defines the legislative powers of Congress, although grants of congressional authority are also found elsewhere in the Constitution.

Bicameralism

The most fundamental change in the institution of Congress brought about by the Constitution was to make it a bicameral, or two-house, body. Under the Articles of Confederation, the Congress was unicameral and each state delegation had only one vote. During the Constitutional Convention of 1787, there was near unanimity on the need for a bicameral Congress, although delegates were divided over the mechanisms of representation in the two houses. Eventually, they compromised on a plan calling for popular election of the members of the House and election of senators by the state legislatures. This plan remained in effect until 1913, when the Seventeenth Amendment was ratified, instituting direct popular election of senators.

Under the Constitution, each state is represented in the Senate by two senators. Thus the size of the Senate has grown from 26 members (two from each of the thirteen original states) to 100 members today. Each state, regardless of its population, is entitled to at least one representative in the House. Beyond this threshold level of representation, House seats are allocated among the states on the basis of population. Members of the House are elected from districts within their respective states. Originally, the House consisted of 65 members; today, that number is 435. Although the drawing of House district lines is left to the state legislatures, the Supreme Court held in *Wesberry v. Sanders* (1964) that House districts must be equal in population so that one person's vote in a congressional election is worth as much as another's. This ruling necessitates the redrawing of House district lines every ten years, after the census. This process, known as **reapportionment**, is fraught with political and legal implications (see Chapter 13).

Bicameralism is an important part of the system of checks and balances established by the Constitution. Because majorities in both houses must agree on a bill before it can become law, it is more difficult for Congress to act precipitously. This is precisely what the Framers had in mind: They wanted to make the process of governance more deliberate in order to prevent transitory public passions from prompting the legislature to adopt ill-considered and unwise legislation.

Qualifications of Members of Congress

Article I specifies qualifications for members of the House and the Senate. All members of Congress must reside (at least officially) within the state they represent. Members of the House must be at least 25 years of age; members of the Senate must be 30. Representatives must have been citizens of the United States for at least seven years; for senators, the citizenship requirement is nine years. No member of Congress may simultaneously hold a position in the executive branch, save for temporary diplomatic duties. According to Article I, Section 5, "Each house shall be the Judge of the . . . Qualifications of its own Members," but the Supreme Court has held that members may be denied seats only if they fail to meet the qualifications specified in Article I (see *Powell v. McCormack* [1969]).

Congressional Terms

The original constitutional provisions regarding congressional terms remain unchanged. Members of the House serve two-year terms; senators hold their offices for six-year terms. Unlike the president, who is limited to two consecutive terms in office by the Twenty-second Amendment, members of Congress may be reelected to an unlimited number of terms.

By the mid-1990s, a movement to limit the number of terms to which members of Congress could be elected had gained considerable momentum. Two basic alternatives were advanced. One called for states to act independently to limit the terms of their congressional delegations; the other provided for nationwide term limits through a federal constitutional amendment. In the pivotal case of *U.S. Term Limits, Inc. v. Thornton* (1995), a sharply divided Supreme Court struck down congressional term limits enacted by the state of Arkansas. In 1992, Arkansas voters had amended their state constitution to limit the number of elections in which one person could run for the U.S. Senate or House of Representatives. Arkansas defended the measure as an exercise of its constitutional authority to determine the "Times, Places and Manner of holding Elections" (U.S. Constitution, Article I, Section 4). The immediate effect of this decision was to invalidate term limits provisions previously adopted by twenty-three states.

Writing for a five-member majority, Justice John Paul Stevens concluded that the federal Constitution's enumeration of the qualifications of members of Congress was exclusive. He observed that the Framers intended "that neither Congress nor the States should possess the power to supplement the exclusive qualifications set forth in [Article I]." Stevens further observed that "[a]llowing individual states to craft their own qualifications for Congress would . . . erode the structure envisioned by the Framers." Justices Kennedy, Souter, Ginsburg, and Breyer joined this opinion.

In dissent, Justice Clarence Thomas, supported by Chief Justice Rehnquist and Justices O'Connor and Scalia, presented a lengthy argument in favor of state authority to prescribe eligibility requirements for congressional candidates beyond the basic requirements enumerated in the Constitution. Thomas sought to revive the long-abandoned notion that the states, rather than the "undifferentiated people of the nation as a whole," are the ultimate source of federal authority. He found "nothing in the Constitution [that] deprives the people of each state of the power to prescribe eligibility requirements for candidates who seek to represent them in Congress. . . . And where the Constitution is silent, it raises no bar to action by the states or the people."

Immediately after the *Thornton* decision was announced, supporters of term limits pledged renewed efforts to adopt a constitutional amendment to limit the tenure of members of Congress. Subsequent efforts to achieve the requisite congressional support for such a measure have failed. By the end of the twentieth century, enthusiasm for term limits had waned. Regardless of what one thinks of the desirability of limiting congressional terms, as a practical matter a constitutional amendment to accomplish this end is highly unlikely.

Immunities of Members of Congress

The **Speech** or **Debate Clause** (Article I, Section 6) provides that members of Congress "shall in all Cases, except Treason, Felony and Breach of the Peace, be privileged from Arrest during their Attendance at the Session of their respective Houses, and in going to and returning from the same; and for any Speech or Debate in either House, they shall not be questioned in any other Place." These protections reflect the Framers' concern over possible harassment of legislators by executive officials, a concern inherited from the English political experience.

The Speech or Debate Clause provides a degree of **immunity** to members of Congress against criminal prosecution. In *United States v. Johnson* (1966), for example, the Court held that the Speech or Debate Clause insulated members from having their speeches in Congress used as evidence against them in criminal prosecutions. However, in *United States v. Brewster* (1972), the Court said that newsletters mailed to constituents were outside the sphere of legislative activity and could therefore be used as evidence in a criminal case. The Speech or Debate Clause also provides a degree of immunity from civil suits. In *Hutchinson v. Proxmire* (1979), the Supreme Court held that a senator could not be sued for libel for statements he made on the Senate floor. He could, however, be sued for allegedly libelous statements contained in press releases and newsletters to his constituents.

TO SUMMARIZE:

- Bicameralism, the division of the Congress into two chambers, contributes significantly to the system of checks and balances. This division makes it more difficult for lawmakers to rush to judgment on volatile public issues.

- The qualifications of members of Congress are spelled out in the Constitution in Article I, Sections 2 and 3. According to Article I, Section 5, "Each house shall be the Judge of the . . . Qualifications of its own Members," but the Supreme Court has held that members may be denied seats only if they fail to meet the qualifications specified in Article I.
- Members of the House serve two-year terms; senators hold their offices for six-year terms. Unlike the president, who is limited to two consecutive terms in office by the Twenty-second Amendment, members of Congress may be reelected to an unlimited number of terms. The Supreme Court has ruled that states may not limit the terms of their congressional delegations. According to this interpretation, congressional term limits would require an amendment to the federal Constitution.
- The Speech or Debate Clause (Article I, Section 6) provides immunity to members of Congress against criminal prosecution for actions within the sphere of legislative activity. It also provides a degree of immunity from civil suits.

CONSTITUTIONAL SOURCES OF CONGRESSIONAL POWER

The enumerated powers of Congress are found in Article I and in provisions scattered throughout the Constitution. For example, Article I, Section 2, grants the House of Representatives the power to return articles of impeachment, and Section 3 gives the Senate the power to try impeachments and remove individuals from public office. Under Senate Rule XI, a committee of senators hears the evidence against an individual who has been impeached and reports evidence to the full Senate, which then votes on the matter of conviction. In *Nixon v. United States* (1993), the Supreme Court dismissed a challenge to this procedure brought by a federal district judge who had been impeached and convicted. Writing for the Court, Chief Justice Rehnquist observed that "judicial involvement in impeachment proceedings . . . would eviscerate the 'important constitutional check' placed on the Judiciary by the Framers."

Article I, Section 8

Most of the **enumerated powers** of Congress are located in **Article I, Section 8**, which consists of seventeen brief paragraphs enumerating specific powers followed by a general clause permitting Congress to "make all Laws which shall be necessary and proper for carrying into Execution the foregoing Powers, and all other Powers vested by this Constitution in the Government of the United States." The powers enumerated in Article I, Section 8, authorize Congress to lay and collect taxes; borrow money; regulate commerce among the states; control immigration and naturalization; regulate bankruptcy; coin money; fix standards of weights and measures; establish post offices and post roads; grant patents and copyrights; establish tribunals "inferior to the Supreme Court"; declare war; raise and support an army and a navy; regulate the militia when called into service; and perform other more restricted functions.

In reading Article I, Section 8, note that, although Congress is empowered to "provide for the common Defence and general Welfare of the United States," there is no general grant of **police power** to Congress. The power to make any and all laws deemed necessary for the protection of the public health, safety, welfare, and morals is thus reserved to the states under the Tenth Amendment. Yet Congress in fact exercises substantial police power by linking laws to the specific powers contained in Section 8. For example, Congress may not be not empowered to prohibit prostitution per se, but it may make it a crime to transport persons across state lines for "immoral purposes" by drawing on its broad power to regulate "commerce among the states" (see *Hoke v. United States* [1913]).

Other Enumerated Powers

Article I, Section 9, authorized Congress to abolish the importation of slaves into the United States, but only after 1808, in deference to the slave-trading states of the Deep South. Congress did act to ban the slave trade in 1808, although the institution of slavery remained legal until the Thirteenth Amendment was ratified in 1865.

Section 9 also permits Congress to suspend the writ of habeas corpus in cases of rebellion or national emergency. It is unclear whether this power is vested in Congress alone. At the outset of the Civil War, President Abraham Lincoln suspended habeas corpus in parts of the Union where secessionist sentiment was strong. Congress, which was not in session at the time, ratified Lincoln's action a few months later.

Article II confers on the Senate the power to participate in the treaty making process and to approve or reject presidential appointments of ambassadors, federal judges, and "all other Officers of the United States whose Appointments are not herein otherwise provided for" (Article II, Section 2, clause 2).

Article III authorizes Congress to define the jurisdiction of the lower federal courts and to regulate the appellate jurisdiction of the Supreme Court. As *Ex parte McCardle* (1869) demonstrates, this power is anything but trivial (see Chapter 1).

Article IV empowers Congress to implement uniform procedures under the clause providing that "[f]ull Faith and Credit shall be given in each State to the public Acts, Records, and judicial Proceedings of every other State" (Article IV, Section 1). Section 3 of this article authorizes Congress to admit new states to the Union, provided that it respects the territorial integrity of existing states. The same section confers on Congress the power to regulate and dispose of "the Territory or other Property belonging to the United States."

Article V grants Congress authority to propose constitutional amendments and specifies their mode of ratification—that is, by state legislatures or conventions. It is significant that neither the courts nor the executive branch plays a role in proposing constitutional amendments; this important function is vested solely in the Congress.

Several constitutional amendments confer additional powers on Congress. Of particular importance, the Sixteenth Amendment permits Congress to "lay and collect taxes on incomes from whatever source derived, without apportionment among the states." This amendment nullified an earlier Supreme Court decision striking down an income tax levied by Congress (see *Pollock v. Farmers' Loan and Trust Company* [1895], discussed in Chapter 1).

A number of constitutional amendments endow Congress with the power to legislate in support of civil rights and liberties. For example, the Civil War Amendments—Thirteen, Fourteen, and Fifteen—authorize Congress to enforce civil rights through "appropriate legislation." These rights include freedom from slavery and involuntary servitude (Amendment Thirteen); the enjoyment of the privileges and immunities of national citizenship (Amendment Fourteen); guarantees against state deprivation or denial of due process or equal protection of law (Amendment Fourteen); and prohibition of governmental interference with the right to vote "on account of race, color, or previous condition of servitude" (Amendment Fifteen, Section 1). The Nineteenth Amendment removes sex as a qualification for voting, and the Twenty-sixth Amendment lowers the voting age in state and federal elections to 18. Both amendments contain clauses permitting Congress to enforce their terms by "appropriate legislation." The Twenty-third and Twenty-fourth Amendments, which, respectively, give the

District of Columbia representation in the Electoral College and abolish poll taxes in federal elections, are likewise subject to congressional enforcement.

The Doctrine of Implied Powers

It is obvious that Congress today exercises far more powers than are specifically enumerated in the Constitution. Over the years, the American people have come to expect, even demand, as much. Yet one may argue that Congress has remained within the scope of powers delegated to it by the Constitution. The linchpin of this argument is the Necessary and Proper Clause (Article I, Section 8, clause 18) and the related doctrine of **implied powers.** In fact, the Necessary and Proper Clause is today, along with the Commerce, Taxing, and Spending Clauses, one of the key sources of congressional power.

The theory of implied powers originated with Alexander Hamilton, an advocate of strong centralized government. In Hamilton's view, the term **necessary** in the Necessary and Proper Clause referred to powers that could be appropriately exercised by Congress. In constitutional law, Hamilton's interpretation first appeared in an opinion by Chief Justice John Marshall in the obscure case of *United States v. Fisher* (1805). But the doctrine was firmly established in the landmark case of *M'Culloch v. Maryland* (1819), which ranks second only to *Marbury v. Madison* (1803) in importance in American constitutional law. It is important not only in relation to the powers of Congress but also in terms of federalism, the division of power between the national and state governments (see Chapter 5).

***M'Culloch v. Maryland* (1819)**   *M'Culloch v. Maryland* grew out of a conflict between national and state authority in the area of monetary policy. In 1791, Congress had granted a twenty-year charter to the Bank of the United States. In 1816, five years after the charter expired, Congress established the Second Bank of the United States, once again with a twenty-year charter. For a variety of reasons, including its heavy speculation and alleged fraudulent practices, the bank soon became the center of political controversy. Eight states passed legislation designed to prevent or discourage the bank from doing business within their jurisdictions. Maryland did so by levying an annual tax of $15,000 on any bank not chartered by the state (a tax that applied only to the Second Bank of the United States); a penalty of $500 was imposed for each violation of the tax measure. James W. M'Culloch, cashier of the Baltimore branch, violated the Maryland statute by refusing to pay the tax, and a judgment was rendered against him by the Baltimore County Court. Agreeing on a statement of facts, the Maryland attorney general and federal officials converted this legal action into a test case on the constitutionality of the state law and, ultimately, of the bank itself. Critics of the bank argued that Congress had no constitutional warrant to charter a national bank and that, in any event, the states were well within their authority to impose a tax on the bank's operations.

The Maryland Court of Appeals upheld the state's tax on the national bank, and the U.S. Supreme Court took the case at M'Culloch's behest. The greatest lawyers of their day, including Daniel Webster, argued the case for nine days before the Supreme Court. In a strong show of support for the national government, the Supreme Court unanimously reversed the Maryland Court of Appeals.

Chief Justice Marshall's Opinion of the Court in *M'Culloch* is widely regarded as a judicial tour de force not unlike *Marbury v. Madison*. In *M'Culloch*, Marshall asserted that although none of the enumerated powers of Congress explicitly authorized the incorporation of a bank, the Necessary and Proper Clause provided the textual basis for Congress's action. In keeping with his general view of the Constitution as an adaptable instrument of government, Marshall construed the Necessary and Proper Clause broadly, concluding that it was not confined merely to authority that was indispensable to the exercise of the enumerated powers. Rather, it was sufficient for Congress to adopt "appropriate" means to carry out its legitimate objectives. Among these were the powers to tax, to coin and borrow money, and to regulate commerce. In Marshall's view, the establishment of a national bank was an appropriate means of achieving these broad objectives and was, accordingly, permissible under the Necessary and Proper Clause. Marshall provided a detailed exposition of the doctrine of implied powers, concluding with the following statement:

> Let the end be legitimate, let it be within the scope of the Constitution, and all means which are plainly adapted to that end, which are not prohibited, but consist with the letter and spirit of the Constitution, are constitutional.

"Strict constructionists" and proponents of states' rights were outraged by the *M'Culloch* decision. In an action uncharacteristic of a distinguished jurist, Judge Spencer Roane of Virginia went so far as to publish a series of newspaper columns attacking the *M'Culloch* decision. In his only public response to criticism of the Court during his chief justiceship, John Marshall wrote two essays that were published in the *Philadelphia Union* under the pseudonym "A Friend to the Union." In these essays, Marshall attacked his critics and defended his reasoning in the *M'Culloch* case. Unlike Roane's articles, Marshall's essays were not widely circulated and seemed to have had little effect on the controversy following *M'Culloch*.

In state legislatures around the country, there were calls for constitutional amendments to restrict the Supreme Court's power of judicial review and reverse the Court's decision in *M'Culloch v. Maryland*. None of these proposals, however, was taken seriously in Congress, which was preoccupied at that time with the slavery issue and the debate over the Missouri Compromise of 1820. Thus, the *M'Culloch* decision, with its expansive interpretation of congressional power, remained intact.

Implied Powers: Congress Unbound?

Under the doctrine of implied powers, scarcely any area exists in which Congress is absolutely barred from acting, since most problems have a conceivable relationship to the broad powers and objectives contained in the Constitution. Thomas Jefferson, an opponent of the doctrine of implied powers, perceived as much in 1790 when, as secretary of state, he opposed the establishment of the First Bank of the United States. In a memorandum to President Washington, Jefferson wrote: "To take a single step beyond the boundaries thus specially drawn around the powers of Congress is to take possession of a boundless field of power, no longer susceptible of any definition." Today, the powers of Congress, while not exactly "boundless," are certainly far greater than most of the founders could have imagined. On the other hand, as we shall see later in this chapter, the conservative majority on the contemporary Supreme Court appears to be determined to reestablish limitations on congressional authority.

TO SUMMARIZE:

- The powers of Congress may be divided into two categories: enumerated and implied.

- Enumerated powers of Congress, such as the taxing and spending powers and the power to regulate interstate commerce, are set forth in Article I, Section 8, and other provisions of the Constitution.
- Implied powers are justified by the Necessary and Proper Clause of Article I, Section 8. The doctrine of implied powers was established by the Supreme Court in *M'Culloch v. Maryland* (1819).

THE POWER TO INVESTIGATE

Article I does not explicitly refer to the power of Congress to conduct investigations. Nevertheless, Congress has conducted hundreds of investigations over the years and called thousands of witnesses to testify. Sometimes these investigations have been great public events, such as the Watergate hearings of 1973 and 1974, which led to the demise of the Nixon presidency. More often, they have involved more mundane questions of public policy, such as consumer product safety or the regulation of the airline industry.

One of the important functions of legislative investigations is **oversight**—Congress serving as a watchdog over the actions of executive and regulatory agencies. This function has become increasingly important in the modern era, as Congress has created so many agencies and delegated to them broad powers within their areas of expertise. In a democracy, it is vital that the people's elected representatives keep tabs on the activities of a powerful, unelected government bureaucracy (for elaboration on this theme, see Chapter 4).

What is the source of Congress's **power to investigate?** There are several theories. The first is that Congress inherited this power from the English Parliament at the time of the Declaration of Independence in 1776. This theory views the power to investigate as inherent in any duly constituted legislature. Under this theory, Congress's power to investigate does not depend on any grant of authority in the Constitution (for a treatment of the general theme of inherited powers, see *United States v. Curtiss-Wright Export Corporation* [1936], reprinted and discussed in Chapter 3).

A second theory is that congressional investigations may be justified under the doctrine of implied powers. In this argument, the power to investigate is seen as both necessary and proper to the exercise of Congress's most basic function—crafting legislation. Investigation is a necessary means of obtaining information about the issues and subjects around which Congress is considering legislation. In fact Professor (later President) Woodrow Wilson went so far as to assert that "[t]he informing function of Congress should be preferred even to its legislative function."

Finally, Congress's power to conduct investigations may be justified under a theory of an evolving system of checks and balances. Under this theory, the system of checks and balances enumerated by the Framers was incomplete in that it failed to grant Congress the power to investigate, since investigation is an obvious means whereby Congress can check the other branches. In this argument, Congress was justified in asserting the power to investigate for the same reason that the Supreme Court was justified in assuming the power to rule on the constitutionality of legislation.

The Supreme Court Recognizes Congress's Power to Investigate

Congress conducted a number of important investigations during the early and mid-1800s. These included an inquiry into the Lewis and Clark exploration of the Louisiana Territory acquired during the Jefferson administration and an investigation of John Brown's abortive raid on the federal arsenal at Harper's Ferry in 1859. The Supreme Court did not, however, address the constitutionality of the investigative power until its decision in *Kilbourn v. Thompson* (1881). The *Kilbourn* case involved a House of Representatives investigation into the collapse of the Jay Cooke banking firm, with which the United States had deposited funds. In the course of the investigation, Hallet Kilbourn was called to testify and bring with him documents pertaining to his "real estate pool" and its dealings with the Jay Cooke company. Kilbourn refused both to testify and to produce the records. He was cited for contempt of Congress and was jailed for forty-five days. Upon his release from custody, Kilbourn sued John G. Thompson, the House sergeant-at-arms, for false imprisonment. Reviewing a lower court decision in Thompson's favor, the Supreme Court held that, although Congress possessed the power to investigate, the power must be exercised in furtherance of the legislative function. Justice Samuel F. Miller wrote for a unanimous bench that Congress could not employ its power of investigation to accomplish functions that were reserved to the other branches of government. In this case, the House had no intent to legislate; its inquiry into the Jay Cooke company was entirely investigatory in nature. Thus, Kilbourn's contempt citation and imprisonment were invalid.

The *Kilbourn* decision established the basic policy of the Supreme Court toward legislative investigations: The power to investigate is a necessary auxiliary of the legislative function. Yet the implied power to investigate is not unlimited. It must be exercised only in relation to potential legislation. Of course, today, there are few areas in which Congress may not potentially legislate; thus, there are few areas off limits to congressional investigation. Still, an investigation purely for its own sake is subject to judicial challenge.

Compulsory Process

When a congressional committee wishes to obtain testimony, it issues a **subpoena** to an individual. If it wishes to obtain documents for its inspection, it issues a *subpoena duces tecum*. A subpoena is often referred to as a **compulsory process,** because the individual is compelled to comply or risk being held in **contempt of Congress.** The Supreme Court upheld Congress's power to enforce a subpoena in *McGrain v. Daugherty* (1927), a case stemming from a Senate investigation into the Teapot Dome scandal during the administration of President Warren G. Harding. There, the Court stated that "the power of inquiry—with the process to enforce it—is an essential and appropriate auxiliary to the legislative function."

The Rights of Individuals Called before Congressional Committees

Congress's power to conduct investigations and compel witnesses to disclose information is generally regarded as both necessary and proper, but the power is certainly subject to abuse. Individuals who are called to testify before congressional committees may under certain circumstances legitimately refuse to answer questions. The Fifth Amendment protection against compulsory self-incrimination applies to legislative investigations, as well as to police interrogations and questioning in a court of law. An individual may legitimately refuse to answer questions if the answers to such questions might reveal criminal wrongdoing on his or her part. Yet, like a court of law, Congress may grant immunity to a witness to circumvent the Fifth Amendment. A witness who is granted immunity from prosecution has no grounds to invoke the Fifth Amendment, since the danger of self-incrimination has been removed. This was the case during the Iran-Contra investigation, when Oliver North was granted immunity in exchange for his testimony before Congress. Under the grant of immunity, federal prosecutors were barred from using North's testimony before Congress as evidence against him in a subsequent criminal prosecution. Under the grant of immunity, North ultimately avoided criminal liability.

In addition to the protection against compulsory self-incrimination, a person called to testify before Congress enjoys certain protections under the Due Process Clause of the Fifth Amendment. In particular, one is entitled to know the subject matter of the investigation. Moreover, questions must be pertinent to that subject (see *Watkins v. United States* [1957]).

Perhaps the best example of the abuse of the investigatory power occurred during the early days of the Cold War, when suspicions of Communist subversion verged on hysteria. In the 1950s, the House Un-American Activities Committee (HUAC) sought to expose Communist infiltration and corruption by subjecting suspected Communists to far-ranging and probing questions about their beliefs, affiliations, activities, and relationships. In the climate of near-hysteria over Communist subversion, the admonitions in *Kilbourn v. Thompson* about the proper scope and function of the investigatory power were all but forgotten. Individuals who invoked their constitutional immunity against compulsory self-incrimination in refusing to answer the committee's questions were branded "Fifth Amendment Communists."

In *Watkins v. United States* (1957), the Supreme Court reversed a conviction for contempt of Congress in a case where a witness had refused to answer questions put to him by HUAC. John Watkins answered questions about his own beliefs and activities but refused to "name names" of other suspected Communists. The Supreme Court reversed Watkins's conviction primarily on procedural grounds, holding that he had been denied due process of law. The Court also expressed concern that First Amendment values were being threatened by HUAC's public hearings.

Critics of HUAC hoped the Court's decision in *Watkins* signaled a desire on the part of the Court to limit congressional investigations on First Amendment grounds. In Congress, however, critics of *Watkins* and similar Warren Court decisions introduced legislation to remove the Court's appellate jurisdiction in cases where persons are held in contempt of Congress. The Court evidently took note of these efforts and soon backed away from its First Amendment concerns regarding congressional investigations. In *Barenblatt v. United States* (1959), the Court upheld a conviction for contempt of Congress, holding that the public interest in exposing Communist infiltration outweighed a witness's First Amendment rights in refusing to answer questions. The *Barenblatt* decision went a long way toward deflating Court-curbing efforts and rehabilitating the Court's standing in Congress. Since 1959, the Court has continued to show deference to congressional investigations and has generally refused to allow uncooperative witnesses to invoke the protections of the First Amendment (see, for example, *Wilkinson v. United States* [1961] and *Eastland v. United States Servicemen's Fund* [1975]).

TO SUMMARIZE:

- Although it is not explicitly provided for in the Constitution, Congress's power to investigate has been recognized by the Supreme Court as an essential auxiliary of the legislative process.

- Congress's power to investigate includes the power to issue subpoenas and to hold in contempt persons who refuse to cooperate with legitimate investigations.
- The Supreme Court has held that the power to investigate is not unlimited; investigations must be related to a legitimate legislative purpose.
- Investigations must conform to standards of procedural due process. Although witnesses called to testify before Congress may rely on their Fifth Amendment privilege against compulsory self-incrimination, Congress may compel testimony by granting immunity.

REGULATION OF INTERSTATE COMMERCE

The Articles of Confederation contained no provision granting Congress **power to regulate interstate commerce.** Thus Congress during this "critical period" could do nothing to control growing commercial rivalries among the thirteen largely independent states. This deficiency led the Framers of the Constitution to adopt Article I, Section 8, clause 3, which provides that "Congress shall have Power . . . to regulate Commerce with foreign Nations, and among the several States, and with the Indian Tribes." The Commerce Clause is important both as a source of national power and as an implicit restriction on state power.

Early Interpretation of the Commerce Clause

During the first century following adoption of the Constitution, Congress made little use of the Commerce Clause as a source of positive power. It is true that this clause served as partial authority for the creation of the Second Bank of the United States, as upheld in *M'Culloch v. Maryland* (1819). The range of potential congressional power was thus recognized at an early date. Nevertheless, during the nineteenth century the Commerce Clause served primarily as a barrier against state legislation. Neither the states nor the national government engaged in extensive regulation of commerce during this early period, but most of the governmental activity that did occur emanated from the states. It was in this setting that the first major Commerce Clause case, *Gibbons v. Ogden* (1824), reached the Supreme Court.

Gibbons v. Ogden   Like many other areas of constitutional analysis, the starting point in the interpretation of the Commerce Clause is found in one of Chief Justice John Marshall's opinions. As in *Marbury v. Madison* (1803) and *M'Culloch v. Maryland* (1819), Marshall's opinion in the *Gibbons* case is one of those fundamental statements of constitutional jurisprudence that has grown in influence with the passage of time. Marshall and his colleagues on the Supreme Court of the early 1800s had the advantage of addressing major questions of constitutional law for the first time, unguided—but also unencumbered—by the weight of precedent. Marshall, far more than any other jurist of his era, displayed the ability to use this advantage effectively.

At issue in *Gibbons v. Ogden* was the constitutionality of New York's grant of a steamboat monopoly to Robert Fulton and Robert Livingston. Aaron Ogden succeeded to the ownership of the Fulton-Livingston interest, which extended to commercial steamboat traffic between New York and New Jersey. Thomas Gibbons challenged this exclusive grant on the ground that it interfered with the power of Congress to regulate commerce among the states. Gibbons was licensed under federal law to engage in the "coasting" trade-commerce and navigation in coastal waters—and he contended that this authorization gave him the right to transact business of an interstate nature within the boundaries of New York, irrespective of that state's monopoly grant to others. Marshall and his colleagues agreed with Gibbons.

In the course of declaring the New York steamboat monopoly unconstitutional, Marshall wrote expansively about the scope of congressional power embodied in the Commerce Clause. In this instance, an obvious conflict existed between the federal licensing provision and the state grant of monopoly. Invoking the Supremacy Clause of Article VI of the Constitution, Marshall resolved this conflict in favor of the national government. He went on to assert that the power of Congress over commerce among the states was plenary—that is, full and complete—and subject to no competing exercise of state power in the same area. The federal law under which Gibbons operated was a modest exercise of that plenary power, but it was enough to warrant invalidation of the state law because the monopoly granted by the state interfered with the commercial privileges provided by the federal government.

It was clear from Marshall's perspective that Congress had acted well within its constitutional authority. In fact, Marshall defined the phrase "commerce among the several states" so broadly, and spoke in such sweeping terms about the power of Congress to regulate it, that his opinion came to be read as an endorsement of regulatory authority on a grand scale—far beyond anything dreamed of in the 1820s. Marshall acknowledged that commerce among the states was "restricted to that commerce which concerns more states than one." Nevertheless, it encompassed a vast range of relationships and transactions summed up in the phrase "commercial intercourse." When Marshall spoke of commerce as intercourse, he included more than the isolated movement of an article of trade from a point in one state to a point in another state. He had in mind commercial activity within and between states and maintained that realistic distinctions could not be automatically equated with state lines. Marshall recognized that some commerce might be altogether internal, or intrastate, in nature; but because that type of commerce was not at issue in this case, he did not elaborate on its precise meaning.

In asserting that the power of Congress under the Commerce Clause was plenary and superior to any competing state power, Marshall skirted one vitally important question: Would state legislation affecting commerce among the states be constitutional in the absence of any conflicting federal law? In a concurring opinion, Justice William Johnson answered this question in the negative. In his view, the power of Congress was not only plenary but also exclusive; he maintained that the states were absolutely barred from legislating in this broad area. Johnson was not supported in this view by other members of the Court, and his interpretation has never been adopted by a Court majority. However, the Court has generally recognized the exclusive power of Congress to regulate commerce "with foreign Nations . . . and with the Indian Tribes."

Justice Johnson's statement endorsing exclusive congressional control of commerce among the states served to sharpen the underlying issue in *Gibbons v. Ogden* and in a long line of cases decided since that decision. The basic issue is this: If the power of Congress is plenary, as Marshall and his colleagues in *Gibbons* maintained, does the failure of Congress to regulate a particular aspect of commerce mean that this aspect is not to be regulated at all? And if the answer to this question is no (as the Court has subsequently indicated), then does it follow that the states are free to regulate commerce in any area not already covered by federal legislation? Broadly speaking, and with varying degrees of imprecision, the Supreme Court has also answered this question in the negative. As Chapter 5 will explain, the states may, in the absence of conflicting federal law, regulate certain **local aspects of interstate commerce.** But even when no conflict with federal law exists, those aspects of interstate commerce that require uniform nationwide regulation cannot be touched by the states. The problem that remains unresolved to the present day is where to draw the line between permissible and impermissible state regulation of commerce in specific cases. It was not necessary in *Gibbons v. Ogden* to explore that problem; but as demands for greater governmental regulation at state and national levels increased, the issue became more and more perplexing.

Gibbons v. Ogden furnished John Marshall with an opportunity to lay down an all-encompassing definition of national power under the Commerce Clause. The decision was widely acclaimed by business leaders because it placed restrictions on state grants of commercial monopoly, thus encouraging competitive commercial and industrial activity at a time when the national government played no significant role in regulating business. To the advocate of private enterprise in the 1820s, it no doubt seemed safe enough to talk in the abstract about broad national power to regulate commerce, especially if such discussion provided a justification for curbing state regulation. Until late in the nineteenth century, that is precisely what the national commerce power symbolized.

During this period, the states, under an expanding definition of their police power, adopted an increasing number and variety of economic regulations, many of which were aimed at large corporations with growing political clout, especially in the post-Civil War era. Some of these laws came into conflict with the power of Congress to regulate commerce—not so much the actual exercise of that power but the potential power that, according to the Supreme Court, Congress alone could exert (see *Wabash, St. Louis & Pacific Railway Company v. Illinois* [1886]).

Congress Exercises the Commerce Power

As the popular demand for economic regulation increased and restrictions on state power multiplied, the national government came under greater pressure to limit the concentration of corporate influence and reduce what many Americans regarded as economic injustice and exploitation. Strong commercial interests countered this pressure to some extent, but ultimately Congress responded by passing the **Interstate Commerce Act of 1887** and the **Sherman Antitrust Act of 1890**. The first of these measures established the Interstate Commerce Commission (ICC), granting this independent agency limited authority to regulate railroads engaged in commerce among the states. The Sherman Act was aimed at controlling on a national scale the concentration of economic power in the form of monopolies or "combinations in restraint of trade," as the statute phrased it.

Both the ICC and the Sherman Act represented the beginning of a national counterpart to state police power. Both rested squarely on the Commerce Clause and both encountered rough sledding in the Supreme Court for a number of years. By 1890, the Court had come under the influence of an economic philosophy that stressed the values of individual and corporate freedom and minimized the legitimate sphere of governmental regulation. Although the Court never fully subscribed to the doctrine of *laissez-faire*, most of its members, including several former corporation lawyers, were sympathetic to this perspective. This view was reflected in changing interpretations of the Commerce Clause, the Tenth Amendment, and the Due Process Clauses of the Fifth and Fourteenth Amendments. Until the judicial revolution of 1937, the Court accorded great importance to the protection of property and other business-related rights against growing regulatory efforts at all levels of government. This subject is discussed more fully in Chapter 7, but it is important to recognize at this point that the restrictive view of the Commerce Clause, characteristic of Supreme Court decisions of the late nineteenth and early twentieth centuries, was part of a larger pattern of constitutional interpretation.

The Supreme Court and the Commerce Clause: 1895–1937

The first major change in Commerce Clause interpretation as applied to the exercise of national power came in the 1895 case of *United States v. E. C. Knight Company*. The decision resulted from the federal government's effort to break up a powerful sugar monopoly by invoking the Sherman Antitrust Act. In this initial interpretation of the act, a Supreme Court majority held that its regulatory provisions, as applied to the manufacture of sugar, went beyond the proper scope of the commerce power.

Commerce Distinguished from Production   By contrast with John Marshall's broad perspective in *Gibbons v. Ogden*, Chief Justice Melville Fuller, writing for the majority in *E. C. Knight*, emphasized the boundaries of the commerce power. He acknowledged the "evils" of monopoly and conceded that the E. C. Knight Company was indeed engaged in monopolistic practices in the manufacture of refined sugar. He also recognized a connection between the control of the manufacture of "a given thing" and "control of its disposition." But he brushed aside the obvious relationship between commerce and manufacturing, maintaining that it was secondary, not primary, in nature. The connection, in his view, was incidental and indirect. Fuller did not clearly indicate why such a distinction should be made or precisely where the line should be drawn. He simply asserted that "commerce succeeds to manufacture and is not a part of it." Under their police power, states were free to regulate monopolies, but the national government had no general police power under the Commerce Clause. He thus accorded a narrow interpretation to the enumerated powers of Congress. Only if the business activity in question was itself a "monopoly of commerce" could the national government suppress it. This formal distinction between commerce and manufacturing, adopted over the strong dissent of Justice John M. Harlan (the elder), temporarily gutted the Sherman Act without rendering it unconstitutional *per se*. If the government could move only against the post-manufacturing phases of monopolistic activity, and not against the entire enterprise, its hands were effectively tied.

The Court followed similar reasoning in *Hammer v. Dagenhart* (1918), invalidating by a 5-to-4 margin federal restrictions on child labor. The manufacture of goods by children, even when those goods were clearly destined for shipment in interstate commerce, was not a part of commerce and could not be regulated by Congress. Here the Court, over the incisive dissent of Justice Oliver Wendell Holmes, added the observation that there was nothing harmful in the manufactured goods themselves, implying that such a showing would have been necessary to justify their prohibition in interstate commerce.

Interestingly, the Court had upheld several equally far-reaching exercises of congressional power under the Commerce Clause between the *E. C. Knight* and *Dagenhart* decisions. In fact, some of these statutes imposed severe criminal penalties in addition to the civil remedies exclusively applied in the latter case. For example, Congress enacted laws imposing fines and imprisonment for participation in lotteries and prostitution. Activities of this sort, unlike child labor and business monopoly, were widely regarded as immoral. And when it came to punishing what most people believed to be sinful behavior, the Commerce Clause was seen as an appropriate weapon (see, for example, *Champion v. Ames* [1903], upholding the federal antilottery statute, and *Hoke v. United States* [1913], sustaining a federal law penalizing the transportation of women across state lines for "immoral purposes"). Throughout this period, the Court was also willing to uphold national legislation designed to protect consumers against adulterated food and the improper processing, packaging, and branding of meat shipped across state lines (see *Hipolite Egg Company v. United States* [1911], in which the Court upheld the Pure Food and Drug Act).

Commerce and Transportation   In the field of transportation, particularly the regulation of railroad freight rates, the scope of national power under the Commerce Clause developed in accordance with the broad language of *Gibbons v. Ogden*. Even intrastate rates might be regulated by the ICC if states created rate structures that discriminated against interstate carriers in favor of their local competitors. This was the situation in the Shreveport Rate Case (*Houston, East & West Texas Railway Company v. United States*, 1914). The Texas Railroad Commission permitted three railroads to charge lower rates for intrastate shipments in east Texas than for interstate shipments of comparable distances in the same geographical area. The impact of this arrangement was to generate business among East Texas cities at the expense of Shreveport, Louisiana, a commercial center naturally linked to cities such as Dallas. The Louisiana Railroad Commission began administrative proceedings before the Interstate Commerce Commission, challenging the differential rate structures. The ICC established uniform maximum rates for interstate and intrastate movement of freight and ordered the three railroads to cease their discriminatory practices. In a 7-to-2 decision the Supreme Court affirmed the decree of a specialized tribunal, the Commerce Court, upholding the ICC decision. In his opinion for the majority, Associate Justice (later Chief Justice) Charles Evans Hughes declared that Congress is authorized

> to supply the needed correction where the relation between intrastate and interstate rates presents the evil to be corrected, and this it may do completely, by reason of its control over the interstate carrier in all matters having such a close and substantial relation to interstate commerce that it is necessary or appropriate to exercise the control for the government of that commerce. . . . Congress is entitled to maintain its own standard as to these rates, and to forbid any discriminatory action . . . which will obstruct the freedom of movement of interstate traffic over their lines in accordance with the terms it establishes.

The "Stream of Commerce" Doctrine   In spite of broad interpretation of the commerce power in the field of transportation, however, prior to the late 1930s the Court resisted congressional efforts to expand the Commerce Clause as a nonselective basis of national police power. Instead, the Court developed several concepts designed to assist it in defining the outer limits of the commerce power. We identify only two of the most prominent of these to illustrate the elusiveness and complexity of constitutional development in this field of congressional regulation. The first of these concepts, the **stream of commerce doctrine**, was first articulated by Justice Holmes in the 1905 decision of *Swift and Company v. United States*. There, the Court held that the power of the national government under the Sherman Act extended to "conspiracies in restraint of trade" among a combination of Chicago meatpackers. Even though the challenged activities—the buying and selling of cattle in Chicago—were local in nature, Holmes found that they were in the "current of commerce" among the states. The same rationale was applied by Chief Justice William Howard Taft seventeen years later in a decision upholding federal regulation under the Packers and Stockyards Act of 1921 (*Stafford v. Wallace* [1922]).

Direct versus Indirect Effects on Interstate Commerce   The second concept is a presumed distinction between the direct and indirect effects of a particular regulation on commerce. In a number of cases during this period, the Court indicated that even though the activity in question might not be defined as commerce *per se*, it could still be regulated if it had a direct effect on interstate commerce. It followed that a mere indirect effect would not alone be sufficient to justify the exercise of congressional power. Although the **direct–indirect test** was usually applied in such a way as to sustain the regulation under review, the Court used this distinction as a means of indicating that congressional authority was subject to limitation. For example, when the National Industrial Recovery Act, a major piece of New Deal legislation, was declared unconstitutional in *Schechter Poultry Corporation v. United States* (1935), one of the principal conclusions reached by the Court was that what the government sought to regulate had only an indirect effect on interstate commerce. (The other principal constitutional basis of the decision, a violation of the rule against congressional delegation of authority, is discussed in Chapter 4.)

Expansion of Federal Regulatory Power   The **distinction between manufacturing and commerce** was reaffirmed in principle and extended to the differentiation between mining and commerce in the 1936 case of *Carter v. Carter Coal Company*. Thus a Supreme Court majority from the mid-1890s through the mid-1930s treated the commerce power of Congress as inherently limited in nature. Then came the confrontation between President Franklin D. Roosevelt and the "nine old men." In the aftermath of Roosevelt's effort to pack the Supreme Court in 1937, the Court moved away from a defense of private enterprise and toward an affirmation of broad regulatory power, both national and state. One very important aspect of this transition was a return to John Marshall's expansive definition of congressional power under the Commerce Clause. As a result, the Commerce Clause came to be recognized as a source of far-reaching national police power.

Post–New Deal Interpretation of the Commerce Clause

Under President Franklin Roosevelt's leadership, the Democratic Congress of the middle and late 1930s enacted sweeping legislation to replace, and in some instances amplify, measures that the Supreme Court had invalidated prior to 1937. Areas such as labor-management relations, agriculture, social insurance, and national resource development became focal points of national policy—and the Commerce Clause figured prominently as a constitutional source for most of the new legislation. Beginning with its decision upholding the National Labor Relations Act (*National Labor Relations Board v. Jones & Laughlin Steel Corporation* [1937]), the reoriented Supreme Court swept away distinctions between commerce and manufacturing, between direct and indirect burdens on commerce, and between activities that directly or indirectly affected commerce.

The post–New Deal perspective on the Commerce Clause is well illustrated by the case of *Wickard v. Filburn* (1942). At issue was the constitutionality of a federal acreage allotment for wheat. On their face, the questions might have seemed easy to resolve in light of the expanded power of Congress in the post–New Deal era. But the specific violation revolved around a farmer who has raised a wheat crop in excess of the prescribed allotment, not for sale or distribution in interstate commerce but for his own consumption. Writing for a unanimous Court, Justice Robert H. Jackson concluded:

> Even if appellant's activity be local and though it may not be regarded as commerce, it may still, whatever its nature, be reached by Congress if it exerts a substantial economic effect on interstate commerce, and this irrespective of whether such effect is what might at some earlier time have been defined as "direct" or "indirect."

A comparison between the sweeping language of *Wickard v. Filburn* and the restrictive view of Chief Justice Fuller in *E. C. Knight* illustrates the extent to which a single clause of the Constitution is subject to contrasting interpretations. Under the modern interpretation of the Commerce Clause, the federal government is permitted to play a very active role in the regulation of economic activity. This is seen in the enforcement of antitrust laws, the control over farm commodities, the supervision of financial markets, the oversight of labor-management relations, and the regulation of various transportation industries. It is also seen in areas of "commerce" that fall outside conventional regulation of business, such as civil rights legislation applicable to places of public accommodation.

The Commerce Clause and Civil Rights

In the 1960s, Congress relied on the Commerce Clause as a basis for vast legislative undertakings, some of them well beyond the field of economic regulation. The most important illustration of the commerce power as a source of noncommercial legislation is within the area of race relations. In *Heart of Atlanta Motel v. United States* (1964), the Supreme Court unanimously upheld the public accommodations section of the **Civil Rights Act of 1964** as a proper exercise of the commerce power. The motel in question did a substantial volume of business with persons from outside Georgia. The Court ruled that its racially restrictive practices could impede commerce among the states and could therefore be appropriately regulated by Congress. In the companion case of *Katzenbach v. McClung* (1964), the Court went even further by recognizing the power of Congress under the Commerce Clause to bar racial discrimination in a restaurant (Ollie's Barbecue in Birmingham, Alabama) patronized almost entirely by local customers. The Court found a connection with interstate commerce in the purchase of food and equipment from sources outside Alabama.

Under such a broad definition, it is questionable whether any local enterprise that opens its doors to the public could remain outside the scope of the Commerce Clause. Today, few businesses attempt to challenge the applicability of the Civil Rights Act, because racial segregation in places of business has become socially, as well as legally, unacceptable.

Environmental Protection

Since the 1960s, government at all levels has been under pressure to do more to protect natural resources and combat pollution. Relying to a great extent on its powers under the Commerce Clause, Congress has enacted sweeping laws designed to promote conservation and protect the natural environment and workers from the adverse effects of an industrialized economy. Some of the more important federal laws in this regard are the Clean Air Act, the Endangered Species Act, and the Occupational Safety and Health Act. These acts involve broad delegations of power from Congress to regulatory agencies, which raises a constitutional question in and of itself (see Chapter 4).

Federal environmental legislation has generally been favorably received in the Supreme Court. For example, in *Hodel v. Virginia Surface Mining and Reclamation Association, Inc.* (1981), the Supreme Court upheld a federal statute aimed at reducing the environmental impact of surface coal mining by establishing uniform national standards on the industry. The Court said that Congress could reasonably conclude that unregulated surface mining could "adversely affect the public welfare by destroying or diminishing the utility of land." Similarly, in *Federal Energy Regulatory Commission v. Mississippi* (1982), the Court upheld an act of Congress regulating local electric power transmissions, taking note of the impact of local electric power generation and transmission on the national supply of electrical power. Finally, in *Preseault v. Interstate Commerce Commission* (1990), the Court upheld a federal statute permitting local governments to convert abandoned railroad rights-of-way for purposes of recreation and conservation. The Court said that the law furthered a legitimate objective under the Commerce Clause—preservation of railroad rights-of-way for possible future reactivation.

The Supreme Court has gone so far as to hold that certain federal laws passed under the aegis of the Commerce Clause are so comprehensive and are of such overriding national importance as to preempt state and local legislation in a given area. By way of illustration, the Court has held that the federal Noise Control Act of 1972 preempts a city from adopting its own aircraft noise abatement ordinance (see *Burbank v. Lockheed Air Terminal* [1973]). Clearly, the Supreme Court has given Congress broad latitude to use the Commerce Clause as a basis for environmental legislation.

The Commerce Clause and Federal Criminal Law

The expansive scope of the modern interpretation of the Commerce Clause has also facilitated increased federal activity in the enactment and enforcement of criminal law, an area traditionally left to the states. For example, in 1970, Congress enacted the Organized Crime Control Act, Title IX of which is titled "Racketeer Influenced and Corrupt Organizations" (RICO). The **RICO Act**, as it is widely known, essentially prohibits infiltration of organized crime into organizations or enterprises engaged in interstate commerce. The act permits the Federal Bureau of Investigation and other federal law enforcement agencies to become more involved in the investigation of organized crime, even into activities that are ostensibly confined to local areas.

In *Perez v. United States* (1971), the Supreme Court upheld Title II of the Consumer Credit Protection Act, a federal statute aimed at loan-sharking. Even though loan-sharking is primarily a local activity, the Court held that Congress could reasonably have concluded that it is a major revenue source for organized crime, which is a national problem with a detrimental impact on interstate commerce. In a dissenting opinion, Justice Potter Stewart observed that the Framers of the Constitution never intended for the national government to define as a crime and prosecute such wholly local activity through the enactment of federal criminal laws:

> [I]t is not enough to say that some loan sharking is a national problem, for all crime is a national problem. It is not enough to say that some loan sharking has interstate characteristics, for any crime may have an interstate setting.

The interpretation of the Commerce Clause, like that of other constitutional provisions, is undertaken, in large part, to facilitate the achievement of practical political goals and to preserve the continuity of legal doctrine. Because substantial segments of the American public have demanded that the national government become increasingly active in such areas as economic regulation, civil rights, and environmental and crime control, the Commerce Clause has been stretched far beyond the intentions or expectations of the Framers of the Constitution.

The Rehnquist Court's Restriction of Congressional Powers under the Commerce Clause

In *United States v. Lopez* (1995), a closely divided Supreme Court invalidated the Gun-Free School Zones Act of 1990, a federal statute criminalizing the possession of a firearm in or within 1,000 feet of a school. As constitutional authority for this statute,

Congress had relied on its power to regulate interstate commerce. Writing for the majority, Chief Justice Rehnquist, joined by Justices O'Connor, Scalia, Kennedy, and Thomas, asserted that the Gun-Free School Zones Act was "a criminal statute that by its terms [had] nothing to do with 'commerce' or any sort of enterprise, however broadly one might define those terms." Rehnquist observed that "if we were to accept the Government's arguments, we are hard-pressed to posit any activity by an individual that Congress is without power to regulate."

Joined by three of his colleagues, Justice Breyer took sharp exception to the majority's characterization of the issue, insisting that the statute was "well within the scope of the commerce power as this Court has understood that power over the past half-century." Breyer cited numerous studies in support of his contention that Congress had a rational basis for concluding that gun-related violence in and near schools affected commerce.

In a concurring opinion, however, Justice Thomas commented that at oral argument, the government's lawyer was asked whether there are any limits to what Congress may regulate under the Commerce Clause. Thomas noted that "the government was at a loss for words." In taking Justice Breyer's dissent to task, Thomas further observed that "the principal dissent insists that there are limits, but it cannot even muster one example."

Without question, the Court's decision in the *Lopez* case represents a sharp deviation from the familiar pattern of modern (post-1937) Commerce Clause decisions. Almost without exception, these decisions have reflected the Court's expansive view of the clause as a source of far-reaching congressional power. Under modern interpretation, traditional constitutional distinctions between national and local responsibilities of government have largely disappeared. Chief Justice Rehnquist addressed this broad question in his *Lopez* opinion, reminding Congress that under the Constitution it exercises enumerated powers, and that enumeration implies limitation. Without suggesting that any of the Court's modern Commerce Clause decisions should be overruled, Rehnquist insisted that the Court in this instance go no further in approving congressional expansion of the commerce power. By recognizing the existence of outer limits on this power, he sought to preserve a meaningful distinction between national and local authority.

The *Lopez* ruling generated widespread commentary. One question posed by many scholars was whether *Lopez* represented a significant departure from the Court's long-established Commerce Clause jurisprudence. Some saw the decision as a sea change in the Court's jurisprudence; others saw the decision as an anomaly. The Court's controversial decision in *United States v. Morrison* (2000), striking down a provision of the Violence against Women Act of 1994, suggested that *Lopez* was not simply an aberration. The same five-member majority that decided *Lopez* found that Congress had no power under the Commerce Clause (or the Fourteenth Amendment) to provide a federal civil remedy to victims of gender-motivated violence. Any such remedy, said the Court, must come from the states. Not surprisingly, the four dissenters were dismayed that the Court would circumscribe congressional power to deal with what many would characterize as a national epidemic of domestic violence.

The Tenth Amendment and the Commerce Clause

The **Tenth Amendment** reserves to the states those powers not delegated to the national government. With the decision in *United States v. Darby* (1941), the Tenth Amendment for all intents and purposes vanished as a significant restraint on the commerce power. In *Darby*, the Court unanimously upheld the Fair Labor Standards

Act of 1938. The *Darby* decision explicitly overruled *Hammer v. Dagenhart*, rejecting the former ruling's narrow interpretation of the Commerce Clause, as well as its reliance on the Tenth Amendment.

In the 1976 case of *National League of Cities v. Usery*, the Court appeared to resurrect the Tenth Amendment as it struck down provisions of the 1974 amendments to the Fair Labor Standards Act extending minimum wage coverage to most state and local government employees. Writing for the Court, Justice William Rehnquist concluded that the national commerce power must yield to the Tenth Amendment when the former infringes on "traditional aspects of state sovereignty." In a sharp dissent, Justice Brennan assailed the *Usery* ruling as an irresponsible departure from modern views regarding the national commerce power and federal–state relations. A number of legal scholars endorsed this view, but others praised the decision as a welcome reassertion of the principle of federalism.

Controversy over *Usery* continued into the 1980s, until the decision was overruled in *Garcia v. San Antonio Metropolitan Transit Authority* (1985). Again the court was divided 5 to 4. Justice Harry A. Blackmun, who had concurred in the *Usery* ruling, switched sides and delivered the majority opinion in *Garcia*. Supported by Justices Brennan, White, Marshall, and Stevens, he concluded that the attempt to draw the boundaries of state regulatory immunity in terms of "traditional governmental function" is not only unworkable but is "inconsistent with established principles of federalism." In a lengthy dissent, Justice Lewis Powell, joined by Chief Justice Burger and Justices Rehnquist and O'Connor, deplored what he characterized as the Court's abrupt departure from precedent and its reduction of the Tenth Amendment to "meaningless rhetoric when Congress acts pursuant to the Commerce Clause." He maintained that this decision "reflects a serious misunderstanding, if not an outright rejection, of the history of our country and the intention of the Framers of the Constitution." (The *Usery* and *Garcia* cases are further discussed and reprinted in Chapter 5).

The Court Limits the Brady Bill   In 1997 the Supreme Court gave new life to the Tenth Amendment in striking down a controversial piece of legislation based on the Commerce Clause. In *Printz v. United States*, the Court invalidated a key provision of the Brady Bill, which required the attorney general to establish a national system to conduct instant background checks on prospective gun buyers. The popular name of the statute was a reference to Jim Brady, President Ronald Reagan's press secretary who was disabled after being shot by John Hinckley in the 1981 assassination attempt on the president. The disputed provision required local law enforcement officers to perform background checks on prospective handgun purchasers. According to Justice Scalia's opinion for the sharply divided Court, this provision violated "the very principle of separate state sovereignty," which Scalia characterized as "one of the Constitution's structural protections of liberty." Scalia observed that "the power of the Federal Government would be augmented immeasurably if it were able to impress into its service—and at no cost to itself—the police officers of the 50 States."

Despite the Rehnquist Court's decisions in *Printz, Morrison,* and *Lopez,* however, the Commerce Clause remains a deep reservoir of legislative power. The expansive scope of the Commerce Clause under modern interpretation might surprise, even shock, many of the Framers of the Constitution. Until recently, however, it had become an accepted feature of the contemporary constitutional order. Recent decisions by the Rehnquist Court show that very little in constitutional law should be considered to be settled with finality.

TO SUMMARIZE:

- During the nineteenth century, the Commerce Clause served primarily as a barrier against state legislation, such as the monopoly invalidated by the Supreme Court in *Gibbons v. Ogden* (1824).
- In *Gibbons v. Ogden*, Chief Justice John Marshall took a broad view of congressional power under the Commerce Clause, but stopped short of concluding that this power belongs exclusively to the national government.
- In the late nineteenth and early twentieth centuries, a conservative Supreme Court adopted a restrictive view of the Commerce Clause and invalidated or limited a number of federal laws regulating various aspects of the economy.
- The Commerce Clause figured prominently in the confrontation between the Court and President Franklin Roosevelt over the constitutionality of the New Deal.
- With its sudden turnaround in 1937, the Court began to take an expansive view of the Commerce Clause and permitted Congress wide latitude in the area of economic policy making.
- Under a view that prevailed between 1937 and 1995, the Commerce Clause provided the basis for federal laws dealing with the environment, civil rights and criminal law, and economic policy.
- In recent decisions, the Rehnquist Court has made it clear that Congress power under the Commerce Clause is not unlimited—that there must be a reasonable connection between Congress's policy objective and interstate commerce.

TAXING AND SPENDING POWERS

If the absence of power to regulate commerce stifled economic growth under the Articles of Confederation, the inability to tax and resulting limits on the ability to spend threatened the continued existence of the national government itself. The Framers of the Constitution proposed to remedy these weaknesses by providing in the very first clause of Article I, Section 8, the following enumerated powers: "to lay and collect Taxes, Duties, Imposts and Excises, to pay the Debts and provide for the common Defence and general Welfare of the United States." The federal taxing power was significantly expanded by the ratification of the Sixteenth Amendment (the income tax amendment) in 1913 (see Chapter 1). The vast taxing and spending powers exercised by the national government today are based on the broad language of Article I, Section 8, as supplemented by the Sixteenth Amendment.

Taxation as a Source of Congressional Power

We must distinguish between two important functions related to taxation—namely, raising revenue and regulation. It is in the second of these areas that the more enduring and important questions of constitutional interpretation have been debated. Although the modern Supreme Court accords wide latitude to both the revenue-raising and regulatory aspects of national taxation, it is at least theoretically more likely to entertain constitutional objections to the latter.

The **taxing power** is independent of any of the specific regulatory powers listed in other provisions of the Constitution. However, through linkage with the Necessary and Proper Clause, this power can be used far beyond the supposed limits of its own enumeration to implement various regulatory programs. In other words, the taxing power is not confined to the objectives set forth in Article I, Section 8, clause 1—that is, those of paying the debt and providing "for the common Defence and general Welfare of the United States." Congress, as Justice Felix Frankfurter pointed out, may also "make an oblique use of the taxing power in relation to activities with which it may deal directly, as, for instance, commerce between the states" (*United States v. Kahriger* [1953], dissenting opinion).

The national taxing power, like the taxing power of the states, is exercised on the people directly. But within strict limits, the national government and the states may also tax each other, provided that fundamental considerations of sovereignty are observed. Sovereignty is an exceedingly elusive concept, and its meaning in this context is determined by the Supreme Court on a case-by-case basis. The doctrine of **reciprocal immunity** has historically imposed some limits on intergovernmental taxation. Although those limits still exist in theory, as a practical matter they are seldom recognized (see Chapter 5).

The Constitution distinguishes between direct and indirect taxes but leaves those vague categories largely undefined. Two separate provisions in Article I specify that direct taxes shall be apportioned among the states on the basis of population (Section 2, clause 3, and Section 9, clause 4). The second of these provisions refers to "Capitation or other direct Tax," suggesting that the Framers had in mind a distinction between direct taxes, such as those imposed on persons without regard to particular activities, and indirect taxes, such as those levied on businesses, goods, services, and various privileges. Nevertheless, the distinction between direct and indirect taxes was and is a muddy one. Fortunately, it is of little constitutional significance today. It figured prominently in the income tax controversy of the 1890s, but the relevance of the distinction in this field was rendered moot by passage of the Sixteenth Amendment in 1913. Most constitutional issues in the field of taxation have involved levies on various aspects of business. The indirect nature of such taxes can be seen in the capacity of the individuals and corporations taxed to pass the burden on to consumers of the product or service in question. The only limitation the Constitution imposes on indirect taxes is that of geographic uniformity: They must be "uniform throughout the United States"—that is, uniform in their application among the states, not identical as applied to each person taxed.

Federal Taxation as a Means of Regulation

The Supreme Court has always given wide latitude to the taxing power as a source of regulatory authority when used in combination with other enumerated powers. The case of *Veazie Bank v. Fenno* (1869) provides a classic example. There, the court upheld a tax of 10 percent on notes issued by state banks, a measure designed by the federal government to drive this unstable form of currency out of existence. In the Court's view, it was significant that the tax was linked with the congressional power to regulate currency, a power that emanates from several provisions in Article I, Section 8.

Historically, the Court has expressed less certainty about the use of the taxing power as an independent regulatory device. By the mid-1930s, two conflicting lines of constitutional precedent bearing on this question had emerged, one endorsing and the other denying broad constitutional authority.

In *McCray v. United States* (1904), a divided Court upheld an act under which Congress, responding to pressure from the dairy industry, levied a tax of ten cents a pound on oleomargarine colored to look like butter. In contrast, there was a tax of only one-fourth cent per pound on uncolored oleomargarine. The majority conceded that both the Fifth Amendment's Due Process Clause and the Tenth Amendment's recognition of the states' reserved powers imposed limits on the taxing power of Congress. But, according to Justice (later Chief Justice) Edward D. White, who wrote the majority opinion, those limits had not been breached by this tax.

According to Justice White, if it were "plain to the judicial mind" that the taxing power was not being used to raise revenue "but solely for the purpose of destroying rights" implicit in constitutional principles of freedom and justice, courts would be duty bound to declare that Congress had acted beyond the authority conferred by the Constitution. The difference between the abuse of legislative power and the exercise of reasonable discretion was simply a matter of judgment, to be made in each case. Applying this elusive standard, White concluded that "the manufacture of artificially colored oleomargarine may be prohibited by a free government without a violation of fundamental rights."

Note that, unlike other exercises of the national police power early in the twentieth century, this law was not clearly identified with the promotion of public health, safety, or morality. At best, it discouraged the deceptive marketing of a food product with which the dairy industry did not want to compete.

The *McCray* decision served as a precedent for using the taxing power to regulate the sale of narcotics and firearms (*United States v. Doremus* [1919], *Sonzinsky v. United States* [1937]). But the *McCray* rationale was not applied to the regulation of child labor (*Bailey v. Drexel Furniture Company* [1922]) or to the regulation of agricultural production (*United States v. Butler* [1936]). In the *Doremus* and *Sonzinsky* cases, the Court chose to recognize the validity of the revenue-raising features of the taxation in question and to view their regulatory aspects as consistent with the constitutional exercise of legislative power. In the *Bailey* and *Butler* cases, the Court did just the opposite, choosing to view the taxes not as revenue measures (although they obviously produced revenue), but as penalties or coercive regulations infringing on either individual liberty or the reserved powers of the states.

In *Bailey* (better known as the child labor tax case), Chief Justice William Howard Taft maintained that Congress through the taxing power was attempting to regulate an activity properly within the scope of state authority. He noted the Court's previous recognition of state autonomy regarding the control of child labor (*Hammer v. Dagenhart*), concluding that Congress could not accomplish through the taxing power an objective previously denied it as an unconstitutional exercise of the commerce power. The tax amounted to 10 percent of the annual net income of mills, factories, mines, and quarries employing children under certain ages. This act singled out certain employment practices for tax purposes, just as the oleomargarine law singled out a particular marketing practice. Both were designed to discourage specific activities through the application of differential tax burdens. Yet the Court viewed one as an appropriate revenue measure and the other as an impermissible use of the taxing power.

The Court also invalidated the Agricultural Adjustment Act of 1933, as, among other things, an unconstitutional exercise of the taxing power. *United States v. Butler* thus nullified a major component of Franklin D. Roosevelt's New Deal program. The decision rejected congressional use of the taxing power as a basis for regulating agricultural production. In fact, the Court's condemnation of the processing tax at issue in this case is, to this day, the last repudiation of national legislative authority based on the distinction between the regulatory and revenue-raising features of a federal tax. In this respect, the *Butler* decision simply reiterated the rationale applied in the child labor tax case, but its constitutional importance is greater because it provided the Court with its first clear opportunity to consider the scope of the spending power as well.

The Spending Power of Congress

The source of the **spending power** is, of course, found in the same clause of the Constitution that grants Congress the power to tax. The provision simply states: "Congress shall have Power To . . . pay the Debts and provide for the common Defence and general Welfare of the United States." The latter phrase—known as the General Welfare Clause (not to be confused with the "general welfare" provision in the Preamble to the Constitution)—has been used in combination with other enumerated powers since *United States v. Butler* as a basis for the establishment of vast governmental programs.

Under the Agricultural Adjustment Act of 1933, proceeds from the processing tax were used to pay farmers in exchange for their promises to reduce crop acreage. Thus, the scheme of regulation at issue embodied both taxing and spending features and rested squarely on Article I, Section 8, clause 1, as its constitutional source. Justice Owen J. Roberts, writing one of his most influential majority opinions, recognized that Congress could use appropriations for regulatory purposes by making them conditional—that is, by withholding them until the potential recipients either performed or failed to perform specified actions. In this way, the spending power could serve the same indirect regulatory function as the taxing power. He found the act objectionable primarily because both its taxing and spending aspects sought to regulate agricultural production, an area then regarded as reserved to the states by the Tenth Amendment. His detailed analysis of the spending power, however, did not necessarily point to this result.

Justice Roberts adopted the view widely held by constitutional scholars that the General Welfare Clause was not an unrestricted grant of power but was linked to the taxing power granted in the same constitutional provision. According to this view, the General Welfare Clause conferred no independent regulatory power as such but only a power to spend. However, he rejected the narrow interpretation advanced by James Madison that the taxing and spending power was to be exercised only in furtherance of other enumerated congressional powers. He reasoned that each of the other enumerated powers incidentally involved the expenditure of money and that if the provisions of Section 8, Clause 1 were to be used only in combination with them, the taxing and spending power was "mere tautology." Roberts accepted the broader alternative view first articulated by Alexander Hamilton and later endorsed by Justice Joseph Story in his influential *Commentaries on the Constitution*. Under this interpretation, the taxing and spending power, although not unrestricted, is subject to limitations found within the General Welfare Clause itself, rather than in other enumerated powers. Thus, Roberts, in effect, recognized an independent source of congressional power to tax and spend but at the same time attempted to place internal limits on that power. He was drawing what he regarded as a crucial distinction between special, enumerated powers and a broad unrestricted grant of national authority. Considerations of classical federalism—the division of power between the national government and the states—were of key importance in his analysis. This is evident from the structure of his detailed and elaborate opinion. After commenting on the internal limits of the taxing and spending power, he shifted abruptly to a consideration of the regulatory scheme contemplated by the Agricultural Adjustment Act, concluding that it violated the reserved powers of the states.

Justice Roberts's opinion has a quality of ambivalence, reflecting his apparent uncertainty about the emergence of sweeping regulatory power at the national level—an uncertainty shared by several other justices during this chaotic period in the Court's history. In any event, his interpretation of the General Welfare Clause proved untenable as a workable standard for assessing the constitutionality of other federal programs based on the taxing and spending power.

Dissenting in *Butler*, Justice Harlan Fiske Stone accused the majority of second-guessing Congress on the "wisdom" of the Agricultural Adjustment Act, remarking caustically: "Courts are not the only agency of government that must be assumed to have the capacity to govern." Stone's call for judicial self-restraint became a central theme of majority opinions in the fields of commerce and fiscal policy from 1937 forward.

The Modern Approach

Beginning with two 1937 decisions upholding the newly enacted Social Security and unemployment compensation programs, the Court abandoned the *Butler* rationale (*Chas. C. Steward Machine Company v. Davis* and *Helvering v. Davis*). In the *Steward Machine Company* case, the Court upheld the unemployment compensation features of the Social Security Act of 1935. Justice Benjamin N. Cardozo's majority opinion recognized extensive congressional power to tax and spend based on an interpretation of the General Welfare Clause as a source of plenary power. Cardozo asserted: "The subject matter of taxation open to the power of the Congress is as comprehensive as that open to the power of the states."

In *Mulford v. Smith* (1939), the Court underscored this expansive view of national economic policy making power by upholding a second Agricultural Adjustment Act that, for all practical purposes, was as far reaching as the 1933 statute that had been struck down by the "nine old men" in *United States v. Butler* (1936).

A more recent illustration of the broad spending powers of the modern Congress involves the effort to persuade the states to raise their legal drinking ages. In 1984, Congress adopted an act directing the secretary of transportation to withhold federal highway funds from states whose drinking age was lower than 21. South Dakota brought suit, attacking the right of the federal government to impose this condition on the receipt of federal funds. In *South Dakota v. Dole* (1987), the Supreme Court rejected the state's challenge, saying that "the condition imposed by Congress is directly related to one of the main purposes for which highway funds are expended—safe interstate travel."

Individual Rights as Restraints on the Taxing and Spending Powers

The potential limits imposed by various provisions of the Bill of Rights remain important in determining the extent of the taxing and spending powers. Due process standards place significant procedural requirements on all legislation, including taxing and spending measures. As a practical matter, however, the Fifth Amendment protection against compulsory self-incrimination has served as the primary constitutional basis in recent years for invalidating the exercise of such power. Justice Black first articulated this source of constitutional restraint in a dissenting opinion in a case sustaining the "wagering tax" provisions of the Revenue Act of 1951 (*United States v. Kahriger* [1953]). He read the registration provisions of the act as requiring persons to confess that they were engaged in the illegal "business of gambling." In his view, such compulsion, however indirect, was condemned by the Fifth Amendment.

In the years following the *Kahriger* decision, the Supreme Court, under the leadership of Chief Justice Earl Warren, greatly expanded the constitutional rights of persons accused of crimes. Consistent with this trend, Justice Black's dissenting view was adopted by a Court majority in 1968, and *Kahriger* was expressly overruled (*Marchetti v. United States* and *Grosso v. United States*). Writing for the Court in *Marchetti*, Justice

Harlan was careful to distinguish between the scope of the taxing power, which he did not wish to diminish, and the specific individual safeguards of the Fifth Amendment, which he sought to recognize. The issue was "whether the methods employed by Congress in the Federal Wagering Tax statutes [were] in this situation consistent with the limitations created by the privilege against self-incrimination." Because the registration requirements forced gamblers to expose their own illegal activities, he concluded that the Fifth Amendment was violated.

The Court made it clear in a 1976 decision, however, that the protection against compulsory self-incrimination does not come into play automatically—one must positively assert the right (*Garber v. United States*). Thus, it rejected a defendant's contention that the introduction into evidence of his income tax return, which listed his occupation as that of "professional gambler," violated his immunity against compulsory self-incrimination. In another attempt to strike a balance between procedural safeguards and substantive powers, the Court recognized that the taxing power cannot be used in such a way as to undermine Fourth Amendment restrictions against unreasonable searches and seizures. Thus, in *General Motors Leasing Corporation v. United States* (1977), it held that a warrantless entry into a business office under the purported authority of the Internal Revenue Code was, under the circumstances, a violation of the Fourth Amendment.

TO SUMMARIZE:

- The broad taxing and spending powers of the federal government are based on Article I, Section 8, clause 1, as supplemented by the Sixteenth Amendment.
- Historically, the most important limitations on the federal taxing power focused on the distinction between taxation as a means of revenue enhancement and taxation for purposes of regulation. Today, this distinction has been virtually abolished.
- Like the commerce and taxing powers, Congress's spending power has been greatly expanded since the constitutional revolution of 1937. It has even been interpreted to allow Congress to place reasonable conditions on states' use of federal grant money.

CONGRESSIONAL ENFORCEMENT OF CIVIL RIGHTS AND LIBERTIES

A number of constitutional amendments provide for congressional enforcement of various rights through "appropriate legislation." All three Civil War Amendments (Thirteen, Fourteen, and Fifteen) contain such provisions, and Congress frequently relied on this enforcement authority in developing civil rights legislation during the Reconstruction Era. For example, the Civil Rights Act of 1866, based on the Thirteenth Amendment's enforcement provision, sought to remove vestiges of slavery perpetuated in the "Black Codes" that had been enacted in Southern states to lessen the full force of the amendment. The 1866 legislation provided, among other things, that all citizens were to be accorded the same right "as enjoyed by white citizens" to have access to the courts, to enter into enforceable contracts, and to buy and sell real estate.

In 1968, the Supreme Court held that the Civil Rights Act of 1866 prohibited racial discrimination in the sale of private housing (see *Jones v. Alfred H. Mayer Company*). Shortly thereafter, Congress adopted the Fair Housing Act, which prohibits racial discrimination in the rental and sale of private residences where such transactions are handled by agents or brokers (transactions by private individuals are not covered).

The Fair Housing Act strengthens the prohibition of racial discrimination in housing transactions by authorizing the Department of Housing and Urban Development to refer cases of racial discrimination to the Justice Department for possible prosecution.

The Voting Rights Act of 1965

Aside from the Civil Rights Act of 1964 (discussed previously in connection with the Commerce Clause), the most significant modern legislation in the field of civil rights is the **Voting Rights Act of 1965.** This far-reaching statute (reenacted in 1982 in spite of initial reservations by the Reagan administration) authorizes the attorney general to suspend voting tests and assign federal voting registrars and poll watchers to any state or political subdivision in which fewer than 50 percent of the voting age population was registered as of a certain specified date (November 1, 1964, under the original act).

In a civil action originating in the U.S. Supreme Court, South Carolina challenged the constitutionality of the Voting Rights Act (*South Carolina v. Katzenbach* [1966]). The Court, in an opinion by Chief Justice Warren, rejected this challenge, concluding that Congress had established an ample factual basis for the legislation and that the provisions in question "are a valid means for carrying out the commands of the Fifteenth Amendment." Warren stated that "the basic test to be applied in a case involving Section 2 of the Fifteenth Amendment [the enforcement section] is the same as in all cases concerning the express powers of Congress with relation to the reserved powers of the states." Warren was relying specifically on Chief Justice Marshall's formulation of implied powers in *M'Culloch v. Maryland*.

The Voting Rights Act met this basic standard of rationality and was thus deemed an "appropriate" mode for enforcing the Fifteenth Amendment command that "the right of citizens of the United States to vote shall not be denied or abridged by the United States or by any state on account of race, color, or previous condition of servitude."

In *Katzenbach v. Morgan* (1966), the Supreme Court upheld another provision of the Voting Rights Act of 1965 as an "appropriate" exercise of constitutional power to enforce the equal protection guarantee of the Fourteenth Amendment. The section in question provided that no person completing the sixth grade in an accredited non-English-language Puerto Rican school can be denied the right to vote through inability to read or write English. John P. and Christine Morgan, registered voters in New York City, challenged this section on the ground that it prohibited enforcement of the requirement that New York's English literacy test be passed in order to register to vote. In an earlier decision, the Supreme Court had held that a similar North Carolina literacy requirement did not violate the Equal Protection Clause of the Fourteenth Amendment (*Lassiter v. Northampton County Board of Elections* [1959]). The New York attorney general argued that Congress could not prohibit the implementation of a state law by invoking the enforcement provision of the Fourteenth Amendment unless the judicial branch determined that the state law violated the Constitution. Justice Brennan, writing for a 7-to-2 majority, disagreed, observing that such an interpretation would "depreciate both constitutional resourcefulness and congressional responsibility for implementing the Amendment." The central question, as he viewed it, was not whether the Supreme Court itself regarded English literacy tests as unconstitutional but whether Congress could "prohibit the enforcement of the state law by legislating under Section 5 of the Fourteenth Amendment." Thus the Court's task was "limited to determining whether such legislation is, as required by Section 5, appropriate legislation to enforce the Equal Protection Clause."

Justice Brennan maintained that the authors of the Fourteenth Amendment intended through Section 5 to give Congress **enforcement power under the Fourteenth Amendment** comparable to the "broad powers expressed in the Necessary and Proper Clause." Again the Court relied on *M'Culloch v. Maryland*, finding that the challenged section of the Voting Rights Act was "appropriate" legislation because it met the rationality standard articulated by Chief Justice Marshall in that landmark decision.

The remedy that Congress chose to provide in protecting the voting rights of non-English-speaking Puerto Ricans could be justified on the basis of two alternative theories: (1) It might provide these persons with a "political weapon" that could be used to fight discriminatory practices by government (a rationale similar to that employed in *South Carolina v. Katzenbach*), or (2) Congress might have concluded that New York's English literacy test requirement violated the Equal Protection Clause of the Fourteenth Amendment, regardless of the Supreme Court's previous position on this issue. The importance of this justification is that it in effect recognizes Congress as a "constitutional interpreter." The implications of this rationale have fascinated legal scholars, some of whom regard *Morgan* as potentially undercutting the authority of the Supreme Court as a final interpreter of the Constitution. Moreover, if Congress has the power to define the scope of constitutional protections, as Brennan's opinion suggests, it logically follows that Congress might at some time narrow, rather than broaden, such protections. In his dissenting opinion, Justice Harlan expressed concern about this possibility. He maintained that Congress could define constitutional rights "so as, in effect, to dilute the equal protection and due process decisions of this Court." However, the *Morgan* decision is confined to the enforcement of rights explicitly recognized in provisions of the Constitution—in this instance, the Equal Protection Clause of the Fourteenth Amendment. Nevertheless, it serves to remind us that other branches of the national government have important roles to play in defining and implementing constitutional rights.

The Religious Freedom Restoration Act

In Chapter 1 we discussed the Religious Freedom Restoration Act of 1993 (RFRA), which Congress enacted as a response to the Supreme Court's 1990 decision in *Employment Division v. Smith*. In *Smith*, the Court departed from modern precedent and adopted a more restrictive interpretation of the Free Exercise Clause of the First Amendment. In passing RFRA, Congress sought to restore the *status quo ante*—to return the law in this area to what it was prior to the *Smith* decision. In adopting this statute, Congress was again invoking its broad powers under Section 5 of the Fourteenth Amendment. Although the Fourteenth Amendment does not expressly protect freedom of religion, the Supreme Court said long ago that freedom of religion is one of those fundamental rights incorporated within the broad term "liberty" in Section 1 of the Fourteenth Amendment (see *Hamilton v. Regents of the University of California* [1934]). Logically, then, Congress may use its legislative power to protect all of the freedoms the courts have recognized as essential to "a scheme of ordered liberty," to quote the Supreme Court's opinion in *Palko v. Connecticut* (1937).

In striking down RFRA (see *City of Boerne v. Flores* [1997]), the Supreme Court was not concerned with the fact that Congress was using its legislative authority in furtherance of a right not explicitly protected by the Fourteenth Amendment. Rather, the Court objected to Congress's attempt to use a simple statute to vitiate the Court's previous interpretation of the First Amendment. In *Boerne*, the Court made clear that it, not the Congress, is the final interpreter of the Constitution. Under *Boerne*, congressional enforcement powers under the Fourteenth Amendment may not be used in contravention of the Court's interpretation of the Constitution.

Critics of *Boerne* question whether it can be reconciled with the expansive view of congressional power under Section 5 of the Fourteenth Amendment that the Court advanced in *Katzenbach v. Morgan*. Remember, however, that the Fourteenth Amendment was adopted shortly after the Civil War primarily to protect the civil rights of African-Americans. The Voting Rights Act upheld in *Morgan* was consistent with this great objective. The Religious Freedom Restoration Act, on the other hand, was designed to reassert liberties that the Supreme Court itself had not recognized until the modern era. Viewed in this historical perspective, therefore, *Katzenbach v. Morgan* may not be fundamentally inconsistent with the *City of Boerne* decision. Nevertheless, *Boerne* has spawned a lively constitutional debate over the scope of congressional power under Section 5 of the Fourteenth Amendment.

The Violence against Women Act

As we noted above in our discussion of the Commerce Clause, the Supreme Court in *United States v. Morrison* (2000) struck down a federal statutory provision allowing victims of gender-motivated violence to sue their victimizers in federal court. The disputed provision was based not solely on the Commerce Clause, however, but also on Congress's authority under Section 5 of the Fourteenth Amendment. In striking down the provision, the Court noted that it was "directed not at any State or state actor, but at individuals who have committed criminal acts motivated by gender bias." Applying the **state action doctrine** first articulated in 1883 (see, for example, *The Civil Rights Cases*, discussed and excerpted in Chapter 12), the Court held that the Fourteenth Amendment does not empower Congress to provide remedies for injuries inflicted upon individuals by other individuals. In the view of the Court's conservative majority, protecting individuals from violence is the function of the states.

TO SUMMARIZE:

- Section 5 of the Fourteenth Amendment allows Congress to adopt "appropriate legislation" to protect and enforce civil rights and liberties.
- The Supreme Court's jurisprudence reflects a degree of ambivalence as to the precise scope of congressional enforcement powers in this area.

CONCLUSION

From the foregoing discussion it is clear that Congress has many sources of constitutional authority. Some of these are quite explicit, as the list of enumerated powers in Article I, Section 8, makes clear. Others are implicit, open ended, and subject to no complete or conclusive definition. These implied powers are fully recognized, however, in the Necessary and Proper Clause and in the enforcement provisions of several constitutional amendments, most notably the Thirteenth, Fourteenth, and Fifteenth Amendments. Within this broad range of explicit and implicit powers, Congress has been accorded broad latitude to address the major problems, needs, and goals of the nation, as perceived by succeeding generations of Americans during two centuries of constitutional history. As recent decisions of the Supreme Court indicate, however, Congress's power is by no means unlimited.

KEY TERMS

distributive articles
reapportionment
bicameralism
Speech or Debate Clause
immunity
enumerated powers
Article I, Section 8
police power
implied powers

oversight
power to investigate
subpoena
compulsory process
contempt of Congress
power to regulate interstate
    commerce
local aspects of interstate
    commerce

Interstate Commerce Act of
    1887
Sherman Antitrust Act of 1890
stream of commerce doctrine
direct–indirect test
distinction between
    manufacturing and
    commerce
Civil Rights Act of 1964

RICO Act
Tenth Amendment
taxing power
reciprocal immunity
spending power
Voting Rights Act of 1965
enforcement power under the
    Fourteenth Amendment
state action doctrine

FOR FURTHER READING

Baker, Leonard. *Back to Back: The Duel between FDR and the Supreme Court.* New York: Macmillan, 1967.

Bamberger, Michael A. *Reckless Legislation: How Lawmakers Ignore the Constitution.* Piscataway, N.J.: Rutgers University Press, 2000.

Beck, Carl. *Contempt of Congress.* New Orleans: Hauser Press, 1959.

Benson, Paul R., Jr. *The Supreme Court and the Commerce Clause, 1937–1970.* Cambridge, Mass.: Dunellen, 1970.

Fisher, Louis. *The Politics of Shared Power: Congress and the Executive.* Washington, D.C.: Congressional Quarterly Press, 1987.

Fisher, Louis. *Constitutional Conflicts between Congress and the President* (4th ed.). Lawrence: University Press of Kansas, 1997.

Frankfurter, Felix. *The Commerce Clause under Marshall, Taney and Waite.* Chapel Hill: University of North Carolina Press, 1971.

Goodman, Walter. *The Committee: The Extraordinary Career of the House Committee on Un-American Activities.* New York: Farrar, Straus and Giroux, 1968.

Gunther, Gerald (ed.). *John Marshall's Defense of M'Culloch v. Maryland.* Stanford, Calif.: Stanford University Press, 1969.

Hamilton, James. *The Power to Probe: A Study of Congressional Investigations.* New York: Random House, 1976.

Pyle, Christopher H., and Richard M. Pious (eds.). *The President, Congress and the Constitution: Power and Legitimacy in American Politics.* New York: Free Press, 1984.

Warren, Charles. *Congress, the Constitution, and the Supreme Court.* New York: Little, Brown, 1935.

White, G. Edward. *The Constitution and the New Deal.* Cambridge, Mass.: Harvard University Press, 2000.

Wilson, Woodrow. *Congressional Government.* Boston: Houghton Mifflin, 1885.

Wood, Stephen B. *Constitutional Politics in the Progressive Era: Child Labor and the Law.* Chicago: University of Chicago Press, 1968.

INTERNET RESOURCES

Name of Resource	Description	URL
U.S. Government Printing Office—Congress page	Various congressional informational resources	http://www.access.gpo.gov/congress/
Library of Congress—"Thomas"	Extensive collection of congressional documents	http://thomas.loc.gov/
C-SPAN Online	Gavel-to-gavel coverage of the U.S. House and other public affairs programming	http://capwiz.com/c-span/home/
Congressional Quarterly	Congressional news, general background information on members of Congress, information about bills sponsored, speeches made, roll call votes, etc.	http://www.cq.com/

Case

U.S. TERM LIMITS, INC. V. THORNTON

514 U.S. 779; 115 S.Ct. 1842; 131 L.Ed. 2d 881 (1995)
Vote: 5–4

An amendment to the Arkansas Constitution (Amendment 73)
prohibited persons who had already served three terms in the
U.S. House of Representatives or two terms in the U.S. Senate
from running for Congress. The Arkansas Supreme Court struck
down the amendment.

Justice Stevens delivered the opinion of the Court.

. . .[T]he constitutionality of Amendment 73 depends critically on the resolution of two distinct issues. The first is whether the Constitution forbids States from adding to or altering the qualifications specifically enumerated in the Constitution. The second is, if the Constitution does so forbid, whether the fact that Amendment 73 is formulated as a ballot access restriction rather than as an outright disqualification is of constitutional significance. Our resolution of these issues draws upon our prior resolution of a related but distinct issue: whether Congress has the power to add to or alter the qualifications of its Members.

Twenty-six years ago, in *Powell v. McCormack* . . . (1969), we reviewed the history and text of the Qualifications Clauses in a case involving an attempted exclusion of a duly elected Member of Congress. The principal issue was whether the power granted to each House in Art. I, § 5, to judge the Qualifications of its own Members includes the power to impose qualifications other than those set forth in the text of the Constitution. In an opinion by Chief Justice Warren for eight Members of the Court, we held that it does not. . . .

Our reaffirmation of *Powell* does not necessarily resolve the specific questions presented in these cases. For petitioners argue that whatever the constitutionality of additional qualifications for membership imposed by Congress, the historical and textual materials discussed in *Powell* do not support the conclusion that the Constitution prohibits additional qualifications imposed by States. In the absence of such a constitutional prohibition, petitioners argue, the Tenth Amendment and the principle of reserved powers require that States be allowed to add such qualifications. . . .

Petitioners argue that the Constitution contains no express prohibition against state-added qualifications, and that Amendment 73 is therefore an appropriate exercise of a State's reserved power to place additional restrictions on the choices that its own voters may make. We disagree for two independent reasons. First, we conclude that the power to add qualifications is not within the original powers of the States, and thus is not reserved to the States by the Tenth Amendment. Second, even if States possessed some original power in this area, we conclude that the Framers intended the Constitution to be the exclusive source of qualifications for members of Congress, and that the Framers thereby divested States of any power to add qualifications. . . .

Contrary to petitioners' assertions, the power to add qualifications is not part of the original powers of sovereignty that the Tenth Amendment reserved to the States. Petitioners' Tenth Amendment argument misconceives the nature of the right at issue because that Amendment could only reserve that which existed before. . . .

With respect to setting qualifications for service in Congress, no such right existed before the Constitution was ratified. The contrary argument overlooks the revolutionary character of the government that the Framers conceived. Prior to the adoption of the Constitution, the States had joined together under the Articles of Confederation. In that system, the States retained most of their sovereignty, like independent nations bound together only by treaties. . . . After the Constitutional Convention convened, the Framers were presented with, and eventually adopted a variation of, a plan not merely to amend the Articles of Confederation but to create an entirely new National Government with a National Executive, National Judiciary, and a National Legislature. . . . In adopting that plan, the Framers envisioned a uniform national system, rejecting the notion that the Nation was a collection of States, and instead creating a direct link between the National Government and the people of the United States. . . . In that National Government, representatives owe primary allegiance not to the people of a State, but to the people of the Nation. . . .

It is surely no coincidence that the context of federal elections provides one of the few areas in which the Constitution expressly requires action by the States, namely that "[t]he Times, Places and Manner of holding Elections for Senators and Representatives, shall be prescribed in each State by the Legislature thereof." This duty parallels the duty under Article II that "Each State shall appoint, in such Manner as the Legislature thereof may direct, a Number of Electors." . . . These Clauses are express delegations of power to the States to act with respect to federal elections.

This conclusion is consistent with our previous recognition that, in certain limited contexts, the power to regulate the incidents of the federal system is not a reserved power of the States, but rather is delegated by the Constitution. Thus, we have noted that [w]hile, in a loose sense, the right to vote for representatives in Congress is sometimes spoken of as a right derived from the states, . . . this statement is true only in the sense that the states are authorized by the Constitution, to legislate on the subject as provided by § 2 of Art. I. . . .

In short, as the Framers recognized, electing representatives to the National Legislature was a new right, arising from the Constitution itself. The Tenth Amendment thus provides no basis for concluding that the States possess reserved power to add qualifications to those that are fixed in the Constitution. Instead, any state power to set the qualifications for membership in Congress must derive not from the reserved powers of state sovereignty, but rather from the delegated powers of national sovereignty. In the absence of any constitutional delegation to the States of power to add qualifications to those enumerated in the Constitution, such a power does not exist. . . .

Congress' subsequent experience with state-imposed qualifications provides further evidence of the general consensus on the lack of state power in this area. In *Powell,* we examined that experience and noted that during the first 100 years of its existence, Congress strictly limited its power to judge the qualifications of its members to those enumerated in the Constitution. . . .

We recognize, as we did in *Powell,* that congressional practice has been erratic and that the precedential value of congressional exclusion cases is quite limited. . . . Nevertheless, those incidents lend support to the result we reach today.

Our conclusion that States lack the power to impose qualifications vindicates the same fundamental principle of our representative democracy that we recognized in *Powell,* namely that the people should choose whom they please to govern them. . . .

As we noted earlier, the *Powell* Court recognized that an egalitarian ideal that election to the National Legislature should be open to all people of merit provided a critical foundation for the Constitutional structure. This egalitarian theme echoes throughout the constitutional debates. . . .

. . . [W]e believe that state-imposed qualifications, as much as congressionally imposed qualifications, would undermine the second critical idea recognized in *Powell:* that an aspect of sovereignty is the right of the people to vote for whom they wish. Again, the source of the qualification is of little moment in assessing the qualification's restrictive impact.

Finally, state-imposed restrictions, unlike the congressionally imposed restrictions at issue in *Powell,* violate a third idea central to this basic principle: that the right to choose representatives belongs not to the States, but to the people. . . .

Permitting individual States to formulate diverse qualifications for their representatives would result in a patchwork of state qualifications, undermining the uniformity and the national character that the Framers envisioned and sought to ensure. . . . Such a patchwork would also sever the direct link that the Framers found so critical between the National Government and the people of the United States. . . .

Petitioners argue that, even if States may not add qualifications, Amendment 73 is constitutional because it is not such a qualification, and because Amendment 73 is a permissible exercise of state power to regulate the Times, Places and Manner of Holding Elections. We reject these contentions.

Unlike §§ 1 and 2 of Amendment 73, which create absolute bars to service for long-term incumbents running for state office, § 3 merely provides that certain Senators and Representatives shall not be certified as candidates and shall not have their names appear on the ballot. They may run as write-in candidates and, if elected, they may serve. Petitioners contend that only a legal bar to service creates an impermissible qualification, and that Amendment 73 is therefore consistent with the Constitution. . . .

We need not decide whether petitioners' narrow understanding of qualifications is correct because, even if it is, Amendment 73 may not stand. As we have often noted, . . . "[c]onstitutional rights would be of little value if they could be . . . indirectly denied." . . . The Constitution nullifies sophisticated as well as simpleminded modes of infringing on Constitutional protections. . . .

In our view, Amendment 73 is an indirect attempt to accomplish what the Constitution prohibits Arkansas from accomplishing directly. As the plurality opinion of the Arkansas Supreme Court recognized, Amendment 73 is an effort to dress eligibility to stand for Congress in ballot access clothing, because the intent and the effect of Amendment 73 are to disqualify congressional incumbents from further service. . . . We must, of course, accept the State Court's view of the purpose of its own law: we are thus authoritatively informed that the sole purpose of § 3 of Amendment 73 was to attempt to achieve a result that is forbidden by the Federal Constitution. Indeed, it cannot be seriously contended that the intent behind Amendment 73 is other than to prevent the election of incumbents. The preamble of Amendment 73 states explicitly: "[T]he people of Arkansas . . . herein limit the terms of elected officials." Sections 1 and § 2 create absolute limits on the number of terms that may be served. There is no hint that § 3 was intended to have any other purpose. . . .

Petitioners make the . . . argument that Amendment 73 merely regulates the Manner of elections, and that the Amendment is therefore a permissible exercise of state power under Article I, § 4, cl. 1 (the Elections Clause) to regulate the Times, Places and Manner of elections. We cannot agree.

A necessary consequence of petitioners' argument is that Congress itself would have the power to make or alter a measure such as Amendment 73. . . . That the Framers would have approved of such a result is unfathomable. As our decision in *Powell* and our discussion above make clear, the Framers were particularly concerned that a grant to Congress of the authority to set its own qualifications would lead inevitably to congressional self-aggrandizement and the upsetting of the delicate constitutional balance. . . . Petitioners would have us believe, however, that even as the Framers carefully circumscribed congressional power to set qualifications, they intended to allow Congress to achieve the same result by simply formulating the regulation as a ballot access restriction under the Elections Clause. We refuse to adopt an interpretation of the Elections Clause that would so cavalierly disregard what the Framers intended to be a fundamental constitutional safeguard.

Moreover, petitioners' broad construction of the Elections Clause is fundamentally inconsistent with the Framers' view of that Clause. The Framers intended the Elections Clause to grant States authority to create procedural regulations, not to provide States with license to exclude classes of candidates from federal office. . . .

The merits of term limits, or rotation, have been the subject of debate since the formation of our Constitution, when the Framers unanimously rejected a proposal to add such limits to the Constitution. The cogent arguments on both sides of the question that were articulated during the process of ratification largely retain their force today. Over half the States have adopted measures that impose such limits on some offices either directly or indirectly, and the Nation as a whole, notably by constitutional amendment, has imposed a limit on the number of terms that the President may serve. Term limits, like any other qualification for office, unquestionably restrict the ability of voters to vote for whom they wish. On the other hand, such limits may provide for the infusion of fresh ideas and new perspectives, and may decrease the likelihood that representatives will lose touch with their constituents. It is not our province to resolve this long-standing debate.

We are, however, firmly convinced that allowing the several States to adopt term limits for congressional service would effect a fundamental change in the constitutional framework. Any such change must come not by legislation adopted either by Congress or by an individual State, but rather as have other important changes in the electoral process—through the Amendment procedures set forth in Article V. The Framers decided that the qualifications for service in the Congress of the United States be fixed in the Constitution and be uniform throughout the Nation. That decision reflects the Framers' understanding that Members of Congress are chosen by separate constituencies, but that they become, when elected, servants of the people of the United States. They are not merely delegates appointed by separate, sovereign States; they occupy offices that are integral and essential components of a single National Government. In the absence of a properly passed constitutional amendment, allowing individual States to craft their own qualifications for Congress would thus erode the structure envisioned by the Framers, a structure that was designed, in the words of the Preamble to our Constitution, to form a more perfect Union. . . .

Justice Kennedy, concurring. . . .

Justice Thomas, with whom the *Chief Justice, Justice O'Connor,* and *Justice Scalia* join, dissenting.

It is ironic that the Court bases today's decision on the right of the people to "choose whom they please to govern them." . . . Under our Constitution, there is only one State whose people have the right to "choose whom they please" to represent Arkansas in Congress. The Court holds, however, that neither the elected legislature of that State nor the people themselves (acting by ballot initiative) may prescribe any qualifications for those representatives. The majority therefore defends the right of the people of Arkansas to "choose whom they please to govern them" by invalidating a provision that won nearly 60% of the votes cast in a direct election and that carried every congressional district in the State.

I dissent. Nothing in the Constitution deprives the people of each State of the power to prescribe eligibility requirements for the candidates who seek to represent them in Congress. The Constitution is simply silent on this question. And where the Constitution is silent, it raises no bar to action by the States or the people. . . .

I take it to be established, then, that the people of Arkansas do enjoy "reserved" powers over the selection of their representatives in Congress. Purporting to exercise those reserved powers, they have agreed among themselves that the candidates covered by § 3 of Amendment 73—those whom they have already elected to three or more terms in the House of Representatives or to two or more terms in the Senate—should not be eligible to appear on the ballot for reelection, but should nonetheless be returned to Congress if enough voters are sufficiently enthusiastic about their candidacy to write in their names. Whatever one might think of the wisdom of this arrangement, we may not override the decision of the people of Arkansas unless something in the Federal Constitution deprives them of the power to enact such measures.

The majority settles on "the Qualifications Clauses" as the constitutional provisions that Amendment 73 violates. . . . Because I do not read those provisions to impose any unstated prohibitions on the States, it is unnecessary for me to decide whether the majority is correct to identify Arkansas' ballot-access restriction with laws fixing true term limits or otherwise prescribing "qualifications" for congressional office. . . .

. . . [T]oday's decision reads the Qualifications Clauses to impose substantial implicit prohibitions on the States and the people of the States. I would not draw such an expansive negative inference from the fact that the Constitution requires Members of Congress to be a certain age, to be inhabitants of the States that they represent, and to have been United States citizens for a specified period. Rather, I would read the Qualifications Clauses to do no more than what they say. I respectfully dissent.

Case

M'CULLOCH V. MARYLAND

4 Wheat. (17 U.S.) 316; 4 L.Ed. 579 (1819)
Vote: 7–0

In 1818, the Maryland legislature imposed a tax on all banks not chartered by the state. The act imposed an annual fee of $15,000 payable in advance or a 2 percent tax on the value of notes issued by such banks. A penalty of $500 was imposed for each violation of this tax measure, which, as everyone recognized, was aimed squarely at the Bank of the United States. M'Culloch, the cashier of the Baltimore branch of the Bank of the United States, refused to comply with the state law. A lower court judgment against M'Culloch was upheld by the Maryland Court of Appeals.

Mr. Chief Justice Marshall delivered the opinion of the Court.

. . . The first question made in the cause is, has Congress power to incorporate a bank? . . . The power now contested was exercised by the first Congress elected under the present Constitution. . . . Its principle was completely understood, and was opposed with equal zeal and ability. After being resisted, first in the fair and open field of debate, and afterwards in the executive cabinet, . . . it became a law. The original act was permitted to expire; but a short experience of the embarrassments to which the refusal to revive it exposed the government, convinced those who were most prejudiced against the measure of its necessity and induced the passage of the present law. . . .

This government is acknowledged by all to be one of enumerated powers. The principle, that it can exercise only the powers granted to it, would seem too apparent to have required to be enforced by all those arguments which its enlightened friends, while it was depending before the people, found it necessary to urge. That principle is now

universally admitted. But the question respecting the extent of the powers actually granted, is perpetually arising, and will probably continue to arise, as long as our system shall exist.

In discussing these questions, the conflicting powers of the general and state governments must be brought into view, and the supremacy of their respective laws, when they are in opposition, must be settled.

If any one proposition could command the universal assent of mankind, we might expect it would be this—that the government of the Union, though limited in its powers, is supreme within its sphere of action. This would seem to result necessarily from its nature. It is the government of all; its powers are delegated by all; it represents all, and acts for all. Though any one state may be willing to control its operations, no state is willing to allow others to control them. The nation, on those subjects on which it can act, must necessarily bind its component parts. But this question is not left to mere reason; the people have, in express terms, decided it by saying, "this Constitution, and the laws of the United States, which shall be made in pursuance thereof," . . . "shall be the supreme law of the land," and by requiring that the members of the state legislatures, and the officers of the executive and judicial departments of the states shall take the oath of fidelity to it.

The government of the United States, then, though limited in its powers, is supreme; and its laws, when made in pursuance of the Constitution, form the supreme law of the land, "anything in the Constitution or laws of any state to the contrary notwithstanding." Among the enumerated powers, we do not find that of establishing a bank or creating a corporation. But there is no phrase in the instrument which, like the Articles of Confederation, excludes incidental or implied powers; and which requires that everything granted shall be expressly and minutely described. Even the 10th Amendment, which was framed for the purpose of quieting the excessive jealousies which had been excited, omits the word "expressly," and declares only that the powers "not delegated to the United States, nor prohibited to the states, are reserved to the states or to the people:" thus leaving the question, whether the particular power which may become the subject of contest has been delegated to the one government, or prohibited to the other, to depend on a fair construction of the whole instrument. . . . A constitution, to contain an accurate detail of all the subdivisions of which its great powers will admit, and of all the means by which they may be carried into execution, would partake of a prolixity of a legal code, and could scarcely be embraced by the human mind. It would probably never be understood by the public. Its nature, therefore, requires, that only its great outlines should be marked, its important objects designated, and the minor ingredients which compose those objects be deduced from the nature of the objects themselves. . . . In considering this question, then, we must never forget that it is a constitution we are expounding.

Although, among the enumerated powers of government, we do not find the word "bank" or "incorporation," we find the great powers to lay and collect taxes; to borrow money; to regulate commerce; to declare and conduct a war; and to raise and support armies and navies. The sword and the purse, all the external relations, and no inconsiderable portion of the industry of the nation, are entrusted to its government. . . . [I]t may with great reason be contended, that a government, entrusted with such ample powers, on the due execution of which the happiness and prosperity of the nation so vitally depends, must also be entrusted with ample means for their execution. The power being given, it is the interest of the nation to facilitate its execution. It can never be their interest, and cannot be presumed to have been their intention, to clog and embarrass its execution by withholding the most appropriate means. . . .

The government which has a right to do an act, and has imposed on it the duty of performing that act, must, according to the dictates of reason, be allowed to select the means; and those who contend that it may not select any appropriate means, that one particular mode of effecting the object is excepted, take upon themselves the burden of establishing that exception. But the Constitution of the United States has not left the right of Congress to employ the necessary means for the execution of the powers conferred on the government to general reasoning. To its enumeration of powers is added that of making "all laws which shall be necessary and proper, for carrying into execution the foregoing powers, and all other powers vested by this Constitution, in the government of the United States, or in any department thereof." The counsel for the

State of Maryland have urged various arguments, to prove that this clause, though in terms a grant of power, is not so in effect. . . . In support of this proposition, they have found it necessary to contend, that this clause was inserted for the purpose of conferring on Congress the power of making laws. That, without it, doubts might be entertained whether Congress could exercise its powers in the form of legislation.

But could this be the object for which it was inserted? A government is created by the people, having legislative, executive, and judicial powers. Its legislative powers are vested in a Congress. . . . That a legislature, endowed with legislative powers, can legislate, is a proposition too self-evident to have been questioned.

But the argument on which most reliance is placed, is drawn from the peculiar language of this clause. Congress is not empowered by it to make all laws, which may have relation to the powers conferred on the government, but such only as may be "necessary and proper" for carrying them into execution. The word "necessary" is considered as controlling the whole sentence, and as limiting the right to pass laws for the execution of the granted powers, to such as are indispensable, and without which the power would be nugatory. That it excludes the choice of means, and leaves to Congress, in each case, that only which is most direct and simple. Is it true that this is the sense in which the word "necessary" is always used? Does it always import an absolute physical necessity, so strong that one thing, to which another may be termed necessary, cannot exist without the other? We think it does not. . . . To employ the means necessary to an end, is generally understood as employing any means calculated to produce the end, and not as being confined to those single means, without which the end would be entirely unattainable. Such is the character of human language, that no word conveys to the mind, in all situations, one single definite idea. . . .

It is, we think, impossible to compare the sentence which prohibits a state from laying "imposts or duties on imports or exports, except what may be absolutely necessary for executing its inspection laws," with that which authorizes Congress "to make all laws which shall be necessary and proper for carrying into execution" the powers of the general government, without feeling a conviction that the convention understood itself to change materially the meaning of the word "necessary," by prefixing the word "absolutely." This word, then, like others, is used in various senses; and, in its construction, the subject, the context, the intention of the person using them, are all to be taken into view.

Let this be done in the case under consideration. The subject is the execution of those great powers on which the welfare of a nation essentially depends. It must have been the intention of those who gave these powers, to insure, as far a human prudence could insure, their beneficial execution. This could not be done by confiding the choice of means to such narrow limits as not to leave it in the power of Congress to adopt any which might be appropriate, and which were conducive to the end. This provision is made in a Constitution intended to endure for ages to come, and, consequently, to be adapted to the various crises of human affairs. . . .

The result of the most careful and attentive consideration bestowed upon this clause is, that if it does not enlarge, it cannot be construed to restrain the powers of Congress, or to impair the right of the legislature to exercise its best judgment in the selection of measures to carry into execution the constitutional powers of the government. If no other motive for its insertion can be suggested, a sufficient one is found in the desire to remove all doubts respecting the right to legislate on the vast mass of incidental powers which must be involved in the Constitution, if that instrument be not a splendid bauble.

We admit, as all must admit, that the powers of the government are limited, and that its limits are not to be transcended. But we think the sound construction of the Constitution must allow to the national legislature that discretion, with respect to the means by which the powers it confers are to be carried into execution, which will enable the body to perform the high duties assigned to it, in the manner most beneficial to the people. Let the end be legitimate, let it be within the scope of the Constitution, and all means which are appropriate, which are plainly adapted to that end, which are not prohibited, but consist with the letter and spirit of the Constitution, are constitutional.

That a corporation must be considered as a means not less usual, not of higher dignity, not more requiring a particular specification than other means, has been sufficiently proved. . . . [W]e find no reason to suppose that a constitution, omitting, and wisely omitting, to enumerate all the means for carrying into execution the great powers vested in government, ought to have specified this. . . .

If a corporation may be employed indiscriminately with other means to carry into execution the powers of the government, no particular reason can be assigned for excluding the use of a bank, if required for its fiscal operations. To use one, must be within the discretion of Congress, if it be an appropriate mode of executing the powers of government. That it is a convenient, a useful, and essential instrument in the prosecution of its fiscal operations, is not now a subject of controversy.

. . . [W]ere its necessity less apparent, none can deny its being an appropriate measure; and if it is, the degree of its necessity, as has been very justly observed, is to be discussed in another place. Should Congress, in the execution of its powers, adopt measures which are prohibited by the Constitution; or should Congress, under the pretext of executing its powers pass laws for the accomplishment of objects not entrusted to the government, it would become the painful duty of this tribunal, should a case requiring such a decision come before it, to say that such an act was not the law of the land. But where the law is not prohibited, and is really calculated to effect any of the objects entrusted to the government, to undertake here to inquire into the degree of its necessity, would be to pass the line which circumscribes the judicial department, and to tread on legislative ground. This court disclaims all pretensions to such a power. . . .

After the most deliberate consideration, it is the unanimous and decided opinion of this court that the act to incorporate the bank of the United States is a law made in pursuance of the Constitution, and is a part of the supreme law of the land. . . .

It being the opinion of the court that the act incorporating the bank is constitutional, . . . we proceed to inquire: Whether the state of Maryland may, without violating the Constitution, tax that branch?

That the power of taxation is one of vital importance; that it is retained by the states; that it is not abridged by the grant of a similar power to the government of the Union; that it is to be concurrently exercised by the two governments: are truths which have never been denied. But, such is the paramount character of the Constitution that its capacity to withdraw any subject from the action of even this power, is admitted. The states are expressly forbidden to lay any duties on imports or exports, except what may be absolutely necessary for executing their inspection laws. If the obligation of this prohibition must be conceded—if it may restrain a state from the exercise of its taxing power on imports and exports—the same paramount character would seem to restrain, as it certainly may restrain, a state from such other exercise of this power, as is in its nature incompatible with, and repugnant to, the constitutional laws of the Union. . . .

This great principle is, that the Constitution and the laws made in pursuance thereof are supreme; that they control the constitution and laws of the respective states, and cannot be controlled by them. From this, which may be almost termed an axiom, other propositions are deduced as corollaries, on the truth or error of which, and on their application to this case the cause has been supposed to depend. These are, 1st. that a power to create implies a power to preserve. 2d. That a power to destroy, if wielded by a different hand, is hostile to, and incompatible with these powers to create and to preserve. 3d. That where this repugnancy exists, that authority which is supreme must control, not yield to that over which it is supreme. . . .

That the power to tax involves the power to destroy; that the power to destroy may defeat and render useless the power to create; that there is a plain repugnance, in conferring on one government a power to control the constitutional measures of another, which other, with respect to those very measures, is declared to be supreme over that which exerts the control, are propositions not to be denied. . . .

If the states may tax one instrument, employed by the government in the execution of its powers, they may tax any and every other instrument. They may tax the mail; they may tax the mint; they may tax patent-rights; they may tax all the means employed by the government, to an excess which would defeat all the ends of government. This was not intended by the American people. . . .

The question is, in truth, a question of supremacy; and if the right of the states to tax the means employed by the general government be conceded, the declaration that the Constitution, and the laws made in pursuance thereof, shall be the supreme law of the land, is an empty and unmeaning declaration. . . .

It has also been insisted, that, as the power of taxation in the general and state governments is acknowledged to be concurrent, every argument which would sustain the right of the general government to tax banks chartered by the states, will equally sustain the right of the states to tax banks chartered by the general government.

But the two cases are not on the same reason. The people of all the states have created the general government, and have conferred upon it the general power of taxation. The people of all the states, and the states themselves, are represented in Congress, and, by their representatives, exercise this power. When they tax the chartered institutions of the states, they tax their constituents; and these

taxes must be uniform. But, when a state taxes the operations of the government of the United States, it acts upon institutions created, not by their own constituents, but by people over whom they claim no control. It acts upon the measures of a government created by others as well as themselves, for the benefit of others in common with themselves. The difference is that which always exists, and always must exist, between the action of the whole on a part, and the action of a part on the whole—between the laws of a government declared to be supreme, and those of a government which, when in opposition to those laws, is not supreme. But if the full application of this argument could be admitted, it might bring into question the right of Congress to tax the state banks, and could not prove the right of the states to tax the Bank of the United States.

The court has bestowed on this subject its most deliberate consideration. The result is a conviction that the states have no power, by taxation or otherwise, to retard, impede, burden, or in any manner control the operations of the constitutional laws enacted by Congress to carry into execution the powers vested in the general government. This is, we think, the unavoidable consequence of that supremacy which the Constitution has declared.

We are unanimously of opinion that the law passed by the legislature of Maryland, imposing a tax on the Bank of the United States, is unconstitutional and void.

This opinion does not deprive the states of any resources which they originally possessed. It does not extend to a tax paid by the real property of the bank, in common with the other real property within the state, nor to a tax imposed on the interest which the citizens of Maryland may hold in this institution, in common with other property of the same description throughout the state. But this is a tax on the operations of the bank, and is, consequently, a tax on the operation of an instrument of the Union to carry its powers into execution. Such a tax must be unconstitutional. . . .

Case

WATKINS V. UNITED STATES

354 U.S. 178; 77 S.Ct. 1173; 1 L.Ed. 2d 1273 (1957)
Vote: 6–1

John Watkins was subpoenaed to testify before the House Committee on Un-American Activities. After answering the committee's questions about his past association with the Communist Party, Watkins refused to say whether certain other named individuals were members of the party. Watkins protested the

committee's questions, saying, "I do not believe that such questions are relevant to the work of this committee nor do I believe that this committee has the right to undertake the public exposure of persons because of their past activities." For his refusal to cooperate, Watkins was convicted of contempt of Congress.

Mr. Chief Justice Warren delivered the opinion of the Court.

. . . We start with several basic premises on which there is general agreement. The power of the Congress to conduct investigations is inherent in the legislative process. That power is broad. It encompasses inquiries concerning the administration of existing laws as well as proposed or possible needed statutes. It includes surveys of defects in our social, economic or political system for the purpose of enabling the Congress to remedy them. It comprehends probes into departments of the Federal Government to expose corruption, inefficiency or waste. But broad as is this power of inquiry, it is not unlimited. There is no general authority to expose the private affairs of individuals without justification in terms of the functions of the Congress. . . . Nor is the Congress a law enforcement or trial agency. These are functions of the executive and judicial departments of government. No inquiry is an end in itself; it must be related to and in furtherance of a legitimate task of the Congress. Investigations conducted solely for the personal aggrandizement of the investigators or to "punish" those investigated are indefensible. It is unquestionably the duty of all citizens to cooperate with the Congress in its efforts to obtain the facts needed for intelligent legislative action. It is their unremitting obligation to respond to subpoenas, to respect the dignity of the Congress and its committees and to testify fully with respect to matters within the province of proper investigation. This, of course, assumes that the constitutional rights of witnesses will be respected by the Congress as they are in a court of justice. The Bill of Rights is applicable to investigations as to all forms of governmental action. Witnesses cannot be compelled to give evidence against themselves. They cannot be subjected to unreasonable search and seizure. Nor can the First Amendment freedoms of speech, press, religion, or political belief and association be abridged. . . .

In the decade following World War II, there appeared a new kind of congressional inquiry unknown in prior periods of American history. Principally this was the result of the various investigations into the threat of subversion of the United States Government, but other subjects of congressional interest also contributed to the changed scene. This new phase of legislative inquiry involved a broadscale intrusion into the lives and affairs of private citizens. It brought before the courts novel questions of the appropriate limits of congressional inquiry. Prior cases . . . had defined the scope of investigative power in terms of the inherent limitations of the sources of that power. In the recent cases, the emphasis shifted to problems of accommodating the interests of the Government with the rights and privileges of individuals. The central theme was the application of the Bill of Rights as a restraint upon the assertion of governmental power in this form.

It was during this period that the Fifth Amendment privilege against self-incrimination was frequently invoked and recognized as a legal limit upon the authority of a committee to require that a witness answer its questions. Some early doubts as to the applicability of that privilege before a legislative committee never matured. When the matter reached this Court, the Government did not challenge in any way that the Fifth Amendment protection was available to the witness, and such a challenge could not have prevailed. . . .

A far more difficult task evolved from the claim by witnesses that the committee's interrogations were infringements upon the freedoms of the First Amendment. Clearly, an investigation is subject to the command that the Congress shall make no law abridging freedom of speech or press or assembly. While it is true that there is no statute to be reviewed, and that an investigation is not a law, nevertheless an investigation is part of law-making. It is justified solely as an adjunct to the legislative process. The First Amendment may be invoked against infringement of the protected freedoms by law or by law-making.

Abuses of the investigative process may imperceptibly lead to abridgment of protected freedoms. The mere summoning of a witness and compelling him to testify, against his will, about his beliefs, expressions or associations is a measure of governmental interference. And when those forced revelations concern matters that are unorthodox, unpopular, or even hateful to the general public, the reaction in the life of the witness may be disastrous. This effect is even more harsh when it is past beliefs, expressions or associations that are disclosed and judged by current standards rather than those contemporary with the matters exposed. Nor does the witness alone suffer the consequences. Those who are identified by witnesses and thereby placed in the same glare of publicity are equally subject to public stigma, scorn and obloquy. Beyond that, there is the more subtle and immeasurable effect upon those who tend to adhere to the most orthodox and uncontroversial views and associations in order to avoid a similar fate at some future time. That this impact is partly the result of non-governmental activity by private persons cannot relieve the investigators of their responsibility for initiating the reaction. . . .

We have no doubt that there is no congressional power to expose for the sake of exposure. The public is, of course, entitled to be informed concerning the workings of its government. That cannot be inflated into a general power to expose where the predominant result can only be an invasion of the private rights of individuals. But a solution to our problem is not to be found in testing the motives of committee members for this purpose. Such is not our function. Their motives alone would not vitiate an investigation which had been instituted by a House of Congress if that assembly's legislative purpose is being served.

. . . The theory of a committee inquiry is that the committee members are serving as the representatives of the parent assembly in collecting information for a legislative purpose. Their function is to act as the eyes and ears of the Congress in obtaining facts upon which the full legislature can act. To carry out this mission, committees and subcommittees, sometimes one Congressman, are endowed with the full power of the Congress to compel testimony. In this case, only two men exercised that authority in demanding information over petitioner's protest. An essential premise in this situation is that House or Senate shall have instructed the committee members on what they are to do with the power delegated to them. It is the responsibility of the Congress, in the first instance, to insure that compulsory process is used only in furtherance of a legislative purpose. That requires that the instructions to an investigating committee spell out that group's jurisdiction and purpose with sufficient particularity. Those instructions are embodied in the authorizing resolution. That document is the committee's charter. Broadly drafted and loosely worded, however, such resolutions can leave tremendous latitude to the discretion of the investigators. The more vague the committee's charter is, the greater becomes the possibility that the committee's specific actions are not in conformity with the will of the parent House of Congress.

The authorizing resolution of the Un-American Activities Committee was adopted in 1938. . . . Several years later, the Committee was made a standing organ of the House with the same mandate. It defines the Committee's authority as follows:

> The Committee on Un-American Activities, as a whole or by subcommittee, is authorized to make from time to time investigations of (i) the extent, character, and objects of un-American propaganda activities in the United States, (ii) the diffusion within the United States of subversive and un-American propaganda that is instigated from foreign countries or of a domestic origin and attacks the principle of the form of government as guaranteed by our Constitution, and (iii) all other questions in relation thereto that would aid Congress in any necessary remedial legislation.

It would be difficult to imagine a less explicit authorizing resolution. Who can define the meaning of "un-American"? What is that single, solitary "principle of the form of government as guaranteed by our Constitution"? . . .

Combining the language of the resolution with the construction it has been given, it is evident that the preliminary control of the Committee exercised by the House of Representatives is slight or non-existent. No one could reasonably deduce from the charter the kind of investigation that the Committee was directed to make. As a result, we are asked to engage in a process of retroactive rationalization. Looking backward from the events that transpired, we are asked to uphold the Committee's actions unless it appears that they were clearly not authorized by the charter. As a corollary to this inverse approach, the Government urges that we must view the matter hospitably to the power of the Congress—that if there is any legislative purpose which might have been furthered by the kind of disclosure sought, the witness must be punished for withholding it. No doubt every reasonable indulgence of legality must be accorded to the actions of a coordinate branch of our Government. But such deference cannot yield to an unnecessary and unreasonable dissipation of precious constitutional freedoms.

The Government contends that the public interest at the core of the investigations of the Un-American Activities Committee is the need by the Congress to be informed of efforts to overthrow the Government by force and violence so that adequate legislative safeguards can be erected. From this core, however, the Committee can radiate outward infinitely to any topic thought to be related in some way to armed insurrection. The outer reaches of this domain are known only by the content of "un-American activities." . . . A third dimension is added when the investigators turn their attention to the past to collect minutiae on remote topics, on the hypothesis that the past may reflect upon the present. . . .

It is, of course, not the function of this Court to prescribe rigid rules for the Congress to follow in drafting resolutions establishing investigating committees. That is a matter peculiarly within the realm of the legislature, and its decisions will be accepted by the courts up to the point where their own duty to enforce the constitutionally protected rights of individuals is affected. An excessively broad charter, like that of the House Un-American Activities Committee, places the courts in an untenable position if they are to strike a balance between the public need for a particular interrogation and the right of citizens to carry on their affairs free from unnecessary governmental interference. . . .

Since World War II, the Congress has practically abandoned its original practice of utilizing the coercive sanction of contempt proceedings at the bar of the House. The sanction there imposed is imprisonment by the House until the recalcitrant witness agrees to testify or disclose the matters sought, provided that the incarceration does not extend beyond adjournment. The Congress has instead invoked the aid of the federal judicial system in protecting itself against contumacious conduct. It has become customary to refer these matters to the United States Attorneys for prosecution under criminal law. . . .

. . . [In such cases] the courts must accord to the defendants every right which is guaranteed to defendants in all other criminal cases. Among these is the right to have available, through a sufficiently precise statute, information revealing the standard of criminality before the commission of the alleged offense. Applied to persons prosecuted under [the statute] . . . this raises a special problem in that the statute defines the crime as refusal to answer "any question pertinent to the question under inquiry." Part of the standard of criminality, therefore, is the pertinency of the questions propounded to the witness.

The problem attains proportion when viewed from the standpoint of the witness who appears before a congressional committee. He must decide at the time the questions are propounded whether or not to answer. . . . An erroneous determination on his part, even if made in the utmost good faith, does not exculpate him if the court should later rule that the questions were pertinent to the question under inquiry.

It is obvious that a person compelled to make this choice is entitled to have knowledge of the subject to which the interrogation is deemed pertinent. That knowledge must be available with the same degree of explicitness and clarity that the Due Process Clause requires in the expression of any element of a criminal offense. The "vice of vagueness" must be avoided here as in all other crimes. There are several sources that can outline the "question under inquiry" in such a way that the rules against vagueness are satisfied. The authorizing resolution, the remarks of the chairman or members of the committee, or even the nature of the proceedings themselves might sometimes make the topic clear. This case demonstrates, however, that these sources often leave the matter in grave doubt.

. . . [Watkins] was not accorded a fair opportunity to determine whether he was within his rights in refusing to answer, and his conviction is necessarily invalid under the Due Process Clause of the Fifth Amendment.

We are mindful of the complexities of modern government and the ample scope that must be left to the Congress as the sole constitutional depository of legislative power. Equally mindful are we of the indispensable function, in the exercise of that power, of congressional investigations. The conclusions we have reached in this case will not prevent the Congress, through its committees, from obtaining any information it needs for the proper fulfillment of its role in our scheme of government. The legislature is free to determine the kinds of data that should be collected. It is only those investigations that are conducted by use of compulsory process that give rise to a need to protect the rights of individuals against illegal encroachment. That protection can be readily achieved through procedures which prevent the separation of power from responsibility and which provide the constitutional requisites of fairness for witnesses. A measure of added care on the part of the House and the Senate in authorizing the use of compulsory process and by their committees in exercising that power would suffice. That is a small price to pay if it serves to uphold the principles of limited, constitutional government without constricting the power of the Congress to inform itself.

The judgment of the Court of Appeals is reversed, and the case is remanded to the District Court with instructions to dismiss the indictment. . . .

Mr. Justice Burton and *Mr. Justice Whittaker* took no part in the consideration or decision of this case.

Mr. Justice Frankfurter, concurring. . . .

Mr. Justice Clark, dissenting.

As I see it the chief fault in the majority opinion is its mischievous curbing of the informing function of the Congress. While I am not versed in its procedures, my experience in the executive branch of the government leads me to believe that the requirements laid down in the opinion for the operation of the committee system of inquiry are both unnecessary and unworkable. . . .

It may be that at times the House Committee on Un-American Activities has, as the Court says, "conceived of its task in the grand view of its name." And, perhaps, as the Court indicates, the rules of conduct placed upon the Committee by the House admit of individual abuse and unfairness. But that is none of our affair. So long as the object of a legislative inquiry is legitimate and the questions propounded are pertinent thereto, it is not for the courts to interfere with the committee system of inquiry. To hold otherwise would be an infringement on the power given the Congress to inform itself, and thus a trespass upon the fundamental American principle of separation of powers. The majority has substituted the judiciary as the grand inquisitor and supervisor of congressional investigations. It has never been so. . . .

Case

BARENBLATT V. UNITED STATES

360 U.S. 109; 79 S.Ct. 1081; 3 L.Ed. 2d 1115 (1959)
Vote: 5–4

As part of its investigation into Communist infiltration into the education system, the House Un-American Activities Committee subpoenaed Lloyd Barenblatt, a former college professor. Barenblatt appeared before the committee but refused to answer its questions, which dealt primarily with his political beliefs and associations. Barenblatt based his refusal not on the self-incrimination clause of the Fifth Amendment, but on the First Amendment protections of political speech and association. Barenblatt was convicted of contempt of Congress.

Mr. Justice Harlan delivered the opinion of the Court.

. . . The precise constitutional issue confronting us is whether the Subcommittee's inquiry into petitioner's past or present membership in the Communist Party transgressed the provisions of the First Amendment, which of course reach and limit congressional investigations. . . . The Court's past cases establish sure guides to decision. Undeniably, the First Amendment in some circumstances protects an individual from being compelled to disclose his associational relationships. However, the protections of the First Amendment, unlike a proper claim of the privilege against self-incrimination under the Fifth Amendment, do not afford a witness the right to resist inquiry in all circumstances. Where First Amendment rights are asserted to bar governmental interrogation, resolution of the issue always involves a balancing by the courts of the competing private and public interests at stake in the particular circumstances shown. These principles were recognized in the Watkins Case. . . .

The first question is whether this investigation was related to a valid legislative purpose, for Congress may not constitutionally require an individual to disclose his political relationships or other private affairs except in relation to such a purpose. . . .

That Congress has wide power to legislate in the field of Communist activity in this Country, and to conduct appropriate investigations in aid thereof, is hardly debatable. The existence of such power has never been questioned by this Court, and it is sufficient to say, without particularization, that Congress has enacted or considered in this field a wide range of legislative measures, not a few of which have stemmed from recommendations of the very Committee whose actions have been drawn in question here. In the last analysis this power rests on the right of self-preservation, "the ultimate value of any society." . . . Justification for its exercise in turn rests on the long and widely accepted view that the tenets of the Communist Party include the ultimate overthrow of the Government of the United States by force and violence, a view which has been given formal expression by the Congress. . . .

. . . To suggest that because the Communist Party may also sponsor peaceable political reforms the constitutional issues before us should not be judged as if that Party were just an ordinary political party from the standpoint of national security, is to ask this Court to blind itself to world affairs which have determined the whole course of our national policy since the close of World War II, . . . and to the vast burdens which these conditions have entailed for the entire Nation.

We think that investigatory power in this domain is not to be denied Congress solely because the field of education is involved. . . . Indeed we do not understand the petitioner here to suggest that Congress in no circumstances may inquire into Communist activity in the field of education. Rather, his position is in effect that this particular investigation was aimed not at the revolutionary aspects but at the theoretical classroom discussion of communism.

In our opinion this position rests on a too constricted view of the nature of the investigatory process, and is not supported by a fair assessment of the record before us. An investigation of advocacy of or preparation for overthrow certainly embraces the right to identify a witness as a member of the Communist Party . . . and to inquire into the various manifestations of the Party's tenets. The strict requirements of a prosecution under the Smith Act, . . . are not the measure of the permissible scope of a congressional investigation into "overthrow," for of necessity the investigatory process must proceed step by step. Nor can it fairly be concluded that this investigation was directed at controlling what is being taught at our universities rather than at overthrow. The statement of the Subcommittee Chairman at the opening of the investigation evinces no such intention, and so far as this record reveals nothing thereafter transpired which would justify our holding that the thrust of the investigation later changed. The record discloses considerable testimony concerning the foreign domination and revolutionary purposes and efforts of the Communist Party. That there was also testimony on the abstract philosophical level does not detract from the dominant theme of this investigation—Communist infiltration furthering the alleged ultimate purpose of overthrow. And certainly the conclusion would not be justified that the questioning of petitioner would have exceeded permissible bounds had he not shut off the Subcommittee at the threshold.

Nor can we accept the further contention that this investigation should not be deemed to have been in furtherance of a legislative purpose because the true objective of the Committee and of the Congress was purely "exposure." So long as Congress acts in pursuance of its constitutional power, the Judiciary lacks authority to intervene on the basis of the motives which spurred the exercise of that power. "It is of course, true," . . . "that if there be no authority in the judiciary to restrain a lawful exercise of power by another department of the government, where a wrong motive or purpose has impelled to the exertion of the power, that abuses of a power conferred may be temporarily effectual. The remedy for this, however, lies, not in the abuse by the judicial authority of its functions, but in the people, upon whom, after all, under our institutions, reliance must be placed for the correction of abuses committed in the exercise of a lawful power." These principles of course apply as well to committee investigations into the need for legislation as to the enactments which such investigations may produce. . . . Thus, in stating in the Watkins Case . . . that "there is no congressional power to expose for the sake of exposure," we at the same time declined to inquire into the "motives of committee members," and recognized that their "motives alone would not vitiate an investigation which had been instituted by a House of Congress if that assembly's legislative purpose is being served." Having scrutinized this record we cannot say that the unanimous panel of the Court of Appeals which first considered this case was wrong in concluding that "the primary purposes of the inquiry were in aid of legislative processes." Certainly this is not a case like *Kilbourn v. Thompson* . . . , where "the House of Representatives not only exceeded the limit of its own authority, but assumed a power which could only be properly exercised by another branch of government, because it was in its nature clearly judicial." The constitutional legislative power of Congress in this instance is beyond question.

Finally, the record is barren of other factors which in themselves might sometimes lead to the conclusion that the individual interests at stake were not subordinate to those of the state. There is no indication in this record that the Subcommittee was attempting to pillory witnesses. Nor did petitioner's appearance as a witness follow from indiscriminate dragnet procedures, lacking in probable cause for belief that he possessed information which might be helpful to the Subcommittee. And the relevancy of the questions put to him by the Subcommittee is not open to doubt.

We conclude that the balance between the individual and the governmental interests here at stake must be struck in favor of the latter, and that therefore the provisions of the First Amendment have not been offended.

We hold that petitioner's conviction for contempt of Congress discloses no infirmity and that the judgment of the Court of Appeals must be Affirmed.

Mr. Justice Black, with whom *Chief Justice Warren* and *Mr. Justice Douglas* concur, dissenting. . . .

Mr. Justice Brennan, dissenting.

. . . I would reverse this conviction. It is sufficient that I state my complete agreement with my Brother Black that no purpose for the investigation of Barenblatt is revealed by the record except exposure purely for the sake of exposure. This is not a purpose to which Barenblatt's rights under the First Amendment can validly be subordinated. An investigation in which the processes of law-making and law-evaluating are submerged entirely in exposure of individual behavior—in adjudication, of a sort, through the exposure process—is outside the constitutional pale of congressional inquiry. . . .

Case

GIBBONS V. OGDEN

9 Wheat. (22 U.S.) 1; 6 L.Ed. 23 (1824)
Vote: 6–0

Aaron Ogden held an exclusive right to navigate steamboats in New York waters, a monopoly granted by the New York state legislature. Gibbons held a "coasting license" from the federal government. When Gibbons began operating a steamboat ferry service between New York and New Jersey, Ogden obtained an injunction in the New York courts.

Mr. Chief Justice Marshall delivered the opinion of the Court.

[Gibbons] contends that [New York's injunction] is erroneous, because the laws [of New York] which purport to give the exclusive privilege (to Ogden to navigate steamboats on New York waters) are repugnant to the Constitution and laws of the United States.

They are said to be repugnant . . . to that clause in the Constitution which authorizes Congress to regulate commerce. . . .

The words are: "Congress shall have power to regulate commerce with foreign nations, and among the several states, and with the Indian tribes."

The subject to be regulated is commerce; and our Constitution being, as was aptly said at the bar, one of enumeration, and not of definition, to ascertain the extent of the power it becomes necessary to settle the meaning of the word. The counsel for [Ogden] would limit it to traffic, to buying and selling, or the interchange of commodities, and do not admit that it comprehends navigation. This would restrict a general term, applicable to many objects, to one of its significations. Commerce, undoubtedly, is traffic, but it is something more; it is intercourse. It describes the commercial intercourse between nations, and parts of nations, in all its branches, and is regulated by prescribing rules for carrying on that intercourse. The mind can scarcely conceive a system for regulating commerce between nations, which shall exclude all laws concerning navigation, which shall be silent on the admission of the vessels of the one nation into the ports of the other, and be confined to prescribing rules for the conduct of individuals, in the actual employment of buying and selling or of barter.

If commerce does not include navigation, the government of the Union has no direct power over that subject, and can make no law prescribing what shall constitute American vessels, or requiring that they shall be navigated by American seamen. Yet this power has been exercised from the commencement of the government, has been exercised with the consent of all, and has been understood by all to be a commercial regulation. All America understands, and has uniformly understood, the word "commerce" to comprehend navigation. It was so understood, and must have been so understood, when the constitution was framed. The power over commerce, including navigation, was one of the primary objects for which the people of America adopted their government, and must have been contemplated in forming it. The convention must have used the word in that sense; because all have understood it in that sense, and the attempt to restrict it comes too late. . . .

The word used in the Constitution, then, comprehends, and has been always understood to comprehend, navigation within its meaning; and a power to regulate navigation is as expressly granted as if that term had been added to the word "commerce."

To what commerce does this power extend? The Constitution informs us, to commerce "with foreign nations, and among the several states, and with the Indian tribes."

It has, we believe, been universally admitted that these words comprehend every species of commercial intercourse between the United States and foreign nations. No sort of trade can be carried on between this country and any other, to which this power does not extend. It has been truly said, that commerce, as the word is used in the Constitution, is a unit, every part of which is indicated by the term.

If this be the admitted meaning of the word, in its application to foreign nations, it must carry the same meaning throughout the sentence, and remain a unit, unless there be some plain intelligible cause which alters it.

The subject to which the power is next applied, is to commerce "among the several states." The word "among" means intermingled with. A thing which is among others, is intermingled with them. Commerce among the states cannot stop at the external boundary line of each state, but may be introduced into the interior.

It is not intended to say that these words comprehend that commerce which is completely internal, which is carried on between man and man in a state, or between different parts of the same state, and which does not extend to or affect other states. Such a power would be inconvenient, and is certainly unnecessary.

Comprehensive as the word "among" is, it may very properly be restricted to that commerce which concerns more states than one. The phrase is not one which would probably have been selected to indicate the completely interior traffic of a state, because it is not an apt phrase for that purpose; and the enumeration of the particular classes of commerce to which the power was to be extended, would not have been made had the intention been to extend the power to every description. The enumeration presupposes something not enumerated; and that something, if we regard the language or the subject of the sentence, must be the exclusively internal commerce of a state. The genius and character of the whole government seem to be, that its action is to be applied to all the external concerns of the nation, and to those internal concerns which affect the states generally; but not to those which are completely within a particular state, which do not affect other states, and with which it is not necessary to interfere, for the purpose of executing some of the general powers of the government. The completely internal commerce of a state, then, may be considered as reserved for the state itself.

But, in regulating commerce with foreign nations the power of Congress does not stop at the jurisdictional lines of the several states. It would be a very useless power if it could not pass those lines. The commerce of the United States with foreign nations, is that of the whole United States. Every district has a right to participate in it. The deep streams which penetrate our country in every direction, pass through the interior of almost every state in the Union, and furnish the means of exercising this right. If

Congress has the power to regulate it, that power must be exercised whenever the subject exists. If it exists within the states, if a foreign voyage may commence or terminate at a port within a state, then the power of Congress may be exercised within a state. . . .

We are now arrived at the inquiry, What is this power? It is the power to regulate; that is, to prescribe the rule by which commerce is to be governed. This power, like all others vested in Congress, is complete in itself, may be exercised to its utmost extent, and acknowledges no limitations, other than are prescribed in the Constitution. These are expressed in plain terms, and do not affect the questions which arise in this case, or which have been discussed at the bar. If, as has always been understood, the sovereignty of Congress, though limited to specified objects, is plenary as to those objects, the power over commerce with foreign nations, and among the several States, is vested in Congress as absolutely as it would be in a single government, having in its constitution the same restrictions on the exercise of the power as are found in the Constitution of the United States. The wisdom and the discretion of Congress, their identity with the people, and the influence which their constituents possess at election, are, in this, as in many other instances, as that, for example, of declaring war, the sole restraints on which they have relied, to secure them from its abuse. They are the restraints on which the people must often rely solely, in all representative governments.

The power of Congress, then, comprehends navigation within the limits of every state in the Union; so far as that navigation may be, in any manner, connected with "commerce with foreign nations, or among the several states, or with the Indian tribes." It may, of consequence, pass the jurisdictional line of New York, and act upon the very waters to which the prohibition now under consideration applies.

But it has been urged with great earnestness, that although the power of Congress to regulate commerce with foreign nations, and among the several states, be coextensive with the subject itself, and have no other limits than are prescribed in the Constitution, yet the states may severally exercise the same power within their respective jurisdictions. In support of this argument, it is said that they possessed it as an inseparable attribute of sovereignty, before the formation of the Constitution, and still retain it, except so far as they have surrendered it by that instrument; that this principle results from the nature of the government, and is secured by the Tenth Amendment; that an affirmative grant of power is not exclusive, unless in its own nature it be such that the continued exercise of it by the former possessor is inconsistent with the grant, and that this is not of that description.

[Gibbons] conceding these postulates, except the last, contends that full power to regulate a particular subject, implies the whole power, and leaves no residuum; that a grant of the whole is incompatible with the existence of a right in another to any part of it. . . .

In discussing the question, whether this [commerce] power is still in the states, in the case under consideration, we may dismiss from it the inquiry, whether it is surrendered by the mere grant to Congress, or is retained until Congress shall exercise the power. We may dismiss that inquiry, because it has been exercised, and the regulations which Congress deemed it proper to make, are now in full operation. The sole question is, can a state regulate commerce with foreign nations and among the states, while Congress is regulating it? . . .

In our complex system, presenting the rare and difficult scheme of one general government, whose action extends over the whole, but which possesses only certain enumerated powers, and of numerous state governments, which retain and exercise all powers not delegated to the Union, contests respecting power must arise. Were it even otherwise, the measures taken by the respective governments to execute their acknowledged powers, would often be of the same description, and might, sometimes, interfere. This, however, does not prove that the one is exercising, or has a right to exercise, the powers of the other. . . .

Since, . . . in exercising the power of regulating their own purely internal affairs, whether of trading or police, the states may sometimes enact laws, the validity of which depends on their interfering with, and being contrary to, an act of Congress passed in pursuance of the Constitution, the court will enter upon the inquiry, whether the laws of New York, as expounded by the highest tribunal of that state, have, in their application to this case, come into collision with an act of Congress, and deprived a citizen of a right to which that act entitles him. Should this collision exist, it will be immaterial whether those laws were passed in virtue of a concurrent power "to regulate commerce with foreign nations and among the several states," or in virtue of a power to regulate their domestic trade and police. In one case and the other, the acts of New York must yield to the law of Congress; and the decision sustaining the privilege they confer, against a right given by a law of the Union, must be erroneous. . . .

. . . [It] has been contended that if a law, passed by a state in the exercise of its acknowledged sovereignty, comes into conflict with a law passed by Congress in pursuance of the Constitution, they affect the subject, and each other, like equal opposing powers. But the framers of our constitution foresaw this state of things, and provided for it, by declaring the supremacy not only of itself, but of the laws made in pursuance of it. The nullity of any act, inconsistent with the Constitution, is produced by the declaration that the Constitution is the supreme law. The appropriate application of that part of the clause which confers the same supremacy on laws and treaties, is to such acts of the state legislatures as do not transcend their powers, but, though enacted in the execution of acknowledged state powers, interfere with, or are contrary to the laws of Congress, made in pursuance of the Constitution, or some treaty made under the authority of the United States. In every such case, the act of Congress, or the treaty, is supreme; and the law of the state, though enacted in the exercise of powers not controverted, must yield to it. . . .

. . . To the court it seems very clear, that the whole act on the subject of the coasting trade, according to those principles which govern the construction of statutes, implies, unequivocally, an authority to licensed vessels to carry on the coasting trade. . . .

If the power reside in Congress, as a portion of the general grant to regulate commerce, then acts applying that power to vessels generally, must be construed as comprehending all vessels. If none appear to be excluded by the language of the act, none can be excluded by construction. Vessels have always been employed to a greater or less extent in the transportation of passengers, and have never been supposed to be, on that account, withdrawn from the control or protection of Congress. . . .

. . . The real and sole question seems to be, whether a steam machine, in actual use, deprives a vessel of the privileges conferred by a license.

In considering this question, the first idea which presents itself, is that the laws of Congress, for the regulation of commerce, do not look to the principle by which vessels are moved. That subject is left entirely to individual discretion; and, in that vast and complex system of legislative enactment concerning it, which embraces everything that the legislature thought it necessary to notice, there is not, we believe, one word respecting the peculiar principle by which vessels are propelled through the water, except what may be found in a single act, granting a particular privilege to steamboats. With this exception, every act, either prescribing duties, or granting privileges, applies to every vessel, whether navigated by the instrumentality of wind or fire, of sails or machinery. . . .

This act demonstrates the opinion of Congress, that steamboats may be enrolled and licensed, in common with vessels using sails. They are, of course, entitled to the same privileges, and can no more be restrained from navigating waters, and entering ports which are free to such vessels, than if they were wafted on their voyage by the winds, instead of being propelled by the agency of fire. The one element may be as legitimately used as the other, for every commercial purpose authorized by the laws of the Union; and the act of a state inhibiting the use of either to any vessel having a license under the act of Congress, comes, we think, in direct collision with the act. . . .

Mr. Justice Johnson [concurring].

. . . The "power to regulate commerce," here meant to be granted, was that power to regulate commerce which previously existed in the states. But what was that power? The states were, unquestionably, supreme, and each possessed that power over commerce which is acknowledged to reside in every sovereign state. . . . The power of a sovereign state over commerce, therefore, amounts to nothing more than a power to limit and restrain it at pleasure. And since the power to prescribe the limits to its freedom necessarily implies the power to determine what shall remain unrestrained, it follows that the power must be exclusive; it can reside but in one potentate; and hence, the grant of this power carries with it the whole subject, leaving nothing for the state to act upon. . . .

It is impossible, with the views which I entertained of the principle on which the commercial privileges of the people of the United States, among themselves, rests, to concur in the view which this Court takes of the effect of the coasting license in this cause. I do not regard it as the foundation of the right set up in behalf of [Gibbons]. If there was any one object riding over every other in the adoption of the Constitution, it was to keep the commercial intercourse among the states free from all invidious and partial restraints. And I cannot overcome the conviction, that if the licensing act was repealed tomorrow, the rights of [Gibbons] to a reversal of the decision complained of, would be as strong as it is under this license. . . .

Case

HAMMER V. DAGENHART

247 U.S. 251; 38 S.Ct. 529; 62 L.Ed. 1101 (1918)
Vote: 5–4

In 1916 Congress enacted a statute prohibiting the interstate shipment of goods produced at factories employing children under the age of 14 or permitting children between the ages of 14 and 16 to work more than eight hours a day or more than six days a week. The question before the Supreme Court is whether this prohibition is a valid regulation of interstate commerce.

Mr. Justice Day delivered the opinion of the Court.

A bill was filed in the United States district court for the western district of North Carolina by a father in his own behalf and as next friend of his two minor sons, one under the age of fourteen years and the other between the ages of fourteen and sixteen years, employees in a cotton mill at Charlotte, North Carolina, to enjoin the enforcement of the act of Congress intended to prevent interstate commerce in the products of child labor. . . .

The district court held the act unconstitutional. . . . This appeal brings the case here. . . .

The power essential to the passage of this act, the government contends, is found in the commerce clause of the Constitution, which authorizes Congress to regulate commerce with foreign nations and among the states.

. . . [The commerce] power is one to control the means by which commerce is carried on, which is directly the contrary of the assumed right to forbid commerce from moving and thus destroy it as to particular commodities. But it is insisted that adjudged cases in this court establish the doctrine that the power to regulate given to Congress incidentally includes the authority to prohibit the movement of ordinary commodities, and therefore that the subject is not open for discussion. The cases demonstrate the contrary. They rest upon the character of the particular subjects dealt with and the fact that the scope of governmental authority, state or national, possessed over them, is such that the authority to prohibit is, as to them, but the exertion of the power to regulate.

. . . [It has been held that] Congress might pass a law having the effect to keep the channels of commerce free from use in the transportation of tickets used in the promotion of lottery schemes; . . . [to prohibit] the introduction into the states by means of interstate commerce of impure food and drugs; . . . [to forbid] transportation of a woman in interstate commerce for the purpose of prosti-

tution; . . . [to prohibit] the transportation of women in interstate commerce for the purposes of debauchery and kindred purposes; . . . [and to bar] the transportation of intoxicating liquors. . . .

In each of these instances the use of interstate transportation was necessary to the accomplishment of harmful results. In other words, although the power over interstate transportation was to regulate, that could only be accomplished by prohibiting the use of the facilities of interstate commerce to effect the evil intended.

This element is wanting in the present case. The thing intended to be accomplished by this statute is the denial of the facilities of interstate commerce to those manufacturers in the states who employ children within the prohibited ages. The act in its effect does not regulate transportation among the states, but aims to standardize the ages at which children may be employed in mining and manufacturing within the states. The goods shipped are of themselves harmless. The act permits them to be freely shipped after thirty days from the time of their removal from the factory. When offered for shipment, and before transportation begins, the labor of their production is over, and the mere fact that they were intended for interstate commerce transportation does not make their production subject to Federal control under the commerce power.

Commerce "consists of intercourse and traffic . . . and includes the transportation of persons and property, as well as the purchase, sale and exchange of commodities." The making of goods and the mining of coal are not commerce, nor does the fact that these things are to be afterwards shipped, or used in interstate commerce, make their production a part thereof. . . .

Over interstate transportation, or its incidents, the regulatory power of Congress is ample, but the production of articles intended for interstate commerce is a matter of local regulation. . . . If it were otherwise, all manufacture intended for interstate shipment would be brought under Federal control to the practical exclusion of the authority of the states—a result certainly not contemplated by the framers of the Constitution when they vested in Congress the authority to regulate commerce among the states. . . .

It is further contended that the authority of Congress may be exerted to control interstate commerce in the shipment of child-made goods because of the effect of the circulation of such goods in other states where the evil of this class of labor has been recognized by local legislation, and the right to thus employ child labor has been more rigorously restrained than in the state of production. In other words, that the unfair competition thus engendered may be controlled by closing the channels of interstate commerce to manufacturers in those states where the local laws do not meet what Congress deems to be the more just standard of other states.

There is no power vested in Congress to require the states to exercise their police power so as to prevent possible unfair competition. Many causes may co-operate to give one state, by reason of local laws or conditions, an economic advantage over others. The commerce clause was not intended to give to Congress a general authority to equalize such conditions. . . .

The grant of power to Congress over the subject of interstate commerce was to enable it to regulate such commerce, and not to give it authority to control the states in their exercise of the police power over local trade and manufacture.

The grant of authority over a purely Federal matter was not intended to destroy the local power always existing and carefully reserved to the states in the 10th Amendment to the Constitution.

Police regulations relating to the internal trade and affairs of the states have been uniformly recognized as within such control. . . .

That there should be limitations upon the right to employ children in mines and factories in the interest of their own and the public welfare, all will admit. That such employment is generally deemed to require regulation is shown by the fact that the brief of counsel states that every state in the Union has a law upon the subject, limiting the right to thus employ children. In North Carolina, the state wherein is located the factory in which the employment was had in the present case, no child under twelve years of age is permitted to work. . . .

In interpreting the Constitution it must never be forgotten that the nation is made up of states, to which are entrusted the powers of local government. And to them and to the people the powers not expressly delegated to the national government are reserved. The power of the states to regulate their purely internal affairs by such laws as seem wise to the local authority is inherent, and has never been surrendered to the general government. . . . To sustain this statute would not be, in our judgment, a recognition of the lawful exertion of congressional authority over interstate commerce, but would sanction an invasion by the Federal power of the control of a matter purely local in its character, and over which no authority has been delegated to Congress in conferring the power to regulate commerce among the states.

We have neither authority nor disposition to question the motives of Congress in enacting this legislation. The purposes intended must be attained consistently with constitutional limitations, and not by an invasion of the powers of the states. This court has no more important function than that which devolves upon it the obligation to preserve inviolate the constitutional limitations upon the exercise of authority, Federal and state, to the end that each may continue to discharge, harmoniously with the other, the duties entrusted to it by the Constitution.

. . . [T]he act in a twofold sense is repugnant to the Constitution. It not only transcends the authority delegated to Congress over commerce, but also exerts a power as to a purely local matter to which the Federal authority does not extend. The far-reaching result of upholding the act cannot be more plainly indicated than by pointing out that if Congress can thus regulate matters entrusted to local authority by prohibition of the movement of commodities in interstate commerce, all freedom of commerce will be at an end, and the power of the state over local matters may be eliminated, and thus our system of government be practically destroyed.

For these reasons we hold that this law exceeds the constitutional authority of Congress. It follows that the decree of the District Court must be affirmed.

Mr. Justice Holmes, dissenting.

. . . [I]f an act is within the powers specifically conferred upon Congress, it seems to me that it is not made any less constitutional because of the indirect effects that it may have, however obvious it may be that it will have those effects; and that we are not at liberty upon such grounds to hold it void.

The first step in my argument is to make plain what no one is likely to dispute—that the statute in question is within the power expressly given to Congress if considered only as to its immediate effects, and that if invalid it is so only upon some collateral ground. The statute confines itself to prohibiting the carriage of certain goods in interstate or foreign commerce. Congress is given power to regulate such commerce in unqualified terms. It would not be argued today that the power to regulate does not include the power to prohibit. Regulation means the prohibition of something, and when interstate commerce is the matter to be regulated I cannot doubt that the regulations may prohibit any part of such commerce that Congress sees fit to forbid. . . .

The question, then is narrowed to whether the exercise of its otherwise constitutional power by Congress can be pronounced unconstitutional because of its possible reaction upon the conduct of the states in a matter upon which I have admitted that they are free from direct control. I should have thought that that matter had been disposed of so fully as to leave no room for doubt. I should have thought that the most conspicuous decisions of this court had made it clear that the power to regulate commerce and other constitutional powers could not be cut down or qualified by the fact that it might interfere with the carrying out of the domestic policy of any state. . . .

The notion that prohibition is any less prohibition when applied to things now thought evil I do not understand. But if there is any matter upon which civilized countries have agreed—far more unanimously than they have with regard to intoxicants, and some other matters over which this country is now emotionally aroused—it is the evil of premature and excessive child labor. I should have thought that if we were to introduce our own moral conceptions where, in my opinion, they do not belong, this was pre-eminently a case for upholding the exercise of all its powers by the United States.

But I had thought that the propriety of the exercise of a power admitted to exist in some cases was for the consideration of Congress alone, and that this court always had disavowed the right to intrude its judgment upon questions of policy or morals. It is not for this court to pronounce when prohibition is necessary to regulation if it ever may be necessary—to say that it is permissible as against strong drink, but not as against the product of ruined lives.

The act does not meddle with anything belonging to the states. They may regulate their internal affairs and their domestic commerce as they like. But when they seek to send their products across the state line they are no longer within their rights. If there were no Constitution and no Congress their power to cross the line would depend upon their neighbors. Under the Constitution such commerce belongs not to the states, but to Congress to regulate. It may carry out its views of public policy whatever indirect effect they may have upon the activities of the states. Instead of being encountered by a prohibitive tariff at her boundaries, the state encounters the public policy of the United States which it is for Congress to express. The public policy of the United States is shaped with a view to the benefit of the nation as a whole. . . . The national welfare as understood by Congress may require a different attitude within its sphere from that of some self-seeking state. It seems to me entirely constitutional for Congress to enforce its understanding by all the means at its command.

Mr. Justice McKenna, Mr. Justice Brandeis, and *Mr. Justice Clarke* concur in this opinion.

Case

CARTER V. CARTER COAL COMPANY

298 U.S. 238; 56 S.Ct. 855; 80 L.Ed. 1160 (1936)
Vote: 5–4

The Bituminous Coal Act of 1935 created a national commission with authority to regulate wages and prices for the coal industry. A 15 percent tax was levied on all coal sold at the mine, and producers who accepted the federal regulations were entitled to a 90 percent rebate of assessed taxes. Carter, a stockholder in the Carter Coal Company, brought suit seeking to enjoin the company from paying the tax or complying with the code.

Mr. Justice Sutherland delivered the opinion of the Court.

. . . The proposition, often advanced and as often discredited, that the power of the federal government inherently extends to purposes affecting the nation as a whole with which the states severally cannot deal or cannot adequately deal, and the related notion that Congress, entirely apart from the powers delegated by the Constitution, may enact laws to promote the general welfare, have never been accepted but always definitely rejected by this court. . . .

. . . [T]he general purposes which the act recites . . . are beyond the power of Congress except so far, and only so far, as they may be realized by an exercise of some specific power granted by the Constitution. . . . [W]e shall find no grant of power which authorized Congress to legislate in respect of these general purposes unless it be found in the commerce clause—and this we now consider. . . .

. . . [T]he word "commerce" is the equivalent of the phrase "intercourse for the purposes of trade." Plainly, the incidents leading up to and culminating in the mining of coal do not constitute such intercourse. The employment of men, the fixing of their wages, hours of labor and working conditions, the bargaining in respect of these things—whether carried on separately or collectively—each and all constitute intercourse for the purposes of production, not of trade. The latter is a thing apart from the relation of employer and employee, which in all producing occupations is purely local in character. Extraction of coal from the mine is the aim and the completed result of local activities. Commerce in the coal mined is not brought into being by force of these activities, but by negotiations, agreements, and circumstances entirely apart from production. Mining brings the subject matter of commerce into existence. Commerce disposes of it.

. . . [T]he effect of the labor provisions of the act, including those in respect of minimum wages, wage agreements, collective bargaining, and the Labor Board and its powers, primarily falls upon production and not upon commerce; and confirms the further resulting conclusion that production is a purely local activity. It follows that none of these essential antecedents of production constitutes a transaction in or forms any part of interstate commerce. . . . Everything which moves in interstate commerce has had a local origin. Without local production somewhere, interstate commerce, as now carried on, would practically disappear. Nevertheless, the local character of mining, or manufacturing and of crop growing is a fact, and remains a fact, whatever may be done with the products. . . .

That the production of every commodity intended for interstate sale and transportation has some effect upon interstate commerce may be, if it has not already been, freely granted; and we are brought to the final and decisive inquiry, whether here that effect is direct, as the "preamble" recites, or indirect. The distinction is not formal, but substantial in the highest degree, as we pointed out in the *Schechter* case. . . .

Whether the effect of a given activity or condition is direct or indirect is not always easy to determine. The word "direct" implies that the activity or condition invoked or blamed shall operate proximately—not mediately, remotely, or collaterally—to produce the effect. It connotes the absence of an efficient intervening agency or condition. And the extent of the effect bears no logical relation to its character. The distinction between a direct and an indirect effect turns, not upon the magnitude of either the cause or the effect, but entirely upon the manner in which the effect has been brought about. If the production by one man of a single ton of coal intended for interstate sale and shipment, and actually so sold and shipped, affects interstate commerce indirectly, the effect does not become direct by multiplying the tonnage, or increasing the number of men employed, or adding to the expense or complexities of the business, or by all combined. It is quite true that rules of law are sometimes qualified by considerations of degree, as the government argues. But the matter of degree has no bearing upon the question here, since the question is not—What is the extent of the local activity or condition, or the extent of the effect produced upon interstate commerce? but—What is the relation between the activity or condition and the effect?

Much stress is put upon the evils which come from the struggle between employers and employees over the matter of wages, working conditions, the right of collective bargaining, etc., and the resulting strikes, curtailment and irregularity of production and effect on prices; and it is insisted that interstate commerce is greatly affected thereby. But, in addition to what has just been said, the conclusive answer is that the evils are all local evils over which the federal government has no legislative control. The relation of employer and employee is a local relation. . . . And the controversies and evils, which it is the object of the act to regulate and minimize, are local controversies and evils affecting local work undertaken to accomplish that local result. Such effect as they may have upon commerce, however extensive it may be, is secondary and indirect. An increase in the greatness of the effect adds to its importance. It does not alter its character. . . .

. . . [We] now declare, that the want of power on the part of the federal government is the same whether the wages, hours or service, and working conditions, and the bargaining about them, are related to production before interstate commerce has begun, or to sale and distribution after it has ended. . . .

Separate opinion of *Mr. Chief Justice Hughes* [dissenting].

The power to regulate interstate commerce embraces the power to protect that commerce from injury, whatever may be the source of the dangers which threaten it, and to adopt any appropriate means to that end. . . . Congress thus has adequate authority to maintain the orderly conduct of interstate commerce and to provide for the peaceful settlement of disputes which threaten it. . . . But Congress may not use this protective authority as a pretext for the exertion of power to regulate activities and relations within the States which affect interstate commerce only indirectly. . . .

But . . . [t]he Act also provides for the regulation of the prices of bituminous coal sold in interstate commerce and prohibits unfair methods of competition in interstate commerce. Undoubtedly transactions in carrying on interstate commerce are subject to the federal power to regulate that commerce and the control of charges and the protection of fair competition in that commerce are familiar illustrations of the exercise of the power, as the Interstate Commerce Act, the Packers and Stockyards Act, and the Anti-Trust Acts abundantly show. . . .

. . . The marketing provisions in relation to interstate commerce can be carried out as provided in Part II without regard to the labor provisions contained in Part III. That fact, in the light of the congressional declaration of separability, should be considered of controlling importance.

In this view, the Act, and the Code for which it provides, may be sustained in relation to the provisions for marketing in interstate commerce, and the decisions of the courts below, so far as they accomplish that result, should be affirmed.

Mr. Justice Cardozo . . . [dissenting].

. . . I am satisfied that the Act is within the power of the central government in so far as it provides for minimum and maximum prices upon sales of bituminous coal in the transactions of interstate commerce and in those of intrastate commerce where interstate commerce is directly or intimately affected. Whether it is valid also in other provisions that have been considered and condemned in the opinion of the Court, I do not find it necessary to determine at this time. Silence must not be taken as importing acquiescence. . . .

I am authorized to state that Mr. Justice Brandeis and Mr. Justice Stone join in this opinion.

Case

NATIONAL LABOR RELATIONS BOARD V. JONES & LAUGHLIN STEEL CORPORATION

301 U.S. 1; 57 S.Ct. 615; 81 L.Ed. 893 (1937)
Vote: 5–4

In this case the Court considers the constitutionality of the National Labor Relations Act of 1935, which recognized the right of workers to organize and bargain collectively with management. The act also created the National Labor Relations Board (NLRB), which was empowered to issue "cease and desist" orders to prevent unfair labor practices.

Mr. Chief Justice Hughes delivered the opinion of the Court.

In a proceeding under the National Labor Relations Act of 1935, the National Labor Relations Board found that the respondent, Jones & Laughlin Steel Corporation, had violated the Act by engaging in unfair labor practices affecting commerce. . . . The unfair labor practices charged were that the corporation was discriminating against members of the union with regard to hire and tenure of employment, and was coercing and intimidating its employees in order to interfere with their self-organization. The discriminatory and coercive action alleged was the discharge of certain employees.

The National Labor Relations Board, sustaining the charge, ordered the corporation to cease and desist from such discrimination and coercion, to offer reinstatement to ten of the employees named, to make good their losses in pay, and to post for thirty days notices that the corporation would not discharge or discriminate against members, or those desiring to become members, of the labor union. As the corporation failed to comply, the Board petitioned the Circuit Court of Appeals to enforce the order. The court denied the petition, holding that the order lay beyond the range of federal power. . . . We granted certiorari.

The scheme of the National Labor Relations Act . . . may be briefly stated. The first section sets forth findings with respect to the injury to commerce resulting from the denial by employers of the right of employees to organize and from the refusal of employers to accept the procedure of collective bargaining. There follows a declaration that it is the policy of the United States to eliminate these causes of obstruction to the free flow of commerce. The Act then defines the terms it uses, including the terms "commerce" and "affecting commerce." . . . It creates the National Labor Relations Board and prescribes its organization. . . . It sets forth the right of employees to self-organization and to bargain collectively through representatives of their own choosing. . . . It defines "unfair labor practices." . . . It lays down rules as to the representation of employees for the purpose of collective bargaining. . . . The Board is empowered to prevent the described unfair labor practices affecting commerce and the Act prescribes the procedure to that end. The Board is authorized to petition designated courts to secure the enforcement of its orders. The findings of the Board as to the facts, if supported by evidence, are to be conclusive. If either party on application to the court shows that additional evidence is material and that there were reasonable grounds for the failure to adduce such evidence in the hearings before the Board, the court may order the additional evidence to be taken. Any person aggrieved by a final order of the Board may obtain a review in the designated courts with the same procedure as in the case of an application by the Board for the enforcement of its order. . . . The Board has broad powers of investigation. . . . Interference with members of the Board or its agents in the performance of their duties is punishable by fine and imprisonment. . . . Nothing in the Act is to be construed to interfere with the right to strike. . . .

The procedure in the instant case followed the statute. . . .

Contesting the ruling of the Board, [Jones & Laughlin] argues (1) that the Act is in reality a regulation of labor relations and not of interstate commerce; [and] (2) that the act can have no application to the respondent's relations with its production employees because they are not subject to regulation by the federal government. . . .

First. The scope of the Act.—The Act is challenged in its entirety as an attempt to regulate all industry, thus invading the reserved powers of the States over their local concerns. It is asserted that the references in the Act to interstate and foreign commerce are colorable at best; that the Act is not a true regulation of such commerce or of matters which directly affect it but on the contrary has the fundamental object of placing under the compulsory supervision of the federal government all industrial labor relations within the nation. . . .

If this conception of terms, intent and consequent inseparability were sound, the Act would necessarily fall by reason of the limitation upon the federal power which inheres in the constitutional grant, as well as because of the explicit reservation of the Tenth Amendment. . . . The authority of the federal government may not be pushed to such an extreme as to destroy the distinction, which the commerce clause itself establishes, between commerce "among the several States" and the internal concerns of a State. That distinction between what is national and what is local in the activities of commerce is vital to the maintenance of our federal system. . . .

But we are not at liberty to deny effect to specific provisions, which Congress has constitutional power to enact, by superimposing upon them inferences from general legislative declarations of an ambiguous character, even if found in the same statute. The cardinal principle of statutory construction is to save and not to destroy. We have repeatedly held that as between two possible interpretations of a statute, by one of which it would be unconstitutional and by the other valid, our plain duty is to adopt that which will save the act. . . .

We think it clear that the National Labor Relations Act may be construed so as to operate within the sphere of constitutional authority. . . .

There can be no question that the commerce . . . contemplated by the Act . . . is interstate and foreign commerce in the constitutional sense. The Act also defines the term "affecting commerce." . . .

This definition is one of exclusion as well as inclusion. The grant of authority to the Board does not purport to extend to the relationship between all industrial employees and employers. Its terms do not impose collective bar-

gaining upon all industry regardless of effects upon interstate or foreign commerce. It purports to reach only what may be deemed to burden or obstruct that commerce and, thus qualified, it must be construed as contemplating the exercise or control within constitutional bounds. It is a familiar principle that acts which directly burden or obstruct interstate or foreign commerce, or its free flow, are within the reach of the congressional power. Acts having that effect are not rendered immune because they grow out of labor disputes.

. . . It is the effect upon commerce, not the source of the injury, which is the criterion. . . . Whether or not particular action does affect commerce in such a close and intimate fashion as to be subject to federal control, and hence to lie within the authority conferred upon the Board, is left by the statute to be determined as individual cases arise. We are thus to inquire whether in the instant case the constitutional boundary has been passed.

Second. The unfair labor practices in question. . . .

. . . [I]n its present application, the statute goes no further than to safeguard the right of employees to self-organization and to select representatives of their own choosing for collective bargaining or other mutual protection without restraint or coercion by their employer. That is a fundamental right. Employees have as clear a right to organize and select their representatives for lawful purposes as the respondent has to organize its business and select its own officers and agents. Discrimination and coercion to prevent the free exercise of the right of employees to self-organization and representation is a proper subject for condemnation by competent legislative authority. Long ago we stated the reason for labor organizations. We said that they were organized out of the necessities of the situation; that a single employee was helpless in dealing with an employer; that he was dependent ordinarily on his daily wage for the maintenance of himself and family; that if the employer refused to pay him the wages that he thought fair, he was nevertheless unable to leave the employ and resist arbitrary and unfair treatment; that union was essential to give laborers opportunity to deal on an equality with their employer. . . . Fully recognizing the legality of collective action on the part of employees in order to safeguard their proper interests, we said that Congress was not required to ignore this right but could safeguard it. Congress could seek to make appropriate collective action of employees an instrument of peace rather than of strife. We said that such collective action would be a mockery if representation were made futile by interference with freedom of choice. Hence the prohibition by Congress of interference with the selection of representatives for the purpose of negotiation and conference between employers and employees, "instead of being an invasion of the constitutional right of either, was based on the recognition of the rights of both." . . .

Third. The application of the Act to employees engaged in production.—The principle involved.—Respondent [Jones & Laughlin Steel Corporation] says that whatever may be said of employees engaged in interstate commerce, the industrial relations and activities in the manufacturing department . . . are not subject to federal regulation. The argument rests upon the proposition that manufacturing in itself is not commerce. . . .

. . . The various parts of respondent's enterprise are described as interdependent and as thus involving "a great movement of iron ore, coal and limestone along well-defined paths to the steel mills, thence through them, and thence in the form of steel products into the consuming centers of the country—a definite and well-understood course of business." It is urged that these activities constitute a "stream" or "flow" of commerce . . . and that industrial strife at [the central manufacturing plant of Jones & Laughlin] would cripple the entire movement. . . .

We do not find it necessary to determine whether these features of [Jones & Laughlin's] business dispose of the asserted analogy to the "stream of commerce" cases. The instances in which that metaphor has been used are but particular, and not exclusive, illustrations of the protection power which the Government invokes in support of the present Act. The congressional authority to protect interstate commerce from burdens and obstructions is not limited to transactions which can be deemed to be an essential part of a "flow" of interstate or foreign commerce. Burdens and obstructions may be due to injurious action springing from other sources. The fundamental principle is that the power to regulate commerce is the power to enact "all appropriate legislation" for "its protection and advancement"; . . . to adopt measures "to promote its growth and insure its safety"; . . . "to foster, protect, control and restrain." . . . That power is plenary and may be exerted to protect interstate commerce "no matter what the source of the dangers which threaten it." . . . Although activities may be intrastate in character when separately considered, if they have such a close and substantial relation to interstate commerce that their control is essential or appropriate to protect that commerce from burdens and obstructions, Congress cannot be denied the power to exercise that control. . . . Undoubtedly the scope of this power must be considered in the light of our dual system of government and may not be extended so as to embrace effects upon interstate commerce so indirect and remote that to embrace them, in view of our complex society, would effectually obliterate the distinction between what is national and what is local and create a completely centralized government. . . . The question is necessarily one of degree. . . .

That intrastate activities, by reason of close and intimate relation to interstate commerce, may fall within federal control is demonstrated in the case of carriers who are engaged in both interstate and intrastate transportation. There federal control has been found essential to secure the freedom of interstate traffic from interference or unjust discrimination and to promote the efficiency of the interstate service. . . . It is manifest that intrastate rates deal primarily with a local activity. But in rate-making they bear such a close relation to interstate rates that effective control of the one must embrace some control over the other. . . .

The close and intimate effect which brings the subject within the reach of federal power may be due to activities in relation to productive industry although the industry when separately viewed is local. . . .

It is . . . apparent that the fact that the employees here concerned were engaged in production is not determinative. The question remains as to the effect upon interstate commerce of the labor practice involved. In the *Schechter* case, . . . we found that the effect there was so remote as to be beyond the federal power. To find "immediacy or directness" there was to find it "almost everywhere," a result inconsistent with the maintenance of our federal system. In the *Carter* case, . . . the Court was of the opinion that the provisions of the statute relating to production were invalid upon several grounds—that there was improper delegation of legislative power, and that the requirements not only went beyond any sustainable measure of protection of interstate commerce but were also inconsistent with due process. These cases are not controlling here.

Fourth. Effects of the unfair labor practice in respondent's enterprise.

. . . [T]he stoppage of [Jones & Laughlin's] operations by industrial strife would have a most serious effect upon interstate commerce. In view of respondent's far-flung activities, it is idle to say that the effect would be indirect or remote. It is obvious that it would be immediate and might be catastrophic. We are asked to shut our eyes to the plainest facts of our national life and to deal with the question of direct and indirect effects in an intellectual vacuum. Because there may be but indirect and remote effects upon interstate commerce in connection with a host of local enterprises throughout the country, it does not follow that other industrial activities do not have such a close and intimate relation to interstate commerce as to make the presence of industrial strife a matter of the most urgent national concern. When industries organize themselves on a national scale, making their relation to interstate commerce the dominant factor in their activities, how can it be maintained that their industrial labor relations constitute a forbidden field into which Congress may not enter when it is necessary to protect interstate commerce from the paralyzing consequences of industrial war? We have often said that interstate commerce itself is a practical conception. It is equally true that interferences with that commerce must be appraised by a judgment that does not ignore actual experience.

Experience has abundantly demonstrated that the recognition of the right of employees to self-organization and to have representatives of their own choosing for the purpose of collective bargaining is often an essential condition of industrial peace. Refusal to confer and negotiate has been one of the most prolific causes of strife. This is such an outstanding fact in the history of labor disturbances that it is a proper subject of judicial notice and requires no citation of instances. . . .

These questions have frequently engaged the attention of Congress and have been the subject of many inquiries. The steel industry is one of the great basic industries of the United States, with ramifying activities affecting interstate commerce at every point. . . . It is not necessary again to detail the facts as to respondent's enterprise. Instead of being beyond the pale, we think that it presents in a most striking way the close and intimate relation which a manufacturing industry may have to interstate commerce and we have no doubt that Congress had constitutional authority to safeguard the right of [Jones & Laughlin's] employees to self-organization and freedom in the choice of representatives for collective bargaining. . . .

Our conclusion is that the order of the Board was within its competency and that the act is valid as here applied. The judgment of the Circuit Court of Appeals is reversed and the cause is remanded for further proceedings in conformity with this opinion.

Reversed.

Mr. Justice McReynolds [joined by *Mr. Justice Van Devanter*, *Mr. Justice Sutherland* and *Mr. Justice Butler*] delivered the following dissenting opinion.

. . . Considering [the statute's] far-reaching import . . ., the departure from what we understand has been consistently ruled here, and the extraordinary power confirmed to a Board of three [the NLRB], the obligation to present our views becomes plain. . . .

Any effect on interstate commerce by the discharge of employees shown here, would be indirect and remote in the highest degree, as consideration of the facts will show. In [this case] ten men out of ten thousand were dis-

charged. . . . The immediate effect in the factory may be to create discontent among all those employed and a strike may follow, which, in turn, may result in reducing production, which ultimately may reduce the volume of goods moving in interstate commerce. By this chain of indirect and progressively remote events we finally reach the evil with which it is said the legislation under consideration undertakes to deal. A more remote and indirect interference with interstate commerce or a more definite invasion of the powers reserved to the states is difficult, if not impossible, to imagine.

The Constitution still recognizes the existence of states with indestructible powers; the Tenth Amendment was supposed to put them beyond controversy.

We are told that Congress may protect the "stream of commerce" and that one who buys raw material without the state, manufactures it therein, and ships the output to another state is in that stream. Therefore it is said he may be prevented from doing anything which may interfere with its flow.

This, too, goes beyond the constitutional limitations heretofore enforced. If a man raises cattle and regularly delivers them to a carrier for interstate shipment, may Congress prescribe the conditions under which he may employ or discharge helpers on the ranch? The products of a mine pass daily into interstate commerce; many things are brought to it from other states. Are the owners and the miners within the power of Congress in respect of the miners' tenure and discharge? May a mill owner be prohibited from closing his factory or discontinuing his business because to do so would stop the flow of products to and from his plant in interstate commerce? May employees in a factory be restrained from quitting work in a body because this will close the factory and thereby stop the flow of commerce? May arson of a factory be made a Federal offense whenever this would interfere with such flow? If the business cannot continue with the existing wage scale, may Congress command a reduction? If the ruling of the Court just announced is adhered to, these questions suggest some of the problems certain to arise. And if this theory of a continuous "stream of commerce" as now defined is correct, will it become the duty of the Federal Government hereafter to suppress every strike which by possibility may cause a blockage in that stream? . . . Moreover, since Congress has intervened, are labor relations between most manufacturers and their employees removed from all control by the State? . . . There is no ground on which reasonably to hold that refusal by a manufacturer, whose raw materials come from states other than that of his factory and whose products are regularly carried to other states, to bargain collectively with employees in his manufacturing plant, directly affects interstate commerce. In such business, there is not one but two distinct movements or streams in interstate transportation. The first brings in raw material and there ends. Then follows manufacture, a separate and local activity. Upon completion of this, and not before, the second distinct movement or stream in interstate commerce begins and the products go to their states. Such is the common course for small as well as large industries. It is unreasonable and unprecedented to say the commerce clause confers upon Congress power to govern relations between employers and employees in these local activities. . . . In Schechter's case we condemned as unauthorized by the commerce clause the assertion of federal power in respect of commodities which had come to rest after interstate transportation. And, in Carter's case, we held Congress lacked power to regulate labor relations in respect of commodities before interstate commerce has begun.

It is gravely stated that experience teaches that if any employer discourages membership in "any organization of any kind . . . in which employees participate, and which exists for the purpose in whole or in part of dealing with employers concerning grievances, labor disputes, wages, rates of pay, hours of employment or conditions of work," discontent may follow and this in turn may lead to a strike, and as the outcome of the strike there may be a block in the stream of interstate commerce. Therefore Congress may inhibit the discharge. Whatever effect any cause of discontent may ultimately have upon commerce is far too indirect to justify Congressional regulations. Almost anything—marriage, birth, death—may in some fashion affect commerce. That Congress has power by appropriate means, not prohibited by the Constitution, to prevent direct and material interference with the conduct of interstate commerce is settled doctrine. But the interference struck at must be direct and material, not some mere possibility contingent on wholly uncertain events; and there must be no impairment of rights guaranteed. . . . The right to contract is fundamental and includes the privilege of selecting those with whom one is willing to assume contractual relations. This right is unduly abridged by the act now upheld. A private owner is deprived of power to manage his own property by freely selecting those to whom his manufacturing operations are to be entrusted. We think this cannot lawfully be done in circumstances like those here disclosed.

It seems clear to us that Congress has transcended the powers granted.

Case

UNITED STATES V. DARBY

312 U.S. 100; 61 S.Ct. 451; 85 L.Ed. 609 (1941)
Vote: 9–0

The Fair Labor Standards Act of 1938 established minimum wages and maximum working hours for employees of industries whose products were shipped in interstate commerce. Fred Darby, owner of the Darby Lumber Company in Statesboro, Georgia, was indicted for violating the statute. Darby demurred to the indictment on the ground that in passing the law Congress had exceeded its powers under the Commerce Clause and had infringed on the powers reserved to the states by the Tenth Amendment.

Mr. Justice Stone delivered the opinion of the Court.

The two principal questions raised by the record in this case are, first, whether Congress has constitutional power to prohibit the shipment in interstate commerce of lumber manufactured by employees whose wages are less than a prescribed minimum or whose weekly hours of labor at that wage are greater than a prescribed maximum, and, second, whether it has power to prohibit the employment of workmen in the production of goods "for interstate commerce" at other than prescribed wages and hours. . . .

The Fair Labor Standards Act [FLSA] set up a comprehensive legislative scheme for preventing the shipment in interstate commerce of certain products and commodities produced in the United States under labor conditions as respects wages and hours which fail to conform to standards set up by the Act. Its purpose, as we judicially know from the declaration of policy . . . is to exclude from interstate commerce goods produced for the commerce and to prevent their production for interstate commerce, under conditions detrimental to the maintenance of the minimum standards of living necessary for health and general well-being; and to prevent the use of interstate commerce as the means of competition in the distribution of goods so produced, and as the means of spreading and perpetuating such substandard labor conditions among the workers of the several states. . . .

. . . [T]he statute . . . prohibits certain specified acts and punishes willful violation of it by a fine of not more than $10,000 and punishes each conviction after the first by imprisonment of not more than six months or by the specified fine or both. . . . [The act makes it unlawful to ship in interstate commerce goods produced by employees working for less than a minimum wage of twenty-five cents per hour or for more than forty-four hours a week.]

The indictment charges that [Darby] is engaged, in the state of Georgia, in the business of acquiring raw materials, which he manufactures into finished lumber with the intent, when manufactured, to ship it in interstate commerce to customers outside the state, and that he does in fact so ship a large part of the lumber so produced. There are numerous counts charging [him] with the shipment in interstate commerce from Georgia to points outside the state of lumber in the production of which, for interstate commerce, [Darby] has employed workmen at less than the prescribed minimum wage or more than the prescribed maximum hours without payment to them of any wage for overtime. . . .

The case comes here on assignments by the Government that the district court erred in so far as it held that Congress was without constitutional power to penalize the acts set forth in the indictment, and [Darby] seeks to sustain the decision below on the grounds that the prohibition by Congress of those Acts is unauthorized by the commerce clause. . . .

The prohibition of shipment of the proscribed goods in interstate commerce. [The FLSA] prohibits, and the indictment charges, the shipment in interstate commerce, of goods produced for interstate commerce by employees whose wages and hours of employment do not conform to the requirements of the Act. . . . [T]he only question arising under the commerce clause with respect to such shipments is whether Congress has the constitutional power to prohibit them.

While manufacture is not of itself interstate commerce the shipment of manufactured goods interstate is such commerce and the prohibition of such shipment by Congress is indubitably a regulation of the commerce. The power to regulate commerce is the power "to prescribe the rule by which commerce is governed." . . . It extends not only to those regulations which aid, foster and protect the commerce, but embraces those which prohibit it. . . . It is conceded that the power of Congress to prohibit transportation in interstate commerce includes noxious articles, . . . and articles such as intoxicating liquor or convict made goods, traffic in which is forbidden or restricted by the laws of the state of destination. . . .

But it is said that the present prohibition falls within the scope of none of these categories; that while the prohibition is nominally a regulation of the commerce its motive or purpose is regulation of wages and hours of persons engaged in manufacture, the control of which has been reserved to the states and upon which Georgia and some of the states of destination have placed no restriction; that the effect of the present statute is not to exclude the prescribed articles from interstate commerce in aid of state regulation, . . . but instead, under the guise of a regulation of interstate commerce, it undertakes to regulate wages and hours within the state contrary to the policy of the state which has elected to leave them unregulated.

The power of Congress over interstate commerce "is complete in itself, may be exercised to its utmost extent, and acknowledges no limitations other than are prescribed in the Constitution." . . . That power can neither be enlarged nor diminished by the exercise or nonexercise of state power. . . . Congress, following its own conception of public policy concerning the restrictions which may appropriately be imposed on interstate commerce, is free to exclude from the commerce articles whose use in the states for which they are destined it may conceive to be injurious to the public health, morals or welfare, even though the state has not sought to regulate their use. . . .

Such regulation is not a forbidden invasion of state power merely because either its motive or its consequence is to restrict the use of articles of commerce within the states of destination and is not prohibited unless by other constitutional provisions. It is no objection to the assertion of power to regulate interstate commerce that its exercise is attended by the same incidents which attend the exercise of the police power of the states. . . .

The motive and purpose of the present regulation are plainly to make effective the Congressional conception of public policy that interstate commerce should not be made the instrument of competition in the distribution of goods produced under substandard labor conditions, which competition is injurious to the commerce and to the states from and to which the commerce flows. The motive and purpose of a regulation of interstate commerce are matters for the legislative judgment upon the exercise of which the Constitution places no restriction and over which the courts are given no control. . . . Whatever their motive and purpose, regulations of commerce which do not infringe some constitutional prohibition are within the plenary power conferred on Congress by the Commerce Clause. Subject only to that limitation, presently to be considered, we conclude that the prohibition of the shipment interstate of goods produced under the forbidden substandard labor conditions is within the constitutional authority of Congress.

In the more than a century which has elapsed since the decision of *Gibbons v. Ogden,* these principles of constitutional interpretation have been so long and repeatedly recognized by this Court as applicable to the Commerce Clause, that there would be little occasion for repeating them now were it not for the decision of this Court twenty-two years ago in *Hammer v. Dagenhart.* . . . In that case it was held by a bare majority of the Court over the powerful and now classic dissent of Mr. Justice Holmes setting forth the fundamental issues involved that Congress was without power to exclude the products of child labor from interstate commerce. The reasoning and conclusion of the Court's opinion there cannot be reconciled with the conclusion which we have reached, that the power of Congress under the Commerce Clause is plenary to exclude any article from interstate commerce subject only to the specific prohibitions of the Constitution.

Hammer v. Dagenhart has not been followed. The distinction on which the decision was rested that Congressional power to prohibit interstate commerce is limited to articles which in themselves have some harmful or deleterious property—a distinction which was novel when made and unsupported by any provision of the Constitution— has long since been abandoned. . . . The thesis of the opinion that the motive of the prohibition or its effect to control in some measure the use or production within the states of the article thus excluded from the commerce can operate to deprive the regulation of its constitutional authority has long since ceased to have force. . . .

The conclusion is inescapable that *Hammer v. Dagenhart* was a departure from the principles which have prevailed in the interpretation of the Commerce Clause both before and since the decision and that such vitality, as a precedent, as it then had has long since been exhausted. It should be and now is overruled.

Validity of the wage and hour requirements. . . . [W]e must at the outset determine whether the particular acts charged in the courts, . . . as they were construed below, constitute "production for commerce" within the meaning of the statute. As the Government seeks to apply the statute in the indictment, and as the court below construed the phrase "produced for interstate commerce," it embraces at least the case where an employer engaged, as is [Darby], in the manufacture and shipment of goods in filling orders of extrastate customers, manufactures his product with the intent or expectation that according to the normal course of his business all or some part of it will be selected for shipment to those customers.

Without attempting to define the precise limits of the phrase, we think the acts alleged in the indictment are within the sweep of the statute. The obvious purpose of the Act was not only to prevent the interstate transportation of the proscribed product, but to stop the initial step toward transportation, production with the purpose of so transporting it. Congress was not unaware that most manufacturing businesses shipping their product in interstate commerce make it in their shops without reference to its ultimate destination and then after manufacture select

some of it for shipment interstate and some intrastate according to the daily demands of their business, and that it would be practically impossible, without disrupting manufacturing businesses, to restrict the prohibited kind of production to the particular pieces of lumber, cloth, furniture or the like which later move in interstate rather than intrastate commerce. . . .

There remains the question whether such restriction on the production of goods for commerce is a permissible exercise of the commerce power. The power of Congress over interstate commerce is not confined to the regulation of commerce among the states. It extends to those activities intrastate which so affect interstate commerce or the exercise of the power of Congress over it as to make regulation of them appropriate means to the attainment of a legitimate end, the exercise of the granted power of Congress to regulate interstate commerce. . . .

While this Court has many times found state regulations of interstate commerce, when uniformity of its regulation is of national concern, to be incompatible with the Commerce Clause even though Congress has not legislated on the subject, the Court has never implied such restraint on state control over matters intrastate not deemed to be regulations of interstate commerce or its instrumentalities even though they affect the commerce. . . . In the absence of Congressional legislation on the subject state laws which are not regulations of the commerce itself or its instrumentalities are not forbidden even though they affect interstate commerce. . . . But it does not follow that Congress may not by appropriate legislation regulate intrastate activities where they have a substantial effect on interstate commerce. . . .

Congress, having by the present Act adopted the policy of excluding from interstate commerce all goods produced for the commerce which do not conform to the specified labor standards, it may choose the means reasonably adapted to the attainment of the permitted end, even though they involve control of intrastate activities. Such legislation has often been sustained with respect to powers, other than the commerce power granted to the national government, when the means chosen, although not themselves within the granted power, were nevertheless deemed appropriate aids to the accomplishment of some purpose within an admitted power of the national government. . . . A familiar like exercise of power is the regulation of intrastate transactions which are so commingled with or related to interstate commerce that all must be regulated if the interstate commerce is to be effectively controlled. . . .

. . . [T]he evils aimed at by the [FLSA] are the spread of substandard labor conditions through the use of the facilities of interstate commerce for competition by the goods so produced with those produced under the prescribed or better labor conditions; and the consequent dislocation of the commerce itself caused by the impairment or destruction of local businesses by competition made effective through interstate commerce. The Act is thus directed at the suppression of a method or kind of competition in interstate commerce which it has in effect condemned as "unfair," as the Clayton Act has condemned other "unfair methods of competition" made effective through interstate commerce. . . .

The means adopted . . . for the protection of interstate commerce by the suppression of the production of the condemned goods for interstate commerce is so related to the commerce and so affects it as to be within the reach of the commerce power. . . . Congress, to attain its objective in the suppression of nationwide competition in interstate commerce by goods produced under substandard labor conditions, has made no distinction as to the volume or amount of shipments in the commerce or of production for commerce by any particular shipper or producer. It recognized that in present day industry, competition by a small part may affect the whole and that the total effect of the competition of many small producers may be great. . . . The legislation aimed at a whole embraces all its parts. . . .

Our conclusion is unaffected by the Tenth Amendment which provides: "The powers not delegated to the United States by the Constitution nor prohibited by it to the states are reserved to the states respectively or to the people." The amendment states but a truism that all is retained which has not been surrendered. There is nothing in the history of its adoption to suggest that it was more than declaratory of the relationship between the national and state governments as it had been established by the Constitution before the amendment or that its purpose was other than to allay fears that the new national government might seek to exercise powers not granted, and that the states might not be able to exercise fully their reserved powers. . . .

From the beginning and for many years the amendment has been construed as not depriving the national government of authority to resort to all means for the exercise of a granted power which are appropriate and plainly adapted to the permitted end. . . . Whatever doubts may have arisen of the soundness of that conclusion they have been put at rest by the decisions under the Sherman Act and the National Labor Relations Act. . . .

The Act is sufficiently definite to meet constitutional demands. One who employs persons, without conforming to the prescribed wage and hour conditions, to work on goods which he ships or expects to ship across state lines, is warned that he may be subject to the criminal penalties of the Act. No more is required. . . .

Reversed.

Case

HEART OF ATLANTA MOTEL V. UNITED STATES

379 U.S. 241; 85 S.Ct. 348; 13 L.Ed. 2d 258 (1964)
Vote: 9–0

In The Civil Rights Cases *(1883) The Supreme Court held that Congress cannot use its power to enforce the Fourteenth Amendment to outlaw racial discrimination by privately owned places of public accommodation unless there is some significant degree of official state action supporting the discriminatory practices. Thus, in the 1964 Civil Rights Act, Congress sought to prohibit racial discrimination by hotels, restaurants, and other public facilities by invoking its broad authority to regulate interstate commerce. The constitutionality of this approach is before the Supreme Court in this case.*

Mr. Justice Clark delivered the opinion of the Court.

. . . Appellant owns and operates the Heart of Atlanta Motel which has 216 rooms available to transient guests. The motel is located on Courtland Street, two blocks from downtown Peachtree Street. It is readily accessible to interstate highways 75 and 85 and state highways 23 and 41. Appellant solicits patronage from outside the State of Georgia through various national advertising media, including magazines of national circulation; it maintains over 50 billboards and highway signs within the State, soliciting patronage for the motel; it accepts convention trade from outside Georgia and approximately 75% of its registered guests are from out of State. Prior to passage of the [Civil Rights Act of 1964] the motel had followed a practice of refusing to rent rooms to Negroes, and it alleged that it intended to continue to do so. In an effort to perpetuate that policy this suit was filed.

The appellant contends that Congress in passing [the Civil Rights Act] exceeded its power to regulate commerce under Art. I, Sec. 8, cl. 3, of the Constitution of the United States. . . .

The sole question posed is, therefore, the constitutionality of the Civil Rights Act of 1964 as applied to these facts. The legislative history of the Act indicates that Congress based the Act on Sec. 5 and the Equal Protection Clause of the Fourteenth Amendment as well as its power to regulate interstate commerce under Art. I, Sec. 8, cl. 3, of the Constitution.

The Senate Commerce Committee made it quite clear that the fundamental object of Title II was to vindicate "the deprivation of personal dignity that surely accompanies denials of equal access to public establishments." At the same time, however, it noted that such an objective has been and could be readily achieved "by congressional action based on the commerce power of the Constitution." . . . Our study of the legislative record, made in the light of prior cases, has brought us to the conclusion that Congress possessed ample power in this regard, and we have therefore not considered the other grounds relied upon. This is not to say that the remaining authority upon which it acted was not adequate, a question upon which we do not pass, but merely that since the commerce power is sufficient for our decision here we have considered it alone. . . .

While the Act as adopted carried no congressional findings, the record of its passage through each house is replete with evidence of the burdens that discrimination by race or color places upon interstate commerce. . . . This testimony included the fact that our people have become increasingly mobile with millions of people of all races traveling from State to State; that Negroes in particular have been the subject of discrimination in transient accommodations, having to travel great distances to secure the same; that often they have been unable to obtain accommodations and have had to call upon friends to put them up overnight, . . . and that these conditions had become so acute as to require the listing of available lodging for Negroes in a special guidebook which was itself "dramatic testimony to the difficulties" Negroes encounter in travel. . . . These exclusionary practices were found to be nationwide, the Under Secretary of Commerce testifying that there is "no question that this discrimination in the North still exists to a large degree" and in the West and Midwest as well. . . . This testimony indicated a qualitative as well as quantitative effect on interstate travel by Negroes. The former was the obvious impairment of the Negro traveler's pleasure and convenience that resulted when he continually was uncertain of finding lodging. As for the latter, there was evidence that this uncertainty stemming from racial discrimination had the effect of discouraging travel on the part of a substantial portion of the Negro community. . . . This was the conclusion not only of the Under Secretary of Commerce but also of the Administrator of the Federal Aviation Agency who wrote the Chairman of the Senate Commerce Committee that it was his "belief that air commerce is adversely affected by the denial to a substantial segment of the traveling public of adequate and desegregated public accommodations." . . . [T]he voluminous testimony presents overwhelming evidence that discrimination by hotels and motels impedes interstate travel.

The power of Congress to deal with these obstructions depends on the meaning of the Commerce Clause. . . . [T]he determinative test of the exercise of power by the Congress under the Commerce Clause is simply whether the activity sought to be regulated is "commerce which concerns more States than one" and has a real and substantial relation to the national interest. Let us now turn to this facet of the problem.

That the "intercourse" of which the Chief Justice spoke included the movement of persons through more States than one was settled as early as 1849, in the Passenger Cases, . . . where Mr. Justice McLean stated: "That the transportation of passengers is a part of commerce is not now an open question." . . .

The same interest in protecting interstate commerce which led Congress to deal with segregation in interstate carriers and the white-slave traffic has prompted it to extend the exercise of its power to gambling, . . . to deceptive practices in the sale of products, . . . to fraudulent security transactions, . . . to misbranding of drugs, . . . to wages and hours, . . . to members of labor unions, . . . to crop control, . . . to discrimination against shippers, . . . to the protection of small business from injurious price cutting, . . . to resale price maintenance, . . . to professional football, . . . and to racial discrimination by owners and managers of terminal restaurants. . . .

That Congress was legislating against moral wrongs in many of these areas rendered its enactments no less valid. In framing Title II of this Act Congress was also dealing with what it considered a moral problem. But that fact does not detract from the overwhelming evidence of the disruptive effect that racial discrimination has had on commercial intercourse. It was this burden which empowered Congress to enact appropriate legislation, and, given this basis for the exercise of its power, Congress was not restricted by the fact that the particular obstruction to interstate commerce with which it was dealing was also deemed a moral and social wrong.

It is said that the operation of the motel here is of a purely local character. But, assuming this to be true, "[i]f it is interstate commerce that feels the pinch, it does not matter how local the operation which applies the squeeze." . . . Thus the power of Congress to promote interstate commerce also included the power to regulate the local incidents thereof, including local activities in both the States of origin and destination, which might have a substantial and harmful effect upon that commerce. One need only examine the evidence which we have discussed above to see that Congress may—as it has—prohibit racial discrimination by motels serving travelers, however "local" their operations may appear. . . .

We, therefore, conclude that the action of the Congress in the adoption of the Act as applied here to a motel which concededly serves interstate travelers is within the power granted it by the Commerce Clause of the Constitution, as interpreted by this Court for 140 years. It may be argued that Congress could have pursued other methods to eliminate the obstructions it found in interstate commerce caused by racial discrimination. But this is a matter of policy that rests entirely with the Congress, not with the courts. How obstructions in commerce may be removed—what means are to be employed—is within the sound and exclusive discretion of the Congress. It is subject only to one caveat—that the means chosen by it must be reasonably adapted to the end permitted by the Constitution. We cannot say that its choice here was not so adapted. The Constitution requires no more.

Mr. Justice Black, concurring. . . .

Mr. Justice Douglas, concurring.

Though I join the Court's opinion, I am somewhat reluctant here . . . to rest solely on the Commerce Clause. My reluctance is not due to any conviction that Congress lacks power to regulate commerce in the interests of human rights. It is rather my belief that the right of people to be free of state action that discriminates against them because of race, like the "right of persons to move freely from State to State" . . . "occupies a more protected position in our constitutional system than does the movement of cattle, fruit, steel, and coal across state lines." . . .

Hence I would prefer to test on the assertion of legislative power contained in Sec. 5 of the Fourteenth Amendment which states: "The Congress shall have power to enforce, by appropriate legislation, the provisions of this article"—a power which the Court concedes was exercised at least in part in this Act.

A decision based on the Fourteenth Amendment would have a more settling effect, making unnecessary litigation over whether a particular customer is an interstate traveler. Under my construction, the Act would apply to all customers in all the enumerated places of public accommodation. And that construction would put an end to all obstructionist strategies and finally close one door on a bitter chapter in American history. . . .

Case

Katzenbach v. McClung

379 U.S. 294; 85 S.Ct. 377; 13 L.Ed. 2d 290 (1964)
Vote: 9–0

In this companion case to Heart of Atlanta Motel v. United States, *the Court considers the constitutionality of Title II of the Civil Rights Act of 1964 as applied to a restaurant in Birmingham, Alabama.*

Mr. Justice Clark delivered the opinion of the Court.

Ollie's Barbecue is a family-owned restaurant . . . specializing in barbecued meats and homemade pies, with a seating capacity of 220 customers. It is located on a state highway 11 blocks from an interstate highway . . . and a somewhat greater distance from railroad and bus stations. The restaurant caters to a family and white-collar trade with a take-out service for Negroes. It employs 36 persons, two-thirds of whom are Negroes.

In the 12 months preceding the passage of the Act, the restaurant purchased locally approximately $150,000 worth of food, $69,683 or 46% of which was meat that it bought from a local supplier who had procured it from outside the State. The district Court expressly found that a substantial portion of the food served in the restaurant had moved in interstate commerce. The restaurant has refused to serve Negroes in its dining accommodations since its original opening in 1927, and since July 2, 1964, it has been operating in violation of the Act. The court below concluded that if it were required to serve Negroes it would lose a substantial amount of business.

. . . The activities that are beyond the reach of Congress are "those which are completely within a particular State, which do not affect other states, and with which it is not necessary to interfere, for the purpose of executing some of the general powers of the government." *Gibbons v. Ogden* . . . (1824). This rule is as good today as it was when

Chief Justice Marshall laid it down almost a century and a half ago.

This Court has held time and again that this power extends to activities of retail establishments, including restaurants, which directly or indirectly burden or obstruct interstate commerce. . . .

Nor are the cases holding that interstate commerce ends when goods come to rest in the State of destination apposite here. That line of cases has been applied with reference to state taxation or regulation but not in the field of federal regulation. . . .

Here, as there, Congress has determined for itself that refusals of service to Negroes have imposed burdens both upon the interstate flow of food and upon the movement of products generally. Of course, the mere fact that Congress has said when particular activity shall be deemed to affect commerce does not preclude further examination by this Court. But where we find that the legislators, in light of the facts and testimony before them, have a rational basis for finding a chosen regulatory scheme necessary to the protection of commerce, our investigation is at an end. The only remaining question—one answered in the affirmative by the court below—is whether the particular restaurant either serves or offers to serve interstate travelers or serves food a substantial portion of which has moved in interstate commerce. . . .

Confronted as we are with the facts laid before Congress, we must conclude that it had a rational basis for finding that racial discrimination in restaurants had a direct and adverse effect on the free flow of interstate commerce. . . .

The power of Congress in this field is broad and sweeping; where it keeps within its sphere and violates no express constitutional limitation it has been the rule of this Court, going back almost to the founding days of the Republic, not to interfere. The Civil Rights Act of 1964, as here applied, we find to be plainly appropriate in the resolution of what the Congress found to be a national commercial problem of the first magnitude. We find it in no violation of any express limitations of the Constitution and we therefore declare it valid. . . .

Case

United States v. Lopez

514 U.S. 549; 115 S.Ct. 1624; 131 L.Ed. 2d 626 (1995)
Vote: 5–4

In enacting the Gun-Free School Zones Act of 1990, Congress made it a federal offense "for any individual knowingly to possess a firearm at a place that the individual knows, or has reasonable cause to believe, is a school zone." A twelfth grade student in San Antonio, Texas, was convicted under the statute after he was found to be carrying a concealed .38-caliber handgun and five bullets at school. The Court of Appeals for the Fifth Circuit reversed respondent's conviction, holding the act was invalid because Congress had exceeded its authority under the Commerce Clause. The Supreme Court granted certiorari.

Chief Justice Rehnquist delivered the opinion of the Court.

We start with first principles. The Constitution creates a Federal Government of enumerated powers. . . . As James Madison wrote, "[t]he powers delegated by the proposed Constitution to the federal government are few and defined. Those which are to remain in the State governments are numerous and indefinite." . . . This constitutionally mandated division of authority "was adopted by the Framers to ensure protection of our fundamental liberties." . . . "Just as the separation and independence of the coordinate branches of the Federal Government serves to prevent the accumulation of excessive power in any one branch, a healthy balance of power between the States and the Federal Government will reduce the risk of tyranny and abuse from either front." . . .

. . . [W]e have identified three broad categories of activity that Congress may regulate under its commerce power. . . . First, Congress may regulate the use of the channels of interstate commerce. . . . Second, Congress is empowered to regulate and protect the instrumentalities of interstate commerce, or persons or things in interstate commerce, even though the threat may come only from intrastate activities. . . . For example, the destruction of an aircraft or . . . thefts from interstate shipments. Finally, Congress' commerce authority includes the power to regulate those activities having a substantial relation to interstate commerce, i.e., those activities that substantially affect interstate commerce. . . .

Within this final category, admittedly, our case law has not been clear whether an activity must "affect" or "substantially affect" interstate commerce in order to be within Congress' power to regulate it under the Commerce Clause. . . . We conclude, consistent with the great

3 tests

weight of our case law, that the proper test requires an analysis of whether the regulated activity "substantially affects" interstate commerce.

We now turn to consider the power of Congress, in the light of this framework, to enact [the challenged statute]. The first two categories of authority may be quickly disposed of: [the challenged statute] is not a regulation of the use of the channels of interstate commerce, nor is it an attempt to prohibit the interstate transportation of a commodity through the channels of commerce; nor can [the challenged statute] be justified as a regulation by which Congress has sought to protect an instrumentality of interstate commerce or a thing in interstate commerce. Thus, if [the challenged statute] is to be sustained, it must be under the third category as a regulation of an activity that substantially affects interstate commerce.

First, we have upheld a wide variety of congressional Acts regulating intrastate economic activity where we have concluded that the activity substantially affected interstate commerce. Examples include the regulation of intrastate coal mining; . . . intrastate extortionate credit transactions, . . . restaurants utilizing substantial interstate supplies, . . . inns and hotels catering to interstate guests, . . . and production and consumption of home-grown wheat. . . . These examples are by no means exhaustive, but the pattern is clear. Where economic activity substantially affects interstate commerce, legislation regulating that activity will be sustained. . . .

. . . [The challenged statute] is a criminal statute that by its terms has nothing to do with "commerce" or any sort of economic enterprise, however broadly one might define those terms. [It] is not an essential part of a larger regulation of economic activity, in which the regulatory scheme could be undercut unless the intrastate activity were regulated. It cannot, therefore, be sustained under our cases upholding regulations of activities that arise out of or are connected with a commercial transaction, which viewed in the aggregate, substantially affects interstate commerce. . . .

The Government's essential contention . . . is that we may determine here that [the challenged statute] is valid because possession of a firearm in a local school zone does indeed substantially affect interstate commerce. . . . The Government argues that possession of a firearm in a school zone may result in violent crime and that violent crime can be expected to affect the functioning of the national economy in two ways. First, the costs of violent crime are substantial, and, through the mechanism of insurance, those costs are spread throughout the population. . . . Second, violent crime reduces the willingness of individuals to travel to areas within the country that are perceived to be unsafe. . . . The Government also argues that the presence of guns in schools poses a substantial threat to the educational process by threatening the learning environment. A handicapped educational process, in turn, will result in a less productive citizenry. That, in turn, would have an adverse effect on the Nation's economic well-being. As a result, the Government argues that Congress could rationally have concluded that [the challenged statute] substantially affects interstate commerce.

We pause to consider the implications of the Government's arguments. The Government admits, under its "costs of crime" reasoning, that Congress could regulate not only all violent crime, but all activities that might lead to violent crime, regardless of how tenuously they relate to interstate commerce. . . . Similarly, under the Government's "national productivity" reasoning, Congress could regulate any activity that it found was related to the economic productivity of individual citizens: family law (including marriage, divorce, and child custody), for example. Under the theories that the Government presents in support of [the challenged statute], it is difficult to perceive any limitation on federal power, even in areas such as criminal law enforcement or education where States historically have been sovereign. Thus, if we were to accept the Government's arguments, we are hard-pressed to posit any activity by an individual that Congress is without power to regulate. . . .

For instance, if Congress can, pursuant to its Commerce Clause power, regulate activities that adversely affect the learning environment, then, *a fortiori*, it also can regulate the educational process directly. Congress could determine that a school's curriculum has a "significant" effect on the extent of classroom learning. As a result, Congress could mandate a federal curriculum . . . because what is taught in local schools has a significant "effect on classroom learning," . . . and that, in turn, has a substantial effect on interstate commerce. . . .

To uphold the Government's contentions here, we would have to pile inference upon inference in a manner that would bid fair to convert congressional authority under the Commerce Clause to a general police power of the sort retained by the States. Admittedly, some of our prior cases have taken long steps down that road, giving great deference to congressional action. . . . The broad language in these opinions has suggested the possibility of additional expansion, but we decline here to proceed any further. To do so would require us to conclude that the Constitution's enumeration of powers does not presuppose something not enumerated . . . and that there never will be a distinction between what is truly national and what is truly local. This we are unwilling to do. . . .

Justice Kennedy, with whom Justice O'Connor joins, concurring. . . .

Justice Thomas, concurring. . . .

Justice Stevens, dissenting. . . .

Justice Souter, dissenting. . . .

Justice Breyer, with whom *Justice Stevens*, *Justice Souter*, and *Justice Ginsburg* join, dissenting.

The issue in this case is whether the Commerce Clause authorizes Congress to enact a statute that makes it a crime to possess a gun in, or near, a school. . . . In my view, the statute falls well within the scope of the commerce power as this Court has understood that power over the last half-century.

In reaching this conclusion, I apply three basic principles of Commerce Clause interpretation. First, the power to "regulate Commerce . . . among the several States" . . . encompasses the power to regulate local activities insofar as they significantly affect interstate commerce. . . . Second, in determining whether a local activity will likely have a significant effect upon interstate commerce, a court must consider, not the effect of an individual act . . ., but rather the cumulative effect of all similar instances (i.e., the effect of all guns possessed in or near schools). . . . Third, the Constitution requires us to judge the connection between a regulated activity and interstate commerce, not directly, but at one remove. Courts must give Congress a degree of leeway in determining the existence of a significant factual connection between the regulated activity and interstate commerce—both because the Constitution delegates the commerce power directly to Congress and because the determination requires an empirical judgment of a kind that a legislature is more likely than a court to make with accuracy. The traditional words "rational basis" capture this leeway. . . . Thus, the specific question before us, as the Court recognizes, is not whether the "regulated activity sufficiently affected interstate commerce," but, rather, whether Congress could have had "a rational basis" for so concluding. . . .

Applying these principles to the case at hand, we must ask whether Congress could have had a rational basis for finding a significant (or substantial) connection between gun-related school violence and interstate commerce. Or, to put the question in the language of the explicit finding that Congress made when it amended this law in 1994: Could Congress rationally have found that "violent crime in school zones," through its effect on the "quality of education," significantly (or substantially) affects "interstate" or "foreign commerce"? . . . As long as one views the com-

merce connection, not as a "technical legal conception," but as "a practical one," . . . the answer to this question must be yes. Numerous reports and studies—generated both inside and outside government—make clear that Congress could reasonably have found the empirical connection that its law, implicitly or explicitly, asserts. . . .

For one thing, reports, hearings, and other readily available literature make clear that the problem of guns in and around schools is widespread and extremely serious. These materials report, for example, that four percent of American high school students (and six percent of inner-city high school students) carry a gun to school at least occasionally, . . . that 12 percent of urban high school students have had guns fired at them, . . . that 20 percent of those students have been threatened with guns, . . . and that, in any 6-month period, several hundred thousand schoolchildren are victims of violent crimes in or near their schools. . . . And, they report that this widespread violence in schools throughout the Nation significantly interferes with the quality of education in those schools . . . . Based on reports such as these, Congress obviously could have thought that guns and learning are mutually exclusive. . . . And, Congress could therefore have found a substantial educational problem—teachers unable to teach, students unable to learn—and concluded that guns near schools contribute substantially to the size and scope of that problem.

Having found that guns in schools significantly undermine the quality of education in our Nation's classrooms, Congress could also have found, given the effect of education upon interstate and foreign commerce, that gun-related violence in and around schools is a commercial, as well as a human, problem. Education, although far more than a matter of economics, has long been inextricably intertwined with the Nation's economy. . . .

The economic links I have just sketched seem fairly obvious. Why then is it not equally obvious, in light of those links, that a widespread, serious, and substantial physical threat to teaching and learning also substantially threatens the commerce to which that teaching and learning is inextricably tied? That is to say, guns in the hands of six percent of inner-city high school students and gun-related violence throughout a city's schools must threaten the trade and commerce that those schools support. The only question, then, is whether the latter threat is (to use the majority's terminology) "substantial." And, the evidence of (1) the extent of the gun-related violence problem, . . . (2) the extent of the resulting negative effect on classroom learning, . . . and (3) the extent of the consequent negative commercial effects, . . . when taken together, indicate a threat to trade and commerce that is "substantial." At the very least, Congress could rationally have concluded that the links are "substantial."

Specifically, Congress could have found that gun-related violence near the classroom poses a serious economic threat (1) to consequently inadequately educated workers who must endure low paying jobs, . . . and (2) to communities and businesses that might (in today's "information society") otherwise gain, from a well-educated work force, an important commercial advantage, . . . of a kind that location near a railhead or harbor provided in the past. . . .

In sum, to find this legislation within the scope of the Commerce Clause would permit "Congress . . . to act in terms of economic . . . realities." . . . It would interpret the Clause as this Court has traditionally interpreted it, with the exception of one wrong turn subsequently corrected . . . . Upholding this legislation would do no more than simply recognize that Congress had a "rational basis" for finding a significant connection between guns in or near schools and (through their effect on education) the interstate and foreign commerce they threaten. For these reasons, I would reverse the judgment of the Court of Appeals. . . .

Case

UNITED STATES V. MORRISON

529 U.S. 598; 120 S.Ct. 1740; 146 L.Ed. 2d 658 (2000)
Vote: 5–4

In this case, the Supreme Court considers the constitutionality of a provision of the Violence against Women Act of 1994, which authorized victims of "gender-motivated violence" to sue their assailants for damages in federal court. The case stemmed from an alleged rape of a female student, Christy Brzonkala, by two Virginia Tech University football players, Antonio Morrison and James Crawford. Dissatisfied with the outcome of disciplinary proceedings conducted by the university, Brzonkala brought suit against the two players in the U.S. District Court for the Western District of Virginia. The defendants moved to dismiss the case on the ground that the civil remedies provision of the Violence against Women Act (§ 13981) was unconstitutional. The U.S. Justice Department intervened to defend the constitutionality of the statute. Thus the Supreme Court decision in this case is reported as United States v. Morrison. *The federal district court granted the defendants' motion to dismiss, holding that Congress did not have the power under Commerce Clause or the Fourteenth Amendment to enact the civil remedies provision of the statute. A three-judge panel of the U.S. Court of Appeals for the Fourth Circuit reversed, but the court, sitting en banc, upheld the district court's decision. The Supreme Court granted certiorari to consider the constitutional question.*

Chief Justice Rehnquist delivered the opinion of the Court.

. . . As we observed in [*United States v.*] *Lopez* [1995], modern Commerce Clause jurisprudence has "identified three broad categories of activity that Congress may regulate under its commerce power." . . . "First, Congress may regulate the use of the channels of interstate commerce." . . . "Second, Congress is empowered to regulate and protect the instrumentalities of interstate commerce, or persons or things in interstate commerce, even though the threat may come only from intrastate activities." . . . "Finally, Congress' commerce authority includes the power to regulate those activities having a substantial relation to interstate commerce, . . . i.e., those activities that substantially affect interstate commerce.". . .

Petitioners do not contend that these cases fall within either of the first two of these categories of Commerce Clause regulation. They seek to sustain § 13981 as a regulation of activity that substantially affects interstate commerce. Given § 13981's focus on gender-motivated violence wherever it occurs (rather than violence directed at the instrumentalities of interstate commerce, interstate markets, or things or persons in interstate commerce), we agree that this is the proper inquiry. . . .

With these principles underlying our Commerce Clause jurisprudence as reference points, the proper resolution of the present cases is clear. Gender-motivated crimes of violence are not, in any sense of the phrase, economic activity. While we need not adopt a categorical rule against aggregating the effects of any noneconomic activity in order to decide these cases, thus far in our Nation's history our cases have upheld Commerce Clause regulation of intrastate activity only where that activity is economic in nature. . . .

Like the Gun-Free School Zones Act at issue in *Lopez*, § 13981 contains no jurisdictional element establishing that the federal cause of action is in pursuance of Congress' power to regulate interstate commerce. Although *Lopez* makes clear that such a jurisdictional element would lend support to the argument that § 13981 is sufficiently tied to interstate commerce, Congress elected to cast

§ 13981's remedy over a wider, and more purely intrastate, body of violent crime.

In contrast with the lack of congressional findings that we faced in *Lopez,* § 13981 *is* supported by numerous findings regarding the serious impact that gender-motivated violence has on victims and their families. . . . But the existence of congressional findings is not sufficient, by itself, to sustain the constitutionality of Commerce Clause legislation. As we stated in *Lopez,* " '[S]imply because Congress may conclude that a particular activity substantially affects interstate commerce does not necessarily make it so.' " . . . Rather, " '[w]hether particular operations affect interstate commerce sufficiently to come under the constitutional power of Congress to regulate them is ultimately a judicial rather than a legislative question, and can be settled finally only by this Court.' " . . .

In these cases, Congress' findings are substantially weakened by the fact that they rely so heavily on a method of reasoning that we have already rejected as unworkable if we are to maintain the Constitution's enumeration of powers. Congress found that gender-motivated violence affects interstate commerce "by deterring potential victims from traveling interstate, from engaging in employment in interstate business, and from transacting with business, and in places involved in interstate commerce; . . . by diminishing national productivity, increasing medical and other costs, and decreasing the supply of and the demand for interstate products." . . .

Given these findings and petitioners' arguments, the concern that we expressed in *Lopez* that Congress might use the Commerce Clause to completely obliterate the Constitution's distinction between national and local authority seems well founded. . . . The reasoning that petitioners advance seeks to follow the but-for causal chain from the initial occurrence of violent crime (the suppression of which has always been the prime object of the States' police power) to every attenuated effect upon interstate commerce. If accepted, petitioners' reasoning would allow Congress to regulate any crime as long as the nationwide, aggregated impact of that crime has substantial effects on employment, production, transit, or consumption. Indeed, if Congress may regulate gender-motivated violence, it would be able to regulate murder or any other type of violence since gender-motivated violence, as a subset of all violent crime, is certain to have lesser economic impacts than the larger class of which it is a part.

Petitioners' reasoning, moreover, will not limit Congress to regulating violence but may, as we suggested in *Lopez,* be applied equally as well to family law and other areas of traditional state regulation since the aggregate effect of marriage, divorce, and childrearing on the national economy is undoubtedly significant. Congress

may have recognized this specter when it expressly precluded § 13981 from being used in the family law context. . . . Under our written Constitution, however, the limitation of congressional authority is not solely a matter of legislative grace. . . .

We accordingly reject the argument that Congress may regulate noneconomic, violent criminal conduct based solely on that conduct's aggregate effect on interstate commerce. The Constitution requires a distinction between what is truly national and what is truly local. . . . In recognizing this fact we preserve one of the few principles that has been consistent since the Clause was adopted. The regulation and punishment of intrastate violence that is not directed at the instrumentalities, channels, or goods involved in interstate commerce has always been the province of the States. . . .

Because we conclude that the Commerce Clause does not provide Congress with authority to enact § 13981, we address petitioners' alternative argument that the section's civil remedy should be upheld as an exercise of Congress' remedial power under § 5 of the Fourteenth Amendment. As noted above, Congress expressly invoked the Fourteenth Amendment as a source of authority to enact § 13981.

The principles governing an analysis of congressional legislation under § 5 are well settled. Section 5 states that Congress may " 'enforce,' by 'appropriate legislation' the constitutional guarantee that no State shall deprive any person of 'life, liberty or property, without due process of law,' nor deny any person 'equal protection of the laws.' " . . . Section 5 is "a positive grant of legislative power," . . . that includes authority to "prohibit conduct which is not itself unconstitutional and [to] intrud[e] into 'legislative spheres of autonomy previously reserved to the States.'" . . .

However, "[a]s broad as the congressional enforcement power is, it is not unlimited." . . .

As our cases have established, state-sponsored gender discrimination violates equal protection unless it "serves important governmental objectives" and . . . the discriminatory means employed are "substantially related to the achievement of those objectives." . . .

However, the language and purpose of the Fourteenth Amendment place certain limitations on the manner in which Congress may attack discriminatory conduct. These limitations are necessary to prevent the Fourteenth Amendment from obliterating the Framers' carefully crafted balance of power between the States and the National Government. . . . Foremost among these limitations is the time-honored principle that the Fourteenth Amendment, by its very terms, prohibits only state action. "[T]he principle has become firmly embedded in our constitutional law that the action inhibited by the first section of the Fourteenth Amendment is only such action as may fairly be said to be that of the States. That Amendment erects no shield against merely private conduct, however discriminatory or wrongful." . . .

. . .Section 13981 is not aimed at proscribing discrimination by officials which the Fourteenth Amendment might not itself proscribe; it is directed not at any State or state actor, but at individuals who have committed criminal acts motivated by gender bias. . . .

For these reasons, we conclude that Congress' power under § 5 does not extend to the enactment of § 13981.

Petitioner Brzonkala's complaint alleges that she was the victim of a brutal assault. But Congress' effort in § 13981 to provide a federal civil remedy can be sustained neither under the Commerce Clause nor under § 5 of the Fourteenth Amendment. If the allegations here are true, no civilized system of justice could fail to provide her a remedy for the conduct of respondent Morrison. But under our federal system that remedy must be provided by the Commonwealth of Virginia, and not by the United States. The judgment of the Court of Appeals is affirmed.

Justice Thomas, concurring.

The majority opinion correctly applies our decision in *United States* v. *Lopez* . . . and I join it in full. I write separately only to express my view that the very notion of a "substantial effects" test under the Commerce Clause is inconsistent with the original understanding of Congress' powers and with this Court's early Commerce Clause cases. By continuing to apply this rootless and malleable standard, however circumscribed, the Court has encouraged the Federal Government to persist in its view that the Commerce Clause has virtually no limits. Until this Court replaces its existing Commerce Clause jurisprudence with a standard more consistent with the original understanding, we will continue to see Congress appropriating state police powers under the guise of regulating commerce.

Justice Souter, with whom ***Justice Stevens, Justice Ginsburg,*** and ***Justice Breyer*** join, dissenting.

. . . Our cases, which remain at least nominally undisturbed, stand for the following propositions. Congress has the power to legislate with regard to activity that, in the aggregate, has a substantial effect on interstate commerce. . . . The fact of such a substantial effect is not an issue for the courts in the first instance, . . . but for the Congress, whose institutional capacity for gathering evidence and taking testimony far exceeds ours. By passing legislation, Congress indicates its conclusion, whether explicitly or not, that facts support its exercise of the commerce power. The business of the courts is to review the congressional

assessment, not for soundness but simply for the rationality of concluding that a jurisdictional basis exists in fact. . . . . Any explicit findings that Congress chooses to make, though not dispositive of the question of rationality, may advance judicial review by identifying factual authority on which Congress relied. Applying those propositions in these cases can lead to only one conclusion.

One obvious difference from *United States* v. *Lopez* . . . (1995), is the mountain of data assembled by Congress, here showing the effects of violence against women on interstate commerce. Passage of the Act in 1994 was preceded by four years of hearings, which included testimony from physicians and law professors; from survivors of rape and domestic violence; and from representatives of state law enforcement and private business. The record includes reports on gender bias from task forces in 21 States, and we have the benefit of specific factual findings in the eight separate Reports issued by Congress and its committees over the long course leading to enactment. . . .

. . . Congress found that "crimes of violence motivated by gender have a substantial adverse effect on interstate commerce, by deterring potential victims from traveling interstate, from engaging in employment in interstate business, and from transacting with business, and in places involved, in interstate commerce . . . [,] by diminishing national productivity, increasing medical and other costs, and decreasing the supply of and the demand for interstate products. . . ." . . .

Congress thereby explicitly stated the predicate for the exercise of its Commerce Clause power. Is its conclusion irrational in view of the data amassed? True, the methodology of particular studies may be challenged, and some of the figures arrived at may be disputed. But the sufficiency of the evidence before Congress to provide a rational basis for the finding cannot seriously be questioned. . . .

The Act would have passed muster at any time between *Wickard* [v. *Filburn*] in 1942 and *Lopez* in 1995, a period in which the law enjoyed a stable understanding that congressional power under the Commerce Clause, complemented by the authority of the Necessary and Proper Clause, . . . extended to all activity that, when aggregated, has a substantial effect on interstate commerce. . . .

Chief Justice Marshall's seminal opinion in *Gibbons* v. *Ogden* . . . construed the commerce power from the start with "a breadth never yet exceeded." . . . In particular, it is worth noting, the Court in *Wickard* did not regard its holding as exceeding the scope of Chief Justice Marshall's view of interstate commerce; *Wickard* applied an aggregate effects test to ostensibly domestic, noncommercial farming consistently with Chief Justice Marshall's indication that the commerce power may be understood by its exclusion of subjects, among others, "which do not affect other States." . . . This plenary view of the power has either prevailed or been acknowledged by this Court at every stage of our jurisprudence. . . .

Since adherence to . . . formalistically contrived confines of commerce power in large measure provoked the judicial crisis of 1937, one might reasonably have doubted that Members of this Court would ever again toy with a return to the days before *NLRB v. Jones & Laughlin Steel Corp.* . . . (1937), which brought the earlier and nearly disastrous experiment to an end. And yet today's decision can only be seen as a step toward recapturing the prior mistakes. Its revival of a distinction between commercial and noncommercial conduct is at odds with *Wickard,* which repudiated that analysis, and the enquiry into commercial purpose, first intimated by the *Lopez* concurrence, . . . is cousin to the intent-based analysis employed in *Hammer* [*v. Dagenhart* (1918)] but rejected for Commerce Clause purposes in *Heart of Atlanta Motel* and [*United States v.*] *Darby.*

Why is the majority tempted to reject the lesson so painfully learned in 1937? . . .

The Court finds it relevant that the statute addresses conduct traditionally subject to state prohibition under domestic criminal law, a fact said to have some heightened significance when the violent conduct in question is not itself aimed directly at interstate commerce or its instrumentalities. . . . Again, history seems to be recycling, for the theory of traditional state concern as grounding a limiting principle has been rejected previously, and more than once. . . .

. . . Today's majority . . . finds no significance whatever in the state support for the Act based upon the States' acknowledged failure to deal adequately with gender-based violence in state courts, and the belief of their own law enforcement agencies that national action is essential.

The National Association of Attorneys General supported the Act unanimously, . . . and Attorneys General from 38 States urged Congress to enact the Civil Rights Remedy, representing that "the current system for dealing with violence against women is inadequate." . . . It was against this record of failure at the state level that the Act was passed to provide the choice of a federal forum in place of the state-court systems found inadequate to stop gender-biased violence. . . . The Act accordingly offers a federal civil rights remedy aimed exactly at violence against women, as an alternative to the generic state tort causes of action found to be poor tools of action by the state task forces. . . . As the 1993 Senate Report put it, "The Violence Against Women Act is intended to respond both to the underlying attitude that this violence is somehow less serious than other crime and to the resulting failure of our criminal justice system to address such violence. Its goals are both symbolic and practical. . . ." . . .

The collective opinion of state officials that the Act was needed continues virtually unchanged, and when the Civil Rights Remedy was challenged in court, the States came to its defense. Thirty-six of them and the Commonwealth of Puerto Rico have filed an *amicus* brief in support of petitioners in these cases, and only one State has taken respondents' side. It is, then, not the least irony of these cases that the States will be forced to enjoy the new federalism whether they want it or not. For with the Court's decision today, Antonio Morrison . . . has "won the states' rights plea against the states themselves." . . .

All of this convinces me that today's ebb of the commerce power rests on error, and at the same time leads me to doubt that the majority's view will prove to be enduring law. . . .

Justice Breyer, with whom *Justice Stevens* joins, and with whom *Justice Souter* and *Justice Ginsburg* join as to Part I-A, dissenting. . . .

Case

UNITED STATES V. BUTLER

297 U.S. 1; 56 S.Ct. 312; 80 L.Ed. 477 (1936)
Vote: 6–3

In this case the Court considers the constitutionality of the Agricultural Adjustment Act of 1933, the purpose of which was to reduce surpluses in various agricultural commodities by reg-
ulating their production. In essence, farmers were paid to stop producing wheat, cotton, tobacco, corn, rice, milk, and hogs. These payments were financed by excise taxes to be paid by companies that processed or packaged these commodities. A federal district judge upheld the tax provisions of the act; the Court of Appeals reversed. The United States asked the Supreme Court to grant certiorari.

Mr. Justice Roberts delivered the opinion of the Court.

. . . The tax can only be sustained by ignoring the avowed purpose and operation of the act, and holding it a measure merely laying an excise upon processors to raise revenue for the support of government. Beyond cavil the sole object of the legislation is to restore the purchasing power of agricultural products to a parity with that prevailing in an earlier day; to take money from the processor and bestow it upon farmers who will reduce their acreage for the accomplishment of the proposed end, and, meanwhile, to aid these farmers during the period required to bring the prices of their crops to the desired level.

The tax plays an indispensable part in the plan of regulation. . . . A tax automatically goes into effect for a commodity when the Secretary of Agriculture determines that rental or benefit payments are to be made for reduction of production of that commodity. The tax is to cease when rental or benefit payments cease. The rate is fixed with the purpose of bringing about crop-reduction and price-raising. . . . If the Secretary finds the policy of the act will not be promoted by the levy of the tax for a given commodity, he may exempt it. . . . The whole revenue from the levy is appropriated in aid of crop control; none of it is made available for general governmental use. The entire agricultural adjustment program . . . is to become inoperative when, in the judgment of the President, the national economic emergency ends. . . .

The statute not only avows an aim foreign to the procurement of revenue for the support of government, but by its operation shows the exaction laid upon processors to be the necessary means for the intended control of agricultural production. . . .

We conclude that the act is one regulating agricultural production; that the tax is a mere incident of such regulation and that [Butler has] standing to challenge the legality of the exaction.

It does not follow that as the act is not an exertion of the taxing power and the exaction not a true tax, the statute is void or the exaction uncollectible. . . . [I]f this is an expedient regulation by Congress, of a subject within one of its granted powers, "and the end to be attained is one falling within that power, the act is not void, because, within a loose and more extended sense than was used in the Constitution," the exaction is called a tax. . . .

There should be no misunderstanding as to the function of this court in such a case. It is sometimes said that the court assumes a power to overrule or control the action of the people's representatives. This is a misconception. The Constitution is the supreme law of the land ordained and established by the people. All legislation must conform to the principles it lays down. When an act of Congress is appropriately challenged in the courts as not conforming to the constitutional mandate the judicial branch of the Government has only one duty—to lay the article of the Constitution which is invoked beside the statute which is challenged and to decide whether the latter squares with the former. All the court does, or can do, is to announce its considered judgment upon the question. The only power it has, if such it may be called, is the power of judgment. This court neither approves nor condemns any legislative policy. Its delicate and difficult office is to ascertain and declare whether the legislation is in accordance with, or in contravention of, the provisions of the Constitution; and, having done that, its duty ends.

The question is not what power the federal Government ought to have but what powers in fact have been given by the people. . . . Each State has all governmental powers save such as the people, by their Constitution, have conferred upon the United States, denied to the States, or reserved to themselves. The federal union is a government of delegated powers. It has only such as are expressly conferred upon it and such as are reasonably to be implied from those granted. In this respect we differ radically from nations where all legislative power, without restriction or limitation, is vested in a parliament or other legislative body subject to no restrictions except the discretion of its members.

Article I, Section 8, of the Constitution vests sundry powers in the Congress. . . . The clause thought to authorize the legislation—the first—confers upon the Congress power "to lay and collect Taxes, Duties, Imposts and Excises, to pay the Debts and provide for the common Defence and general Welfare of the United States. . . ." It is not contended that this provision grants power to regulate agricultural production upon the theory that such legislation would promote the general welfare. The Government concedes that the phrase "to provide for the general welfare" qualifies the power "to lay and collect taxes." The view that the clause grants power to provide for the general welfare, independently of the taxing power, has never been authoritatively accepted. Mr. Justice Story points out that if it were adopted "it is obvious that under color of the generality of the words, to 'provide for the common defence and general welfare,' the government of the United States is, in reality, a government of general and unlimited powers, notwithstanding the subsequent enumeration of specific powers." The true construction undoubtedly is that the only thing granted is the power to tax for the purpose of providing funds for payment of the nation's debts and making provision for the general welfare.

Nevertheless the Government asserts that warrant is found in this clause for the adoption of the Agricultural Adjustment Act. The argument is that Congress may appropriate and authorize the spending of moneys for the "general welfare"; that the phrase should be liberally construed to cover anything conducive to national welfare; that decision as to what will promote such welfare rests with Congress alone, and the courts may not review its determination; and finally that the appropriation under attack was in fact for the general welfare of the United States.

The Congress is expressly empowered to lay taxes to provide for the general welfare. Funds in the Treasury as a result of taxation may be expected only through appropriation. . . . They can never accomplish the objects for which they were collected unless the power to appropriate is as broad as the power to tax. The necessary implication from the terms of the grant is that the public funds may be appropriated "to provide for the general welfare of the United States.". . .

Since the foundation of the nation, sharp differences of opinion have persisted as to the true interpretation of the phrase. Madison asserted it amounted to no more than a reference to the other powers enumerated in the subsequent clauses of the same section; that, as the United States is a government of limited and enumerated powers, the grant of power to tax and spend for the general national welfare must be confined to the enumerated legislative fields committed to the Congress. In this view the phrase is mere tautology, for taxation and appropriation are or may be necessary incidents of the exercise of any of the enumerated legislative powers. Hamilton, on the other hand, maintained the clause confers a power separate and distinct from those later enumerated, is not restricted in meaning by the grant of them, and Congress consequently has a substantive power to tax and to appropriate, limited only by the requirement that it shall be exercised to provide for the general welfare of the United States. Each contention has had the support of those whose views are entitled to weight. This court has noticed the question, but has never found it necessary to decide which is the true construction. Mr. Justice Story, in his Commentaries, espouses the Hamiltonian position. We shall not review the writings of public men and commentators or discuss the legislative practice. Study of all these leads us to conclude that the reading advocated by Mr. Justice Story is the correct one. While, therefore, the power to tax is not unlimited, its confines are set in the clause which confers it, and not in those of Section 8 which bestow and define the legislative powers of the Congress. It results that the power of Congress to authorize expenditure of public moneys for public purposes is not limited by the direct grants of legislative power found in the Constitution. But the adoption of the broader construction leaves the power to spend subject to limitations.

. . .We are not now required to ascertain the scope of the phrase "general welfare of the United States" or to determine whether an appropriation in aid of agriculture falls within it. Wholly apart from that question, another principle embedded in our Constitution prohibits the enforcement of the Agricultural Adjustment Act. The act invades the reserved rights of the states. It is a statutory plan to regulate and control agricultural production, a matter beyond the powers delegated to the federal government. The tax, the appropriation of the funds raised, and the direction for their disbursement, are but parts of the plan. They are but means to an unconstitutional end.

From the accepted doctrine that the United States is a government of delegated powers, it follows that those not expressly granted, or reasonably to be implied from such as are conferred, are reserved to the states or to the people. To forestall any suggestion to the contrary, the Tenth Amendment was adopted. The same proposition, otherwise stated, is that powers not granted are prohibited. None to regulate agricultural production is given, and therefore legislation by Congress for that purpose is forbidden.

It is an established principle that the attainment of a prohibited end may not be accomplished under the pretext of the exertion of powers which are granted. . . .

The power of taxation, which is expressly granted, may, of course, be adopted as a means to carry into operation another power also expressly granted. But resort to the taxing power to effectuate an end which is not legitimate, not within the scope of the Constitution, is obviously inadmissible. . . .

Third. If the taxing power may not be used as the instrument to enforce a regulation of matters of state concern with respect to which the Congress has no authority to interfere, may it, as in the present case, be employed to raise the money necessary to purchase a compliance which the Congress is powerless to command? The Government asserts that whatever might be said against the validity of the plan, if compulsory, it is constitutionally sound because the end is accomplished by voluntary cooperation. There are two sufficient answers to the contention. The regulation is not in fact voluntary. The farmer, of course, may refuse to comply, but the price of such refusal is the loss of benefits. The amount offered is intended to be sufficient to exert pressure on him to agree to the proposed regulation. The power to confer or withhold unlimited benefits is the power to coerce or destroy. If the cotton grower elects not to accept the benefits, he will receive less for his crops; those who receive payment will be able to undersell him. The result may well be financial ruin. . . . This is coercion by economic pressure. The asserted power of choice is illusory.

But if the plan were one for purely voluntary cooperation it would stand no better so far as federal power is concerned. At best it is a scheme for purchasing with federal funds submission to federal regulation of a subject reserved to the states. . . .

Congress has no power to enforce its commands on the farmer to the ends sought by the Agricultural Adjustment Act. It must follow that it may not indirectly accomplish those ends by taxing and spending to purchase compliance. The Constitution and the entire plan of our government negate any such use of the power to tax and to spend as the act undertakes to authorize. It does not help to declare that local conditions throughout the nation have created a situation of national concern; for this is but to say that whenever there is a widespread similarity of local conditions, Congress may ignore constitutional limitations upon its own powers and usurp those reserved to the states. If, in lieu of compulsory regulation of subjects within the states' reserved jurisdiction, which is prohibited, the Congress could invoke the taxing and spending power as a means to accomplish the same end, clause 1 of Sec. 8 of Article I would become the instrument for total subversion of the governmental powers reserved to the individual states. . . .

Hamilton himself, the leading advocate of broad interpretation of the power to tax and to appropriate for the general welfare, never suggested that any power granted by the Constitution could be used for the destruction of local self-government in the states. Story countenances no such doctrine. It seems never to have occurred to them, or to those who have agreed with them, that the general welfare of the United States, . . . might be served by obliterating the constituent members of the Union. But to this fatal conclusion the doctrine contended for would inevitably lead. And its sole premise is that, though the makers of the Constitution, in erecting the federal government, intended sedulously to limit and define its powers, so as to reserve to the states and the people sovereign power, to be wielded by the states and their citizens and not be invaded by the United States, they nevertheless by a single clause gave power to the Congress to tear down the barriers, to invade the states' jurisdiction, and to become a parliament of the whole people, subject to no restrictions save such as are self-imposed. The argument when seen in its true character and in the light of the inevitable results must be rejected. . . .

Mr. Justice Stone [joined by **Mr. Justice Brandeis** and **Mr. Justice Cardozo**], dissenting.

. . . The Constitution requires that public funds shall be spent for a defined purpose, the promotion of the general welfare. . . . The power of Congress to spend is inseparable from persuasion to action over which Congress has no legislative control. Congress may not command that the science of agriculture be taught in state universities. But if it would aid the teaching of that science by grants to state institutions, it is appropriate, if not necessary, that the grant be on the condition . . . that it be used for the intended purpose. Similarly it would seem to be compliance with the Constitution, not violation of it, for the government to take and the university to give a contract that the grant would be so used. It makes no difference that there is a promise to do an act which the condition is calculated to induce. Condition and promise are alike valid since both are in furtherance of the national purpose for which the money is appropriated.

These effects upon individual action, which are but incidents of the authorized expenditure of government money, are pronounced to be themselves a limitation upon the granted power, and so the time-honored principle of constitutional interpretation that the granted power includes all those which are incident to it is reversed. . . .

. . . The spending power of Congress is in addition to the legislative power and not subordinate to it. This independent grant of the power of the purse, and its very nature, involving in its exercise the duty to insure expenditure within the granted power, presuppose freedom of selection among diverse ends and aims, and the capacity to impose such conditions as will render the choice effective. It is a contradiction in terms to say that there is power to spend for the national welfare, while rejecting any power to impose conditions reasonably adapted to the attainment of the end which alone would justify the expenditure.

The limitation now sanctioned must lead to absurd consequences. The government may give seeds to farmers, but may not condition the gift upon their being planted in places where they are most needed or even planted at all. The government may give money to the unemployed, but may not ask that those who get shall give labor in return, or even use it to support their families. It may give money to sufferers from earthquake, fire, tornado, pestilence or flood, but may not impose conditions—health precautions designed to prevent the spread of disease, or induce the movement of population to safer or more sanitary areas. All that, because it is purchased regulation infringing state powers, must be left for the states, who are unable or unwilling to supply the necessary relief. . . . Do all its activities collapse because, in order to effect the permissible purpose, in myriad ways the money is paid out upon terms and conditions which influence action of the recipients within the states, which Congress cannot command? The answer would seem plain. If the expenditure is for a national public purpose, that purpose will not be thwarted because payment is on condition which will advance that purpose. The action which Congress induces by payments of money to promote the general welfare, but which it does not command or coerce, is but an incident to a specifically granted power, but a permissible means to a legitimate end. If appropriation in aid of a program of curtailment of agricultural production is constitutional, and it is not denied that it is, payment to farmers on condition that they reduce their crop acreage is constitutional. It is not any the less so because the farmer at his own option promises to fulfill the condition.

That the governmental power of the purse is a great one is not now for the first time announced. Every student of the history of government and economics is aware of its magnitude and of its existence in every civilized government. Both were well understood by the framers of the Constitution when they sanctioned the grant of the spending power to the federal government, and both were recognized by Hamilton and Story, whose views of the spending power as standing on a parity with the other powers specifically granted, have hitherto been generally accepted. The suggestion that it must now be curtailed by judicial fiat because it may be abused by unwise use hardly rises to the dignity of argument. So may judicial power be abused. "The power to tax is the power to destroy," but we do not, for that reason, doubt its existence, or hold that its efficacy is to be restricted by its incidental or collateral effects upon the states. . . . The power to tax and spend is not without constitutional restraints. One restriction is that the purpose must be truly national. Another is that it may not be used to coerce action left to state control. Another is the conscience and patriotism of Congress and the Executive. . . .

A tortured construction of the Constitution is not to be justified by recourse to extreme examples of reckless congressional spending which might occur if courts could not prevent—expenditures which, even if they could be thought to effect any national purpose, would be possible only by action of a legislature lost to all sense of public responsibility. Such suppositions are addressed to the mind accustomed to believe that it is the business of courts to sit in judgment on the wisdom of legislative action. Courts are not the only agency of government that must be assumed to have the capacity to govern. Congress and the courts both unhappily may falter or be mistaken in the performance of their constitutional duty. But interpretation of our great charter of government which proceeds on any assumption that the responsibility for the preservation of our institution is the exclusive concern of any one of the three branches of government, or that it alone can save them from destruction, is far more likely, in the long run, "to obliterate the constituent members" of "an indestructible union of indestructible states" than the frank recognition of that language, even of a constitution, may mean what it says: that the power to tax and spend includes the power to relieve a nation-wide economic maladjustment by conditional gifts of money. . . .

Case

STEWARD MACHINE COMPANY V. DAVIS

301 U.S. 548; 57 S.Ct. 883; 81 L.Ed. 1279 (1937)
Vote: 5–4

Here the Court considers the validity of the Social Security Act of 1935. The Charles C. Steward Machine Company brought suit to challenge the requirement that firms with eight or more employees pay a 1 percent payroll tax as partial funding for the Social Security system.

Mr. Justice Cardozo delivered the opinion of the Court.

. . . [Steward Machine Company] paid a tax in accordance with the [Social Security Act], filed a claim for refund with the Commissioner of Internal Revenue, and sued to recover the payment ($46.14), asserting a conflict between the statute and the Constitution of the United States. . . . An important question of constitutional law being involved, we granted certiorari. . . .

The Social Security Act . . . is divided into eleven separate titles, of which only titles IX and III are so related to this case as to stand in need of summary. . . . [Under Title IX] every employer (with stated exceptions) is to pay for each calendar year "an excise tax, with respect to having individuals in his employ," the tax to be measured by prescribed percentages of the total wages payable by the employer during the calendar year with respect to such employment. . . . Under [Title III] certain sums of money are "authorized to be appropriated for the purpose of assisting the states in the administration of their unemployment compensation laws. . . ." The appropriations when made were not specifically out of the proceeds of the employment tax, but out of any moneys in the Treasury. Other sections of the title prescribe the method by which the payments are to be made to the state . . . and also certain conditions to be established. . . . They are designed to give assurance to the Federal Government that the moneys granted by it will not be expended for purposes alien to the grant, and will be used in the administration of genuine unemployment compensation laws.

The assault on the statute proceeds on an extended front. Its assailants take the ground that the tax is not an excise; that it is not uniform throughout the United States as excises are required to be; that its exceptions are so many and arbitrary as to violate the Fifth Amendment; that its purpose was not revenue, but an unlawful invasion of the reserved powers of the states; and that the states in submitting to it have yielded to coercion and have abandoned governmental functions which they are not permitted to surrender. . . .

First: The tax, which is described in the statute as an excise, is laid with uniformity throughout the United States as a duty, an impost or an excise upon the relation of employment.

1. We are told that the relation of employment is one so essential to the pursuit of happiness that it may not be burdened with a tax. Appeal is made to history. From the precedents of colonial days we are supplied with illustrations of excises common in the colonies. They are said to have been bound up with the enjoyment of particular commodities. . . .

. . . Doubtless there were many excises in colonial days and later that were associated, more or less intimately, with the enjoyment or the use of property. This would not prove, even if no others were then known, that the forms then accepted were not subject to enlargement. . . . But in truth other excises were known, and known since early times. . . . Our colonial forebears knew more about ways of taxing than some of their descendants seem to be willing to concede. The historical prop failing, the prop or fancied prop of principle remains. We learn that employment for lawful gain is a "natural" or "inherent" or "inalienable" right, and not a "privilege" at all. But natural rights, so called, are as much subject to taxation as rights of less importance. An excise is not limited to vocations or activities that may be prohibited altogether. It is not limited to those that are the outcome of a franchise. It extends to vocations or activities pursued as of common right. What the individual does in the operation of a business is amenable to taxation just as much as what he owns, at all events if the classification is not tyrannical or arbitrary. . . .

The subject matter of taxation open to the power of Congress is as comprehensive as that open to the power of the states, though the method of apportionment may at times be different. . . . The statute books of the states are strewn with illustrations of taxes laid on occupations pursued of common right. We find no basis for a holding that the power in that regard which belongs by accepted practice to the legislatures of the states, has been denied by the Constitution to the Congress of the nation.

2. The tax being an excise, its imposition must conform to the canon of uniformity. There has been no departure from this requirement. According to the settled doctrine the uniformity exacted is geographical, not intrinsic. . . .

Second: The excise is not invalid under the provisions of the Fifth Amendment by force of its exemptions.

The statute does not apply . . . to employers of less than eight. It does not apply to agricultural labor, or domestic service in a private home or to some other classes of less importance. [Steward Machine Company] contends that the effect of these restrictions is an arbitrary discrimination vitiating the tax.

The Fifth Amendment unlike the Fourteenth has no equal protection clause. . . . But even the states, though subject to such a clause, are not confined to a formula of rigid uniformity in framing measures of taxation. . . . They may tax some kinds of property at one rate, and others at another, and exempt others altogether. . . . They may lay an excise on the operations of a particular kind of business, and exempt some other kind of business closely akin thereto. . . . If this latitude of judgment is lawful for the states, it is lawful . . . in legislation by the Congress, which is subject to restraints less narrow and confining. . . .

The classifications and exemptions directed by the statute now in controversy have support in considerations of policy and practical convenience that cannot be condemned as arbitrary. The classifications and exemptions would therefore be upheld if they had been adopted by a state and the provisions of the Fourteenth Amendment were invoked to annul them. . . . The act of Congress is therefore valid, so far at least as its system of exemptions is concerned, and this though we assume that discrimination, if gross enough, is equivalent to confiscation and subject under the Fifth Amendment to challenge and annulment.

Third: The excise is not void as involving the coercion of the States in contravention of the Tenth Amendment or of restrictions implicit in our federal form of government. The proceeds of the excise when collected are paid into the Treasury at Washington, and thereafter are subject to appropriation like public moneys generally. . . . No presumption can be indulged that they will be misapplied or wasted. Even if they were collected in the hope or expectation that some other and collateral good would be furthered as an incident, that without more would not make the act invalid. . . .

To draw the line intelligently between duress and inducement there is need to remind ourselves of facts as to the problem of unemployment that are now matters of common knowledge. . . . Of the many available figures a few only will be mentioned. During the years 1929 to 1936, when the country was passing through a cyclical depression, the number of the unemployed mounted to unprecedented heights. Often the average was more than 10 million; at times a peak was attained of 16 million or more. Disaster to the breadwinner means disaster to dependents. Accordingly the roll of the unemployed, itself formidable enough, was only a partial roll of the destitute or needy. The fact developed quickly that the states were unable to give the requisite relief. The problem had become national in areas and dimensions. There was need of help from the nation if the people were not to starve. It is too late today for the argument to be heard with tolerance that in a crisis so extreme the use of the moneys of the nation to relieve the unemployed and their dependents is a use for any purpose narrower than the promotion of the general welfare. . . .

In the presence of this urgent need for some remedial expedient, the question is to be answered whether the expedient adopted has overleapt the bounds of power. The assailants of the statute say that its dominant end and aim is to drive the state legislatures under the whip of economic pressure into the enactment of unemployment compensation laws at the bidding of the central government. Supporters of the statute say that its operation is not constraint, but the creation of a larger freedom, the states and the nation joining in a cooperative endeavor to avert a common evil. . . .

The Social Security Act is an attempt to find a method by which all these public agencies may work together to a common end. Every dollar of the new taxes will continue in all likelihood to be used and needed by the nation as long as states are unwilling, whether through timidity or for other motives, to do what can be done at home. At least the inference is permissible that Congress so believed, though retaining undiminished freedom to spend the money as it pleased. On the other hand fulfillment of the home duty will be lightened and encouraged by crediting the taxpayer upon his account with the Treasury of the nation to the extent that his contributions under the laws of the locality have simplified or diminished the problem of relief and the probable demand upon the resources of the fisc. . . .

Who then is coerced through the operation of this statute? Not the taxpayer. He pays in fulfillment of the mandate of the local legislature. Not the state. Even now she does not offer a suggestion that in passing the unemployment law she was affected by duress. . . . For all that appears she is satisfied with her choice, and would be sorely disappointed if it were now to be annulled. The difficulty with the petitioner's contention is that it confuses motive with coercion. "Every tax is in some measure regulatory. To some extent it interposes an economic impediment to the activity taxed as compared with others not taxed." . . . In like manner, every rebate from a tax when conditioned upon conduct is in some measure a temptation. But to hold that motive or temptation is equivalent to coercion is to plunge the law in endless difficulties. The outcome of such a doctrine is the acceptance of a philosophical determinism by which choice becomes impossible. Till now the law has been guided by a robust common sense which assumes the freedom of the will as a working hypothesis in the solution of its problems. The wisdom of the hypothesis has illustration in this case. Nothing in the case suggests the exertion of a power akin to undue influence, if we assume that such a concept can ever be applied with fitness to the relations between state and nation. Even on that assumption the location of the point at which pressure turns into compulsion, and ceases to be inducement, would be a question of degree—at times, perhaps, of fact. . . .

In ruling as we do, we leave many questions open. We do not say that a tax is valid, when imposed by act of Congress, if it is laid upon the condition that a state may escape its operation through the adoption of a statute unrelated in subject matter to activities fairly within the scope of national policy and power. No such question is before us. . . .

Fourth: The statute does not call for a surrender by the states of powers essential to their quasi-sovereign existence. . . .

Separate [dissenting] opinion of *Mr. Justice McReynolds.*

That portion of the Social Security legislation here under consideration, I think, exceeds the power granted to Congress. It unduly interferes with the orderly government of the State by her own people and otherwise offends the Federal Constitution. . . .

The doctrine thus announced and often repeated, I had supposed was firmly established. Apparently the States remained really free to exercise governmental powers, not delegated or prohibited, without interference by the Federal Government through threats of punitive measures or offers of seductive favors. Unfortunately, the decision just announced opens the way for practical annihilation of this theory. . . .

No defense is offered for the legislation under review upon the basis of emergency. The hypothesis is that hereafter it will continuously benefit unemployed members of a class. Forever, so far as we can see, the States are expected to function under federal direction concerning an internal matter. By the sanction of this adventure, the door is open for progressive inauguration of others of like kind under which it can hardly be expected that the States will retain genuine independence of action. And without independent States a Federal Union as contemplated by the Constitution becomes impossible. . . .

Ordinarily, I must think, a denial that the challenged action of Congress and what has been done under it amount to coercion and impair freedom of government by the people of the State would be regarded as contrary to practical experience. Unquestionably our federate plan of government confronts an enlarged peril.

Separate [dissenting] opinion of *Mr. Justice Sutherland* [joined by *Mr. Justice Van Devanter*].

. . . If we are to survive as the United States, the balance between the powers of the nation and those of the states must be maintained. There is grave danger in permitting it to dip in either direction, danger—if there were no other—in the precedent thereby set for further departures from the equipoise. The threat implicit in the present encroachment upon the administrative functions of the states is that of greater encroachments, and encroachments upon other functions, will follow.

For the foregoing reasons, I think the judgment below should be reversed. . . .

Mr. Justice Butler [dissenting]. . . .

Case

SOUTH DAKOTA V. DOLE

483 U.S. 203; 107 S.Ct. 2793; 97 L.Ed. 2d 171 (1987)
Vote: 7–2

In this case the Court considers whether Congress may withhold federal highway funds from states that refuse to raise the legal drinking age to 21.

Chief Justice Rehnquist delivered the opinion of the Court.

Petitioner South Dakota permits persons 19 years of age or older to purchase beer containing up to 3.2% alcohol . . . . In 1984 Congress enacted 23 U.S.C. Sec. 158 ("Sec. 158"), which directs the Secretary of Transportation to withhold a percentage of federal highway funds otherwise allocable from States "in which the purchase or public possession of any alcoholic beverage by a person who is less than twenty-one years of age is lawful." The State sued in United States District Court seeking a declaratory judgment that Sec. 158 violates the constitutional limitations on congressional exercise of the spending power and violates the Twenty-first Amendment to the United States Constitution. The District Court rejected the State's claims, and the Court of Appeals for the Eighth Circuit affirmed. . . .

In this Court, the parties direct most of their efforts to defining the proper scope of the Twenty-first Amendment. Relying on our statement in *California Retail Liquor Dealers Assn. v. Midcal Aluminum, Inc.* . . . (1980), that the "Twenty-First Amendment grants the States virtually complete con-

trol over whether to permit importation or sale of liquor and how to structure the liquor distribution system," South Dakota asserts that the setting of minimum drinking ages is clearly within the "core powers" reserved to the States under Sec. 2 of the Amendment. . . . Section 158, petitioner claims, usurps that core power. The Secretary in response asserts that the Twenty-first Amendment is simply not implicated by Sec. 158; the plain language of Sec. 2 confirms the States' broad power to impose restrictions on the sale and distribution of alcoholic beverages but does not confer on them any power to permit sales that Congress seeks to prohibit. . . . That Amendment, under this reasoning, would not prevent Congress from affirmatively enacting a national minimum drinking age more restrictive than that provided by the various state laws; and it would follow *a fortiori* that the indirect inducement involved here is compatible with the Twenty-first Amendment.

These arguments present questions of the meaning of the Twenty-first Amendment, the bounds of which have escaped precise definition. . . . Despite the extended treatment of the question by the parties, however, we need not decide in this case whether that Amendment would prohibit an attempt by Congress to legislate directly a national minimum drinking age. Here, Congress has acted indirectly under its spending power to encourage uniformity in the States' drinking ages. As we explain below, we find this legislative effort within constitutional bounds even if Congress may not regulate drinking ages directly.

The Constitution empowers Congress to "lay and collect Taxes, Duties, Imposts, and Excises, to pay the Debts and provide for the common Defense and general Welfare of the United States." Art. I, Sec. 8, c. 1. Incident to this power, Congress may attach conditions on the receipt of federal moneys upon compliance by the recipient with federal statutory and administrative directives. . . . The breadth of this power was made clear in *United States v. Butler* . . . (1936), where the court, resolving a longstanding debate over the scope of the Spending Clause, determined that "the power of Congress to authorize expenditure of public moneys for public purposes is not limited by the direct grants of legislative power found in the Constitution." Thus, objectives not thought to be within Article I's enumerated legislative fields . . . may nevertheless be attained through the use of the spending power and the condition grant of federal funds.

The spending power is of course not unlimited, . . . but is instead subject to several general restrictions articulated in our cases. The first of these limitations is derived from the language of the Constitution itself; the exercise of the spending power must be in pursuit of "the general welfare." . . . In considering whether a particular expenditure is intended to serve general public purposes, courts should defer substantially to the judgment of Congress . . . . Second, we have required that if Congress desires to condition the States' receipt of federal funds, it "must do so unambiguously . . . , enabl[ing] the States to exercise their choice knowingly, cognizant of the consequences of their participation." . . . Third, our cases have suggested (without significant elaboration) that conditions on federal grants might be illegitimate if they are unrelated "to the federal interest in particular national projects or programs." . . .

South Dakota does not seriously claim that Sec. 158 is inconsistent with any of the first three restrictions mentioned above. We can readily conclude that the provision is designed to serve the general welfare, especially in light of the fact that "the concept of welfare or the opposite is shaped by Congress. . . ." . . . Congress found that the differing drinking ages in the States created particular incentives for young persons to combine their desire to drink with their ability to drive, and that this interstate problem required a national solution. The means it chose to address this dangerous situation were reasonably calculated to advance the general welfare. The conditions upon which States receive the funds, moreover, could not be more clearly stated by Congress. . . . And the State itself, rather than challenging the germaneness of the condition to federal purposes, admits that it "has never contended that the congressional action was . . . unrelated to a national concern in the absence of the Twenty-First Amendment." . . . Indeed, the condition imposed by Congress is directly related to one of the main purposes for which highway funds are expended—safe interstate travel. . . . This goal of the interstate highway system had been frustrated by varying drinking ages among the States. A presidential commission appointed to study alcohol-related accidents and fatalities on the Nation's highways concluded that the lack of uniformity in the states' drinking ages created "an incentive to drink" because "young persons commut[e] to border States where the drinking age is lower." . . . By enacting Sec. 158, Congress conditioned the receipt of federal funds in a way reasonably calculated to address this particular impediment to a purpose for which the funds are expended.

The remaining question about the validity of Sec. 158—and the basic point of disagreement between the parties—is whether the Twenty-first Amendment constitutes an "independent constitutional bar" to the conditional grant of federal funds. . . . Petitioner, relying on its view that the Twenty-first Amendment prohibits direct regulation of drinking ages by Congress, asserts that "Congress may not use the spending power to regulate that which it is prohibited from regulating directly under the Twenty-first Amendment." . . . But our cases show that this "independent constitutional bar" limitation on the spending power is not of the kind petitioner suggests. *United States v. Butler,* . . . for example, established that the constitutional limitations on Congress when exercising its spending power are less exacting than those on its authority to regulate directly.

We have also held that a perceived Tenth Amendment limitation on congressional regulation of state affairs did not concomitantly limit the range of conditions legitimately placed on federal grants. . . .

These cases establish that the "independent constitutional bar" limitation on the spending power is not, as petitioner suggests, a prohibition on the indirect achievement of objectives which Congress is not empowered to achieve directly. Instead, we think that the language in our earlier opinions stands for the unexceptionable proposition that the power may not be used to induce the States to engage in activities that would themselves be unconstitutional. Thus, for example, a grant of federal funds conditioned on invidiously discriminatory state action or the infliction of cruel and unusual punishment would be an illegitimate exercise of the Congress' broad spending power. But no such claim can be or is made here. Were South Dakota to succumb to the blandishments offered by Congress and raise its drinking age to 21, the State's action in so doing would not violate the constitutional rights of anyone.

Our decisions have recognized that in some circumstances the financial inducement offered by Congress might be so coercive as to pass the point at which "pressure turns into compulsion." *Steward Machine Co. v. Davis*. . . . Here, however, Congress has directed only that a State desiring to establish a minimum drinking age lower than 21 lose a relatively small percentage of certain federal highway funds. Petitioner contends that the coercive nature of this program is evident from the degree of success it has achieved. We cannot conclude, however, that a conditional grant of federal money of this sort is unconstitutional simply by reason of its success in achieving the congressional objective.

When we consider, for a moment, that all South Dakota would lose if she adheres to her chosen course as to a suitable minimum drinking age is 5% of the funds otherwise obtainable under specified highway grant programs, the argument as to coercion is shown to be more rhetoric than fact. . . .

Here Congress has offered relatively mild encouragement to the States to enact higher minimum drinking ages than they would otherwise choose. But the enactment of such laws remains the prerogative of the States not merely in theory but in fact. Even if Congress might lack the power to impose a national minimum drinking age directly, we conclude that encouragement to state action found in Sec. 158 is a valid use of the spending power. Accordingly, the judgment of the Court of Appeals is affirmed.

Justice Brennan, dissenting. . . .

Justice O'Connor, dissenting.

The Court today upholds the National Minimum Drinking Age Amendment . . . as a valid exercise of the Spending Power conferred by Article I, Sec. 8. But Sec. 158 is not a condition on spending reasonably related to the expenditure of federal funds and cannot be justified on that ground. Rather, it is an attempt to regulate the sale of liquor, an attempt that lies outside Congress' power to regulate commerce because it falls within the ambit of Sec. 2 of the Twenty-First Amendment.

My disagreement with the Court is relatively narrow on the Spending Power issue; it is a disagreement about the application of a principle rather than a disagreement on the principle itself. I agree with the Court that Congress may attach conditions on the receipt of federal funds to further "the federal interest in particular national projects or programs." . . . I also subscribe to the established proposition that the reach of the Spending Power "is not limited by the direct grants of legislative power found in the Constitution." . . . Finally, I agree that there are four separate types of limitations on the Spending Power: the expenditure must be for the general welfare, . . . the conditions imposed must be unambiguous, . . . they must be reasonably related to the purpose of the expenditure, . . . and the legislation may not violate any independent constitutional prohibition. . . . Insofar as two of these limitations are concerned, the Court is clearly correct that Sec. 158 is wholly unobjectionable. Establishment of a national minimum drinking age certainly fits within the broad concept of the general welfare and the statute is entirely unambiguous. I am also willing to assume *arguendo* that the Twenty-first Amendment does not constitute an "independent constitutional bar" to a spending condition. . . .

But the Court's application of the requirement that the condition imposed be reasonably related to the purpose for which the funds are expended, is cursory and unconvincing. We have repeatedly said that Congress may condition grants under the Spending Power only in ways reasonably related to the purpose of the federal program. . . . In my view, establishment of a minimum drinking age of 21 is not sufficiently related to interstate highway construction to justify so conditioning funds appropriated for that purpose. . . .

When Congress appropriates money to build a highway, it is entitled to insist that the highway be a safe one. But it is not entitled to insist as a condition of the use of highway funds that the State impose or change regulations in other areas of the State's social and economic life because of an attenuated or tangential relationship to highway use or safety. Indeed, if the rule were otherwise, the Congress could effectively regulate almost any area of a State's social, political, or economic life on the theory that use of the interstate transportation system is somehow enhanced. If, for example, the United States were to condition highway moneys upon moving the state capital, I suppose it might argue that interstate transportation is facilitated by locating local governments in places easily accessible to interstate highways—or, conversely, that highways might become overburdened if they had to carry traffic to and from the state capital. In my mind, such a relationship is hardly more attenuated than the one which the Court finds to support Sec. 158. . . .

The appropriate inquiry, then, is whether the spending requirement or prohibition is a condition on a grant or whether it is regulation. The difference turns on whether the requirement specifies in some way how the money should be spent, so that Congress' intent in making the grant will be effectuated. Congress has no power under the Spending Clause to impose requirements on a grant that go beyond specifying how the money should be spent. A requirement that is not such a specification is not a condition, but a regulation, which is valid only if it falls within one of Congress' delegated regulatory powers. . . .

This approach harks back to *United States v. Butler*, . . . the last case in which this Court struck down an Act of

Congress as beyond the authority granted by the Spending Clause. The Butler Court saw the Agricultural Adjustment Act for what it was—an exercise of regulatory, not spending, power. The error in *Butler* was not the Court's conclusion that the Act was essentially regulatory, but rather its crabbed view of the extent of Congress' regulatory power under the Commerce Clause. The Agricultural Adjustment Act was regulatory but it was regulation that today would likely be considered within Congress' Commerce Power. . . .

While *Butler*'s authority is questionable insofar as it assumes that Congress has no regulatory power over farm production, its discussion of the Spending Power and its description of both the power's breadth and its limitations remains sound. The Court's decision in *Butler* also properly recognizes the gravity of the task of appropriately limiting the Spending Power. If the Spending Power is to be limited only by Congress' notion of the general welfare, the reality, given the vast financial resources of the Federal Government, is that the Spending Clause gives "power to the Congress to tear down the barriers, to invade the state's jurisdiction, and to become a parliament of the whole people, subject to no restrictions save such as are self-imposed." . . . This, of course, as *Butler* held, was not the Framers' plan and it is not the meaning of the Spending Clause. . . .

The immense size and power of the Government of the United States ought not obscure its fundamental character. It remains a Government of enumerated powers. . . . Because [Sec. 158] cannot be justified as an exercise of any power delegated to the Congress, it is not authorized by the Constitution. The Court errs in holding it to be the law of the land, and I respectfully dissent.

Case

South Carolina v. Katzenbach

383 U.S. 301; 86 S.Ct. 803; 15 L.Ed. 2d 769 (1966)
Vote: 8–1

The Voting Rights Act of 1965 brought the power of the federal government to bear on traditional practices designed to keep minorities from participating in the electoral process. The act utilized a triggering formula to target those areas in which voting discrimination was most egregious. In such areas, the act abolished literacy tests, waived poll taxes that had accumulated, and forbade the state from implementing new voting requirements until they were found by the federal courts or the U.S. attorney general to be nondiscriminatory. Additionally, the act called for federal examiners to supervise the conduct of elections. Finally, the statute authorized civil and criminal penalties for those who interfere with the rights guaranteed by the act. In this case, the state of South Carolina challenged the constitutionality of various provisions of the Voting Rights Act.

Mr. Chief Justice Warren delivered the opinion of the Court.

. . . The Voting Rights Act of 1965 reflects Congress' firm intention to rid the country of racial discrimination in voting. The heart of the Act is a complex scheme of stringent remedies aimed at areas where voting discrimination has been most flagrant. . . .

These provisions of the Voting Rights Act of 1965 are challenged on the fundamental ground that they exceed the powers of Congress and encroach on an area reserved to the States by the Constitution. . . . Has Congress exercised its powers in an appropriate manner with relation to the states?

The ground rules for resolving this question are clear. The language and purpose of the Fifteenth Amendment, the prior decisions construing its several provisions, and the general doctrines of constitutional interpretation, all point to one fundamental principle. As against the reserved powers of the States, Congress may use any rational means to effectuate the constitutional prohibition of racial discrimination in voting. . . .

Section 1 of the Fifteenth Amendment declares that "[t]he right of citizens of the United States to vote shall not be denied or abridged on account of race, color or previous condition of servitude." This declaration has always been treated as self-executing and has repeatedly been construed, without further legislative specification, to invalidate state voting qualifications or procedures which are discriminatory on their face or in practice. . . . [Here the Court cites numerous cases to illustrate its point.] The gist of the matter is that the Fifteenth Amendment supersedes contrary exertions of state power. "When a State exercises power wholly within the domain of state interest, it is insulated from federal judicial review. But such insulation is not carried over when state power is used as an instrument for circumventing a federally protected right." . . .

South Carolina contends that the cases cited above [omitted] are precedents only for the authority of the judiciary to strike down state statutes and procedures—that to allow an exercise of this authority by Congress would be to rob the courts of their rightful constitutional role. On the contrary, Section 2 of the Fifteenth Amendment expressly declares that "Congress shall have the power to enforce this article by appropriate legislation." By adding this authorization, the Framers indicated that Congress was to be chiefly responsible for implementing the rights created in Section 1. . . .

Congress has repeatedly exercised these powers in the past, and its enactments have repeatedly been upheld. . . . On the rare occasions where the Court has found an unconstitutional exercise of these powers, in its opinion Congress had attacked evils not comprehended by the Fifteenth Amendment. . . .

The basic test to be applied in a case involving Section 2 of the Fifteenth Amendment is the same in all cases concerning the express powers of Congress with relation to the reserved powers of the States. Chief Justice Marshall laid down the classic formulation, 50 years before the Fifteenth Amendment was ratified.

> Let the end be legitimate, let it be within the scope of the constitutional, and all means which are appropriate, which are plainly adapted to that end, which are not prohibited, but consist with the letter and spirit of the Constitution, are constitutional. . . .

We therefore reject South Carolina's argument that Congress may appropriately do no more than to forbid violations of the Fifteenth Amendment in general terms . . . . Congress exercised its authority . . . in an inventive manner when it adopted the Voting Rights Act of 1965. First: the measure prescribes remedies for voting discrimination which go into effect without any need for prior adjudication. This was clearly a legitimate response to the problem, for which there is ample precedent under other constitutional provisions. . . . Congress had found that case-by-case litigation was inadequate to combat widespread and persistent discrimination in voting, because of the inordinate amount of time and energy required to overcome the obstructionist tactics invariably encountered in these lawsuits. After enduring nearly a century of systematic resistance to the Fifteenth Amendment, Congress might well shift the advantage of time and inertia from the perpetrators of the evil to its victims. . . .

Second: The Act intentionally confines these remedies to a small number of states and political subdivisions which in most instances were familiar to Congress by name. This, too, was a permissible method of dealing with the problem. Congress had learned that substantial voting discrimination presently occurs in certain sections of the country, and it knew no way of accurately forecasting whether the evil might spread elsewhere in the future. In acceptable legislative fashion, Congress chose to limit its attention to the geographic areas where immediate action seemed necessary. . . . The doctrine of the equality of States, invoked by South Carolina, does not bar this approach, for that doctrine applies only to the terms upon which States are admitted to the Union, and not to the remedies for local evils which have subsequently appeared. . . .

We now consider the related question of whether the specific States and political subdivisions . . . were an appropriate target for the new remedies. . . .

To be specific, the new remedies of the Act are imposed on three States—Alabama, Louisiana, and Mississippi—in which federal courts have repeatedly found substantial voting discrimination. Section 4(b) of the Act also embraces two other States—Georgia and South Carolina—plus large portions of a third State—North Carolina—for which there was more fragmentary evidence of recent voting discrimination mainly adduced by the Justice Department and the Civil Rights Commission. All these areas were appropriately subjected to the new remedies. . . .

The areas listed above, for which there was evidence of actual voting discrimination, share two characteristics incorporated by Congress into the coverage formula: the use of tests and devices for voter registration, and a voting rate in the 1964 presidential election at least 12 points below the national average. Tests and devices are relevant to voting discrimination because of their long history as a tool for perpetrating the evil; a low voting rate is pertinent for the obvious reason that widespread disenfranchisement must inevitably affect the number of actual voters. Accordingly, the coverage formula is rational in both practice and theory. It was therefore permissible to impose the new remedies on the few remaining States and their political subdivisions covered by the formula. . . .

We now arrive at consideration of the specific remedies prescribed by the Act for areas included within the coverage formula. South Carolina assails the temporary suspension of existing voting qualifications. . . . The record shows that in most of the States covered by the Act, including South Carolina, various tests and devices have been instituted with the purpose of disenfranchising Negroes, have been framed in such a way to facilitate this aim, and have been administered in a discriminatory fashion for many years. Under these circumstances, the Fifteenth Amendment has clearly been violated. . . .

The Act suspends literacy tests and similar devices for a period of five years from the last occurrence of substantial voting discrimination. This was a legitimate response to the problem, for which there is ample precedent in Fifteenth Amendment cases. . . . Underlying the response was the feeling that States and political subdivisions which had been allowing white illiterates to vote for years could not sincerely complain about "dilution" of their electorates through the registration of Negro illiterates. Congress knew that continuance of the tests and devices in use at the present time, no matter how fairly administered in the future, would freeze the effect of past discrimination in favor of unqualified white registrants. Congress permissibly rejected the alternative of requiring a complete re-registration of all voters, believing that this would be too harsh on whites who had enjoyed the franchise for their entire adult lives. . . .

The Act suspends voting regulations pending scrutiny by federal authorities to determine whether their use would violate the Fifteenth Amendment. This may have been an uncommon exercise of Congressional power, as South Carolina contends, but the Court has recognized that exceptional conditions can justify legislative measures not otherwise appropriate. . . . Under the compulsion of these unique circumstances, Congress responded in a permissibly decisive manner. . . .

The Act authorizes the appointment of federal examiners to list qualified applicants who are thereafter entitled to vote, subject to an expeditious challenge procedure. This was clearly an appropriate response to the problem, closely related to remedies authorized in prior cases. . . . In

many of the political subdivisions covered by . . . the Act, voting officials have persistently employed a variety of procedural tactics to deny Negroes the franchise, often in direct defiance or evasion of federal court decrees. Congress realized that merely to suspend voting rules which have been misused or are subject to misuse might leave this localized evil undisturbed. . . .

After enduring nearly a century of widespread resistance to the Fifteenth Amendment, Congress has marshaled an array of potent weapons against the evil, with authority by the Attorney General to employ them effectively. Many of the areas affected by this development have indicated their willingness to abide by any restraints legitimately imposed upon them. We here hold that the portions of the Voting Rights Act properly before us are a valid means for carrying out the commands of the Fifteenth Amendment. Hopefully, millions of non-white Americans will now be able to participate for the first time on an equal basis in the government under which they live. . . .

The bill of complaint is dismissed.

Justice Black, concurring [in part] and dissenting [in part]. . . .

Case

CITY OF BOERNE V. FLORES

521 U.S. 507; 117 S.Ct. 2157; 138 L.Ed. 2d 624 (1997)
Vote: 6–3

In this case a decision by local authorities to deny a church a building permit was challenged under the Religious Freedom Restoration Act of 1993 (RFRA). The Court concludes Congress exceeded its authority in enacting the RFRA. The case raises the question of Congress's role in interpreting the Bill of Rights.

Justice Kennedy delivered the opinion of the Court.

. . . Congress enacted RFRA in direct response to the Court's decision in *Employment Div., Dept. of Human Resources of Ore. v. Smith* (1990). There we considered a Free Exercise Clause claim brought by members of the Native American Church who were denied unemployment benefits when they lost their jobs because they had used peyote. Their practice was to ingest peyote for sacramental purposes, and they challenged an Oregon statute of general applicability which made use of the drug criminal. In evaluating the claim, we declined to apply the balancing test set forth in *Sherbert v. Verner* (1963), under which we

would have asked whether Oregon's prohibition substantially burdened a religious practice and, if it did, whether the burden was justified by a compelling government interest. . . .

The application of the *Sherbert* test, the *Smith* decision explained, would have produced an anomaly in the law, a constitutional right to ignore neutral laws of general applicability. The anomaly would have been accentuated, the Court reasoned, by the difficulty of determining whether a particular practice was central to an individual's religion. We explained, moreover, that it "is not within the judicial ken to question the centrality of particular beliefs or practices to a faith, or the validity of particular litigants' interpretations of those creeds. . . ."

These points of constitutional interpretation were debated by Members of Congress in hearings and floor debates. Many criticized the Court's reasoning, and this disagreement resulted in the passage of RFRA. . . .

RFRA prohibits "[g]overnment" from "substantially burden[ing]" a person's exercise of religion even if the burden results from a rule of general applicability unless the government can demonstrate the burden "(1) is in furtherance of a compelling governmental interest; and (2) is the least restrictive means of furthering that compelling governmental interest." . . .

Congress relied on its Fourteenth Amendment enforcement power in enacting the most far reaching and substantial of RFRA's provisions, those which impose its requirements on the States. . . .

The parties disagree over whether RFRA is a proper exercise of Congress' § 5 power "to enforce" by "appropriate legislation" the constitutional guarantee that no State shall deprive any person of "life, liberty, or property, without due process of law" nor deny any person "equal protection of the laws."

In defense of the Act respondent contends, with support from the United States as *amicus,* that RFRA is permissible enforcement legislation. Congress, it is said, is only protecting by legislation one of the liberties guaranteed by the Fourteenth Amendment's Due Process Clause, the free exercise of religion, beyond what is necessary under *Smith.* It is said the congressional decision to dispense with proof of deliberate or overt discrimination and instead concentrate on a law's effects accords with the settled understanding that § 5 includes the power to enact legislation designed to prevent as well as remedy constitutional violations. It is further contended that Congress' § 5 power is not limited to remedial or preventive legislation. . . .

Legislation which deters or remedies constitutional violations can fall within the sweep of Congress' enforcement power even if in the process it prohibits conduct which is not itself unconstitutional and intrudes into "legislative spheres of autonomy previously reserved to the States." . . . For example, the Court upheld a suspension of literacy tests and similar voting requirements under Congress' parallel power to enforce the provisions of the Fifteenth Amendment . . . as a measure to combat racial discrimination in voting, . . . despite the facial constitutionality of the tests. . . . We have also concluded that other measures protecting voting rights are within Congress' power to enforce the Fourteenth and Fifteenth Amendments, despite the burdens those measures placed on the States. . . .

It is also true, however, that "[a]s broad as the congressional enforcement power is, it is not unlimited." . . . In assessing the breadth of § 5's enforcement power, we begin with its text. Congress has been given the power "to enforce" the "provisions of this article." We agree with respondent, of course, that Congress can enact legislation under § 5 enforcing the constitutional right to the free exercise of religion. . . .

Congress' power under § 5, however, extends only to "enforc[ing]" the provisions of the Fourteenth Amendment. The Court has described this power as "remedial." The design of the Amendment and the text of § 5 are inconsistent with the suggestion that Congress has the power to decree the substance of the Fourteenth Amendment's restrictions on the States. Legislation which alters the meaning of the Free Exercise Clause cannot be said to be enforcing the Clause. Congress does not enforce a constitutional right by changing what the right is. It has been given the power "to enforce," not the power to determine what constitutes a constitutional violation. Were it not so, what Congress would be enforcing would no longer be, in any meaningful sense, the "provisions of [the Fourteenth Amendment]."

While the line between measures that remedy or prevent unconstitutional actions and measures that make a substantive change in the governing law is not easy to discern, and Congress must have wide latitude in determining where it lies, the distinction exists and must be observed. There must be a congruence and proportionality between the injury to be prevented or remedied and the means adopted to that end. Lacking such a connection, legislation may become substantive in operation and effect. History and our case law support drawing the distinction, one apparent from the text of the Amendment.

The Fourteenth Amendment's history confirms the remedial, rather than substantive, nature of the Enforcement Clause. . . .

The remedial and preventive nature of Congress' enforcement power, and the limitation inherent in the power, were confirmed in our earliest cases on the Fourteenth Amendment. . . .

. . . Although the specific holdings of these early cases might have been superseded or modified, . . . their treatment of Congress' § 5 power as corrective or preventive, not definitional, has not been questioned. . . .

Any suggestion that Congress has a substantive, non-remedial power under the Fourteenth Amendment is not supported by our case law. . . .

If Congress could define its own powers by altering the Fourteenth Amendment's meaning, no longer would the Constitution be "superior paramount law, unchangeable by ordinary means." It would be "on a level with ordinary legislative acts, and, like other acts, . . . alterable when the legislature shall please to alter it." . . . Under this approach, it is difficult to conceive of a principle that would limit congressional power. . . . Shifting legislative majorities could change the Constitution and effectively circumvent the difficult and detailed amendment process contained in Article V.

We now turn to consider whether RFRA can be considered enforcement legislation under § 5 of the Fourteenth Amendment.

Respondent contends that RFRA is a proper exercise of Congress' remedial or preventive power. The Act, it is said, is a reasonable means of protecting the free exercise of religion as defined by *Smith*. It prevents and remedies laws which are enacted with the unconstitutional object of targeting religious beliefs and practices. . . . To avoid the difficulty of proving such violations, it is said, Congress can simply invalidate any law which imposes a substantial burden on a religious practice unless it is justified by a compelling interest and is the least restrictive means of accomplishing that interest. If Congress can prohibit laws with discriminatory effects in order to prevent racial discrimination in violation of the Equal Protection Clause, . . . then it can do the same, respondent argues, to promote religious liberty.

While preventive rules are sometimes appropriate remedial measures, there must be a congruence between the means used and the ends to be achieved. The appropriateness of remedial measures must be considered in light of the evil presented. . . . Strong measures appropriate to address one harm may be an unwarranted response to another, lesser one. A comparison between RFRA and the Voting Rights Act is instructive. In contrast to the record which confronted Congress and the judiciary in the voting rights cases, RFRA's legislative record lacks examples of modern instances of generally applicable laws passed because of religious bigotry. The history of persecution in this country detailed in the hearings mentions no episodes occurring in the past 40 years. . . .

. . . The absence of more recent episodes stems from the fact that, as one witness testified, "deliberate persecution is not the usual problem in this country." . . . Rather, the emphasis of the hearings was on laws of general applicability which place incidental burdens on religion. . . .

Regardless of the state of the legislative record, RFRA cannot be considered remedial, preventive legislation, if those terms are to have any meaning. RFRA is so out of proportion to a supposed remedial or preventive object that it cannot be understood as responsive to, or designed to prevent, unconstitutional behavior. It appears, instead, to attempt a substantive change in constitutional protections. Preventive measures prohibiting certain types of laws may be appropriate when there is reason to believe that many of the laws affected by the congressional enactment have a significant likelihood of being unconstitutional. . . . Remedial legislation under § 5 "should be adapted to the mischief and wrong which the [Fourteenth] [A]mendment was intended to provide against." . . .

RFRA is not so confined. Sweeping coverage ensures its intrusion at every level of government, displacing laws and prohibiting official actions of almost every description and regardless of subject matter. RFRA's restrictions apply to every agency and official of the Federal, State, and local Governments. RFRA applies to all federal and state law, statutory or otherwise, whether adopted before or after its enactment. RFRA has no termination date or termination mechanism. Any law is subject to challenge at any time by any individual who alleges a substantial burden on his or her free exercise of religion.

The reach and scope of RFRA distinguish it from other measures passed under Congress' enforcement power, even in the area of voting rights. . . .

The stringent test RFRA demands of state laws reflects a lack of proportionality or congruence between the means adopted and the legitimate end to be achieved. If an objector can show a substantial burden on his free exercise, the State must demonstrate a compelling governmental interest and show that the law is the least restrictive means of furthering its interest. Claims that a law substantially burdens someone's exercise of religion will often be difficult to contest. . . . Requiring a State to demonstrate a compelling interest and show that it has adopted the least restrictive means of achieving that interest is the most demanding test known to constitutional law. If " 'compelling interest' really means what it says . . . many laws will not meet the test. . . . [The test] would open the prospect of constitutionally required religious exemptions from civic obligations of almost every conceivable kind." Laws valid under *Smith* would fall under RFRA without regard to whether they had the object of stifling or punishing free exercise. We make these observations not to reargue the position of the majority in *Smith* but to illustrate the substantive alteration of its holding attempted by RFRA. Even assuming RFRA would be interpreted in effect to mandate some lesser test, say one equivalent to intermediate scrutiny, the statute nevertheless would require searching judicial scrutiny of state law with the attendant likelihood of invalidation. This is a considerable congressional intrusion into the States' traditional prerogatives and general authority to regulate for the health and welfare of their citizens. . . .

When Congress acts within its sphere of power and responsibilities, it has not just the right but the duty to make its own informed judgment on the meaning and force of the Constitution. This has been clear from the early days of the Republic. In 1789, when a Member of the House of Representatives objected to a debate on the constitutionality of legislation based on the theory that "it would be officious" to consider the constitutionality of a measure that did not affect the House, James Madison explained that "it is incontrovertibly of as much importance to this branch of the Government as to any other, that the constitution should be preserved entire. It is our duty." Were it otherwise, we would not afford Congress the presumption of validity its enactments now enjoy.

Our national experience teaches that the Constitution is preserved best when each part of the government respects both the Constitution and the proper actions and determinations of the other branches. When the Court has interpreted the Constitution, it has acted within the province of the Judicial Branch, which embraces the duty to say what the law is. . . .

When the political branches of the Government act against the background of a judicial interpretation of the Constitution already issued, it must be understood that in later cases and controversies the Court will treat its precedents with the respect due them under settled principles, including *stare decisis*, and contrary expectations must be disappointed. RFRA was designed to control cases and controversies, such as the one before us; but as the provisions of the federal statute here invoked are beyond congressional authority, it is this Court's precedent, not RFRA, which must control.

It is for Congress in the first instance to "determin[e] whether and what legislation is needed to secure the guarantees of the Fourteenth Amendment," and its conclusions are entitled to much deference. . . . Congress' discretion is not unlimited, however, and the courts retain the power, as they have since *Marbury v. Madison*, to determine if Congress has exceeded its authority under the Constitution. Broad as the power of Congress is under the Enforcement Clause of the Fourteenth Amendment, RFRA contradicts vital principles necessary to maintain separation of powers and the federal balance. The judgment of the Court of Appeals sustaining the Act's constitutionality is reversed. . . .

Justice Stevens, concurring. . . .

Justice Scalia, with whom *Justice Stevens* joins, concurring in part.

Justice O'Connor, with whom *Justice Breyer* joins . . . dissenting.

I dissent from the Court's disposition of this case. I agree with the Court that the issue before us is whether the Religious Freedom Restoration Act (RFRA) is a proper exercise of Congress' power to enforce § 5 of the Fourteenth Amendment. But as a yardstick for measuring the constitutionality of RFRA, the Court uses its holding in *Employment Div., Dept. of Human Resources of Ore. v. Smith* (1990), the decision that prompted Congress to enact RFRA as a means of more rigorously enforcing the Free Exercise

Clause. I remain of the view that *Smith* was wrongly decided, and I would use this case to reexamine the Court's holding there. . . .

The Court's analysis of whether RFRA is a constitutional exercise of Congress' § 5 power, . . . is premised on the assumption that *Smith* correctly interprets the Free Exercise Clause. This is an assumption that I do not accept. I continue to believe that *Smith* adopted an improper standard for deciding free exercise claims. . . .

Stare decisis concerns should not prevent us from revisiting our holding in *Smith*. . . . I believe that, in light of both our precedent and our Nation's tradition of religious liberty, *Smith* is demonstrably wrong. Moreover, it is a recent decision. As such, it has not engendered the kind of reliance on its continued application that would militate against overruling it. . . .

Accordingly, I believe that we should reexamine our holding in *Smith,* and do so in this very case. In its place, I would return to a rule that requires government to justify any substantial burden on religiously motivated conduct by a compelling state interest and to impose that burden only by means narrowly tailored to achieve that interest. . . .

Justice Souter, dissenting.

To decide whether the Fourteenth Amendment gives Congress sufficient power to enact the Religious Freedom Restoration Act, the Court measures the legislation against the free exercise standard of *Employment Div., Dept. of Human Resources of Ore. v. Smith* (1990). . . . I have serious doubts about the precedential value of the *Smith* rule and its entitlement to adherence. . . . But without briefing and argument on the merits of that rule. . . . I am not now prepared to join Justice O'Connor in rejecting it or the majority in assuming it to be correct. In order to provide full adversarial consideration, this case should be set down for reargument permitting plenary reexamination of the issue. Since the Court declines to follow that course, our free exercise law remains marked by an "intolerable tension," . . . and the constitutionality of the Act of Congress to enforce the free exercise right cannot now be soundly decided. I would therefore dismiss the writ of certiorari as improvidently granted, and I accordingly dissent from the Court's disposition of this case.

Justice Breyer, dissenting. . . .

3

CONSTITUTIONAL UNDERPINNINGS OF THE PRESIDENCY

"There is an idea, which is not without its advocates, that a vigorous executive is inconsistent with the genius of republican government. . . . Energy in the executive is the leading character in the definition of good government. It is essential to the protection of the community against foreign attacks; it is not less essential to the steady administration of the laws, to the protection of property . . . ; [and] to the security of liberty against the enterprises and assaults of ambition, of faction and anarchy."

—ALEXANDER HAMILTON, *THE FEDERALIST*, No. 70

Alexander Hamilton: Apostle of presidential power

INTRODUCTION

The Constitution devotes considerably more attention to Congress than to the other branches of government. Most of the Framers expected Congress to be the dominant element of the new national government because, as James Madison recognized in *The Federalist,* No. 51, "in republican government, the legislative authority necessarily predominates." Perhaps Madison's observation was true of a small republic in the late eighteenth century. It does not, however, apply to the experience of the United States after more than two centuries of constitutional development. Without question, the dominant tendency of American constitutional history has been to concentrate power in the executive branch.

The expansion of presidential power has occurred despite a Constitution that provides little to the president by way of specific, enumerated powers. Throughout history, presidents have taken advantage of opportunities to enhance the power of the executive branch, opportunities afforded by crises such as the Civil War, two world wars, the Great Depression, and, more recently, the Cold War. The tendency of presidents to seize power to cope with the exigencies of their times is what led noted constitutional scholar Edward S. Corwin to remark that "the history of the Presidency has been a history of aggrandizement."

In the 1970s, in the wake of the Vietnam and Watergate debacles, some observers perceived a significant decline in presidential power and prestige. If a decline occurred, it was short-lived. In the 1980s, the Reagan and Bush administrations regained for the presidency a position comparable to the preeminence that it held prior to the late 1960s. The allegations of misconduct that plagued Bill Clinton's two terms had no lasting negative effect on the presidency. George W. Bush was able to assert effective leadership immediately upon assuming the office of president, in spite of the prolonged and intense battle resulting in his controversial victory in the 2000 election. The devastating terrorist attacks on the World Trade Center and the Pentagon on September 11, 2001, instantly enhanced the power and prestige of the presidency, as evidenced by the overwhelming bipartisan congressional and popular support extended to President Bush. While still depending to some extent on the performance and character of the occupant of the office, the power and prestige of the presidency are largely institutionalized.

STRUCTURAL ASPECTS OF THE PRESIDENCY

Some delegates to the Constitutional Convention of 1787 favored a multiple executive, in which power would be exercised simultaneously by three or more individuals. Others insisted on limiting the president to a single term of seven years or to two three-year terms. Still others maintained that the president, in concert with the Supreme Court, should function as a "council of revision," which would in effect pass on the constitutionality of acts of Congress. The Framers, who had recently participated in a successful revolution against the British crown, were understandably wary of creating an executive institution that could "degenerate" into a monarchy. Widespread recognition that George Washington would assume a central role of leadership greatly reduced these fears. In fact, Washington's daily presence as the presiding officer at the Constitutional Convention probably contributed to the decision to create a single executive.

Presidential Terms

Ultimately, the Framers not only vested power in a single executive, elected for a term of four years, but also refused to limit the number of terms the president might serve. Washington, as the first president, displayed both the leadership and self-restraint that the American people expected. He established an important precedent by refusing to seek a third term, a tradition that survived until Franklin D. Roosevelt was elected to a third term in 1940, followed by a fourth term in 1944. Roosevelt died in office in 1945, and the Republican Party gained control of both houses of Congress after the 1946 elections. Reacting to Roosevelt's break with tradition, Congress then proposed the **Twenty-second Amendment**, ratified in 1951, prohibiting future presidents from being elected to more than two terms. In the aftermath of Ronald Reagan's popular first term and landslide reelection in 1984, some political activists began to urge repeal of the Twenty-second Amendment. The Iran-Contra affair and other problems effectively diverted attention from this issue during Reagan's second term.

The Electoral College

Contemporary Americans look to the quadrennial presidential elections as symbols of a deep national commitment to democracy. Yet the Framers of the Constitution, far less sanguine about democracy, provided for an indirect method of presidential selection. Under this arrangement, each state was authorized to appoint as many electors as it had senators and representatives in Congress (Article II, Section 1). This **Electoral College**, as it came to be called, was empowered to choose the president, and the person receiving the second highest number of votes would serve as vice president. The Framers assumed that the electors would act independently of the people in making their selections. But with the advent of the two-party system in the late 1790s the electors soon lost this independent role.

The controlling influence of party identity was underscored dramatically in the presidential election of 1800. A large majority of the electors supported the Jeffersonian Republican Party and dutifully cast their votes for Thomas Jefferson and his running mate, Aaron Burr. The resulting tie vote in the Electoral College threw the election into the House of Representatives, which after a contentious political battle ultimately elected Thomas Jefferson. In the aftermath of this awkward incident, the Twelfth Amendment was adopted in 1804, placing the offices of president and vice president on separate ballots. The effect of this change was that each party developed its own presidential and vice-presidential "tickets," to which designated slates of electors were pledged. With rare exception, the presidential candidate receiving a plurality of the popular vote in a given state automatically received that state's entire electoral vote. Thus, the Electoral College as a deliberative body became a vestigial organ of American government within less than twenty years after its creation.

Although the Electoral College has lost its significance as a decision making body, it retains tremendous importance in that it represents a highly controversial method of electing the president. To win the presidency, a candidate must receive a majority of electoral votes. These votes are allocated among the states based on the size of states' congressional delegations. Thus, each state has two electoral votes for its two U.S. senators plus a number of electoral votes corresponding to the number of its U.S. representatives. The total number of electoral votes is 538, which equals the total number of U.S. senators (100), the total number of members of the House of Representatives (435), plus three electoral votes assigned to the District of Columbia. Because the candidate who wins a plurality of the popular vote in a given state wins all of that state's electoral votes (except in Maine and Nebraska, which allocate electoral votes by the outcome of popular vote within congressional districts), it is possible for a candidate who receives fewer votes in the aggregated national popular vote to win the presidency. Students of American history know that this in fact occurred in 1876 and 1888, when the winning candidates, Rutherford B. Hayes and Benjamin Harrison, received fewer popular votes than their principal rivals, Samuel Tilden and Grover Cleveland. One does not have to be an historian to know that this same anomaly occurred in the presidential election of 2000, when Republican George W. Bush edged Democrat Al Gore in the electoral vote despite Gore's "victory" in the national popular vote.

Long a subject of academic debate, the Electoral College system became a national issue in the wake of the disputed presidential election of 2000. Critics claim that the system is undemocratic, a vestige of eighteenth century elitism. But the Electoral College is not without defenders. Some argue that it is consistent with the federal system and helps to ensure that small states will not be ignored by candidates seeking only to amass individual votes. Abolition of the Electoral College would obviously require a constitutional amendment, which is, of course, difficult to accomplish even when public support is strong. Given that the Electoral College is currently a partisan issue, with Republicans defending the institution and Democrats calling for its abolition, it is unlikely that a proposed amendment could muster the necessary two-thirds majority in either house of Congress. If it did, it would be even more unlikely that three-fourths of the states would support ratification. It appears that the Electoral College is destined to remain a controversial feature of the American electoral system for the foreseeable future.

Presidential Succession and Disability

The constitutional problem of presidential succession has troubled generations of Americans. The problem first arose in 1841, when President William Henry Harrison died after only a month in office. The immediate question was whether Vice President John Tyler would assume the full duties and powers of the office for the remaining forty-seven months of Harrison's term or serve merely as an acting president. Unwilling to settle for less than the full measure of presidential authority, Tyler set an important precedent by successfully assuming full presidential powers. The eight other individuals who have succeeded to the office because of the death or resignation of an incumbent president have followed this practice.

The related problem of presidential disability has proved more perplexing. Several presidents have been temporarily disabled during their terms of office, with resulting uncertainty and confusion as to the locus of actual decision making authority. For example, President Woodrow Wilson was seriously disabled by a stroke in 1919 and for a number of weeks was totally incapable of performing his official duties. No constitutional provision existed at that time for the temporary replacement of a disabled president. The result was that Wilson's wife, Edith, took on much of the responsibility of the office, an arrangement that evoked sharp criticism.

The problem of presidential disability is addressed by the **Twenty-fifth Amendment,** ratified in 1967. This amendment, proposed in the aftermath of the assassination of President John F. Kennedy, establishes, among other things, a procedure under which the vice president may assume the role of acting president during periods of presidential disability. The amendment provides alternative means for determining presidential disability. Section 3 allows the president to transmit to Congress a written declaration that he is unable to discharge the duties of the office, upon which the vice president assumes the role of acting president. The vice president continues in this role unless and until the president is able to transmit a declaration to the contrary. If, however, the president is unable or unwilling to acknowledge the inability to perform the duties of the office, the vice president and a majority of the Cabinet members are authorized to make this determination.

Removal of the Chief Executive

The ultimate constitutional sanction against the abuse of presidential power is **impeachment** and removal from office. The Constitution, in Article II, Section 4, states:

> The President, Vice-President and all civil Officers of the United States shall be removed from Office on Impeachment for, and Conviction of, *Treason, Bribery or other high Crimes and Misdemeanors* [emphasis added].

Only twice in our history have presidents been impeached, although neither was removed from office. President Andrew Johnson was impeached by the House of Representatives in 1868 but narrowly escaped conviction by the Senate. Bill Clinton was impeached late in 1998 but was acquitted by the Senate by a fairly comfortable margin.

Andrew Johnson was impeached for overtly political reasons, stemming from his clash with Congress over Reconstruction policy. His ultimate acquittal may have been influenced by the fact that he had not committed indictable offenses, although many in Congress were willing to interpret the "high crimes and misdemeanors" language in the Constitution quite broadly!

Although there were certainly political motivations behind the impeachment of Bill Clinton, there were serious accusations of misconduct on the president's part. On December 11, 1998, the House Judiciary Committee (voting 21–16) approved four articles of impeachment. These articles alleged that President Clinton:

  I. Gave "perjurious, false and misleading testimony" before a federal grand jury

 II. Obstructed justice by delaying, impeding, covering up, and concealing the existence of evidence in the Paula Jones sexual harassment case

III. Provided "perjurious, false and misleading testimony" in the Paula Jones case

IV. Misused and abused his office by making perjurious statements to Congress in his answers to questions posed by the Judiciary Committee

On December 19, the full House, voting basically along party lines, adopted two of these articles. The article accusing the president of "perjurious, false and misleading testimony" before the federal grand jury was adopted by a vote of 228 to 206. The article alleging obstructing justice in the Paula Jones case was adopted by a vote of 221 to 212.

On February 12, 1999, the Senate voted to acquit President Clinton on both articles of impeachment. The article alleging "perjurious testimony" garnered fifty-five votes, well short of the two-thirds majority necessary for removal. Did the Senate conclude that there was insufficient evidence that the president committed the offenses alleged in the articles of impeachment? Or did senators conclude that the offenses were simply not grave enough to warrant the president's removal from office? Senators who voted to acquit were divided between these two perspectives.

The important constitutional question raised by the Clinton impeachment is: What constitutes "high crimes and misdemeanors"? The prevailing view appears to be that this phrase refers to criminal misconduct alone. But others would argue that a president could be removed from office for abusing power, subverting the Constitution, or even bringing the presidency into disrepute, regardless of whether indictable offenses have been committed.

Although tthey were made moot by the president's voluntary departure, similar questions surrounded the possible impeachment of Richard Nixon. Members of the House Judiciary Committee vigorously debated the meaning of "high crimes and misdemeanors." A majority of the committee's members seemed to believe Nixon could be impeached for "undermining the integrity of office, disregard of constitutional duties and oath of office, arrogation of power, abuse of the governmental process, and adverse impact on the system of government." On the other hand, Nixon's defenders held that the president could be impeached only for specific offenses against the criminal law, offenses for which he could be indicted by a grand jury (for example, obstruction of justice). In light of information currently available regarding Nixon's role in the Watergate scandal, it seems that he could have been impeached, and convicted, under either interpretation of the Constitution.

Is the question of what constitutes "high crimes and misdemeanors" solely a matter for the determination of the House and Senate, or is it appropriately a subject for judicial review? The Supreme Court has not been called on to render an authoritative construction of the "high crimes and misdemeanors" language of Article II. Should it be asked to do so in the future, the Court might well refuse by labeling the issue a "political question." It has been suggested, however, that in light of *Powell v. McCormack* (1969), the Court could define "high crimes and misdemeanors." In *Powell*, the Court refused to view as "political" the question of whether Congress could exclude one of its members for reasons other than residency, age, or citizenship. From a formal legal standpoint, this argument is compelling, but the Court's decisions reflect more than legal arguments. Realistically, the Court could severely jeopardize the delicate balance of its coequal status were it to intervene between president and Congress in an impeachment controversy. Judicial self-restraint would counsel doing otherwise.

TO SUMMARIZE:

- The Constitution vests presidential power in a single executive elected for a term of four years. The Twenty-second Amendment, ratified in 1951, prohibits the election of any person to more than two consecutive terms.
- The Framers of the Constitution provided for the election of the president, not by the people directly, but by the Electoral College. Today the Electoral College is a vestigial body that merely ratifies the outcome of the popular election. It remains possible, however, for a candidate who receives fewer popular votes than a rival to be elected president by receiving a majority of the electoral vote. If one candidate fails to receive a majority in the Electoral College, the election is conducted by the House of Representatives.
- Persons who have succeeded to the presidency through the death or resignation of the elected incumbent have exercised the full powers of the office. The problem of presidential disability is addressed by the Twenty-fifth Amendment, ratified in

1967. This amendment provides a procedure under which the vice president may assume the role of acting president during periods of presidential disability.

- According to Article II, Section 4, the president, as well as the vice president and other civil officers of the United States, may be impeached by the House of Representatives and removed from office by the Senate for the commission of "Treason, Bribery, or other high Crimes and Misdemeanors." It is debatable whether the phrase "high Crimes and Misdemeanors" is limited to indictable offenses, but it is unlikely that the Supreme Court will render an interpretation of this language.

THEORIES OF PRESIDENTIAL POWER

Article II, Section 1, of the Constitution provides that the "executive Power shall be vested in a President of the United States." Sections 2 and 3 enumerate specific powers granted to the president. These include authority to appoint judges and ambassadors, veto legislation, call Congress into special session, grant pardons, and serve as commander in chief of the armed forces. Each of these designated powers is obviously a part of "executive power," but that general term is not defined in Article II. Thus, it is debatable whether the opening statement of Article II is merely a summary of powers later enumerated in the article or, as many have argued, an independent grant of power to the president.

Enumerated and Inherent Powers

In the early days of the republic, James Madison and Alexander Hamilton engaged in the first of what was to be a long series of sharp disagreements among constitutional theorists about the proper scope of presidential power. Madison argued that presidential power is restricted to those powers specifically enumerated in Article II. By contrast, Hamilton argued for a transcendent conception of presidential power. Believing the opening statement in Article II to be a grant of power in its own right, he stated that "the difficulty of a complete enumeration of all cases of executive authority would naturally dictate the use of general terms and would render it improbable that a specification of certain particulars was designed as a substitute for the term [executive power]." Thus, Hamilton held that "the general doctrine of our Constitution . . . is that the executive power of the nation is vested in the President; subject only to the exceptions and qualifications which are expressed in that instrument." For Madison, if new exercises of power could be continually justified by invoking **inherent executive power**, "no citizen could any longer guess at the character of the government under which he lives; the most penetrating jurist would be unable to scan the extent of constructive prerogative." These competing theories correspond to very different notions of the proper role of the president in the newly created national government. While Madison envisaged a passive role for the president, who would faithfully execute the laws adopted by Congress, Hamilton viewed the presidency in more activist terms.

The Stewardship Theory of Presidential Power

The debate over the scope of presidential power was by no means confined to the early years of the republic. A vigorous argument occurred early in the twentieth century between those who espoused the **stewardship theory** and those who embraced the **constitutional theory** of presidential power. The constitutional theory, derived from Madison's ideas, finds its best and most succinct expression in the words of President William Howard Taft. In his view, the president can "exercise no power which cannot be fairly and reasonably traced to some specific grant of power or justly implied and included within such express grant as proper and necessary to its exercise." The stewardship theory, the modern counterpart to Hamilton's perspective, was best encapsulated by President Theodore Roosevelt. In his view, the Constitution permits the president "to do anything that the needs of the nation [demand] unless such action [is] forbidden by the Constitution or the laws." According to this perspective, the president is a steward of the people empowered to do anything deemed necessary, short of what is expressly prohibited by the Constitution, in the pursuit of the general welfare for which he is primarily responsible.

American constitutional history has, for the most part, vindicated the views of Alexander Hamilton and Theodore Roosevelt. Although some observers advocate scaling down the modern presidency, few really expect such diminution to occur. The exigencies of modernization, the complexities of living in a technological age, and the need for the United States as a superpower to speak to other nations with a unified voice and to respond quickly to threats to the national security have forced us to recognize the stewardship presidency as both necessary and legitimate. The inherent vagueness of Article II has facilitated this recognition.

The Supreme Court Legitimates Stewardship

For the most part, the Supreme Court has been willing to allow expansion of executive power over constitutional objections. It would be somewhat naive to expect the Court to stem the flow of power into the executive branch, given the fundamental economic, social, technological, and military needs that have promoted the stewardship presidency. There are cases in which the Court has invalidated particular exercises of executive power—for example, the steel seizure case (*Youngstown Sheet & Tube Company v. Sawyer* [1952]) and the Nixon tapes case (*United States v. Nixon* [1974])—but the overall trend has been to legitimize the "history of aggrandizement."

Because the Supreme Court generally reacts to issues arising elsewhere, it is odd that one of the first instances in which the Court grappled with abstract notions of executive power was a case that involved the not so abstract issue of the justices' personal safety (*In re Neagle* [1890]). In 1890, a federal marshal named David Neagle was charged with first degree murder by the state of California for having killed a man while attempting to protect the life of a Supreme Court justice. At that time, justices were required to "ride circuit"; that is, while the Supreme Court was not in session, they had to travel extensively over particular geographic areas to conduct trials and hear appeals. During one such excursion to California, the life of Justice Stephen J. Field was threatened by a disgruntled litigant (and prominent member of the California bar) named David Terry. Learning of this threat, the U.S. attorney general assigned Neagle to accompany Justice Field when he next rode circuit in California. Upon Field's return to that state, he encountered David Terry in a restaurant. Terry struck Justice Field, whereupon Neagle shot Terry dead. Interestingly, no weapon was found on Terry's corpse, raising the question of whether Neagle's response to the attack had been excessive. In any event, Neagle was promptly arrested by California authorities acting on a complaint from the wife of the deceased. Neagle then brought a federal habeas corpus action in order to challenge his arrest and prosecution. Under federal law, Neagle could secure release if he could show that he had acted "in pursuance of a law of the United States."

Unfortunately for Neagle, his assignment to protect Justice Field was not based on any statutory authority. However, the Supreme Court held that the attorney general's order assigning Neagle to protect Justice Field was tantamount to federal law. Opting essentially for the stewardship view of presidential power, the Court reasoned that the president was not "limited to enforcement of acts of Congress . . . according to their express terms." Rather, because the Constitution vests the government and particularly the executive with the obligation to protect "the peace of the United States," the executive is authorized to do whatever is necessary to fulfill that obligation (and this authorization is equivalent to a law). The president can and must take action to secure the peace, and he appropriately did so in the Neagle case. Thus, Neagle was held to be immune to prosecution by the state of California. In reaching this decision, the Court opted for Alexander Hamilton's broad view of executive power: This power stems not only from specific statutory authorizations or enumerations in Article II of the Constitution—it also derives from the power to protect the public safety implicit in the very nature of executive power.

The Outer Limits of Stewardship

Although the Supreme Court had several opportunities to elaborate on the scope of inherent executive power after *In re Neagle* (see, for example, *In re Debs* [1895], *United States v. Midwest Oil Company* [1915], and *Korematsu v. United States* [1944]), it did not deal with the issue in any real depth until the steel seizure case of 1952 (*Youngstown Sheet & Tube Company v. Sawyer*). In December 1951, President Harry S. Truman was informed that negotiations between labor and management in the steel industry had broken down. Concerned about the possible consequences of a stoppage in steel production, both for the domestic economy and for the Korean War effort, Truman acted to delay a strike by referring the issue to the Wage Stabilization Board for further negotiation. By April 1952, it became clear that negotiations were fruitless, and the workers announced their plans to strike. To prevent this, Truman ordered Secretary of Commerce Charles Sawyer to seize the steel mills and maintain full production. Not surprisingly, this action was challenged in the courts, and very soon the issue was before the Supreme Court.

Much to President Truman's chagrin, the Supreme Court (splitting 6–3) refused to allow the government to seize and operate the steel plants. Writing for the Court, Justice Hugo Black rejected inherent executive power as a justification for Truman's order. This reflected Justice Black's strong inclination to adhere closely to the language of the Constitution, an inclination characteristic of the interpretivist approach to constitutional adjudication. In a separate concurrence, Justice Robert Jackson took a position more characteristic of the historic mainstream of the Court. Jackson recognized an inherent executive power transcending particular enumerations in Article II but nevertheless found Truman's action to be impermissible. Noting that Congress had already considered and rejected legislation permitting such an executive order, Jackson wrote, "when the President takes measures incompatible with the expressed or implied will of Congress, his power is at its lowest ebb."

From the various opinions rendered in the steel seizure case, it is clear that several justices were swayed by the fact that Truman acted not only without congressional approval but irrespective of implied disapproval. When it was considering the Taft-Hartley bill a few years earlier, Congress had rejected an amendment that would have given the president a power similar to that exercised by Truman in seizing the steel mills. Thus, the steel seizure case was by no means a wholesale repudiation of the stewardship theory of presidential power. Rather, it was a reminder that the steward's authority is neither entirely self-derived nor without limitation. Moreover, the decision served notice to the chief executive that his actions, at least those in the domestic sphere, are subject to judicial scrutiny.

Another important instance in which the Court imposed limits on the stewardship presidency was in the Pentagon papers case of 1971 (*New York Times Company v. United States,* discussed and reprinted in Chapter 8). In the most celebrated case arising from the Vietnam controversy, the Court refused to issue an injunction against newspapers that had come into possession of the Pentagon papers, a set of classified documents detailing the history of American strategy in Vietnam. Basing his position on inherent executive power and not on any act of Congress, President Richard M. Nixon sought to restrain the press from disclosing classified information that, he argued, would be injurious to the national security. The Court, obviously skeptical of the alleged threat to national security and sensitive to the values protected by the First Amendment, refused to defer to the president.

It is interesting to speculate whether the results reached in the steel seizure case and Pentagon papers case would have been different in other sociopolitical contexts. If the nation had been engaged in a world war, rather than in limited and divisive conflicts in Korea and Vietnam, it is hard to believe that the Court would have been willing to challenge such assertions of inherent executive power. One must realize that Supreme Court decisions on executive power, as on other constitutional issues, are influenced not simply by legal principles but by complex political forces as well.

TO SUMMARIZE:

- The executive power of the president is formally recognized in Article II of the Constitution, but "executive power" is not defined.
- Under the "stewardship" theory, derived from the writings of Alexander Hamilton, executive power is broadly interpreted to include any actions or initiatives not specifically prohibited by the Constitution. Under the "constitutional" theory, traced to James Madison, any exercise of presidential power must be traceable to a specific grant of authority in the Constitution.
- The stewardship theory has prevailed in the twentieth century and, subject to a few significant limitations, the Supreme Court has legitimated this theory.

THE VETO POWER

Under Article I, Section 7, "[e]very Bill" and "[e]very Order, Resolution or Vote to which the Concurrence of the Senate and the House of Representatives may be necessary" must be presented to the president for approval. There are but three exceptions to this **presentment requirement:** It is not applicable to actions involving a single house, such as the adoption of procedural rules; it does not apply to concurrent resolutions, such as those establishing joint committees or setting a date for adjournment; finally, it does not apply to constitutional amendments proposed by the Congress. Until 1983, there was another category of congressional decisions not subject to presidential approval. The so-called legislative veto was a device whereby one or both houses of Congress passed resolutions to veto certain decisions made in the executive branch. In the case of *Immigration and Naturalization Service v. Chadha* (1983), the Supreme Court invalidated the legislative veto partly on the ground that it violated the presentment requirement of Article I. (The *Chadha* decision is discussed and reprinted in Chapter 4.)

The Pocket Veto

The president has ten days (not counting Sundays) in which to consider legislation presented for approval. The president has several options: (1) Sign the bill into law, which is what usually occurs; (2) **veto** the bill, which can be overridden by a two-thirds majority of both houses of Congress; or (3) neither sign nor veto the bill, thus allowing it to become law automatically after ten days. A major exception applies, however, to the third option: If Congress adjourns before the ten days have expired and the president still has not signed the bill, it is said to have been subjected to a **pocket veto.** The beauty of the pocket veto (at least from the president's standpoint) is that it deprives Congress of the chance to override a formal veto. This device was first used by President James Madison in 1812. The pocket veto has been controversial since its inception. The crucial question is: What constitutes an adjournment of Congress? In the pocket veto case (*Okanogan Indians v. United States* [1929]), the Supreme Court upheld President Calvin Coolidge's authority to pocket-veto a bill between sessions of the same Congress. The Court held that "adjournment" means any congressional break that prevents the return of a bill within the requisite ten-day period.

Questions have persisted about whether adjournments between sessions of the same Congress do in fact prevent the president from returning a bill within the ten-day period. The issue was dramatized during Congress's holiday recess in November 1983, when President Reagan pocket-vetoed a bill linking U.S. aid to El Salvador to that country's progress in the area of human rights. Representative Michael Barnes, the sponsor of the bill, and thirty-two other House Democrats filed suit challenging the president's action. According to these plaintiffs, Congress's break between sessions had not really prevented the president from returning the bill because both the House and Senate had appointed officers to receive presidential messages, and it was possible to reconvene the Congress in short order at the call of the leadership.

Although the administration won the lawsuit at the district court level, a panel of the Court of Appeals for the District of Columbia Circuit reversed, splitting 2 to 1. According to the court of appeals, the holiday recess had not really prevented the president from returning the bill, either signed or vetoed, during the required ten-day period (see *Barnes v. Kline* [1985]). Until the Supreme Court addresses the issue, uncertainty will remain as to whether a pocket veto is limited to the final adjournment of a given Congress or is permissible between sessions of the same Congress and, if the latter, under what circumstances.

The Line-Item Veto

Tradition dictates that the president must accept or veto a bill as a whole. Recent presidents, including Ronald Reagan, George Bush (the elder), and Bill Clinton, called for a constitutional amendment providing the president with a **line-item veto**, a power exercised by many state governors. Supporters of this measure argue that such a veto would allow the president to control unnecessary federal spending. The line-item veto allows the president to defeat the congressional tactic of attaching disagreeable riders to bills the president basically supports. In 1996, Congress passed a statute giving the president line-item veto authority. Because it was accomplished via statute, rather than a constitutional amendment, critics of the line-item veto attacked the constitutionality of the new law. In fact, members of Congress who had opposed the measure went to federal court in an attempt to have the law declared unconstitutional. In the spring of 1997, the federal district court in Washington, D.C., obliged. After an expedited review, the Supreme Court reversed, saying that the members of Congress who challenged the law lacked standing to sue (see *Raines v. Byrd* [1997], reprinted in Chapter 1). However, in *Clinton v. City of New York* (1998), the Court reached the merits of the dispute and declared the line-item veto law unconstitutional. The Court concluded that the law permitted the president to in effect amend duly enacted legislation.

TO SUMMARIZE:

- The president's veto power is a major check on legislative authority.
- Under Article I, Section 7, "[e]very Bill" and "[e]very Order, Resolution or Vote to which the Concurrence of the Senate and the House of Representatives may be necessary" must be presented to the president within ten days for approval.
- The presentment requirement does not apply to (1) actions involving a single house, (2) concurrent resolutions, and (3) proposed constitutional amendments.
- If Congress adjourns before ten days have expired and the president has not signed a bill, it has been subjected to a pocket veto and cannot become law unless duly enacted in a subsequent session of Congress.
- Presidents have favored a constitutional amendment granting them line-item veto authority. In 1996, Congress opted instead for a statute giving the president this authority. In 1998, the Supreme Court declared this approach unconstitutional.

THE POWER OF IMPOUNDMENT

Another controversial presidential power is that of **impoundment,** or the refusal to allow expenditure of funds appropriated by Congress. The first instance occurred in 1803, when President Jefferson withheld $50,000 that Congress had allocated to build gunboats to defend the Mississippi River. Jefferson's purpose was merely to delay the expenditure, primarily because the Louisiana Purchase, which was transacted shortly after Congress appropriated the money for gunboats, minimized the need for defenses along the Mississippi. During the remainder of the nineteenth century, presidents rarely invoked Jefferson's precedent. In 1905, Congress gave the president statutory authority to engage in limited impoundments to avoid departmental deficits. And in 1921, Congress extended this authority to allow the president to withhold funds to save money should Congress authorize more than was needed to secure its goals. Although Congress provided for a limited power of impoundment, these concessions to the president did not significantly undermine Congress's basic "power of the purse."

President Franklin D. Roosevelt consistently spent less than Congress appropriated. After Roosevelt, presidents increasingly used impoundment to pursue policy goals. Presidents Truman, Eisenhower, and Johnson used impoundment in the area of defense spending, justifying their actions on the basis of the president's role as commander in chief. Although these actions produced some criticism in Congress, they were not of sufficient magnitude to produce legislation or constitutional litigation.

Richard Nixon, however, extended the power of impoundment beyond limits acceptable to either Court or Congress. Nixon not only used impoundment to suit his fiscal preferences, but he also attempted to dismantle certain programs of which he disapproved. The most notorious example was his attempt to shut down the Office of Economic Opportunity (OEO) by refusing to spend any of the funds Congress had designated for it. (Congressional and public pressures forced Nixon to capitulate on the OEO issue.) In one of his far-reaching uses of the impoundment power, Nixon ordered the head of the Environmental Protection Agency, Russell Train, to withhold a substantial amount of money allocated for sewage treatment plants under the Water Pollution Control Act of 1972. Particularly disturbing to some members of Congress was the fact that Nixon had originally vetoed the act and Congress had overridden the veto. Thus, Nixon was seeking to have his way, a two-thirds majority of Congress to the contrary notwithstanding, by using the power to impound funds. In *Train v. City of New York* (1975), the Supreme Court invalidated Nixon's impoundment effort, concluding that the president did not possess a "seemingly limitless power to with-hold funds from allotment and obligation."

The Budget and Impoundment Act of 1974

Prior to the Court's decision in the *Train* case, Congress adopted the Congressional Budget and Impoundment Control Act of 1974. Although the act recognizes a limited presidential power to impound funds, it requires the president to inform Congress of the reasons for an intended impoundment and provides for a bicameral legislative veto to prevent the president from proceeding. However, the Supreme Court's decision in *Immigration and Naturalization Service v. Chadha* (1983) rendered the legislative veto provision of the impoundment act presumptively unconstitutional (see Chapter 4).

TO SUMMARIZE:

- "Impoundment" refers to the president's power to disallow expenditure of funds appropriated by Congress. Although not explicitly enumerated in the Constitution, the exercise of this power dates from the Jefferson administration.
- Responding to perceived abuse of this power, Congress has sought to impose limits on such presidential action through passage of the Congressional Budget and Impoundment Control Act of 1974. The act requires the president to inform Congress of the reasons for an intended impoundment and provides for a bicameral legislative veto to prevent the president from proceeding. The legislative veto component of this statute is rendered presumptively unconstitutional by *Immigration and Naturalization Service v. Chadha* (1983).

APPOINTMENT AND REMOVAL POWERS

Long before the advent of the modern stewardship presidency, it was obvious that presidents could not be expected to fulfill their duties alone. As presidential power has expanded, so too has the size and complexity of the executive branch. Originally, Congress provided for three cabinet departments—state, war, and treasury—to assist the president in the execution of policy. Today, there are fourteen cabinet departments, as well as a plethora of agencies, boards, and commissions in the executive establishment. In 1790 fewer than a thousand employees worked for the executive branch; today that number has grown to more than 2 million. Although almost all of these are civil service employees, the president directly appoints more than 3,000 upper-level officials. The power to appoint these officials, as well as federal judges and ambassadors, emanates from Article II, Section 2, which provides that the president

> shall nominate, and by and with the Advice and Consent of the Senate, shall appoint Ambassadors, other public Ministers and Consuls, Judges of the supreme Court, and all other Officers of the United States, whose Appointments are not herein otherwise provided for, which shall be established by Law; but the Congress may by Law vest the Appointment of such inferior Officers, as they think proper, in the President alone, in the Courts of Law, or in the Heads of Departments.

Thus, the Constitution permits some upper-level officials in the executive branch to be selected solely at the discretion of the president and some to be appointed solely by the heads of departments, while the ostensibly more important federal officials are to be appointed by the president with the advice and consent of the Senate. In the case of appointments requiring senatorial consent, the president nominates a candidate, awaits Senate approval by majority vote, and then commissions the confirmed nominee as an "officer of the United States."

The Supreme Court has made it clear that this process of nomination, approval, and commission is mandatory and that the nomination aspect of the process belongs solely to the president. Thus, in *Buckley v. Valeo* (1976), the Court struck down a section of the Federal Election Campaign Act of 1972 that provided Congress with a role in the nomination of members of the newly created Federal Election Commission.

In *Morrison v. Olson* (1988), the Court upheld a provision of the Ethics in Government Act of 1978 under which a "Special Division" of the U.S. Court of Appeals for the District of Columbia is empowered to appoint special prosecutors to investigate allegations of misconduct involving high government officials. The Court held that the special prosecutor is an "inferior officer" whose appointment may be assigned to the courts under Article II, Section 2.

The Removal Problem

Although the Constitution is reasonably clear on the subject of the presidential **appointment power**, the issue of the **removal power** has been rather problematic. Obviously, the president has a strong interest in being able to remove those appointees whose performance displeases him. However, the Constitution addresses the question of removal only in the context of the cumbersome impeachment process. It is unlikely that the Framers intended that administrative officials whose performance is unacceptable to the president be subject to removal only by impeachment. Given the difficulty of this method of removal, such a limitation could paralyze government.

Most observers agree that officers of the United States can be removed by means other than impeachment—except for judges, whose life tenure (assuming good behavior) is guaranteed by the Constitution. The problem is the role of Congress in the removal of executive officers. Given that the Constitution requires senatorial consent for certain presidential appointments, is it not reasonable to expect Congress to play a role in the removal of such officials? The Supreme Court first dealt with the question of the president's removal powers in *Myers v. United States* (1926).

The *Myers* case arose when President Woodrow Wilson removed Frank Myers, a Portland, Oregon, postmaster, before his term had expired. In removing Myers, Wilson ignored provisions of an 1876 act of Congress requiring Senate approval for the removal of postmasters. Consequently, Myers brought suit to recover wages lost between the time he was fired and the time his term was to expire. In a lengthy opinion for the Court, Chief Justice William Howard Taft (himself a former president) held that the removal of Myers was valid and that the senatorial consent provisions were unconstitutional. Taft's opinion stated that, given the president's constitutional duty to faithfully execute the laws, it would be unreasonable to expect an administration to retain an official on whom it could no longer count to follow orders. The upshot of the *Myers* decision is that purely executive officials performing purely executive functions may be removed at will by the president, unchecked by the Congress.

Dicta in Taft's opinion in *Myers* suggested that the president might also remove at will officials appointed to serve in the independent regulatory agencies, such as the Interstate Commerce Commission. This assertion contradicted the statutes establishing such commissions, which provided that the executive show cause (that is, malfeasance or neglect of duty) before removing commissioners. After all, the motivation behind the creation of such commissions was to allow for government by experts free of partisan political concerns. Inevitably, the Supreme Court was to decide whether Congress could limit presidential removal power as applied to independent regulatory agencies.

In *Humphrey's Executor v. United States* (1935), the Supreme Court considered whether President Franklin D. Roosevelt could fire a member of the Federal Trade Commission (FTC) solely on policy grounds. In 1931, President Herbert Hoover reappointed William Humphrey to serve on the FTC. According to an act of Congress, Humphrey's seven-year term was subject to presidential curtailment only for malfeasance, inefficiency, or neglect of duty. When Roosevelt took office, he fired Humphrey, believing that the goals of his administration would be better served by people of his own choosing. Although Humphrey died shortly after his removal, the executor of his estate brought suit to recover wages lost between the time of removal and the time of his death.

In *Humphrey's Executor,* the Supreme Court narrowed Chief Justice Taft's broad view of executive removal powers expressed in the *Myers* case. The Court maintained the view that purely executive officials performing purely executive functions could be removed at will by the president. However, in the case of regulatory commissions like the FTC, Congress had created a quasi-legislative body designed to perform tasks independent of executive control. Thus, said the Court, Congress could regulate the removal of such officials. At the time, some observers viewed the *Humphrey's Executor* decision as a politically motivated departure from the *Myers* precedent. They saw *Humphrey's Executor* as part of the larger struggle between the Court and Roosevelt. Although in 1935 this interpretation was quite plausible, a subsequent decision by the Court indicates that the *Humphrey* case was by no means an anomaly created by transitory political forces.

The Supreme Court expanded on the *Humphrey* rationale in *Wiener v. United States* (1958) by holding that the unique nature of independent agencies requires that removal must be for cause, whether or not Congress has so stipulated. The case involved a member of the War Claims Commission who had been appointed by President Harry S. Truman and who was removed for partisan reasons by President Dwight D. Eisenhower. Noting the adjudicatory character of the commission, the Court stated that "it must be inferred that Congress did not wish to have hang over the Commission the Damocles' sword of removal by the President for no other reason than that he preferred to have on the Commission men of his own choosing."

Thus, the Court's decisions hold that the legality of presidential removal of an official in the executive branch depends on the nature of the duties performed by the official in question. Officials performing purely executive functions may be removed by the president at will; those performing quasi-legislative or quasi-judicial functions can be removed by the president only for cause. Although Congress may determine the basis for removal of such officials, the ultimate power to remove officials in the executive branch belongs to the president. Adhering to this principle, the Court in *Bowsher v. Synar* (1986) held that Congress could not grant executive powers to the comptroller general, since that official was removable by Congress. (For further discussion of this decision, see Chapter 4.)

TO SUMMARIZE:

- Under Article II, Section 2, the president appoints, with the consent of the Senate, federal judges, ambassadors, and officials in the executive branch not designated part of the civil service.
- The most important constitutional questions in this area deal with the scope of presidential authority to remove appointed officials without Senate approval. Officials performing purely executive functions may be removed by the president at will; those performing quasi-legislative or quasi-judicial functions can be removed only for cause.

THE POWER TO GRANT PARDONS

President Gerald Ford's full and unconditional pardon of former President Richard Nixon following the Watergate affair may have been politically unwise, but it was unquestionably constitutional. Article II, Section 2, states that the president shall have the power to "grant reprieves and pardons for offenses against the United States, except in cases of impeachment." Although impeachment proceedings were initiated against Nixon, his sudden resignation foreclosed any possibility of impeachment, let alone conviction by the Senate. Thus, Ford acted constitutionally in issuing the pardon to Nixon. (Lest there be doubt about Nixon's culpability in the Watergate scandal, note that the acceptance of a **presidential pardon** is tantamount to an admission of guilt, for one cannot be pardoned unless one has committed an offense.)

Although President Ford issued a full pardon in the Nixon case, the president may also issue "conditional" pardons. In *Schick v. Reed* (1974), the Supreme Court said:

> The plain purpose of the broad [pardoning] power conferred . . . was to allow . . . the President to "forgive" the convicted person in part or entirely, to reduce a penalty a specified number of years, or to alter it with conditions which are themselves constitutionally unobjectionable.

Maurice Schick had been convicted of murder and sentenced to death by a military tribunal. Subsequently, President Eisenhower commuted Schick's sentence to life imprisonment on the condition he be ineligible for parole. However, in *Furman v. Georgia* (1972), the Supreme Court ruled that the death penalty was in certain instances unconstitutional (see Chapter 10). Consequently, Schick went back to court arguing in light of the Court's capital punishment decision, which had been applied retroactively, that his own original death sentence was unconstitutional and that, accordingly, the no-parole provision should likewise be set aside. The Court disagreed, holding that the conditional pardon was lawful when issued and that the later decision in *Furman* did not alter its validity.

An unqualified presidential pardon fully restores any civil rights forfeited on conviction of the crime. In *Ex parte Garland* (1867), the Court held that a pardon restores an individual's innocence as though a crime had never been committed. In the Garland case, this meant that one who had fought for the Confederacy could practice law before the Supreme Court without the need to take an oath that he had not volun-tarily borne arms against the United States. The Court held that a full pardon by Pres-ident Andrew Johnson absolved Garland of the need to take such an oath.

Although a president has seemingly unlimited authority to grant pardons, it is con-ceivable that a president might commit an impeachable offense by improperly grant-ing a pardon to a contributor. This issue was raised in January 2001 as President Clin-ton granted a number of very controversial "midnight pardons" as he was leaving office. One of them was to a billionaire named Marc Rich, who was living in Switzer-land to avoid prosecution for federal tax violations. Rich's ex-wife Denise was a friend and benefactor to President and Mrs. Clinton. Critics charged that President Clinton in effect "sold" a pardon, which would be a violation of federal law. In a subsequent congressional investigation of the matter, Denise Rich asserted her Fifth Amendment privilege against self-incrimination. The Bush administration declined to investigate the matter and the controversy subsided. Had the incident taken place prior to the impeachment episode of 1998, there might well have been another article of impeachment adopted against President Clinton.

Amnesties

Although the presidential pardon was traditionally thought to be a private transac-tion between the president and the recipient, this did not prevent President Jimmy Carter from granting an **amnesty** that was, in effect, a blanket pardon to those who were either deserters or draft evaders during the Vietnam War. President Carter's amnesty was not challenged in the courts; neither was it criticized on constitutional grounds, although many considered it to be an insult to those who had fought and died in Vietnam. It should be noted that amnesties have traditionally been granted by Congress to those who deserted or evaded service in America's wars.

TO SUMMARIZE:

- Under Article II, Section 2, the president shall have the power to "grant Reprieves and Pardons for Offenses against the United States, except in Cases of Impeach-ment."
- Although acceptance of a pardon is tantamount to an admission of guilt, a pardon restores an individual's innocence as though the crime had never been committed.
- Presidents may also grant amnesties that are, in effect, blanket pardons. These typ-ically apply to persons who have illegally avoided military service.

EXECUTIVE PRIVILEGE

Beginning with George Washington, presidents have asserted a right to withhold information from Congress and the courts. Known as executive privilege, this "right" has been defended as inherent in executive power. Indeed, it must be defended as such because it is nowhere mentioned in the Constitution. Scholars are divided over whether the Framers envisaged such a power in the presidency, but the point is moot in light of two centuries of history, as well as explicit Supreme Court recognition, sup-porting this power.

Although the term **executive privilege** was coined during the Eisenhower administration of the 1950s, the practice dates from 1792. In that year, President

Washington refused to provide the House of Representatives certain documents it had requested relative to the bewildering defeat of military forces under General Arthur St. Clair by the Ohio Indians. Washington again asserted the privilege in 1795 when the House requested information dealing with the negotiation of the Jay Treaty with England. A few years later, President Thomas Jefferson, once a sharp critic of George Washington's imperious approach to the presidency, would rely on inherent executive power in defying a *subpoena duces tecum* issued during the trial of Aaron Burr for treason in 1807. Later presidents invoked executive privilege primarily to maintain the secrecy of information related to national security. Presidents Truman, Eisenhower, Kennedy, and Johnson all found occasion to invoke the doctrine to protect the confidentiality of their deliberations. However, the power of executive privilege did not become a major point of contention until the Nixon presidency.

The Watergate Tapes Controversy

During his first term (1969-1973), President Nixon invoked executive privilege on four separate occasions; others in the Nixon administration did so in more than twenty instances. But after his landslide reelection in 1972, Nixon and his lieutenants routinely employed executive privilege to evade queries from Congress regarding the Watergate break-in and subsequent cover-up.

Although Nixon was able to use executive privilege to withhold information requested by Congress, he was unable to avoid a *subpoena duces tecum* issued by the federal courts at the request of Watergate special prosecutor Leon Jaworski. Earlier, Nixon had fired Archibald Cox, Jaworski's predecessor, when Cox refused to back down in his efforts to subpoena the infamous tapes on which Nixon had recorded conversations with principals in the Watergate scandal. In an episode that became known as the "Saturday Night Massacre," Nixon fired Attorney General Elliot Richardson and Assistant Attorney General William Ruckelshaus, both of whom refused to follow the president's order to dismiss Cox. Ultimately, Cox was dismissed on the order of Robert H. Bork, who was solicitor general at the time. Although there was no question of Nixon's constitutional authority to dismiss Cox—who was, after all, an employee of the Justice Department—the dismissal was politically disastrous: The Saturday Night Massacre led Congress to consider the possibility of impeachment of the president. Succeeding Cox, Leon Jaworski pursued the Watergate investigation with alacrity. When the federal district court denied Nixon's motion to quash a new *subpoena duces tecum* obtained by Jaworski, the question of executive privilege went before the Supreme Court.

When *United States v. Nixon* reached the Supreme Court, Justice William Rehnquist, who had served in the Justice Department during Nixon's first term, recused himself. In deciding the Nixon tapes case, the other eight justices unanimously ordered that the subpoenaed tapes be surrendered. The opinion of the Court was authored by Chief Justice Warren E. Burger, Nixon's first Supreme Court appointee. Recognizing the legitimacy of executive privilege, Burger nevertheless concluded that the demands of due process of law outweighed the presidential interest in confidentiality in this case. Burger refused to view executive privilege as affording absolute presidential immunity from the judicial process. Thus, the Court asserted the primacy of the rule of law over the power of the presidency. Although Nixon was reportedly tempted to defy the Court's ruling, wiser counsel prevailed, and the tapes were produced. Shortly thereafter, recognizing the inevitable, Richard Nixon resigned the presidency in disgrace.

TO SUMMARIZE:

- Although "executive privilege" is not mentioned in the Constitution, presidents since George Washington have asserted a right to withhold information from Congress and the courts.
- In *United States v. Nixon* (1974), the Supreme Court accorded constitutional status to executive privilege, but rejected the proposition that the privilege is absolute.

PRESIDENTIAL IMMUNITY

In addition to a limited power of executive privilege, the Supreme Court has held that presidents enjoy nearly absolute immunity against private civil suits involving claims stemming from official presidential actions. Not surprisingly, the recent cases in which the Court was asked to decide the scope of **presidential immunity** stemmed from controversies that began during the Nixon administration. Morton Halperin, a political scientist, was a staff member of the National Security Council during the Nixon administration. After learning that his home telephone had been illegally wiretapped, Halperin brought suit seeking monetary damages against Nixon, his secretary of state, Henry Kissinger, and his attorney general, John Mitchell. In *Kissinger v. Halperin* (1981), the Court divided 4–4 (Justice Rehnquist not participating), thus letting stand a lower federal court decision upholding President Nixon's susceptibility to lawsuit.

In *Nixon v. Fitzgerald* (1982), the Court was able to reach majority agreement on the question of presidential immunity. The case involved A. Ernest Fitzgerald, a former management analyst with the Air Force. Fitzgerald had attracted much attention in 1968 when he embarrassed the Department of Defense by revealing huge cost overruns on the C-5A transport plane. In 1970, Fitzgerald was dismissed, ostensibly as part of a departmental reorganization. Later, the Civil Service Commission found that Fitzgerald had been illegally removed for his whistle-blowing on the Pentagon. Following the commission's decision, Fitzgerald filed suit in federal court. On appeal, the Supreme Court held that the president was entitled to absolute immunity against private civil suits, at least those stemming from the president's official actions during his time in the White House. Writing for the Court, Justice Lewis Powell opined that "[b]ecause of the singular importance of the President's duties, diversion of his energies by concern with private lawsuits would raise unique risks to the effective functioning of government." Justice Byron White dissented:

> Attaching absolute immunity to the office of the President, rather than to particular activities the President might perform, places the President above the law. It is a reversion to the old notion that the King can do no wrong.

Immunity for Private Misconduct?

In a widely anticipated decision fraught with political ramifications, the Supreme Court in 1997 made it abundantly clear that a sitting president is not above the law. In *Clinton v. Jones*, the Court permitted a sexual harassment suit to proceed against President Bill Clinton, despite the administration's claim that allowing the suit to go forward would hamper the president's performance of his official duties. The lawsuit was brought by Paula Jones, a former Arkansas state employee who claimed that Bill Clinton had made an offensive sexual advance toward her when he was governor of

Arkansas. The federal district court denied the president's motion to dismiss on immunity grounds, but postponed the trial until after Clinton left office. In what was clearly a major blow to President Clinton, the Supreme Court upheld the district court's refusal to dismiss the case on grounds of immunity, but reversed on the question of delaying the trial. Writing for a unanimous Court, Justice Stevens made it clear that the Constitution does not provide a sitting president immunity from civil suits arising from the president's private conduct. While that holding did not come as a great surprise to the Clinton administration, the Court's refusal to delay the trial until after Bill Clinton left office sent shock waves through the White House. The decision meant that President Clinton had to suffer an indignity that no other president has suffered—being designated as the defendant in a trial alleging private misconduct. The lurid nature of the charges made the prospect all the more unsettling. Still, the Supreme Court was widely hailed for placing the law above the interests of a sitting president.

TO SUMMARIZE:

- The Supreme Court has held that presidents enjoy broad immunity against civil suits involving claims stemming from their official actions.
- In *Clinton v. Jones* (1997), the Court held that presidential immunity does not extend to suits involving the president's private conduct.

FOREIGN POLICY AND INTERNATIONAL RELATIONS

Scholars have written of the "two presidencies." One presidency, concerned with domestic affairs, is severely limited by the Constitution, the Supreme Court, and Congress. The other presidency, that involving foreign affairs and international relations, is less susceptible to constitutional and political constraints. Although the thesis may have been overstated, the basic point is valid. Throughout American history, Congress, the courts, and the American public have been highly deferential to the president in the conduct of foreign policy. A serious reading of the Constitution indicates to some commentators that the Framers intended for Congress to play a greater role in the foreign policy process; however, the exigencies of history, more than the intentions of the Framers, determine the roles played by the institutions of government.

Another factor contributing to presidential dominance of foreign policy is the distinctive structures of Congress and the executive branch. Congress is composed of 535 members, each representing either a state or localized constituency. On the other hand, the president represents a national constituency. Is it not reasonable that the president alone should speak for the nation in the international arena?

The "Sole Organ" in the Field of International Relations?

In *United States v. Curtiss-Wright Export Corporation* (1936), the Supreme Court placed its stamp of approval on presidential primacy in the realm of foreign affairs. In May 1934, Congress had adopted a joint resolution authorizing the president to prohibit U.S. companies from selling munitions (under such limitations and exceptions as the president might determine) to the warring nations of Paraguay and Bolivia. Additionally, Congress provided for criminal penalties for those violating presidential prohibitions. Shortly after this resolution was adopted, President Roosevelt issued an executive order imposing an embargo on arms sales to the belligerent countries. In 1936, the Curtiss-Wright Export Corporation was indicted for conspiring to sell arms to Bolivia in violation of the embargo. Curtiss-Wright sought to avoid prosecution by arguing that Congress had unconstitutionally delegated its lawmaking power to the president, because the resolution allowed the president to make the specific rules controlling arms shipments.

Despite the fact that just one year earlier it had taken a tough stand on the issue of delegation of legislative power (see *Schechter Poultry Corporation v. United States* [1935], discussed and reprinted in Chapter 4), the Court refused to find anything unconstitutional in the *Curtiss-Wright* case. The Court distinguished between two classes of power—domestic and foreign—and held that the rule against legislative delegation applied only to the former. Furthermore, the Court suggested that the president would have inherent power to impose such an embargo, even without an authorizing resolution from Congress. Expounding on presidential primacy in foreign affairs, the Court referred to the president as the "sole organ of the federal government in the field of international relations." Justice George Sutherland's opinion in *Curtiss-Wright* went so far as to assert that this class of presidential power transcended the Constitution itself.

Even assuming that it is possible to draw a neat distinction between domestic powers and those pertaining to foreign affairs, many scholars would challenge the Court's sweeping endorsement of **presidential power to make foreign policy.** Few would argue that, in making and executing the foreign policy of this nation, the president is subject to no constitutional limitations. Clearly, though, the degree of freedom afforded the president in the field of foreign policy has been substantial indeed. For example, in *Haig v. Agee* (1981), the Court upheld the Reagan administration's decision to revoke the passport of a former agent of the Central Intelligence Agency (CIA) whose activities in foreign countries were deemed a threat to national security. And in *Regan v. Wald* (1984), the Court sustained the Reagan administration's unilateral restrictions on travel to Cuba. Writing for the Court in *Haig v. Agee,* Chief Justice Burger invoked the expansive view of presidential authority in the field of foreign affairs taken by the Court in *Curtiss-Wright.* And, according to Justice Rehnquist's majority opinion in *Regan v. Wald,* matters involving "the conduct of foreign relations . . . are so entirely entrusted to the political branches of government as to be largely immune from judicial inquiry or interference."

The Iran-Contra Scandal   In the wake of Vietnam and Watergate, and fueled by revelations about covert CIA activities during the 1960s, Congress in the 1970s adopted a series of laws limiting presidential power to employ covert means of pursuing foreign policy objectives. In the 1980s, when Congress learned of CIA efforts to support the Contras battling to overthrow the Marxist government of Nicaragua, it adopted the Boland Amendments, a series of measures restricting the use of U.S. funds to aid the Contras. The Reagan administration attempted an end run around the Boland Amendments by secretly selling weapons to Iran and using the profits to aid the Contras. When the operation was uncovered, an outraged Congress conducted an investigation that included the testimony of Lt. Col. Oliver North, a staff member of the National Security Council who was heavily involved in the covert operation. In a later criminal trial, North was convicted of perjury and obstruction of justice. (His conviction was overturned on appeal in 1991. The appeals court held that prosecutors had illegally introduced evidence covered by the grant of immunity under which North had testified before Congress.)

Although the Iran-Contra affair was a blow to the credibility and prestige of the Reagan administration, it remains shrouded in legal uncertainty. It is not clear whether the administration actually violated the Boland Amendments, although there is little doubt that it sought to undermine the policy objective behind them. Second, given the Supreme Court's pronouncements in *United States v. Curtiss-Wright,* there is a serious question about the extent to which Congress may exercise control over presidential actions in the foreign policy sphere. Clearly, Congress may impose restrictions on the expenditure of government funds, since Congress possesses the power of the purse. But can Congress prevent the president from carrying out a foreign policy objective through "creative enterprises," such as the deal to sell weapons to Iran?

Troubling constitutional questions involving the allocation of powers in the field of foreign policy are unlikely to be resolved in the courts of law. Rather, as "political questions," they are apt to be resolved in the court of public opinion. As the underwhelming public response to the Iran-Contra scandal demonstrates, the American people are not particularly squeamish about broad presidential latitude in the foreign policy arena.

Specifics of Conducting Foreign Affairs

Although presidential authority in international relations rests in large part on inherent executive power, the Constitution also enumerates specific powers important in the everyday management of foreign affairs. Article II, Section 3, authorizes the president to receive ambassadors and emissaries from foreign nations. In effect, this provides the president the power to recognize the legitimate governments of foreign nations. This power is of obvious importance in international relations, as attested by Roosevelt's recognition of the Soviet government in the 1930s, Truman's recognition of Israel, Kennedy's severance of ties with Cuba, and Carter's recognition of the People's Republic of China.

Treaties In addition to the authority to recognize foreign governments, the president is empowered by Article II to make treaties with foreign nations, subject to the consent of the Senate. A **treaty** is an agreement between two or more nations containing promises to behave in specified ways. The atmospheric nuclear test-ban treaty negotiated under President Kennedy's leadership, the SALT I treaty reached with the Soviets during the Nixon presidency, and the Panama Canal treaty negotiated during the Carter administration illustrate the foreign policy importance of the treaty making power.

A constitutional problem has arisen from the fact that the terms of a treaty can affect the domestic policy of the nation. This issue was addressed by the Supreme Court in *Missouri v. Holland* (1920). The case stemmed from a treaty between the United States and Canada designed to protect migratory birds. The treaty required both nations to pass laws restricting the hunting of certain species of fowl during their migrations between the United States and Canada. In 1918, Congress adopted a statute to effectuate the treaty. The state of Missouri brought suit, claiming ownership of the protected birds while they were within its borders and that, accordingly, Congress had usurped the powers reserved to the states by the Tenth Amendment. The Supreme Court, rejecting Missouri's claim of ownership, held the statute valid under the Elastic Clause of Article I, Section 8: "If the treaty is valid there can be no dispute about the validity of the statute . . . as a necessary and proper means to execute the powers of the Government." Addressing the ultimate validity of the treaty, the Court held that "acts of Congress are the supreme law of the land only when made in pursuance of the Constitution, while treaties are declared to be so when made under the authority of the United States." Thus, the Court at once upheld both a treaty and a related statute that probably would not have been upheld in the absence of the treaty.

Missouri v. Holland dramatized the close connection between the foreign and domestic spheres of power and underscored potential problems inherent in a government whose domestic authority supposedly emanates from a constitution but whose power to deal with foreign nations is preconstitutional or metaconstitutional in nature. Indeed, the holding in *Missouri v. Holland* raised the possibility of using treaties as a means of expanding the legislative powers of the national government. In response to the argument that reliance on treaties might override the limitations of the Constitution, Senator John Bricker (R-Ohio) proposed a constitutional amendment in the early 1950s that would have nullified any treaty provision conflicting with the Constitution. The Bricker amendment was never submitted to the states for ratification, falling one vote short of the necessary two-thirds majority in the Senate. Nevertheless, interest in the amendment remained strong throughout the decade. Despite the failure of the Bricker amendment, the fears that motivated its supporters have not been borne out by subsequent experience.

Executive Agreements Support for the Bricker proposal was not based wholly on fears that the treaty power would be used to strengthen the national government at the expense of the states. The amendment also sought to curtail the increasing presidential tendency to bypass Congress altogether through the use of **executive agreements.** Like treaties, executive agreements require certain national commitments. However, such agreements are negotiated solely between heads of state acting independently of their legislative bodies. Most of these agreements involve minor matters of international concern, such as specification of the details of postal relations or the use of radio airwaves. In recent years, however, the executive agreement has emerged as an important tool of foreign policy making. This development was legitimated by the Supreme Court in *United States v. Belmont* (1937) and *United States v. Pink* (1942). Both cases challenged the domestic aspects of the Litvinov Agreements that Franklin Roosevelt had struck with Joseph Stalin without any authorization or approval from the Senate. In addition to providing the Soviet Union with formal recognition, the agreements granted Soviet claims involving Russian companies that had been nationalized but whose assets were in the hands of U.S. banks. A legal controversy arose, however, when the state of New York refused to allow the transfer of assets to the Soviet government. The Supreme Court ultimately overruled the state (*United States v. Belmont*), holding that the executive agreement was legally equivalent to a treaty and thus the supreme law of the land, New York's policy notwithstanding.

The *Belmont* and *Pink* decisions, combined with the inherent uncertainty of treaty ratification, had the effect of making executive agreements all the more enticing to presidents. As the Senate's role in foreign policy making declined, support increased in Congress for the provision of the Bricker amendment that required congressional authorization of executive agreements before they could have any domestic effect. However, during the late 1950s and early 1960s, many of the forces motivating this proposal had diminished with shifts in international concern, changes in domestic public opinion, and the electoral defeat of Senator Bricker. Although there was some talk during and after the Vietnam War of reviving the Bricker amendment, no formal proposals were forthcoming.

Perhaps the most dramatic recent use of the executive agreement was President Carter's agreement with Iran that secured the release of fifty-two American hostages in early 1981. The agreement negated all attachments against Iranian assets in the United States and transferred claims against Iran from American to international tribunals. In *Dames & Moore v. Regan* (1981), the Supreme Court upheld the validity of Carter's executive agreement. The Court found in the Emergency Powers Act of 1977 sufficient presidential authority to cancel attachments against Iranian assets. Finding no statutory authority for the transfer of claims to international tribunal, the Court held that Congress had tacitly approved the president's actions by its traditional pattern of acquiescence to executive agreements. Thus, merely by use, a power arguably in conflict with the Constitution may gain legitimacy.

TO SUMMARIZE:

- In *United States v. Curtiss-Wright Export Corporation* (1936), the Supreme Court recognized presidential primacy in the realm of foreign affairs. By clear implication, the Court greatly circumscribed the role of Congress in this area. Although controversial, this view has not been repudiated by the Court.
- Presidents have authority to make treaties with foreign nations with the advice and consent of the Senate. The broad scope of this power was endorsed by the Supreme Court in *Missouri v. Holland* (1920).
- Presidents often use executive agreements as an alternative to treaties. Unlike treaties, executive agreements do not require the concurrence of the Senate. Valid executive agreements are legally equivalent to treaties.

WAR POWERS

Presidential dominance in international affairs is not limited to or based on the formalities of recognizing and striking agreements with other governments. Integral to the president's foreign policy role is the tremendous power of the U.S. military, over which the Constitution makes the president **commander in chief.** Force is often threatened, and sometimes used, to protect U.S. allies and interests, maintain national security against possible attack, or defend the nation against actual attack. The success of American foreign policy would be severely limited if the Constitution curbed the nation's ability to respond effectively to threats against its interests or security. On the other hand, the Constitution was designed as a limitation on the power of our government. Should not such limitations apply (as Justice Black said in the Pentagon papers case) "to prevent the government from deceiving the people and sending them off to distant lands to die of foreign fevers and foreign shot and shell"?

The Framers of the Constitution did attempt to provide some limitation on the war making power, as they did with respect to government power generally, by dividing power between the president and Congress. Although Article II recognizes the president as commander in chief, Article I provides Congress with the authority to declare war. Certainly the military conflicts in Vietnam and Korea qualify as wars, yet in neither case was there a formal declaration by Congress.

Presidential power to commit military forces to combat situations has a long heritage. It was first exercised at the international level in 1801, when Thomas Jefferson sent the U.S. Marines to "the shores of Tripoli" to root out the Barbary pirates. In 1846, James K. Polk sent American troops to instigate a war with Mexico that Congress formally approved by declaring war. In 1854, Franklin Pierce authorized a show of American force that led to the total destruction of an entire city in Central America. In none of these instances, however, did the Supreme Court have the opportunity to decide the scope of the president's power as commander in chief.

The Court's opportunity came in 1863 in *The Prize Cases*. These cases involved the disposition of vessels captured by the Union navy during the blockade of Southern ports ordered by President Abraham Lincoln in the absence of a congressional declaration of war. Under existing laws of war, the captured vessels would become the property of the Union navy only if the conflict were a declared war. Given the extremely sensitive politics of the day, the Court could do nothing but find the seizures to be legal, even though Congress had not formally declared war against the Confederacy. The Court held that "the President is not only authorized, but bound to resist force. He does not initiate the war, but is bound to accept the challenge without waiting for any special legislative authority." Additionally, Justice Robert C. Grier noted that the "President was bound to meet [the Civil War] in the shape it presented itself, without waiting for the Congress to baptize it with a name; and no name given to it by him or them could change the fact." In *The Prize Cases,* the Court acknowledged the necessity of deferring to the president's decisions in times of crisis.

The Vietnam War

President Lincoln's unprecedented exercise of war powers presaged President Lyndon Johnson's actions in Vietnam a century later. Absent a formal declaration of war by Congress, the Johnson administration maintained that inherent presidential power essentially includes the power to deploy American forces abroad and commit them to military operations when the president decides such action is necessary. Of course, many commentators disagreed with this assessment.

In the Gulf of Tonkin Resolution of 1964, Congress did give limited authority to the president to take whatever actions were necessary to defend the government of South Vietnam and American interests and personnel in the region. The resolution was adopted in response to an alleged attack on American ships operating near North Vietnam. Later evidence indicated that the attack was exaggerated at the very least and was perhaps contrived to force Congress to sanction the growing American involvement in Southeast Asia. It was not long before the war was expanded far beyond anything envisioned by Congress in 1964. In a later development in the Vietnam War, President Nixon's covert war in Cambodia certainly fell beyond any authority granted the president by the Gulf of Tonkin Resolution. Amid the harsh strains of sometimes violent antiwar protest, calmer voices began to be heard questioning the legality of the war effort.

During the Vietnam era, the Supreme Court had ample opportunity to rule on the constitutionality of the war and the concomitant use of presidential power, but it declined to do so, viewing the issue as a "political question" (see *Massachusetts v. Laird* [1970]). The Court drew some criticism for this deferential posture. However, it is likely that the Court would have been more criticized if it had chosen to review the constitutionality of the Vietnam War—and it certainly would have been—had its ruling been adverse to the president. It is beyond question that the influence of the Court over the conduct of wars, foreign or domestic, is minimal at best. The philosophy of judicial self-restraint dictates that the Court maintain a low profile on such issues.

The War Powers Resolution

As the Supreme Court's unwillingness to address the issue became clear, Congress began to question the unbridled conception of **presidential war powers**. In 1973, Congress adopted the **War Powers Resolution** over the veto of President Nixon. The act was designed to limit the president's unilateral power to send troops into foreign combat. It requires the president to make a full report to Congress when sending troops into foreign areas, limits the duration of troop commitment without congressional authorization, and provides a veto mechanism whereby Congress can force the recall of troops at any time.

Given the Supreme Court's decision in *Immigration and Naturalization Service v. Chadha* (1983), the legislative veto provision of the War Powers Resolution is presumptively unconstitutional (see Chapter 4). Yet the provision remains on the books. Since Congress has not yet invoked the War Powers Resolution, the courts have had no occasion to address the specific question of its constitutionality. It is unlikely that the War Powers Resolution will ever be subjected to judicial review, as it is unlikely that it will ever be invoked against the president. Even if it were invoked and litigation resulted, it is probable that the courts would view the matter as a "political question."

Aside from the question of its constitutionality, the War Powers Resolution is probably not an effective constraint on the presidential war power. It can be viewed as little more than a symbolic gesture of defiance from a Congress displeased with the conduct of the Vietnam War. The existence of the War Powers Act did not prevent President Reagan from employing military force in pursuit of his foreign policy objectives. Reagan sent the U.S. Marines into Beirut and even used naval gunfire against the rebels in the Lebanese civil war. Reagan employed U.S. troops to topple the Marxist government of Grenada. And he ordered an air strike on Libya to punish the Khadaffi regime for its support of international terrorism. Although President Reagan chose to comply with the War Powers Act in all three cases by notifying Congress of his actions, he still made the decisions to send troops into hostile situations. Congressional disapproval would have made no difference in the cases of Grenada and Libya; the hostilities had practically ceased by the time Congress was notified.

The Persian Gulf War of 1991

Soon after Saddam Hussein's Iraq invaded and annexed tiny Kuwait in August 1990, President Bush (the elder) ordered military forces into Saudi Arabia in a defensive posture. When it became clear that Iraq had no intention of leaving Kuwait, Bush ordered a massive buildup of forces in the region and began to threaten the use of force to remove Iraqi troops from Kuwait. Bush's critics soon suggested that the War Powers Act had been triggered because American troops were in a situation of imminent hostility. Yet Congress did not attempt to "start the clock" under the War Powers Act. When the president did finally decide to move against Iraq in January 1991, he first obtained a resolution from Congress supporting the use of force. Had Bush refused to obtain congressional approval, it would have been interesting to see whether and how Congress would have asserted itself. There is little question, however, that Bush's decision to seek congressional approval ultimately enhanced political support for the war. The war was executed with overwhelming force, resulting in minimal losses to allied forces. Iraq, which suffered enormous losses in both life and property, capitulated quickly. In the wake of the war, President Bush's approval ratings soared to levels not seen since the end of World War II. Presidential popularity is a volatile phenomenon, however, and Bush's approval ratings dropped steadily during the remainder of 1991.

Confronting Terrorism in the Twenty-first Century

For several decades, countries around the globe have been coping with various forms of terrorism. Prior to 1993, the United States did not experience terrorism on its soil. The World Trade Center bombing of 1993, the Oklahoma City bombing of 1995, and the horrendous attacks on the World Trade Center and the Pentagon in September 2001 demonstrated America's vulnerability to terrorism. The events of September 2001, in which more than 3,000 people were killed, led President George W. Bush to proclaim a "war on terrorism." Some members of Congress called for a formal declaration of war against the terrorist organizations responsible for the September attacks. Others questioned the appropriateness of a declaration of war where no nation-state had been identified as the enemy. Responding quickly, the Bush administration sought and immediately obtained a congressional resolution authorizing the use of military force. This resolution, adopted on September 14, 2001, passed the Senate and House by votes of 98-0 and 420-1, respectively. The resolution authorized the president to

> use all necessary and appropriate force against those nations, organizations, or persons he determines planned, authorized, committed, or aided the terrorist attacks that occurred on September 11, 2001, or harbored such organizations or persons, in order to prevent any future acts of international terrorism against the United States by such nations, organizations or persons.

The resolution went far toward removing any serious questions about the legality of using military power in response to the crisis. By October 2001, American forces were in action against Osama bin Laden's al-Qaeda forces in Afghanistan and the Taliban government that provided sanctuary to these forces. President Bush asked the nation to brace for a protracted war against terrorism, a war that would be waged on numerous fronts and potentially in several countries.

Domestic Affairs during Wartime

Although there is a serious constitutional question over who has the power to make war, an equally difficult question arises over the extent of presidential power in the domestic sphere during wartime. Does the president's inherent power and duty to protect national security override express constitutional limitations and the rights of citizens? The Supreme Court's answer to the question has been mixed.

Civil War Cases One of the early cases raising the question of individual rights versus presidential power during wartime was *Ex parte Merryman* (1861). Although it was not a Supreme Court decision, it did involve Chief Justice Roger B. Taney, acting in his capacity as circuit judge. John Merryman, a resident of Maryland, was a well-known advocate of secession. Fearing that Merryman's statements and potential actions would adversely affect the Union cause, military officials arrested him under the authority of a presidential directive. As a civilian, Merryman asserted that his arrest and detention by the military were illegal. He sought a writ of habeas corpus from Chief Justice Taney, who was "riding circuit" in Baltimore at the time. Earlier, President Lincoln had issued an order authorizing military commanders to suspend habeas corpus, thus facilitating military arrest and detention of civilians. However, Chief Justice Taney believed that only Congress could suspend the habeas corpus privilege (see Article I, Section 9). Taney issued the writ ordering Merryman's release, but it was ignored at Fort McHenry, where Merryman was in custody. Infuriated, Taney wrote an indignant letter to the president. The letter was widely publicized in the press. Although Lincoln never replied directly to Taney, he did ask Congress for legislation suspending habeas corpus, and in 1863, Congress complied with this request. Eventually, Merryman was turned over to civilian authorities.

Although the *Merryman* case never reached the Supreme Court, the justices eventually had an opportunity to rule on the constitutional limits of executive power during wartime. Lambdin P. Milligan, a civilian residing in Indiana, was an active collaborator with the Confederacy. In 1864, he was arrested and tried for treason by a military commission established by order of President Lincoln. Milligan was convicted and sentenced to death, but the sentence was not carried out. In 1866, some time after hostilities had ceased, the Supreme Court reviewed the conviction. Its landmark decision in *Ex parte Milligan* was a ringing endorsement of civil liberties. The Supreme Court took note of the fact that the civilian courts were open and operating in Indiana when Milligan was arrested and tried by the military. In ordering Milligan's release, the Court condemned Lincoln's directive establishing military jurisdiction over civilians outside of the immediate war area. It strongly affirmed the fundamental right of a civilian to be tried in a regular court of law, with all the procedural safeguards that characterize the criminal process. It must be remembered that this strong assertion of constitutional principles occurred a year after the close of the Civil War and the assassination of Abraham Lincoln. Viewed in this light, *Ex parte Milligan* may be more aptly described as an admission of judicial weakness during time of war than as a bold pronouncement of constitutional limits on presidential power.

The "Relocation" of Japanese-Americans Early in the Second World War, President Roosevelt issued orders authorizing the establishment of "military areas" from which ostensibly dangerous persons could be expelled or excluded. Congressional legislation supported Roosevelt's orders by establishing criminal penalties for violators. Under these executive and congressional mandates, General J. L. DeWitt, who headed the Western Defense Command, proclaimed a curfew and issued an order excluding all Japanese-Americans from a designated West Coast military area. The exclusion order led first to the imprisonment of some 120,000 persons in barbed wire-enclosed "assembly centers." Later, these persons were removed to "relocation centers" in rural areas as far inland as Arkansas. Although these actions were defended at the time on grounds of military necessity, overwhelming evidence indicates that they were in fact based on the view that all Japanese-Americans were "subversive" members of an "enemy race." In spite of the blatant racism reflected in these policies, the Supreme Court upheld both the curfew and the exclusion order (*Hirabayashi v. United States* [1943] and *Korematsu v. United States* [1944]). While recognizing that racial classifications are inherently suspect (a term discussed in detail in Chapter 12), a majority of the justices concluded that, under the pressure of war, the government had a compelling interest justifying such extreme measures. The *Korematsu* case stands for the sobering proposition that in time of war, the Supreme Court will defer to presidential assessments of threats to national security, whether real or imaginary.

It has now been well established that the forced relocation of thousands of Japanese-Americans was not justified on grounds of military necessity and was motivated chiefly by racial animus. In 1988, Congress belatedly acknowledged the government's responsibility for this gross miscarriage of justice by awarding reparations to survivors of the internment camps. Yet, after the terrorist attacks on America in September 2001, many began to wonder whether such extreme measures might someday be employed again. How far would President Bush and the military go in the prosecution of the war on terrorism? Would the American people support infringements of the constitutional rights of Americans suspected of aiding or supporting terrorists? If so, would the courts resist such measures?

Peacetime Threats to National Security

During peacetime, presidential responses to perceived domestic threats to the national security are not as likely to win judicial approval. A good example is the

Supreme Court's decision in *United States v. U.S. District Court* (1972). Reflecting Richard Nixon's deep-seated suspicions of the motives and affiliations of political opponents, the government had engaged in extensive wiretapping and other forms of electronic surveillance directed at U.S. citizens. The Supreme Court held that these activities, which were conducted without probable cause or judicial approval, offended the Fourth Amendment prohibition against unreasonable searches. The Court rejected the Nixon administration's argument that inherent executive power permitted the government to take these actions to obtain intelligence regarding foreign agents acting in the domestic sphere. In 1978, Congress buttressed the Court's decision by adopting the Foreign Intelligence Surveillance Act, which requires government agents to obtain a search warrant before subjecting U.S. citizens to electronic surveillance for the purpose of gathering foreign intelligence.

TO SUMMARIZE:

- Although Article I grants Congress the authority to declare war, Article II recognizes the president as commander in chief.
- Historically, this role has enabled presidents to commit military forces abroad without congressional approval.
- Congress attempted to limit presidential authority in this area by enacting the War Powers Resolution in 1973. Although the Supreme Court has never ruled on the matter, the constitutionality of the War Powers Resolution has been widely questioned.
- Another difficult constitutional question involves the extent of presidential power in the domestic sphere during wartime, especially as it relates to the rights of American citizens. The Supreme Court has given mixed answers to this question.

CONCLUSION

American constitutional development has witnessed the transformation of the presidency into the most powerful executive position in the world. The American president possesses awesome powers, most notably the authority to command the world's most formidable military. Yet the presidency is not without constitutional and statutory constraints, as dictated by the principle of checks and balances. Ultimately, though, the power of the presidency is less determined by congressional or judicial action than by public opinion and world events.

Although the presidency occasionally experiences setbacks—as in the aftermath of the Iran-Contra scandal of 1986 and 1987—such reverses tend to be short-lived. The American people simply demand too much from the presidency to allow it to sink to a position of institutional inferiority. The Hamiltonian conception of the presidency has become institutionalized to the extent that neither the personality of the occupant nor the occasional crisis of credibility can produce any significant dismantling of the office.

As America wages war on terrorism, the presidency emerges once again as the preeminent branch of American government. Whether this preeminence is maintained will depend more on the vicissitudes of world events and the tides of American public opinion than on the decisions of courts of law.

KEY TERMS

Twenty-second Amendment
Electoral College
Twenty-fifth Amendment
impeachment
inherent executive power
stewardship theory
constitutional theory

presentment requirement
veto
pocket veto
line-item veto
impoundment
appointment power
removal power

presidential pardon
amnesty
executive privilege
presidential immunity
presidential power to make
  foreign policy
treaty

executive agreements
commander in chief
presidential war powers
War Powers Resolution

FOR FURTHER READING

Berger, Raoul. *Impeachment: The Constitutional Problems.* Cambridge, Mass.: Harvard University Press, 1973.

Berger, Raoul. *Executive Privilege.* Cambridge, Mass.: Harvard University Press, 1974.

Bessette, Joseph, and Jeffrey Tulis. *The Presidency in the Constitutional Order.* Baton Rouge: Louisiana State University Press, 1981.

Corwin, Edward S., et al., *The President: Office and Powers* (5th ed.). New York: New York University Press, 1984.

Crabb, Cecil V. *Invitation to Struggle: Congress, the President, and Foreign Policy* (4th ed.). Washington, D.C.: Congressional Quarterly Press, 1992.

Ely, John Hart. *War and Responsibility: Constitutional Lessons of Vietnam and Its Aftermath.* Cambridge, Mass.: Harvard University Press, 1993.

Fisher, Louis. *Presidential Spending Power.* Princeton, N.J.: Princeton University Press, 1975.

Gerhardt, Michael J. *The Federal Appointments Process: A Constitutional and Historical Analysis.* Durham, N.C.: Duke University Press, 2001.

Henkin, Louis (ed.). *Foreign Affairs and the United States Constitution.* New York: Oxford University Press, 1996.

Keynes, Edward. *Undeclared War: Twilight Zone of Constitutional Power.* University Park: Pennsylvania State University Press, 1982.

Levy, Leonard, and Louis Fisher (eds.). *The Encyclopedia of the American Presidency.* New York: Simon and Schuster, 1993.

Longley, Lawrence D., and Alan G. Braun. *The Politics of Electoral College Reform* (2nd ed.). New Haven, Conn.: Yale University Press, 1975.

McPherson, James M. *Abraham Lincoln and the Second American Revolution.* New York: Oxford University Press, 1991.

Randall, J. G. *Constitutional Problems under Lincoln* (rev. ed.). Urbana: University of Illinois Press, 1951.

Robinson, Greg. *By Order of the President : FDR and the Internment of Japanese Americans.* Cambridge, Mass.: Harvard University Press, 2001.

Schlesinger, Arthur. *The Imperial Presidency.* Boston: Houghton-Mifflin, 1973.

Sirica, John. *To Set the Record Straight: The Break-In, the Tapes, the Conspirators, the Pardon.* New York: Norton, 1979.

Westin, Alan. *The Anatomy of a Constitutional Law Case.* New York: Macmillan, 1958.

INTERNET RESOURCES

Name of Resource	Description	URL
The White House	Information on the president and vice president, events and tours at the White House, press releases, e-mail addresses, etc.; also includes links to offices within the Executive Office of the President	http://www.whitehouse.gov
Grolier Online's the American Presidency	Online history of presidents, the presidency, presidential politics, etc.	http://gi.grolier.com/presidents/preshome.html
The Center for the Study of the Presidency	An educational institution devoted to the study of the presidency and other aspects of American government and politics	http://www.cspresidency.org/
Center for Congressional and Presidential Studies	A teaching, research, and study program at American University focusing on the relationship between Congress and the presidency	http://auvm.american.edu/academic.depts/spa/ccps
Center for Presidential Studies, Policy & Governance	A research center in the Bush School of Government and Public Service at Texas A&M University	http://bush.tamu.edu/cps

Case

YOUNGSTOWN SHEET & TUBE COMPANY V. SAWYER

343 U.S. 579; 72 S.Ct. 863; 96 L.Ed. 1153 (1952)
Vote: 6–3

Mr. Justice Black delivered the opinion of the Court.

We are asked to decide whether the President was acting within his constitutional power when he issued an order directing the Secretary of Commerce to take possession of and operate most of the Nation's steel mills. The mill owners argue that the President's order amounts to lawmaking, a legislative function which the Constitution has expressly confided to the Congress and not to the President. The Government's position is that the order was made on findings of the President that his action was necessary to avert a national catastrophe which would inevitably result from a stoppage of steel production, and that in meeting this grave emergency the President was acting within the aggregate of his constitutional powers as the Nation's Chief Executive and the Commander in Chief of the Armed Forces of the United States. The issue emerges here from the following series of events:

In the latter part of 1951, a dispute arose between the steel companies and their employees over terms and conditions that should be included in new collective bargaining agreements. Long-continued conferences failed to resolve the dispute. On December 18, 1951, the employees' representative, United Steelworkers of America, C.I.O., gave notice of an intention to strike when the existing bargaining agreements expired on December 31. The Federal Mediation and Conciliation Service then intervened in an effort to get labor and management to agree. This failing, the President on December 22, 1951, referred the dispute to the Federal Wage Stabilization Board to investigate and make recommendations for fair and equitable terms of settlement. This Board's report resulted in no settlement. On April 4, 1952, the Union gave notice of a nation-wide strike called to begin at 12:01 A.M., April 9. The indispensability of steel as a component of substantially all weapons and other war materials led the President to believe that the proposed work stoppage would immediately jeopardize our national defense and that governmental seizure of the steel mills was necessary in order to assure the continued availability of steel. Reciting these considerations for his action, the President, a few hours before the strike was to begin, issued Executive Order 10340. . . . The order directed the Secretary of Commerce to take possession of most of the steel mills and keep them running. The Secretary immediately issued his own possessory orders, calling upon the presidents of the various seized companies to serve as operating managers for the United States. They were directed to carry on their activities in accordance with regulations and directions of the Secretary. The next morning the President sent a message to Congress reporting his action. . . . Twelve days later he sent a second message. . . . Congress has taken no action.

Obeying the Secretary's orders under protest, the companies brought proceedings against him in the District Court. Their complaints charged that the seizure was not authorized by an Act of Congress or by any constitutional provisions. The District Court was asked to declare the orders of the President and the Secretary invalid and to issue preliminary and permanent injunctions restraining their enforcement. Opposing the motion for preliminary injunctions, the United States asserted that a strike disrupting steel production for even a brief period would so endanger the well-being and safety of the Nation that the President had "inherent power" to do what he had done— power "supported by the Constitution, by historical precedent, and by court decisions." The Government also contended that in any event no preliminary injunction should be issued because the companies had made no showing that their available legal remedies were inadequate or that their injuries from seizure would be irreparable. Holding against the Government on all points, the District Court on April 30 issued a preliminary injunction restraining the Secretary from "continuing the seizure and possession of the plants . . . and from acting under the purported authority of Executive Order No. 10340." . . . On the same day the Court of Appeals stayed the District Court's injunction. . . . Deeming it best that the issues raised be promptly decided by this Court, we granted certiorari on May 3 and set the cause for argument on May 12. . . .

The President's power, if any, to issue the order must stem either from an act of Congress or from the Constitution itself. There is no statute that expressly authorizes the President to take possession of property as he did here. Nor is there any act of Congress to which our attention has been directed from which such a power can fairly be implied. Indeed, we do not understand the Government to rely on statutory authorization for this seizure. There are two statutes which do authorize the President to take both personal and real property under certain conditions. However, the Government admits that these conditions were not met and that the President's order was not rooted in either of the statutes. The Government refers to the seizure provisions of one of these statutes . . . (the Defense Production Act) as "much too cumbersome, involved, and time-consuming for the crisis which was at hand."

Moreover, the use of the seizure technique to solve labor disputes in order to prevent work stoppages was not only unauthorized by any congressional enactment; prior to this controversy, Congress had refused to adopt that method of settling labor disputes. When the Taft-Hartley Act was under consideration in 1947, Congress rejected an amendment which would have authorized such governmental seizures in cases of emergency. Apparently it was thought that the technique of seizure, like that of compulsory arbitration, would interfere with the process of collective bargaining. Consequently, the plan Congress adopted in that Act did not provide for seizure under any circumstances. Instead, the plan sought to bring about settlements by use of the customary devices of mediation, conciliation, investigation by boards of inquiry, and public reports. In some instances temporary injunctions were authorized to provide cooling-off periods. All this failing, unions were left free to strike after a secret vote by employees as to whether they wished to accept their employers' final settlement offer.

It is clear that if the President had authority to issue the order he did, it must be found in some provision of the Constitution. And it is not claimed that express constitutional language grants this power to the President. The contention is that presidential power should be implied from the aggregate of his powers under the Constitution. Particular reliance is placed on provisions in Article II which say that "The executive Power shall be vested in a President . . . "; that "he shall take Care that the Laws be faithfully executed"; and that he "shall be Commander in Chief of the Army and Navy of the United States."

The order cannot properly be sustained as an exercise of the President's military power as Commander in Chief of the Armed Forces. The Government attempts to do so by citing a number of cases upholding broad powers in military commanders engaged in day-to-day fighting in a theater of war. Such cases need not concern us here. Even though "theater of war" be an expanding concept, we cannot with faithfulness to our constitutional system hold that the Commander in Chief of the Armed Forces has the ultimate power as such to take possession of private property in order to keep labor disputes from stopping production. This is a job for the Nation's lawmakers, not for its military authorities.

Nor can the seizure order be sustained because of the several constitutional provisions that grant executive power to the President. In the framework of our Constitu-

tion, the President's power to see that the laws are faithfully executed refutes the idea that he is to be a lawmaker. The Constitution limits his functions in the lawmaking process to the recommending of laws he thinks wise and the vetoing of laws he thinks bad. And the Constitution is neither silent nor equivocal about who shall make laws which the President is to execute. The first section of the first article says that "All legislative Powers herein granted shall be vested in a Congress of the United States. . . ." After granting many powers to the Congress, Article I goes on to provide that Congress may "make all Laws which shall be necessary and proper for carrying into Execution the foregoing Powers, and all other Powers vested by this Constitution in the Government of the United States, or in any Department or Officer thereof."

The President's order does not direct that a congressional policy be executed in a manner prescribed by Congress—it directs that a presidential policy be executed in a manner prescribed by the President. The preamble of the order itself, like that of many statutes, sets out reasons why the President believes certain policies should be adopted, proclaims these policies as rules of conduct to be followed, and again, like a statute, authorizes a government official to promulgate additional rules and regulations consistent with the policy proclaimed and needed to carry that policy into execution. The power of Congress to adopt such public policies as those proclaimed by the order is beyond question. It can make laws regulating the relationships between employers and employees, prescribing rules designed to settle labor disputes, and fixing wages and working conditions in certain fields of our economy. The Constitution does not subject this lawmaking power of Congress to presidential or military supervision or control.

It is said that other Presidents without congressional authority have taken possession of private business enterprises in order to settle labor disputes. But even if this be true, Congress has not thereby lost its exclusive constitutional authority to make laws necessary and proper to carry out the powers vested by the Constitution "in the Government of the United States, or any Department or Officer thereof."

The Founders of this Nation entrusted the lawmaking power to the Congress alone in both good and bad times. It would do no good to recall the historical events, the fears of power and the hopes for freedom that lay behind their choice. Such a review would but confirm our holding that this seizure order cannot stand. . . .

Mr. Justice Frankfurter [concurring]. . . .

Mr. Justice Douglas, concurring. . . .

Mr. Justice Jackson, concurring in the judgment and opinion of the Court.

That comprehensive and undefined presidential powers hold both practical advantages and grave dangers for the country will impress anyone who has served as legal adviser to a President in time of transition and public anxiety. While an interval of detached reflection may temper teachings of that experience, they probably are a more realistic influence on my views than the conventional materials of judicial decision which seem unduly to accentuate doctrine and legal fiction. . . . The tendency is strong to emphasize transient results upon policies—such as wages or stabilization—and lose sight of enduring consequences upon the balanced power structure of our Republic.

A judge, like an executive advisor, may be surprised at the poverty of really useful and unambiguous authority applicable to concrete problems of executive power as they actually present themselves. Just what our forefathers did envision, or would have envisioned had they foreseen modern conditions, must be divined from materials almost as enigmatic as the dreams Joseph was called upon to interpret for Pharaoh. A century and a half of partisan debate and scholarly speculation yields no net result but only supplies more or less apt quotations from respected sources on each side of any question. They largely cancel each other. And other decisions are indecisive because of the judicial practice of dealing with the largest questions in the most narrow way.

The actual art of governing under our Constitution does not and cannot conform to judicial definitions of the power of any of its branches based on isolated clauses or even single Articles torn from context. While the Constitution diffuses power the better to secure liberty, it also contemplates that practice will integrate the dispersed powers into a workable government. It enjoins upon its branches separateness but interdependence, autonomy but reciprocity. Presidential powers are not fixed but fluctuate, depending upon their disjunction or conjunction with those of Congress. We may well begin by a somewhat over-simplified grouping of practical situations in which a President may doubt, or others may challenge, his powers, and by distinguishing roughly the legal consequences of this factor of relativity.

1. When the President acts pursuant to an express or implied authorization of Congress, his authority is at its maximum, for it includes all that he possesses in his own right plus all that Congress can delegate. In these circumstances, and in these only, may he be said (for what it may be worth) to personify the federal sovereignty. . . .

2. When the President acts in absence of either a congressional grant or denial of authority, he can only rely upon his own independent power, but there is a zone of twilight in which he and Congress may have concurrent authority, or in which its distribution is uncertain. . . . In this area, any actual test of power is likely to depend on the imperatives of events and contemporary imponderables rather than on abstract theories of law.

3. When the President takes measures incompatible with the expressed or implied will of Congress, his power is at its lowest ebb, for then he can rely only upon his own constitutional powers minus any constitutional powers of Congress over the matter. . . . Presidential claim to a power at once so conclusive and preclusive must be scrutinized with caution, for what is at stake is the equilibrium established by our constitutional system.

Into which of these classifications does this executive seizure of the steel industry fit? It is eliminated from the first by admission, for it is conceded that no congressional authorization exists for this seizure. . . .

Can it then be defended under flexible tests available to the second category? It seems clearly eliminated from that class because Congress has not left seizure of private property an open field but has covered it by three statutory policies inconsistent with this seizure. . . .

This leaves the current seizure to be justified only by the severe tests under the third grouping. . . . In short, we can sustain the President only by holding that seizure of such strike-bound industries is within his domain and beyond control by Congress. Thus, this Court's first review of such seizures occurs under circumstances which leave presidential power most vulnerable to attack and in the least favorable of possible constitutional postures.

I did not suppose, and I am not persuaded, that history leaves it open to question, at least in the courts, that the executive branch, like the Federal Government as a whole, possesses only delegated powers. . . . Some clauses could be made almost unworkable, as well as immutable, by refusal to indulge some latitude of interpretation of changing times. I have heretofore, and do now, give to the enumerated powers the scope and elasticity afforded by what seem to be reasonable, practical implications instead of the rigidity dictated by a doctrinaire textualism. . . .

[One] clause on which the Government . . . relies is that "The President shall be Commander in Chief of the Army and Navy of the United States. . . ." These cryptic words have given rise to some of the most persistent controversies in our constitutional history. Of course, they imply something more than an empty title. . . .

That military powers of the Commander in Chief were not to supersede representative government of internal affairs seems obvious from the Constitution and from elementary American history. . . .

We should not use this occasion to circumscribe, much less to contract, the lawful role of the President as Commander in Chief. I should indulge the widest latitude of interpretation to sustain his exclusive function to command the instruments of national force, at least when turned against the outside world for the security of our society. But, when it is turned inward, not because of rebellion but because of a lawful economic struggle between industry and labor, it should have no such indulgence. His command power is not such an absolute as might be implied from that office in a militaristic system but is subject to limitations consistent with a constitutional Republic whose law and policy-making branch is a representative Congress. The purpose of lodging dual titles in one man was to insure that the civilian would control the military, not to enable the military to subordinate the presidential office. No penance would ever expiate the sin against free government of holding that a President can escape control of executive powers by law through assuming his military role. What the power of command may include I do not try to envision, but I think it is not a military prerogative, without support of law, to seize persons or property because they are important or even essential for the military and naval establishment. . . .

The Solicitor General lastly grounds support of the seizure upon nebulous, inherent powers never expressly granted but said to have accrued to the office from the customs and claims of preceding administrations. The plea is for a resulting power to deal with a crisis or an emergency according to the necessities of the case, the unarticulated assumption being that necessity knows no law.

Loose and irresponsible use of adjectives colors all nonlegal and much legal discussion of presidential powers. "Inherent" powers, "implied" powers, "incidental" powers, "war" powers and "emergency" powers are used, often interchangeably and without fixed or ascertainable meanings.

The vagueness and generality of the clauses that set forth presidential powers afford a plausible basis for pressures within and without an administration for presidential action beyond that supported by those whose responsibility it is to defend his actions in court. . . .

In view of the ease, expedition and safety with which Congress can grant and has granted large emergency powers, certainly ample to embrace this crisis, I am quite unimpressed with the argument that we should affirm possession of them without statute. Such power either has no beginning or it has no end. If it exists, it need submit to no legal restraint. I am not alarmed that it would plunge us straightway into dictatorship, but it is at least a step in that wrong direction.

As to whether there is imperative necessity for such powers, it is relevant to note the gap that exists between the President's paper powers and his real powers. The Constitution does not disclose the measure of the actual controls wielded by the modern presidential office. That instrument must be understood as an eighteenth-century sketch of a government hoped for, not as a blueprint of the Government that is. Vast accretions of federal power, eroded from that reserved by the States, have magnified the scope of presidential activity. Subtle shifts take place in the centers of real power that do not show on the face of the Constitution. . . .

But I have no illusion that any decision by this Court can keep power in the hands of Congress if it is not wise and timely in meeting its problems. . . . We may say that power to legislate for emergencies belongs in the hands of Congress, but only Congress itself can prevent power from slipping through its fingers. . . .

Mr. Justice Burton, concurring. . . .

Mr. Justice Clark, concurring in the judgment of the Court. . . .

Mr. Chief Justice Vinson, with whom *Mr. Justice Reed* and *Mr. Justice Minton* join, dissenting.

. . . In passing upon the question of Presidential powers in this case, we must first consider the context in which those powers were exercised.

Those who suggest that this is a case involving extraordinary powers should be mindful that these are extraordinary times. A world not yet recovered from devastation of World War II has been forced to face the threat of another and more terrifying global conflict.

Accepting in full measure its responsibility in the world community, the United States was instrumental in securing adoption of the United Nations Charter. . . . In 1950, when the United Nations called upon member nations "to render every assistance" to repel aggression in Korea, the United States furnished its vigorous support. . . .

Further efforts to protect the free world from aggression are found in the congressional enactments of the Truman Plan for assistance to Greece and Turkey and the Marshall Plan for economic aid needed to build up the strength of our friends in Western Europe. In 1949, the Senate approved the North Atlantic Treaty under which each member nation agrees that an armed attack against one is an armed attack against all. . . . The concept of mutual security recently has been extended by treaty to friends in the Pacific. . . .

Even this brief review of our responsibilities in the world community discloses the enormity of our undertaking. Success of these measures may, as has often been observed, dramatically influence the lives of many generations of the world's peoples yet unborn. Alert to our responsibilities, which coincide with our own self-preservation through mutual security, Congress has enacted a large body of implementing legislation. . . .

[Chief Justice Vinson here discusses these legislative acts as well as the seizure authorizations included in the statutes. In addition, he chronicles instances of seizures, both based on these statutes and deriving their legitimacy from other sources.]

Focusing now on the situation confronting the President on the night of April 8, 1952, we cannot but conclude that the President was performing his duty under the Constitution to "take Care that the Laws be faithfully executed." . . .

The President reported to Congress the morning after the seizure that he acted because a work stoppage in steel production would immediately imperil the safety of the Nation by preventing execution of the legislative programs for procurement of military equipment. And, while a shutdown could be averted by granting the price concessions requested by [Youngstown Sheet & Tube Company], granting such concessions would disrupt the price stabilization program also enacted by Congress. Rather than fail to execute either legislative program, the President acted to execute both.

Much of the argument in this case has been directed at straw men. We do not now have before us the case of a President acting solely on the basis of his own notions of the public welfare. Nor is there any question of unlimited executive power in this case. The President himself closed the door to any such claim when he sent his Message to Congress stating his purpose to abide by any action of Congress, whether approving or disapproving his seizure action. Here, the President immediately made sure that Congress was fully informed of the temporary action he had taken only to preserve the legislative programs from destruction until Congress could act.

The absence of a specific statute authorizing seizure of the steel mills as a mode of executing the laws—both the military procurement program and the anti-inflation program—has not until today been thought to prevent the President from executing the laws. . . . Flexibility as to mode of execution to meet critical situations is a matter of practical necessity. . . .

[A]s of December 22, 1951, the President had a choice between alternate procedures for settling the threatened strike in the steel mills: one route [the Taft-Hartley Act] created to deal with peacetime disputes; the other route [the Defense Production Act] specially created to deal with disputes growing out of the defense and stabilization program. There is no question of bypassing a statutory procedure because both of the routes available to the President in December were based upon statutory authorization. Both routes were available in the steel dispute. The Union, by refusing to abide by the defense and stabilization program, could have forced the President to invoke Taft-Hartley at that time to delay the strike a maximum of 80 days. Instead, the Union agreed to cooperate with the defense program and submit the dispute to the Wage Stabilization Board [WSB]. . . .

When the President acted on April 8, he had exhausted the procedures for settlement available to him. Taft-Hartley was a route parallel to, not connected with, the WSB procedure. The strike had been delayed 99 days as contrasted with the maximum delay of 80 days under Taft-Hartley. There had been a hearing on the issue in dispute and bargaining which promised settlement up to the very hour before seizure had broken down. Faced with immediate national peril through stoppage in steel production on the one hand and faced with destruction of the wage and price legislative programs on the other, the President took temporary possession of the steel mills as the only course open to him consistent with his duty to take care that the laws be faithfully executed.

. . . The President's action has thus far been effective, not in settling the dispute, but in saving the various legislative programs at stake from destruction until Congress could act in the matter.

The diversity of views expressed in the six opinions of the majority, the lack of reference to authoritative precedent, the repeated reliance upon prior dissenting opinions, the complete disregard of the uncontroverted facts showing the gravity of the emergency and the temporary nature of the taking all serve to demonstrate how far afield one must go to affirm the order of the District Court.

The broad executive power granted by Article II to an officer on duty 365 days a year cannot, it is said, be invoked to avert disaster. Instead, the President must confine himself to sending a message to Congress recommending action. Under this messenger-boy concept of the Office, the President cannot even act to preserve legislative programs from destruction so that Congress will have something left to act upon. There is no judicial finding that the executive action was unwarranted because there was in fact no basis for the President's finding of the existence of an emergency for, under this view, the gravity of the emergency and the immediacy of the threatened disaster are considered irrelevant as a matter of law.

Seizure of [the steel companies'] property is not a pleasant undertaking. Similarly unpleasant to a free country are the draft which disrupts the home and military procurement which causes economic dislocation and compels adoption of price controls, wage stabilization and allocation of materials. The President informed Congress that even a temporary Government operation of [the steel mills] was "thoroughly distasteful" to him, but was necessary to prevent immediate paralysis of the mobilization program. Presidents have been in the past, and any man worthy of the Office should be in the future, free to take at least interim action necessary to execute legislative programs essential to survival of the Nation. A sturdy judiciary should not be swayed by the unpleasantness or unpopularity of necessary executive action, but must independently determine for itself whether the President was acting, as required by the Constitution, to "take Care that the Laws be faithfully executed."

As the District Judge stated, this is no time for "timorous" judicial action. But neither is this a time for timorous executive action. Faced with the duty of executing the defense programs which Congress had enacted and the disastrous effects that any stoppage in steel production would have on these programs, the President acted to preserve those programs by seizing the steel mills. There is no question that the possession was other than temporary in character and subject to congressional direction—either approving, disapproving or regulating the manner in which the mills were to be administered and returned to the owners. The President immediately informed Congress of his action and clearly stated his intention to abide by the legislative will. No basis for claims of arbitrary action, unlimited powers or dictatorial usurpation of congressional power appears from the facts of this case. On the contrary, judicial, legislative and executive precedents throughout our history demonstrate that in this case the President acted in full conformity with his duties under the Constitution. Accordingly, we would reverse the order of the District Court.

Case

CLINTON V. CITY OF NEW YORK

524 U.S. 417; 118 S.Ct. 2091; 141 L.Ed. 2d 393 (1998)
Vote: 6–3

In 1996 Congress enacted legislation authorizing the President to exercise a line-item veto over spending. In Raines v. Byrd (1997), the Supreme Court ruled that members of Congress who opposed the line-item veto law lacked standing to challenge its constitutionality. In the instant case, the Court holds that different plaintiffs, whose interests were adversely affected by President Clinton's exercise of the item veto, have standing to sue. Moreover, the Court declares the statute invalid under the Presentment Clause (Article I, Section 7, clause 2) of the Constitution.

Justice Stevens delivered the opinion of the Court.

. . . The Line Item Veto Act gives the President the power to "cancel in whole" three types of provisions that have been signed into law: "(1) any dollar amount of discretionary budget authority; (2) any item of new direct spending; or (3) any limited tax benefit." . . .

The Act requires the President to adhere to precise procedures whenever he exercises his cancellation authority. In identifying items for cancellation he must consider the legislative history, the purposes, and other relevant information about the items. . . . He must determine, with respect to each cancellation, that it will "(i) reduce the Federal budget deficit; (ii) not impair any essential Government functions; and (iii) not harm the national interest." . . . Moreover, he must transmit a special message to Congress notifying it of each cancellation within five calendar days (excluding Sundays) after the enactment of the canceled provision. . . . It is undisputed that the President meticulously followed these procedures in these cases.

A cancellation takes effect upon receipt by Congress of the special message from the President. . . . If, however, a "disapproval bill" pertaining to a special message is enacted into law, the cancellations set forth in that message become "null and void." . . . The Act sets forth a detailed expedited procedure for the consideration of a "disapproval bill," . . . but no such bill was passed for either of the cancellations involved in these cases.

A majority vote of both Houses is sufficient to enact a disapproval bill. The Act does not grant the President the authority to cancel a disapproval bill, . . . but he does, of course, retain his constitutional authority to veto such a bill.

The effect of a cancellation is plainly stated in § 691e, which defines the principal terms used in the Act. With respect to both an item of new direct spending and a limited tax benefit, the cancellation prevents the item "from having legal force or effect." . . .

Thus, under the plain text of the statute, the two actions of the President that are challenged in these cases prevented one section of the Balanced Budget Act of 1997 and one section of the Taxpayer Relief Act of 1997 "from having legal force or effect." The remaining provisions of those statutes, with the exception of the second canceled item in the latter, continue to have the same force and effect as they had when signed into law.

In both legal and practical effect, the President has amended two Acts of Congress by repealing a portion of each. "[R]epeal of statutes, no less than enactment, must conform with Art. I." . . . There is no provision in the Constitution that authorizes the President to enact, to amend, or to repeal statutes. Both Article I and Article II assign responsibilities to the President that directly relate to the lawmaking process, but neither addresses the issue presented by these cases. The President "shall from time to time give to the Congress Information on the State of the Union, and recommend to their Consideration such Measures as he shall judge necessary and expedient. . . ." . . . Thus, he may initiate and influence legislative proposals. Moreover, after a bill has passed both Houses of Congress, but "before it become[s] a Law," it must be presented to the President. If he approves it, "he shall sign it, but if not he shall return it, with his Objections to that House in which it shall have originated, who shall enter the Objections at large on their Journal, and proceed to reconsider it." . . .

His "return" of a bill, which is usually described as a "veto," is subject to being overridden by a two-thirds vote in each House.

There are important differences between the President's "return" of a bill pursuant to Article I, § 7, and the exercise of the President's cancellation authority pursuant to the Line Item Veto Act. The constitutional return takes place before the bill becomes law; the statutory cancellation occurs after the bill becomes law. The constitutional return is of the entire bill; the statutory cancellation is of only a part. Although the Constitution expressly authorizes the President to play a role in the process of enacting statutes, it is silent on the subject of unilateral presidential action that either repeals or amends parts of duly enacted statutes.

There are powerful reasons for construing constitutional silence on this profoundly important issue as equivalent to an express prohibition. The procedures governing the enactment of statutes set forth in the text of Article I were the product of the great debates and compromises that produced the Constitution itself. Familiar historical materials provide abundant support for the conclusion that the power to enact statutes may only "be exercised in accord with a single, finely wrought and exhaustively considered, procedure." . . . Our first President understood the text of the Presentment Clause as requiring that he either "approve all the parts of a Bill, or reject it in toto."

What has emerged in these cases from the President's exercise of his statutory cancellation powers, however, are truncated versions of two bills that passed both Houses of Congress. They are not the product of the "finely wrought" procedure that the Framers designed.

. . . [W]e express no opinion about the wisdom of the procedures authorized by the Line Item Veto Act. Many members of both major political parties who have served in the Legislative and the Executive Branches have long advocated the enactment of such procedures for the purpose of "ensur[ing] greater fiscal accountability in Washington." . . .

The text of the Act was itself the product of much debate and deliberation in both Houses of Congress and that precise text was signed into law by the President. We do not lightly conclude that their action was unauthorized by the Constitution. . . .

We have, however, twice had full argument and briefing on the question and have concluded that our duty is clear.

If there is to be a new procedure in which the President will play a different role in determining the final text of what may "become a law," such change must come not by legislation but through the amendment procedures set forth in Article V of the Constitution. . . .

Justice Kennedy, concurring. . . .

Justice Breyer, with whom *Justice O'Connor* and *Justice Scalia* join as to Part III, dissenting.

. . . In my view the Line Item Veto Act does not violate any specific textual constitutional command, nor does it violate any implicit Separation of Powers principle. Consequently, I believe that the Act is constitutional. . . .

The Court believes that the Act violates the literal text of the Constitution. A simple syllogism captures its basic reasoning:

Major Premise: The Constitution sets forth an exclusive method for enacting, repealing, or amending laws. . . . Minor Premise: The Act authorizes the President to "repea[l] or amen[d]" laws in a different way, namely by announcing a cancellation of a portion of a previously enacted law. . . . Conclusion: The Act is inconsistent with the Constitution. . . .

I find this syllogism unconvincing, however, because its Minor Premise is faulty. When the President "canceled" the two appropriation measures now before us, he did not repeal any law nor did he amend any law. He simply followed the law, leaving the statutes, as they are literally written, intact. . . .

Because I disagree with the Court's holding of literal violation, I must consider whether the Act nonetheless violates Separation of Powers principles. . . . There are three relevant Separation of Powers questions here: (1) Has Congress given the President the wrong kind of power, i.e., "non-Executive" power? (2) Has Congress given the President the power to "encroach" upon Congress' own constitutionally reserved territory? (3) Has Congress given the President too much power, violating the doctrine of "nondelegation?" . . . [W]ith respect to this Act, the answer to all these questions is "no."

In sum, I recognize that the Act before us is novel. In a sense, it skirts a constitutional edge. But that edge has to do with means, not ends. The means chosen do not amount literally to the enactment, repeal, or amendment of a law. Nor, for that matter, do they amount literally to the "line item veto" that the Act's title announces. Those means do not violate any basic Separation of Powers principle. They do not improperly shift the constitutionally foreseen balance of power from Congress to the President. Nor, since they comply with Separation of Powers principles, do they threaten the liberties of individual citizens. They represent an experiment that may, or may not, help representative government work better. The Constitution, in my view, authorizes Congress and the President to try novel methods in this way. Consequently, with respect, I dissent.

Justice Scalia, with whom *Justice O'Connor* joins, and with whom *Justice Breyer* joins as to Part III, concurring in part and dissenting in part. . . .

Case

UNITED STATES V. NIXON

418 U.S. 683; 94 S.Ct. 3090; 41 L.Ed. 2d 1039 (1974)

Vote: 8–0

In this celebrated decision that spelled the end of the Nixon presidency, the Supreme Court considers the scope of executive privilege.

Mr. Chief Justice Burger delivered the opinion of the Court.

. . . [This case presents] for review the denial of a motion, filed on behalf of the President of the United States, . . . to quash a third-party *subpoena duces tecum* issued by the United States District Court for the District of Columbia. . . . The subpoena directed the President to produce certain tape recordings and documents relating to his conversations with aides and advisers. The court rejected the President's claims of absolute executive privilege, of lack of jurisdiction. . . . The President appealed to the Court of Appeals. We granted the United States' petition for certiorari before judgment . . . because of the public importance of the issues presented and the need for their prompt resolution. . . .

. . . [W]e turn to the claim that the subpoena should be quashed because it demands "confidential conversations between a President and his close advisers that it would be inconsistent with the public interest to produce." . . . The first contention is a broad claim that the separation of powers doctrine precludes judicial review of a President's claim of privilege. The second contention is that if he does not prevail on the claim of absolute privilege, the court should hold as a matter of constitutional law that the privilege prevails over the *subpoena duces tecum*.

In the performance of assigned constitutional duties each branch of the Government must initially interpret the Constitution, and the interpretation of its power by any branch is due great respect from the others. The President's counsel, as we have noted, reads the Constitution as providing an absolute privilege of confidentiality for all presidential communications. Many decisions of this Court, however, have unequivocally reaffirmed the holding of *Marbury v. Madison* . . . that "[i]t is emphatically the province and duty of the judicial department to say what the law is." . . .

No holding of the Court has defined the scope of judicial power specifically relating to the enforcement of a subpoena for confidential presidential communications for use in a criminal prosecution, but other exercises of powers by the Executive Branch and the Legislative Branch have been found invalid as in conflict with the Constitution. . . . Since this Court has consistently exercised the power to construe and delineate claims arising under express powers, it must follow that the Court has authority to interpret claims with respect to powers alleged to derive from enumerated powers.

Our system of government "requires that federal courts on occasion interpret the Constitution in a manner at variance with the construction given the document by another branch." . . .

Notwithstanding the deference each branch must accord the others, the "judicial power of the United States" vested in the federal courts by Art. III, Sec. 1 of the

Constitution can no more be shared with the Executive Branch than the Chief Executive, for example, can share with the Judiciary the veto power, or the Congress share with the Judiciary the power to override a Presidential veto. Any other conclusion would be contrary to the basic concept of separation of powers and the checks and balances that flow from the scheme of a tripartite government. . . . We therefore reaffirm that it is the province and the duty of this Court "to say what the law is" with respect to the claim of privilege presented in this case. . . .

In support of his claim of absolute privilege, the President's counsel urges two grounds, one of which is common to all governments and one of which is peculiar to our system of separation of powers. The first ground is the valid need for protection of communications between high government officials and those who advise and assist them in the performance of their manifold duties; the importance of this confidentiality is too plain to require further discussion. Human experience teaches that those who expect public dissemination of their remarks may well temper candor with a concern for appearances and for their own interests to the detriment of the decisionmaking process. Whatever the nature of the privilege of confidentiality of presidential communications in the exercise of Art. II powers, the privilege can be said to derive from the supremacy of each branch within its own assigned area of constitutional duties. Certain powers and privileges flow from the nature of enumerated powers; the protection of confidentiality of Presidential communications has similar constitutional underpinnings.

The second ground asserted by the President's counsel in support of the claim of absolute privilege rests on the doctrine of separation of powers. Here it is argued that the independence of the Executive Branch within its own sphere . . . insulates a president from a judicial subpoena in an ongoing criminal prosecution, and thereby protects confidential presidential communications.

However, neither the doctrine of separation of powers, nor the need for confidentiality of high level communications, without more, can sustain an absolute, unqualified presidential privilege of immunity from judicial process under all circumstances. The President's need for complete candor and objectivity from advisers calls for great deference from the courts. However, when the privilege depends solely on the broad, undifferentiated claim of public interest in the confidentiality of such conversations, a confrontation with other values arises. Absent a claim of need to protect military, diplomatic or sensitive national security secrets, we find it difficult to accept the argument that even the very important interest in confidentiality of presidential communications is significantly diminished by production of such material for in camera inspection with all the protection that a district court will be obliged to provide.

The impediment that an absolute, unqualified privilege would place in the way of the primary constitutional duty of the Judicial Branch to do justice in criminal prosecutions would plainly conflict with the function of the courts under Art. III. In designing the structure of our Government and dividing and allocating the sovereign power among three co-equal branches, the Framers of the Constitution sought to provide a comprehensive system, but the separate powers were not intended to operate with absolute independence. . . . To read the Art. II powers of the President as providing an absolute privilege as against a subpoena essential to enforcement of criminal statutes on no more than a generalized claim of the public interest in confidentiality of nonmilitary and nondiplomatic discussions would upset the constitutional balance of "a workable government" and gravely impair the role of the courts under Art. III.

Since we conclude that the legitimate needs of the judicial process may outweigh presidential privilege, it is necessary to resolve those competing interests in a manner that preserves the essential functions of each branch. The right and indeed the duty to resolve that question does not free the judiciary from according high respect to the representations made on behalf of the President. . . .

The expectation of a President to the confidentiality of his conversations and correspondence, like the claim of confidentiality of judicial deliberations, for example, has all the values to which we accord deference for the privacy of all citizens and added to those values the necessity for protection of the public interest in candid, objective, and even blunt or harsh opinions in presidential decision making. A President and those who assist him must be free to explore alternatives in the process of shaping policies and making decisions and to do so in a way many would be unwilling to express except privately. These are the considerations justifying a presumptive privilege for presidential communications. The privilege is fundamental to the operation of government and inextricably rooted in the separation of powers under the Constitution. . . .

But this presumptive privilege must be considered in light of our historic commitment to the rule of law. . . . We have elected to employ an adversary system of criminal justice in which the parties contest all issues before a court of law. The need to develop all relevant facts in the adversary system is both fundamental and comprehensive. The ends of criminal justice would be defeated if judgments were to be founded on a partial or speculative presentation of the facts. The very integrity of the judicial system and public confidence in the system depend on full disclosure of all the facts, within the framework of the rules of evidence. To ensure that justice is done, it is imperative to the function of courts that compulsory process be available for the production of evidence needed either by the prosecution or by the defense. . . .

In this case the President challenges a subpoena served on him as a third party requiring the production of materials for use in a criminal prosecution on the claim that he has a privilege against disclosure of confidential communications. He does not place his claim of privilege on the ground they are military or diplomatic secrets. As to these areas of Art. II duties the courts have traditionally shown the utmost deference to presidential responsibilities. . . . No case of the Court, however, has extended this high degree of deference to a President's generalized interest in confidentiality. Nowhere in the Constitution, as we have noted earlier, is there any explicit reference to a privilege of confidentiality, yet to the extent this interest relates to the effective discharge of a President's powers, it is constitutionally based.

The right to the production of all evidence at a criminal trial similarly has constitutional dimensions. The Sixth Amendment explicitly confers upon every defendant in a criminal trial the right "to be confronted with the witnesses against him" and "to have compulsory process for obtaining witnesses in his favor." Moreover, the Fifth Amendment also guarantees that no person shall be deprived of liberty without due process of law. It is the manifest duty of the courts to vindicate those guarantees and to accomplish that it is essential that all relevant and admissible evidence be produced.

In this case we must weigh the importance of the general privilege of confidentiality of presidential communications in performance of his responsibilities against the inroads of such a privilege on the fair administration of criminal justice. The interest in preserving confidentiality is weighty indeed and entitled to great respect. However, we cannot conclude that advisers will be moved to temper the candor of their remarks by the infrequent occasions of disclosure because of the possibility that such conversations will be called for in the context of a criminal prosecution.

On the other hand, the allowance of the privilege to withhold evidence that is demonstrably relevant in a criminal trial would cut deeply into the guarantee of due process of law and gravely impair the basic function of the courts. A President's acknowledged need for confidentiality in the communications of his office is general in nature, whereas the constitutional need for production of relevant evidence in a criminal proceeding is specific and central to the fair adjudication of a particular criminal case in the administration of justice. Without access to specific facts a criminal prosecution may be totally frustrated. The President's broad interest in confidentiality of communications will not be vitiated by disclosure of a limited number of conversations preliminarily shown to have some bearing on the pending criminal cases.

We conclude that when the ground for asserting privilege as to subpoenaed materials sought for use in a criminal trial is based only on the generalized interest in confidentiality, it cannot prevail over the fundamental demands of due process of law in the fair administration of criminal justice. The generalized assertion of privilege must yield to the demonstrated, specific need for evidence in a pending criminal trial. . . .

[*Justice Rehnquist* did not participate in this decision.]

Case

CLINTON V. JONES

520 U.S. 681; 117 S.Ct. 1636; 137 L.Ed. 2d 945 (1997)
Vote: 9–0

In this case the Court considers the issue of presidential immunity in the context of a sexual harassment suit brought against President Bill Clinton, stemming from alleged conduct while he was governor of Arkansas.

Justice Stevens delivered the opinion of the Court.

This case raises a constitutional and a prudential question concerning the Office of the President of the United States. Respondent, a private citizen, seeks to recover damages from the current occupant of that office based on actions allegedly taken before his term began. The President submits that in all but the most exceptional cases the Constitution requires federal courts to defer such litigation until his term ends and that, in any event, respect for the office warrants such a stay. Despite the force of the arguments supporting the President's submissions, we conclude that they must be rejected.

Petitioner, William Jefferson Clinton, was elected to the Presidency in 1992, and re-elected in 1996. His term of office expires on January 20, 2001. In 1991 he was the Governor of the State of Arkansas. Respondent, Paula

Corbin Jones, is a resident of California. In 1991 she lived in Arkansas, and was an employee of the Arkansas Industrial Development Commission.

On May 6, 1994, she commenced this action in the United States District Court for the Eastern District of Arkansas by filing a complaint naming petitioner and Danny Ferguson, a former Arkansas State Police officer, as defendants. The complaint alleges two federal claims, and two state law claims over which the federal court has jurisdiction because of the diverse citizenship of the parties. As the case comes to us, we are required to assume the truth of the detailed but as yet untested factual allegations in the complaint.

Those allegations principally describe events that are said to have occurred on the afternoon of May 8, 1991, during an official conference held at the Excelsior Hotel in Little Rock, Arkansas. The Governor delivered a speech at the conference; respondent working as a state employee staffed the registration desk. She alleges that Ferguson persuaded her to leave her desk and to visit the Governor in a business suite at the hotel, where he made "abhorrent" sexual advances that she vehemently rejected. She further claims that her superiors at work subsequently dealt with her in a hostile and rude manner, and changed her duties to punish her for rejecting those advances. Finally, she alleges that after petitioner was elected President, Ferguson defamed her by making a statement to a reporter that implied she had accepted petitioner's alleged overtures, and that various persons authorized to speak for the President publicly branded her a liar by denying that the incident had occurred.

Respondent seeks actual damages of $75,000, and punitive damages of $100,000. Her complaint contains four counts. The first charges that petitioner, acting under color of state law, deprived her of rights protected by the Constitution. . . . The second charges that petitioner and Ferguson engaged in a conspiracy to violate her federal rights, also actionable under federal law. . . . The third is a state common law claim for intentional infliction of emotional distress, grounded primarily on the incident at the hotel. The fourth count, also based on state law, is for defamation, embracing both the comments allegedly made to the press by Ferguson and the statements of petitioner's agents. Inasmuch as the legal sufficiency of the claims has not yet been challenged, we assume, without deciding, that each of the four counts states a cause of action as a matter of law. With the exception of the last charge, which arguably may involve conduct within the outer perimeter of the President's official responsibilities,

it is perfectly clear that the alleged misconduct of petitioner was unrelated to any of his official duties as President of the United States and, indeed, occurred before he was elected to that office.

In response to the complaint, petitioner promptly advised the District Court that he intended to file a motion to dismiss on grounds of Presidential immunity, and requested the court to defer all other pleadings and motions until after the immunity issue was resolved. . . .

The District Judge denied the motion to dismiss on immunity grounds and ruled that discovery in the case could go forward, but ordered any trial stayed until the end of petitioner's Presidency. . . .

Both parties appealed. A divided panel of the Court of Appeals affirmed the denial of the motion to dismiss, but because it regarded the order postponing the trial until the President leaves office as the "functional equivalent" of a grant of temporary immunity, it reversed that order. . . .

The President, represented by private counsel, filed a petition for certiorari. The Solicitor General, representing the United States, supported the petition, arguing that the decision of the Court of Appeals was "fundamentally mistaken" and created "serious risks for the institution of the Presidency." In her brief in opposition to certiorari, respondent argued that this "one-of-a-kind case is singularly inappropriate" for the exercise of our certiorari jurisdiction because it did not create any conflict among the Courts of Appeals, it "does not pose any conceivable threat to the functioning of the Executive Branch," and there is no precedent supporting the President's position.

While our decision to grant the petition expressed no judgment concerning the merits of the case, it does reflect our appraisal of its importance. The representations made on behalf of the Executive Branch as to the potential impact of the precedent established by the Court of Appeals merit our respectful and deliberate consideration. . . .

Petitioner's principal submission that "in all but the most exceptional cases," . . . the Constitution affords the President temporary immunity from civil damages litigation arising out of events that occurred before he took office cannot be sustained on the basis of precedent.

Only three sitting Presidents have been defendants in civil litigation involving their actions prior to taking office. Complaints against Theodore Roosevelt and Harry Truman had been dismissed before they took office; the dismissals were affirmed after their respective inaugurations. Two companion cases arising out of an automobile accident were filed against John F. Kennedy in 1960 during the Presidential campaign. After taking office, he unsuccessfully argued that his status as Commander in Chief gave him a right to a stay under the Soldiers' and Sailors' Civil Relief Act of 1940. . . . The motion for a stay was denied by the District Court, and the matter was settled out of court. Thus, none of those cases sheds any light on the constitutional issue before us.

The principal rationale for affording certain public servants immunity from suits for money damages arising out of their official acts is inapplicable to unofficial conduct. In cases involving prosecutors, legislators, and judges we have repeatedly explained that the immunity serves the public interest in enabling such officials to perform their designated functions effectively without fear that a particular decision may give rise to personal liability. . . .

. . . [W]hen defining the scope of an immunity for acts clearly taken within an official capacity, we have applied a functional approach. "Frequently our decisions have held that an official's absolute immunity should extend only to acts in performance of particular functions of his office." . . . Hence, for example, a judge's absolute immunity does not extend to actions performed in a purely administrative capacity. . . . As our opinions have made clear, immunities are grounded in "the nature of the function performed, not the identity of the actor who performed it." . . .

Petitioner's effort to construct an immunity from suit for unofficial acts grounded purely in the identity of his office is unsupported by precedent.

Petitioner's strongest argument supporting his immunity claim is based on the text and structure of the Constitution. He does not contend that the occupant of the Office of the President is "above the law," in the sense that his conduct is entirely immune from judicial scrutiny. The President argues merely for a postponement of the judicial proceedings that will determine whether he violated any law. His argument is grounded in the character of the office that was created by Article II of the Constitution, and relies on separation of powers principles that have structured our constitutional arrangement since the founding.

As a starting premise, petitioner contends that he occupies a unique office with powers and responsibilities so vast and important that the public interest demands that he devote his undivided time and attention to his public duties. He submits that given the nature of the office the doctrine of separation of powers places limits on the authority of the Federal Judiciary to interfere with the Executive Branch that would be transgressed by allowing this action to proceed.

We have no dispute with the initial premise of the argument. . . .

It does not follow, however, that separation of powers principles would be violated by allowing this action to proceed. The doctrine of separation of powers is concerned with the allocation of official power among the three co-equal branches of our Government. The Framers "built into the tripartite Federal Government . . . a self-executing safeguard against the encroachment or aggrandizement of one branch at the expense of the other." . . . Thus, for example, the Congress may not exercise the judicial power to revise final judgments, . . . or the executive power to manage an airport. . . . Similarly, the President may not exercise the legislative power to authorize the seizure of private property for public use. . . . And, the judicial power to decide cases and controversies does not include the provision of purely advisory opinions to the Executive, or permit the federal courts to resolve nonjusticiable questions. Of course the lines between the powers of the three branches are not always neatly defined. . . . But in this case there is no suggestion that the Federal Judiciary is being asked to perform any function that might in some way be described as "executive." Respondent is merely asking the courts to exercise their core Article III jurisdiction to decide cases and controversies. Whatever the outcome of this case, there is no possibility that the decision will curtail the scope of the official powers of the Executive Branch. The litigation of questions that relate entirely to the unofficial conduct of the individual who happens to be the President poses no perceptible risk of misallocation of either judicial power or executive power.

Rather than arguing that the decision of the case will produce either an aggrandizement of judicial power or a narrowing of executive power, petitioner contends that as a by-product of an otherwise traditional exercise of judicial power burdens will be placed on the President that will hamper the performance of his official duties. We have recognized that "[e]ven when a branch does not arrogate power to itself . . . the separation-of-powers doctrine requires that a branch not impair another in the performance of its constitutional duties." . . . As a factual matter, petitioner contends that this particular case as well as the potential additional litigation that an affirmance of the Court of Appeals judgment might spawn may impose an unacceptable burden on the President's time and energy, and thereby impair the effective performance of his office.

Petitioner's predictive judgment finds little support in either history or the relatively narrow compass of the issues raised in this particular case. As we have already noted, in the more than 200-year history of the Republic, only three sitting Presidents have been subjected to suits for their private actions. . . . If the past is any indicator, it seems unlikely that a deluge of such litigation will ever engulf the Presidency. As for the case at hand, if properly managed by the District Court, it appears to us highly unlikely to occupy any substantial amount of petitioner's time.

Of greater significance, petitioner errs by presuming that interactions between the Judicial Branch and the Executive, even quite burdensome interactions, necessarily rise to the level of constitutionally forbidden impairment of the Executive's ability to perform its constitutionally mandated functions. . . . The fact that a federal court's exercise of its traditional Article III jurisdiction may significantly burden the time and attention of the Chief Executive is not sufficient to establish a violation of the Constitution. Two long-settled propositions, first announced by Chief Justice Marshall, support that conclusion.

First, we have long held that when the President takes official action, the Court has the authority to determine whether he has acted within the law. Perhaps the most dramatic example of such a case is our holding that President Truman exceeded his constitutional authority when he issued an order directing the Secretary of Commerce to take possession of and operate most of the Nation's steel mills in order to avert a national catastrophe. . . . Despite the serious impact of that decision on the ability of the Executive Branch to accomplish its assigned mission, and the substantial time that the President must necessarily have devoted to the matter as a result of judicial involvement, we exercised our Article III jurisdiction to decide whether his official conduct conformed to the law. Our holding was an application of the principle established in *Marbury v. Madison* . . . (1803), that "[i]t is emphatically the province and duty of the judicial department to say what the law is." . . .

Second, it is also settled that the President is subject to judicial process in appropriate circumstances. Although Thomas Jefferson apparently thought otherwise, Chief Justice Marshall, when presiding in the treason trial of Aaron Burr, ruled that a *subpoena duces tecum* could be directed to the President. . . . We unequivocally and emphatically endorsed Marshall's position when we held that President Nixon was obligated to comply with a subpoena commanding him to produce certain tape recordings of his conversations with his aides. . . . Sitting Presidents have responded to court orders to provide testimony and other information with sufficient frequency that such interactions between the Judicial and Executive Branches can scarcely be thought a novelty. . . .

If the Judiciary may severely burden the Executive Branch by reviewing the legality of the President's official conduct, and if it may direct appropriate process to the President himself, it must follow that the federal courts have power to determine the legality of his unofficial conduct. The burden on the President's time and energy that is a mere by-product of such review surely cannot be considered as onerous as the direct burden imposed by judicial review and the occasional invalidation of his official actions. We therefore hold that the doctrine of separation of powers does not require federal courts to stay all private actions against the President until he leaves office.

The reasons for rejecting such a categorical rule apply as well to a rule that would require a stay "in all but the most exceptional cases." . . . Indeed, if the Framers of the Constitution had thought it necessary to protect the President from the burdens of private litigation, we think it far more likely that they would have adopted a categorical rule than a rule that required the President to litigate the question whether a specific case belonged in the "exceptional case" subcategory. In all events, the question whether a specific case should receive exceptional treatment is more appropriately the subject of the exercise of judicial discretion than an interpretation of the Constitution. Accordingly, we turn to the question whether the District Court's decision to stay the trial until after petitioner leaves office was an abuse of discretion.

The Court of Appeals described the District Court's discretionary decision to stay the trial as the "functional equivalent" of a grant of temporary immunity. . . . Concluding that petitioner was not constitutionally entitled to such an immunity, the court held that it was error to grant the stay. . . . Although we ultimately conclude that the stay should not have been granted, we think the issue is more difficult than the opinion of the Court of Appeals suggests.

Strictly speaking the stay was not the functional equivalent of the constitutional immunity that petitioner claimed, because the District Court ordered discovery to proceed. Moreover, a stay of either the trial or discovery might be justified by considerations that do not require the recognition of any constitutional immunity. The District Court has broad discretion to stay proceedings as an incident to its power to control its own docket. . . . As we have explained, "[e]specially in cases of extraordinary public moment, [a plaintiff] may be required to submit to delay not immoderate in extent and not oppressive in its consequences if the public welfare or convenience will thereby be promoted." . . . Although we have rejected the argument that the potential burdens on the President violate separation of powers principles, those burdens are appropriate matters for the District Court to evaluate in its management of the case. The high respect that is owed to the office of the Chief Executive, though not justifying a rule of categorical immunity, is a matter that should inform the conduct of the entire proceeding, including the timing and scope of discovery. Nevertheless, we are persuaded that it was an abuse of discretion for the District Court to defer the trial until after the President leaves office. Such a lengthy and categorical stay takes no account whatever of the respondent's interest in bringing the case to trial. The complaint was filed within the statutory limitations period albeit near the end of that period and delaying trial would increase the danger of prejudice resulting from the loss of evidence, including the inability of witnesses to recall specific facts, or the possible death of a party.

The decision to postpone the trial was, furthermore, premature. The proponent of a stay bears the burden of establishing its need. . . . In this case, at the stage at which the District Court made its ruling, there was no way to assess whether a stay of trial after the completion of discovery would be warranted. Other than the fact that a trial may consume some of the President's time and attention, there is nothing in the record to enable a judge to assess the potential harm that may ensue from scheduling the trial promptly after discovery is concluded. We think the District Court may have given undue weight to the concern that a trial might generate unrelated civil actions that could conceivably hamper the President in conducting the duties of his office. If and when that should occur, the court's discretion would permit it to manage those actions in such fashion (including deferral of trial) that interference with the President's duties would not occur. But no such impingement upon the President's conduct of his office was shown here.

We add a final comment on two matters that are discussed at length in the briefs: the risk that our decision will generate a large volume of politically motivated harassing and frivolous litigation, and the danger that national security concerns might prevent the President from explaining a legitimate need for a continuance.

We are not persuaded that either of these risks is serious. Most frivolous and vexatious litigation is terminated at the pleading stage or on summary judgment, with little if any personal involvement by the defendant. . . . Moreover, the availability of sanctions provides a significant deterrent to litigation directed at the President in his unofficial capacity for purposes of political gain or harassment. History indicates that the likelihood that a significant number of such cases will be filed is remote. Although scheduling problems may arise, there is no rea-

son to assume that the District Courts will be either unable to accommodate the President's needs or unfaithful to the tradition especially in matters involving national security of giving "the utmost deference to Presidential responsibilities." Several Presidents, including petitioner, have given testimony without jeopardizing the Nation's security. . . . In short, we have confidence in the ability of our federal judges to deal with both of these concerns.

If Congress deems it appropriate to afford the President stronger protection, it may respond with appropriate legislation. . . .

As petitioner notes in his brief, Congress has enacted more than one statute providing for the deferral of civil litigation to accommodate important public interests. . . . If the Constitution embodied the rule that the President advocates, Congress, of course, could not repeal it. But our holding today raises no barrier to a statutory response to these concerns.

The Federal District Court has jurisdiction to decide this case. Like every other citizen who properly invokes that jurisdiction, respondent has a right to an orderly disposition of her claims. Accordingly, the judgment of the Court of Appeals is affirmed.

Justice Breyer, concurring in the judgment.

I agree with the majority that the Constitution does not automatically grant the President an immunity from civil lawsuits based upon his private conduct. Nor does the "doctrine of separation of powers . . . require federal courts to stay" virtually "all private actions against the President until he leaves office." . . . Rather, as the Court of Appeals stated, the President cannot simply rest upon the claim that a private civil lawsuit for damages will "interfere with the constitutionally assigned duties of the Executive Branch . . . without detailing any specific responsibilities or explaining how or the degree to which they are affected by the suit." . . . To obtain a postponement the President must "bea[r] the burden of establishing its need." . . .

In my view, however, once the President sets forth and explains a conflict between judicial proceeding and public duties, the matter changes. At that point, the Constitution permits a judge to schedule a trial in an ordinary civil damages action (where postponement normally is possible without overwhelming damage to a plaintiff) only within the constraints of a constitutional principle—a principle that forbids a federal judge in such a case to interfere with the President's discharge of his public duties. I have no doubt that the Constitution contains such a principle applicable to civil suits, based upon Article II's vesting of the entire "executive Power" in a single individual, implemented through the Constitution's structural separation of powers, and revealed both by history and case precedent.

I recognize that this case does not require us now to apply the principle specifically, thereby delineating its contours; nor need we now decide whether lower courts are to apply it directly or categorically through the use of presumptions or rules of administration. Yet I fear that to disregard it now may appear to deny it. I also fear that the majority's description of the relevant precedents deemphasizes the extent to which they support a principle of the President's independent authority to control his own time and energy. . . . Further, if the majority is wrong in predicting the future infrequency of private civil litigation against sitting Presidents, . . . acknowledgement and future delineation of the constitutional principle will prove a practically necessary institutional safeguard. . . . [T]he Constitution's text, history, and precedent support this principle of judicial noninterference with Presidential functions in ordinary civil damages actions.

The Constitution states that the "executive Power shall be vested in a President." . . . This constitutional delegation means that a sitting President is unusually busy, that his activities have an unusually important impact upon the lives of others, and that his conduct embodies an authority bestowed by the entire American electorate. He (along with his constitutionally subordinate Vice President) is the only official for whom the entire Nation votes, and is the only elected officer to represent the entire Nation both domestically and abroad.

This constitutional delegation means still more. Article II makes a single President responsible for the actions of the Executive Branch in much the same way that the entire Congress is responsible for the actions of the Legislative Branch, or the entire Judiciary for those of the Judicial Branch. It thereby creates a constitutional equivalence between a single President, on the one hand, and many legislators, or judges, on the other.

The Founders created this equivalence by consciously deciding to vest Executive authority in one person rather than several. They did so in order to focus, rather than to spread, Executive responsibility thereby facilitating accountability. They also sought to encourage energetic, vigorous, decisive, and speedy execution of the laws by placing in the hands of a single, constitutionally indispensable, individual the ultimate authority that, in

respect to the other branches, the Constitution divides among many. . . .

For present purposes, this constitutional structure means that the President is not like Congress, for Congress can function as if it were whole, even when up to half of its members are absent, . . . It means that the President is not like the Judiciary, for judges often can designate other judges, e.g., from other judicial circuits, to sit even should an entire court be detained by personal litigation. It means that, unlike Congress, which is regularly out of session, . . . the President never adjourns.

More importantly, these constitutional objectives explain why a President, though able to delegate duties to others, cannot delegate ultimate responsibility or the active obligation to supervise that goes with it. And the related constitutional equivalence between President, Congress, and the Judiciary, means that judicial scheduling orders in a private civil case must not only take reasonable account of, say, a particularly busy schedule, or a job on which others critically depend, or an underlying electoral mandate. They must also reflect the fact that interference with a President's ability to carry out his public responsibilities is constitutionally equivalent to interference with the ability of the entirety of Congress, or the Judicial Branch, to carry out their public obligations. . . .

. . . Case law, particularly, *Nixon v. Fitzgerald,* strongly supports the principle that judges hearing a private civil damages action against a sitting President may not issue orders that could significantly distract a President from his official duties. . . .

This case is a private action for civil damages in which, as the District Court here found, it is possible to preserve evidence and in which later payment of interest can compensate for delay. The District Court in this case determined that the Constitution required the postponement of trial during the sitting President's term. It may well be that the trial of this case cannot take place without significantly interfering with the President's ability to carry out his official duties. Yet, I agree with the majority that there is no automatic temporary immunity and that the President should have to provide the District Court with a reasoned explanation of why the immunity is needed; and I also agree that, in the absence of that explanation, the court's postponement of the trial date was premature. For those reasons, I concur in the result.

Case

UNITED STATES V. CURTISS-WRIGHT EXPORT CORPORATION

299 U.S. 304; 57 S.Ct. 216; 81 L.Ed. 255 (1936)
Vote: 7–1

In this case the Court considers the constitutionality of a particular delegation of power from Congress to the president. The case is interesting in light of Schechter Poultry Corporation v. United States (1935), in which the Court enunciated a broad rule against delegations of power by Congress. More relevant to the issues addressed in this chapter, though, is Justice Sutherland's discussion of the powers of the presidency in the field of foreign affairs.

Mr. Justice Sutherland delivered the opinion of the Court.

On January 27, 1936, an indictment was returned in the court below, the first count of which charges that [Curtiss-Wright], beginning with the 29th of May, 1934, conspired to sell in the United States certain arms of war, namely fifteen machine guns, to Bolivia, a country then engaged in armed conflict in the Chaco, in violation of the Joint Resolution of Congress approved May 28, 1934, and the provisions of a proclamation issued on the same day by the President of the United States pursuant to authority conferred by . . . the resolution. . . . [The United States District Court for the Southern District of New York sustained Curtiss-Wright's demurrer to the indictment, and the federal government appealed directly to the Supreme Court.]

The Joint Resolution . . . follows:

Resolved by the Senate and House of Representatives of the United States of America in Congress assembled, that if the President finds that the prohibition of the sale of arms and munitions of war in the United States to those countries now engaged in armed conflict in the Chaco may contribute to the reestablishment of peace between those countries, and if after consultation with the governments of other American Republics and with their cooperation, as well as that of such other governments as he may deem necessary, he makes proclamation to that effect, it shall be unlawful to sell, except under such limitations and exceptions as the President prescribes, any arms or munitions of war in any place in the United States to the countries

now engaged in that armed conflict, or to any person, company, or association acting in the interest of either country, until otherwise ordered by the President or by Congress.

. . . Whoever sells any arms or munitions of war in violation of section 1 shall, on conviction, be punished by a fine not exceeding $10,000 or by imprisonment not exceeding two years, or both.

The President's proclamation [May 28, 1934] . . . after reciting the terms of the Joint Resolution [barred the sale of arms to Bolivia and Paraguay]. . . .

On November 14, 1935, this proclamation was revoked. . . .

. . . It is contended that by the Joint Resolution, the going into effect and continued operation of the resolution was conditioned (a) upon the President's judgment as to its beneficial effect upon the reestablishment of peace between the countries engaged in armed conflict in the Chaco; (b) upon the making of a proclamation, which was left to his unfettered discretion, thus constituting an attempted substitution of the President's will for that of Congress; (c) upon the making of a proclamation putting an end to the operation of the resolution, which again was left to the President's unfettered discretion; and (d) further, that the extent of its operation in particular cases was subject to limitation and exception by the President, controlled by no standard. In each of these particulars, [Curtiss-Wright urges] that Congress abdicated its essential functions and delegated them to the Executive.

Whether, if the Joint Resolution had related solely to internal affairs it would be open to the challenge that it constituted an unlawful delegation of legislative power to the Executive, we find it unnecessary to determine. The whole aim of the resolution is to affect a situation entirely external to the United States, and falling within the category of foreign affairs. The determination which we are called to make, therefore, is whether the Joint Resolution, as applied to that situation, is vulnerable to attack under the rule that forbids a delegation of the law-making power. In other words, assuming (but not deciding) that the challenged delegation, if it were confined to internal affairs, would be invalid, may it nevertheless be sustained on the ground that its exclusive aim is to afford a remedy for a hurtful condition within foreign territory?

It will contribute to the elucidation of the question if we first consider the differences between the powers of the Federal government in respect of foreign or external affairs and those in respect of domestic or internal affairs. That there are differences between them, and that these differences are fundamental, may not be doubted.

The two classes of powers are different, both in respect of their origin and their nature. The broad statement that the Federal government can exercise no powers except those specifically enumerated in the Constitution, and such implied powers as are necessary and proper to carry into effect the enumerated powers, is categorically true only in respect of our internal affairs. In that field, the primary purpose of the Constitution was to carve from the general mass of legislative powers then possessed by the states such portions as it was thought desirable to vest in the Federal government, leaving those not included in the enumerations still in the states. . . . That this doctrine applies only to powers which the states had, is self-evident. And since the states severally never possessed international powers, such powers could not have been carved from the mass of state powers but obviously were transmitted to the United States from some other source. During the colonial period, those powers were possessed exclusively by and were entirely under the control of the Crown. By the Declaration of Independence, "the Representatives of the United States of America" declared the United [not the several] Colonies to be free and independent states, and as such to have "full Power to levy War, conclude Peace, contract Alliances, establish Commerce and to do all other Acts and Things which Independent States may of right do."

As a result of the separation from Great Britain by the colonies, acting as a unit, the powers of external sovereignty passed from the Crown not to the colonies severally, but to the colonies in their collective and corporate capacity as the United States of America. Even before the Declaration, the colonies were a unit in foreign affairs, acting through a common agency—namely the Continental Congress, composed of delegates from the thirteen colonies. That agency exercised the powers of war and peace, raised an army, created a navy, and finally adopted the Declaration of Independence. Rulers come and go; governments end and forms of government change; but sovereignty survives. A political society cannot endure without a supreme will somewhere. Sovereignty is never held in suspense. When, therefore, the external sovereignty of Great Britain in respect of the colonies ceased, it immediately passed to the Union. . . .

The union existed before the Constitution, which was ordained and established among other things to form "a more perfect Union." Prior to that event, it is clear that the Union, declared by the Articles of Confederation to be "perpetual," was the sole possessor of external sovereignty, and in the Union it remained without change save in so far as the Constitution in express terms qualified its exercise. . . .

It results that the investment of the Federal government with the powers of external sovereignty did not depend upon the affirmative grants of the Constitution. The powers to declare and wage war, to conclude peace, to make treaties, to maintain diplomatic relations with other sovereignties, if they had never been mentioned in the Constitution, would have vested in the Federal government as necessary concomitants of nationality. . . .

Not only . . . is the federal power over external affairs in origin and in essential character different from that over internal affairs, but participation in the exercise of power is significantly limited. In this vast external realm, with its important, complicated, delicate and manifold problems, the President alone has the power to speak or listen as a representative of the nation. He makes treaties with the advice and consent of the Senate; but he alone negotiates. Into the field of negotiation the Senate cannot intrude; and Congress itself is powerless to invade it. . . .

It is important to bear in mind that we are here dealing not alone with an authority vested in the President by an exertion of legislative power, but with such an authority plus the very delicate, plenary and exclusive power of the President as the sole organ of the federal government in the field of international relations—a power which does not require as a basis for its exercise an act of Congress, but which, of course, like every other governmental power, must be exercised in subordination to the applicable provisions of the Constitution. It is quite apparent that if, in the maintenance of our international relations, embarrassment—perhaps serious embarrassment—is to be avoided and success for our aims achieved, congressional legislation which is to be made effective through negotiation and inquiry within the international field must often accord to the President a degree of discretion and freedom from statutory restriction which would not be admissible were domestic affairs alone involved. Moreover, he, not Congress, has the better opportunity of knowing the conditions which prevail in foreign countries, and especially is this true in time of war. He has his confidential sources of information. He has his agents in the form of diplomatic, consular and other officials. Secrecy in respect of information gathered by them may be highly necessary, and the premature disclosure of it productive of harmful results. . . .

The marked difference between foreign affairs and domestic affairs in this respect is recognized by both houses of Congress in the very form of their requisitions for information from the executive departments. In the case of every department except the Department of State, the resolution directs the official to furnish the information. In the case of the State Department, dealing with foreign affairs, the President is requested to furnish the information "if not incompatible with public interest." A statement that to furnish the information is not compatible with the public interest rarely, if ever, is questioned.

When the President is to be authorized by legislation to act in respect of a matter intended to affect a situation in foreign territory, the legislator properly bears in mind the important consideration that the form of the President's action—or, indeed, whether he shall act at all—may well depend, among other things, upon the nature of the confidential information which he has or may thereafter receive, or upon the effect which his action may have upon our foreign relations. This consideration, in connection with what we have already said on the subject, disclosed the unwisdom of requiring Congress in this field of governmental power to lay down narrowly definite standards by which the President is to be governed. . . .

In the light of the foregoing observations, it is evident that this court should not be in haste to apply a general rule which will have the effect of condemning legislation like that under review as constituting an unlawful delegation of legislative power. The principles which justify such legislation find overwhelming support in the unbroken legislative practice which has prevailed almost from the inception of the national government to the present day. . . .

Practically every volume of the United States Statutes contains one or more acts or joint resolutions of Congress authorizing action by the President in respect of subjects affecting foreign relations, which either leave the exercise of the power to his unrestricted judgment, or provide a standard far more general than that which has always been considered requisite with regard to domestic affairs. . . .

The result of holding that the joint resolution here under attack is void and unenforceable as constituting an unlawful delegation of legislative power would be to stamp this multitude of comparable acts and resolutions as likewise invalid. And while this court may not and should not, hesitate to declare acts of Congress, however many times repeated, to be unconstitutional if beyond all rational doubt it finds them to be so, an impressive array of legislation such as we have just set forth, enacted by nearly every Congress from the beginning of our national existence to the present day, must be given unusual weight, in the process of reaching a correct determination of the problem. A legislative practice such as we have here, evidenced not by only occasional instances, but marked by the movement of a steady stream for a century and half of time, goes a long way in the direction of proving the presence of unassailable ground for the constitutionality of the practice, to be found in the origin and history of the power involved, or in its nature, or on both combined. . . .

The uniform, long-continued and undisputed legislative practice just disclosed rests upon an admissible view of the Constitution which, even if the practice found far less support in principle than we think it does, we should not feel at liberty at this late day to disturb.

. . . It is enough to summarize by saying that, both upon principle and in accordance with precedent, we conclude there is sufficient warrant for the broad discretion vested in the President to determine whether the enforcement of the statute will have a beneficial effect upon the reestablishment of peace in the affected countries; whether he shall make proclamation to bring the resolution into operation; whether and when the resolution shall cease to operate and to make proclamation accordingly; and to prescribe limitations and exceptions to which the enforcement of the resolution shall be subject. . . .

The judgment of the court below must be reversed and the cause remanded for further proceedings in accordance with the foregoing opinion.

Reversed.

Mr. Justice McReynolds does not agree. He is of opinion that the court below reached the right conclusion and its judgment ought to be affirmed.

Mr. Justice Stone took no part in the consideration or decision of this case.

Case

DAMES & MOORE V. REGAN

453 U.S. 654; 101 S.Ct. 2972; 69 L.Ed. 2d 918 (1981)
Vote: 8–1

In November 1979, Iranian revolutionaries seized the American Embassy in Tehran and took the embassy personnel hostage. In response, President Jimmy Carter issued an order blocking the removal or transfer of all Iranian assets in this country. On January 20, 1981, the hostages were released as part of an agreement worked out between the Carter administration and the revolutionary government of Iran. The agreement called for the creation of a special tribunal to resolve through binding arbitration a number of legal disputes between American firms and the Islamic Republic of Iran. Dames & Moore, an American firm, had won a substantial judgment against Iran in a breach of contract lawsuit in federal district court. In response to the agreement between the United States and Iran, the federal district court stayed execution of the judgment in the Dames & Moore case. In April 1981, Dames & Moore filed suit in district court, seeking to prevent enforcement of the executive orders and Treasury Department regulations implementing the agreement with Iran.

Justice Rehnquist delivered the opinion of the Court.

As we . . . turn to the factual and legal issues in this case, we freely confess that we are obviously deciding only one more episode in the never-ending tension between the President exercising the executive authority in a world that presents each day some new challenge with which he must deal, and the Constitution under which we all live and which no one disputes embodies some sort of system of checks and balances. . . .

The parties and the lower courts, confronted with the instant questions, have all agreed that much relevant analysis is contained in *Youngstown Sheet & Tube Co. v. Sawyer,* 343 U.S. 579 (1952). Justice Black's opinion for the Court in that case, involving the validity of President Truman's effort to seize the country's steel mills in the wake of a nationwide strike, recognized that "[t]he President's power, if any, to issue the order must stem either from an act of Congress or from the Constitution itself." . . . Justice Jackson's concurring opinion elaborated in a general way the consequences of different types of interaction between the two democratic branches in assessing Presidential authority to act in any given case. When the President acts pursuant to an express or implied authorization from Congress, he exercises not only his powers but also those

delegated by Congress. In such a case, the executive action would be supported by the strongest of presumptions and the widest latitude of judicial interpretation, and the burden of persuasion would rest heavily upon any who might attack it. . . . When the President acts in the absence of congressional authorization, he may enter "a zone of twilight in which he and Congress may have concurrent authority, or in which its distribution is uncertain." . . . In such a case, the analysis becomes more complicated, and the validity of the President's action, at least so far as separation of powers principles are concerned, hinges on a consideration of all the circumstances which might shed light on the views of the Legislative Branch toward such action, including "congressional inertia, indifference or quiescence." . . . Finally, when the President acts in contravention of the will of Congress, "his power is at its lowest ebb," and the Court can sustain his actions "only by disabling the Congress from acting upon the subject." . . .

Although we have in the past found, and do today find, Justice Jackson's classification of executive actions into three general categories analytically useful, we should be mindful of Justice Holmes' admonition . . . that "[t]he great ordinances of the Constitution do not establish and divide fields of black and white." . . . Justice Jackson himself recognized that his three categories represented "a somewhat over-simplified grouping," . . . and it is doubtless the case that executive action in any particular instance falls not neatly in one of three pigeonholes, but rather at some point along a spectrum running from explicit congressional authorization to explicit congressional prohibition. This is particularly true as respects cases such as the one before us, involving responses to international crises the nature of which Congress can hardly have been expected to anticipate in any detail. . . .

Because the President's action in nullifying the attachments and ordering the transfer of the assets was taken pursuant to specific congressional authorization (the International Emergency Economic Powers Act), it is supported by the strongest of presumptions and the widest latitude of judicial interpretation, and the burden of persuasion would rest heavily upon any who might attack it. . . . Under the circumstances of this case, we cannot say that petitioner has sustained that heavy burden. A contrary ruling would mean that the Federal Government as a whole lacked the power exercised by the President . . . and that we are not prepared to say.

Although we have concluded that the [International Emergency Economic Powers Act] constitutes specific congressional authorization to the President to nullify the attachments and order the transfer of Iranian assets, there remains the question of the President's authority to suspend claims pending in American courts. Such claims have, of course, an existence apart from the attachments which accompanied them. In terminating these claims through Executive Order No. 12294, the President purported to act under authority of both the IEEPA and . . . the so-called "Hostage Act." . . .

We conclude that, although the IEEPA authorized the nullification of the attachments, it cannot be read to authorize the suspension of the claims. The claims of American citizens against Iran are not, in themselves, transactions involving Iranian property or efforts to exercise any rights with respect to such property. An *in personam* lawsuit, although it might eventually be reduced to judgment and that judgment might be executed upon, is an effort to establish liability and fix damages, and does not focus on any particular property within the jurisdiction. The terms of the IEEPA therefore do not authorize the President to suspend claims in American courts. This is the view of all the courts which have considered the question. . . .

. . . Although the broad language of the Hostage Act suggests it may cover this case, there are several difficulties with such a view. The legislative history indicates that the Act was passed in response to a situation unlike the recent Iranian crisis. Congress in 1868 was concerned with the activity of certain countries refusing to recognize the citizenship of naturalized Americans traveling abroad and repatriating such citizens against their will. . . . These countries were not interested in returning the citizens in exchange for any sort of ransom. This also explains the reference in the Act to imprisonment "in violation of the rights of American citizenship." Although the Iranian hostage-taking violated international law and common decency, the hostages were not seized out of any refusal to recognize their American citizenship—they were seized precisely because of their American citizenship. The legislative history is also somewhat ambiguous on the question whether Congress contemplated Presidential action such as that involved here, or rather simply reprisals directed against the offending foreign country and its citizens. . . .

Concluding that neither the IEEPA nor the Hostage Act constitutes specific authorization of the President's action suspending claims, however, is not to say that these statutory provisions are entirely irrelevant to the question of the validity of the President's action. We think both statutes highly relevant in the looser sense of indicating congressional acceptance of a broad scope for executive action in circumstances such as those presented in this case. . . . [T]he IEEPA delegates broad authority to the President to act in times of national emergency with respect to property of a foreign country. The Hostage Act similarly indicates congressional willingness that the President have broad discretion when responding to the hostile acts of foreign sovereigns. . . .

Although we have declined to conclude that the IEEPA or the Hostage Act directly authorizes the President's suspension of claims for the reasons noted, we cannot ignore the general tenor of Congress' legislation in this area in trying to determine whether the President is acting alone, or at least with the acceptance of Congress. As we have noted, Congress cannot anticipate and legislate with regard to every possible action the President may find it necessary to take, or every possible situation in which he might act. Such failure of Congress specifically to delegate authority does not, "especially . . . in the areas of foreign policy and national security," imply "congressional disapproval" of action taken by the Executive. . . . On the contrary, the enactment of legislation closely related to the question of the President's authority in a particular case which evinces legislative intent to accord the President broad discretion may be considered to "invite measures on independent presidential responsibility." . . . At least this is so where there is no contrary indication of legislative intent and when, as here, there is a history of congressional acquiescence in conduct of the sort engaged in by the President. It is to that history which we now turn.

Not infrequently in affairs between nations, outstanding claims by nationals of one country against the government of another country are "sources of friction" between the two sovereigns. . . . To resolve these difficulties, nations have often entered into agreements settling the claims of their respective nationals. As one treatise writer puts it, international agreements settling claims by nationals of one state against the government of another "are established international practice reflecting traditional international theory." . . . Consistent with that principle, the United States has repeatedly exercised its sovereign authority to settle the claims of its nationals against foreign countries. Though those settlements have sometimes been made by treaty, there has also been a longstanding practice of settling such claims by executive agreement, without the advice and consent of the Senate. Under such agreements, the President has agreed to renounce or extinguish claims of United States nationals against foreign governments in return for lump-sum payments or the establishment of arbitration procedures. To be sure, many of these settlements were encouraged by the United States claimants themselves, since a claimant's only hope of obtaining any payment at all might lie in having his Government negotiate a diplomatic settlement on his behalf. But it is also undisputed that the United States has sometimes disposed of the claims of its citizens without their consent, or even without consultation with them, usually without exclusive regard for their interests, as distinguished from those of the nation as a whole. . . . It is clear that the practice of settling claims continues today. Since 1952, the President has entered into at least 10 binding settlements with foreign nations, including an $80 million settlement with the People's Republic of China.

Crucial to our decision today is the conclusion that Congress has implicitly approved the practice of claim settlement by executive agreement. . . .

In addition to congressional acquiescence in the President's power to settle claims, prior cases of this Court have also recognized that the President does have some measure of power to enter into executive agreements without obtaining the advice and consent of the Senate. In *United States v. Pink,* 315 U.S. 203 (1942), for example, the Court upheld the validity of the Litvinov Assignment, which was part of an Executive Agreement whereby the Soviet Union assigned to the United States amounts owed to it by American nationals so that outstanding claims of other American nationals could be paid. The Court explained that the resolution of such claims was integrally connected with normalizing United States' relations with a foreign state. . . .

. . . [Dames & Moore] insists that the President, by suspending its claims, has circumscribed the jurisdiction of the United States courts in violation of Art. III of the Constitution. We disagree. In the first place, we do not believe that the President has attempted to divest the federal courts of jurisdiction. [The] Executive Order purports only to "suspend" the claims, not divest the federal court of "jurisdiction." . . .

In light of all of the foregoing—the inferences to be drawn from the character of the legislation Congress has enacted in the area, such as the IEEPA and the Hostage Act, and from the history of acquiescence in executive claims settlement—we conclude that the President was authorized to suspend pending claims pursuant to [the] Executive Order. . . .

. . . In light of the fact that Congress may be considered to have consented to the President's action in suspending claims, we cannot say that action exceeded the President's powers.

Our conclusion is buttressed by the fact that the means chosen by the President to settle the claims of American nationals provided an alternative forum, the Claims Tribunal which is capable of providing meaningful relief. The Solicitor General also suggests that the provision of the Claims Tribunal will actually enhance the opportunity for

claimants to recover their claims, in that the Agreement removes a number of jurisdictional and procedural impediments faced by claimants in United States courts. . . . Although being overly sanguine about the chances of United States claimants before the Claims Tribunal would require a degree of naivete which should not be demanded even of judges, the Solicitor General's point cannot be discounted. Moreover, it is important to remember that we have already held that the President has the statutory authority to nullify attachments and to transfer the assets out of the country. The President's power to do so does not depend on his provision of a forum whereby claimants can recover on those claims. The fact that the President has provided such a forum here means that the claimants are receiving something in return for the suspension of their claims, namely, access to an international tribunal before which they may well recover something on their claims. Because there does appear to be a real "settlement" here, this case is more easily analogized to the more traditional claim settlement cases of the past.

Just as importantly, Congress has not disapproved of the action taken here. Though Congress has held hearings on the Iranian Agreement itself, Congress has not enacted legislation, or even passed a resolution, indicating its displeasure with the Agreement. Quite the contrary, the relevant Senate committee has stated that the establishment of the Tribunal is "of vital importance to the United States. . . ." We are thus clearly not confronted with a situation in which Congress has in some way resisted the exercise of Presidential authority.

Finally, we reemphasize the narrowness of our decision. We do not decide that the President possesses plenary power to settle claims, even as against foreign governmental entities. . . . But where, as here, the settlement of claims has been determined to be a necessary incident to the resolution of a major foreign policy dispute between our country and another, and where, as here, we can conclude that Congress acquiesced in the President's action, we are not prepared to say that the President lacks the power to settle such claims. . . .

We do not think it appropriate at the present time to address petitioner's contention that the suspension of claims, if authorized, would constitute a taking of property in violation of the Fifth Amendment to the United States Constitution in the absence of just compensation. Both petitioner and the Government concede that the question whether the suspension of the claims constitutes a taking is not ripe for review. . . .

Justice Stevens, concurring in part.

In my judgment, the possibility that requiring this petitioner to prosecute its claim in another forum will constitute an unconstitutional "taking" is so remote that I would not address the jurisdictional question considered in . . . the Court's opinion. However, I join the remainder of the opinion.

Justice Powell, concurring in part and dissenting in part.

I join the Court's opinion except its decision that the nullification of the attachments did not effect a taking of property interests giving rise to claims for just compensation. . . .

. . . The Government must pay just compensation when it furthers the Nation's foreign policy goals by using as "bargaining chips" claims lawfully held by a relatively few persons and subject to the jurisdiction of our courts. The extraordinary powers of the President and Congress upon which our decision rests cannot, in the circumstances of this case, displace the Just Compensation Clause of the Constitution.

Case

THE PRIZE CASES

2 Black (67 U.S.) 635; 17 L.Ed. 459 (1863)
Vote: 5–4

A few days after the Confederate attack on Fort Sumter but before Congress had formally recognized the existence of civil war, President Abraham Lincoln ordered a blockade of Southern ports. Owners of ships seized by the blockade brought suit in federal court challenging the legality of the president's order. From adverse judgments in the lower courts, the owners took an appeal to the Supreme Court.

Mr. Justice Grier.

. . . By the Constitution, Congress alone has the power to declare a national or foreign war. It cannot declare war against a State, or any number of States, by virtue of any clause in the Constitution. . . .

If a war be made by invasion of a foreign nation, the President is not only authorized but bound to resist force by force. He does not initiate the war, but is bound to accept the challenge without waiting for any special legislative authority. . . .

This greatest of civil wars was not gradually developed by popular commotion, tumultuous assemblies, or local unorganized insurrections. However long may have been its previous conception, it nevertheless sprung forth suddenly from the parent brain, a Minerva in the full panoply of war. The President was bound to meet it in the shape it presented itself, without waiting for Congress to baptize it with a name; and no name given to it by him or them could change the fact.

It is not the less a civil war, with belligerent parties in hostile array, because it may be called an "insurrection" by one side, and the insurgents be considered as rebels or traitors. It is not necessary that the independence of the revolted province or State be acknowledged in order to constitute it a party belligerent in a war according to the law of nations. Foreign nations acknowledge it as war by a declaration of neutrality. The condition of neutrality cannot exist unless there be two belligerent parties. . . .

As soon as the news of the attack on Fort Sumter, and the organization of a government by the seceding States, assuming to act as belligerents, could become known in Europe, to wit, on the 13th of May, 1861, the Queen of England issued her proclamation of neutrality, "recognizing hostilities as existing between the Government of the United States of America and certain States styling themselves the Confederate States of America." This was immediately followed by similar declarations or silent acquiescence by other nations.

After such an official recognition by the sovereign, a citizen of a foreign State is stopped to deny the existence of a war with all its consequences as regards neutrals. They cannot ask a Court to affect a technical ignorance of the existence of a war, which all the world acknowledges to be the greatest civil war known in the history of the human race, and thus cripple the arm of the Government and paralyze its power by subtle definitions and ingenious sophisms. . . .

Whether the President in fulfilling his duties, as Commander-in-chief, in suppressing an insurrection, has met with such armed hostile resistance, and a civil war of such alarming proportions as will compel him to accord to them the character of belligerents, is a question to be decided by him, and this Court must be governed by the decisions and acts of the political department of the Government to which this power was entrusted. "He must determine what degree of force the crisis demands." The proclamation of blockade is itself official and exclusive evidence to the Court that a state of war existed which demanded and authorized a recourse to such a measure, under the circumstances peculiar to the case. . . .

If it were necessary to the technical existence of a war, that it should have a legislative sanction, we find it in almost every act passed at the extraordinary session of the Legislature of 1861, which was wholly employed in enacting laws to enable the Government to prosecute the war with vigor and efficiency. And finally, in 1861, we find Congress . . . in anticipation of such astute objections, passing an act "approving legalizing, and making valid all the acts, proclamations, and orders of the President, as if they had been issued and done under the precious express authority and direction of the Congress of the United States."

Without admitting that such an act was necessary under the circumstances, it is plain that if the President had in any manner assumed powers which it was necessary should have the authority or sanction of Congress . . . this ratification has operated to perfectly cure the defect. . . .

The objection made to this act of ratification, that it is *ex post facto,* and therefore unconstitutional and void, might possibly have some weight on the trial of an indictment in a criminal Court. But precedents from that source cannot be received as authoritative in a tribunal administering public and international law.

On this first question, therefore, we are of the opinion that the President had a right . . . to institute a blockade of ports in possession of the States in rebellion, which neutrals are bound to regard.

We come now to the consideration of the second question. What is included in the term "enemies' property"?

The appellants contend that the term "enemy" is properly applicable to those only who are subjects or citizens of a foreign State at war with our own. . . .

They contend, also, that insurrection is the act of individuals and not of a government or sovereignty; that the individuals engaged are subjects of law. That confiscation of their property can be effected only under a municipal law. That by the law of the land such confiscation cannot take place without the conviction of the owner of some offense, and finally that the secession ordinances are nullities and ineffectual to release any citizen from his allegiance to the national Government, and consequently that the Constitution and Laws of the United States are still operative over persons in all the States for punishment as well as protection.

This argument rests on the assumption of two propositions, each of which is without foundation on the established law of nations. It assumes that where a civil war

exists, the party belligerent claiming to be sovereign, cannot, for some unknown reason, exercise the rights of belligerents, although the revolutionary party may. Being sovereign, he can exercise only sovereign rights over the other party. The insurgent may be killed on the battle-field or by the executioner; his property on land may be confiscated under the municipal law; but the commerce on the ocean, which supplies the rebels with means to support the war, cannot be made the subject of capture under the laws of war, because it is "unconstitutional." Now, it is a proposition never doubted, that the belligerent party who claims to be sovereign, may exercise both belligerent and sovereign rights. . . . Treating the other party as a belligerent and using only the milder modes of coercion which the law of nations has introduced to mitigate the rigors of war, cannot be a subject of complaint by the party to whom it is accorded as a grace or granted as a necessity. We have shown that a civil war such as that now waged between the Northern and Southern States is properly conducted according to the humane regulations of public law as regards capture on the ocean.

Under the very peculiar Constitution of this Government, although the citizens owe supreme allegiance to the Federal government, they owe also a qualified allegiance to the State in which they are domiciled. Their persons and property are subject to its laws.

Hence, in organizing this rebellion, they have acted as States claiming to be sovereign over all persons and property within their respective limits, and asserting a right to absolve their citizens from their allegiance to the Federal Government. Several of these States have combined to form a new confederacy, claiming to be acknowledged by the world as a sovereign State. Their right to do so is now being decided by wager of battle. . . .

Mr. Justice Nelson, dissenting.

. . . The truth is, this idea of the existence of any necessity for clothing the President with the war power, under the Act of 1795, is simply a monstrous exaggeration; for, besides having the command of the whole of the army and navy, Congress can be assembled within any thirty days, if the safety of the country requires that the war power shall be brought into operation.

The Acts of 1795 and 1807 did not, and could not under the Constitution, confer on the President the power of declaring war against a State of this Union, or of deciding that war existed, and upon the ground authorize the capture and confiscation of the property of every citizen of the State whenever it was found on the waters. The laws of war . . . convert every citizen of the hostile State into a public enemy, and treat him accordingly, whatever may have been his previous conduct. This great power over the business and property of the citizen is reserved to the legislative department by the express words of the Constitution. It cannot be delegated or surrendered to the Executive. Congress alone can determine whether war exists or would be declared; and until they have acted, no citizen of the State can be punished in his person or property, unless he has committed some offence against a law of Congress passed before the act was committed, which made it a crime, and defined the punishment. The penalty of confiscation for the acts of others with which he had no concern cannot lawfully be inflicted.

Mr. Justice Taney, Mr. Justice Catron, and *Mr. Justice Clifford* concurred in the dissenting opinion of *Mr. Justice Nelson.*

Case

KOREMATSU V. UNITED STATES

323 U.S. 214; 65 S.Ct. 193; 89 L.Ed. 194 (1944)
Vote: 6–3

In this case the Court considers the constitutionality of an executive order under which the military "relocated" thousands of Japanese-Americans from their homes on the West Coast during the Second World War.

Mr. Justice Black delivered the opinion of the Court.

The petitioner [Korematsu], an American citizen of Japanese descent, was convicted in a federal district court for remaining in San Leandro, California, a "Military Area," contrary to Civilian Exclusion Order No. 34 . . . which directed that after May 9, 1942, all persons of Japanese ancestry should be excluded from that area. No question was raised as to [Korematsu's] loyalty to the United States. The Circuit Court of Appeals affirmed, and the importance of the constitutional question involved caused us to grant certiorari.

It should be noted, to begin with, that all legal restrictions which curtail the civil rights of a single racial group are immediately suspect. That is not to say that all such restrictions are unconstitutional. It is to say that courts must subject them to the most rigid scrutiny. Pressing public necessity may sometime justify the existence of such restrictions; racial antagonism never can.

In the instant case prosecution of [Korematsu] was begun by information charging violation of an Act of Congress, of March 21, 1942, . . . which provides that . . . "whoever shall enter, remain in, leave, or commit any act in any military area or military zone prescribed, under the authority of an Executive order of the President, . . . contrary to the restrictions applicable to any such area or zone . . . shall, if it appears that he knew or should have known of the existence and extent of the restrictions or order and that his act was in violation thereof, be guilty of a misdemeanor and upon conviction shall be liable to a fine of not to exceed $5,000 or to imprisonment for not more than one year, or both, for each offense."

Exclusion Order No. 34, which [Korematsu] knowingly and admittedly violated, was one of a number of military orders and proclamations, all of which were substantially based upon Executive Order No. 9066. . . . That order, issued after we were at war with Japan, declared that "the successful prosecution of the war requires every possible protection against espionage and against sabotage to national-defense material, national-defense premises, and national-defense utilities." . . .

One of the series of orders and proclamations, a curfew order, . . . subjected all persons of Japanese ancestry in prescribed West Coast military areas to remain in their residences from 8 P.M. to 6 A.M. As is the case with the exclusion order here, that prior curfew order was designed as a "protection against espionage and against sabotage." In *Hirabayashi v. United States* . . . we sustained a conviction obtained for violation of the curfew order. . . .

The 1942 Act was attacked in the *Hirabayashi* case as an unconstitutional delegation of power; it was contended that the curfew order and other orders on which it rested were beyond the war powers of the Congress, the military authorities and of the President, as Commander in Chief of the Army; and finally that to apply the curfew order against none but citizens of Japanese ancestry amounted to a constitutionally prohibited discrimination solely on account of race. . . .

In the light of the principles we announced in the *Hirabayashi* case, we are unable to conclude that it was beyond the war power of Congress and the Executive to exclude those of Japanese ancestry from the West Coast war area at the time they did. True, exclusion from the area in which one's home is located is a far greater deprivation than constant confinement to the home from 8 P.M. to 6 A.M. Nothing short of apprehension by the proper military authorities of the gravest imminent danger to the public safety can constitutionally justify either. But exclusion from a threatened area, no less than curfew, has a definite and close relationship to the prevention of espionage and sabotage. The military authorities, charged with the primary responsibility of defending our shores, concluded that curfew provided inadequate protection and ordered exclusion. They did so, as pointed out in our *Hirabayashi* opinion, in accordance with Congressional authority to the military to say who should, and who should not, remain in the threatened areas.

In this case [Korematsu] challenges the assumptions upon which we rested our conclusions in the *Hirabayashi* case. He also urges that by May 1942, when Order No. 34 was promulgated, all danger of Japanese invasion of the West Coast had disappeared. After careful consideration of these contentions we are compelled to reject them.

Here, as in the *Hirabayashi* case, . . . ". . . we cannot reject as unfounded the judgment of the military authorities and of Congress that there were disloyal members of that population, whose number and strength could not be precisely and quickly ascertained. We cannot say that the war-making branches of the Government did not have grounds for believing that in a critical hour such persons could not readily be isolated and separately dealt with, and constituted a menace to the national defense and safety, which demanded that prompt and adequate measures be taken to guard against it." . . .

Like curfew, exclusion of those of Japanese origin was deemed necessary because of the presence of an unascertained number of disloyal members of the group, most of whom we have no doubt were loyal to this country. It was because we could not reject the finding of the military authorities that it was impossible to bring about an immediate segregation of the disloyal from the loyal that we sustained the validity of the curfew order as applying to the whole group. In the instant case, temporary exclusion of the entire group was rested by the military on the same ground. The judgment that exclusion of the entire group was for the same reason a military imperative answers the contention that the exclusion was in the nature of group punishment based on antagonism to those of Japanese origin. That there were members of the group who retained loyalties to Japan has been confirmed by investigations made subsequent to the exclusion. Approximately five thousand American citizens of Japanese ancestry refused to swear unqualified allegiance to the United States and to renounce allegiance to the Japanese Emperor, and several thousand evacuees requested repatriation to Japan.

We uphold the exclusion order as of the time it was made and when [Korematsu] violated it. . . . In doing so, we are not unmindful of the hardships imposed by it upon a large group of American citizens. . . . But hardships are part of war, and war is an aggregation of hardships. All cit-

izens alike, both in and out of uniform, feel the impact of war in greater or lesser measure. Citizenship has its responsibilities as well as its privileges, and in time of war the burden is always heavier. Compulsory exclusion of large groups of citizens from their homes, except under circumstances of direst emergency and peril, is inconsistent with our basic governmental institutions. But when under conditions of modern warfare our shores are threatened by hostile forces, the power to protect must be commensurate with the threatened danger. . . .

It is said that we are dealing here with the case of imprisonment of a citizen in a concentration camp solely because of his ancestry, without evidence or inquiry concerning his loyalty and good disposition towards the United States. Our task would be simple, our duty clear, were this a case involving the imprisonment of a loyal citizen in a concentration camp because of racial prejudice. Regardless of the true nature of the assembly and relocation centers—and we deem it unjustifiable to call them concentration camps with all the ugly connotations that term implies—we are dealing specifically with nothing but an exclusion order. To cast this case into outlines of racial prejudice, without reference to the real military dangers which were presented, merely confused the issue. Korematsu was not excluded from the Military Area because of hostility to him or his race. He was excluded because we are at war with the Japanese Empire, because the properly constituted military authorities feared an invasion of our West Coast and felt constrained to take proper security measures, because they decided that the military urgency of the situation demanded that all citizens of Japanese ancestry be segregated from the West Coast temporarily, and finally, because Congress, reposing its confidence in this time of war in our military leaders—as inevitably it must— determined that they should have the power to do just this. There was evidence of disloyalty on the part of some, the military authorities considered that the need for action was great, and time was short. We cannot—by availing ourselves of the calm perspective of hindsight— now say that at that time these actions were unjustified.

Affirmed.

Mr. Justice Frankfurter, concurring. . . .

Mr. Justice Roberts [dissenting]. . . .

Mr. Justice Murphy, dissenting.

. . . The judicial test of whether the Government, on a plea of military necessity, can validly deprive an individual of any of his constitutional rights is whether the deprivation is reasonably related to a public danger that is so "immediate, imminent, and impending" as not to admit of delay and not to permit the intervention of ordinary constitutional processes to alleviate the danger. . . . Civilian Exclusion Order No. 34, banishing from a prescribed area of the Pacific Coast "all persons of Japanese ancestry, both alien and non-alien," clearly does not meet that test. Being an obvious racial discrimination, the order deprives all those within its scope of the equal protection of the laws as guaranteed by the Fifth Amendment. It further deprives these individuals of their constitutional rights to live and work where they will, to establish a home where they choose and to move about freely. In excommunicating them without benefit of hearings, this order also deprives them of all their constitutional rights to procedural due process. Yet no reasonable relation to an "immediate, imminent, and impending" public danger is evident to support this racial restriction which is one of the most sweeping and complete deprivations of constitutional rights in the history of this nation in the absence of martial law. . . .

That this forced exclusion was the result in good measure of [the] erroneous assumption of racial guilt rather than bona fide military necessity is evidenced by the Commanding General's Final Report on the evacuation from the Pacific Coast area. In it he refers to all individuals of Japanese descent as "subversive," as belonging to "an enemy race" whose "racial strains are undiluted," and as constituting "over 112,000 potential enemies . . . at large today" along the Pacific Coast. In support of this blanket condemnation of all persons of Japanese descent, however, no reliable evidence is cited to show that such individuals were generally disloyal, or had generally so conducted themselves in this area as to constitute a special menace to defense installations or war industries, or had otherwise by their behavior furnished reasonable ground for their exclusion as a group.

Justification for the exclusion is sought, instead, mainly upon questionable racial and sociological grounds not ordinarily within the realm of expert military judgment, supplemented by certain semi-military conclusions drawn from an unwarranted use of circumstantial evidence. . . .

The main reasons relied upon by those responsible for the forced evacuation, therefore, do not prove a reasonable relations between the group characteristics of Japanese Americans by people with racial and economic prejudices—the same people who have been among the foremost advocates of the evacuation. A military judgment based upon such racial and sociological considerations is not entitled to the great weight ordinarily given the judgments based upon strictly military considerations. . . .

The military necessity which is essential to the validity of the evacuation order thus resolves itself into a few intimations that certain individuals actively aided the enemy, from which it is inferred that the entire group of Japanese Americans could not be or remain loyal to the United States. . . . But to infer that examples of individual disloyalty prove group disloyalty and justify discriminatory action against the entire group is to deny that under our system of law individual guilt is the sole basis for deprivation of rights. . . . To give constitutional sanction to that inference in this case, however well-intentioned may have been the military command on the Pacific Coast, is to adopt one of the cruelest of the rationales used by our enemies to destroy the dignity of the individual and to encourage and open the door to discriminatory actions against other minority groups in the passions of tomorrow.

No adequate reason is given for the failure to treat these Japanese Americans on an individual basis by holding investigations and hearings to separate the loyal from the disloyal, as was done in the case of persons of German and Italian ancestry. . . .

I dissent, therefore, from this legalization of racism. Racial discrimination in any form and in any degree has no justifiable part whatever in our democratic way of life. It is unattractive in any setting but it is utterly revolting among a free people who have embraced the principles set forth in the Constitution of the United States. All residents of this nation are kin in some way by blood or culture to a foreign land. Yet they are primarily and necessarily a part of the new and distinct civilization of the United States. They must accordingly be treated at all times as the heirs of the American experiment and as entitled to all the rights and freedoms guaranteed by the Constitution.

Mr. Justice Jackson, dissenting.

. . . [I]f any fundamental assumption underlies our system, it is that guilt is personal and not inheritable. Even if all of one's antecedents had been convicted of treason, the Constitution forbids its penalties to be visited upon him, for it provides that "no attainder of treason shall work corruption of blood, or forfeiture except during the life of the person attainted." But here is an attempt to make an otherwise innocent act a crime merely because this prisoner is the son of parents as to whom he had no choice, and belongs to a race from which there is no way to resign. If Congress in peace-time legislation should enact such a criminal law, I should suppose this Court would refuse to enforce it. . . .

It would be impracticable and dangerous idealism to expect or insist that each specific military command in an area of probable operations will conform to conventional tests of constitutionality. When an area is so beset that it must be put under military control at all, the paramount consideration is that its measures be successful, rather than legal. The armed services must protect a society, not merely its Constitution. The very essence of the military job is to marshal physical force to remove every obstacle to its effectiveness, to give it every strategic advantage. Defense measures will not, and often should not, be held within the limits that bind civil authority in peace. . . .

But if we cannot confine military expedients by the Constitution, neither would I distort the Constitution to approve all that the military may deem expedient. That is what the Court appears to be doing, whether consciously or not. . . .

. . . [O]nce a judicial opinion rationalizes . . . an order [such as the Civilian Exclusion Order] to show that it conforms to the Constitution, or rather rationalizes the Constitution to show that the Constitution sanctions such an order, the Court for all time has validated the principle of racial discrimination in criminal procedure and of transplanting American citizens. The principle then lies about like a loaded weapon ready for the hand of any authority that can bring forward a plausible claim of an urgent need. Every repetition imbeds that principle more deeply in our law and thinking and expands it to new purposes. All who observe the work of courts are familiar with what Judge Cardozo described as "the tendency of a principle to expand itself to the limit of its logic." A military commander may overstep the bounds of constitutionality, and it is an incident. But if we review and approve, that passing incident becomes the doctrine of the Constitution. There it has a generative power of its own, and all that it creates will be in its own image. Nothing better illustrates this danger than does the Court's opinion in this case. . . .

I should hold that a civil court cannot be made to enforce an order which violates constitutional limitations even if it is a reasonable exercise of military authority. The courts can exercise only the judicial power, can apply only law, and must abide by the Constitution, or they cease to be civil courts and become instruments of military policy. . . . My duties as a justice as I see them do not require me to make a military judgment as to whether General DeWitt's evacuation and detention program was a reasonable military necessity. I do not suggest that the courts should have attempted to interfere with the Army in carrying out its task. But I do not think they may be asked to execute a military expedient that has no place in law under the Constitution.

I would reverse the judgment and discharge the prisoner.

4

THE CONSTITUTION AND THE MODERN ADMINISTRATIVE STATE

"The hydraulic pressure inherent within each of the separate Branches to exceed the outer limits of its power, even to accomplish desirable objectives, must be resisted."
—CHIEF JUSTICE WARREN E. BURGER, WRITING FOR THE COURT IN
IMMIGRATION AND NATURALIZATION SERVICE V. CHADHA (1983)

Warren E. Burger: Chief Justice, 1969–1986

INTRODUCTION

Even a cursory examination of American constitutional history reveals that the role of the national government has changed dramatically in the two centuries since the Constitution was adopted. In the early days of the republic, the role of the national government essentially followed Jefferson's dictum that "that government is best which governs least." For the most part, the national government left such functions as social welfare and education to state and local governments and concerned itself with the regulation of foreign trade, internal improvements such as canals and post roads, and the protection of the national security. State and local governments, in turn, tended to leave matters of social welfare and education to neighborhoods, churches, and families. Perhaps most fundamentally, individuals were regarded as responsible for their own problems as well as their own good fortune. For many years, the national government was seen neither as "big brother" nor *parens patriae*.

In the wake of post-Civil War industrialization and the emergence of an economy dominated by giant corporations, the limited role of the national government began to change. A new ethos emerged, one in which government assumed primary responsibility for solving social problems. With the passage of the Interstate Commerce Act in 1887 and the concomitant establishment of the Interstate Commerce Commission, the relatively unobtrusive government envisaged by the founders began to evolve in the direction of ever more complex and intrusive regulation. The era of Progressive reform and the subsequent New Deal contributed mightily to the growth of such regulation. The years elapsing since the New Deal have witnessed the institutionalization of the **modern administrative state.** The administrative state is the sum total of all the agencies, departments, and commissions that comprise the contemporary federal government.

Whereas classical liberals such as John Locke and Thomas Jefferson espoused minimal government as consistent with the ideal of individual freedom, liberal theorists of the late nineteenth and early twentieth centuries sought to justify a broader role for government. Social theorists such as John Dewey advocated an expanded governmental role in part to realize the ideal of socioeconomic equality in an industrialized economy in which gross disparities existed between rich and poor. For modern liberal economists such as John Maynard Keynes, a greater degree of government intervention was necessary to smooth off the rough edges of the business cycle in order to avoid the wild swings between periods of dramatic growth and periods of recession or even depression. According to the Keynesian perspective—dominant during the New Deal era—the very survival of capitalism depended on successful governmental management of the economy. In the decades following the New Deal, the American intellectual community, as exemplified in the work of the economist John Kenneth Galbraith, embraced the concept of "proactive" government—that is, government committed to progress through regulation, redistribution, and planning.

Today, in spite of the conservative reaction of the 1980s and 1990s, the national government is regarded by most Americans as responsible for the social and economic well-being of the nation. No doubt, this expanded role of government has been reinforced by the ideas of Dewey, Keynes, and Galbraith. As a practical matter, however, the influence of pluralist politics has been even more conspicuous. One need only consider the success of numerous interest groups in shaping, perpetuating, and often enlarging government programs created (in theory) to advance the public interest. Students of American politics have long recognized that government regulators are apt to be more influenced by the interests of those who are to be regulated than by abstract notions of responsible government.

The existence of the modern administrative state poses serious questions of constitutional law—questions involving the foundational principles of limited government, the rule of law, separation of powers, federalism, and individual liberty. This chapter is concerned primarily with separation of powers, the problems of legislative and judicial oversight of the federal bureaucracy, and the relationship between bureaucratic power and individual rights.

THE DELEGATION OF LEGISLATIVE POWER

The expansive role now played by the national government renders the legislative task of Congress considerably more difficult. In an increasingly complex society characterized by technological sophistication and economic interdependence, the sheer magnitude of problems demanding congressional attention and the practical difficulties of regulation obviously limit the ability of Congress to legislate comprehensively, much less effectively. Indeed, this complexity and attendant impracticability, coupled with the pluralistic politics of the legislative process, make it difficult for Congress to fashion rules that can be enforced with any degree of certainty or predictability. At the same time, the deliberate, tortoise-like pace of the legislative process makes it all but impossible for Congress to respond promptly to changing objective conditions, making meaningful, relevant regulations almost inconceivable. Thus, given the expansive scope of government, the nature of the legislative process, and the fact that many of the subjects of regulation are both complex and esoteric, Congress has come to rely more and more on "experts" for the development as well as the implementation of regulations. These experts are found in a host of government departments, commissions, agencies, boards, and bureaus that comprise the modern administrative state.

Through a series of broad delegations of legislative power, Congress has transferred to the **federal bureaucracy** much of the responsibility for making and enforcing the rules and regulations deemed necessary for a technological society. The Food and Drug Administration (FDA), the Nuclear Regulatory Commission (NRC), the Federal Aviation Administration (FAA), the Occupational Safety and Health Administration (OSHA), the Environmental Protection Agency (EPA), and the Securities and Exchange Commission (SEC) are just a few of the myriad government agencies to which Congress has delegated broad authority to make public policy.

Frequently, the enabling legislation creating these agencies provides little more than vague generalities to guide agency **rule making.** For example, in 1970 Congress gave OSHA the power to make rules that are "reasonably necessary or appropriate to provide safe and healthful employment and places of employment." The rules promulgated by OSHA as "necessary" or "appropriate" take on all the force of law.

A more recent example of legislative delegation is seen in the Americans with Disabilities Act (ADA) of 1990. The ADA, which built on the existing body of federal civil rights law, mandates the elimination of discrimination against individuals with disabilities. A number of federal agencies—including the Department of Justice, the Department of Transportation, the Equal Employment Opportunity Commission (EEOC), and the Federal Communications Commission (FCC)—are given extensive regulatory and enforcement powers under the act. As one of the many regulations that have been adopted in support of the statute, the Department of Justice published in the *Federal Register* a final rule prohibiting discrimination on the basis of disability in the provision of state and local government services.

Twenty-nine pages of the *Federal Register* of July 26, 1991, are devoted to this one rule. Hundreds of pages of the *Federal Register* are devoted to regulations implementing this act alone.

It is argued that broad delegations of legislative power are necessary so that agencies can develop the programs required to deal with targeted problems. These delegations of power may be to a great extent desirable or even inevitable, but they do raise serious questions of constitutional theory.

Concern for Representative Government

Although various factors have prompted Congress to delegate degrees of legislative power to the executive branch and to the **independent agencies**, the practice does not comport well with a traditional understanding of the Constitution. Specifically, two constitutional values are arguably infringed by legislative delegation. The first is the principle of representative government that lies within the grant of legislative power to Congress, whose members are chosen by the people. The constitutional grant of legislative power to an elected institution reflects the fundamental national commitment to the idea of democracy, albeit in a form limited by constitutional strictures. The **delegation of legislative power** to unelected bureaucrats can be viewed as antithetical to the ideal of **representative government**.

Concern for the Separation of Powers

Furthermore, delegation is difficult to square with the principle of **separation of powers** implicit in the very structure of the Constitution. Article I vests all legislative power in the Congress. Thus, when Congress delegates legislative power to the executive branch, it can be viewed as violating the implicit constitutional principles of representative government and separation of powers, as well as the express language of Article I. In *J. W. Hampton & Company v. United States* (1928), Chief Justice William Howard Taft recognized the constitutional problem raised by legislative delegation:

> [I]n carrying out that Constitutional division into three branches it is a breach of the national fundamental law if Congress gives up its legislative power and transfers it to the President, or to the judicial branch, or if by law attempts to vest itself of either executive or judicial power.

Taft's essential point was that if the Constitution imposes meaningful limitations on government, then Congress must be very careful in transferring its own power to the other branches. On the other hand, we have already noted the radical change to a political ethos in which active, affirmative government is regarded as legitimate and even essential. Is it possible to have both an effective separation of powers and proactive government? As our system has evolved, the primary responsibility for reconciling political reality with constitutional principle has come to rest with the Supreme Court. Unfortunately, the Court has seldom been able to harmonize theory and reality in this context. Thus, it can be argued that the Court's decisions do not reflect a coherent constitutional theory justifying the modern administrative state.

Delegation in the Context of Foreign Affairs

The Supreme Court first encountered the issue of delegation of legislative power in *Brig Aurora v. United States* (1813). The case arose in connection with American efforts to remain neutral during the Napoleonic Wars. One measure designed to ensure this neutrality was the Non-Intercourse Act of 1809. The act granted to the president the power to impose an embargo against either Great Britain or France, depending on the president's determination of specific facts. If the president found that either nation ceased "to violate neutral commerce" involving American ships, he was free to impose an embargo on the remaining offender. President James Madison determined that France was the first to comply and thus initiated an embargo against Great Britain. The Supreme Court sustained the act against a constitutional challenge, holding that the president's role was merely one of fact finding, rather than lawmaking. Thus, in the Court's view, no unconstitutional delegation of power had taken place.

The Supreme Court handed down a similar ruling some eighty years later in *Field v. Clark* (1892). In this case, the Court upheld the Tariff Act of 1890, which imposed tariffs on certain imports if, in the president's judgment, the exporting country placed "reciprocally unequal and unreasonable" tariffs on American products. Here again the Court viewed the president's role as one of fact finder, rather than lawmaker, and thus upheld the challenged act. Speaking for the majority, Justice John M. Harlan (the elder) noted that:

> The Act . . . does not in any real sense invest the President with the power of legislation. . . . Legislative power was exercised when Congress declared that [enforcement of the tariffs] should take effect upon a named contingency.

In 1928, however, the Court sustained "contingency" tariff legislation that not only allowed presidential discretion as to when to apply a tariff but also granted the president the power to alter the tariff rate. In *J. W. Hampton & Company v. United States,* the Court expanded the permissible scope of legislative delegations by holding that:

> If Congress shall lay down by legislative act an intelligible principle to which the person or body authorized to fix such rates is directed to conform, such legislative action is not a forbidden delegation of legislative power.

It should be noted that the challenged delegations in *Brig Aurora, Field v. Clark,* and *Hampton* dealt primarily with foreign affairs. In *United States v. Curtiss-Wright Export Corporation* (1936) (discussed and reprinted in the previous chapter), the Supreme Court made it clear that delegations of legislative power in the field of foreign affairs must be assessed on different grounds from delegations involving domestic matters. Since the executive branch has been recognized as "the sole organ of the Federal government in the field of international relations," no clear standards govern delegations of power to the president in this area. In *Zemel v. Rusk* (1965), the Court elaborated on this view by saying that "Congress—in giving the Executive broad authority over matters of foreign affairs—must of necessity paint with a brush broader than that it customarily wields in domestic affairs."

Delegation in the Domestic Context

Although the Supreme Court has expressed more reservations about congressional delegation in the domestic sphere, the end result has been essentially the same—that is, to rationalize and uphold vast transfers of power from Congress to other branches and agencies of government. Implicitly acknowledging this "bottom-line" similarity, the Court has applied the **intelligible principle standard** of the *Hampton* case in assessing delegations of congressional power on the domestic side, as well as in foreign policy contexts. In fact, this parallel appeared in the Court's earliest decisions regarding delegation in the domestic sphere.

The first challenge to such a delegation of power occurred in *Wayman v. Southard* (1825). There, the Supreme Court upheld a congressional grant of power to the Court to determine its own rules of procedure. Given his desire to maximize the independence and power of the Supreme Court, it is not surprising that Chief Justice John Marshall held this delegation to be constitutional. In Marshall's view, the transfer of power was justified because (1) the subject was of "less interest" to the Congress than to the Court, and (2) the Court was merely "filling in the details" of a more general congressional provision. Of Marshall's two justifications, the latter survived to guide subsequent Court decisions in this area. This was essentially the position taken by the Court in the *Hampton* case, when the Court allowed delegations as long as executive discretion was guided by an "intelligible principle."

In two significant cases during the New Deal era, the Supreme Court demonstrated that the **nondelegation doctrine** could be more than a mere exhortation to Congress. In *Panama Refining Company v. Ryan* (1935) and *Schechter Poultry Corporation v. United States* (1935), the Court struck down provisions of the National Industrial Recovery Act (NIRA) on grounds of nondelegability. In *Panama v. Ryan,* also known as the hot oil case, the Court invalidated the NIRA's grant of power to President Franklin D. Roosevelt to exclude from interstate commerce oil produced in violation of state regulation. In striking down this provision, the Court noted that the Congress requires "flexibility and practicality . . . to perform its function in laying down principles and establishing standards." The Court also acknowledged that Congress often must delegate to "selected instrumentalities the making of subordinate rules within prescribed limits and the determination of facts to which the policy as declared by the legislature is to apply." Yet, while it was willing to allow limited delegations of power to the executive branch, the majority in the hot oil case viewed the NIRA as granting broad legislative power to the president, "without standard or rule, to be dealt with as he pleased." As such, it was an unacceptable delegation.

In *Schechter,* commonly known as the sick chicken case, the Court invalidated a key section of the NIRA that allowed the executive branch to promulgate "codes of fair competition" for a broad range of industries. These codes, developed in some cases in cooperation with targeted industries, were enforceable by criminal and civil penalties established by Congress. The Schechter Poultry Corporation was convicted on several counts of violating the Live Poultry Code developed by the National Recovery Administration (NRA). The development of this code was obviously based on a broad delegation of legislative power. The crucial issue was whether the delegation was accompanied by standards sufficiently clear to pass constitutional muster.

Although the preamble of the National Industrial Recovery Act had announced such general purposes as curbing unfair competition, increasing productivity, and otherwise rehabilitating industry, the grant of power to establish codes did not carry standards satisfactory to the Court. Rather, the Court asserted that the NIRA granted "virtually unfettered" discretion to the president to enact "laws for the government of trade and industry throughout the country." As such, the NIRA could not pass the nondelegation test.

The Permissiveness of the Modern Court   The *Panama Refining Company* and *Schechter* cases stand out as the only two instances in which the Supreme Court has invalidated federal statutes on grounds that Congress impermissibly delegated its lawmaking power to the executive branch. It must be recognized that these cases were part and parcel of a larger battle between the Court and the Roosevelt administration over the New Deal. Many of the Court's critics were inclined to see the decisions in *Panama Refining Company* and *Schechter* as political attacks on the New Deal, rather than neutral applications of a legitimate constitutional principle. It is note-worthy that since the mid-1930s, the Court has not invoked the nondelegation doctrine to strike down any act of Congress, despite many sweeping delegations of power to the executive branch.

The permissiveness of the post-New Deal Supreme Court in this area was clearly manifested in *Yakus v. United States* (1944). Here, the Court upheld the Emergency Price Control Act of 1942, which established the Office of Price Administration and vested it with wide latitude to control prices and rents. The Court's decision in *Yakus* might be viewed as turning on the temporary nature of the act and the fact that the nation was at war. Subsequent decisions have made it clear, however, that *Yakus* was no fluke but rather represented a trend of judicial tolerance toward congressional del-egations of power.

Perhaps the best example of the permissive approach the Court has taken toward legislative delegation is *Arizona v. California* (1963). In this case, the Court sustained an extremely vague delegation of power to the Secretary of the Interior under the Boulder Canyon Act of 1928. The act gave the secretary almost unlimited discretion to allocate the water of the Colorado River (which had been dammed to create reser-voirs) among seven states. In making such allocations, the secretary was to follow leg-islative priorities indicated in the act: "first, for river regulation, improvement of nav-igation and flood control; second, for irrigation and domestic uses and satisfaction of present perfected rights . . . ; and third, for [electrical] power." On the basis of these guidelines, it was difficult to determine whether the secretary was in fact acting within the "principles" established by Congress. The Court, however, gave Congress the benefit of the doubt, although not without a sharp dissent from Justice John M. Harlan (the younger). "Under the Court's construction of the Act," wrote Harlan, "Congress has made a gift to the Secretary of almost one million, five hundred thou-sand acre feet of water a year, to allocate virtually as he pleases. . . ." No doubt aware of the inherent vagueness of the delegation it had sustained, the Court suggested that if the Secretary of the Interior acted in a fashion not consistent with congressional intent, Congress could reduce his power through subsequent legislation. Certainly this is not the approach to legislative delegations manifested in the *Hampton, Panama Refining Company,* and *Schechter* decisions.

In the 1970s, some members of the Court seemed ready to put the antidelegation doctrine to rest once and for all. For example, in *National Cable Association v. United States* (1974), Justice Thurgood Marshall's concurring opinion characterized the anti-delegation rule as a remnant of a bygone era, the period before the "constitutional revolution" of 1937. According to Justice Marshall, the antidelegation rule "is surely as moribund as the substantive due process approach of the same era." Marshall's comments notwithstanding, a number of scholars have called for the revival of the nondelegation doctrine. In his influential book *The End of Liberalism* (1979), political scientist Theodore Lowi made a strong argument for resurrection of the *Schechter* rule.

In the early 1980s, certain members of the Supreme Court in fact indicated a desire to scrutinize legislative delegations more carefully. For example, in *Industrial Union Department v. American Petroleum Institute* (1980), the Court considered a challenge to an OSHA regulation that limited workers' exposure to benzene, a toxic chemical. Under law, OSHA was empowered to set exposure limits for toxic agents in the work-place so as to ensure "to the extent feasible" that employees would not suffer adverse health effects. The parties to the case differed on the meaning of the phrase "to the extent feasible." The American Petroleum Institute argued that the law required OSHA to demonstrate that the benefits of the regulation outweighed its costs. A four-member plurality of the Court did not reach this issue, however, because OSHA had not made the necessary determination that benzene posed a significant health risk at the prohibited level of exposure. In a concurring opinion, Justice William Rehnquist opined that the statutory provisions before the Court offended the nondelegation doctrine. The plurality, as well as the four dissenters, avoided the delegation issue altogether.

The very next term, in *American Textile Manufacturers Institute v. Donovan* (1981), the Court sustained an OSHA "cotton dust" regulation against a challenge from the textile industry. Here, Justice Rehnquist dissented, joined by Chief Justice Warren Burger. Rehnquist reiterated his view that the OSHA Act of 1970 "unconstitutionally delegated to the Executive Branch the authority to make the 'hard policy choices' properly the task of the legislature." Rehnquist elaborated:

> In believing . . . [the challenged provision of the OSHA statute] . . . amounts to an unconstitutional delegation . . . , I do not mean to suggest that Congress, in enacting a statute, must resolve all ambiguities or must "fill in all the blanks." Even the neophyte student of government realizes that legislation is the art of compromise, and that an important, controversial bill is seldom enacted by Congress in the form in which it is first introduced. It is not unusual for the various factions supporting or opposing a proposal to accept some departure from the language they would prefer. . . . But that sort of compromise is a far cry from this case, where Congress simply abdicated its responsibility for the making of a fundamental and most difficult policy choice.

In *Bowsher v. Synar* (1986), the Supreme Court was provided an excellent opportunity to revitalize the *Schechter* rule. The case raised the question of legislative delegation in the context of the spending power of Congress, clearly one of the most important legislative functions. In coping with the politically sensitive issue of the massive federal deficit, Congress adopted the Balanced Budget and Emergency Deficit Control Act of 1985, popularly known as the Gramm-Rudman-Hollings Act. This legislation required automatic cuts in federal spending in order to achieve a balanced budget. A constitutionally dubious provision of the law required such cuts to be made by the comptroller general if Congress proved unwilling or unable to legislate such cuts within a given timetable. Arguably, this represented a delegation of Congress's spending power to an unaccountable bureaucrat. To use language from Justice Rehnquist's dissent in *American Textile Manufacturers v. Donovan,* it could be argued that Congress, in delegating spending authority to the comptroller general, had "simply abdicated its responsibility for the making of a fundamental and most difficult policy choice."

Only a few hours after President Reagan signed Gramm-Rudman-Hollings into law, a legal challenge was filed in federal court by Oklahoma Representative Mike Synar, joined by eleven other members of Congress. Their major objection to Gramm-Rudman-Hollings was the delegation of legislative power to unelected bureaucrats. While Representative Synar ultimately won his lawsuit, the rationale adopted by the Supreme Court for invalidating the key provision of Gramm-Rudman-Hollings was quite different from that advanced by the plaintiff. Rather than holding that Congress had unconstitutionally delegated its spending power, the Court ruled 7 to 2 that since the comptroller general was an agent of Congress, not of the executive branch, Congress had encroached on the president's duty to "faithfully execute the laws." In the final opinion of his judicial career, Chief Justice Burger expressed the Court's view:

> Congress has consistently viewed the Comptroller General as an officer of the Legislative Branch. Over the years, the Comptrollers General have also viewed themselves as part of the Legislative Branch. . . . [W]e see no escape from the conclusion that, because

Congress had retained removal authority over the Comptroller General, he may not be entrusted with executive powers.

Thus, the Court's rationale was nearly the inverse of the argument made by Representative Synar. According to the Court, the Gramm-Rudman-Hollings provision was flawed not because it delegated legislative power to unelected officials but because it vested an agent of Congress with powers of implementation properly belonging to the executive branch. In other words, the Court managed to invalidate Gramm-Rudman-Hollings on separation of powers grounds without invoking the antidelegation doctrine. In adopting this approach, the Court was simply following the *Ashwander* rules (see Chapter 1), which counsel the justices to adopt the narrowest possible grounds in striking down legislation. Had the Court chosen the broader nondelegation rationale, the entire statutory basis of the modern administrative state might have been called into question. Obviously, some critics of bureaucratic government would like nothing better. But given the realities of modern society, it seems highly unlikely that the Supreme Court will move very far in that direction.

The Court's long-standing reluctance to invoke the nondelegation doctrine was reaffirmed in its 1989 ruling upholding Congress's creation of the U.S. Sentencing Commission and recognizing the constitutionality of detailed sentencing guidelines promulgated by the commission in 1987 (*Mistretta v. United States* [1989]). Eight members of the Court rejected the argument that Congress had impermissibly delegated its power to prescribe ranges of criminal sentences that federal judges were required to impose on persons convicted of crimes. The Court also rejected the argument that Congress had violated the separation of powers principle by placing the sentencing commission within the judicial branch and authorizing it to establish legally binding sentencing guidelines. In a lone dissent, Justice Antonin Scalia asserted that the separation of powers principle had been violated, concluding that the new sentencing commission amounted to a "junior varsity Congress with extensive lawmaking power."

The contemporary Court's unwillingness to revive the nondelegation doctrine is illustrated by a 2001 decision upholding the broad regulatory authority of the Environmental Protection Agency. The EPA is perhaps the most powerful of the independent regulatory agencies of the federal government. Congress has delegated enormous responsibility to the EPA to deal with matters of air pollution, water pollution, environmental reclamation, and the transportation and disposal of hazardous chemicals and waste products. Accordingly, the EPA has long been a target for those who believe that the courts should more strictly apply the nondelegation doctrine. In *Whitman v. American Trucking Associations* (2001), the Supreme Court was afforded such an opportunity. The American Trucking Associations and other business interests challenged new EPA limits on ozone and soot, arguing, among other things, that the Clean Air Act under which EPA promulgated the regulations constituted an impermissible delegation of legislative power. To the surprise of many observers, the Court was unanimous in rejecting the challenge to the EPA's authority. Writing for the Court, Justice Scalia observed that "[t]he scope of discretion [the challenged provision] allows is in fact well within the outer limits of our nondelegation precedents." Some Court watchers were surprised by Scalia's position, given his dissent in *Mistretta*. Quoting his *Mistretta* dissent, Scalia noted that "a certain degree of discretion, and thus of lawmaking, inheres in most executive or judicial action." The *Whitman* decision suggests strongly that the nondelegation doctrine, while officially viable, is not likely to be invoked to upset the institutional arrangements that have come to characterize the modern administrative state.

TO SUMMARIZE:

- Through a series of broad delegations of legislative power, Congress has transferred to the federal bureaucracy much of the responsibility for making and enforcing rules and regulations. Such delegations have been criticized on constitutional grounds. The nondelegation doctrine holds that Congress may not delegate the legislative power vested in it by the Constitution.
- In *Schechter Poultry Corporation v. United States* (1935), the Court struck down the National Industrial Recovery Act of 1933 on the ground that Congress had improperly delegated its legislative power to the executive branch. Since then, despite numerous opportunities, the Court has declined to invoke the nondelegation doctrine to invalidate any act of Congress.
- The position of the contemporary Supreme Court on the nondelegation doctrine is well illustrated by its unanimous decision in *Whitman v. American Trucking Associations* (2001), in which the Court upheld the Environmental Protection Agency's broad regulatory authority conferred by the Clean Air Act.

CONGRESSIONAL CONTROL OF ADMINISTRATIVE ACTIONS

Although Congress has found it necessary or expedient to delegate much of its legislative authority to the executive branch, it has attempted to maintain control over executive decisions arising out of the exercise of delegated authority. It must be realized that executive agencies in many cases do not merely promulgate but also implement and enforce regulations, the traditional concept of separation of powers notwithstanding. Thus, Congress, through a variety of mechanisms, has attempted to retain control over agency discretion. These attempts include informal means as well as more formal mechanisms, such as attaching riders to agency appropriations bills, conducting **oversight hearings**, and reducing agency budgets. Of course, if Congress is extremely dissatisfied with the performance of a particular agency, it may rewrite the statute that created the agency in the first instance. By amending the appropriate statute(s), Congress may enlarge or contract the agency's jurisdiction, as well as the nature and scope of its rule making authority.

The Legislative Veto

One of the more interesting, and certainly the most controversial, of the mechanisms by which Congress has sought to control the bureaucracy is the **legislative veto.** In existence since the early 1930s, the legislative veto is a device whereby Congress, one house of Congress, or even one congressional committee can "veto" agency decisions made pursuant to delegated authority. A legislative veto provision is written into the original act delegating legislative power to an executive agency. While such original legislation is adopted in the ordinary fashion, involving bicameral passage and presentment to the president, legislative veto resolutions are not subject to the formal requirements of Article I. For example, the seminal case of *Immigration and Naturalization Service v. Chadha* (1983) involved a resolution adopted by the House of Representatives reversing a deportation decision reached by the Immigration and Naturalization Service. This veto resolution was based on authority given to both houses of Congress by the Immigration and Nationality Act of 1952. As allowed under the act, the House veto resolution was neither submitted to the Senate nor presented to the president for approval. Indeed, the Supreme Court cited these reasons in striking down this legislative veto in the *Chadha* case.

The *Chadha* Case   In *Chadha,* the Supreme Court majority chose to view the veto as a legislative act subject to the requirements of Article I. In adopting this approach, the Court not only invalidated the veto provision actually before it but rendered some 230 similar statutory provisions presumptively unconstitutional. Thus, the *Chadha* case can be viewed as the most sweeping exercise of judicial review in the history of the Supreme Court.

Reacting to the breadth of the majority opinion, Justice Lewis Powell wrote a concurring opinion in which he parted company with the Court's rationale. Like the majority, Powell found the legislative veto at issue invalid but for an entirely different reason. For him, the provision was unconstitutional not because it violated the Presentment Clause and the principle of bicameralism but because it authorized Congress to exercise a power that could not properly be considered "legislative" in nature. Powell viewed the exercise of the veto by the House as more judicial in character, in that the House was essentially deciding on the interests of particular individuals (such as Mr. Chadha), rather than making legislative pronouncements on policy questions. In Powell's view, judicial self-restraint dictated the narrower approach, leaving as an open question the constitutionality of other legislative veto provisions, such as that contained in the War Powers Resolution (see Chapter 3).

In his dissenting opinion, Justice Byron White defended the legislative veto as an innovation in keeping with the notion of checks and balances. White regarded the legislative veto as an "indispensable political invention" and saw its invalidation as "regrettable."

The *Chadha* decision places the Court in an anomalous situation with respect to the modern administrative state. On one hand, the Court permits broad and vague delegations of power from Congress to the executive branch, notwithstanding obvious constitutional problems. On the other hand, it refuses to allow Congress to create a device by which it may check the exercise of the very power it delegated. How can the Court be so permissive in its interpretation of the Constitution on the delegation issue and so strict on the issue of the legislative veto? It is clear that the Court is not operating from a coherent theoretical perspective in this area of constitutional law.

Although the *Chadha* decision can be faulted on several grounds, it should not be viewed as tremendously destructive of congressional oversight of the executive bureaucracy. Several mechanisms (discussed earlier) allow Congress to exercise a measure of control. But *Chadha* did represent a symbolic loss for the Congress and, by the same token, a symbolic victory for the executive branch and, in particular, the presidency. Indeed, one might view the *Chadha* case as representing a "hidden agenda" to rebuild a presidency "damaged" by such decisions as *United States v. Nixon* (1974) and *Train v. City of New York* (1975) (see Chapter 3). It is also interesting, and perhaps somewhat surprising, that the Court chose to announce the *Chadha* ruling at the height of anti-Court attacks in Congress aimed at the curtailment of the Court's appellate jurisdiction in certain constitutional areas.

A further indication of the limited practical effect of the *Chadha* decision is seen in the retention of the many legislative veto provisions in existing legislation and the inclusion of legislative veto provisions in a number of statutes passed since *Chadha* was decided. Some of these provisions require executive agencies to obtain approval of certain actions by congressional committees. Others authorize Congress to approve or disapprove agency decisions made pursuant to delegated authority. Thus, although presumptively invalid, the legislative veto survives, at least in the statute books.

Additional Separation of Powers Concerns

Some observers saw the legislative veto (*Chadha*) and Gramm-Rudman-Hollings (*Bowsher*) decisions as exceptions to the Supreme Court's generally permissive view of the separation of powers requirement. They pointed to decisions of the late 1980s upholding congressional establishment of special prosecutors (see *Morrison v. Olson* [1988]) and creation of a sentencing commission (see *Mistretta v. United States* [1989]) as signifying a return to the view that the principle of separation of powers imposed no serious limitation on the authority of Congress. However, in the 1991 decision of *Metropolitan Washington Airports Authority (MWAA) v. Citizens for the Abatement of Aircraft Noise (CAAN)*, the Court made it clear that the separation of powers requirement is not to be taken lightly.

In *MWAA v. CAAN*, the Court held that Congress had violated the separation of powers principle by authorizing the establishment of a board of review, consisting exclusively of members of Congress, with authority to veto decisions made by MWAA, an entity created by a compact between Virginia and Washington, D.C. The Court, in effect, saw the board of review as an agent of Congress and was not impressed by the formal requirement that board members act "in their individual capacities as representatives of airport users nationwide." Relying heavily on *Chadha* and *Bowsher,* the Court struck down an arrangement in which Congress was seeking to exercise control over an ostensibly independent regulatory entity through nonlegislative means. The MWAA case suggests that, contrary to the expectations of some scholars, the *Chadha* and *Bowsher* decisions were not mere anomalies. The Court continued to recognize the separation of powers principle as an important and practical limitation on the prerogatives of Congress.

TO SUMMARIZE:

- Congress retains control over agency discretion by attaching riders to agency appropriations bills, conducting oversight hearings, reducing agency budgets, and rewriting enabling legislation.
- The legislative veto, a modern device used to control agency actions, was declared unconstitutional in *Immigration and Naturalization Service v. Chadha* (1983).
- *Chadha* and other decisions suggest that Congress may not attempt to control an independent regulatory entity through nonlegislative means.

JUDICIAL OVERSIGHT OF THE BUREAUCRACY

Like Congress, the federal courts play an important role in supervising the federal bureaucracy. A fundamental question arising in many cases is whether an agency has acted beyond the scope of its authority as defined by Congress. For example, in *National Association for the Advancement of Colored People v. Federal Power Commission* (1976), the Supreme Court said that the Federal Power Act and the Natural Gas Act did not endow the Federal Power Commission (FPC) with the authority to promulgate a rule requiring the electrical power industry to follow nondiscriminatory employment practices. Writing for the Court, Justice Potter Stewart said:

> The question is not whether Congress could authorize the Federal Power Commission to combat such discrimination. It clearly could. The question is simply whether or to what extent Congress did grant the Commission such authority. . . . [T]he parties point to nothing in the Acts or their legislative histories to indicate that the elimination of employment discrimination was one of the purposes that Congress had in mind when it enacted this legislation.

Naturally, if Congress had wished to provide the FPC with the authority to promulgate rules against employment discrimination, it could merely have amended the statutes that created the agency and defined its authority. In 1977, Congress abolished the FPC and assigned its regulatory functions to a new agency, the Federal Energy Regulatory Commission.

A more recent example of the Court's willingness to limit bureaucratic authority by recognizing limitations imposed by statutory provisions is *Food and Drug Administration v. Brown & Williamson Tobacco Corporation* (2000). In 1996, the FDA promulgated regulations designed to limit young people's access to tobacco products. These regulations were immediately challenged by the tobacco industry. Affirming a court of appeals decision, the Supreme Court held in a 5–4 ruling that the FDA did not have statutory authority to adopt the regulations at issue. Writing for the Court, Justice Sandra Day O'Connor acknowledged that tobacco use is "one of the most troubling public health problems facing our Nation today," but concluded that Congress did not intend for the FDA to exercise authority over tobacco products. O'Connor observed:

> Regardless of how serious the problem an administrative agency seeks to address, . . . it may not exercise its authority "in a manner that is inconsistent with the administrative structure that Congress enacted into law." . . . And although agencies are generally entitled to deference in the interpretation of statutes that they administer, a reviewing "court, as well as the agency, must give effect to the unambiguously expressed intent of Congress."

Due Process of Law

In addition to the substantive issues of agency jurisdiction and rule making authority, there are significant procedural questions regarding administrative actions. Not only are federal regulatory agencies empowered to promulgate rules, they also have substantial powers to enforce those rules, as well as **quasi-judicial authority** to provide hearings and issue binding orders in individual cases. It is important that agency decisions follow procedural guidelines so as to prevent arbitrary and capricious action and to safeguard the rights of parties.

Federal agency procedures are generally based on statutory requirements, most notably the **Administrative Procedure Act** (APA) of 1946. The APA has been called the "Magna Carta of administrative law." It deals with the two basic types of agency decision making—rule making and adjudication—and specifies proper procedures for each. In addition, the Supreme Court has applied the Due Process Clauses of the Fifth and Fourteenth Amendments when it has found statutory procedures inadequate to ensure fairness or to protect the fundamental rights of individuals.

Before a federal court will review any agency decision, threshold criteria such as "standing to sue," "exhaustion of remedies," and "ripeness" must be met (see

Chapter 1). Assuming a federal court decides to review an administrative decision, it will generally attempt to dispose of the case on statutory grounds (for example, by interpreting the Administrative Procedure Act) instead of reaching the constitutional due process issue.

In regard to agency rule making, the Supreme Court has tended to rely on the Administrative Procedure Act as an adequate framework for agency procedures. For example, in *Vermont Yankee Nuclear Power Corporation v. Natural Resources Defense Council, Inc.* (1978), the Supreme Court considered the adequacy of procedures used by the Atomic Energy Commission (now the Nuclear Regulatory Commission) for the licensure of nuclear power plants. Of particular concern was the agency's procedure in promulgating a rule governing spent nuclear fuel. The procedure in question included the scheduling of hearings prior to adoption of the rule, as required by the APA. These hearings were somewhat informal, however, and did not include full adjudicatory procedures, such as discovery and cross-examination. The Court of Appeals for the District of Columbia Circuit held that the existing procedure was inadequate under the Due Process Clause of the Fifth Amendment. The Supreme Court reversed without a dissenting vote. In his opinion for the Court, Justice Rehnquist sharply criticized the court of appeals decision, complaining that "this sort of unwarranted judicial examination of perceived procedural shortcomings of a rulemaking proceeding can do nothing but seriously interfere with that process prescribed by Congress."

During the 1970s, the Supreme Court seemed more willing to apply constitutional due process requirements in cases where agency decisions affected the economic interests of specific individuals. In such cases, the Court must make two determinations. First, it must decide whether the Due Process Clause is applicable. Administrative decisions are constrained by the Due Process Clause only if they in some meaningful way deprive an individual of "life, liberty, or property." Second, assuming the Due Process Clause does apply, the Court must determine what "process" is due in order to ensure fundamental fairness.

The "New Property" Decisions   In *Goldberg v. Kelly* (1970), the Supreme Court held that the Fourteenth Amendment Due Process Clause required a state agency to provide an evidentiary hearing before terminating a person's welfare benefits after the agency determined that the individual was no longer eligible for such benefits. However, Justice Brennan's opinion for the Court failed to clarify the nature of the individual's interest (that is, life, liberty, or property) that gave rise to due process rights. Most commentators have assumed that the welfare entitlements involved in *Goldberg v. Kelly* were viewed by the Court as property interests, hence the term **new property** is often used to describe statutory entitlements.

In *Goss v. Lopez* (1975), the Court continued along the path it paved in *Goldberg v. Kelly*. Here the Court, splitting 5 to 4, held that the ten-day suspension of a student from a public school constituted deprivation of property within the meaning of the Due Process Clause. Thus, the school was required to provide elementary procedural safeguards. The dissenting justices objected to the extension of constitutional protection to an interest they regarded as insubstantial in character.

A series of decisions in the early 1970s extended due process protections to a wide variety of claimants, including employees, automobile drivers, prisoners, and debtors. Eventually, something approaching a counterrevolution was to take place in this area of constitutional law. The first signal of this change came in 1976. In *Mathews v. Eldridge*, the Court upheld procedures under which Social Security disability benefits could be initially terminated without a prior evidentiary hearing. George Eldridge, who had been disabled due to "chronic anxiety and back strain," was informed by an official letter that, according to medical reports, his disability no longer existed and that benefit payments would be terminated. Although agency procedures required ample notification and an evidentiary hearing prior to final termination, the payments could be stopped initially without a hearing. Provision was also made for retroactive payments to any recipient whose disability was later determined not to have ended. Eldridge, who was concerned with the initial decision to terminate payments, relied on *Goldberg v. Kelly* in arguing that the Due Process Clause required an evidentiary hearing before any termination of benefits.

Writing for the Court in *Mathews v. Eldridge*, Justice Lewis Powell conceded the existence of a property interest in Social Security benefits and thus the applicability of the Due Process Clause. But Powell said that "due process is flexible and calls for such procedural protections as the particular situation demands." In other words, the degree of procedural safeguards required by the Constitution depends on how much one stands to lose. In this case, the Court distinguished Social Security from welfare benefits and held that the "potential deprivation . . . is generally likely to be less" when Social Security payments are denied than when welfare benefits are terminated. In this way, the Court significantly narrowed the potential application of *Goldberg v. Kelly* without formally overruling it. In *Mathews*, the Court was willing to regard the existing agency procedures as adequate safeguards. To a litigant in Eldridge's position, the distinction between termination of Social Security and welfare benefits was purely academic. Nevertheless, from the Court's perspective, it was irrelevant that the initial termination of Eldridge's benefits resulted in the foreclosure of his mortgage and repossession of his furniture, forcing him and his family to share one bed. For better or worse, such considerations are generally not permitted to influence the Court in its development and application of constitutional principles.

The Supreme Court's recent decisions in this area are mixed, but the trend seems to be toward limiting the scope of due process protections (see, for example, *Federal Deposit Insurance Corporation v. Meyer* [1994]). The doctrinal coherence that was beginning to emerge in the early 1970s has given way to an ad hoc approach. No single set of constitutional principles has gained dominance. As a result, the prediction of outcomes in individual cases in this area is particularly difficult.

TO SUMMARIZE:

- The judicial branch oversees the federal bureaucracy, ensuring that agency decisions conform to applicable provisions of law. Ultimately, the Due Process Clause of the Fifth Amendment provides a basis for judicial review of the adequacy of agency procedures.
- The early Burger Court expanded due process rights of beneficiaries of federal programs, viewing statutory entitlements as a form of "property" within the meaning of the Fifth Amendment. The later Burger Court and the Rehnquist Court have contracted, or simply refused to expand, due process rights of individuals vis-à-vis federal agencies.

AGENCY ACTIONS AND OTHER INDIVIDUAL RIGHTS

The vast power entrusted to the modern administrative state increases the likelihood that government actions will impinge on individual interests that are protected by the Bill of Rights. For example, FCC regulations of broadcast media have often been challenged on First Amendment grounds (see Chapter 8). In the 1930s and 1940s, the most obvious impact of enlarged governmental regulation was on property rights. But it soon became clear that no neat distinction could be drawn between these rights and other personal rights guaranteed by the Constitution. All constitutional rights may, under some circumstances, give way to compelling public interests. The difficulty, of course, lies in determining which public interests are truly compelling. When agency actions are challenged as violations of individual rights, courts must weigh the magnitude of the alleged violation against the public interest the agency is serving.

Fourth Amendment Concerns

Many administrative practices pose threats to rights protected by the Fourth, Fifth, and Sixth Amendments. One of the more controversial examples involves the Immigration and Naturalization Service (INS), which routinely detains without hearings or the benefit of counsel persons suspected of entering this country illegally. In *Wong Wing v. United States* (1896), the Supreme Court ruled that individuals can be detained by immigration authorities without hearings as long as the purpose of the detention is not punitive. For the most part, however, the Court has refrained from reviewing federal immigration laws for compliance with substantive constitutional rights.

INS detentions of suspected illegal aliens are not the only administrative actions that threaten constitutionally protected liberties. **Administrative searches** of industrial plants are routinely conducted by such regulatory bodies as the Environmental Protection Agency (EPA) and the Occupational Safety and Health Administration (OSHA). Traditionally, the Supreme Court has been more permissive toward administrative searches directed at business and industry than toward police searches directed at private individuals. For example, in *Frank v. Maryland* (1959) and *Ohio ex rel. Eaton v. Price* (1960), the Supreme Court found no violation of the Fourth Amendment when administrative searches were conducted without notice and without search warrants. In the 1960s and 1970s, the Court became stricter, holding that, as a general rule, warrants must be obtained to justify administrative searches (see, for example, *Camara v. Municipal Court* [1967], overruling *Frank v. Maryland*).

Following this stricter approach, in *Marshall v. Barlow's, Inc.* (1978), the Supreme Court struck down a provision of the Occupational Health and Safety Act of 1970 that allowed OSHA to conduct warrantless searches of the workplace. However, the Court was careful to point out that to obtain administrative search warrants, OSHA inspectors did not have to meet the same strict standards of probable cause that govern the issuance of warrants in criminal investigations. In *Donovan v. Dewey* (1981), the Court refused to invalidate a provision of the Federal Mine Safety and Health Act of 1977 that allowed the Department of Labor to conduct warrantless inspections of mines. The Court attempted to distinguish the case from *Barlow's*, but it seems clear that a majority of the justices preferred the more permissive approach of the pre-*Camara* period.

Another recent case that epitomizes a permissive approach to the Fourth Amendment as it relates to regulatory agency searches is *Dow Chemical Company v. United States* (1986). Here, the EPA, acting without a warrant, had employed a commercial aerial photographer to take pictures of a Dow chemical plant from an altitude of 1,200 feet. When Dow learned of the photographic flyover, it filed suit in federal court, claiming that the EPA had violated its reasonable expectation of privacy. Splitting 5 to 4, the Supreme Court rejected Dow's claim, holding that the flyover was not a "search" within the meaning of the Fourth Amendment.

Self-Incrimination Concerns

The Self-Incrimination Clause of the Fifth Amendment is another provision of the Bill of Rights potentially endangered by administrative actions. Essentially, this clause protects the individual from being forced to divulge incriminating information. Although the obvious application of the Self-Incrimination Clause is to criminal investigations, the Supreme Court has held that the protection applies in any governmental context that might ultimately lead to criminal prosecution (see *Murphy v. Waterfront Commission* [1964]). However, the Court has distinguished between verbal testimony and physical evidence, holding that the immunity against self-incrimination applies only to the former. Consequently, businesses have no real Fifth Amendment protections in the instance of compulsory production of incriminating business records. As a result of the winnowing of the Self-Incrimination Clause, businesspersons can be compelled to disclose their records to the scrutiny of government agencies. Justice William J. Brennan consistently dissented from this view of the Fifth Amendment, arguing that business records fall within the "zone of privacy" protected by the Self-Incrimination Clause (see, for example, *Andresen v. Maryland* [1976], dissenting opinion).

Public Access to Agency Information

Other potential objections to the actions of the modern administrative state involve access to the tremendous stockpile of information maintained by various government agencies. Although the Supreme Court has never held such access to be a matter of constitutional right, Congress has created a statutory right of public access under the **Freedom of Information Act** and a right of individual access under the Privacy Act. Although these acts do create exemptions for certain types of secret information, such as sensitive national security material, they nevertheless represent a significant attempt to open up the process of modern governance to the ordinary citizen.

Bureaucratic Support for Civil Rights and Liberties

Lest one assume that all actions of the federal bureaucracy are inimical to civil rights and liberties, we should point out that, in recent decades, the federal government has created programs that foster them. For example, the Civil Rights Division of the Department of Justice is responsible for enforcing the extensive civil rights legislation adopted since the late 1950s—most notably the Civil Rights Act of 1964, the Voting Rights Act of 1965, and the Americans with Disabilities Act of 1990. Other agencies, such as the Department of Labor and the EEOC, also exercise important responsibilities in enforcing federal policies against job discrimination. Additionally, in 1974, Congress created the Legal Services Corporation to provide legal assistance to indigent persons involved in civil cases.

TO SUMMARIZE:

- When agency actions are challenged as violations of individual rights, courts must weigh the magnitude of the violation against the public interest the agency is serving.
- The Supreme Court has been more permissive toward administrative searches directed at business and industry than toward police searches of private homes.
- A number of federal agencies have an important role to play in enforcing civil rights and liberties.

CONCLUSION

The sociologist Max Weber argued that bureaucracy exists in the modern world because it is the most rational way of organizing efforts toward the achievement of collective goals. Whether or not Weber was right, bureaucracy is an inextricable component of modern government. Clearly, bureaucracy is here to stay, whether one considers the federal government, the governments of the fifty states, or the governments of the nation's major cities. However, the essence of American constitutionalism is that government derives its powers from and must operate within the limitations of the Constitution, the supreme law of the land. The existence of the mammoth federal bureaucracy and similar, if smaller, bureaucracies in all fifty states poses serious problems of constitutional theory. These problems include the delegation of legislative power and the means of legislative and judicial oversight of administrative decision making.

In grappling with these issues, the Supreme Court has not developed a coherent constitutional theory. But one must recognize that no area of constitutional law is fully coherent. In the nature of things political, the Court's decisions are bound to reflect the untidy realities of politics more than the neatness of syllogisms. Yet it is in this particular realm of constitutional law that the eighteenth century ideals of limited government and the rule of law seem to be most out of sync with the realities of twenty-first century political life. As the primary mechanism for fitting constitutional principles with political realities, the Supreme Court faces an especially formidable task in addressing questions of bureaucratic power.

KEY TERMS

modern administrative state	delegation of legislative power	nondelegation doctrine	Administrative Procedure Act
federal bureaucracy	representative government	oversight hearings	new property
rule making	separation of powers	legislative veto	administrative searches
independent agencies	intelligible principle standard	quasi-judicial authority	Freedom of Information Act

FOR FURTHER READING

Barber, Sotirios A. *The Constitution and the Delegation of Congressional Power*. Chicago: University of Chicago Press, 1975.

Carter, Lief H., and Christine B. Harrington. *Administrative Law and Politics: Cases and Comments* (3rd ed.). New York: Longman, 2000.

Davis, Kenneth C. *Discretionary Justice*. Baton Rouge: Louisiana State University Press, 1969.

Dodd, Lawrence C., and Richard L. Schott. *Congress and the Administrative State*. New York: Wiley, 1979.

Epstein, Richard A. *Takings: Private Property and the Power of Eminent Domain*. Cambridge, Mass.: Harvard University Press, 1985.

Fisher, Louis. *The Politics of Shared Power: Congress and the Executive*. Washington, D.C.: Congressional Quarterly Press, 1987.

Harris, Joseph. *Congressional Control of Administration*. New York: Doubleday, 1965.

Lowi, Theodore J. *The End of Liberalism* (2nd ed.). New York: Norton, 1979.

Rohr, John A. *To Run a Constitution: The Legitimacy of the Administrative State*. Lawrence: University Press of Kansas, 1986.

Shapiro, Martin. *Who Guards the Guardians? Judicial Control of Administration*. Athens: University of Georgia Press, 1988.

Sunstein, Cass R. *After the Rights Revolution: Reconceiving the Regulatory State*. Cambridge, Mass.: Harvard University Press, 1990.

Warren, Kenneth F. *Administrative Law in the American Political System* (3rd edition). Englewood Cliffs, N.J.: Prentice-Hall, 1996.

Case

J. W. HAMPTON & COMPANY V. UNITED STATES

276 U.S. 394; 48 S.Ct. 348; 72 L.Ed. 624 (1928)
Vote: 9–0

In this case, the Court considers the issue of congressional delegation of legislative power in the context of a "flexible tariff provision."

Mr. Chief Justice Taft delivered the opinion of the Court.

J. W. Hampton, Jr. & Company made an importation into New York of barium dioxide which the collector of customs assessed at the dutiable rate of 6 cents per pound. This was 2 cents per pound more than that fixed by statute. . . . The rate was raised by the collector by virtue of the proclamation of the President . . . issued under . . . authority of . . . the Tariff Act of September 21, 1922, . . . which is the so-called flexible tariff provision. Protest was made and an appeal was taken. . . . The case came . . . before the United States customs court. . . . A majority held the action constitutional. Thereafter the case was appealed to the United States court of customs appeals. On the 16th day of October, 1926, the Attorney General certified that in his opinion the case was of such importance as to render expedient its review by this court. Thereafter the judgment of the United States customs court was affirmed. . . . On a petition to this court for certiorari, . . . the writ was granted. . . .

The issue here is as to the constitutionality of [the Tariff Act] upon which depends the authority for the proclamation of the President and for 2 of the 6 cents per pound duty collected from [J. W. Hampton]. The contention of the taxpayers is . . . that the section is invalid in that it is a delegation to the President of the legislative power, which by Article 1, Sec. 1 of the Constitution, is vested in

Congress, the power being that declared in Sec. 8 of Article 1, that the Congress shall have power to lay and collect taxes, duties, imposts, and excises. . . .

. . . It seems clear what Congress intended by [the act]. Its plan was to secure by law the imposition of customs duties on articles of imported merchandise which should equal the difference between the cost of producing in a foreign country the articles in question and laying them down for sale in the United States, and the cost of producing and selling like or similar articles in the United States, so that the duties not only secure revenue but at the same time enable domestic producers to compete on terms of equality with foreign producers in the markets of the United States. It may be that it is difficult to fix with exactness this difference, but the difference which is sought in the statute is perfectly clear and perfectly intelligible. Because of the difficulty in practically determining what that difference is, Congress seems to have doubted that the information in its possession was such as to enable it to make the adjustment accurately, and also to have apprehended that with changing conditions the difference might vary in such a way that some readjustments would be necessary to give effect to the principle on which the statute proceeds. To avoid such difficulties, Congress adopted . . . the method of describing with clearness what its policy and plan was and then authorizing a member of the executive branch to carry out its policy and plan and to find the changing difference from time to time and to make the adjustments necessary to conform the duties to the standard underlying that policy and plan. As it was a matter of great importance, it concluded to give by statute to the President . . . the function of determining the difference as it might vary. . . .

The well-known maxim *delegata potestas non potest delegari* ["that which is delegated cannot be redelegated"], applicable to the law of agency in the general and common law, is well understood and has had wider application in the construction of our Federal and state Constitutions than it has in private law. Our Federal Constitution and state Constitutions of this country divide the governmental power into three branches. The first is the legislative, the second is the executive, and the third is the judicial, and the rule is that in the actual administration of the government Congress or the legislature should exercise the legislative power, the President or the state executive, the governor, the executive power, and the courts or the judiciary the judicial power, and in carrying out that constitutional division into three branches it is a breach of the national fundamental law if Congress gives up its legislative power and transfers it to the President, or to the judicial branch, or if by law it attempts to invest itself or its members with either executive power or judicial power. This is not to say that the three branches are not coordinate parts of one government and that each in the field of its duties may not invoke the action of the two other branches in so far as the action invoked shall not be an assumption of the constitutional field of action of another branch. In determining what it may do in seeking assistance from another branch, the extent and character of that assistance must be fixed according to common sense and the inherent necessities of the governmental coordination.

The field of Congress involves all and many varieties of legislative action, and Congress had found it frequently necessary to use officers of the executive branch, within definite limits, to secure the exact effect intended by its acts of legislation, by vesting discretion in such officers to make public regulations interpreting a statute and directing the details of its execution, even to the extent of providing for penalizing a breach of such regulations. . . .

Congress may feel itself unable conveniently to determine exactly when its exercise of the legislative power should become effective, because dependent on future conditions, and it may leave the determination of such time to the decision of an executive. . . .

[O]ne of the great functions conferred on Congress by the Federal Constitution is the regulation of interstate commerce and rates to be exacted by interstate carriers for the passenger and merchandise traffic. The rates to be fixed are myriad. If Congress were to be required to fix every rate, it would be impossible to exercise the power at all. Therefore, common sense requires that in the fixing of such rates, Congress may provide a Commission, as it does, called the Interstate Commerce Commission, to fix those rates, after hearing evidence and argument concerning them from interested parties, all in accord with a general rule that Congress first lays down that rates shall be just and reasonable considering the service given and not discriminatory. . . .

It is conceded by counsel that Congress may use executive officers in the application and enforcement of a policy declared in law by Congress and authorize such officers in the application of the congressional declaration to enforce it by regulation equivalent to law. But it is said that this never has been permitted to be done where Congress has exercised the power to levy taxes and fix customs duties. The authorities make no such distinction. The same principle that permits Congress to exercise its rate-making power in interstate commerce by declaring the rule which shall prevail in the legislative fixing of rates, and enables it to remit to a rate-making-body created in accordance with its provisions the fixing of such rates, justifies a similar provision for the fixing of customs duties on imported merchandise. If Congress shall lay down by legislative act an intelligible principle to which the person or body authorized to fix such rates is directed to conform, such legislative action is not a forbidden delegation of legislative power. If it is thought wise to vary the customs duties according to changing conditions of production at home and abroad, it may authorize the Chief Executive to carry out this purpose. . . .

Case

SCHECHTER POULTRY CORPORATION V. UNITED STATES

295 U.S. 495; 55 S.Ct. 837; 79 L.Ed. 1570 (1935)
Vote: 9–0

In this landmark case, the Supreme Court considers the constitutionality of the National Industrial Recovery Act of 1933. The Court considers two issues: (1) whether the act constitutes

an impermissible delegation of power from Congress to the executive; and (2) whether the act is a valid exercise of Congress's power to regulate interstate commerce. In this excerpt, only the former issue is addressed.

Mr. Chief Justice Hughes delivered the opinion of the Court.

[Schechter Poultry Corporation et al.] were convicted in the District Court of the United States for the Eastern District of New York on eighteen counts of an indictment charging violations of what is known as the "Live Poultry Code," and on an additional count for conspiracy to commit such violations. . . .

The Circuit Court of Appeals sustained the conviction on the conspiracy count and on sixteen counts for violation of the code. . . . On the respective applications of the defendants . . . this Court granted writs of certiorari. . . .

The "Live Poultry Code" was promulgated under Sec. 3 of the National Industrial Recovery Act. That section . . . authorizes the President to approve "codes of fair competition." Such a code may be approved for a trade or industry, upon application by one of more trade or industrial associations or groups, if the President finds (1) that such associations or groups "impose no inequitable restrictions on admission to membership therein and are truly representative," and (2) that such codes are not designed "to promote monopolies or to eliminate or oppress small enterprises and will not operate to discriminate against them, and will tend to effectuate the policy" . . . of the act. Such codes "shall not permit monopolies or monopolistic practices." As a condition of his approval, the President may "impose such conditions (including requirements for the making of reports and the keeping of accounts) for the protection of consumers, competitors, employees and others, and in furtherance of the public interest, and may provide such exceptions to an exemption from the provisions of such code as the President in his discretion deems necessary to effectuate the policy herein declared." Where such a code has not been approved, the President may prescribe one, either on his own motion or on complaint. Violation of any provision of a code (so approved or prescribed) "in any transaction in or affecting interstate or foreign commerce" is made a misdemeanor punishable by a fine of not more than $500 for each offense, and each day the violation continues is to be deemed a separate offense.

The "Live Poultry Code" was approved by the President on April 13, 1934. . . .

The declared purpose is "To effect the policies of title I of the National Industrial Recovery Act." . . .

The code fixes the number of hours for workdays. It provides that no employee, with certain exceptions, shall be permitted to work in excess of forty (40) hours in any one week, and that no employee, save as stated, "shall be paid in any pay period less than at the rate of fifty (50) cents per hour." . . . [The code also limits child labor practices and creates administrative procedures for the execution of the code's provisions.]

Of the eighteen counts of the indictment upon which the defendants were convicted, aside from the count for conspiracy, two counts charged violations of the minimum wage and maximum hour provisions of the code; . . . ten

counts, respectively, were that [Schechter, in selling] to retail dealers and butchers, had permitted "selections of individual chickens taken from particular coops and half coops."

Of the other six counts, one charged the sale to a butcher of an unfit chicken; two counts charged the making of sales without having the poultry inspected or approved in accordance with regulations or ordinances of the City of New York; two counts charged the making of false reports or the failure to make reports relating to the range of daily prices and volume and sales for certain periods; and the remaining count was for sales to slaughterers or dealers who were without licenses required by the ordinances and regulations of the City of New York.

First. Two preliminary points are stressed by the government with respect to the appropriate approach to the important questions presented. We are told that the provision of the statute authorizing the adoption of codes must be viewed in the light of the grave national crisis with which Congress was confronted. Undoubtedly, the conditions to which power is addressed are always to be considered when the exercise of power is challenged. Extraordinary conditions may call for extraordinary remedies. But the argument necessarily stops short of an attempt to justify action which lies outside the sphere of constitutional authority. Extraordinary conditions do not create or enlarge constitutional power. The Constitution establishes a national government with powers deemed to be adequate, as they have proved to be both in war and peace, but these powers of the national government are limited by the constitutional grants. Those who act under these grants are not at liberty to transcend the imposed limits because they believe that more or different power is necessary. . . .

The further point is urged that the national crisis demanded a broad and intensive co-operative effort by those engaged in trade and industry, and that this necessary co-operation was sought to be fostered by permitting them to initiate the adoption of codes. But the statutory plan is not simply one for voluntary effort. It does not seek merely to endow voluntary trade or industrial associations or groups with privileges or immunities. It involves the coercive exercise of the law-making power. The codes of fair competition which the statute attempts to authorize are codes of laws. If valid, they place all persons within their reach under the obligation of positive law, binding equally those who assent and those who do not assent. Violations of the provisions of the codes are punishable as crimes.

Second. The question of the delegation of legislative power [:] . . . the Constitution provides that "all legislative powers herein granted shall be vested in a Congress of the United States, which shall consist of a Senate and House of

Representatives." . . . And the Congress is authorized "to make all laws which shall be necessary and proper for carrying into execution" its general power. . . . The Congress is not permitted to abdicate or to transfer to others the essential legislative functions with which it is thus vested. We have repeatedly recognized the necessity of adapting legislation to complex conditions involving a host of details with which the National Legislature cannot deal directly. We point out in the Panama Ref. Co. Case [*Panama Refining Company v. Ryan* (1935)] that the Constitution has never been regarded as denying to Congress the necessary resources of flexibility and practicality, which will enable it to perform its function in laying down policies and establishing standards, while leaving to selected instrumentalities the making of subordinate rules within prescribed limits and the determination of facts to which the policy as declared by the Legislature is to apply. But . . . the constant recognition of the necessity and validity of such provisions, and the wide range of administrative authority which has been developed by means of them, cannot be allowed to obscure the limitations of the authority to delegate, if our constitutional system is to be maintained. . . .

Accordingly, we look to the statute to see whether Congress has overstepped these limitations—whether Congress in authorizing "Codes of Fair Competition" has itself established the standards of legal obligation, thus performing its essential legislative function, or, by the failure to enact such standards, has attempted to transfer that function to others. . . .

What is meant by "fair competition" as the term is used in the act? Does it refer to a category established in the law, and is the authority to make codes limited accordingly? Or is it used as a convenient designation for whatever set of laws the formulators of a code for a particular trade or industry may propose and the President may himself prescribe, as being wise and beneficent provisions for the government of the trade or industry in order to accomplish the broad purposes of rehabilitation, correction and expansion which are stated [in the act]?

The act does not define "fair competition." "Unfair competition" as known to the common law is a limited concept. Primarily, and strictly, it relates to the palming off of one's goods as those of a rival trader. . . . In recent years its scope has been extended. It has been held to apply to misappropriation as well as misrepresentation, to the selling of anther's goods as one's own—to misappropriation of what equitably belongs to a competitor. . . . Unfairness in competition has been predicated on acts which lie outside the ordinary course of business and are tainted by fraud, or coercion, or conduct otherwise prohibited by law. . . . But it is evident that in its widest range "unfair competition," as it has been understood in the law,

does not reach the objectives of the codes which are authorized by the National Industrial Recovery Act. The codes may, indeed, cover conduct which existing law condemns, but they are not limited to conduct of that sort. The government does not contend that the act contemplates such a limitation. It would be opposed both to the declared purposes of the act and to its administrative construction.

The Federal Trade Commission Act . . . introduces the expression "unfair methods of competition," which were declared to be unlawful. That was an expression new in the law. Debate apparently convinced the sponsors of the legislation that the words "unfair competition," in the light of their meaning at common law, were too narrow. We have said that the substituted phrase has a broader meaning; that it does not admit of precise definition, its scope being left to judicial determination as controversies arise. . . . What are "unfair methods of competition" are thus to be determined in particular competitive conditions and of what is found to be a specific and substantial public interest. . . . To make this possible Congress set up a special procedure. A commission, a quasi-judicial body, was created. Provision was made for formal complaint, for notice and hearing, for appropriate findings of fact supported by adequate evidence, and for judicial review to give assurance that the action of the Commission is taken within its statutory authority. . . .

In providing for codes, the National Industrial Recovery Act dispenses with this administrative procedure and with any administrative procedure of an analogous character. But the difference between the code plan of the Recovery Act and the scheme of the Federal Trade Commission Act lies not only in procedure but in subject matter. We cannot regard the "fair competition" of the codes as antithetical to the "unfair methods of competition" of the Federal Trade Commission Act. The "fair competition" of the codes has a much broader range and a new significance. The Recovery Act provides that it shall not be construed to impair the powers of the Federal Trade Commission, but, when a code is approved, its provisions are to be the "standards of fair competition" for the trade or industry concerned, and any violation of such standards in any transaction in or affecting interstate or foreign commerce is to be deemed "an unfair method of competition" within the meaning of the Federal Trade Commission Act. . . .

For a statement of the authorized objectives and content of the "codes of fair competition" we are referred repeatedly to the "declaration of policy" in . . . the Recovery Act. Thus, the approval of a code by the President is conditioned on his finding that it "will tend to effectuate the policy of this title." . . . The President is authorized to impose such conditions "for the protection of consumers, competitors, employees and others, and in furtherance of the public interest, and may provide such exceptions to and exemptions from the provisions of such code as the President in his discretion deems necessary to effectuate the policy herein declared." . . . The "policy herein declared" is manifestly that set forth. . . . That declaration embraces a broad range of objectives. Among them we find the elimination of "unfair competitive practices." But even if this clause were to be taken to relate to practices which fall under the ban of existing law, either common law or statute, it is still only one of the authorized aims described. . . . It is there declared to be "the policy of Congress"—to remove obstructions to the free flow of interstate and foreign commerce which tend to diminish the amount thereof; and to provide for the general welfare by promoting the organization of industry for the purpose of co-operative action among trade groups, to induce and maintain united action of labor and management under adequate governmental sanctions and supervision, to eliminate unfair competitive practices, to promote the fullest possible utilization of the present productive capacity of industries, to avoid undue restriction of production (except as may be temporarily required), to increase the consumption of industrial and agricultural products by increasing purchasing power, to reduce and rehabilitate industry and to conserve natural resources.

. . . [Under these provisions], whatever "may tend to effectuate" these general purposes may be included in the "codes of fair competition." We think the conclusion is inescapable that the authority sought to be conferred . . . was not merely to deal with "unfair competitive practices" which offend against existing law, and could be the subject of judicial condemnation without further legislation, or to create administrative machinery for the application of established principles of law to particular instances of violation. Rather, the purpose is clearly disclosed to authorize new and controlling prohibitions through codes of laws which would embrace what the formulators would propose, and what the President would approve, or prescribe, as wise and beneficent measures for the government of trades and industries in order to bring about their rehabilitation, correction and development, according to the general declaration of policy. . . . Codes of laws of this sort are styled "codes of fair competition." . . .

The question, then, turns upon the authority which . . . the Recovery Act vests in the President to approve or prescribe. . . . Congress cannot delegate legislative power to the President to exercise an unfettered discretion to make whatever laws he thinks may be needed or advisable for the rehabilitation and expansion of trade or industry. . . .

Accordingly we turn to the Recovery Act to ascertain what limits have been set to the exercise of the President's discretion. First, the President, as a condition of approval, is required to find that the trade or industrial associations or groups which propose a code "impose no inequitable restrictions on admission to membership" and are "truly representative." That condition, however, relates only to the status of the initiators of the new laws and not to the permissible scope of such laws. Second, the President is required to find that the code is not "designed to promote monopolies or to eliminate or oppress small enterprises and will not operate to discriminate against them." And to this is added a proviso that the code "shall not permit monopolies or monopolistic practices." But these restrictions leave virtually untouched the field of policy envisaged . . . and in what wide field of legislative possibilities the proponents of a code, refraining from monopolistic designs, may roam at will and the President may approve or disapprove their proposals as he may see fit. "That is the precise effect of the further finding that the President is to make—that the code will tend to effectuate the policy of this title." While this is called a finding, it is really but a statement of an opinion as to the general effect upon the promotion of trade or industry of a scheme of laws. These are the only findings which Congress has made essential in order to put into operation a legislative code having the aims described in the "Declaration of Policy."

Nor is the breadth of the President's discretion left to the necessary implications of this limited requirement as to his findings. As already noted, the President in approving a code may impose his own conditions, adding to or taking from what is proposed, as "in his discretion" he thinks necessary "to effectuate the policy" declared by the act. Of course, he has no less liberty when he prescribes a code on his own motion or on complaint, and he is free to prescribe one if a code has not been approved. The act provides for the creation by the President of administrative agencies to assist him, but the action or reports of such agencies, or of his other assistants—their recommendations and findings in relation to the making of codes—have no sanction beyond the will of the President, who may accept, modify or reject them as he pleases. . . .

To summarize and conclude upon this point: . . . the Recovery Act is without precedent. It supplies no standards for any trade, industry or activity. It does not undertake to prescribe rules of conduct to be applied to particular states of fact determined by appropriate administrative procedure. Instead of prescribing rules of conduct, it authorizes the making of codes to prescribe them. For that legislative undertaking, Sec. 3 sets up no standards, aside from the statement of the general aims of rehabilitation, correction and expansion. . . . In view of the scope of that broad declaration, and of the nature of the few restrictions that are imposed, the discretion of the President in approving or prescribing codes, and thus enacting laws for the government of trade and industry throughout the country, is virtually unfettered. We think that the code-making authority thus conferred is an unconstitutional delegation of legislative power. . . .

[The Court also considered Commerce Clause questions and concluded that the attempted regulation of intrastate activities exceeded the constitutional grant of power to regulate interstate commerce.]

Mr. Justice Cardozo, concurring.

The delegated power of legislation which has found expression in this code is not canalized within banks that keep it from overflowing. It is unconfined and vagrant. . . .

. . . Here, in the case before us, is an attempted delegation not confined to any single act nor to any class or group of acts identified or described by reference to a standard. Here in effect is a roving commission to inquire into evils and upon discovery correct them. . . .

. . . This is delegation running riot. No such plenitude of power is susceptible of transfer. The statute, however, aims

at nothing less, as one can learn both from its terms and from the administrative practice under it. Nothing less is aimed at by the code now submitted to our scrutiny. . . .

The code does not confine itself to the suppression of methods of competition that would be classified as unfair according to accepted business standards or accepted norms of ethics. It sets up a comprehensive body of rules to promote the welfare of the industry, if not the welfare of the nation, without reference to standards, ethical or commercial, that could be known or predicted in advance of its adoption. . . . Even if the statute itself had fixed the meaning of fair competition by way of contrast with practices that are oppressive or unfair, the code outruns the bounds of the authority conferred. What is excessive is not sporadic or superficial. It is deep-seated and pervasive. The licit and illicit sections are so combined and welded as to be incapable of severance without destructive mutilation. . . .

I am authorized to state that Mr. Justice Stone joins in this opinion.

Case

Mistretta v. United States

488 U.S. 361; 109 S.Ct. 647; 102 L.Ed. 2d 714 (1989)

Vote: 8–1

Under the Sentencing Reform Act of 1984 Congress abolished the system of indeterminate criminal sentencing and parole previously applied in federal cases. Indeterminate sentencing and parole had long been criticized because of wide disparities among similarly situated defendants both in the sentences imposed by judges and in the actual time of imprisonment served prior to release on parole. One of the most controversial provisions of the Sentencing Reform Act called for the establishment of the U.S. Sentencing Commission, an independent body of seven voting members within the judicial branch. All members of the commission were to be appointed by the president, with Senate approval, and were subject to removal by the president for "neglect of duty," "malfeasance in office," or "other good cause." The statute required that at least three members of the sentencing commission be federal judges, chosen from a list of six recommended to the president by the Judicial Conference of the United States. The commission was empowered to promulgate binding sentencing guidelines that federal judges were required to follow. These guidelines prescribed ranges of determinate sentences for all types of federal

offenses and defendants, according to detailed specified factors. A federal grand jury returned a three-count indictment against John Mistretta, resulting from his alleged distribution of cocaine. Mistretta moved to have the sentencing guidelines ruled unconstitutional on the grounds that they represented an excessive delegation of authority by Congress and that they violated the principle of separation of powers. The district court denied his motion and upheld the guidelines. Mistretta then agreed to plead guilty to one count of the indictment (conspiracy to distribute) in exchange for the prosecutors' willingness to dismiss the other two counts. Accepting this negotiated guilty plea, the trial judge applied the sentencing guidelines over Mistretta's constitutional objections and sentenced him to a prison term of eighteen months. Mistretta filed a notice of appeal to the U.S. Court of Appeals for the Eighth Circuit, but both he and the government later petitioned the Supreme Court for certiorari, thus obtaining review by the High Court prior to judgment by the court of appeals. The Court's willingness to grant this expedited review underscored its recognition of the importance of constitutional questions posed by the Sentencing Reform Act.

Justice Blackmun delivered the Opinion of the Court.

. . . Petitioner argues that in delegating the power to promulgate sentencing guidelines for every federal criminal offense to an independent Sentencing Commission,

Congress has granted the Commission excessive legislative discretion in violation of the constitutionally based nondelegation doctrine. We do not agree.

The nondelegation doctrine is rooted in the principle of separation of powers that underlies our tripartite system of Government. The Constitution provides that "[a]ll legislative Powers herein granted shall be vested in a Congress of the United States," . . . and we long have insisted that "the integrity and maintenance of the system of government ordained by the Constitution" mandate that Congress generally cannot delegate its legislative power to another Branch. . . . We also have recognized, however, that the separation-of-powers principle, and the nondelegation doctrine in particular, do not prevent Congress from obtaining the assistance of its coordinate Branches. . . .

. . . [O]ur jurisprudence has been driven by a practical understanding that in our increasingly complex society, replete with ever changing and more technical problems, Congress simply cannot do its job absent an ability to delegate power under broad general directives. . . .

. . . In light of our approval of these broad delegations, we harbor no doubt that Congress' delegation of authority to the Sentencing Commission is sufficiently specific and detailed to meet constitutional requirements. Congress charged the Commission with three goals: to "assure the meeting of the purposes of sentencing as set forth" in the Act; to "provide certainty and fairness in meeting the purposes of sentencing, avoiding unwarranted sentencing disparities among defendants with similar records . . . while maintaining sufficient flexibility to permit individualized sentences," where appropriate; and to "reflect, to the extent practicable, advancement in knowledge of human behavior as it relates to the criminal justice process." . . . Congress further specified four "purposes" of sentencing that the Commission must pursue in carrying out its mandate: "to reflect the seriousness of the offense, to promote respect for the law, and to provide just punishment for the offense"; "to afford adequate deterrence to criminal conduct"; "to protect the public from further crimes of the defendant"; and "to provide the defendant with needed . . . correctional treatment." . . .

In addition, Congress prescribed the specific tool—the guidelines system—for the Commission to use in regulating sentencing. More particularly, Congress directed the Commission to develop a system of "sentencing ranges" applicable "for each category of offense involving each category of defendant." . . . Congress instructed the Commission that these sentencing ranges must be consistent with pertinent provisions of Title 18 of the United States Code and could not include sentences in excess of the statutory maxima. Congress also required that for sentences of imprisonment, "the maximum of the range established for such a term shall not exceed the minimum of that range by more than the greater of 25 percent or 6 months, except that, if the minimum term of the range is 30 years or more, the maximum may be life imprisonment." . . . Moreover, Congress directed the Commission to use current average sentences "as a starting point" for its structuring of the sentencing ranges. . . .

To guide the Commission in its formulation of offense categories, Congress directed it to consider seven factors: the grade of the offense; the aggravating and mitigating circumstances of the crime; the nature and degree of the harm caused by the crime; the community view of the gravity of the offense; the public concern generated by the crime; the deterrent effect that a particular sentence may have on others; and the current incidence of the offense. . . . Congress set forth 11 factors for the Commission to consider in establishing categories of defendants. These include the offender's age, education, vocational skills, mental and emotional condition, physical condition (including drug dependence), previous employment record, family ties and responsibilities, community ties, role in the offense, criminal history, and degree of dependence upon crime for a livelihood. . . . Congress also prohibited the Commission from considering the "race, sex, national origin, creed, and socioeconomic status of offenders," . . . and instructed that the guidelines should reflect the "general inappropriateness" of considering certain other factors, such as current unemployment, that might serve as proxies for forbidden factors. . . .

In addition to these overarching constraints, Congress provided even more detailed guidance to the Commission about categories of offenses and offender characteristics. Congress directed that guidelines require a term of confinement at or near the statutory maximum for certain crimes of violence and for drug offenses, particularly when committed by recidivists. . . . Congress further directed that the Commission assure a substantial term of imprisonment for an offense constituting a third felony conviction, for a career felon, for one convicted of a managerial role in a racketeering enterprise, for a crime of violence by an offender on release from a prior felony conviction, and for an offense involving a substantial quantity of narcotics. . . . Congress also instructed "that the guidelines reflect . . . the general appropriateness of imposing a term of imprisonment" for a crime of violence that resulted in serious bodily injury. On the other hand, Congress directed that guidelines reflect the general inappropriateness of imposing a sentence of imprisonment "in cases in which the defendant is a first offender who has not been convicted of a crime of violence or an otherwise serious offense." . . . Congress also enumerated various aggravating and mitigating circumstances, such as, respectively, multiple offenses or substantial assistance to the Government, to be reflected in the guidelines. . . . In other words, although Congress granted the Commission substantial discretion in formulating guidelines, in actuality it legislated a full hierarchy of punishment—from near maximum imprisonment, to substantial imprisonment, to some imprisonment, to alternatives—and stipulated the most important offense and offender characteristics to place defendants within these categories.

We cannot dispute petitioner's contention that the Commission enjoys significant discretion in formulating guidelines. The Commission does have discretionary authority to determine the relative severity of federal crimes and to assess the relative weight of the offender characteristics that Congress listed for the Commission to consider. . . . The Commission also has significant discretion to determine which crimes have been punished too leniently, and which too severely. . . . Congress has called upon the Commission to exercise its judgment about which types of crimes and which types of criminals are to be considered similar for the purposes of sentencing.

But our cases do not at all suggest that delegations of this type may not carry with them the need to exercise judgment on matters of policy. . . .

. . . The Act sets forth more than merely an "intelligible principle" or minimal standards. One court has aptly put it: "The statute outlines the policies which prompted establishment of the Commission, explains what the Commission should do and how it should do it, and sets out specific directives to govern particular situations." . . .

Developing proportionate penalties for hundreds of different crimes by a virtually limitless array of offenders is precisely the sort of intricate, labor-intensive task for which delegation to an expert body is especially appropriate. Although Congress has delegated significant discretion to the Commission to draw judgments from its analysis of existing sentencing practice and alternative sentencing models, "Congress is not confined to that method of executing its policy which involves the least possible delegation of discretion to administrative officers." . . . We have no doubt that in the hands of the Commission "the criteria which Congress has supplied are wholly adequate for carrying out the general policy and purpose" of the Act. . . .

We conclude that in creating the Sentencing Commission—an unusual hybrid in structure and authority—Congress neither delegated excessive legislative power nor upset the constitutionally mandated balance of powers among the coordinate Branches. The Constitution's structural protections do not prohibit Congress from delegating to an expert body located within the Judicial Branch the intricate task of formulating sentencing guidelines consis-

tent with such significant statutory direction as is present here. Nor does our system of checked and balanced authority prohibit Congress from calling upon the accumulated wisdom and experience of the Judicial Branch in creating policy on a matter uniquely within the ken of judges. Accordingly, we hold that the Act is constitutional.

The judgment of United States District Court for the Western District of Missouri is affirmed. . . .

Justice Scalia, dissenting.

While the products of the Sentencing Commission's labors have been given the modest name "Guidelines," . . . they have the force and effect of laws, prescribing the sentences criminal defendants are to receive. A judge who disregards them will be reversed. . . . I dissent from today's decision because I can find no place within our constitutional system for an agency created by Congress to exercise no governmental power other than the making of laws. . . . Today's decision follows the regrettable tendency of our recent separation-of-powers jurisprudence . . . to treat the Constitution as though it were no more than a generalized prescription that the functions of the Branches should not be commingled too much—how much is too much to be determined, case-by-case, by this Court. The Constitution is not that. Rather, as its name suggests, it is a prescribed structure, a framework, for the conduct of Government. In designing that structure, the Framers themselves considered how much commingling was, in the generality of things, acceptable, and set forth their conclusions in the document. That is the meaning of the statements concerning acceptable commingling made by Madison in defense of the proposed Constitution, and now routinely used as an excuse for disregarding it. When he said, as the Court correctly quotes, that separation of power "d[oes] not mean that these [three] departments ought to have no partial agency in, or no control over the acts of each other," . . . his point was that the commingling specifically provided for in the structure that he and his colleagues had designed—the Presidential veto over legislation, the Senate's confirmation of executive and judicial officers, the Senate's ratification of treaties, the Congress' power to impeach and remove executive and judicial officers—did not violate a proper understanding of separation of powers. He would be aghast, I think, to hear those words used as justification for ignoring that carefully designed structure so long as, in the changing view of the Supreme Court from time to time, "too much commingling" does not occur. Consideration of the degree of commingling that a particular disposition produces may be appropriate at the margins where the outline of the framework itself is not clear; but it seems to me far from a marginal question whether our constitutional structure allows for a body which is not the Congress, and yet exercises no governmental powers except the making of rules that have the effect of laws.

I think the Court errs, in other words, not so much because it mistakes the degree of commingling, but because it fails to recognize that this case is not about commingling, but about the creation of a new Branch altogether, a sort of junior-varsity Congress. It may well be that in some circumstances such a Branch would be desir-

able; perhaps the agency before us here will prove to be so. But there are many desirable dispositions that do not accord with the constitutional structure we live under. And in the long run the improvisation of a constitutional structure on the basis of currently perceived utility will be disastrous.

I respectfully dissent from the Court's decision, and would reverse the judgment of the District Court.

Case

WHITMAN V. AMERICAN TRUCKING ASSOCIATIONS

531 U.S. 457; 121 S.Ct. 903; 149 L.Ed. 2d 1 (2001)

Vote: 9–0

In this case the Supreme Court considers whether a provision of the Clean Air Act (CAA) is an impermissible delegation of legislative power to the Environmental Protection Agency.

Justice Scalia delivered the opinion of the Court.

. . . Section 109(a) of the CAA . . . requires the Administrator of the EPA to promulgate national ambient air quality standards [NAAQS] for each air pollutant for which "air quality criteria" have been issued. . . . Once a NAAQS has been promulgated, the Administrator must review the standard (and the criteria on which it is based) "at five-year intervals" and make "such revisions . . . as may be appropriate." . . .

These cases arose when, on July 18, 1997, the Administrator revised the NAAQS for particulate matter (PM) and ozone. . . . American Trucking Associations, Inc., and its co-respondents—which include, in addition to other private companies, the States of Michigan, Ohio, and West Virginia—challenged the new standards in the Court of Appeals for the District of Columbia Circuit. . . .

Section 109(b)(1) of the CAA instructs the EPA to set "ambient air quality standards the attainment and maintenance of which in the judgment of the Administrator, based on [the] criteria [documents of § 108] and allowing an adequate margin of safety, are requisite to protect the public health." . . . The Court of Appeals held that this section as interpreted by the Administrator did not provide an "intelligible principle" to guide the EPA's exercise of authority in setting NAAQS. "[The] EPA," it said, "lack[ed] any determinate criteria for drawing lines. It has failed to

state intelligibly how much is too much." . . . The court hence found that the EPA's interpretation (but not the statute itself) violated the nondelegation doctrine. . . . We disagree.

In a delegation challenge, the constitutional question is whether the statute has delegated legislative power to the agency. Article I, § 1, of the Constitution vests "[a]ll legislative Powers herein granted . . . in a Congress of the United States." This text permits no delegation of those powers, . . . and so we repeatedly have said that when Congress confers decision making authority upon agencies *Congress* must "lay down by legislative act an intelligible principle to which the person or body authorized to [act] is directed to conform." . . . We have never suggested that an agency can cure an unlawful delegation of legislative power by adopting in its discretion a limiting construction of the statute.

. . . The idea that an agency can cure an unconstitutionally standardless delegation of power by declining to exercise some of that power seems to us internally contradictory. The very choice of which portion of the power to exercise—that is to say, the prescription of the standard that Congress had omitted—would *itself* be an exercise of the forbidden legislative authority. Whether the statute delegates legislative power is a question for the courts, and an agency's voluntary self-denial has no bearing upon the answer.

We agree with the Solicitor General that the text of § 109(b)(1) of the CAA at a minimum requires that "[f]or a discrete set of pollutants and based on published air quality criteria that reflect the latest scientific knowledge, [the] EPA must establish uniform national standards at a level that is requisite to protect public health from the adverse effects of the pollutant in the ambient air." . . . Requisite, in turn, "mean[s] sufficient, but not more than necessary." . . .

These limits on the EPA's discretion are strikingly similar to the ones we approved in *Touby v. United States* (1991), which permitted the Attorney General to designate a drug as a controlled substance for purposes of criminal drug enforcement if doing so was "necessary to avoid an imminent hazard to the public safety." . . . They also resemble the Occupational Safety and Health Act provision requiring the agency to "set the standard which most adequately assures, to the extent feasible, on the basis of the best available evidence, that no employee will suffer any impairment of health"—which the Court upheld in *Industrial Union Dept., AFL-CIO v. American Petroleum Institute* (1980), and which even then-Justice Rehnquist, who alone in that case thought the statute violated the nondelegation doctrine, . . . would have upheld if, like the statute here, it did not permit economic costs to be considered. . . .

The scope of discretion § 109(b)(1) allows is in fact well within the outer limits of our nondelegation precedents. In the history of the Court we have found the requisite "intelligible principle" lacking in only two statutes, one of which provided literally no guidance for the exercise of discretion, and the other of which conferred authority to regulate the entire economy on the basis of no more precise a standard than stimulating the economy by assuring "fair competition." See *Panama Refining Co. v. Ryan* (1935); *A. L. A. Schechter Poultry Corp. v. United States*, (1935). We have, on the other hand, upheld the validity of § 11(b)(2) of the Public Utility Holding Company Act of 1935, 49 Stat. 821, which gave the Securities and Exchange Commission authority to modify the structure of holding company systems so as to ensure that they are not "unduly or unnecessarily complicate[d]" and do not "unfairly or inequitably distribute voting power among security holders." *American Power & Light Co. v. SEC* (1946). We have approved the wartime conferral of agency power to fix the prices of commodities at a level that "'will be generally fair and equitable and will effectuate the [in some respects conflicting] purposes of th[e] Act.'" *Yakus v. United States* (1944). And we have found an "intelligible principle" in various statutes authorizing regulation in the "public interest." . . . In short, we have "almost never felt qualified to second-guess Congress regarding the permissible degree of policy judgment that can be left to those executing or applying the law." . . .

It is true enough that the degree of agency discretion that is acceptable varies according to the scope of the power congressionally conferred. . . . While Congress need not provide any direction to the EPA regarding the manner in which it is to define "country elevators," which are to be exempt from new-stationary-source regulations governing grain elevators, . . . it must provide substantial guidance on setting air standards that affect the entire national economy. But even in sweeping regulatory schemes we have never demanded, as the Court of Appeals did here, that statutes provide a "determinate criterion" for saying "how much [of the regulated harm] is too much." . . .

In *Touby*, for example, we did not require the statute to decree how "imminent" was too imminent, or how "necessary" was necessary enough, or even—most relevant here—how "hazardous" was too hazardous. . . . It is therefore not conclusive for delegation purposes that, as respondents argue, ozone and particulate matter are "nonthreshold" pollutants that inflict a continuum of adverse health effects at any airborne concentration greater than zero, and hence require the EPA to make judgments of degree. "[A] certain degree of discretion, and thus of lawmaking, inheres in most executive or judicial action." . . . Section 109(b)(1) of the CAA, which to repeat we interpret as requiring the EPA to set air quality standards at the level that is "requisite"—that is, not lower or higher than is necessary—to protect the public health with an adequate margin of safety, fits comfortably within the scope of discretion permitted by our precedent.

We therefore reverse the judgment of the Court of Appeals remanding for reinterpretation that would avoid a supposed delegation of legislative power. . . .

Justice Thomas, concurring.

I agree with the majority that § 109's directive to the agency is no less an "intelligible principle" than a host of other directives that we have approved. . . . I write separately, however, to express my concern that there may nevertheless be a genuine constitutional problem with § 109, a problem which the parties did not address.

The parties to this case who briefed the constitutional issue wrangled over constitutional doctrine with barely a nod to the text of the Constitution. Although this Court since 1928 has treated the "intelligible principle" requirement as the only constitutional limit on congressional grants of power to administrative agencies, . . . the Constitution does not speak of "intelligible principles." Rather, it speaks in much simpler terms: "*All* legislative Powers herein granted shall be vested in a Congress." . . . I am not convinced that the intelligible principle doctrine serves to prevent all cessions of legislative power. I believe that there are cases in which the principle is intelligible and yet the significance of the delegated decision is simply too great for the decision to be called anything other than "legislative."

As it is, none of the parties to this case has examined the text of the Constitution or asked us to reconsider our precedents on cessions of legislative power. On a future day, however, I would be willing to address the question whether our delegation jurisprudence has strayed too far from our Founders' understanding of separation of powers.

Justice Stevens, with whom *Justice Souter* joins, concurring in part and concurring in the judgment.

Section 109(b)(1) delegates to the Administrator of the Environmental Protection Agency (EPA) the authority to promulgate national ambient air quality standards (NAAQS). . . . [T]he Court convincingly explains why the Court of Appeals erred when it concluded that § 109 effected "an unconstitutional delegation of legislative power." . . . I wholeheartedly endorse the Court's result and endorse its explanation of its reasons, albeit with the following caveat.

The Court has two choices. We could choose to articulate our ultimate disposition of this issue by frankly acknowledging that the power delegated to the EPA is "legislative" but nevertheless conclude that the delegation is constitutional because adequately limited by the terms of the authorizing statute. Alternatively, we could pretend, as the Court does, that the authority delegated to the EPA is somehow not "legislative power." Despite the fact that there is language in our opinions that supports the Court's articulation of our holding, I am persuaded that it would be both wiser and more faithful to what we have actually done in delegation cases to admit that agency rulemaking authority is "legislative power."

The proper characterization of governmental power should generally depend on the nature of the power, not on the identity of the person exercising it. . . . If the NAAQS that the EPA promulgated had been prescribed by Congress, everyone would agree that those rules would be the product of an exercise of "legislative power." The same characterization is appropriate when an agency exercises rulemaking authority pursuant to a permissible delegation from Congress.

My view is not only more faithful to normal English usage, but is also fully consistent with the text of the Constitution. In Article I, the Framers vested "All legislative Powers" in the Congress, . . . just as in Article II they vested the "executive Power" in the President, . . . Those provisions do not purport to limit the authority of either recipient of power to delegate authority to others. . . .

It seems clear that an executive agency's exercise of rulemaking authority pursuant to a valid delegation from Congress is "legislative." As long as the delegation provides a sufficiently intelligible principle, there is nothing inherently unconstitutional about it. Accordingly, . . . I would hold that when Congress enacted § 109, it effected a constitutional delegation of legislative power to the EPA.

Justice Breyer, concurring in part and concurring in the judgment. . . .

Case

IMMIGRATION AND NATURALIZATION SERVICE V. CHADHA

462 U.S. 919; 103 S.Ct. 2764; 77 L.Ed. 2d 317 (1983)

Vote: 7–2

In this case the Court considers the constitutionality of a one-house legislative veto provision contained in the Immigration and Nationality Act of 1952.

Chief Justice Burger delivered the opinion of the Court.

. . . Chadha is an East Indian who was born in Kenya and holds a British passport. He was lawfully admitted to the United States in 1966 on a non-immigrant student visa. His visa expired on June 30, 1972. On October 11, 1973, the District Director of the Immigration and Naturalization Service ordered Chadha to show cause why he should not be deported for having "remained in the United States for a longer time than permitted." . . . [A]

deportation hearing was held before an immigration judge on January 11, 1974. Chadha conceded that he was deportable for overstaying his visa and the hearing was adjourned to enable him to file an application for suspension of deportation. . . . Section 244(a)(1) provides:

(a) As hereinafter prescribed in this section, the Attorney General may, in his discretion, suspend deportation and adjust the status to that of an alien lawfully admitted for permanent residence, in the case of an alien who applies to the Attorney General for suspension of deportation and—

(1) is deportable under any law of the United States except the provisions specified in paragraph (2) of this subsection; has been physically present in the United States for a continuous period of not less than seven years immediately preceding the date of such application, and proves that during all of such period he was and is a person of good moral character; and is a person whose deportation would, in the opinion of the

Attorney General, result in extreme hardship to the alien or to his spouse, parent, or child, who is a citizen of the United States, or an alien lawfully admitted for permanent residence.

After Chadha submitted his application for suspension of deportation, the deportation hearing was resumed on February 7, 1974. On the basis of evidence adduced at the hearing, affidavits submitted with the application, and the results of a character investigation conducted by the INS, the immigration judge, on June 25, 1974, ordered that Chadha's deportation be suspended. The immigration judge found that Chadha met the requirements of 244(a)(1): he had resided continuously in the United States for over seven years, was of good moral character, and would suffer "extreme hardship" if deported.

Pursuant to 244(c)(1) of the Act, the immigration judge suspended Chadha's deportation and a report of the suspension was transmitted to Congress. Section 244(c)(1) provides:

> Upon application by any alien who is found by the Attorney General to meet the requirements of subsection (a) of this section the Attorney General may in his discretion suspend deportation of such alien. If the deportation of any alien is suspended under the provisions of this subsection, a complete and detailed statement of the facts and pertinent provisions of law in the case shall be reported to the Congress with the reasons for such suspension. Such reports shall be submitted on the first day of each calendar month in which Congress is in session.

Once the Attorney General's recommendation for suspension of Chadha's deportation was conveyed to Congress, Congress had the power under § 244(c)(2) of the Act, to veto the Attorney General's determination that Chadha should not be deported. Section 244(c)(2) provides:

> (2) In the case of an alien specified in paragraph (1) of subsection (a) of this subsection—if during the session of the Congress at which a case is reported, or prior to the close of the session of the Congress next following the session at which a case is reported, either the Senate or the House of Representatives passes a resolution stating in substance that it does not favor the suspension of such deportation, the Attorney General shall thereupon deport such alien or authorize the alien's voluntary departure at his own expense under the order of deportation in the manner provided by law. If, within the time above specified, neither the Senate nor the House of Representatives shall pass such a resolu-

tion, the Attorney General shall cancel deportation proceedings.

The June 25, 1974, order of the immigration judge suspending Chadha's deportation remained outstanding as a valid order for a year and a half. For reasons not disclosed by the record, Congress did not exercise the veto authority reserved to it under 244(c)(2), until the first session of the 94th Congress. This was the final session in which Congress, pursuant to 244(c)(2), could act to veto the Attorney General's determination that Chadha should not be deported. The session ended on December 19, 1975. Absent Congressional action, Chadha's deportation proceedings would have been cancelled after this date and his status adjusted to that of a permanent resident alien.

On December 12, 1975, Representative Eilberg, Chairman of the Judiciary Subcommittee on Immigration, Citizenship, and International Law, introduced a resolution opposing "the granting of permanent residence in the United States to [six] aliens," including Chadha. . . . The resolution was referred to the House Committee on the Judiciary. On December 16, 1975, the resolution was discharged from further consideration by the House Committee on the Judiciary and submitted to the House of Representatives for a vote. The resolution had not been printed and was not made available to other Members of the House prior to or at the time it was voted on. . . . So far as the record before us shows, the House consideration of the resolution was based on Representative Eilberg's statement from the floor that

> [i]t was the feeling of the committee, after reviewing 340 cases, that the aliens contained in the resolution [Chadha and five others] did not meet these statutory requirements, particularly as it relates to hardship; and it is the opinion of the committee that their deportation should not be suspended. . . .

The resolution was passed without debate or recorded vote. Since the House action was pursuant to 244(c)(2), the resolution was not treated as an Article I legislative act; it was not submitted to the Senate or presented to the President for his action.

After the House veto of the Attorney General's decision to allow Chadha to remain in the United States, the immigration judge reopened the deportation proceedings to implement the House order deporting Chadha. Chadha moved to terminate the proceedings on the ground that § 244(c)(2) is unconstitutional. The immigration judge held that he has no authority to rule on the constitutional validity of 244(c)(2). On November 8, 1976, Chadha was ordered deported pursuant to the House action.

Chadha appealed the deportation order to the Board of Immigration Appeals again contending that § 244(c)(2) is unconstitutional. The Board held that it had "no power to declare unconstitutional an act of Congress" and Chadha's appeal was dismissed. . . .

Pursuant to 106(a) of the Act, Chadha filed a petition for review of the deportation order in the United States Court of Appeals for the Ninth Circuit. The Immigration and Naturalization Service agreed with Chadha's position before the Court of Appeals and joined him in arguing that § 244(c)(2) is unconstitutional. In light of the importance of the question, the Court of Appeals invited both the Senate and the House of Representatives to file briefs *amici curiae.*

After full briefing and oral argument, the Court of Appeals held that the House was without constitutional authority to order Chadha's deportation; accordingly it directed the Attorney General "to cease and desist from taking any steps to deport this alien based upon the resolution enacted by the House of Representatives." . . . The essence of its holding was that § 244(c)(2) violates the constitutional doctrine of separation of powers.

We granted certiorari . . . and we now affirm.

. . . We turn now to the question whether action of one House of Congress under § 244(c)(2) violates strictures of the Constitution. We begin, of course, with the presumption that the challenged statute is valid. Its wisdom is not the concern of the courts; if a challenged action does not violate the Constitution, it must be sustained. . . .

By the same token, the fact that a given law or procedure is efficient, convenient, and useful in facilitating functions of government, standing alone, will not save it if it is contrary to the Constitution. Convenience and efficiency are not the primary objectives—or the hallmarks—of democratic government and our inquiry is sharpened rather than blunted by the fact that Congressional veto provisions are appearing with increasing frequency in statutes which delegate authority to executive and independent agencies:

Since 1932, when the first veto provision was enacted into law, 295 congressional veto-type procedures have been inserted in 196 different statutes as follows: from 1932 to 1939, five statutes were affected; from 1940–49, nineteen statutes; between 1950–59, thirty-four statutes; and from 1960–69, forty-nine. From the years 1970 through 1975, at least one hundred sixty-three such provisions were included in eighty-nine laws. . . .

Justice White undertakes to make a case for the proposition that the one-House veto is a useful "political inven-tion," and we need not challenge that assertion. We can even concede this utilitarian argument although the long-range political wisdom of this "invention" is arguable. It has been vigorously debated and it is instructive to compare the views of the protagonists. But policy arguments supporting even useful "political inventions" are subject to the demands of the Constitution which defines powers and, with respect to this subject, sets out just how those powers are to be exercised.

Explicit and unambiguous provisions of the Constitution prescribe and define the respective functions of the Congress and of the Executive in the legislative process. Since the precise terms of those familiar provisions are critical to the resolution of this case, we set them out verbatim. Art. I provides:

All legislative Powers herein granted shall be vested in a Congress of the United States, which shall consist of a Senate and a House of Representatives. . . . Every Bill which shall have passed the House of Representatives and the Senate, shall, before it becomes a Law, be presented to the President of the United States; . . .

Every Order, Resolution, or Vote to which the Concurrence of the Senate and House of Representatives may be necessary (except on a question of Adjournment) shall be presented to the President of the United States; and before the Same shall take Effect, shall be approved by him, or being disapproved by him, shall be repassed by two thirds of the Senate and House of Representatives, according to the Rules and Limitations prescribed in the Case of a Bill.

These provisions of Art. I are integral parts of the constitutional design for the separation of powers. We have recently noted that "[t]he principle of separation of powers was not simply an abstract generalization in the minds of the Framers: it was woven into the documents that they drafted in Philadelphia in the summer of 1787." . . . Just as we relied on the textual provision of Art. II, Sec. 2, cl. 2, to vindicate the principle of separation of powers . . ., we find that the purposes underlying the Presentment Clauses, Art. I, Sec. 7, cls. 2, 3, and the bicameral requirement of Art. I, Sec. 1 and 7, cl. 2, guide our resolution of the important question presented in this case. The very structure of the articles delegating and separating powers under Arts. I, II, and III exemplify the concept of separation of powers and we now turn to Art. I.

The records of the Constitutional Convention reveal that the requirement that all legislation be presented to the President before becoming law was uniformly accepted by the Framers. Presentment to the President and the Presidential veto were considered so imperative that the draftsmen took special pains to assure that these requirements could not be circumvented. During the final debate on Art. I, Sec. 7, cl. 2, James Madison expressed concern that it might easily be evaded by the simple expedient of calling a proposed law a "resolution" or "vote" rather than a "bill." As a consequence, Art. I, Sec. 7, cl. 3, was added.

The decision to provide the President with a limited and qualified power to nullify proposed legislation by veto was based on the profound conviction of the Framers that the powers conferred on Congress were the powers to be most carefully circumscribed. It is beyond doubt that law-making was a power to be shared by both Houses and the President. . . .

The President's role in the law-making process also reflects the Framers' careful efforts to check whatever propensity a particular Congress might have to enact oppressive, improvident, or ill-considered measures.

The bicameral requirement of Art. I, Sec. 1, 7 was of scarcely less concern to the Framers than was the Presidential veto and indeed the two concepts are interdependent. By providing that no law could take effect without the concurrence of the prescribed majority of the Members of both Houses, the Framers reemphasized their belief, already remarked upon in connection with the Presentment Clauses, that legislation should not be enacted unless it has been carefully and fully considered by the Nation's elected officials. . . .

However familiar, it is useful to recall that apart from their fear that special interests could be favored at the expense of public needs, the Framers were also concerned, although not of one mind, over the apprehensions of the smaller states. Those states feared a commonality of interest among the larger states would work to their disadvantage; representatives of the larger states, on the other hand, were skeptical of a legislature that could pass laws favoring a minority of the people. It need hardly be repeated here that the Great Compromise, under which one House was viewed as representing the people and the other the states, allayed the fears of both the large and small states.

We see therefore that the Framers were acutely conscious that the bicameral requirement and the Presentment Clauses would serve essential constitutional functions. The President's participation in the legislative process was to protect the Executive Branch from Congress and to protect the whole people from improvident laws. The division of the Congress into two distinctive bodies assures that the legislative power would be exercised only after opportunity for full study and debate in separate settings. The President's unilateral veto power, in turn, was limited by the power of two thirds of both Houses of Congress to overrule a veto thereby precluding final arbitrary action of one person. . . . [This] represents the Framers' decision that the legislative power of the Federal government be exercised in accord with a single, finely wrought and exhaustively considered, procedure.

. . . The Constitution sought to divide the delegated powers of the new federal government into three defined categories, legislative, executive and judicial, to assure, as nearly as possible, that each Branch of government would confine itself to its assigned responsibility. The hydraulic pressure inherent within each of the separate Branches to exceed the outer limits of its power, even to accomplish desirable objectives, must be resisted.

Although not "hermetically" sealed from one another, the powers delegated to the three Branches are functionally identifiable. When any Branch acts, it is presumptively exercising the power the Constitution has delegated to it. When the Executive acts, it presumptively acts in an executive or administrative capacity as defined in Art. II. And when, as here, one House of Congress purports to act, it is presumptively acting within its assigned sphere.

Beginning with this presumption, we must nevertheless establish that the challenged action under § 244(c)(2) is of the kind to which the procedural requirements of Art. I, Sec. 7 apply. Not every action taken by either House is subject to the bicameralism and presentment requirements of Art. I. Whether actions taken by either House are, in law and fact, an exercise of legislative power depends not on their form but upon "whether they contain matter which is properly to be regarded as legislative in its character and effect." . . .

Examination of the action taken here by one House pursuant to § 244(c)(2) reveals that it was essentially legislative in purpose and effect. In purporting to exercise power defined in Art. I, Sec. 8, cl. 4 to "establish an uniform Rule of Naturalization," the House took action that had the purpose and effect of altering the legal rights, duties and relations of persons, including the Attorney General, Executive Branch officials and Chadha, all outside the legislative branch. Section 244(c)(2) purports to authorize one House of Congress to require the Attorney General to deport an individual alien whose deportation otherwise would be cancelled under 244. The one-House veto operated in this case to overrule the Attorney General and mandate Chadha's deportation; absent the House action, Chadha would remain in the United States. Congress has acted and its action has altered Chadha's status.

The legislative character of the one-House veto in this case is confirmed by the character of the Congressional action it supplants. Neither the House of Representatives nor the Senate contends that, absent the veto provision in § 244(c)(2), either of them, or both of them acting together, could effectively require the Attorney General to deport an alien once the Attorney General, in the exercise of legislatively delegated authority, had determined the alien should remain in the United States. Without the challenged provision in 244(c)(2), this could have been achieved, if at all, only by legislation requiring deportation. Similarly, a veto by one House of Congress under § 244(c)(2) cannot be justified as an attempt at amending the standards set out in 244(a)(1), or as a repeal of 244 as applied to Chadha. Amendment and repeal of statutes, no less than enactment, must conform with Art. I.

The nature of the decision implemented by the one-House veto in this case further manifests its legislative character. After long experience with the clumsy, time-consuming private bill procedure, Congress made a deliberate choice to delegate to the Executive Branch, and specifically to the Attorney General, the authority to allow deportable aliens to remain in this country in certain specified circumstances. It is not disputed that this choice to delegate authority is precisely the kind of decision that can be implemented only in accordance with the procedures set out in Art. I. Disagreement with the Attorney General's decision on Chadha's deportation—that is, Congress' decision to deport Chadha—no less than Congress' original choice to delegate to the Attorney General the authority to make that decision, involves determinations of policy that Congress can implement in only one way; bicameral passage followed by presentment to the President. Congress must abide by its delegation of authority until that delegation is legislatively altered or revoked.

Finally, we see that when the Framers intended to authorize either House of Congress to act alone and outside of its prescribed bicameral legislative role, they narrowly and precisely defined the procedure for such action. There are but four provisions in the Constitution, explicit and unambiguous, by which one House may act alone with the unreviewable force of law, not subject to the President's veto:

(a) The House of Representatives alone was given the power to initiate impeachments. Art. I, Sec. 2, cl. 6;

(b) The Senate alone was given the power to conduct trials following impeachment on charges initiated by the House and to convict following trial. Art. I, Sec. 3, cl. 5;

(c) The Senate alone was given final unreviewable power to approve or to disapprove presidential appointments. Art. II, Sec. 2, cl. 2;

(d) The Senate alone was given unreviewable power to ratify treaties negotiated by the President. Art. II, Sec. 2, cl. 2.

Clearly, when the Draftsmen sought to confer special powers on one House, independent of the other House, or of the President, they did so in explicit, unambiguous terms. Those carefully defined exceptions from presentment and bicameralism underscore the difference between the legislative functions of Congress and other unilateral but important and binding one-House acts provided for in the Constitution. These exceptions are narrow, explicit, and separately justified; none of them authorize the action challenged here. On the contrary, they provide further support for the conclusion that Congressional authority is not to be implied and for the conclusion that the veto provided for in § 244(c)(2) is not authorized by the constitutional design of the powers of the Legislative Branch.

Since it is clear that the action by the House under § 244(c)(2) was not within any of the express constitutional exceptions authorizing one House to act alone, and equally clear that it was an exercise of legislative power, that action was subject to the standards prescribed in Article I. The bicameral requirement, the Presentment Clauses, the President's veto, and Congress' power to override a veto were intended to erect enduring checks on each Branch and to protect the people from the improvident exercise of power by mandating certain prescribed steps. To preserve those checks, and maintain the separation of powers, the carefully defined limits on the power of each Branch must not be eroded. To accomplish what has been attempted by one House of Congress in this case requires action in conformity with the express procedures of the Constitution's prescription for legislative action: passage by a majority of both Houses and presentment to the President.

The veto authorized by § 244(c)(2) doubtless has been in many respects a convenient shortcut; the "sharing" with the Executive by Congress of its authority over aliens in this manner is, on its face, an appealing compromise. In purely practical terms, it is obviously easier for action to be taken by one House without submission to the President; but it is crystal clear from the records of the Convention, contemporaneous writings and debates, that the Framers ranked other values higher than efficiency. The records of the Convention and debates in the States preceding ratification underscore the common desire to define and limit the exercise of the newly created federal powers affecting the states and the people. There is unmistakable expression of a determination that legislation by the national Congress be a step-by-step, deliberate and deliberative process.

The choices we discern as having been made in the Constitutional Convention impose burdens on governmental processes that often seem clumsy, inefficient, even unworkable, but those hard choices were consciously made by men who had lived under a form of government that permitted arbitrary governmental acts to go unchecked. There is no support in the Constitution or decisions of this Court for the proposition that the cumbersomeness and delays often encountered in complying with explicit Constitutional standards may be avoided, either by the Congress or by the President. With all the obvious flaws of delay, untidiness, and potential for abuse, we have not yet found a better way to preserve freedom than by making the exercise of power subject to the carefully crafted restraints, spelled out in the Constitution.

. . . We hold that the Congressional veto provision in § 244(c)(2) is severable from the Act and that it is unconstitutional. Accordingly, the judgment of the Court of Appeals is affirmed.

Justice Powell, concurring in the judgment.

The Court's decision, based on the Presentment Clauses, Art. I, Sec. 7, cl. 2 and 3, apparently will invalidate every use of the legislative veto. The breadth of this holding gives one pause. Congress has included the veto in literally hundreds of statutes, dating back to the 1930s. Congress clearly views this procedure as essential to controlling the delegation of power to administration agencies. One reasonably may disagree with Congress' assessment of the veto's utility, but the respect due its judgment as a coordinate branch of Government cautions that our holding should be no more extensive than necessary to decide this case. In my view, the case may be decided on a narrower ground. When Congress finds that a particular person does not satisfy the statutory criteria for permanent residence in this country it has assumed a judicial function in violation of the principle of separation of powers. Accordingly, I concur only in the judgment. . . .

Justice White, dissenting.

Today the Court not only invalidates § 244(c)(2) of the Immigration and Nationality Act, but also sounds the death knell for nearly 200 other statutory provisions in which Congress has reserved a "legislative veto." For this reason, the Court's decision is of surpassing importance. And it is for this reason that the Court would have been well-advised to decide the case, if possible, on the narrower grounds of separation of powers, leaving for full consideration the constitutionality of other congressional review statutes operating on such varied matters as war

powers and agency rulemaking, some of which concern the independent regulatory agencies.

The prominence of the legislative veto mechanism in our contemporary political system and its importance to Congress can hardly be overstated. It has become a central means by which Congress secures the accountability of executive and independent agencies. Without the legislative veto, Congress is faced with a Hobson's choice: either to refrain from delegating the necessary authority, leaving itself with a hopeless task of writing laws with the requisite specificity to cover endless special circumstances across the entire policy landscape, or in the alternative, to abdicate its lawmaking function to the executive branch and independent agencies. To choose the former leaves major national problems unresolved; to opt for the latter risks unaccountable policymaking by those not elected to fill that role. Accordingly, over the past five decades, the legislative veto has been placed in nearly 200 statutes. The device is known in every field of governmental concern: reorganization, budgets, foreign affairs, war powers, and regulation of trade, safety, energy, the environment and the economy.

The legislative veto developed initially in response to the problems of reorganizing the sprawling government structure created in response to the Depression.

. . . [T]he legislative veto is more than "efficient, convenient, and useful." . . . It is an important if not indispensable political invention that allows the President and Congress to resolve major constitutional and policy differences, assures the accountability of independent regulatory agencies, and preserves Congress' control over lawmaking. Perhaps there are other means of accommodation and accountability, but the increasing reliance of Congress upon the legislative veto suggests that the alternatives to which Congress must now turn are not entirely satisfactory.

The history of the legislative veto also makes clear that it has not been a sword with which Congress has struck out to aggrandize itself at the expense of the other branches—the concerns of Madison and Hamilton. Rather, the veto has been a means of defense, a reservation of ultimate authority necessary if Congress is to fulfill its designated role under Article I as the nation's lawmaker. While the President has often objected to particular legislative vetoes, generally those left in the hands of congressional committees, the Executive has more often agreed to legislative review as the price for a broad delegation of authority. To be sure, the President may have preferred unrestricted power, but that could be precisely why Congress thought it essential to retain a check on the exercise of delegated authority.

For all the reasons, the apparent sweep of the Court's decision today is regrettable. The Court's Article I analysis appears to invalidate all legislative vetoes irrespective of form or subject. Because the legislative veto is commonly found as a check upon rulemaking by administrative agencies and upon broad-based policy decisions of the Executive Branch, it is particularly unfortunate that the Court reaches its decision in a case involving the exercise of a veto over deportation decisions regarding particular individuals. Courts should always be wary of striking statutes as unconstitutional; to strike an entire class of statutes based on consideration of a somewhat atypical and more-readily indictable exemplar of the class is irresponsible.

If the legislative veto were as plainly unconstitutional as the Court strives to suggest, its broad ruling today would be more comprehensible. But, the constitutionality of the legislative veto is anything but clear-cut. The issue divides scholars, courts, attorneys general, and the two other branches of the National Government. If the veto devices so flagrantly disregarded the requirements of Article I as the Court today suggests, I find it incomprehensible that Congress, whose members are bound by oath to uphold the Constitution, would have placed these mechanisms in nearly 200 separate laws over a period of 50 years.

I do not suggest that all legislative vetoes are necessarily consistent with separation of powers principles. A legislative check on an inherently executive function, for example that of initiating prosecutions, poses an entirely different question. But the legislative veto device here—and in many other settings—is far from an instance of legislative tyranny over the Executive. It is a necessary check on the unavoidably expanding power of the agencies, both executive and independent, as they engage in exercising authority delegated by Congress.

I regret that I am in disagreement with my colleagues on the fundamental questions that this case presents. But even more I regret the destructive scope of the Court's holding. It reflects a profoundly different conception of the Constitution than that held by the courts which sanctioned the modern administrative state. Today's decision strikes down in one fell swoop provisions in more laws enacted by Congress than the Court has cumulatively invalidated in its history. I fear it will now be more difficult "to insure that the fundamental policy decisions in our society will be made not by an appointed official but by the body immediately responsible to the people." . . . I must dissent.

Justice Rehnquist, dissenting. . . .

Case

GOLDBERG V. KELLY

397 U.S. 254; 90 S.Ct. 1011; 25 L.Ed. 2d 287 (1970)

Vote: 5–3

A group of welfare recipients from New York City brought suit challenging an action by a state agency terminating their benefits without a prior evidentiary hearing. They claimed that the agency's action violated the Due Process Clause of the Fourteenth Amendment.

Mr. Justice Brennan delivered the opinion of the Court.

The constitutional issue to be decided . . . is the narrow one whether the Due Process Clause requires that the recipient be afforded an evidentiary hearing before the termination of benefits. . . .

The constitutional challenge cannot be answered by an argument that public assistance benefits are "a 'privilege' and not a 'right.'" . . . Relevant constitutional restraints apply as much to the withdrawal of public assistance benefits as to disqualification for unemploy-

ment compensation, . . . or to denial of a tax exemption, . . . or to discharge from public employment. . . . The extent to which procedural due process must be afforded the recipient is influenced by the extent to which he may be "condemned to suffer grievous loss," . . . depends upon whether the recipient's interest in avoiding that loss outweighs the governmental interest in summary adjudication. Accordingly, . . . "consideration of what procedures due process may require under any given set of circumstances must begin with a determination of the precise nature of the government function involved as well as of the private interest that has been affected by governmental action." . . .

It is true, of course, that some governmental benefits may be administratively terminated without affording the recipient a pre-termination evidentiary hearing. But we agree . . . that when welfare is discontinued, only a pre-termination evidentiary hearing provides the recipient with procedural due process. For qualified recipients, welfare provides the means to obtain essential food, clothing, housing, and medical care. . . . Thus the crucial factor in this context—a factor not present in the case of the blacklisted government contractor, the discharged government employee, the taxpayer denied a tax exemption, or virtually anyone else whose governmental entitlements are ended—is that termination of aid pending resolution of a controversy over eligibility may deprive an eligible recipient of the very means by which to live while he waits. Since he lacks independent resources, his situation becomes immediately desperate. His need to concentrate upon finding the means for daily subsistence, in turn, adversely affects his ability to seek redress from the welfare bureaucracy.

Moreover, important governmental interests are promoted by affording recipients a pre-termination evidentiary hearing. From its founding the Nation's basic commitment has been to foster the dignity and well-being of all persons within its borders. We have come to recognize that forces not within the control of the poor contribute to their poverty. This perception, against the background of our traditions, has significantly influenced the development of the contemporary public assistance system. Welfare, by meeting the basic demands of subsistence, can help bring within the reach of the poor the same opportunities that are available to others to participate meaningfully in the life of the community. At the same time, welfare guards against the societal malaise that may flow from a widespread sense of unjustified frustration and insecurity. Public assistance, then, is not mere charity, but a means to "promote the general Welfare, and secure the Blessings of Liberty to ourselves and our Posterity." The same governmental interests that counsel the provision of welfare, counsel as well its uninterrupted provision to those eligible to receive it; pre-termination evidentiary hearings are indispensable to that end.

Appellant does not challenge the force of these considerations but argues that they are outweighed by countervailing governmental interests in conserving fiscal and administrative resources. These interests, the argument goes, justify the delay of any evidentiary hearing until after discontinuance of the grants. Summary adjudication protects the public fisc by stopping payments promptly upon discovery of reason to believe that a recipient is no longer eligible. Since most terminations are accepted without challenge, summary adjudication also conserves both the fisc and administrative time and energy by reducing the number of evidentiary hearings actually held.

We agree . . . however, that these governmental interests are not overriding in the welfare context. The requirement of a prior hearing doubtless involves some greater expense, and the benefits paid to ineligible recipients pending decision at the hearing probably cannot be recouped, since these recipients are likely to be judgment-proof. But the State is not without weapons to minimize these increased costs. Much of the drain on fiscal and administrative resources can be reduced by developing procedures for prompt pre-termination hearings and by skillful use of personnel and facilities. Indeed, the very provision for a post-termination evidentiary hearing in New York's Home Relief program is itself cogent evidence that the State recognizes the primacy of the public interest in correct eligibility determinations and therefore in the provision of procedural safeguards. Thus, the interest of the eligible recipient in uninterrupted receipt of public assistance, coupled with the State's interest that his payments not be erroneously terminated, clearly outweighs the State's competing concern to prevent any increase in its fiscal and administrative burdens. . . .

The city's procedures presently do not permit recipients to appear personally with or without counsel before the official who finally determines continued eligibility. Thus a recipient is not permitted to present evidence to that official orally, or to confront or cross-examine adverse witnesses. These omissions are fatal to the constitutional adequacy of the procedures.

The opportunity to be heard must be tailored to the capacities and circumstances of those who are to be heard. It is not enough that a welfare recipient may present his position to the decision maker in writing or secondhand through his caseworker. Written submissions are an unrealistic option for most recipients, who lack the educational attainment necessary to write effectively and who cannot obtain professional assistance. Moreover, written submissions do not afford the flexibility of oral presentations; they do not permit the recipient to mold his argument to the issues the decision maker appears to regard as important. Particularly where credibility and veracity are at issue, as they must be in many termination proceedings, written submissions are a wholly unsatisfactory basis for decision. The secondhand presentation to the decision maker by the caseworker has its own deficiencies; since the caseworker usually gathers the facts upon which the charge of ineligibility rests, the presentation of the recipient's side of the controversy cannot safely be left to him. Therefore a recipient must be allowed to state his position orally. Informal procedures will suffice; in this context due process does not require a particular order of proof or mode of offering evidence.

In almost every setting where important decisions turn on questions of fact, due process requires an opportunity to confront and cross-examine adverse witnesses. . . .

Welfare recipients must therefore be given an opportunity to confront and cross-examine the witnesses relied on by the department. . . .

Finally, the decisionmaker's conclusion as to a recipient's eligibility must rest solely on the legal rules and evidence adduced at the hearing. . . . To demonstrate compliance with this elementary requirement, the decision maker should state the reasons for his determination and indicate the evidence he relied on, . . . though his statement need not amount to a full opinion or even formal findings of fact and conclusions of law. And, of course, an impartial decision maker is essential. . . . We agree with the District Court that prior involvement in some aspects of a case will not necessarily bar a welfare official from acting as a decision maker. He should not, however, have participated in making the determination under review.

Mr. Chief Justice Burger, dissenting. . . .

Mr. Justice Stewart, dissenting. . . .

Mr. Justice Black, dissenting.

In the last half century the United States, along with many, perhaps most, other nations of the world, has moved far toward becoming a welfare state, that is, a nation that for one reason or another taxes its most affluent people to help support, feed, clothe, and shelter its less fortunate citizens. The result is that today more than nine million men, women, and children in the United States receive some kind of state or federally financed public assistance in the form of allowances or gratuities, generally paid them periodically, usually by the week, month, or quarter. Since these gratuities are paid on the basis of need, the list of recipients is not static, and some people go off the lists and others are added from time to time. These ever-changing lists put a constant administrative burden on government and it certainly could not have reasonably anticipated that this burden would include the additional procedural expense imposed by the Court today. . . .

The procedure required today as a matter of constitutional law finds no precedent in our legal system. Reduced to its simplest terms, the problem in this case is similar to that frequently encountered when two parties have an ongoing legal relationship that requires one party to make periodic payments to the other. Often the situation arises where the party "owing" the money stops paying it and justifies his conduct by arguing that the recipient is not legally entitled to payment. The recipient can, of course, disagree and go to court to compel payment. But I know of no situation in our legal system in which the person alleged to owe money to another is required by law to continue making payments to a judgment-proof claimant without the benefit of any security or bond to insure that these payments can be recovered if he wins his legal argument. Yet today's decision in no way obligates the welfare recipient to pay back any benefits wrongfully received during the pre-termination evidentiary hearings or post

any bond, and in all "fairness" it could not do so. These recipients are by definition too poor to post a bond or to repay the benefits that, as the majority assumes, must be spent as received to insure survival.

The Court apparently feels that this decision will benefit the poor and needy. In my judgment the eventual result will be just the opposite. While today's decision requires only an administrative, evidentiary hearing, the inevitable logic of the approach taken will lead to constitutionally imposed, time-consuming delays of a full adversary process of administrative and judicial review. In the next case the welfare recipients are bound to argue that cutting off benefits before judicial review of the agency's decision is also a denial of due process. Since, by hypothesis, termination of aid at that point may still "deprive an eligible recipient of the very means by which to live while he waits," . . . I would be surprised if the weighing process did not compel the conclusion that termination without full judicial review would be unconscionable. After all, at each step, as the majority seems to feel, the issue is only one of weighing the government's pocketbook against the actual survival of the recipient, and surely that balance must always tip in favor of the individual. Similarly today's decision requires only the opportunity to have the benefit of counsel at the administrative hearing, but it is difficult to believe that the same reasoning process would not require the appointment of counsel, for otherwise the right to counsel is a meaningless one since these people are too poor to hire their own advocates. . . . Thus the end result of today's decision may well be that the government, once it decides to give welfare benefits, cannot reverse that decision until the recipient has had the benefits of full administrative and judicial review, including, of course, the opportunity to present his case to this Court. Since this process will usually entail a delay of several years, the inevitable result of such a constitutionally imposed burden will be that the government will not put a claimant on the rolls initially until it has made an exhaustive investigation to determine his eligibility. While this Court will perhaps have insured that no needy person will be taken off the rolls without a full "due process" proceeding, it will also have insured that many will never get on the rolls, or at least that they will remain destitute during the lengthy proceedings followed to determine initial eligibility.

. . . The operation of a welfare state is a new experiment for our Nation. For this reason, among others, I feel that new experiments in carrying out a welfare program should not be frozen into our constitutional structure. They should be left, as are other legislative determinations, to the Congress and the legislatures that the people elect to make our laws.

Case

MATHEWS V. ELDRIDGE

424 U.S. 319; 96 S.Ct. 893; 47 L.Ed. 2d 18 (1976)

Vote: 6–2

Here the Court considers the scope of constitutional due process protections in the context of termination of Social Security disability benefits.

Mr. Justice Powell delivered the opinion of the Court.

The issue in this case is whether the Due Process Clause of the Fifth Amendment requires that prior to the termination of Social Security disability benefit payments the recipient be afforded an opportunity for an evidentiary hearing.

Cash benefits are provided to workers during periods in which they are completely disabled under the disability insurance program created by the 1956 amendments to . . . the Social Security Act. . . . Eldridge was first awarded benefits in June 1968. In March 1972, he received a questionnaire from the state agency charged with monitoring his medical condition. Eldridge completed the questionnaire, indicating that his condition had not improved and identifying the medical sources, including physicians, from whom he had received treatment recently. The state agency then obtained reports from his physician and a psychiatric consultant. After considering these reports and other information in his file the agency informed Eldridge by letter that it has made a tentative determination that his disability had ceased in May 1972. The letter included a statement of reasons for the proposed termination of benefits, and advised Eldridge that he might request reasonable time in which to obtain and submit additional information pertaining to his condition.

In his written response, Eldridge disputed one characterization of his medical condition and indicated that the agency already had enough evidence to establish his disability. The state agency then made its final determination that he had ceased to be disabled in May 1972. This determination was accepted by the Social Security Administration (SSA), which notified Eldridge in July that his benefits would terminate after that month. The notification also advised him of his right to seek reconsideration by the state agency of this initial determination within six months.

Instead of requesting reconsideration Eldridge commenced this action challenging the constitutional validity of the administrative procedures established by the Secretary of Health, Education, and Welfare for assessing whether there exists a continuing disability. He sought an immediate reinstatement of benefits pending a hearing on the issue of his disability. . . . The secretary moved to dismiss on the grounds that Eldridge's benefits had been terminated in accordance with valid administrative regulations and procedures and that he had failed to exhaust available remedies. . . .

. . . [The] District Court held that prior to termination of benefits Eldridge had to be afforded an evidentiary hearing of the type required for welfare beneficiaries under . . . the Social Security Act. . . . [T]he Court of Appeals for the Fourth Circuit affirmed. . . . We reverse. . . .

Procedural due process imposes constraints on governmental decisions which deprive individuals of "liberty" or "property" interests within the meaning of the Due Process Clause of the Fifth or Fourteenth Amendment. The Secretary does not contend that procedural due process is inapplicable to terminations of Social Security disability benefits. He recognizes, as has been implicit in our prior decisions, . . . that the interest of an individual in continued receipt of these benefits is a statutorily created "property" interest protected by the Fifth Amendment. . . . Rather, the Secretary contends that the existing administration procedures . . . provide all the process that is constitutionally due before a recipient can be deprived of that interest.

This Court consistently has held that some form of hearing is required before an individual is finally deprived of a property interest. . . . The "right to be heard before being condemned to suffer grievous loss of any kind, even though it may not involve the stigma and hardships of a criminal conviction, is a principle basic to our society." . . . The fundamental requirement of due process is the opportunity to be heard "at a meaningful time and in a meaningful manner." . . . Eldridge agrees that the review procedures available to a claimant before the initial determination of ineligibility becomes final would be adequate if disability benefits were not terminated until after the evidentiary hearing stage of the administrative process. The dispute centers upon what process is due prior to the initial termination of benefits, pending review.

In recent years this Court increasingly has had occasion to consider the extent to which due process requires an evidentiary hearing prior to the deprivation of some type of property interest even if such a hearing is provided thereafter. In only one case, *Goldberg v. Kelly*, . . . has the Court held that a hearing closely approximating a judicial trial is necessary. In other cases requiring some type of pretermination hearing as a matter of constitutional right the Court has spoken sparingly about the requisite procedures. . . .

These decisions underscore the truism that "'[d]ue process,' unlike some legal rules, is not a technical conception with a fixed content unrelated to time, place, and circumstances." . . . "[D]ue process is flexible and calls for such procedural protections as the particular situation demands." . . . Accordingly, resolution of the issue whether the administrative procedures provided here are constitutionally sufficient requires analysis of the governmental and private interests that are affected. . . . More precisely, our prior decisions indicate that identification of the specific dictates of due process generally requires consideration of three distinct factors: first, the private interest that will be affected by the official action; second, the risk of an erroneous deprivation of such interest through the procedures used, and the probable value, if any, of additional or substitute procedural safeguards; and finally, the Government's interest, including the function involved and the fiscal and administrative burdens that the additional or substitute procedural requirement would entail. . . .

Despite the elaborate character of the administrative procedures provided by the Secretary, the courts below held them to be constitutionally inadequate, concluding that due process requires an evidentiary hearing prior to termination. In light of the private and governmental interests at stake here and the nature of the existing procedures, we think this was error.

Since a recipient whose benefits are terminated is awarded full retroactive relief if he ultimately prevails, his sole interest is in the uninterrupted receipt of this course of income pending final administrative decision on his claim. . . .

Only in *Goldberg* has the Court held that due process requires an evidentiary hearing prior to a temporary deprivation. It was emphasized there that welfare assistance is given to persons on the very margin of subsistence. . . . Eligibility for disability benefits, in contrast, is not based upon financial need. Indeed, it is wholly unrelated to the worker's income or support from many other sources, such as earnings of other family members, workmen's compensation awards, tort claims awards, savings, private insurance, public or private pensions, veterans' benefits, food stamps, public assistance, or the "many other important programs, both public and private, which contain provisions for disability payments affecting a substantial portion of the work force." . . .

As *Goldberg* illustrates, the degree of potential deprivation that may be created by a particular decision is a factor to be considered in assessing the validity of any administrative decisionmaking process. . . . The potential deprivation here is generally likely to be less than in *Goldberg*, although the degree of difference can be overstated. . . .

[T]o remain eligible for benefits a recipient must be "unable to engage in substantial gainful activity." . . .

As we recognized last Term, . . . "the possible length of wrongful deprivation of . . . benefits [also] is an important factor in assessing the impact of official action on the private interests." The Secretary concedes that the delay between a request for a hearing before an administrative law judge and a decision on the claim is currently between 10 and 11 months. Since a terminated recipient must first obtain a reconsideration decision as a prerequisite to invoking his right to an evidentiary hearing, the delay between the actual cut off of benefits and final decision after a hearing exceeds one year.

In view of the torpidity of this administrative review process, . . . and the typically modest resources of the family unit of the physically disabled worker, the hardship imposed upon the erroneously terminated disability recipient may be significant. Still, the disabled worker's need is likely to be less than that of a welfare recipient. In addition to the possibility of access to private resources, other forms of government assistance will become available where the termination of disability benefits places a worker or his family below the subsistence level. . . . In view of these potential sources of temporary income, there is less reason here than in *Goldberg* to depart from the ordinary principle, established by our decisions, that something less than an evidentiary hearing is sufficient prior to adverse administrative action.

An additional factor to be considered here is the fairness and reliability of the existing pretermination procedures, and the probable value, if any, of additional procedural safeguards. Central to the evaluation of any administrative process is the nature of the relevant inquiry. . . . In order to remain eligible for benefits the disabled worker must demonstrate by means of "medically acceptable clinical and laboratory diagnostic techniques" . . . that he is unable "to engage in any substantial gainful activity by reason of any medically determinable physical or mental impairment." . . . In short, a medical assessment of the worker's physical or mental condition is required. This is a more sharply focused and easily documented decision than the typical determination of welfare entitlement. In the latter case, a wide variety of information may be deemed relevant, and issues of witness credibility and veracity often are critical to the decisionmaking process. . . .

By contrast, the decision whether to discontinue disability benefits will turn, in most cases, upon "routine, standard, and unbiased medical reports by physician specialists," . . . concerning a subject whom they have personally examined. . . . To be sure, credibility and veracity may be a factor in the ultimate disability assessment in some cases. But procedural due process rules are shaped by the risk of error inherent in the truthfinding process as applied to the generality of cases, not the rare exceptions. The potential value of an evidentiary hearing, or even oral presentation to the decisionmaker, is substantially less in this context than in *Goldberg*. . . .

A further safeguard against mistake is the policy of allowing the disability recipient's representative full access to all information relied upon by the state agency. In addition, prior to the cutoff of benefits the agency informs the recipient of its tentative assessment, the reasons therefore, and provides a summary of the evidence that it considers most relevant. Opportunity is then afforded the recipient to submit additional evidence or arguments, enabling him to challenge directly the accuracy of information in his field as well as the correctness of the agency's tentative conclusions. These procedures . . . enable the recipient to "mold" his argument to respond to the precise issues which the decisionmaker regards as crucial. . . .

In striking the appropriate due process balance the final factor to be assessed is the public interest. This includes the administrative burden and other societal costs that would be associated with requiring, as a matter of constitutional right, an evidentiary hearing upon demand in all cases prior to the termination of disability benefits. The most visible burden would be the incremental cost resulting from the increased number of hearings and the expense of providing benefits to ineligible recipients pending decision. No one can predict the extent of the increase, but the fact that full benefits would continue until after such hearings would assure the exhaustion in most cases of this attractive option. Nor would the theoretical right of the Secretary to recover undeserved benefits result, as a practical matter, in any substantial offset of the added outlay of public funds. . . . [E]xperience with the constitutionalizing of government procedures suggests that the ultimate additional cost in terms of money and administrative burden would not be insubstantial.

Financial cost alone is not a controlling weight in determining whether due process requires a particular procedural safeguard prior to some administrative decision. But the Government's interest, and hence that of the public, in conserving scarce fiscal and administrative recourses, is a factor that must be weighed. At some point the benefit of an additional safeguard to the individual affected by the administrative action and to society, in terms of increased assurance that the action is just, may be outweighed by the cost. Significantly, the cost of protecting those whom the preliminary administrative process had identified as likely to be found undeserving may in the end come out of the pockets of the deserving since resources available for any particular program of social welfare are not unlimited. . . .

But more is implicated in cases of this type than ad hoc weighing of fiscal and administrative burdens against the interests of a particular category of claimants. The ultimate balance involves a determination as to when, under our constitutional system, judicial-type procedures must be imposed upon administrative action to assure fairness. We reiterate the wise admonishment of Mr. Justice Frankfurter that differences in the origin and function of administrative agencies "preclude wholesale transplantation of the rules of procedure, trial, and review which have evolved from the history and experience of courts." . . . The judicial model of an evidentiary hearing is neither a required, nor even the most effective, method of decisionmaking in all circumstances. The essence of due process is the requirement that "a person in jeopardy of serious loss [be given] notice of the case against him and opportunity to meet it." . . . All that is necessary is that the procedures be tailored, in light of the decision to be made, to "the capacity and circumstances of those who are to be heard," . . . to insure that they are given a meaningful opportunity to present their case. In assessing what process is due in this case, substantial weight must be given to the good-faith judgments of the individuals charged by Congress with the administration of social welfare programs that the procedures they have provided assure fair consideration of the entitlement claims of individuals. . . . This is especially so where, as here, the prescribed procedures not only provide the claimant with an effective process for asserting his claim prior to any administrative action, but also assure a right to an evidentiary hearing, as well as to subsequent judicial review, before the denial of his claim becomes final. . . .

We conclude that an evidentiary hearing is not required prior to the termination of disability benefits and that the present administrative procedures fully comport with due process.

The judgment of the Court of Appeals is reversed.

Mr. Justice Brennan, with whom ***Mr. Justice Marshall*** concurs, dissenting.

. . . I agree with the District Court and the Court of Appeals that, prior to termination of benefits, Eldridge must be afforded an evidentiary hearing of the type required for welfare beneficiaries. . . . I would add that the Court's consideration that a discontinuance of disability benefits may cause the recipient to suffer only a limited deprivation is no argument. It is speculative. Moreover, the very legislative determination to provide disability benefits, without any prerequisite determination of need in fact, presumes a need by the recipient which is not this Court's function to denigrate. Indeed, in the present case, it is indicated that because disability benefits were terminated there was a foreclosure upon the Eldridge home and the family's furniture was repossessed, forcing Eldridge, his wife and children to sleep in one bed. . . . Finally, it is also no argument that a worker, who has been placed in the untenable position of having been denied disability benefits, may still seek other forms of public assistance.

Mr. Justice Stevens took no part in the consideration or decision of this case.

Case

DOW CHEMICAL COMPANY V. UNITED STATES

476 U.S. 227; 106 S.Ct. 1819; 90 L.Ed. 2d 226 (1986)
Vote: 5–4

In this case, the Supreme Court reviews a court of appeals decision upholding the Environmental Protection Agency's aerial observation of a chemical plant complex. The key question is whether the EPA action constituted a search within the meaning of the Fourth Amendment.

Chief Justice Burger delivered the opinion of the Court.

. . . Petitioner Dow Chemical Co. operates a 2,000-acre facility manufacturing chemicals at Midland, Michigan. The facility consists of numerous covered buildings, with manufacturing equipment and piping conduits located between the various buildings exposed to visual observation from the air. At all times, Dow has maintained elaborate security around the perimeter of the complex barring ground-level public views of these areas. It also investigates any low-level flights by aircraft over the facility. Dow has not undertaken, however, to conceal all manufacturing equipment within the complex from aerial views. Dow maintains that the cost of covering its exposed equipment would be prohibitive.

In early 1978, enforcement officials of EPA, with Dow's consent, made an on-site inspection of two power plants in this complex. A subsequent EPA request for a second inspection, however, was denied, and EPA did not thereafter seek an administrative search warrant. Instead, EPA employed a commercial aerial photographer, using a standard floor-mounted, precision aerial mapping camera, to take photographs of the facility from altitudes of 12,000, 3,000, and 1,200 feet. At all times the aircraft was lawfully within navigable airspace. . . .

EPA did not inform Dow of this aerial photography, but when Dow became aware of it, Dow brought suit in the District Court alleging that EPA's action violated the Fourth Amendment and was beyond EPA's statutory investigative authority. The District Court granted Dow's motion for summary judgment on the grounds that EPA had no authority to take aerial photographs and that doing so was a search violating the Fourth Amendment. EPA was permanently enjoined from taking aerial photographs of Dow's premises and from disseminating, releasing, or copying the photographs already taken. . . .

The District Court accepted the parties' concession that EPA's "quest for evidence" was a "search," . . . and limited its analysis to whether the search was unreasonable under *Katz v. United States* . . . (1967). Proceeding on the assumption that a search in Fourth Amendment terms had been conducted, the court found that Dow manifested an expectation of privacy in its exposed plant areas because it intentionally surrounded them with buildings and other enclosures. . . .

The District Court held that this expectation of privacy was reasonable, as reflected in part by trade secret protections restricting Dow's commercial competitors from aerial photography of these exposed areas. . . . The court emphasized that use of "the finest precision aerial camera available" permitted EPA to capture on film "a great deal more than the human eye could ever see." . . .

The Court of Appeals reversed. . . . It recognized that Dow indeed had a subjective expectation of privacy in certain areas from ground-level intrusions, but the court was not persuaded that Dow had a subjective expectation of being free from aerial surveillance since Dow had taken no precautions against such observation, in contrast to its elaborate ground-level precautions. . . . The court rejected the argument that it was not feasible to shield any of the critical parts of the exposed plant areas from aerial surveys. The Court of Appeals, however, did not explicitly reject the District Court's factual finding as to Dow's subjective expectations.

. . . Viewing Dow's facility to be more like the "open field" in *Oliver v. United States* . . . (1984), than a home or an office, [the court of appeals] held that the common-law curtilage doctrine did not apply to a large industrial complex of closed buildings connected by pipes, conduits, and other exposed manufacturing equipment. The Court of Appeals looked to "the peculiarly strong concepts of intimacy, personal autonomy and privacy associated with the home" as the basis for the curtilage protection. The court did not view the use of sophisticated photographic equipment by EPA as controlling.

The Court of Appeals then held that EPA clearly acted within its statutory powers even absent express authorization for aerial surveillance, concluding that the delegation of general investigative authority to EPA, similar to that of other law enforcement agencies, was sufficient to support the use of aerial photography. . . .

The photographs at issue in this case are essentially like those commonly used in mapmaking. Any person with an airplane and an aerial camera could readily duplicate them. In common with much else, the technology of photography has changed in this century. These developments have enhanced industrial processes, and indeed all areas of life; they have also enhanced law enforcement techniques. Whether they may be employed by competitors to penetrate trade secrets is not a question presented in this case. Governments do not generally seek to appropriate trade secrets of the private sector, and the right to be free of appropriation of trade secrets is protected by law.

Dow nevertheless relies heavily on its claim that trade secret laws protect it from any aerial photography of this industrial complex by its competitors, and that this protection is relevant to our analysis of such photography under the Fourth Amendment. That such photography might be barred by state law with regard to competitors, however, is irrelevant to the questions presented here. State tort law governing unfair competition does not define the limits of the Fourth Amendment. . . . The Government is seeking these photographs in order to regulate, not to compete with, Dow. If the Government were to use the photographs to compete with Dow, Dow might have a Fifth Amendment "taking" claim. Indeed, Dow alleged such a claim in its complaint, but the District Court dismissed it without prejudice. But even trade secret laws would not bar all forms of photography of this industrial complex; rather, only photography with an intent to use any trade secrets revealed by the photographs may be proscribed. Hence, there is no prohibition of photographs taken by a casual passenger on an airliner, or those taken by a company producing maps for its mapmaking purposes.

Dow claims first that EPA has no authority to use aerial photography to implement its statutory authority for "site inspection" under 114(a) of the Clean Air Act . . .;

second, Dow claims EPA's use of aerial photography was a "search" of an area that, notwithstanding the large size of the plant, was within an "industrial curtilage" rather than an "open field," and that it had a reasonable expectation of privacy from such photography protected by the Fourth Amendment. . . .

Congress has vested in EPA certain investigatory and enforcement authority, without spelling out precisely how this authority was to be exercised in all the myriad circumstances that might arise in monitoring matters relating to clean air and water standards. When Congress invests an agency with enforcement and investigatory authority, it is not necessary to identify explicitly each and every technique that may be used in the course of executing the statutory mission. Aerial observation authority, for example, is not usually expressly extended to police for traffic control, but it could hardly be thought necessary for a legislative body to tell police that aerial observation could be employed for traffic control of a metropolitan area, or to expressly authorize police to send messages to ground highway patrols that a particular over-the-road truck was traveling in excess of 55 miles per hour. Common sense and ordinary human experience teach that traffic violators are apprehended by observation.

Regulatory or enforcement authority generally carries with it all the modes of inquiry and investigation traditionally employed or useful to execute the authority granted. Environmental standards such as clean air and clean water cannot be enforced only in libraries and laboratories, helpful as those institutions may be.

Under 114(a)(2), the Clean Air Act provides that "upon presentation of . . . credentials," EPA has a "right of entry to, upon, or through any premises." . . . Dow argues this limited grant of authority to enter does not authorize any aerial observation. In particular, Dow argues that unannounced aerial observation deprives Dow of its right to be informed that an inspection will be made or has occurred, and its right to claim confidentiality of the information contained in the places to be photographed. . . . It is not claimed that EPA has disclosed any of the photographs outside the agency.

Section 114(a), however, appears to expand, not restrict, EPA's general powers to investigate. Nor is there any suggestion in the statute that the powers conferred by this section are intended to be exclusive. There is no claim that EPA is prohibited from taking photographs from a ground-level location accessible to the general public. EPA, as a regulatory and enforcement agency, needs no explicit statutory provision to employ methods of observation commonly available to the public at large: we hold that the use of aerial observation and photography is within EPA's statutory authority. . . .

We turn now to Dow's contention that taking aerial photographs constituted a search without a warrant, thereby violating Dow's rights. Under this contention, however, Dow concedes that a simple flyover with naked-eye observation, or the taking of a photograph from a nearby hillside overlooking such a facility, would give rise to no Fourth Amendment problem. . . .

Dow plainly has a reasonable, legitimate, and objective expectation of privacy within the interior of its covered buildings, and it is equally clear that expectation is one society is prepared to observe. . . . Moreover, it could hardly be expected that Dow would erect a huge cover over a 2,000-acre tract. In contending that its entire enclosed plant complex is an "industrial curtilage," Dow argues that its exposed manufacturing facilities are analogous to the curtilage surrounding a home because it has taken every possible step to bar access from ground level.

The Court of Appeals held that whatever the limits of an "industrial curtilage" barring ground-level intrusions into Dow's private areas, the open areas exposed here were more analogous to "open fields" than to a curtilage for purposes of aerial observation. In *Oliver*, the Court described the curtilage of a dwelling as "the area to which extends the intimate activity associated with the 'sanctity of a man's home and the privacies of life.' " The intimate activities associated with family privacy and the home and its curtilage simply do not reach the outdoor areas or spaces between structures and buildings of a manufacturing plant.

Admittedly, Dow's enclosed plant complex, like the area in *Oliver*, does not fall precisely with the "open fields" doctrine. The area at issue here can perhaps be seen as falling somewhere between "open fields" and curtilage, but lacking some of the critical characteristics of both. Dow's inner manufacturing areas are elaborately secured to ensure they are not open or exposed to the public from the ground. Any actual physical entry by EPA into any enclosed area would raise significantly different questions, because "the businessman, like the occupant of a residence, has a constitutional right to go about his business free from unreasonable official entries upon his private commercial property." The narrow issue raised by Dow's claim of search and seizure, however, concerns aerial observation of a 2,000-acre outdoor manufacturing facility without physical entry.

We pointed out in *Donovan v. Dewey* . . . (1981), that the Government has "greater latitude to conduct warrantless inspections of commercial property" because "the expectation of privacy that the owner of commercial property enjoys in such property differs significantly from the sanctity accorded an individual's home." We emphasized that unlike a homeowner's interest in his dwelling, the interest of the owner of commercial property is not one in being free from any inspections." And with regard to regulatory inspections, we have held that "[w]hat is observable by the public is observable without a warrant, by the Government inspector as well."

. . . Here, EPA was not employing some unique sensory device that, for example, could penetrate the walls of buildings and record conversations in Dow's plants, offices, or laboratories, but rather a conventional, albeit precise, commercial camera commonly used in mapmaking. The Government asserts it has not yet enlarged the photographs to any significant degree, but Dow points out that simple magnification permits identification of objects such as wires as small as $1/2$-inch diameter.

It may well be, as the Government concedes, that surveillance of private property by using highly sophisticated surveillance equipment not generally available to the public, such as satellite technology, might be constitutionally proscribed absent a warrant. But the photographs here are not so revealing of intimate details as to raise constitutional concerns. Although they undoubtedly give EPA more detailed information than naked-eye views, they remain limited to an outline of the facility's buildings and equipment. The mere fact that human vision is enhanced somewhat, at least to the degree here, does not give rise to constitutional problems.

An electronic device to penetrate walls or windows so as to hear and record confidential discussions of chemical formulae or other trade secrets would raise very different and far more serious questions; other protections such as trade secret laws are available to protect commercial activities from private surveillance by competitors.

We conclude that the open areas of an industrial plant complex with numerous plant structures spread over an area of 2,000 acres are not analogous to the curtilage of a dwelling, [because they are] open to the view and observation of persons in aircraft lawfully in the public airspace immediately above or sufficiently near the area for the reach of cameras.

We hold that the taking of aerial photographs of an industrial plant complex from navigable airspace is not a search prohibited by the Fourth Amendment. . . .

Justice Powell, with whom *Justice Brennan, Justice Marshall*, and *Justice Blackmun* join, . . . dissenting in part.

The Fourth Amendment protects private citizens from arbitrary surveillance by their Government. For nearly 20 years, this Court has adhered to a standard that ensured that Fourth Amendment rights would retain their vitality as technology expanded the Government's capacity to commit unsuspected intrusions into private areas and activities. Today, in the context of administrative aerial photography of commercial premises, the Court retreats from that standard. It holds that the photography was not a Fourth Amendment "search" because it was not accompanied by a physical trespass and because the equipment used was not the most highly sophisticated form of technology available to the Government. Under this holding, the existence of an asserted privacy interest apparently will be decided solely by reference to the manner of surveillance used to intrude on that interest. Such an inquiry will not protect Fourth Amendment rights, but rather will permit their gradual decay as technology advances. . . .

I would reverse the decision of the Court of Appeals. EPA's aerial photography penetrated into a private commercial enclave, an area in which society has recognized that privacy interests legitimately may be claimed. The photographs captured highly confidential information that Dow had taken reasonable and objective steps to preserve as private. Since the Clean Air Act does not establish a defined and regular program of warrantless inspections, see *Marshall v. Barlow's, Inc.* . . . (1978), EPA should have sought a warrant from a neutral judicial officer. The Court's holding that the warrantless photography does not constitute an unreasonable search within the meaning of the Fourth Amendment is based on the absence of any physical trespass—a theory disapproved in a line of cases beginning with the decision in *Katz v. United States.* . . . . These cases have provided a sensitive and reasonable means of preserving interests in privacy cherished by our society. The Court's decision today cannot be reconciled with our precedents or with the purpose of the Fourth Amendment.

5

THE DYNAMICS OF THE FEDERAL SYSTEM

" 'Our Federalism' . . . is a system in which there is sensitivity to the legitimate interests of both State and National Governments, and in which the National Government, anxious though it may be to vindicate and protect federal rights and federal interests, always endeavors to do so in ways that will not unduly interfere with the legitimate activities of the States. It should never be forgotten that this slogan, 'Our Federalism,' born in the early struggling days of our Union of States, occupies a highly important place in our Nation's history and its future."

—JUSTICE HUGO L. BLACK, WRITING FOR THE COURT IN

   YOUNGER V. HARRIS (1971)

Hugo L. Black: Associate Justice, 1937–1971

INTRODUCTION

In a **federal system**, power is divided between a central government and a set of regional governments. A **unitary system**, by contrast, vests all authority in the central government. In the American context, federalism refers to the division of power between the national government on the one hand and the state and local governments on the other.

Federalism is one of the two basic structural characteristics of the American constitutional system, the other being separation of powers among branches of the national government. During the two centuries since the republic was founded, the relationship between the national government and the states has changed dramatically. Today, there is no question of the dominance of the national government in most areas of policy making. Yet states remain viable actors in the political system and in recent years may have become even more important. Thus, as a constitutional principle, federalism retains considerable vitality.

As an applied principle of government, federalism requires an ongoing effort by legislators, chief executives, and judges to balance many competing interests and values—among them individual liberty and public order, local diversity and the national interest, limited government, and social justice. This chapter examines the constitutional basis and evolving meaning of federalism, giving special attention to the contribution of the U.S. Supreme Court in defining the relationships and marking the boundaries between national and state functions.

DEVELOPMENT OF THE FEDERAL SYSTEM

Prior to the ratification of the Constitution of 1787, the United States was a confederation of sovereign states. Each state was vested with the necessary powers of government, limited only by the terms of state constitutions and the traditional common law rights and immunities of individuals. States had broad taxing and spending powers, of course, but they also issued their own currency and regulated the terms of their commercial relationships with other states and foreign countries. Moreover, the states possessed police power: the authority to make laws to protect the public safety, health, and welfare, and even to foster the morality of their citizens.

There was never any real prospect that the Constitution of 1787 would provide for a unitary system. The states existed as autonomous political entities from the time of the American Revolution and were not about to surrender to the national government rights and powers to which they had become accustomed. Moreover, there was widespread fear of concentrating too much power in the national government. The smaller states, in particular, were concerned about how their interests would be protected under the new Constitution. The solution was twofold. First, all states would enjoy equal representation in the U.S. Senate. Second, the national government would be one of definite and limited powers. In addition, the **Tenth Amendment**, ratified in 1791, specifically recognized the reserved powers of the states:

> The powers not delegated to the United States by the Constitution, nor prohibited by it to the States, are reserved to the States respectively, or to the people.

National Supremacy versus States' Rights

Although the Supremacy Clause of Article VI recognized the primacy of national authority in areas of national activity, those areas were specifically enumerated, for the most part, with the implication (made explicit in the Tenth Amendment) that the states retained autonomy in other areas. The original Constitution, however, was ambiguous on the question of where ultimate sovereign power resided. Federalist Party leaders, including Alexander Hamilton, John Marshall, and John Adams, argued eloquently that the issue must be resolved in favor of the national government.

The Democratic-Republicans, most notably James Madison and Thomas Jefferson, argued on behalf of **states' rights.** In proposing the Virginia and Kentucky Resolution of 1798, Jefferson went so far as to argue that the "sovereign and independent states" had the right to nullify acts of Congress that they deemed to be unconstitutional. This was the origin of the doctrines of **nullification** and **interposition**, later employed by the New England states during the War of 1812 and by South Carolina in opposition to federal tariff legislation in 1832. These doctrines were most fully developed in the writings of the South Carolina statesman and political theorist John C. Calhoun. Theories of nullification and interposition later provided a rationale for the **secession** of eleven southern states in 1860 and 1861. States' rights doctrines even figured prominently in the desegregation battles of the 1950s and 1960s.

Chisholm v. Georgia   The U.S. Supreme Court rendered its first major constitutional decision in 1793. The case, *Chisholm v. Georgia*, dealt specifically with the issue of state sovereignty. An essential aspect of sovereignty in the Anglo-American tradition has been **sovereign immunity**, the doctrine that the government may be sued only with its consent. As previously noted, Article III of the Constitution granted to federal courts jurisdiction over "controversies between a state and citizens of another state." In response to criticism from the Anti-Federalists, proponents of the Constitution argued that this provision did not authorize a private individual to sue a state without its consent.

Nevertheless, shortly after the Constitution was adopted, several such suits were filed in federal court. One of these cases was *Chisholm v. Georgia,* an original action brought in the Supreme Court by two South Carolina citizens who, as executors of the estate of a British decedent, sought to recover property confiscated by the state of Georgia during the Revolution. Georgia refused to appear in the case but filed a strong protest denying the Court's jurisdiction. In addition, a resolution was introduced in the Georgia legislature asserting that federal judicial authority to entertain such suits "would effectually destroy the retained sovereignty of the states."

By a 4-to-1 majority, the Supreme Court rejected Georgia's argument, strongly endorsing the authority of the federal judiciary in relation to the states. This decision drew an intense reaction from states' rights advocates. The result was adoption of the **Eleventh Amendment** in 1798, in effect barring a citizen from suing a state government in a federal court without the state's consent. Specifically, the amendment provides:

> The judicial power of the United States shall not be construed to extend to any suit in law or equity, commenced or prosecuted against one of the United States by Citizens of another State, or by Citizens or Subjects of any Foreign State.

Although ratification of the Eleventh Amendment was a major victory for states' rights forces, the amendment has not proved to be an insurmountable barrier to federal court review of most state policies. As noted in Chapter 2, the Fourteenth Amendment authorizes Congress to enforce certain basic civil rights guarantees against the states. Congress has used this power to limit the states' sovereign immunity with respect to certain civil rights lawsuits. However, since the mid-1990s, a determined five-member majority of the Rehnquist Court has placed substantial limits on the power of Congress to abrogate state sovereign immunity. (This topic is discussed more fully later in the chapter, in the section titled "Resurgence of the Tenth and Eleventh Amendments.")

The Marshall Court Establishes National Supremacy

Although *Chisholm v. Georgia* was overruled by the Eleventh Amendment, the Supreme Court continued to embrace a nationalist point of view. This was largely due to President John Adams's appointment of John Marshall, an ardent Federalist, to be chief justice in 1801. Chief Justice Marshall provided one of the most forceful statements of **national supremacy** in *M'Culloch v. Maryland* (1819), in which he and his colleagues broadly interpreted the Necessary and Proper Clause as conferring on Congress the implied power to establish a national bank (see Chapter 2). The Court not only expanded congressional powers but also struck a blow against states' rights by invalidating a Maryland law imposing a tax on the Baltimore branch of the bank.

Marshall developed his theory of national power in large part as a constitutional rationale for limiting the broad authority reserved to the states. His Court invalidated various state commercial and financial restrictions opposed by business interests, citing infringements on federal authority. But federal power was largely dormant during the Marshall era. Marshall did not anticipate a vigorous national regulatory policy, and in fact no such policy emerged until well into the twentieth century. Thus, Marshall's nationalism went hand in hand with the growth of private enterprise. By placing restrictions on state power in the name of abstract principles of national supremacy, the Marshall Court helped clear the way for early commercial and industrial expansion.

As this economic development proceeded, basic changes took place within the political environment. Jacksonian democracy, with its emphasis on broader political participation (at least by white males), swept away most of the property qualifications for voting that had existed when the Constitution was written. With this drive toward greater political equality, economic privilege also came under attack, primarily in state legislatures. Laws were passed providing for debtor relief and more extensive regulation of business. The Court moderated its earlier negative position as it reviewed more and more legislation of this kind. This developing trend was apparent even before Marshall's death in 1835. For example, over his solitary dissent, the Court upheld an Ohio law making bankruptcy procedures available to persons who assumed debts after its passage (*Ogden v. Saunders* [1827]). A similar law, applicable to all debtors regardless of whether their obligations were incurred before or after its passage, had been declared unconstitutional by the Marshall Court a few years earlier (*Sturges v. Crowninshield* [1819]). In 1829, Marshall joined his colleagues in upholding the authority of a state to drain disease-infested marshlands as a public health measure (*Willson v. Black-Bird Creek Marsh Company* [1829]). The dam constructed for this purpose interfered with commercial navigation. Nevertheless, the Court recognized that, as a basic aspect of the state's police power, the public health objective was controlling. This decision was a limited, but significant, victory for proponents of state regulation.

The Taney Court: Renewed Emphasis on States' Rights

During the time Marshall's successor, Roger B. Taney, served as chief justice (1836–1864), the **police powers of the states** continued to expand. In addition to protecting public health and safety, the police power was also used as a justification for safeguarding the morals and general welfare of the community (see, for example, *New York v. Miln* [1837]). Moreover, the Taney Court came to recognize state power to regulate certain aspects of interstate commerce, a power that the Federalists earlier had argued was the exclusive domain of the national government (see *Cooley v. Board of Port Wardens* [1852], discussed later in this chapter).

Slavery and the Civil War

Despite the Supreme Court's attempts to harmonize federal and state power, a conflict was brewing that would forever change the character of American federalism. The source of the conflict was the "peculiar institution" of slavery, an institution so divisive that it had threatened to derail the Constitutional Convention of 1787. During the early and middle nineteenth century, the integrity of the Union was preserved by a series of fragile congressional compromises defining the extent of slavery in the states and federal territories.

By far the most significant decision of the Taney Court was *Scott v. Sandford* (1857), in which the Court severely limited the power of the federal government to regulate slavery in the territories (see Chapter 1). Sharp regional divisions, aggravated by the Court's defense of slavery, ultimately split the nation into two armed camps. Southern states, under the banner of states' rights, asserted the right to secede from the Union and ultimately backed this assertion with the use of force. The Union, under the leadership of President Abraham Lincoln, resolved to prevent secession by any means necessary. The resulting Civil War was by far the greatest bloodbath in American history. After the loss of more than 620,000 lives and the destruction of billions of dollars worth of property, it was settled once and for all that a state could not secede from the Union.

With its decision in *Texas v. White* (1869), handed down four years after General Robert E. Lee's surrender at Appomattox, the Supreme Court added its constitutional endorsement to the new order by solemnly proclaiming that a state could not withdraw from the Union without violating the basic law. Perhaps the Court contributed a measure of legal authority to the military verdict of the Civil War, but in doing so (after the fact), it merely underscored the limits of judicial power to deal with questions that profoundly divide the American people.

The Civil War Amendments

The ratification of the Thirteenth, Fourteenth, and Fifteenth Amendments in 1865, 1868, and 1870, respectively, had a significant impact on federalism. These amendments were designed primarily to protect the civil rights of the former slaves. As a means to that end, the **Civil War Amendments** imposed prohibitions on the state governments and authorized Congress to pass legislation in support of these prohibitions. Beginning with passage of the Civil Rights Act of 1866, Congress has used its powers under the Civil War Amendments to enact far-ranging civil rights legislation, including the Civil Rights Act of 1964 and the Voting Rights Act of 1965. Moreover, in a long series of decisions beginning in 1897, the Supreme Court held that various provisions of the Bill of Rights are enforceable against the states under the Fourteenth Amendment. The creation and extension of the **doctrine of incorporation** eventually resulted in increased federal judicial supervision of state and local policies.

The Heyday of Dual Federalism: 1890–1937

The constitutional changes wrought by the Civil War did not impede the further growth of state police power. The rapid accumulation and concentration of corporate wealth, stimulated by the upheaval and dislocation of war, drew an even more active regulatory response from state legislatures during the 1860s and 1870s. Only with the rise of organized labor in the 1880s and the appearance of the Populist Party in the 1890s did a marked change in the permissive view toward state regulatory power take place. Identifying with an economic establishment that saw the specter of socialism in these movements, the Supreme Court began to use the Due Process Clause of the Fourteenth Amendment and the Commerce Clause as justifications for restricting the police power of the states.

This tendency was but one aspect of a far larger trend of constitutional interpretation through which the Court set limits on regulatory power at all levels of government. Although it placed restrictions on state police power, the Court also imposed similar curbs on the emerging national police power by invoking the Tenth Amendment and the Due Process Clause of the Fifth Amendment, the latter provision applying directly to the national government. This development contributed to the growing influence of **dual federalism** after 1890. A good example of this perspective can be seen in *Hammer v. Dagenhart* (1918) (discussed and reprinted in Chapter 2), in which the Supreme Court invoked the Tenth Amendment in striking down a federal law restricting the use of child labor in factories. Writing for the Court, Justice William R. Day characterized the statute as "an invasion by the federal power" into an area reserved to the states by the Tenth Amendment.

Proponents of the dual federalism perspective not only sought a balance between state and national power, but they also contemplated a kind of constitutional "twilight zone" into which neither the states nor the national government could intrude. Dual federalism reflected the Jeffersonian view that the best government is that which governs least. From 1890 to 1937, the Supreme Court was often receptive to this view and, as a consequence, struck down a great number of laws, both federal and state, that interfered with the operations of the free market.

The Constitutional Revolution of 1937

Dual federalism remained a major factor in American constitutional development until the beginning of the constitutional revolution of 1937 (see Chapters 1 and 2). But it was by no means the only factor at work during the half century preceding its eventual eclipse. Accelerated industrial growth and urbanization increased the impetus toward centralized governmental authority. As we noted in Chapter 2, the Court sanctioned piecemeal extension of national power under the Commerce Clause, particularly to protect conventional morality, public health, and safety. Thus, even during the period before the New Deal, the growing number of problems demanding a national response threatened to upset the balance implicit in dual federalism.

Following its 1937 confrontation with President Franklin D. Roosevelt, the Court began to sanction the exercise of national regulatory power and social welfare programs of broad scope. The Fourteenth Amendment was no longer interpreted as a restriction on state regulatory power, and the Tenth Amendment virtually disappeared as a limitation on national authority. Dual federalism eventually gave way to **cooperative federalism**, a system of shared powers that has become an essential feature of American government and politics since the late 1930s. Supreme Court decisions upholding the Social Security Act of 1935 (*Helvering v. Davis* [1937] and *Steward Machine Company v. Davis* [1937]) and the Fair Labor Standards Act of 1938 (*United States v. Darby Lumber Company* [1941]) represented this trend.

Cooperative federalism was a prominent feature of the Social Security Act. The dissenting justices in *Steward Machine Company* contended that the tax credits allowed to employers who contributed to state unemployment funds had the effect of forcing the states to participate in the Social Security program and that such coercion violated the Tenth Amendment. The argument did not prevail, and with the passage of time, it became apparent that cooperative arrangements between nation and state would proliferate. The traditional model of two distinct spheres of government, characteristic of dual federalism, gave way to what has been aptly described as "marble cake" federalism, due to the blending of national and state functions and responsibilities.

Coercive Federalism   Today federal and state agencies work together in a variety of programmatic areas, including law enforcement, social welfare, housing, education, and health care. However, due to its fiscal superiority and constitutional supremacy, the federal government plays the dominant role in this "cooperative" relationship. Indeed, the term **coercive federalism** is sometimes used to refer to the tendency for the national government to use its considerable fiscal resources to pressure the states into adopting policies the federal government prefers but is unable to impose directly. An excellent example of coercive federalism in seen in *South Dakota v. Dole* (1987) (discussed and reprinted in Chapter 2), in which the Court allowed Congress to use federal highway grants to the states as a means of persuading the states to raise their legal drinking age to 21.

TO SUMMARIZE:

- With the adoption of the Constitution of 1787, the United States was converted from a confederation to a federal republic.
- Under Chief Justice John Marshall, the Supreme Court firmly established the principle of national supremacy embodied in Article VI of the Constitution.
- The Taney Court, more favorably inclined toward states' rights, accommodated the growing demand for governmental regulation by expanding the doctrine of the state police power.
- Precipitating the crisis of the Civil War was the constitutional question of whether states could secede from the Union. Ultimately the issue was resolved on the battlefield in favor of national unity and against secession.
- Although the state police power continued to develop during the immediate post-Civil War era, the emphasis shifted in the 1890s toward dual federalism, a perspective that provided a basis for the Court to limit both state and national regulatory power.
- One result of the constitutional revolution of 1937 was that dual federalism was replaced by cooperative federalism, which emphasizes the expansion of regulatory authority at all levels of government.
- In some instances the federal government uses its superior position to coerce the states into enacting policies the federal government cannot mandate directly.

NATIONAL PREEMPTION OF STATE LAW

In a long line of decisions, the Supreme Court has held that national law preempts—that is, supersedes—state law if considerations of national policy warrant it, as long as those considerations are consistent either with enumerated powers or broader national interests. In these cases the Court relies, of course, on the Supremacy Clause, under which national law trumps conflicting state law. A classic example of **federal preemption** is provided by *Pennsylvania v. Nelson* (1956), in which the Court struck down a state law criminalizing sedition against the national government. As the Court made clear in *Nelson,* a state law may be struck down, even where there is no explicit conflict with federal law, if the Court finds that Congress has legitimately occupied the field.

Questions in this area call for careful balancing of important state and national interests. Problems arise when Congress fails to make its purpose explicit—which is often the case. The Court must then draw inferences based on the presumed objectives of federal law and the supposed impact of related state action. For example, in *Burbank v. Lockheed Air Terminal* (1973), the Supreme Court held that a local aircraft noise abatement ordinance was preempted by the federal Noise Control Act of 1972, even though the latter contained no specific preemptive language and there was no evidence that the ordinance placed a heavy burden on interstate commerce. Relying on the **Supremacy Clause,** Justice William O. Douglas emphasized the potential safety hazard that could result if a "significant number of municipalities" adopted similar ordinances. The Noise Control Act established a "comprehensive scheme" of aircraft noise regulation, including a role for the Environmental Protection Agency. In the Court's opinion, it was the "pervasive nature" of this federal regulatory pattern that preempted the Burbank ordinance. The four dissenting justices cited considerations of federalism in support of their view that the ordinance should be upheld. They maintained that the "basic constitutional division of legislative competence between the states and Congress" was consistent with democratic values and that this principle should be followed. The dissenters preferred to view the ordinance as a routine exercise of police power and thought the inquiry should be confined to the facts of the case, unaffected by speculation about the possible effect of such an ordinance if adopted by other cities.

More recently, in *California v. Federal Energy Regulatory Commission* (1990), the Supreme Court held that state regulations imposing minimum flow rates on rivers used to generate hydroelectric power were preempted by the Federal Power Act. In *Nantahala Power and Light Company v. Thornburg* (1986), another case involving the Federal Energy Regulatory Commission (FERC), the Court invoked the preemption doctrine to prohibit states from deviating from federal standards in setting intrastate rates for the sale of electrical power. Likewise, in *Mississippi Power and Light Company v. Mississippi ex rel. Moore* (1988), the Court held that FERC regulations preempted a state's authority to set rates in the area of electrical power.

The field of energy policy has tended to be one in which the Court has taken a strongly nationalistic posture. Nevertheless, in the controversial area of nuclear power, two significant preemption decisions of the 1980s were resolved in favor of the states. In *Pacific Gas and Electric Company v. State Energy Resources Conservation and Development Commission* (1983), the Supreme Court upheld a California statute imposing a moratorium on the certification of nuclear power plants, pending state approval of an effective method of nuclear waste disposal. The Court found that the state moratorium was not preempted by the Atomic Energy Act of 1954. In his majority opinion, Justice Byron White noted that the federal Nuclear Regulatory Commission (NRC) has "exclusive jurisdiction to license the transfer, delivery, receipt, acquisition, possession, and use of nuclear materials." But the NRC does not have authority over "the generation of electricity itself, or over the economic question whether a particular plant should be built." Finding it "inconceivable that Congress would have left a regulatory vacuum," White inferred that Congress intended for the states to exercise economic judgments, including assessment of nuclear waste disposal methods.

In 1984, in the highly publicized Karen Silkwood case (*Silkwood v. Kerr-McGee Corporation*), the Supreme Court upheld a state law that permitted punitive damages in a lawsuit stemming from an incident in which a nuclear power worker was exposed to a lethal dose of radiation. The Court reaffirmed its earlier holding that state efforts to regulate the safety of nuclear power were preempted by federal law but held that the punitive damages rule at issue was primarily economic in character. The *Pacific Gas and Electric* and *Silkwood* cases allow the states more regulatory leeway in a controversial field traditionally dominated by the federal government. It is reasonable to suppose that increased public concern over the safety of nuclear power and skepticism about the federal government's ability to ensure nuclear safety had some impact on the Court's willingness to accommodate increased regulatory activity at the state level.

In spite of the *Silkwood* and *Pacific Gas and Electric* cases, recent decisions indicate that the preemption doctrine continues to stand as a major limitation on state regulatory authority. During the 2000 term, for example, the Supreme Court handed down no fewer than three decisions reinforcing the preemption doctrine (see *Buckman Company v. Plaintiff's Legal Committee* [2001]; *Egelhoff v. Egelhoff* [2001]; and *Lorillard Tobacco Company v. Reilly* [2001]). In the most prominent of the these cases, the Rehnquist Court was unwilling to accommodate the states in the area of cigarette advertising; in the *Lorillard* case, decided June 28, 2001, the Court held that the Federal Cigarette Labeling and Advertising Act (FCLAA) preempted Massachusetts regulations governing the sale and advertisement of tobacco products. Emphasizing the narrowness of the Court's holding, Justice Sandra Day O'Connor's majority opinion observed:

> Although the FCLAA prevents States and localities from imposing special requirements or prohibitions based on smoking and health with respect to the advertising or promotion of cigarettes, that language still leaves significant power in the hands of States to impose generally applicable zoning regulations and to regulate conduct.

(The *Lorillard* case also addressed a First Amendment question involving commercial speech. For discussion of this aspect of the case, see Chapter 8.)

TO SUMMARIZE:

- Relying on the Supremacy Clause of Article VI, the Supreme Court has held that national law preempts state law if considerations of national policy warrant it, as long as those considerations are consistent either with enumerated powers or broader national interests.
- Congress can preempt state law through explicit statutory language or by implication. In reviewing preemption claims, the Court engages in statutory interpretation, seeking to determine, either through the specific language of the federal statute or the intent of Congress, whether state policy has been preempted.

RESURGENCE OF THE TENTH AND ELEVENTH AMENDMENTS

As previously noted, the Tenth Amendment virtually disappeared as a limitation on the powers of the national government in the wake of the constitutional revolution of 1937. Yet in 1976, the Supreme Court resurrected the Tenth Amendment in a controversial 5–4 decision. In *National League of Cities v. Usery,* the Court struck down the 1974 amendments to the Fair Labor Standards Act that extended the federal minimum wage to state and local government employees. Writing for the Court, Justice William Rehnquist opined that the Tenth Amendment prohibits

Congress from infringing on "traditional aspects of state sovereignty." In a stinging dissent, Justice William Brennan accused the majority of an irresponsible departure from modern principles of constitutional law. Brennan's dissent was vindicated in 1985, when a sharply divided Court overruled *National League of Cities* (*Garcia v. San Antonio Metropolitan Transit Authority* [1985]). With the *Garcia* decision, many assumed that the revitalization of the Tenth Amendment had ended. Throughout the 1980s, the Court continued to narrowly interpret the Tenth Amendment's restrictions on national power. In *South Carolina v. Baker* (1988), in upholding a federal tax on interest from unregistered state and local bonds, the Court concluded that protections afforded by the Tenth Amendment are "structural, not substantive." Writing for the majority, Justice Brennan explained that the states "must find their protection from congressional regulation through the national political process, not through judicially defined spheres of unregulated state activity." Brennan found that "nothing in *Garcia* or the Tenth Amendment authorizes courts to second-guess the substantive basis for congressional legislation."

It is true that the Court in *Garcia* recognized the importance of the national political process in protecting the autonomy of the states. Still, the *Garcia* majority examined the question of whether the political process offered sufficient protection to state interests threatened by the minimum wage legislation at issue in that case. In *South Carolina v. Baker,* on the other hand, the Court made no such inquiry. South Carolina did not allege that it was barred from participation in the political process or that "it was singled out in a way that left it politically isolated and powerless." As the majority viewed the case, this purely procedural question was the only relevant Tenth Amendment concern. As thus interpreted, the Tenth Amendment offered no protection to the states other than their right to take part in national politics. The Supreme Court evidently assumed, rightly or wrongly, that such participation alone is a sufficient means of protecting state interests.

Yet Another Revival of the Tenth Amendment

In 1992 the Supreme Court gave new life to the Tenth Amendment when it struck down the "take title" provision of the Low-Level Radioactive Waste Policy Amendments Act of 1985. Under this act, states that had not created nuclear waste disposal sites were required to "take title and possession" of any such waste generated inside the state if requested by those who owned or generated it. The Court, dividing 6 to 3 in *New York v. United States,* concluded that "no matter how powerful the federal interest involved, the Constitution simply does not give Congress the authority to require the states to regulate."

Five years later, the Court went one step further in reviving the Tenth Amendment when it struck down a key provision of the Brady Bill. In *Printz v. United States* (1997), the Court invalidated a federal requirement that local law enforcement officers perform background checks on prospective handgun purchasers. According to Justice Antonin Scalia's opinion for the sharply divided Court, this federal requirement violated "the very principle of separate state sovereignty." Dissenting, Justice John Paul Stevens observed that "[i]f Congress believes that such a statute will benefit the people of the Nation, and serve the interests of cooperative federalism better than an enlarged federal bureaucracy, we should respect both its policy judgment and its appraisal of its constitutional power." *Printz* and *New York v. United States* signaled the Rehnquist Court's strong determination to reshape the federal balance. This determination soon manifested itself in the rediscovery of the Eleventh Amendment as a significant limitation on Congressional power in relation to the states.

The Eleventh Amendment Redux

A direct response to the Supreme Court's decision in *Chisholm v. Georgia* (discussed earlier), the Eleventh Amendment bars citizens of one state from suing governments of other states in federal court. Although the Eleventh Amendment does not expressly forbid suits by citizens against their own states, the Supreme Court, maintaining that state sovereign immunity transcends the Eleventh Amendment, extended this constitutional restriction to bar such actions (*Hans v. Louisiana* [1890]).

In the modern era, the Court recognized the power of Congress under Section 5 of the Fourteenth Amendment to authorize private lawsuits against states in federal courts. Thus Congress was permitted to abrogate the states' sovereign immunity in order to vindicate individual rights protected by the Fourteenth Amendment (see *Fitzpatrick v. Bitzer* [1976]). In 1989 the Court went a step further by recognizing that Congress had similar authority under the Commerce Clause of Article I, Section 8. In *Pennsylvania v. Union Gas Company* (1989), a five-member majority concluded that Congress has the authority under the Commerce Clause to abrogate the sovereign immunity of the states.

The retirements of liberal Justices William Brennan and Thurgood Marshall in the early 1990s led to a reconsideration of congressional authority to abrogate state sovereign immunity. Beginning in the mid-1990s, a more conservative Court, dividing 5–4, overturned *Pennsylvania v. Union Gas Company*. Thus, in *Seminole Tribe of Florida v. Florida* (1996), the Court struck down a provision of the Indian Gaming Regulatory Act that allowed Indian tribes to bring federal lawsuits against states to require them to engage in good faith negotiations to establish "Tribal-State Gaming Compacts." Speaking for the Court, Chief Justice Rehnquist asserted that: "Even when the Constitution vests in Congress complete law-making authority over a particular area [in this instance, the power to regulate commerce with the Indian tribes], the Eleventh Amendment prevents congressional authorization of suits by private parties against unconsenting states."

The *Seminole Tribe* decision barred Congress from authorizing suits brought against states in federal court. But what about suits brought against states in their own courts? In *Alden v. Maine* (1999), the Court extended the logic of *Seminole Tribe* to prohibit Congress from authorizing such actions. Again dividing 5–4, the Court, speaking this time through Justice Anthony Kennedy, held that congressional authority under the Commerce Clause "does not include the power to subject nonconsenting States to private suits for damages in state courts."

On the same day that it decided *Alden v. Maine,* the Court handed down two rulings placing similar restrictions on the authority of Congress to abrogate state sovereign immunity with respect to infringment of trademarks and patents (see *Florida Prepaid Post-Secondary Education Expense Board v. College Savings Bank* [1999]; *College Savings Bank v. Florida Prepaid Post-Secondary Education Expense Board* [1999]). Thus by the turn of the new century, the Supreme Court had effectively prohibited Congress from abolishing state sovereign immunity as a means of implementing its enumerated powers under Article I.

As noted in Chapter 2, the Court held in *City of Boerne v. Flores* (1997) that the power of Congress to enforce the Fourteenth Amendment must be consistent with judicial interpretation of the substantive protections of that amendment. In *Kimel v. Board of Regents* (2000), the Court reiterated this position in the context of an attempt by Congress to abrogate state sovereign immunity. The Court did not disturb its holding in *Fitzpatrick v. Bitzer* that Congress may abrogate state sovereign immunity as a means of protecting Fourteenth Amendment rights. However, the Court in *Kimel* held that in attempting to protect state employees from age discrimination, Congress had prohibited state action that did not violate of the Equal Protection Clause of the Fourteenth Amendment. (*Kimel* and related cases are discussed in Chapter 12.)

TO SUMMARIZE:

- In the wake of the constitutional revolution of 1937, the Tenth Amendment virtually disappeared as a meaningful limitation on the power of the national government. In recent years a more conservative Supreme Court has revitalized the Tenth Amendment, holding that it prohibits Congress from mandating that the states enact particular policies.
- In the modern era, the Supreme Court has recognized the power of Congress under Section 5 of the Fourteenth Amendment to authorize private lawsuits against states in federal courts. The Court has maintained that position, but has emphasized that it is the role of the courts, not Congress, to determine the substantive protections of the Fourteenth Amendment.
- In the 1970s and 1980s, the Court also recognized Congress's power to abrogate state sovereign immunity as a means of implementing its enumerated powers under Article I. In recent years, however, a more conservative Court has repudiated this position, thus greatly restricting congressional power in this area and redefining somewhat the federal-state relationship.
- The Court's recent effort to resuscitate the Tenth and Eleventh Amendments is one of its most important contributions to American constitutional development and reflects the broader political trend toward devolving power from the national government to the states.

JUDICIAL FEDERALISM

Another distinctive aspect of American federalism is the relationship between the federal and state court systems. As we noted in Chapter 1, every state maintains its own system of trial and appellate courts responsible for adjudicating issues of state law. The decision of the highest state court with respect to matters of state law, including interpretation of the state constitution, is final and, accordingly, unreviewable by the federal courts. Ultimately, a complete understanding of American constitutional law must take into account the myriad state court decisions involving matters of state, as opposed to federal, constitutional interpretation.

Of course, in matters of federal constitutional law, the U.S. Supreme Court speaks with finality. This principle was firmly established by two significant decisions of the Marshall era (see *Martin v. Hunter's Lessee* [1816] and *Cohens v. Virginia* [1821], both of which are discussed in Chapter 1). In *Cohens v. Virginia,* the Supreme Court held that its constitutional jurisdiction extended to state criminal cases in which a federal question was involved.

The most notable development in the history of **judicial federalism** was the ratification in 1868 of the Fourteenth Amendment with its broad restrictions on state power. The Fourteenth Amendment has been interpreted to extend most of the prohibitions of the Bill of Rights to actions of state and local governments (for an extensive discussion of the incorporation doctrine, see Chapter 6). The application of the Bill of Rights to the states allows for increased federal judicial supervision of state courts, especially in cases dealing with the rights of the criminally accused (see Chapter 10). Nevertheless, state courts and laws are normally afforded considerable deference by federal courts in areas of the law not affected by provisions of the federal Constitution.

The federal Constitution establishes a minimum level of protection for individual rights to which states must adhere. State courts are free, however, to interpret their respective state constitutions to provide higher levels of protection to individuals within their jurisdictions. For example, the constitutions of several states (for example, Alaska and Florida) contain provisions explicitly protecting individual privacy. State court decisions interpreting these provisions typically provide a greater degree of protection for individual privacy than is afforded by the federal courts under the implicit guarantee of privacy in the federal Constitution (see Chapter 11).

The Supreme Court has recognized that federal courts should not overrule state court decisions recognizing broader individual rights than those afforded by the federal Constitution as long as such decisions are based on **independent state grounds.** Indeed, in *Michigan v. Long* (1983), the Court said that if a state court decision "indicates clearly and expressly that it is alternatively based on bona fide separate, adequate, and independent grounds, we, of course, will not undertake to review the decision." *Michigan v. Long* effectively invited the state courts to consider the parallel provisions of their state constitutions independently. Many state courts have accepted this invitation.

For example, in *In re T.W.* (1989), the Florida Supreme Court struck down as a violation of the right of privacy a statute that required parental consent in cases where minors sought abortions. The constitutionality of a similar law had been upheld on federal grounds by the U.S. Supreme Court in *Planned Parenthood v. Ashcroft* (1983). In *T.W.,* the Florida Supreme Court made it clear that it was basing its decision on an amendment to the Florida Constitution that (unlike the federal constitution) explicitly protects the right of privacy. Similarly, in *Powell v. State* (1988), the Georgia Supreme Court ruled that the state law prohibiting sodomy was in violation of the right to privacy guaranteed by the Georgia Constitution. What is interesting about this decision is that in *Bowers v. Hardwick* (1986), the U.S. Supreme Court had upheld the same statute against a challenge based on the federal Constitution. (Both *Bowers v. Hardwick* and *Powell v. State* are discussed and reprinted in Chapter 11.)

TO SUMMARIZE:

- The U.S. Constitution and the federal statutes that are consistent with the Constitution take precedence over conflicting state laws or state constitutions.
- State courts are free to interpret their respective state constitutions and statutes as they see fit as long as these interpretations do not conflict with federal law or the federal Constitution.
- State courts may recognize greater protections for individual rights and liberties under their respective state constitutions than are provided by the federal Constitution.
- In recent years, state courts have recognized broader constitutional protections with respect to individual privacy than are provided by the federal Constitution.
- Federal courts will generally not overrule state court decisions that rest on adequate, independent state grounds.

THE SCOPE OF STATE POWER TO REGULATE COMMERCE

In the preceding sections of this chapter, we have surveyed the historical development and contemporary characteristics of American federalism. We turn now to a more detailed examination of the interplay between state and national power in a major area of policy making: the regulation of commerce.

As described in Chapter 2, the power of Congress to regulate commerce among the states is vast, but far from exclusive. The constitutional language granting this power is general and open-ended. One of the Supreme Court's most important responsibilities has been to decide how this general language relates to the exercise of state power in an endless variety of regulatory settings. No definitive rulings fixing the limits of state authority or drawing a precise line of demarcation between national and state power have emerged. The process of constitutional interpretation is heavily influenced by changes in the perceived needs and interests of society. Nowhere is this influence better illustrated than in the regulation of commerce. Cases in this area also vividly illustrate the Court's important function in policing the boundaries of our federal system.

The Commerce Clause as drafted in 1787 represented an attempt to address problems faced by a growing national economy saddled with commercial rivalries among largely independent states. But this affirmative grant of authority to Congress was not accompanied by an explicit negation of state power. Although it forbids the states to tax imports and exports (unless specifically authorized by Congress), the Constitution is silent on the nature and extent of state power to regulate commerce. We know that some of the Framers of the Constitution assumed that the commerce power was indivisible—that is, an exclusive grant of power to the national government. But experience, coupled with the logical and political implications of federalism, soon made it clear that this inflexible position was unworkable. Nevertheless, the Commerce Clause placed substantial implied limits on state power. Over the years, those limits have been defined and redefined, not only by the Supreme Court but also by Congress.

Gibbons v. Ogden

The first major decision of the Supreme Court involving state versus federal regulation of commerce was *Gibbons v. Ogden* (1824). The *Gibbons* case resulted from an attempt by the state of New York to create and protect a monopoly issued to a private steamboat company. A competing company, operating under a federal license, was enjoined by a New York court from operating on waters within the borders of New York state (for an extensive discussion of *Gibbons,* see Chapter 2). The Supreme Court held that (1) the licensure of steamboats by the federal government was a valid exercise of the national power to regulate interstate commerce and (2) the attempt by New York to enforce a steamboat monopoly within its waters was a violation of the Supremacy Clause.

In terms of federalism, the thrust of *Gibbons v. Ogden* was that states could not impede the efforts of Congress to regulate commerce among the states. But the Court stopped short of holding that states had no power whatsoever to regulate interstate commerce. Suppose Congress has not acted on a matter covered by state commercial legislation. Or suppose state law merely complements existing national policy. Under such circumstances, are the states free to act, even if their actions have an impact on interstate commerce? The *Gibbons* decision left these questions unanswered.

The *Cooley* Case

It was not until 1852 that the Supreme Court made a serious effort to resolve the issue of **state power to regulate interstate commerce.** Before that time, the Court had upheld various state laws directly or indirectly affecting interstate commerce, ruling that they were appropriate exercises of the police power. But the concept of interstate commerce was too all-embracing and the demand for state regulatory activity too strong for the Court to avoid the issue indefinitely. Ultimately, it reached the Taney Court in *Cooley v. Board of Port Wardens* (1852). Justice Benjamin R. Curtis wrote the opinion of the Court, recognizing that the Commerce Clause did not automatically bar all state regulation in this field. At issue was the constitutionality of a Pennsylvania law requiring ships entering or leaving the port of Philadelphia to hire local harbor pilots. This was admittedly a regulation of both interstate and foreign commerce. Nevertheless, it was upheld because it dealt with a "subject" of commerce "imperatively demanding that diversity, which alone can meet the local necessities of navigation." Curtis reasoned that the term *commerce* covered a multitude of subjects, some requiring national uniformity in their regulation, others calling for the diversity of local control. Because the Constitution did not explicitly prohibit the states from regulating, and because Congress in 1789 had purported to authorize state regulation of pilots, he concluded that the law in question was valid. This distinction between local and national aspects of interstate commerce, although far from clear-cut, was a significant contribution to constitutional interpretation. While its application in *Cooley* was expressly limited to the facts of that case, the principle applied soon achieved the status of constitutional doctrine.

The Supreme Court's attempt to strike a balance between the values of local diversity and national uniformity has been apparent in hundreds of decisions rendered since *Cooley*. The justices have developed more sophisticated terminology than the local-national dichotomy used by Justice Curtis. But his perception of the complex problem of promoting commerce in a federal system remains important to this day.

State Regulation of Interstate Commerce: Divergent Perspectives

Except for the Court's general inclination to take a more critical view of economic regulation between the late 1880s and late 1930s, no consistent historical pattern has emerged in this field since the *Cooley* case. From time to time, the Court has attempted to classify state regulations with respect to their "direct" or "indirect" effect on interstate commerce or the degree to which they "burden" or "discriminate against" it. The **direct-indirect test** has not been in vogue since the late 1930s, but even when it was used, the Court seemed more concerned about the basic distinction between commercial regulations per se and police power legislation aimed at protecting the health, safety, and general welfare of the community. The Court has become less concerned than was Justice Curtis with the subject of commerce being regulated and more concerned with the means by which the regulation is implemented.

This approach has produced results in different cases that are difficult to reconcile. For instance, in *South Carolina Highway Department v. Barnwell Brothers* (1938), the Supreme Court sustained a South Carolina statute prescribing maximum weights and widths of trucks using the highways of the state. This measure imposed a substantial burden on interstate commerce, but the Court, through Justice Harlan F. Stone, reasoned that the countervailing safety considerations were more important. Stone pointed to the extensive control states had traditionally exerted over their public roads. He also pointed out that the highway regulation fell with equal weight on intrastate and interstate truckers—that it did not, in other words, single out businesses engaged in interstate commerce and impose added burdens on them to the advantage of intrastate economic interests. Still, the decision depended heavily on a view of state autonomy in building, maintaining, and controlling highways that was debatable even in 1938 and is open to far more serious challenge now that a nationally subsidized interstate highway system is well established.

In sharp contrast to its decision in *Barnwell,* the Court in *Southern Pacific Railroad Company v. Arizona* (1945) invalidated a law limiting the lengths of passenger and freight trains traveling through the state to fourteen and seventy cars, respectively. The regulation imposed a substantial burden on interstate commerce, but Arizona defended it as an appropriate safety measure and pointed to the absence of conflicting federal legislation on the subject. The Supreme Court, in a sharply divided decision, declared the law unconstitutional. Justice Stone, who had been elevated to chief justice in 1941, again wrote the majority opinion. He concluded that "as a safety measure" the law afforded "slight and dubious advantage, if any, over unregulated train lengths." Accordingly, the "serious burden" imposed on interstate commerce was not justified. On the other hand, before this decision was rendered, the Court had upheld a number of railroad safety measures adopted by the states, including Arkansas's "full crew" laws. These regulations fixed the minimum number of employees required to serve on trains traveling designated distances within the state. The statutes were again sustained more than twenty years after the *Southern Pacific* decision, even though they were no longer relevant to the issue of safety. As enacted in 1903 and 1907, they included the requirement for firemen to be present on each train. By 1966, coal-burning steam engines had been replaced by diesel power, and the continued requirement of a fireman was justified, if at all, only as a means of providing local employment. Nevertheless, the Court, in an opinion by Justice Hugo Black, who had dissented in the *Southern Pacific* case, was willing to defer to state policy. Even if the laws were no longer justifiable as safety measures, Black maintained that it was up to the legislature, not the Court, to change them (*Brotherhood of Locomotive Engineers v. Chicago, Rock Island & Pacific Railroad Company* [1966]).

Cases Involving the Trucking Industry   Although the Supreme Court has continued to express deference toward state efforts to promote highway safety, it has from time to time invalidated statutes in this area when the "burden" on interstate commerce appears to outweigh the safety benefits of the regulation. Thus, in *Bibb v. Navajo Freight Lines* (1959), the Court struck down as a burden on interstate commerce an Illinois law requiring the use of contoured mudguards on trucks traversing the state's highways. A more recent example is *Kassel v. Consolidated Freightways Corporation* (1981), in which the Court struck down, as a violation of the Commerce Clause, an Iowa statute prohibiting the use of 65-foot-long double-trailer trucks on its highways. The justices, however, could not agree on a rationale for their decision. A plurality of four (Powell, White, Blackmun, and Stevens) expressed the view that the Iowa statute imposed an unreasonable burden on interstate commerce, given the absence of "any significant countervailing safety interest." In a concurring opinion, Justice Brennan, joined by Justice Marshall, maintained that the Iowa legislation was protectionist in nature. He found that the primary intent underlying the statute was not to promote safety but "to discourage interstate truck traffic on Iowa's highways." Justice Rehnquist, in a dissenting opinion supported by Chief Justice Burger and Justice Stewart, took issue with Brennan's view, arguing that the statute was without doubt "a valid highway safety regulation and thus entitled to the strongest presumption of validity against Commerce Clause challenges." He maintained that Iowa's regulation of truck lengths was rational and that the safety benefits were more than slight. The "true problem" with this decision, as Rehnquist viewed it, was that the plurality and concurring opinions gave the states "no guidance whatsoever . . . as to whether their laws are valid or how to defend them."

The Nation as an Economic Unit

Any state regulation of interstate commerce aimed squarely at promoting local business interests by curtailing competition from out-of-state firms is unlikely to survive a constitutional challenge that reaches the Supreme Court. Those who drafted the Commerce Clause recognized the importance of promoting a national economy, and successive generations of Supreme Court justices have not lost sight of that objective. Although the Commerce Clause does not place explicit limits on state power, it contains a clear negative implication—states may not discriminate against interstate commerce unless they can show that their actions serve legitimate local purposes that could not be served by alternative nondiscriminatory means. This negative component is often labeled the "dormant Commerce Clause."

The 1949 decision in *H. P. Hood and Sons v. Du Mond* provides a good illustration of the dormant Commerce Clause. In *Hood,* the Supreme Court invalidated a New York administrative decision that denied Hood and Sons, a Massachusetts corporation, permission to increase from three to four the number of milk processing plants it operated in New York. Writing for the majority, Justice Robert Jackson viewed this limitation on Hood's source of supply as a form of economic isolationism that the state was not free to impose. It made no difference in principle that New York placed a ceiling, rather than an absolute ban, on Hood's activities within the state. "Our system, fostered by the Commerce Clause," Jackson asserted, "is that every farmer and every craftsman shall be encouraged to produce by the certainty that he will have free access to every market in the nation." Here, as in the *Southern Pacific* case, the absence of national legislation on the matter at issue was not the controlling factor. The state had acted simply to protect local interests, and that action, the Court found, was inconsistent with the Commerce Clause.

The Supreme Court has been equally skeptical of state regulations that pressure out-of-state businesses into moving the center of their operations to the regulating state. Even when such coercive measures are defended as legitimate health laws, the Court is not easily persuaded. In *Dean Milk Company v. Madison* (1951), for instance, the Court struck down a purported local health ordinance prohibiting the sale of milk if it came from a farm more than 25 miles from Madison, Wisconsin, or was bottled more than 5 miles from the central square of the city. Clearly this measure discriminated against interstate commerce, something the Court was unwilling to condone, even for health purposes, if "reasonable, nondiscriminatory alternatives, adequate to conserve legitimate local interests" were available. In this instance, the Court believed such alternatives could be found.

In 1976, the Court invalidated a Mississippi regulation under which the board of health prohibited the sale of milk from another state unless Mississippi milk could be marketed there. The mandatory nature of this reciprocity was held to be an undue burden on interstate commerce and was not justified either as a health measure or as a provision promoting free trade among the states (*Great Atlantic and Pacific Tea Company v. Cottrell* [1976]).

Interstate Waste Disposal   In recent decades, state and local governments have struggled with the increasingly serious problem of disposing of household and industrial waste materials. In the landmark case of *Philadelphia v. New Jersey* (1978), the Supreme Court invalidated a state law prohibiting the importation of most solid and liquid waste materials from other states. Brushing aside the alleged environmental dangers posed by overuse of New Jersey's limited landfill space, the Court, through Justice Potter Stewart, concluded that however justifiable the objectives of the law might be, the method employed to achieve them could not discriminate against articles of interstate commerce (in this instance, garbage) "unless there is some reason, apart from their origin, to treat them differently." The Court saw this attempt to bar out-of-state access to New Jersey's privately owned landfill sites, while leaving them open to in-state users, as simply another example of **parochial legislation** tending to promote state **economic protectionism** at the expense of national interests. The problem of preserving adequate landfill space was by no means unique to New Jersey. And yet, in the Court's view, the state was attempting through this legislation "to isolate itself from a problem common to many by erecting a barrier against the movement of interstate trade."

In *Chemical Waste Management, Inc. v. Hunt* (1992), the Supreme Court relied on *Philadelphia v. New Jersey* in striking down Alabama's $72 per ton fee on the disposal of out-of-state hazardous waste. However, the Court left open the possibility that such a fee could be valid if based on the increased cost of disposing of waste from other states. But in *Oregon Waste Systems v. Department of Environmental Quality* (1994), the Court invalidated a surcharge placed on the importation of out-of-state waste by the state of Oregon. Splitting 7 to 2, the Court had little difficulty reaching the conclusion that the surcharge discriminated against interstate commerce. Dissenting, Chief Justice Rehnquist chided the Court for limiting "the dwindling options available to States as they contend with the environmental, health, safety, and political challenges posed by the problem of solid waste disposal in modern society."

Regulation of Alcoholic Beverages

In 1984, the Court, by a 5-to-3 margin (Justice Brennan did not participate) invalidated a provision of the Hawaii liquor tax exempting certain locally produced alcoholic beverages (*Bacchus Imports, Ltd. v. Dias*). Writing for the majority, Justice White reasoned that although "a State may enact laws pursuant to its police powers that have the purpose and effect of encouraging domestic industry, . . . [the] Commerce Clause stands as a limitation on the means by which a state can constitutionally seek to achieve that goal." He found it "irrelevant to the Commerce Clause inquiry that the motivation of the legislature was the desire to aid the makers of the locally produced beverage rather than to harm out-of-state producers." The exemption at issue violated the Commerce Clause "because it had both the purpose and effect of discriminating in favor of local products." The Court rejected a challenge to the tax exemption based on Section 2 of the **Twenty-first Amendment**, recognizing the power of the states to regulate the importation and sale of "intoxicating liquors" within their borders. (The Twenty-first Amendment repealed the Eighteenth Amendment, which had prohibited the "manufacture, sale, or transportation of intoxicating liquors" within the United States.)

In dissent, Justice Stevens, joined by Justices Rehnquist and O'Connor, maintained that the Commerce Clause argument was "squarely foreclosed by the Twenty-first Amendment." Stevens asserted that since adoption of this amendment in 1933, the Court had "consistently reaffirmed" the view that the states may regulate commerce in intoxicating liquors "unconfined by ordinary limitations imposed . . . by the Commerce Clause and other constitutional provisions."

The Supreme Court followed a line of reasoning similar to that of *Bacchus* in striking down state laws designed to keep local liquor and beer prices in line with prices charged in neighboring states. In *Healy v. Beer Institute* (1989), for example, the Court invalidated Connecticut's "beer price affirmation" statute as a violation of the Commerce Clause. This act required brewers and importers of beer to post monthly prices for each brand of beer they intended to sell in Connecticut and to affirm that these prices were no higher than prices in bordering states at the time of posting. Writing for the Court, Justice Harry Blackmun found that this law had the effect of controlling commercial activity entirely outside Connecticut. He maintained that "the practical effect of this affirmation law, in conjunction with the many other beer pricing and affirmation laws that have been or might be enacted throughout the country, is to create just the kind of competing and interlocking local economic regulation that the Commerce Clause was meant to preclude." As in previous cases, the Court rejected the argument that because this regulation involved alcoholic beverages, it was justified under the Twenty-first Amendment. (For further discussion of this issue, see *Brown-Forman Distillers Corporation v. New York State Liquor Authority* [1986].)

State Attempts to Conserve Their Natural Resources

The Supreme Court is unlikely even to permit a state to conserve its privately controlled natural resources if the conservation effort affords preferential treatment to local consumers. In a 1923 decision, for example, the Court invalidated a West Virginia law requiring local natural gas producers to give priority to the orders of in-state, as opposed to out-of-state, customers (*Pennsylvania v. West Virginia*). Of course, a state can assume ownership and direct control of its natural resources without violating the Commerce Clause. But if a state seeks to regulate privately owned businesses, even those engaged in the sale of scarce natural resources, the federal courts are almost certain to condemn the policy if it results in local favoritism.

For a long time, the Supreme Court recognized an exception to this general restriction by permitting the states to exercise broad control over interstate shipment of wild animals and fish for commercial sale. But in *Hughes v. Oklahoma* (1979), this exception was abolished. Here, the Court struck down a statute providing that minnows other than those produced in licensed hatcheries could not be sold outside Oklahoma. The law was presumably designed to protect the state's "natural" minnow population, but the Court rejected this rationale. Writing for the majority, Justice Brennan concluded that "challenges under the Commerce Clause to state regulations of wild animals should be considered according to the same general rule applied to state regulations of other natural resources." The *Hughes* decision requires courts to scrutinize state laws restricting the import and export of animals and fish. It does not, however, create an insurmountable obstacle to such legislation. For example, in *Maine v. Taylor* (1986), the Supreme Court upheld a state law prohibiting the importation of live bait fish. The Court accepted Maine's argument that the restriction was necessary to protect the state's valuable fisheries from parasites and nonnative species of fish.

The "Market Participant" Exception

Despite its critical view of state economic protectionism, the Supreme Court has upheld state regulation designed to promote noneconomic objectives, even when such regulations inhibit economic competition—as long as the state is a "market participant." For example, in a sharply divided ruling, the Court upheld a Maryland law authorizing the state to pay a bounty to junk processors for the hulks of abandoned automobiles (*Hughes v. Alexandria Scrap Corporation* [1976]). To receive the bounty, a dealer had to furnish documentation of title. However, the documentation requirements were more demanding for out-of-state processors. A Virginia processor challenged the law as a violation of both the Commerce and the Equal Protection Clauses of the Fourteenth Amendment. Justice Lewis Powell, writing for the majority, conceded that the law had the practical effect of channeling economic benefits to in-state processors. Nevertheless, he concluded that "[n]othing in the purposes animating the Commerce Clause forbids a state, in the absence of congressional action, from participating in the market and exercising the right to favor its own citizens over others." In a dissenting opinion, Justice Brennan, joined by Justices White and Marshall, denied that this law differed from the kind of economic protectionism struck down in previous cases. He maintained that the Maryland bounty was an obvious discrimination against interstate commerce.

The **market participant exception** recognized in *Alexandria Scrap* was reaffirmed in the 1980 case of *Reeves, Inc. v. Stake*. Here, the Court, by a 5-to-4 margin, upheld a South Dakota policy under which all in-state customers were supplied first with cement produced by a state-operated plant. Adhering closely to the reasoning in *Alexandria Scrap*, Justice Blackmun, writing for the majority, stated that "the Commerce Clause responds principally to state taxes and regulatory measures impeding free private trade in the national marketplace." He found "no indication of a constitutional plan to limit the ability of the states themselves to operate freely in the free market."

Three years later, in *White v. Massachusetts Council of Construction Employers, Inc.* (1983), the Court held that the Commerce Clause did not bar implementation of an executive order requiring that at least 50 percent of the workers on all city-funded construction projects be residents of Boston. In his majority opinion, Justice Rehnquist reasoned that "[i]f the city is a market participant, then the Commerce Clause establishes no barrier to conditions such as these which the city demands for its participation." The Court, however, refused to apply the market participant exception to an Alaska law requiring that any timber taken from state-owned land be at least partially processed before being removed from the state (*South-Central Timber Development, Inc. v. Wunnicke* [1984]).

Continuing Controversy over the Dormant Commerce Clause

The contemporary Supreme Court remains sharply divided over interpretation of the Commerce Clause as a limitation on state regulatory power. This point is well illustrated by the 1997 decision in *Camps Newfound/Owatonna v. Town of Harrison*. Here a five-member majority, speaking through Justice Stevens, held unconstitutional a state law granting preferential tax treatment to charities that extended benefits to in-state, as distinguished from out-of-state, residents. In an attempt to justify this stringent application of the dormant Commerce Clause, Justice Stevens observed that "[t]he history of our Commerce Clause jurisprudence has shown that even the smallest scale discrimination can interfere with the project of our federal Union." In a vigorous dissenting opinion, Justice Scalia, joined by Chief Justice Rehnquist and Justices Thomas and Ginsburg, maintained that the Court had gone too far:

> We have often said that the purpose of our negative commerce clause jurisprudence is to create a national market. . . . In our zeal to advance this policy, however, we must take care not to overstep our mandate, for the Commerce Clause was not intended "to cut the States off from legislating on all subjects relating to the health, life, and safety of their citizens, though the legislation might indirectly affect the commerce of the country."

It is clear from this decision and others reviewed in this section that the Court has been unable to articulate a bright-line standard defining the scope of state regulatory power in relation to national commerce. Of course, the complexity of this subject makes it virtually impossible to achieve such clarity.

TO SUMMARIZE:

- The Commerce Clause is both a source of national power and a limitation of state power.
- Although states are permitted to regulate local aspects of interstate commerce, they may not engage in economic protectionism.
- In balancing competing interests in this area, the Supreme Court encourages the continued growth of a strong national economy while acknowledging state responsibility to protect the health, safety, and general welfare of the citizenry.
- The inherent tension between legitimate state and national interests within a federal system is well illustrated by the continuing controversy over state regulatory power in the field of commerce.

STATE TAXING POWER

By contrast with the regulation of commerce, state power to tax was well established when the Constitution was drafted in 1787. The grant of taxing authority to Congress in Article I, Section 8, clause 1, did not withdraw or transfer this power from the states. Taxation simply became one of those **concurrent powers** exercised broadly by both spheres of government. Of course, the authority to tax at the local level is derived from the states. Cities, counties, and other units of local government are created and may be abolished by the states, and the scope of their taxing power is largely determined either by state constitutional provisions or by statutes—always subject, however, to federal constitutional requirements.

Routine aspects of state and local taxation do not often raise serious federal constitutional problems. The states have retained broad discretion under the federal Constitution to tap a variety of revenue sources that have widened as governmental services and costs have increased. It is only when states or their local subdivisions use taxation to block or undermine a federal constitutional principle or objective that state taxing power is likely to be limited by the Supreme Court. One such principle is the promotion of a national economy, embodied in such provisions as the Commerce Clause and the restriction on state taxation of imports and exports (see Article I, Section 10). A state tax that unfairly burdens interstate commerce to the advantage of local economic interests is vulnerable to constitutional attack. The foregoing discussion of state power to regulate commerce touched on this aspect of state taxation. Two additional problems are posed by the federal relationship, both of which have their origins in constitutional principles and reflect the gradual expansion of governmental power. These problem areas are intergovernmental tax immunity and the scope of state taxing power under the Imports-Exports Clause.

Intergovernmental Tax Immunity

First, we examine the doctrine of **intergovernmental tax immunity**. *In M'Culloch v. Maryland* (1819), Chief Justice Marshall asserted that Congress has not only an implied power to establish a national bank but also that a state cannot use its taxing authority to undermine that power. Marshall refused to sanction a state tax having the potential to destroy an entity constitutionally created by the national government. As he put it, characteristically "the power to tax involves the power to destroy." But in Marshall's view, this reasoning did not apply in reverse—that is, it provided no justification for imposing restrictions on national taxing power when that power interfered with lawful state objectives. But whether Marshall acknowledged it or not, the logic of his argument cut both ways.

As the doctrine of dual federalism emerged in the aftermath of the Civil War, the argument in favor of state immunity from national taxation gained support. In 1871, the Supreme Court embraced this doctrine in *Collector v. Day,* holding that the salary of a Massachusetts judge was immune from the federal income tax levied during the Civil War. The judge's salary was treated as an "instrumentality" of state government protected by the Tenth Amendment, just as the Bank of the United States had been viewed as an instrumentality of the national government protected by the Supremacy Clause. This reasoning was later applied to exempt from state as well as federal income taxes the salaries of many employees at all levels of government. Precisely why these salaries should be afforded special protection was never made clear, but the broader principle of intergovernmental tax immunity, which *Collector v. Day* established, followed logically from the assumptions underlying classical federalism.

For a number of years, the doctrine of intergovernmental tax immunity flourished in American constitutional law. The Court expanded the doctrine in the famous income tax case of 1895 by holding, among other things, that Congress could not tax income generated by state and local government securities (see *Pollock v. Farmers' Loan and Trust Company*). Although the *Pollock* decision was in large part overruled by the Sixteenth Amendment, adopted in 1913, this restriction on federal taxation remained in effect for many years. The exemption was finally challenged in 1982, when Congress imposed a tax on the interest from unregistered, long-term bonds issued by state and local governments. The state of South Carolina brought an original action in the Supreme Court attacking the constitutionality of this measure (*South Carolina v. Baker* [1988]). In upholding the tax, the Court concluded that neither the Tenth Amendment nor the doctrine of intergovernmental tax immunity prevented Congress from taxing this important source of state and local revenue. *South Carolina v. Baker* thus finally overruled the last remaining vestige of the *Pollock* decision.

Intergovernmental tax immunity had its heyday during the 1920s. In 1922, for example, the Court went so far as to strike down a state tax on income accruing to a company from oil lands it had leased from Indian tribes. Because these lands were classified as federal property, the Court concluded that the oil company, as lessee, was an instrumentality of the United States, carrying out the government's "duties to the Indians" (*Gillespie v. Oklahoma* [1922]). In a 1928 case, the states were barred from taxing royalties derived from national patents on the ground that such a tax would discourage national efforts to promote science and invention (*Long v. Rockwood*).

With growing demands for additional tax sources in response to the Great Depression, these highly restrictive decisions were overruled (*Fox Film Corporation v. Doyal* [1932]). In 1939, the Supreme Court overruled *Collector v. Day* and its progeny, thus removing the tax exemptions previously applied to the salaries of state and federal employees (*Graves v. New York ex rel. O'Keefe*). Justice Harlan Stone, who, along with Justices Oliver Wendell Holmes and Louis Brandeis, had been on the dissenting side during the heyday of reciprocal tax immunity, assumed a leading role in articulating the new approach. He rejected the rigid logic of dual federalism and recognized the practical demands imposed by two legally distinct governments, both obviously requiring more revenue to perform their expanding duties.

Neither the states nor the national government can tax essential governmental functions performed by the other. This is as true today as it was in the 1920s. The problem is determining just what constitutes an essential function of government. Presumably, Congress could not impose a tax on the publication of statutes enacted by a state legislature. Nor could a state levy a tax on the the Supreme Court case reporter, *United States Reports*. But once we move away from such extreme and improbable situations, the answers are not found as easily. For example, although a state may not tax federal property directly, it can place a privilege tax on an individual or corporation using federal property and may base the tax on the value of such property (*United States v. City of Detroit* [1958]). States may also tax federal contractors, even if the burden of the tax is absorbed in the contract price and thus in effect is passed on to the government (*Alabama v. King & Boozer* [1941]). On the other hand, the Supremacy Clause broadly protects functions of the national government from regulation through the imposition of state taxes or exercise of the state police power (*United States v. Georgia Public Service Commission* [1963]).

Basically, the Supreme Court has attempted to maximize the discretion of the taxing authority without impairing the performance of essential activities of government. Formal doctrine is less useful to the Court in making specific determinations in this field than practical assessments of political or economic reality. The gradual decline of reciprocal tax immunity since the 1930s illustrates the veracity of Justice Oliver Wendell Holmes's famous observation that the "life of the law has not been logic; it has been experience."

A modern example of the erosion of reciprocal tax immunity is provided by the 1978 decision in *Massachusetts v. United States*. Here, the Court upheld the imposition of a federal aircraft registration tax on a state-owned helicopter used exclusively for police work. It is difficult to think of a more basic governmental function than that of law enforcement, but the Court readily found the tax valid as a "user fee." Writing for the majority, Justice Brennan concluded:

> A nondiscriminatory taxing measure that operates to defray the cost of a federal program by recovering a fair approximation of each beneficiary's share of the cost is surely no more offensive to the constitutional scheme than is either a tax on the income earned by state employees or a tax on a State's sale of bottled water [see *New York v. United States* (1946)]. . . . There is no danger that such measures will not be based on benefits conferred or that they will function as regulatory devices unduly burdening essential state activities.

With respect to both federal and state taxation, the emphasis today is on enlarging, not restricting, available sources of revenue. This point is illustrated by the decision in *United States v. County of Fresno* (1977), in which the Court upheld a local property tax on U.S. Forestry Service employees whose houses were rented from the government. The tax was imposed only on those renting from owners (in this instance, the federal government) who were themselves exempt from taxation. Justice White, for the majority, found the tax to be nondiscriminatory, concluding that since it fell on individuals and not government, it was no impediment to the work of the Forestry Service. On the other hand, in *Davis v. Michigan Department of Treasury* (1989), the Court struck down a state law exempting state but not federal retirement benefits from state income taxes. The Court concluded that no significant differences existed between the two classes of retirees that would justify exempting one but not the other from state taxation.

The Imports-Exports Clause

Article I, Section 10, clause 2, of the Constitution provides: "No State shall, without the Consent of the Congress, lay any Imposts or Duties on Imports or Exports, except what may be absolutely necessary for executing its inspection Laws." Like the Commerce Clause, the **Imports-Exports Clause** was intended to promote broad national economic interests and minimize the negative influence of parochial state policies. In addition, the Imports-Exports Clause was designed to bar discrimination against both the shipment of goods into the United States from foreign countries and the shipment of American goods destined for foreign markets. Another aim of this clause was to remove the unfair advantage that seaboard states with ports of entry would otherwise have over interior states. Given the legal characteristics of the federal system, however, the Imports-Exports Clause was also theoretically applicable to goods imported from or exported to other states. Despite occasional tendencies to accord it this broad interpretation, this clause has usually been confined to the movement of goods between foreign countries and the United States.

The first question the Supreme Court considered in limiting the scope of state taxing power turned on the definition of the word *import* in this clause. At what point, for state taxation purposes, does a commodity imported from a foreign country lose its distinct character as an import and thereby become subject to a state's general taxing power? Chief Justice Marshall considered this question in the 1827 case of *Brown v. Maryland*. Maryland required that importers and sellers of goods in designated forms pay a license fee of $50. The state imposed a financial penalty for failure to comply with this requirement. Four sellers of foreign merchandise challenged the Maryland law as violative of the Imports-Exports Clause and the Commerce Clause. The Marshall Court declared the law unconstitutional on both grounds. The chief justice interpreted the Imports-Exports Clause as a broad restriction on state power. The fee at issue in this case was aimed exclusively at imports and, on the basis of his analysis, was clearly a violation of the Constitution. But Marshall went one step further and considered a question not directly at issue in this case: When does a commodity moving into a state from a foreign jurisdiction lose its distinct character as an import? He answered as follows:

> When the importer has so acted upon the thing imported, that it has become incorporated and mixed up with the mass of property within the country, it has perhaps lost its distinctive character as an import, and has become subject to the taxing power of the state; but while remaining the property of the importer, in his warehouse, in the original form or package in which it was imported, a tax upon it is too plainly a duty on imports to escape the prohibition in the Constitution.

Because the law at issue did not apply to sellers of domestic goods, it was plainly discriminatory and could have been invalidated without reference to this "original package" test. But the state attorney general, Roger B. Taney (Marshall's successor as chief justice on the Supreme Court), argued that a simple invalidation of the license fee through strict construction of the language of the Imports-Exports Clause could permanently insulate imported goods from state and local taxation. Marshall's development of the **original package doctrine,** with its emphasis on a cutoff point beyond which the states would be free to tax, appears to have come in response to Taney's argument.

The Rise and Fall of the Original Package Doctrine   In 1872, the original package dictum was accorded formal constitutional status, providing the basis for invalidating a nondiscriminatory property tax on imported goods that, although no longer in the "stream of commerce," remained in their original packages (*Low v. Austin*). The original package doctrine had the appeal of apparent simplicity, and over time it acquired the aura accorded to many of the pronouncements of Chief Justice Marshall. But as many scholars pointed out, the doctrine was both mechanical and inconsistent with the purpose of the Imports-Exports Clause, which was simply to prevent discriminatory state taxation on goods moving from or to foreign markets.

Generally speaking, the development of American law relies heavily on precedent. Although less pronounced in constitutional law than in most other legal subfields, *stare decisis* is a powerful factor in the decision making process. Perhaps this explains the durability of the original package doctrine. However, with advances in technology and great increases in the volume of foreign trade, the doctrine became untenable. By the 1940s, legal scholars were calling for its abandonment. They urged the substitution of a simple test focusing on the question of whether a given state tax is discriminatory. Finally, in the 1976 case of *Michelin Tire Corporation v. Wages,* the Supreme Court adopted this position. It overruled *Lowe v. Austin* and upheld a nondiscriminatory Georgia tax on tires and tubes imported from France and Canada. Writing for the majority, Justice Brennan took note of the extensive criticism of the original package doctrine and of its departure from the intent of the Framers. He then concluded:

> Our independent study persuades us that a nondiscriminatory *ad valorem* property tax is not the type of state exaction which the Framers of the Constitution or the Court in *Brown* [*v. Maryland*] had in mind as being an "impost" or duty and the *Lowe v. Austin's* reliance upon the *Brown* dictum to reach the contrary conclusion was misplaced.

In this way, the Court managed to nullify the original package doctrine without challenging John Marshall's initial statement of the formula, thus according deference to judicial tradition while at the same time overruling a troublesome constitutional precedent.

Other Taxation Issues

The Supreme Court has encountered other constitutional problems in determining the scope of state taxing power. These include issues of multiple taxation, the proper basis of assessment, the degree of burden that will be permitted on interstate commerce, and the procedural requirements of due process of law. This chapter, however, is concerned only with the more salient aspects of American federalism and cannot elaborate on these additional questions of state taxation. Like its national counterpart, state taxation serves regulatory as well as revenue-raising purposes. For example, certain state-imposed license fees may be upheld even though they apply to interstate as well as intrastate business activities. The question in such cases is whether the state is acting within the proper scope of its police power. The Supreme Court has not invalidated a state tax merely because of its regulatory effect. The Court has been far more concerned with whether a given tax discriminates against interstate or foreign commerce or whether it inhibits an essential function of the national government. The constitutional scope of the state taxing power is strongly influenced, even in an age of cooperative federalism, by the central objective of balancing state and national interests.

TO SUMMARIZE:

- When states use taxation to block or undermine a federal constitutional principle or objective, such state taxing power is likely to be limited by the Supreme Court.
- A state tax that unfairly burdens interstate commerce to the advantage of local economic interests is vulnerable to constitutional attack.
- Until the late 1930s, the doctrine of intergovernmental tax immunity served as a basis for limiting both state and federal taxing authority. As a practical matter, the doctrine no longer limits federal taxing power and only rarely restricts state taxing authority.

- The Imports-Exports Clause limits state power to tax imports and exports and was intended to promote broad national economic interests and minimize the negative influence of parochial state policies. Chief Justice John Marshall developed the original package doctrine in an effort to place tangible limits on state taxing power over imports. The vast growth of commercial activity in combination with the revolution in transportation rendered this doctrine obsolete, and the Supreme Court formally repudiated it in 1976.

INTERSTATE RELATIONS

In addition to interaction between the national government and the states, American federalism encompasses relations among the states. This interstate dimension is addressed primarily by Article IV of the Constitution, with its Full Faith and Credit, Privileges and Immunities, and Rendition provisions. The Framers also provided, in Article I, Section 10, clause 3, that the states could not, without congressional consent, "enter into any Agreement or Compact" with other states or with foreign powers.

The Full Faith and Credit Clause

The Constitution requires that each state give "[f]ull Faith and Credit . . . to the public Acts, Records, and judicial Proceedings of every other State" (Article IV, Section 1, clause 1). In addition to asserting this general principle, the **Full Faith and Credit Clause** grants Congress the power to "prescribe the Manner in which such Acts, Records and Proceedings shall be proved, and the Effect thereof." To that end, Congress passed legislation in 1790 and 1804 providing for the authentication and effect of public records. As a result of this early legislation and occasional minor changes over the years, the principle of full faith and credit has become an integral part of our legal system.

The most difficult and important questions in this area have involved the extent to which valid final judgments by state courts are enforceable in other states. One brief illustration of the complexity characterizing this area is provided by the Supreme Court's decision in *Estin v. Estin* (1948). Here, the Court recognized a "divisible" divorce decree. Under this approach, a state must accord validity to a divorce granted by another state but is not bound by another state's decision on such related matters as alimony, child custody, and division of property.

The Controversy over Same-Sex Marriage   The Full Faith and Credit Clause has long been interpreted to require states to recognize marriage licenses issued by other states. In the late 1990s, an issue emerged over whether states would have to recognize same-sex marriages licensed by other states. Although no state has yet recognized same-sex marriage, several states have come close to doing so. Vermont permits same-sex couples to enter into "civil unions" that have all the legal rights and duties associated with marriage. This appears to avoid the issue of recognition by other states, as civil unions are not technically marriages. In 1996 the Hawaii Supreme Court invalidated that state's ban on same-sex marriage, but this decision was effectively overturned in 1999 when voters in that state overwhelmingly approved a constitutional amendment reserving to the legislature the power to limit marriages to opposite-sex couples. Many other states have enacted laws reaffirming the traditional conception of marriage. Still, gay rights activists are pushing for courts and legislatures around the country to legalize same-sex marriage and many believe that it is only a matter of time before this happens. If and when it does, are other states obligated to recognize such unions? In 1996 Congress passed and in 1997 President Bill Clinton signed the Defense of Marriage Act. The act provides:

> No State, territory, or possession of the United States, or Indian tribe, shall be required to give effect to any public act, record, or judicial proceeding of any other State, territory, possession, or tribe respecting a relationship between persons of the same sex that is treated as a marriage under the laws of such other State, territory, possession, or tribe, or a right or claim arising from such relationship.

The Defense of Marriage Act did not end the controversy, however. Critics charge that Congress has no power to relieve states of their obligations under the Full Faith and Credit Clause. It is likely that the courts will address this question in the not too distant future.

The Privileges and Immunities Clause

The principle of full faith and credit is insufficient to promote harmonious interstate relations. Recognition of another state's "Acts, Records, and judicial Proceedings" would be of little consequence if the states were free to favor their own citizens over those of other states. To preclude this possibility, the Framers provided in Section 2, clause 1, of Article IV that "Citizens of each State shall be entitled to all Privileges and Immunities of Citizens in the several States." This **Privileges and Immunities Clause** should not be confused with a similar provision in the Fourteenth Amendment declaring "No state shall make or enforce any law which shall abridge the privileges or immunities of citizens of the United States." Whereas the Fourteenth Amendment protects privileges and immunities of national citizenship only, Article IV is directed to state citizenship (see *The Slaughter-House Cases* [1873]). In spite of its open-ended language, this provision was until recently accorded a narrow judicial interpretation.

The first major decision interpreting Article IV's Privileges and Immunities Clause established this narrow construction but identified a number of fundamental rights embraced by the provision (*Corfield v. Coryell* [1823]). In this circuit court ruling, Supreme Court Justice Bushrod Washington argued that the clause protects only those privileges and immunities "which are, in their nature, fundamental; which belong of right to the citizens of all free governments." For Washington, these fundamentals included "the right of a citizen of one state to pass through or reside in any other state . . . ; to claim the benefit of the writ of habeas corpus; to institute and maintain actions of any kind in the courts of the state; to take, hold, and dispose of property; and an exemption from higher taxes or impositions than are paid by other citizens of the state."

Justice Washington's list of **fundamental rights** is limited by comparison with the scope of constitutional protections today. Nevertheless, the logic underlying his position could be extended to include many rights guaranteed by other constitutional provisions. Indeed, the Privileges and Immunities Clause is closely related to such concepts as equal protection and due process, as well as to the negative implications of the Commerce Clause.

The Supreme Court has not elaborated on the "fundamental rights" formulation of *Corfield v. Coryell*. Rather, it directed its attention to the question of whether states are granting equality of rights to citizens of other states relative to their own citizens. However, the Privileges and Immunities Clause has never been interpreted to preclude all differential treatment of out-of-state citizens. On occasion, the Court has allowed even discrimination involving fundamental rights if it could be shown that such discrimination could not be "reasonably . . . characterized as hostile to the rights of citizens of other states" (*Blake v. McClung* [1898]). As a result, differential state standards governing the practice of certain professions are not barred by the Privileges and Immunities Clause: Out-of-state physicians, lawyers, and other professionals may be required to prove their competency on the basis of higher standards than those applied to their in-state counterparts. Tuition rates at public colleges and universities are typically lower for in-state students. Out-of-state residents are charged more for hunting and fishing licenses than are in-state residents. Such discrepancies are generally accepted as justifiable because they advance legitimate state interests.

On this basis, the Supreme Court upheld Iowa's one-year residency requirement as a prerequisite to obtaining a divorce (*Sosna v. Iowa* [1975]). Similar durational residency requirements had been struck down as applied to welfare benefits, voting, and publicly financed health care (see, for example, *Shapiro v. Thompson* [1969] and *Dunn v. Blumstein* [1972]). The state-imposed restrictions in those cases were justified only by budgetary and record-keeping concerns. These interests were regarded as less important than the constitutional claims of individuals burdened by the residency requirements. By contrast, Iowa could justify its residency requirement for divorce on grounds other than budgetary constraints and administrative convenience. "A decree of divorce," said Justice Rehnquist for the majority, "is not a matter in which the only interested parties are the state as a sort of 'grantor' and a plaintiff . . . in the role of 'grantee.' " He continued by observing:

> Both spouses are obviously interested in the proceedings, since it will affect their marital status and very likely their property rights. Where a married couple has minor children, a decree of divorce would usually include provisions for their custody and support. With consequences of such moment riding on a divorce decree issued by its courts, Iowa may insist that one seeking to initiate such a proceeding have the modicum of attachment to the state required here.

Thus, a state must show that its differential treatment of in-state and out-of-state residents serves some reasonable purpose.

Alaska's failure to justify such differential treatment led the Court in 1978 to strike down a statute requiring employers to give preferential treatment to in-state residents (*Hicklin v. Orbeck*). Specifically, the law required "the employment of qualified Alaska residents" in preference to out-of-state residents, in connection with "all oil and gas leases, easements or right-of-way permits for oil or gas pipeline purposes . . . to which the state is a party." Alaska began to enforce this act seriously in 1975, when construction on the Trans-Alaska Pipeline was reaching its peak. As a result, Hicklin and other nonresidents who had previously worked on this project "were prevented from obtaining pipeline-related work." The Court unanimously invalidated Alaska's preferential requirement as a violation of the Privileges and Immunities Clause of Article IV. Writing for the Court, Justice Brennan concluded that this law was "an attempt to force virtually all businesses that benefit in some way from the economic ripple effect of Alaska's decision to develop her oil and gas resources to bias their employment practices in favor of the state's residents."

We have already noted the close relationship between the Privileges and Immunities Clause and the Commerce Clause. But this relationship does not mean that the two clauses are entirely equivalent in impact. Thus, a state policy that survives scrutiny under the Commerce Clause may be invalidated under Article IV, Section 2. This point is well illustrated by the 1984 decision of *United Building and Construction*

Trades v. Camden. At issue was the question of whether the Privileges and Immunities Clause was violated by a Camden, New Jersey, city ordinance requiring that a minimum of 40 percent of persons employed under city construction contracts be Camden residents. The New Jersey Supreme Court held that because the ordinance was written in terms of municipal rather than state residency, it was not subject to the Privileges and Immunities Clause. Without ruling on the constitutionality of the ordinance, the Supreme Court reversed. In his majority opinion, Justice Rehnquist concluded that the local character of the ordinance did not "somehow place it outside the scope of the Clause." The ordinance in question had state approval, but even if it had been "adopted solely by Camden, the hiring preference would still have to comport" with this constitutional provision.

Distinguishing the Camden decision from *White v. Massachusetts Council of Construction Employers* (1983), discussed earlier, Rehnquist asserted that the Commerce and the Privileges and Immunities Clauses "have different aims and set different standards for state conduct." The "market participant" rationale applied in *White* was not controlling in the *Camden* case. In supporting this conclusion, Rehnquist reasoned as follows:

> The Commerce Clause is an implied restraint upon state regulatory powers. Such powers must give way before the superior authority of Congress to legislate on (or leave unregulated) matters involving interstate commerce. When the state acts solely as a market participant, no conflict between state regulation and federal regulatory authority can arise. . . . The Privileges and Immunities Clause, on the other hand, imposes a direct restraint on state action in the interests of interstate harmony. . . . It is discrimination against out-of-state residents on matters of fundamental concern which triggers the Clause, not regulation affecting interstate commerce.

The Rendition Clause

The Full Faith and Credit Clause does not extend to criminal offenses; that is, no state need enforce the criminal laws of another state or respect those laws as a defense in a prosecution. This position has its roots in the Anglo-American concept of due process, which requires trial in the district where the crime was committed. Complete reliance on this tradition could have permitted any of the states to become havens of refuge for fugitives from other states. The Framers therefore included a **Rendition Clause** in Section 2 of Article IV:

> A Person charged in any State with Treason, Felony, or other Crime, who shall flee from Justice, and be found in another State, shall on Demand of the executive Authority of the State from which he fled, be delivered up, to be removed to the State having Jurisdiction of the Crime.

Pursuant to this clause, Congress in 1793 passed legislation delineating the manner of rendition and obligating governors to comply with the extradition requirements. Those provisions, both statutory and constitutional, were presumed to cover any and all violations of a state's criminal law and required a governor to deliver a fugitive to the "requesting" state, even if the fugitive's acts would not have been criminal in the governor's state. This requirement was upheld in the 1861 case of *Kentucky v. Dennison.* Ohio Governor William Dennison had refused to comply with Kentucky's demand that he surrender a black defendant charged in Kentucky with aiding the escape of slaves. The Supreme Court unanimously held that although Dennison had a duty to comply with Kentucky's demand, this duty was unenforceable. This anomalous aspect of the *Dennison* case was eventually overruled by a 1987 Supreme Court decision holding that a federal judge can require a governor to perform "the ministerial duty" of delivering a fugitive upon a proper demand from another state (*Puerto Rico v. Branstad*).

Interstate Compacts

The Full Faith and Credit, Privileges and Immunities, and Rendition Clauses were obviously designed to minimize friction among the states. By contrast, the Compacts Clause, although stated in negative terms, was more positive in that it paved the way for the states, with congressional consent, to enter into agreements among themselves. The relevant language of Article I, Section 10, clause 3, provides that "[n]o State shall, without the Consent of Congress, . . . enter into any Agreement or Compact with another State, or with a foreign Power." Over the years, many such agreements have been entered into with generally beneficial results. New York and New Jersey, for example, have cooperated in administering the New York Port Authority. Other states have developed **interstate agreements** for the regulation of oil and gas, the management of water resources, and the like. Despite the constitutional requirement of congressional approval, the Court has sustained several interstate agreements not explicitly sanctioned by Congress.

This was the result in the 1978 case of *U.S. Steel Corporation v. Multistate Tax Commission.* In 1967, a multistate tax compact went into effect among seven states. By 1978, some twenty-three states had participated at various times, some remaining affiliated, others withdrawing. The purpose of this compact was to reduce the inefficiency inherent in the separate single-state administration of taxes levied on multistate businesses. The compact established a commission to carry out a number of related functions. U.S. Steel and other large corporations, believing that the commission's activities worked to their disadvantage, challenged the constitutionality of the compact, alleging that it unreasonably burdened interstate commerce. However, the Supreme Court sustained the compact in spite of the absence of explicit congressional consent.

In *Multistate Tax Commission,* the Supreme Court relied principally on the precedent of *Virginia v. Tennessee* (1893). There, the Court had sustained a compact between Virginia and Tennessee that resolved a border dispute, finding that Congress had tacitly approved the arrangement. In this early decision, Justice Stephen J. Field, speaking for the Court, added that not all compacts required even tacit approval. Approval was unnecessary if the compact did not tend to "increase the political power of the states which may encroach upon or interfere with the just supremacy of the United States." The Court applied this rationale in *Multistate Tax Commission.* Justice Powell, writing for the majority, reasoned that because the taxing authority remained in the hands of each state and because all regulations promulgated by the commission were ineffectual until state statutes authorized them, the compact did not expand state power at the expense of federal authority. Indeed, the compact gave no single state any greater power than it possessed independently. Accordingly, the compact was no greater burden on interstate commerce than were state taxes on multistate businesses previously sustained as constitutional.

Interstate compacts that are granted congressional approval function as the legal equivalent of federal treaties and statutes—that is, they are the supreme law of the land. Once approved, the terms of the compact are binding on all parties, preventing a state from unilaterally withdrawing and from using its internal domestic policy to avoid compliance with the terms of the compact. This policy is well illustrated by the case of *West Virginia ex rel. Dyer v. Sims* (1951). There, the Supreme Court overruled the West Virginia Supreme Court's holding that West Virginia's commitments under an interstate compact were invalid because they conflicted with the state constitution.

TO SUMMARIZE:

- The Full Faith and Credit Clause of Article IV, Section 1, of the Constitution requires each state to recognize and enforce the public acts, records, and judicial proceedings of other states. The most difficult questions in this area involve the extent to which final judgments of state courts are enforceable in other states.
- The Privileges and Immunities Clause of Article IV, Section 2, of the Constitution embodies the principle that states cannot show favoritism to their own citizens at the expense of persons from other states. A state must show that any differential treatment serves a reasonable and legitimate purpose.
- Article IV, Section 2, also provides for extradition of accused criminals who flee across state lines. The process begins upon the request of the governor of the state from which the fugitive has fled. A federal judge can require a governor to perform the duty of delivering a fugitive upon a proper demand from another state.
- The qualified prohibition against interstate compacts contained in Article I, Section 10, clause 3, of the Constitution has not prevented the states from entering into numerous agreements designed to promote their mutual interests. The Supreme Court has upheld interstate compacts even in the absence of explicit congressional approval.

CONCLUSION

Taking into account both the constitutional basis and the political dimensions of American federalism, it is possible to identify five basic characteristics of this system of government.

1. *The continuing division of legal authority between two levels of government: national and state.* Each level has an independent mechanism of government through which it enacts, interprets, and administers law. Considerable overlapping occurs, of course, but the structure of two legally distinct spheres of government—each with its own constitution, legislature, chief executive, judiciary, and administrative bureaucracy—remains intact.
2. *Direct simultaneous authority over persons within their jurisdictions.* The national government and the states exercise authority over persons within their jurisdictions. Dual citizenship is a fundamental part of the federal system, and rights, privileges, and immunities derive from both types of citizenship.
3. *National supremacy.* Both the Supremacy Clause of Article VI and the Fourteenth Amendment mandate the subordination of state to national authority in instances where the national government is constitutionally empowered to act.
4. *Cooperative federalism.* The modern era has been characterized by a high level of interaction between federal and state authorities. Today, the national government and the states work cooperatively in the areas of law enforcement, domestic security, education, highway construction, public health, social welfare, and environmental protection, among others. While the term "cooperative federal-

ism" is often used to describe these relationships, the role of the national government is clearly dominant.

5. *The Supreme Court as "umpire of the federal system."* Throughout its history, the Supreme Court has played a leading role in allocating constitutional power between the national government and the states and in refereeing interstate relations. Federalism encompasses a set of complex and dynamic relationships between the states and the national government and among the states themselves. These relationships are defined and redefined through the process of judicial interpretation. In performing its role as **umpire of the federal system**, the Supreme Court has attempted over the years to give expression to the contending values of national unity and local diversity.

Although the role of the national government became dominant during the second half of the twentieth century, the states continue to be viable and important governmental entities. They have by no means become mere administrative units of the national government. Indeed, as a result of the "Reagan Revolution" of the 1980s and the Republican Congress's "devolution" of power to the states in the 1990s, states have had to shoulder greater policy making and fiscal responsibilities.

Since the mid-1990s, the Supreme Court, in a series of closely divided and highly controversial decisions, has buttressed the constitutional standing of the states within the federal system. Whether the recent reallocation of power toward the states represents a long-term trend remains to be seen. American federalism, after all, is highly dynamic.

KEY TERMS

federal system	police powers of the states	state power to regulate interstate commerce	Imports-Exports Clause
unitary system	Civil War Amendments	direct-indirect test	original package doctrine
Tenth Amendment	doctrine of incorporation	parochial legislation	Full Faith and Credit Clause
states' rights	dual federalism	economic protectionism	Privileges and Immunities Clause
nullification	cooperative federalism	Twenty-first Amendment	fundamental rights
interposition	coercive federalism	market participant exception	Rendition Clause
secession	federal preemption	concurrent powers	interstate agreements
sovereign immunity	Supremacy Clause	intergovernmental tax immunity	umpire of the federal system
Eleventh Amendment	judicial federalism		
national supremacy	independent state grounds		

FOR FURTHER READING

Beer, Samuel H. *To Make a Nation: The Rediscovery of American Federalism.* Cambridge, Mass.: Harvard University Press, 1993.

Berger, Raoul. *Federalism: The Founders' Design.* Norman: University of Oklahoma Press, 1987.

Bowman, Ann O., and Richard C. Kearney. *The Resurgence of the States.* Englewood Cliffs, N.J.: Prentice Hall, 1986.

Calhoun, John C. *A Disquisition on Government.* New York: Bobbs-Merrill, 1953.

Conlan, Timothy. *New Federalism: Intergovernmental Reform from Nixon to Reagan.* Washington, D.C.: Brookings Institution, 1988.

Corwin, Edward S. *The Commerce Clause versus States' Rights.* Princeton, N.J.: Princeton University Press, 1936.

Elazar, Daniel. *American Federalism: The View from the States* (3rd ed.). New York: Harper and Row, 1984.

Elkins, Stanley, and Eric McKitrick. *The Age of Federalism.* New York: Oxford University Press, 1994.

May, Christopher N., and Allan Ides. *Constitutional Law: National Power and Federalism: Examples and Explanations.* New York: Aspen Publishers, 1998.

Porter, Mary, and G. Allan Tarr (eds.). *State Supreme Courts: Policymakers in the Federal System.* Westport, Conn.: Greenwood Press, 1982.

Pritchett, C. Herman. *Constitutional Law of the Federal System.* Englewood Cliffs, N.J.: Prentice-Hall, 1984.

Redish, Martin H. *The Constitution as Political Structure.* New York: Oxford University Press, 1995.

Riker, William. *Federalism: Origin, Operation, Significance.* Boston: Little, Brown, 1964.

Walker, David B. *The Rebirth of Federalism* (2nd ed.). Chatham, N.J.: Chatham House, 2000.

Williams, Robert F. *State Constitutional Law: Cases and Materials* (3rd ed.). New York: Matthew Bender & Co., 1999.

INTERNET RESOURCES

Name of Resource	Description	URL
Legal Information Institute	A list of state statutes available on the Internet	http://www.law.cornell.edu/topics.state_statutes.html
Publius: The Journal of Federalism	A scholarly journal devoted to issues of federalism	http://www.lafayette.edu/publius
The Federalism Project (American Enterprise Institute)	Provides a conservative perspective	http://www.federalismproject.org
Center for the Study of Federalism (Temple University)	Academic institute dedicated to the study of federalism	http://www.temple.edu/federalism

Case

CHISHOLM V. GEORGIA

2 Dall. (2. U.S.) 419; 1 L.Ed. 440 (1793)
Vote: 4–1

In 1777, the state of Georgia authorized two state commissioners to purchase supplies from Robert Farquhar, a merchant based in Charleston, South Carolina. Although the supplies were delivered, Farquhar never received payment. After Farquhar's death, the executor of his estate, Alexander Chisholm, brought a federal lawsuit against the state of Georgia to force payment of the claim. Relying on the ancient doctrine of sovereign immunity, Georgia responded that it could not be sued without its own consent, even by a citizen of another state proceeding in a federal tribunal. The Chisholm case was decided by the Supreme Court on February 18, 1793. Dividing 4 to 1, the Court rejected the state's contention of immunity. In keeping with the common practice of the day, all five justices rendered opinions seriatim. Chief Justice John Jay and Associate Justices James Wilson, John Cushing, and John Blair wrote opinions concurring in the judgment. Justice James Iredell produced a dissenting opinion. (Although Congress in 1792 had increased the size of the Court to six justices, Justice William Paterson did not begin service on the Court until March 1793.)

Only Justice Wilson's concurrence and Justice Iredell's dissent are excerpted here.

Wilson, Justice:

This is a case of uncommon magnitude. One of the parties to it is a state; certainly respectable, claiming to be sovereign. The question to be determined is whether this state, so respectable, and whose claim soars so high, is amenable to the jurisdiction of the supreme court of the United States? This question, important in itself, will depend on others, more important still; and, may, perhaps, be ultimately resolved into one, no less radical than this—"do the people of the United States form a nation?" . . .

To the Constitution of the United States the term "sovereign" is totally unknown. There is but one place where it could have been used with propriety. But, even in that place it would not, perhaps, have comported with the delicacy of those who ordained and established that constitution. They might have announced themselves "sovereign people of the United States." But serenely conscious of the fact, they avoided the ostentatious declaration. . . .

In one sense, the term "sovereign" has for its correlative, [the term] "subject." In this sense, the term can receive no application; for it has no object in the Constitution of the United States. Under that constitution there are citizens, but no subjects. "Citizens of the United States." "Citizens of another state." "Citizens of different states." "A state or citizen thereof." The term "subject" occurs indeed, once in the instrument; but to make the contrast strongly, the epithet "foreign" is prefixed. In this sense, I presume the state of Georgia has no claim upon her own citizens: In this sense, I am certain, she can have no claim upon the citizens of another state. . . .

As a judge of this court, I know, and can decide upon the knowledge, that the citizens of Georgia, when they acted upon the large scale of the union, as part of the "People of the United States," did not surrender the supreme or sovereign power to that state; but, as to the purposes of the union, retained it to themselves. As to the purposes of the union, therefore, Georgia is not a sovereign state. . . .

. . . "The people of the United States" are the first personages introduced [in the Constitution]. Who were those people? They were the citizens of thirteen states, each of which had a separate constitution and government, and all of which were connected together by Articles of Confederation. To the purposes of public strength and felicity that confederacy was totally inadequate. A requisition on the several states terminated its legislative authority; executive or judicial authority it had none. In order, therefore, to form a more perfect union, to establish justice, to insure domestic tranquility, to provide for common defense, and to secure the blessings of liberty, those people, among whom were the people of Georgia, ordained and established the present constitution. By that constitution, legislative power is vested, executive power is vested, judicial power is vested.

The question now opens fairly to our view, could the people of those states, among whom were those of Georgia, bind those states, and Georgia, among the others, by the legislative, executive, and judicial power so vested? If the principles on which I have founded myself are just and true, this question must, unavoidably, receive an affirmative answer. If those States were the work of those people, those people, and that I may apply the case closely, the people of Georgia, in particular, could alter, as they pleased, their former work; to any given degree, they could diminish as well as enlarge it. Any or all of the former State powers they could extinguish or transfer. The inference which necessarily results is, that the constitution ordained and established by those people; and still closely to apply the case, in particular, by the people of Georgia, could vest jurisdiction or judicial power over those states, and over the state of Georgia in particular.

The next question . . . is—Has the constitution done so? Did those people mean to exercise this, their undoubted power? These questions may be resolved,

either by fair and conclusive deductions, or by direct and explicit declarations. In order, ultimately, to discover, whether the people of the United States intended to bind those states by the judicial power vested by the national constitution, a previous inquiry will naturally be: Did those people intend to bind those states by the legislative power vested by that constitution? The Articles of Confederation, it is well known, did not operate upon individual citizens, but operated only upon states. This defect was remedied by the national constitution, which as all allow, has an operation on individual citizens. But if an opinion, which some seem to entertain, be just; the defect remedied, on one side, was balanced by a defect introduced on the other: for they seem to think, that the present constitution operates only on individual citizens, and not on states. This opinion, however, appears to be altogether unfounded. When certain laws of the states are declared to be "subject to the revision and control of the congress"; it cannot, surely be contended, that the legislature power of the national government was meant to have no operation on the several states. The fact, incontrovertibly established in one instance, proves the principle in all other instances, to which the facts will be found to apply. We may then infer, that the people of the United States intended to bind the several states, by the legislative power of the national government. . . .

Whoever considers, in a combined and comprehensive view, the general texture of the constitution, will be satisfied that the people of the United States intended to form themselves into a nation for national purposes. They instituted, for such purposes, a national government complete in all its parts, with powers legislative, executive and judiciary; and in all those powers extending over the whole nation. Is it congruous that, with regard to such purposes, any man or body of men, any person, natural or artificial, should be permitted to claim successfully an entire exemption from the jurisdiction of the national government? Would not such claims, crowned with success, be repugnant to our very existence as a nation? When so many trains of deduction, coming from different quarters, converge and unite at last in the same point, we may safely conclude, as the legitimate result of this constitution, that the State of Georgia is amenable to the jurisdiction of this court. . . .

Iredell, Justice [dissenting]:

Every state in the union in every instance where its sovereignty has not been delegated to the United States, I consider to be as completely sovereign, as the United States are in respect to the powers surrendered. The United States are sovereign as to all the powers of government actually surrendered. Each state in the union is sovereign as to all the powers reserved. It must necessarily be so, because the United States have no claim to any authority but such as the states have surrendered to them. Of course the part not surrendered must remain as it did before. The powers of the general government, either of a legislative or executive nature, or which particularly concerns treaties with foreign powers, do for the most part (if not wholly) affect individuals, and not states. They require no aid from any state authority. This is the great leading distinction between the old articles of confederation, and the present constitution. The judicial power is of a peculiar kind. It is indeed commensurate with the ordinary legislative and executive powers of the general government, and the power which concerns treaties. But it also goes further. . . .

So far as states under the constitution can be made legally liable to [the federal courts] . . . , so far to be sure they are subordinate to the authority of the United States, and their individual sovereignty is in this respect limited. But it is limited no farther than the necessary execution of such authority requires. The authority extends only to the decision of controversies in which a state is a party, and providing laws necessary for that purpose. That surely can refer only to such controversies in which a state can be a party; it can be determined, according to the principles [of law] I have supported, in no other manner than by a reference either to preexistent laws, or laws passed under the constitution and in conformity to it.

Whatever be the true construction of the constitution in this particular; whether it is to be construed as intending merely a transfer of jurisdiction from one tribunal to another, or as authorizing the legislature to provide laws for the decision of all possible controversies in which a state may be involved with an individual, without regard to any prior exception; yet it is certain that the legislature [in passing the Judiciary Act of 1789] has in fact proceeded upon the former supposition and not upon the latter. . . . [I]n instances like this before the court, this court hath a concurrent jurisdiction only; the present being one of those cases where by the judicial act this court hath original but not exclusive jurisdiction. This court, therefore, under that act, can exercise no authority in such instances but such authority as from the subject matter of it may be exercised in some other court.—There are no courts with which a concurrence can be suggested but the circuit courts, or courts of the different states. With the former it cannot be, for admitting that the Constitution is not to have a restrictive operation, so as to confine all cases in which a state is a party exclusively to the supreme court (an opinion to which I am strongly inclined), yet there are no words in the definition of the powers of the circuit court which give a color to an opinion, that where a suit is brought against a state by a citizen of another state, the circuit court could exercise any jurisdiction at all. If they could, however, such a jurisdiction, by the very terms of their authority, could only be concurrent with the courts of the several States. It follows, therefore, unquestionably, I think, that looking at the act of Congress, which I consider is on this occasion the limit of our authority . . . , we can exercise no authority in the present instance consistently with the clear intention of the act, but such a proper state court would have been at least competent to exercise at the same time the act was passed. . . .

Case

NATIONAL LEAGUE OF CITIES V. USERY

426 U.S. 833; 96 S.Ct. 2465; 49 L.Ed. 2d 245 (1976)
Vote: 5–4

Here the Court considers whether Congress may, consistent with the Tenth Amendment, extend the federal minimum wage to employees of state and local governments.

Mr. Justice Rehnquist delivered the opinion of the Court.

Nearly 40 years ago Congress enacted the Fair Labor Standards Act, and required employers covered by the Act to pay their employees a minimum hourly wage and to pay them at one and one-half times their regular rate of pay for hours worked in excess of 40 during a work week. . . . This Court unanimously upheld the Act as a valid exercise of congressional authority under the commerce power in *United States v. Darby*. . . .

The original Fair Labor Standards Act passed in 1938 specifically excluded the States and their political subdivisions from its coverage. In 1974, however, Congress enacted the most recent of a series of broadening amendments to the Act. By these amendments Congress has extended the minimum wage and maximum hour provisions to almost all public employees employed by the States and by their various political subdivisions. Appellants in these cases include individual cities and States, the National League of Cities, and the National Governors' Conference; they brought an action . . . which challenged the validity of the 1974 amendments. They asserted in effect when Congress sought to apply the Fair Labor Standards Act provisions virtually across the board to employees of state and municipal governments it "infringed a constitutional prohibition" running in favor of the States as States. The gist of their complaint was not that the conditions of employment of such public employees were beyond the scope of the commerce power had those employees been employed in the private sector, but that the established constitutional doctrine of intergovernmental immunity consistently recognized in a long series of our cases affirmatively prevented the exercise of this authority in the manner which Congress chose in the 1974 amendments. . . .

[The League] in no way challenge[s] . . . the breadth of authority granted Congress under the commerce power. Their contention, on the contrary, is that when Congress seeks to regulate directly the activities of States as public employers, it transgresses an affirmative limitation on the exercise of its power akin to other commerce power affirmative limitations contained in the Constitution. Congressional enactments which may be fully within the grant of legislative authority contained in the Commerce Clause may nonetheless be invalid because [they are] found to offend against the right to trial by jury contained in the Sixth Amendment . . . or the Due Process Clause of the Fifth Amendment. . . . [The League's] essential contention is that the 1974 amendments to the Act, while undoubtedly within the scope of the Commerce Clause, encounter a similar constitutional barrier because they are to be applied directly to the States and subdivisions of States as employers.

This Court has never doubted that there are limits upon the power of Congress to override state sovereignty, even when exercising its otherwise plenary powers to tax or to regulate commerce which are conferred by Art. I of the Constitution. . . . [T]he Court [has] recognized that an express declaration of this limitation is found in the Tenth Amendment. . . .

. . . It is one thing to recognize the authority of Congress to enact laws regulating individual businesses necessarily subject to the dual sovereignty of the government of the Nation and of the State in which they reside. It is quite another to uphold a similar exercise of congressional authority directed, not to private citizens, but to the States as States. We have repeatedly recognized that there are attributes of sovereignty attaching to every state government which may not be impaired by Congress, not

because Congress may lack an affirmative grant of legislative authority to reach the matter, but because the Constitution prohibits it from exercising the authority in that manner. . . .

One undoubted attribute of state sovereignty is the States' power to determine the wages which shall be paid to those whom they employ in order to carry out their governmental functions, what hours those persons will work, and what compensation will be provided where these employees may be called upon to work overtime. The question we must resolve here, then, is whether these determinations are "functions essential to separate and independent existence," . . . so that Congress may not abrogate the States' otherwise plenary authority to make them. . . .

Quite apart from the substantial costs imposed upon the States and their political subdivisions, the Act displaces state policies regarding the manner in which they will structure delivery of those governmental services which their citizens require. The Act, speaking directly to the States qua States, requires that they shall pay all but an extremely limited minority of their employees the minimum wage rates currently chosen by Congress. It may well be that as a matter of economic policy it would be desirable that States, just as private employers, comply with these minimum wage requirements. But it cannot be gainsaid that the federal requirement directly supplants the considered policy choices of the States' elected officials and administrators as to how they wish to structure pay scales in state employment. The State might wish to employ persons with little or no training, or those who wish to work on a casual basis, or those who for some other reason do not possess minimum employment requirements, and pay them less than the federally prescribed minimum wage. It may wish to offer part-time or summer employment to teenagers at a figure less than the minimum wage, and if unable to do so may decline to offer such employment at all. But the Act would forbid such choices by the States. The only "discretion" left to them under the Act is either to attempt to increase their revenue to meet the additional financial burden imposed upon them by paying congressionally prescribed wages to their existing complement of employees, or to reduce that complement to a number which can be paid the federal minimum wage without increasing revenue.

This dilemma presented by the minimum wage restrictions may seem not immediately different from that faced by private employers, who have long been covered by the Act and who must find ways to increase their gross income if they are to pay higher wages while maintaining current earnings. The difference, however, is that a State is not merely a factor in the "shifting economic arrangements" of the private sector of the economy, . . . but is itself a coordinate element in the system established by the Framers for governing our Federal Union.

This congressionally imposed displacement of state decisions may substantially restructure traditional ways in which the local governments have arranged their affairs. Although at this point many of the actual effects under the proposed amendments remain a matter of some dispute among the parties, enough can be satisfactorily anticipated for an outline discussion of their general import. The requirement imposing premium rates upon any employment in excess of what Congress has decided is appropriate for a governmental employee's workweek, for example, appears likely to have the effect of coercing the States to structure work periods in some employment areas, such as police and fire protection, in a manner substantially different from practices which have long been commonly accepted among local governments of this Nation. . . .

Our examination of the effect of the 1974 amendments, as sought to be extended to the States and their political subdivisions, satisfies us that both the minimum wage and the maximum hour provisions will impermissibly interfere with the integral governmental functions of these bodies. . . . If Congress may withdraw from the States the authority to make those fundamental employment decisions upon which their systems for performance of these functions must rest, we think there would be little left of the States' "separate and independent existence." . . . Thus, even if appellants may have overestimated the effect which the Act will have upon their current levels and patterns of governmental activity, the dispositive factor is that Congress has attempted to exercise its Commerce Clause authority to prescribe minimum wages and maximum hours to be paid by the States in their capacities as sovereign governments. In so doing, Congress has sought to wield its power in a fashion that would impair the States' "ability to function effectively in a federal system." . . . This exercise of congressional authority does not comport with the federal system of government embodied in the Constitution. We hold that insofar as the challenged amendments operate to directly displace the States' freedom to structure integral operations in areas of traditional governmental functions, they are not within the authority granted Congress by Art. I, Sec. 8, cl. 3. . . .

Mr. Justice Blackmun, concurring. . . .

Mr. Justice Brennan, with whom *Mr. Justice White* and *Mr. Justice Marshall* join, dissenting.

. . . My Brethren do not successfully obscure today's patent usurpation of the role reserved for the political process by their purported discovery in the Constitution of a restraint derived from sovereignty of the States on Congress' exercise of the commerce power. . . . [T]here is no restraint based on state sovereignty requiring or permitting judicial enforcement anywhere expressed in the Constitution; our decisions over the last century and a half have explicitly rejected the existence of any such restraint on the commerce power. . . .

We are left with a catastrophic judicial body blow at Congress' power under the Commerce Clause. Even if Congress may nevertheless accomplish its objectives—for example, by conditioning grants of federal funds upon compliance with federal minimum wage and overtime standards . . . —there is an ominous portent of disruption of our constitutional structure implicit in today's mischievous decision. I dissent.

Mr. Justice Stevens, dissenting.

The Court holds that the Federal Government may not interfere with a sovereign State's inherent right to pay a substandard wage to the janitor at the state capitol. The principle on which the holding rests is difficult to perceive.

The Federal Government may, I believe, require the State to act impartially when it hires or fires the janitor, to withhold taxes from his paycheck, to observe safety regulations when he is performing his job, to forbid him from burning too much soft coal in the capitol furnace, from dumping untreated refuse in an adjacent waterway, from overloading a state-owned garbage truck, or from driving either the truck or the governor's limousine over 55 miles an hour. Even though these and many other activities of the capitol janitor are activities of the State qua State, I have no doubt that they are subject to federal regulation. . . .

My disagreement with the wisdom of this legislation may not, of course, affect my judgment with respect to its validity. On this issue there is no dissent from the proposition that the Federal Government's power over the labor market is adequate to embrace these employees. Since I am unable to identify a limitation on that federal power that would not also invalidate federal regulation of state activities that I consider unquestionably permissible, I am persuaded that this statute is valid. Accordingly, with respect and a great deal of sympathy for the views expressed by the Court, I dissent from its constitutional holding.

Case

GARCIA V. SAN ANTONIO METROPOLITAN TRANSIT AUTHORITY

469 U.S. 528; 105 S.Ct. 1005; 83 L.Ed. 2d 1016 (1985)
Vote: 5–4

In National League of Cities v. Usery the Court held that Congress may not enforce the minimum wage and overtime provisions of the Fair Labor Standards Act (FLSA) against the states "in areas of traditional governmental functions." Here the Court reconsiders this decision.

Justice Blackmun delivered the opinion of the Court.

. . . Although *National League of Cities* supplied some examples of "traditional governmental functions," it did not offer a general explanation of how a "traditional" function is to be distinguished from a "nontraditional" one. Since then, federal and state courts have struggled with the task, thus imposed, of identifying a traditional function for purposes of state immunity under the Commerce Clause.

In the present cases, a Federal District Court concluded that municipal ownership and operation of a mass-transit system is a traditional governmental function and thus, under *National League of Cities,* is exempt from the obligations imposed by the FLSA. Faced with the identical question, three Federal Courts of Appeals and one state appellate court have reached the opposite conclusion.

Our examination of this "function" standard applied in these and other cases over the last eight years now persuades us that the attempt to draw the boundaries of state regulatory immunity in terms of "traditional governmental function" is not only unworkable but is inconsistent with established principles of federalism and, indeed, with those very federalism principles on which *National League of Cities* purported to rest. That case, accordingly, is overruled.

The history of public transportation in San Antonio, Tex., is characteristic of the history of local mass transit in the United States generally. Passenger transportation for hire within San Antonio originally was provided on a private basis by a local transportation company. In 1913, the Texas Legislature authorized the State's municipalities to regulate vehicles providing carriage for hire. . . . Two years later, San Antonio enacted an ordinance setting forth franchising, insurance, and safety requirements for passenger vehicles operated for hire. The city continued to rely on

such publicly regulated private mass transit until 1959, when it purchased the privately owned San Antonio Transit Company and replaced it with a public authority known as the San Antonio Transit System (SATS). SATS operated until 1978, when the city transferred its facilities and equipment to appellee San Antonio Metropolitan Transit Authority (SAMTA), a public mass-transit authority organized on a countywide basis. . . . SAMTA currently is the major provider of transportation in the San Antonio metropolitan area; between 1978 and 1980 alone, its vehicles traveled over 26 million route miles and carried over 63 million passengers.

As did other localities, San Antonio reached the point where it came to look to the Federal Government for financial assistance in maintaining its public mass transit. SATS managed to meet its operating expenses and bond obligations for the first decade of its existence without federal or local financial aid. By 1970, however, its financial position had deteriorated to the point where federal subsidies were vital for its continued operation. SATS' general manager that year testified before Congress that "if we do not receive substantial help from the Federal Government, San Antonio may . . . join the growing ranks of cities that have inferior [public] transportation or may end up with no [public] transportation at all." . . .

The principal federal program to which SATS and other mass-transit systems looked for relief was the Urban Mass Transportation Act of 1964 (UMTA), . . . which provides substantial federal assistance to urban mass-transit programs. . . . UMTA now authorizes the Department of Transportation to fund 75 percent of the capital outlays and up to 50 percent of the operating expenses of qualifying mass-transit programs. . . . SATS received its first UMTA subsidy, a $4.1 million capital grant, in December 1970. From then until February 1980, SATS and SAMTA received over $51 million in UMTA grants—more than $31 million in capital grants, over $20 million in operating assistance, and a minor amount in technical assistance. During SAMTA's first two fiscal years, it received $12.5 million in UMTA operating grants, $26.8 million from sales taxes, and only $10.1 million from fares. Federal subsidies and local sales taxes currently account for about 75 percent of SAMTA's operating expenses.

The present controversy concerns the extent to which SAMTA may be subjected to the minimum-wage and overtime requirements of the FLSA. When the FLSA was enacted in 1938, its wage and overtime provisions did not apply to local mass-transit employees or, indeed, to employees of state and local governments. . . . In 1961, Congress extended minimum-wage coverage to employees of any private mass-transit carrier whose annual gross revenue was not less than $1 million. . . . Five years later, Congress extended FLSA coverage to state and local-government employees for the first time by withdrawing the minimum-wage and overtime exemptions from public hospitals, schools, and mass-transit carriers whose rates and services were subject to state regulation. . . . At the same time, Congress eliminated the overtime exemption for all mass-transit employees other than drivers, operators, and conductors. . . . The application of the FLSA to public schools and hospitals was ruled to be within Congress' power under the Commerce Clause. . . .

The FLSA obligations of public mass-transit systems like SATS were expanded in 1974 when Congress provided for the progressive repeal of the surviving overtime exemption for mass-transit employees. . . . Congress simultaneously brought the States and their subdivisions further within the ambit of the FLSA by extending FLSA coverage to virtually all state and local-government employees. . . .

Appellees have not argued that SAMTA is immune from regulation under the FLSA on the ground that it is a local transit system engaged in intrastate commercial activity. In a practical sense, SAMTA's operations might well be characterized as "local." Nonetheless, it long has been settled that Congress' authority under the Commerce Clause extends to intrastate economic activities that affect interstate commerce. . . . Were SAMTA a privately owned and operated enterprise, it could not credibly argue that Congress exceeded the bounds of its Commerce Clause powers in prescribing minimum wages and overtime rates for SAMTA's employees. Any constitutional exemption from the requirements of the FLSA therefore must rest on SAMTA's status as a governmental entity rather than on the "local" nature of its operations.

The prerequisites for governmental immunity under *National League of Cities* were summarized by this Court in *Hodel* [v. *Virginia Surface Mining and Reclamation Association*]. . . . Under that summary, four conditions must be satisfied before a state activity may be deemed immune from a particular federal regulation under the Commerce Clause. First, it is said that the federal statute at issue must regulate "the 'States as States.'" Second, the statute must "address matters that are indisputably 'attribute[s] of state sovereignty.'" Third, state compliance with the federal obligation must "directly impair [the States'] ability 'to structure integral operations in areas of traditional governmental functions.'" Finally, the relation of state and

federal interests must not be such that "the nature of the federal interest . . . justifies state submission." . . .

The controversy in the present cases has focused on the third *Hodel* requirement—that the challenged federal statute trenches on "traditional governmental functions." The District Court voiced a common concern: "Despite the abundance of adjectives, identifying which particular state functions are immune remains difficult." . . . Just how troublesome the task has been is revealed by the results reached in other federal cases. . . .

Thus far, this Court itself has made little headway in defining the scope of the governmental functions deemed protected under *National League of Cities*. In that case the Court set forth examples of protected and unprotected functions, . . . but provided no explanation of how those examples were identified. . . .

The central theme of *National League of Cities* was that the States occupy a special position in our constitutional system and that the scope of Congress' authority under the Commerce Clause must reflect that position. Of course, the Commerce Clause by its specific language does not provide any special limitation on Congress' actions with respect to the States. . . . It is equally true, however, that the text of the Constitution provides the beginning rather than the final answer to every inquiry into questions of federalism, for "[b]ehind the words of the constitutional provisions are postulates which limit and control." . . . *National League of Cities* reflected the general conviction that the Constitution precludes "the National Government [from] devour[ing] the essentials of state sovereignty." . . . In order to be faithful to the underlying federal premises of the Constitution, courts must look for the "postulates which limit and control."

What has proved problematic is not the perception that the Constitution's federal structure imposes limitations on the Commerce Clause, but rather the nature and content of those limitations. One approach to defining the limits on Congress' authority to regulate the States under the Commerce Clause is to identify certain underlying elements of political sovereignty that are deemed essential to the States' "separate and independent existence." . . . This approach obviously underlay the Court's use of the "traditional governmental function" concept in *National League of Cities*. It also has led to the separate requirement that the challenged federal statute "address matters that are indisputably 'attribute[s] of state sovereignty.'" . . . In *National League of Cities* itself, for example, the Court concluded that decisions by a State concerning the wages and hours of its employees are an "undoubted attribute of state sovereignty." . . . The opinion did not explain what aspects of such decisions made them such an "undoubted attribute," and the Court since then has remarked on the uncertain scope of the concept. . . . The point of the inquiry, however, has remained to single out particular features of a State's internal governance that are deemed to be intrinsic parts of state sovereignty.

We doubt that courts ultimately can identify principled constitutional limitations on the scope of Congress' Commerce Clause powers over the States merely by relying on *a priori* definitions of state sovereignty. In part, this is because of the elusiveness of objective criteria for "fundamental" elements of state sovereignty, a problem we have witnessed in the search for "traditional governmental functions." There is, however, a more fundamental reason: the sovereignty of the States is limited by the Constitution itself. A variety of sovereign powers, for example, are withdrawn from the States by Article I, Sec. 10. Section 8 of the same Article works an equally sharp contraction of state sovereignty by authorizing Congress to exercise a wide range of legislative powers and (in conjunction with the Supremacy Clause of Article VI) to displace contrary state legislation. . . . By providing for final review of questions of federal law in this Court, Article III curtails the sovereign power of the States' judiciaries to make authoritative determinations of law. . . . Finally, the developed application, through the Fourteenth Amendment, of the greater part of the Bill of Rights to the States limits the sovereign authority that States otherwise would possess to legislate with respect to their citizens and to conduct their own affairs.

The States unquestionably do "retai[n] a significant measure of sovereign authority." . . . They do so, however, only to the extent that the Constitution has not divested them of their original powers and transferred those powers to the Federal Government. . . .

. . . [T]o say that the Constitution assumes the continued role of the States is to say little about the nature of that role. Only recently, this Court recognized that the purpose of the constitutional immunity recognized in *National League of Cities* is not to preserve "a sacred province of state autonomy." . . . With rare exceptions, like the guarantee, in Article IV, 3, of state territorial integrity, the Constitution does not carve out express elements of state sovereignty that Congress may not employ its delegated powers to displace. . . . The power of the Federal Government is a "power to be respected" as well, and the fact that the States remain sovereign as to all powers not vested in Congress or denied them by the Constitution offers no guidance about where the frontier between state and federal power lies. In short, we have no license to employ freestanding conceptions of state sovereignty when measuring congressional authority under the Commerce Clause.

When we look for the States' "residuary and inviolable sovereignty" . . . in the shape of the constitutional scheme rather than in predetermined notions of sovereign power, a different measure of state sovereignty emerges. Apart from the limitation on federal authority inherent in the delegated nature of Congress' Article I powers, the principal means chosen by the Framers to ensure the role of the States in the federal system lies in the structure of the Federal Government itself. It is no novelty to observe that the composition of the Federal Government was designed in large part to protect the States from overreaching by Congress. The Framers thus gave the States a role in the selection both of the Executive and the Legislative Branches of the Federal Government. The States were vested with indirect influence over the House of Representatives and the Presidency by their control of electoral qualifications and their role in presidential elections. . . . They were given more direct influence in the Senate, where each State received equal representation and each Senator was to be selected by the legislature of his State. . . . The significance attached to the States' equal representation in the Senate is underscored by the prohibition of any constitutional amendment divesting a State of equal representation without the State's consent. . . .

The extent to which the structure of the Federal Government itself was relied on to insulate the interests of the States is evident in the views of the Framers. James Madison explained that the Federal Government "will partake sufficiently of the spirit [of the States], to be disinclined to invade the rights of the individual States, or the prerogatives of their governments. . . ." . . . In short, the Framers chose to rely on a federal system in which special restraints on federal power over the States inhered principally in the workings of the National Government itself, rather than in discrete limitations on the objects of federal authority. State sovereign interests, then, are more properly protected by procedural safeguards inherent in the structure of the federal system than by judicially created limitations on federal power. . . .

This analysis makes clear that Congress' action in affording SAMTA employees the protections of the wage and hour provisions of the FLSA contravened no affirmative limit on Congress' power under the Commerce Clause. The judgment of the District Court therefore must be reversed.

Of course, we continue to recognize that the States occupy a special and specific position in our constitutional system and that the scope of Congress' authority under the Commerce Clause must reflect that position. But the principal and basic limit on the federal commerce power is that inherent in all congressional action—the built-in restraints that our system provides through state participation in federal governmental action. The political process ensures that laws that unduly burden the States will not be promulgated. In the factual setting of these cases the internal safeguards of the political process have performed as intended.

These cases do not require us to identify or define what affirmative limits the constitutional structure might impose on federal action affecting the States under the Commerce Clause. . . .

Though the separate concurrence providing the fifth vote in *National League of Cities* was "not untroubled by certain possible implications" of the decision, . . . the Court in that case attempted to articulate affirmative limits on the Commerce Clause power in terms of core governmental functions and fundamental attributes of state sovereignty. But the model of democratic decisionmaking the Court there identified underestimated, in our view, the solicitude of the national political process for the continued vitality of the States. Attempts by other courts since then to draw guidance from this model have proved it both impracticable and doctrinally barren. In sum, in *National League of Cities* the Court tried to repair what did not need repair.

We do not lightly overrule recent precedent. We have not hesitated, however, when it has become apparent that a prior decision has departed from a proper understanding of congressional power under the Commerce Clause. . . . Due respect for the reach of congressional power within the federal system mandates that we do so now.

National League of Cities v. Usery . . . is overruled. The judgment of the District Court is reversed, and these cases are remanded to that court for further proceedings consistent with this opinion.

Justice Powell, with whom the **Chief Justice, Justice Rehnquist**, and **Justice O'Connor** join, dissenting. . . .

Justice Rehnquist, dissenting. . . .

Justice O'Connor, with whom **Justice Powell** and **Justice Rehnquist** join, dissenting.

. . . The last two decades have seen an unprecedented growth of federal regulatory activity, as the majority itself acknowledges. . . . In 1954, one could speak of a "burden of persuasion on those favoring national intervention" in asserting that "National action has . . . always been regarded as exceptional in our polity, an intrusion to be justified by some necessity, the special rather than the ordinary case." . . . Today, as federal legislation and coercive grant programs have expanded to embrace innumerable activities that were once viewed as local, the burden of persuasion has surely shifted, and the extraordinary

has become ordinary. . . . For example, recently the Federal Government has, with this Court's blessing, undertaken to tell the States the age at which they can retire their law enforcement officers, and the regulatory standards, procedures, and even the agenda which their utilities commissions must consider and follow. . . . The political process has not protected against these encroachments on state activities, even though they directly impinge on a State's ability to make and enforce its laws. With the abandonment of *National League of Cities,* all that stands between the remaining essentials of state sovereignty and Congress is the latter's underdeveloped capacity for self-restraint.

The problems of federalism in an integrated national economy are capable of more responsible resolution than holding that the States as States retain no status apart from that which Congress chooses to let them retain. The proper resolution, I suggest, lies in weighing state autonomy as a factor in the balance when interpreting the means by which Congress can exercise its authority on the States as States. It is insufficient, in assessing the validity of congressional regulation of a State pursuant to the commerce power, to ask only whether the same regulation would be valid if enforced against a private party. That reasoning, embodied in the majority opinion, is inconsistent with the spirit of our Constitution. It remains relevant that a State is being regulated, as *National League of Cities* and every recent case have recognized. . . . As far as the Constitution is concerned, a State should not be equated with any private litigant. . . . Instead, the autonomy of a State is an essential component of federalism. If state autonomy is ignored in assessing the means by which Congress regulates matters affecting commerce, then federalism becomes irrelevant simply because the set of activities remaining beyond the reach of such a commerce power "may well be negligible." . . .

It has been difficult for this Court to craft bright lines defining the scope of the state autonomy protected by *National League of Cities.* Such difficulty is to be expected whenever constitutional concerns as important as federalism and the effectiveness of the commerce power come into conflict. Regardless of the difficulty, it is and will remain the duty of this Court to reconcile these concerns in the final instance. That the Court shuns the task today by appealing to the "essence of federalism" can provide scant comfort to those who believe our federal system requires something more than a unitary, centralized government. I would not shirk the duty acknowledged by *National League of Cities* and its progeny, and I share Justice Rehnquist's belief that this Court will in time again assume its constitutional responsibility. . . .

Case

PRINTZ V. UNITED STATES

521 U.S. 898; 117 S.Ct. 2365; 138 L.Ed. 2d 914 (1997)
Vote: 5–4

Here the Court considers the validity of provisions of the Brady Handgun Violence Prevention Act requiring state and local law enforcement officers to conduct background checks on prospective handgun purchasers.

Justice Scalia delivered the opinion of the Court.

. . . In 1993, Congress amended the [Gun Control Act of 1968] by enacting the Brady Act. The Act requires the Attorney General to establish a national instant background check system by November 30, 1998 . . . and immediately puts in place certain interim provisions until that system becomes operative. Under the interim provisions, a firearms dealer who proposes to transfer a handgun must first: (1) receive from the transferee a statement (the Brady Form), . . . containing the name, address and date of birth of the proposed transferee along with a sworn statement that the transferee is not among any of the classes of prohibited purchasers, . . . (2) verify the identity of the transferee by examining an identification document, . . . and (3) provide the "chief law enforcement officer" (CLEO) of the transferee's residence with notice of the contents (and a copy) of the Brady Form. . . . With some exceptions, the dealer must then wait five business days before consummating the sale, unless the CLEO earlier notifies the dealer that he has no reason to believe the transfer would be illegal. . . .

The Brady Act creates two significant alternatives to the foregoing scheme. A dealer may sell a handgun immediately if the purchaser possesses a state handgun permit issued after a background check, . . . or if state law provides for an instant background check. . . . In States that have not rendered one of these alternatives applicable to all gun purchasers, CLEOs are required to perform certain duties. When a CLEO receives the required notice of a proposed transfer from the firearms dealer, the CLEO must "make a reasonable effort to ascertain within 5 business days whether receipt or possession would be in violation of the law, including research in whatever State and local record keeping systems are available and in a national system designated by the Attorney General." . . . The Act does not require the CLEO to take any particular action if he determines that a pending transaction would be unlawful; he may notify the firearms dealer to that effect, but is not

required to do so. If, however, the CLEO notifies a gun dealer that a prospective purchaser is ineligible to receive a handgun, he must, upon request, provide the would be purchaser with a written statement of the reasons for that determination. . . . Moreover, if the CLEO does not discover any basis for objecting to the sale, he must destroy any records in his possession relating to the transfer, including his copy of the Brady Form. . . . Under a separate provision of the GCA, any person who "knowingly violates [the section of the GCA amended by the Brady Act] shall be fined under this title, imprisoned for no more than 1 year, or both." . . .

Petitioners Jay Printz and Richard Mack, the CLEOs for Ravalli County, Montana, and Graham County, Arizona, respectively, filed separate actions challenging the constitutionality of the Brady Act's interim provisions. In each case, the District Court held that the provision requiring CLEOs to perform background checks was unconstitutional, but concluded that that provision was severable from the remainder of the Act, effectively leaving a voluntary background check system in place. . . . A divided panel of the Court of Appeals for the Ninth Circuit reversed, finding none of the Brady Act's interim provisions to be unconstitutional. . . . We granted certiorari. . . .

From the description set forth above, it is apparent that the Brady Act purports to direct state law enforcement officers to participate, albeit only temporarily, in the administration of a federally enacted regulatory scheme. Regulated firearms dealers are required to forward Brady Forms not to a federal officer or employee, but to the CLEOs, whose obligation to accept those forms is implicit in the duty imposed upon them to make "reasonable efforts" within five days to determine whether the sales reflected in the forms are lawful. While the CLEOs are subjected to no federal requirement that they prevent the sales determined to be unlawful (it is perhaps assumed that their state law duties will require prevention or apprehension), they are empowered to grant, in effect, waivers of the federally prescribed 5 day waiting period for handgun purchases by notifying the gun dealers that they have no reason to believe the transactions would be illegal.

The petitioners here object to being pressed into federal service, and contend that congressional action compelling state officers to execute federal laws is unconstitutional. Because there is no constitutional text speaking to this precise question, the answer to the CLEOs' challenge must be sought in historical understanding and practice, in the structure of the Constitution, and in the jurisprudence of this Court. We treat those three sources, in that order, in this and the next two sections of this opinion.

Petitioners contend that compelled enlistment of state executive officers for the administration of federal programs is, until very recent years at least, unprecedented. The Government contends, to the contrary, that the earliest Congresses enacted statutes that required the participation of state officials in the implementation of federal laws. . . .

The Government observes that statutes enacted by the first Congresses required state courts to record applications for citizenship, . . . to transmit abstracts of citizenship applications and other naturalization records to the Secretary of State, . . . and to register aliens seeking naturalization and issue certificates of registry. . . . It may well be, however, that these requirements applied only in States that authorized their courts to conduct naturalization proceedings. . . .

These early laws establish, at most, that the Constitution was originally understood to permit imposition of an obligation on state judges to enforce federal prescriptions, insofar as those prescriptions related to matters appropriate for the judicial power. That assumption was perhaps implicit in one of the provisions of the Constitution, and was explicit in another. In accord with the so called Madisonian Compromise, Article III, § 1, established only a Supreme Court, and made the creation of lower federal courts optional with the Congress—even though it was obvious that the Supreme Court alone could not hear all federal cases throughout the United States. . . . And the Supremacy Clause, Art. VI, cl. 2, announced that "the Laws of the United States . . . shall be the supreme Law of the Land; and the Judges in every State shall be bound thereby." It is understandable why courts should have been viewed distinctively in this regard; unlike legislatures and executives, they applied the law of other sovereigns all the time. The principle underlying so called "transitory" causes of action was that laws which operated elsewhere created obligations in justice that courts of the forum state would enforce. . . . The Constitution itself, in the Full Faith and Credit Clause, Art. IV, § 1, generally required such enforcement with respect to obligations arising in other States. . . .

For these reasons, we do not think the early statutes imposing obligations on state courts imply a power of Congress to impress the state executive into its service. Indeed, it can be argued that the numerousness of these statutes, contrasted with the utter lack of statutes imposing obligations on the States' executive (notwithstanding the attractiveness of that course to Congress), suggests an assumed absence of such power. The only early federal law the Government has brought to our attention that imposed duties on state executive officers is the Extradition Act of 1793, which required the "executive authority" of a State to cause the arrest and delivery of a fugitive from justice upon the request of the executive authority of the State from which the fugitive had fled. . . . That was in direct implementation, however, of the Extradition Clause of the Constitution itself. . . .

Not only do the enactments of the early Congresses, as far as we are aware, contain no evidence of an assumption that the Federal Government may command the States' executive power in the absence of a particularized constitutional authorization, they contain some indication of precisely the opposite assumption. On September 23, 1789—the day before its proposal of the Bill of Rights, . . . the First Congress enacted a law aimed at obtaining state assistance of the most rudimentary and necessary sort for the enforcement of the new Government's laws: the holding of federal prisoners in state jails at federal expense. Significantly, the law issued not a command to the States' executive, but a recommendation to their legislatures. Congress "recommended to the legislatures of the several States to pass laws, making it expressly the duty of the keepers of their gaols, to receive and safe keep therein all prisoners committed under the authority of the United States," and offered to pay 50 cents per month for each prisoner. . . . Moreover, when Georgia refused to comply with the request, . . . Congress's only reaction was a law authorizing the marshal in any State that failed to comply with the Recommendation of September 23, 1789, to rent a temporary jail until provision for a permanent one could be made. . . .

In addition to early legislation, the Government also appeals to other sources we have usually regarded as indicative of the original understanding of the Constitution. It points to portions of *The Federalist* which reply to criticisms that Congress's power to tax will produce two sets of revenue officers—for example, "Brutus's" assertion in his letter to the *New York Journal* of December 13, 1787, that the Constitution "opens a door to the appointment of a swarm of revenue and excise officers to prey upon the honest and industrious part of the community, eat up their substance, and riot on the spoils of the country." . . . "Publius" responded that Congress will probably "make use of the State officers and State regulations, for collecting" federal taxes. . . . The Government also invokes the *Federalist*'s more general observations that the Constitution would "enable the [national] government to employ the ordinary magistracy of each [State] in the execution of its laws," . . . and that it was "extremely probable that in other instances, particularly in the organization of the judicial power, the officers of the States will be clothed in the correspondent authority of the Union," . . . But none of these statements necessarily implies—what is the critical point here—that Congress could impose these responsibilities without the consent of the States. They appear to rest on the natural assumption that the States would consent to allowing their officials to assist the Federal Government, . . . an assumption proved correct by the extensive mutual assistance the States and Federal Government voluntarily provided one another in the early days of the Republic, . . . including voluntary federal implementation of state law. . . .

To complete the historical record, we must note that there is not only an absence of executive commandeering statutes in the early Congresses, but there is an absence of them in our later history as well, at least until very recent years. . . .

The Government points to a number of federal statutes enacted within the past few decades that require the participation of state or local officials in implementing federal regulatory schemes. Some of these are connected to federal funding measures, and can perhaps be more accurately described as conditions upon the grant of federal funding than as mandates to the States; others, which require only the provision of information to the Federal Government, do not involve the precise issue before us here, which is the forced participation of the States' executive in the actual administration of a federal program. We of course do not address these or other currently operative enactments that are not before us; it will be time enough to do so if and when their validity is challenged in a proper case. For deciding the issue before us here, they are of little relevance. Even assuming they represent assertion of the very same congressional power challenged here, they are of such recent vintage that they are no more probative than the statute before us of a constitutional tradition that lends meaning to the text. Their persuasive force is far outweighed by almost two centuries of apparent congressional avoidance of the practice. . . .

The constitutional practice we have examined above tends to negate the existence of the congressional power asserted here, but is not conclusive. We turn next to consideration of the structure of the Constitution, to see if we can discern among its "essential postulate[s]," . . . a principle that controls the present cases.

It is incontestible that the Constitution established a system of "dual sovereignty." . . . Although the States surrendered many of their powers to the new Federal Government, they retained "a residuary and inviolable sovereignty." . . . This is reflected throughout the Constitution's text . . . including (to mention only a few examples) the prohibition on any involuntary reduction or combination of a State's territory, Art. IV, § 3; the Judicial Power Clause, Art. III, § 2, and the Privileges and Immunities Clause, Art.

IV, § 2, which speak of the "Citizens" of the States; the amendment provision, Article V, which requires the votes of three fourths of the States to amend the Constitution; and the Guarantee Clause, Art. IV, § 4, which "presupposes the continued existence of the states and . . . those means and instrumentalities which are the creation of their sovereign and reserved rights." . . . Residual state sovereignty was also implicit, of course, in the Constitution's conferral upon Congress of not all governmental powers, but only discrete, enumerated ones, Art. I, § 8, which implication was rendered express by the Tenth Amendment's assertion that "[t]he powers not delegated to the United States by the Constitution, nor prohibited by it to the States, are reserved to the States respectively, or to the people."

The Framers' experience under the Articles of Confederation had persuaded them that using the States as the instruments of federal governance was both ineffectual and provocative of federal state conflict. . . . "The Framers explicitly chose a Constitution that confers upon Congress the power to regulate individuals, not States." . . . The great innovation of this design was that our citizens would have two political capacities, one state and one federal, each protected from incursion by the other—"a legal system unprecedented in form and design, establishing two orders of government, each with its own direct relationship, its own privity, its own set of mutual rights and obligations to the people who sustain it and are governed by it." . . . The Constitution thus contemplates that a State's government will represent and remain accountable to its own citizens. . . .

This separation of the two spheres is one of the Constitution's structural protections of liberty. . . .

. . . The power of the Federal Government would be augmented immeasurably if it were able to impress into its service—and at no cost to itself—the police officers of the 50 States. . . .

Finally, and most conclusively in the present litigation, we turn to the prior jurisprudence of this Court. Federal commandeering of state governments is such a novel phenomenon that this Court's first experience with it did not occur until the 1970's, when the Environmental Protection Agency promulgated regulations requiring States to prescribe auto emissions testing, monitoring and retrofit programs, and to designate preferential bus and carpool lanes. The Courts of Appeals for the Fourth and Ninth Circuits invalidated the regulations on statutory grounds in order to avoid what they perceived to be grave constitutional issues, . . . and the District of Columbia Circuit invalidated the regulations on both constitutional and statutory grounds. . . . After we granted certiorari to review the statutory and constitutional validity of the regulations, the Government declined even to defend them, and instead rescinded some and conceded the invalidity of those that remained, leading us to vacate the opinions below and remand for consideration of mootness. . . .

. . . [L]ater opinions of ours have made clear that the Federal Government may not compel the States to implement, by legislation or executive action, federal regulatory programs. . . .

When we were at last confronted squarely with a federal statute that unambiguously required the States to enact or administer a federal regulatory program, our decision should have come as no surprise. At issue in *New York v. United States,* 505 U.S. 144 (1992), were the so called "take title" provisions of the Low Level Radioactive Waste Policy Amendments Act of 1985, which required States either to enact legislation providing for the disposal of radioactive waste generated within their borders, or to take title to, and possession of the waste—effectively requiring the States either to legislate pursuant to Congress's directions, or to implement an administrative solution. . . . We concluded that Congress could constitutionally require the States to do neither. . . . "The Federal Government," we held, "may not compel the States to enact or administer a federal regulatory program." . . .

Even assuming, moreover, that the Brady Act leaves no "policymaking" discretion with the States, we fail to see how that improves rather than worsens the intrusion upon state sovereignty. Preservation of the States as independent and autonomous political entities is arguably less undermined by requiring them to make policy in certain fields than . . . by "reduc[ing] [them] to puppets of a ventriloquist Congress." . . . It is an essential attribute of the States' retained sovereignty that they remain independent and autonomous within their proper sphere of authority. . . . It is no more compatible with this independence and autonomy that their officers be "dragooned" . . . into administering federal law, than it would be compatible with the independence and autonomy of the United States that its officers be impressed into service for the execution of state laws.

Finally, the Government puts forward a cluster of arguments that can be grouped under the heading: "The Brady Act serves very important purposes, is most efficiently administered by CLEOs during the interim period, and places a minimal and only temporary burden upon state officers." There is considerable disagreement over the extent of the burden, but we need not pause over that detail. Assuming all the mentioned factors were true, they might be relevant if we were evaluating whether the incidental application to the States of a federal law of general applicability excessively interfered with the functioning of state governments. . . . But where, as here, it is the whole object of the law to direct the functioning of the state executive, and hence to compromise the structural framework of dual sovereignty, such a "balancing" analysis is inappropriate. It is the very principle of separate state sovereignty that such a law offends, and no comparative assessment of the various interests can overcome that fundamental defect. . . .

We . . . conclude categorically . . . [that] "[t]he Federal Government may not compel the States to enact or administer a federal regulatory program." . . . The mandatory obligation imposed on CLEOs to perform background checks on prospective handgun purchasers plainly runs afoul of that rule.

What we have said makes it clear enough that the central obligation imposed upon CLEOs by the interim provisions of the Brady Act—the obligation to "make a reasonable effort to ascertain within 5 business days whether receipt or possession [of a handgun] would be in violation of the law, including research in whatever State and local record keeping systems are available and in a national system designated by the Attorney General," . . . is unconstitutional. Extinguished with it, of course, is the duty implicit in the background check requirement that the CLEO accept notice of the contents of, and a copy of, the completed Brady Form, which the firearms dealer is required to provide to him. . . .

. . . Congress cannot compel the States to enact or enforce a federal regulatory program. Today we hold that Congress cannot circumvent that prohibition by conscripting the State's officers directly. The Federal Government may neither issue directives requiring the States to address particular problems, nor command the States' officers, or those of their political subdivisions, to administer or enforce a federal regulatory program. It matters not whether policymaking is involved, and no case by case weighing of the burdens or benefits is necessary; such commands are fundamentally incompatible with our constitutional system of dual sovereignty. Accordingly, the judgment of the Court of Appeals for the Ninth Circuit is reversed.

Justice O'Connor, concurring. . . .

Justice Thomas, concurring. . . .

The Court today properly holds that the Brady Act violates the Tenth Amendment in that it compels state law enforcement officers to "administer or enforce a federal regulatory program." . . . Although I join the Court's opinion in full, I write separately to emphasize that the Tenth Amendment affirms the undeniable notion that under our Constitution, the Federal Government is one of enumerated, hence limited, powers. . . . Accordingly, the Federal Government may act only where the Constitution authorizes it to do so. . . .

Justice Stevens, with whom ***Justice Souter, Justice Ginsburg***, and ***Justice Breyer*** join, dissenting.

When Congress exercises the powers delegated to it by the Constitution, it may impose affirmative obligations on executive and judicial officers of state and local governments as well as ordinary citizens. This conclusion is firmly supported by the text of the Constitution, the early history of the Nation, decisions of this Court, and a correct understanding of the basic structure of the Federal Government.

These cases do not implicate the more difficult questions associated with congressional coercion of state legislatures. . . . Nor need we consider the wisdom of relying on local officials rather than federal agents to carry out aspects of a federal program, or even the question whether such officials may be required to perform a federal function on a permanent basis. The question is whether Congress, acting on behalf of the people of the entire Nation, may require local law enforcement officers to perform certain duties during the interim needed for the development of a federal gun control program. It is remarkably similar to the question, heavily debated by the Framers of the Constitution, whether the Congress could require state agents to collect federal taxes. Or the question whether Congress could impress state judges into federal service to entertain and decide cases that they would prefer to ignore.

Indeed, since the ultimate issue is one of power, we must consider its implications in times of national emergency. Matters such as the enlistment of air raid wardens, the administration of a military draft, the mass inoculation of children to forestall an epidemic, or perhaps the threat of an international terrorist, may require a national response before federal personnel can be made available to respond. If the Constitution empowers Congress and the President to make an appropriate response, is there anything in the Tenth Amendment, "in historical understanding and practice, in the structure of the Constitution, [or] in the jurisprudence of this Court," . . . that forbids the enlistment of state officers to make that response effective? More narrowly, what basis is there in any of those sources for concluding that it is the Members of this Court, rather than the elected representatives of the people, who should determine whether the Constitution contains the unwritten rule that the Court announces today?

Perhaps today's majority would suggest that no such emergency is presented by the facts of these cases. But such a suggestion is itself an expression of a policy judg-

ment. And Congress' view of the matter is quite different from that implied by the Court today.

The Brady Act was passed in response to what Congress described as an "epidemic of gun violence." . . . The Act's legislative history notes that 15,377 Americans were murdered with firearms in 1992, and that 12,489 of these deaths were caused by handguns. . . . Congress expressed special concern that "[t]he level of firearm violence in this country is, by far, the highest among developed nations." . . . The partial solution contained in the Brady Act, a mandatory background check before a handgun may be purchased, has met with remarkable success. Between 1994 and 1996, approximately 6,600 firearm sales each month to potentially dangerous persons were prevented by Brady Act checks; over 70% of the rejected purchasers were convicted or indicted felons. . . . Whether or not the evaluation reflected in the enactment of the Brady Act is correct as to the extent of the danger and the efficacy of the legislation, the congressional decision surely warrants more respect than it is accorded in today's unprecedented decision.

The text of the Constitution provides a sufficient basis for a correct disposition of this case. Article I, § 8, grants the Congress the power to regulate commerce among the States. Putting to one side the revisionist views expressed by Justice Thomas in his concurring opinion in *United States v. Lopez* (1995), there can be no question that that provision adequately supports the regulation of commerce in handguns effected by the Brady Act. Moreover, the additional grant of authority in that section of the Constitution "[t]o make all Laws which shall be necessary and proper for carrying into Execution the foregoing Powers" is surely adequate to support the temporary enlistment of local police officers in the process of identifying persons who should not be entrusted with the possession of handguns. In short, the affirmative delegation of power in Article I provides ample authority for the congressional enactment.

Unlike the First Amendment, which prohibits the enactment of a category of laws that would otherwise be authorized by Article I, the Tenth Amendment imposes no restriction on the exercise of delegated powers. . . .

The Amendment confirms the principle that the powers of the Federal Government are limited to those affirmatively granted by the Constitution, but it does not purport to limit the scope or the effectiveness of the exercise of powers that are delegated to Congress. . . . Thus, the Amendment provides no support for a rule that immunizes local officials from obligations that might be imposed on ordinary citizens. Indeed, it would be more reasonable to infer that federal law may impose greater duties on state officials than on private citizens because another provision of the Constitution requires that "all executive and judicial Officers, both of the United States and of the several States, shall be bound by Oath or Affirmation, to support this Constitution." . . .

It is appropriate for state officials to make an oath or affirmation to support the Federal Constitution because, as explained in *The Federalist,* they "have an essential agency in giving effect to the federal Constitution." . . . There can be no conflict between their duties to the State and those owed to the Federal Government because Article VI unambiguously provides that federal law "shall be the supreme Law of the Land," binding in every State. . . . Thus, not only the Constitution, but every law enacted by Congress as well, establishes policy for the States just as firmly as do laws enacted by state legislatures.

There is not a clause, sentence, or paragraph in the entire text of the Constitution of the United States that supports the proposition that a local police officer can ignore a command contained in a statute enacted by Congress pursuant to an express delegation of power enumerated in Article I.

Indeed, the historical materials strongly suggest that the Founders intended to enhance the capacity of the federal government by empowering it—as a part of the new authority to make demands directly on individual citizens—to act through local officials. . . .

The provision of the Brady Act that crosses the Court's newly defined constitutional threshold is more comparable to a statute requiring local police officers to report the identity of missing children to the Crime Control Center of the Department of Justice than to an offensive federal command to a sovereign state. If Congress believes that such a statute will benefit the people of the Nation, and serve the interests of cooperative federalism better than an enlarged federal bureaucracy, we should respect both its policy judgment and its appraisal of its constitutional power. . . .

Justice Souter, dissenting. . . .

Justice Breyer, with whom *Justice Stevens* joins, dissenting. . . .

Case

ALDEN V. MAINE

527 U.S. 706; 119 S.Ct. 2240; 144 L.Ed. 2d 636 (1999)
Vote: 5–4

In Seminole Tribe of Florida v. Florida (1996), the Supreme Court held that Congress does not have authority under Article I of the Constitution to abrogate states' sovereign immunity with respect to suits filed in federal courts. In this case the Supreme Court considers whether Congress has authority to abrogate states' sovereign immunity with respect to suits filed in state courts.

Justice Kennedy delivered the opinion of the Court.

In 1992, petitioners, a group of probation officers, filed suit against their employer, the State of Maine, in the United States District Court for the District of Maine. The officers alleged the State had violated the overtime provisions of the Fair Labor Standards Act of 1938 (FLSA) . . . and sought compensation and liquidated damages. While the suit was pending, this Court decided *Seminole Tribe of Fla. v. Florida* (1996), which made it clear that Congress lacks power under Article I to abrogate the States' sovereign immunity from suits commenced or prosecuted in the federal courts. Upon consideration of *Seminole Tribe,* the District Court dismissed petitioners' action, and the

Court of Appeals affirmed. . . . Petitioners then filed the same action in state court. The state trial court dismissed the suit on the basis of sovereign immunity, and the Maine Supreme Judicial Court affirmed. . . .

The Maine Supreme Judicial Court's decision conflicts with the decision of the Supreme Court of Arkansas . . . and calls into question the constitutionality of the provisions of the FLSA purporting to authorize private actions against States in their own courts without regard for consent. . . . In light of the importance of the question presented and the conflict between the courts, we granted certiorari. . . .The United States intervened as a petitioner to defend the statute.

We hold that the powers delegated to Congress under Article I of the United States Constitution do not include the power to subject nonconsenting States to private suits for damages in state courts. We decide as well that the State of Maine has not consented to suits for overtime pay and liquidated damages under the FLSA. On these premises we affirm the judgment sustaining dismissal of the suit.

I

The Eleventh Amendment makes explicit reference to the States' immunity from suits "commenced or prosecuted against one of the United States by Citizens of another State, or by Citizens or Subjects of any Foreign

State." . . . We have, as a result, sometimes referred to the States' immunity from suit as "Eleventh Amendment immunity." The phrase is convenient shorthand but something of a misnomer, for the sovereign immunity of the States neither derives from nor is limited by the terms of the Eleventh Amendment. Rather, as the Constitution's structure, and its history, and the authoritative interpretations by this Court make clear, the States' immunity from suit is a fundamental aspect of the sovereignty which the States enjoyed before the ratification of the Constitution, and which they retain today (either literally or by virtue of their admission into the Union upon an equal footing with the other States) except as altered by the plan of the Convention or certain constitutional Amendments.

A

Although the Constitution establishes a National Government with broad, often plenary authority over matters within its recognized competence, the founding document "specifically recognizes the States as sovereign entities." . . . Various textual provisions of the Constitution assume the States' continued existence and active participation in the fundamental processes of governance. . . . The limited and enumerated powers granted to the Legislative, Executive, and Judicial Branches of the National Government, moreover, underscore the vital role reserved to the States by the constitutional design. . . . Any doubt regarding the constitutional role of the States as sovereign entities is removed by the Tenth Amendment, which, like the other provisions of the Bill of Rights, was enacted to allay lingering concerns about the extent of the national power. The Amendment confirms the promise implicit in the original document: "The powers not delegated to the United States by the Constitution, nor prohibited by it to the States, are reserved to the States respectively, or to the people." . . .

The federal system established by our Constitution preserves the sovereign status of the States in two ways. First, it reserves to them a substantial portion of the Nation's primary sovereignty, together with the dignity and essential attributes inhering in that status. The States "form distinct and independent portions of the supremacy, no more subject, within their respective spheres, to the general authority than the general authority is subject to them, within its own sphere." . . .

Second, even as to matters within the competence of the National Government, the constitutional design secures the founding generation's rejection of "the concept of a central government that would act upon and through the States" in favor of "a system in which State and Federal Governments would exercise concurrent authority over the people—who were, in Hamilton's words, 'the only proper objects of government.' " . . . In this the founders achieved a deliberate departure from the Articles of Confederation: Experience under the Articles had "exploded on all hands" the "practicality of making laws, with coercive sanctions, for the States as political bodies." . . .

The States thus retain "a residuary and inviolable sovereignty." . . . They are not relegated to the role of mere provinces or political corporations, but retain the dignity, though not the full authority, of sovereignty.

B

The generation that designed and adopted our federal system considered immunity from private suits central to sovereign dignity. When the Constitution was ratified, it was well established in English law that the Crown could not be sued without consent in its own courts. . . .

Although the American people had rejected other aspects of English political theory, the doctrine that a sovereign could not be sued without its consent was universal in the States when the Constitution was drafted and ratified. . . .

The ratification debates, furthermore, underscored the importance of the States' sovereign immunity to the American people. Grave concerns were raised by the provisions of Article III which extended the federal judicial power to controversies between States and citizens of other States or foreign nations. . . .

The leading advocates of the Constitution assured the people in no uncertain terms that the Constitution would not strip the States of sovereign immunity. . . .

Although the state conventions which addressed the issue of sovereign immunity in their formal ratification documents sought to clarify the point by constitutional amendment, they made clear that they . . . understood the Constitution as drafted to preserve the States' immunity from private suits. . . .

Despite the persuasive assurances of the Constitution's leading advocates and the expressed understanding of the only state conventions to address the issue in explicit terms, this Court held [in *Chisholm v. Georgia*], just five years after the Constitution was adopted, that Article III authorized a private citizen of another State to sue the State of Georgia without its consent. . . .

The Court's decision "fell upon the country with a profound shock." . . .

The States, in particular, responded with outrage to the decision. . . .

An initial proposal to amend the Constitution was introduced in the House of Representatives the day after *Chisholm* was announced; the proposal adopted as the

Eleventh Amendment was introduced in the Senate promptly following an intervening recess. . . . Congress turned to the latter proposal with great dispatch; little more than two months after its introduction it had been endorsed by both Houses and forwarded to the States. . . .

Each House spent but a single day discussing the Amendment, and the vote in each House was close to unanimous. . . . All attempts to weaken the Amendment were defeated. . . .

Not only do the ratification debates and the events leading to the adoption of the Eleventh Amendment reveal the original understanding of the States' constitutional immunity from suit, they also underscore the importance of sovereign immunity to the founding generation. Simply put, "The Constitution never would have been ratified if the States and their courts were to be stripped of their sovereign authority except as expressly provided by the Constitution itself." . . .

II

. . . Whether Congress has authority under Article I to abrogate a State's immunity from suit in its own courts is . . . a question of first impression. In determining whether there is "compelling evidence" that this derogation of the States' sovereignty is "inherent in the constitutional compact" . . . we continue our discussion of history, practice, precedent, and the structure of the Constitution. . . .

. . . [W]hile the Eleventh Amendment by its terms addresses only "the Judicial power of the United States," nothing in *Chisholm,* the catalyst for the Amendment, suggested the States were not immune from suits in their own courts. . . .

In light of the language of the Constitution and the historical context, it is quite apparent why neither the ratification debates nor the language of the Eleventh Amendment addressed the States' immunity from suit in their own courts. The concerns voiced at the ratifying conventions, the furor raised by *Chisholm,* and the speed and unanimity with which the Amendment was adopted, moreover, underscore the jealous care with which the founding generation sought to preserve the sovereign immunity of the States. To read this history as permitting the inference that the Constitution stripped the States of immunity in their own courts and allowed Congress to subject them to suit there would turn on its head the concern of the founding generation—that Article III might be used to circumvent state-court immunity. In light of the historical record it is difficult to conceive that the Constitution would have been adopted if it had been understood to strip the States of immunity from suit in their own courts and cede to the Federal Govern-

ment a power to subject nonconsenting States to private suits in these fora. . . .

As it is settled doctrine that neither substantive federal law nor attempted congressional abrogation under Article I bars a State from raising a constitutional defense of sovereign immunity in federal court . . . our decisions suggesting that the States retain an analogous constitutional immunity from private suits in their own courts support the conclusion that Congress lacks the Article I power to subject the States to private suits in those fora. . . .

Our final consideration is whether a congressional power to subject nonconsenting States to private suits in their own courts is consistent with the structure of the Constitution. We look both to the essential principles of federalism and to the special role of the state courts in the constitutional design.

Although the Constitution grants broad powers to Congress, our federalism requires that Congress treat the States in a manner consistent with their status as residuary sovereigns and joint participants in the governance of the Nation. . . .

Petitioners contend that immunity from suit in federal court suffices to preserve the dignity of the States. Private suits against nonconsenting States, however, present "the indignity of subjecting a State to the coercive process of judicial tribunals at the instance of private parties". . . regardless of the forum. Not only must a State defend or default but also it must face the prospect of being thrust, by federal fiat and against its will, into the disfavored status of a debtor, subject to the power of private citizens to levy on its treasury or perhaps even government buildings or property which the State administers on the public's behalf.

In some ways, of course, a congressional power to authorize private suits against nonconsenting States in their own courts would be even more offensive to state sovereignty than a power to authorize the suits in a federal forum. Although the immunity of one sovereign in the courts of another has often depended in part on comity or agreement, the immunity of a sovereign in its own courts has always been understood to be within the sole control of the sovereign itself. . . . A power to press a State's own courts into federal service to coerce the other branches of the State, furthermore, is the power first to turn the State against itself and ultimately to commandeer the entire political machinery of the State against its will and at the behest of individuals. . . . Such plenary federal control of state governmental processes denigrates the separate sovereignty of the States.

It is unquestioned that the Federal Government retains its own immunity from suit not only in state tribunals but also in its own courts. In light of our constitutional system recognizing the essential sovereignty of the States, we are reluctant to conclude that the States are not entitled to a reciprocal privilege.

Underlying constitutional form are considerations of great substance. Private suits against nonconsenting States—especially suits for money damages—may threaten the financial integrity of the States. It is indisputable that, at the time of the founding, many of the States could have been forced into insolvency but for their immunity from private suits for money damages. Even today, an unlimited congressional power to authorize suits in state court to levy upon the treasuries of the States for compensatory damages, attorney's fees, and even punitive damages could create staggering burdens, giving Congress a power and a leverage over the States that is not contemplated by our constitutional design. The potential national power would pose a severe and notorious danger to the States and their resources.

A general federal power to authorize private suits for money damages would place unwarranted strain on the States' ability to govern in accordance with the will of their citizens. Today, as at the time of the founding, the allocation of scarce resources among competing needs and interests lies at the heart of the political process. While the judgment creditor of the State may have a legitimate claim for compensation, other important needs and worthwhile ends compete for access to the public fisc. Since all cannot be satisfied in full, it is inevitable that difficult decisions involving the most sensitive and political of judgments must be made. If the principle of representative government is to be preserved to the States, the balance between competing interests must be reached after deliberation by the political process established by the citizens of the State, not by judicial decree mandated by the Federal Government and invoked by the private citizen. . . .

Congress cannot abrogate the States' sovereign immunity in federal court; were the rule to be different here, the National Government would wield greater power in the state courts than in its own judicial instrumentalities. . . .

In light of history, practice, precedent, and the structure of the Constitution, we hold that the States retain immunity from private suit in their own courts, an immunity beyond the congressional power to abrogate by Article I legislation. . . .

III

The constitutional privilege of a State to assert its sovereign immunity in its own courts does not confer upon the State a concomitant right to disregard the Constitution or valid federal law. The States and their officers are bound by obligations imposed by the Constitution and by federal statutes that comport with the constitutional design. We are unwilling to assume the States will refuse to honor the Constitution or obey the binding laws of the United States. The good faith of the States thus provides an important assurance that "[t]his Constitution, and the Laws of the United States which shall be made in Pursuance thereof . . . shall be the supreme Law of the Land." . . .

Sovereign immunity, moreover, does not bar all judicial review of state compliance with the Constitution and valid federal law. Rather, certain limits are implicit in the constitutional principle of state sovereign immunity.

The first of these limits is that sovereign immunity bars suits only in the absence of consent. Many States, on their own initiative, have enacted statutes consenting to a wide variety of suits. The rigors of sovereign immunity are thus "mitigated by a sense of justice which has continually expanded by consent the suability of the sovereign." . . . Nor, subject to constitutional limitations, does the Federal Government lack the authority or means to seek the States' voluntary consent to private suits. . . .

The States have consented, moreover, to some suits pursuant to the plan of the Convention or to subsequent constitutional amendments. In ratifying the Constitution, the States consented to suits brought by other States or by the Federal Government. . . . A suit which is commenced and prosecuted against a State in the name of the United States by those who are entrusted with the constitutional duty to "take Care that the Laws be faithfully executed," . . . differs in kind from the suit of an individual: While the Constitution contemplates suits among the members of the federal system as an alternative to extralegal measures, the fear of private suits against nonconsenting States was the central reason given by the founders who chose to preserve the States' sovereign immunity. Suits brought by the United States itself require the exercise of political responsibility for each suit prosecuted against a State, a control which is absent from a broad delegation to private persons to sue nonconsenting States.

We have held also that in adopting the Fourteenth Amendment, the people required the States to surrender a portion of the sovereignty that had been preserved to them by the original Constitution, so that Congress may authorize private suits against nonconsenting States pursuant to its §5 enforcement power. . . . By imposing explicit limits on the powers of the States and granting Congress the power to enforce them, the Amendment "fundamentally altered the balance of state and federal power struck by the Constitution." . . . When Congress enacts appropriate legislation to enforce this Amendment, . . . federal interests are paramount, and Congress may assert an authority over the States which would be otherwise unauthorized by the Constitution. . . .

The second important limit to the principle of sovereign immunity is that it bars suits against States but not lesser entities. The immunity does not extend to suits prosecuted against a municipal corporation or other governmental entity which is not an arm of the State. . . . Nor does sovereign immunity bar all suits against state officers. Some suits against state officers are barred by the rule that sovereign immunity is not limited to suits which name the State as a party if the suits are, in fact, against the State. . . . The rule, however, does not bar certain actions against state officers for injunctive or declaratory relief. . . . Even a suit for money damages may be prosecuted against a state officer in his individual capacity for unconstitutional or wrongful conduct fairly attributable to the officer himself, so long as the relief is sought not from the state treasury but from the officer personally. . . .

IV

The sole remaining question is whether Maine has waived its immunity. . . . To the extent Maine has chosen to consent to certain classes of suits while maintaining its immunity from others, it has done no more than exercise a privilege of sovereignty concomitant to its constitutional immunity from suit. The State, we conclude, has not consented to suit.

V

This case at one level concerns the formal structure of federalism, but in a Constitution as resilient as ours form mirrors substance. Congress has vast power but not all power. When Congress legislates in matters affecting the States, it may not treat these sovereign entities as mere prefectures or corporations. Congress must accord States the esteem due to them as joint participants in a federal system, one beginning with the premise of sovereignty in both the central Government and the separate States. Congress has ample means to ensure compliance with valid federal laws, but it must respect the sovereignty of the States.

In apparent attempt to disparage a conclusion with which it disagrees, the dissent attributes our reasoning to natural law. We seek to discover, however, only what the Framers and those who ratified the Constitution sought to accomplish when they created a federal system. We appeal to no higher authority than the Charter which they wrote and adopted. Theirs was the unique insight that freedom is enhanced by the creation of two governments, not one. We need not attach a label to our dissenting colleagues' insistence that the constitutional structure adopted by the founders must yield to the politics of the moment. Although the Constitution begins with the principle that sovereignty rests with the people, it does not follow that the National Government becomes the ultimate, preferred mechanism for expressing the people's will. The States exist as a refutation of that concept. In choosing to ordain and establish the Constitution, the people insisted upon a federal structure for the very purpose of rejecting the idea that the will of the people in all instances is expressed by the central power, the one most remote from their control. The Framers of the Constitution did not share our dissenting colleagues' belief that the Congress may circumvent the federal design by regulating the States directly when it pleases to do so, including by a proxy in which individual citizens are authorized to levy upon the state treasuries absent the States' consent to jurisdiction.

The case before us depends upon these principles. The State of Maine has not questioned Congress' power to prescribe substantive rules of federal law to which it must comply. Despite an initial good-faith disagreement about the requirements of the FLSA, it is conceded by all that the State has altered its conduct so that its compliance with federal law cannot now be questioned. The Solicitor General of the United States has appeared before this Court, however, and asserted that the federal interest in compensating the States' employees for alleged past violations of federal law is so compelling that the sovereign State of Maine must be stripped of its immunity and subjected to suit in its own courts by its own employees. Yet, despite specific statutory authorization, . . . the United States apparently found the same interests insufficient to justify sending even a single attorney to Maine to prosecute this litigation. The difference between a suit by the United States on behalf of the employees and a suit by the employees implicates a rule that the National Government must itself deem the case of sufficient importance to take action against the State; and history, precedent, and the structure of the Constitution make clear that, under the plan of the Convention, the States have consented to suits of the first kind but not of the second. The judgment of the Supreme Judicial Court of Maine is

Affirmed.

Justice Souter, with whom ***Justice Stevens, Justice Ginsburg***, and ***Justice Breyer*** join, dissenting.

. . .Today's issue arises naturally in the aftermath of the decision in *Seminole Tribe*. The Court holds that the Constitution bars an individual suit against a State to enforce a federal statutory right under the Fair Labor Standards Act of 1938 (FLSA) . . . when brought in the State's courts over its objection. In thus complementing its earlier decision, the Court of course confronts the fact that the state forum renders the Eleventh Amendment beside the point, and it has responded by discerning a simpler and more straightforward theory of state sovereign immunity than it found in *Seminole Tribe*: a State's sovereign immunity from all individual suits is a "fundamental aspect" of state sovereignty "confirm[ed]" by the Tenth Amendment. . . . As a consequence, *Seminole Tribe*'s contorted reliance on the Eleventh Amendment and its background was presumably unnecessary; the Tenth would have done the work with an economy that the majority in *Seminole Tribe* would have welcomed. Indeed, if the Court's current reasoning is correct, the Eleventh Amendment itself was unnecessary. Whatever Article III may originally have said about the federal judicial power, the embarrassment to the State of Georgia occasioned by attempts in federal court to enforce the State's war debt could easily have been avoided if only the Court that decided *Chisholm v. Georgia* (1793), had understood a State's inherent, Tenth Amendment right to be free of any judicial power, whether the court be state or federal, and whether the cause of action arise under state or federal law.

The sequence of the Court's positions prompts a suspicion of error, and skepticism is confirmed by scrutiny of the Court's efforts to justify its holding. There is no evidence that the Tenth Amendment constitutionalized a concept of sovereign immunity as inherent in the notion of statehood, and no evidence that any concept of inherent sovereign immunity was understood historically to apply when the sovereign sued was not the font of the law. Nor does the Court fare any better with its subsidiary lines of reasoning, that the state-court action is barred by the scheme of American federalism, a result supposedly confirmed by a history largely devoid of precursors to the action considered here. The Court's federalism ignores the accepted authority of Congress to bind States under the FLSA and to provide for enforcement of federal rights in state court. The Court's history simply disparages the capacity of the Constitution to order relationships in a Republic that has changed since the founding.

On each point the Court has raised it is mistaken, and I respectfully dissent from its judgment.

I

The Court rests its decision principally on the claim that immunity from suit was "a fundamental aspect of the sovereignty which the States enjoyed before the ratification of the Constitution," . . . an aspect which the Court understands to have survived the ratification of the Constitution in 1788 and to have been "confirm[ed]" and given constitutional status, . . . by the adoption of the Tenth Amendment in 1791. If the Court truly means by "sovereign immunity" what that term meant at common law, . . . its argument would be insupportable. While sovereign immunity entered many new state legal systems as a part of the common law selectively received from England, it was not understood to be indefeasible or to have been given any such status by the new National Constitution, which did not mention it. . . . Had the question been posed, state sovereign immunity could not have been thought to shield a State from suit under federal law on a subject committed to national jurisdiction by Article I of the Constitution. Congress exercising its conceded Article I power may unquestionably abrogate such immunity. I set out this position at length in my dissent in *Seminole Tribe* and will not repeat it here.

The Court does not, however, offer today's holding as a mere corollary to its reasoning in *Seminole Tribe*, substituting the Tenth Amendment for the Eleventh as the occasion demands, and it is fair to read its references to a "fundamental aspect" of state sovereignty as referring not to a prerogative inherited from the Crown, but to a conception necessarily implied by statehood itself. The conception is thus not one of common law so much as of natural law, a universally applicable proposition discoverable by reason. . . .

. . . There is almost no evidence that the generation of the Framers thought sovereign immunity was fundamental in the sense of being unalterable. Whether one looks at the period before the framing, to the ratification controversies, or to the early republican era, the evidence is the same. Some Framers thought sovereign immunity was an obsolete royal prerogative inapplicable in a republic; some thought sovereign immunity was a common-law power defeasible, like other common-law rights, by statute; and perhaps a few thought, in keeping with a natural law view distinct from the common-law conception, that immunity was inherent in a sovereign because the body that made a law could not logically be bound by it. Natural law thinking on the part of a doubtful few will not, however, support the Court's position. . . .

If the natural law conception of sovereign immunity as an inherent characteristic of sovereignty enjoyed by the States had been broadly accepted at the time of the founding, one would expect to find it reflected somewhere in the five opinions delivered by the Court in *Chisholm v. Georgia* (1793). Yet that view did not appear in any of them. And since a bare two years before *Chisholm*, the Bill of Rights had been added to the original Constitution, if the Tenth Amendment had been understood to give federal constitutional status to state sovereign immunity so as to endue it with the equivalent of the natural law conception, one would be certain to find such a development mentioned somewhere in the *Chisholm* writings. In fact, however, not one of the opinions espoused the natural law view, and not one of them so much as mentioned the Tenth Amendment. . . .

It is clear enough that the Court has no historical predicate to argue for a fundamental or inherent theory of sovereign immunity as limiting authority elsewhere conferred by the Constitution or as imported into the Constitution by the Tenth Amendment. But what if the facts were otherwise and a natural law conception of state sovereign immunity in a State's own courts were implicit in the Constitution? On good authority, it would avail the State nothing, and the Court would be no less mistaken than it is already in sustaining the State's claim today. . . .

II

The Court's rationale for today's holding based on a conception of sovereign immunity as somehow fundamental to sovereignty or inherent in statehood fails for the lack of any substantial support for such a conception in the thinking of the founding era. The Court cannot be counted out yet, however, for it has a second line of argument looking not to a clause-based reception of the natural law conception or even to its recognition as a "background principle," . . . but to a structural basis in the Constitution's creation of a federal system. Immunity, the Court says, "inheres in the system of federalism established by the Constitution," . . . its "contours [being] determined by the founders' understanding, not by the principles or limitations derived from natural law." . . . Again, "[w]e look both to the essential principles of federalism and to the special role of the state courts in the constitutional design." . . . That is, the Court believes that the federal constitutional structure itself necessitates recognition of some degree of state autonomy broad enough to include sovereign immunity from suit in a State's own courts, regardless of the federal source of the claim asserted against the State. If one were to read the Court's federal structure rationale in isolation from the preceding portions of the opinion, it would appear that the Court's position on state sovereign immunity might have been rested entirely on federalism alone. If it had been, however, I would still be in dissent, for the Court's argument that state court sovereign immunity on federal questions is inherent in the very concept of federal structure is demonstrably mistaken. . . .

. . . Once "the atom of sovereignty" had been split, . . . the general scheme of delegated sovereignty as between the two component governments of the federal system was clear, and was succinctly stated by Chief Justice Marshall: "In America, the powers of sovereignty are divided between the government of the Union, and those of the States. They are each sovereign, with respect to the objects committed to it, and neither sovereign with respect to the objects committed to the other." . . .

Hence the flaw in the Court's appeal to federalism. The State of Maine is not sovereign with respect to the national objective of the FLSA. It is not the authority that promulgated the FLSA, on which the right of action in this case depends. That authority is the United States acting through the Congress, whose legislative power under Article I of the Constitution to extend FLSA coverage to state employees has already been decided, . . . and is not contested here.

Nor can it be argued that because the State of Maine creates its own court system, it has authority to decide what sorts of claims may be entertained there, and thus in effect to control the right of action in this case. Maine has created state courts of general jurisdiction; once it has done so, the Supremacy Clause of the Constitution, . . . which requires state courts to enforce federal law and state-court judges to be bound by it, requires the Maine courts to entertain this federal cause of action. Maine has advanced no "valid excuse" . . . for its courts' refusal to hear federal-law claims in which Maine is a defendant, and sovereign immunity cannot be that excuse, simply because the State is not sovereign with respect to the subject of the claim against it. . . .

It is equally puzzling to hear the Court say that "federal power to authorize private suits for money damages would place unwarranted strain on the States' ability to govern in accordance with the will of their citizens." . . . So long as the citizens' will, expressed through state legislation, does not violate valid federal law, the strain will not be felt; and to the extent that state action does violate federal law, the will of the citizens of the United States already trumps that of the citizens of the State: the strain then is not only expected, but necessarily intended.

Least of all does the Court persuade by observing that "other important needs" than that of the "judgment creditor" compete for public money. . . . The "judgment creditor" in question is not a dunning bill-collector, but a citizen whose federal rights have been violated, and a constitutional structure that stints on enforcing federal rights out of an abundance of delicacy toward the States has substituted politesse in place of respect for the rule of law.

III

If neither theory nor structure can supply the basis for the Court's conceptions of sovereign immunity and federalism, then perhaps history might. The Court apparently believes that because state courts have not historically entertained Commerce Clause-based federal-law claims against the States, such an innovation carries a presumption of unconstitutionality. . . .

Today, however, in light of *Garcia,* (overruling *National League of Cities v. Usery,* [1976]), the law is settled that federal legislation enacted under the Commerce Clause may bind the States without having to satisfy a test of undue incursion into state sovereignty. . . . Because the commerce power is no longer thought to be circumscribed, the dearth of prior private federal claims entertained against the States in state courts does not tell us anything, and reflects nothing but an earlier and less expansive application of the commerce power.

Least of all is it to the point for the Court to suggest that because the Framers would be surprised to find States subjected to a federal-law suit in their own courts under the commerce power, the suit must be prohibited by the Constitution. . . . The Framers' intentions and expectations count so far as they point to the meaning of the Constitution's text or the fair implications of its structure, but they do not hover over the instrument to veto any application of its principles to a world that the Framers could not have anticipated.

If the Framers would be surprised to see States subjected to suit in their own courts under the commerce power, they would be astonished by the reach of Congress under the Commerce Clause generally. The proliferation of Government, State and Federal, would amaze the Framers, and the administrative state with its reams of regulations would leave them rubbing their eyes. But the Framers' surprise at, say, the FLSA, or the Federal Communications Commission, or the Federal Reserve Board is no threat to the constitutionality of any one of them. . . .

IV [omitted]

V

The Court has swung back and forth with regrettable disruption on the enforceability of the FLSA against the States, but if the present majority had a defensible position one could at least accept its decision with an expectation of stability ahead. As it is, any such expectation would be naive. The resemblance of today's state sovereign immunity to the *Lochner* era's industrial due process is striking. The Court began this century by imputing immutable constitutional status to a conception of economic self-reliance that was never true to industrial life and grew insistently fictional with the years, and the Court has chosen to close the century by conferring like status on a conception of state sovereign immunity that is true neither to history nor to the structure of the Constitution. I expect the Court's late essay into immunity doctrine will prove the equal of its earlier experiment in laissez-faire, the one being as unrealistic as the other, as indefensible, and probably as fleeting.

Case

COOLEY V. BOARD OF PORT WARDENS

12 How. (53 U.S.) 299; 13 L.Ed. 996 (1852)

Vote: 7–2

The controversy that led to this landmark constitutional decision began when Aaron Cooley violated a Pennsylvania law by first failing to hire pilots and then refusing to pay pilotage fees on two of his ships at the port of Philadelphia. The Board of Port Wardens successfully sued him in a local trial court, and this judgment was affirmed by the Pennsylvania Supreme Court. Cooley brought his case to the U.S. Supreme Court, challenging the pilotage law on several constitutional grounds. The following excerpts from Justice Curtis's majority opinion deal with the question of whether this law violated the Commerce Clause.

Mr. Justice Curtis delivered the opinion of the Court.

. . . That the power to regulate commerce includes the regulation of navigation, we consider settled. And when we look to the nature of the service performed by pilots, to the relations which that service and its compensations bear to navigation between the several States, and between the ports of the United States and foreign countries, we are brought to the conclusion, that the regulation of the qualifications of pilots, of the modes and times of offering and rendering their services, of the responsibilities which shall rest upon them, of the powers they shall possess, of the compensation they may demand, and of the penalties by which their rights and duties may be enforced, do constitute regulations of navigation, and consequently of commerce, within the just meaning of this clause of the Constitution.

The power to regulate navigation is the power to prescribe rules in conformity with which navigation must be carried on. It extends to the persons who conduct it, as well as to the instruments used. Accordingly, the first Congress assembled under the Constitution passed laws, requiring the masters of ships and vessels of the United States to be citizens of the United States, and established many rules for the government and regulation of officers and seamen. . . . These have been from time to time added to and changed, and we are not aware that their validity has been questioned.

Now, a pilot, so far as respects the navigation of the vessel in that part of the voyage which is his pilotage ground, is the temporary master charged with the safety of the vessel and cargo, and of the lives of those on board, and intrusted with command of the crew. He is not only one of the persons engaged in navigation, but he occupies a most important and responsible place among those thus engaged. And if Congress has power to regulate the seamen who assist the pilot in the management of the vessel, a power never denied, we can perceive no valid reason why the pilot should be beyond the reach of the same power. . . .

Nor should it be lost sight of, that this subject of the regulation of pilots and pilotage has an intimate connection with, and an important relation to, the general subject of commerce with foreign nations and among the several States, over which it was one main object of the Constitution to create a national control. . . .

It becomes necessary, to consider whether this law of Pennsylvania, being a regulation of commerce, is valid.

The Act of Congress of the 7th of August, 1789, . . . is as follows:

> That all pilots in the bays, inlets, rivers, harbors, and ports of the United States, shall continue to be regulated in conformity with the existing laws of the States, respectively, wherein such pilots may be, or with such laws as the States may respectively hereafter enact for the purpose, until further legislative provision shall be made by Congress.

If the law of Pennsylvania, now in question, had been in existence at the date of this Act of Congress, we might hold it to have been adopted by Congress, and thus made a law of the United States, and so valid. Because this Act does, in effect, give the force of an Act of Congress, to the then existing state laws on this subject, so long as they should continue unrepealed by the State which enacted them.

But the law on which these actions are founded was not enacted till 1803. What effect, then, can be attributed to so much of the Act of 1789 as declares that pilots shall continue to be regulated in conformity "with such laws as the States may respectively hereafter enact for the purpose, until further legislative provision shall be made by Congress"?

If the States were divested of the power to legislate on this subject by the grant of the commercial power to Congress, it is plain this Act could not confer upon them power thus to legislate. If the Constitution excluded the States from making any law regulating commerce, certainly Congress cannot regrant, or in any manner reconvey to the States that power. . . . [W]e are brought directly and unavoidably to the consideration of the question, whether the grant of the commercial power to Congress, did *per se* deprive the States of all power to regulate pilots. This question has never been decided by this court, nor, in our judgment, has any case depending upon all the considerations which must govern this one, come before this court. The grant of commercial power to Congress does not contain any terms which expressly exclude the States from exercising an authority over its subject matter. If they are excluded it must be because the nature of the power, thus granted Congress, requires that a similar authority should not exist in the States. If it were conceded on the one side, that the nature of this power, like that to legislate for the District of Columbia, is absolutely and totally repugnant to the existence of similar power in the States, probably no one would deny that the grant of the power to Congress, as effectually and perfectly excludes the States from all future legislation on the subject, as if express words has been used to exclude them. And on the other hand, if it were admitted that the existence of this power in Congress, like the power of taxation, is compatible with the existence of a similar power in the states, then it would be in conformity with the contemporary exposition of the Constitution . . . and with the judicial construction, given from time to time by this court, after the most deliberate consideration, to hold that the mere grant of such a power to Congress, did not imply a prohibition on the States to exercise the same power; that it is not the mere existence of such a power, but its exercise by Congress, which may be incompatible with the exercise of the same power by the States, and that the States may legislate in the absence of congressional regulations. . . .

. . . [W]hen the nature of a power like this is spoken of, when it is said that the nature of the power requires that it should be exercised exclusively by Congress, it must be intended to refer to the subjects of that power, and to say they are of such a nature as to require exclusive legislation by Congress. Now, the power to regulate commerce, embraces a vast field, containing not only many, but exceedingly various subjects, quite unlike in their nature, some imperatively demanding a single uniform rule, operating equally on the commerce of the United States in every port; and some, like the subject now in question, as imperatively demanding that diversity, which alone can meet the local necessities of navigation.

Either absolutely to affirm, or deny, that the nature of this power requires exclusive legislation by Congress, is to lose sight of the nature of the subjects of this power, and to assert concerning all of them, what is really applicable but to a part. Whatever subjects of this power are in their nature national, or admit only of one uniform system, or plan of regulation, may justly be said to be of such a nature as to require exclusive legislation by Congress. That this cannot be affirmed of laws for the regulation of pilots and pilotage is plain. The Act of 1789 contains a clear and authoritative declaration by the first Congress, that the nature of this subject is such, that until Congress should find it necessary to exert its power, it should be left to the legislation of the States; that it is local and not national; that it is likely to be the best provided for, not by one system, or plan of regulations, but by as many as the legislative discretion of the several States should deem applicable to the local peculiarities of the port within their limits. . . .

It is the opinion of a majority of the court that the mere grant to Congress of the power to regulate commerce, did not deprive the States of power to regulate pilots, and that although Congress has legislated on this subject, its legislation manifests an intention, with a single exception, not to regulate this subject, but to leave its regulation to the several States. To these precise questions, which are all we are called on to decide, this opinion must be understood to be confined. It does not extend to the question what other subjects, under the commercial power, are within the exclusive control of Congress, or may be regulated by the States in the absence of all congressional legislation; nor to the general question how far any regulation of a subject by Congress may be deemed to operate as an exclusion of all legislation by the States upon the same subject. We decide the precise questions before us, upon what we deem sound principles, applicable to this particular subject in the state in which the legislation of Congress has left it. We go no farther. . . .

We are of opinion that this state law was enacted by virtue of a power, residing in the State to legislate; that it is not in conflict with any law of Congress; that it does not interfere with any system which Congress has established by making regulations, or by intentionally leaving individuals to their own unrestricted action; that this law is therefore valid, and the judgment of the Supreme Court of Pennsylvania in each case must be affirmed.

Messrs. Justices McLean and *Wayne* dissented. *Mr. Justice Daniel*, although he concurred in the judgment of the court, yet dissented from its reasoning.

Mr. Justice Daniel:

I agree with the majority in their decision, that the judgments of the Supreme Court of Pennsylvania in these cases should be affirmed, though I cannot go with them in the process or argument by which their conclusion has been reached. . . . The true question here is, whether the power to enact pilot laws is appropriate and necessary, or rather most appropriate and necessary to the state or the federal governments. It being conceded that this power has been exercised by the States from their very dawn of existence; that it can be practically and beneficially applied by the local authorities only; it being conceded, as it must be, that the power to pass pilot laws, as such, has not been in any express terms delegated to Congress, and does not necessarily conflict with the right to establish commercial regulations, I am forced to conclude that this is an original and inherent power in the States, and not one to be merely tolerated, or held subject to the sanction of the federal government.

Case

SOUTH CAROLINA HIGHWAY DEPARTMENT V. BARNWELL BROTHERS

303 U.S. 177; 58 S.Ct. 510; 82 L.Ed. 734 (1938)

Vote: 7–0

In this case the Court considers the scope of state power to regulate interstate commerce in the context of a state law restricting the weight and size of trucks operating on state highways. Students should compare this decision to Southern Pacific v. Arizona. Are the cases distinguishable? Can these decisions be reconciled?

Mr. Justice Stone delivered the opinion of the Court.

The Act of the General Assembly of South Carolina . . . prohibits use on the state highways of motor trucks and "semi-trailer motor trucks" whose width exceeds 90 inches, and whose weight including load exceeds 20,000 pounds. . . . The principal question for decision is whether these prohibitions impose an unconstitutional burden upon interstate commerce.

The district court of three judges, after hearing evidence, . . . enjoined the enforcement of the weight provision against interstate motor carriers on the specified highways, and also the width limitation of 90 inches, except in the case of vehicles exceeding 96 inches in width. . . .

The trial court rested its decision that the statute unreasonably burdens interstate commerce, upon findings, not assailed here, that there is a large amount of motor truck traffic passing interstate in the southeastern part of the United States, which would normally pass over the highways of South Carolina, but which will be barred from the state by the challenged restrictions if enforced, and upon its conclusion that, when viewed in the light of their effect upon interstate commerce, these restrictions are unreasonable.

South Carolina has built its highways and owns and maintains them. It has received from the federal government, in aid of its highway improvements, money grants which have been expended upon the highways to which the injunction applies. . . .

While the constitutional grant to Congress of power to regulate interstate commerce has been held to operate of its own force to curtail state power in some measure, it did not forestall all state action affecting interstate commerce. Ever since *Wilson v. Black Bird Creek Marsh Co.* . . . it has been recognized that there are matters of local concern, the regulation of which unavoidably involves some regulation of interstate commerce but which, because of their local character and their number and diversity, may never be fully dealt with by Congress. Notwithstanding the commerce clause, such regulation in the absence of Congressional action has for the most part been left to the states by the decisions of this Court, subject to the other applicable constitutional restraints.

The commerce clause, by its own force, prohibits discrimination against interstate commerce, whatever its form or method, and the decisions of this Court have recognized that there is scope for its like operation when state legislation nominally of local concern is in point of fact aimed at interstate commerce, or by its necessary operation is a means of gaining a local benefit by throwing the attendant burdens on those without the state. . . .

But the present case affords no occasion for saying that the bare possession of power by Congress to regulate the interstate traffic forces the states to conform to standards which Congress might, but has not adopted, or curtails their power to take measures to insure the safety and conservation of their highways which may be applied to like traffic moving intrastate. Few subjects of state regulation are so peculiarly of local concern as is the use of state highways. There are few matters, local regulation of which is so inseparable from a substantial effect on interstate commerce. Unlike the railroads, local highways are built, owned and maintained by the state or its municipal subdivisions. The state has a primary and immediate concern in their safe and economical administration. The present regulations, or any others of like purpose, if they are to accomplish their end, must be applied alike to interstate and intrastate traffic both moving in large volume over the highways. The fact that they affect alike shippers in interstate and intrastate commerce in large number within as well as without the state is a safeguard against their abuse.

From the beginning it has been recognized that a state can, if it sees fit, build and maintain its own highways, canals and railroads and that in the absence of Congressional action their regulation is peculiarly within its competence, even though interstate commerce is materially affected. . . . Congress not acting, state regulation of intrastate carriers has been upheld regardless of its effect upon interstate commerce. . . . With respect to the extent and nature of the local interests to be protected and the unavoidable effect upon interstate and intrastate commerce alike, regulations of the use of the highways are akin to local regulation of rivers, harbors, piers and docks, quarantine regulations, and game laws, which, Congress not acting, have been sustained even though they materially interfere with interstate commerce.

The nature of the authority of the state over its own highways has often been pointed out by this Court. It may not, under the guise of regulation, discriminate against interstate commerce. But "in the absence of national legislation especially covering the subject of interstate commerce, the state may rightly prescribe uniform regulations adapted to promote safety upon its highways and the conservation of their use applicable alike to vehicles moving in interstate commerce and those of its own citizens." . . . This Court has often sustained the exercise of that power although it has burdened or impeded interstate commerce. It has upheld weight limitations lower than those presently imposed, applied alike to motor traffic moving interstate and intrastate. . . . Restrictions favoring passenger traffic over the carriage of interstate merchandise by truck have been similarly sustained, . . . as has the exaction of a reasonable fee for the use of the highways. . . .

In each of these cases regulation involves a burden on interstate commerce. But so long as the state action does not discriminate, the burden is one which the Constitution permits because it is an inseparable incident of the exercise of a legislative authority, which, under the Constitution, has been left to the states.

Congress, in the exercise of its plenary power to regulate interstate commerce, may determine whether the burdens imposed on it by state regulation, otherwise permissible, are too great, and may, by legislation designed to secure uniformity or in other respect to protect the national interest in the commerce, curtail to some extent the state's regulatory power. But that is a legislative, not a judicial function, to be performed in the light of the congressional judgment of what is appropriate regulation of interstate commerce, and the extent to which, in that field, state power and local interests should be required to yield to the national authority and interest. In the absence of such legislation the judicial function, under the commerce clause . . . stops with the inquiry whether the state legislature in adopting regulations such as the present has acted within its province, and whether the means of regulation chosen are reasonably adapted to the end sought. . . .

. . . [C]ourts do not sit as legislatures, either state or national. They cannot act as Congress does when, after weighing all the conflicting interests, state and national, it determines when and how much the state regulatory power shall yield to the larger interests of a national commerce. And in reviewing a state highway regulation where Congress has not acted, a court is not called upon, as are state legislatures, to determine what, in its judgment, is the most suitable restriction to be applied of those that are possible, or to choose that one which in its opinion is best adapted to all the diverse interests affected. . . . When the action of a legislature is within the scope of its power, fairly debatable questions as to its reasonableness, wisdom and propriety are not for the determination of courts, but for the legislative body, on which rest the duty and responsibility of decision. . . . This is equally the case when the legislative power is one which may legitimately place an incidental burden on interstate commerce. It is not any the less a legislative power committed to the states because it affects interstate commerce, and courts are not any the more entitled, because interstate commerce is affected, to substitute their own for the legislative judgment. . . .

Since the adoption of one weight or width regulation, rather than another, is a legislative not a judicial choice, its constitutionality is not to be determined by weighing in the judicial scales and merits of the legislative choice and rejecting it if the weight of evidence presented in court appears to favor a different standard. . . . Being a legislative judgment it is presumed to be supported by facts known to the legislature unless facts judicially known or proved preclude that possibility. Hence, in reviewing the present determination we examine the record, not to see whether the findings of the court below are supported by evidence, but ascertain upon the whole record whether it is possible to say that the legislative choice is without rational basis. . . . Not only does the record fail to exclude that possibility, but it shows affirmatively that there is adequate support for the legislative judgment.

. . . The fact that many states have adopted a different standard is not persuasive. The conditions under which highways must be built in the several states, their construction and the demands made upon them, are not uniform. The road-building art, as the record shows, is far from having attained a scientific certainty and precision, and scientific precision is not the criterion for the exercise of the constitutional regulatory power of the states. . . . The legislature, being free to exercise its own judgment, is not bound by that of other legislatures. It would hardly be contended that if all the states had adopted a single standard, none, in the light of its own experience and in the exercise of its judgment upon all the complex elements which enter into the problem, could change it.

The regulatory measures taken by South Carolina are within its legislative power . . . and the resulting burden on interstate commerce is not forbidden.

Mr. Justice Cardozo and *Mr. Justice Reed* took no part in the consideration or decision of this case.

Case

SOUTHERN PACIFIC RAILROAD COMPANY V. ARIZONA

325 U.S. 761; 65 S.Ct. 1515; 89 L.Ed. 1915 (1945)

Vote: 7–2

Here the Court again considers the scope of state power to regulate interstate commerce. The issue is the validity of an Arizona law limiting trains to fourteen passenger cars or seventy freight cars. Before reading this case, students should review the Court's decision in South Carolina Highway Department v. Barnwell Brothers.

Mr. Chief Justice Stone delivered the opinion of the Court.

The Arizona Train Limit Law of May 16, 1912, . . . makes it unlawful for any person or corporation to operate within the state a railroad train of more than fourteen passenger or seventy freight cars, and authorizes the state to recover a money penalty for each violation of the Act. The questions for decision are whether Congress has, by legislative enactment, restricted the power of the states to regulate the length of interstate trains as a safety measure and, if not, whether the statute contravenes the commerce clause of the federal Constitution.

Although the Commerce Clause conferred on the national government power to regulate commerce, its possession of the power does not exclude all state power of regulation. Ever since *Wilson v. Black Bird Creek Marsh Co.* [1829] . . . it has been recognized that, in the absence of conflicting legislation by Congress, there is a residuum of power in the state to make laws governing matters of local concern which nevertheless in some measure affect interstate commerce or even, to some extent, regulate it. . . . Thus the states may regulate matters which, because of their number and diversity, may never be adequately dealt with by Congress. . . . When the regulation of matters of local concern is local in character and effect, and its impact on the national commerce does not seriously interfere with its operation, and the consequent incentive to deal with them nationally is slight, such regulation has been generally held to be within state authority. . . .

But ever since *Gibbons v. Ogden* . . . the states have not been deemed to have authority to impede substantially the free flow of commerce from state to state, or to regulate those phases of the national commerce which, because of the need of national uniformity, demand that their regulation, if any, be prescribed by a single authority. . . . Whether or not this long recognized distribution of power between the national and the state governments is predicated upon the implications of the Commerce Clause itself . . . or upon the presumed intention of Congress, where Congress has not spoken, . . . the result is the same.

In the application of these principles some enactments may be found to be plainly within and others plainly without state power. But between these extremes lies the infinite variety of cases, in which regulation of local matters may also operate as a regulation of commerce, in which reconciliation of the conflicting claims of state and national power is to be attained only by some appraisal and accommodation of the competing demands of the state and national interests involved. . . .

For a hundred years it has been accepted constitutional doctrine that the Commerce Clause, without the aid of congressional legislation, thus affords some protection from state legislation inimical to the national commerce, and that in such cases, where Congress has not acted, this Court, and not the state legislature, is under the Commerce Clause the final arbiter of the competing demands of state and national interests. . . .

Congress has undoubted power to redefine the distribution of power over interstate commerce. It may either permit the states to regulate the commerce in a manner which would otherwise not be permissible . . . or exclude state regulation even of matters of peculiarly local concern which nevertheless affect interstate commerce. . . .

But in general Congress has left it to the courts to formulate the rules thus interpreting the Commerce Clause in its application, doubtless because it has appreciated the destructive consequences to the commerce of the nation if their protection were withdrawn . . . and has been aware

that in their application state laws will not be invalidated without the support of relevant factual material which will "afford a sure basis" for an informed judgment. . . . Meanwhile, Congress has accommodated its legislation, as have the states, to these rules as an established feature of our constitutional system. There has thus been left to the states wide scope for the regulation of matters of local state concern, even though it in some measure affects the commerce, provided it does not materially restrict the free flow of commerce across state lines, or interfere with it in matters with respect to which uniformity of regulation is of predominant national concern.

Hence the matters for ultimate determination here are the nature and extent of the burden which the state regulation of interstate trains, adopted as a safety measure, imposes on interstate commerce, and whether the relative weights of the state and national interests involved are such as to make inapplicable the rule, generally observed, that the free flow of interstate commerce and its freedom from local restraints in matters requiring uniformity of regulation are interests safeguarded by the commerce clause from state interference.

While this Court is not bound by the findings of the state court, and may determine for itself the facts of a case upon which an asserted federal right depends, . . . the facts found by the state trial court showing the nature of the interstate commerce involved, and the effect upon it of the train limit law, are not seriously questioned. Its findings with respect to the need for and effect of the statute as a safety measure, although challenged in some particulars which we do not regard as material to our decision, are likewise supported by evidence.

The findings show that the operation of long trains . . . is standard practice over the main lines of the railroads of the United States, and that, if the length of trains is to be regulated at all, national uniformity in the regulation adopted, such as only Congress can prescribe, is practically indispensable to the operation of an efficient and economical national railway system. . . . Outside of Arizona, where the length of trains is not restricted, [Southern Pacific] runs a substantial proportion of long trains. In 1939 on its comparable route for through traffic through Utah and Nevada from 66 to 85% of its freight trains were over 70 cars in length and over 43% of its passenger trains included more than fourteen passenger cars.

In Arizona, approximately 93% of the freight traffic and 95% of the passenger traffic is interstate. Because of the Train Limit Law [Southern Pacific] is required to haul over 30% more trains in Arizona than would otherwise have been necessary. The record shows a definite relationship between operating costs and the length of trains, the increase in length resulting in a reduction of operating costs per car. The additional cost of operation of trains complying with the Train Limit Law in Arizona amounts for the two railroads traversing that state to about $1,000,000 a year. The reduction in train lengths also impedes efficient operation. . . .

The unchallenged findings leave no doubt that the Arizona Train Limit Law imposes a serious burden on the interstate commerce conducted by [Southern Pacific]. It materially impedes the movement of . . . interstate trains through that state and interposes a substantial obstruction to the national policy proclaimed by Congress, to promote adequate, economical and efficient railway transportation service. . . . Enforcement of the law in Arizona, while train lengths remain unregulated or are regulated by varying standards in other states, must inevitably result in an impairment of uniformity of efficient railroad operation because the railroads are subjected to regulation which is not uniform in its application. Compliance with a state statute limiting train lengths requires interstate trains of a length lawful in other states to be broken up and reconstituted as they enter each state according as it may impose varying limitations upon train lengths. The alternative is for the carrier to conform to the lowest train limit restriction of any of the states through which its trains pass, whose laws thus control the carriers' operations both within and without the regulating state.

If one state may regulate train lengths, so may all the others, and they need not prescribe the same maximum limitation. The practical effect of such regulation is to control train operations beyond the boundaries of the state exacting it because of the necessity of breaking up and reassembling long trains at the nearest terminal points before entering and after leaving the regulating state. The serious impediment to the free flow of commerce by the local regulation of train lengths and the practical necessity that such regulation, if any, must be prescribed by a single body having a nation-wide authority are apparent.

We think, as the trial court found, that the Arizona Train Limit Law, viewed as a safety measure, affords at most slight and dubious advantage, if any, over unregulated train lengths. . . . Its undoubted effect on the commerce is the regulation, without securing uniformity, of the length of trains operated in interstate commerce, which lack is itself a primary cause of preventing the free flow of commerce by delaying it and by substantially increasing its cost and impairing its efficiency. In these respects the case differs from those where a state, by regulatory measures affecting the commerce, has removed or reduced safety hazards without substantial interference with the interstate movement of trains. Such are measures

abolishing the car stove, . . . requiring locomotives to be supplied with electric headlights, . . . providing for full train crews, . . . and for the equipment of freight trains with cabooses. . . .

The principle that, without controlling congressional action, a state may not regulate interstate commerce so as substantially to affect its flow or deprive it of needed uniformity in its regulation is not to be avoided by "simply invoking the convenient apologetics of the police power." . . .

. . . [W]e have pointed out that when a state goes beyond safety measures which are permissible because only local in their effect upon interstate commerce and "attempts to impose particular standards as to structure, design, equipment and operation [of vessels plying interstate] which in the judgment of its authorities may be desirable but pass beyond what is plainly essential to safety and seaworthiness, the State will encounter the principle that such requirements, if imposed at all, must be through the action of Congress which can establish a uniform rule. Whether the state in a particular matter goes too far must be left to be determined when the precise question arises."

Here we conclude that the state does go too far. Its regulation of train lengths, admittedly obstructive to interstate train operation, and having a seriously adverse effect on transportation efficiency and economy, passes beyond what is plainly essential for safety since it does not appear that it will lessen rather than increase the danger of accident. . . .

South Carolina Highway Department v. Barnwell . . . was concerned with the power of the state to regulate the weight and width of motor cars passing interstate over its highways, a legislative field over which the state has a far more extensive control than over interstate railroads. In that case . . . we were at pains to point out that there are few subjects of state regulation affecting interstate commerce which are so peculiarly of local concern as is the use of the state's highways. Unlike the railroads local highways are built, owned and maintained by the state or its municipal subdivisions. The state is responsible for their safe and economical administration. Regulations affecting the safety of their use must be applied alike to intrastate and interstate traffic. The fact that they affect alike shippers in interstate and intrastate commerce in great numbers, within as well as without the state, is a safeguard against regulatory abuses. Their regulation is akin to quarantine measures, game laws, and like local regulations of rivers, harbors, piers, and docks, with respect to which the state has exceptional scope for the exercise of its regulatory power, and which, Congress not acting, have been sustained even though they materially interfere with interstate commerce. . . .

The contrast between the present regulation and . . . the highway safety regulation in point of the nature of the subject of regulation and the state's interest in it, illustrate and emphasize the considerations which enter into a determination of the relative weights of state and national interests where state regulating affecting interstate commerce is attempted. Here examination of all the relevant factors makes it plain that the state interest is outweighed by the interest of the nation in an adequate, economical and efficient railway transportation service, which must prevail.

Mr. Justice Rutledge concurs in the result.

Mr. Justice Black, dissenting.

. . . The determination of whether it is in the interest of society for the length of trains to be governmentally regulated is a matter of public policy. Someone must fix that policy—either the Congress, or the state, or the courts. A century and a half of constitutional history and government admonishes this Court to leave that choice to the elected legislative representatives of the people themselves, where it properly belongs both on democratic principles and the requirements of efficient government.

There have been many sharp divisions of this Court concerning its authority, in the absence of congressional enactment, to invalidate state laws as violating the Commerce Clause. . . . That discussion need not be renewed here, because even the broadest exponents of judicial power in this field have not heretofore expressed doubt as to a state's power, absent a paramount congressional declaration, to regulate interstate trains in the interest of safety. . . .

. . . Congress could when it pleased establish a uniform rule as to the length of trains. Congress knew about the Arizona law. It is common knowledge that the Interstate Commerce Committees of the House and the Senate keep in close and intimate touch with the affairs of railroads and other national means of transportation. Every year brings forth new legislation which goes through those Committees, much of it relating to safety. The attention of the members of Congress and of the Senate has been focused on the particular problem of the length of railroad trains. We cannot assume that they were ignorant of the commonly known fact that a long train might be more dangerous in some territories and on some particular types of railroad. The history of congressional consideration of this problem leaves little if any room to doubt that the choice of Congress to leave the state free in this field was a deliberate choice, which was taken with a full knowledge of the complexities of the problems and the probable need for diverse regulations in different localities. I am therefore compelled to reach the conclusion that today's decision is the result of the belief of a majority of this Court that both the legislature of Arizona and the Congress made wrong policy decisions in permitting a law to stand which limits the length of railroad trains. . . .

When we finally get down to the gist of what the Court today actually decides, it is this: Even though more railroad employees will be injured by "slack actions" movements on long trains than on short trains, there must be no regulation of this danger in the absence of "uniform regulations." That means that no one can legislate against this danger except the Congress; and even though the Congress is perfectly content to leave the matter to the different state legislatures, this Court, on the ground of "lack of uniformity," will require it to make an express avowal of that fact before it will permit a state to guard against that admitted danger.

We are not left in doubt as to why, as against the potential peril of injuries to employees, the Court tips the scales on the side of "uniformity." For the evil it finds in a lack of uniformity is that it (1) delays interstate commerce, (2) increases its cost and (3) impairs its efficiency. All three of these boil down to the same thing, and that is that running shorter trains would increase the cost of railroad operations. The "burden" on commerce reduces itself to mere cost because there was no finding, and no evidence to support a finding that by the expenditure of sufficient sums of money, the railroads could not enable themselves to carry goods and passengers just as quickly and efficiently with short trains as with long trains. Thus the conclusion that a requirement for long trains will "burden interstate commerce" is a mere euphemism for the statement that a requirement for long trains will increase the cost of railroad operations.

This record in its entirety leaves me with no doubt whatever that many employees have been seriously injured and killed in the past, and that many more are likely to be so in the future, because of "slack movement" in trains. . . . It may be that offsetting dangers are possible in the operation of short trains. The balancing of these probabilities, however, is not in my judgment a matter for judicial determination, but one which calls for legislative consideration. Representatives elected by the people to make their laws, rather than judges appointed to interpret those laws, can best determine the policies which govern the people. That at least is the basic principle on which our democratic society rests. I would affirm the judgment of the Supreme Court of Arizona.

Mr. Justice Douglas, dissenting. . . .

Case

PHILADELPHIA V. NEW JERSEY

437 U.S. 617; 98 S.Ct. 2531; 57 L.Ed. 2d 475 (1978)

Vote: 7–2

In this case the Court considers whether a New Jersey law prohibiting the importation of waste products originating outside the state violates the Commerce Clause.

Mr. Justice Stewart delivered the opinion of the Court.

. . . The statutory provision . . . took effect in early 1974. . . . Apart from . . . narrow exceptions, . . . New Jersey closed its borders to all waste from other States.

Immediately affected by these developments were the operators of private landfills in New Jersey, and several cities in other States that had agreements with these operators for waste disposal. They brought suit against New Jersey and its Department of Environmental Protection in state court, attacking the statute and regulations on a number of state and federal grounds. . . . [T]he trial court declared the law unconstitutional because it discriminated against interstate commerce. The New Jersey Supreme Court . . . reversed. It found that [the statute] advanced vital health and environmental objectives with no economic discrimination against, and with little burden upon, interstate commerce, and that the law was therefore permissible under the Commerce Clause of the Constitution. . . .

The state court reached this conclusion in an attempt to reconcile modern Commerce Clause concepts with several old cases of this Court holding that States can prohibit the importation of some objects because they "are not legitimate subjects of trade and commerce." . . . These articles include items "which, on account of their existing condition, would bring in and spread disease, pestilence, and death, such as rags or other substances infected with the germs of yellow fever or the virus of small-pox, or cattle or meat or other provisions that are diseased or decayed, or otherwise, from their condition and quality, unfit for human use or consumption." . . . The state court found that . . . the state regulations banned only "those wastes which can [not] be put to effective use," and therefore those wastes were not commerce at all, unless "the mere transportation and disposal of valueless waste between states constitutes interstate commerce within the meaning of the constitutional provision." . . .

We think the state court misread our cases, and thus erred in assuming that they require a two-tiered definition of commerce. . . . All objects of interstate trade merit Commerce Clause protection; none is excluded by definition at the outset. . . . Hence, we reject the state court's suggestion that the banning of "valueless" out-of-state wastes . . . implicates no constitutional protection. Just as Congress has power to regulate the interstate movement of these wastes, States are not free from constitutional scrutiny when they restrict that movement. . . .

The opinions of the Court through the years have reflected an alertness to the evils of "economic isolation" and protectionism, while at the same time recognizing that incidental burdens on interstate commerce may be unavoidable when a State legislates to safeguard the health and safety of its people. Thus, where simple economic protectionism is effected by state legislation, a virtually *per se* rule of invalidity has been erected. . . . The clearest example of such legislation is a law that overtly blocks the flow of interstate commerce at a State's borders. . . . But where other legislative objectives are credibly advanced and there is no patent discrimination against interstate trade, the Court has adopted a much more flexible approach. . . . The crucial inquiry . . . must be directed to determining whether [the New Jersey statute] is basically a protectionist measure, or whether it can fairly be viewed as a law directed to legitimate local concerns, which effects upon interstate commerce that are only incidental.

. . . [Philadelphia] strenuously contend[s] that [New Jersey's law], "while outwardly cloaked 'in the currently fashionable garb of environmental protection,' . . . is actually no more than a legislative effort to suppress competition and stabilize the cost of solid waste disposal for New Jersey residents. . . ."

[New Jersey], on the other hand, [denies that its law] was motivated by financial concerns or economic protectionism. . . .

This dispute about ultimate legislative purpose need not be resolved, because its resolution would not be relevant to the constitutional issue to be decided in this case. Contrary to the evident assumption of . . . the parties, the evil of protectionism can reside in legislative means as well as legislative ends. Thus, it does not matter whether the ultimate aim of [the statute] is to reduce the waste disposal costs of New Jersey residents or to save remaining open lands from pollution, for we assume New Jersey has every right to protect its residents' pocketbooks as well as their environment. And it may be assumed as well that

New Jersey may pursue those ends by slowing the flow of all waste into the State's remaining landfills, even though interstate commerce may incidentally be affected. But whatever New Jersey's ultimate purpose, it may not be accomplished by discriminating against articles of commerce coming from outside the State unless there is some reason, apart from their origin, to treat them differently. Both on its face and in its plain effect, [New Jersey's law] violates this principle of nondiscrimination.

The Court has consistently found parochial legislation of this kind to be constitutionally invalid, whether the ultimate aim of the legislation was to assure a steady supply of milk by erecting barriers to allegedly ruinous outside competition, . . . or to create jobs by keeping industry within the State, . . . or to preserve the State's financial resources from depletion by fencing out indigent immigrants. . . . In each of these [instances], a presumably legitimate goal was sought to be achieved by the illegitimate means of isolating the State from the national economy. . . .

The New Jersey law at issue in this case falls squarely within the area that the Commerce Clause puts off-limits to state regulation. On its face, it imposes on out-of-state commercial interests the full burden of conserving the State's remaining landfill space. . . . [T]he State has overtly moved to slow or freeze the flow of commerce for protectionist reasons. . . . What is crucial is the attempt by one State to isolate itself from a problem common to many by erecting a barrier against the movement of interstate trade.

[New Jersey argues] that not all laws which facially discriminate against out-of-state commerce are forbidden protectionist regulations. In particular, they point to quarantine laws, which this Court has repeatedly upheld even though they appear to single out interstate commerce for special treatment. . . . [In New Jersey's view, the statute] is analogous to such health-protective measures, since it reduces the exposure of New Jersey residents to the allegedly harmful effects of landfill sites.

It is true that certain quarantine laws have not been considered forbidden protectionist measures, even though they were directed against out-of-state commerce. . . . But those quarantine laws banned the importation of articles such as diseased livestock that required destruction as soon as possible because their very movement risked contagion and other evils. Those laws thus did not discriminate against interstate commerce as such, but simply prevented traffic in noxious articles, whatever their origin.

The New Jersey statute is not such a quarantine law. There has been no claim here that the very movement of waste into or through New Jersey endangers health, or that waste must be disposed of as soon and as close to its point of generation as possible. The harms caused by waste are said to arise after its disposal in landfill sites, and at that point, as New Jersey concedes, there is no basis to distinguish out-of-state waste from domestic waste. If one is inherently harmful, so is the other. Yet New Jersey has banned the former while leaving its landfill sites open to the latter. The New Jersey law blocks the importation of waste in an obvious effort to saddle those outside the State with the entire burden of slowing the flow of refuse into New Jersey's remaining landfill sites. That legislative effort is clearly impermissible under the Commerce Clause of the Constitution.

Today, cities in Pennsylvania and New York find it expedient or necessary to send their waste into New Jersey for disposal, and New Jersey claims the right to close its borders to such traffic. Tomorrow, cities in New Jersey may find it expedient or necessary to send their waste into Pennsylvania or New York for disposal, and those States might then claim the right to close their borders. The Commerce Clause will protect New Jersey in the future, just as it protects her neighbors now, from efforts by one State to isolate itself in the stream of interstate commerce from a problem shared by all.

The judgment is reversed.

Mr. Justice Rehnquist, with whom the *Chief Justice* joins, dissenting.

The question presented in this case is whether New Jersey must . . . continue to receive and dispose of solid waste from neighboring States, even though these will inexorably increase . . . health problems. . . . The Court answers this question in the affirmative. New Jersey must either prohibit all landfill operations, leaving itself to cast about for a presently nonexistent solution to the serious problem of disposing of the waste generated within its own borders, or it must accept waste from every portion of the United States, thereby multiplying the health and safety problems which would result if it dealt only with such wastes generated within the State. Because past precedents establish that the Commerce Clause does not present [New Jersey] with such a Hobson's choice, I dissent. . . .

. . . The physical fact of life that New Jersey must somehow dispose of its own noxious items does not mean that it must serve as a depository for those of every other State. . . . New Jersey should be free under our past precedents to prohibit the importation of solid waste because of the health and safety problems that such waste poses to its citizens. The fact that New Jersey continues to, and indeed must continue to, dispose of its own solid waste does not mean that New Jersey may not prohibit the importation of even more solid waste into the State. I simply see no way to distinguish solid waste, on the record of this case, from germ-infected rags, diseased meat, and other noxious items. . . .

. . . I do not see why a State may ban the importation of items whose movement risks contagion, but cannot ban the importation of items which, although they may be transported into the State without undue hazard, will then simply pile up in an ever increasing danger to the public's health and safety. The Commerce Clause was not drawn with a view to having the validity of state laws turn on such pointless distinctions.

. . . The fact that New Jersey has left its landfill sites open for domestic waste does not, of course, mean that solid waste is not innately harmful. Nor does it mean that New Jersey prohibits importation of solid waste for reasons other than the health and safety of its population. New Jersey must out of sheer necessity treat and dispose of its solid waste in some fashion. . . . It does not follow that New Jersey must, under the Commerce Clause, accept solid waste . . . from outside its borders and thereby exacerbate its problems.

. . . Because I find no basis for distinguishing the laws under challenge here from our past cases upholding state laws that prohibit the importation of items that could endanger the population of the State, I dissent.

Case

OREGON WASTE SYSTEMS V. DEPARTMENT OF ENVIRONMENTAL QUALITY

511 U.S. 93; 114 S.Ct. 1345; 128 L.Ed. 2d 13 (1994)

Vote: 7–2

In Chemical Waste Management, Inc. v. Hunt (1992), the Supreme Court held that the Commerce Clause prohibited the state of Alabama from imposing a higher fee on the disposal of hazardous waste from other states than on the disposal of identical waste from Alabama. The Court's opinion suggested, however, that a surcharge might be acceptable if it was based on the increased costs of handling out-of-state waste. In the present case, the Court considers whether Oregon's allegedly cost-based surcharge on the disposal of out-of-state waste violates the Commerce Clause.

Justice Thomas delivered the opinion of the Court.

. . . Like other States, Oregon comprehensively regulates the disposal of solid wastes within its borders. Respondent Oregon Department of Environmental Quality oversees the State's regulatory scheme by developing and executing plans for the management, reduction, and recycling of solid wastes. To fund these and related activities, Oregon levies a wide range of fees on landfill operators. . . . In 1989, the Oregon Legislature imposed an additional fee, called a "surcharge," on "every person who disposes of solid waste generated out-of-state in a disposal site or regional disposal site." . . . The amount of that surcharge was left to respondent Environmental Quality Commission (Commission) to determine through rulemaking, but the legislature did require that the resulting surcharge "be based on the costs to the State of Oregon and its political subdivisions of disposing of solid waste generated out-of-state which are not otherwise paid for" under specified statutes. . . . At the conclusion of the rulemaking process, the Commission set the surcharge on out-of-state waste at $2.25 per ton.

In conjunction with the out-of-state surcharge, the legislature imposed a fee on the in-state disposal of waste generated within Oregon. . . . The in-state fee, capped by statute at $0.85 per ton (originally $0.50 per ton), is considerably lower than the fee imposed on waste from other States. . . . Subsequently, the legislature conditionally extended the $0.85 per ton fee to out-of-state waste, in addition to the $2.25 per ton surcharge, . . . with the proviso that if the surcharge survived judicial challenge, the $0.85 per ton fee would again be limited to in-state waste. . . .

The anticipated court challenge was not long in coming. Petitioners, Oregon Waste Systems, Inc. (Oregon Waste) and Columbia Resource Company (CRC), joined by Gilliam County, Oregon, sought expedited review of the out-of-state surcharge in the Oregon Court of Appeals. Oregon Waste owns and operates a solid waste landfill in Gilliam County, at which it accepts for final disposal solid waste generated in Oregon and in other States. CRC, pursuant to a 20-year contract with Clark County, in neighboring Washington State, transports solid waste via barge from Clark County to a landfill in Morrow County, Oregon. Petitioners challenged the administrative rule establishing the out-of-state surcharge and its enabling statutes under both state law and the Commerce Clause of the United States Constitution. The Oregon Court of Appeals upheld the statutes and rule. . . .

The State Supreme Court affirmed. . . .

We granted certiorari, . . . because the decision below conflicted with a recent decision of the United States Court of Appeals for the Seventh Circuit. We now reverse.

The Commerce Clause provides that "[t]he Congress shall have Power . . . [t]o regulate Commerce . . . among the several States." . . . Though phrased as a grant of regulatory power to Congress, the Clause has long been understood to have a "negative" aspect that denies the States the power unjustifiably to discriminate against or burden the interstate flow of articles of commerce. . . . The Framers granted Congress plenary authority over interstate commerce "in the conviction that in order to succeed, the new Union would have to avoid the tendencies toward economic Balkanization that had plagued relations among the Colonies and later among the States under the Articles of Confederation." . . . "This principle that our economic unity is the Nation, which alone has the gamut of powers necessary to control of the economy, . . . has as its corollary that the states are not separable economic units." . . .

Consistent with these principles, we have held that the first step in analyzing any law subject to judicial scrutiny under the negative Commerce Clause is to determine whether it "regulates evenhandedly with only 'incidental' effects on interstate commerce, or discriminates against interstate commerce." . . . As we use the term here, "discrimination" simply means differential treatment of in-state and out-of-state economic interests that benefits the former and burdens the latter. If a restriction on commerce is discriminatory, it is virtually *per se* invalid. . . . By contrast, nondiscriminatory regulations that have only incidental effects on interstate commerce are valid unless "the burden imposed on such commerce is clearly excessive in relation to the putative local benefits." . . .

In *Chemical Waste* [*Management v. Hunt* (1992)], we easily found Alabama's surcharge on hazardous waste from other States to be facially discriminatory because it imposed a higher fee on the disposal of out-of-state waste than on the disposal of identical in-state waste. . . . We deem it equally obvious here that Oregon's $2.25 per ton surcharge is discriminatory on its face. The surcharge subjects waste from other States to a fee almost three times greater than the $0.85 per ton charge imposed on solid in-state waste. The statutory determinant for which fee applies to any particular shipment of solid waste to an Oregon landfill is whether or not the waste was "generated out-of-state." . . . It is well-established, however, that a law is discriminatory if it "tax[es] a transaction or incident more heavily when it crosses state lines than when it occurs entirely within the State." . . .

Respondents argue, and the Oregon Supreme Court held, that the statutory nexus between the surcharge and "the [otherwise uncompensated] costs to the State of Ore-

gon and its political subdivisions of disposing of solid waste generated out-of-state," . . . necessarily precludes a finding that the surcharge is discriminatory. We find respondents' narrow focus on Oregon's compensatory aim to be foreclosed by our precedents. As we reiterated in *Chemical Waste,* the purpose of, or justification for, a law has no bearing on whether it is facially discriminatory. . . . Consequently, even if the surcharge merely recoups the costs of disposing of out-of-state waste in Oregon, the fact remains that the differential charge favors shippers of Oregon waste over their counterparts handling waste generated in other States. In making that geographic distinction, the surcharge patently discriminates against interstate commerce.

Because the Oregon surcharge is discriminatory, the virtually *per se* rule of invalidity provides the proper legal standard here. . . . As a result, the surcharge must be invalidated unless respondents can "sho[w] that it advances a legitimate local purpose that cannot be adequately served by reasonable nondiscriminatory alternatives." . . . Our cases require that justifications for discriminatory restrictions on commerce pass the "strictest scrutiny." . . . The State's burden of justification is so heavy that "facial discrimination by itself may be a fatal defect." . . .

At the outset, we note two justifications that respondents have *not* presented. No claim has been made that the disposal of waste from other States imposes higher costs on Oregon and its political subdivisions than the disposal of in-state waste. Also, respondents have not offered any safety or health reason unique to nonhazardous waste from other States for discouraging the flow of such waste into Oregon. . . . Consequently, respondents must come forward with other legitimate reasons to subject waste from other States to a higher charge than is levied against waste from Oregon. . . .

Respondents' principal defense of the higher surcharge on out-of-state waste is that it is a "compensatory tax" necessary to make shippers of such waste pay their "fair share" of the costs imposed on Oregon by the disposal of their waste in the State. In *Chemical Waste* we noted the possibility that such an argument might justify a discriminatory surcharge or tax on out-of-state waste. . . . In making that observation, we implicitly recognized the settled principle that interstate commerce may be made to "pay its way." . . . "It was not the purpose of the Commerce Clause to relieve those engaged in interstate commerce from their just share of state tax burden[s]." . . . Nevertheless, one of the central purposes of the Clause was to prevent States from "exacting *more* than a just share" from interstate commerce. . . .

At least since our decision in *Hinson v. Lott* . . . (1868), these principles have found expression in the "compensatory" or "complementary" tax doctrine. Though our cases sometimes discuss the concept of the compensatory tax as if it were a doctrine unto itself, it is merely a specific way of justifying a facially discriminatory tax as achieving a legitimate local purpose that cannot be achieved through nondiscriminatory means. . . . Under that doctrine, a facially discriminatory tax that imposes on interstate commerce the rough equivalent of an identifiable and "substantially similar" tax on intrastate commerce does not offend the negative Commerce Clause. . . .

To justify a charge on interstate commerce as a compensatory tax, a State must, as a threshold matter, "identify . . . the [intrastate tax] burden for which the State is attempting to compensate." . . . Once that burden has been identified, the tax on interstate commerce must be shown roughly to approximate—but not exceed—the amount of the tax on intrastate commerce. . . . Finally, the events on which the interstate and intrastate taxes are imposed must be "substantially equivalent"; that is, they must be sufficiently similar in substance to serve as mutually exclusive "prox[ies]" for each other. . . .

Although it is often no mean feat to determine whether a challenged tax is a compensatory tax, we have little difficulty concluding that the Oregon surcharge is not such a tax. Oregon does not impose a specific charge of at least $2.25 per ton on shippers of waste generated in Oregon, for which the out-of-state surcharge might be considered compensatory. In fact, the only analogous charge on the disposal of Oregon waste is $0.85 per ton, approximately one-third of the amount imposed on waste from other States. . . . Respondents' failure to identify a specific charge on intrastate commerce equal to or exceeding the surcharge is fatal to their claim. . . .

Respondents argue that, despite the absence of a specific $2.25 per ton charge on in-state waste, intrastate commerce does pay its share of the costs underlying the surcharge through general taxation. Whether or not that is true is difficult to determine, as "[general] tax payments are received for the general purposes of the [government], and are, upon proper receipt, lost in the general revenues." . . . Even assuming, however, that various other means of general taxation, such as income taxes, could serve as an identifiable intrastate burden roughly equivalent to the out-of-state surcharge, respondents' compensatory tax argument fails because the in-state and out-of-state levies are not imposed on substantially equivalent events.

The prototypical example of substantially equivalent taxable events is the sale and use of articles of trade. . . . In fact, use taxes on products purchased out of state are the only taxes we have upheld in recent memory under the compensatory tax doctrine. . . . Indeed, the very fact that

in-state shippers of out-of-state waste, such as Oregon Waste, are charged the out-of-state surcharge even though they pay Oregon income taxes refutes respondents' argument that the respective taxable events are substantially equivalent. . . . We conclude that, far from being substantially equivalent, taxes on earning income and utilizing Oregon landfills are "entirely different kind[s] of tax[es]." . . . We are no more inclined here . . . to "plunge . . . into the morass of weighing comparative tax burdens" by comparing taxes on dissimilar events. . . .

Respondents' final argument is that Oregon has an interest in spreading the costs of the in-state disposal of Oregon waste to all Oregonians. That is, because all citizens of Oregon benefit from the proper in-state disposal of waste from Oregon, respondents claim it is only proper for Oregon to require them to bear more of the costs of disposing of such waste in the State through a higher general tax burden. At the same time, however, Oregon citizens should not be required to bear the costs of disposing of out-of-state waste, respondents claim. The necessary result of that limited cost-shifting is to require shippers of out-of-state waste to bear the full costs of in-state disposal, but to permit shippers of Oregon waste to bear less than the full cost.

We fail to perceive any distinction between respondents' contention and a claim that the State has an interest in reducing the costs of handling in-state waste. Our cases condemn as illegitimate, however, any governmental interest that is not "unrelated to economic protectionism," . . . and regulating interstate commerce in such a way as to give those who handle domestic articles of commerce a cost advantage over their competitors handling similar items produced elsewhere constitutes such protectionism. . . . To give controlling effect to respondents' characterization of Oregon's tax scheme as seemingly benign cost-spreading would require us to overlook the fact that the scheme necessarily incorporates a protectionist objective as well. . . .

Respondents counter that if Oregon is engaged in any form of protectionism, it is "resource protectionism," not economic protectionism. It is true that by discouraging the flow of out-of-state waste into Oregon landfills, the higher surcharge on waste from other States conserves more space in those landfills for waste generated in Oregon. Recharacterizing the surcharge as resource protectionism hardly advances respondents' cause, however. Even assuming that landfill space is a "natural resource," "a State may not accord its own inhabitants a preferred right of access over consumers in other States to natural resources located within its borders." . . .

We recognize that the States have broad discretion to configure their system of taxation as they deem appropriate. . . . All we intimate here is that their discretion in this regard, as in all others, is bounded by any relevant limitations of the Federal Constitution, in this case the negative Commerce Clause. Because respondents have offered no legitimate reason to subject waste generated in other States to a discriminatory surcharge approximately three times as high as that imposed on waste generated in Oregon, the surcharge is facially invalid under the negative Commerce Clause. Accordingly, the judgment of the Oregon Supreme Court is reversed, and the cases are remanded for further proceedings not inconsistent with this opinion. . . .

Chief Justice Rehnquist, with whom **Justice Blackmun** joins, dissenting.

. . . The State of Oregon responsibly attempted to address its solid waste disposal problem through enactment of a comprehensive regulatory scheme for the management, disposal, reduction, and recycling of solid waste. For this Oregon should be applauded. The regulatory scheme included a fee charged on out-of-state solid waste. The Oregon Legislature directed the Commission to determine the appropriate surcharge "based on the costs . . . of disposing of solid waste generated out-of-state." . . . The Commission arrived at a surcharge of $2.25 per ton compared to the $0.85 per ton charged on in-state solid waste. . . . The surcharge works out to an increase of about $0.14 per week for the typical out-of-state solid waste producer. . . . This seems a small price to pay for the right to deposit your "garbage, rubbish, refuse . . .; sewage sludge, septic tank and cesspool pumpings or other sludge; . . . manure, . . . dead animals, [and] infectious waste" on your neighbors. . . .

Nearly 20 years ago, we held that a State cannot ban all out-of-state waste disposal in protecting themselves from hazardous or noxious materials brought across the State's borders. . . . Two terms ago in *Chemical Waste Management, Inc. v. Hunt* . . . (1992), in striking down the State of Alabama's $72 per ton fee on the disposal of out-of-state hazardous waste, the Court left open the possibility that such a fee could be valid if based on the cost of disposing of waste from other States. . . . Once again, however, as in *Philadelphia* [*v. New Jersey*] and *Chemical Waste Management*, the Court further cranks the dormant Commerce Clause ratchet against the States by striking down such cost-based fees, and by so doing ties the hands of the States in addressing the vexing national problem of solid waste disposal. I dissent. . . .

The State of Oregon is not prohibiting the export of solid waste from neighboring States; it is only asking that those neighbors pay their fair share for the use of Oregon landfill sites. I see nothing in the Commerce Clause that compels less densely populated States to serve as the low-cost dumping grounds for their neighbors, suffering the attendant risks that solid waste landfills present. The Court, deciding otherwise, further limits the dwindling options available to States as they contend with the environmental, health, safety, and political challenges posed by the problem of solid waste disposal in modern society. . . .

PART 2

CIVIL RIGHTS AND LIBERTIES

Robert H. Jackson: Associate Justice, 1941–1954

"Government of limited power need not be anemic government. Assurance that rights are secure tends to diminish fear and jealousy of strong government, and by making us feel safe to live under it makes for its better support. Without promise of a limiting Bill of Rights it is doubtful if our Constitution could have mustered enough strength to enable its ratification. To enforce those rights today is not to choose weak government over strong government. It is only to adhere as a means of strength to individual freedom of mind in preference to officially disciplined uniformity for which history indicates a disappointing and disastrous end."

—JUSTICE ROBERT H. JACKSON, WRITING FOR THE COURT IN *WEST VIRGINIA BOARD OF EDUCATION V. BARNETTE* (1943)

6

CONSTITUTIONAL SOURCES OF CIVIL RIGHTS AND LIBERTIES

Thurgood Marshall:
Associate Justice, 1967–1991

"[H]istory makes clear that constitutional principles of equality, like constitutional principles of liberty, property, and due process, evolve over time; what once was a 'natural' and 'self-evident' ordering later comes to be seen as an artificial and invidious constraint on human potential and freedom."

—JUSTICE THURGOOD MARSHALL, CONCURRING IN THE JUDGMENT IN *CITY OF CLEBURNE V. CLEBURNE LIVING CENTER* (1985)

"By extending constitutional protection to an asserted right or liberty interest, we, to a great extent, place the matter outside the arena of public debate and legislative action. We must therefore 'exercise the utmost care whenever we are asked to break new ground in this field,' . . . lest the liberty protected by the Due Process Clause be subtly transformed into the policy preferences of the members of this Court."

—CHIEF JUSTICE WILLIAM H. REHNQUIST, WRITING FOR THE COURT IN *WASHINGTON V. GLUCKSBERG* (1997)

William H. Rehnquist:
Associate Justice, 1972–1986;
Chief Justice, 1986–

INTRODUCTION

One of the principal objectives of the U.S. Constitution, as stated in its preamble, is "to secure the Blessings of Liberty to ourselves and our Posterity." The Framers of the Constitution thus recognized the protection of individual liberty as a fundamental goal of constitutional government. Paraphrasing John Locke, the Declaration of Independence (1776) had declared the **unalienable rights** of man to be "life, liberty and the pursuit of happiness." Other more specific rights, including trial by jury and freedom of speech, were generally embraced by Americans, legacies of the Magna Carta (1215) and the English Bill of Rights (1689). The Framers of the Constitution sought to protect these rights by creating a system of government that would be inherently restricted in power and, hence, limited in its ability to transgress the rights of the individual.

The founders were heavily influenced by the theory of **natural rights**, in which rights are seen as inherently belonging to individuals, not as created by government. According to this view, individuals have the right to do whatever they please unless (1) they interfere with the rights of others or (2) government is constitutionally empowered to act to restrict the exercise of that freedom. The founders thus conceived of the powers of government as mere islands in a vast sea of individual rights. This was especially true of the newly created national government, which was limited to the exercise of delegated powers. The original Constitution thus contained no provision guaranteeing freedom of religion, because the Constitution gave the federal government no authority to regulate religion. Yet the Framers did recognize certain rights, at least indirectly, by enumerating specific limitations on the national government and the states.

During the debate over ratification of the Constitution, a consensus emerged that the Constitution should be more explicit as to the rights of individuals. Reflecting this consensus, the First Congress in 1789 adopted the Bill of Rights, which was ratified in 1791. This prompt response by Congress and the States underscored the strong national commitment to individual freedom.

Liberty, however, is only one aspect of constitutional rights. Equally critical in a constitutional democracy is the ideal of **equality.** Although the Framers of the original Constitution were less interested in equality than in liberty, the Constitution has come to be considerably more egalitarian over the years, both through formal amendment and through judicial interpretation. In its constitutional sense, equality means that all citizens are considered to be equal before the law, equal before the state, and equal in their possession of rights. The term **civil rights**, as distinct from **civil liberties**, is generally used to denote citizens' equality claims, as distinct from their liberty claims.

The subject matter of civil rights and liberties is far ranging, touching on most contemporary social, political, and economic issues. School prayer, gay rights, abortion, doctor-assisted suicide, and affirmative action are a few of the more salient policy questions the courts have addressed in recent years in disputes over the meaning of particular civil rights and liberties protections. The Supreme Court's rulings on such issues comprise a major aspect of contemporary American constitutional law and, accordingly, are the subject of Part II of this textbook.

RIGHTS RECOGNIZED IN THE ORIGINAL CONSTITUTION

As noted, the original, unamended Constitution contained few explicit protections of individual rights. This was not because the Framers did not value rights, but because they thought it unnecessary to deal with them explicitly. Significantly, most of the state constitutions adopted during the American Revolution contained fairly detailed bills of rights placing limits on state and local governments. The Framers did not anticipate the growth of a pervasive national government and thus did not regard the extensive enumeration of individual rights in the federal Constitution as critical. They did, however, recognize a few important safeguards in the original Constitution.

Circumscribing the Crime of Treason

The Framers of the Constitution, having recently participated in a successful revolution, were understandably sensitive to the prospect that government could employ the crime of **treason** to stifle **political dissent**. Thus, they provided in Article III, Section 3, that "Treason against the United States, shall consist only in levying War against them, or in adhering to their Enemies, giving them Aid and Comfort." To protect citizens against unwarranted prosecution for treason, the Framers further specified that "[n]o Person shall be convicted of Treason unless on the Testimony of two Witnesses to the same overt Act, or on Confession in open Court."

Prohibition of Religious Tests for Public Office

Article VI of the Constitution provides, among other things, that "no religious Test shall ever be required as a Qualification to any Office or public Trust under the United States." This clause means, in effect, that personal views regarding religion may not officially qualify or disqualify one for public service. The prohibition against **religious tests** reflects the Framers' commitment to the idea that government ought to be neutral with respect to matters of religion, a view that was strongly reinforced by adoption of the **Establishment Clause** of the First Amendment (see Chapter 9).

Habeas Corpus

Article I, Section 9, of the Constitution states that "the Privilege of the Writ of Habeas Corpus shall not be suspended, unless when in Cases of Rebellion or Invasion the public Safety may require it." Grounded in English common law, the writ of habeas corpus gives effect to the all-important right of the individual not to be held in unlawful custody. Specifically, **habeas corpus** ("you have the body") enables a court to review a custodial situation and order the release of an individual who is found to have been illegally incarcerated. This right has many applications, but the most common is in the criminal context, in which an individual is arrested and held in custody but denied due process of law. In adopting the habeas corpus provision of Article I, Section 9, the Framers wanted not only to recognize the right but also to limit its suspension to emergency situations. The Constitution is ambiguous as to which branch of government has the authority to suspend the writ of habeas corpus during emergencies. As noted in Chapter 3, early in the Civil War President Lincoln authorized military commanders to suspend the writ. Congress ultimately confirmed the president's action through legislation. During the Second World War, the writ of habeas corpus was suspended in the territory of Hawaii.

The writ of habeas corpus is an important element in modern criminal procedure. As a result of legislation passed by Congress in 1867 and subsequent judicial interpretation of that legislation, a person convicted of a crime in a state court and sentenced to state prison may petition a federal district court for habeas corpus relief. This permits a federal court to review the constitutional correctness of the arrest, trial, and sentencing of a state prisoner.

Under Chief Justice Earl Warren, the Supreme Court broadened the scope of federal habeas corpus review of state criminal convictions by permitting prisoners to raise issues in federal court that they did not raise in their state appeals (see, for example, *Fay v. Noia* [1963]). The more conservative Burger and Rehnquist Courts significantly restricted state prisoners' access to federal habeas corpus (see, for example, *Stone v. Powell* [1976] and *McCleskey v. Zant* [1991]). Nevertheless, the continuing controversy over federal habeas corpus review of state criminal convictions prompted Congress to place further restrictions on the availability of the writ. The Antiterrorism and Effective Death Penalty Act of 1996 curtailed habeas corpus petitions by state prisoners who have already filed such petitions in federal court. Of course, because Congress initially provided this jurisdiction to the federal courts by statute, Congress may modify or abolish this jurisdiction if it so desires. It is unlikely, though, that Congress would eliminate federal habeas review of state criminal cases altogether (for further discussion, see Chapter 10).

Ex Post Facto Laws

Article I, Section 9, of the Constitution prohibits Congress from passing *ex post facto* **laws.** Article I, Section 10, imposes the same prohibition on state legislatures. *Ex post facto* laws (literally, "after the fact") are laws passed after the occurrence of an act that alter the legal status or consequences of that act. In *Calder v. Bull* (1798), the Supreme Court held that the *ex post facto* clauses applied to criminal but not to civil laws. According to Justice Samuel Chase's opinion in that case, impermissible *ex post facto* laws are those that "create or aggravate . . . [a] crime; or increase the punishment, or change the rules of evidence, for the purpose of conviction." Retrospective laws dealing with civil matters are thus not prohibited by the *ex post facto* clauses.

In two cases decided during the late nineteenth century, *Kring v. Missouri* (1883) and *Thompson v. Utah* (1898), the Supreme Court broadened the definition of *ex post facto* laws to prohibit certain changes in criminal procedure that might prove disadvantageous to the accused. However, in *Collins v. Youngblood* (1990), the Supreme Court overruled these precedents and returned to the definition adopted in *Calder v. Bull*. For an act to be invalidated as an *ex post facto* law, two key elements must exist. First, the act must be retroactive—it must apply to events that occurred before its passage. Second, it must seriously disadvantage the accused, not merely by changes in procedure but by means that render conviction more likely or punishment more severe.

Judicial decisions relying on the Ex Post Facto Clause are uncommon today. But during its 1999 term, the Supreme Court handed down a ruling in this area. In *Carmell v. Texas* (2000), the Court reversed convictions on four sexual assault charges. The convictions were for assaults that occurred in 1991 and 1992, when Texas law provided that a defendant could not be convicted merely on the testimony of the victim unless he or she was under age 14. At the time of the alleged assaults, the victim was 14 or 15. The law was later amended to extend the "child victim exception" to victims under 18 years old. Carmell was convicted under the amended law, which the Supreme Court held to be an *ex post facto* law. Writing for the Court, Justice Stevens observed that "[u]nder the law in effect at the time the acts were committed, the prosecution's case was legally insufficient . . . unless the State could produce both the victim's testimony *and* corroborative evidence."

Bills of Attainder

Article I, Sections 9 and 10, also prohibit Congress and the states, respectively, from adopting bills of attainder. A **bill of attainder** is a legislative act that imposes punishment on a person without benefit of a trial in a court of law.

Perhaps the best known cases involving bills of attainder are the test oath cases of 1867. In *Ex parte Garland*, the Court struck down an 1865 federal statute forbidding attorneys from practicing before federal courts unless they took an oath that they had not supported the Confederacy during the Civil War. In *Cummings v. Missouri* (1866), the Court voided a provision of the Missouri Constitution that required a similar oath of all persons who wished to be employed in a variety of occupations, including the ministry. Cummings, a Catholic priest, had been fined $500 for preaching without having taken the oath. The Court found that these laws violated both the bill of attainder and *ex post facto* provisions of Article I.

Since World War II, the Supreme Court has declared only two acts of Congress invalid as bills of attainder. The first instance was *United States v. Lovett* (1946), in which the Court struck down a rider to an appropriations measure that prohibited three named federal employees from receiving compensation from the government. The three individuals had been branded by the House Un-American Activities Committee as "subversives." The Court said that legislative acts "that apply either to named individuals or to easily ascertainable members of a group in such a way as to inflict punishment on them without a judicial trial are bills of attainder prohibited by the Constitution."

In *United States v. Brown* (1965), the Court invalidated a law that prohibited members of the Communist Party from serving as officers in trade unions, saying that Congress had inflicted punishment on "easily ascertainable members of a group." Four justices dissented, however, citing a number of legislative prohibitions on members of the Communist Party that the Court had previously upheld (see, for example, *American Communications Association v. Douds* [1950]).

The Supreme Court considered an interesting bill of attainder issue in *Nixon v. Administrator of General Services* (1977). In this case, former President Richard Nixon challenged the Presidential Recordings and Materials Preservation Act of 1974, in which Congress had placed control of Nixon's presidential papers and recordings in the hands of the General Services Administration, an agency of the federal government. Nixon argued that the law singled him out for punishment by depriving him of the traditional right of presidents to control their own presidential papers. The Court ruled 7 to 2 that the act was not a bill of attainder, concluding that Congress's purpose in passing the law was not punitive.

The Contracts Clause

After the Revolutionary War, the thirteen states comprising the newly formed Union experienced a difficult period of political and economic instability. Numerous citizens, especially farmers, defaulted on their loans. Many were imprisoned under the harsh debtor laws of the period. Some state legislatures adopted laws to alleviate the plight of debtors. Cheap paper money was made legal tender; bankruptcy laws were adopted; in some states, creditors' access to the courts was restricted; some states prohibited imprisonment for debt. These policies, while commonplace today, were at that time anathema to the wealthy. Members of the creditor class believed that serious steps had to be taken to prevent the states from abrogating debts and interfering with contracts generally.

It is fair to say that one of the motivations behind the Constitutional Convention of 1787 was the desire to secure overriding legal protection for contracts. Thus, Article I, Section 10, prohibits states from passing laws "impairing the Obligation of Contracts." The **Contracts Clause** must be included among the provisions of the original Constitution that protect individual rights—in this case, the right of individuals to be free from governmental interference with their contractual relationships.

By protecting contracts, Article I, Section 10, performed an important function in the early years of American economic development. Historically, the Contracts Clause was an important source of litigation in the federal courts. In modern times, it is seldom interpreted to impose significant limits on the states in the field of economic regulation. (The Contracts Clause is discussed more fully in Chapter 7.)

TO SUMMARIZE:

- Apart from the provisions of the first ten amendments, various provisions of Article I, Sections 9 and 10, recognize individual rights by placing restrictions on the federal government and the states, respectively.
- The specific provisions defining and limiting the crime of treason apply only to the federal government, as does the prohibition against religious tests for holding public office.
- The protection of the writ of habeas corpus also applies specifically to the federal government and, in effect, may not be suspended except in cases of national emergency.
- Two provisions of the original Constitution protect certain individual rights against both federal and state encroachment. These are the prohibitions of *ex post facto* laws and bills of attainder.
- The Contracts Clause of Article I, Section 10, imposes limitations on state interference with contractual rights and obligations. In the early years of the republic, this provision served as a major basis for federal judicial protection of private property rights.

THE BILL OF RIGHTS

As previously noted, the original Constitution contained little by way of explicit protection of individual rights. In *The Federalist*, No. 84, Alexander Hamilton argued that since the Constitution provided for limited government through enumerated powers, a Bill of Rights was unnecessary. In rebuttal, Anti-Federalists argued that the Necessary and Proper Clause of Article I, Section 8, could be used to justify expansive government power that might threaten individual liberties. As we saw in Chapter 5, the Anti-Federalists were definitely on target.

The omission of a bill of rights from the original Constitution was regarded as a major defect by numerous critics and even threatened to derail ratification in some states. Thomas Jefferson, who had not participated in the Constitutional Convention due to his diplomatic duties in France, was among the most influential critics. In a letter to his close friend James Madison, Jefferson argued, "You must specify your liberties, and put them down on paper." Madison, the acknowledged father of the Constitution, thought it unwise and unnecessary to enumerate individual rights, but Jefferson's view eventually prevailed. Honoring a "gentleman's agreement" designed to secure ratification of the Constitution in several key states, the 1st Congress considered a proposed bill of rights drafted by Madison.

Madison's original bill of rights called for limitations on the states as well as the federal government, but this proposal was defeated by states' rights advocates in Congress. Twelve amendments to the Constitution were adopted by Congress in September 1789. Although two of these amendments were rejected by the states, the other ten were ratified in November 1791 and were added to the Constitution as the Bill of Rights.

The First Amendment

The **First Amendment** provides a number of crucial guarantees of freedom. The Establishment Clause prohibits Congress from making laws "respecting an establishment of religion," while the **Free Exercise Clause** enjoins the national government from "prohibiting the free exercise thereof." These first two clauses demonstrate the fundamental character of the founders' devotion to freedom of religion. Today, the Religion Clauses remain both important and controversial, involving such emotional issues as prayer and the teaching of "creation science" in the public schools. (The Religion Clauses of the First Amendment are examined in Chapter 9.)

The First Amendment also protects **freedom of speech** and **freedom of the press**, often referred to jointly as **freedom of expression.** One can argue that freedom of expression is the most vital freedom in a democracy, in that it permits the free flow of information between the people and their government. Certainly the authors of the Bill of Rights were aware of its fundamental importance, which is why the freedoms of speech and press were placed in the First Amendment. Finally, the First Amendment protects the "right of the people peaceably to assemble and petition the Government for a redress of grievances." Freedom of assembly remains an important right, and one that is often controversial, such as when an extremist group such as the Ku Klux Klan stages a public rally. The freedom to petition government tends to be less controversial but no less important. Today, it is referred to as "lobbying," the principal activity of interest groups. (The freedoms of speech, press, and assembly are examined in Chapter 8.)

The Second Amendment

Most Americans believe that the Constitution protects their **right to keep and bear arms.** Yet the **Second Amendment** refers not only to the keeping and bearing of arms but also to the need for a **well-regulated militia.** The Second Amendment provides: "A well-regulated Militia, being necessary to the security of a free State, the right of the people to keep and bear Arms, shall not be infringed." In *United States v. Cruikshank* (1875), the Supreme Court held that the Second Amendment guaranteed states the right to maintain militias but did not guarantee to individuals the right to possess guns. Subsequently, in *United States v. Miller* (1939), the Court upheld a federal law banning the interstate transportation of certain firearms. Miller, who had been arrested for transporting a double-barreled sawed-off shotgun from Oklahoma to Arkansas, sought the protection of the Second Amendment. The Court rejected Miller's argument, asserting that "we cannot say that the Second Amendment guarantees the right to keep and bear such an instrument." In *Lewis v. United States* (1980), the Court reaffirmed the *Miller* precedent. In upholding a federal gun control act, the Court said:

> These legislative restrictions on the use of firearms are neither based on constitutionally suspect criteria, nor do they trench upon any constitutionally protected liberties. . . . [T]he Second Amendment guarantees no right to keep and bear a firearm that does not have "some reasonable relationship to the preservation or efficiency of a well regulated militia."

As currently interpreted, the Second Amendment does not pose a significant constitutional barrier to the enactment or enforcement of gun control laws, whether passed by Congress, state legislatures, or local governments. However, other constitutional provisions may limit Congressional action in this area. See, for example, the discussion of *Printz v. United States* (1997) in Chapter 5. In *Printz*, the Supreme Court struck down provisions of the Brady Handgun Violence Prevention Act requiring state and local law enforcement officers to conduct background checks on prospective handgun purchasers. The Court said these provisions infringed state sovereignty as protected by the Tenth Amendment.

The Third Amendment

The **Third Amendment** prohibits military authorities from quartering troops in citizens' homes without their consent. This was a matter of serious concern to the founders, because English troops had been forcibly billeted in colonists' homes during the Revolutionary War. Today, the Third Amendment is little more than an historical curiosity, since it has not been the subject of any significant litigation.

The Fourth Amendment

The **Fourth Amendment** protects citizens from **unreasonable searches and seizures** conducted by police and other government agents. Reflecting a serious concern of the founders, the Fourth Amendment remains extremely important today, especially in light of the pervasiveness of crime and the national war on drugs. In the twentieth century, the Fourth Amendment was the source of numerous important Supreme Court decisions and generated a tremendous and complex body of legal doctrine. For example, in *Katz v. United States* (1967), the Supreme Court under Chief Justice Warren expanded the scope of Fourth Amendment protection to include **wiretapping,** an important tool of modern law enforcement. The Burger and Rehnquist Courts have been decidedly more conservative in this area, facilitating police efforts to ferret out crime. (The Fourth Amendment as it relates to criminal justice is examined in some depth in Chapter 10.)

Drug Testing The Fourth Amendment is not limited to the areas of law enforcement and criminal justice. In recent years, courts have been called on to interpret the Fourth Amendment in the context of statutes and regulations imposing various **drug testing** requirements. In *Skinner v. Railway Labor Executives' Association* (1989), the U.S. Supreme Court upheld federal regulations requiring drug and alcohol testing of railroad employees involved in train accidents. The Court has also sustained a Customs Service policy requiring drug tests for persons seeking positions as customs inspectors (see *National Treasury Employees Union v. Von Raab* [1989]). As yet, the Supreme Court has not addressed the issue of general, random drug testing of public employees. It has, however, invalidated a policy under which all political candidates were required to submit to drug testing as a condition of qualifying for the ballot (see *Chandler v. Miller* [1997]).

The Fifth Amendment

The **Fifth Amendment** contains a number of important provisions involving the rights of persons accused of crime. It requires the federal government to obtain an **indictment** from a **grand jury** before trying someone for a major crime. It also prohibits **double jeopardy**—that is, being tried twice for the same offense. Additionally, the Fifth Amendment protects persons against **compulsory self-incrimination,** which is what is commonly meant by the phrase "taking the Fifth." (Fifth Amendment rights of the accused are dealt with in Chapter 10.)

The Fifth Amendment also protects people against arbitrary use of **eminent domain,** the power of government to take private property for public use. The Just Compensation Clause forbids government from taking private property without paying **just compensation** to the owner (see Chapter 7).

Finally, the Fifth Amendment prohibits the federal government from depriving persons of life, liberty, or property without **due process of law.** A virtually identical clause is found in the **Fourteenth Amendment**, which applies specifically to the states. The Due Process Clauses have implications both for civil and criminal cases, as well as for a variety of relationships between citizen and government. Due process may be the broadest and most basic protection afforded by the Constitution. (The concept of due process is more fully explicated later in this chapter, as part of the discussion of the Fourteenth Amendment.)

The Sixth Amendment

The **Sixth Amendment** is concerned exclusively with the rights of the accused. It requires, among other things, that people accused of crimes be provided a **"speedy and public trial,** by an impartial jury." The right of **trial by jury** is one of the most cherished rights in the Anglo-American tradition, predating the Magna Carta of 1215. The Sixth Amendment also grants defendants the right to confront, or cross-examine, witnesses for the prosecution and the right to have "compulsory process" (the power of **subpoena**) to require favorable witnesses to appear in court. Significantly, considering the incredible complexity of the criminal law, the Sixth Amendment guarantees that accused persons have the "Assistance of Counsel" for their defense. The Supreme Court has regarded the **right to counsel** as crucial to a fair trial, holding that defendants who are unable to afford private counsel must be afforded counsel at public expense (*Gideon v. Wainwright* [1963]). (Sixth Amendment rights in the context of criminal justice are examined in Chapter 10.)

The Seventh Amendment

The **Seventh Amendment** guarantees the right to a jury trial in federal civil suits "at common law" where the amount at issue exceeds $20. Originally, it was widely assumed that the Seventh Amendment required jury trials only in traditional common law cases—for example, actions for libel, wrongful death, and trespass. But over the years, the Supreme Court expanded the scope of the Seventh Amendment to encompass civil suits seeking enforcement of statutory rights. For example, in *Curtis v. Loether* (1974), an African-American woman brought suit against a number of white defendants, charging them with refusing to rent her an apartment in violation of the Fair Housing Act of 1968. The defendants requested a trial by jury, but the district court ruled that the Seventh Amendment did not apply to lawsuits seeking to enforce the rights created by the Fair Housing Act. In reversing the district court, the Supreme Court said:

> The Seventh Amendment does apply to actions enforcing statutory rights, and requires a jury trial on demand, if the statute creates legal rights and remedies, enforceable in an action for damages in the ordinary courts of law. . . . We recognize . . . the possibility that jury prejudice may deprive a victim of discrimination of the verdict to which he or she is entitled. Of course, the trial judge's power to direct a verdict, to grant judgment notwithstanding the verdict, or to grant a new trial provides substantial protection against this risk.

Although it does apply to suits enforcing statutory rights, the Seventh Amendment does not apply to the adjudication of certain issues by administrative or regulatory agencies. In *Thomas v. Union Carbide* (1985), the Supreme Court said that the Seventh Amendment does not provide the right to a jury trial where Congress "has created a 'private' right that is so closely integrated into a public regulatory scheme as to be a matter appropriate for agency resolution with limited involvement by the Article III judiciary."

Under current interpretation, the Seventh Amendment does not require the traditional common law twelve-person jury in civil trials. In *Colgrove v. Battin* (1973), the

Supreme Court held that a six-person jury was sufficient to try a civil case in federal court. The defendant in the case argued that the Seventh Amendment's reference to "suits at common law" required federal courts to adopt the traditional common law jury. The Supreme Court, dividing 5 to 4, disagreed. Writing for the Court, Justice William Brennan said:

> Consistently with the historical objective of the Seventh Amendment, our decisions have defined the jury right preserved in cases covered by the Amendment, as "the substance of the common-law right of trial by jury, as distinguished from mere matters of form or procedure. . . ." The Amendment, therefore, does not bind the federal courts to the exact procedural incidents or details of jury trial according to the common law in 1791.

In a lengthy dissent, Justice Thurgood Marshall stressed the need for fidelity to the traditions of the common law:

> Since some definition of "jury" must be chosen, I would . . . rely on the fixed bounds of history which the Framers, by drafting the Seventh Amendment, meant to "preserve. . . ." It may well be that the number 12 is no more than a "historical accident" and is "wholly without significance." . . . But surely there is nothing more significant about the number six, or three or one. The line must be drawn somewhere, and the difference between drawing it in the light of history and drawing it on an ad hoc basis is, ultimately, the difference between interpreting a constitution and making it up as one goes along.

The controversy over the appropriate size of the jury in federal civil trials parallels the issue of jury size in criminal cases, a question examined in Chapter 10.

The Eighth Amendment

The **Eighth Amendment** protects persons accused of crimes from being required to post **excessive bail** to secure **pretrial release**. In *Stack v. Boyle* (1951), the Supreme Court held that bail is excessive if it is higher than is necessary to ensure a defendant's appearance for trial. But in *United States v. Salerno* (1987), a case involving the prosecution of an organized crime figure, the Court said that the Eighth Amendment does not require that defendants be released on bail, only that, if the court grants bail, it must not be "excessive." (The issue of **pretrial detention** is discussed more thoroughly in Chapter 10.)

The Eighth Amendment also forbids the imposition of **excessive fines** and the infliction of **cruel and unusual punishments** on persons convicted of crimes. Originally thought to proscribe torture, the Cruel and Unusual Punishments Clause now figures prominently in the ongoing national debate over the death penalty (see Chapter 10). Writing for the Supreme Court in *Trop v. Dulles* (1958), Chief Justice Earl Warren observed that the Cruel and Unusual Punishments Clause "must draw its meaning from the evolving standards of decency that mark the progress of a maturing society." In the *Trop* case, a soldier had lost his citizenship after being found guilty of desertion from the U.S. Army. The Supreme Court restored Trop's citizenship, noting that "[t]he civilized nations of the world are in virtual unanimity that statelessness is not to be imposed as punishment for a crime."

Civil Forfeitures   Federal law provides for forfeiture of the proceeds of a variety of criminal activities. Most controversial are the federal law provisions allowing **forfeiture** of property used in illicit drug activity. Under federal law a "conveyance," which includes aircraft, motor vehicles, and vessels, is subject to forfeiture if it is used to transport controlled substances. Real estate may be forfeited if it is used to commit or facilitate commission of a drug-related felony. Many states have similar statutes. Though technically such forfeitures are civil, not criminal, sanctions, the Supreme Court has recognized that forfeiture constitutes significant punishment and is thus subject to constitutional limitations under the Eighth Amendment. In *Austin v. United States* (1993), the Court said that forfeiture "constitutes 'payment to a sovereign as punishment for some offense' . . . and, as such, is subject to the limitations of the Eighth Amendment's Excessive Fines Clause." However, the Court left it to state and lower federal courts to determine the tests of "excessiveness" in the context of forfeiture.

The Ninth Amendment

The **Ninth Amendment** was included in the Bill of Rights as a solution to a problem raised by James Madison—namely, that the specification of particular liberties might suggest that individuals possessed only those specified. The Ninth Amendment makes it clear that individuals retain a reservoir of rights and liberties beyond those listed in the Constitution: "The enumeration in the Constitution, of certain rights, shall not be construed to deny or disparage others retained by the people." This amendment reflects the dominant thinking of late eighteenth century America: Individual rights precede and transcend the power of government; individuals possess all rights except those that have been surrendered to government for the protection of the public good. Yet prior to 1965, the Ninth Amendment had little significance in constitutional law. In the words of Justice Potter Stewart:

> The Ninth Amendment, like its companion the Tenth, which this Court has held "states but a truism that all is retained which has not been surrendered, . . ." was framed by James Madison and adopted by the States simply to make clear that the adoption of the Bill of Rights did not alter the plan that the Federal government was to be a government of express and limited powers, and that all rights and powers not delegated to it were retained by the people and the individual States. (*Griswold v. Connecticut* [1965] [dissenting opinion])

But in *Griswold v. Connecticut* (1965), a Supreme Court majority, in recognizing a constitutional right of privacy (discussed more fully in Chapter 11), relied in part on the Ninth Amendment. Here, the Court invalidated a Connecticut statute that made it a crime to use birth control devices. In dissent, Justice Stewart expressed dismay, observing that "the idea that a federal court could ever use the Ninth Amendment to annul a law passed by the elected representatives of the people of the State of Connecticut would have caused James Madison no little wonder."

Although they have seldom relied explicitly on the Ninth Amendment, federal and state courts have over the years recognized a number of rights that Americans take for granted but which are not specifically enumerated in the Constitution. The right to marry, to determine how one's children are to be reared and educated, to choose one's occupation, to start a business, to travel freely across state lines, to sue in the courts, and to be presumed innocent of a crime until proven guilty are all examples of individual rights that have been recognized as "constitutional," despite their absence from the text of the Constitution. Quite often these rights have been recognized under the broad Due Process Clauses of the Fifth and Fourteenth Amendments.

The Tenth Amendment

The Bill of Rights is generally considered to be the first ten amendments to the Constitution. But the Tenth Amendment is of a fundamentally different character from the nine amendments that precede it. The Tenth Amendment provides: "The powers not delegated to the United States by the Constitution, nor prohibited by it to the

States, are reserved to the States respectively, or to the people." Unlike other provisions of the Bill of Rights, and despite its reference to "the people," the Tenth Amendment recognizes the powers of the states vis-à-vis the federal government and does not directly address individual rights. However, the Framers of the Constitution and Bill of Rights believed that the federal structure guaranteed by the Tenth Amendment was conducive to the maintenance of freedom generally.

TO SUMMARIZE:

- The omission of a more detailed enumeration of rights from the original Constitution was regarded in many quarters as a major deficiency and even threatened to undermine ratification of the Constitution.
- The first ten amendments to the Constitution, known today as the Bill of Rights, were adopted by Congress in 1789 and ratified by the states in 1791. Most of these amendments (the First, Fourth, Fifth, Sixth, Eighth, and Ninth) are of fundamental importance in the field of civil rights and liberties and are discussed in detail in later chapters.
- The Second Amendment protects the "right to keep and bear Arms" but does so in the context of a "well-regulated Militia." The Supreme Court has never interpreted this amendment as conferring a broad personal right to possess and use firearms. Indeed, the Court has upheld federal statutes regulating the sale, possession, and use of certain weapons.
- The Third Amendment, which prohibits the nonconsensual quartering of troops in private homes, has never been the subject of significant constitutional adjudication.
- The Seventh Amendment, which guarantees the common law right to a jury trial in a civil suit, has been expanded to include civil suits seeking enforcement of statutory rights. Under prevailing interpretation, the Seventh Amendment permits some variation from the use of the traditional twelve-member jury in a civil trial.
- The Tenth Amendment, often referred to as the "states' rights" amendment, applies to matters of federalism and is not directly related to individual rights and liberties.

THE FOURTEENTH AMENDMENT

Without question, the most important amendment to the Constitution outside of the Bill of Rights is the Fourteenth Amendment. Ratified in 1868, the principal objective of the Fourteenth Amendment was to protect the civil rights and liberties of African-Americans. Although slavery had been formally abolished by the **Thirteenth Amendment**, ratified in 1865, questions remained about the legal status of the former slaves. Recall from Chapter 1 that in *Scott v. Sandford* (1857), the Supreme Court not only defended the institution of slavery but indicated that blacks were not citizens of the United States and possessed "no rights or privileges but such as those who held the power and the Government might choose to grant them." Section 1 of the Fourteenth Amendment made clear that *Scott v. Sandford* was no longer the law of the land:

> All persons born or naturalized in the United States, and subject to the jurisdiction thereof, are citizens of the United States and of the State wherein they reside. No State shall make or enforce any law which shall abridge the privileges or immunities of citizens of the United States; nor shall any State deprive any person of life, liberty, or property, without due process of law; nor deny to any person within its jurisdiction the equal protection of the laws.

The federal courts have relied heavily on the **Equal Protection Clause** of Section 1 in advancing the civil rights of African-Americans and other minority groups. The "case of the century," *Brown v. Board of Education* (1954), in which the Supreme Court abolished racial segregation in the public schools, was based squarely on the Equal Protection Clause. The Equal Protection Clause has provided the basis on which the Supreme Court has invalidated a number of state laws discriminating among persons, not only on the basis of race, but on the basis of gender and other characteristics (see Chapter 12). The Court has also relied upon the Equal Protection Clause in seeking to ensure fundamental fairness in the political process (see, for example, *Reynolds v. Sims* [1964]). The most dramatic example of the use of the Equal Protection Clause in this context was the Court's decision in Bush v. Gore (2000) (discussed and reprinted in Chapter 13), in which the Court effectively determined the outcome of the 2000 presidential election.

Section 5 of the Fourteenth Amendment grants to Congress the power to enforce the broad provisions of Section 1 through "appropriate legislation." Congress has relied on Section 5 in passing civil rights legislation, such as the landmark Voting Rights Act of 1965, which forbids racial discrimination in matters of voting and representation (see Chapter 13).

Although the principal purpose of the Fourteenth Amendment was to protect the rights of African-Americans, it has come to be regarded as a broad shield against actions by state and local governments that would infringe on individual rights and liberties. Of particular importance in this context is the **Due Process Clause.**

Due Process of Law

In its most generic sense, due process refers to the exercise of governmental power under the rule of law with due regard for the rights and interests of individuals. The concept of **procedural due process** embraces government's obligation to provide **fair notice** and a **fair hearing** to individuals before depriving them of "life, liberty, or property." Thus, for example, the Supreme Court relied on the Due Process Clause of the Fourteenth Amendment in a landmark decision revolutionizing the juvenile justice system, holding that juveniles must be afforded certain procedural protections before they can be judged "delinquent" and sent to a reformatory (*In re Gault* [1967]). Similarly, the Supreme Court has invoked due process to say that police may not use methods that "shock the conscience" in attempting to gather evidence of criminal wrongdoing (*Rochin v. California* [1952]).

Historically, the concept of due process was extremely important in defending private property rights from government regulation (see Chapter 7). More recently, the courts have recognized government employment and government benefits as "property interests" subject to the requirements of due process. Thus, while there is no constitutional right to receive welfare assistance, government may not terminate a person's welfare benefits without observing certain procedural safeguards (see, for example, *Goldberg v. Kelly* [1970]).

Substantive Due Process   In addition to providing procedural protections against arbitrary and capricious government action, due process has been held to impose substantive limits on government policies as well. Under the concept of **substantive due process,** government is barred from enforcing policies that are irrational, unfair, unreasonable, or unjust, even if such policies do not run counter to other specific constitutional prohibitions.

For almost fifty years (roughly 1890–1937), the Supreme Court relied on substantive due process to invalidate a variety of state and federal laws regulating aspects of economic life (see Chapter 7). For example, in *Lochner v. New York* (1905), the Court struck down a state law setting maximum working hours in bakeries. The Court held that the restriction violated both the employer's and the employee's **liberty of contract**, a right not specifically enumerated in the Constitution but held to be embraced within the substantive prohibitions of the Due Process Clause of the Fourteenth Amendment. While the liberty of contract version of substantive due process has been repudiated by the modern Supreme Court, substantive due process lives on under the rubric of the constitutional **right of privacy.**

The Right of Privacy

First recognized in *Griswold v. Connecticut* (1965), the right of privacy is not found in any specific provision of the Bill of Rights. Nevertheless, the Supreme Court has held that privacy is among the **fundamental rights** enforceable against the state governments via the Due Process Clause of the Fourteenth Amendment. As previously noted, in *Griswold* the right of privacy was invoked to invalidate a state law prohibiting the use of birth control devices. Eight years later, in *Roe v. Wade* (1973), the right of privacy was held to be broad enough to include a woman's decision to have an abortion, touching off a constitutional debate that continues to rage. In the popular debate over *Roe*, the issue tends to be the desirability of legalized abortion. Yet the scholarly debate over *Roe v. Wade* focuses to a greater extent on the legitimacy of substantive due process as a constitutional doctrine. (The right of privacy and its application to a variety of issues, including abortion, gay rights, and euthanasia, are discussed in Chapter 11.)

The Fourteenth Amendment and State Action

Normally one thinks of the Fourteenth Amendment, as well as the provisions of the Bill of Rights, as placing constraints on government action. The Supreme Court has said on numerous occasions, the first being in *The Civil Rights Cases* (1883), that the prohibitions of the Fourteenth Amendment apply to state action but not to actions by private individuals or corporations. (This important doctrine of constitutional law is discussed at some length in Chapter 12.) However, an action that is ostensibly private in character may be treated as "state action" within the purview of the Fourteenth Amendment if there is a "close nexus" between the state and the private actor. Thus, for example, the Supreme Court in 1944 invalidated the Texas Democratic Party's whites-only primary election, even though the party was not, strictly speaking, an agency of the state (see *Smith v. Allwright* [1944], discussed and reprinted in Chapter 13).

Can Inaction Be "State Action"?   In modern times, the **state action doctrine** has been criticized as being too restrictive. Indeed, some have argued that the Fourteenth Amendment should be interpreted to impose an affirmative duty on government to protect persons against harm in some circumstances. This argument was made in dramatic form in the 1989 case of *DeShaney v. Winnebago Social Services*. There, the Supreme Court, dividing 6 to 3, held that a social services agency, regardless of its prior knowledge of the danger, did not violate the Fourteenth Amendment by failing to protect a child from his abusive father.

Writing for the majority, Chief Justice Rehnquist noted that the Court had previously recognized a state's constitutional obligation to protect the safety and well-being of those within its custody, including mentally retarded persons in state institutions. But this "affirmative duty to protect" did not arise "from the state's knowledge of [Joshua's] predicament or from its expressions of its intent to help him." Since the state had no constitutional duty to protect Joshua from his father, its failure to do so, although calamitous, did not constitute a violation of the Due Process Clause.

In a dissenting opinion, Justice Harry Blackmun excoriated the Court for its "sterile formalism." Blackmun asserted that the "broad and stirring clauses of the Fourteenth Amendment" were "designed, at least in part, to undo the formalistic legal reasoning that infected antebellum jurisprudence." Blackmun preferred a "sympathetic reading" of the Fourteenth Amendment that recognized that "compassion need not be exiled from the province of judging."

The Incorporation of the Bill of Rights

One of the most important impacts of the Fourteenth Amendment has been the effective "nationalization" of the Bill of Rights. There is little doubt that, at the time of its ratification in 1791, the Bill of Rights was widely perceived as imposing limitations only on the powers and actions of the national government. This is suggested by the first clause of the First Amendment, which begins, "Congress shall make no law. . . ." The Court held as much in 1833 in the case of *Barron v. Baltimore*, when it refused to permit a citizen to sue a local government for violating his property rights under the Just Compensation Clause of the Fifth Amendment. Speaking for the Court, Chief Justice John Marshall said:

> We are of the opinion, that, the provision in the Fifth Amendment to the Constitution, declaring that private property shall not be taken for public use without just compensation is intended solely as a limitation on the power of the United States, and is not applicable to the legislation of the states.

The ratification of the Fourteenth Amendment in 1868 provided an opportunity for the Supreme Court to reconsider the relationship between the Bill of Rights and state and local governments. As we have seen, Section 1 of the Fourteenth Amendment imposed broad restrictions on state power, requiring the states to provide equal protection of the law to all persons, to respect the "privileges and immunities" of citizens of the United States, and, most importantly, to protect the "life, liberty, and property" of all persons. More to the point, the Fourteenth Amendment enjoined states from depriving persons of these basic rights "without due process of law." Although there is no conclusive evidence that the authors of the Fourteenth Amendment intended for it to "incorporate" the Bill of Rights and thus make the latter applicable to actions of state and local governments, plaintiffs in federal cases began to make this argument fairly soon after the amendment was ratified.

Initially, the Supreme Court was not favorably disposed toward the **doctrine of incorporation**. In *Hurtado v. California* (1884), the Court rejected the argument that the grand jury procedure required in federal criminal cases by the Fifth Amendment was an essential feature of due process and thus required in state criminal cases by the Fourteenth Amendment. Today, the *Hurtado* decision remains good law; states are not required by the federal Constitution to use grand juries to bring criminal charges, although many still do.

Selective Incorporation   The fact that the *Hurtado* decision remains valid indicates that the Supreme Court has never accepted the argument that the Fourteenth Amendment incorporates the Bill of Rights *en toto*. The Court has, however, endorsed a doctrine of **selective incorporation** by which most of the provisions of the Bill of Rights have been extended to limit actions of the state and local governments. The process of selective incorporation began in 1897 in the case of *Chicago, Burlington, & Quincy Railroad Company v. Chicago*. There, a conservative Court concerned about protecting private enterprise against a rising tide of government interventionism held that the Due Process Clause of the Fourteenth Amendment imposed on state and local governments the same obligation to respect private property that the Fifth Amendment imposed on the federal government. The Court said that when a state or local government takes private property under its power of eminent domain, it must provide just compensation to the owner. Thus, the Court had "incorporated" the Just Compensation Clause of the Fifth Amendment into the Due Process Clause of the Fourteenth Amendment.

The doctrine of incorporation was next applied to First Amendment freedoms, specifically the freedoms of speech and press. In *Gitlow v. New York* (1925), the Supreme Court said that "we may and do assume that freedom of speech and of the press—which are protected by the First Amendment from abridgment by Congress— are among the fundamental personal rights and "liberties" protected by the due process clause of the Fourteenth Amendment from impairment by the states." This dictum was soon followed by decisions in which the Court relied on the doctrine of incorporation to invalidate state actions abridging the freedoms of speech and press. In *Fiske v. Kansas* (1927), the Court invalidated a state statute that prohibited mere advocacy of violent action, finding it to be a violation of freedom of speech. Four years later, in *Near v. Minnesota* (1931), the Court struck down a state law that permitted **censorship** of "malicious, scandalous and defamatory" periodicals, finding it to be a clear violation of freedom of the press. In the wake of these and related decisions, state and local policies impinging on freedom of expression became subject to challenge in the courts under the same First Amendment standards that applied to federal legislation.

In *Palko v. Connecticut* (1937), the Supreme Court refused to incorporate the Double Jeopardy Clause of the Fifth Amendment into the Due Process Clause of the Fourteenth. To merit incorporation, said Justice Benjamin N. Cardozo, a provision of the Bill of Rights must be essential to "a scheme of ordered liberty." Cardozo's majority opinion suggested that the First Amendment freedoms that had been previously incorporated represented "the matrix, the indispensable condition, of nearly every other form of freedom." The Double Jeopardy Clause, in Cardozo's view, lay on "a different plane of social and moral values."

Following *Palko v. Connecticut*, the doctrine of incorporation became the subject of an intense debate among the justices of the Supreme Court. In *Cantwell v. Connecticut* (1940), the Court incorporated the Free Exercise of Religion Clause of the First Amendment. Similarly, in *Everson v. Board of Education* (1947), the Court extended the Establishment Clause to the states under the Fourteenth Amendment (for more discussion of both cases and clauses, see Chapter 9). Yet in *Adamson v. California* (1947) and in *Rochin v. California* (1952), the Court refused to extend the Fifth Amendment privilege against compulsory self-incrimination to state criminal trials. The Court's highly selective approach to incorporation of the Bill of Rights drew the particular ire of Justices Hugo Black and William O. Douglas.

In the 1960s, the views of Justices Black and Douglas as to the applicability of the Bill of Rights to state criminal prosecutions came to be supported by a majority of justices on the Supreme Court. Indeed, one of the priorities of the Court under the leadership of Chief Justice Warren was to increase the legal protections afforded to persons accused of crimes, both in state and federal court. In a series of landmark decisions, the Warren Court incorporated nearly all of the relevant provisions of the Bill of Rights into the Due Process Clause of the Fourteenth Amendment and thus made them applicable to state criminal cases (see Table 6.1).

In one of the most significant of these decisions, *Duncan v. Louisiana* (1968), the Court made the ancient right of trial by jury applicable to defendants in state criminal cases.

TABLE 6.1	Chronology of Incorporation of the Bill of Rights	
Year	**Issue and Amendment Involved**	**Case**
1897	Just compensation (V)	*Chicago, Burlington & Quincy RR v. Chicago*
1927	Speech (I)	*Fiske v. Kansas*
1931	Press (I)	*Near v. Minnesota*
1937	Assembly and petition (I)	*De Jonge v. Oregon*
1940	Free exercise of religion (I)	*Cantwell v. Connecticut*
1947	Separation of church and state (I)	*Everson v. Board of Education*
1948	Public trial (VI)	*In re Oliver*
1949	Unreasonable searches and seizures (IV)	*Wolf v. Colorado*
1962	Cruel and unusual punishment (VIII)	*Robinson v. California*
1963	Right to counsel (VI)	*Gideon v. Wainwright*
1964	Compulsory self-incrimination (V)	*Malloy v. Hogan*
1965	Confrontation of hostile witnesses (VI)	*Pointer v. Texas*
1966	Impartial jury (VI)	*Parker v. Gladden*
1967	Confrontation of favorable witnesses	*Washington v. Texas*
1967	Speedy trial (VI)	*Klopfer v. North Carolina*
1968	Jury trial in nonpetty criminal cases (VI)	*Duncan v. Louisiana*
1969	Double jeopardy (V)	*Benton v. Maryland*

In a concurring opinion joined by Justice Douglas, Justice Black expressed his satisfaction with what the Court had done under the mantle of selective incorporation:

> I believe as strongly as ever that the Fourteenth Amendment was intended to make the Bill of Rights applicable to the States. I have been willing to support the selective incorporation doctrine, however, as an alternative, although perhaps less historically supportable than complete incorporation. . . . [M]ost importantly for me, the selective incorporation process has the virtue of having already worked to make most of the Bill of Rights protections applicable to the States.

The process of selective incorporation of the Bill of Rights may have reached its terminus in 1969. In that year, in *Benton v. Maryland*, the Supreme Court overruled its earlier decision in *Palko v. Connecticut* and decided, after all, that the Double Jeopardy Clause of the Fifth Amendment warranted incorporation into the Fourteenth Amendment. The *Benton* case marks the latest and perhaps last instance of a provision of the Bill of Rights being extended to state action via the Fourteenth Amendment. As of 1998, the only provisions of the Bill of Rights that had not been absorbed into the Fourteenth Amendment were the Second, Third, and Seventh Amendments, the Fifth Amendment grand jury clause, and the Eighth Amendment prohibitions against "excessive fines" and "excessive bail."

The principal thrust of the process of selective incorporation is that today, with few exceptions, policies of state and local government are subject to judicial scrutiny under the same standards that the Bill of Rights imposes on the federal government. Thus, for example, the prohibition of the First Amendment against establishment of religion applies with the same force to a school board in rural Arkansas as it does to the Congress of the United States. Likewise, the Eighth Amendment injunction against cruel and unusual punishments applies equally to high-profile federal prosecutions for treason and to sentences imposed by local courts for violations of city or county ordinances. Note, however, that in a few instances, such as those governed by the Sixth Amendment right to trial by jury, the Supreme Court has been willing to give the states slightly greater latitude than the federal government in complying with Bill of Rights requirements (for further discussion, see Chapter 10).

TO SUMMARIZE:

- Beyond the Bill of Rights, the Fourteenth Amendment (1868) is the most important constitutional amendment in the field of civil rights and liberties. This amendment places broad restrictions on the power of states to infringe on the rights and liberties of citizens.
- The Equal Protection Clause of Section 1 of the Fourteenth Amendment serves as the primary basis for protecting the civil rights of minority groups against discriminatory state action.
- The Due Process Clause of Section 1 is the most far-reaching provision of the Fourteenth Amendment. This clause prohibits states from depriving persons of life, liberty, or property without due process of law. The courts have distinguished between two aspects of due process: procedural and substantive.
- Procedural due process, which embodies the requirements of notice and hearing, requires fundamental fairness in governmental proceedings against individuals.
- Substantive due process prohibits government from enforcing policies that are deemed unreasonable, unfair or unjust, even if they do not violate specific constitutional prohibitions. The right of privacy can be seen as a contemporary manifestation of substantive due process.
- In a long series of cases beginning in the late nineteenth century, the Supreme Court has held that the Due Process Clause of the Fourteenth Amendment incorporates most of the provisions of the Bill of Rights, thus making them applicable to the states.

AMENDMENTS PROTECTING VOTING RIGHTS

While the Fourteenth Amendment is the broadest, and most important, source of protection for civil rights and liberties outside of the Bill of Rights, a number of other constitutional amendments address specific civil rights issues. These amendments (Fifteenth, Nineteenth, Twenty-fourth, and Twenty-sixth) focus on the **right to vote**, which is arguably the most essential right in a democracy. The original Constitution left the matter of voting rights to the states. In 1787, voting in the United States was confined for the most part to "freeholders"—that is, white male landowners above the age of 21. As our society has become progressively more democratic, the Constitution has been amended to make the franchise more inclusive.

The Fifteenth Amendment

Like the Thirteenth and Fourteenth Amendments, the **Fifteenth Amendment** (ratified in 1870) was an outgrowth of the Civil War. Unlike the Fourteenth Amendment, however, the Fifteenth Amendment is targeted fairly narrowly, its only concern being the denial of voting rights in state and federal elections on grounds of race. As in the Thirteenth and Fourteenth Amendments, Section 5 of the Fifteenth Amendment grants Congress the power to adopt "appropriate legislation" to enforce its guarantees. Almost a century later, Congress employed its enforcement powers under Section 5 in adopting the landmark Voting Rights Act of 1965. Among other things, the act allowed the federal government to actively supervise electoral systems in states where racial discrimination had been pervasive. It also granted individuals the right to sue in federal court to challenge features of state and local elections deemed to be discriminatory. Without question, the Voting Rights Act of 1965 has had an enormous impact on ending racial discrimination in this area. (The issue of voting rights is examined in detail in Chapter 13.)

The Nineteenth Amendment

Like most African-Americans, women were originally excluded from participation in elections in this country. In 1848, a delegation of women, including the famous suffragist Elizabeth Cady Stanton, met at Seneca Falls, New York, to address the "social, civil, and religious conditions and rights of woman." The Seneca Falls Convention adopted a resolution stating that "it is the duty of the women of this country to secure to themselves their sacred right to the elective franchise." Securing the franchise would not be easy. In 1872, Susan B. Anthony was prosecuted for attempting to vote in the presidential election. Three years later, the Supreme Court rebuffed a woman seeking to cast a ballot in a Missouri election, saying that "the Constitution of the United States does not confer the right of suffrage upon anyone" (*Minor v. Happersett* [1875]). In the last decades of the nineteenth century, a few states changed their statutes to permit female suffrage. By 1912, nine states had extended the franchise to include women. In 1918, President Woodrow Wilson took a stand in favor of women's suffrage. Following Wilson's lead, Congress adopted a constitutional amendment granting women the right to vote and submitted it to the states for ratification. In 1920, the **Nineteenth Amendment** was added to the Constitution:

> The right of the citizens of the United States to vote shall not be denied or abridged by the United States or by any State on account of sex. Congress shall have the power, by appropriate legislation, to enforce the provision of this article.

In one fell swoop, the size of the potential electorate was doubled! Political participation by women did not, as some critics feared, radically alter the political system or its public policy outputs.

The Twenty-fourth Amendment

Although formally granted the right to vote by the Fifteenth Amendment, many African-Americans were still effectively disenfranchised by practices such as **grandfather clauses**, **literacy tests**, the **"white primary,"** and poll taxes (see Chapter 13). The **poll tax** was a fee required as a condition for voting. Typically, the unpaid fees would accumulate from election to election, posing an ever greater economic impediment to voting. Poll taxes had been common in the United States at the time the Constitution was adopted but fell into disuse by the mid-nineteenth century. They were resurrected after the ratification of the Fifteenth Amendment as a means of preventing African-Americans, most of whom were poor, from voting. In *Breedlove v. Suttles* (1937), the Supreme Court ruled that poll taxes, in and of themselves, did not violate the Fourteenth or Fifteenth Amendments. The *Breedlove* decision gave impetus to a movement to abolish the poll tax, and by 1960, poll taxes existed in only five southern states. The Twenty-fourth Amendment, ratified in 1964, outlawed poll taxes as a requirement to vote in federal elections. A year later, the Supreme Court extended this policy when it overturned Breedlove and struck down poll taxes in state elections as well (*Harper v. Virginia State Board of Elections* [1966]) (see Chapter 13).

The Twenty-sixth Amendment

During the 1960s, young people, galvanized primarily by the Vietnam War, began to assert themselves politically. Often, political participation by the young was unconventional, taking the form of demonstrations and protests. Many youth leaders argued that if 18-year-olds were old enough to be drafted into military service and placed in combat, they were also old enough to cast a ballot. This line of argument was not new; it had persuaded Georgia and Kentucky to lower the minimum voting age to 18 during the Second World War.

In 1970, Congress passed a measure lowering the voting age from 21 to 18 in both state and federal elections. The Supreme Court, however, declared this measure unconstitutional in *Oregon v. Mitchell* (1970). Dividing 5 to 4, the Court held that, although Congress possessed the authority to lower the voting age in federal elections, it could not by simple statute lower the voting age in state elections. This decision prompted Congress to adopt the **Twenty-sixth Amendment**, which was ratified by the states in record time—five weeks. Unlike women, however, young people have not taken full advantage of the extension of the franchise. People aged 18 to 21 are considerably less likely to vote than their elders.

TO SUMMARIZE:

- The right to vote, one of the most essential rights in a democracy, has been protected and enlarged by several amendments to the Constitution as interpreted by the Supreme Court.
- The Fifteenth Amendment (1870) prohibits racial discrimination in defining and implementing the right to vote and empowers Congress to enact legislation to achieve this purpose.
- The Nineteenth Amendment (1920) removes gender as a qualification for voting.
- The Twenty-fourth Amendment (1964) prohibits the imposition of a poll tax as a precondition for voting in federal elections. In 1966, the Supreme Court interpreted the Equal Protection Clause of the Fourteenth Amendment to extend this prohibition to state elections as well.
- The Twenty-sixth Amendment (1971) lowered the voting age to 18 in both state and federal elections.

STANDARDS OF REVIEW IN CIVIL RIGHTS AND LIBERTIES CASES

The Supreme Court has developed several different standards of review in determining the constitutionality of laws affecting civil rights and liberties. These standards can be categorized as **minimal scrutiny, heightened scrutiny,** and **strict scrutiny.**

Minimal Scrutiny: The Rational Basis Test

Minimal scrutiny, the most lenient standard of judicial review, typically involves the application of the **rational basis test.** In *Massachusetts Board of Retirement v. Murgia* (1976), the Supreme Court said that a law that touches on a constitutionally protected interest must, at a minimum, be "rationally related to furthering a legitimate government interest." For example, a state law that prohibits performing surgery without a license impinges on constitutionally protected interests by depriving laypersons of their right to make contracts freely and discriminating against those unable or unwilling to obtain a license. Yet the prohibition is obviously a rational means of advancing the state's legitimate interests in public health and safety. There is no doubt that, if it were challenged, the prohibition would withstand judicial review.

In applying the rational basis test, courts begin with a strong presumption that the challenged law or policy is valid. The burden of proof is on the party making the challenge to show that the law or policy is unconstitutional. To carry this burden, the party must demonstrate that there is no rational basis for the law or policy. Since this is a difficult showing to make, application of the rational basis test usually leads to a judgment sustaining the constitutionality of the challenged law or policy.

Strict Scrutiny: The Compelling Government Interest Test

When a law or policy impinges on a right explicitly protected by the Constitution, such as the right to vote, it is subjected to a more searching judicial scrutiny. This approach also applies in the case of unenumerated rights that the courts have identified as fundamental, such as the right of privacy (see *Roe v. Wade* [1973]) and the right of interstate travel (see *Shapiro v. Thompson* [1969]). Strict judicial scrutiny is also warranted in cases involving forms of discrimination, such as that based on race, that have been held to be "inherently suspect" (see *Korematsu v. United States* [1944]).

Under strict scrutiny, the ordinary **presumption of constitutionality** is reversed, which means, in effect, that the challenged law or policy is presumed to be unconstitutional. The burden shifts to the government (local, state, or federal) to show that the law or policy furthers a **compelling government interest.** Moreover, the government must show that the law is **narrowly tailored** to achieve this interest. This is a heavy burden for the government to carry. Consequently, most laws subjected to strict judicial scrutiny are declared unconstitutional. However, the application of strict scrutiny is not necessarily tantamount to a declaration of unconstitutionality. For example, in *New York v. Ferber* (1982), the Supreme Court upheld a child pornography law that impinged on the First Amendment freedom of expression because, in the view of the Court, the law served a compelling interest in protecting children from the abuse typically associated with the pornography industry.

Intermediate Scrutiny

To further complicate matters, the Supreme Court has developed an intermediate level of review, often referred to as heightened scrutiny. This standard has been most important in reviewing claims of gender-based discrimination under the Equal Protection Clause of the Fourteenth Amendment.

TO SUMMARIZE:

- The Supreme Court utilizes several distinctive standards of review in determining the constitutionality of laws affecting civil rights and liberties.
- The most lenient standard, *minimal scrutiny*, utilizes the rational basis test. Here the ordinary presumption of constitutionality applies, placing the burden of persuasion on the party challenging the law. To pass muster under this standard, a law need merely be rationally related to the furtherance of a legitimate government interest.
- The most stringent standard of review, *strict scrutiny*, applies in cases of racial discrimination and where other fundamental rights are at stake. Here the burden of

persuasion rests with the government to show that the law serves a compelling interest and is narrowly tailored to that end.

- The Court has identified an intermediate standard of review, often termed *heightened scrutiny*, which has been applied primarily in the area of sex discrimination.

THE IMPORTANCE OF STATE CONSTITUTIONS

In trying to understand constitutional law as it relates to civil rights and liberties, we must not ignore the role of the state constitutions and courts in protecting individual rights. Under our federal system of government, the highest court of each state possesses the authority to interpret with finality its state constitution and statutes. Since every state constitution contains language protecting individual rights and liberties, many state court decisions implicate both state and federal constitutional provisions. Under the relevant language of their constitutions and statutes, state courts are free to recognize greater (but not lesser) protections of individual rights than are provided by the U.S. Constitution as interpreted by the federal courts. For example, in *In re T. W.* (1989), the Florida Supreme Court struck down as a violation of the right of privacy a statute that required parental consent in cases where minors sought abortions. The constitutionality of a similar law had been upheld on federal grounds by the U.S. Supreme Court in *Planned Parenthood v. Ashcroft* (1983). In *T. W.*, the Florida Supreme Court made it clear that it was basing its decision on an amendment to the Florida constitution that (unlike the federal Constitution) explicitly protects the right of privacy. Similarly, in *State v. Kam* (1988), the Hawaii Supreme Court adopted an interpretation of its state constitution that affords considerably broader protection to pornography than that provided by the U.S. Constitution. These decisions, and many others like them, mean that a study of civil rights and liberties must encompass the provisions of state constitutions that parallel those of the U.S. Constitution.

TO SUMMARIZE:

- Under our system of federalism, the U.S. Constitution provides a base level of protection for civil rights and liberties applicable at every level of government.
- Under their respective constitutions, as interpreted by their courts, states may provide higher levels of protection for individual rights than are recognized in the federal Constitution as interpreted by the federal courts.

CONCLUSION

This chapter has provided a broad survey of the constitutional sources of protection for civil rights and liberties. As manifestations of the ideals of liberty and equality, civil rights and liberties are regarded as indispensable features of American democracy. Yet individual rights exist in constant tension with majority rule, another essential feature of democracy. Individual rights must be balanced wisely against compelling societal interests, such as public order, national defense, and the general welfare. The task of achieving this balance rests primarily with the courts, most notably the U.S. Supreme Court. The remaining chapters of this book are devoted to an examination of the Supreme Court's jurisprudence in several key areas of civil rights and liberties.

KEY TERMS

unalienable rights	well-regulated militia	Seventh Amendment	selective incorporation
natural rights	Third Amendment	Eighth Amendment	censorship
liberty	Fourth Amendment	excessive bail	right to vote
equality	unreasonable searches and	pretrial release	Fifteenth Amendment
civil rights	seizures	pretrial detention	Nineteenth Amendment
civil liberties	wiretapping	excessive fines	grandfather clause
treason	drug testing	cruel and unusual punishments	literacy tests
political dissent	Fifth Amendment	forfeiture	white primary
religious tests	indictment	Ninth Amendment	poll tax
Establishment Clause	grand jury	Thirteenth Amendment	Twenty-sixth Amendment
habeas corpus	double jeopardy	Equal Protection Clause	minimal scrutiny
ex post facto laws	compulsory self-incrimination	Due Process Clause	heightened scrutiny
bill of attainder	eminent domain	procedural due process	strict scrutiny
Contracts Clause	just compensation	fair notice	rational basis test
First Amendment	due process of law	fair hearing	presumption of
Free Exercise Clause	Fourteenth Amendment	substantive due process	constitutionality
freedom of speech	Sixth Amendment	liberty of contract	compelling government interest
freedom of the press	speedy and public trial	right of privacy	narrowly tailored
freedom of expression	trial by jury	fundamental rights	
right to keep and bear arms	subpoena	state action doctrine	
Second Amendment	right to counsel	doctrine of incorporation	

FOR FURTHER READING

Abraham, Henry J., and Barbara A. Perry. *Freedom and the Court: Civil Rights and Liberties in the United States* (7th ed.). New York: Oxford University Press, 1998.

Amar, Akhil Reed. *The Bill of Rights: Creation and Reconstruction.* New Haven, Conn.: Yale University Press, 2000.

Biskupic, Joan, and Elder Witt. *The Supreme Court and Individual Rights* (3rd ed.). Washington, D.C.: Congressional Quarterly Press, 1997.

Dworkin, Ronald. *Taking Rights Seriously.* Cambridge, Mass.: Harvard University Press, 1978.

Hensley, Thomas R., Christopher E. Smith, and Joyce A. Baugh. *Changing Supreme Court: Constitutional Rights and Liberties.* Belmont, Calif.: Wadsworth, 1996.

Levy, Leonard D. *Origins of the Bill of Rights* (Contemporary Law Series). New Haven, Conn.: Yale University Press, 1999.

Perry, Michael. *The Constitution, the Courts, and Human Rights.* New Haven, Conn.: Yale University Press, 1982.

Sarat, Austin, and Thomas R. Kearns. *Legal Rights: Historical and Philosophical Perspectives.* Ann Arbor: University of Michigan Press, 1996.

Tarr, G. Alan, and Ellis Katz (eds.). *Federalism and Rights.* Lanham, Md.: Rowman and Littlefield, 1996.

Walker, Samuel. *In Defense of American Liberties: A History of the ACLU* (2nd ed.). Carbondale: Southern Illinois University Press, 1999.

INTERNET RESOURCES

Name of Resource	Description	URL
American Civil Liberties Union	The premier civil rights/civil liberties interest group	http://www.aclu.org/
National Rifle Association	The leading organization dedicated to promoting the right to keep and bear arms	http://www.nra.org/
The American Civil Rights Union	A conservative counterpart to the ACLU	http://www.civilrightsunion.org/
The Institute for Justice	A libertarian alternative to the ACLU	http://www.ij.org/

Case

CARMELL V. TEXAS

529 U.S. 513; 120 S.Ct. 1620; 146 L.Ed. 2d 577 (2000)
Vote: 5–4

Carmell was convicted in a Texas court of sexual assault, aggravated sexual assault, and indecency with a child. Evidence showed that between 1991 and 1995 Carmell committed various sex acts with his stepdaughter, beginning when she was 12. Carmell was sentenced to life in prison on two convictions for aggravated sexual assault and twenty years in prison on thirteen other counts. Four of these convictions were for sexual assaults that occurred in 1991 and 1992, when Texas law provided that a defendant could not be convicted merely on the testimony of the victim unless she was under age 14. At the time of the assaults in question, the victim was 14 or 15. The law was later amended to extend the "child victim exception" to victims under 18 years old. Carmell was convicted under the amended law (Article 38.07). Here the Supreme Court considers whether this is an impermissible ex post facto law.

Justice Stevens delivered the opinion of the Court.

. . . In *Calder v. Bull*, Justice Chase stated that . . . the phrase "*ex post facto*" referred only to certain types of criminal laws. Justice Chase catalogued those types as follows:

1st. Every law that makes an action done before the passing of the law, and which was *innocent* when done, criminal; and punishes such action. 2d. Every law that *aggravates* a *crime*, or makes it *greater* than it was, when committed. 3d. Every law that *changes the punishment*, and inflicts a *greater punishment*, than the law annexed to the crime, when committed. 4th. Every law that alters the *legal* rules of *evidence*, and receives less, or different, testimony, than the law required at the time of the commission of the offence, *in order to convict the offender.*"

It is the fourth category that is at issue in petitioner's case.

This Court, moreover, has repeatedly endorsed this understanding, including, in particular, the fourth category . . . .

Article 38.07 is unquestionably a law "that alters the legal rules of evidence, and receives less, or different, testimony, than the law required at the time of the commission of the offence, in order to convict the offender." Under the law in effect at the time the acts were committed, the prosecution's case was legally insufficient and petitioner was entitled to a judgment of acquittal, unless the State could produce both the victim's testimony *and* corroborative evidence. The amended law, however, changed the quantum of evidence necessary to sustain a conviction; under the new law, petitioner could be (and was) convicted on the victim's testimony alone, without any corroborating evidence. Under any commonsense understanding of *Calder's* fourth category, Article 38.07 plainly fits. Requiring only the victim's testimony to convict, rather than the victim's testimony plus other corroborating evidence is surely "less testimony required to convict" in any straightforward sense of those words. . . .

The fourth category, so understood, resonates harmoniously with one of the principal interests that the *Ex Post Facto* Clause was designed to serve, fundamental justice. . . .

. . . A law reducing the quantum of evidence required to convict an offender is as grossly unfair as, say, retrospectively eliminating an element of the offense, increasing the punishment for an existing offense, or lowering the burden of proof. . . . In each of these instances, the government subverts the presumption of innocence by reducing the number of elements it must prove to overcome that presumption; by threatening such severe punishment so as to induce a plea to a lesser offense or a lower sentence; or by making it easier to meet the threshold for overcoming the presumption. Reducing the quantum of evidence necessary to meet the burden of proof is simply another way of achieving the same end. All of these legislative changes, in a sense, are mirror images of one another. In each instance, the government refuses, after the fact, to play by its own rules, altering them in a way that is advantageous only to the State, to facilitate an easier conviction. There is plainly a fundamental fairness interest, even apart from any claim of reliance or notice, in having the government abide by the rules of law it establishes to govern the circumstances under which it can deprive a person of his or her liberty or life. . . .

The United States as *amicus* asks us to revisit the accuracy of the fourth category as an original matter. None of its reasons for abandoning the category is persuasive.

. . . [W]e hold that the petitioner's convictions on counts 7 through 10, insofar as they are not corroborated by other evidence, cannot be sustained under the *Ex Post Facto* Clause, because Texas' amendment to Article 38.07 falls within *Calder*'s fourth category. It seems worth remembering, at this point, Joseph Story's observation about the Clause: "If the laws in being do not punish an offender, let him go unpunished; let the legislature, admonished of the defect of the laws, provide against the commission of future crimes of the same sort. The escape of one delinquent can never produce so much harm to the community, as may arise from the infraction of a rule, upon which the purity of public justice, and the existence of civil liberty, essentially depend." . . . And, of course, nothing in the *Ex Post Facto* Clause prohibits Texas' *prospective* application of its amendment. Accordingly, the judgment of the Texas Court of Appeals is reversed, and the case is remanded for further proceedings not inconsistent with this opinion.

Justice Ginsburg, with whom **The Chief Justice, Justice O'Connor**, and **Justice Kennedy** join, dissenting.

The Court today holds that the amended version of Article 38.07 of the Texas Code of Criminal Procedure reduces the amount of proof necessary to support a sexual assault conviction, and that its retroactive application therefore violates the *Ex Post Facto* Clause. In so holding, the Court misreads both the Texas statute and our precedents concerning the *Ex Post Facto* Clause. Article 38.07 is not, as the Court would have it, most accurately characterized as a "sufficiency of the evidence rule"; it is in its essence an evidentiary provision dictating the circumstances under which the jury may credit victim testimony in sexual offense prosecutions. The amended version of Article 38.07 does nothing more than accord to certain victims of sexual offenses full testimonial stature, giving them the same undiminished competency to testify that Texas extends to witnesses generally in the State's judicial proceedings. Our precedents make clear that such a witness competency rule validly may be applied to offenses committed before its enactment. I therefore dissent.

. . . [I]t is well settled (or was until today) that retroactive changes to rules concerning the admissibility of evidence and the competency of witnesses to testify cannot be *ex post facto*. Because Article 38.07 is in both function and purpose a rule of admissibility, . . . its retroactive application does not violate the *Ex Post Facto* Clause. That conclusion comports perfectly with the dual purposes that underlie the Clause: ensuring fair notice so that individuals can rely on the laws in force at the time they engage in conduct, and sustaining the separation of powers while preventing the passage of vindictive legislation. The Court today thus not only brings about an "undefined enlargement of the *Ex Post Facto* Clause," . . . that conflicts with established precedent, it also fails to advance the Clause's fundamental purposes. For these reasons, I dissent.

Case

DeShaney v. Winnebago Social Services

489 U.S. 189; 109 S.Ct. 998; 103 L.Ed. 2d 249 (1989)
Vote: 6–3

This case dramatizes the tension between law and justice that is inherent in a constitutional system that seeks to "establish justice" and maintain the "rule of law." At issue is whether the failure of a state agency to take action constitutes "state action" for the purposes of the Fourteenth Amendment.

Following his parents' divorce, 1-year-old Joshua DeShaney was placed in the custody of his father, who soon established legal residence in Winnebago County, Wisconsin. Two years later, county social workers began to receive reports that the father was physically abusing the child. When Joshua was 4 years old, his father beat him so severely as to inflict permanent brain damage, leaving the child profoundly retarded and institutionalized for life. Joshua's mother brought suit on her son's behalf under 42 U.S. Code, Section 1983, seeking monetary damages from the state, arguing that the state agency's failure to protect her son constituted an abridgment of his rights under the Fourteenth Amendment.

Chief Justice Rehnquist delivered the opinion of the Court.

. . . The Due Process Clause of the Fourteenth Amendment provides that "[n]o State shall . . . deprive any person of life, liberty, or property, without due process of law." Petitioners contend that the State deprived Joshua of his liberty interest in "free[dom] from . . . unjustified intrusions on personal security," . . . by failing to provide him with adequate protection against his father's violence. The claim is one invoking the substantive rather than procedural component of the Due Process Clause; petitioners do not claim that the State denied Joshua protection without according him appropriate procedural safeguards . . . but that it was categorically obligated to protect him in these circumstances.

But nothing in the language of the Due Process Clause itself requires the State to protect the life, liberty, and property of its citizens against invasion by private actors. The Clause is phrased as a limitation on the State's power to act, not as a guarantee of certain minimal levels of safety and security. It forbids the State itself to deprive individuals of life, liberty, or property without "due process of law," but its language cannot fairly be extended to impose an affirmative obligation on the State to ensure that those interests do not come to harm through other means. Nor does history support such an expansive reading of the constitutional text. Like its counterpart in the Fifth Amendment, the Due Process Clause of the Fourteenth Amendment was intended to prevent government "from abusing [its] power, or employing it as an instrument of oppression. . . ." Its purpose was to protect the people from the State, not to ensure that the State protected them from each other. The Framers were content to leave the extent of governmental obligation in the latter area to the democratic political processes.

Consistent with these principles, our cases have recognized that the Due Process Clauses generally confer no affirmative right to governmental aid, even where such aid may be necessary to secure life, liberty, or property interests of which the government itself may not deprive the individual. . . . If the Due Process Clause does not require the State to provide its citizens with particular protective services, it follows that the State cannot be held liable under the Clause for injuries that could have been averted had it chosen to provide them. As a general matter, then, we conclude that a State's failure to protect an individual against private violence simply does not constitute a violation of the Due Process Clause.

Petitioners contend, however, that even if the Due Process Clause imposes no affirmative obligation on the State to provide the general public with adequate protective services, such a duty may arise out of certain "special relationships" created or assumed by the State with respect to particular individuals. . . . Petitioners argue that such a "special relationship" existed here because the State knew that Joshua faced a special danger of abuse at his father's hands, and specifically proclaimed, by word and by deed, its intention to protect him against that danger. . . . Having actually undertaken to protect Joshua from this danger—which petitioners concede the State played no part in creating—the State acquired an affirmative "duty," enforceable through the Due Process Clause, to do so in a reasonably competent fashion. Its failure to discharge that duty, so the argument goes, was an abuse of governmental power that so "shocks the conscience," . . . as to constitute a substantive due process violation. . . .

We reject this argument. It is true that in certain limited circumstances the Constitution imposes upon the State affirmative duties of care and protection with respect to particular individuals. . . .

. . . While the State may have been aware of the dangers that Joshua faced in the free world, it played no part in their creation, nor did it do anything to render him any more vulnerable to them. That the State once took temporary custody of Joshua does not alter the analysis, for when it returned him to his father's custody, it placed him in no worse position than that in which he would have been had it not acted at all; the State does not become the permanent guarantor of an individual's safety by having once offered him shelter. Under these circumstances, the State had no constitutional duty to protect Joshua. . . .

Judges and lawyers, like other humans, are moved by natural sympathy in a case like this to find a way for Joshua and his mother to receive adequate compensation for the grievous harm inflicted upon them. But before yielding to that impulse, it is well to remember once again that the harm was inflicted not by the State of Wisconsin, but by Joshua's father. The most that can be said of the state functionaries in this case is that they stood by and did nothing when suspicious circumstances dictated a more active role for them. In defense of them it must also be said that had they moved too soon to take custody of the son away from the father, they would likely have been met with charges of improperly intruding into the parent-child relationship. . . .

The people of Wisconsin may well prefer a system of liability which would place upon the State and its officials the responsibility for failure to act in situations such as the present one. They may create such a system, if they do not have it already, by changing the tort law of the State in accordance with the regular law-making process. But they should not have it thrust upon them by this Court's expansion of the Due Process Clause of the Fourteenth Amendment. . . .

Justice Brennan, with whom *Justice Marshall* and *Justice Blackmun* join, dissenting. . . .

Justice Blackmun, dissenting.

Today, the Court purports to be the dispassionate oracle of the law, unmoved by "natural sympathy." But, in this pretense, the Court itself retreats into a sterile formalism which prevents it from recognizing either the facts of the case before it or the legal norms that should apply to those facts. As Justice Brennan demonstrates, the facts here involve not mere passivity, but active state intervention in the life of Joshua DeShaney—intervention that triggered a fundamental duty to aid the boy once the State learned of the severe danger to which he was exposed.

The Court fails to recognize this duty because it attempts to draw a sharp and rigid line between action and inaction. But such formalistic reasoning has no place in the interpretation of the broad and stirring clauses of the Fourteenth Amendment. Indeed, I submit that these clauses were designed, at least in part, to undo the formalistic legal reasoning that infected antebellum jurisprudence, which the late Professor Robert Cover analyzed so effectively in his significant work entitled *Justice Accused* (1975).

Like the antebellum judges who denied relief to fugitive slaves, the Court today claims that its decision, however harsh, is compelled by existing legal doctrine. On the contrary, the question presented by this case is an open one and our Fourteenth Amendment precedents may be read more broadly or narrowly depending upon how one chooses to read them. Faced with the choice, I would adopt a "sympathetic" reading, one which comports with dictates of fundamental justice and recognizes that compassion need not be exiled from the province of judging. . . .

Poor Joshua! Victim of repeated attacks by an irresponsible, bullying, cowardly, and intemperate father, and abandoned by respondents who placed him in a dangerous predicament and who knew or learned what was going on, and yet did essentially nothing except, as the Court revealing observes, . . . "dutifully recorded these incidents in [their] files." It is a sad commentary upon American life, and constitutional principles—so full of late patriotic fervor and proud proclamations about "liberty and justice for all," that this child, Joshua DeShaney, now is assigned to live out the remainder of his life profoundly retarded. Joshua and his mother, as petitioners here, deserve—but now are denied by this Court—the opportunity to have the facts of their case considered in the light of the constitutional protection that 42 U.S.C. Sec. 1983 is meant to provide.

Case

BARRON V. BALTIMORE

7 Pet. (32 U.S.) 243; 8 L.Ed. 672 (1833)
Vote: 7–0

Like the cases that follow in this chapter, Barron v. Baltimore deals with the issue of whether the protections of the Bill of Rights are applicable to actions of the states and their local subdivisions. The case stemmed from an incident in which the city of Baltimore diverted the flow of certain streams, causing silt to be deposited in front of John Barron's wharf, making it unusable. Barron brought suit in state court, claiming that since the City's action amounted to a taking of private property, he was entitled to "just compensation" under the Fifth Amendment to the U.S. Constitution. The trial court agreed and awarded Barron $4,500. After this judgment was reversed by a state appellate court, Barron appealed to the U.S. Supreme Court on a writ of error.

Mr. Chief Justice Marshall delivered the Opinion of the Court:

. . . The plaintiff in error [Barron] contends that [this case] comes within that clause in the Fifth Amendment to the Constitution which inhibits the taking of private property for public use without just compensation. He insists that this amendment, being in favor of the liberty of the citizen, ought to be so construed as to restrain the legislative power of a State, as well as that of the United States. If this proposition be untrue, the Court can take no jurisdiction of the cause.

The question thus presented is, we think, of great importance, but not of much difficulty.

The Constitution was ordained and established by the people of the United States for themselves, for their own government, and not for the government of the individual States. Each State established a constitution for itself, and in that constitution provided such limitations and restrictions on the powers of its particular government as its judgment dictated. The people of the United States framed such a government for the United States as they supposed best adapted to their situation, and best calculated to promote their interests. The powers they conferred on this government were to be exercised by itself; and the limitations on power, if expressed in general terms, are naturally, and, we think, necessarily applicable to the government created by the instrument. They are limitations of power granted in the instrument itself; not of distinct governments, framed by different persons and for different purposes.

If this proposition be correct, the Fifth Amendment must be understood as restraining the power of the general government, not as applicable to the States. In their several constitutions they have imposed such restrictions on their respective governments as their own wisdom suggested; such as they deemed most proper for themselves. It is a subject on which they judge exclusively, and with which others interfere no farther than they are supposed to have a common interest.

The counsel for the plaintiff in error insists that the Constitution was intended to secure the people of the several States against the undue exercise of power by their respective State governments; as well as against that which might be attempted by their general government. In support of this argument he relies on the inhibitions contained in the tenth section of the first article.

We think that section affords a strong if not a conclusive argument in support of the opinion already indicated by the Court.

The preceding section contains restrictions which are obviously intended for the exclusive purpose of restraining the exercise of power by the departments of the general government. Some of them use language applicable only to Congress, others are expressed in general terms. The third clause, for example, declares that "no bill of attainder or *ex post facto* law shall be passed." No language can be more general; yet the demonstration is complete that it applies solely to the government of the United States. In addition to the general arguments furnished by the instrument itself, some of which have been already suggested, the succeeding section, the avowed purpose of which is to restrain State legislation, contains in terms the very prohibition. It declares that "no State shall pass any bill of attainder or *ex post facto* law." This provision then,

of the ninth section, however comprehensive its language, contains no restriction on State legislation.

The ninth section having enumerated, in the nature of a bill of rights, the limitations intended to be imposed on the powers of the general government, the tenth proceeds to enumerate those which were to operate on the State legislatures. These restrictions are brought together in the same section, and are by express words applied to the States. . . .

. . . It would be tedious to recapitulate the several limitations on the powers of the States which are contained in this section. They will be found, generally, to restrain State legislation on subjects entrusted to the government of the Union, in which the citizens of all the States are interested. In these alone were the whole people concerned. The question of their application to States is not left to construction. It is averred in positive words.

If the original Constitution, in the ninth and tenth sections of the first article, draws this plain and marked line of discrimination between the limitations it imposes on the powers of the general government and on those of the States; if in every inhibition intended to act on State power, words are employed which directly express that intent, some strong reason must be assigned for departing from this safe and judicious course in framing the amendments, before that departure can be assumed.

We search in vain for that reason. . . .

We are of opinion that the provision in the Fifth Amendment to the Constitution, declaring that private property shall not be taken for public use without just compensations, is intended solely as a limitation on the exercise of power by the government of the United States, and is not applicable to the legislation of the States. We are therefore of opinion that there is no repugnancy between the several acts of the General Assembly of Maryland, given in evidence by the defendants at the trial of this cause in the court of that State, and the Constitution of the United States. . . .

Case

HURTADO V. CALIFORNIA

110 U.S. 516; 4 S.Ct. 111; 28 L.Ed. 232 (1884)
Vote: 7–1

Here the Court considers whether the grand jury requirement of the Fifth Amendment is applicable to state criminal prosecutions by way of the Fourteenth Amendment. The facts are contained in Justice Matthews's majority opinion.

Mr. Justice Matthews delivered the Opinion of the Court:

The Constitution of the State of California adopted in 1879, in article I, section 8, provides as follows:

Offenses heretofore required to be prosecuted by indictment shall be prosecuted by information after examination and commitment by a magistrate, or by indictment, with or without such examination and commitment, as may be prescribed by law. A grand jury shall be drawn and summoned at least once a year in each county.

Various provisions of the [California] Penal Code regulate proceedings before the examining and committing magistrate in cases of persons arrested and brought before them upon charges of having committed public offenses. These require, among other things, that the testimony of the witnesses shall be reduced to writing in the form of deposition; and section 872 declares that if it appears from the examination that a public offense has been committed, and there is sufficient cause to believe the defendant guilty thereof, the magistrate must indorse on the depositions an order, signed by him, to that effect, describing the general nature of the offense committed, and ordering that the defendant be held to answer thereto. Sec. 809 of the Penal Code is as follows.

When a defendant has been examined and committed, as provided in section 872 of this Code, it shall be the duty of the district attorney, within thirty days thereafter, to file in the superior court of the county in which the offense is triable, an information charging the defendant with such offense. The information shall be in the name of the people of the State of California, and subscribed by the district attorney, and shall be in form like an indictment for the same offense.

In pursuance of the foregoing provision of the Constitution, and of the several sections of the Penal Code of California, the District Attorney of Sacramento County, on the 20th day of February, 1882, made and filed an information against the plaintiff in error, charging him with the crime of murder in the killing of one Jose Antonio Stuardo. Upon this information and without any previous investigation of the cause by any grand jury, the plaintiff in error was arraigned on the 22d day of March, 1882, and pleaded not guilty. A trial of the issue was thereafter had, and on May 7, 1882, the jury rendered its verdict, in which it found the plaintiff in error guilty of murder in the first degree.

On the 5th day of July, 1882, the Superior Court of Sacramento County, in which the plaintiff in error had been tried, rendered its judgment upon said verdict, that the said Joseph Hurtado, plaintiff in error, be punished by the infliction of death, and the day of his execution was fixed for the 20th day of July, 1882. From this judgment an appeal was taken, and the Supreme Court of the State of California affirmed the judgment.

The proposition of law we are asked to affirm is, that an indictment or presentment by a grand jury, as known to the common law of England, is essential to that "due process of law," when applied to prosecutions for felonies, which is secured and guarantied by this provision of the Constitution of the United States, and which accordingly it is forbidden to the States respectively to dispense with in the administration of criminal law.

We are to construe this phrase in the 14th Amendment by the *usus loquendi* of the Constitution itself. The same words are contained in the 5th Amendment. That article makes specific and express provision for perpetuating the institution of the grand jury, so far as relates to prosecutions, for the most aggravated crimes under the laws of the United States. It declares that "[n]o person shall be held to answer for a capital or otherwise infamous crime, unless on a presentment or indictment of a grand jury, except in cases arising in the land or naval forces, or in the militia when in actual service in time of war or public danger; nor shall any person be subject for the same offense to be twice put in jeopardy of life or limb; nor shall he be compelled in any criminal case to be a witness against himself." It then immediately adds: "nor be deprived of life, liberty or property, without due process of law." According to a recognized canon of interpretation, especially applicable to formal and solemn instruments of constitutional law, we are forbidden to assume, without clear reason to the contrary, that any part of this most important Amendment is superfluous. The natural and obvious inference is, that in the sense of the Constitution, "due process of law" was not meant or intended to include, *ex vi termini*, the institution and procedure of a grand jury in any case. The conclusion is equally irresistible, that when the same phrase was employed in the 14th Amendment to restrain the action of the States, it was used in the same sense and with no greater extent; and that if in the adoption of that Amendment it had been part of its purpose to perpetuate the institution of the grand jury in all the States, it would have embodied, as did the 5th Amendment, express declarations to that effect. Due process of law in the latter refers to that law of the land, which derives its authority from the legislative powers conferred upon Congress by the Constitution of the United States, exercised within the limits therein prescribed, and interpreted according to the principles of the common law. In the 14th Amendment, by parity of reason, it refers to that law of the land in each State, which derives its authority from the inherent and reserved powers of the State, exerted within the limits of those fundamental principles of liberty and justice which lie at the base of all our civil and political institutions, and the greatest security for which resides in the right of the people to make their own laws, and alter them at their pleasure.

For these reasons, finding no error therein, the judgment of the Supreme Court of California is affirmed.

Mr. Justice Harlan, dissenting.

. . . "Due process of law," within the meaning of the national Constitution, does not import one thing with reference to the powers of the States, and another with reference to the powers of the general government. If particular proceedings conducted under the authority of the general government, and involving life, are prohibited, because not constituting that due process of law required by the Fifth Amendment of the Constitution of the United States, similar proceedings, conducted under the authority of a State, must be deemed illegal as not being due process of law within the meaning of the Fourteenth Amendment. What, then, is the meaning of the words, "due process of law" in the latter amendment? . . .

According to the settled usages and modes of proceeding existing under the common and statute law of England at the settlement of this country, information in capital cases was not consistent with the "law of the land," or with "due process of law." Such was the understanding of the patriotic men who established free institutions upon this continent. Almost the identical words of Magna Charta were incorporated into most of the State Constitutions before the adoption of our national Constitution. When they declared, in substance, that no person should be deprived of life, liberty or property, except by the judgment of his peers of the law of the land, they intended to assert his right to the same guaranties that were given in the mother country by the great charter and the laws passed in furtherance of its fundamental principles. . . .

But it is said that the framers of the Constitution did not suppose that due process of law necessarily required

for a capital offence the institution and procedure of a grand jury, else they would not in the same amendment prohibiting the deprivation of life, liberty, or property, without due process of law, have made specific and express provision for a grand jury where the crime is capital or otherwise infamous; therefore, it is argued, the requirement by the Fourteenth Amendment of due process of law in all proceedings involving life, liberty, and property, without specific reference to grand juries in any case whatever, was not intended as a restriction upon the power which it is claimed the States previously had, so far as the express restrictions of the national Constitution are concerned, to dispense altogether with grand juries.

This line of argument, it seems to me, would lead to results which are inconsistent with the vital principles of republican government. If the presence in the Fifth Amendment of a specific provision for grand juries in capital cases, alongside the provision for due process of law in proceedings involving life, liberty, or property, is held to prove that "due process of law" did not, in the judgment of the framers of the Constitution, necessarily require a grand jury in capital cases, inexorable logic would require it to be, likewise, held that the right not to be put twice in jeopardy of life and limb for the same offense, nor compelled in a criminal case to testify against one's self—rights and immunities also specifically recognized in the Fifth Amendment—were not protected by that due process of law required by the settled usages and proceedings existing under the common and statute law of England at the settlement of this country. More than that, other amendments of the Constitution proposed at the same time, expressly recognize the right of persons to just compensation for private property taken for public use; their right, when accused of crime, to be informed of the nature and cause of the accusation against them, and to a speedy and public trial, by an impartial jury of the State and district wherein the crime was committed: to be confronted by the witnesses against them; and to have compulsory process for obtaining witnesses in their favor. Will it be claimed that these rights were not secured by the "law of the land" or by "due process of law," as declared and established at the foundation of our government? Are they to be excluded from the enumeration of the fundamental principles of liberty and justice, and, therefore, not embraced by "due process of law?" If the argument of my brethren be sound, those rights—although universally recognized at the establishment of our institutions as secured by that due process of law which for centuries had been the foundation of Anglo-Saxon liberty—were not deemed by our fathers as essential in the due process of law prescribed by our Constitution; because—such seems to be the argument—had they been regarded as involved in due process of law they would not have been specifically and expressly provided for, but left to the protection given by the general clause forbidding the deprivation of life, liberty, or property without due process of law. Further, the reasoning of the opinion indubitably leads to the conclusion that but for the specific provisions made in the Constitution for the security of the personal rights enumerated, the general inhibition against deprivation of life, liberty and property without due process of law would not have prevented Congress from enacting a statute in derogation of each of them. . . .

Mr. Justice Field did not take part in the decision of this case.

Case

CHICAGO, BURLINGTON, & QUINCY RAILROAD COMPANY V. CHICAGO

166 U.S. 226; 17 S.Ct. 581; 41 L.Ed. 979 (1897)
Vote: 7–1

This case arose when the city of Chicago sought to widen Rockwell Street between West Eighteenth and West Nineteenth Streets. To obtain the land necessary to widen the street, the city used its power of eminent domain, taking part of the right-of-way owned by the Chicago, Burlington, & Quincy Railroad. A state trial court awarded the railroad company a mere $1 as "just compensation" for the condemned parcels of land. The railroad took the case to the U.S. Supreme Court on a writ of error. Although the Court ruled in favor of the city, its opinion made new law by extending the Just Compensation Clause of the Fifth Amendment to state action under the Fourteenth Amendment.

Mr. Justice Harlan delivered the opinion of the Court.

. . . [A] state may not, by any of its agencies, disregard the prohibitions of the 14th Amendment. Its judicial authorities may keep within the letter of the statute prescribing forms of procedure in the courts and give the parties the fullest opportunity to be heard, and yet it might be that its final action would be inconsistent with that Amendment. In determining what is due process of law, regard must be had to substance, not to form. This court, referring to the 14th Amendment, has said: "Can a state make anything due process of law which, by its own legislation, it chooses to declare such? To affirm this is to hold that the prohibition to the states is of no avail, or has no application where the invasion of private rights is effected under the forms of state legislation. . . ." The same question could be propounded, and the same answer could be made, in reference to judicial proceedings inconsistent with the requirement of due process of law. If compensation for private property taken for public use is an essential element of due process of law as ordained by the 14th Amendment, then the final judgment of a state court, under the authority of which the property is in fact taken, is to be deemed the act of the state within the meaning of that Amendment.

It is proper now to inquire whether the due process of law enjoined by the 14th Amendment requires compensation to be made or adequately secured to the owner of private property taken for public use under the authority of a state.

. . . [A] statute declaring in terms, without more, that the full and exclusive title to a described piece of land belonging to one person should be and is hereby vested in another person, would, if effectual, deprive the former of his property without due process of law, within the meaning of the 14th Amendment. . . . Such an enactment would not receive judicial sanction in any country having a written Constitution distributing the powers of government among three coordinate departments, and committing to the judiciary, expressly or by implication, authority to enforce the provisions of such Constitution. It would be treated, not as an exertion of legislative power, but as a sentence—an act of spoliation. Due protection of the rights of property has been regarded as a vital principle of republican institutions. The requirement that the property shall not be taken for public use without just compensation is but "an affirmance of a great doctrine established by the common law for the protection of private property. It is founded in natural equity, and is laid down as a principle of universal law. Indeed, in a free government almost all other rights would become worthless if the government possessed an uncontrollable power over the private fortune of every citizen." . . .

. . . We have examined all the questions of law arising on the record of which this court may take cognizance, and which, in our opinion, are of sufficient importance to require notice at our hands, and finding no error, the judgment [of the state court] is affirmed.

Mr. Justice Brewer, dissenting:

I dissent from the judgment in this case. I approve that which is said in the first part of the opinion as to the potency of the 14th Amendment to restrain action by a state through either its legislative, executive or judicial departments, which deprives a party of his property rights without due compensation. . . .

It is disappointing after reading so strong a declaration of the protecting reach of the 14th Amendment and the power and duty of this court in enforcing it as against action by a state by any of its officers or agencies, to find sustained a judgment, depriving a party—even though a railroad corporation—of valuable property without any, or, at least only nominal, compensation. . . .

The Chief Justice took no part in the consideration or decision of this case.

Case

PALKO V. CONNECTICUT

302 U.S. 319; 58 S.Ct. 149; 82 L.Ed. 288 (1937)
Vote: 8–1

Here the Court sets forth a test for determining which provisions of the Bill of Rights are applicable to the states via the Fourteenth Amendment.

Mr. *Justice Cardozo* delivered the opinion of the Court.

A statute of Connecticut permitting appeals in criminal cases to be taken by the state is challenged by appellant as an infringement of the Fourteenth Amendment of the Constitution of the United States. Whether the challenge should be upheld is now to be determined. . . .

The argument for appellant is that whatever is forbidden by the Fifth Amendment is forbidden by the Fourteenth also. The Fifth Amendment, which is not directed to the states, but solely to the federal government, creates immunity from double jeopardy. No person shall be "subject for the same offense to be twice put in jeopardy of life or limb." The Fourteenth Amendment ordains, "nor shall any state deprive any person of life, liberty, or property, without due process of law." To retry a defendant, though under one indictment and only one, subjects him, it is said, to double jeopardy in violation of the Fifth Amendment, if the prosecution is one on behalf of the United States. From this the consequence is said to follow that there is a denial of life or liberty without due process of law, if the prosecution is one on behalf of the People of a State. . . .

We do not find it profitable to mark the precise limits of the prohibition of double jeopardy in federal prosecutions. . . .

We have said that in appellant's view the Fourteenth Amendment is to be taken as embodying the prohibitions of the Fifth. His thesis is even broader. Whatever would be a violation of the original Bill of Rights (Amendments 1 to 8) if done by the federal government is now equally unlawful by force of the Fourteenth Amendment if done by a state. There is no such general rule.

The Fifth Amendment provides, among other things, that no person shall be held to answer for a capital or otherwise infamous crime unless on presentment or indictment of a grand jury. This court has held that, in prosecutions by a state, presentment or indictment by a grand jury may give way to informations at the instance of a public officer. . . . The Fifth Amendment provides also that no person shall be compelled in any criminal case to be a witness against himself. This court has said that, in prosecutions by a state, the exemption will fail if the state elects to end it. . . . The Sixth Amendment calls for a jury trial in criminal cases and the Seventh for a jury trial in civil cases at common law where the value in controversy shall exceed twenty dollars. This court has ruled that consistently with those amendments trial by jury may be modified by a state or abolished altogether. . . .

On the other hand, the Due Process Clause of the Fourteenth Amendment may make it unlawful for a state to abridge by its statutes the freedom of speech which the First Amendment safeguards against encroachment by the Congress . . . or the right of peaceable assembly, without which speech would be unduly trammeled or the right of one accused of crime to the benefit of counsel. . . . In these and other situations immunities that are valid as against the federal government by force of the specific pledges of particular amendments have been found to be implicit in the concept of ordered liberty, and thus, through the Fourteenth Amendment, become valid as against the states.

The line of division may seem to be wavering and broken if there is a hasty catalogue of the cases on the one side and the other. Reflection and analysis will induce a different view. There emerges the perception of a rationalizing principle which gives to discrete instances a proper order and coherence. The right to trial by jury and the immunity from prosecution except as the result of an indictment may have value and importance. Even so, they are not of the very essence of a scheme of ordered liberty. To abolish them is not to violate a "principle of justice so rooted in the traditions and conscience of our people as to be ranked as fundamental. . . ." Few would be so narrow or provincial as to maintain that a fair and enlightened system of justice would be impossible without them. What is true of jury trials and indictments is true also, as the cases show, of the immunity from compulsory self-incrimination. . . . This too might be lost, and justice still be done. Indeed, today as in the past there are students of our penal system who look upon the immunity as a mischief rather than a benefit, and who would limit its scope or destroy it altogether. No doubt there would remain the need to give protection against torture, physical or mental. . . . Justice, however, would not perish if the accused were subject to a duty to respond to orderly inquiry. . . .

We reach a different plane of social and moral values when we pass to the privileges and immunities that have been taken over from the earlier articles of the federal Bill of Rights and brought within the Fourteenth Amendment by a process of absorption. These in their origin were effective against the federal government alone. If the Fourteenth Amendment has absorbed them, the process of absorption has had its source in the belief that neither liberty nor justice would exist if they were sacrificed. . . . This is true, for illustration, of freedom of thought and speech. Of that freedom one may say that it is the matrix, the indispensable condition, of nearly every other form of freedom. With rare aberrations a pervasive recognition of that truth can be traced in our history, political and legal. So it has come about that the domain of liberty, withdrawn by the Fourteenth Amendment from encroachment by the states, has been enlarged by latter-day judgments to include liberty of the mind as well as liberty of action. The extension became, indeed, a logical imperative when once it was recognized, as long ago it was, that liberty is something more than exemption from physical restraint, and that even in the field of substantive rights and duties the legislative judgment, if oppressive and arbitrary, may be overridden by the courts. . . . Fundamental too in the concept of due process, and so in that of liberty, is the thought that condemnation shall be rendered only after trial. . . . The hearing, moreover, must be a real one, not a sham or a pretense. . . . For that reason, ignorant defendants in a capital case were held to have been condemned unlawfully when in truth, though not in form, they were refused the aid of counsel. . . . The decision did not turn upon the fact that the benefit of counsel would have been guaranteed to the defendants by the provisions of the Sixth Amendment if they had been prosecuted in a federal court. The decision turned upon the fact that in the particular situation laid before us in the evidence the benefit of counsel was essential to the substance of a hearing.

Our survey of the cases serves, we think, to justify the statement that the dividing line between them, if not unfaltering throughout its course, has been true for the most part to a unifying principle. On which side of the line the case made out by the appellant has appropriate location must be the next inquiry and the final one. Is that kind of double jeopardy to which the statute has subjected him a hardship so acute and shocking that our polity will not endure it? Does it violate those "fundamental principles of liberty and justice which lie at the base of all our civil and political institutions"? . . . The answer surely must be "no." What the answer would have to be if the state were permitted after a trial free from error to try the accused over again or to bring another case against him, we have no occasion to consider. We deal with the statute before us and no other. The state is not attempting to wear the accused out by a multitude of cases with accumulated trials. It asks no more than this, that the case against him shall go on until there shall be a trial free from the corrosion of substantial legal error. . . . This is not cruelty at all, nor even vexation in any immoderate degree. If the trial had been infected with error adverse to the accused, there might have been review at his instance, and as often as necessary to purge the vicious taint. A reciprocal privilege, subject at all times to the discretion of the presiding judge . . . has now been granted to the state. There is here no seismic innovation. The edifice of justice stands, in its symmetry, to many, greater than before. . . .

The judgment is affirmed.

Mr. Justice Butler dissents.

Case

ADAMSON V. CALIFORNIA

332 U.S. 46; 67 S.Ct. 1672; 91 L.Ed. 1903 (1947)
Vote: 5–4

In Twining v. New Jersey (1908), the Court held that the Fifth Amendment protection against compulsory self-incrimination did not have to be honored in state criminal trials. The Court revisits this question in the instant case. The student should pay close attention to the different theories of Fourteenth Amendment due process espoused in the various opinions in this case.

Mr. Justice Reed delivered the opinion of the Court.

The appellant, Adamson, a citizen of the United States, was convicted, without recommendation for mercy, by a jury in a Superior Court of the State of California of murder in the first degree. After considering the same objections to the conviction that are pressed here, the sentence of death was affirmed by the Supreme Court of the state. The provisions of California law which were challenged . . . as invalid under the Fourteenth Amendment . . . permit the failure of a defendant to explain or to deny evidence against him to be commented upon by court and by counsel and to be considered by court and jury. The defendant did not testify. As the trial court gave its instructions and the District Attorney argued the case in accordance with the constitutional and statutory provisions just referred to, we have for decision the question of their constitutionality.

The appellant was charged in the information with former convictions for burglary, larceny and robbery and pursuant to 1025, California Penal Code, answered that he had suffered the previous convictions. This answer barred allusion to these charges of convictions on the trial. Under California's interpretation of Sec. 1025 of the Penal Code and Sec. 2051 of the Code of Civil Procedure, however, if the defendant, after answering affirmative charges alleging prior convictions, takes the witness stand to deny or explain away other evidence that has been introduced "the commission of these crimes could have been revealed to the jury on cross-examination to impeach his testimony." This forces an accused who is a repeat offender to choose between the risk of having his prior offenses disclosed to the jury or having it draw harmful inferences from uncontradicted evidence that can only be denied or explained by the defendant.

In the first place, appellant urges that the provision of the Fifth Amendment that no person "shall be compelled in any criminal case to be a witness against himself" is a fundamental national privilege or immunity protected against state abridgment by the Fourteenth Amendment or a privilege or immunity secured, through the Fourteenth Amendment, against deprivation by state action because it is a personal right, enumerated in the federal Bill of Rights.

Secondly, appellant relies upon the due process of law clause of the Fourteenth Amendment to invalidate the provisions of the California law and as applied (a) because comment on failure to testify is permitted, (b) because appellant was forced to forego testimony in person because of danger of disclosure of his past convictions through cross-examination and (c) because the presumption of innocence was infringed by the shifting of the burden of proof to appellant in permitting comment on his failure to testify.

We shall assume, but without any intention thereby of ruling upon the issue, that permission by law to the court, counsel and jury to comment upon and consider the failure of defendant "to explain or to deny by his testimony any evidence or facts in the case against him" would infringe defendant's privilege against self-incrimination under the Fifth Amendment if this were a trial in a court of the United States under a similar law. Such an assumption does not determine appellant's rights under the Fourteenth Amendment. It is settled law that the clause of the Fifth Amendment, protecting a person against being compelled to be a witness against himself, is not made effective by the Fourteenth Amendment as a protection against state action on the ground that freedom from testimonial compulsion is a right of national citizenship, or because it is a personal privilege or immunity secured by the Federal Constitution as one of the rights of man that are listed in the Bill of Rights.

The reasoning that leads to those conclusions starts with the unquestioned premise that the Bill of Rights, when adopted, was for the protection of the individual against the federal government and its provisions were inapplicable to similar actions done by the states. . . . With the adoption of the Fourteenth Amendment, it was suggested that the dual citizenship recognized by its first sentence, secured for citizens' federal protection for their elemental privileges and immunities of state citizenship. *The Slaughter-House Cases* decided, contrary to the suggestion, that these rights, as privileges and immunities of state citizenship, remained under the sole protection of the state governments. This Court, without the expression of a contrary view upon that phase of the issues before the Court, has approved this determination. The power to free defendants in state trials from self-incrimination was specifically determined to be beyond the scope of the privileges and immunities clause of the Fourteenth Amendment in *Twining v. New Jersey.* . . .

We reaffirm the conclusion of the *Twining and Palko* Cases that protection against self-incrimination is not a privilege or immunity of national citizenship.

A right to a fair trial is a right admittedly protected by the due process clause of the Fourteenth Amendment. Therefore, appellant argues, the due process clause of the Fourteenth Amendment protects his privilege against self-incrimination. The due process clause of the Fourteenth Amendment, however, does not draw all the rights of the federal Bill of Rights under its protection. That contention was made and rejected in *Palko v. Connecticut.* . . . It was rejected with citation of the cases excluding several of the rights, protected by the Bill of Rights, against infringement by the National Government. Nothing has been called to our attention that either the framers of the Fourteenth Amendment or the states that adopted it intended its due process clause to draw within its scope the earlier amendments to the Constitution. *Palko* held that such provisions of the Bill of Rights as were "implicit in the concept of ordered liberty," became secure from state interference by the clause. But it held nothing more.

For a state to require testimony from an accused is not necessarily a breach of a state's obligation to give a fair trial. Therefore, we must examine the effect of the California law applied in this trial to see whether the comment on failure to testify violates the protection against state action that the due process clause does grant to an accused. The due process clause forbids compulsion to testify by fear of hurt, torture or exhaustion. So our inquiry is directed, not at the broad question of the constitutionality of compulsory testimony from the accused under the due process clause, but to the constitutionality of the provision of the California law that permits comment upon his failure to testify. It is, of course, logically possible that while an accused might be required, under appropriate penalties, to submit himself as a witness without a violation of due process, comment by judge or jury on inferences to be drawn from his failure to testify, in jurisdictions where an accused's privilege against self-incrimination is protected, might deny due process. For example, a statute might declare that a permitted refusal to testify would compel an acceptance of the truth of the prosecution's evidence.

Generally, comment on the failure of an accused to testify is forbidden in American jurisdictions. This arises from state constitutional or statutory provisions similar in character to the federal provisions. . . . California, however, is one of a few states that permit limited comment upon a defendant's failure to testify. That permission is narrow. The California law authorizes comment by court

and counsel upon the "failure of the defendant to explain or to deny by his testimony any evidence or facts in the case against him." This does not involve any presumption, rebuttable or irrebuttable, either of guilt or of the truth of any fact, that is offered in evidence. It allows inferences to be drawn from proven facts. Because of this clause, the court can direct the jury's attention to whatever evidence there may be that a defendant could deny and the prosecution can argue as to inferences that may be drawn from the accused's failure to testify. California has prescribed a method for advising the jury in the search for truth. However sound may be the legislative conclusion that an accused should not be compelled in any criminal case to be a witness against himself, we see no reason why comment should not be made upon his silence. It seems quite natural that when a defendant has opportunity to deny or explain facts and determines not to do so, the prosecution should bring out the strength of the evidence by commenting upon defendant's failure to explain or deny it. The prosecution evidence may be of facts that may be beyond the knowledge of the accused. If so, his failure to testify would have little if any weight. But the facts may be such as are necessarily in the knowledge of the accused. In that case a failure to explain would point to an inability to explain.

Appellant sets out the circumstances of this case, however, to show coercion and unfairness in permitting comment. The guilty person was not seen at the place and time of the crime. There was evidence, however, that entrance to the place or room where the crime was committed might have been obtained through a small door. It was freshly broken. Evidence showed that six fingerprints on the door were petitioner's. Certain diamond rings were missing from the deceased's possession. There was evidence that appellant, sometime after the crime, asked an unidentified person whether the latter would be interested in purchasing a diamond ring. As has been stated, the information charged other crimes to appellant and he admitted them. His argument here is that he could not take the stand to deny the evidence against him because he would be subjected to a cross-examination as to former crimes to impeach his veracity and the evidence so produced might well bring about his conviction. Such cross-examination is allowable in California. Therefore, appellant contends the California statute permitting comment denies him due process.

It is true that if comment were forbidden, an accused in this situation could remain silent and avoid evidence of former crimes and comment upon his failure to testify. We are of the view, however, that a state may control such a situation in accordance with its own ideas of the most efficient administration of criminal justice. The purpose of due process is not to protect an accused against a proper conviction but against an unfair conviction. When evidence is before a jury that threatens conviction, it does not seem unfair to require him to choose between leaving the adverse evidence unexplained and subjecting himself to impeachment through disclosures of former crimes. Indeed, this is a dilemma with which any defendant may be faced. If facts, adverse to the defendant, are proven by the prosecution, there may be no way to explain them favorably to the accused except by a witness who may be vulnerable to impeachment on cross-examination. The defendant must then decide whether or not to use such a witness. The fact that the witness may also be the defendant makes the choice more difficult but a denial of due process does not emerge from the circumstances. . . .

Mr. Justice Frankfurter, concurring.

. . . [T]he issue is not whether an infraction of one of the specific provisions of the first eight Amendments is disclosed by the record. The relevant question is whether the criminal proceedings which resulted in conviction deprived the accused of the due process of law to which the United States Constitution entitled him. Judicial review of that guaranty of the Fourteenth Amendment inescapably imposes upon this Court an exercise of judgment upon the whole course of the proceedings in order to ascertain whether they offend those canons of decency and fairness which express the notions of justice of English-speaking peoples even toward those charged with the most heinous offenses. These standards of justice are not authoritatively formulated anywhere as though they were prescriptions in a pharmacopoeia. But neither does the application of Due Process Clause imply that judges are wholly at large. The judicial judgment in applying the Due Process Clause must move within the limits of accepted notions of justice and is not to be based upon the idiosyncracies of a merely personal judgment. The fact that judges among themselves may differ whether in a particular case a trial offends accepted notions of justice is not disproof that general rather than idiosyncratic standards are applied. An important safeguard against such merely individual judgment is an alert deference to the judgment of the State court under review.

Mr. Justice Black [joined by Mr. Justice Douglas], dissenting.

This decision reasserts a constitutional theory spelled out in Twining v. New Jersey . . . that this Court is endowed by the Constitution with boundless power under "natural law" periodically to expand and contract constitutional standards to conform to the Court's conception of what at a particular time constitutes "civilized decency" and "fundamental liberty and justice." Invoking this Twining rule, the Court concludes that although comment upon testi-

mony in a federal court would violate the Fifth Amendment, identical comment in a state court does not violate today's fashion in today's decency and fundamentals and is therefore not prohibited by the Federal Constitution as amended.

The Twining Case was the first, and it is the only, decision of this Court, which has squarely held that states were free, notwithstanding the Fifth and Fourteenth Amendments, to extort evidence from one accused of crime. I agree that if Twining be reaffirmed, the result reached might appropriately follow. But I would not reaffirm the Twining decision. I think that decision and the "natural law" theory of the Constitution upon which it relies degrade the constitutional safeguards of the Bill of Rights and simultaneously appropriate for this Court a broad power which we are not authorized by the Constitution to exercise.

Whether this Court ever will, or whether it now should, in the light of past decisions, give full effect to what the Amendment was intended to accomplish is not necessarily essential to a decision here. However that may be, our prior decisions, including Twining, do not prevent our carrying out that purpose, at least to the extent of making applicable to the states, not a mere part, as the Court has, but the full protection of the Fifth Amendment's provision against compelling evidence from an accused to convict him of crime. And I further contend that the "natural law" formula which the Court uses to reach its conclusion in this case should be abandoned as an incongruous excrescence on our Constitution. I believe that formula to be itself a violation of our Constitution, in that it subtly conveys to courts, at the expense of legislatures, ultimate power over public policies in fields where no specific provision of the Constitution limits legislative power.

I cannot consider the Bill of Rights to be an outworn 18th Century "strait jacket" as the Twining opinion did. Its provisions may be thought outdated abstractions by some. And it is true that they were designed to meet ancient evils. But they are the same kind of human evils that have emerged from century to century wherever excessive power is sought by the few at the expense of the many. In my judgment the people of no nation can lose their liberty so long as a Bill of Rights like ours survives and its basic purposes are conscientiously interpreted, enforced and respected so as to afford continuous protection against old, as well as new, devices and practices which might thwart those purposes. I fear to see the consequences of the Court's practice of substituting its own concepts of decency and fundamental justice for the language of the Bill of Rights as its point of departure in interpreting and enforcing that Bill of Rights. If the choice must be between the selective process of the Palko decision applying some of the Bill of Rights to the States, or the Twining rule applying none of them, I would choose the *Palko* selective process. But rather than accept either of these choices, I would follow what I believe was the original purpose of the Fourteenth Amendment—to extend to all the people of the nation the complete protection of the Bill of Rights. To hold that this Court can determine what, if any provisions of the Bill of Rights will be enforced, and if so to what degree, is to frustrate the great design of a written Constitution.

Conceding the possibility that this Court is now wise enough to improve on the Bill of Rights by substituting natural law concepts for the Bill of Rights, I think the possibility is entirely too speculative to agree to take that course. I would therefore hold in this case that the full protection of the Fifth Amendment's proscription against compelled testimony must be afforded by California. This I would do because of reliance upon the original purpose of the Fourteenth Amendment. . . .

Mr. Justice Murphy, with whom *Mr. Justice Rutledge* concurs, dissenting.

. . . I agree that the specific guarantees of the Bill of Rights should be carried over intact into the first section of the Fourteenth Amendment. But I am not prepared to say that the latter is entirely and necessarily limited by the Bill of Rights. Occasions may arise where a proceeding falls so far short of conforming to fundamental standards of procedure as to warrant constitutional condemnation in terms of a lack of due process despite the absence of a specific provision in the Bill of Rights.

The point, however, need not be pursued here inasmuch as the Fifth Amendment is explicit in its provision that no person shall be compelled in any criminal case to be a witness against himself. That provision, as Mr. Justice Black demonstrates, is a constituent part of the Fourteenth Amendment.

Moreover, it is my belief that this guarantee against self-incrimination has been violated in this case. Under California law, the judge or prosecutor may comment on the failure of the defendant in a criminal trial to explain or deny any evidence or facts introduced against him. As interpreted and applied in this case, such a provision compels a defendant to be a witness against himself in one of two ways:

1. If he does not take the stand, his silence is used as the basis for drawing unfavorable inferences against him as to matters which he might reasonably be expected to explain. Thus he is compelled, through his silence, to testify against himself. And silence can be as effective in this situation as oral statements.

2. If he does take the stand, thereby opening himself to cross-examination, so as to overcome the effects of the provision in question, he is necessarily compelled to testify against himself. In that case, his testimony on cross-examination is the result of the coercive pressure of the provision rather than his own volition.

Much can be said pro and con as to the desirability of allowing comment on the failure of the accused to testify. But policy arguments are to no avail in the face of a clear constitutional command. This guarantee of freedom from self-incrimination is grounded on a deep respect for those who might prefer to remain silent before their accusers. "It is not every one who can safely venture on the witness stand though entirely innocent of the charge against him. Excessive timidity, nervousness when facing others and attempting to explain transactions of a suspicious character, and offenses charged against him, will often confuse and embarrass him to such a degree as to increase rather than remove prejudices against him. It is not every one, however honest, who would, therefore, willingly be placed on the witness stand."

We are obliged to give effect to the principle of freedom from self-incrimination. That principle is as applicable where the compelled testimony is in the form of silence as where it is composed of oral statements. Accordingly, I would reverse the judgment below.

Case

ROCHIN V. CALIFORNIA

342 U.S. 165; 72 S.Ct. 205; 96 L.Ed. 183 (1952)
Vote: 8–0

Here, the Court again considers the meaning of the Due Process Clause of the Fourteenth Amendment and the relationship of the Bill of Rights to the states. Again, the specific issue is that of compulsory self-incrimination. The facts are contained in Justice Frankfurter's majority opinion.

Mr. Justice Frankfurter delivered the opinion of the Court.

Having "some information that [the petitioner] was selling narcotics," three deputy sheriffs of the County of Los Angeles, on the morning of July 1, 1949, made for the two-story dwelling house in which Rochin lived with his mother, common-law wife, brothers and sisters. Finding the outside door open, they entered and then forced open the door to Rochin's room on the second floor. Inside they found petitioner sitting partly dressed on the side of the bed, upon which his wife was lying. On a "night stand" beside the bed the deputies spied two capsules. When asked "Whose stuff is this?" Rochin seized the capsules and put them in his mouth. A struggle ensued, in the course of which the three officers "jumped upon him" and attempted to extract the capsules. The force they applied proved unavailing against Rochin's resistance. He was handcuffed and taken to a hospital. At the direction of one of the officers a doctor forced an emetic solution through a tube into Rochin's stomach against his will. This "stomach pumping" produced vomiting. In the vomited matter were found two capsules which proved to contain morphine.

Rochin was brought to trial before a California Superior Court, sitting without a jury, on the charge of possessing "a preparation of morphine" in violation of the California Health and Safety Code. . . . Rochin was convicted and sentenced to sixty days' imprisonment. The chief evidence against him was the two capsules. They were admitted over petitioner's objection, although the means of obtaining them was frankly set forth in the testimony by one of the deputies, substantially as here narrated.

On appeal, the District Court of Appeal affirmed the conviction, despite the finding that the officers "were guilty of unlawfully breaking into and entering defendant's room and were guilty of unlawfully assaulting and battering defendant while in the room," and "were guilty of unlawfully assaulting, battering, torturing and falsely imprisoning the defendant at the alleged hospital." . . .

This Court granted certiorari, because a serious question is raised as to the limitations which the Due Process Clause of the Fourteenth Amendment imposes on the conduct of criminal proceedings by the States. . . .

In our federal system the administration of criminal justice is predominantly committed to the care of the States. The power to define crimes belongs to Congress only as an appropriate means of carrying into execution its limited grant of legislative powers. Broadly speaking, crimes in the United States are what the laws of the individual States make them, subject to the limitations of Art. 1 [sec.] 10 [cl. 1], in the original Constitution, prohibiting bills of attainder and ex post facto laws, and of the Thirteenth and Fourteenth Amendments.

These limitations, in the main, concern not restrictions upon the powers of the States to define crime, except in the restricted area where federal authority has preempted the field, but restrictions upon the manner in which the States may enforce their penal codes. Accordingly, in reviewing a State criminal conviction under a claim of right guaranteed by the Due Process Clause of the Fourteenth Amendment, . . . "we must be deeply mindful of the responsibilities of the States for the enforcement of criminal laws, and exercise with due humility our merely negative function in subjecting convictions from state courts to the very narrow scrutiny which the Due Process Clause of the Fourteenth Amendment authorizes." Due process of law is not to be turned into a destructive dogma against the States in the administration of their systems of criminal justice.

However, this Court too has its responsibility. Regard for the requirements of the Due Process Clause "inescapably imposes upon this Court an exercise of judgment upon the whole course of the proceedings [resulting in a conviction] in order to ascertain whether they offend those canons of decency and fairness which express the notions of justice of English-speaking peoples even toward those charged with the most heinous offenses." . . . These standards of justice are not authoritatively formulated anywhere as though they were specifics. Due process of law is a summarized constitutional guarantee of respect for those personal immunities which, as Mr. Justice Cardozo twice wrote for the Court, are "so rooted in the traditions and conscience of our people as to be ranked as fundamental," . . . or are "implicit in the concept of ordered liberty." . . .

The vague contours of the Due Process Clause do not leave judges at large. We may not draw on our merely personal and private notions and disregard the limits that bind judges in their judicial function. Even though the concept of due process of law is not final and fixed, these limits are derived from considerations that are fused in the whole nature of our judicial process. The Due Process Clause places upon this Court the duty of exercising a judgment, within the narrow confines of judicial power in reviewing State convictions, upon interests of society pushing in opposite directions.

Due process of law thus conceived is not to be derided as resort to a revival of "natural law." To believe that this judicial exercise of judgment could be avoided by freezing "due process of law" at some fixed stage of time or thought is to suggest that the most important aspect of constitutional adjudication is a function for inanimate machines and not for judges, for whom the independence safeguarded by Article 3 of the Constitution was designed and who are presumably guided by established standards of judicial behavior. Even cybernetics has not yet made that haughty claim. To practice the requisite detachment and to achieve sufficient objectivity no doubt demands of judges the habit of self-discipline and self-criticism, incertitude that one's own views are incontestable and alert tolerance toward views not shared. They are precisely the qualities society has a right to expect from those entrusted with ultimate judicial power.

Restraints on our jurisdiction are self-imposed only in the sense that there is from our decisions no immediate appeal short of impeachment or constitutional amendment. But that does not make due process of law a matter of judicial caprice. The faculties of the Due Process Clause may be indefinite and vague, but the mode of their ascertainment is not self-willed. In each case "due process of law" requires an evaluation based on a disinterested inquiry pursued in the spirit of science, on a balanced order of facts exactly and fairly stated, on the detached consideration of conflicting claims. . . .

Applying these general considerations to the circumstances of the present case, we are compelled to conclude that the proceedings by which this conviction was obtained do more than offend some fastidious squeamishness or private sentimentalism about combating crime too energetically. This is conduct that shocks the conscience. Illegally breaking into the privacy of the petitioner, the struggle to open his mouth and remove what was there, the forcible extraction of his stomach's contents—this course of proceeding by agents of government to obtain evidence is bound to offend even hardened sensibilities. They are methods too close to the rack and the screw to permit of constitutional differentiation.

It has long since ceased to be true that due process of law is heedless of the means by which otherwise relevant and credible evidence is obtained. This was not true even before the series of recent cases enforced the constitutional principle that the States may not base convictions upon confessions, however much verified, obtained by coercion. These decisions are not arbitrary exceptions to the comprehensive right of States to fashion their own rules of evidence for criminal trials. They are not sports in our constitutional law but applications of a general principle. They are only instances of the general requirement that States in their prosecutions respect certain decencies of civilized conduct. Due process of law, as a historic and generative principle, precludes defining, and thereby confining, these standards of conduct more precisely than to say that convictions cannot be brought about by methods that offend "a sense of justice." It would be a stultification of the responsibility which the course of constitutional history has cast upon this Court to hold that in order to convict a man the police cannot extract by force what is in his mind but can extract what is in his stomach.

To attempt in this case to distinguish what lawyers call "real evidence" from verbal evidence is to ignore the reasons for excluding coerced confessions. Use of involuntary verbal confessions in State criminal trials is constitutionally obnoxious not only because of their unreliability. They are inadmissible under the Due Process Clause even though statements contained in them may be independently established as true. Coerced confessions offend the community's sense of fair play and decency. So here, to sanction the brutal conduct which naturally enough was condemned by the court whose judgment is before us, would be to afford brutality the cloak of law. Nothing would be more calculated to discredit law and thereby to brutalize the temper of a society.

Mr. Justice Minton took no part in the consideration or decision of this case.

Mr. Justice Black, concurring.

Adamson v. California . . . sets out reasons for my belief that state as well as federal courts and law enforcement officers must obey the Fifth Amendment's command that "No person . . . shall be compelled in any criminal case to be a witness against himself." I think a person is compelled to be a witness against himself not only when he is compelled to testify, but also when as here, incriminating evidence is forcibly taken from him by a contrivance of modern science. . . .

Some constitutional provisions are stated in absolute and unqualified language such, for illustration, as the First Amendment stating that no law shall be passed prohibiting the free exercise of religion or abridging the freedom of speech or press. Other constitutional provisions do require courts to choose between competing policies, such as the Fourth Amendment which, by its terms, necessitates a judicial decision as to what is an "unreasonable" search or seizure. There is, however, no express constitutional language granting judicial power to invalidate every state law of every kind deemed "unreasonable" or contrary to the Court's notion of civilized decencies; yet the constitutional philosophy used by the majority has, in the past, been used to deny a state the right to fix the price of gasoline, and even the right to prevent bakers from palming off smaller for larger loaves of bread. These cases, and others, show the extent to which the evanescent standards of the majority's philosophy have been used to nullify state legislative programs passed to suppress evil economic practices. What paralyzing role this same philosophy will play in the future economic affairs of this country is impossible to predict. Of even graver concern, however, is the use of the philosophy to nullify the Bill of Rights. I long ago concluded that the accordion-like qualities of this philosophy must inevitably imperil all the individual liberty safeguards specifically enumerated in the Bill of Rights. Recent decisions of this Court sanctioning abridgment of the freedom of speech and press have strengthened this conclusion.

Mr. Justice Douglas, concurring.

. . . As an original matter it might be debatable whether the provision in the Fifth Amendment that no person "shall be compelled in any criminal case to be a witness against himself" serves the ends of justice. Not all civilized legal procedures recognize it. But the choice was made by the Framers, a choice which sets a standard for legal trials in this country. The Framers made it a standard of due process for prosecutions by the Federal Government. If it is a requirement of due process for a trial in the federal courthouse, it is impossible for me to say it is not a requirement of due process for a trial in the state courthouse. That was the issue recently surveyed in *Adamson v. California*. . . . The Court rejected the view that compelled testimony should be excluded and held in substance that the accused in a state trial can be forced to testify against himself. I disagree. Of course an accused can be compelled to be present at the trial, to stand, to sit, to turn this way or that, and to try on a cap or a coat. But I think that words taken from his lips, capsules taken from his stomach, blood taken from his veins are all inadmissible provided they are taken from him without his consent. They are inadmissible because of the command of the Fifth Amendment.

That is an unequivocal, definite and workable rule of evidence for state and federal courts. But we cannot in fairness free the state courts from that command and yet excoriate them for flouting the "decencies of civilized conduct" when they admit the evidence. That is to make the rule turn not on the Constitution but on the idiosyncrasies of the judges who sit here. . . .

Case

DUNCAN V. LOUISIANA

391 U.S. 145; 88 S.Ct. 1444; 20 L.Ed. 2d 491 (1968)
Vote: 7–2

This case raises the question of whether, and under what circumstances, the Due Process Clause of the Fourteenth Amendment incorporates the Sixth Amendment guarantee of trial by jury in a criminal case. The facts are set forth in Justice White's majority opinion.

Mr. Justice White delivered the opinion of the Court.

Appellant, Gary Duncan, was convicted of simple battery in the Twenty-fifth Judicial District Court of Louisiana. Under Louisiana law simple battery is a misdemeanor, punishable by a maximum of two years' imprisonment and a $300 fine. Appellant sought trial by jury, but because the Louisiana Constitution grants jury trials only in cases in which capital punishment or imprison-

ment at hard labor may be imposed, the trial judge denied the request. Appellant was convicted and sentenced to serve 60 days in the parish prison and pay a fine of $150. Appellant sought review in the Supreme Court of Louisiana, asserting that the denial of jury trial violated rights guaranteed to him by the United States Constitution. The Supreme Court, finding "[n]o error of law in the ruling complained of," denied appellant a writ of certiorari. . . . [A]ppellant sought review in this Court, alleging that the Sixth and Fourteenth Amendments to the United States Constitution secure the right to jury trial in state criminal prosecutions where a sentence as long as two years may be imposed. . . .

Appellant was 19 years of age when tried. While driving on Highway 23 in Plaquemines Parish on October 18, 1966, he saw two younger cousins engaged in a conversation by the side of the road with four white boys. Knowing his cousins, Negroes who had recently transferred to a formerly all-white high school, had reported the occurrence of racial incidents at the school, Duncan stopped the car, got out, and approached the six boys. At trial the white boys and white onlooker testified, as did appellant and his cousins. The testimony was in dispute on many points, but the witnesses agreed that appellant and the white boys spoke to each other, that appellant encouraged his cousins to break off the encounter and enter his car, and that appellant was about to enter the car himself for the purpose of driving away with his cousins. The whites testified that just before getting in the car appellant slapped Herman Landry, one of the white boys, on the elbow. The Negroes testified that appellant had not slapped Landry, but had merely touched him. The trial judge concluded that the State had proved beyond a reasonable doubt that Duncan had committed simple battery, and found him guilty. . . .

The Fourteenth Amendment denies the States the power to "deprive any person of life, liberty, or property, without due process of law." In resolving conflicting claims concerning the meaning of this spacious language, the Court has looked increasingly to the Bill of Rights for guidance; many of the rights guaranteed by the first eight Amendments to the Constitution have been held to be protected against state action by the Due Process Clause of the Fourteenth Amendment. That clause now protects the right to compensation for property taken by the State; the rights of speech, press, and religion covered by the First Amendment; the Fourth Amendment rights to be free from unreasonable searches and seizures and to have excluded from criminal trials any evidence illegally seized; the right guaranteed by the Fifth Amendment to be free of compelled self-incrimination; and the Sixth Amendment rights to counsel, to a speedy and public trial, to confrontation of opposing witnesses, and to compulsory process for obtaining witnesses.

The test for determining whether a right extended by the Fifth and Sixth Amendments with respect to federal criminal proceedings is also protected against state action by the Fourteenth Amendment has been phrased in a variety of ways in the opinions of this Court. The question has been asked whether a right is among those "fundamental principles of liberty and justice which lie at the base of all our civil and political institutions," . . . whether it is "basic in our system of jurisprudence," . . . and whether it is "a fundamental right, essential to a fair trial." . . . The claim before us is that the right to trial by jury guaranteed by the Sixth Amendment meets these tests. The position of Louisiana, on the other hand, is that the Constitution imposes upon the States no duty to give a jury trial in any criminal case, regardless of the seriousness of the crime or the size of the punishment which may be imposed. Because we believe that trial by jury in criminal cases is fundamental to the American

scheme of justice, we hold that the Fourteenth Amendment guarantees a right of jury trial in all criminal cases which—were they to be tried in a federal court—would come within the Sixth Amendment's guarantee. Since we consider the appeal before us to be such a case, we hold that the Constitution was violated when appellant's demand for jury trial was refused.

The history of trial by jury in criminal cases has been frequently told. It is sufficient for present purposes to say that by the time our Constitution was written, jury trial in criminal cases had been in existence in England for several centuries and carried impressive credentials traced by many to Magna Charta [1215]. . . .

Jury trial came to America with English colonists, and received strong support from them. Royal interference with the jury trial was deeply resented. . . .

The constitution adopted by the original States guaranteed jury trial. Also, the constitution of every State entering the Union thereafter in one form or another protected the right to jury trial in criminal cases.

Even such skeletal history is impressive support for considering the right to jury in criminal cases to be fundamental to our system of justice, an importance frequently recognized in the opinions of this Court. . . .

Jury trial continues to receive strong support. The laws of every State guarantee a right to jury trial in serious criminal cases; no State has dispensed with it; nor are there significant movements underway to do so. Indeed, the three most recent state constitutional revisions, in Maryland, Michigan, and New York, carefully preserved the right of the accused to have the judgment of a jury when tried for a serious crime.

We are aware of prior cases in this Court in which the prevailing opinion contains statements contrary to our holding today that the right to jury trial in serious criminal cases is a fundamental right and hence must be recognized by the States as part of their obligation to extend due process of law to all persons within their jurisdiction. . . . None of these cases, however, dealt with a State which had purported to dispense entirely with a jury trial in serious criminal cases. . . .

The guarantees of jury trial in the Federal and State Constitutions reflect a profound judgment about the way in which law should be enforced and justice administered. A right to jury trial is granted to criminal defendants in order to prevent oppression by the Government. . . .

The State of Louisiana urges that holding that the Fourteenth Amendment assures a right to jury trial will cast doubt on the integrity of every trial conducted without a jury. Plainly, this is not the import of our holding. Our conclusion is that in the American States, as in the federal judicial system, a general grant of jury trial for serious offenses is a fundamental right, essential for preventing miscarriages of justice and for assuring that fair trials are provided for all defendants. We would not assert, however, that every criminal trial—or any particular trial—held before a judge alone is unfair or that a defendant may never be as fairly treated by a judge as he would be by a jury. Thus we hold no constitutional doubts about the practices, common in both federal and state courts, of accepting waivers of jury trial and prosecuting petty crimes without extending a right to jury trial. However, the fact is that in most places more trials for serious crimes are to juries than to a court alone; a great many defendants prefer the judgment of a jury to that of a court. Even where defendants are satisfied with bench trials, the right to a jury trial very likely serves its intended purpose of making judicial or prosecutorial unfairness less likely.

Louisiana's final contention is that even if it must grant jury trials in serious criminal cases, the conviction before us is valid and constitutional because here the petitioner was tried for simple battery and was sentenced to only 60 days in the parish prison. We are not persuaded. It is doubtless true that there is a category of petty crimes or offenses which is not subject to the Sixth Amendment jury trial provision and should not be subject to the Fourteenth Amendment jury trial requirement here applied to the States. Crimes carrying possible penalties up to six months do not require a jury trial if they otherwise qualify as petty offenses. . . . The question, then, is whether a crime carrying such a penalty is an offense which Louisiana may insist on trying without a jury.

We think not. So-called petty offenses were tried without juries both in England and in the Colonies and have always been held to be exempt from the otherwise comprehensive language of the Sixth Amendment's jury trial provisions. There is no substantial evidence that the Framers intended to depart from this established common-law practice, and the possible consequences to defendants from convictions for petty offenses have been thought insufficient to outweigh the benefits to efficient law enforcement and simplified judicial administration resulting from the availability of speedy and inexpensive nonjury adjudications. These same considerations compel the same result under the Fourteenth Amendment. Of course the boundaries of the petty offense category have always been ill defined, if not ambulatory. . . .

. . . We need not, however, settle in this case the exact location of the line between petty offenses and serious crimes. It is sufficient for our purposes to hold that a crime punishable by two years in prison is, based on past and contemporary standards in this country, a serious crime and not a petty offense. Consequently appellant was entitled to a jury trial and it was error to deny it. . . .

Mr. Justice Fortas, concurring.

. . . [A]lthough I agree with the decision of the Court, I cannot agree with the implication . . . that the tail must go with the hide: that when we hold, influenced by the Sixth Amendment, that "due process" requires that the States accord the right of jury trial for all but petty offenses, we automatically import all of the ancillary rules which have been or may hereafter be developed incidental to the right to jury trial in the federal courts. I see no reason whatever, for example, to assume that our decision today should require us to impose federal requirements such as unanimous verdicts or a jury of 12 upon the States. We may well conclude that these and other features of federal jury practice are by no means fundamental—that they are not essential to due process of law—and that they are not obligatory on the States.

I would make these points clear today. Neither logic nor history nor the intent of the draftsmen of the Fourteenth Amendment can possibly be said to require that the Sixth Amendment or its jury trial provision be applied to the States together with the total gloss that this Court's decisions have supplied. The draftsmen of the Fourteenth Amendment intended what they said, not more or less: that no State shall deprive any person of life, liberty, or property without due process of law. It is ultimately the duty of this Court to interpret, to ascribe specific meaning to this phrase. There is no reason whatever for us to conclude that, in so doing, we are bound slavishly to follow not only the Sixth Amendment but all of its bag and baggage, however securely or insecurely affixed they may be by law and precedent to federal proceedings. To take this course, in my judgment, would be not only unnecessary but mischievous because it would inflict a serious blow upon the principle of federalism. The Due Process Clause commands us to apply its great standard to state court proceedings to assure basic fairness. It does not command us rigidly and arbitrarily to impose the exact pattern of federal proceedings upon the 50 States. On the contrary, the Constitution's command, in my view, is that in our insistence upon state observance of due process, we should, so far as possible, allow the greatest latitude for state differences. It requires, within the limits of the lofty basic standards that it prescribes for the States as well as the Federal Government, maximum opportunity for diversity and minimal imposition of uniformity of methods and detail upon the States. Our Constitution sets up a federal union, not a monolith. . . .

Mr. Justice Black, with whom *Mr. Justice Douglas* joins, concurring.

The Court today holds that the right to trial by jury guaranteed defendants in criminal cases in federal courts by Art. III of the United States Constitution and by the Sixth Amendment is also guaranteed by the Fourteenth

Amendment to defendants tried in state courts. With this holding I agree for reasons given by the Court. I also agree because of reasons given in my dissent in *Adamson v. California*. . . . I am very happy to support this selective process through which our Court has since the *Adamson* case held most of the specific Bill of Rights' protections applicable to the States to the same extent they are applicable to the Federal Government. Among these are the right to trial by jury decided today, the right against compelled self-incrimination, the right to counsel, the right to compulsory process for witnesses, the right to confront witnesses, the right to a speedy and public trial, and the right to be free from unreasonable searches and seizures. . . .

. . . I believe as strongly as ever that the Fourteenth Amendment was intended to make the Bill of Rights applicable to the States. I have been willing to support the selective incorporation doctrine, however, as an alternative, although perhaps less historically supportable than complete incorporation. The selective incorporation process, if used properly, does limit the Supreme Court in the Fourteenth Amendment field to specific Bill of Rights' protections only and keeps judges from roaming at will in their own notions of what policies outside the Bill of Rights are desirable and what are not. And, most importantly for me, the selective incorporation process has the virtue of having already worked to make most of the Bill of Rights' protections applicable to the States.

Mr. Justice Harlan, whom **Mr. Justice Stewart** joins, dissenting.

. . . The question before us is not whether jury trial is an ancient institution, which it is; nor whether it plays a significant role in the administration of criminal justice, which it does; nor whether it will endure, which it shall. The question in this case is whether the State of Louisiana, which provides trial by jury for all felonies, is prohibited by the Constitution from trying charges of simple battery to the court alone. In my view, the answer to that question, mandated alike by our constitutional history and by the longer history of trial by jury, is clearly "no."

The States have always borne primary responsibility for operating the machinery of criminal justice within their borders, and adapting it to their particular circumstances. In exercising this responsibility, each State is compelled to conform its procedures to the requirements of the Federal Constitution. The Due Process Clause of the Fourteenth Amendment requires that those procedures be fundamentally fair in all respects. It does not, in my view, impose or encourage nationwide uniformity for its own sake; it does not command adherence to forms that happen to be old; and it does not impose on the State the rules that may be in force in the federal courts except where such rules are also found to be essential to basic fairness.

The Court's approach to this case is an uneasy and illogical compromise among the views of various Justices on how the Due Process Clause should be interpreted. The Court does not say that those who framed the Fourteenth Amendment intended to make the Sixth Amendment applicable to the States, and the Court concedes that it finds nothing unfair about the procedure by which the present appellant was tried. Nevertheless, the Court reverses his conviction: it holds, for some reason not apparent to me, that the Due Process Clause incorporates the particular clause of the Sixth Amendment that requires trial by jury in federal criminal cases—including, as I read its opinion, the sometimes trivial accompanying baggage of judicial interpretation in federal contexts. I have raised my voice many times before against the Court's continuing undiscriminating insistence upon fastening on the States federal notions of criminal justice, and I must do so again in this instance. With all respect, the Court's approach and its reading of history are altogether topsy-turvy. . . .

Apart from the approach taken by the absolute incorporationists, I can see only one method of analysis that has any internal logic. That is to start with the words "liberty" and "due process of law" and attempt to define them in a way that accords with American traditions and our system of government. This approach, involving a much more discriminating process of adjudication than does "incorporation," is, albeit difficult, the one that was followed throughout the 19th and most of the present century. It entails a "gradual process of judicial inclusion and exclusion," seeking, with due recognition of constitutional tolerance for state experimentation and disparity, to ascertain those "immutable principles . . . of free government which no member of the Union may disregard." . . .

7

PROPERTY RIGHTS AND ECONOMIC FREEDOM

"The great and chief end . . . of Men's uniting into Commonwealths, and putting themselves under Government, is the preservation of their property."

—JOHN LOCKE, *SECOND TREATISE OF GOVERNMENT*

John Locke: The English philosopher whose ideas exerted profound influence on the American founders

INTRODUCTION

The twin pillars of any **capitalist economy** are **private property** and **contracts**. For a capitalist system to flourish, it is imperative that there be legal protection for private property and legal enforcement of contracts. Unquestionably, the protection of private property and contractual relationships was particularly important to the Framers of the Constitution. This chapter focuses on historic Supreme Court decisions balancing individual **property rights** and claims of **economic freedom** against the **police power**, both of the states and the national government, to protect the health, safety, and general welfare of the community. The term *property rights* includes the ownership, acquisition, and use of private property. The term *economic freedom* more accurately indicates the cluster of rights associated with private enterprise.

The Influence of John Locke

Americans of the eighteenth century, including those who wrote the Constitution and Bill of Rights, generally accepted the theory of **natural rights** as expounded by the English philosopher John Locke. According to Locke, basic rights to life, liberty, and property were grounded in natural law. As such they were universal and timeless, transcending government and human law. According to Locke's theory of the **social contract**, individuals living originally in a "state of nature" (anarchy) subordinated themselves to civil government in exchange for the protection of fundamental rights to life, liberty, and property. Government in turn was limited in the means by which it could interfere with the exercise of individual rights.

Of course, the very existence of social order presumed some loss of personal and economic freedom. To protect individual rights and advance the public good, government might restrict liberty and might even take private property for public use. But in the latter instance, it would have to provide just compensation to the previous owner, and in limiting individual liberty, it would be required to act reasonably. In short, under this social contract theory, governmental restrictions would be balanced against the high priority afforded to individual rights.

This Lockean perspective is reflected in the Contracts Clause (Article I, Section 10) of the Constitution. It is also easily recognized in the Due Process Clauses of the Fifth and Fourteenth Amendments, as well as in the Fifth Amendment provision that private property shall not be "taken for public use without just compensation." As with other general provisions of the Constitution, the Supreme Court assumed principal responsibility for interpreting such phrases as "just compensation," "due process of law," and "impairment of the obligation of contracts." The interpretation of these broad phrases defined the central theme of American constitutional lawmaking during roughly the first 150 years of Supreme Court history.

Early Judicial Perspectives

The *ex post facto* law provisions (Article I, Sections 9 and 10) of the original Constitution had the potential to protect property rights against governmental encroachment. But, as noted in Chapter 6, the Supreme Court held in *Calder v. Bull* (1798) that the *ex post facto* limitation applied only to retroactive criminal statutes and not to laws affecting property rights or contractual obligations. Two of the four opinions filed in this case contain important dicta on the sources of individual rights and limitations on government. These opinions, written by Justices Samuel Chase and James Iredell, merit additional attention at this point in our discussion. Without designating any specific constitutional limitations, Justice Chase asserted that "certain vital principles in our free republican governments . . . will determine and overrule an apparent and flagrant abuse of legislative power." A legislative act "contrary to the great first principles of the social compact," he continued, "cannot be considered a rightful exercise of legislative authority."

Chase's opinion in *Calder v. Bull* was grounded in natural rights theory. Although this perspective has never achieved dominance on the Supreme Court as a standard for determining the validity of governmental acts, it has occasionally influenced judicial interpretation of the nature and scope of individual rights. By contrast, Justice Iredell's opinion in *Calder* maintained that courts could not invalidate legislation "merely because it is, in their judgment, contrary to the principles of natural justice." If legislatures cross explicit constitutional boundaries, however, "they violate a fundamental law, which must be our guide, whenever we are called upon, as judges, to determine the validity of a legislative act." Iredell's emphasis on the written Constitution as the ultimate standard for determining the validity of legislation soon became the dominant view among the justices.

The Age of Conservative Activism

Throughout most of the nineteenth century the Supreme Court sought to balance competing public and private interests in its property-related jurisprudence. However, in the face of a rising tide of state and federal economic legislation, the Court of the late nineteenth and early twentieth centuries became more adamant in its defense of what was loosely termed **laissez-faire capitalism.** Although the Framers of the Constitution attached great importance to the protection of property, it is doubtful that most of them would have subscribed to the doctrines by which the Supreme Court attempted to protect economic individualism. In a series of controversial decisions between the late 1880s and the late 1930s, the Court invoked the constitutional protections of private property and economic freedom to strike down numerous laws designed to regulate economic activity. This period of conservative activism came to an abrupt end with the constitutional revolution of 1937, brought about by a confrontation between the Court and the elected branches over the constitutionality of President Roosevelt's New Deal programs (see Chapters 1 and 2).

Modern Judicial Perspectives on Economic Freedom

Since 1937, the Supreme Court has largely deferred to other branches of government in the field of economic regulation. The post-New Deal Court's self-restraint in the economic area was juxtaposed with a more liberal activism on behalf of cultural, political, or human rights largely outside the field of economic activity. Until recently the Court has been much more concerned with matters of free expression, the rights of the accused, personal privacy, and racial and sexual equality (areas of Supreme Court activity discussed in subsequent chapters). Beginning in the late 1990s, however, a sharply divided Court manifested greater interest in balancing the claims of private property and private enterprise against governmental regulation, especially in the field of environmental protection.

One must recognize that private property and private enterprise are widely shared and deeply held cultural values in the United States. Especially in the wake of the decline of communism and socialism around the world, public policy in this country is unlikely to threaten these values. Thus, the need for judicial protection of property rights may be substantially less now than in the early days of the republic or even during the Great Depression. Nevertheless, judicial protection of private property and free enterprise played an extremely important part in the development of American constitutional law and in the institutional history of the Supreme Court.

THE CONTRACTS CLAUSE

The **Contracts Clause** of Article I, Section 10, forbids states from passing laws "impairing the obligation of contracts." Historically, this clause was extremely important in the protection of economic freedom and private property. Like many important constitutional provisions, the Contracts Clause was first given life during the era of Chief Justice John Marshall (1801–1835).

Key Decisions of the Marshall Court

In *Fletcher v. Peck* (1810), the Supreme Court invalidated as a violation of the Contracts Clause an act of the Georgia legislature that rescinded the state's sale of land to private investors. To reach this result, it was necessary for Chief Justice Marshall, who wrote the Court's opinion, to conclude that a grant is a contract. In Marshall's view, Georgia's original grant of land carried with it an implied contractual obligation not to assert a right to reclaim the land. Once this land passed into the hands of "innocent third parties" who bought it from the original purchasers, the state could not repeal the original sale, even if it could be proved that the initial grant had been obtained by bribing members of the legislature. As Marshall and his colleagues saw it, "absolute rights" had been established under the contract—that is, they had become "vested" in the subsequent purchasers. But because the state itself was a party to the contract, how could its obligations be enforced? In Marshall's view, Georgia had a moral obligation accorded the status of law, but he was equivocal as to the ultimate source of legal authority. He concluded that Georgia was "restrained" from passing the rescinding act "either by general principles, which are common to our free institutions, or by the particular provisions of the Constitution of the United States." This ambivalence underscores the continuing influence of the "natural rights" approach adopted by Justice Chase in *Calder v. Bull*. Whereas Marshall at least recognized the appropriateness of applying constitutional provisions to protect contractual obligations, Justice William Johnson, in a concurring opinion, opted for the "natural justice" approach exclusively:

> I do not hesitate to declare that a state does not possess the power of revoking its own grants. But I do it on a general principle on the reason and nature of things, a principle which will impose laws even on the deity.

The Dartmouth College Case   *Fletcher v. Peck* greatly broadened the scope and potential application of the Contracts Clause. But the Court's decision nine years later in *Dartmouth College v. Woodward* (1819) had far greater influence on economic development in the nineteenth century United States. The Court held in essence that a corporate charter was a contract, the terms of which could not be changed materially by the state without violating the Constitution. The charter in question had been issued in 1769 by the British crown for the creation of Dartmouth College. This corporate charter authorized a self-perpetuating twelve-member board of trustees to govern the college. With the American Revolution, the state of New Hampshire succeeded to the rights and obligations of the crown provided by the charter. The college soon became embroiled in state politics, leading to an attempt in 1816 to convert it from a private institution into a state university. This objective was to be accomplished by placing the college under a board of overseers appointed by the governor pursuant to state legislation. The ousted trustees sued to recover the charter, seal, and records of the college and in this way directly challenged the authority of New Hampshire to enact the legislation. Again speaking for the Court, Chief Justice Marshall determined that the charter was a valid contract and that the legislature's attempt to modify the governing structure of the college violated Article I, Section 10, of the Constitution. No specific language in the original charter required this rigid limitation on the state's power to amend it almost half a century after the charter was granted by King George III and at a time when none of the original parties to the contract remained on the scene. Nevertheless, Marshall found that the challenged legislation violated the spirit if not the letter of the Contracts Clause. Marshall indicated that any ambiguity in the charter should be construed in favor of "the adventurers" and against the state.

Although Dartmouth College was created as a charitable educational institution, the broad principle that Marshall enunciated in this case was soon applied to profit-seeking corporations. The *Dartmouth College* decision came at a time when business corporations in such fields as insurance, canal building, and road construction were beginning to proliferate. These companies and their financial backers were tangibly aided by an interpretation of the Contracts Clause that gave corporate charters firm constitutional protection.

The Marshall Court also interpreted the Contracts Clause as a protection of creditor interests against some forms of state regulation. In the same year that it decided the *Dartmouth College* case, the Court, in *Sturges v. Crowninshield* (1819), struck down a New York bankruptcy law under which debtors could obtain relief from financial obligations previously incurred. Speaking through Marshall once again, the Court found that this measure amounted to an impairment of the obligation of contracts. Marshall himself went so far as to assert, eight years later, that the Contracts Clause barred state bankruptcy laws that applied to debts incurred *after* their passage. But on this occasion, the legislation was upheld by a majority of his brethren, leaving Marshall to record his only dissenting opinion in a constitutional case (*Ogden v. Saunders* [1827]).

The Contribution of the Taney Court

In spite of the expanded protection of property and business interests through early interpretation of the Contracts Clause, the demand for state economic regulation continued to grow. As noted in Chapter 5, the Marshall Court itself began to provide limited recognition to the state police power, and Marshall's successor, Roger B. Taney, significantly extended this recognition. The *Dartmouth College* case logically implied that corporations chartered by the state could conduct their business free of governmental regulation. This laissez-faire approach could not survive for long, even in the preindustrial United States of the early nineteenth century. Counterpressures, reflected in the rise of Jacksonian democracy, were too strong to permit the continuation of such limitations on state regulatory power.

The judicial pendulum began to swing back in the other direction with the Taney Court's 1837 decision in the case of *Charles River Bridge Company v. Warren Bridge Company*. In 1785, the Massachusetts legislature had granted a corporate charter to the Charles River Bridge Company that authorized it to build a privately owned bridge between Boston and Charlestown and to collect tolls from persons using the bridge. This highly profitable arrangement, granted for a period of seventy years, was threatened by the legislature's incorporation of the Warren Bridge Company in 1828 with authorization to build a competing bridge nearby. Within a short time, the bridge built by Warren Bridge was to become free to the public as a part of the Massachusetts highway system. The Charles River Bridge Company challenged the 1828 act as a violation of the 1785 charter, which allegedly implied "that the legislature would not authorize another bridge, and especially a free one," alongside the original bridge. Rejecting this contention, Chief Justice Taney construed the language of the charter literally. He concluded that no rights were "taken from the public, or given to the corporation, beyond those which the words of the charter, by their natural and proper construction, [purported] to convey." By contrast with Marshall's approach in the *Dartmouth College* case, Taney was unwilling to restrict legislative authority on the basis of implicit contractual rights. The Court's position was effectively summed up in Taney's assertion that "[w]hile the rights of private property are sacredly guarded, we must not forget that the community also has rights, and that the happiness and well-being of every citizen depends on their faithful preservation."

Later Developments

The decline of the Contracts Clause as a bulwark of **vested rights** began with the *Charles River Bridge* case. Some forty years later, in *Stone v. Mississippi* (1880), the Supreme Court refused to extend Contracts Clause protection to a chartered lottery company subsequently prohibited from selling lottery tickets in Mississippi. By the late 1880s, the **Due Process Clause of the Fourteenth Amendment** had supplanted the Contracts Clause as a source of constitutional restraint on state regulation of business.

The extent of the demise of the Contracts Clause in the twentieth century is well illustrated by the decision in the Minnesota mortgage moratorium case (*Home Building and Loan Association v. Blaisdell* [1934]). Here, by a 5-to-4 vote, the Court upheld a state law, passed in 1933 in the depths of the Great Depression, that authorized the postponement of mortgage foreclosures for periods not to extend beyond May 1, 1935. Chief Justice Charles Evans Hughes, writing for the majority, emphasized the qualified nature of the Contracts Clause as a limitation on state power. He concluded that "the reservation of the reasonable exercise of the protective power of the state is read into all contracts."

In summary, the Contracts Clause figured prominently in the Supreme Court's protection of vested property rights during the early part of the nineteenth century. Although its influence began to be undermined by the expanding doctrine of state police power during the Taney era, the Contracts Clause remained a significant weapon in defense of property interests until supplanted by the development of **substantive due process** in the late 1800s. The Supreme Court invoked the Contracts Clause in invalidating state legislation in some seventy-five cases prior to 1890. But the Contracts Clause has not been a major restraint on state regulatory power for more than a century. Nevertheless, it is not a dead letter and is still occasionally invoked as a constitutional limitation. For example, in 1977, the Court held that a New Jersey statute violated the Contracts Clause because it impaired the state's obligation to holders of bonds issued by the Port Authority of New York and New Jersey (*United States Trust Company v. New Jersey*). Similarly, in *Allied Structural Steel Company v. Spannaus* (1978), the Court invalidated under the Contracts Clause Minnesota's attempt to regulate a company's pension fund. Writing for a five-member majority, Justice Stewart observed: "If the Contracts Clause is to retain any meaning at all, . . . it must be understood to impose *some* limits on the power of a State to abridge existing contractual relationships" [emphasis in the original].

Any expectation in the wake of these cases that the Contracts Clause would reemerge as a significant limitation on state regulatory authority has thus far been unfulfilled. Since the late 1970s, the Court has shown no inclination to further reinvigorate the Contracts Clause. For example, in *Energy Reserves Group v. Kansas Power & Light* (1983), the Court, rejecting a Contracts Clause challenge to a state law regulating natural gas prices, recognized that the prohibition of laws impairing the obligation of contracts must be balanced against a state's "inherent police power to safeguard the vital interests of its people." The Court said that the first question is "whether the state law has, in fact, operated as a substantial impairment of a contractual relationship." If so, the state must advance a "significant and legitimate public purpose" to justify the impairment. In the *Kansas Power & Light* case and other recent Contracts Clause decisions, the Court has found that this requirement has been satisfied.

TO SUMMARIZE:

- During the Marshall era (1801–1835), the Contracts Clause of Article I, Section 10, served as a significant limitation on state interference with private property rights. In particular, John Marshall's opinion for the Court in *Dartmouth College v. Woodward* (1819),which recognized that corporate charters were protected by the Contracts Clause, had great influence on nineteenth century economic development.
- With the rise of the state police power during the Taney era (1836–1864), the Court began to narrow the scope of protection afforded by the Contracts Clause. In the pivotal case of *Charles River Bridge Company v. Warren Bridge Company* (1837), Chief Justice Taney effectively subordinated traditional contract rights to the interests of the community in a rapidly changing society.
- By the time of the Great Depression, as illustrated by the Court's decision in *Home Building and Loan Association v. Blaisdell* (1934), the Contracts Clause no longer stood as a significant impediment to state regulatory power in the economic realm. This remains true today despite a short-lived effort in the late 1970s to resuscitate a more restrictive interpretation of the Contracts Clause as a limitation on state power.

THE RISE AND FALL OF ECONOMIC DUE PROCESS

State police power continued to develop through the Civil War and Reconstruction, but the protection of property rights, especially in the context of business activity, remained a prime concern of American judges, including members of the U.S. Supreme Court. Due process as a substantive limitation on governmental authority began to emerge in the 1850s, but its potential was not fully realized until some years after adoption of the Fourteenth Amendment. With the exception of the *Dred Scott* case, in which congressional regulation of slavery in the territories was held to deprive slave owners of property without due process of law (see Chapter 1), the **Fifth Amendment Due Process Clause** was not invoked, prior to the Civil War, as a substantive limitation on federal authority. This is not surprising, since the national government did not play an active role in the field of economic regulation until very late in the nineteenth century.

Origins of Substantive Due Process

It is generally agreed that substantive due process as a limitation on *state* economic regulation originated in an 1856 decision of the New York Court of Appeals (the state's highest court). In *Wynehamer v. New York,* that court held that a state criminal statute prohibiting the sale of liquor curtailed the economic liberty of a Buffalo tavern owner who had been prosecuted for violating its provisions. The court of appeals held that the state police power could not be used to deprive the tavern owner of his liberty to practice his livelihood, a liberty protected by the due process clause of the New York constitution.

Following adoption of the Fourteenth Amendment, lawyers representing business interests in opposition to growing state regulation began to emphasize substantive due process arguments. These arguments drew heavily on an influential legal treatise entitled *Constitutional Limitations,* written by a Michigan judge, Thomas M. Cooley. First published in 1868, the year in which the Fourteenth Amendment was ratified, Cooley's treatise went through several editions in the late 1800s and had a significant impact on the constitutional jurisprudence of the laissez-faire era.

As noted in previous chapters, substantive due process focuses on the reasonable-ness of legislation. By contrast with the more familiar procedural aspect, which emphasizes such elements as notice and the right to a fair hearing (in other words, *how* government should operate in relation to the individual), substantive due process stresses *what* government may or may not do.

Early Supreme Court Resistance to Economic Due Process

For a number of years following the adoption of the Fourteenth Amendment, most members of the Supreme Court resisted the **economic due process** approach. Thus, in *The Slaughterhouse Cases* (1873), a narrowly divided Court upheld Louisiana's grant of a monopoly in the slaughtering business in and around New Orleans. Although officially designated as "An Act to Protect the Health of the City of New Orleans," the law was not in any meaningful sense a health measure. Its only apparent effect was to deprive more than a thousand persons of their right to engage in the slaughtering trade. A number of these individuals filed suit, maintaining that the state had con-ferred "odious and exclusive privileges upon a small number of persons at the expense of the great body of the community of New Orleans."

In rejecting this contention, the Supreme Court, in an opinion by Justice Samuel F. Miller, narrowly interpreted Fourteenth Amendment restrictions on state author-ity. Miller virtually read out of the Fourteenth Amendment the provision that says: "No State shall make or enforce any law which shall abridge the privileges or immu-nities of citizens of the United States." This language, he said, extended only to rights held by Americans as citizens of the nation, as distinguished from their rights as state citizens.

In addition to this restrictive view of the Privileges and Immunities Clause, Justice Miller found no deprivation of rights under the Due Process and Equal Protection Clauses. He identified the central purpose of the Fourteenth Amendment as the pro-tection of the civil rights of former slaves, although he was unwilling to say that no one else was entitled to this protection. In a strong dissenting opinion, Justice Stephen J. Field took issue with Miller's narrow interpretation of the Privileges and Immunities Clause: "The privileges and immunities designated," he maintained, "are those which of right belong to the citizens of all free governments." Over the years, many scholars have sharply criticized Justice Miller's narrow interpretation of the Privileges and Immunities Clause (see, for example, John Hart Ely, *Democracy and Dis-trust,* 1980, and Charles L. Black, *A New Birth of Freedom: Human Rights Named and Unnamed,* 1999). With few exceptions, however, the Supreme Court has adhered to Justice Miller's narrow interpretation of the Privileges and Immunities Clause. A broader interpretation might have enabled the Court to develop a more plausible basis for protecting individual rights than that provided by the Due Process Clause. (For an indication that the Rehnquist Court may be reconsidering the Privileges and Immunities Clause, see *Saenz v. Roe* [1999], where the Court, relying in part on the Privileges and Immunities Clause, struck down a California restriction on welfare ben-efits for new residents.)

Justice Joseph L. Bradley's dissenting opinion in *The Slaughterhouse Cases* antici-pated the Court's later development of the Due Process Clause as the basis for pro-tecting property rights. While agreeing with Justice Field's position regarding the broad protection that should be afforded by the Privileges and Immunities Clause, Bradley went one important step further, by expressing the view that a law which prohibits a large class of citizens from adopting a lawful employment previously adopted, does deprive them of liberty as well as property, without due process of law. Their right of choice is a portion of their liberty; their occupation is their property.

Business Affected with a Public Interest   Four years later, the Court again sustained a broad exercise of the state police power, in this instance an act of the Illinois legislature fixing maximum storage rates charged by grain elevators and public warehouses and requiring licenses to operate these facilities. This legislation grew out of the granger movement, in which thousands of farmers sought protection against excessive freight rates charged by railroads and other businesses involved in the distribution of agricultural commodities. Chief Justice Morrison R. Waite, writing for a seven-member majority in *Munn v. Illinois* (1877), sustained the rate regulation under the English common law doctrine of **business affected with a public interest.** Like common carriers, innkeepers, and other persons directly serving the public, Waite reasoned, the owners of grain elevators were equally subject to regulation under this standard. Sounding a note that aroused the anger of business leaders, Waite acknowledged that such regulatory power was subject to abuse but admonished that, in such instances, "the people must resort to the polls, and not to the courts."

Dissenting in *Munn,* Justice Field contended that the regulation violated due process. He maintained that under our system of government, the legislature lacked power "to fix the price which anyone shall receive for his property of any kind." He also argued that "there is hardly any enterprise or business engaging the attention and labor of any considerable portion of the community in which the public has not an interest in the sense in which that term is used by the Court." This was a prescient observation in view of the Court's rejection, almost half a century later, of the distinction between "private" businesses and those "affected with a public interest" (*Nebbia v. New York* [1934]).

Ironically, once the concept of substantive due process came to be recognized by a Court majority as a basis for invalidating economic legislation, the Court began to apply Waite's rationale negatively. For example, regulations of labor-management disputes, theater ticket scalping, and the rates charged by private employment agencies were ruled unconstitutional on the ground that the businesses involved were not "affected with a public interest" (see, for example, *Charles Wolff Packing Company v. Court of Industrial Relations* [1923], *Tyson v. Banton* [1927], and *Ribnik v. McBride* [1928]).

The Court Reflects Growing Corporate Influence

Powerful corporate interests reacted sharply and decisively to the *Munn* decision. In fact, the American Bar Association was organized for the immediate purpose of leading the counterattack. In 1882, former Senator Roscoe Conkling, in an argument before the Supreme Court, unveiled his "conspiracy theory" of the Fourteenth Amendment. Conkling had participated as a member of the joint congressional committee that drafted the Fourteenth Amendment in 1866. Referring selectively to a previously undisclosed journal of committee proceedings, Conkling maintained in essence that those who drafted the amendment intended for the word "person," as used in the Equal Protection and Due Process clauses, to include corporations. Later research established that Conkling's "conspiracy theory" was of dubious validity, if not an outright fraud. But in the 1880s, the theory was eagerly received and widely supported by those who sought to justify the protection of economic rights under the

Fourteenth Amendment. In 1886, the Supreme Court announced without discussion that the Equal Protection Clause did apply to corporations (*Santa Clara County v. Southern Pacific Railroad*). This conclusion extended logically to the Due Process Clause as well.

Changes in Supreme Court personnel also influenced the shift toward economic due process. Chief Justice Waite, who had written the majority opinion in the *Munn* case, died in 1888 and was succeeded by Melville W. Fuller. In 1890, David J. Brewer, a nephew of Justice Field, took the seat on the high bench vacated by Justice Stanley Matthews. These and other appointees, drawn largely from the ranks of corporation lawyers, were receptive to the limited government approach implicit in substantive due process. During this period, under the leadership of Chief Justice Fuller, the Court significantly curtailed national authority through a restrictive interpretation of the commerce and taxing powers (see Chapter 2). Theories of economic individualism, especially the **Social Darwinism** of Herbert Spencer and William Graham Sumner, were very much in vogue during the period and obviously had some impact on the justices.

The Court's changing mood was signaled clearly by Justice John Marshall Harlan (the elder) in 1887. Writing for the Court in upholding a Kansas law prohibiting the sale of certain alcoholic beverages, he warned that not all exercises of the state police power would be automatically approved: "The Courts are not bound by mere forms, nor are they to be misled by mere pretenses. They are at liberty— indeed, are under a solemn duty—to look at the substance of things" (*Mugler v. Kansas* [1887]).

Economic Due Process Comes of Age

The first major shift in the Court's position came in 1890 with the decision that a state legislature could not authorize a commission to set railroad rates with finality. Such rate making, the Court concluded, must be subject to judicial review (*Chicago, Milwaukee, & St. Paul Railway Company v. Minnesota*). In 1897, the Court invalidated Louisiana's effort to regulate out-of-state insurance companies transacting business in the state. Writing for the Court, Justice Rufus Peckham found this regulation to be an infringement of the **liberty of contract** protected by the Fourteenth Amendment Due Process Clause (*Allgeyer v. Louisiana* [1897]). ("Liberty of contract," as used by the Court in this and many subsequent due process cases, should not be confused with the Contracts Clause of Article I, Section 10, discussed earlier in this chapter.)

Lochner v. New York: **The Apotheosis of Economic Due Process**   Justice Peckham used the same rationale eight years later in what has become the best known case of the early twentieth century: *Lochner v. New York* (1905). In *Lochner,* the Court, dividing 5 to 4, struck down a state law specifying a maximum sixty-hour workweek for bakery employees. Seven years earlier, the Court had upheld, as a proper exercise of the police power, an act of the Utah legislature establishing an eight-hour workday for employees in "mines . . . smelters and all other institutions for the reduction or refining of ores or metals" (*Holden v. Hardy* [1898]). The Utah statute was recognized as a reasonable health measure, but the majority in *Lochner* found no such justification for limiting working hours "in the occupation of a baker." "To the common understanding," Peckham opined, "the trade of a baker has never been regarded as an unhealthy one." However, the Court's fundamental objection to the legislation was that it was a "meddlesome interference" with business. The majority gave no consideration to the relative bargaining power of employers and employees in the baking industry. They simply regarded the law as an unjustified infringement on

"the right to labor, and with the right of free contract on the part of the individual, either as employer or employee."

Justice Harlan and his celebrated colleague Oliver Wendell Holmes, Jr., filed powerful dissenting opinions in the *Lochner* case. While Harlan pursued a conventional line of analysis, Justice Holmes attacked the majority for reading laissez-faire theory into the Constitution:

> This case is decided upon an economic theory which a large part of the country does not entertain. If it were a question whether I agreed with that theory, I should desire to study it further and long before making up my mind. But I do not conceive that to be my duty, because I strongly believe that my agreement or disagreement has nothing to do with the right of a majority to embody their opinions in law. . . . The Fourteenth Amendment does not enact Mr. Herbert Spencer's *Social Statics*.

Constitutional scholars have widely accepted Justice Holmes's charge that the ruling in *Lochner* was little more than an expression of the economic policy preferences of the Court's conservative majority. In recent years, however, revisionist scholars have challenged the Holmesian view. In his 1993 book, *The Constitution Besieged: The Rise and Decline of Lochner Era Police Powers Jurisprudence,* Howard Gillman argues that the *Lochner* decision "represented a serious principled effort to maintain one of the central distinctions in nineteenth-century constitutional law—the distinction between valid economic regulation, on the one hand, and invalid class legislation on the other—during a period of unprecedented class conflict." Thus, in Gillman's view, the Court invalidated the bakery statute in *Lochner* not because it regulated business per se, but because it took sides in an emerging class conflict.

The Heyday of Economic Due Process

Although the philosophical perspective underlying the *Lochner* ruling remained influential for a number of years, its practical effect was short-lived. In 1908, the Court upheld an Oregon act limiting the workday to ten hours for women in designated occupational fields (*Muller v. Oregon*). In this case, attorney (later Associate Justice) Louis D. Brandeis submitted a novel brief in support of the legislation, presenting extensive sociological and medical data in support of the state's contention that the limitation of working hours was directly related to the promotion of the health and welfare of women. The **Brandeis brief**, which added a new dimension to constitutional argumentation, underscored the relationship between legal principles and research in the social and biological sciences. Following the *Muller* precedent, the Court in 1917 sustained the constitutionality of a maximum-hours limitation for men as well as women employed in mills and factories (*Bunting v. Oregon*). This decision amounted to the de facto overruling of *Lochner,* but the Court did not specifically refer to the latter case.

The Court's willingness to sustain maximum-hours laws did not carry over into other areas of labor legislation. A federal law outlawing **yellow dog contracts** (employment contracts in which workers agree not to join unions) was invalidated in 1908 as a violation of the Due Process Clause of the Fifth Amendment (*Adair v. United States*). Seven years later, in *Coppage v. Kansas* (1915), the Court voided a similar state provision as a violation of the freedom of contract protected by the Fourteenth Amendment. In these cases, the Court seemed unconcerned with the blatant inequality in the bargaining positions of individual nonunion employees and corporate employers. Indeed, in the Court's view, it was unreasonable for the legislature to interfere with the "natural order" of inequalities, no matter how great the resulting disparities between employer and employee.

Wages proved to be as invulnerable to legislative regulation as yellow dog contracts. Thus, in 1923 a divided Court struck down a congressional measure authorizing the setting of minimum wages for women and minors employed in the District of Columbia (*Adkins v. Children's Hospital*). The stated purposes of the minimum wage were to provide women with " 'the necessary cost of living,' . . . to maintain them in good health and to protect their morals." As in *Lochner,* the government's perceived interference with liberty of contract was held to violate due process—in this instance, the Fifth Amendment's restriction on federal authority. Writing for the majority, Justice George Sutherland noted that the law was demeaning to women, especially in light of the drive toward political equality that had resulted, shortly before this decision, in ratification of the Nineteenth Amendment, which removed sex as a qualification for voting. But the real object of Sutherland's concern is unmistakably apparent from the following excerpt from his majority opinion:

> The law takes account of the necessities of only one party to the contract. It ignores the necessities of the employer by compelling him to pay not less than a certain sum, not only whether the employee is capable of earning it, but irrespective of the ability of his business to sustain the burden, generously leaving him, of course, the privilege of abandoning his business as an alternative of going on at a loss.

During the 1920s, Chief Justice William Howard Taft often supported the Court's limitation of regulatory authority by way of substantive due process (see, for example, his majority opinion in *Charles Wolff Packing Company v. Court of Industrial Relations* [1923]). However, Taft dissented in the *Adkins* case. In an opinion supported by Justice Edward T. Sanford, Taft expressed his belief that because no meaningful distinction could be drawn between minimum wage and maximum hours legislation and since the latter had been upheld in the *Muller* and *Bunting* cases, the Washington, D.C., minimum wage should be sustained. This view was further supported, he maintained, by the fact that the law upheld in *Bunting* contained a time-and-a-half provision for overtime pay. He emphasized, moreover, that "it is not the function of this Court to hold congressional acts invalid simply because they are passed to carry out economic views which the Court believes to be unwise or unsound."

Justice Holmes wrote a separate dissenting opinion, asserting that the power of Congress to enact minimum wage legislation seemed "absolutely free from doubt." Holmes sharply criticized the Court's development of what he called the "dogma" of liberty of contract. The word *contract,* he pointed out, is not mentioned in the Due Process Clause. Holmes viewed contract merely as "an example of doing what you want to do, embodied in the word liberty. But pretty much all law," he added, "consists in forbidding men to do some things that they want to do, and contract is no more exempt from law than other acts."

Substantive due process as a restriction on economic legislation continued to flourish through the 1920s and into the 1930s. It was an integral part of the Supreme Court's intellectual defense of business interests in general. This judicial philosophy also produced a number of rulings limiting the application of the antitrust acts as restrictions on corporate behavior while extending these restrictions to such labor practices as strikes and secondary boycotts (see, for example, *Loewe v. Lawlor* [1908], *Duplex Printing Company v. Deering* [1921], and *Bedford Cut Stone Company v. Journeymen Stone Cutters' Association* [1927]). The Court strongly resisted efforts during this period to restrict child labor and to regulate agricultural and industrial production. Apparently economic liberties, although not officially designated as "preferred freedoms," were accorded paramount importance and often prevailed over countervailing demands for socioeconomic regulation.

Patterns of Supreme Court decision making, especially in complex areas of constitutional law, often do not follow unwavering lines of analytical precision or logical consistency. As we have noted, during the period marked by such decisions as *Lochner* and *Adkins,* the Court did not always invalidate challenged regulatory legislation. The Court still adhered (officially, at least) to the principle of the presumptive validity of legislation and, as a result, many regulatory measures were upheld during the heyday of economic due process. Nevertheless, enough state and federal measures were invalidated to retard serious efforts at economic and social reform.

The Decline of Economic Due Process

The Great Depression of the 1930s, with its crippling effect on employment, industrial production, and the economic well-being of millions of people, forced the Supreme Court to rethink its constitutional commitment to limited government in the field of economic policy. It did so in a variety of issue areas between the mid-1930s and the early 1940s. With this reappraisal came the Court's repudiation of substantive due process as a restriction on the regulation of business.

This fundamental change in the Court's posture was signaled by two key decisions in 1934. As previously indicated, in that year, the Court upheld the Minnesota Mortgage Moratorium Act, finding that its provisions did not violate the Contracts Clause (*Home Building and Loan Association v. Blaisdell*). Although this decision did not turn on the meaning of due process, its implications for the Court's interpretation of liberty of contract under the Fifth and Fourteenth Amendments were unmistakable.

The due process issue was confronted directly in *Nebbia v. New York* (1934), in which the Court upheld by a 5-to-4 margin the power of a state to regulate the retail price of milk. Concluding that this price regulation did not violate due process, Justice Owen J. Roberts emphasized the breadth of legislative power in relation to economic matters: "It is clear that there is no closed class or category of businesses affected with a public interest." Since the *Munn* case, the Court had gradually narrowed the category of businesses thus "affected" and had established a substantial constitutional barrier against state regulation in a number of areas. In fact, during the decade or so immediately prior to the *Nebbia* decision, very few businesses other than public utilities and places of public accommodation were subject to price control with full judicial approval. Consequently, the Court's obliteration of the category of "business affected with a public interest" represented a significant turning point in constitutional development. In effect, the Court was saying in *Nebbia* that all businesses, irrespective of their supposed relationship to the public interest, are subject to regulation.

This stern repudiation of judicial activism in the field of economic liberties drew a scathing dissent from Justice James C. McReynolds, supported by Justices Willis Van Devanter, George Sutherland, and Pierce Butler. The fixing of retail prices as a means of stabilizing production was, in McReynolds's view, "not regulation, but management, control, dictation," amounting to "deprivation of the fundamental right which one has to conduct his own affairs honestly and along customary lines." He strongly suggested that the Court's decision amounted to a declaration that "rights guaranteed by the Constitution exist only so long as supposed public interest does not require their extinction." McReynolds asserted that adoption of this view "would put an end to liberty under the Constitution."

The "end to liberty" feared by Justice McReynolds was postponed in the field of economic rights for another three years. In fact, in 1936, the Court reaffirmed its controversial *Adkins* ruling by striking down a New York minimum wage law for women (*Morehead v. New York ex rel. Tipaldo*). In this decision, the majority simply reiterated the "liberty of contract" rationale, but the decision was given added significance because it coincided with the Court's invalidation of major New Deal legislation (see, for example, *United States v. Butler* [1936] and *Carter v. Carter Coal*

Company [1936], both of which are discussed and reprinted in Chapter 2). In seeking Supreme Court review of a New York Court of Appeals decision invalidating this minimum wage statute, attorneys failed to ask specifically for reconsideration of the *Adkins* precedent. Rather, they sought to distinguish the New York minimum wage law from the congressional act invalidated in *Adkins*. Writing for a five-member majority, Justice Butler seized on this omission and considered only the question of whether the two cases were distinguishable. He found that they were not and thus struck down the New York law.

In dissenting opinions, Chief Justice Charles Evans Hughes and Justice Harlan Fiske Stone (supported by Justices Brandeis and Benjamin Cardozo) maintained that the two laws were, in fact, distinguishable. More significantly, however, they criticized the Court for its refusal to reconsider the validity of *Adkins,* especially in light of the country's experience during the Great Depression. Justice Stone chastised his colleagues in the majority for reading their own economic views into the Constitution.

It is not for the courts to resolve doubts about whether the remedy by wage regulation is as efficacious as many believe, or is better than some other, or is better even than the blind operation of uncontrolled economic forces. The legislature must be free to choose unless government is to be rendered impotent. The Fourteenth Amendment has no more embedded in the Constitution our preference for some particular set of economic beliefs than it has adopted, in the name of liberty, the system of theology that we may happen to approve.

West Coast Hotel Company v. Parrish: A Sudden Turnaround

Ten months later in *West Coast Hotel Company v. Parrish* (1937), the Supreme Court, again by a 5-to-4 vote (Justice Roberts having changed sides), dramatically overruled the *Adkins* and *Tipaldo* decisions. Although the votes of the justices had occurred in conference several weeks before President Franklin Roosevelt unveiled his controversial Court-packing plan on February 5, 1937, most political observers and the public in general regarded the *Parrish* decision, announced on March 29, as a clear indication that the Court had caved in to pressure from a popular presidential administration. Justice Roberts later claimed he had voted with the majority in *Tipaldo* simply because he believed that the only question presented in that case was whether the New York minimum wage law could be distinguished from the provision struck down in *Adkins*. Whatever the true motivations of Justice Roberts, his change of position in this and several other major constitutional decisions in the spring of 1937 figured prominently in the constitutional revolution that to this day marks the single most important transition in Supreme Court history.

In *West Coast Hotel Company v. Parrish,* the Court considered the constitutionality of a Washington State minimum wage law enacted in 1913. Chief Justice Hughes delivered the majority opinion. He noted that in upholding the minimum wage, the Washington Supreme Court had "refused to regard the decision in the *Adkins* case as determinative." Such a ruling, Hughes declared, "demands on our part a reexamination" of the *Adkins* case. This reexamination began with the dismantling of the liberty of contract doctrine on which *Adkins* was based. Hughes pointed out that this freedom is not absolute. Moreover, "the liberty safeguarded is liberty in a social organization which requires the protection of law against the evils which menace the health, safety, morals, and welfare of the people." Thus, constitutional liberty is "necessarily subject to the restraints of due process, and regulation which is reasonable in relation to its subject and is adopted in the interests of the community is due process."

Hughes enumerated a wide array of state laws in the field of employer-employee relations previously upheld by the Supreme Court. Then, after quoting approvingly from the dissenting opinions of Chief Justice Taft and Justice Holmes in *Adkins,* he branded that decision as "a departure from the true application of the principles governing the regulation by the state of the relation of employer and employed."

In further support of the formal overruling of *Adkins* and in repudiation of the philosophy it represented, Hughes took judicial notice of "the unparalleled demands for relief" arising during the Great Depression and still very much in evidence at the time of this decision. Interestingly, no Brandeis brief had been filed in the *Parrish* case, primarily because this approach had failed in the *Tipaldo* case the previous year. Acknowledging the absence in the record of statistical data establishing the need for minimum wage legislation, Hughes nevertheless had no doubt, based on "common knowledge," that the state of Washington had "encountered the same social problem . . . present elsewhere." The state, he concluded, was free to correct the abusive practices of "unconscionable employers" who selfishly disregard the public interest.

West Coast Hotel Company v. Parrish marked the end of an era in American constitutional law. Although the fact might not have been fully recognized at the time, substantive due process as a limitation on governmental power in the field of economic regulation was dead. Justice Sutherland, the author of the *Adkins* majority opinion, sounded a defensive, subdued note in a dissenting opinion. For him, the Constitution had a fixed meaning that did not change "with the ebb and flow of economic events." He attempted, with little success, to distinguish between the "judicial function" of constitutional interpretation and "the power of amendment under the guise of interpretation." "To miss the point of difference between the two," he said, "is to miss all that the phrase 'supreme law of the land' stands for and to convert what was intended as inescapable and enduring mandates into mere moral reflections." That was precisely what the critics of the *Lochner-Adkins-Tipaldo* approach charged that the Court had been doing. But Sutherland insisted that "[i]f the Constitution, intelligently and reasonably construed in the light of these principles, stands in the way of desirable legislation, the blame must rest upon that instrument, and not upon the Court for enforcing it according to its terms."

Personnel changes, beginning only a few months after announcement of the *Parrish* decision, soon resulted in the replacement of all four dissenting justices in that case. The newly constituted "Roosevelt Court" continued the trend begun in *Parrish* and in other 1937 decisions upholding far-reaching economic and social legislation (see, for example, *National Labor Relations Board v. Jones & Laughlin Steel Corporation* [1937] and *Steward Machine Company v. Davis* [1937], both of which are discussed and reprinted in Chapter 2). In 1939, the Court upheld the second Agricultural Adjustment Act (*Mulford v. Smith*), and in 1941, it sustained sweeping federal regulatory power in the areas of employer-employee relations by sustaining the Fair Labor Standards Act (*United States v. Darby,* reprinted in Chapter 2). The constitutional revolution begun by the *Parrish* case in 1937 thus applied directly not only to due process interpretation but also to other key provisions of the Constitution, including the Commerce Clause, the taxing and spending power, and the Tenth Amendment.

The Court Gives Carte Blanche to Legislatures in the Economic Regulation Field   For more than half a century, no significant state or federal regulation of business or labor-management relations has been struck down on due process grounds. The 1963 decision in *Ferguson v. Skrupa* is representative of the modern approach in this area. Here, the Supreme Court, in an opinion by Justice Hugo Black, upheld the validity of a Kansas statute conferring a virtual monopoly on the legal profession to engage in the business of "debt adjusting." Black noted that the doctrine prevailing in the *Lochner-Coppage-Adkins* line of cases authorizing courts to invalidate laws because of a belief that the legislature acted unwisely "has long since been discarded." The Court, he continued, had "returned to the original constitutional proposition that courts do not substitute their social and economic beliefs for the judgment of legislative bodies, who are elected to pass laws." Once again, we see how the "original" meaning of the Constitution can mean diametrically opposing things to various Supreme Court justices. In any event, for Justice Black, objections to the law on grounds of social utility should be addressed by the legislature, not the courts. "Whether the legislature takes for its textbook Adam Smith, Herbert Spencer, Lord Keynes, or some other," Black concluded, "is no concern of ours." He also found no violation of the Equal Protection Clause of the Fourteenth Amendment in the legislative decision to provide lawyers a monopoly in the field of debt adjusting.

For the most part, the Supreme Court during the last four decades has followed the approach taken in the *Skrupa* case. Substantive due process has virtually disappeared as a barrier to economic policy making by Congress and state legislatures. However, as a constitutional doctrine, substantive due process is anything but dead. It lives on in recent Court decisions recognizing various noneconomic rights under the Fifth and Fourteenth Amendments, especially the constitutional right of privacy (see Chapter 11).

TO SUMMARIZE:

- In the late nineteenth century, as the Supreme Court came under the influence of social Darwinism and the economic doctrine of laissez-faire, the Due Process Clause of the Fourteenth Amendment served as the basis for invalidating state economic regulation. The Court developed a substantive interpretation of due process in which "liberty of contract" prevailed over competing claims based on state police power. In the leading case of *Lochner v. New York* (1905), a sharply divided Court followed this approach in striking down a New York law limiting working hours in bakeries. Critics of this decision argued that the Court was merely reading its own economic theory into the Constitution.
- After three decades in which the Court used the liberty of contract doctrine to invalidate numerous state laws dealing with conditions of employment and related matters, the Court finally yielded to political pressures stemming from the Great Depression and the New Deal. In *West Coast Hotel Company v. Parrish* (1937), the Court overturned precedent in upholding a state law establishing a minimum wage for working women.
- Since 1937 the Supreme Court has steadfastly refused to invoke the Due Process Clause as a substantive limitation on the power of government to regulate the economy.

EQUAL PROTECTION AND ECONOMIC REGULATION

Our discussion has thus far focused on the substantive interpretation of due process in the protection of private enterprise. Note, however, that during the heyday of economic due process, the Court occasionally read similar protections into the **Equal Protection Clause** of the Fourteenth Amendment. For example, in *Yick Wo v. Hopkins* (1886), the Court invalidated a San Francisco ordinance requiring owners of laundries housed in wooden buildings to obtain permission from the Board of Supervisors to continue operation of their businesses. The Court found that the ordinance was being administered to the serious detriment of Chinese immigrants. Whereas all of the affected Chinese laundry owners were denied licenses by the Board of Supervisors, nearly all non-Chinese applicants were granted licenses. Writing for the Court, Justice Stanley Matthews observed: "No reason whatever, except the will of the Supervisors, is assigned why they [the Chinese laundry owners] should not be permitted to carry on, in the accustomed manner, their harmless and useful occupation, on which they depend for a livelihood."

Similarly, in 1915, the Court struck down an Arizona law requiring that a minimum of 80 percent of any company's workforce had to consist of American citizens (*Truax v. Raich*). In these cases, the Court was especially concerned with the adverse impact of discriminatory legislation on the conduct of business.

Equal protection, like due process, disappeared as an important limitation on state economic regulatory power after the mid-1930s. It was used, however, in the late 1950s, to strike down a provision of an Illinois law exempting the American Express Company from the requirement that any firm selling or issuing money orders in the state obtain a license and submit to state regulation (*Morey v. Doud* [1957]). The effect of the discrimination here was not reasonably related to the underlying regulatory purpose of the statute. This ruling is an isolated exception to the modern Court's unwillingness to invalidate economic regulation on Fourteenth Amendment grounds.

TO SUMMARIZE:

- During the age of laissez-faire activism, the Court on occasion also used the Equal Protection Clause of the Fourteenth Amendment to limit state economic regulation. In the post–New Deal era, equal protection, like due process, has virtually disappeared as a restraint on state regulatory power in this area.

PROPERTY RIGHTS AND THE "TAKINGS" ISSUE

The final provision of the Fifth Amendment states that "nor shall private property be taken for public use without just compensation." In *Barron v. Baltimore* (1833), the Supreme Court held that the **Just Compensation Clause**, like the other provisions of the Bill of Rights, was applicable only to the acts and policies of the national government. However, in 1897, this clause became the first provision of the Bill of Rights to be incorporated into the Fourteenth Amendment and thus made applicable to the states (*Chicago, Burlington, & Quincy Railroad v. Chicago*). (For further discussion of the **doctrine of incorporation** and these important cases, see Chapter 6.) The salient legal questions raised by the Just Compensation Clause are these: (1) What constitutes a "taking" of private property? (2) What constitutes a "public use"? and (3) What constitutes "just compensation"?

Although the "takings" concept has sometimes been interpreted literally to refer only to a physical appropriation of private property by the government, there are circumstances in which a regulation may be so severe as to constitute a **taking**. The basic problem is to determine the point at which a regulation goes beyond the legitimate scope of the police power and becomes an exercise of the power of **eminent domain**. The dominant view is that the distinction between a valid regulation and the taking of property is one of degree. Justice Holmes stated this rule in the 1922 case of *Pennsylvania Coal Company v. Mahon*. Under a duly executed deed, the coal company claimed rights to mine coal under the land on which Mahon's dwelling was located. Mahon claimed, however, that irrespective of the deed, these rights were superseded by a Pennsylvania statute preventing the mining of coal in such a way as to cause the subsidence of specified types of improved land, including that on which his house was located. The issue was whether this exercise of the state's police power amounted to a "taking" of the coal company's property without just compensation. Writing for the Court, Holmes concluded that it did, and that the company was entitled to compensation. "The general rule," he declared, "is that while property may be regulated to a certain extent, if regulation goes too far it will be recognized as a taking."

Although the general concept remains valid, the value of the *Mahon* case as a precedent has been substantially diminished by the Supreme Court's decision in *Keystone Bituminous Coal Association v. DeBenedictis* (1987). Dividing 5 to 4, the Court held that a more recent Pennsylvania law designed to prevent subsidence damage from coal mining did not on its face violate either the Takings Clause or the Contracts Clause.

As the *Keystone* case suggests, the modern Court tends to give a narrow interpretation to the rights protected by the Takings Clause. Thus, in *Hawaii Housing Authority v. Midkiff* (1984), the Court ruled unanimously that the state of Hawaii had not violated the Public Use Clause by adopting a policy for the redistribution of land as a means of reducing the high concentration of ownership by a small number of individuals. After extensive hearings, the legislature had discovered in the mid-1960s that, whereas the state and federal governments owned almost 49 percent of the land in Hawaii, 47 percent of the total was in the hands of seventy-two private landowners. On the heavily populated island of Oahu, twenty-two landowners held 72.5 percent of the **fee simple** titles. The legislature concluded that such concentrated land ownership was responsible for skewing the state's real estate market in the area of home ownership, that it inflated land prices, and that it was detrimental to the public welfare.

Writing for the Supreme Court, Justice Sandra Day O'Connor found ample precedent for the exercise of such regulatory power. O'Connor acknowledged that there had to be a legitimate public purpose for taking land, even where, as here, compensation was provided. "But where the exercise of the eminent domain power is rationally related to a conceivable public purpose, the Court has never held a compensated taking to be proscribed by the Public Use Clause." O'Connor concluded that on this basis, the Hawaii land reform policy was clearly constitutional. The regulation of oligopoly and "the evils associated with it is a classic exercise of a state's police powers." The Court would inquire only as to the rationality of the act, not its wisdom or desirability as public policy. O'Connor concluded that the legislature passed this act "not to benefit a particular class of identifiable individuals, but to attack certain perceived evils of concentrated property ownership in Hawaii—a legitimate public purpose."

The Takings Issue under the Rehnquist Court

In a move generally applauded by conservatives, the Rehnquist Court has shown renewed interest in the Takings Clause as a basis for protecting property rights. For example, in *First English Evangelical Lutheran Church v. County of Los Angeles* (1987), the Court reviewed an ordinance that prohibited the reconstruction of privately owned buildings destroyed by a flood. The prohibition applied to a parcel of land owned by the Evangelical Lutheran Church, which filed a lawsuit seeking compensation for the loss it would sustain in not being able to continue to use its land as a campground. Dividing 6 to 3, the Court found that the ordinance at issue "denied appellant all use of its property for a considerable period of years" and held that "invalidation of the ordinance without payment of fair value for the use of the property during this period of time would be a constitutionally insufficient remedy."

In another California case, the Supreme Court considered a state agency ruling that required owners of beachfront property to grant an **easement** to allow public beach access as a condition for obtaining a building permit. In *Nollan v. California Coastal Commission* (1987), the Court struck down this requirement by a 5-to-4 vote. Speaking through Justice Antonin Scalia, the Court said that the state's justification for the law was

> simply an expression of the . . . [state's] belief that the public interest will be served by a continuous strip of publicly accessible beach along the coast. The [Coastal] Commission may well be right that it is a good idea, but that does not establish that the Nollans (and other coastal residents) alone can be compelled to contribute to its realization. Rather, California is free to advance its "comprehensive program," if it wishes, by using its power of eminent domain. . . , but if it wants an easement across the Nollans' property, it must pay for it.

In a bitter dissent, Justice William Brennan castigated the Court's "narrow view" of the case, saying that its "reasoning is hardly suited to the complex reality of natural resource protection in the 20th century." Brennan concluded by expressing hope "that today's decision is an aberration, and that a broader vision ultimately prevails."

In another important decision involving eminent domain, the Court in 1994 held that state and local governments that refuse to allow land development unless an owner dedicates part of the land for public use must prove that the required conditions are related to the impact of the proposed development. In *Dolan v. City of Tigard,* the Court split 5 to 4 in holding that a city had taken private property without just compensation where the city was unwilling to grant a development permit because the owner refused to dedicate part of the land to a public use. According to Chief Justice Rehnquist's majority opinion, government must show a rough proportionality between the required set-aside of land and the harm that will be caused by the new development. Rehnquist observed that the Takings Clause of the Fifth Amendment should no longer be "relegated to the status of a poor relation" among the provisions of the Bill of Rights. Dissenting from the decision were the Court's liberals: Justices Blackmun, Stevens, Souter, and Ginsburg.

The decisions in *Nollan* and *Tigard* were warmly welcomed by advocates of renewed judicial protection for property rights. On the other hand, these decisions were severely criticized by environmentalists, planners, and others who believe in regulation of private property for the general welfare. As a result of the Rehnquist Court's renewed interest in the takings issue, the volume of litigation in this area has increased substantially.

The *PruneYard* Case: Freedom of Expression versus Private Control of Property   The decision in *PruneYard Shopping Center v. Robins* (1980) illustrates how property rights may be at odds with the freedom of expression and how, in such instances, the modern Court is likely to strike a balance in favor of the latter. Our discussion of this case leads logically into the examination of freedom of expression in Chapter 8. The privately owned PruneYard Shopping Center in Campbell, California, had a policy prohibiting on its premises all "expressive activity" not directly related to its commercial purposes. In accordance with this policy, the shopping center had excluded several high school students who were seeking signatures for a petition opposing a United Nations resolution against Zionism. The California Supreme Court interpreted a state constitutional provision as granting the students a right to engage in this activity on the shopping center's property.

In an opinion by Justice Rehnquist, the U.S. Supreme Court rejected the shopping center owner's allegations that his federally protected property rights and freedom of speech had been violated. The Court found no violation of the constitutional guarantee against the taking of private property without just compensation. Although Rehnquist recognized that "one of the essential sticks in the bundle of property rights is the right to exclude others," he found "nothing to suggest that preventing [the shopping center] from prohibiting this activity will unreasonably impair the value or use of [the] property as a shopping center." The students were orderly and had limited their activities to the "common area" of the shopping center. PruneYard had failed to show that its "right to exclude others" was "so essential to the use or economic value of [its] property that the state-authorized limitation of it amounted to a 'taking.'" In addition, Rehnquist found that the state constitutional provision granting the right of access satisfied the test of rationality established in such cases as *Nebbia v. New York* (1934). Moreover, the state could reasonably conclude that recognizing a right of access furthered its "asserted interest in promoting more expansive rights of free speech and petition than [those] conferred by the Federal Constitution." This opinion, written by one of the most conservative justices, underscores the extent to which the modern Court defers to state policies limiting economic freedom.

TO SUMMARIZE:

- The Takings Clause of the Fifth Amendment, enforceable against the states through the Fourteenth Amendment, restricts government's use of the power of eminent domain. Government can take private property only for a "public use" and only with "just compensation" to the previous owner. The "taking" of private property is not limited to its physical appropriation, but includes regulatory measures that effectively deprive the owner of the enjoyment, use, or control of the property.
- Throughout most of the twentieth century, the Takings Clause did not serve as a significant limitation on governmental power. However, in recent years the Rehnquist Court has found occasion to remind public policy makers, especially at the local level, that this constitutional guarantee retains some practical force.

CONCLUSION

For almost a century and a half, the U.S. Supreme Court extended significant constitutional protection to property rights and economic freedom. The balance between these rights and the exercise of the police power shifted to some extent from period to period. The Marshall Court, primarily through the Contracts Clause, erected major safeguards for "vested rights." Coincident with the subsequent rise of Jacksonian democracy, these rights began to give way to the state police power. This trend continued from the beginning of the Taney era in the late 1830s into the 1880s. With significant personnel changes on the Court and the rising influence of corporate business interests, the Court began to interpret various provisions of the Constitution, particularly the Due Process Clauses of the Fifth and Fourteenth Amendments, as substantive limitations on economic legislation. This orientation, with its emphasis on "liberty of contract," became more pronounced around the turn of the twentieth century and, despite growing criticism from dissenting justices and legal commentators, continued to have a powerful influence on constitutional interpretation until the Supreme Court's confrontation with the Great Depression and the New Deal.

Because private property and free enterprise are deeply ingrained cultural values, there is little need for heightened judicial protection of these institutions. Nevertheless, it should be recognized that American judges at all levels continue to accord great weight to the protection of private property and contractual rights. Congress, the state legislatures, and local governments are unlikely to enact measures that seriously undermine economic freedom. At the same time, substantial political support exists for economic policy measures that regulate the economy "around the margins." A strong consensus exists in support of public policy designed to foster competition, reduce inequalities, stabilize the business cycle, and protect the environment, the consumer, and the worker. Facing a political consensus, the modern Supreme Court has generally acceded to these departures from laissez-faire capitalism.

During the 1980s, conservative theorists displeased with the policies of the modern regulatory state, most notably Bernard Seigan and Richard Epstein, urged the Supreme Court to resurrect its former commitment to private property and private enterprise. As yet, there is little evidence that the Court is interested in moving very far in that direction. For now, battles over government regulation of the economy appear to be more in the province of the constitutional historian than the constitutional lawyer. Of course, given the vicissitudes of American constitutional politics, nothing in the law should be considered settled once and for all.

The Modern Concern for Noneconomic Rights

As the last vestiges of laissez-faire disappeared from the Court's majority opinions, the justices began to give significantly greater attention to the protection of cultural and political freedoms, especially as exercised by members of racial and religious minorities outside the mainstream of American life. Consistent with this reorientation, the Court also began to recognize broader constitutional safeguards for persons accused of crime.

To a greater or lesser degree, the Court has continued to emphasize individual rights largely outside the economic sphere. Some observers have criticized the Court for having withdrawn so completely from the defense of property interests, but even the Court's most conservative members seem disinclined to reassert the laissez-faire-oriented judicial activism of the 1920s. Of course, the Supreme Court cannot successfully pursue a course of constitutional interpretation far removed from the prevailing national political consensus. At the same time, the Court should not be expected to relinquish its position of coequality as a branch of the national government. During the past half century, it has found ample opportunity to shape constitutional interpretation in many areas directly affecting the lives of the American people. The remaining chapters of this book will examine the Court's performance in the most important of these areas.

KEY TERMS

capitalist economy	laissez-faire capitalism	economic due process	Just Compensation Clause
private property	Contracts Clause	business affected with a public	doctrine of incorporation
contracts	vested rights	interest	taking
property rights	Due Process Clause of the	social Darwinism	eminent domain
economic freedom	Fourteenth Amendment	liberty of contract	fee simple
police power	substantive due process	Brandeis brief	easement
natural rights	Fifth Amendment Due Process	yellow dog contracts	
social contract	Clause	Equal Protection Clause	

FOR FURTHER READING

Ackerman, Bruce. *Private Property and the Constitution*. New Haven, Conn.: Yale University Press, 1977.

Black, Charles L., Jr., *A New Birth of Freedom: Human Rights Named and Unnamed*. New Haven, Conn.: Yale University Press, 1999.

Conant, Michael. *The Constitution and Capitalism*. St. Paul, Minn.: West, 1974.

Corwin, Edward S. *Liberty against Government*. Baton Rouge: Louisiana State University Press, 1948.

Dorn, James A., and Henry G. Manne (eds.). *Economic Liberties and the Judiciary*. Fairfax, Va.: George Mason University Press, 1987.

Ely, James W., Jr. (ed.). *Property Rights in American History* (6 vols.). New York: Garland, 1997.

Ely, John Hart. *Democracy and Distrust*. Cambridge, Mass.: Harvard University Press, 1980.

Epstein, Richard A. *Takings: Private Property and the Power of Eminent Domain*. Cambridge, Mass.: Harvard University Press, 1985.

Gillman, Howard. *The Constitution Besieged: The Rise and Decline of Lochne-Era Police Powers Jurisprudence*. Durham, N.C.: Duke University Press, 1993.

Kens, Paul. *Judicial Power and Reform Politics: The Anatomy of Lochner v. New York*. Lawrence: University of Kansas Press, 1990.

Keynes, Edward. *Liberty, Property, and Privacy: Toward a Jurisprudence of Substantive Due Process*. University Park: Pennsylvania State University Press, 1996.

Mendelson, Wallace. *Capitalism, Democracy, and the Supreme Court*. New York: Appleton-Century-Crofts, 1960.

Nedelsky, Jennifer. *Private Property and the Limits of American Constitutionalism: The Madisonian Framework and Its Legacy*. Chicago: University of Chicago Press, 1990.

Seigan, Bernard H. *Economic Liberties and the Constitution*. Chicago: University of Chicago Press, 1980.

Wright, Benjamin F. *The Contracts Clause of the Constitution*. Cambridge, Mass.: Harvard University Press, 1938.

INTERNET RESOURCES

Name of Resource	Description	URL
American Enterprise Institute	Conservative policy research organization that emphasizes economic issues	http://www.aei.org/
American Land Rights Association	An organization dedicated to protecting private property rights, especially in rural areas	http://www.landrights.org/
Cato Institute	A leading libertarian think tank	http://www.cato.org/
Center for Democratic Values	Think tank sponsored by the Democratic Socialists of America	http://www.igc.org/cdv/
Defenders of Property Rights	A legal foundation devoted to protecting private property rights	http://www.defendersproprights.org/
Public Citizen	A pro-consumer, pro-democracy group founded by Ralph Nader	http://www.citizen.org/

Case

DARTMOUTH COLLEGE V. WOODWARD

4 Wheat. (17 U.S.) 518; 4 L.Ed. 629 (1819)
Vote: 6–1

Dartmouth College was originally chartered by King George III in 1769. Under the royal charter, the trustees of the College were "forever" granted the right to govern the institution as they saw fit. However, in 1816, the New Hampshire legislature attempted to take control of the college, believing its royal charter was no longer valid. Naturally, the trustees turned to the courts for protection. Failing in the state judiciary, they appealed to the U.S. Supreme Court on a writ of error.

The opinion of the Court was delivered by . . . [*Chief Justice Marshall*].

. . . It can require no argument to prove, that the circumstances of this case constitute a contract. An application is made to the crown for a charter to incorporate a religious and literary institution. In the application, it is stated, that large contributions have been made for the object, which will be conferred on the corporation, as soon as it shall be created. The charter is granted, and on its faith the property is conveyed. Surely, in this transaction every ingredient of a complete and legitimate contract is to be found. The points for consideration are, 1. Is this contract protected by the Constitution of the United States? 2. Is it impaired by the acts under which the defendant holds? . . .

. . . [I]t appears that Dartmouth College is an eleemosynary institution, incorporated for the purpose of perpetuating the application of the bounty of the donors to the specified objects of that bounty; that its trustees or governors were originally named by the founder, and invested with the power of perpetuating themselves; that they are not public officers, nor is it a civil institution, participating in the administration of government; but a charity school, or a seminary of education, incorporated for the preservation of its property, and the perpetual application of that property to the objects of its creation. . . .

This is plainly a contract to which the donors, the trustees, and the Crown (to whose rights and obligations New Hampshire succeeds) were the original parties. It is a contract made on a valuable consideration. It is a contract on the faith of which real and personal estate has been conveyed to the corporation. It is then a contract within the letter of the Constitution, and within its spirit also, unless the fact that the property is invested by the donors in trustees, for the promotion of religion and education,

for the benefit of persons who are perpetually changing, though the objects remain the same, shall create a particular exception, taking this case out of the prohibition contained in the Constitution.

It is more than possible that the preservation of rights of this description was not particularly in the view of the framers of the Constitution, when the clause under consideration was introduced into that instrument. It is probable that interferences of more frequent recurrence, to which the temptation was stronger, and of which the mischief was more extensive, constituted the great motive for imposing this restriction on the state legislatures. But although a particular and a rare case may not, in itself, be of sufficient magnitude to induce a rule, yet it must be governed by the rule, when established, unless some plain and strong reason for excluding it can be given. It is not enough to say, that this particular case was not in the mind of the Convention when the article was framed, nor of the American people when it was adopted. It is necessary to go further, and to say that, had this particular case been suggested, the language would have been so varied as to exclude it, or it would have been made a special exception. The case being within the words of the rule, must be within its operation likewise, unless there be something in the literal construction so obviously absurd or mischievous, or repugnant to the general spirit of the instrument, as to justify those who expound the Constitution in making it an exception.

On what safe and intelligible ground can this exception stand? There is no expression in the Constitution, no sentiment delivered by its contemporaneous expounders, which would justify us in making it. In the absence of all authority of this kind, is there, in the nature and reason of the case itself, that which would sustain a construction of the Constitution not warranted by its words? Are contracts of this description of a character to excite so little interest that we must exclude them from the provisions of the Constitution, as being unworthy of the attention of those who framed the instrument? Or does public policy so imperiously demand their remaining exposed to legislative alteration as to compel us, or rather permit us to say, that these words, which were introduced to give stability to contracts, and which in their plain import comprehend this contract, must yet be so construed as to exclude it? . . .

If the insignificance of the object does not require that we should exclude contracts respecting it from the protection of the Constitution, neither, as we conceive, is the policy of leaving them subject to legislative alteration so apparent, as to require a forced construction of that instrument, in order to effect it. These eleemosynary institutions do not fill the place, which would otherwise be occupied by government, but that which would otherwise remain vacant. They are complete acquisitions to literature. They are donations to education; donations, which any government must be disposed rather to encourage than to discountenance. It requires no very critical examination of the human mind, to enable us to determine, that one great inducement to these gifts is the conviction felt by the giver, that the disposition he makes of them is immutable. It is probable, that no man was, and that no man ever will be, the founder of a college, believing at the time, that an act of incorporation constitutes no security for the institution; believing, that it is immediately to be deemed a public institution, whose funds are to be governed and applied, not by the will of the donor, but by the will of the legislature. All such gifts are made in the pleasing, perhaps delusive hope, that the charity will flow forever in the channel which the givers have marked out for it. If every man finds in his own bosom strong evidence of the universality of this sentiment, there can be but little reason to imagine, that the framers of our Constitution were strangers to it, and that, feeling the necessity and policy of giving permanence and security to contracts, of withdrawing them from the influence of legislative bodies, whose fluctuating policy and repeated interferences, produced the most perplexing and injurious embarrassments, they still deemed it necessary to leave these contracts subject to those interferences. The motives for such an exception must be very powerful, to justify the construction which makes it. . . .

We next proceed to the inquiry, whether its obligation has been impaired by those acts of the legislature of New Hampshire, to which the special verdict refers? . . .

It has been already stated, that the act "to amend the charter, and enlarge and improve the corporation of Dartmouth College," increases the number of trustees to twenty-one, gives the appointment of the additional members to the executive of the state, and creates a board of overseers, to consist of twenty-five persons, of whom twenty-one are also appointed by the executive of New Hampshire, who have power to inspect and control the most important acts of the trustees.

On the effect of this law [of 1816], two opinions cannot be entertained. Between acting directly, and acting through the agency of trustees and overseers, no essential difference is perceived. The whole power of governing the college is transferred from trustees appointed according to the will of the founder, expressed in the charter, to the executive of New Hampshire. The management and application of the funds of this eleemosynary institution, which are placed by the donors in the hands of trustees named in the charter, and empowered to perpetuate themselves, are placed by this act under the control of the government of the state. The will of the state is substituted for the will of the donors, in every essential operation of the college. This is not an immaterial change. The founders of the college contracted, not merely for the perpetual application of the funds which they gave, to the objects for which those funds were given; they contracted, also, to secure that application by the Constitution of the corporation. They contracted for a system which should, as far as human foresight can provide, retain forever the government of the literary institution they had formed, in the hands of persons approved by themselves. This system is totally changed. The charter of 1769 exists no longer. It is reorganized; and reorganized in such a manner as to convert a literary institution, moulded according to the will of its founders, and placed under the control of private literary men, into a machine entirely subservient to the will of government. This may be for the advantage of literature in general; but it is not according to the will of the donors, and is subversive of that contract on the faith of which their property was given. . . .

It results from this opinion, that the acts of the legislature of New Hampshire, which are stated in the special verdict found in this cause, are repugnant to the Constitution of the United States; and that the judgment on this special verdict ought to have been for the plaintiffs. The judgment of the State Court must therefore be reversed.

Mr. Justice Duvall dissented.

Case

CHARLES RIVER BRIDGE COMPANY V. WARREN BRIDGE COMPANY

11 Pet. (36 U.S.) 420; 9 L.Ed. 773 (1837)
Vote: 5–2

This decision was one of the Taney Court's most important contributions to American constitutional development. The case grew out of a dispute involving rival companies in the business of building and operating bridges. The constitutional issue stemmed from the fact that both companies were operating under charters granted them by a state legislature. In 1785, the Massachusetts legislature incorporated the Charles River Bridge Company for forty years, for the purpose of building and operating a toll bridge over the Charles River between Boston and Cambridge. In 1792, the legislature extended the term of the charter to seventy years. In 1828, the legislature chartered another company, the Warren Bridge Company, and authorized it to build another bridge three hundred yards from the Charles River Bridge. The Charles River Bridge Company then brought suit, arguing that the legislature had implicitly granted it an exclusive right to operate a bridge in the area throughout the life of its charter. According to the Charles River Bridge Company, the grant of the charter to the Warren Bridge Company was an impairment of the obligation of contracts, forbidden by Article I, Section 10, of the Constitution. The state courts rejected this argument, and the Supreme Court took the case on a writ of error.

Mr. Chief Justice Taney delivered the opinion of the Court.

. . . This brings us to the act of the legislature of Massachusetts, of 1785, by which the plaintiffs were incorporated by the name of "The Proprietors of the Charles River Bridge"; and it is here, and in the law of 1792, prolonging their charter, that we must look for the extent and nature of the franchise conferred upon the plaintiffs.

Much has been said in the argument of the principles of construction by which this law is to be expounded, and what undertakings, on the part of the state, may be implied. The Court think[s] there can be no serious difficulty on that head. It is the grant of certain franchises by the public to a private corporation, and in a matter where the public interest is concerned. The rule of construction in such cases is well settled, both in England and by the decisions of our own tribunals. . . . In the case of the *Proprietors of the Stourbridge Canal v. Wheely* and others, the Court say[s], "The canal having been made under an act of Parliament, the rights of the plaintiffs are derived entirely

from that act. This, like many other cases, is a bargain between a company of adventurers and the public, the terms of which are expressed in the statute; and the rule of construction, in all such cases, is now fully established to be this; that any ambiguity in the terms of the contract must operate against the adventurers, and in favor of the public, and the plaintiffs can claim nothing that is not clearly given them by the act." And the doctrine thus laid down is abundantly sustained by the authorities referred to in this decision. . . .

. . . The argument in favour of the proprietors of the Charles River bridge, is . . . that the power claimed by the state, if it exists, may be so used as to destroy the value of the franchise they have granted to the corporation. . . . The existence of the power does not, and cannot depend upon the circumstance of its having been exercised or not.

. . . [T]he object and end of all government is to promote the happiness and prosperity of the community by which it is established, and it can never be assumed, that the government intended to diminish its power of accomplishing the end for which it was created. And in a country like ours, free, active, and enterprising, continually advancing in numbers and wealth, new channels of communication are daily found necessary, both for travel and trade; and are essential to the comfort, convenience and prosperity of the people. A state ought never to be presumed to surrender this power, because, like the taxing power, the whole community have an interest in preserving it undiminished. And when a corporation alleges that a state has surrendered, for seventy years, its power of improvement and public accommodation, in a great and important line of travel, along which a vast number of its citizens must daily pass, the community have a right to insist, in the language of this court above quoted, "that its abandonment ought not to be presumed in a case in which the deliberate purpose of the state to abandon it does not appear." The continued existence of a government would be of no great value, if by implications and presumptions it was disarmed of the powers necessary to accomplish the ends of its creation, and the functions it was designed to perform, transferred to the hands of privileged corporations. The rule of construction announced by the court was not confined to the taxing power; nor is it so limited in the opinion delivered. On the contrary, it was distinctly placed on the ground that the interests of the community were concerned in preserving, undiminished, the power then in question; and whenever any power of the state is said to be surrendered and diminished, whether it be the taxing power or any other affecting the public interest, the same principle applies, and the rule of construction must be the same. No one will question that the interests of the great body of the people of the state would, in this instance, be affected by the surrender of this great line of travel to a single corporation, with the right to exact toll, and exclude competition for seventy years. While the rights of private property are sacredly guarded, we must not forget that the community also have rights, and that the happiness and well-being of every citizen depends on their faithful preservation.

Adopting the rule of construction above stated as the settled one, we proceed to apply it to the charter of 1785, to the proprietors of the Charles River bridge. This act of incorporation is in the usual form, and the privileges such as are commonly given to corporations of that kind. It confers on them the ordinary faculties of a corporation, for the purpose of building the bridge; and establishes certain rates of toll, which the company are authorized to take. This is the whole grant. There is no exclusive privilege given to them over the waters of Charles River, above or below their bridge; no right to erect another bridge themselves, nor to prevent other persons from erecting one. No engagement from the state, that another shall not be erected; and no undertaking not to sanction competition, nor to make improvements that may diminish the amount of its income. Upon all these subjects, the charter is silent, and nothing is said in it about a line of travel, so much insisted on in the argument, in which they are to have exclusive privileges. . . .

. . . In short, all the franchises and rights of property, enumerated in the charter, and there mentioned to have been granted to it, remain unimpaired. But its income is destroyed by the Warren bridge; which, being free, draws off the passengers and property which would have gone over it, and renders their franchise of no value. This is the gist of the complaint. For it is not pretended, that the erection of the Warren bridge would have done them any injury, or in any degree affected their right of property, if it had not diminished the amount of their tolls. In order, then, to entitle themselves to relief, it is necessary to show, that the legislature contracted not to do the act of which they complain; and that they impaired, or in other words, violated, that contract by the erection of the Warren bridge.

The inquiry, then, is, does the charter contain such a contract on the part of the state? Is there any such stipulation to be found in that instrument? It must be admitted on all hands, that there is none; no words that even relate to another bridge, or to the [diminution] of their tolls, or to the line of travel. If a contract on that subject can be gathered from the charter, it must be by implication; and cannot be found in the words used. Can such an agreement be implied? The rule of construction before stated is an answer to the question; in charters of this description, no rights are taken from the public, or given

to corporations, beyond those which the words of the charter, by their natural and proper construction, purport to convey. There are no words which import such a contract as the plaintiffs in error contend for, and none can be implied. . . .

Indeed, the practice and usage of almost every state in the Union, old enough to have commenced the work of internal improvement, is opposed to the doctrine contended for on the part of the plaintiffs in error. Turnpike roads have been made in succession, on the same line of travel; the later ones interfering materially with the profits of the first. These corporations have, in some instances, been utterly ruined by the introduction of newer and better modes of transportation and traveling. In some cases, railroads have rendered the turnpike roads on the same line of travel so entirely useless, that the franchise of the turnpike corporation is not worth preserving. Yet in none of these cases have the corporations supposed that their privileges were invaded, or any contract violated on the part of the state. Amid the multitude of cases which have occurred, and have been daily occurring for the last forty or fifty years, this is the first instance in which such an implied contract has been contended for, and this court called upon to infer it, from an ordinary act of incorporation, containing nothing more than the usual stipulations and provisions to be found in every such law. The absence of any such controversy, when there must have been so many occasions to give rise to it, proves that neither states, nor individuals, nor corporations, ever imagined that such a contract could be implied from such charters. It shows, that the men who voted for these laws never imagined that they were forming such a contract; and if we maintain that they have made it, we must create it by a legal fiction, in opposition to the truth of the fact, and the obvious intention of the party. We cannot deal thus with the rights reserved to the states; and by legal intendments and mere technical reasoning, take away from them any portion of that power over their own internal police and improvement, which is not necessary to their well-being and prosperity.

And what would be the fruits of this doctrine of implied contracts, on the part of the states, and of property in a line of travel by a corporation if it should now be sanctioned by this court? To what results would it lead us? If it is to be found in the charter to this bridge, the same process of reasoning must discover it, in the various acts which have been passed, within the last forty years, for turnpike companies. And what is to be the extent of the privileges of exclusion on the different sides of the road? The counsel who have so ably argued this case, have not attempted to define it by any certain boundaries. How far must the new improvement be distant from the old one? How near may you approach, without invading its rights in the privileged line? If this court should establish the principles now contented for, what is to become of the numerous railroads established on the same line of travel with turnpike companies; and which have rendered the franchises of the turnpike corporations of no value? Let it once be understood, that such charters carry with them these implied contracts, and give this unknown and undefined prosperity in a line of traveling; and you will soon find the old turnpike corporations awakening from their sleep and calling upon this court to put down the improvements which have taken their place. The millions of property which have been invested in railroads and canals, upon lines of travel which had been before occupied by turnpike corporations, will be put in jeopardy. We shall be thrown back to the improvements of the last century, and obliged to stand still, until the claims of the old turnpike corporations shall be satisfied; and they shall consent to permit these states to avail themselves of the lights of modern science, and to partake of the benefit of those improvements which are now adding to the wealth and prosperity, and the convenience and comfort, of every other part of the civilized word. Nor is this all. This court will find itself compelled to fix, by some kind of arbitrary rule, the width of this new kind of property in a line of travel; for if such a right of property exists, we have no

lights to guide us in marking out its extent, unless, indeed, we resort to the old feudal grants, and to the exclusive rights of ferries, by prescription, between towns; and are prepared to decide that when a turnpike road from one town to another, had been made, no railroad or canal, between these two points, could afterwards be established. This court are not prepared to sanction principles which must lead to such results. . . .

The judgment of the supreme judicial court of the commonwealth of Massachusetts, dismissing the plaintiffs' bill, must therefore, be affirmed with costs.

Mr. Justice McLean delivered an opinion [concurring in the judgment] holding that the case should be dismissed for want of jurisdiction.

Mr. Justice Story, dissenting. . . .

. . . Upon the whole, my judgment is that the act of the legislature of Massachusetts granting the charter of Warren Bridge, is an act impairing the obligation of the prior contract and grant to the proprietors of Charles River bridge; and, by the Constitution of the United States, it is, therefore, utterly void. I am for reversing the decree of the state court for further proceedings. . . .

Mr. Justice Thompson concurred in this [dissenting] opinion. . . .

Case

HOME BUILDING AND LOAN ASSOCIATION V. BLAISDELL

290 U.S. 398; 54 S.Ct. 231; 78 L.Ed. 413 (1934)
Vote: 5–4

In 1933, the Minnesota legislature adopted an act designed to prevent the foreclosure of mortgages on real estate during the economic emergency produced by the Great Depression. The Mortgage Moratorium Act authorized courts to extend the redemption periods of mortgages in order to prevent foreclosures. The act was to remain in effect only during the emergency period and in no case beyond May 1, 1935.

Mr. Chief Justice Hughes delivered the opinion of the Court.

. . . The state court upheld the statute as an emergency measure. Although conceding that the obligations of the mortgage contract were impaired, the court decided that what it thus described as an impairment was, notwith-

standing the Contracts Clause of the Federal Constitution, within the police power of the state as that power was called into exercise by the public economic emergency which the legislature had found to exist. . . .

In determining whether the provision for this temporary and conditional relief exceeds the power of the state by reason of the clause in the Federal Constitution prohibiting impairment of the obligations of contracts, we must consider the relation of emergency to constitutional power, the historical setting of the Contracts Clause, the development of the jurisprudence of this Court in the construction of that clause, and the principles of construction which we may consider to be established.

Emergency does not create power. Emergency does not increase granted power or remove or diminish the restrictions imposed upon power granted or reserved. The Constitution was adopted in a period of grave emergency. Its grants of power to the Federal Government and its limitations of the power of the states were determined in the light of emergency, and they are not altered by emergency. What power was thus granted and what limitations were thus imposed are questions which have always been, and always will be, the subject of close examination under our constitutional system.

While emergency does not create power, emergency may furnish the occasion for the exercise of power. "Although an emergency may not call into life a power which has never lived, nevertheless emergency may afford a reason for the exertion of a living power already enjoyed." . . . The constitutional question presented in the light of an emergency is whether the power possessed embraces the particular exercise of it in response to particular conditions. Thus, the war power of the federal government is not created by the emergency of war, but it is a power to wage war successfully, and thus it permits the harnessing of the entire energies of the people in a supreme co-operative effort to preserve the nation. But even the war power does not remove constitutional limitations safeguarding essential liberties. When the provisions of the Constitution, in grant or restriction, are specific, so particularized as not to admit a state to have more than two Senators in the Congress, or permit the election of a President by a general popular vote without regard to the number of electors to which the states are respectively entitled, or permit the states to "coin money" or to "make anything but gold and silver coin a tender in payment of debts." But, where constitutional grants and limitations of power are set forth in general clauses, which afford a broad outline, the process of construction is essential to fill in the details. That is true of the Contracts Clause. . . .

In the construction of the Contracts Clause, the debates in the Constitutional Convention are of little aid. But the reasons which led to the adoption of that clause, and of the other prohibitions of Section 10 of Article I, are not left in doubt, and have frequently been described with eloquent emphasis. The widespread distress following the revolutionary period, and the plight of debtors had called forth in the state an ignoble array of legislative schemes for the defeat of creditors and the invasion of contractual obligations. Legislative interferences had been so numerous and extreme that the confidence essential to prosperous trade had been undermined and the utter destruction of credit was threatened. "The sober people of America" were convinced that some "thorough reform" was needed which would "inspire a general prudence and industry, and give a regular course to the business of society." . . .

The inescapable problems of construction have been: What is a contract? What are the obligations of contracts? What constitutes impairment of these obligations? What residuum of power is there still in the states, in relation to the operation of contracts, to protect the vital interests of the community? Questions of this character, "of no small nicety and intricacy, have vexed the legislative halls, as well as the judicial tribunals, with an uncounted variety and frequency of litigation and speculation." . . .

It is manifest . . . that there has been a growing appreciation of public needs and of the necessity of finding ground for a rational compromise between individual rights and public welfare. . . . Pressure of a constantly increasing density of population, the interrelation of the activities of our people and the complexity of our economic interests, have inevitably led to an increased use of the organization of society in order to protect the very bases of individual opportunity. Where, in earlier days, it was thought that only the concerns of individuals or of classes were involved, and that those of the state itself were touched only remotely, it has later been found that the fundamental interests of the state are directly affected; and that the question is no longer merely that of one party to a contract as against another, but of the use of reasonable means to safeguard the economic structure upon which the good of all depends.

It is no answer to say that this public need was not apprehended a century ago, or to insist that what the provision of the Constitution meant to the vision of that day it must mean to the vision of our time. If by the statement that what the Constitution meant at the time of its adoption it means today, it is intended to say that the great clauses of the Constitution must be confined to the interpretation which the framers, with the conditions and outlook of their time, would have placed upon them, the statement carries its own refutation. It was to guard against such a narrow conception that Chief Justice Marshall uttered the memorable warning: "We must never forget, that it is a *constitution* we are expounding"; . . . "a constitution intended to endure for ages to come, and, consequently, to be adapted to the various *crises* of human affairs." . . . When we are dealing with the words of the Constitution, . . . "we must realize that they have called into life a being the development of which could not have been foreseen completely by the most gifted of its begetters. . . . The case before us must be considered in the light of our whole experience and not merely in that of what was said a hundred years ago." . . .

Nor is it helpful to attempt to draw a fine distinction between the intended meaning of the words of the Constitution and their intended application. When we consider the Contracts Clause and the decisions which have expounded it in harmony with the essential reserved power of the states to protect the security of their peoples, we find no warrant for the conclusion that the clause has been warped by these decisions from its proper significance or that the founders of our government would have interpreted the clause differently had they had occasion to assume that responsibility in the conditions of the later day. The vast body of law which has been developed was unknown to the fathers, but it is believed to have preserved the essential content and the spirit of the Constitution. With a growing recognition of public needs and the relation of individual right to public security, the Court has sought to prevent the perversion of the clause through its use as an instrument to throttle the capacity of the states to protect their fundamental interests. . . .

We are of the opinion that the Minnesota statute as here applied does not violate the Contracts Clause of the Federal Constitution. Whether the legislation is wise or unwise as a matter of policy is a question with which we are not concerned. . . .

Mr. Justice Sutherland, dissenting.

Few questions of greater moment than that just decided have been submitted for judicial inquiry during this generation. He simply closes his eyes to the necessary implications of the decision who fails to see in it the potentiality of future gradual but ever-advancing encroachments upon the sanctity of private and public contracts. The effect of the Minnesota legislation, though serious enough in itself, is of trivial significance compared with the far more serious and dangerous inroads upon the limitations of the Constitution which are almost certain to ensue as a consequence naturally following any step beyond the boundaries fixed by that instrument. And those of us who are thus apprehensive of the effect of this decision would, in a matter so important, be neglectful of our duty should we fail to spread upon the permanent records of the court the reasons which move us to the opposite view.

A provision of the Constitution, it is hardly necessary to say, does not admit of two distinctly opposite interpretations. It does not mean one thing at one time and an entirely different thing at another time. If the Contract Impairment Clause, when framed and adopted, meant that the terms of a contract for the payment of money could not be altered . . . by a state statute enacted for the relief of hardly pressed debtors to the end and with the effect of postponing payment or enforcement during and because of an economic or financial emergency, it is but to state the obvious to say that it means the same now. This view, at once so rational in its application to the written word, and so necessary to the stability of constitutional principles, though from time to time challenged, has never, unless recently, been put within the realm of doubt by the decisions of this Court. . . .

The provisions of the federal Constitution, undoubtedly, are pliable in the sense that in appropriate cases they have the capacity of bringing within their grasp every new condition which falls within their meaning. But their *mean-*

ing is changeless; it is only their *application* which is extensible. . . . Constitutional grants of power and restrictions upon the exercise of power are not flexible as the doctrines of the common law are flexible. These doctrines, upon the principles of the common law itself, modify or abrogate themselves whenever they are or whenever they become plainly unsuited to different or changed conditions. . . .

The whole aim of construction, as applied to a provision of the Constitution, is to discover the meaning, to ascertain and give effect to the intent, of its framers and the people who adopted it. . . . And if the meaning be at all doubtful, the doubt should be resolved, wherever reasonably possible to do so, in a way to forward the evident purpose with which the provision was adopted. . . .

An application of these principles to the question under review removes any doubt, if otherwise there would be any, that the Contract Impairment Clause denies to the several states the power to mitigate hard consequences resulting to debtors from financial or economic exigencies by an impairment of the obligation of contracts of indebtedness. A candid consideration of the history and circumstances which led up to and accompanied the framing and adoption of this clause will demonstrate conclusively that it was framed and adopted with the specific and studied purpose of preventing legislation designed to relieve debtors especially in time of financial distress. Indeed, it is not probable that any other purpose was definitely in the minds of those who composed the framers' convention or the ratifying state conventions which followed, although the restriction has been given a wider application upon principles clearly stated by Chief Justice Marshall in the Dartmouth College Case. . . .

The present exigency is nothing new. From the beginning of our existence as a nation, periods of depression, of industrial failure, of financial distress, of unpaid and unpayable indebtedness, have alternated with years of plenty. The vital lesson that expenditure beyond income begets poverty, that public or private extravagance, financed by promises to pay, either must end in complete or partial repudiation or the promises be fulfilled by self-denial and painful effort, though constantly taught by bitter experience, seems never to be learned; and the attempt by legislative devices to shift the misfortune of debtor to the shoulders of the creditor without coming into conflict with the Contract Impairment Clause has been persistent and oft-repeated.

The defense of the Minnesota law is made upon grounds which were discountenanced by the makers of the Constitution and have many times been rejected by this court. That defense should not now succeed, because it constitutes an effort to overthrow the constitutional provision by an appeal to facts and circumstances identical with those which brought it into existence. With due regard for the process of logical thinking, it legitimately cannot be urged that conditions which produced the rule may now be invoked to destroy it.

. . . The opinion concedes that emergency does not create power, or increase granted power, or remove or diminish restrictions upon power granted or reserved. It then proceeds to say, however, that while emergency does not create power, it may furnish the occasion for the exercise of power. I can only interpret what is said on that subject as meaning that while an emergency does not diminish a restriction upon power it furnishes an occasion for diminishing it; and this, as it seems to me, is merely to say the same thing by the use of another set of words, with the effect of affirming that which has just been denied.

It is quite true that an emergency may supply the occasion for the exercise of power, depending upon the nature of the power and the intent of the Constitution with respect thereto. The emergency of war furnishes an occasion for the exercise of certain of the war powers. This the Constitution contemplates, since they cannot be exercised upon any other occasion. The existence of another kind of emergency authorizes the United States to protect each of the states of the Union against domestic violence. . . . But we are here dealing not with a power granted by the federal Constitution, but with the state policy power, which exists in its own right. Hence the question is not whether an emergency furnishes the occasion for the exercise of that state power, but whether an emergency furnishes an occasion for the relaxation of the restrictions upon the power imposed by the Contract Impairment Clause, and the difficulty is that the Contract Impairment Clause forbids state action under any circumstances, if it have the effect of impairing the obligation of contracts.

That clause restricts every state power in the particular specified, no matter what may be the occasion. It does not contemplate that an emergency shall furnish an occasion for softening the restriction or making it any the less a restriction upon state action in that contingency than it is under strictly normal conditions.

The Minnesota statute either impairs the obligation of contracts or it does not. If it does not, the occasion to which it relates becomes immaterial, since then the passage of the statute is the exercise of a normal, unrestricted, state power and requires no special occasion to render it effective. If it does, the emergency no more furnishes a proper occasion for its exercise than if the emergency were nonexistent. And so, while, in form, the suggested distinction seems to put us forward in a straight line, in reality it simply carries us back in a circle, like bewildered travelers lost in a wood, to the point where we parted company with the view of the state court. . . .

I quite agree with the opinion of the Court that whether the legislation under review is wise or unwise is a matter with which we have nothing to do. Whether it is likely to work well or work ill presents a question entirely irrelevant to the issue. The only legitimate inquiry we can make is whether it is constitutional. If it is not, its virtues, if it have any, cannot save it; if it is, its faults cannot be invoked to accomplish its destruction. If the provisions of the Constitution be not upheld when they pinch as well as when they comfort, they may as well be abandoned. Being unable to reach any other conclusion than that the Minnesota statute infringes the constitutional restrictions under review, I have no choice but to say so.

I am authorized to say that *Mr. Justice Van Devanter,* *Mr. Justice McReynolds* and *Mr. Justice Butler* concur in this opinion.

Case

THE SLAUGHTERHOUSE CASES

16 Wall. (83 U.S.) 36; 21 L.Ed. 394 (1873)
Vote: 5–4

In 1869, the Louisiana legislature granted to a slaughterhouse company a monopoly for the city of New Orleans. A number of independent butchers sought injunctions against the monopoly. Unable to secure injunctions in the state courts, they turned to the Supreme Court, which granted review pursuant to a writ of error.

Mr. Justice Miller . . . delivered the opinion of the Court.

The plaintiffs . . . allege that the statute is a violation of the Constitution of the United States in these several particulars:

That it creates an involuntary servitude forbidden by the thirteenth article of amendment;

That it abridges the privileges and immunities of citizens of the United States;

That it denies to the plaintiffs the equal protection of the laws; and,

That it deprives them of their property without due process of law; contrary to the provisions of the first section of the fourteenth article of amendment.

This court is thus called upon for the first time to give construction to these articles.

. . . On the most casual examination of the language of [the Thirteenth, Fourteenth, and Fifteenth] amendments, no one can fail to be impressed with the one pervading purpose found in them all, lying at the foundation of each, and without which none of them would have been even suggested; we mean the freedom of the slave race, the security and firm establishment of that freedom, and the protection of the newly-made freeman and citizen from the oppressions of those who had formerly exercised unlimited dominion over him. It is true that only the Fifteenth Amendment, in terms, mentions the negro by speaking of his color and his slavery. But it is just as true that each of the other articles was addressed to the grievances of that race, and designed to remedy them as the Fifteenth.

We do not say that no one else but the negro can share in this protection. Both the language and spirit of these articles are to have their fair and just weight in any question of construction. Undoubtedly while negro slavery alone was in the mind of the congress which proposed the thirteenth article, it forbids any other kind of slavery, now or hereafter. If Mexican peonage or the Chinese cooly labor system shall develop slavery of the Mexican or Chinese race within our territory, this amendment may safely be trusted to make it void. And so if other rights are assailed by the States which properly and necessarily fall within the protection of these articles, that protection will apply, though the party interested may not be of African descent. But what we do say, and what we wish to be understood is, that in any fair and just construction of any section or phrase of these amendments, it is necessary to look to the purpose which we have said was the pervading spirit of them all, the evil which they were designed to remedy, and the process of continued addition to the Constitution, until that purpose was supposed to be accomplished, as far as constitutional law can accomplish it. . . .

The next observation is more important in view of the arguments of counsel in the present case. It is, that the distinction between citizenship of the United States and citizenship of a State is clearly recognized and established. Not only may a man be a citizen of the United States without being a citizen of a State, but an important element is necessary to convert the former into the latter. He must reside within the State to make him a citizen of it, but it is only necessary that he should be born or naturalized in the United States to be a citizen of the Union.

It is quite clear, then, that there is a citizenship of the United States, and a citizenship of a State, which are distinct from each other, and which depend upon different characteristics of circumstance in the individual.

We think this distinction and its explicit recognition in this amendment of great weight in this argument, because the next paragraph of this same section, which is the one mainly relied on by the plaintiffs in error, speaks only of privileges and immunities of citizens of the United States, and does not speak of those of citizens of the several States. The argument, however, in favor of the plaintiffs rests wholly on the assumption that the citizenship is the same, and the privileges and immunities guaranteed by the clause are the same.

The language is, "No State shall make or enforce any law which shall abridge the privileges or immunities of citizens of the United States." It is a little remarkable, if this clause was intended as a protection to the citizen of a State against the legislative power of his own State, that the [words] *citizen of the State* should be left out when it is so carefully used, and used in contradistinction to citizens of the United States, in the very sentence which precedes it. It is too clear for argument that the change in phraseology was adopted understandingly and with a purpose.

Of the privileges and immunities of the citizen of the United States, and of the privileges and immunities of the citizen of the States, and what they respectively are, we will presently consider; but we wish to state here that it is only the former which are placed by this clause under the protection of the Federal Constitution, and that the latter, whatever they may be, are not intended to have any additional protection by this paragraph of the amendment.

If, then, there is a difference between the privileges and immunities belonging to a citizen of the United States as such, and those belonging to the citizen of the State as such the latter must rest for their security and protection where they have heretofore rested; for they are not embraced by this paragraph of the amendment. . . .

Fortunately we are not without judicial construction of this clause of the Constitution, the first and the leading case on the subject is that of *Corfield v. Coryell,* . . . decided by Mr. Justice Washington in the Circuit Court for the District of Pennsylvania in 1823. "The inquiry," he says, is,

[W]hat are the privileges and immunities of citizens of the several States? We feel no hesitation in confining these expressions to those privileges and immunities which are fundamental; which belong of right to the citizens of all free governments, and which have at all times been enjoyed by citizens of the several States which compose this Union, from the time of their becoming free, independent, and sovereign. What these fundamental principles are, it would be more tedious than difficult to enumerate. They may all, however, be comprehended under the following general heads: protection by the government, with the right to acquire and possess property of every kind, to such restraints as the government may pre-scribe for the general good of the whole. . . .

It would be the vainest show of learning to attempt to prove by citations of authority, that up to the adoption of the recent amendments, no claim or pretense was set up that those rights depended on the Federal government for their existence or protection, beyond the very few express limitations which the Federal Constitution imposed upon the States—such, for instance, as the prohibition against *ex post facto* laws, bills of attainder, and laws impairing the obligation of contracts. But with the exception of these and a few other restrictions, the entire domain of the privileges and immunities of the citizens of the States, and without that of the Federal government. Was it the purpose of the Fourteenth Amendment, by the simple declaration that no States should make or enforce any law which abridge the privileges and immunities of citizens of the United States, to transfer the security and protection of all the civil rights which we have mentioned, from the states to the Federal government? And where it is declared that Congress shall have the power to enforce that article, was it intended to bring within the power of Congress the entire domain of civil rights heretofore belonging exclusively to the States?

All this and more must follow, if the proposition of the plaintiffs in error be sound. For not only are these rights subject to the control of Congress whenever in its discretion any of them are supposed to be abridged by State legislation, but that body may also pass laws in advance, limiting and restricting the exercise of legislative power of the States, in their most ordinary and usual functions, as in its judgment it may think proper on all such subjects. And still further, such a construction followed by the reversal of the judgments of the Supreme Court of Louisiana in these cases, would constitute this court a perpetual censor upon all legislation of the States, on the civil rights of their own citizens, with authority to nullify such as it did not approve as consistent with those rights, as they existed at the time of the adoption of this amendment. The argument we admit is not always the most conclusive which is drawn from the consequences urged against the adoption of a particular construction of an instrument. But when, as in the case before us, these consequences are so serious, so far-reaching and pervading, so great a departure from the structure and spirit of our institutions; when the effect is to fetter and degrade the State governments by subjecting them to the control of Congress, in the exercise of powers heretofore universally conceded to them of the most ordinary and fundamental character; when in fact it radically changes the whole theory of the relations of the State and Federal governments to each other and of both of these govern-

ments to the people; the argument has a force that is irresistible, in the absence of language which expresses such a purpose too clearly to admit of doubt.

We are convinced that no such results were intended by the Congress which proposed these amendments, nor by the legislatures of the States which ratified them.

Having shown that the privileges and immunities relied on in the argument are those which belong to citizens of the States as such, and that they are left to the State governments for security and protection, and not by this article placed under the special care of the Federal government, we may hold ourselves excused from defining the privileges and immunities of citizens of the United States which no State can abridge, until some case involving those privileges may make it necessary to do so.

But lest it be said that no such privileges and immunities are to be found if those we have been considering are excluded, we venture to suggest some which owe their existence to the Federal government, its National character, its Constitution, or its laws.

One of these is well described in the case of *Crandall v. Nevada.* . . . It is said to be the right of the citizens of this great country, protected by implied guarantees of its Constitution, "to come to the seat of government to assert any claim he may have upon that government, to transact any business he may have with it, to seek its protection, to share its offices, to engage in administering its functions. He has the right of free access to its seaports, through which all operations of foreign commerce are conducted, to the subtreasuries, land offices, and courts of justice in the several States." And quoting from the language of Chief Justice Taney in another case, it is said "that for all the great purposes for which the Federal government was established, we are one people, with one common country, we are all citizens of the United States"; and it is, as such citizens, that their rights are supported in this court in *Crandall v. Nevada.* . . .

The argument has not been much pressed in these cases that the defendant's charter deprives the plaintiffs of their property without due process of law, or that it denies to them the equal protection of the law. The first of these paragraphs has been in the Constitution since the adoption of the fifth amendment, as a restraint upon the Federal power. It is also to be found in some form of expression in the constitutions of nearly all the States, as a restraint upon the power of the States. This law, then, has practically been the same as it now is during the existence of the government, except so far as the present amendment may place the restraining power over the States in this matter in the hands of the Federal government.

We are not without judicial interpretation, therefore, both State and National, of the meaning of this clause. And it is sufficient to say that under no construction of that provision that we have ever seen, or any that we deem admissible, can the restraint imposed by the state of Louisiana upon the exercise of their trade by the butchers of New Orleans be held to be a deprivation of property within the meaning of that provision.

"Nor shall any State deny to any person within its jurisdiction the equal protection of the laws."

In the light of the history of these amendments, and the pervading purpose of them, which we have already discussed, it is not difficult to give a meaning to this clause. The existence of laws in the states where the newly emancipated negroes resided, which discriminated with gross injustice and hardship against them as a class, was the evil to be remedied by this clause, and by it such laws are forbidden.

If, however, the states did not conform their laws to its requirements, then by the fifth section of the article of amendment Congress was authorized to enforce it by suitable legislation. We doubt very much whether any action of a State not directed by way of discrimination against the negroes as a class, or on account of their race, will ever be held to come within the purview of this provision. It is so clearly a provision for that race and that emergency, that a strong case would be necessary for its application to any other. But as it is a State that is to be dealt with, and not alone the validity of its laws, we may safely leave that matter until congress shall have exercised its power, or some case of State oppression, by denial of equal justice in its courts, shall have claimed a decision at our hands. We find no such case in the one before us, and do not deem it necessary to go over the argument again, as it may have relation to this particular clause of the amendment. . . .

The judgments of the Supreme Court of Louisiana in these cases are affirmed.

Mr. Justice Field, dissenting:

. . . The question presented is . . . one of the gravest importance, not merely to the parties here, but to the whole country. It is nothing less than the question whether the recent amendments to the Federal Constitution protect the citizens of the United States against the deprivation of their common rights by State legislation. In my judgment the Fourteenth Amendment does afford such protection, and was so intended by the Congress which framed and the States which adopted it.

The amendment does not attempt to confer any new privileges or immunities upon citizens, or to enumerate or define those already existing. It assumes that there are such privileges and immunities which belong of right to citizens as such, and ordains that they shall not be abridged by State legislation. If this inhibition has no reference to privileges and immunities of this character, but only refers, as held by the majority of the court in their opinion, to such privileges and immunities as were before its adoption specially designated in the Constitution or necessarily implied as belonging to citizens of the United States, it was a vain and idle enactment, which accomplished nothing, and most unnecessarily excited Congress and the people on its passage. With privileges and immunities thus designated or implied no State could ever have interfered by its laws and no new constitutional provision was required to inhibit such interference. The supremacy of the Constitution and the laws of the United States always controlled any State legislation of that character. But if the amendment refers to the natural and inalienable rights which belong to all citizens, the inhibition has a profound significance and consequence.

What, then, are the privileges and immunities which are secured against abridgment by State legislation? . . .

The terms, privileges and immunities, are not new in the Amendment; they were in the Constitution before the Amendment was adopted. They are found in the second section of the fourth article, which declares that "the citizens of each State shall be entitled to all privileges and immunities of citizens in the several States," and they have been the subject of frequent consideration in judicial decisions. . . . The privileges and immunities designated are those which of right belong to the citizens of all free governments. Clearly among these must be placed the right to pursue a lawful employment in a lawful manner, without other restraint than such as equally affects all persons. . . .

This equality of right, with exemption from all disparaging and partial enactments, in the lawful pursuits of life, throughout the whole country, is the distinguishing privilege of citizens of the United States. To them, everywhere, all pursuits, all professions, all avocations are open without other restrictions than such as are imposed equally upon all others of the same age, sex, and condition. The State may prescribe such regulations for every pursuit and calling of life as will promote the public health, secure the good order and advance the general prosperity of society, but when once prescribed, the pursuit or calling must be free to be followed by every citizen who is within the conditions designated, and will conform to the regulations. This is the fundamental idea upon which our institutions rest, and unless adhered to in the legislation of the country our government will be a republic only in name. The Fourteenth Amendment, in my judgment, makes it essential to the validity of the legislation of every State that this equality of right should be respected. How widely this equality has been departed from, how entirely rejected and trampled upon by the act of Louisiana, I have already shown. And it is to me a matter of profound regret that its validity is recognized by a majority of this court, for by it the right of free labor, one of the most sacred and imprescriptible rights of man, is violated. . . .

I am authorized by the *Chief Justice, Mr. Justice Swayne,* and *Mr. Justice Bradley,* to state that they concur with me in this dissenting opinion.

Mr. Justice Bradley, dissenting.

. . . The right of a State to regulate the conduct of its citizens is undoubtedly a very broad and extensive one, and not to be lightly restricted. But there are certain fundamental rights which this right of regulation cannot infringe. It may prescribe the manner of their exercise, but it cannot subvert the rights themselves. . . .

The granting of monopolies, or exclusive privileges to individuals or corporations, is an invasion of the right of another to choose a lawful calling, and an infringement of personal liberty. It was so felt by the English nation as far back as the reigns of Elizabeth and James. A fierce struggle for the suppression of such monopolies, and for abolishing the prerogative of creating them, was made and was successful. . . . And ever since that struggle no English-speaking people have ever endured such an odious badge of tyranny. . . .

Can the Federal courts administer relief to citizens of the United States whose privileges and immunities have been abridged by a State? Of this I entertain no doubt. Prior to the Fourteenth Amendment this could not be done, except in a few instances, for the want of the requisite authority. . . .

Admitting, therefore, that formerly the States were not prohibited from infringing any fundamental privileges and immunities of citizens of the United States, except in a few specified cases, that cannot be said now, since the adoption of the Fourteenth Amendment. In my judgment, it was the intention of the people of this country in adopting that amendment to provide National security against violation by the States of the fundamental rights of the citizen. . . .

In my view, a law which prohibits a large class of citizens from adopting a lawful employment, or from following a lawful employment previously adopted, does deprive them of liberty as well as property, without due process of law. Their right of choice is a portion of their liberty; their occupation is their property. Such a law also deprives those citizens of the equal protection of the laws, contrary to the last clause of the section. . . .

Mr. Justice Swayne, dissenting. . . .

Case

LOCHNER V. NEW YORK

198 U.S. 45; 25 S.Ct. 539; 49 L.Ed. 937 (1905)
Vote: 5–4

Joseph Lochner, a bakery owner in Utica, New York, was fined $50 for violating a state law that limited employment in bakeries to ten hours a day and sixty hours a week. After the state appellate courts upheld his conviction, Lochner obtained review in the U.S. Supreme Court on a writ of error.

Mr. Justice Peckham delivered the opinion of the Court.

The indictment . . . charges that the plaintiff in error violated . . . the labor law of the state of New York, in that he wrongfully and unlawfully required and permitted an employee working for him to work more than sixty hours in one week. . . . The mandate of the statute, that "no employee shall be required or permitted to work," is the substantial equivalent of an enactment that "no employee shall contract or agree to work," more than ten hours per day; and, as there is no provision for special emergencies, the statute is mandatory in all cases. It is not an act merely fixing the number of hours which shall constitute a legal day's work, but an absolute prohibition upon the employer permitting, under any circumstances, more than ten hours work to be done in his establishment. The employee may desire to earn the extra money which would arise from his working more than the prescribed time, but this statute forbids the employer from permitting the employee to earn it.

The statute necessarily interferes with the right of contract between the employer and employees, concerning the number of hours in which the latter may labor in the bakery of the employer. The general right to make a contract in relation to his business is part of the liberty of the individual protected by the 14th Amendment of the Federal Constitution. . . . Under that provision no state can deprive any person of life, liberty, or property without due process of law. The right to purchase or to sell labor is part of the liberty protected by this amendment, unless there are circumstances which exclude the right. There are, however, certain powers, existing in the sovereignty of each state in the Union, somewhat vaguely termed police powers, the exact description and limitation which have not been attempted by the courts. Those powers, broadly stated, and without, at present, any attempt at a more specific limitation, relate to the safety, health, morals, and general welfare of the public. Both property and liberty are held on such reasonable conditions as may be imposed by the governing power of the state in the exercise of those powers, and with such conditions the 14th Amendment was not designed to interfere. . . .

The state, therefore, has power to prevent the individual from making certain kinds of contracts, and in regard to them the Federal Constitution offers no protection. If the contract be one which the state, in the legitimate exercise of its police power, has the right to prohibit, it is not prevented from prohibiting it by the 14th Amendment. Contracts in violation of a statute, for immoral purposes, or to do any other unlawful act, could obtain no protection from the Federal Constitution, as coming under the liberty of person or of free contract. Therefore, when the state, by its legislature, in the assumed exercise of its police powers, has passed an act which seriously limits the right to labor or the right of contract in regard to their means of livelihood between persons who are *sui juris* (both employer and employee), it becomes of great importance to determine which shall prevail—the right of the individual to labor for such time as he may choose, or the right of the state to prevent the individual from laboring, or from entering into any contract to labor, beyond a certain time prescribed by the state.

This court has recognized the existence and upheld the exercise of the police powers of the states in many cases which might fairly be considered as border ones, and it has, in the course of its determination of questions regarding the asserted invalidity of such statutes, on the ground of their violation of the rights secured by the Federal Constitution, been guided by rules of a very liberal nature, the application of which has resulted, in numerous instances, in upholding the validity of state statutes thus assailed. Among the later cases where the state law has been upheld by this court is that of *Holden v. Hardy.* . . . A provision in the act of the legislature of Utah was there under consideration, the act limiting the employment of workmen in all underground mines or workings, to eight hours per day, "except in cases of emergency, where life or property is in imminent danger." It also limited the hours of labor in smelting and other institutions for the reduction or refining of ores or metals to eight hours per day, except in like cases of emergency. The act was held to be a valid exercise of the police powers of the state. . . .

It must, of course, be conceded that there is a limit to the valid exercise of the police power by the state. There is no dispute concerning this general proposition. Otherwise the 14th Amendment would have no efficacy and the legislatures of the states would have unbounded power, and it would be enough to say that any piece of legislation was enacted to conserve the morals, the health, or the safety of the people; such legislation would be valid, no matter

how absolutely without foundation the claim might be. The claim of the police power would be a mere pretext—become another and delusive name for the supreme sovereignty of the state to be exercised free from constitutional restraint. This is not contended for. In every case that comes before this court, therefore, where legislation of this character is concerned, and where the protection of the Federal Constitution is sought, the question necessarily arises. Is this a fair, reasonable, and appropriate exercise of the police power of the state, or is it an unreasonable, unnecessary, and arbitrary interference with the right of the individual to his personal liberty, or to enter into those contracts in relation to labor which may seem to him appropriate or necessary for the support of himself and his family? Of course the liberty of contract relating to labor includes both parties to it. The one has as much right to purchase as the other to sell labor.

This is not a question of substituting the judgment of the court for that of the legislature. If the act be within the power of the state it is valid, although the judgment of the court might be totally opposed to the enactment of such a law. But the question would still remain: Is it within the police power of the state? And that question must be answered by the court.

The question whether this act is valid as a labor law, pure and simple, may be dismissed in a few words. There is no reasonable ground for interfering with the liberty of person or the right of free contract, by determining the hours of labor, in the occupation of a baker. There is no contention that bakers as a class are not equal in intelligence and capacity to men in other trades or manual occupations, or that they are not able to assert their rights and care for themselves without the protecting arm of the state, interfering with their independence of judgment and of action. They are in no sense wards of the state. Viewed in the light of a purely labor law, with no reference whatever to the question of health, we think that a law like the one before us involves neither the safety, the morals, nor the welfare, of the public, and that interest of the public is not in the slightest degree affected by such an act. The law must be upheld, if at all, as a law pertaining to the health of the individual engaged in the occupation of a baker. It does not affect any other portion of the public than those who are engaged in that occupation. Clean and wholesome bread does not depend upon whether the baker works but ten hours per day or only sixty hours a week. The limitation of the hours of labor does not come within the police power on that ground.

It is a question of which of two powers or rights shall prevail—the power of the state to legislate or the right of the individual to liberty of person and freedom of contract. The mere assertion that the subject relates, though but in a remote degree, to the public health, does not necessarily render the enactment valid. The act must have a more direct relation, as a means to an end, and the end itself must be appropriate and legitimate, before an act can end, and the end itself must be appropriate and legitimate, before an act can be held to be valid which interferes with the general right of an individual to be free in his person and in his power to contract in relation to his own labor. . . .

We think the limit of the police power has been reached and passed in this case. There is, in our judgment, no reasonable foundation for holding this to be necessary or appropriate as a health law to safeguard the public health, or the health of the individuals who are following the trade of a baker. If this statute be valid, and if, therefore, a proper case is made out in which to deny the right of an individual, *sui juris,* as employer or employee, to make contracts for the labor of the latter under the protection of the provisions of the Federal Constitution, there would seem to be no length to which legislation of this nature might not go. . . .

We think that there can be no fair doubt that the trade of a baker, in and of itself, is not an unhealthy one to that degree which would authorize the legislature to interfere with the right to labor, and with the right of free contract on the part of the individual, either as employer or employee. In looking through statistics regarding all trades and occupations, it may be true that the trade of a baker does not appear to be as healthy as some other trades, and is also vastly more healthy than still others. To the common understanding the trade of a baker has never been regarded as an unhealthy one. Very likely physicians would not recommend the exercise of that or of any other trade as a remedy for ill health. Some occupations are more healthy than others, but we think there are none which might not come under the power of the legislature to supervise and control the hours of working therein, if the mere fact that the occupation is not absolutely and perfectly healthy is to confer that right upon the legislative department of the government. . . .

. . . Statutes of the nature of that under review, limiting the hours in which grown and intelligent men may labor to earn their living, are mere meddlesome interferences with the rights of the individual, and they are not saved from condemnation by the claim that they are passed in the exercise of the police power and upon the subject of the health of the individual whose rights are interfered with, unless there be some fair ground, reasonable in and of itself, to say that there is material danger to the public health or to the health of the employees if the hours of labor are not curtailed. If this be not clearly the case, the individuals whose rights are thus made the subject of legislative interference are under the protection of the Federal Constitution regarding their liberty of contract as well as of person, and the legislature of the State has no power to limit their right as proposed in this statute. All that it could properly do has been done by it with regard to the conduct of bakeries, as provided for in the other sections of the act above set forth. These several sections provide for the inspection of the premises where the bakery is carried on, with regard to furnishing proper wash-rooms and water-closets, apart from the bake-room, also with regard to providing proper drainage, plumbing and painting; the sections, in addition, provide for the height of the ceiling, the cementing or tiling of floors, where necessary in the opinion of the factory inspector, and for other things of that nature; alterations are also provided for and are to be made where necessary in the opinion of the inspector, in order to comply with the provisions of the statute. These various sections may be wise and valid regulations, and they certainly go to the full extent of providing for the cleanliness and the healthiness, so far as possible, of the quarters in which bakeries are to be conducted. Adding to all these requirements a prohibition to enter into any contract of labor in a bakery for more than a certain number of hours a week is, in our judgment, so wholly beside the matter of a proper, reasonable and fair provision as to run counter to that liberty of person and of free contract provided for in the Federal Constitution.

It is impossible for us to shut our eyes to the fact that many of the laws of this character, while passed under what is claimed to be the police power for the purpose of protecting the public health or welfare, are, in reality, passed from other motives. We are justified in saying so when, from the character of the law and the subject upon which it legislates, it is apparent that the public health or welfare bears but the most remote relation to the law. The purpose of a statute must be determined from the natural and legal effect of the language employed; and whether it is or is not repugnant to the Constitution of the United States must be determined from the natural effect of such statutes when put into operation, and not from their proclaimed purpose. . . .

It is manifest to us that the limitation of the hours of labor as provided for in this section of the statute under which the indictment was found, and the plaintiff in error convicted, has no such direct relation to, and no such substantial effect upon, the health of the employee, as to justify us in regarding the section as really a health law. It seems to us that the real object and purpose were simply to regulate the hours of labor between the master and his employees . . . in a private business, not dangerous in any degree to morals, or in any real and substantial degree to the health of the employees. Under such circumstances the freedom of master and employee to contract with each other in relation to their employment, and in defining the same, cannot be prohibited or interfered with, without violating the Federal Constitution.

The judgment of the Court of Appeals of New York, as well as that of the Supreme Court and of the County Court of Oneida County, must be reversed and the case remanded to County Court for further proceedings not inconsistent with this opinion.

Reversed.

Mr. Justice Harlan [with whom *Mr. Justice White* and *Mr. Justice Day* concurred], dissenting:

. . . It is plain that this statute was enacted in order to protect the physical well-being of those who work in bakery and confectionery establishments. It may be that the statute had its origin, in part, in the belief that employers and employees in such establishments were not upon an equal footing, and that the necessities of the latter often compelled them to submit to such exactions as unduly taxed their strength. Be this as it may, the statute must be taken as expressing the belief of the people of New York that, as a general rule, and in the case of the average man, labor in excess of sixty hours during a week in such establishments may endanger the health of those who thus labor. Whether or not this be wise legislation it is not the province of the court to inquire. Under our system of government the courts are not concerned with the wisdom or policy of legislation. So that, in determining the question of power to interfere with liberty of contract, the court may inquire whether the means devised by the state are germane to an end which may be lawfully accomplished and have a real or substantial relation to the protection of health, as involved in the daily work of the persons, male and female, engaged in bakery and confectionery establishments. But when this inquiry is entered upon I find it impossible, in view of common experience, to say that there is here no real or substantial relation between the means employed by the state and the end sought to be accomplished by its legislation. Nor can I say that the statute has no appropriated or direct connection with that protection to health which each state owes to her citizens; or that it is not promotive of the health of the employees in question; or that the regulation prescribed by the state is utterly unreasonable and extravagant or wholly arbitrary. Still less can I say that the statute is, beyond question, a plain, palpable invasion of rights secured by the fundamental law. Therefore I submit that this court will transcend its functions if it assumes to annul the statute of New York. It must be remembered that this statute does not apply to all kinds of business. It applies only to work in bakery and confectionery establishments, in which, as all know, the air constantly breathed by workmen is not as

pure and healthful as that to be found in some other establishments or out of doors. . . .

. . . [T]he state is not amenable to the judiciary, in respect of its legislative enactments, unless such enactments are plainly, palpably, beyond all question, inconsistent with the Constitution of the United States. We are not to presume that the state of New York has acted in bad faith. Nor can we assume that its legislature acted without due deliberation, or that it did not determine this question upon the fullest attainable information and for the common good. We cannot say that the state has acted without reason, nor ought we to proceed upon the theory that its action is a mere sham. Our duty, I submit, is to sustain the statute as not being in conflict with the Federal Constitution, for the reason—and such is an all-sufficient reason—it is not shown to be plainly and palpably inconsistent with that instrument. Let the state alone in the management of its purely domestic affairs, so long as it does not appear beyond all question that it has violated the Federal Constitution. This view necessarily results from the principle that the health and safety of the people of a state are primarily for the state to guard and protect.

I take leave to say that the New York statute, in the particulars here involved, cannot be held to be in conflict with the 14th Amendment, without enlarging the scope of the amendment far beyond its original purpose, and without bringing under the supervision of this court matters which have been supposed to belong exclusively to the legislative departments of the several states . . . to guard the health and safety of their citizens. . . .

Mr. Justice Holmes, dissenting:

. . . This case is decided upon an economic theory which a large part of the country does not entertain. If it were a question whether I agreed with that theory, I should desire to study it further and long before making up my mind. But I do not conceive that to be my duty, because I strongly believe that my agreement or disagreement has nothing to do with the right of a majority to embody their opinions in law. It is settled by various decisions of this court that . . . state laws may regulate life in many ways which are as legislators might think as injudicious, or if you like as tyrannical, as this, and which, equally with this, interfere with the liberty to contract. Sunday laws and usury laws are ancient examples. A more modern one is the prohibition of lotteries. The liberty of the citizen to do as he likes so long as he does not interfere with the liberty of others to do the same, which has been a shibboleth for some well-known writers, is interfered with by school laws, by the post office, by every state or municipal institution which takes his money for purposes thought desirable, whether he likes it or not. The

14th Amendment does not enact Mr. Herbert Spencer's *Social Statics*. . . . But a Constitution is not intended to embody a particular economic theory, whether of paternalism and the organic relation of the citizen to the state or of laissez faire. It is made for people of fundamentally differing views, and the accident of finding certain opinions natural and familiar, or novel, and even shocking, ought not to conclude our judgment upon the question whether statutes embodying them conflict with the Constitution of the United States.

General propositions do not decide concrete cases. The decision will depend on a judgment or intuition more subtle than any articulate major premise. But I think that the proposition just stated, if it is accepted, will carry us far toward the end. Every opinion tends to become a law. I think that the word "liberty," in the 14th Amendment, is perverted when it is held to prevent the natural outcome of a dominant opinion, unless it can be said that a rational and fair man necessarily would admit that the statute proposed would infringe fundamental principles as they have been understood by the traditions of our people and our law. It does not end research to show that no such sweeping condemnation can be passed upon the statute before us. A reasonable man might think it a proper measure on the score of health. Men whom I certainly could not pronounce unreasonable would uphold it as a first installment of a general regulation of the hours of work. Whether in the latter aspect it would be open to the charge of inequality I think it unnecessary to discuss.

Case

ADKINS V. CHILDREN'S HOSPITAL

261 U.S. 525; 43 S.Ct. 394; 67 L.Ed. 785 (1923)
Vote: 5–3

In 1918, Congress created a board and empowered it to set minimum wages for women and children working in the District of Columbia. Children's Hospital obtained an injunction to prevent Adkins and other board members from enforcing the minimum wage. Adkins et al. appealed to the Supreme Court.

Mr. Justice Sutherland delivered the opinion of the Court.

. . . The judicial duty of passing upon the constitutionality of an act of Congress is one of great gravity and delicacy. The statute here in question has successfully borne the scrutiny of the legislative branch of the government, which, by enacting it, has affirmed its validity; and that determination must be given great weight. This Court, by an unbroken line of decisions from Chief Justice Marshall to the present day, has steadily adhered to the rule that every possible presumption is in favor of the validity of an act of Congress until overcome beyond rational doubt. But if, by clear and indubitable demonstration, a statute be opposed to the Constitution, we have no choice but to say so. The Constitution, by its own terms, is the supreme law of the land, emanating from the people, the repository of ultimate sovereignty under our form of government. A congressional statute, on the other hand, is the act of an agency of this sovereign authority, and, if it conflict with the Constitution, must fall; for that which is not supreme must yield to that which is. . . .

The statute now under consideration is attacked upon the ground that it authorizes an unconstitutional interference with the freedom of contract included within the guarantees of the due process clause of the Fifth Amendment. That the right to contract about one's affairs is a part of the liberty of the individual protected by this clause is settled by the decisions of this Court, and is no longer open to question. . . . Within this liberty are contracts of employment of labor. In making such contracts, generally speaking, the parties have an equal right to obtain from each other the best terms they can as the result of private bargaining. . . .

There is, of course, no such thing as absolute freedom of contract. It is subject to a great variety of restraints. But freedom of contract is, nevertheless, the general rule and restraint the exception; and the exercise of legislative authority to abridge it can be justified only by the existence of exceptional circumstances. Whether these circumstances exist in the present case constitutes the question to be answered. . . .

In the *Muller* Case the validity of an Oregon statute, forbidding the employment of any female in certain industries more than ten hours during any one day, was upheld. The decision proceeded upon the theory that the difference between the sexes may justify a different rule respecting hours of labor in the case of women than in the case of men. It is pointed out that these consist in differences of physical structure, especially in respect of the maternal functions, and also in the fact that historically woman has always been dependent upon man, who has established his control by superior physical strength. . . . But the ancient inequality of the sexes, otherwise than physical as suggested in the *Muller* Case has continued "with diminishing intensity." In view of the great—not to say revolutionary—changes which have taken place since that utterance, in the contractual, political, and civil status of women, culminating in the Nineteenth Amendment, it is not unreasonable to say that these differences have now come almost, if not quite, to the vanishing point. In this aspect of the matter, while the physical differences must be recognized in appropriate cases, and legislation fixing hours or conditions of work may properly taken them into account, we cannot accept the doctrine that women of mature age, *sui juris,* require or may be subjected to restrictions upon their liberty of contract which could not lawfully be imposed in the case of men under similar circumstances. To do so would be to ignore all the implications to be drawn from the present-day trend of legislation, as well as that of common thought and usage, by which woman is accorded emancipation from the old doctrine that she must be given special protection or be subjected to special restraint in her contractual and civil relationships. In passing, it may be noted that the instant statute applies in the case of a woman employer contracting with a woman employee as it does when the former is a man.

The essential characteristics of the statute now under consideration, which differentiate it from the laws fixing hours of labor, will be made to appear as we proceed. It is sufficient now to point out that the latter . . . deal with incidents of the employment having no necessary effect upon the heart of the contract; that is, the amount of wages to be paid and received. A law forbidding work to continue beyond a given number of hours leaves the parties free to contract about wages and thereby equalize whatever additional burdens may be imposed upon the employer as a result of the restrictions as to hours, by an adjustment in respect of the amount of wages. Enough has been said to show that the authority to fix hours of labor cannot be exercised except in respect of those occupations where work of long-continued duration is detrimental to health. This Court has been careful in every case where the question has been raised, to place its decision upon this limited authority of the legislature to regulate hours of labor, and to disclaim any purpose to uphold the legislation as fixing wages, thus recognizing an essential difference between the two. It seems plain that these decisions afford no real support for any form of law establishing minimum wages.

If now, in the light furnished by the foregoing exceptions to the general rule forbidding legislative interference with freedom of contract, we examine and analyze the statute in question, we shall see that it differs from them in every material respect. . . . It is simply and exclusively a price-fixing law, confined to adult women (for we are not now considering the provisions relating to minors), who are legally as capable of contracting for themselves as men. It forbids two parties having lawful capacity under penalties as to the employer to freely contract with one another in respect of the price for which one shall render service to the other in a purely private employment where both are willing, perhaps anxious, to agree, even though the consequences may be to oblige one to surrender a desirable engagement, and the other to dispense with the services of a desirable employee. . . .

The standard furnished by the statute for the guidance of the board is so vague as to be impossible of practical application with any reasonable degree of accuracy. What is sufficient to supply the necessary cost of living for a woman worker and maintain her in good health and protect her morals is obviously not a precise or unvarying sum—not even approximately so. The amount will depend upon a variety of circumstances: The individual temperament, habits of thrift, care, ability to buy necessaries intelligently, and whether the woman lives alone or with her family. To those who practice economy, a given sum will afford comfort, while to those of contrary habit the same sum will be wholly inadequate. The cooperative economies of the family group are not taken into account, though they constitute an important consideration in estimating the cost of living, for it is obvious that the individual expense will be less in the case of a member of a family than in the case of one living alone. The relation between earnings and morals is not capable of standardization. It cannot be shown that well-paid women safeguard their morals more carefully than those who are poorly paid. Morality rests upon other considerations than wages; and there is, certainly, no such prevalent connection between the two as to justify a broad attempt to adjust the latter with reference to the former. . . .

The law takes account of the necessities of only one party to the contract. It ignores the necessities of the employer by compelling him to pay not less than a certain sum, not only whether the employee is capable of earning it, but irrespective of the ability of his business to sustain the burden, generously leaving him, of course, the privilege of abandoning his business as an alternative for going on at a loss. Within the limits of the minimum sum, he is precluded, under penalty of fine and imprisonment, from adjusting compensation to the differing merits of his employees. It compels him to pay at least the sum fixed in any event, because the employee needs it, but requires no service of equivalent value from the employee. . . . To the extent that the sum fixed exceeds the fair value of the services rendered, it amounts to a compulsory exaction from the employer for the support of a partially indigent person, for whose condition there rests upon him no peculiar responsibility, and therefore, in effect, arbitrarily shifts to his shoulders a burden which, if it belongs to anybody, belongs to society as a whole.

The feature of this statute which, perhaps more than any other, puts upon it the stamp of invalidity is that it exacts from the employer an arbitrary payment for a purpose and upon a basis having no causal connection with his business, or the contract, or the work the employee engages to do. . . . The ethical right of every worker, man or woman, to a living wage, may be conceded. One of the declared and important purposes of trade organizations is to secure it. And with that principle and with every legitimate effort to realize it in fact, no one can quarrel; but the fallacy of the proposed method of attaining it is that it assumes that every employer is bound, at all events to furnish it. The moral requirement, implicit in every contract of employment, *viz.,* that the amount to be paid and the service to be rendered shall bear to each other some relation of just equivalence, is completely ignored. . . . Certainly the employer, by paying a fair equivalent for the service rendered, though not sufficient to support the employee, has neither caused nor contributed to her poverty. On the contrary, to the extent of what he pays, he has relieved it. In principle, there can be no difference between the case of selling labor and the case of selling goods. If one goes to the butcher, the baker, or grocer to buy food, he is morally entitled to obtain the worth of his money, but he is not entitled to more. If what he gets is worth what he pays, he is not justified in demanding more simply because he needs more; and the shopkeeper, having dealt fairly and honestly in that transaction, is not concerned in any peculiar sense with the question of his customer's necessities. . . . But a statute which prescribes payment without regard to any of these things, and solely with relation to circumstances apart from the contract of employment, the business affected by it, and the work done under it, is so clearly the product of a naked, arbitrary exercise of power, that it cannot be allowed to stand under the Constitution of the United States.

We are asked, upon the one hand, to consider the fact that several states have adopted similar statutes, and we are invited, upon the other hand, to give weight to the fact that three times as many states, presumably as well informed and as anxious to promote the health and morals of their people, have refrained from enacting such legislation. We have also been furnished with a large number of printed opinions approving the policy of the minimum wage, and our own reading has disclosed a large number to the contrary. These are all proper enough for the consideration of the lawmaking bodies, since their tendency is to establish the desirability or undesirability of the legislation; but they reflect no legitimate light upon the question of its validity, and that is what we are called upon to decide. The elucidation of that question cannot be aided by counting heads.

It is said that great benefits have resulted from the operation of such statutes, not alone in the District of Columbia, but in the several states where they have been in force. A mass of reports, opinions of special observers and students of the subject, and the like, has been brought before us in support of this statement, all of which we have found interesting but only mildly persuasive. That the earnings of women now are greater than they were formerly, and that conditions affecting women have become better in other respects, may be conceded; but convincing indications of the logical relation of these desirable changes to the law in question are significantly lacking. They may be, and quite probably are, due to other causes. . . .

Finally, it may be said that if, in the interest of the public welfare, the police power may be invoked to justify the fixing of a minimum wage, it may, when the public welfare is thought to require it, be invoked to justify a maximum wage. The power to fix high wages connotes, by like course of reasoning, the power to fix low wages. If, in the face of the guarantees of the Fifth Amendment, this form of legislation shall be legally justified, the field for the operation of the police power will have been widened to a great and dangerous degree. If, for example, in the opinion of future lawmakers, wages in the building trades shall become so high as to preclude people of ordinary means from building and owning homes, an authority which sustains the minimum wage will be invoked to support a maximum wage for building laborers and artisans, and the same argument which has been here urged to strip the employer of his constitutional liberty of contract in one direction will be utilized to strip the employee of his constitutional liberty of contract in the opposite direction. A wrong decision does not end with itself: it is a precedent, and, with the swing of sentiment, its bad influence may run from one extremity of the arc to the other.

It has been said that legislation of the kind now under review is required in the interest of social justice, for whose ends freedom of contract may lawfully be subjected to restraint. The liberty of the individual to do as he pleases, even in innocent matters, is not absolute. It must frequently yield to the common good, and the line beyond which the power of interference may not be pressed is neither definite nor unalterable, but may be made to move, within limits not well defined, with changing need and circumstance. Any attempt to fix a rigid boundary would be unwise as well as futile. But, nevertheless, there are limits to the power, and when these have been passed, it becomes the plain duty of the courts, in the proper exercise of their authority, to so declare. To sustain the individual freedom of action contemplated by the Constitution is not to strike down the common good, but to exalt it; for surely the good of society as a whole cannot be better served than by the preservation against arbitrary restraint of the liberties of its constituent members.

It follows from what has been said that the act in question passes the limit prescribed by the Constitution, and, accordingly, the decrees of the court below are affirmed.

Mr. Justice Brandeis took no part in the consideration or decision of these cases.

Mr. Chief Justice Taft, dissenting.

. . . The boundary of the police power, beyond which its exercise becomes an invasion of the guaranty of liberty under the Fifth and Fourteenth Amendments to the Constitution, is not easy to mark. Our Court has been laboriously engaged in pricking out a line in successive cases. We must be careful, it seems to me, to follow that line as well as we can, and not to depart from it by suggesting a distinction that is formal rather than real.

Legislatures, in limiting freedom of contract between employee and employer by a minimum wage, proceed on the assumption that employees in the class receiving least pay are not upon a full level of equality of choice with their employer, and in their necessitous circumstances are prone to accept pretty much anything that is offered. They are peculiarly subject to the overreaching of the harsh and greedy employer. The evils of the sweating system and of the long hours and low wages which are characteristic of it are well known. Now, I agree that it is a disputable question in the field of political economy how far a statutory requirement of maximum hours or minimum wages may be a useful remedy for these evils, and whether it may not make the case of the oppressed employee worse than it was before. But it is not the function of this Court to hold congressional acts invalid simply because they are passed to carry out economic views which the Court believes to be unwise or unsound. . . .

The right of the legislature under the Fifth and Fourteenth Amendments to limit the hours of employment on the score of the health of the employee, it seems to me, has been firmly established. As to that, one would think, the line had been pricked out so that it has become a well-formulated rule. . . . In [*Bunting v. Oregon*] . . . this Court sustained a law limiting the hours of labor of any person, whether man or woman, working in any mill, factory, or manufacturing establishment, to ten hours a day, with a proviso as to further hours [allowing limited overtime at one and one-half times the regular wage]. . . . The law covered the whole field of industrial employment, and certainly covered the case of persons employed in bakeries. Yet the opinion in the *Bunting* Case does not mention the *Lochner* Case. No one can suggest any constitutional distinction between employment in a bakery and one in any other kind of a manufacturing establishment which should make a limit of hours in the one invalid, and the same limit in the other permissible. It is impossible for me to reconcile the *Bunting* Case and the *Lochner* Case, and I have always supposed that the *Lochner* Case was thus overruled *sub silentio*. Yet the opinion of the Court herein in support of its conclusion quotes from the opinion in the *Lochner* Case as one which has been sometimes distinguished, but never overruled. Certainly there was no attempt to distinguish it in the *Bunting* Case.

However, the opinion herein does not overrule the *Bunting* Case in express terms, and therefore I assume that the conclusion in this case rests on the distinction between a minimum of wages and a maximum of hours in the limiting of liberty to contract. I regret to be at variance with the court as to the substance of this distinction. In absolute freedom of contract the one term is as important as the other, for both enter equally into the consideration given and received; a restriction as to one is not any greater in essence than the other, and is of the same kind. One is the multiplier and the other the multiplicand.

If it be said that long hours of labor have a more direct effect upon the health of the employee than the low wage, there is very respectable authority from those observers, disclosed in the record and in the literature on the subject, quoted at length in the briefs, that they are equally harmful in this regard. Congress took this view, and we cannot say it was not warranted in so doing. . . .

I am authorized to say that *Mr. Justice Sanford* concurs in this opinion.

Mr. Justice Holmes, dissenting.

The question in this case is the broad one, whether Congress can establish minimum rates of wages for women in the District of Columbia, with due provision for special circumstances, or whether we must say that Congress has no power to meddle with the matter at all. To me, notwithstanding the deference due to the prevailing judgment of the Court, the power of Congress seems absolutely free from doubt. The end—to remove conditions leading to ill health, immorality, and the deterioration of the race—no one would deny to be within the scope of constitutional legislation. The means are means that have the approval of Congress, of many states, and of those governments from which we have learned our greatest lessons. When so many intelligent persons, who have studied the matter more than any of us can, have thought that the means are effective and are worth the price, it seems to me impossible to deny that the belief reasonably may be held by reasonable men. If the law encountered no other objection than that the means bore no relation to the end, or that they cost too much, I do not suppose that anyone would venture to say that it was bad. I agree, of course, that a law answering the foregoing requirements might be invalidated by specific provisions of the Constitution. For instance, it might take private property without just compensation. But, in the present instance, the only objection that can be urged is found within the vague contours of the Fifth Amendment, prohibiting the depriving any person of liberty or property without due process of law. To that I turn.

The earlier decisions upon the same words in the Fourteenth Amendment began within our memory, and went no farther than an unpretentious assertion of the liberty to follow the ordinary callings. Later that innocuous generality was expanded into the dogma, Liberty of Contract. Contract is not specifically mentioned in the text that we have to construe. It is merely an example of doing what you want to do, embodied in the word "liberty." But pretty much all law consists in forbidding men to do some things that they want to do, and contract is no more exempt from law than other acts. Without enumerating all the restrictive laws that have been upheld, I will mention a few that seem to me to have interfered with liberty of contract quite as seriously and directly as the one before us. Usury laws

prohibit contracts by which a man receives more than so much interest for the money that he lends. Statutes of frauds restrict many contracts to certain forms. Some Sunday laws prohibit practically all contracts during one-seventh of our whole life. Insurance rates may be regulated. Finally, women's hours of labor may be fixed. . . . And the principle was extended to men, with the allowance of a limited overtime, to be paid for "at the rate of time and one half of the regular wage," in *Bunting v. Oregon*. . . .

I confess that I do not understand the principle on which the power to fix a minimum for the wages of women can be denied by those who admit the power to fix a maximum for their hours of work. I fully assent to the proposition that here, as elsewhere, the distinctions of the law are distinctions of degree; but I perceive no difference in the kind or degree of interference with liberty, the only matter with which we have any concern, between the one case and the other. The bargain is equally affected whichever half you regulate. *Muller v. Oregon* [1908], I take it, is as good law today as it was in 1908. It will need more than the Nineteenth Amendment to convince me that there are no differences between men and women, or that legislation cannot take those differences into account. I should not hesitate to take them into account if I thought it necessary to sustain this act. . . . But after *Bunting v. Oregon* . . . I had supposed that it was not necessary, and that *Lochner v. New York* . . . would be allowed a deserved repose. . . .

Case

WEST COAST HOTEL COMPANY V. PARRISH

300 U.S. 379; 57 S.Ct. 578; 81 L.Ed. 703 (1937)
Vote: 5–4

In May 1935, Elsie Parrish was discharged from her job as a chambermaid at the Cascadian Hotel (owned by the West Coast Hotel Company) in Wenatchee, Washington. She had originally been employed in the late summer of 1933 at a wage rate of 22 cents per hour. At the time of her dismissal, Parrish was being paid 25 cents an hour, still well below the $14.50 weekly minimum set by the Industrial Welfare Committee pursuant to a state minimum wage law passed in 1913. Elsie Parrish and her husband, Ernest, promptly sued the West Coast Hotel Company for $216.19, the amount by which the minimum wage exceeded her actual earnings during the period of her employment. Although the Parrishes lost at the trial level (the judge held that the case was controlled by Adkins v. Children's Hospital), they appealed to the state supreme court

which, in spite of Adkins, sustained the Washington minimum wage statute. The U.S. Supreme Court agreed to review their case in the late fall of 1936.

Mr. Chief Justice Hughes delivered the opinion of the Court.

This case presents the question of the constitutional validity of the minimum wage law of the state of Washington. . . . It provides:

Sec. 1. The welfare of the State of Washington demands that women and minors be protected from conditions of labor which have a pernicious effect on their health and morals. The State of Washington, therefore, exercising herein its police and sovereign power declares that inadequate wages and unsanitary conditions of labor exert such pernicious effect.

Sec. 2. It shall be unlawful to employ women or minors in any industry or occupation within the State of Washington under conditions of labor detrimental to their health or morals; and it shall be unlawful to employ women workers in any industry within the State of Washington at wages which are not adequate for their maintenance.

Sec. 3. There is hereby created a commission to be known as the "Industrial Welfare Commission" for the State of Washington, to establish such standards of wages and conditions of labor for women and minors employed within the State of Washington, as shall be held hereunder to be reasonable and not detrimental to health and morals, and which shall be sufficient for the decent maintenance of women. . . .

The appellant conducts a hotel. The appellee Elsie Parrish was employed as a chambermaid and (with her husband) brought this suit to recover the difference between the wages paid her and the minimum wage fixed pursuant to the state law. The minimum wage was $14.50 per week of 48 hours. The appellant challenged the act as repugnant to the due process clause of the Fourteenth Amendment of the Constitution of the United States. The Supreme Court of the State, reversing the trial court, sustained the statute and directed judgment for the plaintiffs. . . .

The appellant relies upon the decision of the Court in *Adkins v. Children's Hospital* . . . which held invalid the District of Columbia Minimum Wage Act, which was attacked under the Due Process Clause of the Fifth Amendment. On the argument at bar, counsel for the appellees attempted to distinguish the *Adkins* case upon the ground that the appellee was employed in a hotel and that the business of an innkeeper was affected with a public interest. That effort at distinction is obviously futile, as it appears that in one of the cases ruled by the *Adkins* opinion the employee was a woman employed as an elevator operator in a hotel. . . .

The recent case of *Morehead v. New York ex rel. Tipaldo* . . . came here on certiorari to the New York court, which had held the New York minimum wage act for women to be invalid. A minority of this Court thought that the New York statute was distinguishable in a material feature from that involved in the *Adkins* case, and that for that and other reasons the New York statute should be sustained. But the Court of Appeals of New York had said that it found no material difference between the two statutes, and this Court held that the "meaning of the statute" as fixed by the decision of the state court "must be accepted here as if the meaning had been specifically expressed in the enactment." . . . That view led to the affirmance by this Court of the judgment in the *Morehead* case, as the Court considered that the only question before it was whether the *Adkins* case was distinguishable and that reconsideration of that decision had not been sought. . . .

We think that the question which was not deemed to be open in the *Morehead* case is open and is necessarily pre-

sented here. The Supreme Court of Washington has upheld the minimum wage statute of that State. It has decided that the statute is a reasonable exercise of the police power of the State. In reaching that conclusion the state court has invoked principles long established by this Court in the application of the Fourteenth Amendment. The state court has refused to regard the decision in the *Adkins* case as determinative and has pointed to our decisions both before and since that case as justifying its position. We are of the opinion that this ruling of the state court demands on our part a reexamination of the *Adkins* case. The importance of the question, in which many States having similar laws are concerned, the close division by which the decision in the *Adkins* case was reached, and the economic conditions which have supervened, and in the light of which the reasonableness of the exercise of the protective power of the State must be considered, make it not only appropriate, but we think imperative, that in deciding the present case the subject should receive fresh consideration. . . .

The principle which must control our decision is not in doubt. The constitutional provision invoked is the due process clause of the Fourteenth Amendment governing the States, as the due process clause invoked in the *Adkins* case governed Congress. In each case the violation alleged by those attacking minimum wage regulation for women is deprivation of freedom of contract. What is this freedom? The Constitution does not speak of freedom of contract. It speaks of liberty and prohibits the deprivation of liberty without due process of law. In prohibiting that deprivation the Constitution does not recognize an absolute and uncontrollable liberty. Liberty in each of its phases has its history and connotation. But the liberty safeguarded is liberty in a social organization which requires the protection of law against the evils which menace the health, safety, morals and welfare of the people. Liberty under the Constitution is thus necessarily subject to the restraints of due process, and regulation which is reasonable in relation to its subject and is adopted in the interests of the community is due process.

This essential limitation of liberty in general governs freedom of contract in particular. More than twenty-five years ago we set forth the applicable principle in these words, after referring to the cases where the liberty guaranteed by the Fourteenth Amendment had been broadly described:

> But it was recognized in the cases cited, as in many others, that freedom of contract is a qualified and not an absolute right. There is no absolute freedom to do as one wills or to contract as one chooses. The guaranty of liberty does not withdraw from legislative supervision that wide department of activity which consists of the making of contracts, or

deny to government the power to provide restrictive safeguards. Liberty implies the absence of arbitrary restraint, not immunity from reasonable regulations and prohibitions imposed in the interests of the community. . . .

This power under the Constitution to restrict freedom of contract has had many illustrations. That it may be exercised in the public interest with respect to contracts between employer and employee is undeniable. . . .

The point that has been strongly stressed that adult employees should be deemed competent to make their own contracts was decisively met nearly forty years ago in *Holden v. Hardy* . . . where we pointed out the inequality in the footing of the parties. . . . "In other words, the proprietors lay down the rules and the laborers are practically constrained to obey them." . . .

And we added that the fact "that both parties are of full age and competent to contract does not necessarily deprive the state of the power to interfere where the parties do not stand upon an equality, or where the public health demands that one party to the contract shall be protected against himself." . . .

It is manifest that this established principle is peculiarly applicable in relation to the employment of women in whose protection the State has a special interest. That phase of the subject received elaborate consideration in *Muller v. Oregon* . . . where the constitutional authority of the State to limit the working hours of women was sustained. We emphasized the consideration that "woman's physical structure and the performance of maternal functions place her at a disadvantage in the struggle for subsistence" and that her physical well-being "becomes an object of public interest and care in order to preserve the strength and vigor of the race." We emphasized the need of protecting women against oppression despite her possession of contractual rights. We said that "though limitations upon personal and contractual rights may be removed by legislation, there is that in her disposition and habits of life which will operate against a full assertion of those rights. She will still be where some legislation to protect her seems necessary to secure a real equality of right." Hence she was "properly placed in a class by herself, and legislation designed for her protection may be sustained even when like legislation is not necessary for men and could not be sustained." We concluded that the limitations which the statute there in question "placed upon her contractual powers, upon her right to agree with her employer as to the time she shall labor" were "not imposed solely for her benefit, but also largely for the benefit of all." . . .

. . . [T]he dissenting Justices in the *Adkins* case [argued] that the minimum wage statute [should] be sustained. The validity of the distinction made by the Court between a minimum wage and a maximum of hours in limiting liberty of contract was especially challenged. . . . That challenge persists and is without any satisfactory answer. As Chief Justice Taft observed: "In absolute freedom of contract the one term is as important as the other, for both enter equally into the consideration given and received, a restriction as to the one is not greater in essence than the other and is of the same kind. One is the multiplier and the other the multiplicand." And Mr. Justice Holmes, while recognizing that "the distinctions of the law are distinctions of degree," could "perceive no difference in the kind or degree of interference with liberty, the only matter with which we have any concern, between the one case and the other. The bargain is equally affected whichever half you regulate." . . .

The minimum wage to be paid under the Washington statute is fixed after full consideration by representatives of employers, employees and the public. It may be assumed that the minimum wage is fixed in consideration of the services that are performed in the particular occupations under normal conditions. Provision is made for special licenses at less wages in the case of women who are incapable of full service. . . .

The statement of Mr. Justice Holmes in the *Adkins* case is pertinent:

> This statute does not compel anybody to pay anything. It simply forbids employment at rates below those fixed as the minimum requirement of health and right living. It is safe to assume that women will not be employed at even the lowest wages allowed unless they earn them, or unless the employer's business can sustain the burden. In short the law in its character and operation is like hundreds of so-called police laws that have been upheld. . . .

We think that the views thus expressed are sound and that the decision in the *Adkins* case was a departure from the true application of the principles governing the regulation by the State of the relation of employer and employed. . . .

With full recognition of the earnestness and vigor which characterize the prevailing opinion in the *Adkins* case, we find it impossible to reconcile that ruling with these well-considered declarations. What can be closer to the public interest than the health of women and their protection from unscrupulous and overreaching employers? And if the protection of women is a legitimate end of the exercise of state power, how can it be said that the requirement of the payment of a minimum wage fairly fixed in order to meet the very necessities of existence is not an admissible means to that end? The legislature of the State was clearly entitled to consider the situation of women in employment, the fact that they are in the class receiving the least pay, that their bargaining power is relatively weak, and that they are the ready victims of those who would take advantage of their necessitous circumstances. The legislature was entitled to adopt measures to reduce the evils of the "sweating system," the exploiting of workers at wages so low as to be insufficient to meet the bare cost of living, thus making their very helplessness the occasion of a most injurious competition. The legislature had the right to consider that its minimum wage requirements would be an important aid in carrying out its policy of protection. The adoption of similar requirements by many States evidences a deep-seated conviction both as to the presence of the evil and as to the means adapted to check it. Legislative response to that conviction cannot be regarded as arbitrary or capricious, and that is all we have to decide. Even if the wisdom of the policy be regarded as debatable and its effects uncertain, still the legislature is entitled to its judgment. . . .

Affirmed.

Mr. Justice Sutherland [joined by Justices *Van Devanter, McReynolds* and *Butler*], dissenting.

The principles and authorities relied upon to sustain the judgment, were considered in *Adkins v. Children's Hospital* and *Morehead v. New York ex rel. Tipaldo;* and their lack of application to cases like the one in hand was pointed out. A sufficient answer to all that is now said will be found in the opinions of the Court in those cases. Nevertheless, in the circumstances, it seems well to restate our reasons and conclusions. . . .

It is urged that the question involved should now receive fresh consideration, among other reasons, because of "the economic conditions which have supervened";

but the meaning of the Constitution does not change with the ebb and flow of economic events. We frequently are told in more general words that the Constitution must be construed in the light of the present. If by that it is meant that the Constitution is made up of living words that apply to every new condition which they include, the statement is quite true. But to say, if that be intended, that the words of the Constitution mean today what they did not mean when written—that is, that they do not apply to a situation now to which they would have applied then—is to rob that instrument of the essential element which continues it in force as the people have made it until they, and not their official agents, have made it otherwise. . . .

The judicial function is that of interpretation; it does not include the power of amendment under the guise of interpretation. To miss the point of difference between the two is to miss all that the phrase "supreme law of the land" stands for and to convert what was intended as inescapable and enduring mandates into mere moral reflections.

If the Constitution, intelligently and reasonably construed in the light of these principles, stands in the way of desirable legislation, the blame must rest upon that instrument, and not upon the Court for enforcing it according to its terms. The remedy in that situation—and the only true remedy—is to amend the Constitution. . . .

Coming, then, to a consideration of the Washington statute, it first is to be observed that it is in every substantial respect identical with the statute involved in the *Adkins* case. Such vices as existed in the latter are present in the former. And if the *Adkins* case was properly decided, as we who join in this opinion think it was, it necessarily follows that the Washington statute is invalid. . . .

Case

FERGUSON V. SKRUPA

372 U.S. 726; 83 S.Ct. 1028; 10 L.Ed. 2d 93 (1963)
Vote: 9–0

In this case the Court repudiates substantive due process as a barrier to economic regulation. The pertinent facts and issues are contained in Justice Black's opinion for the Court.

Mr. Justice Black delivered the opinion of the Court.

In this case . . . we are asked to review the judgment of a three-judge District Court enjoining, as being in violation of the Due Process Clause of the Fourteenth Amendment, a Kansas statute making it a misdemeanor for any

person to engage "in the business of debt adjusting" except as an incident to "the lawful practice of law in this state." The statute defines "debt adjusting" as "the making of a contract, express or implied, with a particular debtor whereby the debtor agrees to pay a certain amount of money periodically to the person engaged in the debt adjusting business who shall for a consideration distribute the same among certain specified creditors in accordance with a plan agreed upon."

The complaint, filed by appellee Skrupa doing business as "Credit Advisor," alleged that Skrupa was engaged in the business of "debt adjusting" as defined by the statute, that his business was a "useful and desirable" one, that his business activities were not "inherently immoral or dangerous" or in any way contrary to the public welfare, and that therefore the business could not be "absolutely prohibited" by Kansas. The three-judge court heard evidence by Skrupa tending to show the usefulness and desirability of his business and evidence by the state officials tending to show that "debt adjusting" lends itself to grave abuses against distressed debtors, particularly in the lower income brackets, and that these abuses are of such gravity that a number of States have strictly regulated "debt adjusting" or prohibited it altogether. The court found that Skrupa's business did fall within the Act's proscription and concluded, one judge dissenting, that the Act was prohibitory, not regulatory, but that even if construed in part as regulatory it was an unreasonable regulation of a "lawful business," which the court held amounted to a violation of the Due Process Clause of the Fourteenth Amendment. The court accordingly enjoined enforcement of the statute.

Under the system of government created by the Constitution, it is up to legislatures, not courts, to decide on the wisdom and utility of legislation. There was a time then the Due Process Clause was used by this Court to strike down laws which were thought unreasonable, that is, unwise or incompatible with some particular economic or social philosophy. In this manner the Due Process Clause was used, for example, to nullify laws prescribing maximum hours for work in bakeries, *Lochner v. New York,* . . . outlawing "yellow dog" contracts, *Coppage v. Kansas,* . . . setting minimum wages for women, *Adkins v. Children's Hospital,* . . . and fixing the weight of loaves of bread, *Jay Burns Baking Co. v. Bryan.* . . . This intrusion by the judiciary into the realm of legislative value judgments was strongly objected to at the time, particularly by Mr. Justice Holmes and Mr. Justice Brandeis. . . .

The doctrine that prevailed in *Lochner, Coppage, Adkins, Burns,* and like cases—that due process authorizes courts to hold laws unconstitutional when they believe the legislature has acted unwisely—has long since been discarded. We have returned to the original constitutional proposition that courts do not substitute their social and economic beliefs for the judgment of legislative bodies, who are elected to pass laws. As this Court stated in a unanimous opinion in 1941, "We are not concerned . . . with the wisdom, need, or appropriateness of the legislation." Legislative bodies have broad scope to experiment with economic problems, and this Court does not sit to "subject the State to an intolerable supervision hostile to the basic principles of our Government and wholly beyond the protection which the general clause of the Fourteenth Amendment was intended to secure." It is now settled that States "have power to legislate against what are found to be injurious practices in their internal commercial and business affairs, so long as their laws do not run afoul of some specific federal constitutional prohibition or of some valid federal law."

. . . We conclude that the Kansas Legislature was free to decide for itself that legislation was needed to deal with the business of debt adjusting. Unquestionably, there are arguments showing that the business of debt adjusting has social utility, but such arguments are properly addressed to the legislature, not to us. We refuse to sit as a "super-legislature to weigh the wisdom of legislation," and we emphatically refuse to go back to the time when courts used the Due Process Clause "to strike down state laws, regulatory of business and industrial conditions, because they may be unwise, improvident, or out of harmony with a particular school of thought." Nor are we able or willing to draw lines by calling a law "prohibitory" or "regulatory." Whether the legislature takes for its textbook Adam Smith, Herbert Spencer, Lord Keynes, or some other is no concern of ours. The Kansas debt adjusting statute may be wise or unwise. But relief, if any be needed, lies not with us but with the body constituted to pass laws for the State of Kansas.

Nor is the statute's exception of lawyers a denial of equal protection of the laws to nonlawyers. Statutes create many classifications which do not deny equal protection; it is only "invidious discrimination" which offends the Constitution. If the State of Kansas wants to limit debt adjusting to lawyers, the Equal Protection Clause does not forbid. We also find no merit in the contention that the Fourteenth Amendment is violated by the failure of the Kansas statute's title to be as specific as appellee thinks it ought to be under the Kansas constitution.

Reversed.

Mr. Justice Harlan concurs in the judgment on the ground that this state measure bears a rational relation to a constitutionally permissible objective. . . .

Case

HAWAII HOUSING AUTHORITY V. MIDKIFF

467 U.S. 229; 104 S.Ct. 2321; 81 L.Ed. 2d 186 (1984)
Vote: 8–0

In this case the Court considers whether the state of Hawaii may use its power of eminent domain to redistribute land previously held by a small minority of large landowners. The constitutional question is whether the state's "taking" is justified by a valid "public use."

Justice O'Connor delivered the opinion of the Court.

. . . The starting point for our analysis of the Act's constitutionality is the Court's decision in *Berman v. Parker* [1954]. . . . In *Berman,* the Court held constitutional the District of Columbia Redevelopment Act of 1945. That Act provided both for the comprehensive use of the eminent domain power to redevelop slum areas and for the possible sale or lease of the condemned lands to private interests. In discussing whether the takings authorized by that Act were for a "public use," . . . the Court stated

> We deal, in other words, with what traditionally has been known as the police power. An attempt to define its reach or trace its outer limits is fruitless, for each case must turn on its own facts. The definition is essentially the product of legislative determinations addressed to the purposes of government, purposes neither abstractly nor historically capable of complete definition. Subject to specific constitutional limitations, when the legislature has spoken, the public interest has been declared in terms well-nigh conclusive. In such cases the legislature, not the judiciary, is the main guardian of the public needs to be served by social legislation, whether it be Congress legislating concerning the District of Columbia . . . or the States legislating concerning local affairs. . . . This principle admits of no exception merely because the power of eminent domain is involved. . . .

The "public use" requirement is thus coterminous with the scope of a sovereign's police powers.

There is, of course, a role for courts to play in reviewing a legislature's judgment of what constitutes a public use, even when the eminent domain power is equated with the police power. But the Court in *Berman* made clear that it is "an extremely narrow" one. The Court in *Berman* cited with approval the Court's decision in *Old Dominion Co. v. United States* [1925], . . . which held that deference to the legislature's "public use" determination is required "until

it is shown to involve an impossibility." The *Berman* Court also cited to *United States ex rel. TVA v. Welch* [1946], . . . which emphasized that "[a]ny departure from this judicial restraint would result in courts deciding on what is and is not a governmental function and in their invalidating legislation on the basis of their view on that question at the moment of decision, a practice which has proved impracticable in other fields." In short, the Court has made clear that it will not substitute its judgment for a legislature's judgment as to what constitutes a public use "unless the use be palpably without reasonable foundation." . . .

To be sure, the Court's cases have repeatedly stated that "one person's property may not be taken for the benefit of another private person without a justifying public purpose, even though compensation be paid." . . . Thus, in *Missouri Pacific R. Co. v. Nebraska* [1896], . . . where the "order in question was not, and was not claimed to be, . . . a taking of private property for a public use under the right of eminent domain," . . . the Court invalidated a compensated taking of property for lack of a justifying public purpose. But where the exercise of the eminent domain power is rationally related to a conceivable public purpose, the Court has never held a compensated taking to be proscribed by the Public Use Clause. . . .

On this basis, we have no trouble concluding that the Hawaii Act is constitutional. The people of Hawaii have attempted, much as the settlers of the original 13 Colonies did, to reduce the perceived social and economic evils of a land oligopoly traceable to their monarchs. The land oligopoly has, according to the Hawaii Legislature, created artificial deterrents to the normal functioning of the State's residential land market and forced thousands of individual homeowners to lease, rather than buy, the land underneath their homes. Regulating oligopoly and the evils associated with it is a classic exercise of a State's police powers. . . . We cannot disapprove of Hawaii's exercise of this power.

Nor can we condemn as irrational the Act's approach to correcting the land oligopoly problem. The Act presumes that when a sufficiently large number of persons declare that they are willing but unable to buy lots at fair prices the land market is malfunctioning. When such a malfunction is signaled, the Act authorizes HHA to condemn lots in the relevant tract. The Act limits the number of lots any one tenant can purchase and authorizes HHA to use public funds to ensure that the market dilution goals will be achieved. This is a comprehensive and rational approach to identifying and correcting market failure.

Of course, this Act, like any other, may not be successful in achieving its intended goals. But "whether in fact the provision will accomplish its objectives is not the question: the [constitutional requirement] is satisfied if . . . the . . . [state] Legislature rationally could have believed that the [Act] would promote its objective." . . . When the legislature's purpose is legitimate and its means are not irrational, our cases make clear that empirical debates over the wisdom of takings—no less than debates over the wisdom of other kinds of socioeconomic legislation—are not to be carried out in the federal courts. Redistribution of fees simple to correct deficiencies in the market determined by the state legislature to be attributable to land oligopoly is a rational exercise of the eminent domain power. Therefore, the Hawaii statute must pass the scrutiny of the Public Use Clause. . . .

The State of Hawaii has never denied that the Constitution forbids even a compensated taking of property when executed for no reason other than to confer a private benefit on a particular private party. A purely private

taking could not withstand the scrutiny of the public use requirement; it would serve no legitimate purpose of government and would thus be void. But no purely private taking is involved in this case. The Hawaii Legislature enacted its Land Reform Act not to benefit a particular class of identifiable individuals but to attack certain perceived evils of concentrated property ownership in Hawaii—a legitimate public purpose. Use of the condemnation power to achieve this purpose is not irrational. Since we assume for purposes of this appeal that the weighty demand of just compensation has been met, the requirements of the Fifth and Fourteenth Amendments have been satisfied. Accordingly, we reverse the judgment of the Court of Appeals, and remand these cases for further proceedings in conformity with this opinion. . . .

Justice Marshall took no part in the consideration or decision of these cases.

Case

DOLAN V. CITY OF TIGARD

512 U.S. 374; 114 S.Ct. 2309; 129 L.Ed. 2d 304 (1994)
Vote: 5–4

In this case the Supreme Court addresses a city's refusal to grant a building permit unless the property owner agreed to dedicate a portion of her land for flood control and traffic improvements. In deciding the case, the Court considers a question left open in Nollan v. California Coastal Commission (1987) regarding the relationship between the impact of proposed development and the conditions imposed by government on such development.

Chief Justice Rehnquist delivered the opinion of the Court.

. . . The State of Oregon enacted a comprehensive land use management program in 1973. . . . The program required all Oregon cities and counties to adopt new comprehensive land use plans that were consistent with the statewide planning goals. . . . The plans are implemented by land use regulations which are part of an integrated hierarchy of legally binding goals, plans, and regulations. . . . Pursuant to the State's requirements, the city of Tigard, a community of some 30,000 residents on the southwest edge of Portland, developed a comprehensive plan and codified it in its Community Development Code (CDC). The CDC requires property owners in the area zoned Central Business District to comply with a 15% open space and landscaping requirement, which limits total site cov-

erage, including all structures and paving parking to 85% of the parcel. . . . After the completion of a transportation study that identified congestion in the Central Business District as a particular problem, the city adopted a plan for a pedestrian/bicycle pathway intended to encourage alternatives to automobile transportation for short trips. The CDC requires that new development facilitate this plan by dedicating land for pedestrian pathways where provided for in the pedestrian/bicycle pathway plan.

The city also adopted a Master Drainage Plan (Drainage Plan). The Drainage Plan noted that flooding occurred in several areas along Fanno Creek, including areas near petitioner's property. . . . The Drainage Plan also established that the increase in impervious surfaces associated with continued urbanization would exacerbate these flooding problems. To combat these risks, the Drainage Plan suggested a series of improvements to the Fanno Creek Basin, including channel excavation in the area next to petitioner's property. . . . Other recommendations included ensuring that the floodplain remains free of structures and that it be preserved as greenways to minimize flood damage to structures. . . . The Drainage Plan concluded that the cost of these improvements should be shared based on both direct and indirect benefits, with property owners along the waterways paying more due to the direct benefit that they would receive. . . .

Petitioner Florence Dolan owns a plumbing and electric supply store located on Main Street in the Central Business District of the city. The store covers approximately 9,700 square feet on the eastern side of a 1.67 acre parcel, which includes a gravel parking lot. Fanno Creek flows through the southwestern corner of the lot and along its western boundary. The year-round flow of the creek renders the area within the creek's 100-year floodplain virtually unusable for commercial development. The city's comprehensive plan includes the Fanno Creek floodplain as part of the city's greenway system.

Petitioner applied to the city for a permit to redevelop the site. Her proposed plans called for nearly doubling the size of the store to 17,600 square feet, and paving a 39-space parking lot. The existing store, located on the opposite side of the parcel, would be razed in sections as construction progressed on the new building. In the second phase of the project, petitioner proposed to build an additional structure on the northeast side of the site for complementary businesses, and to provide more parking. The proposed expansion and intensified use are consistent with the city's zoning scheme in the Central Business District. . . .

The City Planning Commission granted petitioner's permit application subject to conditions imposed by the city's CDC. The CDC establishes the following standard for site development review approval: "Where landfill and/or development is allowed within and adjacent to the 100-year floodplain, the city shall require the dedication of sufficient open land area for greenway adjoining and within the floodplain. This area shall include portions at a suitable elevation for the construction of a pedestrian/bicycle pathway within the floodplain in accordance with the adopted pedestrian/bicycle plan." . . .

Thus, the Commission required that petitioner dedicate the portion of her property lying within the 100-year floodplain for improvement of a storm drainage system along Fanno Creek and that she dedicate an additional 15-foot strip of land adjacent to the floodplain as a pedestrian/bicycle pathway. The dedication required by that condition encompasses approximately 7,000 square feet, or roughly 10% of the property. In accordance with city practice, petitioner could rely on the dedicated property to meet the 15% open space and landscaping requirement mandated by the city's zoning scheme. . . . The city would bear the cost of maintaining a landscaped buffer between the dedicated area and the new store. . . .

Petitioner requested variances from the CDC standards. Variances are granted only where it can be shown that, owing to special circumstances related to a specific piece of the land, the literal interpretation of the applicable zoning provisions would cause "an undue or unnecessary hardship" unless the variance is granted. . . . Rather than posing alternative mitigating measures to offset the expected impacts of her proposed development, as allowed under the CDC, petitioner simply argued that her

proposed development would not conflict with the policies of the comprehensive plan. . . . The Commission denied the request.

The Commission made a series of findings concerning the relationship between the dedicated conditions and the projected impacts of petitioner's project. First, the Commission noted that "[i]t is reasonable to assume that customers and employees of the future uses of this site could utilize a pedestrian/bicycle pathway adjacent to this development for their transportation and recreational needs." . . . The Commission noted that the site plan has provided for bicycle parking in a rack in front of the proposed building and "[i]t is reasonable to expect that some of the users of the bicycle parking provided for by the site plan will use the pathway adjacent to Fanno Creek if it is constructed." . . . In addition, the Commission found that creation of a convenient, safe pedestrian/bicycle pathway system as an alternative means of transportation "could offset some of the traffic demand on [nearby] streets and lessen the increase in traffic congestion." . . . The Commission went on to note that the required floodplain dedication would be reasonably related to petitioner's request to intensify the use of the site given the increase in the impervious surface. The Commission stated that the "anticipated increased stormwater flow from the subject property to an already strained creek and drainage basin can only add to the public need to manage the stream channel and floodplain for drainage purposes." . . . Based on this anticipated increased stormwater flow, the Commission concluded that "the requirement of dedication of the floodplain area on the site is related to the applicant's plan to intensify development on the site." . . . The Tigard City Council approved the Commission's final order. . . .

Petitioner appealed to the Land Use Board of Appeals (LUBA) on the ground that the city's dedication requirements were not related to the proposed development, and, therefore, those requirements constituted an uncompensated taking of their property under the Fifth Amendment. . . . [This appeal was unsuccessful.]

The Oregon Court of Appeals affirmed, rejecting petitioner's contention that in *Nollan v. California Coastal Commission* . . . we had abandoned the "reasonable relationship" test in favor of a stricter "essential nexus" test. . . . The court decided that both the pedestrian/ bicycle pathway condition and the storm drainage dedication had an essential nexus to the development of the proposed site. . . . Therefore, the court found the conditions to be reasonably related to the impact of the expansion of petitioner's business. . . . We granted certiorari . . . because of an alleged conflict between the Oregon Supreme Court's decision and our decision in *Nollan*.

The Takings Clause of the Fifth Amendment . . . provides: "[N]or shall private property be taken for public use, without just compensation." One of the principal purposes of the Takings Clause is "to bar Government from forcing some people alone to bear public burdens which, in all fairness and justice, should be borne by the public as a whole." . . . Without question, had the city simply required petitioner to dedicate a strip of land along Fanno Creek for public use, rather than conditioning the grant of her permit to redevelop her property on such a dedication, a taking would have occurred. . . . Such public access would deprive petitioner of the right to exclude others, "one of the most essential sticks in the bundle of rights that are commonly characterized as property." . . .

. . . Under the well-settled doctrine of "unconstitutional conditions," the government may not require a person to give up a constitutional right—the right to receive just compensation when property is taken for a public use—in exchange for a discretionary benefit conferred by the government where the property sought has little or no relationship to the benefit. . . .

Petitioner contends that the city has forced her to choose between the building permit and her right under the Fifth Amendment to just compensation for the public easements. Petitioner does not quarrel with the city's authority to exact some forms of dedication as a condition for the grant of a building permit, but challenges the showing made by the city to justify these exactions. She argues that the city has identified "no special benefits" conferred on her, and has not identified any "special quantifiable burdens" created by her new store that would justify the particular dedications required from her which are not required from the public at large.

In evaluating petitioner's claim, we must first determine whether the "essential nexus" exists between the "legitimate state interest" and the permit condition exacted by the city. . . . If we find that a nexus exists, we must then decide the required degree of connection between the exactions and the projected impact of the proposed development. We were not required to reach this question in *Nollan,* because we concluded that the connection did not meet even the loosest standard. . . . Here, however, we must decide this question. . . .

. . . Undoubtedly, the prevention of flooding along Fanno Creek and the reduction of traffic congestion in the Central Business District qualify as the type of legitimate public purposes we have upheld. . . . It seems equally obvious that a nexus exists between preventing flooding along Fanno Creek and limiting development within the creek's 100-year floodplain. Petitioner proposes to double the size of her retail store and to pave her now-gravel parking lot, thereby expanding the impervious surface on the property and increasing the amount of stormwater run-off into Fanno Creek.

The same may be said for the city's attempt to reduce traffic congestion by providing for alternative means of transportation. In theory, a pedestrian/bicycle pathway provides a useful alternative means of transportation for workers and shoppers. . . .

The second part of our analysis requires us to determine whether the degree of the exactions demanded by the city's permit conditions bear the required relationship to the projected impact of petitioner's proposed development. . . .

The city required that the petitioner dedicate "to the city as greenway all portions of the site that fall within the existing 100-year floodplain . . . and all property 15 feet above [the floodplain] boundary." In addition, the city demanded that the retail store be designed so as not to intrude into the greenway area. The city relies on the Commission's rather tentative findings that increased stormwater flow from petitioner's property "can only add to the public need to manage the [floodplain] for drainage purposes" to support its conclusion that the "requirement of dedication of the floodplain area on the site is related to the applicant's plan to intensify development on the site." . . .

The city made the following specific findings relevant to the pedestrian/bicycle pathway: "In addition, the proposed expanded use of this site is anticipated to generate additional vehicular traffic thereby increasing congestion on nearby collector and arterial streets. Creation of a convenient, safe pedestrian/bicycle pathway system as an alternative means of transportation could offset some of the traffic demand on these nearby streets and lessen the increase in traffic congestion." . . .

The question for us is whether these findings are constitutionally sufficient to justify the conditions imposed by the city on petitioner's building permit. Since state courts have been dealing with this question a good deal longer than we have, we turn to representative decisions made by them.

In some States, very generalized statements as to the necessary connection between the required dedication and the proposed development seem to suffice. . . . We think this standard is too lax to adequately protect petitioner's right to just compensation if her property is taken for a public purpose. . . .

A number of state courts have taken an intermediate position, requiring the municipality to show a "reasonable relationship" between the required dedication and the impact of the proposed development. . . .

We think the "reasonable relationship" test adopted by a majority of the state courts is closer to the federal constitutional norm than either of those previously discussed. But we do not adopt it as such, partly because the term "reasonable relationship" seems confusingly similar to the term "rational basis" which describes the minimal level of scrutiny under the Equal Protection Clause of the Fourteenth Amendment. We think a term such as "rough proportionality" best encapsulates what we hold to be the requirement of the Fifth Amendment. No precise mathematical calculation is required, but the city must make some sort of individualized determination that the required dedication is related both in nature and extent to the impact of the proposed development. . . .

It is axiomatic that increasing the amount of impervious surface will increase the quantity and rate of stormwater flow from petitioner's property. . . . Therefore, keeping the floodplain open and free from development would likely confine the pressures on Fanno Creek created by petitioner's development. . . .

. . . As we have noted, [the] right to exclude others is "one of the most essential sticks in the bundle of rights that are commonly characterized as property." . . . It is difficult to see why recreational visitors trampling along petitioner's floodplain easement are sufficiently related to the city's legitimate interest in reducing flooding problems along Fanno Creek, and the city has not attempted to make any individualized determination to support this part of its request. . . .

Admittedly, petitioner wants to build a bigger store to attract members of the public to her property. She also wants, however, to be able to control the time and manner in which they enter. . . . [T]he city wants to impose a permanent recreational easement upon petitioner's property that borders Fanno Creek. Petitioner would lose all rights to regulate the time in which the public entered onto the Greenway, regardless of any interference it might pose with her retail store. Her right to exclude would not be regulated, it would be eviscerated.

If petitioner's proposed development had somehow encroached on existing greenway space in the city, it would have been reasonable to require petitioner to provide some alternative greenway space for the public either on her property or elsewhere. . . . But that is not the case here. We conclude that the findings upon which the city relies do not show the required reasonable relationship between the floodplain easement and the petitioner's proposed new building.

With respect to the pedestrian/bicycle pathway, we have no doubt that the city was correct in finding that the larger retail sales facility proposed by petitioner will increase traffic on the streets of the Central Business District. The city estimates that the proposed development would generate roughly 435 additional trips per day. Dedications for streets, sidewalks, and other public ways are generally reasonable exactions to avoid excessive congestion from a proposed property use. But on the record before us, the city has not met its burden of demonstrating that the additional number of vehicle and bicycle trips generated by the petitioner's development reasonably relate to the city's requirement for a dedication of the pedestrian/bicycle pathway easement. The city simply found that the creation of the pathway "could offset some of the traffic demand . . . and lessen the increase in traffic congestion."

. . . No precise mathematical calculation is required, but the city must make some effort to quantify its findings in support of the dedication for the pedestrian/ bicycle pathway beyond the conclusory statement that it could offset some of the traffic demand generated.

Cities have long engaged in the commendable task of land use planning, made necessary by increasing urbanization particularly in metropolitan areas such as Portland. The city's goals of reducing flooding hazards and traffic congestion, and providing for public greenways, are laudable, but there are outer limits to how this may be done. . . .

Justice Stevens, with whom *Justice Blackmun* and *Justice Ginsburg* join, dissenting.

. . . If the Court proposes to have the federal judiciary micromanage state decisions of this kind, it is indeed extending its welcome mat to a significant new class of litigants. Although there is no reason to believe that state courts have failed to rise to the task, property owners have surely found a new friend today.

The Court has made a serious error by abandoning the traditional presumption of constitutionality and imposing a novel burden of proof on a city implementing an admittedly valid comprehensive land use plan. Even more consequential than its incorrect disposition of this case, however, is the Court's resurrection of a species of substantive due process analysis that it firmly rejected decades ago. . . .

In our changing world one thing is certain: uncertainty will characterize predictions about the impact of new urban developments on the risks of floods, earthquakes, traffic congestion, or environmental harms. When there is doubt concerning the magnitude of those impacts, the public interest in averting them must outweigh the private interest of the commercial entrepreneur. If the government0 can demonstrate that the conditions it has imposed in a land-use permit are rational, impartial and conducive to fulfilling the aims of a valid land-use plan, a strong presumption of validity should attach to those conditions. The burden of demonstrating that those conditions have unreasonably impaired the economic value of the proposed improvement belongs squarely on the shoulders of the party challenging the state action's constitutionality. That allocation of burdens has served us well in the past. The Court has stumbled badly today by reversing it. . . .

Justice Souter, dissenting. . . .

8

EXPRESSIVE FREEDOM AND THE FIRST AMENDMENT

"If there is a bedrock principle underlying the First Amendment, it is that the government may not prohibit the expression of an idea simply because society finds the idea itself offensive or disagreeable."

—JUSTICE WILLIAM BRENNAN, WRITING FOR THE SUPREME COURT IN
    TEXAS V. JOHNSON (1989)

William J. Brennan: Associate Justice, 1956–1990

427

INTRODUCTION

This chapter examines the Supreme Court's development of constitutional doctrine effectively defining **freedom of expression**, which encompasses both **freedom of speech** and **freedom of the press**. To a lesser extent, the chapter deals with **freedom of assembly**, which is an explicit component of the First Amendment, and **freedom of association**, which the courts have recognized as an implicit First Amendment right. We deal separately with the First Amendment freedom of religion in the next chapter. As important as freedom of religion was to the founders of the republic, one can argue that freedom of expression is *the* fundamental freedom in a democracy. Accordingly, our examination of specific civil liberties begins with the expressive freedoms of the First Amendment.

INTERPRETIVE FOUNDATIONS OF EXPRESSIVE FREEDOM

The idea of free speech is a largely modern notion that correlates with the emergence of democracy. To the ancient and medieval world, freedom of speech was unthinkable, especially in religious and political matters. In England the idea of freedom of speech emerged gradually, coincident with the development of parliamentary government. The importance of free speech in galvanizing the American Revolution resulted in specific protections of freedom of speech being incorporated into the constitutions of the new American states.

The constitutional commitment to freedom of the press also has its roots in English history and in American colonial experience, especially during the decades immediately preceding the American Revolution. The mass media of that period, consisting of small independent newspaper and pamphlet publishers, played a vital role in facilitating political debate and in disseminating information. It is worth recalling in this context that the ratification of the Constitution was vigorously debated not only in the state ratifying conventions but in the press as well. The collection of essays known as *The Federalist Papers* first appeared as a series of newspaper articles analyzing and endorsing the new Constitution. Anti-Federalists also made wide use of newspapers to express opposition to ratification.

Despite the obvious importance of freedoms of speech and press in the establishment of American democracy, the U.S. Supreme Court did not pay major attention to these values during the early days of the republic. For a brief period during the administration of President John Adams, the national government sought to suppress public criticism through enforcement of the Sedition Act, passed by Congress in 1798. The Sedition Act prohibited "any false, scandalous and malicious" writing against the national government. A few of Thomas Jefferson's partisans were prosecuted under this statute, and it may have had a **chilling effect** on criticism of the government. Nevertheless, the provision expired on March 3, 1801, just before Jefferson and his newly victorious party took power. Jefferson pardoned those convicted under the statute, and no occasion arose for the Supreme Court to determine its constitutionality.

During the Civil War, a number of limits were imposed on freedom of expression. These included newspaper censorship and the prosecution of some of the more vociferous critics of the Lincoln administration. However, no constitutional challenges raising First Amendment issues reached the Supreme Court.

Incorporation of the Freedoms of Speech and Press

The principal reason that First Amendment controversies did not reach the Supreme Court during the nineteenth century was that, by design, the First Amendment did not apply to the state and local governments. Not until *Gitlow v. New York* (1925) did the Supreme Court recognize that the First Amendment freedoms of speech and press were applicable to the states via the Fourteenth Amendment. In addition to the **incorporation** of the First Amendment, changes in the national political environment brought questions of freedom of speech to the forefront. The national government's efforts to deal with political dissent in the early decades of the twentieth century produced a series of cases that required the Court to interpret the scope of First Amendment protection. By the 1920s, the First Amendment emerged as an important field of constitutional interpretation.

Preferred Freedoms?

In the wake of the constitutional revolution of the late 1930s, the Supreme Court moved away from the protection of private property rights and toward the enhancement of personal freedoms. The First Amendment figured prominently in the Court's newfound emphasis. Writing for the Court in *Palko v. Connecticut* (1937), Justice Benjamin Cardozo characterized freedom of speech as "the matrix, the indispensable condition, of nearly every other form of freedom." During the 1940s several members of the Supreme Court went so far as to suggest that the First Amendment freedoms of speech and press enjoy a "preferred position" in relation to other constitutional guarantees (see, for example, Justice William O. Douglas's majority opinion in *Murdock v. Pennsylvania* [1943]).

Although the Court soon abandoned the **preferred freedoms** language, freedom of expression was accorded high priority during the Warren Court era (1953-1969). The Warren Court established a number of important precedents in this area, and the more conservative Burger and Rehnquist Courts have, for the most part, adhered to these precedents. Clearly, First Amendment questions of increasing complexity and difficulty continue to be among the most important concerns of the Court.

Are the Protections of the First Amendment Absolute?

Although the First Amendment begins with the seemingly absolute injunction, "Congress shall make *no* law . . ." [emphasis added], the Supreme Court has never taken the view that First Amendment protections are absolute in character. Indeed, only a few justices who have served on the Court have argued for an absolutist interpretation. Hugo Black, the best known and most forceful of the First Amendment absolutists, believed that all speech and writing, regardless of its purpose, content, or impact, should be absolutely protected against **censorship** or sanction. Thus Black believed that criminal laws prohibiting **obscenity**, **profanity**, and **seditious speech** were inherently unconstitutional. Justice Black also believed that laws that permitted civil suits for **libel** or **slander** could not be reconciled with the First Amendment.

In Black's view, the First Amendment gives everyone the right to say or write anything, regardless of its impact on other individuals or society in general. However, Justice Black believed that the protections of the First Amendment were limited to **pure speech** and pure writing. In his view, **picketing** and other forms of **expressive conduct** were not covered by the First Amendment.

Although Hugo Black wrote a number of important opinions for the Court on questions of freedom of speech and freedom of the press, most of his colleagues and most of the justices who came after him refused to accept Black's **First Amendment absolutism**. The Court has never taken the position that the protections of the First Amendment are absolute. Indeed, the Court has recognized that certain types of expression, including obscenity, **fighting words**, and **defamation**, are outside the scope of the First Amendment. It has also held that speech that is normally protected by the Constitution might not be protected depending on the circumstances in which it takes place.

On the other hand, the Court has recognized that the protections of the First Amendment are not limited to pure speech and writing. Rather, the First Amendment potentially protects communication of any kind. Protests, demonstrations, performances, advertisements, artistic endeavors—all of these are within the ambit of expression. So too are records, films, videos, software, e-mail, broadcasts, cablecasts, and sites on the Internet. In short, the First Amendment protects communication, regardless of its nature or medium. Whether specific instances of expression merit First Amendment protection or may be censored or sanctioned by government depends on a number of factors that we will examine in this chapter.

Government can infringe on freedom of expression in two ways. It can employ censorship to prevent a specific instance of expression from reaching the public. Alternatively, it can punish someone after the fact, usually through criminal prosecution. We begin our examination of First Amendment doctrine with the principle that limits government censorship prior to expression or publication—the rule against **prior restraint.**

TO SUMMARIZE:

- Constitutional freedoms of expression came of age in the twentieth century. In the 1920s and 1930s, the Supreme Court incorporated freedoms of speech, press, and assembly into the Fourteenth Amendment, thus making them fully applicable to the states as well as the federal government.
- Although a majority of the Court has never regarded the First Amendment freedoms as absolute, these freedoms have come to be regarded as fundamental rights essential to the preservation of a constitutional democracy.

THE PROHIBITION OF PRIOR RESTRAINT

The authors of the Bill of Rights saw the need for the First Amendment because common law, which this nation inherited from England, provided little protection to freedom of expression. However, one common law doctrine has been grafted onto the First Amendment through judicial interpretation. This is the rule against prior restraint. In *Commentaries on the Laws of England,* Vol. IV (1769), William Blackstone stated the rule against prior restraint in the context of freedom of the press: "The liberty of the press is indeed essential to the nature of a free state; but this consists in laying no previous restraints upon publications, and not in freedom from censure for criminal matter when published." In this country, the concept of prior restraint has been of great importance to the Supreme Court in defining both freedom of the press and freedom of speech under the First Amendment. The concept was first discussed by the Court, however, in the context of a dispute over publication of a newspaper.

The Court Adopts the Rule against Prior Restraint

In *Near v. Minnesota* (1931), the Court struck down a state law that permitted public officials to seek an injunction to stop publication of any "malicious, scandalous and defamatory newspaper, magazine or other periodical." The statute was invoked to suppress publication of a small Minneapolis newspaper, the *Saturday Press,* which had strong anti-Semitic overtones and maligned local political officials, particularly the chief of police. The state law provided that once a newspaper was enjoined, further publication was punishable as contempt of court. Writing for the Court in *Near,* Chief Justice Charles Evans Hughes characterized this mode of suppression as "the essence of censorship" and declared it unconstitutional. Note also that with its decision in *Near v. Minnesota,* the Court specifically incorporated the First Amendment freedom of the press into the Due Process Clause of the Fourteenth Amendment, thus making it fully applicable to the states.

In commenting with general approval on the rule against prior restraint, Chief Justice Hughes acknowledged that this restriction is not absolute. It would not, for example, prevent the government in time of war from prohibiting publication of "the sailing dates of transports or the number and location of troops." In these and related situations, national security interests are almost certain to prevail over freedom of the press. But where is the line to be drawn? How far can the "national security" justification be extended in suppressing publication?

The Pentagon Papers Case

The Court revisited the question of prior restraint on the press in the much-heralded Pentagon papers case of 1971 (*New York Times Company v. United States*). Here, the federal government attempted to prevent the *New York Times* and the *Washington Post* from publishing excerpts from a classified study titled "History of U.S. Decision-Making Process on Viet Nam Policy" (the Pentagon papers). By a 6-to-3 vote, the Supreme Court, in a brief *per curiam* opinion, held that the government's effort to block publication of this material amounted to an unconstitutional prior restraint. The majority was simply not convinced that such publication—several years after the events and decisions discussed in the Pentagon papers—constituted a significant threat to national security. The furor produced by this highly publicized case and the great pressure brought to bear on the Court for a speedy decision help explain why no detailed majority opinion was produced. The justices in fact wrote nine separate opinions, advancing a wide variety of rationales for and against application of the prior restraint concept. Excerpts from each of these opinions are reprinted at the end of this chapter, and it is important to consider the constitutional implications of the various arguments.

May the Government Prevent Publication of How to Make a Hydrogen Bomb?

The issue of prior restraint arose again in 1979 in connection with the publication of a magazine article purporting to describe the process of making a hydrogen bomb. The federal government obtained a preliminary injunction against *The Progressive* blocking publication of the article pending a hearing. In the meantime, however, another magazine published a similar article, with no apparent damage to national security. As a result, the case against *The Progressive* was dismissed and the injunction lifted (see *United States v. Progressive* [1979]). *The Progressive*'s hydrogen bomb article was ultimately published in November 1979. In light of the Pentagon papers and *Progressive* cases, we could conclude that, although national security may justify a departure from the rule against prior restraint, in the real world of American constitutional law, such departures tend to be rare and short-lived.

Does the Prior Restraint Doctrine Apply to Student Newspapers?

One notable exception to the protection of press freedom against prior restraint involves the publication of student-operated school newspapers. In *Hazelwood School*

District v. Kuhlmeier (1988), the Supreme Court voted 5 to 3 to uphold a public school principal's decision to excise certain controversial material from the school newspaper. The principal objected to certain articles dealing with divorce and teenage pregnancy on the grounds that they were written in such a way as to permit students to identify classmates who had encountered such difficulties. The student newspaper staff hired a lawyer and challenged the principal's action in federal court. Writing for the majority, Justice Byron White concluded that "educators do not offend the First Amendment by exercising editorial control over the style and content of student speech in school-sponsored expressive activities so long as their actions are reasonably related to legitimate pedagogical concerns." Dissenting, Justice William Brennan accused the majority of eviscerating *Tinker v. Des Moines Independent Community School District* (1969), in which the Court had accorded First Amendment protection to certain expressive activities by students in public schools. According to Brennan, the majority opinion in *Hazelwood* "denudes high school students of much of the First Amendment protection that *Tinker* itself prescribed."

The controversy in *Hazelwood* centered around a student newspaper at a public high school. Would the federal courts permit officials at a state college or university to censor student-run campus newspapers? Could "legitimate pedagogical concerns" at this level ever justify such interference? Most observers doubt the Courts would permit this type of censorship.

TO SUMMARIZE:

- The prohibition of prior restraint has evolved from a technical common law rule regarding the licensing of publications into a broad First Amendment principle that restricts government censorship of expression prior to its utterance.
- The Supreme Court applied the rule against prior restraint most prominently in the Pentagon papers case of 1971. In this case, the Court refused to allow the federal government to bar newspapers from publishing classified documents dealing with the Vietnam War.

THE CLEAR AND PRESENT DANGER DOCTRINE

Even though a specific instance of expression may not be censored prior to its utterance or publication, it may still be subject to sanctions after the fact. Individuals may be subjected to criminal prosecution or civil suit for instances of expression that violate specific legal prohibitions. Whether such instances of expression are protected by the First Amendment depends on a number of factors including the nature of the expression and context in which it takes place.

In *Schenck v. United States* (1919), the first major Supreme Court decision interpreting the scope of free speech, the Court made plain that there are instances in which speech that is normally subject to constitutional protection may be suppressed by the government. Writing for the Court, Justice Oliver Wendell Holmes, Jr., flatly rejected an absolutist interpretation of the First Amendment. In what has become a stock phrase in the American political lexicon, Holmes observed that "the most stringent protection of free speech would not protect a man in falsely shouting fire in a theater, and causing a panic." Holmes went on to articulate the famous **clear and present danger test**, saying that "the question in every case is whether the words used are used in such circumstances and are of such a nature as to create a clear and present danger that they will bring about the substantive evils that Congress has a right to prevent." For example, government has a right, indeed an obligation, to protect the national security. If an instance of expression creates a clear and present danger to national security, then government has the right to prohibit the speech or punish the speaker.

In the *Schenck* case, an official of the Socialist Party was convicted for conspiring to print and circulate leaflets urging resistance to the military draft. The leaflets urged resistance to the draft on the grounds that it violated the Thirteenth Amendment. Although sharply critical of the war effort, Schenck's message was confined to the advocacy of peaceful measures, such as petition for repeal of the draft. Nevertheless, a unanimous Supreme Court believed that Schenck's activities amounted to a clear and present danger. One must remember, though, that Schenck's prosecution occurred during World War I. As Justice Holmes observed, "when a nation is at war many things that might be said in time of peace are such a hindrance to its effort that their utterance will not be endured so long as men fight, and that no court could regard them as protected by any constitutional right."

It is also noteworthy that the Court's decision came down at a time when there was widespread concern about the specter of international communism. For the next four decades, the clear and present danger doctrine competed with other approaches to First Amendment interpretation in the area of political dissent.

The Bad Tendency Test

The standard that Justice Holmes articulated in the *Schenck* case was ignored by a Court majority some eight months later in *Abrams v. United States* (1919). Here, the Court affirmed the convictions of Jacob Abrams, a self-styled "anarchist-Socialist," and several associates for distributing leaflets in New York City urging the "workers of the world" to resist, among other things, American intervention in Russia against the newly formed Bolshevik government. For Justice John H. Clarke, the Court's majority spokesman, it was enough that Abrams was advocating a general strike "in the greatest port of our land" for the purpose of "curtailing the production of ordnance and munitions necessary and essential to the prosecution of the war." In effect, Clarke was reverting to the traditional common law **bad tendency test**, according little importance to the free speech question and focusing on the possibility that Abrams's circular might in some way hinder the war effort.

In a powerful dissenting opinion, Justice Holmes, joined by Justice Louis D. Brandeis, again resorted to the clear and present danger test, but this time he used it as a basis for challenging, rather than endorsing, governmental interference with free speech:

> [T]he ultimate good desired is better reached by free trade in ideas. . . . I think that we should be eternally vigilant against attempts to check the expression of opinions that we loathe and believe to be fraught with death, unless they so imminently threaten immediate interference with the lawful and pressing purposes of the law that an immediate check is required to save the country.

Through the 1920s, a Court majority continued to adhere to the bad tendency test, while Holmes and Brandeis further developed the clear and present danger doctrine as a rationale in support of freedom of expression and association. In *Gitlow v. New York* (1925), the Court upheld a conviction under New York's Criminal Anarchy Act that prohibited advocacy of the overthrow of government "by force or violence." Prior to this decision, the Court had addressed issues of freedom of expression arising from the states strictly on the basis of the Due Process Clause of the Fourteenth Amendment, without specific reference to the First Amendment. In fact, as late as 1922 the Court observed that "the Constitution of the United States imposes upon the States no obligation to convey upon those within their jurisdiction . . . the right of free speech" (*Prudential Insurance Company v. Cheek*).

In 1923, the Court invalidated on due process grounds a Nebraska law prohibiting the teaching of the German language in primary schools (*Meyer v. Nebraska*). Similarly, in *Pierce v. Society of Sisters* (1925), the Court struck down an amendment to the Oregon constitution aimed at prohibiting parents from sending their children to private schools. In the *Meyer* and *Pierce* cases, the Court focused on the deprivation of liberty and property rights protected by the Fourteenth Amendment Due Process Clause. In the *Gitlow* case, however, Justice Edward T. Sanford, writing for the majority, stated without elaboration: "For present purposes we may and do assume that freedom of speech and of the press—which are protected by the First Amendment from abridgment by Congress—are among the fundamental personal rights and 'liberties' protected by the Due Process Clause of the Fourteenth Amendment from impairment by the states." (The Court first invalidated a state law on First Amendment freedom of speech grounds two years later in *Fiske v. Kansas* [1927].)

The incident giving rise to the *Gitlow* case was publication of the "Left Wing Manifesto," a statement of beliefs held by what the Court characterized as the most radical section of the Socialist Party. In essence, the manifesto called for the destruction of established government and its replacement by a "revolutionary dictatorship of the proletariat." In affirming the conviction of Benjamin Gitlow, business manager of *The Revolutionary Age,* the Socialist Party paper that published the "Left Wing Manifesto," Justice Sanford stated the essence of the bad tendency test:

> That a state, in the exercise of its police power, may punish those who abuse [freedom of speech and press] by utterances inimical to the public welfare, tending to corrupt public morals, incite to crime, or disturb the public peace, is not open to question.

Sanford continued:

> The state cannot reasonably be required to measure the danger from every such utterance in the nice balance of a jeweler's scale. A single revolutionary spark may kindle a fire that, smoldering for a time, may burst into a sweeping and destructive conflagration. It cannot be said that the state is acting arbitrarily or unreasonably when, in the exercise of its judgment as to the measures necessary to protect the public peace and safety, it seeks to extinguish the spark without waiting until it has enkindled the flame or blazed into the conflagration.

Again, Justices Holmes and Brandeis dissented. They could find no clear and present danger of an effort "to overthrow the government by force on the part of the admittedly small minority who shared the defendant's views." In response to the contention that the "Left Wing Manifesto" was an incitement, Holmes asserted:

> Every idea is an incitement. It offers itself for belief and if believed it is acted on unless some other belief outweighs it or some failure of energy stifles the movement at its birth. The only difference between the expression of an opinion and an incitement in the narrower sense is the speaker's enthusiasm for the result. Eloquence may set fire to reason. But whatever may be thought of the redundant discourse before us it had no chance of starting a present conflagration. If in the long run the beliefs expressed in proletarian dictatorship are destined to be accepted by the dominant forces of the community, the only meaning of free speech is that they should be given their chance and have their way.

This ringing endorsement of the concept of a **free marketplace of ideas** contrasts sharply with Holmes's earlier deference, in the *Schenck* case, to governmental control of dissident expression. As we have seen in connection with judicial review of economic regulation (in Chapter 7), Holmes was inclined to give wide latitude to legislative discretion in matters of public policy. But his dissent in *Gitlow,* like his dissent in *Abrams v. United States,* reflected a decided shift in emphasis where First Amendment values were concerned. This change was probably influenced by Holmes's association on the Court with Justice Brandeis, a dedicated and articulate defender of civil rights and liberties, and his acquaintance with Harvard University law professor Zechariah Chafee, Jr., a widely recognized authority on the First Amendment.

Brandeis himself had occasion to discuss the clear and present danger formula in a concurring opinion in *Whitney v. California* (1927). In this case, the majority, speaking again through Justice Sanford, adhered to the bad tendency test in affirming the conviction of Charlotte Anita Whitney (a niece of Justice Stephen J. Field) for violating California's Criminal Syndicalism Act. The statute defined "criminal syndicalism" as "any doctrine or precept advocating, teaching or aiding and abetting the commission of crime, sabotage . . . or unlawful acts of force and violence or unlawful methods of terrorism as a means of accomplishing a change in industrial ownership or control, or effecting any political change." Whitney's conviction was based on her participation in the organizing convention of the Communist Labor Party of California. The jury rejected her contention that at this meeting she advocated lawful, nonviolent political reform. She maintained that her conviction was a deprivation of liberty without due process of law, but she did not contend specifically that her participation in organizing the Communist Labor Party constituted no clear and present danger. Sanford rejected the view that the act, as applied in this case, was "an unreasonable or arbitrary exercise of the police power of the state, unwarrantably infringing any right of free speech, assembly, or association, or that those persons are protected by the Due Process Clause who abuse such rights by joining and furthering an organization . . . menacing the peace and welfare of the state."

Because Whitney did not raise the clear and present danger issue, Brandeis and Holmes felt compelled to concur. The jury was presented with evidence of a conspiracy and under the circumstances, they concluded, its verdict should not be disturbed. Nevertheless, Brandeis took sharp issue with the majority's narrow view of the constitutional protection that should be afforded political dissent. The crux of the Brandeis-Holmes position is contained in the following excerpts:

> Those who won our independence believed that the final end of the state was to make men free to develop their faculties; and that in its government the deliberative forces should prevail over the arbitrary. They valued liberty both as an end and as a means. They believed liberty to be the secret of happiness and courage to be the secret of liberty. They believed that . . . public discussion is a political duty; and that this should be a fundamental principle of the American government. . . .

> . . . To justify suppression of free speech there must be reasonable ground to fear that serious evil will result if free speech is practiced. There must be reasonable ground to believe that the danger apprehended is imminent. There must be reasonable ground to believe that the evil to be presented is a serious one.

A Supreme Court majority first used the clear and present danger test in defense of free speech in the 1937 case of *Herndon v. Lowry*. This decision reversed a conviction for violation of a Georgia statute prohibiting "any attempt, by persuasion or otherwise," to incite insurrection. Following this decision, the Court began to apply the clear and present danger test not only to "seditious" speech but to other First Amendment issues as well.

Clear and Probable Danger

The Cold War, which had begun after World War II, deepened after the United States became embroiled in the Korean conflict—and by the early 1950s, McCarthyism, with its emphasis on the "communist menace," had achieved substantial national influence. Against this background of Cold War paranoia, the Supreme Court reviewed and affirmed the convictions of eleven leaders of the American Communist Party in *Dennis v. United States* (1951). Eugene Dennis and his ten codefendants had been convicted after a highly publicized nine-month federal trial for violation of the Internal Security Act of 1940, more commonly known as the Smith Act.

The Smith Act made it a crime "to knowingly or willfully advocate, abet, advise, or teach the duty, necessity, desirability, or propriety of overthrowing or destroying any government in the United States by force or violence." In essence, the defendants' convictions resulted from their activities in organizing and furthering the purposes of the Communist Party in the United States.

The Court of Appeals for the Second Circuit upheld these convictions. In his opinion for that court, Chief Judge Learned Hand substituted a more limited defense of First Amendment freedoms than that of clear and present danger. This doctrine, popularly known as the **clear and probable danger test**, was adopted by Chief Justice Frederick M. Vinson in a plurality opinion announcing the Supreme Court's judgment affirming the convictions. The new standard that Hand articulated required courts in each case to "ask whether the gravity of the 'evil,' discounted by its improbability, justifies such invasion of free speech as is necessary to avoid the danger."

Two members of the *Dennis* majority, Justices Felix Frankfurter and Robert Jackson, wrote separate concurring opinions, neither of which endorsed Hand's formula or the clear and present danger test. Frankfurter maintained that the Court should defer to the legislative balancing of competing interests in the free speech area no less than in other areas of policy making. Jackson differentiated between isolated, localized protest and what he saw as a highly organized conspiracy of international dimensions aimed at subverting American government. He regarded the clear and present danger test as an inadequate standard for assessing a conspiracy of this magnitude. Jackson found "no constitutional right to 'gang up' on the Government."

Justice Black, who dissented along with Justice Douglas, expressed the hope that "in calmer times, when present pressures, passions and fears subside, this or some later Court will restore the First Amendment liberties to the high preferred place where they belong in a free society."

Changes in public opinion and in Supreme Court personnel did in fact result in a gradual movement away from the restrictive First Amendment interpretation symbolized by the *Dennis* decision. Although, as previously indicated, the Court did not resurrect the phrase "preferred position" and did not formally overrule *Dennis*, it narrowed the scope of the Smith Act and offered greater protection to advocacy of ideas, including the forcible overthrow of government. The Court raised evidentiary standards for Smith Act prosecutions and confined its "membership clause" to "active" as distinguished from "nominal" membership in an organization advocating forcible overthrow of the government (see, for example, *Yates v. United States* [1957], *Scales v. United States* [1961], *Noto v. United States* [1961], and *Communist Party v. Subversive Activities Control Board* [1961]).

Ad Hoc Balancing

In the aftermath of *Dennis,* the Court moved away from the clear and present danger test and relied instead on **ad hoc balancing** to determine the limits of First Amendment protection in the area of internal security. This weighing of "competing private and public interests," as Justice John M. Harlan (the younger) phrased it, emphasized the particular circumstances of each case (see *Barenblatt v. United States* [1959], reprinted in Chapter 2). Thus ad hoc balancing in practice amounted to a process of decision making, rather than a clear interpretive doctrine. However, it is doubtful that a standard such as clear and present danger is, on close analysis, any more definite.

The Imminent Lawless Action Standard

In the early twentieth century, many states had adopted statutes prohibiting **criminal syndicalism**, which was, in essence, the crime of advocating political change through violent means. As discussed earlier, in *Whitney v. California* (1927), the Supreme Court had upheld one such law, but by the 1960s the Warren Court was ready to revisit the issue. Thus, in *Brandenburg v. Ohio* (1969), the Court invalidated a criminal syndicalism statute and explicitly overruled *Whitney v. California*. In reversing the conviction of a local Ku Klux Klan leader who had conducted a televised rally near Cincinnati, the Court held that "the constitutional guarantees of free speech and free press do not permit a State to forbid or proscribe advocacy of the use of force or of law violation except where such advocacy is directed to inciting or producing **imminent lawless action** and is likely to incite or produce such action."

The *Brandenburg* standard, with emphasis on imminent lawless action, reaffirmed and refined the clear and present danger test as articulated by Justice Holmes. The Burger Court firmly adhered to this standard in the 1970s and 1980s, as seen in *Hess v. Indiana* (1973), *Communist Party of Indiana v. Whitcomb* (1974), and *National Association for the Advancement of Colored People v. Claiborne Hardware Company* (1982). The Rehnquist Court has not extensively discussed the imminent lawless action standard, but has not given any indication of moving away from it. To the contrary, the Court has indicated a clear willingness to protect political dissent (see, for example, *Texas v. Johnson* [1989], reprinted in this chapter).

In the aftermath of the government's response to the terrorist attacks of September 11, 2001, a number of observers expressed concern about the changing mood of the country regarding political dissent. Will the courts respond to this change in national mood by relaxing First Amendment protections? Will the imminent lawless action standard survive the war on terrorism?

TO SUMMARIZE:

- In *Schenck v. United States* (1919), the Supreme Court, speaking through Justice Holmes, first articulated the famous clear and present danger doctrine. Under this doctrine government may punish expression if it creates a clear and present danger of bringing about conditions that government has authority to prevent. Although the doctrine was first used as a rationale for upholding restrictions on radical political expression, in later years it came to be used as basis for protecting dissent.
- In the decades following the *Schenck* ruling the Court occasionally opted for more restrictive approaches to the First Amendment, including the bad tendency, clear and probable danger, and ad hoc balancing tests. In *Brandenburg v. Ohio* (1969), however, the Court reaffirmed the essential concept of the clear and present danger doctrine but limited its application to expression in situations where there is "imminent lawless action."

FIGHTING WORDS, HATE SPEECH, AND PROFANITY

Does the First Amendment protect expression that is uncivil, vulgar, hateful, or profane? Prior to the 1960s, the Supreme Court took the view that offensive speech was beyond the pale of the First Amendment. In *Chaplinsky v. New Hampshire* (1942), the Court observed that

> [t]here are certain well defined and narrowly limited classes of speech, the prevention and punishment of which have never been thought to raise any constitutional problem.

These include the lewd and obscene, the profane, the libelous, and the insulting or "fighting" words—those which by their very utterance inflict injury or tend to incite an immediate breach of the peace. It has been well observed that such utterances are no essential part of any exposition of ideas, and are of such slight social value as a step to truth that any benefit that may be derived from them is clearly outweighed by the social interest in order and morality.

Fighting Words

The preceding excerpt from *Chaplinsky v. New Hampshire* provides the original statement of the fighting words doctrine. Under *Chaplinsky,* speech could be punished if it inflicted injury or created a danger that the person addressed would resort to violence. The Court probably underestimated the social value of what some would regard as fighting words, and no consideration was given to the question of whether police should be expected to exercise more restraint than the average person in responding to such epithets. For several decades, state courts routinely used the fighting words doctrine and the *Chaplinsky* precedent to justify prosecutions of intemperate street-corner orators for incitement to riot or breach of the peace.

In 1971 the Court significantly narrowed the fighting words exception. In *Cohen v. California* (1971), the Court refused to classify as fighting words the message "Fuck the Draft" emblazoned on the back of a jacket worn by Paul Robert Cohen in the corridors of the Los Angeles County Courthouse. Reversing Cohen's conviction for breach of the peace, the Court, through Justice Harlan, reasoned as follows:

> While the four-letter word displayed by Cohen in relation to the draft is not uncommonly employed in a personally provocative fashion, in this instance it was clearly not "directed to the person of the hearer." . . . No individual actually or likely to be present could reasonably have regarded the words on appellant's jacket as a direct personal insult. Nor do we have here an instance of the exercise of the State's police power to prevent a speaker from intentionally provoking a given group to hostile reaction.

Although the Court still gives formal recognition to the fighting words exception, it has not in recent years found any specific instances of expression to qualify as fighting words.

Hate Speech

During the 1980s, a number of communities adopted laws aimed at protecting African-Americans and other minority groups from so-called **hate crimes**, crimes motivated by racial or other group-related hatred. One such ordinance was enacted by the city of St. Paul, Minnesota:

> Whoever places on public or private property a symbol, object, appellation, characterization or graffiti, including, but not limited to, a burning cross or Nazi swastika, which one knows or has reasonable grounds to know arouses anger, alarm or resentment in others on the basis of race, color, creed, religion or gender commits disorderly conduct and shall be guilty of a misdemeanor.

In the widely publicized case of *R.A.V. v. St. Paul* (1992), the Supreme Court declared the ordinance unconstitutional. Justice Scalia summarized the rationale of the majority as follows:

> Assuming *arguendo,* that all of the expression reached by the ordinance is proscribable under the "fighting words" doctrine, we nonetheless conclude that the ordinance is

facially unconstitutional in that it prohibits otherwise permitted speech solely on the basis of the subjects the speech addresses.

The Court's decision in *R.A.V.* raised serious questions as to whether hate crimes legislation can be made to conform to constitutional standards. Nevertheless, states and communities have a number of legal means at their disposal for combating hate crimes. For example, an individual who burns a cross on someone else's front lawn may be charged with criminal trespass and possibly with malicious mischief or vandalism.

Another approach to deterring hate crimes is enhancing or extending criminal penalties based on characteristics of the crime or the victim. In *Wisconsin v. Mitchell* (1993), the U.S. Supreme Court upheld a Wisconsin statute that increases the severity of punishment if a crime victim is chosen on the basis of race or other designated characteristics. Stressing the fact that the statute was aimed at conduct rather than belief, the Court held that increasing punishment because the defendant targeted the victim on the basis of his race does not infringe the defendant's freedom of conscience protected by the First Amendment. Many commentators, however, thought that *Wisconsin v. Mitchell* could not be squared with the Court's earlier decision in *R.A.V.*

Profanity

Although in *Chaplinsky v. New Hampshire* (1942) the Supreme Court specifically enumerated profanity as being among those categories of speech so lacking in value as not to merit First Amendment protection, this view no longer prevails. As we discussed earlier, in *Cohen v. California* the Supreme Court overturned the conviction of a man who entered a courthouse wearing a jacket emblazoned with the slogan "Fuck the Draft." Speaking for the Court, Justice Harlan opined that

> while the particular four-letter-word being litigated here is perhaps more distasteful than others of its genre, it is nevertheless often true that one man's vulgarity is another's lyric. Indeed, we think it is largely because government officials cannot make principled distinctions in this area that the Constitution leaves matters of taste and style so largely to the individual.

Despite the Supreme Court's decision in *Cohen v. California,* most states and many cities retain laws proscribing profanity. But these laws are seldom enforced and even more rarely challenged in court. One notable exception is the case of the "cussing canoeist" that made national news in 1998. When Timothy Boomer fell from his canoe into Michigan's Rifle River he unleashed a tirade of profanities in a very loud voice. He was convicted of violating a nineteenth century state law that prohibited the utterance of profanity in the presence of children. Boomer was fined $75 and ordered to perform four days of community service. With the assistance of the American Civil Liberties Union, Boomer appealed his conviction to the Michigan Court of Appeals. On April 1, 2002, the Michigan appellate court reversed Boomer's conviction and struck down the statute on which the conviction was based. Writing for the court, Judge William B. Murphy observed that the law, "as drafted, reaches constitutionally protected speech, and it operates to inhibit the exercise of First Amendment rights."

TO SUMMARIZE:

- In the early 1940s, the Court recognized that "fighting words," utterances that are inherently likely to produce a violent reaction, are outside the scope of First

Amendment protection. In recent times, the fighting words doctrine has been honored more in the breach than in the observance.

- A more recent problem is posed by "hate speech" directed at members of targeted groups such as women and minorities. Unless a particular instance of hate speech can be identified with fighting words, defamation, or imminent lawless action, it is likely to be accorded First Amendment protection. Of course, an instance of hate speech that involves criminal conduct such as trespass or assault may be subject to criminal prosecution.
- Although profanity was once recognized as falling outside the scope of First Amendment protection, this view has eroded to the point where profanity is now considered part of ordinary speech. Thus prosecutions for uttering profanity are very rare.

SYMBOLIC SPEECH AND EXPRESSIVE CONDUCT

As *Cohen v. California* and *R.A.V. v. St. Paul* make clear, the protection of the First Amendment is not limited to pure speech. The term **symbolic speech** is applied to a wide range of nonverbal communication that is subject to First Amendment protection. Of course, not every symbol is entitled to constitutional protection; it depends on the circumstances in which the symbol is displayed.

The Flag Salute Controversy

An early example of the modern Court's willingness to protect symbolic speech is provided by the flag salute cases of *Minersville School District v. Gobitis* (1940) and *West Virginia State Board of Education v. Barnette* (1943). (These cases, which also implicate freedom of religion, are discussed more fully in Chapter 9.) In the first of these cases, the Court upheld a local school board directive requiring public school students to salute the American flag as part of the daily class routine. Then, in one of the most dramatic turnabouts in its history, the Court overruled this precedent three years later in the second flag salute case. In *Barnette,* a six-member majority recognized the right of schoolchildren who were members of Jehovah's Witnesses to refrain from participation in the flag salute ritual. Writing for the Court, Justice Robert Jackson observed that "no official, high or petty, can prescribe what shall be orthodox in politics, nationalism, religion, or other matters of opinion or force citizens to confess by word or act their faith therein."

Symbolic Speech in the Vietnam Era

Protests against the Vietnam War produced a number of controversies over symbolic speech. For example, in *United States v. O'Brien* (1968), the Court rejected the First Amendment claim of a Vietnam War protester that publicly burning his draft card was a form of constitutionally protected symbolic speech. David Paul O'Brien, who had burned his Selective Service registration certificate on the steps of the South Boston Courthouse in the presence of a "sizable crowd," was convicted for violation of a federal law providing that an offense was committed by any person "who forges, alters, knowingly destroys, knowingly mutilates, or in any manner changes any such certificate." Chief Justice Earl Warren, writing for a seven-member majority, determined that Congress had ample constitutional authority to prohibit the destruction or mutilation of draft cards. The card, after all, belonged to the government, not to Mr. O'Brien.

A less defiant form of symbolic speech in opposition to the Vietnam War was afforded First Amendment protection in *Tinker v. Des Moines Independent Community*

School District (1969). High school students John Tinker and Christopher Eckhardt, along with Tinker's sister Mary Beth, wore black armbands to school to protest American involvement in the Vietnam War. Anticipating this protest, school officials had adopted a policy that students refusing to remove such armbands would be suspended until they agreed to return to school without them. The Tinkers and Eckhardt refused to remove their armbands when requested and were sent home under suspension. They then brought suit to recover nominal damages and to enjoin school officials from enforcing the regulation. The case eventually reached the Supreme Court, which rejected the lower court's view that the action of school officials was "reasonable" because it was based on fear that a disturbance would result from the wearing of armbands. Writing for the majority, Justice Abe Fortas concluded that the wearing of armbands in this instance "was divorced from actual or potential disruptive conduct" and as such was "closely akin to 'pure speech' which . . . is entitled to comprehensive protection under the First Amendment." For public school officials to justify prohibiting the "particular expression of opinion," Fortas asserted, they must be able to show that such action "was caused by something more than a mere desire to avoid the discomfort and unpleasantness that always accompany an unpopular viewpoint."

Flag Burning

During the same year in which it decided the *Tinker* case, the Court had an opportunity to address the question of whether burning the American flag is entitled to constitutional protection as symbolic speech (*Street v. New York* [1969]). The Court focused on the element of verbal expression also presented in this case, however, and effectively avoided the symbolic speech issue. After learning of the assassination attempt against civil rights leader James Meredith in Mississippi, Sidney Street burned his American flag on a Brooklyn street corner. The arresting officer testified that he heard Street say to a small crowd of onlookers: "We don't need no damn flag." Street was convicted of "malicious mischief" in violation of a New York State statute making it a misdemeanor to "publicly mutilate, deface, defile, or defy, trample upon or cast contempt upon, either by words or act [any flag of the United States]." Because a general verdict was rendered by the trial court, the Supreme Court, in an opinion by Justice Harlan, observed that Street might have been punished for his speech as well as for burning the flag. The Court concluded that under the circumstances, he could not be constitutionally punished for his words alone. Harlan emphasized that the Court was not ruling on the question of whether Street could be punished for flag burning, "even though the burning was an act of protest."

The Warren Court's decision left open the question of whether flag burning per se was a form of symbolic speech protected by the First Amendment. The Rehnquist Court, surprising many observers, answered that question in the affirmative in the highly publicized case of *Texas v. Johnson* (1989). After publicly burning the American flag outside the 1984 Republican National Convention in Dallas, Gregory Johnson was prosecuted under a Texas law prohibiting flag desecration. Johnson was convicted at trial, but his conviction was reversed by the Texas Court of Criminal Appeals, which held that Johnson's conduct was protected by the First Amendment. In an extremely controversial decision, the U.S. Supreme Court agreed, splitting 5 to 4. Perhaps most surprising to Court watchers was the fact that two Reagan appointees, Justices Antonin Scalia and Anthony Kennedy, joined the majority. On the other hand, Justice John Paul Stevens, generally considered a liberal on civil liberties issues, was among the dissenters.

Writing for the Court in *Johnson*, Justice William Brennan observed that "[t]he expressive, overtly political nature of [Johnson's] conduct was both intentional and overwhelmingly apparent." In Brennan's view,

Johnson was convicted for engaging in expressive conduct. The State's interest in preventing breaches of the peace does not support his conviction because Johnson's conduct did not threaten to disturb the peace. Nor does the State's interest in preserving the flag as a symbol of nationhood and national unity justify his criminal conviction for engaging in political expression.

Dissenting, Chief Justice William Rehnquist challenged the majority's conclusion that Johnson's act of flag burning was a form of political speech, saying that "flag burning is the equivalent of an inarticulate grunt or roar that . . . is most likely to be indulged in not to express any particular idea, but to antagonize others." Rehnquist stressed the "unique position" of the flag "as the symbol of our Nation, a uniqueness that justifies a governmental prohibition against flag burning." But for Justice Brennan and the majority, "[t]he way to preserve the flag's special role is not to punish those who feel differently."

In the wake of the *Johnson* decision, conservatives called for a constitutional amendment to place flag burning beyond the pale of First Amendment protection. In an attempt to address the issue by less drastic means, Congress passed the Federal Flag Protection Act of 1989, making flag burning a federal crime. In *United States v. Eichman* (1990), the Court struck down the Flag Protection Act as applied to flag burning as a means of political protest.

Are Nude Performances a Form of Symbolic Speech?

Every state has a prohibition against indecent exposure. Generally, these statutes are applied in situations where individuals expose themselves in public or private to unwilling viewers. But what if the exposure takes place by mutual consent, such as in a nightclub that features nude dancing? Although there is certainly no First Amendment protection for public nudity generally, nudity may acquire constitutional protection in certain contexts. As a part of a play or performance that is not legally obscene, nudity may be considered symbolic speech protected under the First Amendment. In *Doran v. Salem Inn* (1975), the Supreme Court said that "although the customary 'barroom' type of nude dancing may involve only the barest minimum of constitutional protection, . . . this form of entertainment might be entitled to First and Fourteenth Amendment protection under some circumstances."

The Court faced the nude dancing issue squarely in *Barnes v. Glen Theatre, Inc.* (1991). This case involved a constitutional challenge to an Indiana statute requiring that nightclub dancers wear pasties and G-strings. The Court rejected the challenge, splitting 5 to 4. Speaking for a plurality, Chief Justice Rehnquist recognized that nude dancing was "expressive conduct within the outer perimeters of the First Amendment" but held that the state's interest in fostering order and morality justified the minimal burden on free expression associated with requiring dancers to wear pasties and G-strings. Justice Scalia's opinion concurring in the judgment was even more conservative in refusing to recognize any First Amendment protection for such activities. Justice David Souter's concurrence was more narrowly drawn. Like Rehnquist, Souter recognized the applicability of the First Amendment but concluded that the state's interest in eliminating "harmful secondary effects, including the crime associated with adult entertainment," justified the limited restriction on freedom of expression.

The four dissenting justices in *Glen Theatre* (White, Marshall, Blackmun, and Stevens) found the nude dancing at issue in the case to be "communicative activity" squarely within the protection of the First Amendment, saying that "nudity is itself an expressive component of the dance, not merely incidental 'conduct.'" The dissenters quoted approvingly from the Court's previous decision in *Doran v. Salem Inn,* which observed that "while the entertainment afforded by a nude ballet at Lincoln Center to those who can pay the price may differ vastly in content (as viewed by judges) or in quality (as viewed by critics), it may not differ in substance from the dance viewed by the person who . . . wants some 'entertainment' with his beer or shot of rye."

In the wake of the Supreme Court's decision in *Glen Theatre*, states, cities, and counties around the country where nude dancing has been permitted began to consider laws to restrict this activity. In a 2000 decision, *Erie v. Pap's A.M.*, seven members of the Supreme Court voted to uphold an Erie, Pennsylvania, ordinance that effectively prohibited nude dancing. As in *Barnes v. Glen Theatre*, the Court was unable to produce a majority opinion. Writing for a four-member plurality, Justice O'Connor observed that "[t]he requirement that dancers wear pasties and G-strings is a minimal restriction . . . [and] . . . leaves ample capacity to convey the dancer's erotic message."

TO SUMMARIZE:

- Symbolic speech refers to nonverbal communication that is deemed entitled to First Amendment protection.
- The determination of whether a particular symbol is accorded constitutional protection depends on the circumstances surrounding its display.
- The Supreme Court has accorded First Amendment protection to the burning of the American flag as a form of nonviolent political protest.
- Although public nudity in general is not recognized as symbolic speech, nudity as a form of artistic expression may under some circumstances be granted this constitutionally protected status.

DEFAMATION

Defamation of character consists of injuring someone's reputation by making false public statements about that person. Defamation is not a crime, but a tort. The appropriate remedy is a civil suit for damages. Defamation may take two forms. The verbal form is called *slander;* the written form is known as *libel*. From a legal and constitutional perspective, this distinction matters little. As a practical matter, most of the litigation in this area has involved libel, usually alleged to have been committed by newspapers.

As the Court observed in *Chaplinsky v. New Hampshire* (1942), libelous publications have traditionally been outside the scope of First Amendment protection. However, since the mid-1960s, the Supreme Court has in effect made it easier for defendants in libel suits brought by "public persons" to avoid libel judgments. In so doing, the Court has substantially expanded First Amendment freedom in an area traditionally controlled by principles of tort law. This development reflects what Justice Brennan described as "a profound national commitment to the principle that debate on public issues should be uninhibited, robust, and wide-open" (*New York Times Company v. Sullivan* [1964]).

Actual Malice

Prior to the Supreme Court's decision in *New York Times v. Sullivan,* the primary defense in a libel action was proof that the published material was true. The *Sullivan* decision substituted a new rule that afforded far greater protection to published criticism of official conduct. As stated by Justice Brennan, this standard "prohibits a public official from recovering damages for a defamatory falsehood relating to his official conduct unless he proves that the statement was made with '**actual malice**'—

that is, with knowledge that it was false or with reckless disregard of whether it was false or not." As long as there is an "absence of malice" on the part of the press, public officials are barred from recovering damages for the publication of false statements about them.

The *Sullivan* case emerged out of the civil rights struggle of the 1960s. L. B. Sullivan, a city commissioner in Montgomery, Alabama, brought suit against the *New York Times* for its publication of a paid advertisement in which civil rights leaders chastised Montgomery officials for police responses to civil rights demonstrations. The *Sullivan* decision, which broadened protection of the press against libel actions, thus reflected the Warren Court's commitment to protecting free expression by minority groups facing a politically hostile environment.

Libel Suits Brought by "Public Persons"

Although *New York Times v. Sullivan* applied only to cases where public officials sued for libel, the principle was soon expanded to cover a broader category designated as **public figures** (see *Curtis Publishing Company v. Butts* [1967]). This category includes prominent (and not so prominent) public figures, as well as persons who thrust themselves into the glare of publicity. The theory underlying this doctrine is that public figures have sufficient access to the media to defend themselves against false charges and thus do not require the assistance of libel suits. In *Gertz v. Robert Welch, Inc.* (1974), the Supreme Court stated that "public officials and public figures usually enjoy significantly greater access to the channels of effective communication and hence have a more realistic opportunity to counteract false statements than private individuals normally enjoy." The Court went on to discuss the concept of a "public figure":

> In some instances an individual may achieve such pervasive fame or notoriety that he becomes a public figure for all purposes and in all contexts. More commonly, an individual voluntarily injects himself or is drawn into a particular public controversy and thereby becomes a public figure for a limited range of issues. In either case, such persons assume special prominence in the resolution of public questions.

The concept of "public person" has been difficult to apply, but the Supreme Court has made it clear that publicity does not necessarily make a private citizen a public figure for purposes of libel law. For example, in *Time, Inc. v. Firestone* (1976), the Court rejected an attempt by a defendant in a libel suit to characterize Dorothy Firestone, a wealthy Palm Beach socialite, as a public figure merely because she was involved in a highly publicized divorce case. Speaking for the Court, Justice William Rehnquist said that for a plaintiff in a libel suit to be considered a public figure, the alleged defamation must involve a public controversy, not merely a private dispute that has been publicized in the press. While Firestone's divorce may have generated widespread public interest, it did not involve questions of vital public concern. Moreover, Firestone had not sought public attention; it was thrust upon her by an inquiring press.

Reverend Jerry Falwell Takes on *Hustler* Magazine   In one of its more colorful recent cases, *Hustler Magazine v. Falwell* (1988), the Supreme Court reaffirmed the *Sullivan-Gertz* rules. In its November 1983 issue, *Hustler* ran a fictional advertisement titled "Jerry Falwell talks about his first time." The ad, which was a spoof on the popular ad campaign for Campari liqueur, portrayed Rev. Falwell as a hypocritical drunkard whose "first time" involved sex with his mother in an outhouse. At the bottom of the page, in fine print, was the disclaimer "Ad Parody—Not to be Taken Seriously." Nevertheless, Rev. Falwell took the ad very seriously, and brought a federal lawsuit alleging libel and intentional infliction of emotional distress. Given the outrageous nature of the parody, which no reasonable person could have believed to be true, the jury found for *Hustler* on the libel claim. But the jury did rule in Rev. Falwell's favor on the claim of infliction of emotional distress and awarded substantial monetary damages against *Hustler*. In a unanimous decision, the Supreme Court reversed the judgment, holding that Falwell, as a public figure, could not recover damages for infliction of emotional distress without showing that *Hustler* had published a false statement of fact with actual malice. Writing for the Court, Chief Justice Rehnquist observed that

> in the world of debate about public affairs, many things done with motives that are less than admirable are protected by the First Amendment. . . . Thus while such a bad motive may be deemed controlling for purposes of tort liability in other areas of the law, we think the First Amendment prohibits such a result in the area of public debate about public figures.

Invasions of Privacy

Closely related to libel is the concept of invasion of privacy. Many jurisdictions have laws permitting private individuals to sue the press for unwarranted invasions of their privacy. Following its decision in *New York Times Company v. Sullivan,* the Supreme Court began to restrict such lawsuits. The first major decision came in *Time, Inc. v. Hill* (1967). There, the Court set aside a judgment in an **invasion of privacy** suit brought against *Life* magazine. *Life* had published a story about a family that had been held hostage by escaped prisoners. Unfortunately, not all of the statements made in the magazine story were true. Under New York law, family members could sue regardless of whether the story constituted libel. In setting aside the verdict for the plaintiffs, the Supreme Court said that the First Amendment "preclude[s] the application of the New York statute to redress false reports of matters of public interest in the absence of proof that the defendant published the report with knowledge of its falsity or in reckless disregard of the truth."

In a similar vein, the Supreme Court has blocked efforts to restrict the press from reporting the identities of crime victims. In *Cox Broadcasting v. Cohn* (1975), the Court reversed a judgment for the plaintiff in a case in which a television station reported the name of a rape victim. The Court emphasized the fact that the name had been contained in the indictment and was thus a part of the public record. Similarly, in *The Florida Star v. B.J.F.* (1989), the Court overturned a verdict against a newspaper that reported the name of a rape victim. The newspaper had obtained the victim's name from a police report that had been released in violation of state law and the established policy of the police department. The *Cox Broadcasting* and *Florida Star* decisions reflect a commitment to the principle that the press has the right to report information that it lawfully obtains.

TO SUMMARIZE:

- The tort of libel is outside the scope of First Amendment protection. However, since the mid-1960s the Supreme Court has extended First Amendment safeguards to defendants in libel suits brought by "public persons," thus expanding freedom of expression in a field traditionally controlled by principles of tort law.
- Under the rule adopted in *New York Times v. Sullivan* (1964), a public official (a term later expanded to include all "public persons") cannot recover damages for a

"defamatory falsehood" relating to official conduct unless it is proved that the state-ment in question "was made with 'actual malice'—that is, with knowledge that it was false or with reckless disregard of whether it was false or not."

- In general the press is accorded freedom to publish any material lawfully obtained, even though publication may seriously invade the privacy of individuals.

THE INTRACTABLE OBSCENITY PROBLEM

In recent decades sexually explicit magazines, books, videotapes, and films have become increasingly available in the marketplace. To locate such materials, one does not need to go to an "adult" bookstore. Soft-core pornography like *Hustler* is readily available at most convenience stores and magazine stands. Many cable and satellite television companies also provide adult entertainment in varying degrees of explicit-ness. Even **hard-core pornography** is easily obtained in the back rooms of many local video rental stores. The commercial success of such ventures obviously indicates a degree of social acceptance, but many critics continue to regard pornography as an evil that should be curtailed if not eliminated altogether.

Of course, anyone accused of producing or selling obscene materials will argue that the First Amendment protects his or her right to engage in such activities. One of the most difficult tasks the Supreme Court has undertaken in recent decades is that of determining the degree to which the First Amendment protects pornography.

Prior to the Supreme Court's entry into this field in 1957, most American courts adhered to a legal definition of obscenity derived from the 1868 English case of *Regina v. Hicklin.* The *Hicklin* test was "whether the tendency of the matter charged as obscen-ity is to deprave and corrupt those whose minds are open to such immoral influences, and into whose hands a publication of this sort may fall." By the mid-twentieth century, this standard was widely regarded as unduly restrictive of artistic and literary expression. The principal objection to the *Hicklin* test was that it sought to measure obscenity with reference to its supposed impact on the most vulnerable members of society.

The Prurient Interest Test

In *Roth v. United States* (1957), the Supreme Court handed down new legal guidelines for obscenity. Writing for the majority, Justice Brennan expressed the view that obscenity is "utterly without redeeming social importance" and thus entitled to no First Amend-ment protection. Rejecting the essence of the *Hicklin* standard, he stated the new test as "whether to the average person, applying contemporary community standards, the dominant theme of the material taken as a whole appeals to a prurient interest."

Roth v. United States, a federal case, was consolidated with the state case of *Alberts v. California,* thus making the new test applicable to every level of government in the country. But in spite of its uniform applicability and apparent simplicity, the *Roth-Alberts* test drew the Court into an interpretive quagmire from which it has not yet emerged. Virtually every term contained in the new obscenity test proved elusive. The Court could never reach full agreement on what constitutes a **prurient interest.** The term **redeeming social importance** also failed to generate consensus. A majority of the Court, in the years immediately following *Roth,* could not even agree on whether "community" referred to the nation as a whole or to individual states or localities. Although most of the justices believed that hard-core pornography was not entitled to First Amendment protection, they were unable to define its meaning. Justice Pot-ter Stewart's well-known remark "I know it when I see it" (see *Jacobellis v. Ohio* [1964], concurring opinion) points up the difficulty of precise definition in this area.

The *Miller* Test

Partly because of the complexity of the problem and partly as a result of the refusal of Justices Hugo Black and William O. Douglas to recognize the legitimacy of *any* limitations on expression in the obscenity field, the Warren Court was unable to muster a clear majority in support of all aspects of the *Roth-Alberts* test during the 1960s. The Burger Court was also sharply divided but ultimately achieved a bare majority in restating the constitutional test of obscenity. Writing for the Court in *Miller v. California* (1973), Chief Justice Burger stated that "the basic guidelines for the trier of fact" in obscenity cases are as follows:

> (a) whether "the average person, applying contemporary community standards" would find that the work, taken as a whole, appeals to the prurient interest, . . . (b) whether the work depicts or describes, in a patently offensive way, sexual conduct specifically defined by the applicable state law, and (c) whether the work, taken as a whole, lacks serious literary, artistic, political, or scientific value.

The *Miller* test was somewhat more restrictive of free expression than was the original *Roth-Alberts* test as embellished and applied by the Warren Court. The Burger Court explicitly rejected the "utterly without redeeming social value" standard advanced by a minority of justices in the 1960s (see *Memoirs v. Massachusetts* [1966]). Nevertheless, the new guidelines were far from clear. Exactly what is **patently offensive** material? Precisely how does a prurient interest in sex differ from a normal, healthy interest? What constitutes serious literary, artistic, political, or scientific value? And, perhaps most importantly, whose standards are to prevail in making these determinations?

In *Miller,* the Court indicated that the applicable **community standards** under the new test were local or at most statewide standards. But when authorities in Albany, Georgia, purportedly applying "community standards," attempted to ban the movie *Carnal Knowledge,* the Court ruled that the test had been improperly applied. Only material showing "patently offensive hard core sexual conduct" could be proscribed under the new rules (*Jenkins v. Georgia* [1974]).

In 1987, a 5-to-4 majority of the Court modified the "contemporary community standards" yardstick. Writing for the majority in *Pope v. Illinois,* Justice White declared that "the proper inquiry is not whether an ordinary member of any given community would find serious literary, artistic, political and scientific value in allegedly obscene material, but whether a reasonable person would find such value in the material, taken as a whole." Whether this "reasonable person" alternative represents a liberalization of the obscenity test or fosters "intolerable orthodoxy," as Justice John Paul Stevens predicted in a dissenting opinion, it is clear that First Amendment issues in the field of obscenity are far from resolved.

Pornography on the Internet

As a practical matter, one must recognize that pornography has become much more widely available in recent years. This is due to several factors. Most fundamentally, society's attitudes in this area have become more permissive. Second, prosecutions in this area have become increasingly rare. In the absence of a public outcry, prosecutors tend to avoid this area in favor of more "ordinary" types of crime. Finally, one must recognize the effect of the Internet, which has made pornography easily accessible to people who might not wish to enter an adult bookstore or place an order from the back of an adult magazine. The World Wide Web has thousands of sites devoted to "adult entertainment," many of which feature extremely graphic, hard-core pornography. One of the principal concerns about pornography on the Internet is its availability to children.

In 1996, Congress passed the Communications Decency Act, which made it a crime to display "indecent" material on the Internet in a manner that might make it available to minors. In *Reno v. American Civil Liberties Union* (1997), the Court declared this statute unconstitutional on First Amendment grounds. Writing for the Court, Justice Stevens concluded that, with respect to cyberspace, "the interest in encouraging freedom of expression in a democratic society outweighs any theoretical but unproven benefit of censorship." The Court's opinion in *Reno* left open the possibility that a more narrowly tailored statute—that is, one limited to prohibiting *obscenity* as distinct from *indecency*—might pass constitutional muster.

Child Pornography

It is now well established that government may criminalize the production and distribution of material depicting children engaged in sexual activities, irrespective of whether the material meets the legal test of obscenity. In *New York v. Ferber* (1982), the Court held that a state has a compelling interest in protecting children from sexual abuse and found a close connection between such abuse and the use of children in the production of pornographic materials. But in 2002 the Court surprised some observers by limiting government's efforts to ban child pornography. In *Ashcroft v. Free Speech Coalition*, the Court struck down as "overbroad" a provision of federal law that banned virtual child pornography as well as that employing live subjects. Dividing 6 to 3, the Court, speaking through Justice Kennedy, held that the challenged provision of the Child Pornography Prevention Act of 1996 "covers materials beyond the categories recognized in *Ferber* and *Miller*, and the reasons the Government offers in support of limiting the freedom of speech have no justification in our precedents or in the law of the First Amendment."

TO SUMMARIZE:

- The Supreme Court has said that the First Amendment does not protect expression determined to be obscene. The Court has made it clear that obscenity refers only to hard-core pornography that meets a specific legal test.
- Under *Miller v. California* (1973), the definition of obscenity is (a) whether "the average person, applying contemporary community standards" would find that the work, taken as a whole, appeals to the prurient interest, . . . (b) whether the work depicts or describes, in a patently offensive way, sexual conduct specifically defined by the applicable state law, and (c) whether the work, taken as a whole, lacks serious literary, artistic, political, or scientific value.
- In striking down the Communications Decency Act of 1996, the Supreme Court refused to accept the government's argument that "indecent" material on the Internet is subject to regulations similar to those upheld for the broadcast media. Thus the Court recognized the Internet as a form of communication comparable to the printed page.
- It is now well established that government may criminalize the production and distribution of material depicting children engaged in sexual activities, regardless of whether the material meets the legal test of obscenity.

EXPRESSIVE ACTIVITIES IN THE PUBLIC FORUM

Although the Supreme Court has recognized legitimate community interests that may, under some conditions, justify limitations on speech and assembly, it has tended to favor the First Amendment right of groups to assemble and express themselves in the **public forum**, especially for the purpose of communicating a political message. Such expressive activities in the public forum are an essential part of the democratic process.

Civil Rights Demonstrations of the 1960s

Organized public protest against racial segregation in southern and border states was a critical component of the **Civil Rights movement** of the 1950s and 1960s. In many instances these protests resulted in arrests. Several of these cases reached the Supreme Court. In *Edwards v. South Carolina* (1963), for example, the Court reversed breach-of-the-peace convictions of 187 African-American college students who had participated in a peaceful civil rights demonstration on the grounds of the state capitol in Columbia, South Carolina. The Court held that in "arresting, convicting, and punishing" these students, South Carolina had infringed their "constitutionally protected rights of free speech, free assembly, and freedom to petition for redress of their grievances." In his opinion for the majority, Justice Potter Stewart observed that "the Fourteenth Amendment does not permit a state to make criminal the peaceful expression of unpopular views."

In a similar case, *Cox v. Louisiana* (1965), the Court reversed convictions for breach of the peace, obstructing "public passages," and picketing near a courthouse. In this case Rev. B. Elton Cox led 2,000 African-American college students in a peaceful demonstration protesting the jailing of twenty-three fellow students who had been picketing segregated lunch counters in Baton Rouge, Louisiana. When the students refused to comply with a police order to disperse, tear gas was used to break up the demonstration. In *Cox,* the Court held that the convictions for breach of the peace and for obstructing the sidewalk violated Cox's First Amendment freedoms of speech and assembly. The picketing conviction was reversed on due process grounds.

A similar factual pattern was presented in the 1966 case of *Adderley v. Florida,* but this time the Court affirmed the conviction of African-American students who were protesting local practices of racial segregation. Like the situation in *Cox,* the demonstrators were also denouncing the arrests of other students, in this instance students from Florida A & M University who had attempted to integrate movie theaters in Tallahassee. During their demonstration, Harriet Louise Adderley and other students had allegedly blocked a jail driveway not normally used by the public. When they ignored requests to leave this area, they were arrested and charged with violating a state law that prohibited trespass "committed with a malicious and mischievous intent."

In justifying defendants' convictions, Justice Black, writing for a majority of five, found that nothing in the Constitution prevented Florida from "even-handed enforcement of its general trespass statute." Emphasizing the use of the driveway for vehicles providing service to the jail and playing down the symbolic significance of a civil rights protest at the place of incarceration, Black insisted: "The State, no less than a private owner of property, has power to preserve the property under its control for the use to which it is lawfully dedicated."

The *Adderley* decision may be viewed as marking the Warren Court's outer limit of tolerance for public protest. But *Adderley* is perhaps more accurately seen as a concession to public opinion. The decision was rendered at a time of great public concern over a rising tide of crime and violence in America's cities. Perhaps certain justices on the Court saw the *Adderley* case as a good opportunity to make a statement in favor of "law and order," a value that the Warren Court was seldom credited with stressing.

The Civil Rights and antiwar movements of the 1960s were characterized by frequent demonstrations, most of which stayed within constitutional parameters, others of which pressed the limits of constitutional tolerance for public protest. The relatively tranquil decades of the 1970s, 1980s, and 1990s produced fewer cases involving large-scale demonstrations.

Antiabortion Demonstrations

The issue that has consistently produced the most turmoil in the public forum in recent decades has been abortion. "Pro-choice" and "pro-life" activists have often clashed in the streets, screaming at one another and sometimes resorting to violence. Pro-life forces have been particularly aggressive in their public demonstrations, often congregating outside abortion clinics and sometimes harassing women seeking to enter these clinics. On occasion, operators of abortion clinics have gone to court to obtain injunctions limiting pro-lifers' protest activities.

In *Madsen v. Women's Health Center* (1994), the Court upheld a Florida court's injunction that prohibited antiabortion protesters from coming within a 36-foot buffer zone around the entrances to an abortion clinic. The state judge had found that protesters were impeding access to the clinic and harassing clients. In addition to creating a buffer zone that included a section of the public street and sidewalk, the judge banned "singing, chanting, whistling, shouting, yelling, use of bullhorns, auto horns, sound amplification equipment or other sounds or images observable to or within earshot of the patients inside the clinic" between the hours of 7:30 A.M. and noon on Mondays through Saturdays. The injunction was similar to many others that had been issued by state judges around the country to protect abortion clinics and their patrons from the activities of protesters. Judy Madsen, a member of Operation Rescue who had participated in the demonstrations, challenged the constitutionality of the injunction on First Amendment grounds. The Florida Supreme Court upheld the injunction, but in a separate case the Eleventh Circuit Court of Appeals in Atlanta struck it down. By a 6-to-3 vote, the Supreme Court sided with Florida's highest court.

Writing for the majority, Chief Justice Rehnquist concluded that the 36-foot buffer zone "burdens no more speech than necessary to accomplish the governmental interest at stake." Rehnquist noted the state's interests in ensuring public safety and order, promoting the free flow of traffic along streets and sidewalks, protecting a woman's freedom to seek abortion and other pregnancy-related services, and protecting the property rights of all citizens. The Court also upheld the noise restrictions contained in the injunction, noting that "the First Amendment does not demand that patients at a medical facility undertake Herculean efforts to escape the cacophony of political protests." But the Court invalidated other parts of the injunction, holding that the state judge had gone too far in limiting expression. In a stinging dissent, joined by Justices Thomas and Kennedy, Justice Scalia asserted that the entire injunction "departs so far from the established course of our jurisprudence that in any other context it would have been regarded as a candidate for summary reversal."

Six years later, in *Schenck v. Pro-Choice Network* (1997), the Court applied its *Madsen* rationale in upholding an injunction designed to keep demonstrators at least 15 feet from the doorways and driveways of clinics. Consistent with *Madsen,* the Court, however, struck down a provision of the injunction creating a "floating buffer zone" around clients and staff entering and exiting abortion clinics.

What Constitutes a Public Forum?

A key issue for the Court in the last several decades has been defining the concept of public forum. The Supreme Court has recognized that the term *public forum* includes not only streets and parks but any property that government "has opened for use by the public as a place for expressive activity" (*Perry Educational Association v. Perry Local Educators' Association* [1983]). In *United States v. Grace* (1983), the Court recognized that the sidewalks surrounding the Court's own building in Washington, D.C., qualified as a public forum and struck down the federal law forbidding use of that space for picketing or handing out leaflets.

Not every place open to the public constitutes a public forum for purposes of the First Amendment. For example, a privately owned shopping center is not considered a public forum. In *Lloyd Corporation v. Tanner* (1972), the Supreme Court observed that a privately owned shopping center does not "lose its private character merely because the public is generally invited to use it for designated purposes." On the other hand, the Court let stand a California Supreme Court ruling that recognized shopping centers as public forums under the California Constitution (see *PruneYard Shopping Center v. Robins* [1980]). The *PruneYard* decision points up the ability of state courts and state constitutions to grant civil liberties claims transcending those recognized under the federal constitution.

Is an Airport a Public Forum?   The Supreme Court has struggled with the problem of whether an airport is a public forum for the purposes of soliciting, proselytizing, and distributing literature. In *Board of Airport Commissioners v. Jews for Jesus* (1987) and *Lee v. International Society for Krishna Consciousness* (1992), the Court struck down policies that restricted such activities in public airport terminals. Although it relied in both decisions on First Amendment considerations, the Court was unable to reach agreement, however, as to whether an airport is a public forum. Given the prevalence of expressive activities in airports, it is unlikely that the Court will be able to avoid this question forever.

Time, Place, and Manner Regulations

It is well established that reasonable **time, place, and manner regulations** can justify the restriction of First Amendment activities in the public forum. The general rule is that such regulations must be reasonable, narrowly drawn, and **content-neutral.** Applying this standard, the Supreme Court struck down, as unconstitutional on its face, a local ordinance that gave unlimited discretion to the chief of police in forbidding or permitting the use of sound amplification devices, such as loudspeakers on trucks (*Saia v. New York* [1948]). A year later, in *Kovacs v. Cooper,* the Court upheld a narrowly interpreted ordinance prohibiting vehicles on the public streets from operating amplifiers or other instruments emitting "loud and raucous noises."

The requirement of content neutrality is not absolute, but government cannot depart from it without meeting a heavy burden of justification. The Court is likely to invalidate a regulation of this kind unless the government can show that it is necessary to serve a compelling interest and is narrowly drawn to achieve that purpose. The Court applied this standard in declaring unconstitutional the previously noted restriction on picketing on the sidewalks surrounding the Supreme Court building (*United States v. Grace* [1983]).

In *Boos v. Barry* (1988), the Supreme Court struck down a District of Columbia regulation that prohibited the display of signs within 500 feet of a foreign embassy if the message displayed on the signs brought the embassy's government into "disrepute." At the same time, the Court sustained the regulation permitting police to disperse assemblies within 500 feet of embassies. The former regulation was a restriction on the content of a political message; the latter, if applied evenhandedly, was regarded as a legitimate time, place, and manner regulation.

The Special Problem of Zoning Regulations   Time, place, and manner restrictions often take the form of local **zoning** requirements that have the effect of limiting freedom of expression. In the continuing process of First Amendment line drawing, the Supreme Court has had occasion to look closely at a number of these restrictions. In *Heffron v. International Society for Krishna Consciousness* (1981), a majority of five justices upheld a Minnesota "zoning" restriction limiting solicitation at the state fair, as applied to an organization wishing to distribute and sell religious literature and request donations from fair patrons. The regulation, which applied to nonprofit, charitable, and commercial enterprises alike, confined solicitation activities to booths rented on a first-come, first-served basis. The International Society for Krishna Consciousness (ISKCON) maintained that this restriction violated the First and Fourteenth Amendments by interfering with one of its sacred rituals, *sankirtan,* which required the faithful to distribute and sell religious literature and to solicit contributions. Writing for the majority, Justice White left no doubt that he was unimpressed by this line of argument:

> None of our cases suggest that the inclusion of peripatetic solicitation as part of a church ritual entitles church members to solicitation rights in a public forum superior to those members of other religious groups who raise money but do not purport to ritualize the process.

In the majority's view, the regulation at issue was content-neutral and nondiscriminatory in application. Moreover, it served a significant governmental interest, that of maintaining crowd control on the congested state fairgrounds. Justice Brennan, speaking for the four dissenters, saw the First Amendment issue quite differently:

> As soon as a proselytizing member of ISKCON hands out a free copy of the Bhagavad-Gita to an interested listener, or a political candidate distributes his campaign brochure to a potential voter, he becomes subject to arrest and removal from the fairgrounds. This constitutes a significant restriction on First Amendment rights.

Five years later, the Court upheld a zoning ordinance passed by the city of Renton, Washington, prohibiting the location of "adult theaters" within 1,000 feet of residential, church, park, or school property (*Renton v. Playtime Theatres, Inc.* [1986]). Writing for a majority of seven, Justice Rehnquist found that the ordinance was "content-neutral," that it served a "substantial governmental interest," and that it permitted reasonable alternative "avenues of communication." He asserted that the ordinance was a "valid governmental response to the 'admittedly serious problems'
created by adult theaters." The city had not used its zoning power as a "pretext for suppressing expression" but had made areas available for adult theaters and their patrons while "preserving the quality of life in the community at large." Rehnquist concluded: "This, after all, is the essence of zoning."

Again Justice Brennan filed a dissenting opinion, this time supported only by Justice Marshall. Brennan flatly rejected the central premise of the majority opinion when he asserted that "the circumstances here strongly suggest that the ordinance was designed to suppress expression, even that constitutionally protected, and thus was not to be analyzed as a content-neutral time, place and manner restriction." From Justice Brennan's criticism of the Court's analysis in this case, it is clear that the initial characterization of a law, for First Amendment purposes, is all important. Regulations are not automatically classified as reasonable time, place, and manner restrictions simply because the legislative body enacting them uses that rationale. Ultimately, in matters touching freedom of expression, judges must determine whether a given law is to be viewed as primarily a content-neutral time, place, and manner restriction or as a deliberate attempt, under the guise of this rationale, to limit freedom of expression. The Court may apply neat verbal formulas and strive for analytical consistency, but ultimately the question comes down to one of judgment in which intuition and ideology are often decisive factors.

TO SUMMARIZE:

- Because expressive activities in the public forum are an essential part of the democratic process, the Supreme Court has accorded broad First Amendment protection to groups desiring to assemble and express themselves in the public forum.
- Since the 1930s the Supreme Court has had numerous opportunities to interpret the First Amendment in the context of political and social protests. Most notable among these are the civil rights demonstrations of the 1950s and 1960s and the public protests on both sides of the abortion issue since the 1970s.
- The Supreme Court has recognized that the term *public forum* includes not only streets and parks but any property that government "has opened for use by the public as a place for expressive activity."
- Although the Court strongly resists governmental efforts to control the content of expression in the public forum, the justices have repeatedly upheld reasonable "time, place, and manner" regulations on such expression.

ELECTRONIC MEDIA AND THE FIRST AMENDMENT

The authors of the First Amendment could not have foreseen the invention of radio and television, let alone the prevalence of **electronic media** in contemporary society. Nevertheless, because television and radio are used to express ideas in the public forum, most observers would agree that these electronic media deserve First Amendment protection, at least to some extent. Yet since their inception, radio and television have been regulated extensively by the federal government.

To operate a television or radio station, one must obtain a license from the Federal Communications Commission (FCC); to broadcast without a license from the FCC is a federal crime (as operators of "pirate" radio stations have often discovered). In granting licenses, the FCC is authorized to regulate the station's frequency, wattage, and hours of transmission. To a lesser extent, it also has the power to regulate the content of broadcasts. For example, the FCC has developed regulations to keep the airwaves free of "obscene" or "indecent" programming. Moreover, station licenses come up for renewal every three years, and the FCC is invested with tremendous discretion to determine whether a given station has been operating "in the public interest."

Clearly, government regulations that apply to the electronic media would be unconstitutional if applied to books, newspapers, and magazines. The more permissive approach to government regulation of television and radio was originally predicated on the **scarcity theory**, which held that due to the limited number of available broadcast channels, the government must allocate this scarce resource in the public interest. The proliferation of cable TV and radio has undermined the controlling influence of the scarcity doctrine. Moreover, changing societal norms have led to a relaxation of earlier restrictions on sexual content and profanity on radio and TV. Nevertheless, the Supreme Court continues to recognize the FCC's authority to impose restrictions on broadcast media that would not be tolerated if they were applied to the print medium.

Restrictions of "Indecent" Programming on Television and Radio

In a broad regulation that would almost certainly be declared unconstitutional if applied to a magazine or newspaper, the FCC has prohibited radio and television stations, whether public or private, from broadcasting "indecent" or "obscene" programs. In April 1987, the FCC made national news when it threatened not to renew the licenses of certain radio stations in New York and California. These stations were engaged in so-called "shock radio," which featured talk programs that were intentionally tasteless and given to heavy doses of profanity and frequent sexual references. Although the FCC's threats made headlines, there was little talk of litigation to challenge the agency's regulations. The Supreme Court had previously upheld restrictions on indecent broadcasting in *Federal Communications Commission v. Pacifica Foundation* (1978). In that case, the Court reviewed FCC regulations as applied to a radio broadcast of a monologue by comedian George Carlin that examined "seven dirty words you can't say on the radio." Attorneys for the Pacifica Foundation argued that the monologue in question did not meet the legal test of obscenity and therefore could not be banned from the radio by the FCC. Writing for the Court, Justice Stevens disagreed, observing that "when the Commission finds that a pig has entered the parlor, the exercise of its regulatory power does not depend on proof that the pig is obscene."

Indecent Programming on Cable Television   The so-called "Helms amendment" to the Cable Television Consumer Protection and Competition Act of 1992 required cable systems that lease channels to commercial providers of "patently offensive" programming to scramble the signals of those channels and make them available only to subscribers who specifically request access. In *Denver Area Educational Telecommunications Consortium v. Federal Communications Commission* (1996), the Court struck down this provision. Writing for the Court, Justice Breyer observed that the provision was not carefully drafted, failed to consider less intrusive alternatives, and was not a "narrowly or reasonably tailored effort to protect children." In Breyer's view, the provision was "overly restrictive, 'sacrific[ing]' important First Amendment interests for too 'speculative a gain.'" In dissent, Justice Thomas (joined by Scalia and Rehnquist) argued that the requirement that indecent programming be scrambled was supported by the government's compelling interest in protecting children. In Thomas's view, the provision at issue was in keeping with "precedents [which] establish that government may support parental authority to direct the moral upbringing of their children."

Some commentators were disappointed that the Court failed in the *Denver Consortium* decision to articulate a coherent general theory of the First Amendment as it relates to new technology and media. Indeed, the various opinions produced by the justices manifested uncertainty, even confusion, as to the fundamental First Amendment issues involved. This is often the case when the law is confronted by rapid technological change. By 1997, however, the Court achieved greater clarity in addressing the question of whether government could regulate "indecency" on the Internet (see previous discussion of *Reno v. American Civil Liberties Union* [1997]). While recognizing the government's legitimate role in shielding children from inappropriate expression, the Court insisted that this objective cannot justify limiting adults' access to the Internet only to material that is appropriate for children.

Editorializing by Public Television and Radio Stations

Public radio and television, as distinguished from commercial stations and networks, have long been subject to more restrictive government regulations on editorializing. Based on a 1967 act of Congress, the FCC prohibited public radio and television stations from engaging in editorializing altogether. However, in *Federal Communications*

Commission v. League of Women Voters (1984), the Supreme Court declared this ban unconstitutional. Writing for a sharply divided Court, Justice Brennan concluded that the ban failed to meet a **least restrictive means test.** In Brennan's view, the ban "far exceeds what is necessary to protect against the risk of governmental interference or to prevent the public from assuming that editorials by public broadcasting stations represent the official view of government."

The Court's general expansion of freedom of expression since the mid-twentieth century is reflected not only in areas of political, social, and cultural dialogue, but in the Court's growing awareness that we live in an information age. The emergence and dynamic growth of electronic media, most recently the Internet, have stimulated the Court's development of a First Amendment jurisprudence that elevates communication to an almost hallowed status.

TO SUMMARIZE:

- Traditionally the Supreme Court has tolerated more extensive regulation of electronic media than of books, newspapers, and periodicals. This was originally justified by the scarcity theory, an idea that has since been undermined by the proliferation of cable TV and radio.
- The Court has approved the FCC's prohibition against "indecent" content on radio and TV broadcasts, but has resisted the application of such restrictions to cable TV and to the Internet.
- The trend of modern Court decisions is away from governmental control of the content of expression in the media. This is exemplified by the Court's invalidation of an FCC ban on editorializing by public television and radio stations.

COMMERCIAL SPEECH

Prior to the mid-1970s, the Supreme Court regarded the regulation of **commercial speech** (a broad category including but not limited to the advertising of products and services) as simply an aspect of economic regulation, entitled to no special First Amendment protection. In an important 1976 decision, however, the Court struck down Virginia's ban on the advertisement of prescription drug prices (*Virginia State Board of Pharmacy v. Virginia Citizens Consumer Council*). Writing for the Court, Justice Harry Blackmun stated that although reasonable time, place, and manner restrictions on commercial speech are legitimate and although the state is free to proscribe "false and misleading" advertisements, consumers have a strong First Amendment interest in the free flow of information about goods and services available in the marketplace.

A Test for Judging Regulations of Commercial Speech

In his opinion for the Court in *Central Hudson Gas and Electric Corporation v. Public Service Commission of New York* (1980), Justice Lewis Powell articulated the general rationale for First Amendment protection in this area:

> Commercial expression not only serves the economic interest of the speaker, but also assists consumers and furthers the societal interest in the fullest possible dissemination of information. In applying the First Amendment to this area, we have rejected the "highly paternalistic" view that government has complete power to suppress or regulate commercial speech.

In the same opinion, Justice Powell outlined a four-part test for evaluating regulations of commercial speech. To begin with, commercial speech must "concern lawful activity and not be misleading" if it is to be protected under the First Amendment. If this prerequisite is met, then three additional questions must be considered: (1) Is the "asserted governmental interest" in regulation substantial? (2) Does the regulation directly advance the asserted governmental interest? (3) Finally, is the regulation more extensive than is necessary to serve that purpose? This test is an attempt to balance the need for consumer protection on one hand with the value of a free marketplace of ideas on the other.

Conflicting Applications of the Test

In an important decision in 1986, a narrowly divided Supreme Court opted for consumer protection over the free marketplace of ideas. In *Posadas de Puerto Rico Associates v. Tourism Company,* the Court upheld a law prohibiting advertisements inviting residents of the territory of Puerto Rico to gamble legally in local casinos. In his majority opinion, Justice Rehnquist emphasized Puerto Rico's substantial interest in reducing the demand for casino gambling among its citizens and noted that the regulation at issue directly advanced this objective. He maintained that the legislature of Puerto Rico "surely could have prohibited casino gambling by the residents of Puerto Rico altogether." He concluded that this "greater power to completely ban casino gambling necessarily includes the lesser power to ban advertising of casino gambling."

In a strongly worded dissent, Justice Stevens contended that Puerto Rico had not merely banned the advertising of casino gambling, it had "blatantly" discriminated in punishing speech "depending on the publication, audience and words employed." In his view, the challenged prohibition established "a regime of prior restraint" and articulated a "hopelessly vague and unpredictable" standard.

Commercial Advertising of Alcoholic Beverages   Under the Twenty-first Amendment, states have broad authority to regulate the sale of alcoholic beverages. Does this authority extend to the ban of advertising in this area? In *44 Liquormart, Inc. v. Rhode Island* (1996), the Court struck down Rhode Island's "statutory prohibition against advertisements that provide the public with accurate information about retail prices of alcoholic beverages." Speaking for a unanimous Court, Justice Stevens concluded that "such an advertising ban is an abridgment of speech protected by the First Amendment and . . . is not shielded from constitutional scrutiny by the Twenty-first Amendment." In a concurring opinion, Justice Thomas wrote that "[a]ll attempts to dissuade legal choices by citizens by keeping them ignorant are impermissible."

Restrictions on Advertising of Tobacco Products   In 1965, Congress passed the Federal Cigarette Labeling and Advertising Act, which mandates warning labels on cigarette packages. In 1969, Congress adopted the Public Health Cigarette Smoking Act, which prohibits cigarette advertising on any medium of electronic communication under the jurisdiction of the Federal Communications Commission. In 1984, Congress enacted the Comprehensive Smoking Education Act, which, among other things, established a series of strong health warnings to appear in print and billboard advertisements of cigarettes. While these measures have been criticized by libertarians and various interest groups, they have come to be widely accepted—by the courts, by the society, and even by the tobacco industry. In 2001, however, the Supreme Court held that the state of Massachusetts had gone too far in its attempt to regulate advertising of tobacco products. In *Lorillard Tobacco Company v. Reilly,* the Court held that Massachusetts's regulation of cigarette advertising was preempted by federal law. It further held that regulations with respect to other tobacco products (including cigars and smokeless tobacco) violated the First Amendment. Writing for a majority of five, Justice O'Connor observed that "so long as the sale and use of tobacco is lawful for adults, the tobacco industry has a protected interest in communicating information about its products and adult customers have an interest in receiving that information."

Attorney Advertising and Solicitation   Until the late 1970s attorneys were prohibited by their state bar associations from advertising. These prohibitions reflected a desire by the elite elements of the bar to maintain lawyering as a noble and learned profession. But critics of the prohibition, including many newly licensed attorneys, viewed it as an unwarranted restriction on the dissemination of important information in the marketplace. In *Bates v. State Bar of Arizona* (1977), the Supreme Court sided with the critics, and extended First Amendment protection to attorney advertising. As a consequence, it is now common to see ads for legal services on TV, in newspapers, and on buses.

Despite the relaxation of the ban on attorney advertising, many states still maintain restrictions on solicitation by lawyers. For example, the Florida Bar, a state-sanctioned organization, prohibits lawyers from sending targeted direct mail solicitations to personal injury victims and their relatives for thirty days following an accident or disaster. The rule was challenged by a number of personal injury lawyers who argued that it violated the First Amendment. In *Florida Bar v. Went* for It, Inc. (1995), the Court divided 5 to 4 in upholding the challenged restriction. Justice O'Connor delivered the opinion of the Court, concluding that the Florida Bar "has substantial interest both in protecting injured Floridians from invasive conduct by lawyers and in preventing the erosion of confidence in the profession that such repeated invasions have engendered." In an unusually caustic dissent, Justice Kennedy attacked the majority opinion as "a serious departure, not only from our prior decisions involving attorney advertising, but also from the principles that govern the transmission of commercial speech." Kennedy accused the majority of unsettling precedents "at the expense of those victims most in need of legal assistance."

In spite of the somewhat restrictive (some would say paternalistic) ruling in *Florida Bar v. Went for It*, it is clear that a great many commercial messages today are entitled to First Amendment protection that was nonexistent two decades ago. The Supreme Court has even gone so far as to protect commercial interests against "compelled speech." Thus in *United States v. United Foods* (2001), Justice Kennedy, writing for a six-member majority, concluded that a federal assessment on mushroom growers used to fund mushroom advertising violated the First Amendment. The enlargement of freedom of expression in the commercial realm underscores the recognition that First Amendment freedoms are by no means limited to the traditional categories of political debate and social protest, important as these concerns are in a constitutional democracy.

Despite the Court's recognition of commercial speech, this type of expression is still not accorded the degree of First Amendment protection extended to political and social communication. Indeed, numerous restrictions on commercial speech still abound. For example, truth-in-lending laws require creditors to disclose accurate information regarding all the terms of loans. Various state laws prohibit false advertising. In spite of enhanced legal protections of "adult expression," the advertising of adult-oriented material is often restricted. Some scholars have urged the abandonment of any distinction between commercial speech and other forms of expression. Thus far, however, the U.S. Supreme Court has been unwilling to place commercial speech alongside political speech in the hierarchy of First Amendment values.

TO SUMMARIZE:

- Until the mid-1970s, the Supreme Court accorded little if any First Amendment protection to commercial speech. Since that time, however, the Court has not only recognized the First Amendment's application in this area, but has generally narrowed the gap between commercial speech and traditional areas of constitutionally protected expression.
- Under prevailing doctrine, commercial speech must "concern lawful activity and not be misleading" if it is to be protected under the First Amendment. If this prerequisite is met, then three additional questions must be considered: (1) Is the "asserted governmental interest" in regulation substantial? (2) Does the regulation directly advance the asserted governmental interest? (3) Finally, is the regulation more extensive than is necessary to serve that purpose?
- The Twenty-first Amendment, which gives states broad authority to regulate the sale of alcoholic beverages, has not been interpreted to override First Amendment protections of commercial speech as they relate to advertising in this area.
- Despite the Court's recognition of commercial speech, this type of expression is still not accorded the degree of First Amendment protection extended to political and social communication. Indeed, numerous restrictions on commercial speech still abound.

RIGHTS OF PUBLIC EMPLOYEES AND BENEFICIARIES

Government employment, government grants and contracts, even government programs such as Social Security are not constitutional rights but rather benefits that government may eliminate altogether or deny to particular individuals, as long as it provides due process of law. Can government make the enjoyment of such benefits contingent on the surrender of constitutional rights, in particular those rights guaranteed by the First Amendment?

Under the Federal Lobbying (Hatch) Act, federal civil servants are barred from actively participating in political campaigns. The Supreme Court upheld this prohibition in *United States v. Harris* (1954) and again in *United States Civil Service Commission v. National Association of Letter Carriers* (1973). Writing for the Court in the latter decision, Justice White asserted that it was essential that the political influence of federal government workers be limited in order to maintain the concept of a merit-based civil service.

The Court's recent jurisprudence shows greater solicitude for the First Amendment rights of public employees. For example, in *Branti v. Finkel* (1980) the Court said that the First Amendment bars the firing of public prosecutors merely for expressing their political sentiments. Similarly, in *Rankin v. McPherson* (1987), the Court held that a newly hired deputy constable could not be terminated merely for making an intemperate remark about the president. Upon learning of John Hinckley's unsuccessful attempt to assassinate President Reagan in 1981, Ardith McPherson was overheard saying, "If they go for him again, I hope they get him." McPherson, who was at the time a probationary employee, was summarily discharged for making this statement. Writing for the Supreme Court, Justice Thurgood Marshall remarked that "[v]igilance is necessary to ensure that public employers do not use authority over employees to silence discourse, not because it hampers public functions but simply because superiors disagree with the content of employees' speech."

In *United States v. National Treasury Employees Union* (1995), the Court struck down a provision of the Ethics in Government Act that barred federal civil service employees from accepting honoraria for speeches and articles. Although the ban was content-neutral, it applied to all honoraria, even those received for speeches and writings having nothing to do with civil servants' jobs. Writing for the Court, Justice Stevens quoted approvingly from *Pickering v. Board of Education* (1968): "Even though respondents work for the Government, they have not relinquished 'the First Amendment rights they would otherwise enjoy as citizens to comment on matters of public interest.'" The vote was 6 to 3, with Chief Justice Rehnquist and Justices Scalia and Thomas in dissent. Writing for the dissenters, Chief Justice Rehnquist complained that the majority's "application of the First Amendment understates the weight which should be accorded to the governmental justifications for the honoraria ban and overstates the amount of speech which actually will be deterred."

First Amendment Rights of Government Contractors

In *O'Hare Trucking Service v. Northlake* (1996), the Court split 7 to 2 (Scalia and Thomas dissenting) in ruling that independent contractors who do business with government agencies have the same free speech rights as government employees. Writing for the majority, Justice Kennedy stated that "government officials may indeed terminate at-will [contractual] relationships . . . without cause; but it does not follow that this discretion can be exercised to impose conditions on expressing, or not expressing, specific political views." Given the sheer volume of federal, state, and local contracts, and the fact that political favoritism often plays a role in determining which companies obtain contracts, the decision is apt to spawn considerable litigation.

Restricting Abortion Counseling

The decision in *Rust v. Sullivan* (1991) suggests a different perspective on issues in this area. In *Rust*, the Court sustained a federal regulation barring private birth control clinics that receive federal funds from counseling their clients regarding abortion. The Department of Health and Human Services imposed this restriction in 1987 at the direction of the Reagan administration. When the Court upheld the restriction with a 5-to-4 vote in June 1991, abortion rights activists were not the only ones to protest. Civil libertarians, members of the medical profession, and even some supporters of the Bush administration expressed opposition to what they perceived as an attack on free speech.

Critics of the *Rust* decision pointed out that if government could make the receipt of federal funds conditional upon the surrender of First Amendment rights, then all government benefits might be used as devices to limit constitutional rights. For example, people who live in public housing could be asked to surrender their Fourth Amendment rights or face eviction; public defenders could be limited in the defenses they provide to their indigent clients; students could have their choice of occupations dictated by conditions imposed on student loans. The most serious implication of the *Rust* ruling is that public employees, including teachers, might be prohibited from addressing controversial issues or face losing their jobs. The precedential value of *Rust* is open to question, however, given the close division among the justices and subsequent changes in Court personnel.

The NEA Funding Controversy

Since the late 1980s, controversy has surrounded National Endowment for the Arts (NEA) funding of provocative works of art that offend the religious and sexual sensibilities of many people. In 1990, Congress directed the NEA to consider "general standards of decency" in making its funding decisions. During the early stages of the 1992 presidential election campaign, President George Bush (the elder) intensified the dispute by firing NEA Chairman John Frohnmeyer. Is it legitimate for the federal government to censor works of art that it subsidizes through a granting agency like the NEA? In a speech to the National Press Club on March 23, 1992, Frohnmeyer argued that "when the government does support free expression, it must do so with a level playing field—no blacklists and no ideological preconceptions." On the other hand, conservative critics of the NEA argued that the taxpayers have no obligation to support works of art that many people find offensive. In *National Endowment for the Arts v. Finley* (1998), the Supreme Court upheld the decency requirement, construing the statute as more of an exhortation than a restriction on expression.

TO SUMMARIZE:

- Traditionally, public employees (especially in the federal civil service) have operated under a number of constraints on their political activities. Consistent with its expanding recognition of constitutionally protected expression, however, the Supreme Court in recent years has shown greater solicitude for the right of public employees to express themselves on political issues.
- The Court has said that government contractors enjoy the same rights of free expression as those accorded to public employees.
- There is continuing controversy over the extent to which government can condition the provision of benefits on the surrender of First Amendment rights.

FREEDOM OF ASSOCIATION

Although the Constitution makes no explicit reference to freedom of association, the Supreme Court has long recognized association as a "penumbral" or "implicit" constitutional right. Different provisions of the Constitution have been identified as sources for the protection of various types of association, and some associational freedoms are given more protections than others. Intimate associations—for example, those between husband and wife or parent and child—are extensively protected by the constitutional right of privacy (see Chapter 11). On the other hand, economic associations, like property rights, are afforded more limited protection under the Due Process Clauses of the Fifth and Fourteenth Amendments. The right to associate with others for purposes of worship or devotion is obviously implied by the Free Exercise of Religion Clause of the First Amendment (see Chapter 9). Similarly, the First Amendment freedoms of speech, assembly, and petition implicitly protect the right of individuals to associate for political purposes.

Political Association

Political association, like political expression, occupies a high place in the Supreme Court's scheme of constitutional values. But, like political expression, freedom of political association is far from absolute. Thus, in *Scales v. United States* (1961), the Supreme Court was willing to place its stamp of approval on Section 2 of the Smith Act, which impinged on freedom of association by making it a crime merely to belong to the Communist Party. The Court majority saved the constitutionality of Section 2 by interpreting it narrowly so as to apply only to "active" members of the Communist Party who had a "specific intent" to bring about the violent overthrow of the U.S. government. Four members of the Court (Douglas, Black, Warren, and Brennan) dissented, claiming that the majority had in effect legalized guilt by association.

The constitutional controversy over communism and government efforts to rid the country of the "Red menace" greatly diminished during the 1960s. On the other hand, the Civil Rights movement was at that time reaching its apogee. In the struggle for civil rights, the National Association for the Advancement of Colored People (NAACP) was one of the most significant political organizations. The NAACP had aroused tremendous hostility in the South and had occasionally been the target of state government attempts at intimidation and suppression. In *National Association for the Advancement of Colored People v. Alabama* (1958), the Supreme Court found that the state of Alabama had unconstitutionally infringed the NAACP's freedom of association by selectively enforcing a law requiring organizations based outside Alabama to register members' names and addresses with state authorities.

In ruling in favor of the NAACP, the Supreme Court had to distinguish a precedent that cut the other way. In 1928, it had upheld a New York law under which the Ku Klux Klan was forced to disclose its membership list. In that case, *Bryant v. Zimmerman*, the Court had justified the state policy by stressing the violent and unlawful tactics of the Klan. In *NAACP v. Alabama*, the Court stressed the fact that the NAACP used lawful means in seeking its political objectives.

Freedom of Association and the Problem of Discrimination

Today there is very little controversy about the rights of minorities to organize for purposes of litigation and political action. Many states use their legislative powers on behalf of minority groups and women seeking integration into the economic and cultural mainstream. Public accommodations laws have been used to force civic groups and social clubs to extend membership to women and minorities. Freedom of association has often been raised as a constitutional objection to such efforts.

In *Roberts v. United States Jaycees* (1984), a unanimous Supreme Court found that Minnesota's interest in eradicating sex discrimination was sufficiently compelling to justify a decision of its human rights commission requiring local chapters of the Jaycees to admit women. Writing for the Court, Justice Brennan recognized a political dimension to the Jaycees' activities but nevertheless held that the organization's freedom of political association must give way to the superior state interest in abolishing sex discrimination. In *Rotary International v. Rotary Club of Duarte* (1987), the Court extended its decision in the *Jaycees* case to encompass the Rotary Club as well. In 1988, the Court upheld a city ordinance requiring large all-male social clubs to admit women (*New York State Club Association v. City of New York*). The Court's decisions dealing with "private" clubs suggest that freedom of association in that context must yield to the societal interest in eradicating racial and sexual inequality.

Freedom of Association versus Gay Rights

In *Hurley v. Irish-American Gay, Lesbian, and Bisexual Group of Boston* (1995), the Court held that the state of Massachusetts could not prohibit a private organization from excluding a gay rights group from its annual St. Patrick's Day parade. The Massachusetts Supreme Court had ruled against the South Boston Allied War Veterans Council, which organized the parade and refused to permit gay rights groups to participate. The state court held that gay rights groups could not be excluded under Massachusetts's long-standing and broadly construed public accommodations statute. In a unanimous decision, the Supreme Court reversed, saying that the state could not compel the parade's organizers to promote a message of which they disapproved. Writing for the Court, Justice Souter insisted that the decision "rests not on any particular view about the Council's message but on the Nation's commitment to protect freedom of speech."

In *Boy Scouts of America v. Dale* (2000), the Court addressed a much more controversial question involving freedom of association and gay rights. James Dale was dismissed from his position as an assistant scoutmaster when the organization learned that Dale was gay. Dale successfully sued the Boy Scouts in the New Jersey courts, which ultimately ruled that the Boy Scouts had violated a state law prohibiting discriminating on the basis of sexual orientation by places of public accommodation. Dividing 5-4, the U.S. Supreme Court reversed, holding that the Boy Scouts' freedom of association trumped the state's interest in advancing the cause of gay rights. Critics of the decision, and there were many, argued that the Court was giving its sanction to bigotry. But many in the private, not-for-profit sector applauded the Court for protecting a private organization from government control. In an official statement, the Boy Scouts of America commented that the *Dale* decision "affirms our standing as a private association with the right to set its own standards for membership and leadership . . . and allows us to continue our mission of providing character-building experiences for young people, which has been our chartered purpose since our founding."

One of the factors that makes the *Dale* case so problematical is the close relationship that the Boy Scouts have with public schools, fire departments, and other governmental entities. Critics of the *Dale* decision argue that it is unrealistic to view the Scouts as a strictly private organization. Others argue that even if the Scouts are a private group, the compelling public interest in defeating discrimination should prevail over any First Amendment claim. It is fair to say that this issue is far from resolved.

TO SUMMARIZE:

- Although the Constitution does not explicitly provide for freedom of association, the Supreme Court has long recognized association as an implied First Amendment right.
- The Court has balanced the right of individuals to associate freely against legitimate government interests such as the protection of national security and the promotion of social equality. In general, freedom of association will be protected unless the government advances a very strong justification for abridging it.

CONCLUSION

The preceding discussion of major issues involving freedom of expression, assembly, and association, although necessarily selective, underscores several important First Amendment themes. The Supreme Court recognizes no absolutes in this area, but it does operate on the assumption that First Amendment freedoms are of fundamental importance in a democratic society. As a result, the Court generally imposes high standards in determining the constitutionality of legislation challenged on First Amendment grounds. In recent years, a majority of the justices have resisted easy generalizations and uncritical application of neat doctrinal tests in this particularly complex area of constitutional interpretation. In deciding difficult First Amendment cases, the Court attempts to accommodate legitimate government interests in maintaining peace, order, security, decency, and overall quality of life with an open society's vital interest in maintaining a free marketplace of ideas.

KEY TERMS

freedom of expression	libel	clear and probable danger test	patently offensive
freedom of speech	slander	ad hoc balancing	community standards
freedom of the press	pure speech	criminal syndicalism	public forum
freedom of assembly	picketing	imminent lawless action	Civil Rights movement
freedom of association	expressive conduct	hate crimes	time, place, and manner
chilling effect	First Amendment absolutism	symbolic speech	regulations
incorporation	fighting words	actual malice	content-neutral
preferred freedoms	defamation	public figures	zoning
censorship	prior restraint	invasion of privacy	electronic media
obscenity	clear and present danger test	hard-core pornography	scarcity theory
profanity	bad tendency test	prurient interest	least restrictive means test
seditious speech	free marketplace of ideas	redeeming social importance	commercial speech

FOR FURTHER READING

Berns, Walter. *The First Amendment and the Future of American Democracy*. New York: Basic Books, 1976.

Bollinger, Lee. *The Tolerant Society: Freedom of Speech and Extremist Speech in America*. New York: Oxford University Press, 1986.

Downs, D. A. *Nazis in Skokie: Freedom, Communication and the First Amendment*. South Bend, Ind.: Notre Dame University Press, 1985.

Fortas, Abe. *Concerning Dissent and Civil Disobedience*. New York: New American Library, 1968.

Irons, Peter. *May It Please the Court: The First Amendment*. New York: New Press, 1997.

Kalven, Harry, Jr. *A Worthy Tradition: Freedom of Speech in America*. New York: Harper and Row, 1988.

Konefsky, Samuel J. *The Legacy of Holmes and Brandeis: A Study in the Influence of Ideas*. New York: Macmillan, 1956.

Lowenthal, David. *No Liberty for License: The Forgotten Logic of the First Amendment*. Dallas: Spence Publishing, 1997.

Polenberg, Richard. *Fighting Faiths: The Abrams Case, the Supreme Court and Free Speech*. New York: Viking Press, 1987.

Shiffrin, Steven H. *Dissent, Injustice, and the Meanings of America*. Princeton, N.J.: Princeton University Press, 1999.

Walker, Sam. *Hate Speech: The History of an American Controversy*. Lincoln: University of Nebraska Press, 1994.

INTERNET RESOURCES

Name of Resource	Description	URL
The Freedom Forum	A nonpartisan foundation dedicated to freedoms of speech and press	http://www.freedomforum.org/
First Amendment Lawyers Association	An organization of lawyers dedicated to the defense of the First Amendment	http://www.fala.org/
The Thomas Jefferson Center for the Protection of Free Expression	A nonprofit organization located in Charlottesville, Virginia, devoted to the defense of free expression in all its forms	http://www.tjcenter.org/

Case

NEAR V. MINNESOTA

283 U.S. 697; 51 S.Ct. 625; 75 L.Ed. 1357 (1931)
Vote: 5–4

In this seminal case, the Court interprets the First Amendment as imposing a broad prohibition against prior restraints on publication.

Mr. Chief Justice Hughes delivered the opinion of the Court.

Chapter 285 of the Sessions Laws of Minnesota for the year 1925 provides for the abatement, as a public nuisance, of a "malicious, scandalous and defamatory newspaper, magazine or other periodical." . . .

Under this statute . . . the county attorney of Hennepin County brought this action to enjoin the publication of what was described as a "malicious, scandalous and defamatory newspaper, magazine and periodical," known as *The Saturday Press,* published by the defendants in the city of Minneapolis. The complaint alleged that the defendants, on September 24, 1927, and on eight subsequent dates in October and November, 1927, published and circulated editions of that periodical which were "largely devoted to malicious, scandalous and defamatory articles" concerning [various public officials and others]. . . .

The district court . . . found in general terms that the editions in question were "chiefly devoted to malicious, scandalous and defamatory articles," concerning the individuals named. The court further found that the defendants through these publications "did engage in the business of regularly and customarily producing, publishing and circulating a malicious, scandalous and defamatory newspaper," and that "the said publication . . . constitutes a public nuisance under the laws of the state." Judgment was thereupon entered adjudging that "the newspaper, magazine and periodical known as *The Saturday Press,* as a public nuisance, be and is hereby abated. . . ."

The defendant Near appealed from this judgment to the supreme court of the state, . . . asserting his right under the Federal Constitution, and the judgment was affirmed upon the authority of the former decision. . . .

From the judgment as thus affirmed, the defendant Near appeals to this Court.

This statute, for the suppression as a public nuisance of a newspaper or periodical, is unusual, if not unique, and raises questions of grave importance transcending the local interests involved in the particular action. It is no longer open to doubt that the liberty of the press and of speech is within the liberty safeguarded by the Due Process Clause of the Fourteenth Amendment from invasion by state action. It was found impossible to conclude that this essential personal liberty of the citizen was left unprotected by the general guaranty of fundamental rights of persons and property. . . . Liberty of speech and of the press is not an absolute right, and the state may punish its abuse. Liberty, in each of its phases, has its history and connotation and, in the present instance, the inquiry is as to the historic conception of the liberty of the press and whether the statute under review violates the essential attributes of that liberty. . . .

If we cut through mere details of procedure, the operation and effect of the statute in substance is that public authorities may bring the owner or publisher of a newspaper or periodical before a judge upon a charge of conducting a business of publishing scandalous and defamatory matter—in particular that the matter consists of charges against public officers of official dereliction—and unless the owner or publisher is able and disposed to bring competent evidence to satisfy the judge that the charges are true and are published with good motives and for justifiable ends, his newspaper or periodical is suppressed and further publication is made punishable as a contempt. This is of the essence of censorship.

The question is whether a statute authorizing such proceedings in restraint of publication is consistent with the conception of the liberty of the press as historically conceived and guaranteed. In determining the extent of the constitutional protection, it has been generally, if not universally, considered that it is the chief purpose of the guaranty to prevent previous restraints upon publication. The struggle in England, directed against the legislative power of the licenser, resulted in renunciation of the censorship of the press. The liberty deemed to be established was thus described by Blackstone:

> The liberty of the press is indeed essential to the nature of a free state; but this consists in laying no previous restraints upon publications, and not in freedom from censure for criminal matter when published. Every freeman has an undoubted right to lay what sentiments he pleases before the public; to forbid this, is to destroy the freedom of the press; but if he publishes what is improper, mischievous or illegal, he must take the consequences of his own temerity. . . .

The criticism upon Blackstone's statement has not been because immunity from previous restraint upon publication has not been regarded as deserving of special emphasis, but chiefly because that immunity cannot be deemed to exhaust the conception of the liberty guaranteed by state and Federal constitutions. The point of criticism has been "that the mere exemption from previous restraints cannot be all that is secured by the constitutional provisions;" and that "the liberty of the press might be rendered a mockery and a delusion, and the phrase itself a by-word, if, while every man was at liberty to publish what he pleased, the public authorities might nevertheless punish him for harmless publications." . . .

The objection has also been made that the principle as to immunity from previous restraint is stated too broadly, if every such restraint is deemed to be prohibited. That is undoubtedly true; the protection even as to previous restraint is not absolutely unlimited. But the limitation has been recognized only in exceptional cases. "When a nation is at war many things that might be said in time of peace are such a hindrance to its effort that their utterance will not be endured so long as men fight and that no court could regard them as protected by any constitutional right." . . . No one would question but that a government might prevent actual obstruction to its recruiting service or the publication of the sailing dates of transports or the number and location of troops. On similar grounds, the primary requirements of decency may be enforced against obscene publications. The security of the community life may be protected against incitements to acts of violence and the overthrow by force of orderly government.

The constitutional guaranty of free speech does not "protect a man from an injunction against uttering words that may have all the effect of force. . . ."

The exceptional nature of its limitations places in a strong light the general conception that liberty of the press, historically considered and taken up by the Federal Constitution, has meant, principally, although not exclusively, immunity from previous restraints or censorship. The conception of the liberty of the press in this country has broadened with the exigencies of the colonial period and with the efforts to secure freedom from oppressive administration. That liberty was especially cherished for the immunity it afforded from previous restraint of the publication of censure of public officers and charges of official misconduct. . . .

The fact that for approximately one hundred and fifty years there has been almost an entire absence of attempts to impose previous restraints upon publications relating to the malfeasance of public officers is significant of the deep-seated conviction that such restraints would violate constitutional rights. Public officers, whose character and conduct remain open to debate and free discussion in the press, find their remedies for false accusations in actions under libel laws providing for redress and punishment, and not in proceedings to restrain the publication of newspapers and periodicals. . . .

The importance of this immunity has not lessened. While reckless assaults upon public men, and efforts to bring obloquy upon those who are endeavoring faithfully to discharge official duties, exert a baleful influence and deserve the severest condemnation in public opinion, it cannot be said that this abuse is greater, and it is believed to be less, than that which characterized the period in which our institutions took shape. Meanwhile, the administration of government has become more complex, the opportunities for malfeasance and corruption have multiplied, crime has grown to most serious proportions, and the danger of its protection by unfaithful officials and of the impairment of the fundamental security of life and property by criminal alliances and official neglect, emphasizes the primary need of a vigilant and courageous press, especially in great cities. The fact that the liberty of the press may be abused by miscreant purveyors of scandal does not make any the less necessary the immunity of the press from previous restraint in dealing with official misconduct. Subsequent punishment for such abuses as may exist is the appropriate remedy, consistent with constitutional privilege. . . .

The statute in question cannot be justified by reason of the fact that the publisher is permitted to show, before injunction issues, that the matter published is true, and is published with good motives and for justifiable ends. If such a statute, authorizing suppression and injunction on such a basis, is constitutionally valid, it would be equally permissible for the legislature to provide that at any time the publisher of any newspaper could be brought before a court, or even an administrative officer (as the constitutional protection may not be regarded as resting on mere procedural details) and required to produce proof of the truth of his publication, or of what he intended to publish, and of his motives, or stand enjoined. If this can be done, the legislature may provide machinery for determining in the complete exercise of its discretion what are justifiable ends and restrain publication accordingly. And it would be but a step to a complete system of censorship. The recognition of authority to impose previous restraint upon publication in order to protect the community against the circulation of charges of misconduct, and especially of official misconduct, necessarily would carry with it the admission of the authority of the censor against which the constitutional barrier was erected. The preliminary freedom, by virtue of the very reason for its existence, does not depend, as this court has said, on proof of truth. . . .

Equally unavailing is the insistence that the statute is designed to prevent the circulation of scandal which tends to disturb the public peace and to provoke assaults and the commission of crime. Charges of reprehensible conduct, and in particular of official malfeasance, unquestionably create a public scandal, but the theory of the constitutional guaranty is that even a more serious public evil would be caused by authority to prevent publication.

For these reasons we hold the statute, so far as it authorized the proceedings in this action under clause (b) of section one, to be an infringement of the liberty of the press guaranteed by the Fourteenth Amendment. We should add that this decision rests upon the operation and effect of the statute, without regard to the question of the truth of the charges contained in the particular periodical. The fact that the public officers named in this case, and those associated with the charges of official dereliction, may be deemed to be impeccable, cannot affect the conclusion that the statute imposes an unconstitutional restraint upon publication.

Judgment reversed.

Mr. Justice Butler, dissenting:

The decision of the Court in this case declares Minnesota and every other state powerless to restrain by injunction the business of publishing and circulating among the people malicious, scandalous and defamatory periodicals that in due course of judicial procedure have been adjudged to be a public nuisance. It gives to freedom of the press a meaning and a scope not heretofore recognized and construes "liberty" in the Due Process Clause of the Fourteenth Amendment to put upon the states a Federal restriction that is without precedent. . . .

The Minnesota statute does not operate as a previous restraint on publication within the proper meaning of that phrase. It does not authorize administrative control in advance such as was formerly exercised by the licensers and censors but prescribes a remedy to be enforced by a suit in equity. In this case there was previous publication made in the course of the business of regularly producing malicious, scandalous and defamatory periodicals. The business and publications unquestionably constitute an abuse of the right of free press. The statute denounces the things done as a nuisance on the ground, as stated by the state supreme court, that they threaten morals, peace and good order. There is no question of the power of the state to denounce such transgressions. The restraint authorized is only in respect of continuing to do what has been duly adjudged to constitute a nuisance. . . . There is nothing in the statute purporting to prohibit publications that have not been adjudged to constitute a nuisance. It is fanciful to suggest similarity between the granting or enforcement of the decree authorized by this statute to prevent further publication of malicious, scandalous and defamatory articles and the previous restraint upon the press by licensers as referred to by Blackstone and described in the history of the times to which he alludes. . . .

It is well known, as found by the state supreme court, that existing libel laws are inadequate effectively to suppress evils resulting from the kind of business and publications that are shown in this case. The doctrine that measures such as the one before us are invalid because they operate as previous restraints to infringe freedom of press exposes the peace and good order of every community and the business and private affairs of every individual to the constant and protracted false and malicious assaults of any insolvent publisher who may have purpose and sufficient capacity to contrive and put into effect a scheme or program for oppression, blackmail or extortion.

The judgment should be affirmed.

Mr. Justice Van Devanter, Mr. Justice McReynolds, and *Mr. Justice Sutherland,* concur in this opinion.

Case

NEW YORK TIMES COMPANY V. UNITED STATES (THE PENTAGON PAPERS CASE)

403 U.S. 713; 91 S.Ct. 2140; 29 L.Ed. 2d 822 (1971)
Vote: 6–3

In June 1971 Daniel Ellsberg, a disaffected Pentagon employee, turned over to the New York Times *a 7,000–page top secret study titled "History of U.S. Decision-Making Process on Viet Nam Policy." Excerpts from the study, popularly known as the Pentagon papers, appeared in the* New York Times *beginning on June 13, 1971. After the* Times *refused a request to cease publishing excerpts from the study, the Justice Department filed a motion for an injunction in federal court. On Tuesday, June 16, 1971, Judge Harold Gurfein issued the first federal court injunction against a newspaper in this nation's history. Three days later, a federal district court in Washington, D.C., refused to issue a similar injunction against the* Washington Post. *Thereupon, Judge Gurfein lifted the injunction against the* New York Times. *On appeal to the circuit courts, the injunctions were quickly reinstated. The Supreme Court granted certiorari and heard the case immediately.*

PER CURIAM. We granted certiorari in these cases in which the United States seeks to enjoin the *New York Times* and the *Washington Post* from publishing the contents of a classified study entitled "History of U.S. Decision-Making Process on Viet Nam Policy."

"Any system of prior restraints of expression comes to this Court bearing a heavy presumption against its constitutional validity." . . . The Government "thus carries a heavy burden of showing justification for the imposition of such a restraint." . . . The District Court for the Southern District of New York in the *New York Times* case and the District Court for the District of Columbia and the Court of Appeals for the District of Columbia Circuit in the *Washington Post* case held that the Government had not met that burden. We agree.

The judgment of the Court of Appeals for the District of Columbia Circuit is therefore affirmed. The order of the Court of Appeals for the Second Circuit is reversed and the case is remanded with directions to enter a judgment affirming the judgment of the District Court for the Southern District of New York. The stays entered June 25, 1971, by the Court are vacated. The judgments shall issue forthwith.

So ordered.

Mr. Justice Black, with whom *Mr. Justice Douglas* joins, concurring.

. . . I believe that every moment's continuance of the injunctions against these newspapers amounts to a flagrant, indefensible, and continuing violation of the First Amendment. . . . In my view it is unfortunate that some of my Brethren are apparently willing to hold that the publication of news may sometimes be enjoined. Such a holding would make a shambles of the First Amendment. . . .

In seeking injunctions against these newspapers and in its presentation to the Court, the Executive Branch seems to have forgotten the essential purpose and history of the First Amendment. . . .

In the First Amendment the Founding Fathers gave the free press the protection it must have to fulfill its essential role in our democracy. The press was to serve the governed, not the governors. The Government's power to censor the press was abolished so that the press would remain forever free to censure the Government. The press was protected so that it could bare the secrets of government and inform the people. Only a free and unrestrained press can effectively expose deception in government. And paramount among the responsibilities of a free press is the duty to prevent any part of the government from deceiving the people and sending them off to distant lands to die of foreign fevers and foreign shot and shell. In my view, far from deserving condemnation for their courageous reporting, the *New York Times,* the *Washington Post,* and other newspapers should be commended for serving the purpose that the Founding Fathers saw so clearly. In revealing the workings of government that led to the Vietnam war, the newspapers nobly did precisely that which the Founders hoped and trusted they would do. . . .

. . . [W]e are asked to hold that despite the First Amendment's emphatic command, the Executive Branch, the Congress, and the Judiciary can make laws enjoining publication of current news and abridging freedom of the press in the name of "national security." The Government does not even attempt to rely on any act of Congress. Instead it makes the bold and dangerously far-reaching contention that the courts should take it upon themselves to "make" a law abridging freedom of the press in the name of equity, presidential power, and national security, even when the representatives of the people in Congress have adhered to the command of the First Amendment and refused to make such a law. . . . To find that the President has "inherent power" to halt the publication of news by resort to the courts would wipe out the First Amendment and destroy the fundamental liberty and security of the very people the Government hopes to make "secure." No one can read the history of the adoption of the First Amendment without being convinced beyond any doubt that it was injunctions like those sought here that Madison and his collaborators intended to outlaw in this Nation for all time.

The word "security" is a broad, vague generality whose contours should not be invoked to abrogate the fundamental law embodied in the First Amendment. The guarding of military and diplomatic secrets at the expense of informed representative government provides no real security for our Republic. The Framers of the First Amendment, fully aware of both the need to defend a new nation and the abuses of the English and colonial Governments, sought to give this new society strength and security by providing that freedom of speech, press, religion, and assembly should not be abridged. . . .

Mr. Justice Douglas, with whom *Mr. Justice Black* joins, concurring.

. . . The Government says that it has inherent powers to go into court and obtain an injunction to protect the national interest, which in this case is alleged to be national security. *Near v. Minnesota* [1931] . . . repudiated that expansive doctrine in no uncertain terms.

The dominant purpose of the First Amendment was to prohibit the widespread practice of governmental suppression of embarrassing information. It is common knowledge that the First Amendment was adopted against the widespread use of the common law of seditious libel to punish the dissemination of material that is embarrassing to the powers-that-be. . . . The present cases will, I think, go down in history as the most dramatic illustration of that principle. A debate of large proportions goes on in the Nation over our posture in Vietnam. That debate antedated the disclosure of the contents of the present documents. The latter are highly relevant to the debate in progress.

Secrecy in government is fundamentally antidemocratic, perpetuating bureaucratic errors. Open debate and discussion of public issues are vital to our national health. On public questions there should be "uninhibited, robust, and wide-open" debate. . . .

Mr. Justice Brennan, concurring.

. . . I write separately in these cases only to emphasize what should be apparent: that our judgments in the present cases may not be taken to indicate the propriety, in the future, of issuing temporary stays and restraining orders to block the publication of material sought to be suppressed by the Government. So far as I can determine, never before has the United States sought to enjoin a newspaper from publishing information in its possession. The relative novelty of the question presented, the necessary haste with which decisions were reached, the magnitude of the interests asserted, and the fact that all the parties have concentrated their arguments upon the question whether permanent restraints were proper may have justified at least some of the restraints heretofore imposed in these cases. Certainly it is difficult to fault the several courts below for seeking to assure that the issues here involved were preserved for ultimate review by this Court. But even if it be assumed that some of the interim restraints were proper in the two cases before us, that assumption has no bearing upon the propriety of similar judicial action in the future. To begin with, there has now been ample time for reflection and judgment; whatever values there may be in the preservation of novel questions for appellate review may not support any restraints in the future. More important, the First Amendment stands as an absolute bar to the imposition of judicial restraints in circumstances of the kind presented by these cases. . . .

The error that has pervaded these cases from the outset was the granting of any injunctive relief whatsoever, interim or otherwise. The entire thrust of the Government's claim throughout these cases has been that publication of the material sought to be enjoined "could," or "might," or "may" prejudice the national interest in various ways. But the First Amendment tolerates absolutely no prior judicial restraints of the press predicated upon surmise or conjecture that untoward consequences may result. . . .

Mr. Justice Stewart, with whom *Mr. Justice White* joins, concurring.

In the governmental structure created by our Constitution, the Executive is endowed with enormous power in the two related areas of national defense and international relations. This power, largely unchecked by the Legislative and Judicial branches, has been pressed to the very hilt since the advent of the nuclear missile age. For better or for worse, the simple fact is that a President of the United States possesses vastly greater constitutional independence in these two vital areas of power than does, say, a prime minister of a country with a parliamentary form of government.

In the absence of the governmental checks and balances present in other areas of our national life, the only effective restraint upon executive policy and power in the areas of national defense and international affairs may lie in an enlightened citizenry—in an informal and critical public opinion which alone can here protect the values of democratic government. For this reason, it is perhaps here that a press that is alert, aware, and free most vitally serves the basic purpose of the First Amendment. For without an informed and free press there cannot be an enlightened people.

Yet it is elementary that the successful conduct of international diplomacy and the maintenance of an effective national defense require both confidentiality and secrecy. Other nations can hardly deal with this Nation in an atmosphere of mutual trust unless they can be assured that their confidences will be kept. And within our own executive departments, the development of considered and intelligent international policies would be impossible if those charged with their formulation could not communicate with each other freely, frankly, and in confidence. In the area of basic national defense the frequent need for absolute secrecy is, of course, self-evident.

I think there can be but one answer to this dilemma, if dilemma it be. The responsibility must be where the power is. If the Constitution gives the Executive a large degree of unshared power in the conduct of foreign affairs and the maintenance of our national defense, then under the Constitution the Executive must have the largely unshared duty to determine and preserve the degree of internal security necessary to exercise that power successfully. It is an awesome responsibility, requiring judgment and wisdom of a high order. I should suppose that moral, political, and practical considerations would dictate that a very first principle of that wisdom would be an insistence upon avoiding secrecy for its own sake. For when everything is classified, then nothing is classified, and the system becomes one to be disregarded by the cynical or the careless, and to be manipulated by those intent on self-protection or self-promotion. I should suppose, in short, that the hallmark of a truly effective internal security system would be the maximum possible disclosure, recognizing that secrecy can best be preserved only when credibility is truly maintained. But be that as it may, it is clear to me that it is the constitutional duty of the Executive—as a matter of sovereign prerogative and not as a matter of law as the courts know law—through the promulgation and enforcement of executive regulations, to protect the confidentiality necessary to carry out its responsibilities in the fields of international relations and national defense.

This is not to say that Congress and the courts have no role to play. Undoubtedly Congress has the power to enact specific and appropriate criminal laws to protect government property and preserve government secrets. Congress has passed such laws, and several of them are of very colorable relevance to the apparent circumstances of these cases. And if a criminal prosecution is instituted, it will be the responsibility of the courts to decide the applicability of the criminal law under which the charge is brought. Moreover, if Congress should pass a specific law authorizing civil proceedings in this field, the courts would likewise have the duty to decide the constitutionality of such a law as well as its applicability to the facts proved.

But in the cases before us we are asked neither to construe specific regulations nor to apply specific laws. We are asked, instead, to perform a function that the Constitution gave to the Executive, not the Judiciary. We are asked, quite simply, to prevent the publication by two newspapers of material that the Executive Branch insists should not, in the national interest, be published. I am convinced that the Executive is correct with respect to some of the documents involved. But I cannot say that disclosure of any of them will surely result in direct, immediate, and irreparable damage to our Nation or its people. That being so, there can under the First Amendment be but one judicial resolution of the issues before us. I join the judgments of the Court.

Mr. Justice White, with whom *Mr. Justice Stewart* joins, concurring.

I concur in today's judgments, but only because of the concededly extraordinary protection against prior restraints enjoyed by the press under our constitutional system. I do not say that in no circumstances would the First Amendment permit an injunction against publishing information about government plans or operations. Nor, after examining the materials the Government characterizes as the most sensitive and destructive, can I deny that revelation of these documents will do substantial damage to public interests. Indeed, I am confident that their disclosure will have that result. But I nevertheless agree that the United States has not satisfied the very heavy burden that it must meet to warrant an injunction against publication in these cases, at least in the absence of express and appropriately limited congressional authorization for prior restraints in circumstances such as these. . . .

Mr. Justice Marshall, concurring.

. . . It would . . . be utterly inconsistent with the concept of separation of powers for this Court to use its power of contempt to prevent behavior that Congress has specifically declined to prohibit. There would be a similar damage to the basic concept of these coequal branches of Government if when the Executive Branch has adequate authority granted by Congress to protect "national security" it can choose instead to invoke the contempt power of a court to enjoin the threatened conduct. The Constitution provides that Congress shall make laws, the President execute laws, and courts interpret laws. It did not provide for government by injunction in which the courts and the Executive Branch can "make law" without regard to the action of Congress. It may be more convenient for the Executive Branch if it need only convince a judge to prohibit conduct rather than ask the Congress to pass a law, and it may be more convenient to enforce a contempt order than to seek a criminal conviction in a jury trial. Moreover, it may be considered politically wise to get a court to share the responsibility for arresting those who the Executive Branch has probable cause to believe are violating the law. But convenience and political considerations of the moment do not justify a basic departure from the principles of our system of government. . . .

Mr. Chief Justice Burger, dissenting.

. . . I suggest . . . these cases have been conducted in unseemly haste. . . . [T]he chronology of events demonstrat[es] the hectic pressures under which these cases have been processed and I need not restate them. The prompt setting of these cases reflects our universal abhorrence of prior restraint. But prompt judicial action does not mean unjudicial haste.

Here, moreover, the frenetic haste is due in large part to the manner in which the *Times* proceeded from the date it obtained the purloined documents. It seems reasonably clear now that the haste precluded reasonable and deliberate judicial treatment of these cases and was not warranted. The precipitate action of this Court aborting trials not yet completed is not the kind of judicial conduct that ought to attend the disposition of a great issue.

The newspapers make a derivative claim under the First Amendment; they denominate this right as the public "right to know"; by implication, the *Times* asserts a sole trusteeship of that right by virtue of its journalistic "scoop." The right is asserted as an absolute. Of course, the First Amendment right itself is not an absolute, as Justice Holmes so long ago pointed out in his aphorism concerning the right to shout "fire" in a crowded theater if there was no fire. There are other exceptions, some of which Chief Justice Hughes mentioned by way of example in *Near v. Minnesota*. There are no doubt other exceptions no one has had occasion to describe or discuss. Conceivably such exceptions may be lurking in these cases and would have been flushed had they been properly considered in the trial courts, free from unwarranted deadlines and frenetic pressures. An issue of this importance should be tried and heard in a judicial atmosphere conducive to thoughtful, reflective deliberation, especially when haste, in terms of hours, is unwarranted in light of the long period the *Times,* by its own choice, deferred publication.

It is not disputed that the *Times* has had unauthorized possession of the documents for three to four months, during which it has had its expert analysts studying them, presumably digesting them and preparing the material for publication. During all of this time, the *Times* presumably in its capacity as trustee of the public's "right to know," had held up publication for purposes it considered proper and thus public knowledge was delayed. No doubt this was for a good reason; the analysis of 7,000 pages of complex material drawn from a vastly greater volume of material would inevitably take time and the writing of good news stories takes time. But why should the United States Government, from whom this information was illegally acquired by someone, along with all the counsel, trial judges, and appellate judges be placed under needless pressure? After these months of deferral, the alleged "right to know" has somehow and suddenly become a right that must be vindicated instanter.

Would it have been unreasonable since the newspaper could anticipate the Government's objections to release of secret material, to give the Government an opportunity to review the entire collection and determine whether agreement could be reached on publication? Stolen or not, if security was not in fact jeopardized, much of the material could no doubt have been declassified, since it spans a period ending in 1968. With such an approach—one that great newspapers have in the past practiced and stated editorially to be the duty of an honorable press—the newspapers and Government might well have narrowed the area of disagreement as to what was and was not publishable, leaving the remainder to be resolved in orderly litigation, if necessary. To me it is hardly believable that a newspaper long regarded as a great institution in American life would fail to perform one of the basic and simple duties of every citizen with respect to the discovery or possession of stolen property or secret government documents. That duty, I had thought—perhaps naively—was to report forthwith, to responsible public officers. This duty rests on taxi drivers, Justices and the *New York Times.* The course followed by the *Times,* whether so calculated or not, removed any possibility of orderly litigation of the issues. If the action of the judges up to now has been correct, that result is sheer happenstance. . . .

Mr. Justice Harlan, with whom the *Chief Justice* and **Mr. Justice Blackmun** join, dissenting.

. . . Pending further hearings in each case conducted under the appropriate ground rules, I would continue the restraints on publication. I cannot believe that the doctrine prohibiting prior restraints reaches to the point of preventing courts from maintaining the status quo long enough to act responsibly in matters of such national importance as those involved here. . . .

Mr. Justice Blackmun, dissenting.

. . . The First Amendment, after all, is only one part of an entire Constitution. Article II of the great document vests in the Executive Branch primary power over the conduct of foreign affairs and places in that branch the responsibility for the Nation's safety. Each provision of the Constitution is important, and I cannot subscribe to a doctrine of unlimited absolutism for the First Amendment at the cost of downgrading other provisions. . . .

Case

SCHENCK V. UNITED STATES

249 U.S. 47; 39 S.Ct. 247; 63 L.Ed. 470 (1919)
Vote: 9–0

Charles T. Schenck, general secretary of the Socialist Party, was convicted of "causing and attempting to cause insubordination in the military and naval forces of the United States," in violation of the Espionage Act of 1917. The conviction stemmed from the Socialist Party's activities in printing and distributing leaflets attacking American participation in the First World War and urging young men to oppose the military draft.

Mr. Justice Holmes delivered the opinion of the Court:

This is an indictment in three counts. The first charges a conspiracy to violate the Espionage Act of June 15, 1917, . . . by causing and attempting to cause insubordination, etc., in the military and naval forces of the United States, and to obstruct the recruiting and enlistment service of the United States, when the United States was at war with the German Empire; to wit, that the defendant wilfully conspired to have printed and circulated to men who had been called and accepted for military service, a document set forth and alleged to be calculated to cause such insubordination and obstruction. The court alleges overt acts in pursuance of the conspiracy, ending in the distribution of the document set forth. The second count alleges a conspiracy to commit an offense against the United States; to wit, to use the mails for the transmission of matter declared to be non-mailable, . . . to wit, the above-mentioned document, with an averment of the same overt acts. The third count charges an unlawful use of the mails for the transmission of same matter and otherwise as above. The defendants were found guilty on all the counts. They set up the First Amendment to the Constitution, forbidding Congress to make any law abridging the freedom of speech or of the press. . . .

According to the testimony Schenck said he was general secretary of the Socialist party and had charge of the Socialist headquarters from which the documents were sent. He identified a book found there as the minutes of the executive committee of the party. The book showed a resolution of August 13, 1917, that 15,000 leaflets should be printed . . . to be mailed to men who had passed exemption boards, and for distribution. Schenck personally attended to the printing. On August 20 the general secretary's report said, "Obtained new leaflets from the printer and started work addressing envelopes," etc.; and there was a resolve that Comrade Schenck be allowed $125 for sending leaflets through the mail. He said that he had

about fifteen or sixteen thousand printed. There were files of the circular in question in the inner office. . . . Copies were proved to have been sent through the mails to drafted men. Without going into confirmatory details that were proved, no reasonable man could doubt that the defendant Schenck was largely instrumental in sending the circulars about. . . .

The document in question, upon its first printed side, recited the 1st section of the Thirteenth Amendment, said that the idea embodied in it was violated by the Conscription Act, and that a conscript is little better than a convict. In impassioned language it intimated that conscription was despotism in its worst form and a monstrous wrong against humanity, in the interest of Wall Street's chosen few. It said: "Do not submit to intimidation"; but in form at least confined itself to peaceful measures, such as a petition for the repeal of the act. The other and later printed side of the sheet was headed, "Assert Your Rights." It stated reasons for alleging that anyone violated the Constitution when he refused to recognize "your right to assert your opposition to the draft," and went on: "If you do not assert and support your rights, you are helping to deny or disparage rights which it is the solemn duty of all citizens and residents of the United States to retain." It described the arguments on the other side as coming from cunning politicians and a mercenary capitalist press, and even silent consent to the Conscription Law as helping to support an infamous conspiracy. It denied the power to send our citizens away to foreign shores to shoot up the people of other lands, and added that words could not express the condemnation such cold-blooded ruthlessness deserves, etc., etc., winding up, "You must do your share to maintain, support, and uphold the rights of the people of this country." Of course the document would not have been sent unless it had been intended to have some effect, and we do not see what effect it could be expected to have upon persons subject to the draft except to influence them to obstruct the carrying of it out. The defendants do not deny that the jury might find against them on this point.

But it is said, suppose that that was the tendency of this circular, it is protected by the First Amendment to the Constitution. Two of the strongest expressions are said to be quoted respectively from well-known public men. It well may be that the prohibition of laws abridging the freedom of speech is not confined to previous restraints, although to prevent them may have been the main purpose. . . . We admit that in many places and in ordinary times the defendants, in saying all that was said in the circular, would have been within their constitutional rights. But the character of every act depends upon the circumstances in which it is done. . . . The most stringent protection of free speech would not protect a man in falsely shouting fire in a theater, and causing a panic. It does not even protect a man from an injunction against uttering words that may have all the effect of force. . . . The question in every case is whether the words used are used in such circumstances and are of such a nature as to create a clear and present danger that they will bring about the substantive evils that Congress has a right to prevent. It is a question of proximity and degree. When a nation is at war many things that might be said in time of peace are such a hindrance to its effort that their utterance will not be endured so long as men fight, and that no court could regard them as protected by any constitutional right. It seems to be admitted that if an actual obstruction of the recruiting service were proved, liability for words that produced that effect might be enforced. The Statute of 1917 punishes conspiracies to obstruct as well as actual obstruction. If the act (speaking, or circulating a paper), its tendency and the intent with which it is done, are the same, we perceive no ground for saying that success alone warrants making the act a crime. . . .

Case

BRANDENBURG V. OHIO

395 U.S. 444; 89 S.Ct. 1827; 23 L.Ed. 2d 430 (1969)
Vote: 9–0

In Whitney v. California *(1927), the Court upheld a state criminal syndicalism statute. Here the Court reconsiders the constitutionality of such laws. The court also reconsiders the formulation of the clear and present danger test.*

PER CURIAM. The appellant, a leader of a Ku Klux Klan group, was convicted under the Ohio Criminal Syndicalism statute for "advocat[ing] . . . the duty, necessity, or propriety of crime, sabotage, violence, or unlawful methods of terrorism as a means of accomplishing industrial or political reform" and for "voluntarily assembl[ing] with any society, group, or assemblage of persons formed to teach or advocate the doctrines of criminal syndicalism." . . . He was fined $1,000 and sentenced to one to 10 years' imprisonment. The appellant challenged the constitutionality of the criminal syndicalism statute under the First and Fourteenth Amendments to the United States Constitution, but the intermediate appellate court of Ohio affirmed his conviction without opinion. The Supreme Court of Ohio dismissed his appeal. . . . It did not file an opinion or explain its conclusions. Appeal was taken to this Court, and we noted probable jurisdiction. . . . We reverse.

The record shows that a man, identified at trial as the appellant, telephoned an announcer-reporter on the staff of a Cincinnati television station and invited him to come to a Ku Klux Klan "rally" to be held at a farm in Hamilton County. With the cooperation of the organizers, the reporter and a cameraman attended the meeting and filmed the events. Portions of the films were later broadcast on the local station and on a national network.

The prosecution's case rested on the films and on testimony identifying the appellant as the person who communicated with the reporter and who spoke at the rally. The State also introduced into evidence several articles appearing in the film, including a pistol, a rifle, a shotgun, ammunition, a Bible, and a red hood worn by the speaker in the films.

One film showed 12 hooded figures, some of whom carried firearms. They were gathered around a large wooden cross, which they burned. No one was present other than the participants and the newsmen who made the film. Most of the words uttered during the scene were incomprehensible when the film was projected, but scattered phrases could be understood that were derogatory of Negroes and, in one instance, of Jews. Another scene on the same film showed the appellant, in Klan regalia, making a speech. The speech, [in part], was as follows:

. . . We're not a revengent organization, but if our President, our Congress, our Supreme Court, continues to suppress the white, Caucasian race, it's possible that there might have to be some revengeance taken.

The second film showed six hooded figures, one of whom, later identified as the appellant, repeated a speech very similar to that recorded on the first film. The reference to the possibility of "revengeance" was omitted, and one sentence was added: "Personally, I believe the nigger should be returned to Africa, the Jew returned to Israel." Though some of the figures in the films carried weapons, the speaker did not.

The Ohio Criminal Syndicalism Statute was enacted in 1919. From 1917 to 1920, identical or quite similar laws were adopted by 20 States and two territories. . . . In 1927, this Court sustained the constitutionality of California's Criminal Syndicalism Act, the text of which is quite similar to that of the laws of Ohio. . . . The Court upheld that statute on the ground that, without more, "advocating" violent means to effect political and economic change involves such danger to the security of the State that the State may outlaw it.... But [this view] has been thoroughly discredited by later decisions.... These later decisions have fashioned the principle that the constitutional guarantees of free speech and free press do not permit a State to forbid or proscribe advocacy of the use of force or of law violation except where such advocacy is directed to inciting or producing imminent lawless action and is likely to incite or produce such action. As we said in *Noto v. United States,* ... "the mere abstract teaching . . . of the moral propriety or even moral necessity for a resort to force and violence, is not the same as preparing a group for violent action and steeling it to such action." ... A statute which fails to draw this distinction impermissibly intrudes upon the freedoms guaranteed by the First and Fourteenth Amendments. It sweeps within its condemnation speech which our Constitution has immunized from governmental control....

Measured by this test, Ohio's Criminal Syndicalism Act cannot be sustained. The Act punishes persons who "advocate or teach the duty, necessity, or propriety" of violence "as a means of accomplishing industrial or political reform"; or who publish or circulate or display any book or paper containing such advocacy; or who "justify" the commission of violent acts "with intent to exemplify, spread or advocate the propriety of the doctrines of criminal syndicalism"; or who "voluntarily assemble" with a group formed "to teach or advocate the doctrines of criminal syndicalism." ...

. . . [W]e are here confronted with a statute which, by its own words and as applied, purports to punish mere advocacy and to forbid, on pain of criminal punishment, assembly with others merely to advocate the described type of action. Such a statute falls within the condemnation of the First and Fourteenth Amendments. The contrary teaching of *Whitney v. California* . . . cannot be supported and that decision is therefore overruled. . . .

Mr. Justice Black, concurring. . . .

Mr. Justice Douglas, concurring.

. . . I see no place in the regime of the First Amendment for any "clear and present danger" test, whether strict and tight as some would make it, or freewheeling. . . .

The line between what is permissible and not subject to control and what may be made impermissible and subject to regulation is the line between ideas and overt acts.

The example usually given by those who would punish speech is the case of one who falsely shouts fire in a crowded theatre.

This is, however, a classic case where speech is brigaded with action. . . . They are indeed inseparable and a prosecution can be launched for the overt acts actually caused. Apart from rare instances of that kind, speech is, I think, immune from prosecution. Certainly there is no constitutional line between advocacy of abstract ideas . . . and advocacy of political action. . . . The quality of advocacy turns on the depth of the conviction; and government has no power to invade that sanctuary of belief and conscience.

Case

COHEN V. CALIFORNIA

403 U.S. 15; 91 S.Ct. 1780; 29 L.Ed. 2d 284 (1971)
Vote: 5–4

Paul Robert Cohen was convicted in Los Angeles Municipal Court of "maliciously and willfully disturb[ing] the peace" by "offensive conduct" and was sentenced to thirty days in jail. The constitutional question is whether Cohen's conduct constitutes speech as protected by the First Amendment.

Mr. Justice Harlan delivered the opinion of the Court.

. . . On April 26, 1968, the defendant was observed in the Los Angeles County Courthouse in the corridor outside the division 20 of the municipal court wearing a jacket bearing the words "Fuck the Draft" which were plainly visible. There were women and children present in the corridor. The defendant was arrested. The defendant testified that he wore the jacket knowing that the words were on the jacket as a means of informing the public of the depth of his feelings against the Vietnam War and the draft.

The defendant did not engage in, nor threaten to engage in, nor did anyone as the result of his conduct in fact commit or threaten to commit any act of violence. The defendant did not make any loud or unusual noise, nor was there any evidence that he uttered any sound prior to his arrest. . . .

In affirming the conviction the Court of Appeal held that "offensive conduct" means "behavior which has a tendency to provoke others to acts of violence or to in turn disturb the peace," and that the State had proved this element because, on the facts of this case, "[i]t was certainly reasonably foreseeable that such conduct might cause others to rise up to commit a violent act against the person of the defendant or attempt to forcibly remove his jacket." . . .

In order to lay hands on the precise issue which this case involves, it is useful first to canvass various matters which this record does not present.

The conviction quite clearly rests upon the asserted offensiveness of the words Cohen used to convey his message to the public. The only "conduct" which the State sought to punish is the fact of communication. Thus, we deal here with a conviction resting solely upon "speech," . . . not upon any separately identifiable conduct which allegedly was intended by Cohen to be perceived by others as expressive of particular views but which, on its face, does not necessarily convey any message and hence arguably could be regulated without effectively repressing Cohen's ability to express himself. . . . Further, the State certainly lacks power to punish Cohen for the underlying content of the message the inscription conveyed. At least so long as there is no showing of an intent to incite disobedience to or disruption of the draft, Cohen could not, consistently with the First and Fourteenth Amendments, be punished for asserting the evident position on the inutility or immorality of the draft his jacket reflected. . . .

Appellant's conviction, then, rests squarely upon his exercise of the "freedom of speech" protected from arbitrary governmental interference by the Constitution and can be justified, if at all, only as a valid regulation of the manner in which he exercised that freedom, not as a permissible prohibition on the substantive message it conveys. This does not end the inquiry, of course, for the First and Fourteenth Amendments have never been thought to give absolute protection to every individual to speak whenever or wherever he pleases, or to use any form of address in any circumstances that he chooses. In this vein, too, however, we think it important to note that several issues typically associated with such problems are not presented here. . . .

In the first place, Cohen was tried under a statute applicable throughout the entire State. Any attempt to support this conviction on the ground that the statute seeks to preserve an appropriately decorous atmosphere in the courthouse where Cohen was arrested must fall in the absence of any language in the statute that would have put appellant on notice that certain kinds of otherwise permissible speech or conduct would nevertheless, under California law, not be tolerated in certain places. . . .

In the second place, as it comes to us, this case cannot be said to fall within those relatively few categories of instances where prior decisions have established the power of government to deal more comprehensively with certain forms of individual expression simply upon

a showing that such a form was employed. This is not, for example, an obscenity case. Whatever else may be necessary to give rise to the States' broader power to prohibit obscene expression, such expression must be, in some significant way, erotic. . . . It cannot plausibly be maintained that this vulgar allusion to the Selective Service System would conjure up such psychic stimulation in anyone likely to be confronted with Cohen's crudely defaced jacket.

This Court has also held that the States are free to ban the simple use, without a demonstration of additional justifying circumstances, of so-called "fighting words," those personally abusive epithets which, when addressed to the ordinary citizen, are, as a matter of common knowledge, inherently likely to provoke violent reaction. . . . While the four-letter word displayed by Cohen in relation to the draft is not uncommonly employed in a personally provocative fashion, in this instance it was clearly not "directed to the person of the hearer." . . . No individual actually or likely to be present could reasonably have regarded the words on appellant's jacket as a direct personal insult. Nor do we have here an instance of the exercise of the State's police power to prevent a speaker from intentionally provoking a given group to hostile reaction. . . . There is, as noted above, no showing that anyone who saw Cohen was in fact violently aroused or that appellant intended such a result.

Finally, in arguments before this Court much has been made of the claim that Cohen's distasteful mode of expression was thrust upon unwilling or unsuspecting viewers, and that the State might therefore legitimately act as it did in order to protect the sensitive from otherwise unavoidable exposure to appellant's crude form of protest. Of course, the mere presumed presence of unwitting listeners or viewers does not serve automatically to justify curtailing all speech capable of giving offense. . . . While this Court has recognized that government may properly act in many situations to prohibit intrusion into the privacy of the home of unwelcome views and ideas which cannot be totally banned from the public dialogue, . . . we have at the same time consistently stressed that "we are often 'captives' outside the sanctuary of the home and subject to objectionable speech." . . . The ability of government, consonant with the Constitution, to shut off discourse solely to protect others from hearing it is, in other words, dependent upon a showing that substantial privacy interests are being invaded in an essentially intolerable manner. Any broader view of this authority would effectively empower a majority to silence dissidents simply as a matter of personal predilections.

In this regard, persons confronted with Cohen's jacket were in a quite different posture than, say, those subjected to the raucous emissions of sound trucks blaring outside their residences. Those in the Los Angeles courthouse could effectively avoid further bombardment of their sensibilities simply by averting their eyes. And, while it may be that one has a more substantial claim to a recognizable privacy interest when walking through a courthouse corridor than, for example, strolling through Central Park, surely it is nothing like the interest in being free from unwanted expression in the confines of one's own home. Given the subtlety and complexity of the factors involved, if Cohen's "speech" was otherwise entitled to constitutional protection, we do not think the fact that some unwilling "listeners" in a public building may have been briefly exposed to it can serve to justify this breach of the peace conviction where, as here, there was no evidence that persons powerless to avoid appellant's conduct did in fact object to it, and where that portion of the statute upon which Cohen's conviction rests evinces no concern, either on its face or as construed by the California courts, with the special plight of the captive auditor, but, instead, indiscriminately sweeps within its prohibitions all "offensive conduct" that disturbs "any neighborhood or person." . . .

Against this background, the issue flushed by this case stands out in bold relief. It is whether California can excise, as "offensive conduct," one particular scurrilous epithet from the public discourse, either upon the theory of the court below that its use is inherently likely to cause violent reaction or upon a more general assertion that the States, acting as guardians of public morality, may properly remove this offensive word from the public vocabulary.

The rationale of the California court is plainly untenable. At most it reflects an "undifferentiated fear or apprehension of disturbance [which] is not enough to overcome the right to freedom of expression." . . . We have been shown no evidence that substantial numbers of citizens are standing ready to strike out physically at whoever may assault their sensibilities with execrations like that uttered by Cohen. There may be some persons about with such lawless and violent proclivities, but that is an insufficient base upon which to erect, consistently with constitutional values, a governmental power to force persons who wish to ventilate their dissident views into avoiding particular forms of expression. The argument amounts to little more than the self-defeating proposition that to avoid physical censorship of one who has not sought to provoke such a response by a hypothetical coterie of the violent and lawless, the State may more appropriately effectuate that censorship themselves. . . .

Admittedly, it is not so obvious that the First and Fourteenth Amendments must be taken to disable the States from punishing public utterance of this unseemly expletive in order to maintain what they regard as a suitable level of discourse within the body politic. We think, however, that examination and reflection will reveal the shortcomings of a contrary viewpoint.

. . . [W]e cannot overemphasize that, in our judgment, most situations where the State has a justifiable interest in regulating speech will fall within one or more of the various established exceptions, discussed above but not applicable here, to the usual rule that governmental bodies may not prescribe the form or content of individual expression. Equally important to our conclusion is the constitutional backdrop against which our decision must be made. The constitutional right of free expression is powerful medicine in a society as diverse and populous as ours. It is designed and intended to remove governmental restraints from the arena of public discussion, putting the decision as to what views shall be voiced largely into the hands of each of us, in the hope that use of such freedom will ultimately produce a more capable citizenry and more perfect polity and in the belief that no other approach would comport with the premise of individual dignity and choice upon which our political system rests. . . .

To many, the immediate consequence of this freedom may often appear to be only verbal tumult, discord, and even offensive utterance. These are, however, within established limits, in truth necessary side effects of the broader enduring values which the process of open debate permits us to achieve. That the air may at times seem filled with verbal cacophony is, in this sense, not a sign of weakness but of strength. We cannot lose sight of the fact that, in what otherwise might seem a trifling and annoying instance of individual distasteful abuse of a privilege, these fundamental societal values are truly implicated. That is why "[w]holly neutral futilities . . . come under the protection of free speech as fully as do Keats' poems or Donne's sermons," . . . and why "so long as the means are peaceful, the communication need not meet standards of acceptability." . . .

Against this perception of the constitutional policies involved, we discern certain more particularized considerations that peculiarly call for reversal of this conviction. First, the principle contended for by the State seems inherently boundless. How is one to distinguish this from any other offensive word? Surely the State has no right to cleanse public debate to the point where it is grammatically palatable to the most squeamish among us. Yet no readily ascertainable general principle exists for stopping short of that result were we to affirm the judgment below. For, while the particular four-letter word being litigated here is perhaps more distasteful than most others of its genre, it is nevertheless often true that one man's vulgarity is another's lyric. Indeed, we think it is largely because governmental officials cannot make principled distinctions in this area that the Constitution leaves matter of taste and style so largely to the individual.

Additionally, we cannot overlook the fact, because it is well illustrated by the episode involved here, that much linguistic expression serves a dual communicative function: it conveys not only ideas capable of relatively precise detached explication, but otherwise inexpressible emotions as well. In fact, words are often chosen as much for their emotive as their cognitive force. We cannot sanction the view that the Constitution, while solicitous of the cognitive content of individual speech, has little or no regard for that emotive function which, practically speaking, may often be the more important element of the overall message sought to be communicated. Indeed, as Mr. Justice Frankfurter has said, "[o]ne of the prerogatives of American citizenship is the right to criticize public men and measures—and that means not only informed and responsible criticism but the freedom to speak foolishly and without moderation." . . .

Finally, and in the same vein, we cannot indulge the facile assumption that one can forbid particular words without also running a substantial risk of suppressing ideas in the process. Indeed, governments might soon seize upon the censorship of particular words as a convenient guise for banning the expression of unpopular views. We have been able, as noted above, to discern little social benefit that might result from running the risk of opening the door to such grave results.

It is, in sum, our judgment that, absent a more particularized and compelling reason for its actions, the State may not, consistently with the First and Fourteenth Amendments, make the simple public display here involved of this single four-letter expletive a criminal offense. . . .

Mr. Justice Blackmun, with whom the *Chief Justice* and *Mr. Justice Black* join, dissenting.

. . . Cohen's absurd and immature antic, in my view, was mainly conduct and little speech. . . . The California Court of Appeal appears so to have described it, . . . and I cannot characterize it otherwise. Further, the case appears to me to be well within the sphere of *Chaplinsky v. New Hampshire,* . . . where Mr. Justice Murphy, a known champion of First Amendment freedoms, wrote for a unanimous bench. As a consequence, this Court's agonizing over First Amendment values seems misplaced and unnecessary. . . .

Mr. Justice White [dissenting]. . . .

Case

TEXAS V. JOHNSON

491 U.S. 397; 109 S.Ct. 2533; 105 L.Ed. 2d 342 (1989)
Vote: 5–4

After burning an American flag as part of a public protest, Gregory Lee Johnson was convicted of desecrating a flag in violation of Texas law. The Texas Court of Criminal Appeals reversed the conviction, holding that the statute under which Johnson was convicted was unconstitutional as applied to his particular conduct.

Justice Brennan delivered the opinion of the Court.

. . . We must first determine whether Johnson's burning of the flag constituted expressive conduct, permitting him to invoke the First Amendment in challenging his conviction. . . . If his conduct was expressive, we next decide whether the State's regulation is related to the suppression of free expression. . . . If the State's regulation is not related to expression, then the less stringent standard we announced in *United States v. O'Brien* [1968] for regulations of noncommunicative conduct controls. . . . If it is, then we are outside of *O'Brien's* test, and we must ask whether this interest justifies Johnson's conviction under a more demanding standard. . . . A third possibility is that the State's asserted interest is simply not implicated on these facts, and in that event the interest drops out of the picture. . . .

The First Amendment literally forbids the abridgment only of "speech," but we have long recognized that its protection does not end at the spoken or written word. While we have rejected "the view that an apparently limitless variety of conduct can be labeled 'speech' whenever the person engaging in the conduct intends thereby to express an idea," . . . we have acknowledged that conduct may be "sufficiently imbued with elements of communication to fall within the scope of the First and Fourteenth Amendments." . . .

In deciding whether particular conduct possesses sufficient communicative elements to bring the First Amendment into play, we have asked whether "[a]n intent to convey a particularized message was present, and [whether] the likelihood was great that the message was present, and [whether] the likelihood was great that the message would be understood by those who viewed it." Hence, we have recognized the expressive nature of students' wearing of black armbands to protest American military involvement in Vietnam, . . . of the wearing of American military uniforms in a dramatic presentation criticizing American involvement in Vietnam, . . . and of picketing about a wide variety of causes. . . .

Especially pertinent to this case are our decisions recognizing the communicative nature of conduct relating to flags. Attaching a peace sign to the flag, . . . saluting the flag, . . . and displaying a red flag, . . . we have held, all may find shelter under the First Amendment. . . . That we have had little difficulty identifying an expressive element in conduct relating to flags should not be surprising. The very purpose of a national flag is to serve as a symbol of our country; it is, one might say, "the one visible manifestation of two hundred years of nationhood." . . . Pregnant with expressive content, the flag as readily signifies this Nation as does the combination of letters found in "America."

We have not automatically concluded, however, that any action taken with respect to our flag is expressive. Instead, in characterizing such action for First Amendment purposes, we have considered the context in which it occurred.

The State of Texas conceded for purposes of its oral argument in this case that Johnson's conduct was expressive conduct. . . . Johnson burned an American flag as part—indeed, as the culmination—of a political demonstration that coincided with the convening of the Republican Party and its renomination of Ronald Reagan for President. The expressive, overtly political nature of this conduct was both intentional and overwhelmingly apparent. . . .

The government generally has a freer hand in restricting expressive conduct than it has in restricting the written or spoken word. . . . It may not, however, proscribe particular conduct because it has expressive elements. . . . It is, in short, not simply the verbal or nonverbal nature of the expression, but the governmental interest at stake, that helps to determine whether a restriction on that expression is valid. . . .

In order to decide whether *O'Brien*'s test applies here, therefore we must decide whether Texas has asserted an interest in support of Johnson's conviction that is unrelated to the suppression of expression. If we find that an interest asserted by the State is simply not implicated on the facts before us, we need not ask whether *O'Brien*'s test applies. . . . The State offers two separate interests to justify this conviction: preventing breaches of the peace, and preserving the flag as a symbol of nationhood and national unity. We hold that the first interest is not implicated on this record and that the second is related to the suppression of expression. . . .

Texas claims that its interest in preventing breaches of the peace justifies Johnson's conviction for flag desecration. However, no disturbance of the peace actually occurred or threatened to occur because of Johnson's burning of the flag. Although the State stresses the disruptive behavior of the protestors during their march toward City Hall, . . . it admits that no actual breach of the peace "occurred at the time of the flag burning or in response to the flag burning." The State's emphasis on the protestors' disorderly actions prior to arriving at City Hall is not only somewhat surprising given that no charges were brought on the basis of this conduct, but it also fails to show that a disturbance of the peace was a likely reaction to Johnson's conduct. The only evidence offered by the State at trial to show the reaction to Johnson's actions was the testimony of several persons who had been seriously offended by the flag burning.

The State's position, therefore, amounts to a claim that an audience that takes serious offense at particular expression is necessarily likely to disturb the peace and that the expression may be prohibited on this basis. Our precedents do not countenance such a presumption. On the contrary, they recognize that a principal "function of free speech under our system of government is to invite dispute. It may indeed best serve its high purpose when it induces a condition of unrest, creates dissatisfaction with conditions as they are, or even stirs people to anger." . . .

. . . Johnson's expressive conduct [does not] fall within that small class of "fighting words" that are "likely to provoke the average person to retaliation, and thereby cause a breach of the peace." . . . No reasonable onlooker would have regarded Johnson's generalized expression of dissatisfaction with the policies of the Federal Government as a direct personal insult or an invitation to exchange fisticuffs.

We thus conclude that the State's interest in maintaining order is not implicated on these facts. The State need not worry that our holding will disable it from preserving the peace. We do not suggest that the First Amendment forbids a State to prevent "imminent lawless action." . . .

The State also asserts an interest in preserving the flag as a symbol of nationhood and national unity. . . . The State, apparently, is concerned that . . . [flag burning] will lead people to believe either that the flag does not stand for nationhood and national unity, but instead reflects other, less positive concepts, or that the concepts reflected in the flag do not in fact exist, that is, we do not enjoy unity as a Nation. These concerns blossom only when a person's treatment of the flag communicates some message, and thus are related "to the suppression of free expression" within the meaning of *O'Brien*. We are thus outside of *O'Brien*'s test altogether.

It remains to consider whether the State's interest in preserving the flag as a symbol of nationhood and national unity justifies Johnson's conviction.

. . . Johnson was not . . . prosecuted for the expression of just any idea; he was prosecuted for his expression of dissatisfaction with the policies of this country, expression situated at the core of our First Amendment values. . . .

Moreover, Johnson was prosecuted because he knew that his politically charged expression would cause "serious offense." If he had burned the flag as a means of disposing of it because it was dirty or torn, he would not have been convicted of flag desecration under this Texas law: federal law designates burning as the preferred means of disposing of a flag "when it is in such condition that it is no longer a fitting emblem for display," . . . and Texas has no quarrel with this means of disposal. The Texas law is thus not aimed at protecting the physical integrity of the flag in all circumstances, but is designed instead to protect it only against impairments that would cause serious offense to others. . . .

Whether Johnson's treatment of the flag violated Texas law thus depended on the likely communicative impact of his expressive conduct. . . . [T]his restriction on Johnson's expression is content-based.

. . . Johnson's political expression was restricted because of the content of the message he conveyed. We must therefore subject the State's asserted interest in preserving the special symbolic character of the flag to "the most exacting scrutiny." . . .

If there is a bedrock principle underlying the First Amendment, it is that Government may not prohibit the expression of an idea simply because society finds the idea itself offensive or disagreeable. . . .

. . . [N]othing in our precedents suggests that a State may foster its own view of the flag by prohibiting expressive conduct relating to it. . . .

There is, moreover, no indication—either in the text of the Constitution or in our cases interpreting it—that a separate judicial category exists for the American flag alone. Indeed, we would not be surprised to learn that the persons who framed our Constitution and wrote the Amendment that we now construe were not known for their reverence for the Union Jack. The First Amendment does not guarantee that other concepts virtually sacred to our Nation as a whole—such as the principle that discrimination on the basis of race is odious and destructive—will go unquestioned in the marketplace of ideas. . . . We decline, therefore to create for the flag an exception to the joust of principles protected by the First Amendment.

It is not the State's ends, but its means, to which we object. It cannot be gainsaid that there is a special place reserved for the flag in this Nation, and thus we do not doubt that the Government has a legitimate interest in making efforts to "preserv[e] the national flag as an unalloyed symbol of our country." . . . Congress has, for example, enacted precatory regulations describing the proper treatment of the flag . . . and we cast no doubt on the legitimacy of its interest in making such recommendations. To say that the Government has an interest in encouraging proper treatment of the flag, however, is not to say that it may criminally punish a person for burning a flag as a means of political protest. . . .

We are tempted to say . . . that the flag's deservedly cherished place in our community will be strengthened, not weakened, by our holding today. Our decision is a reaffirmation of the principles of freedom and inclusiveness that the flag best reflects, and of the conviction that our toleration of criticism such as Johnson's is a sign and source of our strength.

The way to preserve the flag's special role is not to punish those who feel differently about these matters. It is to persuade them that they are wrong.

. . . [P]recisely because it is our flag that is involved, one's response to the flag-burners may exploit the uniquely persuasive power of the flag itself. We can imagine no more appropriate response to burning a flag than waving one's own, no better way to counter a flag-burner's message than by saluting the flag that burns, no surer means of preserving the dignity even of the flag that burned than by—as one witness here did—according its remains a respectful burial. We do not consecrate the flag by punishing its desecration, for in doing so we dilute the freedom that this cherished emblem represents. . . .

The judgment of the Texas Court of Criminal Appeals is . . . affirmed.

Justice Kennedy, concurring. . . .

Chief Justice Rehnquist, with whom *Justice White* and *Justice O'Connor* join, dissenting.

In holding this Texas statute unconstitutional, the Court ignores Justice Holmes' familiar aphorism that "a page of history is worth a volume of logic." . . . For more than 200 years, the American flag has occupied a unique position as the symbol of our Nation, a uniqueness that justifies a governmental prohibition against flag burning in the way respondent Johnson did here. . . .

Here it may equally well be said that the public burning of the American flag by Johnson was no essential part of any exposition of ideas, and at the same time it had a tendency to incite a breach of the peace. Johnson was free to make any verbal denunciation of the flag that he wished; indeed, he was free to burn the flag in private. He could publicly burn other symbols of the Government or effigies of political leaders. He did lead a march through the streets of Dallas, and conducted a rally in front of the Dallas City Hall. He engaged in a "die-in" to protest nuclear weapons. He shouted out various slogans during the march, including: "Reagan, Mondale which will it be? Either one means World War III"; "Ronald Reagan, killer of the hour, perfect example of US power"; and "red, white and blue, we spit on you, you stand for plunder, you will go under." . . . For none of these acts was he arrested or prosecuted; it was only when he proceeded to burn publicly an American flag stolen from its rightful owner that he violated the Texas statute. . . .

The Court concludes its opinion with a regrettably patronizing civics lecture, presumably addressed to the Members of both Houses of Congress, the members of the 48 state legislatures that enacted prohibitions against flag burning, and the troops fighting under that flag in Vietnam who objected to its being burned: "The way to preserve the flag's special role is not to punish those who feel differently about these matters. It is to persuade them that they are wrong." . . . The Court's role as the final expositor of the Constitution is well established, but its role as a platonic guardian admonishing those responsible to public opinion as if they were truant school children has no similar place in our system of government. The cry of "no taxation without representation" animated those who revolted against the English Crown to found our Nation— the idea that those who submitted to government should have some say as to what kind of laws would be passed. Surely one of the high purposes of a democratic society is to legislate against conduct that is regarded as evil and profoundly offensive to the majority of people—whether it be murder, embezzlement, pollution, or flag burning.

Our Constitution wisely places limits on powers of legislative majorities to act, but the declaration of such limits by this Court "is, at all times, a question of much delicacy which ought seldom, if ever, to be decided in the affirmative, in a doubtful case." . . . Uncritical extension of constitutional protection to the burning of the flag risks the frustration of the very purpose for which organized governments are instituted. The Court decides that the American flag is just another symbol, about which not only must opinions pro and con be tolerated, but for which the most minimal public respect may not be enjoined. The government may conscript men into the Armed Forces where they must fight and perhaps die for the flag, but the government may not prohibit the public burning of the banner under which they fight. I would uphold the Texas statute as applied in this case.

Justice Stevens, dissenting.

. . . A country's flag is a symbol of more than "nationhood and national unity." . . . It also signifies the ideas that characterize the society that has chosen that emblem as well as the special history that has animated the growth and power of those ideas. The fleur-de-lis and the tricolor both symbolized "nationhood and national unity," but they had vastly different meanings. The message conveyed by some flags—the swastika, for example—may survive long after it has outlived its usefulness as a symbol of regimented unity in a particular nation.

So it is with the American flag. It is more than a proud symbol of the courage, the determination, and the gifts of nature that transformed 13 fledgling Colonies into a world power. It is a symbol of freedom, of equal opportunity, of religious tolerance, and of goodwill for other peoples who share our aspirations. The symbol carries its message to dissidents both at home and abroad who may have no interest at all in our national unity or survival.

The value of the flag as a symbol cannot be measured. Even so, I have no doubt that the interest in preserving that value for the future is both significant and legitimate. Conceivably that value will be enhanced by the Court's conclusion that our national commitment to free expression is so strong that even the United States as ultimate guarantor of that freedom is without power to prohibit the desecration of its unique symbol. But I am unpersuaded. The creation of a federal right to post bulletin boards and graffiti on the Washington Monument might enlarge the market for free expression, but at a cost I would not pay. . . .

The Court is . . . quite wrong in blandly asserting that respondent "was prosecuted for his expression of dissatisfaction with the policies of this country, expression situated at the core of our First Amendment values." . . . Respondent was prosecuted because of the method he chose to express his dissatisfaction with those policies. Had he chosen to spray paint—or perhaps convey with a motion picture projector—his message of dissatisfaction on the facade of the Lincoln Memorial, there would be no question about the power of the Government to prohibit his means of expression. The prohibition would be supported by the legitimate interest in preserving the quality of an important national asset. Though the asset at stake in this case is intangible, given its unique value, the same interest supports a prohibition on the desecration of the American flag. . . .

Case

BARNES V. GLEN THEATRE, INC.

501 U.S. 560; 111 S.Ct. 2456; 115 L.Ed. 2d 504 (1991)
Vote: 5–4

Two South Bend, Indiana, establishments that featured all-nude dancing brought suit in the U.S. District Court for the Northern District of Indiana seeking an injunction against enforcement of an Indiana statute prohibiting complete nudity in public places. The district court dismissed the case, concluding that "the type of dancing these plaintiffs wish to perform is not expressive activity protected by the Constitution of the United States." On appeal, the Court of Appeals for the Seventh Circuit reversed, holding that the nude dancing at issue was "expressive conduct protected by the First Amendment." The Supreme Court granted certiorari.

Chief Justice Rehnquist . . . [announced the judgment of the Court and delivered an opinion joined by Justices O'Connor and Kennedy].

. . . The Kitty Kat Lounge, Inc. (Kitty Kat) is located in the city of South Bend. It sells alcoholic beverages and presents "go-go dancing." Its proprietor desires to present "totally nude dancing," but an applicable Indiana statute regulating public nudity requires that the dancers wear "pasties" and a "G-string" when they dance. The dancers are not paid an hourly wage, but work on commission. They receive a 100 percent commission on the first $60 in drink sales during their performances. Darlene Miller, one of the respondents in the action, had worked at the Kitty Kat for about two years at the time this action was brought. Miller wishes to dance nude because she believes she would make more money doing so.

Respondent Glen Theatre, Inc. is an Indiana corporation with a place of business in South Bend. Its primary business is supplying so-called adult entertainment through written and printed materials, movie showings, and live entertainment at the "bookstore" consisting of nude and seminude performances and showings of the female body through glass panels. Customers sit in a booth and insert coins into a timing mechanism that permits them to observe the live nude and seminude dancers for a period of time. One of Glen Theatre's dancers, Gayle Ann Marie Sutro, has danced, modeled, and acted professionally for more than 15 years, and in addition to her performances at the Glen Theatre, can be seen in a pornographic movie at a nearby theater. . . .

Several of our cases contain language suggesting that nude dancing of the kind involved here is expressive con-duct protected by the First Amendment. In *Doran v. Salem Inn, Inc.* . . . (1975), we said: "[A]lthough the customary 'barroom' type of nude dancing may involve only the barest minimum of protected expression, we recognized in *California v. LaRue* . . . (1972), that this form of entertainment might be entitled to First and Fourteenth Amendment protection under some circumstances." In *Schad v. Borough of Mount Ephraim* . . . (1981), we said that "[f]urthermore, as the state courts in this case recognized, nude dancing is not without its First Amendment protections from official regulation." . . . These statements support the conclusion of the Court of Appeals that nude dancing of the kind sought to be performed here is expressive conduct within the outer perimeters of the First Amendment, though we view it as only marginally so. This, of course, does not end our inquiry. We must determine the level of protection to be afforded to the expressive conduct at issue, and must determine whether the Indiana statute is an impermissible infringement of that protected activity.

Indiana, of course, has not banned nude dancing as such, but has proscribed public nudity across the board. The Supreme Court of Indiana has construed the Indiana statute to preclude nudity in what are essentially places of public accommodation such as the Glen Theatre and the Kitty Kat Lounge. In such places, respondents point out, minors are excluded and there are no non-consenting viewers. Respondents contend that while the state may license establishments such as the ones involved here, and limit the geographical area in which they do business, it may not in any way limit the performance of the dances within them without violating the First Amendment. The petitioner contends, on the other hand, that Indiana's restriction on nude dancing is a valid "time, place or manner" restriction under cases such as *Clark v. Community for Creative Non-Violence* . . . (1984).

The "time, place, or manner" test was developed for evaluating restriction on expression taking place on the public property which had been dedicated as a "public forum," . . . although we have on at least one occasion applied it to conduct occurring on private property. . . . In *Clark* we observed that this test has been interpreted to embody much the same standards as those set forth in *United States v. O'Brien* . . . (1968), and we turn, therefore, to the rule enunciated in *O'Brien*. . . .

This Court has held that when "speech" and "nonspeech" elements are combined in the same course of conduct, a sufficiently important governmental interest in regulating the nonspeech element can justify incidental limitation on First Amendment freedoms. To characterize the quality of the governmental interest which must appear, the Court has employed a variety of descriptive terms: compelling; substantial; subordinating; paramount; cogent; strong. Whatever imprecision inheres in these terms, we think it clear that a government regulation is sufficiently justified if it is within the constitutional power of the Government; if it furthers an important or substantial governmental interest; if the governmental interest is unrelated to the suppression of free expression; and if the incidental restriction on alleged First Amendment freedoms is no greater than essential to the furtherance of that interest. . . .

Applying the four-part *O'Brien* test enunciated above, we find that Indiana's public indecency statute is justified despite its incidental limitations on some expressive activity. The public indecency statute is clearly within the constitutional power of the State and furthers substantial governmental interests. It is impossible to discern, other than from the text of the statute, exactly what governmental interest the Indiana legislators had in mind when they enacted this statute, for Indiana does not record legislative history, and the state's highest court has not shed additional light on the statute's purpose. Nonetheless, the statute's purpose of protecting societal order and morality is clear from its text and history. Public indecency statutes of this sort are of ancient origin, and presently exist in at least 47 States. Public indecency, including nudity, was a criminal offense at common law, and this Court recognized the common-law roots of the offense of "gross and open indecency" in *Winters v. New York* . . . (1948). Public nudity was considered an act *malum en se*. . . . Public indecency statutes such as the one before us reflect moral disapproval of people appearing in the nude among strangers in public places.

This public indecency statute follows a long line of earlier Indiana statutes banning all public nudity. The history of Indiana's public indecency statute shows that it predates barroom nude dancing and was enacted as a general prohibition. At least as early as 1831, Indiana has a statute punishing "open and notorious lewdness, or . . . any grossly scandalous and public indecency." . . . A gap during which no statute was in effect was filled by the Indiana Supreme Court in *Ardery v. State* . . . (1877), which held that the court could sustain a conviction for exhibitions of "privates" in the presence of others. The court traced the offense to the Bible story of Adam and Eve. . . . In 1881, a statute was enacted that would remain essentially unchanged for nearly a century:

> Whoever, being over fourteen years of age, makes an indecent exposure of his person in a public place, or in any place where there are other persons to be offended or annoyed thereby, . . . is guilty of public indecency. . . .

The language quoted above remained unchanged until it was simultaneously repealed and replaced with the present statute in 1976. . . .

This and other public indecency statutes were designed to protect morals and public order. The traditional police power of the States is defined as the authority to provide for the public health, safety, and morals, and we have upheld such a basis for legislation. . . .

. . . In *Bowers v. Hardwick* . . . (1986), we said: "The law, however, is constantly based on notion of morality, and if all laws representing essentially moral choices are to be invalidated under the Due Process Clause, the courts will be very busy indeed."

Thus, the public indecency statute furthers a substantial government interest in protecting order and morality.

This interest is unrelated to the suppression of free expression. Some may view restricting nudity on moral grounds as necessarily related to expression. We disagree. It can be argued, of course, that almost limitless types of conduct—including appearing in the nude in public—are "expressive," and in one sense of the word this is true. People who go about in the nude in public may be expressing something about themselves by so doing. But the Court rejected this expansive notion of "expressive conduct" in *O'Brien,* saying:

> We cannot accept the view that an apparently limitless variety of conduct can be labelled "speech" whenever the person engaging in the conduct intends thereby to express an idea. . . .

Respondents contend that even though prohibiting nudity in public generally may not be related to suppressing expression, prohibiting the performance of nude dancing is related to expression because the state seeks to prevent its erotic message. Therefore, they reason that the application of the Indiana statute to the nude dancing in this case violates the First Amendment, because it fails the third part of the *O'Brien* test, viz: the governmental interest must be unrelated to the suppression of free expression.

But we do not think that when Indiana applies its statute to the nude dancing in these nightclubs it is proscribing nudity because of the erotic message conveyed by the dancers. Presumably numerous other erotic performances are presented at these establishments and similar clubs without any interference from the state, so long as the performers wear a scant amount of clothing. Likewise the requirement that the dancers don pasties and a G-string does not deprive the dance of whatever erotic message it conveys; it simply makes the message slightly less graphic. The perceived evil that Indiana seeks to address is not erotic dancing, but public nudity. The appearance of people of all shapes, sizes and ages in the nude at a beach, for example, would convey little if any erotic message, yet the state still seeks to prevent it. Public nudity is the evil the state seeks to prevent, whether or not it is combined with expressive activity.

This conclusion is buttressed by a reference to the facts of *O'Brien*. An act of Congress provided that anyone who knowingly destroyed a selective service registration certificate committed an offense. O'Brien burned his certificate on the steps of the South Boston Courthouse to influence others to adopt his anti-war beliefs. The Court upheld his conviction, reasoning that the continued availability of issued certificates served a legitimate and substantial purpose in the administration of the selective service system. O'Brien's deliberate destruction of his certificate frustrated this purpose and "for this non-communicative aspect of his conduct, and for nothing else, he was convicted." . . . It was assumed that *O'Brien's* act in burning the certificate had a communicative element in it sufficient to bring into play the First Amendment, . . . but it was for the non-communicative element that he was prosecuted. So here with the Indiana statute; while the dancing to which it was applied had a communicative element, it was not the dancing that was prohibited, but simply its being done in the nude.

The fourth part of the *O'Brien* test requires that the incidental restriction on First Amendment freedom be no greater than is essential to the furtherance of the governmental interest. As indicated in the discussion above, the governmental interest served by the text of the prohibition is societal disapproval of nudity in public places and among strangers. The statutory prohibition is not a means to some greater end, but an end in itself. It is without cavil that the public indecency statute is "narrowly tailored"; Indiana's requirement that the dancers wear at least pasties and a G-string is modest, and the bare minimum necessary to achieve the state's purpose.

The judgment of the Court of Appeals accordingly is . . . reversed.

Justice Scalia, concurring in the judgment. . . .

Justice Souter, concurring in the judgment. . . .

Justice White, with whom *Justice Marshall*, *Justice Blackmun*, and *Justice Stevens* join, dissenting.

. . . We are told by the Attorney General of Indiana that . . . the Indiana Supreme Court [has] held that the statute at issue here cannot and does not prohibit nudity as part of some larger form of expression meriting protection when the communication of ideas is involved. . . . Petitioners also state that the evils sought to be avoided by applying the statute in this case would not obtain in the case of theatrical productions such as *Salome* or *Hair*. Nei-

ther is there any evidence that the State has attempted to apply the statute to nudity in performances such as plays, ballets or operas. "No arrests have ever been made for nudity as part of a play or ballet." . . .

Thus, the Indiana statute is not a general prohibition of the type that we have upheld in prior cases. As a result, the Court's and Justice Scalia's simple references to the State's general interest in promoting societal order and morality [are] not sufficient justification for a statute which concededly reaches a significant amount of expressive activity. Instead of applying the *O'Brien* test, we are obligated to carefully examine the reasons the State has chosen to regulate this expressive conduct in a less than general statute. In other words, when the State enacts a law which draws a line between expressive conduct of the same type which is regulated and nonexpressive conduct which is not regulated, *O'Brien* places the burden on the State to justify the distinctions it has made. Closer inquiry as to the purpose of the statute is surely appropriate.

Legislators do not just randomly select certain conduct for proscription; they have reasons and those reasons illuminate the purpose of the law that is passed. Indeed, a law may have multiple purposes. The purpose of forbidding people from appearing nude in parks, beaches, hot dog stands, and like public places is to protect others from offense. But that could not possibly be the purpose of preventing nude dancing in theaters and barrooms since the viewers are exclusively consenting adults who pay money to see these dances. The purpose of the proscription in these contexts is to protect the viewers from what the State believes is the harmful message that nude dancing communicates. . . .

That the performances in the Kitty Kat Lounge may not be high art, to say the least, and may not appeal to the Court, is hardly an excuse for distorting and ignoring settled doctrine. The Court's assessment of the artistic merits of nude dancing performances should not be the determining factor in deciding this case. In the words of Justice Harlan, "it is largely because governmental officials cannot make principled decisions in this area that the Constitution leaves matters of taste and style so largely to the individual." . . . "[W]hile the entertainment afforded by a nude ballet at Lincoln Center to those who can pay the price may differ vastly in content (as viewed by judges) or in quality (as viewed by critics), it may not differ in substance from the dance viewed by the person who . . . wants some 'entertainment' with his beer or shot of rye." . . .

As I see it, our cases require us to affirm absent a compelling state interest supporting the statute. Neither the Court nor the State suggests that the statute could withstand scrutiny under that standard. . . .

Accordingly, I would affirm the judgment of the Court of Appeals, and dissent from this Court's judgment.

Case

NEW YORK TIMES COMPANY V. SULLIVAN

376 U.S. 254; 84 S.Ct. 710; 11 L.Ed. 2d 686 (1964)
Vote: 9–0

In this case the Court determines the extent to which the First Amendment limits a state's power to award damages in a libel suit brought by a public official against critics of his official conduct.

Mr. Justice Brennan delivered the opinion of the Court.

. . . Respondent L. B. Sullivan is one of the three elected Commissioners of the City of Montgomery, Alabama. He testified that he was "Commissioner of Public Affairs and the duties are supervision of the Police Department, Fire Department, Department of Cemetery and Department of Scales." He brought this civil libel action against the four individual petitioners, who are Negroes and Alabama clergymen, and against petitioner the New York Times Company, a New York corporation which publishes the *New York Times,* a daily newspaper. A jury in the Circuit Court of Montgomery County awarded him damages of $500,000, the full amount claimed, against all the petitioners and the Supreme Court of Alabama affirmed. . . .

Respondent's complaint alleged that he had been libeled by statements in a full-page advertisement that was carried in the *New York Times* on March 29, 1960. Entitled "Heed Their Rising Voices," the advertisement began by stating that "As the whole world knows by now, thousands of Southern Negro students are engaged in widespread nonviolent demonstrations in positive affirmation of the right to live in human dignity as guaranteed by the U.S. Constitution and the Bill of Rights." It went on to charge that "in their efforts to uphold these guarantees, they are being met by an unprecedented wave of terror by those who would deny and negate that document which the whole world looks upon as setting the pattern for modern freedom. . . ." Succeeding paragraphs purported to illustrate the "wave of terror" by describing certain alleged events. The text concluded with an appeal for funds for three purposes: support of the student movement, "the struggle for the right-to-vote," and the legal defense of Dr. Martin Luther King, Jr., leader of the movement, against a perjury indictment then pending in Montgomery.

The text appeared over the names of 64 persons, many widely known for their activities in public affairs, religion, trade unions, and the performing arts. Below these names, and under a line reading "We in the south who are struggling daily for dignity and freedom warmly endorse this

appeal," appeared the names of the four individual petitioners and of 16 other persons, all but two of whom were identified as clergymen in various Southern cities. The advertisement was signed at the bottom of the page by the "Committee to Defend Martin Luther King and the Struggle for Freedom in the South," and the officers of the Committee were listed.

Of the 10 paragraphs of text in the advertisement, the third and a portion of the sixth were the basis of respondent's claim of libel. They read as follows:

Third paragraph:

In Montgomery, Alabama, after students sang "My Country, 'Tis of Thee" on the State Capitol steps, their leaders were expelled from school, and truckloads of police armed with shotguns and tear-gas ringed the Alabama State College Campus. When the entire student body protested to state authorities by refusing to re-register, their dining hall was padlocked in an attempt to starve them into submission.

Sixth paragraph:

Again and again the Southern violators have answered Dr. King's peaceful protests with intimidation and violence. They have bombed his home almost killing his wife and child. They have assaulted his person. They have arrested him seven times—for "speeding," "loitering" and similar "offenses." And now they have charged him with "perjury"—a felony under which they could imprison him for ten years. . . .

Although neither of these statements mentions respondent by name, he contended that the word "police" in the third paragraph referred to him as the Montgomery Commissioner who supervised the Police Department, so that he was being accused of "ringing" the campus with police. He further claimed that the paragraph would be read as imputing to the police, and hence to him, the padlocking of the dining hall in order to starve the students into submission. As to the sixth paragraph, he contended that since arrests are ordinarily made by the police, the statement "They have arrested [Dr. King] seven times" would be read as referring to him; he further contended that the "They" who did the arresting would be equated with the "They" who committed the other described acts and with the "Southern violators." Thus, he argued, the paragraph would be read as accusing the Montgomery police, and hence him, of answering Dr. King's protests with "intimidation and violence," bombing his home, assaulting his person, and charging him with perjury. Respondent and six other Montgomery residents testified that they read some of all of the statements as referring to him in his capacity as Commissioner.

It is uncontroverted that some of the statements contained in the two paragraphs were not accurate descriptions of events which occurred in Montgomery. Although Negro students staged a demonstration on the State Capitol steps, they sang the National Anthem and not "My Country, 'Tis of Thee." Although nine students were expelled by the State Board of Education, this was not for leading the demonstration at the Capitol, but for demanding service at a lunch counter in the Montgomery County Courthouse on another day. Not the entire student body, but most of it, had protested the expulsion, not by refusing to register, but by boycotting classes on a single day; virtually all the students did register for the ensuing semester. The campus dining hall was not padlocked on any occasion, and the only students who may have been barred from eating there were the few who had neither signed a preregistration application nor requested temporary meal tickets. Although the police were deployed near the campus in large numbers on three occasions, they did not at any time "ring" the campus, and they were not called to the campus in connection with the demonstration on the State Capitol steps, as the third paragraph implied. Dr. King had not been arrested seven times, but only four; and although he claimed to have been assaulted some years earlier in connection with his arrest for loitering outside a courtroom, one of the officers who made the arrest denied that there was such an assault.

On the premise that the charges in the sixth paragraph could be read as referring to him, respondent was allowed to prove that he had not participated in the events described. Although Dr. King's home had in fact been bombed twice when his wife and child were there, both of these occasions antedated respondent's tenure as Commissioner, and the police were not only not implicated in the bombings, but had made every effort to apprehend those who were. Three of Dr. King's four arrests took place before respondent became Commissioner. Although Dr. King had in fact been indicted (he was subsequently acquitted) on two counts of perjury, each of which carried a possible five-year sentence, respondent had nothing to do with procuring the indictment. . . .

Because of the importance of the constitutional issues involved, we granted the separate petitions for certiorari of the individual petitioners and of the *Times*. . . . We reverse the judgment. We hold that the rule of law applied by the Alabama courts is constitutionally deficient for failure to provide the safeguards for freedom of speech and of the press that are required by the First and Fourteenth Amendments in a libel action brought by a public official against critics of his official conduct. We further hold that under the proper safeguards the evidence presented in this case is constitutionally insufficient to support the judgment for respondent. . . .

Under Alabama law as applied in this case, a publication is "libelous per se" if the words "tend to injure a person . . . in his reputation" or to "bring [him] into public contempt"; the trial court stated that the standard was met if the words are such as to "injure him in his public office, or impute misconduct to him in his office, or want of official integrity, or want of fidelity to a public trust. . . ." The jury must find that the words were published "of and concerning" the plaintiff, but where the plaintiff is a public official his place in the governmental hierarchy is sufficient evidence to support a finding that his reputation has been affected by statements that reflect upon the agency of which he is in charge. Once "libel per se" has been established, the defendant has no defense as to stated facts unless he can persuade the jury that they were true in all their particulars. . . . His privilege of "fair comment" for expressions of opinion depends on the truth of the facts upon which the comment is based. . . . Unless he can discharge the burden of proving truth, general damages are presumed, and may be awarded without proof of pecuniary injury. A showing of actual malice is apparently a prerequisite to recovery of punitive damages, and the defendant may in any event forestall a punitive award by a retraction meeting the statutory requirements. Good motives and belief in truth do not negate an inference of malice, but are relevant only in mitigation of punitive damages if the jury chooses to accord them weight. . . .

The question before us is whether this rule of liability, as applied to an action brought by a public official against critics of his official conduct, abridges the freedom of speech and of the press that is guaranteed by the First and Fourteenth Amendments.

Respondent relies heavily, as did the Alabama courts, on statements of this Court to the effect that the Constitution does not protect libelous publications. Those statements do not foreclose our inquiry here. None of the cases sustained the use of libel laws to impose sanctions upon expression critical of the official conduct of public officials. . . . Like insurrection, contempt, advocacy of unlawful acts, breach of the peace, obscenity, solicitation of legal business, and the various other formulae for the repression of expression that have been challenged in this Court, libel can claim no talismanic immunity from constitutional limitations. It must be measured by standards that satisfy the First Amendment. . . .

[W]e consider this case against the background of a profound national commitment to the principle that debate on public issues should be uninhibited, robust, and wide-open, and that it may well include vehement, caustic, and sometimes unpleasantly sharp attacks on government and public officials. . . .

A rule compelling the critic of official conduct to guarantee the truth of all his factual assertions—and to do so on pain of libel judgments virtually unlimited in amount—leads to a comparable "self-censorship." Allowance of the defense of truth, with the burden of proving it on the defendant, does not mean that only false speech will be deterred. Even courts accepting this defense as an adequate safeguard have recognized the difficulties of adducing legal proofs that the alleged libel was true in all its factual particulars. . . . Under such a rule, would-be critics of official conduct may be deterred from voicing their criticism, even though it is believed to be true and even though it is in fact true, because of doubt whether it can be proved in court or fear of the expense of having to do so. They tend to make only statements which "steer far wider of the unlawful zone." . . . The rule thus dampens the vigor and limits the variety of public debate. It is inconsistent with the First and Fourteenth Amendments.

The constitutional guarantees require, we think, a federal rule that prohibits a public official from recovering damages for a defamatory falsehood relating to his official conduct unless he proves that the statement was made with "actual malice"—that is, with knowledge that it was false or with reckless disregard of whether it was false or not. . . .

Such a privilege for criticism of official conduct is appropriately analogous to the protection accorded a public official when he is sued for libel by a private citizen. . . . The reason for the official privilege is said to be that the threat of damage suits would otherwise "inhibit the fearless, vigorous, and effective administration of policies of government" and "dampen the ardor of all but the most resolute, or the most irresponsible, in the unflinching discharge of their duties." . . . Analogous considerations support the privilege for the citizen-critic of government. It is as much his duty to criticize as it is the official's duty to administer. . . . It would give public servants an unjustified

preference over the public they serve, if critics of official conduct did not have a fair equivalent of the immunity granted to the officials themselves. . . .

We hold today that the Constitution delimits a State's power to award damages for libel in actions brought by public officials against critics of their official conduct. Since this is such an action, the rule requiring proof of actual malice is applicable. While Alabama law apparently requires proof of actual malice for an award of punitive damages, where general damages are concerned malice is "presumed." Such a presumption is inconsistent with the federal rule. . . . Since the trial judge did not instruct the jury to differentiate between general and punitive damages, it may be that the verdict was wholly an award of one or the other. But it is impossible to know, in view of the general verdict returned. Because of this uncertainty, the judgment must be reversed and the case remanded. . . .

Mr. Justice Black, with whom *Mr. Justice Douglas* joins, concurring.

. . . I base my vote to reverse on the belief that the First and Fourteenth Amendments not merely "delimit" a State's power to award damages to "public officials against critics of their official conduct" but completely prohibit a State from exercising such a power. The Court goes on to hold that a State can subject such critics to damages if "actual malice" can be proved against them. "Malice," even as defined by the Court, is an elusive, abstract concept, hard to prove and hard to disprove. The requirement that malice be proved provides at best an evanescent protection for the right critically to discuss public affairs and certainly does not measure up to the sturdy safeguard embodied in the First Amendment. Unlike the Court, therefore, I vote to reverse exclusively on the ground that the *Times* and the individual defendants had an absolute, unconditional constitutional right to publish in the *Times* advertisement their criticisms of the Montgomery agencies and officials. . . .

Case

MILLER V. CALIFORNIA

413 U.S. 15; 93 S.Ct. 2607; 37 L.Ed. 2d 419 (1973)
Vote: 5–4

In this case the Supreme Court sets forth the constitutional standards for determining obscenity. The defendant, Miller, was convicted in the Orange County Superior Court of "knowingly distributing obscene matter," a misdemeanor under California law. The appellate court affirmed his conviction without opinion.

Mr. Chief Justice Burger delivered the opinion of the Court.

. . . Appellant conducted a mass mailing campaign to advertise the sale of illustrated books, euphemistically called "adult" material. After a jury trial, he was convicted of violating California Penal Code [Section] 311.2 (a), a misdemeanor, by knowingly distributing obscene matter, and the Appellate Department, Superior Court of California, County of Orange, summarily affirmed the judgment without opinion. Appellant's conviction was specifically based on his conduct in causing five unsolicited advertising brochures to be sent through the mail in an envelope addressed to a restaurant in Newport Beach, California. The envelope was opened by the manager of the restaurant and his mother. They had not requested the brochures; they complained to the police.

The brochures advertise four books entitled "Intercourse," "Man-Woman," "Sex Orgies Illustrated," and "An Illustrated History of Pornography," and a film entitled "Marital Intercourse." While the brochures contain some descriptive printed material, primarily they consist of pictures and drawings very explicitly depicting men and women in groups of two or more engaging in a variety of sexual activities, with genitals often prominently displayed. . . .

. . . This much has been categorically settled by the Court, that obscene material is unprotected by the First Amendment. . . . "The First and Fourteenth Amendments have never been treated as absolutes." . . . We acknowledge, however, the inherent dangers of undertaking to regulate any form of expression. State statutes designed to regulate obscene materials must be carefully limited. . . . As a result, we now confine the permissible scope of such regulation to works which depict or describe sexual conduct. That conduct must be specifically defined by the applicable state law, as written or authoritatively construed. A state office must also be limited to works which, taken as a whole, appeal to the prurient interest in sex, which portray sexual conduct in a patently offensive way, and which, taken as a whole, do not have serious literary, artistic, political, or scientific value.

The basic guidelines for the trier of fact must be: (a) whether "the average person, applying contemporary community standards" would find that the work, taken as a whole, appeals to the prurient interest, . . . (b) whether the work depicts or describes, in a patently offensive way, sexual conduct specifically defined by the applicable state law, and (c) whether the work, taken as a whole, lacks serious literary, artistic, political, or scientific value. We do not adopt as a constitutional standard the "*utterly* without redeeming social value" test of *Memoirs v. Massachusetts;* . . . that concept has never commanded the adherence of more than three Justices at one time. . . . If a state law that regulates obscene material is thus limited, as written or construed, the First Amendment values applicable to the States through the Fourteenth Amendment are adequately protected by the ultimate power of appellate courts to conduct an independent review of constitutional claims when necessary. . . .

We emphasize that it is not our function to propose regulatory schemes for the States. That must await their concrete legislative efforts. It is possible, however, to give a few plain examples of what a state statute could define for regulation under the second part (b) of the standard announced in this opinion *supra:*

(a) Patently offensive representations or descriptions of ultimate sexual acts, normal or perverted, actual or simulated.

(b) Patently offensive representations or descriptions of masturbation, excretory functions, and lewd exhibition of the genitals.

Sex and nudity may not be exploited without limit by films or pictures exhibited or sold in places of public accommodation any more than live sex and nudity can be exhibited or sold without limit in such public places. At a minimum, prurient, patently offensive depiction or description of sexual conduct must have serious literary, artistic, political, or scientific value to merit First Amendment protection. . . .

Under the holdings announced today, no one will be subject to prosecution for the sale or exposure of obscene materials unless these materials depict or describe patently offensive "hard core" sexual conduct specifically defined by the regulating state law, as written or construed. We are satisfied that these specific prerequisites will provide fair notice to a dealer in such materials that his public and commercial activities may bring prosecution. . . .

It is certainly true that the absence, since *Roth v. United States* of a single majority view of this Court as to proper standards for testing obscenity has placed a strain on both state and federal courts. But today, for the first time since *Roth* was decided in 1957, a majority of this Court has agreed on concrete guidelines to isolate "hard core" pornography from expression protected by the First Amendment. . . .

This may not be an easy road, free from difficulty. But no amount of "fatigue" should lead us to adopt a convenient "institutional" rationale—an absolutist, "anything goes" view of the First Amendment—because it will lighten our burdens. "Such an abnegation of judicial supervision in this field would be inconsistent with our duty to uphold the constitutional guarantees." . . . Nor should we remedy "tension between state and federal courts" by arbitrarily depriving the States of a power reserved to them under the Constitution, a power which they have enjoyed and exercised continuously from before the adoption of the First Amendment to this day. . . .

Under a national Constitution, fundamental First Amendment limitations on the powers of the States do not vary from community to community, but this does not mean that there are, or should or can be, fixed, uniform national standards of precisely what appeals to the "prurient interest" or is "patently offensive." These are essentially questions of fact, and our nation is simply too big and too diverse for this Court to reasonably expect that such standards could be articulated for all 50 States in a single formulation, even assuming the prerequisite consensus exists. When triers of fact are asked to decide whether "the average person, applying contemporary community standards" would consider certain materials "prurient," it would be unrealistic to require that the answer be based on some abstract formulation. The adversary system, with lay jurors as the usual ultimate factfinders in criminal prosecution, has historically permitted triers-of-fact to draw on the standards of their community, guided always by limiting instructions on the law. To require a State to structure obscenity proceedings around evidence of a national "community standard" would be an exercise in futility. . . .

It is neither realistic nor constitutionally sound to read the First Amendment as requiring that the people of Maine or Mississippi accept public depiction of conduct found tolerable in Las Vegas, or New York City. . . . People in different States vary in their tastes and attitudes, and this diversity is not to be strangled by the absolutism of imposed uniformity. . . .

The dissenting Justices sound the alarm of repression. But, in our view, to equate the free and robust exchange of ideas and political debate with commercial exploitation of obscene material demeans the grand conception of the First Amendment and its high purposes in the historic struggle for freedom. It is a "misuse of the great guarantees of free speech and free press." . . . The First Amendment protects works which, taken as a whole, have serious literary, artistic, political or scientific value, regardless of whether the government or a majority of the people approve the ideas these works represent. "The protection given speech and press was fashioned to assure unfettered interchange of *ideas* for the bringing about of political and social changes desired by the people." . . . But the public portrayal of hard core sexual conduct for its own sake, and for the ensuing commercial gain, is a different matter.

One can concede that the "sexual revolution" of recent years may have had useful byproducts in striking layers of prudery from a subject long irrationally kept from needed ventilation. But it does not follow that no regulation of patently offensive "hard core" materials is needed or permissible; civilized people do not allow unregulated access to heroin because it is a derivative of medicinal morphine. . . .

Mr. Justice Douglas, dissenting.

. . . The idea that the First Amendment permits government to ban publications that are "offensive" to some people puts an ominous gloss on freedom of the press. That test would make it possible to ban any paper or any journal or magazine in some benighted place. The First Amendment was designed "to invite dispute," to induce "a condition of unrest," to "create dissatisfactions with conditions as they are," and even to stir "people to anger." . . . The idea that the First Amendment permits punishment for ideas that are "offensive" to the particular judge or jury sitting in judgment is astounding. No greater leveler of speech or literature has ever been designed. To give the power to the censor, as we do today, is to make a sharp and radical break with the traditions of a free society. The First Amendment was not fashioned as a vehicle for dispensing tranquilizers to the people. Its prime function was to keep debate open to "offensive" as well as to "staid" people. The tendency throughout history has been to subdue the individual and to exalt the power of government. The use of the standard "offensive" gives authority to government that cuts the very vitals out of the First Amendment. As is intimated by the Court's opinion, the materials before us may be garbage. But so is much of what is said in political campaigns, in the daily press, on TV or over the radio. By reason of the First Amendment—and solely because of it—speakers and publishers have not been threatened or subdued because their thoughts and ideas may be "offensive" to some. . . .

Mr. Justice Brennan, with whom *Mr. Justice Stewart* and *Mr. Justice Marshall* join, dissenting. . . .

Case

FEDERAL COMMUNICATIONS COMMISSION V. PACIFICA FOUNDATION

438 U.S. 726; 98 S.Ct. 3026; 57 L.Ed. 2d 1073 (1978)
Vote: 5–4

On Tuesday, October 30, 1973, at about 2 P.M., a New York radio station owned by the Pacifica Foundation broadcast a George Carlin monologue on the "seven dirty words you can't say on the radio." Before airing the recording, the station warned listeners of the strong content. The station received no complaints directly from listeners. Several weeks later, a man who claimed that he had heard the monologue while driving in his car with his young son filed a complaint with the Federal Communications Commission. Although it imposed no formal sanctions, the FCC indicated that the complaint would be "associated with the station's license file, and in the event that subsequent complaints are received, the Commission will then decide whether it should utilize any of the available sanctions it has been granted by Congress." Pacifica Foundation appealed the agency's action to the U.S. Court of Appeals, which reversed the FCC.

Justice Stevens delivered the opinion of the Court . . .

. . . Obscene materials have been denied the protection of the First Amendment because their content is so offensive to contemporary moral standards. . . . But the fact that society may find speech offensive is not a sufficient reason for suppressing it. Indeed, if it is the speaker's opinion that gives offense, that consequence is a reason for according it constitutional protection. For it is a central tenet of the First Amendment that the government must remain neutral in the marketplace of ideas. If there were any reason to believe that the Commission's characterization of the Carlin monologue as offensive could be traced to its political content—or even to the fact that it satirized contemporary attitudes about four-letter words—First Amendment protection might be required. But that is simply not this case. These words offend for the same reasons that obscenity offends. This place in the hierarchy of First Amendment values was aptly sketched by Justice Murphy when he said: "Such utterances are no essential part of any exposition of ideas, and are of such slight social value as a step to truth that any benefit that may be derived from them is clearly outweighed by the social interest in order and morality." . . .

Although these words ordinarily lack literary, political, or scientific value, they are not entirely outside the protection of the First Amendment. Some uses of even the most offensive words are unquestionably protected. . . . Indeed, we may assume, *arguendo,* that this monologue would be protected on other contexts. Nonetheless, the constitutional protection accorded to a communication containing such patently offensive sexual and excretory language need not be the same in every context. It is a characteristic of speech such as this that both its capacity to offend and its "social value," to use Justice Murphy's term, vary with the circumstances. Words that are commonplace in one setting are shocking in another. To paraphrase Justice Harlan, one man's lyric is another's vulgarity. . . .

In this case it is undisputed that the content of Pacifica's broadcast was "vulgar," "offensive," and "shocking." Because content of that character is not entitled to absolute constitutional protection under all circumstances, we must consider its context in order to determine whether the Commission's action was constitutionally permissible.

We have long recognized that each medium of expression presents special First Amendment problems. And of all forms of communication, it is broadcasting that has received the most limited First Amendment protection. Thus, although other speakers cannot be licensed except under laws that carefully define and narrow official discretion, a broadcaster may be deprived of his license and his forum if the Commission decides that such an action would serve "the public interest, convenience, and necessity." . . . Similarly, although the First Amendment protects newspaper publishers from being required to print the replies of those whom they criticize, . . . it affords no such protection to broadcasters; on the contrary, they must give free time to the victims of their criticism. . . .

The reasons for these distinctions are complex, but two have relevance to the present case. First, the broadcast media have established a uniquely pervasive presence in the lives of all Americans. Patently offensive, indecent material presented over the airwaves confronts the citizen, not only in public, but also in the privacy of the home, where the individual's right to be left alone plainly outweighs the First Amendment rights of an intruder. . . . Because the broadcast audience is constantly tuning in and out, prior warnings cannot completely protect the listener or viewer from unexpected program content. To say that one may avoid further offense by turning off the radio when he hears indecent language is like saying that the remedy for an assault is to run away after the first blow. One may hang up on an indecent phone call, but that option does not give the caller a constitutional immunity or avoid a harm that has already taken place.

Second, broadcasting is uniquely accessible to children, even those too young to read. . . . Pacifica's broadcast could have enlarged a child's vocabulary in an instant. Other forms of offensive expression may be withheld from the young without restricting the expression at its source. Bookstores and motion picture theaters, for example, may be prohibited from making indecent material available to children. We held in *Ginsberg v. New York* . . . [1968], that the government's interest in the "well-being of its young" and in supporting "parents' claim to authority in their own household" justified the regulation of otherwise protected expression. The ease with which children may obtain access to broadcast material, coupled with the concerns recognized in *Ginsberg*, amply justify special treatment of indecent broadcasting.

It is appropriate, in conclusion, to emphasize the narrowness of our holding. This case does not involve a two-way radio conversation between a cab driver and a dispatcher, or a telecast of an Elizabethan comedy. We have not decided that an occasional expletive in either setting would justify any sanction, or, indeed, that this broadcast would justify a criminal prosecution. The Commission's decision rested entirely on a nuisance rationale under which context is all-important. The concept requires consideration of a host of variables. The time of day was emphasized by the Commission. The content of the program in which the language is used will also affect the composition of the audience, and differences between radio, television, and perhaps closed-circuit transmissions, may also be relevant. As Justice Sutherland wrote, a "nuisance may be merely a right thing in the wrong place—like a pig in the parlor instead of the barnyard." . . . We simply hold that when the Commission finds that a pig has entered the parlor, the exercise of its regulatory power does not depend on proof that the pig is obscene. . . .

Justice Powell, with whom ***Justice Blackmun*** joins, concurring in part.

The issue . . . is whether the Commission may impose civil sanctions on a licensee radio station for broadcasting the monologue at two o'clock in the afternoon. The Commission's primary concern was to prevent the broadcast from reaching the ears of unsupervised children who were likely to be in the audience at that hour. In essence, the Commission sought to "channel" the monologue to hours when the fewest unsupervised children would be exposed

to it. In my view, this consideration provides strong support for the Commission's holding.

The Court has recognized society's right to "adopt more stringent controls on communicative materials available to youths than on those available to adults." . . . This recognition stems in large part from the fact that "a child . . . is not possessed of that full capacity for individual choice which is the presupposition of First Amendment guarantees." . . . At the same time, such speech may have a deeper and more lasting negative effect on a child than on an adult. . . . The Commission properly held that the speech from which society may attempt to shield its children is not limited to that which appeals to the youthful prurient interest. The language involved in this case is as potentially degrading and harmful to children as representations of many erotic acts.

In most instances, the dissemination of this kind of speech to children may be limited without also limiting willing adults' access to it. Sellers of printed and recorded matter and exhibitors of motion pictures and live performances may be required to shut their doors to children, but such a requirement has no effect on adults' access. The difficulty is that such a physical separation of the audience cannot be accomplished in the broadcast media. . . .

In my view, the Commission was entitled to give substantial weight to this difference in reaching its decision in this case.

A second difference, not without relevance, is that broadcasting—unlike most other forms of communication—comes directly into the home, the one place where people ordinarily have the right not to be assaulted by uninvited and offensive sights and sounds. . . . The Commission also was entitled to give this factor appropriate weight in the circumstances of the instant case. This is not to say, however, that the Commission has an unrestricted license to decide what speech, protected in other media, may be banned from the airwaves in order to protect unwilling adults from momentary exposure to it in their homes. Making the sensitive judgments required in these cases is not easy. But this responsibility has been reposed initially in the Commission, and its judgment is entitled to respect. . . .

In short, I agree that on the facts of this case, the Commission's order did not violate respondent's First Amendment rights. . . .

In my view, the result in this case does not turn on whether Carlin's monologue, viewed as a whole, or the words that constitute it, have more or less "value" than a candidate's campaign speech. This is a judgment for each person to make, not one for the judges to impose upon him.

The result turns instead on the unique characteristics of the broadcast media, combined with society's right to protect its children from speech generally agreed to be inappropriate for their years, and with the interest of unwilling adults in not being assaulted by such offensive speech in their homes. Moreover, I doubt whether today's decision will prevent any adult who wishes to receive Carlin's message in Carlin's own words from doing so, and from making for himself a value judgment as to the merit of the message and words.

Justice Brennan, with whom *Justice Marshall* joins, dissenting.

. . . Most parents will undoubtedly find understandable as well as commendable the Court's sympathy with the FCC's desire to prevent offensive broadcasts from reaching the ears of unsupervised children. Unfortunately, the facial appeal of this justification for radio censorship masks its constitutional insufficiency. . . .

Because the Carlin monologue is obviously not an erotic appeal to the prurient interests of children, the Court, for the first time, allows the government to prevent minors from gaining access to materials that are not obscene, and are therefore protected, as to them. It thus ignores our recent admonition that "[s]peech that is neither obscene as to youths nor subject to some other legitimate proscription cannot be suppressed solely to protect the young from ideas or images that a legislative body thinks unsuitable for them." . . . The Court's refusal to follow its own pronouncements is especially lamentable since it has the anomalous subsidiary effect, at least in the radio context at issue here, of making completely unavailable to adults material which may not constitutionally be kept even from children. This result violates in spades the principle of *Butler v. Michigan* . . . (1957). *Butler* involved a challenge to a Michigan statute that forbade the publication, sale, or distribution of printed material "tending to incite minors to violent or depraved or immoral acts, manifestly tending to the corruption of the morals of youth." Although *Roth v. United States* . . . (1957) had not yet been decided, it is at least arguable that the material the statute in *Butler* was designed to suppress could have been constitutionally denied to children. Nevertheless, this Court found the statute unconstitutional. . . .

Where, as here, the government may not prevent the exposure of minors to the suppressed material, the principle of *Butler* applies *a fortiori.* . . .

[N]either . . . the intrusive nature of radio [nor] the presence of children in the listening audience . . . can . . . support the FCC's disapproval of the Carlin monologue. These two asserted justifications are further plagued by a common failing: the lack of principled limits on their use as a basis for FCC censorship. No such limits come readily to mind, and neither of the opinions constituting the Court serve to clarify the extent to which the FCC may assert the privacy and children-in-the-audience rationales as justification for expunging from the airways protected communications the Commission finds offensive. Taken to their logical extreme, these rationales would support the cleansing of public radio of any "four-letter words" whatsoever, regardless of their context. The rationales could justify the banning from radio of a myriad of literary works, novels, poems, and plays by the likes of Shakespeare, Joyce, Hemingway, Ben Jonson, Henry Fielding, Robert Burns, and Chaucer; they could support the suppression of a good deal of political speech, such as the Nixon tapes; and they could even provide the basis for imposing sanctions for the broadcast of certain portions of the Bible. . . .

To insure that the FCC's regulation of protected speech does not exceed these bounds, my Brother Powell is content to rely upon the judgment of the Commission while my Brother Stevens deems it prudent to rely on this Court's ability accurately to assess the worth of various kinds of speech. For my own part, even accepting that this case is limited to its facts, I would place the responsibility and the right to weed worthless and offensive communications from the public airways where it belongs and where, until today, it resided: in a public free to choose those communications worthy of its attention from a marketplace unsullied by the censor's hand. . . .

Justice Stewart, with whom *Justice Brennan, Justice White,* and *Justice Marshall* join, dissenting.

I think that "indecent" should properly be read as meaning no more than "obscene." Since the Carlin monologue concededly was not "obscene," I believe that the Commission lacked statutory authority to ban it. Under this construction of the statute, it is unnecessary to address the difficult and important issue of the Commission's constitutional power to prohibit speech that would be constitutionally protected outside the context of electronic broadcasting. . . .

Case

RENO V. AMERICAN CIVIL LIBERTIES UNION

521 U.S. 844; 117 S.Ct. 2329; 138 L.Ed. 2d 874 (1997)
Vote: 7-2

In this widely publicized case, the Court considers the constitutionality of the Communications Decency Act (CDA), federal legislation enacted to protect minors from "indecent" and "patently offensive" communications on the Internet.

Justice Stevens delivered the opinion of the Court.

. . . Notwithstanding the legitimacy and importance of the congressional goal of protecting children from harmful materials, we agree with the three judge District Court that the statute abridges "the freedom of speech" protected by the First Amendment. . . .

. . . In its appeal, the Government argues that the District Court erred in holding that the CDA violated both the First Amendment because it is overbroad and the Fifth Amendment because it is vague. While we discuss the vagueness of the CDA because of its relevance to the First Amendment overbreadth inquiry, we conclude that the judgment should be affirmed without reaching the Fifth Amendment issue. We begin our analysis by reviewing the principal authorities on which the Government relies. Then, after describing the overbreadth of the CDA, we consider the Government's specific contentions, including its submission that we save portions of the statute either by severance or by fashioning judicial limitations on the scope of its coverage.

In arguing for reversal, the Government contends that the CDA is plainly constitutional under three of our prior decisions: (1) *Ginsberg v. New York* . . . (1968); (2) *FCC v. Pacifica Foundation* . . . (1978); and (3) *Renton v. Playtime Theatres, Inc.,* . . . (1986). A close look at these cases, however, raises—rather than relieves—doubts concerning the constitutionality of the CDA. . . . *[Justice Stevens proceeds to discuss these precedents.]*

These precedents . . . surely do not require us to uphold the CDA and are fully consistent with the application of the most stringent review of its provisions.

In *Southeastern Promotions, Ltd. v. Conrad* . . . (1975), we observed that "[e]ach medium of expression . . . may present its own problems." Thus, some of our cases have recognized special justifications for regulation of the broadcast media that are not applicable to other speakers, see *Red Lion Broadcasting Co. v. FCC* . . . (1969); *FCC v. Pacifica Foundation* . . . (1978). In these cases, the Court relied on the history of extensive government regulation of the broadcast medium; the scarcity of available frequencies at its inception; and its "invasive" nature.

Those factors are not present in cyberspace. Neither before nor after the enactment of the CDA have the vast democratic fora of the Internet been subject to the type of government supervision and regulation that has attended the broadcast industry. Moreover, the Internet is not as "invasive" as radio or television. The District Court specifically found that "[c]ommunications over the Internet do not 'invade' an individual's home or appear on one's computer screen unbidden. Users seldom encounter content 'by accident.'" It also found that "[a]lmost all sexually explicit images are preceded by warnings as to the content," and cited testimony that "'odds are slim' that a user would come across a sexually explicit sight by accident." . . .

Finally, unlike the conditions that prevailed when Congress first authorized regulation of the broadcast spectrum, the Internet can hardly be considered a "scarce" expressive commodity. It provides relatively unlimited, low cost capacity for communication of all kinds. The Government estimates that "[a]s many as 40 million people use the Internet today, and that figure is expected to grow to 200 million by 1999." This dynamic, multifaceted category of communication includes not only traditional print and news services, but also audio, video, and still images, as well as interactive, real time dialogue. Through the use of chat rooms, any person with a phone line can become a town crier with a voice that resonates farther than it could from any soapbox. Through the use of Web pages, mail exploders, and newsgroups, the same individual can become a pamphleteer. As the District Court found, "the content on the Internet is as diverse as human thought." . . . We agree with its conclusion that our cases provide no basis for qualifying the level of First Amendment scrutiny that should be applied to this medium.

Regardless of whether the CDA is so vague that it violates the Fifth Amendment, the many ambiguities concerning the scope of its coverage render it problematic for purposes of the First Amendment. For instance, each of the two parts of the CDA uses a different linguistic form. The first uses the word "indecent," . . . while the second speaks of material that "in context, depicts or describes, in terms patently offensive as measured by contemporary community standards, sexual or excretory activities or organs." Given the absence of a definition of either term, this difference in language will provoke uncertainty among speakers about how the two standards relate to each other and just what they mean.

Could a speaker confidently assume that a serious discussion about birth control practices, homosexuality, the First Amendment issues raised by the Appendix to our *Pacifica* opinion, or the consequences of prison rape would not violate the CDA? This uncertainty undermines the likelihood that the CDA has been carefully tailored to the congressional goal of protecting minors from potentially harmful materials.

The vagueness of the CDA is a matter of special concern for two reasons. First, the CDA is a content based regulation of speech. The vagueness of such a regulation raises special First Amendment concerns because of its obvious chilling effect on free speech. . . . Second, the CDA is a criminal statute. In addition to the opprobrium and stigma of a criminal conviction, the CDA threatens violators with penalties including up to two years in prison for each act of violation. The severity of criminal sanctions may well cause speakers to remain silent rather than communicate even arguably unlawful words, ideas, and images. . . . As a practical matter, this increased deterrent effect, coupled with the "risk of discriminatory enforcement" of vague regulations, poses greater First Amendment concerns. . . .

In contrast to *Miller* [*v. California*] and our other previous cases, the CDA . . . presents a greater threat of censoring speech that, in fact, falls outside the statute's scope. Given the vague contours of the coverage of the statute, it unquestionably silences some speakers whose messages would be entitled to constitutional protection. That danger provides further reason for insisting that the statute not be overly broad. The CDA's burden on protected speech cannot be justified if it could be avoided by a more carefully drafted statute.

We are persuaded that the CDA lacks the precision that the First Amendment requires when a statute regulates the content of speech. In order to deny minors access to potentially harmful speech, the CDA effectively suppresses a large amount of speech that adults have a constitutional right to receive and to address to one another. That burden on adult speech is unacceptable if less restrictive alternatives would be at least as effective in achieving the legitimate purpose that the statute was enacted to serve.

In evaluating the free speech rights of adults, we have made it perfectly clear that "[s]exual expression which is indecent but not obscene is protected by the First Amendment." . . . Indeed, *Pacifica* itself admonished that "the fact that society may find speech offensive is not a sufficient reason for suppressing it." . . .

It is true that we have repeatedly recognized the governmental interest in protecting children from harmful materials. . . . But that interest does not justify an unnecessarily broad suppression of speech addressed to adults. As we have explained, the Government may not "reduc[e] the adult population . . . to . . . only what is fit for children." . . .

In arguing that the CDA does not so diminish adult communication, the Government relies on the incorrect factual premise that prohibiting a transmission whenever it is known that one of its recipients is a minor would not interfere with adult to adult communication. The findings of the District Court make clear that this premise is untenable.

Given the size of the potential audience for most messages, in the absence of a viable age verification process, the sender must be charged with knowing that one or more minors will likely view it. Knowledge that, for instance, one or more members of a 100 person chat group will be minor—and therefore that it would be a crime to send the group an indecent message—would surely burden communication among adults.

The District Court found that at the time of trial existing technology did not include any effective method for a sender to prevent minors from obtaining access to its communications on the Internet without also denying access to adults. The Court found no effective way to determine the age of a user who is accessing material through e mail, mail exploders, newsgroups, or chat rooms. As a practical matter, the Court also found that it would be prohibitively expensive for noncommercial—as well as some commercial—speakers who have web sites to verify that their users are adults. . . . These limitations must inevitably curtail a significant amount of adult communication on the Internet. By contrast, the District Court found that "[d]espite its limitations, currently available user based software suggests that a reasonably effective method by which parents can prevent their children from accessing sexually explicit and other material which parents may believe is inappropriate for their children will soon be widely available." . . .

The breadth of the CDA's coverage is wholly unprecedented. . . . [T]he scope of the CDA is not limited to commercial speech or commercial entities. Its open ended prohibitions embrace all nonprofit entities and individuals posting indecent messages or displaying them on their own computers in the presence of minors. The general, undefined terms "indecent" and "patently offensive" cover large amounts of nonpornographic material with serious educational or other value. Moreover, the "community standards" criterion as applied to the Internet means that any communication available to a nationwide audience will be judged by the standards of the community most likely to be offended by the message. The regulated subject matter includes any of the seven "dirty words" used in the Pacifica monologue, the use of which the Government's expert acknowledged could constitute a felony. . . . It may also extend to discussions about prison rape or safe sexual practices, artistic images that include nude subjects, and arguably the card catalogue of the Carnegie Library. . . .

The breadth of this content based restriction of speech imposes an especially heavy burden on the Government to explain why a less restrictive provision would not be as effective as the CDA. It has not done so. The arguments in this Court have referred to possible alternatives such as requiring that indecent material be "tagged" in a way that facilitates parental control of material coming into their homes, making exceptions for messages with artistic or educational value, providing some tolerance for parental choice, and regulating some portions of the Internet— such as commercial web sites—differently than others, such as chat rooms. Particularly in the light of the absence of any detailed findings by the Congress, or even hearings addressing the special problems of the CDA, we are persuaded that the CDA is not narrowly tailored if that requirement has any meaning at all. . . .

We agree with the District Court's conclusion that the CDA places an unacceptably heavy burden on protected speech, and that the defenses do not constitute the sort of "narrow tailoring" that will save an otherwise patently invalid unconstitutional provision. . . . The CDA, casting a far darker shadow over free speech, threatens to torch a large segment of the Internet community. . . .

In this Court, though not in the District Court, the Government asserts that—in addition to its interest in protecting children—its "[e]qually significant" interest in fostering the growth of the Internet provides an independent basis for upholding the constitutionality of the CDA. . . . The Government apparently assumes that the unregulated availability of "indecent" and "patently offensive" material on the Internet is driving countless citizens away from the medium because of the risk of exposing themselves or their children to harmful material.

We find this argument singularly unpersuasive. The dramatic expansion of this new marketplace of ideas contradicts the factual basis of this contention. The record demonstrates that the growth of the Internet has been and continues to be phenomenal. As a matter of constitutional tradition, in the absence of evidence to the contrary, we presume that governmental regulation of the content of speech is more likely to interfere with the free exchange of ideas than to encourage it. The interest in encouraging freedom of expression in a democratic society outweighs any theoretical but unproven benefit of censorship.

For the foregoing reasons, the judgment of the district court is affirmed.

Justice O'Connor, with whom the *Chief Justice* joins, concurring in the judgment in part and dissenting in part.

. . . I view the Communications Decency Act of 1996 (CDA) as little more than an attempt by Congress to create "adult zones" on the Internet. Our precedent indicates that the creation of such zones can be constitutionally sound. Despite the soundness of its purpose, however, portions of the CDA are unconstitutional because they stray from the blueprint our prior cases have developed for constructing a "zoning law" that passes constitutional muster. . . .

. . . [T]o prevail in a facial challenge, it is not enough for a plaintiff to show "some" overbreadth. Our cases require a proof of "real" and "substantial" overbreadth, . . . and appellees have not carried their burden in this case. In my view, the universe of speech constitutionally protected as to minors but banned by the CDA—i.e., the universe of material that is "patently offensive," but which nonetheless has some redeeming value for minors or does not appeal to their prurient interest—is a very small one. Appellees cite no examples of speech falling within this universe and do not attempt to explain why that universe is substantial "in relation to the statute's plainly legitimate sweep." . . . That the CDA might deny minors the right to obtain material that has some "value," . . . is largely beside the point. While discussions about prison rape or nude art . . . may have some redeeming education value for adults, they do not necessarily have any such value for minors, and . . . minors only have a First Amendment right to obtain patently offensive material that has "redeeming social importance for minors." . . . There is also no evidence in the record to support the contention that "many [e] mail transmissions from an adult to a minor are conversations between family members," . . . and no support for the legal proposition that such speech is absolutely immune from regulation. Accordingly, in my view, the CDA does not burden a substantial amount of minors' constitutionally protected speech.

. . . [T]he constitutionality of the CDA as a zoning law hinges on the extent to which it substantially interferes with the First Amendment rights of adults. Because the rights of adults are infringed only by the "display" provision and by the "indecency transmission" and "specific person" provisions as applied to communications involving more than one adult, I would invalidate the CDA only to that extent. Insofar as the "indecency transmission" and "specific person" provisions prohibit the use of indecent speech in communications between an adult and one or more minors, however, they can and should be sustained. The Court reaches a contrary conclusion, and from that holding that I respectfully dissent.

Case

EDWARDS V. SOUTH CAROLINA

372 U.S. 229; 83 S.Ct. 680; 9 L.Ed. 2d 697 (1963)
Vote: 8–1

In this case the Court considers the issues of freedom of assembly and freedom of speech in the public forum in the context of a civil rights demonstration on the grounds of a state capitol.

Mr. Justice Stewart delivered the opinion of the Court.

The petitioners, 187 in number, were convicted in a magistrate's court in Columbia, South Carolina, of the common-law crime of breach of the peace. . . .

There was no substantial conflict in the trial evidence. Late in the morning of March 2, 1961, the petitioners, high school and college students of the Negro race, met at the Zion Baptist Church in Columbia. From there, at about noon, they walked in separate groups of about 15 to the South Carolina State House grounds, an area of two city blocks open to the general public. Their purpose was "to submit a protest to the citizens of South Carolina, along with the Legislative Bodies of South Carolina, our feelings and our dissatisfaction with the present condition of discriminatory actions against Negroes, in general, and to let them know that we were dissatisfied and that we would like for the laws which prohibited Negro privileges in this State to be removed."

Already on the State House grounds when the petitioners arrived were 30 or more law enforcement officers, who had advance knowledge that the petitioners were coming. Each group of petitioners entered the grounds through a driveway and parking area known in the record as the "horseshoe." As they entered, they were told by the law enforcement officials that "they had a right, as a citizen, to go through the State House grounds, as any other citizen has, as long as they were peaceful." During the next half hour or 45 minutes, the petitioners, in the same small groups, walked single file or two abreast in an orderly way through the grounds, each group carrying placards bearing such messages as "I am proud to be a Negro" and "Down with segregation."

During this time a crowd of some 200 to 300 onlookers had collected in the horseshoe area and on the adjacent sidewalks. There was no evidence to suggest that these onlookers were anything but curious, and no evidence at all of any threatening remarks, hostile gestures, or offensive language on the part of any member of the crowd. The City Manager testified that he recognized some of the onlookers, whom he did not identify, as "possible trouble makers," but his subsequent testimony made clear that nobody among the crowd actually caused or threatened any trouble. There was no obstruction of pedestrian or vehicular traffic within the State House grounds. No vehicle was prevented from entering or leaving the horseshoe area. Although vehicular traffic at a nearby street intersection was slowed down somewhat, an officer was dispatched to keep traffic moving. There were a number of bystanders on the public sidewalks adjacent to the State House grounds, but they all moved on when asked to do so, and there was no impediment of pedestrian traffic. Police protection at the scene was at all times sufficient to meet any foreseeable possibility of disorder.

In the situation and under the circumstances thus described, the police authorities advised the petitioners that they would be arrested if they did not disperse within 15 minutes. Instead of dispersing, the petitioners engaged in what the City manager described as "boisterous," "loud," and "flamboyant" conduct, which, as his later testimony made clear, consisted of listening to a "religious harangue" by one of their leaders, and loudly singing "The Star Spangled Banner" and other patriotic and religious songs, while stamping their feet and clapping their hands. After 15 minutes had passed, the police arrested the petitioners and marched them off to jail.

Upon this evidence the state trial court convicted the petitioners of breach of the peace, and imposed sentences ranging from a $10 fine or five days in jail, to a $100 fine or 30 days in jail. In affirming the judgments, the Supreme Court of South Carolina said that under the law of that State the offense of breach of the peace "is not susceptible for exact definition," but that the "general definition of the offense" is as follows:

In general terms, a breach of the peace is a violation of public order, a disturbance of the public tranquility, by any act or conduct inciting to violence . . . , it includes any violation of any law enacted to preserve peace and good order. It may consist of an act of violence or an act likely to produce violence. It is not necessary that the peace be actually broken to lay the foundation for a prosecution for this offense. If what is done is unjustifiable and unlawful, tending with sufficient directness to break the peace, no more is required. Nor is actual personal violence an essential element in the offense. . . .

By "peace," as used in the law in this connection, is meant the tranquility enjoyed by citizens of a municipality or community where good order reigns among its members, which is the natural right of all persons in political society. . . .

:. . . It has long been established that these First Amendment freedoms are protected by the Fourteenth Amendment from invasion by the States. . . . The circumstances in this case reflect an exercise of these basic constitutional rights in their most pristine and classic form. The petitioners felt aggrieved by laws of South Carolina which allegedly "prohibited Negro privileges in this State." They peaceably assembled at the site of the State Government and there peaceably expressed their grievances "to the citizens of South Carolina, along with the Legislative Bodies of South Carolina." Not until they were told by police officials that they must disperse on pain of arrest did they do more. Even then, they but sang patriotic and religious songs after one of their leaders had delivered a "religious harangue." There was no violence or threat of violence on their part, or on the part of any member of the crowd watching them. Police protection was "ample."

This, therefore, was a far cry from the situation in *Feiner v. New York* [1951], . . . where two policemen were faced with a crowd which was "pushing, shoving, and milling around," . . . where at least one member of the crowd "threatened violence if the police did not act," . . . where "the crowd was pressing closer around petitioner and the officer," . . . and where "the speaker passes the bounds of argument or persuasion and undertakes incitement to riot." . . . And the record is barren of any evidence of "fighting words." . . .

We do not review in this case criminal convictions resulting from the even-handed application of a precise and narrowly drawn regulatory statute evincing a legislative judgment that certain specific conduct be limited or proscribed. If, for example, the petitioners had been convicted upon evidence that they had violated a law regulating traffic, or had disobeyed a law reasonably limiting the periods during which the State House grounds were open to the public, this would be a different case. . . . These petitioners were convicted of an offense so generalized as to be, in the words of the South Carolina Supreme Court, "not susceptible of exact definition." And they were convicted upon evidence which showed no more than that the opinions which they were peaceably expressing were sufficiently opposed to the views of the majority of the community to attract a crowd and necessitate police protection. . . .

Mr. Justice Clark, dissenting.

. . . Beginning, as did the South Carolina courts, with the premise that the petitioners were entitled to assemble and voice their dissatisfaction with segregation, the enlargement of constitutional protection for the conduct here is as fallacious as would be the conclusion that free speech necessarily includes the right to broadcast from a sound truck in the public street. . . . Here the petitioners were permitted without hindrance to exercise their rights of free speech and assembly. Their arrests occurred only after a situation arose in which the law-enforcement officials on the scene considered that a dangerous disturbance was imminent. The County Court found that "[t]he evidence is clear that the officers were motivated solely by a proper concern for the preservation of order and prevention of further interference with traffic upon the public streets and sidewalks." . . .

. . . [I]n *Feiner v. New York* . . . (1951), we upheld a conviction for breach of the peace in a situation no more dangerous than that found here. There the demonstration was conducted by only one person and the crowd was limited to approximately 80, as compared with the present lineup of some 200 demonstrators and 300 onlookers. There the petitioner was "endeavoring to arouse the Negro people against the whites, urging that they rise up in arms and fight for equal rights." . . . Only one person—in a city having an entirely different historical background—was exhorting adults. Here 200 youthful Negro demonstrators were being aroused to a "fever pitch" before a crowd of some 300 people who undoubtedly were hostile. Perhaps their speech was not so animated but in this setting their actions, their placards reading "You may jail our bodies but not our souls" and their chanting of "I Shall Not Be Moved," accompanied by stamping feet and clapping hands, created a much greater danger of riot and disorder. It is my belief that anyone conversant with the almost spontaneous combustion in some Southern communities in such a situation will agree that the [city's] action may well have averted a major catastrophe.

The gravity of the danger here surely needs no further explication. The imminence of that danger has been emphasized at every stage of this proceeding, from the complaints charging that the demonstrations "tended directly to immediate violence" to the State Supreme Court's affirmance on the authority of *Feiner*. . . . This record, then, shows no steps backward from a standard of "clear and present danger." But to say that the police may not intervene until the riot has occurred is like keeping out the doctor until the patient dies. I cannot subscribe to such a doctrine. . . .

Case

ADDERLEY V. FLORIDA

385 U.S. 39; 87 S.Ct. 242; 17 L.Ed. 2d 149 (1966)
Vote: 5–4

In this case the Court reviews the convictions of thirty-two college students who marched onto the premises of the county jail in Tallahassee, Florida, to protest the arrest of other students the previous day. Are the premises of a county jail a public forum?

Mr. Justice Black delivered the opinion of the Court.

Petitioners, Harriett Louise Adderley and 31 other persons, were convicted by a jury in a joint trial in the County Judge's Court of Leon County, Florida, on a charge of "trespass with a malicious and mischievous intent" upon the premises of the county jail contrary to 821.18 of the Florida statutes set out below. Petitioners, apparently all students of the Florida A. & M. University in Tallahassee, had gone from the school to the jail about a mile away, along with many other students, to "demonstrate" at the jail their protests of arrests of other protesting students the day before, and perhaps to protest more generally against state and local policies and practices of racial segregation, including segregation of the jail. The county sheriff, legal custodian of the jail and jail grounds, tried to persuade the students to leave the jail grounds. When this did not work, he notified them that they must leave, that if they did not leave he would arrest them for trespassing, and that if they resisted he would charge them with that as well. Some of the students left but others, including petitioners, remained and they were arrested. On appeal the convictions were affirmed by the Florida Circuit Court and then by the Florida District Court of Appeal. . . . That being the highest state court to which they could appeal, petitioners applied to us for certiorari contending that, in view of petitioners' purpose to protest against jail and other segregation policies, their conviction denied them "rights of free speech, assembly, petition, due process of law and equal protection of the laws as guaranteed by the Fourteenth Amendment to the Constitution of the United States." On this "Question Presented" we granted certiorari. . . .

Petitioners have insisted from the beginning of this case that it is controlled by and must be reversed because of our prior cases of *Edwards v. South Carolina* . . . and *Cox v. Louisiana*. . . . We cannot agree. . . .

Petitioners argue that "petty criminal statutes may not be used to violate minorities' constitutional rights." This

of course is true but this abstract proposition gets us nowhere in deciding this case. . . .

Petitioners here contend that "Petitioners' convictions are based on a total lack of relevant evidence." If true, this would be a denial of due process. . . . Both in the petition for certiorari and in the brief on the merits petitioners state that their summary of the evidence "does not conflict with the facts contained in the Circuit Court's opinion" which was in effect affirmed by the District Court of Appeal. . . . That statement is correct and petitioners' summary of facts, as well as that of the Circuit Court, shows an abundance of facts to support the jury's verdict of guilty in this case.

In summary both these statements show testimony ample to prove this: Disturbed and upset by the arrest of their schoolmates the day before, a large number of Florida A. & M. students assembled on the school grounds and decided to march down to the county jail. Some apparently wanted to be put in jail too, along with the students already there. A group of around 200 marched from the school and arrived at the jail singing and clapping. They went directly to the jail-door entrance where they were met by a deputy sheriff, evidently surprised by their arrival. He asked them to move back, claiming they were blocking the entrance to the jail and fearing that they might attempt to enter the jail. They moved back part of the way, where they stood or sat, singing, clapping and dancing, on the jail driveway and on an adjacent grassy area upon the jail premises. This particular jail entrance and driveway were not normally used by the public, but by the sheriff's department for transporting prisoners to and from the courts several blocks away and by commercial concerns for servicing the jail. Even after their partial retreat, the demonstrators continued to block vehicular passage over this driveway up to the entrance of the jail. Someone called the sheriff who was at the moment apparently conferring with one of the state court judges about incidents connected with prior arrests for demonstrations. When the sheriff returned to the jail, he immediately inquired if all was safe inside the jail and was told it was. He then engaged in a conversation with two of the leaders. He told them that they were trespassing upon jail property and that he would give them 10 minutes to leave or he would arrest them. Neither of the leaders did anything to disperse the crowd, and one of them told the sheriff that they wanted to get arrested. A local minister talked with some of the demonstrators and told them not to enter the jail, because they could not arrest themselves, but just to remain where they were. After about 10 minutes, the sheriff, in a voice loud enough to be heard by all, told the demonstrators that he was the legal custodian of the jail and its premises, that they were trespassing on county property in violation of the law, that they should all leave forthwith or he would arrest them, and that if they attempted to resist arrest, he would charge them with that as a separate offense. Some of the group then left. Others, including all petitioners, did not leave. Some of them sat down. In a few minutes, realizing that the remaining demonstrators had no intention of leaving, the sheriff ordered his deputies to surround those remaining on jail premises and placed them, 107 demonstrators, under arrest. The sheriff unequivocally testified that he did not arrest any persons other than those who were on the jail premises. Of the three petitioners testifying, two insisted that they were arrested before they had a chance to leave, had they wanted to, and one testified that she did not intend to leave. The sheriff again explicitly testified that he did not arrest any person who was attempting to leave.

Under the foregoing testimony the jury was authorized to find that the State had proven every essential element of the crime, as it was defined by the state court. That interpretation is, of course, binding on us, leaving only the question of whether conviction of the state offense, thus defined, unconstitutionally deprives petitioners of their rights to freedom of speech, press, assembly or petition. We hold it does not. The sheriff, as jail custodian, had power, as the state courts have here held, to direct that this large crowd of people get off the grounds. There is not a shred of evidence in this record that this power was exercised, or that its exercise was sanctioned by the lower courts, because the sheriff objected to what was being sung or said by the demonstrators or because he disagreed with the objectives of their protest. The record reveals that he objected only to their presence on that part of the jail grounds reserved for jail uses. There is no evidence at all that on any other occasion had similarly large groups of the public been permitted to gather on this portion of the jail grounds for any purpose. Nothing in the Constitution of the United States prevents Florida from even-handed enforcement of its general trespass statute against those refusing to obey the sheriff's order to remove themselves from what amounted to the curtilage of the jailhouse. The State, no less than a private owner of property, has power to preserve the property under its control for the use to which it is lawfully dedicated. For this reason there is no merit to the petitioners' argument that they had a constitutional right to stay on the property, over the jail custodian's objections, because this "area chosen for the peaceful civil rights demonstration was not only 'reasonable'

but also particularly appropriate. . . ." Such an argument has as its major unarticulated premise the assumption that people who want to propagandize protests or views have a constitutional right to do so whenever and however and wherever they please. That concept of constitutional law was vigorously and forthrightly rejected in . . . *Cox v. Louisiana*. . . . We reject it again. . . .

Mr. Justice Douglas, with whom the *Chief Justice, Mr. Justice Brennan,* and *Mr. Justice Fortas* concur, dissenting.

. . . The jailhouse, like an executive mansion, a legislative chamber, a courthouse, or the statehouse itself . . . is one of the seats of government, whether it be the Tower of London, the Bastille, or a small county jail. And when it houses political prisoners or those who many think are unjustly held, it is an obvious center for protest. The right to petition for the redress of grievances has an ancient history and is not limited to writing a letter or sending a telegram to a congressman; it is not confined to appearing before the local city council, or writing letters to the President or Governor or Mayor. . . .

Conventional methods of petitioning may be, and often have been, shut off to large groups of our citizens. Legislators may turn deaf ears; formal complaints may be routed endlessly through a bureaucratic maze; courts may let the wheels of justice grind very slowly. Those who do not control television and radio, those who cannot afford to advertise in newspapers or circulate elaborate pamphlets may have only a more limited type of access to public officials. Their methods should not be condemned as tactics of obstruction and harassment as long as the assembly and petition are peaceable, as these were.

There is no question that petitioners had as their purpose a protest against the arrest of Florida A. & M. students for trying to integrate public theatres. The sheriff's testimony indicates that he well understood the purpose of the rally. The petitioners who testified unequivocally stated that the group was protesting the arrests, and state and local policies of segregation, including segregation of the jail. This testimony was not contradicted or even questioned. The fact that no one gave a formal speech, that no elaborate handbills were distributed, and that the group was not laden with signs would seem to be immaterial. Such methods are not the *sine qua non* of petitioning for the redress of grievances. The group did sing "freedom" songs. And history shows that a song can be a powerful tool of protest. . . . There was no violence; no threat of violence; no attempted jail break; no storming of a prison; no plan or plot to do anything but protest. The evidence is uncontradicted that the petitioners' conduct did not upset the jailhouse routine; things went on as they normally would. None of the group entered the jail. Indeed, they moved back from the entrance as they were instructed. There was no shoving, no pushing, no disorder or threat of riot. It is said that some of the group blocked part of the driveway leading to the jail entrance. The chief jailer, to be sure, testified that vehicles would not have been able to use the driveway. Never did the students locate themselves so as to cause interference with persons or vehicles going to or coming from the jail. Indeed, it is undisputed that the sheriff and deputy sheriff, in separate cars, were able to drive up the driveway to the parking places near the entrance and that no one obstructed their path. Further, it is undisputed that the entrance to the jail was not blocked. And whenever the students were requested to move they did so. If there was congestion, the solution was a further request to move to lawns or parking areas, not complete ejection and arrest. The claim is made that a tradesman waited inside the jail because some of the protestants were sitting around and leaning on his truck. The only evidence supporting such a conclusion is the testimony of a deputy sheriff that the tradesman "came to the door . . . and then did not leave." His remaining is just as consistent with a desire to satisfy his curiosity as it is with a restraint. Finally, the fact that some of the protestants may have felt their cause so just that they were willing to be arrested for making their protest outside the jail seems wholly irrelevant. A petition is nonetheless a petition, though its futility may make martyrdom attractive.

We do violence to the First Amendment when we permit this "petition for redress of grievances" to be turned into a trespass action. It does not help to analogize this problem to the problem of picketing. Picketing is a form of protest usually directed against private interests. I do not see how rules governing picketing in general are relevant to this express constitutional right to assemble and to petition for redress of grievances. In the first place the jailhouse grounds were not marked with "no trespassing!" signs, nor does respondent claim that the public was generally excluded from the grounds. Only the sheriff's fiat transformed lawful conduct into an unlawful trespass. To say that a private owner could have done the same if the rally had taken place on private property is to speak of a different case, as an assembly and a petition for redress of grievances run to government, not to private proprietors.

The Court forgets that prior to this day our decisions have drastically limited the application of state statutes inhibiting the right to go peacefully on public property to exercise First Amendment rights. . . .

There may be some public places which are so clearly committed to other purposes that their use for the airing of grievances is anomalous. There may be some instances in which assemblies and petitions for redress of grievances are not consistent with other necessary purposes of public property. A noisy meeting may be out of keeping with the serenity of the statehouse or the quiet of the courthouse. No one, for example, would suggest that the Senate gallery is the proper place for a vociferous protest rally. And in other cases it may be necessary to adjust the right to petition for redress of grievances to the other interests inhering in the uses to which the public property is normally put. . . . But this is quite different from saying that all public places are off limits to people with grievances. . . .

Today a trespass law is used to penalize people for exercising a constitutional right. Tomorrow a disorderly conduct statute, a breach-of-the-peace statute, a vagrancy statute will be put to the same end. It is said that the sheriff did not make the arrests because of the views which petitioners espoused. That excuse is usually given, as we know from the many cases involving arrests of minority groups for breaches of the peace, unlawful assemblies, and parading without a permit. The charge against William Penn, who preached a nonconformist doctrine in a street in London, was that he caused "a great concourse and tumult of people" in contempt of the King and "to the great disturbance of his peace." . . . That was in 1670. In modern times, also such arrests are usually sought to be justified by some legitimate function of government. Yet by allowing these orderly and civilized protests against injustice to be suppressed, we only increase the forces of frustration which the conditions of second-class citizenship are generating amongst us.

Case

LORILLARD TOBACCO COMPANY V. REILLY

533 U.S. 525; 121 S.Ct. 2404; 150 L.Ed. 2d 532 (2001)
Vote: 5–4

In 1999, the attorney general of the state of Massachusetts adopted regulations governing the advertising and sale of tobacco products. The regulations prohibited outdoor advertising of cigarettes, cigars, and smokeless tobacco within 1,000 feet of any playground or school. They also required that ads inside stores be at least 5 feet off the floor, away from the usual sight of children. A group of tobacco product manufacturers and retailers brought suit to challenge the legality and constitutionality of these regulations. In the instant case, the Supreme Court holds that the Federal Cigarette Labeling and Advertising Act (FCLAA) preempts the Massachusetts regulations with respect to cigarette advertising. The Court then considers the constitutionality of the remaining regulations.

Justice O'Connor delivered the opinion of the Court.

. . . For over 25 years, the Court has recognized that commercial speech does not fall outside the purview of the First Amendment. . . . Instead, the Court has afforded commercial speech a measure of First Amendment protection commensurate with its position in relation to other constitutionally guaranteed expression. . . . In recognition of the distinction between speech proposing a commercial transaction, which occurs in an area traditionally subject to government regulation, and other varieties of speech, . . . we developed a framework for analyzing regulations of commercial speech that is substantially similar to the test for time, place, and manner restrictions. . . . The analysis contains four elements:

At the outset, we must determine whether the expression is protected by the First Amendment. For commercial speech to come within that provision, it at least must concern lawful activity and not be misleading. Next, we ask whether the asserted governmental interest is substantial. If both inquiries yield positive answers, we must determine whether the regulation directly advances the governmental interest asserted, and whether it is not more extensive than is necessary to serve that interest. . . .

Petitioners urge us to reject the *Central Hudson* analysis and apply strict scrutiny. They are not the first litigants to do so. . . . Admittedly, several Members of the Court have expressed doubts about the *Central Hudson* analysis and whether it should apply in particular cases. . . . But . . . we see no need to break new ground. *Central Hudson*, as applied in our more recent commercial speech cases, provides an adequate basis for decision. . . .

The State's interest in preventing underage tobacco use is substantial, and even compelling, but it is no less true that the sale and use of tobacco products by adults is a legal activity. We must consider that tobacco retailers and manufacturers have an interest in conveying truthful information about their products to adults, and adults have a corresponding interest in receiving truthful information about tobacco products. . . .

In some instances, Massachusetts outdoor advertising regulations would impose particularly onerous burdens on speech. For example, we disagree with the Court of Appeals conclusion that because cigar manufacturers and retailers conduct a limited amount of advertising in comparison to other tobacco products, the relative lack of cigar advertising also means that the burden imposed on cigar advertisers is correspondingly small. . . . If some retailers have relatively small advertising budgets, and use few avenues of communication, then the Attorney General's outdoor advertising regulations potentially place a greater, not lesser, burden on those retailers' speech. Furthermore, to the extent that cigar products and cigar advertising differ from that of other tobacco products, that difference should inform the inquiry into what speech restrictions are necessary.

In addition, a retailer in Massachusetts may have no means of communicating to passersby on the street that it sells tobacco products because alternative forms of advertisement, like newspapers, do not allow that retailer to propose an instant transaction in the way that onsite advertising does. The ban on any indoor advertising that is visible from the outside also presents problems in establishments like convenience stores, which have unique security concerns that counsel in favor of full visibility of the store from the outside. It is these sorts of considerations that the Attorney General failed to incorporate into the regulatory scheme.

We conclude that the Attorney General has failed to show that the outdoor advertising regulations for smokeless tobacco and cigars are not more extensive than necessary to advance the State's substantial interest in preventing underage tobacco use. Justice Stevens urges that the Court remand the case for further development of the factual record. . . . We believe that a remand is inappropriate in this case because the State had ample opportunity to develop a record with respect to tailoring (as it had to justify its decision to regulate advertising), and additional evidence would not alter the nature of the scheme before the Court. . . .

A careful calculation of the costs of a speech regulation does not mean that a State must demonstrate that there is no incursion on legitimate speech interests, but a speech regulation cannot unduly impinge on the speaker's ability to propose a commercial transaction and the adult listeners opportunity to obtain information about products. After reviewing the outdoor advertising regulations, we find the calculation in this case insufficient for purposes of the First Amendment. . . .

Massachusetts has also restricted indoor, point-of-sale advertising for smokeless tobacco and cigars. Advertising cannot be placed lower than five feet from the floor of any retail establishment which is located within a one thousand foot radius of any school or playground. . . .

We conclude that the point-of-sale advertising regulations fail both the third and fourth steps of the *Central Hudson* analysis. A regulation cannot be sustained if it provides only ineffective or remote support for the government's purpose, . . . or if there is little chance that the restriction will advance the State's goal. . . . As outlined above, the State's goal is to prevent minors from using tobacco products and to curb demand for that activity by limiting youth exposure to advertising. The 5 foot rule does not seem to advance that goal. Not all children are less than 5 feet tall, and those who are certainly have the ability to look up and take in their surroundings. . . .

Massachusetts may wish to target tobacco advertisements and displays that entice children, much like floor-level candy displays in a convenience store, but the blanket height restriction does not constitute a reasonable fit with that goal. The Court of Appeals recognized that the efficacy of the regulation was questionable, but decided that [i]n any event, the burden on speech imposed by the provision is very limited. . . . There is no de minimis exception for a speech restriction that lacks sufficient tailoring or justification. We conclude that the restriction on the height of indoor advertising is invalid under *Central Hudson's* third and fourth prongs. . . .

We have observed that tobacco use, particularly among children and adolescents, poses perhaps the single most significant threat to public health in the United States. . . . From a policy perspective, it is understandable for the States to attempt to prevent minors from using tobacco products before they reach an age where they are capable of weighing for themselves the risks and potential benefits of tobacco use, and other adult activities. Federal law, however, places limits on policy choices available to the States.

In this case, Congress enacted a comprehensive scheme to address cigarette smoking and health in advertising and pre-empted state regulation of cigarette advertising that attempts to address that same concern, even with respect to youth. The First Amendment also constrains state efforts to limit advertising of tobacco products, because so long as the sale and use of tobacco is lawful for adults, the tobacco industry has a protected interest in communicating information about its products and adult customers have an interest in receiving that information.

To the extent that federal law and the First Amendment do not prohibit state action, States and localities remain free to combat the problem of underage tobacco use by appropriate means. The judgment of the United States Court of Appeals for the First Circuit is therefore affirmed in part and reversed in part, and the cases are remanded for further proceedings consistent with this opinion. . . .

Justice Kennedy, with whom *Justice Scalia* joins, concurring in part and concurring in the judgment.

The obvious overbreadth of the outdoor advertising restrictions suffices to invalidate them under the fourth part of the test in *Central Hudson Gas* . . . (1980). As a result, in my view, there is no need to consider whether the restrictions satisfy the third part of the test, a proposition about which there is considerable doubt. . . . Neither are we required to consider whether *Central Hudson* should be retained in the face of the substantial objections that can be made to it. . . . My continuing concerns that the test gives insufficient protection to truthful, nonmisleading commercial speech require me to refrain from expressing agreement with the Court's application of the third part of *Central Hudson*. . . . With [this] exception . . . I join the opinion of the Court.

Justice Thomas, concurring in part and concurring in the judgment.

I join the opinion of the Court . . . because I agree that the Massachusetts cigarette advertising regulations are preempted by the Federal Cigarette Labeling and Advertising Act. . . . I also agree with the Court's disposition of the First Amendment challenges to the other regulations at issue here, and I share the Court's view that the regulations fail even the intermediate scrutiny of *Central Hudson Gas & Elec. Corp. v. Public Serv. Comm'n of N.Y.* . . . (1980). At the same time, I continue to believe that when the government seeks to restrict truthful speech in order to suppress the ideas it conveys, strict scrutiny is appropriate, whether or not the speech in question may be characterized as commercial. . . . I would subject all of the advertising restrictions to strict scrutiny and would hold that they violate the First Amendment. . . .

Justice Souter, concurring in part and dissenting in part. . . .

Justice Stevens, with whom *Justice Ginsburg* and *Justice Breyer* join, and with whom *Justice Souter* joins as to Part I, concurring in part, concurring in the judgment in part, and dissenting in part.

This suit presents two separate sets of issues. The first involving preemption is straightforward. The second involving the First Amendment is more complex. Because I strongly disagree with the Court's conclusion that the Federal Cigarette Labeling and Advertising Act of 1965 (FCLAA or Act) . . . precludes States and localities from regulating the location of cigarette advertising, I dissent from Parts IIA and IIB of the Court's opinion. On the First Amendment questions, I agree with the Court both that the outdoor advertising restrictions imposed by Massachusetts serve legitimate and important state interests and that the record does not indicate that the measures were properly tailored to serve those interests. Because the present record does not enable us to adjudicate the merits of those claims on summary judgment, I would vacate the decision upholding those restrictions and remand for trial on the constitutionality of the outdoor advertising regulations. Finally, because I do not believe that either the point-of-sale advertising restrictions or the sales practice restrictions implicate significant First Amendment concerns, I would uphold them in their entirety.

Case

NATIONAL ENDOWMENT FOR THE ARTS V. FINLEY

524 U.S. 569; 118 S. Ct. 2168; 141 L.Ed. 2d 500 (1998)
Vote: 8–1

Here the Court considers a statutory requirement that the National Endowment for the Arts take into account "general standards of decency" in deciding which artistic endeavors will receive public support. In a case brought by performance artist Karen Finley, a federal district judge in California declared the provision unconstitutional under the First Amendment. The Ninth Circuit Court of Appeals affirmed.

Justice O'Connor delivered the opinion of the Court.

The National Foundation on the Arts and Humanities Act, as amended in 1990, requires the Chairperson of the National Endowment for the Arts (NEA) to ensure that "artistic excellence and artistic merit are the criteria by which [grant] applications are judged, taking into consideration general standards of decency and respect for the diverse beliefs and values of the American public." 20 U.S.C. § 954(d)(1). . . .

Since 1965, the NEA has distributed over three billion dollars in grants to individuals and organizations, funding that has served as a catalyst for increased state, corporate, and foundation support for the arts. Congress has recently restricted the availability of federal funding for individual artists, confining grants primarily to qualifying organizations and state arts agencies, and constraining sub-granting. . . . By far the largest portion of the grants distributed in fiscal year 1998 were awarded directly to state arts agencies. In the remaining categories, the most substantial grants were allocated to symphony orchestras, fine arts museums, dance theater foundations, and opera associations. . . .

Throughout the NEA's history, only a handful of the agency's roughly 100,000 awards have generated formal complaints about misapplied funds or abuse of the public's trust. Two provocative works, however, prompted public controversy in 1989 and led to congressional reevaluation of the NEA's funding priorities and efforts to increase oversight of its grant-making procedures. The Institute of Contemporary Art at the University of Pennsylvania had used $30,000 of a visual arts grant it received from the NEA to fund a 1989 retrospective of photographer Robert Mapplethorpe's work. The exhibit, entitled The Perfect Moment, included homoerotic photographs that several Members of Congress condemned as pornographic. . . . Members also denounced artist Andres Serrano's work Piss Christ, a photograph of a crucifix immersed in urine. . . . Serrano had been awarded a $15,000 grant from the Southeast Center for Contemporary Art, an organization that received NEA support.

When considering the NEA's appropriations for fiscal year 1990, Congress reacted to the controversy surrounding the Mapplethorpe and Serrano photographs by eliminating $45,000 from the agency's budget, the precise amount contributed to the two exhibits by NEA grant recipients. Congress also enacted an amendment providing that no NEA funds "may be used to promote, disseminate, or produce materials which in the judgment of [the NEA] may be considered obscene, including but not limited to, depictions of sadomasochism, homoeroticism, the sexual exploitation of children, or individuals engaged in sex acts and which, when taken as a whole, do not have serious literary, artistic, political, or scientific value." . . . The NEA implemented Congress' mandate by instituting a requirement that all grantees certify in writing that they would not utilize federal funding to engage in projects inconsistent with the criteria in the 1990 appropriations bill. That certification requirement was subsequently invalidated as unconstitutionally vague by a Federal District Court . . . and the NEA did not appeal the decision.

In the 1990 appropriations bill, Congress also agreed to create an Independent Commission of constitutional law scholars to review the NEA's grant-making procedures and assess the possibility of more focused standards for public arts funding. The Commission's report, issued in September 1990, concluded that there is no constitutional obligation to provide arts funding, but also recommended that the NEA rescind the certification requirement and cautioned against legislation setting forth any content restrictions. Instead, the Commission suggested procedural changes to enhance the role of advisory panels and a statutory reaffirmation of "the high place the nation accords to the fostering of mutual respect for the disparate beliefs and values among us." . . .

Informed by the Commission's recommendations, and cognizant of pending judicial challenges to the funding limitations in the 1990 appropriations bill, Congress debated several proposals to reform the NEA's grant-making process when it considered the agency's reauthorization in the fall of 1990. . . . Ultimately, Congress adopted . . . a bipartisan compromise between Members opposing any funding restrictions and those favoring some guidance to the agency. In relevant part, [this compromise] became § 954(d)(1). . . .

. . . Respondents raise a facial constitutional challenge to § 954(d)(1), and consequently they confront "a heavy burden" in advancing their claim. . . . Facial invalidation "is, manifestly, strong medicine" that "has been employed by the Court sparingly and only as a last resort." . . . To prevail, respondents must demonstrate a substantial risk that application of the provision will lead to the suppression of speech. . . .

Respondents argue that the provision is a paradigmatic example of viewpoint discrimination because it rejects any artistic speech that either fails to respect mainstream values or offends standards of decency. The premise of respondents' claim is that § 954(d)(1) constrains the agency's ability to fund certain categories of artistic expression. The NEA, however, reads the provision as merely hortatory, and contends that it stops well short of an absolute restriction. Section 954(d)(1) adds "considerations" to the grant-making process; it does not preclude awards to projects that might be deemed "indecent" or "disrespectful," nor place conditions on grants, or even specify that those factors must be given any particular weight in reviewing an application. . . .

Furthermore, like the plain language of § 954(d), the political context surrounding the adoption of the "decency and respect" clause is inconsistent with respondents' assertion that the provision compels the NEA to deny funding on the basis of viewpoint discriminatory criteria. The legislation was a bipartisan proposal introduced as a counterweight to amendments aimed at eliminating the NEA's funding or substantially constraining its grant-making authority. . . .

That § 954(d)(1) admonishes the NEA merely to take "decency and respect" into consideration, and that the legislation was aimed at reforming procedures rather than precluding speech, undercut respondents' argument that the provision inevitably will be utilized as a tool for invidious viewpoint discrimination. In cases where we have struck down legislation as facially unconstitutional, the dangers were both more evident and more substantial. . . .

. . . Thus, we do not perceive a realistic danger that § 954(d)(1) will compromise First Amendment values. As respondents' own arguments demonstrate, the considerations that the provision introduces, by their nature, do not engender the kind of directed viewpoint discrimination that would prompt this Court to invalidate a statute on its face.

Respondents' claim that the provision is facially unconstitutional may be reduced to the argument that the criteria in § 954(d)(1) are sufficiently subjective that the agency could utilize them to engage in viewpoint discrimination. Given the varied interpretations of the criteria and the vague exhortation to "take them into consideration," it seems unlikely that this provision will introduce any greater element of selectivity than the determination of "artistic excellence" itself. And we are reluctant, in any event, to invalidate legislation "on the basis of its hypothetical application to situations not before the Court." . . .

Finally, although the First Amendment certainly has application in the subsidy context, we note that the Government may allocate competitive funding according to criteria that would be impermissible were direct regulation of speech or a criminal penalty at stake. So long as legislation does not infringe on other constitutionally protected rights, Congress has wide latitude to set spending priorities. . . .

Section 954(d)(1) merely adds some imprecise considerations to an already subjective selection process. It does not, on its face, impermissibly infringe on First or Fifth Amendment rights. Accordingly, the judgment of the Court of Appeals is reversed and the case is remanded for further proceedings consistent with this opinion.

Justice Scalia, with whom *Justice Thomas* joins, concurring in the judgment.

"The operation was a success, but the patient died." What such a procedure is to medicine, the Court's opinion in this case is to law. It sustains the constitutionality of

§ 954(d)(1) by gutting it. The most avid congressional opponents of the provision could not have asked for more. I write separately because, unlike the Court, I think that § 954(d)(1) must be evaluated as written, rather than as distorted by the agency it was meant to control. By its terms, it establishes content and viewpoint-based criteria upon which grant applications are to be evaluated. And that is perfectly constitutional. . . .

The nub of the difference between me and the Court is that I regard the distinction between "abridging" speech and funding it as a fundamental divide, on this side of which the First Amendment is inapplicable. The Court, by contrast, seems to believe that the First Amendment, despite its words, has some ineffable effect upon funding, imposing constraints of an indeterminate nature which it announces (without troubling to enunciate any particular test) are not violated by the statute here—or, more accurately, are not violated by the quite different, emasculated statute that it imagines. "[T]he Government," it says, "may allocate competitive funding according to criteria that would be impermissible were direct regulation of speech or a criminal penalty at stake." . . . The government, I think, may allocate both competitive and non-competitive funding ad libitum, insofar as the First Amendment is concerned. Finally, what is true of the First Amendment is also true of the constitutional rule against vague legislation: it has no application to funding. Insofar as it bears upon First Amendment concerns, the vagueness doctrine addresses the problems that arise from government regulation of expressive conduct, . . . not government grant programs. In the former context, vagueness produces an abridgment of lawful speech; in the latter it produces, at worst, a waste of money. I cannot refrain from observing, however, that if the vagueness doctrine were applicable, the agency charged with making grants under a statutory standard of "artistic excellence"—and which has itself thought that standard met by everything from the playing of Beethoven to a depiction of a crucifix immersed in urine—would be of more dubious constitutional validity than the "decency" and "respect" limitations that respondents (who demand to be judged on the same strict standard of "artistic excellence") have the humorlessness to call too vague.

In its laudatory description of the accomplishments of the NEA, . . . the Court notes with satisfaction that "only a handful of the agency's roughly 100,000 awards have generated formal complaints." . . . The Congress that felt it necessary to enact § 954(d)(1) evidently thought it much more noteworthy that any money exacted from American taxpayers had been used to produce a crucifix immersed in urine, or a display of homoerotic photographs. It is no secret that the provision was prompted by, and directed at, the funding of such offensive productions. Instead of banning the funding of such productions absolutely, which I think would have been entirely constitutional, Congress took the lesser step of requiring them to be disfavored in the evaluation of grant applications. The Court's opinion today renders even that lesser step a nullity. For that reason, I concur only in the judgment.

Justice Souter, dissenting.

. . . The decency and respect proviso mandates viewpoint-based decisions in the disbursement of government subsidies, and the Government has wholly failed to explain why the statute should be afforded an exemption from the fundamental rule of the First Amendment that viewpoint discrimination in the exercise of public authority over expressive activity is unconstitutional. . . .

"If there is a bedrock principle underlying the First Amendment, it is that the government may not prohibit the expression of an idea simply because society finds the idea itself offensive or disagreeable." . . . Because this principle applies not only to affirmative suppression of speech, but also to disqualification for government favors, Congress is generally not permitted to pivot discrimination against otherwise protected speech on the offensiveness or unacceptability of the views it expresses. . . .

It goes without saying that artistic expression lies within this First Amendment protection. . . . The constitutional protection of artistic works turns not on the political significance that may be attributable to such productions, though they may indeed comment on the political, but simply on their expressive character, which falls within a spectrum of protected "speech" extending outward from the core of overtly political declarations. Put differently, art is entitled to full protection because our "cultural life," just like our native politics, "rests upon [the] ideal" of governmental viewpoint neutrality. . . . When called upon to vindicate this ideal, we characteristically begin by asking "whether the government has adopted a regulation of speech because of disagreement with the message it conveys. The government's purpose is the controlling consideration." . . . The answer in this case is damning. One need do nothing more than read the text of the statute to conclude that Congress's purpose in imposing the decency and respect criteria was to prevent the funding of art that conveys an offensive message; the decency and respect provision on its face is quintessentially viewpoint based, and quotations from the Congressional Record merely confirm the obvious legislative purpose. In the words of a cosponsor of the bill that enacted the proviso, "[w]orks which deeply offend the sensibilities of significant portions of the public ought not to be supported with public funds."

. . . Another supporter of the bill observed that "the Endowment's support for artists like Robert Mapplethorpe and Andre[s] Serrano has offended and angered many citizens," behooving "Congress . . . to listen to these complaints about the NEA and make sure that exhibits like [these] are not funded again." . . . Indeed, if there were any question at all about what Congress had in mind, a definitive answer comes in the suc-

cinctly accurate remark of the proviso's author, that the bill "add[s] to the criteria of artistic excellence and artistic merit, a shell, a screen, a viewpoint that must be constantly taken into account." . . .

Since the [challenged legislation] is substantially overbroad and carries with it a significant power to chill artistic production and display, it should be struck down on its face.

Case

BOY SCOUTS OF AMERICA V. DALE

530 U.S. 640; 120 S.Ct. 2446; 147 L.Ed. 2d 554 (2000)
Vote: 5–4

James Dale, a former Eagle Scout, was dismissed from his position as an assistant scoutmaster of a New Jersey Boy Scout troop when the organization learned that Dale was openly gay. Dale sued the Boy Scouts in the New Jersey courts, asserting that the organization was in violation of a state statute barring discriminating on the basis of sexual orientation by places of public accommodation.

Chief Justice Rehnquist delivered the opinion of the Court.

. . .The Boy Scouts is a private, not-for-profit organization engaged in instilling its system of values in young people. The Boy Scouts asserts that homosexual conduct is inconsistent with the values it seeks to instill. . . . The New Jersey Supreme Court held that New Jersey's public accommodations law requires that the Boy Scouts admit Dale. This case presents the question whether applying New Jersey's public accommodations law in this way violates the Boy Scouts' First Amendment right of expressive association. We hold that it does.

. . . In *Roberts v. United States Jaycees*, . . . (1984), we observed that "implicit in the right to engage in activities protected by the First Amendment" is "a corresponding right to associate with others in pursuit of a wide variety of political, social, economic, educational, religious, and cultural ends." This right is crucial in preventing the majority from imposing its views on groups that would rather express other, perhaps unpopular, ideas. . . . Government actions that may unconstitutionally burden this freedom may take many forms, one of which is "intrusion into the internal structure or affairs of an association" like a "regulation that forces the group to accept members it does not desire." . . . Forcing a group to accept certain members may impair the ability of the group to express

those views, and only those views, that it intends to express. Thus, "[f]reedom of association . . . plainly presupposes a freedom not to associate." . . .

The forced inclusion of an unwanted person in a group infringes the group's freedom of expressive association if the presence of that person affects in a significant way the group's ability to advocate public or private viewpoints. . . . But the freedom of expressive association, like many freedoms, is not absolute. We have held that the freedom could be overridden "by regulations adopted to serve compelling state interests, unrelated to the suppression of ideas, that cannot be achieved through means significantly less restrictive of associational freedoms." . . .

To determine whether a group is protected by the First Amendment's expressive associational right, we must determine whether the group engages in "expressive association." The First Amendment's protection of expressive association is not reserved for advocacy groups. But to come within its ambit, a group must engage in some form of expression, whether it be public or private.

. . .[T]he general mission of the Boy Scouts is clear: "[T]o instill values in young people." . . . The Boy Scouts seeks to instill these values by having its adult leaders spend time with the youth members, instructing and engaging them in activities like camping, archery, and fishing. During the time spent with the youth members, the scoutmasters and assistant scoutmasters inculcate them with the Boy Scouts' values—both expressly and by example. It seems indisputable that an association that seeks to transmit such a system of values engages in expressive activity. . . .

Given that the Boy Scouts engages in expressive activity, we must determine whether the forced inclusion of Dale as an assistant scoutmaster would significantly affect the Boy Scouts' ability to advocate public or private viewpoints. This inquiry necessarily requires us first to explore, to a limited extent, the nature of the Boy Scouts' view of homosexuality.

The values the Boy Scouts seeks to instill are "based on" those listed in the Scout Oath and Law. . . . The Boy Scouts explains that the Scout Oath and Law provide "a positive moral code for living; they are a list of 'do's' rather than 'don'ts.'" . . . The Boy Scouts asserts that homosexual conduct is inconsistent with the values embodied in the Scout Oath and Law, particularly with the values represented by the terms "morally straight" and "clean."

Obviously, the Scout Oath and Law do not expressly mention sexuality or sexual orientation. . . . And the terms "morally straight" and "clean" are by no means self-defining. Different people would attribute to those terms very different meanings. For example, some people may believe that engaging in homosexual conduct is not at odds with being "morally straight" and "clean." And others may believe that engaging in homosexual conduct is contrary to being "morally straight" and "clean." The Boy Scouts says it falls within the latter category.

The New Jersey Supreme Court analyzed the Boy Scouts' beliefs and found that the "exclusion of members solely on the basis of their sexual orientation is inconsistent with Boy Scouts' commitment to a diverse and 'representative' membership . . . [and] contradicts Boy Scouts' overarching objective to reach 'all eligible youth.'" . . . The court concluded that the exclusion of members like Dale "appears antithetical to the organization's goals and philosophy." . . . But our cases reject this sort of inquiry; it is not the role of the courts to reject a group's expressed values because they disagree with those values or find them internally inconsistent. . . .

The Boy Scouts asserts that it "teach[es] that homosexual conduct is not morally straight," . . . and that it does "not want to promote homosexual conduct as a legitimate form of behavior." . . . We accept the Boy Scouts' assertion. We need not inquire further to determine the nature of the Boy Scouts' expression with respect to homosexuality. But because the record before us contains written evidence of the Boy Scouts' viewpoint, we look to it as instructive, if only on the question of the sincerity of the professed beliefs. . . .

We must then determine whether Dale's presence as an assistant scoutmaster would significantly burden the Boy Scouts' desire to not "promote homosexual conduct as a legitimate form of behavior." . . . As we give deference to an association's assertions regarding the nature of its expression, we must also give deference to an association's view of what would impair its expression. . . . That is not to say that an expressive association can erect a shield against antidiscrimination laws simply by asserting that mere acceptance of a member from a particular group would impair its message. But here Dale, by his own admission, is one of a group of gay Scouts who have "become leaders in their community and are open and honest about their sexual orientation." . . . Dale was the copresident of a gay and lesbian organization at college and remains a gay rights activist. Dale's presence in the Boy Scouts would, at the very least, force the organization to send a message, both to the youth members and the world, that the Boy Scouts accepts homosexual conduct as a legitimate form of behavior. . . .

Having determined that the Boy Scouts is an expressive association and that the forced inclusion of Dale would significantly affect its expression, we inquire whether the application of New Jersey's public accommodations law to require that the Boy Scouts accept Dale as an assistant scoutmaster runs afoul of the Scouts' freedom of expressive association. We conclude that it does.

State public accommodations laws were originally enacted to prevent discrimination in traditional places of public accommodation—like inns and trains. . . . New Jersey's statutory definition of "[a] place of public accommodation" is extremely broad. The term is said to "include, but not be limited to," a list of over 50 types of places. . . . Many on the list are what one would expect to be places where the public is invited. For example, the statute includes as places of public accommodation taverns, restaurants, retail shops, and public libraries. But the statute also includes places that often may not carry with them open invitations to the public, like summer camps and roof gardens. In this case, the New Jersey Supreme Court went a step further and applied its public accommodations law to a private entity without even attempting to tie the term "place" to a physical location. As the definition of "public accommodation" has expanded from clearly commercial entities, such as restaurants, bars, and hotels, to membership organizations such as the Boy Scouts, the potential for conflict between state public accommodations laws and the First Amendment rights of organizations has increased.

. . .We have already concluded that a state requirement that the Boy Scouts retain Dale as an assistant scoutmaster would significantly burden the organization's right to oppose or disfavor homosexual conduct. The state interests embodied in New Jersey's public accommodations law do not justify such a severe intrusion on the Boy Scouts' rights to freedom of expressive association. That being the case, we hold that the First Amendment prohibits the State from imposing such a requirement through the application of its public accommodations law. . . .

. . .We are not, as we must not be, guided by our views of whether the Boy Scouts' teachings with respect to homosexual conduct are right or wrong; public or judicial disapproval of a tenet of an organization's expression does not justify the State's effort to compel the organization to accept members where such acceptance would derogate from the organization's expressive message. "While the law is free to promote all sorts of conduct in place of harmful behavior, it is not free to interfere with speech for no better reason than promoting an approved message or discouraging a disfavored one, however enlightened either purpose may strike the government." . . .

The judgment of the New Jersey Supreme Court is reversed, and the cause remanded for further proceedings not inconsistent with this opinion. . . .

Justice Stevens, with whom *Justice Souter*, **Justice Ginsburg** and *Justice Breyer* join, dissenting.

. . .The majority holds that New Jersey's law violates BSA's right to associate and its right to free speech. But that law does not "impos[e] any serious burdens" on BSA's "collective effort on behalf of [its] shared goals," . . . nor does it force BSA to communicate any message that it does not wish to endorse. New Jersey's law, therefore, abridges no constitutional right of the Boy Scouts. . . .

. . . BSA's claim finds no support in our cases. We have recognized "a right to associate for the purpose of engaging in those activities protected by the First Amendment—speech, assembly, petition for the redress of grievances, and the exercise of religion." . . . And we have acknowledged that "when the State interferes with individuals' selection of those with whom they wish to join in a common endeavor, freedom of association . . . may be implicated." . . . But "[t]he right to associate for expressive purposes is not . . . absolute"; rather, "the nature and degree of constitutional protection afforded freedom of association may vary depending on the extent to which . . . the constitutionally protected liberty is at stake in a given case." . . . Indeed, the right to associate does not mean "that in every setting in which individuals exercise some discrimination in choosing associates, their selective process of inclusion and exclusion is protected by the Constitution." . . . For example, we have routinely and easily rejected assertions of this right by expressive organizations with discriminatory membership policies, such as private schools, law firms, and labor organizations. In fact, until today, we have never once found a claimed right to associate in the selection of members to prevail in the face of a State's antidiscrimination law. To the contrary, we have squarely held that a State's antidiscrimination law does not violate a group's right to associate simply because the law conflicts with that group's exclusionary membership policy. . . .

. . . The evidence before this Court makes it exceptionally clear that BSA has, at most, simply adopted an exclusionary membership policy and has no shared goal of disapproving of homosexuality. BSA's mission statement and federal charter say nothing on the matter; its official membership policy is silent; its Scout Oath and Law—and accompanying definitions—are devoid of any view on the topic; its guidance for Scouts and Scoutmasters on sexuality declare that such matters are "not construed to be Scouting's proper area," but are the province of a Scout's parents and pastor; and BSA's posture respecting religion tolerates a wide variety of views on the issue of homosexuality. Moreover, there is simply no evidence that BSA otherwise teaches anything in this area, or that it instructs Scouts on matters involving homosexuality in ways not conveyed in the Boy Scout or Scoutmaster Handbooks. In short, Boy Scouts of America is simply silent on homosexuality. There is no shared goal or collective effort to foster a belief about homosexuality at all—let alone one that is significantly burdened by admitting homosexuals.

. . .[T]here is "no basis in the record for concluding that admission of [homosexuals] will impede the [Boy Scouts'] ability to engage in [its] protected activities or to disseminate its preferred views" and New Jersey's law "requires no change in [BSA's] creed." . . .

. . .Equally important is BSA's failure to adopt any clear position on homosexuality. BSA's temporary, though ultimately abandoned, view that homosexuality is incompatible with being "morally straight" and "clean" is a far cry from the clear, unequivocal statement necessary to prevail on its claim. Despite the solitary sentences in the 1991 and 1992 policies, the group continued to disclaim any single religious or moral position as a general matter and actively eschewed teaching any lesson on sexuality. It also continued to define "morally straight" and "clean" in the Boy Scout and Scoutmaster Handbooks without any reference to homosexuality. As noted earlier, nothing in our cases suggests that a group can prevail on a right to expressive association if it, effectively, speaks out of both sides of its mouth. A State's antidiscrimination law does not impose a "serious burden" or a "substantial restraint" upon the group's "shared goals" if the group itself is unable to identify its own stance with any clarity.

The majority pretermits this entire analysis. It finds that BSA in fact "teach[es] that homosexual conduct is not morally straight." . . . This conclusion, remarkably, rests entirely on statements in BSA's briefs. . . . Moreover, the majority insists that we must "give deference to an association's assertions regarding the nature of its expression" and "we must also give deference to an association's view of what would impair its expression." . . . So long as the record "contains written evidence" to support a group's bare assertion, "[w]e need not inquire further." . . . Once the organization "asserts" that it engages in particular expression, "[w]e cannot doubt" the truth of that assertion. . . .

This is an astounding view of the law. I am unaware of any previous instance in which our analysis of the scope of a constitutional right was determined by looking at what a litigant asserts in his or her brief and inquiring no further. It is even more astonishing in the First Amendment area, because, as the majority itself acknowledges, "we are obligated to independently review the factual record." . . . It is an odd form of independent review that consists of deferring entirely to whatever a litigant claims. But the majority insists that our inquiry must be "limited," because "it is not the role of the courts to reject a group's expressed values because they disagree with those values or find them internally inconsistent." . . .

But nothing in our cases calls for this Court to do any such thing. An organization can adopt the message of its choice, and it is not this Court's place to disagree with it. But we must inquire whether the group is, in fact, expressing a message (whatever it may be) and whether that message (if one is expressed) is significantly affected by a State's antidiscrimination law. More critically, that inquiry requires our *independent* analysis, rather than deference to a group's litigating posture. Reflection on the subject dictates that such an inquiry is required. . . .

Surely there are instances in which an organization that truly aims to foster a belief at odds with the purposes of a State's antidiscrimination laws will have a First Amendment right to association that precludes forced compliance with those laws. But that right is not a freedom to discriminate at will, nor is it a right to maintain an exclusionary membership policy simply out of fear of what the public reaction would be if the group's membership were opened up. It is an implicit right designed to protect the enumerated rights of the First Amendment, not a license to act on any discriminatory impulse. To prevail in asserting a right of expressive association as a defense to a charge of violating an antidiscrimination law, the organization must at least show it has adopted and advocated an unequivocal position inconsistent with a position advocated or epitomized by the person whom the organization seeks to exclude. If this Court were to defer to whatever position an organization is prepared to assert in its briefs, there would be no way to mark the proper boundary between genuine exercises of the right to associate, on the one hand, and sham claims that are simply attempts to insulate nonexpressive private discrimination, on the other hand. Shielding a litigant's claim from judicial scrutiny would, in turn, render civil rights legislation a nullity, and turn this important constitutional right into a farce. Accordingly, the Court's prescription of total deference will not do. . . .

The only apparent explanation for the majority's holding . . . is that homosexuals are simply so different from the rest of society that their presence alone—unlike any other individual's—should be singled out for special First Amendment treatment. Under the majority's reasoning, an openly gay male is irreversibly affixed with the label "homosexual." That label, even though unseen, communicates a message that permits his exclusion wherever he goes. His openness is the sole and sufficient justification for his ostracism. Though unintended, reliance on such a justification is tantamount to a constitutionally prescribed symbol of inferiority. . . .

. . .Generally, a private person or a private organization has a right to refuse to broadcast a message with which it disagrees, and a right to refuse to contradict or garble its own specific statement at any given place or time by including the messages of others. An expressive association claim, however, normally involves the avowal and advocacy of a consistent position on some issue over time. This is why a different kind of scrutiny must be given to an expressive association claim, lest the right of expressive association simply turn into a right to discriminate whenever some group can think of an expressive object that would seem to be inconsistent with the admission of some person as a member or at odds with the appointment of a person to a leadership position in the group.

. . . Furthermore, it is not likely that BSA would be understood to send any message, either to Scouts or to the world, simply by admitting someone as a member. Over the years, BSA has generously welcomed over 87 million young Americans into its ranks. In 1992 over one million adults were active BSA members. . . . The notion that an organization of that size and enormous prestige implicitly endorses the views that each of those adults may express in a non-Scouting context is simply mind-boggling. Indeed, in this case there is no evidence that the young Scouts in Dale's troop, or members of their families, were even aware of his sexual orientation, either before or after his public statements at Rutgers University. It is equally farfetched to assert that Dale's open declaration of his homosexuality, reported in a local newspaper, will effectively force BSA to send a message to anyone simply because it allows Dale to be an Assistant Scoutmaster. For an Olympic gold medal winner or a Wimbledon tennis champion, being "openly gay" perhaps communicates a message—for example, that openness about one's sexual orientation is more virtuous than concealment; that a homosexual person can be a capable and virtuous person who should be judged like anyone else; and that homosexuality is not immoral—but it certainly does not follow that they necessarily send a message on behalf of the organizations that sponsor the activities in which they excel. The fact that such persons participate in these organizations is not usually construed to convey a message on behalf of those organizations any more than does the inclusion of women, African-Americans, religious minorities, or any other discrete group. Surely the organizations are not forced by antidiscrimination laws to take any position on the legitimacy of any individual's private beliefs or private conduct.

. . .The State of New Jersey has decided that people who are open and frank about their sexual orientation are entitled to equal access to employment as school teachers, police officers, librarians, athletic coaches, and a host of other jobs filled by citizens who serve as role models for children and adults alike. Dozens of Scout units throughout the State are sponsored by public agencies, such as schools and fire departments, that employ such role models. BSA's affiliation with numerous public agencies that comply with New Jersey's law against discrimination cannot be understood to convey any particular message endorsing or condoning the activities of all these people. . . .

Unfavorable opinions about homosexuals "have ancient roots." . . . Like equally atavistic opinions about certain racial groups, those roots have been nourished by sectarian doctrine. . . . Over the years, however, interaction with real people, rather than mere adherence to traditional ways of thinking about members of unfamiliar classes, have modified those opinions. . . .

That such prejudices are still prevalent and that they have caused serious and tangible harm to countless members of the class New Jersey seeks to protect are established matters of fact that neither the Boy Scouts nor the Court disputes. That harm can only be aggravated by the creation of a constitutional shield for a policy that is itself the product of a habitual way of thinking about strangers. As Justice Brandeis so wisely advised, "we must be ever on our guard, lest we erect our prejudices into legal principles."

If we would guide by the light of reason, we must let our minds be bold. I respectfully dissent.

Justice Souter, with whom *Justice Ginsburg* and *Justice Breyer* join, dissenting. . . .

9

RELIGIOUS LIBERTY AND CHURCH-STATE RELATIONS

"We are a people whose institutions presuppose a Supreme Being."

—JUSTICE WILLIAM O. DOUGLAS,

WRITING FOR THE COURT IN *ZORACH V. CLAUSON* (1952)

"[O]ne of the mandates of the First Amendment is to promote a viable, pluralistic society and to keep government neutral, not only between sects, but also between believers and nonbelievers."

—JUSTICE WILLIAM O. DOUGLAS,

DISSENTING IN *WALZ V. TAX COMMISSION* (1970)

William O. Douglas: Associate Justice, 1939–1975

509

INTRODUCTION

Religion is one of the hallmarks of American society. Americans are more likely than people in other Western democracies to hold religious beliefs, affiliate with religious denominations, and attend religious services. Another distinguishing feature of American social life is the great diversity of religious beliefs and practices that coexist peacefully. No other society on earth has such a wide array of creeds and denominations. Despite obvious differences in doctrine and styles of worship, most religions are united by their common belief in a Supreme Being and their commitment to standards of right and wrong. Nevertheless, history and current events teach us that human beings are given to zealotry, intolerance, persecution, and even warfare in the name of God. Peaceful coexistence among competing religious groups is one of the major accomplishments of modern democracy.

The authors of the Bill of Rights were well aware of the excesses that can result when one denomination is established as the official religion and recognized and supported by government. Indeed, a profound thirst for the freedom to worship God in one's own way, without coercion or persecution by government, was one of the principal motivations in the formation of the American colonies. However, nine of the thirteen original American colonies set up official churches and provided them with financial support. In fact, at the time the Bill of Rights was ratified in 1791, Connecticut, Massachusetts, and New Hampshire continued to recognize the Congregational Church as the official, state-sponsored denomination. Nevertheless, opposition to officially established religion ultimately prevailed. The First Amendment to the Constitution provides that "Congress shall make no law respecting an establishment of religion, or prohibiting the free exercise thereof."

That the protection of religious freedom was of fundamental importance is underscored by the fact that the Religion Clauses are listed first among the safeguards contained in the Bill of Rights. These clauses not only reflect the strong desire for religious freedom held by eighteenth-century Americans, but they also protect and foster the religious diversity that exists in America today.

Widespread agreement exists regarding the abstract value of the **Religion Clauses of the First Amendment.** Nevertheless, there is equally broad disagreement about what these clauses specifically require, permit, and forbid. Some of the Supreme Court's least popular decisions are in the realm of government involvement with religion, specifically in the area of **school prayer.** Note, however, that these decisions are often as misunderstood as they are unpopular. This chapter attempts to clarify and explain what the Supreme Court has said in some of its many decisions interpreting the Religion Clauses of the First Amendment. Sadly, too often those who are given to strong opinions on the subject of religion are unwilling or unable to understand clearly what has been decided by the courts. While informed debate over judicial decisions is to be encouraged, criticism based on ignorance is counterproductive.

The Incorporation of the Religion Clauses

In his original draft of the Bill of Rights, James Madison proposed that state as well as federal establishments of religion be prohibited. The First Congress rejected Madison's suggestion in this respect, preferring to allow states to make their own determinations in this area. Thus, the First Amendment proscribed establishments of religion by the national government only. By the late 1940s, the Supreme Court had ruled, however, that the Religion Clauses of the First Amendment were of sufficient importance in a "scheme of ordered liberty" to warrant their application to the states through the Due Process Clause of the Fourteenth Amendment (for a discussion of the doctrine of incorporation, see Chapter 6). The **Free Exercise Clause** was definitively applied to the states in *Cantwell v. Connecticut* (1940); arguably, it had been incorporated in the 1934 case of *Hamilton v. Regents of the University of California*. The **Establishment Clause** was incorporated in *Everson v. Board of Education* (1947). Thus, all levels of government, from local school boards to the U.S. Congress, are now required to abide by the strictures of the Religion Clauses of the First Amendment.

What Constitutes Religion for First Amendment Purposes?

Before one can define "establishment of religion" or "the free exercise thereof," one must understand what is meant by the term *religion*. It comes from the Latin *religare*, which means "to tie down" or "to restrain." Since its appearance in the English language at the beginning of the thirteenth century, the term *religion* has had a distinctly theological connotation. *Webster's Third New International Dictionary of the English Language* (1986) offers seven definitions of the term. The first is "the personal commitment to and serving of God or a god with worshipful devotion. . . ." It goes on to define religion as "a personal awareness or conviction of the existence of a supreme being or of supernatural powers or influences controlling one's own, humanity's, or all nature's destiny. . . ."

In the 1890 case of *Davis v. Beason,* the Supreme Court first had occasion to define religion. In a majority opinion authored by Justice Stephen J. Field, the Court stated that "the term 'religion' has reference to one's view of his relations to his Creator, and to the obligations they impose of reverence for His being and character, and obedience to His will." This conception of religion was strictly theistic, which no doubt mirrored popular attitudes circa 1890. By the 1960s, however, American society had become much more religiously diverse, and nontheistic creeds from Asia, such as Buddhism and Taoism, were beginning to find adherents in this country.

Religion Broadly Defined In 1965, the Supreme Court attempted to define religion in a fashion broad enough to respect the diversity of creeds that coexist in modern America. The definitional problem arose in *United States v. Seeger*, a case involving four men who claimed **conscientious objector** status in refusing to serve in the Vietnam War. In the Universal Military Training and Service Act of 1940, Congress exempted from combat duty anyone "who, by reason of religious training and belief, is conscientiously opposed to participation in war in any form." The act defined "religious training and belief" as training or belief "in a relation to a Supreme Being involving duties superior to those arising from any human relation." Although some organized religions (such as the Quakers) do not approve of participation in war, Daniel Seeger was not a member of any such group. Nevertheless, he sought conscientious objector status on religious grounds. When specifically asked about his belief in a Supreme Being, Seeger stated that "you could call [it] a belief in the Supreme Being or God. These just do not happen to be the words that I use." Forest Peter, another man whose refusal to serve in Vietnam was before the Supreme Court in *Seeger,* claimed that after considerable meditation and reflection "on values derived from the Western religious and philosophical tradition," he determined that it would be "a violation of his moral code to take human life and that he considered this belief superior to any obligation to the state." In deciding the *Seeger* case, the Court avoided a constitutional question by interpreting the statutory definition of religion broadly. Writing for the Court, Justice Tom C. Clark held that

> Congress, in using the expression "Supreme Being" rather than the designation "God," was merely clarifying the meaning of religious tradition and belief so as to embrace all religions and to exclude essentially political, sociological, or philosophical views [and]

the test of belief "in a relation to a Supreme Being" is whether a given belief that is sincere and meaningful occupies a place in the life of its possessor parallel to the orthodox belief in God.

Apparently the Court was persuaded that Seeger, Peter, and the others whose refusal to serve in Vietnam was before the Court possessed such a belief and recognized them as conscientious objectors on religious grounds.

A Working Definition of Religion Subsequent decisions in both federal and state tribunals have expanded the definition of religion adopted by the Supreme Court in the *Seeger* case. Essentially, a creed must meet four criteria to qualify as a religion as this term is used in the First Amendment. First, as noted earlier, there must be a belief in God or some parallel belief that occupies a central place in the believer's life. Second, the religion must involve a moral code that transcends individual belief—it cannot be purely subjective. Third, some associational ties must be involved. That is, there must be some community of people united by common beliefs. Fourth, there must be a demonstrable sincerity of belief. Under these criteria, even nontheistic creeds, such as Taoism or Zen Buddhism, qualify as religions. But frivolous or ridiculous beliefs, such as Stanley Oscar Brown's professed "faith" in Kozy Kitten Cat Food (see *Brown v. Pena* [1977]), fail to meet any of the four criteria. Of course, there is a long continuum between ludicrous beliefs such as Brown's and conventional religions.

RELIGIOUS BELIEF AND THE RIGHT TO PROSELYTIZE

The First Amendment provides virtually absolute protection with respect to individual religious convictions and beliefs. The government may never question a person's beliefs or impose penalties or disabilities based solely on those beliefs. Thus, in *Torcaso v. Watkins* (1961), the Court unanimously struck down a Maryland constitutional provision requiring persons seeking public office to take an oath declaring their belief in God. Likewise, in *McDaniel v. Paty* (1978), the Court was unanimous in holding that states may not bar priests and ministers from serving as delegates to state constitutional conventions.

The Free Exercise Clause obviously protects more than belief—it carries over into the realm of action. But here the protections are somewhat attenuated. Whether specific actions are protected by the First Amendment depends on the character of those actions and the government's rationale for trying to regulate them.

Religious Solicitation

The highest degree of protection is accorded to **religious speech** and other **expressive religious conduct.** Thus, in *Cantwell v. Connecticut* (1940), the Court struck down a state law that prohibited door-to-door solicitation for any religious or charitable cause without prior approval of a state agency. The law was challenged by Newton Cantwell, a member of the Jehovah's Witnesses, a sect committed to active proselytizing. Cantwell and his sons routinely went from door to door or stopped people on the street in order to communicate a message that was highly critical of the Roman Catholic Church and other organized religions. Eventually they were arrested and charged with failure to obtain approval for solicitation under the state law, as well as with common law breach of the peace. The Court reversed the breach-of-the-peace conviction and invalidated the state statute, saying in part:

> In the realm of religious faith, and in that of political belief, sharp differences arise. In both fields the tenets of one man may seem the rankest error to his neighbor. To persuade

others to his point of view, the pleader, as we know, resorts to exaggeration, to vilification of men who have been, or are, prominent in church or state, and even to false statement. But the people of this nation have ordained in the light of history, that, in spite of the probability of excesses and abuses, these liberties are, in the long view, essential to enlightened opinion and right conduct on the part of citizens of a democracy.

Three years later, the Court in *Douglas v. City of Jeanette* (1943) held that police could not prohibit members of the Jehovah's Witnesses from peaceable and orderly proselytizing on Sundays merely because other citizens complained. In another 1943 case involving the Jehovah's Witnesses, *Murdock v. Pennsylvania,* the Court held that a state law requiring the payment of a tax for the privilege of solicitation could not be constitutionally applied to religious solicitation. Writing for the Court, Justice William O. Douglas observed that "a person cannot be compelled to purchase . . . a privilege freely granted by the Constitution."

In still another case involving members of the Jehovah's Witnesses, *Niemotko v. Maryland* (1951), the Supreme Court held unconstitutional a city council's denial of a permit to the Jehovah's Witnesses to use the city park for a public meeting. The city council had refused to grant the permit because the Jehovah's Witnesses' answers to questions about Catholicism, military service, and other issues were "unsatisfactory." A unanimous Supreme Court regarded this denial of the public forum to an unpopular religious group as blatant censorship.

Time, Place, and Manner Regulations

As we saw in the preceding chapter, the First Amendment does not guarantee the right to communicate one's views at all times and places or in any manner that may be desired. Religious expression in the **public forum** is subject to reasonable **time, place, and manner regulations.** Airports, courthouses, and other public buildings may be declared off-limits to all First Amendment activities, as long as particular groups are not singled out. Similarly, religious proselytizing in congested areas may be limited to certain areas so as to maintain the safe and orderly flow of pedestrian and vehicular traffic (see, for example, *Heffron v. Internationa'l Society for Krishna Consciousness* [1981]).

TO SUMMARIZE:

- The First Amendment affords unlimited protection to freedom of belief per se.
- The actions of believers in proselytizing and soliciting contributions are also highly protected by the First Amendment, but are subject to reasonable time, place, and manner restrictions.

UNCONVENTIONAL RELIGIOUS PRACTICES

Although the Supreme Court has consistently defended the right of unpopular religious groups to meet, canvass, solicit, and proselytize in the public forum, it has generally rejected arguments that the Free Exercise Clause allows religious groups to engage in activities that are proscribed as detrimental to public health, safety, or morality. Thus, in 1975, the Court refused to review a lower court decision upholding Tennessee's law prohibiting the handling of poisonous snakes in religious ceremonies (see *State ex rel. Swann v. Pack*). In *Employment Division v. Smith* (1990), the Supreme Court rejected a claim made by members of the Native American Church that their ritualistic use of peyote constituted free exercise of religion.

The Mormon Polygamy Case

The first major pronouncement from the Supreme Court on the subject of **unconventional religious practices** came in *Reynolds v. United States* (1879). In this landmark case, the Court upheld application of the federal antipolygamy statute to a Mormon who claimed it was his religious duty to have several wives. The federal law in question merely adopted the long-standing common-law prohibition against bigamy (the crime of having more than one spouse). Although the law applied to everyone regardless of religion, it is clear from the congressional debates surrounding this legislation that the law was aimed at the Mormons, a highly controversial sect in nineteenth-century America.

The *Reynolds* decision was based on a sharp distinction between belief and conduct. According to Chief Justice Morrison R. Waite, "Congress was deprived of all legislative power over mere opinion, but was left free to reach actions which were in violation of social duties or subversive of good order." Although the Supreme Court has occasionally reiterated the distinction between religious belief and conduct, it has largely repudiated the position taken in *Reynolds* that religious conduct is beyond the pale of the Free Exercise Clause. After all, few if any government policies infringe religious belief per se; rather, they are aimed at particular kinds of actions deemed socially undesirable.

The Warren Court Establishes the Compelling Interest Test

In its post-New Deal expansion of civil liberties, the Court markedly increased the degree of judicial protection of religiously motivated conduct, but this did not mean that religious activity received absolute immunity from government regulation. The Court remained willing to uphold public policies that infringed on religious practices if the government could point to an important secular justification for such infringement. In *Sherbert v. Verner* (1963), the Court said that freedom of religion is a **fundamental right** that could be abridged only if necessary to protect a **compelling government interest**. Although the justices often disagreed over precisely which government interests should be viewed as compelling, this general standard established a strong presumption in favor of the free exercise of religion.

The Oregon Peyote Case

Throughout the 1970s and 1980s, the Supreme Court continued to apply the rationale established in *Sherbert v. Verner* (see, for example, *Thomas v. Review Board* [1981] and *Hobbie v. Unemployment Appeals Division* [1987]). These cases stood for the proposition that, in the absence of a compelling justification, a state could not withhold unemployment compensation from an employee who resigned or was discharged due to unwillingness to depart from religious practices or beliefs that conflicted with job requirements. In 1990, however, a sharply divided Court, in *Employment Division v. Smith,* departed dramatically from this approach and imposed potentially serious limits on the scope of religious freedom protected by the First Amendment.

In *Smith,* a state's interest in prohibiting the use of illicit drugs came into conflict with well-established practices of the Native American Church, a sect outside the Judeo-Christian mainstream of American religion. Two members of this church, Alfred Smith and Galen Black, worked as drug rehabilitation counselors for a private social service agency in Oregon. Along with other church members, Smith and Black ingested peyote, a hallucinogenic drug, at a sacramental ceremony practiced by Native Americans for hundreds of years. Citing their use of peyote as "job-related misconduct," the social service agency fired Smith and Black. Recognizing no exception, even for sacramental purposes, Oregon's controlled substances statute made the possession of peyote a criminal offense. Although Smith and Black were not charged with violation of this law, its existence figured prominently in the Supreme Court's ultimate resolution of the free exercise issue.

Shortly after they were fired, Smith and Black applied for unemployment compensation. The Oregon Employment Appeals Board denied their applications, accepting the employer's explanation that Smith and Black had been discharged for job-related misconduct. The former counselors successfully challenged this administrative ruling in the Oregon Court of Appeals, thus initiating a lengthy and complex judicial struggle that generated several state court decisions and two rulings by the U.S. Supreme Court. On remand from the first of these rulings, the Oregon Supreme Court held that the controlled substance law, as applied in this case, violated the Free Exercise Clause of the First Amendment and that Smith and Black were thus entitled to unemployment compensation.

Reviewing the case for a second time and finally reaching the basic constitutional issue, the U.S. Supreme Court reversed. Justice Antonin Scalia, writing for the majority, ruled that "if prohibiting the exercise of religion . . . is . . . merely the incidental effect of a generally applicable and otherwise valid [criminal] law, the First Amendment has not been offended." According to this reasoning, the Free Exercise Clause would be violated only if a particular religious practice were singled out for proscription. In supporting this holding, Scalia relied heavily on *Reynolds v. United States* (1879), in effect equating Oregon's drug prohibition with the federal antipolygamy statute. He contended that "[t]o make an individual's obligation to obey such a law contingent upon the law's coincidence with his religious beliefs except where the state's interest is compelling . . . contradicts both constitutional tradition and common sense." The legislature, Scalia maintained, is free to make accommodations for religious practices. Such accommodations, however, are not required, no matter how "central" a particular practice might be to one's religious beliefs.

As Justice Sandra Day O'Connor's concurring opinion indicates, Scalia's rejection of the compelling governmental interest test was the most controversial aspect of this decision. Although she supported the Court's judgment that the Free Exercise Clause had not been violated, O'Connor sharply criticized the majority opinion as a dramatic departure "from well-settled First Amendment jurisprudence . . . and . . . [as] incompatible with our Nation's fundamental commitment to individual religious liberty." This part of O'Connor's opinion was supported by Justices Brennan, Marshall, and Blackmun, who dissented from the Court's decision. "The compelling interest test," O'Connor asserted, "effectuates the First Amendment's command that religious liberty is an independent liberty, that it occupies a preferred position, and that the Court will not permit encroachments upon this liberty, whether direct or indirect, unless required by clear and compelling governmental interests 'of the highest order.'"

In a separate dissenting opinion, Justice Harry Blackmun, joined by Justices Brennan and Marshall, charged the majority with "mischaracterizing" precedents and "overturning . . . settled law concerning the Religion Clauses of our Constitution." With evident sarcasm, Blackmun expressed the hope that the Court was "aware of the consequences" and that the result was not a "product of overreaction to the serious problems the country's drug crisis [had] generated." He pointed out that the Native American Church restricted and supervised the sacramental use of peyote. The state thus had no significant health or safety justification for regulating this form of drug use. Blackmun also noted that Oregon had not attempted to prosecute Smith and Black or, for that matter, any other Native Americans for the sacramental use of peyote. He concluded that "Oregon's interest in enforcing its drug laws against religious use of peyote [was] not sufficiently compelling to outweigh respondents' right to the free exercise of their religion."

The Religious Freedom Restoration Act

Negative public reaction to the Court's decision in *Smith,* especially from the religious community, convinced a majority in Congress to pass the **Religious Freedom Restoration Act (RFRA)** of 1993. The RFRA prohibited government at all levels from substantially burdening a person's free exercise of religion, even if such burden resulted from a generally applicable rule, unless the government could demonstrate a compelling interest and that the rule constituted the least restrictive means of furthering that interest. In passing the RFRA, Congress sought to restore the status quo ante—to return the law in this area to what it was prior to the *Smith* decision. In adopting this statute, Congress relied on its broad powers under Section 5 of the Fourteenth Amendment.

In *City of Boerne v. Flores* (1997) the Supreme Court, dividing 6 to 3, declared the RFRA unconstitutional. While conceding that Congress has broad power to enforce the provisions of the Fourteenth Amendment, Justice Kennedy, writing for the majority, concluded that "RFRA contradicts vital principles necessary to maintain separation of powers and the federal balance." In this decision the Court stressed the primacy of its role as interpreter of the Constitution. It was firm and unequivocal in rejecting, on broad institutional grounds, a direct congressional challenge of final judicial authority on a question of constitutional interpretation.

Is Animal Sacrifice "Free Exercise of Religion"?

In 1987, the city of Hialeah, a Miami suburb, passed an ordinance making it a crime to "unnecessarily kill, torment, torture, or mutilate an animal in a public or private ritual or ceremony not for the primary purpose of food consumption." The ordinance came in response to local concern over the sacrificial practices associated with Santeria, a blend of Roman Catholicism and West African religions brought to the Caribbean by East African slaves. Santeria, which literally means "worship of the saints," involves occasional sacrifices of live animals, usually goats or chickens. According to some estimates, there are as many as 70,000 devotees of Santeria in the Miami area, and perhaps as many as one million nationwide. Ernesto Pichardo, a Santeria priest, challenged the Hialeah law as a violation of the First Amendment.

In *Church of the Lukumi Babalu Aye v. City of Hialeah* (1993), the justices unanimously invalidated the Hialeah ordinance. Writing for the Supreme Court, Justice Kennedy observed that "the laws in question were enacted by officials who did not understand, failed to perceive, or chose to ignore the fact that their official actions violated the Nation's essential commitment to religious freedom." Justice Kennedy was careful to point out that the ordinance in question was not a generally applicable criminal prohibition, but rather singled out practitioners of Santeria in that it forbade animal slaughter only insofar as it took place within the context of religious rituals. Thus, the decision in *Lukumi Babalu Aye* is consistent with the Court's decision in *Employment Division v. Smith.*

TO SUMMARIZE:

- In contrast to proselytizing and solicitation of contributions, unconventional religious practices such as polygamy and use of illicit drugs receive far less protection under the Free Exercise Clause.
- Although generally applicable prohibitions that incidentally burden religion are likely to be upheld, prohibitions that single out particular religious groups are less likely to survive constitutional challenge.

PATRIOTIC RITUALS AND CIVIC DUTIES

Some religious groups prefer to live largely in isolation from the mainstream of modern society, pursuing lifestyles and embracing virtues reminiscent of the early nineteenth century. For the most part, they are uninterested in things political, preferring to concentrate on their families' moral and spiritual development. They are generally unwilling to serve in the armed forces, since they are opposed to war in any form. They also avoid displays of nationalism or even citizenship. Sometimes, they refuse to school their children formally beyond the primary grades. To what extent does the First Amendment protect such groups from being forced to observe patriotic rituals and civic duties that are readily observed by most Americans?

The Flag Salute Cases

In *Minersville School District v. Gobitis* (1940), the Supreme Court upheld a local school board requirement that all public school students participate in a daily flag salute program. The requirement had been challenged by a member of the Jehovah's Witnesses whose children were being forced to salute the American flag in violation of their religious training, which held the flag salute to be the worship of a "graven image" (see Exodus 20:4–5). In a dramatic turnabout, the *Gobitis* decision was overruled three years later in *West Virginia State Board of Education v. Barnette* (1943). In the *Gobitis* decision, Justice Felix Frankfurter had justified the compulsory flag salute as an appropriate means for the attainment of national unity, which he viewed as "the basis of national security." Writing for the Court that overruled Frankfurter's position, Justice Robert Jackson stated that "compulsory unification of opinion leads only to the unanimity of the graveyard," obviously referring to the situation in Europe in 1943. For Justice Jackson, "to believe that patriotism will not flourish if patriotic ceremonies are voluntary and spontaneous instead of a compulsory routine is to make an unflattering estimate of the appeal of our institutions to free minds."

Nothing that the Supreme Court has decided since *Barnette* indicates that government has any justification for forcing citizens to make professions of patriotism. The Court has even gone so far as to prohibit the state of New Hampshire from requiring that an automobile display a license plate inscribed with the state's motto "Live Free or Die" if such motto offends the religious sensibilities of the car's owner (see *Wooley v. Maynard* [1977]). Although the Court has not faced the question since 1931 (see *United States v. Bland*), it is interesting to speculate as to whether the current Court would require a religious pacifist who wishes to become a citizen to swear that he or she would "defend the Constitution and the laws of the United States against all enemies, foreign or domestic," which is the oath required of all naturalized citizens. The Court upheld the oath requirement in 1931. Would it do so today?

Free Exercise of Religion and Military Service

Another interesting constitutional question involves conscientious objection to military service, alluded to earlier in the discussion of the *Seeger* case. Although Congress has provided an exemption from military service for religiously motivated conscientious objectors, is such an exemption required by the Free Exercise Clause? In other words, would the Supreme Court permit religiously motivated refusal to serve in combat on constitutional grounds if there were no act of Congress providing such an exemption? On the other hand, is it not possible to argue that, in granting an exemption only to those whose refusal to serve is based on religion, Congress has run afoul of the Establishment Clause? The Court has never squarely addressed these questions.

One of the most controversial Supreme Court decisions in the area of free exercise of religion dealt with military regulations that were alleged to infringe First Amendment rights. In *Goldman v. Weinberger* (1986), the Court upheld an Air Force dress code requirement against the challenge of an Orthodox Jew who was disciplined for wearing a yarmulke while in uniform. Stressing the need for discipline and uniformity in the military, the Court rejected the challenge by a vote of 5 to 4. Writing for the sharply divided Court, Justice William Rehnquist maintained that "when evaluating whether military needs justify a particular restriction on religiously motivated conduct, courts must give great deference to the professional judgment of military authorities concerning the relative importance of a particular military interest."

In *Goldman,* the Supreme Court thus reiterated the position taken five years before that "[j]udicial deference . . . is at its apogee when legislative action under the congressional authority to raise and support armies and make rules and regulations for their governance is challenged" (*Rostker v. Goldberg* [1981]). In response to the *Goldman* decision, Congress passed legislation permitting military personnel to wear religious apparel. However, this legislation authorized the Department of Defense to restrict the wearing of apparel that "would interfere with the performance of . . . military duties" or is "not neat and conservative." As of this writing (April 2002), the Supreme Court has not considered the constitutionality of this legislation.

TO SUMMARIZE:

- The First Amendment prohibits government from compelling individuals to make public affirmations of belief, whether religious or political.
- Because Congress has created a statutory basis for conscientious objection to military service, the Supreme Court has not faced the issue of whether exemptions for conscientious objectors are required by the Free Exercise Clause.
- The Court tends to be deferential to military regulations such as dress codes that impinge upon the free exercise of religion by persons in military service, as long as such regulations do not single out or discriminate against particular religions.

FREEDOM OF RELIGION VERSUS *PARENS PATRIAE*

Our legal traditions recognize government as *parens patriae,* meaning literally "parent of the country." This term refers to the role of government as guardian of persons who are not legally competent to make their own decisions, such as children, the severely retarded, and the mentally ill. Occasionally, the state uses this power to take custody of children who are the victims of neglect or abuse. The state's role as *parens patriae* has sometimes come into conflict with the Free Exercise Clause when parents refuse on religious grounds to allow their children to receive medical treatment. Some devoutly religious persons believe that medical science is blasphemous—that true faith is all that is necessary to promote healing. For example, in a 1983 Tennessee case that attracted wide attention, a fundamentalist preacher refused to allow a hospital to treat his young daughter for cancer. The state intervened as *parens patriae* and secured a court order requiring medical treatment (see *In the Matter of Hamilton* [1983]).

Although some state and federal court decisions have recognized a competent adult's **right to refuse medical treatment** on religious and/or privacy grounds, courts are generally disinclined to uphold such free exercise claims where the health of children is involved. Judges generally assume that children are not sufficiently mature to make rational choices regarding medical treatment and, in some instances, must be protected against the consequences of their parents' unusual religious convictions.

In *Prince v. Massachusetts* (1944), the Supreme Court upheld a child labor law against an attack based on the Free Exercise Clause. The law prohibited boys under age 12 and girls under 18 from selling newspapers on the streets. The law was challenged by a member of the Jehovah's Witnesses whose children normally assisted her in the sale and distribution of religious literature. Dividing 8 to 1, the Court held that the state's role as *parens patriae* in protecting the safety of children overrode Prince's free exercise claim.

Compulsory School Attendance

In *Wisconsin v. Yoder* (1972), the Supreme Court held that a state's compulsory high school attendance law could not be constitutionally applied to members of the Old Order Amish faith, which does not permit secular education beyond the eighth grade. Writing for the Court, Chief Justice Warren E. Burger placed great stress on the fact that the education of the Amish teenager continued in the home, with emphasis on practical skills as well as religious and moral values. Based on Burger's opinion in *Yoder,* it seems unlikely that the Court would grant the Amish an exemption from compulsory primary education. Nor would it grant an exemption to members of a "religion" that strikes the Court as silly, faddish, or insincere.

One wonders whether the Amish would prevail if their case came before the current Supreme Court. After all, compulsory school attendance laws are generally applicable rules. In *Minnesota v. Hershberger* (1990), the Court vacated a state supreme court decision exempting the Amish from compliance with state traffic laws. On the other hand, the Court has long recognized the rights of parents in matters pertaining to the education of their children (see, for example, *Meyer v. Nebraska* [1923]). One can make good arguments for the current Court deciding the compulsory school attendance issue either way.

TO SUMMARIZE:

- Courts have recognized the right of competent adults to refuse medical treatment on religious grounds, but generally do not permit parents to refuse life-saving medical treatment for their minor children.
- The Supreme Court has held that the Free Exercise Clause exempts members of the Old Order Amish faith from compliance with state laws requiring children to attend school beyond the eighth grade. The Court recognized the exceptional circumstances under which this exemption was granted, making it clear that a mere claim of religious liberty is not enough to warrant such special treatment.

THE WALL OF SEPARATION

The Establishment Clause of the First Amendment was adopted in contradiction to the practice, prevalent not only in Europe but among the American colonies, of having official churches supported by taxation. Indeed, as previously noted, some states maintained their established churches well into the nineteenth century. Thus, the concept of "a wall of separation between church and state," as Thomas Jefferson referred to it, was an American invention whose application remained to be worked out in practice. In *Everson v. Board of Education* (1947), the Supreme Court adopted Jefferson's metaphor as encapsulating the meaning of the Establishment Clause.

Competing Interpretations of the Establishment Clause

Since its ratification more than two centuries ago, Americans both on and off the Supreme Court have disagreed sharply over the meaning of the Establishment Clause. One view is that it merely forbids the establishment of an official, state-supported religion. According to this restrictive interpretation, Congress does not run afoul of the First Amendment as long as it refrains from selecting one denomination as the official or preferred religion. However, even the literal language of the First Amendment suggests a broader prohibition. It does not say that Congress shall make no law establishing an official religion; rather, it states that "Congress shall make no law *respecting an establishment of religion*" [emphasis added]. This general language indicates a broader restriction than mere prohibition of an established church. For the most part, the Supreme Court has opted for this broader interpretation.

When polled, most Americans respond approvingly to the abstract concept of **separation of church and state.** Yet there is no consensus on how high or how thick the wall of separation should be. Thus, the Supreme Court's decisions applying this concept to particular situations have been even more controversial than its decisions under the Free Exercise Clause. Many of these controversial decisions involve education, notably prayer in public schools and state aid to private religious schools.

Traditional Government Practices

Potential Establishment Clause questions are implicit in many traditional government practices. For example, consider the practice of Congress and every state legislature of paying a chaplain, usually of a particular Protestant denomination, to lead our representatives in public prayer (see *Marsh v. Chambers* [1983]). What about the inscription "In God We Trust" on American currency? Or the Supreme Court's time-honored practice of opening oral argument with the invocation "God save the United States and this honorable Court"? Or the recognition of America as "one nation under God" in the official pledge of allegiance to the flag? These and other common practices indicate the degree to which religion figures prominently in the public life of this nation. Although many Americans no doubt approve of such official endorsement and invocation of religion, what about the rights of nonbelievers? How far does the First Amendment allow the government to go in recognizing, endorsing, or accommodating religious beliefs? As the controversial Supreme Court decisions interpreting the Establishment Clause demonstrate, the answer to this question is far from clear.

The *Lemon* Test

In 1971, the Court laid down a three-pronged test for determining the constitutionality of policies challenged under the Establishment Clause (see *Lemon v. Kurtzman*). The so-called ***Lemon* test** synthesized various elements of the Court's Establishment Clause jurisprudence as it had evolved during the 1940s, 1950s, and 1960s. Although controversial from its inception, the *Lemon* test has been applied to a broad range of issues involving separation of church and state. Under the *Lemon* test, a challenged policy must meet the following criteria in order to pass muster under the Establishment Clause: (1) it must have a "secular purpose"; (2) it must not have the principal or primary effect of "inhibiting or advancing religion"; and (3) it must avoid an "excessive government entanglement with religion."

It should go without saying that the *Lemon* test does not contain hard and fast criteria for judicial decision making. Rather, like all judicial doctrines, it is subject to some degree of manipulation by those who are predisposed to a particular result. For example, how can the "purpose" of a challenged law be determined with certainty by the courts? How does one distinguish the "principal" or "primary" effects of a law from its secondary or tertiary effects? Finally, how much entanglement between religion and government is "excessive"? During the 1970s and 1980s, the Court was often criticized for inconsistency in its application of the *Lemon* test, leading some scholars to question the value of the test altogether. Since the 1990s, the Court has moved away from a strict application of the *Lemon* test, but has stopped short of repudiating it altogether (see, for example, *Agostini v. Felton* [1997], discussed below and excerpted at the end of the chapter).

TO SUMMARIZE:

- The Supreme Court has adopted Thomas Jefferson's metaphor of a "wall of separation between church and state" as capturing the essential meaning of the Establishment Clause. Since its first decision in this area, however, the Court has sought to balance the idea of separation of church and state with the equally important constitutional commitment to free exercise of religion.
- In *Lemon v. Kurtzman* (1971), the Court fashioned a three-part test for determining whether a particular policy constitutes an establishment of religion. To survive challenge, the policy must have a secular purpose, its principal effect must not be to advance or inhibit religion, and it must avoid excessive entanglement between government and religion.
- The Court has moved away from a strict application of the *Lemon* test but has stopped short of repudiating it altogether.

RELIGION AND PUBLIC EDUCATION

In *Everson v. Board of Education* (1947), the first case in which the Supreme Court applied the Establishment Clause to the states via the Fourteenth Amendment, the issue was whether a local school board could reimburse parents for expenses they incurred in transporting their children to and from Catholic schools. The payments to parents of children in parochial schools were part of a general program under which all parents of children in public schools and nonprofit private schools, regardless of religious affiliation, were entitled to reimbursement for transportation costs. However, it is worth noting that the overwhelming number of children attending nonprofit private schools in this New Jersey school district were enrolled in Catholic schools. Writing for a sharply divided Court, Justice Hugo Black justified the challenged payments on the theory that the school board was merely furthering the state's legitimate interest in getting children, "regardless of their religion, safely and expeditiously to and from accredited schools."

Justice Wiley Rutledge, joined by Justices Felix Frankfurter, Robert Jackson, and Harold Burton, dissented vigorously. Professing sympathy for the economic hardships involved in sending one's children to private, religious schools, Justice Rutledge nevertheless asserted:

> Like St. Paul's freedom, religious liberty with a great price must be bought. And for those who exercise it most fully, by insisting upon religious education for their children mixed with secular, by the terms of our Constitution the price is greater than for others.

The **child benefit theory** articulated in *Everson* has for the most part been maintained. Thus, for example, in *Board of Education v. Allen* (1968), the Supreme Court upheld a New York statute requiring local public school districts to lend textbooks on secular subjects to students in private and parochial schools. And in *Meek v. Pittenger* (1975), the Court reaffirmed this position.

Released Time Programs and Equal Access Policies

To accommodate the religious beliefs of public school students, the Court has upheld **released-time programs,** which allow students to leave campus to attend religious exercises. Distinguishing a 1948 decision in which it struck down an on-campus released-time program (*McCollum v. Board of Education*), the Court in *Zorach v. Clauson* (1952) upheld a New York policy under which public school students who received parental permission left campus to attend religious services while other students attended study hall. Writing for the Court, Justice Douglas stressed the need for governmental accommodation of religious practices, a position from which he would later retreat.

Released-time programs, although constitutionally permissible under *Zorach v. Clauson,* are not in widespread use in public schools today. More common today are policies under which religiously oriented student groups are permitted **equal access** to school facilities. In *Widmar v. Vincent* (1981), the Supreme Court said that public school facilities that have been designated an open forum may not be placed off-limits to religious groups. In *Board of Education v. Mergens* (1990), the Court upheld the Equal Access Act of 1984, in which Congress prohibited public secondary schools that receive federal funds from disallowing meetings of student groups on the basis of "religious, political, philosophical or other content of the speech at such meetings." Three years later, in *Lamb's Chapel v. Center Moriches Union Free School District,* the Court held that the limited public forum approach could not be used to bar a religious organization from a showing a film after school hours dealing with family planning and child-rearing issues, while permitting discussion of these issues by nonreligious groups. According to the Court, the school district rule at issue in this case amounted to viewpoint discrimination in violation of the First Amendment's free speech guarantee. The Court rejected the argument that Lamb's Chapel's after-hours use of school property violated the *Lemon* test. In *Good News Club v. Milford Central School* (2001), the Court went one step further by holding that if a school permits after-hours activities concerning moral or character development, it cannot prohibit activities even if they involve religious instruction of elementary school students.

Government Efforts to Assist Religious Schools

In *Lemon v. Kurtzman* (1971), the Court struck down Pennsylvania and Rhode Island policies providing publicly funded salary supplements to teachers in parochial schools as fostering "excessive entanglement." Similarly, in *Committee for Public Education v. Nyquist* (1973), the Court used the three-pronged test in striking down a New York law that provided various forms of economic aid to parochial schools. Although the released- time programs approved in *Zorach* have not been recently litigated before the Supreme Court, it is highly unlikely such programs could survive a rigorous application of the *Lemon* test.

The Supreme Court reinforced its holdings in *Lemon* and *Nyquist* in two significant decisions of the mid-1980s. In *Aguilar v. Felton* (1985), the Court struck down a New York City program that used federal funds to supplement the salaries of public school teachers who taught remedial courses on the premises of religious schools. Similarly, in *Grand Rapids School District v. Ball* (1985), the Court invalidated a program in which supplementary classes for students in sectarian schools were taught by public school teachers at public expense. Writing for the Court in the *Grand Rapids* case, Justice Brennan observed that "the symbolic union of church and state inherent in the provision of secular, state-provided instruction in the religious school buildings threatens to convey a message of state support for religion to students and to the general public."

Justice Byron White used the occasion to dissent not only from the Court's *Grand Rapids* holding but from the entire thrust of the Court's decisions in the area of state aid to religious schools:

> I am firmly of the belief that the Court's decisions in these cases, like its decisions in *Lemon* and *Nyquist,* are not required by the First Amendment and [are] contrary to the long-range interest of the country. . . . I am satisfied that what the States have sought to do in these cases is well within their authority and is not forbidden by the Establishment Clause.

In 1994 the Court reaffirmed its decisions in *Aguilar* and *Grand Rapids* by striking down a New York law that created a new special school district in a community occupied exclusively by Hassidic Jews. Virtually all of the community's children were being educated in private schools. The new district was established for the purpose of enabling the community to avail itself of public funds for the education of children with disabilities. Under *Aguilar* and *Grand Rapids,* this kind of assistance could not be provided directly to the community's private schools, thus explaining the creation of a new public school district. In *Kiryas Joel School District v. Grumet* (1994), the Court found this arrangement to be an unconstitutional establishment of religion. In this case the Court conspicuously avoided relying on the *Lemon* test, leading commentators to wonder whether this three-pronged formulation was being phased out. Recalling Justice White's dissent in *Grand Rapids,* Justice Scalia, joined by Chief Justice Rehnquist and Justice Thomas, was sharply critical of the Court's decision and indeed of its general approach in this area.

By 1997 a Court majority was willing to give ground in the area of aid to parochial schools. Thus, in *Agostini v. Felton,* a bare majority of justices voted to overturn *Aguilar v. Felton* and corresponding portions of *Grand Rapids School District v. Ball.* In her majority opinion, Justice O'Connor maintained that *Aguilar* was inconsistent with the Court's later Establishment Clause decisions. O'Connor stressed the neutrality of the federally funded remedial instruction and the procedural safeguards surrounding the program. She also noted that this program could not "reasonably be viewed as an endorsement of religion." With the concurrence of Chief Justice Rehnquist and Justices Scalia, Kennedy, and Thomas, Justice O'Connor therefore concluded that "*Aguilar,* as well as the portion of *Ball* addressing Grand Rapids' 'shared time' program, are no longer good law." In dissent, Justices Stevens, Souter, Ginsburg, and Breyer continued to express concern about the difficulty of limiting government assistance in this area to purely secular objectives.

In *Mitchell v. Helms* (2000), the Court, by a 6-to-3 vote, expanded the types of public aid that government may provide to parochial schools. Relying heavily on the *Agostini* precedent, the Court upheld a Louisiana statute permitting state and local governments to lend library books, projectors, televisions, computers, software, and similar equipment to parochial and other private not-for-profit elementary and secondary schools. The six members of the majority could not agree on a single opinion, however. Justice Thomas, in a plurality opinion joined by Chief Justice Rehnquist and Justices Scalia and Kennedy, indicated his willingness to go further than the Court's holding, suggesting that he and his three colleagues in the plurality would be willing to support even broader public assistance to religious schools. His position is summarized in the following statement: "If religious, irreligious and areligious are all eligible for governmental aid, no one would conclude that any indoctrination that any particular recipient conducts has been done at the behest of the government."

In a separate opinion concurring in the judgment only, Justice O'Connor, joined by Justice Breyer, criticized what she viewed as the "unprecedented breadth" of the rule announced by the plurality. She contended that considerations of neutrality alone are not sufficient in determining whether governmental aid to religious schools violates the Establishment Clause. Such factors as "endorsement" of religion should also be taken into account. Thomas's opinion, she maintained, foreshadowed "the approval of direct monetary subsidies to religious organizations, even when they use the money to advance their religious objectives." In dissent, Justice Souter, supported by Justices Stevens and Ginsburg, expressed alarm at the scope of the plurality opinion:

> As a break with consistent doctrine the plurality's new criterion is unequaled in the history of Establishment Clause interpretation. Simple on its face, it appears to take even-handedness neutrality and in practical terms promote it to a single and sufficient test for the establishment [*sic*] constitutionality of school aid.

If evenhanded neutrality were the sole standard for determining the constitutionality of public aid, Souter reasoned, "religious schools could be blessed with government funding as massive as expenditures made for the benefit of their public school counterparts and religious missions would thrive on public money."

Mitchell v. Helms could have the effect of giving virtually all schoolchildren access to the Internet. Some critics have noted that computers, by contrast with textbooks loaned to parochial schools at public expense, can be used in an endless variety of ways, both secular and religious. Barry W. Lynn, executive director of Americans United for Separation of Church and State, observed that as a result of this decision, "religious schools can now have students surf the Internet to read the Bible in religion classes, learn theology from Jerry Falwell, or download crucifixes as screen savers." On the other hand, children in religious schools might well use the Internet to access ideas that run counter to the religious views of their teachers and parents.

The Continuing School Prayer Controversy

Few decisions of the modern Supreme Court have been criticized more intensely than the **school prayer decisions** of the early 1960s. In *Engel v. Vitale* (1962), the Court invalidated a New York Board of Regents policy that established the voluntary recitation of a brief generic prayer by children in the public schools at the start of each school day. Justice Black wrote the opinion for the majority, saying that "in this country it is no part of the business of government to compose official prayers for any group of the American people to recite as part of a religious program carried on by government."

Justice Potter Stewart, the lone dissenter in *Engel v. Vitale,* compared the recitation of the regents' prayer to other official recognitions of God and religion, such as the pledge of allegiance to the flag, the president's oath of office, and the invocation said prior to oral argument in the Supreme Court:

> I do not believe that this Court, or the Congress, or the President has by the actions and practices I have described established an "official religion" in violation of the Constitution. And I do not believe the State of New York has done so in this case. What each has done has been to recognize and to follow the deeply entrenched and highly cherished spiritual traditions of our Nation.

In 1963, the Court reinforced the *Engel* decision in the companion cases of *Abington School District v. Schempp* and *Murray v. Curlett* by striking down the practice of Bible reading and the recitation of the Lord's Prayer in the Pennsylvania and Maryland public schools. Again, only Justice Stewart dissented.

The reaction to the Court's school prayer decisions came fast and furious and, indeed, has still not disappeared. The Court was roundly condemned by religious leaders and conservative members of Congress and through resolutions passed by several state legislatures. Polls have consistently shown that a majority of Americans oppose the Court's ban on school prayer. Even today, the public has lower regard for the Court's work in this area than in other policy areas.

On several occasions, constitutional amendments have been introduced in Congress aimed specifically at overturning the school prayer decisions. In November 1971, one such proposal in the House of Representatives fell only twenty-eight votes short of the two-thirds majority required for constitutional amendments. In the election of 1980, Ronald Reagan capitalized on public sentiment about school prayer by advocating a "school prayer amendment." However, once in office, President Reagan was either unwilling or unable to push this proposal through Congress.

Negative public reaction and widespread noncompliance notwithstanding, the Supreme Court has maintained, although by a shrinking majority, the position articulated in the school prayer cases. For example, in *Stone v. Graham* (1980), the Court invalidated a Kentucky law requiring that the Ten Commandments be posted in all public school classrooms. In *Wallace v. Jaffree* (1985) the Court struck down an Alabama law that required public school students to observe a **moment of silence** "for the purpose of meditation or voluntary prayer" at the start of each school day. In *Lee v. Weisiman* (1992) the Court held unconstitutional the practice of inviting a member of the clergy to deliver a nonsectarian prayer at a public school graduation ceremony. Most recently, in *Santa Fe Independent School District v. Doe* (2000), the Court split 5 to 4 in striking down a public high school's policy of allowing students to elect a chaplain to deliver invocations before football games.

The reaction to the Court's decisions in this area have been predictable. Conservative organizations and religious activists have been harshly critical. In the wake of the *Santa Fe* decision, conservative activist and Republican presidential candidate Gary Bauer said the decision "proves that a majority of the court is at war with the religious tradition of America." On the other hand, civil liberties groups have applauded the Court for these decisions. Barry W. Lynn, of Americans United for Separation of Church and State, said that the *Santa Fe* decision "was a major victory for people who believe that mob rule—majority rule—is not appropriate in matters of religion."

Note that in no case has the Court held that it is unconstitutional for a student to pray voluntarily in the public school classroom, although some school officials have interpreted the Court's position this way. What the Court has said is that it is unconstitutional for the state schools to require, endorse, or sanction prayer, either directly or indirectly. One might think that if this were better understood, some of the public hostility toward the Court's decisions would abate. On the other hand, given the nature and intensity of feelings on this issue, it is unlikely that an accurate public perception of the Court's holdings would diminish the public opprobrium.

The Evolution-Creationism Conflict

With the rapid expansion of public education in the early twentieth century, especially in rural areas dominated by fundamentalist Protestantism, a controversy erupted over the teaching of evolution in the public schools. The controversy achieved national prominence in 1925 when John T. Scopes, a high school biology teacher in Dayton, Tennessee, was prosecuted for teaching evolution in violation of a state law that had been passed earlier that year. Amid a carnival-like atmosphere, the **Scopes trial**—or the "Monkey Trial," as it was caricatured in the press—pitted famous politician and orator William Jennings Bryan against celebrated lawyer Clarence Darrow in a battle royal in the courtroom. Although Darrow outsmarted Bryan in a much-publicized debate over biblical literalism, Scopes was nevertheless convicted of violating the state statute. The Tennessee Supreme Court reversed the conviction on technical grounds, however, preventing the U.S. Supreme Court from having to consider what was potentially the most explosive constitutional question of that decade.

In the wake of the Scopes trial, two states, Arkansas and Mississippi, enacted legislation similar to the Tennessee anti-evolution law. Yet it was not until 1965 that one of these laws was challenged in court. In that year, Susan Epperson, a high school biology teacher in Little Rock, filed a lawsuit challenging the Arkansas statute. Although the Arkansas trial court ruled in favor of Epperson and struck down the anti-evolution law, the state supreme court reversed and reinstated the statute. On certiorari, the U.S. Supreme Court reversed (*Epperson v. Arkansas* [1968]). Writing for the Court, Justice Abe Fortas asserted that Arkansas could not "prevent its teachers from discussing the theory of evolution because it is contrary to the belief of some that the Book of Genesis must be the exclusive source of doctrine as to the origins of man."

The *Epperson* decision put to rest the issue of whether states could prohibit the teaching of evolution in their public schools. But two decades later, the evolution-creationism conflict resurfaced in Louisiana. This time, the question was whether the state could mandate that creationism, or **creation science**, be given equal time in the classroom along with the theory of evolution. In *Edwards v. Aguillard* (1987), the Supreme Court answered this question in the negative. Writing for a majority of seven, Justice Brennan averred that "the primary purpose" of the Louisiana Creationism Act was "to endorse a particular religious doctrine," rather than further the legitimate interests of the state in fostering different points of view in the classroom.

In the wake of such decisions as *Edwards v. Aguillard* and *Epperson v. Arkansas,* as well as the school prayer decisions discussed previously, fundamentalist Christians began to argue that, in its attempt to expunge religious teaching and symbols from the public schools, the Supreme Court had fostered a "religion" of **secular humanism**. According to its detractors, secular humanism is a philosophy emphasizing the view that morality is a human invention and that moral choices are largely matters of personal values. In the view of some fundamentalists, the pervasiveness of secular humanism in public school curricula was highly corrosive to traditional values and institutions.

In 1987, a federal district court barred the use of certain widely used history, social studies, and home economics textbooks in the public schools of Mobile County, Alabama. In essence, the district judge held that these books advanced the "religion" of secular humanism. In embracing this philosophy, the textbooks allegedly ignored or understated the historical and contemporary significance of traditional religion in American life, thus abridging the Free Exercise rights of students holding theistic beliefs. The "teaching" of secular humanism amounted to "a sweeping fundamental belief that must not be promoted by the public schools." Such promotion, the district court concluded, was a violation of the Establishment Clause of the First Amendment. The Court of Appeals for the Eleventh Circuit promptly overruled this novel decision, finding that the "purpose" for using the textbooks in question was "purely secular" (see *Smith v. Board of School Commissioners of Mobile County* [1987]).

In a similar case initiated in 1986, fundamentalist parents in Hawkins County, Tennessee, sued their county school board over the reading curriculum in the local public schools, complaining of the humanist perspective embodied in the curriculum. Although plaintiffs won at trial, the judgment was overruled on appeal by the

Court of Appeals for the Sixth Circuit. The U.S. Supreme Court declined to review the case (*Mozert v. Hawkins County Public Schools* [1988]), thus letting the appeals court's decision stand.

Discrimination against Religious Expression in the Public Educational Arena

If a public school or university subsidizes a variety of student newspapers, can it withhold funds from a particular paper solely because it "promotes or manifests a particular belief in or about a deity or an ultimate reality"? This was the issue before the Court in *Rosenberger v. University of Virginia* (1995). The university denied a subsidy to "Wide Awake: A Christian Perspective at the University of Virginia." The student-publisher of the paper went to court. The Supreme Court found the denial of support violative of free speech, in that the university was discriminating against the paper based on its content. Moreover, the Court rejected the argument that to subsidize the paper, the Uuniversity would be breaching the wall of separation between church and state. Four justices (Souter, Stevens, Ginsburg, and Breyer) dissented, claiming that for the university to provide the subsidy in question would constitute a clear violation of the Establishment Clause. Some observers regarded Justice O'Connor's concurring opinion as somewhat equivocal, leading them to speculate that in a similar case O'Connor might be persuaded to go the other way. It is possible that the *Rosenberger* decision will be limited to its rather unique facts.

TO SUMMARIZE:

- The Supreme Court has struggled with the question of whether various kinds of governmental support for education extending to private, parochial schools can be justified under a general "child benefit" theory or must be barred as a violation of the Establishment Clause.
- The Court has aroused deep and protracted controversy with its persistent efforts to proscribe officially sponsored religious exercises in the public schools. From its school prayer decisions of the early 1960s through its "moment of silence" ruling in 1985 to its 1992 holding regarding commencement exercises, the Court has steadfastly applied a principle of strict separation in this area.
- The Court has also applied the principle of separation of church and state in thwarting state efforts dating from the 1920s to forbid the teaching of evolution and later attempts to promote the teaching of "creation science" in the public schools.

GOVERNMENTAL AFFIRMATIONS OF RELIGIOUS BELIEF

In a religious society such as ours, it is inevitable (and, many would say, desirable) for there to be numerous public affirmations of belief. The Court's decision in *Abington v. Schempp* suggests, however, that government sponsorship of such affirmations may be unconstitutional. Nevertheless, the Supreme Court has been unwilling to hold government-sponsored displays or affirmations of belief to the same standard of **strict neutrality** that underlies the school prayer decisions. For example, in *McGowan v. Maryland* (1961) the Court upheld laws that prohibited certain businesses from operating on Sunday, despite the obvious religious underpinnings of such restrictions. In the Court's view, these **Sunday closing laws** had a secular purpose in that they represented the community's desire for a day of rest and relaxation, independent of any religious significance. The fact that this day of rest happened to be the day of worship for most Christians was merely incidental. Writing for the Court in *McGowan,* Chief Justice Earl Warren noted that

> it is common knowledge that the first day of the week has come to have special signif-icance as a rest day in this country. People of all religions and people with no religion regard Sunday as a time for family activity, for visiting friends and relatives, for late sleeping, for passive and active entertainments, for dining out, and the like.

Perhaps the best example of the Court's unwillingness to extend the holding of *Abington v. Schempp* to its logical conclusion came in *Marsh v. Chambers* (1983). Here, the Court refused to invalidate Nebraska's policy of beginning legislative sessions with prayers offered by a Protestant chaplain retained at the taxpayers' expense. Writing for the Court, Chief Justice Burger made no pretense of applying the strict three-part test laid down in his own majority opinion in *Lemon v. Kurtzman.* Instead, Burger's opinion relied heavily on history and the need for accommodation of popular religious beliefs. In a caustic dissent, Justice Brennan observed that "if any group of law students were asked to apply the principles of *Lemon* to the question of legislative prayer, they would nearly unanimously find the practice to be unconstitutional."

The decision in *Marsh v. Chambers* suggested to some observers that the Supreme Court was prepared to abandon the strict tripartite *Lemon* test for determining establishment of religion. To others, *Marsh* was a mere aberration, based on the pragmatic realization that the Court would inevitably be embarrassed if it were to attempt to strike down a practice that occurs in nearly every legislature in the United States, including the U.S. Congress. This case provides a good illustration of the practical limits of judicial power.

Religious Displays on Public Property

The decision in *Lynch v. Donnelly* (1984) suggests that *Marsh* was more than a mere aberration. In *Lynch,* the Court upheld a city-sponsored nativity scene in Pawtucket, Rhode Island. Chief Justice Burger's majority opinion barely mentioned the *Lemon* test. Again Burger relied on history and the fact that the crèche had become for many a "neutral harbinger of the holiday season," rather than a symbol of Christianity.

Five years later, in the Pennsylvania case of *County of Allegheny v. American Civil Liberties Union* (1989), the Court reexamined the constitutional question posed by traditional holiday displays on public property. Here, the justices considered two separate displays: a crèche prominently situated on the grand staircase inside the county courthouse and an arrangement featuring a Christmas tree and a Hanukkah menorah placed just outside the nearby city—county building. A sign bearing the mayor's name and entitled the slogan "Salute to Liberty" was placed at the foot of the Christmas tree. Justice Blackmun, for a majority of the Court, maintained that the display of the crèche inside the courthouse, with the accompanying words "Gloria in Excelsis Deo," clearly conveyed a religious message. By authorizing the display, the county had, in Blackmun's view, indicated its endorsement of that message. Such endorsement, he concluded, was a violation of the Establishment Clause. By contrast, the Christmas tree and menorah display, in tandem with the mayor's message, was not in the Court's view "an endorsement of religious faith, but simply a recognition of cultural diversity." The overall display conveyed a predominantly secular message and thus did not violate the Establishment Clause.

The Supreme Court's decisions in *Marsh* and *Lynch* indicate that the Burger Court retreated from the strict neutrality of the Warren Court in favor of an approach that might be labeled **accommodation** or **benevolent neutrality**. The *Allegheny County* decision suggested, however, that the Rehnquist Court was seeking a middle ground in this area.

TO SUMMARIZE:

- With respect to the issue of governmental affirmation of popular religious beliefs, the Court has sought a middle ground in which considerations of tradition and established practice are balanced against the principle of church-state separation.

THE PROBLEM OF TAX EXEMPTIONS

Traditionally, church properties have been exempt from local property taxes and church incomes have been exempt from federal and state income taxes. Such exemptions generally are not limited to churches but extend to various private, nonprofit organizations that can be classified as charitable institutions. The existence of **tax exemptions** for churches and religious schools raises questions under both the Establishment and Free Exercise Clauses of the First Amendment. On the one hand, it can be argued that a tax exemption is an indirect subsidy. Arguably, for government to exempt churches and church schools from paying taxes is to subsidize them in violation of the requirement of separation of church and state. On the other hand, one can argue that failure to exempt churches from taxation amounts to an infringement of the Free Exercise Clause, since, as Chief Justice John Marshall pointed out in *M'Culloch v. Maryland* (1819), "the power to tax involves the power to destroy."

The Supreme Court considered the constitutionality of property tax exemptions for churches in the case of *Walz v. Tax Commission* (1970). Frederick Walz brought suit against the New York City Tax Commission, arguing that the commission's grant of property tax exemptions to churches (as allowed by state law) required him to subsidize those churches indirectly. Relying heavily on the long-standing practice of religious tax exemptions and the Court's traditional deference to legislative bodies with regard to the taxing power, the Court found no constitutional violation. Writing for a majority of eight, Chief Justice Burger noted that

> [f]ew concepts are more deeply embedded in the fabric of our national life, beginning with pre-Revolutionary colonial times, than for the government to exercise . . . this kind of benevolent neutrality toward churches and religious exercise generally so long as none was favored over others and none suffered interference.

Dissenting vigorously, Justice Douglas argued for strict government neutrality toward religion as distinct from the Chief Justice's "benevolent neutrality" approach:

> If believers are entitled to public financial support, so are nonbelievers. A believer and nonbeliever under the present law are treated differently because of the articles of their faith. Believers are doubtless comforted that the cause of religion is being fostered by this legislation. Yet one of the mandates of the First Amendment is to promote a viable, pluralistic society and to keep government neutral, not only between sects, but also between believers and nonbelievers.

It is interesting to compare Justice Douglas's dissent in *Walz* with his majority opinion in *Zorach v. Clauson*. In 1952, Douglas had written, apparently in earnest, about the importance of governmental accommodation of religion. In concurring opinions in the school prayer decisions of 1962 and 1963, Douglas indicated that he was reconsidering his position on the Establishment Clause generally. By 1970, his stance had shifted from accommodation to strict neutrality. Justice Douglas's forceful dissent in *Walz* to the contrary notwithstanding, it is unlikely that the Supreme Court would ever invalidate religious tax exemptions. There is simply too much public support for these long-standing policies.

To take advantage of tax exemptions for religious property, a small minority of unscrupulous individuals have established "churches" in their homes after obtaining inexpensive "doctor of divinity" degrees through the mail. For example, in the late 1970s in one small town in New York, nearly 85 percent of the residents became "ministers" and claimed tax-exempt status for their homes. This subterfuge was finally ended through state legislation that was upheld by a later court decision. The U.S. Supreme Court dismissed the appeal, thus allowing the state court decision to stand (*Hardenbaugh v. New York* [1981]).

One of the most controversial Supreme Court decisions of the early 1980s dealt with the question of whether tax-exempt status could be withdrawn from religious schools that practice race discrimination. In *Bob Jones University v. United States* (1983), the Court held that such institutions could indeed be denied their federal income tax exemptions by the Internal Revenue Service (IRS). Prior to 1975, Bob Jones University, a fundamentalist Christian college in South Carolina, had refused to admit African-Americans. After 1975, African-Americans were admitted, but interracial dating and marriage were strictly prohibited. The IRS formally revoked the school's long-standing tax exemption in 1976. Then, in 1982, the Reagan administration announced that the IRS was restoring tax-exempt status to all segregated private schools, claiming that the IRS lacked the authority to remove tax exemptions without specific authorizing legislation from Congress. The Court's 8-to-1 decision in *Bob Jones* repudiated the Reagan administration's view that the IRS lacked authority to revoke the tax-exempt status of religious schools that practice racial discrimination. With regard to the First Amendment issue, the Court held that

> [t]he governmental interest at stake here is compelling. . . . The government has a fundamental, overriding interest in eradicating racial discrimination in education. . . . That governmental interest substantially outweighs whatever burden denial of tax benefits places on petitioners' exercise of their religious beliefs.

The Court's decision in *Bob Jones* implies that tax exemptions for religious enterprises are not a matter of constitutional entitlement—they are granted through governmental benevolence and can be withdrawn for reasons of public policy.

Tuition Tax Credits

A number of states have considered the idea of providing tax credits to parents of children in private and parochial schools. Indeed, in 1982, President Reagan proposed **tuition tax credits** of $500 per child for parents whose children attend private and parochial schools. Although the proposal did not obtain congressional approval, serious questions were raised about its constitutionality. In *Committee for Public Education v. Nyquist* (1973), the Supreme Court had struck down a state tax deduction for parents of children in parochial schools. However, the Court may be moving away from the *Nyquist* decision, at least insofar as it dealt with tax benefits. In 1983, in *Mueller v. Allen,* the Court upheld a Minnesota law that allowed parents of children in private and parochial schools to deduct as much as $700 of school expenses from their incomes subject to state income tax. More recently, in February 2002 the Supreme Court heard arguments in *Zelman v. Simmons-Harris*, a case concerning school vouchers in Cleveland. As this book goes to print, the decision had not yet been announced.

Given the conservatism of the Rehnquist Court, many observers are waiting to see whether the Court will move even further away from *Nyquist*.

TO SUMMARIZE:

- While state and local governments are not constitutionally required to provide tax exemptions for religious institutions, such exemptions have been upheld so long as they extend to all nonprofit charitable entities.
- The Supreme Court has permitted the Internal Revenue Service to revoke tax-exempt status from private schools that engage in racial discrimination in clear violation of fundamental public policy commitments.
- In light of the Court's diverse opinions in the area of government aid to parochial schools, it is an open question whether the Court would approve tuition tax credits to parents of children attending such schools.

CONCLUSION

Although the United States is a decidedly religious nation, much more so than other advanced democracies, it is also committed to **secular government** and religious freedom. These competing values create tensions that can never be fully resolved. Inevitably, constitutional law on the subject of religious liberty remains unsettled, reflecting the evolving views of a maturing society.

The current Supreme Court appears to accord legitimacy to governmental efforts to accommodate traditional religious practices. In this respect, it has followed the initiatives of the Burger Court in such cases as *Widmar v. Vincent* (1981) and *Lynch v. Donnelly* (1984). The Court has been less receptive to unorthodox religious practices, especially if they are perceived to be in conflict with the imperatives of law enforcement (see, for example, *Employment Division v. Smith* [1990]). The ideological impact on the Court resulting from appointments made by Presidents Nixon, Reagan, and Bush (the elder) is apparent in this area. In addition to the influence of partisan judicial appointments, we see the Court responding to a conservative trend in society's attitudes with respect to religion, crime, and deviance. The following chapter examines the changing response of the Supreme Court to constitutional questions dealing specifically with crime and punishment.

KEY TERMS

Religion Clauses of the First Amendment
school prayer
Free Exercise Clause
Establishment Clause
conscientious objector
religious speech
expressive religious conduct
public forum

time, place, and manner regulations
unconventional religious practices
fundamental right
compelling government interest
Religious Freedom Restoration Act (RFRA)
parens patriae

right to refuse medical treatment
separation of church and state
Lemon test
child benefit theory
released-time programs
equal access
school prayer decisions
moment of silence
Scopes trial

creation science
secular humanism
strict neutrality
Sunday closing laws
accommodation
benevolent neutrality
tax exemptions
tuition tax credits
secular government

FOR FURTHER READING

Bellah, Robert, et al. *The Good Society*. New York: Knopf, 1991.

Carter, Lief. *An Introduction to Constitutional Interpretation: Cases in Law and Religion*. New York: Longman, 1991.

Carter, Stephen. *The Culture of Disbelief*. New York: Anchor Books, 1994.

Curry, Thomas J. *The First Freedoms*. New York: Oxford University Press, 1986.

Howe, Mark DeWolfe. *The Garden and the Wilderness: Religion and Government in American Constitutional History*. Chicago: University of Chicago Press, 1985.

Irons, Peter. *The Courage of Their Convictions: Sixteen Americans Who Fought Their Way to the Supreme Court*. New York: Penguin Books, 1990. See, in particular, chapters 1, 7, 9, and 15.

Kauper, Paul. *Religion and the Constitution*. Baton Rouge: Louisiana State University Press, 1964.

Levy, Leonard. *The Establishment Clause: Religion and the First Amendment*. New York: Macmillan, 1986.

Manwaring, David. *Render unto Caesar: The Flag Salute Controversy*. Chicago: University of Chicago Press, 1962.

Miller, William Lee. *The First Liberty: Religion and the American Republic*. New York: Knopf, 1986.

Oaks, Dallin (ed.). *The Wall between Church and State*. Chicago: University of Chicago Press, 1963.

Pfeffer, Leo. *God, Caesar and the Constitution*. Boston: Beacon Press, 1975.

Sorauf, Frank. *The Wall of Separation: The Constitutional Politics of Church and State*. Princeton, N.J.: Princeton University Press, 1976.

Stokes, Anson, and Leo Pfeffer. *Church and State in the United States*. New York: Harper and Row, 1965.

Tussman, Joseph. *The Supreme Court on Church and State*. New York: Oxford University Press, 1962.

INTERNET RESOURCES

Name of Resource	Description	URL
Center for Religious Freedom	Devoted to promotion of religious freedom worldwide	http://www.freedomhouse.org/religion/
Religious Freedom	Site maintained by the Christian Science Committee on Publication	http://www.religious-freedom.org/
Catholic League for Religious and Civil Rights	Site promoting the nation's largest Catholic civil rights organization	http://www.catholicleague.org/
The Christian Coalition	A political organization dedicated to public policies informed by conservative Christian ideas	http://www.cc.org/
Americans United for Separation of Church and State	A site maintained by one of the best known antiestablishmentarian organizations	http://www.au.org/
The Secular Web	A Web site devoted to promoting secular humanism	http://www.secular.org/

Case

WEST VIRGINIA STATE BOARD OF EDUCATION V. BARNETTE

319 U.S. 624; 63 S.Ct. 1178; 87 L.Ed. 1628 (1943)
Vote: 6–3

In Minersville School District v. Gobitis (1940), the Supreme Court, in an 8-to-1 decision, upheld a local school board directive in Minersville, Pennsylvania, requiring public school students and teachers to participate in a flag salute ceremony conducted as a regular part of the daily classroom schedule. This requirement had been challenged by Walter Gobitis, a member of the Jehovah's Witnesses sect, whose children, Lillian and William (ages 12 and 10), were expelled from school for refusing to salute the flag. In upholding the flag salute requirement, the Court rejected Gobitis's contention that it violated First Amendment principles of religious liberty as applied to the states through the Due Process Clause of the Fourteenth Amendment.

Three years later, in a dramatic and highly publicized reversal of its position, the Supreme Court, by a 6-to-3 margin, overruled the Gobitis case by striking down a virtually identical flag salute requirement imposed by the West Virginia Board of Education. The board was acting under authority of a statute passed by the West Virginia legislature in the immediate aftermath of the Gobitis decision. This law required all schools in the state to offer classes in civics, history, and the federal and state constitutions "for the purpose of teaching, fostering, and perpetuating the ideals, principles, and spirit of Americanism, and increasing the knowledge of the organization and machinery of the Government."

Walter Barnette and two other Jehovah's Witnesses, all of whom had children in the public schools, filed suit to enjoin the compulsory flag salute on grounds that it violated a constitutionally protected religious precept contained in the Old Testament (Exodus. 20:4–5) forbidding the worship of "any graven image." Under their reading of the Scriptures, the flag salute constituted such forbidden worship.

Because this decision represents such a swift and decisive overruling of constitutional precedent, it is interesting to compare the alignments of the justices in Gobitis and Barnette. Justice Frankfurter wrote the majority opinion in the Gobitis case, with only Justice Stone dissenting. Justice Jackson, who along with Justice Rutledge joined the Court after that decision was announced, wrote the majority opinion in Barnette. Justices Black, Douglas, and Murphy, all of whom had supported Frankfurter's original majority position, switched sides and supported the majority opinion in Barnette. Justices Frankfurter, Reed, and Roberts dissented in the latter case.

Mr. Justice Jackson delivered the opinion of the Court.

. . . National unity as an end which officials may foster by persuasion and example is not in question. The problem is whether under our Constitution compulsion as here employed is a permissible means for its achievement.

Struggles to coerce uniformity of sentiment in support of some end thought essential to their time and country have been waged by many good as well as by evil men. Nationalism is a relatively recent phenomenon but at other times and places the ends have been racial or territorial security, support of a dynasty or regime, and particular plans for saving souls. As first and moderate methods to attain unity have failed, those bent on its accomplishment must resort to an ever increasing severity. As governmental pressure toward unity becomes greater, so strife becomes more bitter as to whose unity it shall be. Probably no deeper division of our people could proceed from any provocation than from finding it necessary to choose what doctrine and whose program public educational officials shall compel youth to unite in embracing. Ultimate futility of such attempts to compel coherence is the lesson of every such effort from the Roman drive to stamp out Christianity as a disturber of its pagan unity, the Inquisition, as a means to religious and dynastic unity, the Siberian exiles as a means to Russian unity, down to the fast failing efforts of our present totalitarian enemies. Those who begin coercive elimination of dissent soon find themselves exterminating dissenters. Compulsory unification of opinion achieves only the unanimity of the graveyard.

It seems trite but necessary to say that the First Amendment to our Constitution was designed to avoid these ends by avoiding these beginnings. There is no mysticism in the American concept of the State or of the nature or origin of its authority. We set up government by consent of the governed, and the Bill of Rights denies those in power any legal opportunity to coerce that consent. Authority here is to be controlled by public opinion, not public opinion by authority.

The case is made difficult not because the principles of its decision are obscure but because the flag involved is our own. Nevertheless, we apply the limitations of the Constitution with no fear that freedom to be intellectually and spiritually diverse or even contrary will disintegrate the social organization. To believe that patriotism will not flourish if patriotic ceremonies are voluntary and spontaneous instead of a compulsory routine is to make an unflattering estimate of the appeal of our institutions to free minds. We can have intellectual individualism and the rich cultural diversities that we owe to exceptional minds only at the price of occasional eccentricity and abnormal attitudes. When they are so harmless to others or to the State as those we deal with here, the price is not too great. But freedom to differ is not limited to things that do not matter much. That would be a mere shadow of freedom. The test of its substance is the right to differ as to things that touch the heart of the existing order.

If there is any fixed star in our constitutional constellation, it is that no official, high or petty, can prescribe what shall be orthodox in politics, nationalism, religion, or other matters of opinion or force citizens to confess by word or act their faith therein. If there are any circumstances which permit an exception, they do not now occur to us.

We think the action of the local authorities in compelling the flag salute and pledge transcends constitutional limitations on their power and invades the sphere of intellect and spirit which it is the purpose of the First Amendment to our Constitution to reserve from all official control.

The decision of this Court in *Minersville School Dist. v. Gobitis* and the holdings of those few *per curiam* decisions which preceded and foreshadowed it are overruled, and the judgment enjoining enforcement of the West Virginia Regulation is affirmed.

Mr. Justice Roberts and ***Mr. Justice Reed*** adhere to the views expressed by the Court in *Minersville School Dist. v. Gobitis,* . . . and are of the opinion that the judgment below should be reversed.

Mr. Justice Black and ***Mr. Justice Douglas,*** concurring.

We are substantially in agreement with the opinion just read, but since we originally joined with the Court in the *Gobitis* case, it is appropriate that we make a brief statement of reasons for our change of view.

Reluctance to make the Federal Constitution a rigid bar against state regulation of conduct thought inimical to the public welfare was the controlling influence which moved us to consent to the *Gobitis* decision. Long reflection convinced us that although the principle is sound, its application in the particular case was wrong. . . . We believe that the statute before us fails to accord full scope to the freedom of religion secured to the appellees by the First and Fourteenth Amendments. . . .

No well ordered society can leave to the individuals an absolute right to make final decisions, unassailable by the State, as to everything they will or will not do. The First Amendment does not go so far. Religious faiths, honestly held, do not free individuals from responsibility to conduct themselves obediently to laws which are either

imperatively necessary to protect society as a whole from grave and pressingly imminent dangers or which, without any general prohibition, merely regulate time, place or manner of religious activity. Decisions as to the constitutionality of particular laws which strike at the substance of religious tenets and practices must be made by this Court. The duty is a solemn one, and in meeting it we cannot say that a failure, because of religious scruples, to assume a particular physical position and to repeat the words of a patriotic formula creates a grave danger to the nation. Such a statutory exaction is a form of test oath, and the test oath has always been abhorrent in the United States.

Words uttered under coercion are proof of loyalty to nothing but self-interest. Love of country must spring from willing hearts and free minds, inspired by a fair administration of wise laws enacted by the people's elected representatives within the bounds of express constitutional prohibitions. These laws must, to be consistent with the First Amendment, permit the widest toleration of conflicting viewpoints consistent with a society of free men.

Neither our domestic tranquility in peace nor our martial effort in war depend on compelling little children to participate in a ceremony which ends in nothing for them but a fear of spiritual condemnation. If, as we think, their fears are groundless, time and reason are the proper antidotes for their errors. The ceremonial, when enforced against conscientious objectors, more likely to defeat than to serve its high purpose, is a handy implement for disguised religious persecution. As such, it is inconsistent with our Constitution's plan and purpose.

Mr. Justice Murphy, concurring:

. . . Without wishing to disparage the purposes and intentions of those who hope to inculcate sentiments of loyalty and patriotism by requiring a declaration of allegiance as a feature of public education, or unduly belittle the benefits that may accrue therefrom, I am impelled to conclude that such a requirement is not essential to the maintenance of effective government and orderly society. To many it is deeply distasteful to join in a public chorus of affirmation of private belief. By some, including the members of this sect, it is apparently regarded as incompatible with a primary religious obligation and therefore a restriction on religious freedom. Official compulsion to affirm what is contrary to one's religious beliefs is the antithesis of freedom of worship which, it is well to recall, was achieved in this country only after what Jefferson characterized as the "severest contests in which I have ever been engaged." . . .

Mr. Justice Frankfurter, dissenting.

One who belongs to the most vilified and persecuted minority in history is not likely to be insensible to the freedoms guaranteed by our Constitution. Were my purely personal attitude relevant I should wholeheartedly associate myself with the general libertarian views in the Court's opinion, representing as they do the thought and action of a lifetime. But as judges we are neither Jew nor Gentile, neither Catholic nor agnostic. We owe equal attachment to the Constitution and are equally bound by our judicial obligations whether we derive our citizenship from the earliest or the latest immigrants to these shores. As a member of this Court I am not justified in writing my private notions of policy into the Constitution, no matter how deeply I may cherish them or how mischievous I may deem their disregard. The duty of a judge who must decide which of two claims before the Court shall prevail, that of a State to enact and enforce laws within its general competence or that of an individual to refuse obedience because of the demands of his conscience, is not that of the ordinary person. It can never be emphasized too much that one's own opinion about the wisdom or evil of a law should be excluded altogether when one is doing one's duty on the bench. The only opinion of our own even looking in that direction that is material is our opinion whether legislators could in reason have enacted such a law. In the light of all the circumstances, including the history of this question in this Court, it would require more daring than I possess to deny that reasonable legislators could have taken the action which is before us for review. Most unwillingly, therefore, I must differ from my brethren with regard to legislation like this. I cannot bring my mind to believe that the "liberty" secured by the Due Process Clause gives this Court authority to deny to the State of West Virginia the attainment of that which we all recognize as a legitimate legislative end, namely, the promotion of good citizenship, by employment of the means here chosen. . . .

Of course patriotism cannot be enforced by the flag salute. But neither can the liberal spirit be enforced by judicial invalidation of illiberal legislation. Of constant preoccupation with the constitutionality of legislation rather than with its wisdom tends to preoccupation of the American mind with a false value. The tendency of focusing attention on constitutionality is to make constitutionality synonymous with wisdom, to regard a law as all right if it is constitutional. Such an attitude is a great enemy of liberalism. Particularly in legislation affecting freedom of thought and freedom of speech much which should offend a free-spirited society is constitutional. Reliance for the most precious interests of civilization, therefore, must be found outside of their vindication in courts of law. Only a persistent positive translation of the faith of a free society into the convictions and habits and actions of a community is the ultimate reliance against unabated temptations to fetter the human spirit.

Case

WISCONSIN V. YODER

406 U.S. 205; 92 S.Ct. 1526; 32 L.Ed. 2d 15 (1972)
Vote: 6–1

Here the Court considers whether members of the Old Order Amish have a constitutional right to refuse to comply with a state's compulsory high school attendance law.

Mr. Chief Justice Burger delivered the opinion of the Court.

. . . Respondents Jonas Yoder and Wallace Miller are members of the Old Order Amish religion, and respondent Adin Yutzy is a member of the Conservative Amish Mennonite Church. They and their families are residents of Green County, Wisconsin. Wisconsin's compulsory school-attendance law required them to cause their children to attend public or private school until . . . age 16 but the respondents declined to send their children, ages 14 and 15, to public school after they completed the eighth grade. The children were not enrolled in any private school, or within any recognized exception to the compulsory-attendance law, and they are conceded to be subject to the Wisconsin statute.

On complaint of the school district administrator for the public schools, respondents were charged, tried, and convicted of violating the compulsory-attendance law in Green County Court and were fined the sum of $5 each. Respondents defended on the ground that the application of the compulsory-attendance law violated their rights under the First and Fourteenth Amendments. The trial testimony showed that respondents believed, in accordance with the tenets of Old Order Amish communities generally, that their children's attendance at high school, public or private, was contrary to the Amish religion and way of life. They believed that by sending their children to high school, they would not only expose themselves to the danger of the censure of the church community, but, as found by the county court, also endanger their own salvation and that of their children. The State stipulated that respondents' religious beliefs were sincere.

In support of their position, respondents presented as expert witnesses scholars on religion and education whose testimony is uncontradicted. They expressed their opinions on the relationship of the Amish belief concerning school attendance to the more general tenets of their religion, and described the impact that compulsory high school attendance could have on the continued survival of Amish communities as they exist in the United States today. The history of the Amish sect was given in some detail, beginning with the Swiss Anabaptists of the 16th century who rejected institutionalized churches and sought to return to the early, simple, Christian life de-emphasizing material success, rejecting the competitive spirit, and seeking to insulate themselves from the modern world. As a result of their common heritage, Old Order Amish communities today are characterized by a fundamental belief that salvation requires life in a church community separate and apart from the world and worldly influence. This concept of life aloof from the world and its values is central to their faith. . . .

Amish objection to formal education beyond the eighth grade is firmly grounded in these central religious concepts. They object to the high school, and higher education generally, because the values they teach are in marked variance with Amish values and the Amish way of life; they view secondary school education as an impermissible exposure of their children to a "worldly" influence in conflict with their beliefs. The high school tends to emphasize intellectual and scientific accomplishments, self-distinction, competitiveness, worldly success, and social life with other students. Amish society emphasizes informal learning-through-doing; a life of "goodness," rather than a life of intellect; wisdom, rather than technical knowledge, community welfare, rather than competition; and separation from, rather than integration with, contemporary worldly society. . . .

The Amish do not object to elementary education through the first eight grades as a general proposition because they agree that their children must have basic skills in the "three R's" in order to read the Bible, to be good farmers and citizens, and to be able to deal with non-Amish people when necessary in the course of daily affairs. They view such a basic education as acceptable because it does not significantly expose their children to worldly values or interfere with their development in the Amish community during the crucial adolescent period. While Amish accept compulsory elementary education generally, wherever possible they have established their own elementary schools in many respects like the small local schools of the past. In the Amish belief higher learning tends to develop values they reject as influences that alienate man from God. . . .

Although the trial court in its careful findings determined that the Wisconsin compulsory school-attendance law "does interfere with the freedom of the Defendants to act in accordance with their sincere religious belief" it also concluded that the requirement of high school attendance until age 16 was a "reasonable and constitutional" exercise of governmental power, and therefore denied the motion to dismiss the charges. The Wisconsin Circuit Court affirmed the convictions. The Wisconsin Supreme Court, however, sustained respondents' claim under the Free Exercise Clause of the First Amendment and reversed the convictions. A majority of the court was of the opinion that the State had failed to make an adequate showing that its interest in "establishing and maintaining an educational system overrides the defendants' right to the free exercise of their religion." . . .

There is no doubt as to the power of a State, having a high responsibility for education of its citizens, to impose reasonable regulations for the control and duration of basic education. See, e.g., *Pierce v. Society of Sisters* . . . (1925). Providing public schools ranks at the very apex of the function of a State. Yet even this paramount responsibility was, in *Pierce*, made to yield to the right of parents to provide an equivalent education in a privately operated system. There the Court held that Oregon's statute compelling attendance in a public school from age eight to age 16 unreasonably interfered with the interest of parents in directing the rearing of their offspring, including their education in church-operated schools. As that case suggests, the values of parental direction of the religious upbringing and education of their children in their early and formative years have a high place in our society. . . . Thus, a State's interest in universal education, however highly we rank it, is not totally free from a balancing process when it impinges on fundamental rights and interests, such as those specifically protected by the Free Exercise Clause of the First Amendment, and the traditional interest of parents with respect to the religious upbringing of their children so long as they, in the words of *Pierce*, "prepare [them] for additional obligations." . . .

It follows that in order for Wisconsin to compel school attendance beyond the eighth grade against a claim that such attendance interferes with the practice of a legitimate religious belief, it must appear either that the State does not deny the free exercise of religious belief by its requirement, or that there is a state interest of sufficient magnitude to override the interest claiming protection under the Free Exercise Clause. . . .

. . . A way of life, however virtuous and admirable, may not be interposed as a barrier to reasonable state regulation of education if it is based on purely secular considerations; to have the protection of the Religion Clauses, the claims must be rooted in religious belief. Although a determination of what is a "religious" belief or practice entitled to constitutional protection may present a most delicate question, the very concept of ordered liberty precludes allowing every person to make his own standards on matters of conduct in which society as a whole has important interests. . . .

. . . [T]he record in this case abundantly supports the claim that the traditional way of life of the Amish is not merely a matter of personal preference, but one of deep religious conviction, shared by an organized group, and intimately related to daily living. . . .

The impact of the compulsory-attendance law on respondents' practice of the Amish religion is not only severe, but inescapable, for the Wisconsin law affirmatively compels them, under threat of criminal sanction, to perform acts undeniably at odds with fundamental tenets of their religious beliefs. . . . Nor is the impact of the compulsory-attendance law confined to grave interference with important Amish religious tenets from a subjective point of view. It carries with it precisely the kind of objective danger to the free exercise of religion that the First Amendment was designed to prevent. As the record shows, compulsory school attendance to age 16 for Amish children carries with it a very real threat of undermining the Amish community and religious practice as they exist today; they must either abandon belief and be assimilated into society at large, or be forced to migrate to some other and more tolerant region.

In sum, the unchallenged testimony of acknowledged experts in education and religious history, almost 300 years of consistent practice, and strong evidence of a sustained faith pervading and regulating respondents' entire mode of life support the claim that enforcement of the State's requirement of compulsory formal education after the eighth grade would gravely endanger if not destroy the free exercise of respondents' religious beliefs. . . .

Wisconsin concedes that under the Religion Clauses religious beliefs are absolutely free from the State's control, but it argues that "actions," even though religiously grounded, are outside the protection of the First Amendment. But our decisions have rejected the idea that religiously grounded conduct is always outside the protection of the Free Exercise Clause. It is true that activities of individuals, even when religiously based, are often subject to regulation by the States in the exercise of their undoubted power to promote the health, safety, and general welfare, or the Federal government in the exercise of its delegated powers. . . . But to agree that religiously grounded conduct must often be subject to the broad police power of the State is not to deny that there are areas of conduct protected by the Free Exercise Clause of the First Amendment and thus beyond the power of the State to control, even under regulations of general applicability. . . . This case, therefore, does not become easier because respondents were convicted for their "actions" in refusing to send their children to the public high school; in this context belief and action cannot be neatly confined in logic-tight compartments. . . .

Nor can this case be disposed of on the grounds that Wisconsin's requirement for school attendance to age 16 applies uniformly to all citizens of the State and does not, on its face, discriminate against religions or a particular religion, or that it is motivated by legitimate secular concerns. A regulation neutral on its face may, in its application, nonetheless offend the constitutional requirement for governmental neutrality if it unduly burdens the free exercise of religion. . . . The Court must not ignore the danger that an exception from a general obligation of citizenship on religious grounds may run afoul of the Establishment Clause, but that danger cannot be allowed to prevent any exception no matter how vital it may be to the protection of values promoted by the right of free exercise. . . .

The State advances two primary arguments in support of its system of compulsory education. It notes, as Thomas Jefferson pointed out early in our history, that some degree of education is necessary to prepare citizens to participate effectively and intelligently in our open political system if we are to preserve freedom and independence. Further, education prepares individuals to be self-reliant and self-sufficient participants in society. We accept these propositions.

However, the evidence adduced by the Amish in this case is persuasively to the effect that an additional one or two years of formal high school for Amish children in place of their long-established program of informal vocational education would do little to serve those interests. Respondents' experts testified at trial, without challenge, that the value of all education must be assessed in terms of its capacity to prepare the child for life. It is one thing to say that compulsory education for a year or two beyond the eighth grade may be necessary when its goal is the preparation of the child for life in modern society as the majority live, but is quite another if the goal of education be viewed as the preparation of the child for life in the separated agrarian community that is the keystone of the Amish faith. . . .

The State attacks respondents' position as one fostering "ignorance" from which the child must be protected by the State. No one can question the State's duty to protect children from ignorance but this argument does not square with the facts disclosed in the record. Whatever their idiosyncrasies as seen by the majority, this record strongly shows that the Amish community has been a highly successful social unit within our society, even if apart from the conventional "mainstream." Its members are productive and very law-abiding members of society; they reject public welfare in any of its usually modern forms. The Congress itself recognized their self-sufficiency by authorizing exemption of such groups as the Amish from the obligation to pay social security taxes.

It is neither fair nor correct to suggest that the Amish are opposed to education beyond the eighth grade level. What this record shows is that they are opposed to conventional formal education of the type provided by a certified high school because it comes at the child's crucial adolescent period of religious development. . . .

. . . There can be no assumption that today's majority is "right" and the Amish and others like them are "wrong." A way of life that is odd or even erratic but interferes with no rights or interests of others is not to be condemned because it is different.

The State, however, supports its interest in providing an additional one or two years of compulsory high school education to Amish children because of the possibility that some such children will choose to leave the Amish community, and that if this occurs they will be ill-equipped for life. The State argues that if Amish children leave their church they should not be in the position of making their way in the world without the education available in the one or two additional years the State requires. However, on this record, that argument is highly speculative. There is no specific evidence of the loss of Amish adherents by attrition, nor is there any showing that upon leaving the Amish community Amish children, with their practical agricultural training and habits of industry and self-reliance, would become burdens on society because of educational shortcomings. . . .

Insofar as the State's claim rests on the view that a brief additional period of formal education is imperative to enable the Amish to participate effectively and intelligently in our democratic process, it must fall. The Amish alternative to formal secondary school education has enabled them to function effectively in their day-to-day life under self-imposed limitations on relations with the world, and to survive and prosper in contemporary society as a separate, sharply identifiable and highly self-sufficient community for more than 200 years in this country. In itself this is strong evidence that they are capable of fulfilling the social and political responsibilities of citizenship without compelled attendance beyond the eighth grade at the price of jeopardizing their free exercise of religious belief. . . .

Finally, the State . . . argues that a decision exempting Amish children from the State's requirement fails to recognize the substantive right of the Amish child to a secondary education, and fails to give due regard to the power of the State as *parens patriae* to extend the benefit of secondary education to children regardless of the wishes of their parents. . . .

The State's argument proceeds without reliance on any actual conflict between the wishes of parents and children. It appears to rest on the potential that exemption of Amish parents from the requirements of the compulsory-education law might allow some parents to act contrary to the best interests of their children by foreclosing their opportunity to make an intelligent choice between the Amish way of life and that of the outside world. The same argument could, of course, be made with respect to all church schools short of college. There is nothing in the record or in the ordinary course of human experience to suggest that non-Amish parents generally consult with children of ages 14–16 if they are placed in a church school of the parents' faith.

Indeed it seems clear that if the State is empowered, as *parens patriae,* to "save" a child from himself or his Amish parents by requiring an additional two years of compulsory formal high school education, the State will in large measure influence, if not determine, the religious future of the child. [T]his case involves the fundamental interest of parents, as contrasted with that of the State, to guide the religious future and education of their children. . . .

For the reasons stated we hold, with the Supreme Court of Wisconsin, that the First and Fourteenth Amendments prevent the State from compelling respondents to cause their children to attend formal high school to age 16. . . .

Nothing we hold is intended to undermine the general applicability of the State's compulsory school-attendance statutes or to limit the power of the State to promulgate reasonable standards that, while not impairing the free exercise of religion, provide for continuing agricultural vocational education under parental and church guidance by the Old Order Amish or others similarly situated. The States have had a long history of amicable and effective relationships with church-sponsored schools, and there is no basis for assuming that, in this related context, reasonable standards cannot be established concerning the content of the continuing vocational education of Amish children under parental guidance, provided always that state regulations are not inconsistent with what we have said in this opinion.

Affirmed.

Mr. Justice Powell and *Mr. Justice Rehnquist* took no part in the consideration or decision of this case.

Mr. Justice Stewart, with whom *Mr. Justice Brennan* joins, concurring. . . .

Mr. Justice Douglas, dissenting in part.

I agree with the Court that the religious scruples of the Amish are opposed to the education of their children beyond the grade schools, yet I disagree with the Court's conclusion that the matter is within the dispensation of parents alone. The Court's analysis assumes that the only interests at stake in the case are those of the Amish parents on the one hand, and those of the State on the other. The difficulty with this approach is that, despite the Court's claim, the parents are seeking to vindicate not only their own free exercise claims, but also those of their high-school-age children. . . .

. . . Our opinions are full of talk about the power of the parents over the child's education. . . . And we have in the past analyzed similar conflicts between parent and State with little regard for the views of the child. . . . Recent cases, however, have clearly held that the children themselves have constitutionally protectible interests. . . .

On this important and vital matter of education, I think the children should be entitled to be heard. While the parents, absent dissent, normally speak for the entire family, the education of the child is a matter on which the child will often have decided views. He may want to be a pianist or an astronaut or an oceanographer. To do so he will have to break from the Amish tradition.

It is the future of the student, not the future of the parents, that is imperiled by today's decision. If a parent keeps his child out of school beyond the grade school, then the child will be forever barred from entry into the new and amazing world of diversity that we have today. The child may decide that that is the preferred course, or he may rebel. It is the student's judgment, not his parents', that is essential if we are to give full meaning to what we have said about the Bill of Rights and of the right of students to be masters of their own destiny. If he is harnessed to the Amish way of life by those in authority over him and if his education is truncated, his entire life may be stunted and deformed. The child, therefore, should be given an opportunity to be heard before the State gives the exemption which we honor today.

The views of the two children in question were not canvassed by the Wisconsin courts. The matter should be explicitly reserved so that new hearings can be held on remand of the case. . . .

Case

EMPLOYMENT DIVISION V. SMITH

494 U.S. 872; 110 S.Ct. 1595; 108 L.Ed. 2d 876 (1990)

Vote: 6–3

Alfred Smith and Galen Black, both members of the Native American Church, were fired from their jobs as drug rehabilitation counselors on the grounds that they had used peyote during a religious ritual. They were subsequently denied unemployment benefits because they had been discharged for "misconduct." The question before the U.S. Supreme Court is whether the refusal of the state to grant unemployment benefits in this situation constitutes an abridgement of rights under the Free Exercise Clause of the First Amendment.

Justice Scalia delivered the opinion of the Court.

. . . Respondents' claim for relief rests on our decisions in *Sherbert v. Verner* . . . [1963]; *Thomas v. Review Board* . . . [1981]; and *Hobbie v. Unemployment Appeals Comm'n of Florida* . . . [1987], in which we held that a State could not condition the availability of unemployment insurance on an individual's willingness to forego conduct required by his religion. . . . [H]owever, the conduct at issue in those cases was not prohibited by law. . . . [T]hat distinction [is] critical, for "if Oregon does prohibit the religious use of peyote, and if that prohibition is consistent with the Federal Constitution, there is no federal right to engage in that conduct in Oregon," and "the State is free to withhold unemployment compensation from respondents for engaging in work-related misconduct, despite its religious motivation." . . . Now that the Oregon Supreme Court has confirmed that Oregon does prohibit the religious use of peyote, we proceed to consider whether that prohibition is permissible under the Free Exercise Clause. . . .

The free exercise of religion means, first and foremost, the right to believe and profess whatever religious doctrine one desires. Thus, the First Amendment obviously excludes all "governmental regulation of religious beliefs as such." . . .

But the "exercise of religion" often involves not only belief and profession but the performance of (or abstention from) physical acts: assembling with others for a worship service, participating in sacramental use of bread and wine, proselytizing, abstaining from certain foods or certain modes of transportation. It would be true, we think (though no case of ours has involved the point), that a state would be "prohibiting the free exercise [of religion]" . . . if it sought to ban such acts or abstentions only when they are engaged in for religious reasons, or only because of the religious belief that they display. It would doubtless be unconstitutional, for example, to ban the casting of "statues that are to be used for worship purposes," . . . or to prohibit bowing down before a golden calf.

Respondents in the present case, however, seek to carry the meaning of "prohibiting the free exercise [of religion]" one large step further. They contend that their religious motivation for using peyote places them beyond the reach of a criminal law that is not specifically directed at their religious practice, and that is concededly constitutional as applied to those who use the drug for other reasons. They assert, in other words, that "prohibiting the free exercise [of religion]" includes requiring any individual to observe a generally applicable law that requires (or forbids) the performance of an act that his religious belief forbids (or requires). As a textual matter, we do not think the words must be given that meaning. It is no more necessary to regard the collection of a general tax, for example, as "prohibiting the free exercise [of religion]" by those citizens who believe support of organized government to be sinful, than it is to regard the same tax as "abridging the freedom . . . of the press" of those publishing companies that must pay the tax as a condition of staying in business. It is a permissible reading of the text, in the one case as in the other, to say that if prohibiting the exercise of religion (or burdening the activity of printing) is not the object of the tax but merely the incidental effect of a generally applicable and otherwise valid provision, the First Amendment has not been offended. . . .

Our decisions reveal that the latter reading is the correct one. We have never held that an individual's religious beliefs excuse him from compliance with an otherwise valid law prohibiting conduct that the State is free to regulate. . . .

The only decisions in which we have held that the First Amendment bars application of a neutral, generally applicable law to religiously motivated action have involved not the Free Exercise Clause alone, but the Free Exercise Clause in conjunction with other constitutional protections, such as freedom of speech and of the press. . . .

The present case does not present such a hybrid situation, but a free exercise claim unconnected with any communicative activity or parental right. Respondents urge us to hold, quite simply, that when otherwise prohibitable conduct is accompanied by religious convictions, not only the convictions but the conduct itself must be free from governmental regulation. . . .

Respondents argue that even though exemption from generally applicable criminal laws need not automatically be extended to religiously motivated actors, at least the claim for a religious exemption must be evaluated under the balancing test set forth in *Sherbert v. Verner* [1963]. . . . Under the *Sherbert* test, governmental actions that substantially burden a religious practice must be justified by a compelling governmental interest. . . . Applying that test we have, on three occasions, invalidated state unemployment compensation rules that conditioned the availability of benefits upon an applicant's willingness to work under conditions forbidden by his religion. . . . We have never invalidated any governmental action on the basis of the *Sherbert* test except the denial of unemployment compensation. . . .

Even if we were inclined to breathe into *Sherbert* some life beyond the unemployment compensation field, we would not apply it to require exemptions from a generally applicable criminal law. . . .

We conclude today that the sounder approach, and the approach in accord with the vast majority of our precedents, is to hold the test inapplicable to such challenges. The government's ability to enforce generally applicable prohibitions of socially harmful conduct, like its ability to carry out other aspects of public policy, "cannot depend on measuring the effects of a governmental action on a religious objector's spiritual development." . . . To make an individual's obligation to obey such a law contingent upon the law's coincidence with his religious beliefs, except where the State's interest is "compelling"—permitting him, by virtue of his beliefs, "to become a law unto himself," . . . —contradicts both constitutional tradition and common sense.

The "compelling government interest" requirement seems benign, because it is familiar from other fields. But using it as the standard that must be met before the government may accord different treatment on the basis of race, . . . is not remotely comparable to using it for the purpose asserted here. What it produces in those other fields—equality of treatment, and an unrestricted flow of contending speech—are constitutional norms; what it would produce here—a private right to ignore generally applicable laws—is a constitutional anomaly.

Nor is it possible to limit the impact of respondents' proposal by requiring a "compelling state interest" only when the conduct prohibited is "central" to the individual's religion. It is no more appropriate for judges to determine the "centrality" of religious beliefs before applying a "compelling interest" test in the free exercise field, than it would be for them to determine the "importance" of ideas before applying the "compelling interest" test in the free speech field. What principle of law or logic can be brought to bear to contradict a believer's assertion that a particular act is "central" to his personal faith? . . .

If the "compelling interest" test is to be applied at all, then, it must be applied across the board, to all actions thought to be religiously commanded. Moreover, if "compelling interest" really means what it says (and watering it down here would subvert its rigor in the other fields where it is applied), many laws will not meet the test. Any society adopting such a system would be courting anarchy, but that danger increases in direct proportion to the society's diversity of religious beliefs, and its determination to coerce or suppress none of them. . . .

Values that are protected against government interference through enshrinement in the Bill of Rights are not thereby banished from the political process. Just as a society that believes in the negative protection accorded to the press by the First Amendment is likely to enact laws that affirmatively foster the dissemination of the printed word, so also a society that believes in the negative protection accorded to religious belief can be expected to be solicitous of that value in its legislation as well. It is therefore not surprising that a number of States have made an exception to their drug laws for sacramental peyote use. But to say that a nondiscriminatory religious-practice exemption is permitted, or even that it is desirable, is not to say that it is constitutionally required, and that the appropriate occasions for its creation can be discerned by the courts. It may fairly be said that leaving accommodation to the political process will place at a relative disadvantage those religious practices that are not widely engaged in; but that unavoidable consequence of democratic government must be preferred to a system in which each conscience is a law unto itself or in which judges weigh the social importance of all law against the centrality of all religious beliefs. . . .

Because respondent's ingestion of peyote was prohibited under Oregon law, and because that prohibition is constitutional, Oregon may, consistent with the Free Exercise Clause, deny respondents unemployment compensation when their dismissal results from use of the drug. The decision of the Oregon Supreme Court is accordingly reversed. . . .

Justice O'Connor . . . [concurring in the judgment only].

Although I agree with the result the Court reaches in this case, I cannot join its opinion. In my view, today's holding dramatically departs from well-settled First Amendment jurisprudence, appears unnecessary to resolve the question presented, and is incompatible with our Nation's fundamental commitment to individual religious liberty. . . .

[T]he critical question in this case is whether exempting respondents from the State's general criminal prohibition "will unduly interfere with fulfillment of the governmental interest." . . . Although the question is close, I would conclude that uniform application of Oregon's

criminal prohibition is "essential to accomplish" its overriding interest in preventing the physical harm caused by the use of a Schedule I controlled substance. Oregon's criminal prohibition represents that State's judgment that the possession and use of controlled substances, even by only one person, is inherently harmful and dangerous. Because the health effects caused by the use of controlled substances exist regardless of the motivation of the user, the use of such substances, even for religious purposes, violates the very purpose of the law that prohibits them. . . .

For these reasons, I believe that granting a selective exemption in this case would seriously impair Oregon's compelling interest in prohibiting possession of peyote by its citizens. Under such circumstances, the Free Exercise Clause does not require the State to accommodate respondents' religiously motivated conduct. . . .

I would therefore adhere to our established free exercise jurisprudence and hold that the State in this case has a compelling interest in regulating peyote use by its citizens and that accommodating respondents' religiously motivated conduct "will unduly interfere with fulfillment of the governmental interest." . . . Accordingly, I concur in the judgment of the Court.

Justice Blackmun, with whom *Justice Brennan* and *Justice Marshall* join, dissenting.

This Court over the years painstakingly has developed a consistent and exacting standard to test the constitutionality of a state statute that burdens the free exercise of religion. Such a statute may stand only if the law in general, and the State's refusal to allow a religious exemption in particular, are justified by a compelling interest that cannot be served by less restrictive means.

Until today, I thought this was a settled and inviolate principle of this Court's First Amendment jurisprudence. The majority, however, perfunctorily dismisses it as a "constitutional anomaly." As carefully detailed in Justice O'Connor's concurring opinion . . . the majority is able to arrive at this view only by mischaracterizing this Court's precedents. The Court discards leading free exercise cases such as *Cantwell v. Connecticut* . . . (1940), and *Wisconsin v. Yoder* (1972), as "hybrid." . . . The Court views traditional free exercise analysis as somehow inapplicable to criminal prohibitions (as opposed to conditions on the receipt of benefits), and to state laws of general applicability (as opposed, presumably, to laws that expressly single out religious practices). The Court cites cases in which, due to various exceptional circumstances, we found strict scrutiny inapposite, to hint that the Court is aware of the consequences, and that its result is not a product of overreaction to the serious problems the country's drug crisis has generated.

This distorted view of our precedents leads the majority to conclude that strict scrutiny of a state law burdening the free exercise of religion is a "luxury" that a well-ordered society cannot afford, and that the repression of minority religions is an "unavoidable consequence of democratic government." . . . I do not believe the Founders thought their dearly bought freedom from religious persecution a "luxury," but an essential element of liberty—and they could not have thought religious intolerance "unavoidable," for they drafted the Religion Clauses precisely in order to avoid that intolerance.

For these reasons, I agree with Justice O'Connor's analysis of the applicable free exercise doctrine. . . . As she points out, "the critical question in this case is whether exempting respondents from the State's general criminal prohibition: 'will unduly interfere with fulfillment of the governmental interest.'" . . . I do disagree, however, with her specific answer to that question.

The State's interest in enforcing its prohibition, in order to be sufficiently compelling to outweigh a free exercise claim, cannot be merely abstract or symbolic. The State cannot plausibly assert that unbending application of a criminal prohibition is essential to fulfill any compelling interest, if it does not, in fact, attempt to enforce that prohibition. In this case, the State actually has not evinced any concrete interest in enforcing its drug laws against religious users of peyote. Oregon has never sought to prosecute respondents, and does not claim that it has made significant enforcement efforts against other religious users of peyote. The State's asserted interest thus amounts only to the symbolic preservation of an unenforced prohibition. . . .

The State proclaims an interest in protecting the health and safety of its citizens from the dangers of unlawful drugs. It offers, however, no evidence that the religious use of peyote has ever harmed anyone. . . .

The fact that peyote is classified as a Schedule I controlled substance does not, by itself, show that any and all uses of peyote, in any circumstance, are inherently harmful and dangerous. The Federal Government, which created the classifications of unlawful drugs from which Oregon's drug laws are derived, apparently does not find peyote so dangerous as to preclude an exemption for religious use. . . .

The carefully circumscribed ritual context in which respondents used peyote is far removed from the irresponsible and unrestricted recreational use of unlawful drugs. The Native American Church's internal restrictions on, and supervision of, its members' use of peyote substantially obviate the State's health and safety concerns. . . .

Moreover, just as in *Yoder,* the values and interests of those seeking a religious exemption in this case are congruent, to a great degree, with those the State seeks to promote through its drug laws. . . . Not only does the Church's doctrine forbid nonreligious use of peyote; it also generally advocates self-reliance, familial responsibility, and abstinence from alcohol. . . . Far from promoting the lawless and irresponsible use of drugs, Native American Church members' spiritual code exemplifies values that Oregon's drug laws are presumably intended to foster. . . .

Finally, although I agree with Justice O'Connor that courts should refrain from delving into questions of whether, as a matter of religious doctrine, a particular practice is "central" to the religion, I do not think this means that the courts must turn a blind eye to the severe impact of a State's restrictions on the adherents of a minority religion. . . .

If Oregon can constitutionally prosecute them for this act of worship, they, like the Amish, may be "forced to migrate to some other and more tolerant region." *Yoder.* This potentially devastating impact must be viewed in light of the federal policy—reached in reaction to many years of religious persecution and intolerance—of protecting the religious freedom of Native Americans. . . .

The American Indian Religious Freedom Act, in itself, may not create rights enforceable against government action restricting religious freedom, but this Court must scrupulously apply its free exercise analysis to the religious claims of Native Americans, however unorthodox they may be. Otherwise, both the First Amendment and the stated policy of Congress will offer to Native Americans merely an unfulfilled and hollow promise.

For these reasons, I conclude that Oregon's interest in enforcing its drug laws against religious use of peyote is not sufficiently compelling to outweigh respondents' right to the free exercise of their religion. Since the State could not constitutionally enforce its criminal prohibition against respondents, the interests underlying the State's drug laws cannot justify its denial of unemployment benefits. Absent such justification, the State's regulatory interest in denying benefits for religiously motivated "misconduct," is indistinguishable from the state interests this Court has rejected. . . . The State of Oregon cannot, consistently with the Free Exercise Clause, deny respondents unemployment benefits. . . .

Case

CHURCH OF THE LUKUMI BABALU AYE, INC. V. CITY OF HIALEAH

508 U.S. 520;, 113 S.Ct. 2217;, 124 L.Ed. 2d. 472 (1993)
Vote: 9–0

In this case the Court considers a challenge to a set of Hialeah, Florida, ordinances prohibiting animal sacrifice in religious rituals. The ordinances were challenged in federal district court by the Church of the Lukumi Babalu Aye, which practiced animal sacrifice in keeping with the Santeria religion. Unsuccessful in the lower courts, the Cchurch obtained review in the Supreme Court.

Justice Kennedy delivered the opinion of the Court.

. . . This case involves practices of the Santeria religion, which originated in the nineteenth century. When hundreds of thousands of members of the Yoruba people were brought as slaves from eastern Africa to Cuba, their traditional African religion absorbed significant elements of Roman Catholicism. The resulting syncretion, or fusion, is Santeria, "the way of the saints." The Cuban Yoruba express their devotion to spirits, called orishas, through the iconography of Catholic saints. . . .

. . . The basis of the Santeria religion is the nurture of a personal relation with the orishas, and one of the principal forms of devotion is an animal sacrifice. . . .

. . . Sacrifices are performed at birth, marriage, and death rites, for the cure of the sick, for the initiation of new members and priests, and during an annual celebration. Animals sacrificed in Santeria rituals include chickens, pigeons, doves, ducks, guinea pigs, goats, sheep, and turtles. The animals are killed by the cutting of the carotid arteries in the neck. The sacrificed animal is cooked and eaten, except after healing and death rituals. . . .

The prospect of a Santeria church in their midst was distressing to many members of the Hialeah community, and the announcement of the plans to open a Santeria church in Hialeah prompted the city council to hold an emergency public session on June 9. . . .

In September 1987, the city council adopted three substantive ordinances addressing the issue of religious animal sacrifice. Ordinance 87-52 defined "sacrifice" as "to unnecessarily kill, torment, torture, or mutilate an animal in a public or private ritual or ceremony not for the primary purpose of food consumption," and prohibited owning or possessing an animal "intending to use such animal for food purposes." It restricted application of this prohibition, however, to any individual or group that "kills, slaughters or sacrifices animals for any type of ritual, regardless of whether or not the flesh or blood of the animal is to be consumed." The ordinance contained an exemption for slaughtering by "licensed establishment[s]" of animals "specifically raised for food purposes." Declaring, moreover, that the city council "has determined that the sacrificing of animals within the city limits is contrary to the public health, safety, welfare and morals of the community," the city council adopted Ordinance 87-71. That ordinance defined sacrifice as had Ordinance 87-52, and then provided that "[i]t shall be unlawful for any person, persons, corporations or associations to sacrifice any animal within the corporate limits of the City of Hialeah, Florida." The final Ordinance, 87-72, defined "slaughter" as "the killing of animals for food" and prohibited slaughter outside of areas zoned for slaughterhouse use. The ordinance provided an exemption, however, for the slaughter or processing for sale of "small numbers of hogs and/or cattle per week in accordance with an exemption provided in state law." All ordinances and resolutions passed the city council by unanimous vote. Violations of each of the four ordinances were punishable by fines not exceeding $500 or imprisonment not exceeding 60 days, or both. . . .

. . . In addressing the constitutional protection for free exercise of religion, our cases establish the general proposition that a law that is neutral and of general applicability need not be justified by a compelling governmental interest even if the law has the incidental effect of burdening a particular religious practice. . . . Neutrality and general applicability are interrelated, and, as becomes apparent in this case, failure to satisfy one requirement is a likely indication that the other has not been satisfied. A law failing to satisfy these requirements must be justified by a compelling governmental interest and must be narrowly tailored to advance that interest. . . .

At a minimum, the protections of the Free Exercise Clause pertain if the law at issue discriminates against some or all religious beliefs or regulates or prohibits conduct because it is undertaken for religious reasons. . . . Indeed, it was "historical instances of religious persecution and intolerance that gave concern to those who drafted the Free Exercise Clause." . . . These principles, though not often at issue in our Free Exercise Clause cases, have played a role in some. . . .

Although a law targeting religious beliefs as such is never permissible, . . . if the object of a law is to infringe upon or restrict practices because of their religious motivation, the law is not neutral; . . . and it is invalid unless it is justified by a compelling interest and is narrowly tailored to advance that interest. . . .

The record in this case compels the conclusion that suppression of the central element of the Santeria worship service was the object of the ordinances. First, though use of the words "sacrifice" and "ritual" does not compel a finding of improper targeting of the Santeria religion, the choice of these words is support for our conclusion. There are further respects in which the text of the city council's enactments discloses the improper attempt to target Santeria. . . . No one suggests, and on this record it cannot be maintained, that city officials had in mind a religion other than Santeria.

It becomes evident that these ordinances target Santeria sacrifice when the ordinances' operation is considered. Apart from the text, the effect of a law in its real operation is strong evidence of its object. To be sure, adverse impact will not always lead to a finding of impermissible targeting. For example, a social harm may have been a legitimate concern of government for reasons quite apart from discrimination. . . . The subject at hand does implicate, of course, multiple concerns unrelated to religious animosity, for example, the suffering or mistreatment visited upon the sacrificed animals, and health hazards from improper disposal. But the ordinances when considered together disclose an object remote from these legitimate concerns. The design of these laws accomplishes instead a "religious gerrymander," . . . an impermissible attempt to target petitioners and their religious practices.

It is a necessary conclusion that almost the only conduct subject to [the] Ordinances . . . is the religious exercise of Santeria church members. The tests show that they were drafted in tandem to achieve this result. . . .

The legitimate governmental interests in protecting the public health and preventing cruelty to animals could be addressed by restrictions stopping far short of a flat prohibition of all Santeria sacrificial practice. If improper disposal, not the sacrifice itself, is the harm to be prevented, the city could have imposed a general regulation on the disposal of organic garbage. It did not do so. Indeed, counsel for the city conceded at oral argument that, under the ordinances, Santeria sacrifices would be illegal even if they occurred in licensed, inspected, and zoned slaughterhouses. . . . Thus, these broad ordinances prohibit Santeria sacrifice even when it does not threaten the city's interest in the public health. The District Court accepted the argument that narrower regulation would be unenforceable because of the secrecy in the Santeria rituals. . . . It is difficult to understand, however, how a prohibition of the sacrifices themselves, which occur in private, is enforceable if a ban on improper disposal, which occurs in public, is

not. The neutrality of a law is suspect if First Amendment freedoms are curtailed to prevent isolated collateral harms not themselves prohibited by direct regulation. . . .

Under similar analysis, a narrow regulation would achieve the city's interest in preventing cruelty to animals. . . .

Ordinance 87-72—unlike the three other ordinances—does appear to apply to substantial nonreligious conduct and not to be overbroad. For our purposes here, however, the four substantive ordinances may be treated as a group for neutrality purposes. . . .

That the ordinances were enacted "'because of,' not merely 'in spite of,'" their suppression of Santeria religious practice is revealed by the events preceding enactment of the ordinances. Although respondent claimed at oral argument that it had experienced significant problems resulting from the sacrifice of animals within the city before the announced opening of the Church, the city council made no attempt to address the supposed problem before its meeting in June 1987, just weeks after the Church announced plans to open. The minutes and taped excerpts of the June 9 session, both of which are in the record, evidence significant hostility exhibited by residents, members of the city council, and other city officials toward the Santeria religion and its practice of animal sacrifice. The public crowd that attended the June 9 meetings interrupted statements by council members critical of Santeria with cheers and the brief comments of Pichardo with taunts. When Councilman Martinez, a supporter of the ordinances, stated that in prerevolutionary Cuba "people were put in jail for practicing this religion," the audience applauded. . . .

In sum, the neutrality inquiry leads to one conclusion: The ordinances had as their object the suppression of religion. The pattern we have recited discloses animosity to Santeria adherents and their religious practices; the ordinances by their own terms target this religious exercise; the texts of the ordinances were gerrymandered with care to proscribe religious killings of animals but to exclude almost all secular killings, and the ordinances suppress much more religious conduct than is necessary in order to achieve the legitimate ends asserted in their defense. . . .

We turn next to a second requirement of the Free Exercise Clause, the rule that laws burdening religious practice must be of general applicability. . . . All laws are selective to some extent, but categories of selection are of paramount concern when a law has the incidental effect of burdening religious practice. The Free Exercise Clause "protect[s] religious observers against unequal treatment," . . . and inequality results when a legislature decides that the governmental interests it seeks to advance are worthy of being pursued only against conduct with a religious motivation.

The principle that government, in pursuit of legitimate interests, cannot in a selective manner impose burdens only on conduct motivated by religious belief is essential to the protection of the rights guaranteed by the Free Exercise Clause. The principle underlying the general applicability requirement has parallels in our First Amendment jurisprudence. . . . In this case we need not define with precision the standard used to evaluate whether a prohibition is of general application, for these ordinances fall well below the minimum standard necessary to protect First Amendment rights.

Respondents claim that Ordinances 87-40, 87-52, and 87-71 advance two interests: protecting the public health and preventing cruelty to animals. The ordinances are underinclusive for those ends. They fail to prohibit non-religious conduct that endangers these interests in a similar or greater degree than Santeria sacrifice does. The underinclusion is substantial, not inconsequential. Despite the city's proffered interest in preventing cruelty to animals, the ordinances are drafted with care to forbid few killings but those occasioned by religious sacrifice. . . .

We conclude . . . that each of Hialeah's ordinances pursues the city's governmental interests only against conduct motivated by religious belief. The ordinances "ha[ve] every appearance of a prohibition that society is prepared to impose upon [Santeria worshippers] but not upon itself." . . . This precise evil is what the requirement of general applicability is designed to prevent. . . .

A law burdening religious practice that is not neutral or not of general application must undergo the most rigorous of scrutiny. To satisfy the commands of the First Amendment, a law restrictive of religious practice must advance "interests of the highest order" and must be narrowly tailored in pursuit of those interests. . . . A law that targets religious conduct for distinctive treatment or advances legitimate governmental interests only against conduct with a religious motivation will survive strict scrutiny only in rare cases. It follows from what we have already said that these ordinances cannot withstand this scrutiny.

First, even were the governmental interests compelling, the ordinances are not drawn in narrow terms to accomplish those interests. As we have discussed, . . . all four ordinances are overbroad or underinclusive in substantial respects. The proffered objectives are not pursued with respect to analogous non-religious conduct, and those interests could be achieved by narrower ordinances that burdened religion to a far lesser degree. The absence of narrow tailoring suffices to establish the invalidity of the ordinances. . . .

Respondent has not demonstrated, moreover, that, in the context of these ordinances, its governmental interests are compelling. Where government restricts only conduct protected by the First Amendment and fails to enact feasible measures to restrict other conduct producing substantial harm or alleged harm of the same sort, the interest given in justification of the restriction is not compelling. It is established in our strict scrutiny jurisprudence that "a law cannot be regarded as protecting an interest 'of the highest order' . . . when it leaves appreciable damage to that supposedly vital interest unprohibited." . . . As we show above, . . . the ordinances are underinclusive to a substantial extent with respect to each of the interests that respondent has asserted, and it is only conduct motivated by religious conviction that bears the weight of the governmental restrictions. There can be no serious claim that those interests justify the ordinances. . . .

The Free Exercise Clause commits government itself to religious tolerance, and upon even slight suspicion that proposals for state intervention stem from animosity to religion or distrust of its practices, all officials must pause to remember their own high duty to the Constitution and to the rights it secures. Those in office must be resolute in resisting importunate demands and must ensure that the sole reasons for imposing the burdens of law and regulation are secular. Legislators may not devise mechanisms, overt or disguised, designed to persecute or oppress a religion or its practices. The laws here in question were enacted contrary to these constitutional principles, and they are void. . . .

Justice Scalia, with whom the *Chief Justice* joins, concurring in part and concurring in the judgment. . . .

Justice Souter, concurring in part and concurring in the judgment. . . .

Justice Blackmun, with whom *Justice O'Connor* joins, concurring in the judgment. . . .

The Court holds today that the city of Hialeah violated the First and Fourteenth Amendments when it passed a set of restrictive ordinances explicitly directed at petitioners' religious practice. With this holding I agree. I write separately to emphasize that the First Amendment's protection of religion extends beyond those rare occasions on which the government explicitly targets religion (or a particular religion) for disfavored treatment, as is done in this case. In my view, a statute that burdens the free exercise of religion "may stand only if the law is general, and the State's refusal to allow a religious exemption in particular, are justified by a compelling interest that cannot be served by less restrictive means." *Employment Div., Oregon Dept. of Human Resources v. Smith* . . . (1990) (dissenting opinion). The Court, however, applies a different test. It applies the test announced in *Smith,* under which "a law that is neutral and of general applicability need not be justified by a compelling governmental interest even if the law has the incidental effect of burdening a particular religious practice." . . . I continue to believe that *Smith* was wrongly decided, because it ignored the value of religious freedom as an affirmative individual liberty and treated the Free Exercise Clause as no more than an antidiscrimination principle. . . . Thus, while I agree with the result the Court reaches in this case, I arrive at that result by a different route. . . .

Case

EVERSON V. BOARD OF EDUCATION

330 U.S. 1; 67 S.Ct. 504; 91 L.Ed. 711 (1947)
Vote: 5–4

In this case, the seminal decision in the Court's Establishment Clause jurisprudence, the issue is whether the First Amendment prohibits a local school board from reimbursing parents for costs incurred as a result of transporting their children to and from parochial schools.

Mr. Justice Black delivered the opinion of the Court.

A New Jersey statute authorizes its local school districts to make rules and contracts for the transportation of children to and from schools. The appellee, a township board of education, acting pursuant to this statute, authorized reimbursement to parents of money expended by them for the bus transportation of their children on regular buses operated by the public transportation system. Part of this money was for the payment of transportation of some children in the community to Catholic parochial schools. These church schools give their students, in addition to secular education, regular religious instruction conforming to the religious tenets and modes of worship of the Catholic Faith. The superintendent of these schools is a Catholic priest.

The appellant, in his capacity as a district taxpayer, filed suit in a state court challenging the right of the Board to reimburse parents of parochial school students. He contended that the statute and the resolution passed pursuant to it violated both the State and the Federal Constitutions. That court held that the legislature was without power to authorize such payment under the state constitution. . . . The New Jersey Court of Errors and Appeals reversed, holding that neither the statute nor the resolution passed pursuant to it was in conflict with the State constitution or the provisions of the Federal Constitution in issue. . . .

Since there has been no attack on the statute on the ground that a part of its language excludes children attending private schools operated for profit from enjoying State payment for their transportation, we need not consider this exclusionary language; it has no relevancy to any constitutional question here presented. Furthermore, if the exclusion clause had been properly challenged, we do not know whether New Jersey's highest court would construe its statutes as precluding payment of the school transportation of any group of pupils, even those of a private school run for profit. Consequently, we put to one side the question as to the validity of the statute against the claim that it does not authorize payment for the transportation generally of school children in New Jersey. . . .

The New Jersey statute is challenged as a "law respecting the establishment of religion." The First Amendment, as made applicable to the states by the Fourteenth, . . . commands that a state "shall make no law respecting an establishment of religion, or prohibiting the free exercise thereof. . . ." These words of the First Amendment reflected in the minds of early Americans a vivid mental picture of conditions and practices which they fervently wished to stamp out in order to preserve liberty for themselves and for their posterity. Doubtless their goal has not been entirely reached; but so far has the Nation moved toward it that the expression "law respecting the establishment of religion," probably does not so vividly remind present-day Americans of the evils, fears, and political problems that caused that expression to be written into our Bill of Rights. . . .

The meaning and scope of the First Amendment, preventing establishment of religion or prohibiting the free exercise thereof, in the light of its history and the evils it was designed forever to suppress, have been several times elaborated by the decisions of this Court prior to the application of the First Amendment to the states by the Fourteenth. The broad meaning given the Amendment by these earlier cases has been accepted by this Court in its decisions concerning an individual's religious freedom rendered since the Fourteenth Amendment was interpreted to make the prohibitions of the First applicable to state action abridging religious freedom. There is every reason to give the same application and broad interpretation to the "establishment of religion" clause. . . .

The "establishment of religion" clause of the First Amendment means at least this: Neither a state nor the Federal Government can set up a church. Neither can pass laws which aid one religion, aid all religions, or prefer one religion over another. Neither can force nor influence a person to go to or to remain away from church against his will or force him to profess a belief or disbelief in any religion. No person can be punished for entertaining or professing religious beliefs or disbeliefs, for church attendance or nonattendance. No tax in any amount, large or small, can be levied to support any religious activities or institutions, whatever they may be called, or whatever form they may adopt to teach or practice religion. Neither a state nor the Federal Government can, openly or secretly, participate in the affairs of any religious organizations or groups and vice versa. In the words of Jefferson, the clause against establishment of religion by law was intended to erect "a wall of separation between church and State." . . .

We must consider the New Jersey statute in accordance with the foregoing limitations imposed by the First Amendment. But we must not strike that state statute down if it is within the State's constitutional power even though it approaches the verge of that power. . . . New Jersey cannot consistently with the "establishment of religion" clause of the First Amendment contribute tax-raised funds to the support of an institution which teaches the tenets and faith of any church. On the other hand, other language of the amendment commands that New Jersey cannot hamper its citizens in the free exercise of their own religion. Consequently, it cannot exclude individual Catholics, Lutherans, Mohammedans, Baptists, Jews, Methodists, Non-believers, Presbyterians, or the members of any other faith, because of their faith, or lack of it, from receiving the benefits of public welfare legislation. While we do not mean to intimate that a state could not provide transportation only to children attending public schools, we must be careful in protecting the citizens of New Jersey against state-established churches, to be sure that we do not inadvertently prohibit New Jersey from extending its general state law benefits to all its citizens without regard to their religious belief.

Measured by these standards, we cannot say that the First Amendment prohibits New Jersey from spending tax-raised funds to pay the bus fares of parochial school pupils as a part of a general program under which it pays the fares of pupils attending public and other schools. It is undoubtedly true that children are helped to get to church schools. There is even a possibility that some of the children might not be sent to the church schools if the parents were compelled to pay their children's bus fares out of their own pockets when transportation to a public school would have been paid for by the State. The same possibility exists where the state requires a local transit company to provide reduced fares to school children including those attending parochial schools, or where a municipally owned transportation system undertakes to carry all school children free of charge. Moreover, state-paid policemen, detailed to protect children going to and from

church schools from the very real hazards of traffic, would serve much the same purpose and accomplish much the same result as state provisions intended to guarantee free transportation of a kind which the state deems to be best for the school children's welfare. And parents might refuse to risk their children to the serious danger of traffic accidents going to and from parochial schools, the approaches to which were not protected by policemen. Similarly, parents might be reluctant to permit their children to attend schools which the state had cut off from such general government services as ordinary police and fire protection, connections for sewage disposal, public highways and sidewalks. Of course, cutting off church schools from these services, so separate and so indisputably marked off from the religious function, would make it far more difficult for the schools to operate. But such is obviously not the purpose of the First Amendment. That Amendment requires the state to be a neutral in its relations with groups of religious believers and non-believers; it does not require the state to be their adversary. State power is no more to be used so as to handicap religions than it is to favor them.

This Court has said that parents may, in the discharge of their duty under state compulsory education laws, send their children to a religious rather than a public school if the school meets the secular educational requirements which the state has power to impose. . . . It appears that these parochial schools meet New Jersey's requirements. The State contributes no money to the schools. It does not support them. Its legislation, as applied, does no more than provide a general program to help parents get their children, regardless of their religion, safely and expeditiously to and from accredited schools.

The First Amendment has erected a wall between church and state. That wall must be kept high and impregnable. We could not approve the slightest breach. New Jersey has not breached it here. . . .

Mr. Justice Jackson, dissenting.

I find myself, contrary to first impressions, unable to join in this decision. I have a sympathy, though it is not ideological, with Catholic citizens who are compelled by law to pay taxes for public schools, and also feel constrained by conscience and discipline to support other schools for their own children. Such relief to them as this case involves is not in itself a serious burden to taxpayers and I had assumed it to be as little serious in principle. Study of this case convinces me otherwise. The Court's opinion marshals every argument in favor of state aid and puts the case in its most favorable light, but much of its reasoning confirms my conclusions that there are no good grounds upon which to support the present legislation. In fact, the undertones of the opinion, advocating complete and uncompromising separation of Church from State, seem utterly discordant with its conclusion yielding support to their commingling in educational matters. The case which irresistibly comes to mind as the most fitting precedent is that of Julia who, according to Byron's reports, "whispering 'I will ne'er consent,'—consented." . . .

This policy of our Federal Constitution has never been wholly pleasing to most religious groups. They all are quick to invoke its protections; they are all irked when they feel its restraints. This Court has gone a long way, if not an unreasonable way, to hold that public business of such paramount importance as maintenance of public order, protection of the privacy of the home, and taxation may not be pursued by a state in a way that even indirectly will interfere with religious proselytizing. . . .

But we cannot have it both ways. Religious teaching cannot be a private affair when the state seeks to impose regulations which infringe on it indirectly, and a public affair when it comes to taxing citizens of one faith to aid another, or those of no faith to aid all. If these principles seem harsh in prohibiting aid to Catholic education, it must not be forgotten that it is the same Constitution that alone assures Catholics the right to maintain these schools at all when predominant local sentiment would forbid them. . . . Nor should I think that those who have done so well without this aid would want to see this separation between Church and State broken down. If the state may aid these religious schools, it may therefore regulate them. Many groups have sought aid from tax funds only to find that it carried political controls with it. Indeed this Court has declared that "It is hardly lack of due process for the Government to regulate that which it subsidizes." . . .

But in any event, the great purposes of the Constitution do not depend on the approval or convenience of those they restrain. I cannot read the history of the struggle to separate political from ecclesiastical affairs, well summarized in the opinion of Mr. Justice Rutledge in which I generally concur, without a conviction that the Court today is unconsciously giving the clock's hands a backward turn.

Mr. Justice Frankfurter joins in this opinion.

Mr. Justice Rutledge, with whom *Mr. Justice Frankfurter, Mr. Justice Jackson* and *Mr. Justice Burton* agree, dissenting.

. . . No one conscious of religious values can be unsympathetic toward the burden which our constitutional separation puts on parents who desire religious instruction mixed with secular for their children. They pay taxes for others' children's education, at the same time the added cost of instruction for their own. Nor can one happily see benefits denied to children which others receive, because in conscience they or their parents for them desire a different kind of training others do not demand.

But if those feelings should prevail, there would be an end to our historic constitutional policy and command. No more unjust or discriminatory in fact is it to deny attendants at religious schools the cost of their transportation than it is to deny them tuitions, sustenance for their teachers, or any other educational expense which others receive at public cost. . . .

. . . [I]t is only by observing the prohibition rigidly that the state can maintain its neutrality and avoid partisanship in the dissensions inevitable when sect opposes sect over demands for public moneys to further religious education, teaching or training in any form or degree, directly or indirectly. Like St. Paul's freedom, religious liberty with a great price must be bought. And for those who exercise it most fully, by insisting upon religious education for their children mixed with secular, by the terms of our Constitution the price is greater than for others. . . .

Case

ABINGTON SCHOOL DISTRICT V. SCHEMPP

374 U.S. 203; 83 S.Ct. 1560; 10 L.Ed. 2d. 844 (1963)
Vote: 8–1

This is one of the controversial "school prayer decisions" handed down by the Warren Court during the early 1960s. Edward and Sidney Schempp, members of the Unitarian religion and parents of children attending a public high school, brought suit to challenge the official practice of opening the

school day with Bible reading and recitation of the Lord's Prayer. A three-judge panel of the U.S. District Court for the Eastern District of Pennsylvania held the practice unconstitutional under the Establishment Clause of the First Amendment. The school district appealed.

Mr. Justice Clark delivered the opinion of the Court.

. . . On each school day at the Abington Senior High School . . . opening exercises are conducted pursuant to [state law]. The exercises are broadcast into each room in the school building through an intercommunications system and are conducted under the supervision of a teacher by students attending the school's radio and television workshop. Selected students from this course gather each morning in the school's workshop studio for the exercises, which include readings by one of the students of 10 verses of the Holy Bible, broadcast to each room in the building. This is followed by the recitation of the Lord's Prayer, likewise over the intercommunications system, but also by the students in the various classrooms, who are asked to stand and join in repeating the prayer in unison. The exercises are closed with the flag salute and such pertinent announcements as are of interest to the students. Participation in the opening exercises, as directed by the statute, is voluntary. The student reading the verses from the Bible may select the passages and read from any version he chooses, although the only copies furnished by the school are the King James version, copies of which were circulated to each teacher by the school district. During the period in which the exercises have been conducted the King James, the Douay and the Revised Standard versions of the Bible have been used, as well as the Jewish Holy Scriptures. There are no prefatory statements, no questions asked or solicited, no comments or explanations made and no interpretations given at or during the exercises. The students and parents are advised that the student may absent himself from the classroom or, should he elect to remain, not participate in the exercises. . . .

The wholesome "neutrality" of which this Court's cases speak . . . stems from a recognition of the teachings of history that powerful sects or groups might bring about a fusion of governmental and religious functions or a concert or dependency of one upon the other to the end that official support of the State or Federal Government would be placed behind the tenets of one or of all orthodoxies. This the Establishment Clause prohibits. And a further reason for neutrality is found in the Free Exercise Clause, which recognizes the value of religious training, teaching and observance and, more particularly, the right of every person to freely choose his own course with reference thereto, free of any compulsion from the state. This the Free Exercise Clause guarantees. Thus, the two clauses may overlap. . . . [T]he Establishment Clause has been directly considered by this Court eight times in the past score of years and, with only one Justice dissenting on the point, it has consistently held that the clause withdrew all legislative power respecting religious belief or the expression thereof. The test may be stated as follows: what are the purpose and the primary effect of the enactment? If either is the advancement or inhibition of religion then the enactment exceeds the scope of legislative power as circumscribed by the Constitution. That is to say that to withstand the strictures of the Establishment Clause there

must be a secular legislative purpose and a primary effect that neither advances nor inhibits religion. . . . The Free Exercise Clause, likewise considered many times here, withdraws from legislative power, state and federal, the exertion of any restraint on the free exercise of religion. Its purpose is to secure religious liberty in the individual by prohibiting any invasions thereof by civil authority. Hence it is necessary in a free exercise case for one to show the coercive effect of the enactment as it operates against him in the practice of his religion. The distinction between the two clauses is apparent—a violation of the Free Exercise Clause is predicated on coercion while the Establishment Clause violation need not be so attended.

Applying the Establishment Clause principles to the cases at bar we find that the States are requiring the selection and reading at the opening of the school day of verses from the Holy Bible and the recitation of the Lord's Prayer by the students in unison. These exercises are prescribed as part of the curricular activities of students who are required by law to attend school. They are held in the school buildings under the supervision and with the participation of teachers employed in those schools. . . . The trial court . . . has found that such an opening exercise is a religious ceremony and was intended by the State to be so. We agree with the trial court's finding as to the religious character of the exercises. Given that finding, the exercises and the law requiring them are in violation of the Establishment Clause. . . .

The conclusion follows that the laws require religious exercises and such exercises are being conducted in direct violation of the rights of the appellees and petitioners. Nor are these required exercises mitigated by the fact that individual students may absent themselves upon parental request, for that fact furnishes no defense to a claim of unconstitutionality under the Establishment Clause. . . . Further, it is no defense to urge that the religious practices here may be relatively minor encroachments on the First Amendment. The breach of neutrality that is today a trickling stream may all too soon become a raging torrent and, in the words of Madison, "it is proper to take alarm at the first experiment on our liberties." . . .

It is insisted that unless these religious exercises are permitted a "religion of secularism" is established in the schools. We agree of course that the State may not establish a "religion of secularism" in the sense of affirmatively opposing or showing hostility to religion, thus "preferring those who believe in no religion over those who do believe." . . . We do not agree, however, that this decision in any sense has that effect. In addition, it might well be said that one's education is not complete without a study of comparative religion or the history of religion and its relationship to the advancement of civilization. It certainly may be said that the Bible is worthy of study for its literary and historic qualities. Nothing we have said here indicates that such study of the Bible or of religion, when presented objectively as part of a secular program of education, may not be effected consistently with the First Amendment. But the exercises here do not fall into those categories. They are religious exercises, required by the State in violation of the command of the First Amendment that the Government maintain strict neutrality, neither aiding nor opposing religion.

Finally, we cannot accept that the concept of neutrality, which does not permit a State to require a religious exercise even with the consent of the majority of those affected, collides with the majority's right to free exercise of religion. While the Free Exercise Clause clearly prohibits the use of state action to deny the rights of free exercise to anyone, it has never meant that a majority could use the machinery of the State to practice its beliefs. . . .

The place of religion in our society is an exalted one, achieved through a long tradition of reliance on the home, the church and the inviolable citadel of the individual heart and mind. We have come to recognize through bitter experience that it is not within the power of government to invade that citadel, whether its purpose or effect be to aid or oppose, to advance or retard. In the relationship between man and religion, the State is firmly committed to a position of neutrality. Though the application of that rule requires interpretation of a delicate sort, the rule itself is clearly and concisely stated in the words of the First Amendment. Applying that rule to the facts of these cases, we affirm. . . .

Mr. Justice Douglas, concurring. . . .

Mr. Justice Goldberg, with whom *Mr. Justice Harlan* joins, concurring. . . .

Mr. Justice Stewart, dissenting.

I think the records in the two cases before us are so fundamentally deficient as to make impossible an informed or responsible determination of the constitutional issues presented. Specifically, I cannot agree that on these records we can say that the Establishment Clause has necessarily been violated. But I think there exist serious questions under both that provision and the Free Exercise Clause—insofar as each is imbedded in the Fourteenth Amendment—which require the remand of these cases for the taking of additional evidence. . . .

What our Constitution indispensably protects is the freedom of each of us, be he Jew or Agnostic, Christian or Atheist, Buddhist or Freethinker, to believe or disbelieve, to worship or not worship, to pray or keep silent, according to his own conscience, uncoerced and unrestrained by government. It is conceivable that these school boards, or even all school boards, might eventually find it impossible to administer a system of religious exercises during school hours in such a way as to meet this constitutional standard—in such a way as completely to free from any kind of official coercion those who do not affirmatively want to participate. But I think we must not assume that school boards so lack the qualities of inventiveness and good will as to make impossible the achievement of that goal.

I would remand both cases for further hearings.

Case

WALLACE V. JAFFREE

472 U.S. 38; 105 S.Ct. 2479; 86 L.Ed. 2d. 29 (1985)
Vote: 6–3

In 1978, the Alabama legislature passed a law that provided: "At the commencement of the first class each day in the first through the sixth grades in all public schools . . . a period of silence, not to exceed one minute in duration, shall be observed for meditation, and during any such period silence shall be maintained and no activities engaged in." In 1981, this law was amended to authorize the period of silence "for meditation or voluntary prayer." The amended version of the Alabama "moment of silence law" is before the Supreme Court in this case.

Justice Stevens delivered the opinion of the Court.

. . . [T]he narrow question for decision is whether [the challenged law], which authorizes a period of silence for "meditation or voluntary prayer," is a law respecting the establishment of religion within the meaning of the First Amendment.

Appellee Ishmael Jaffree is a resident of Mobile County, Alabama. On May 28, 1982, he filed a complaint on behalf of three of his minor children; two of them were second-grade students and the third was then in kindergarten. The complaint named members of the Mobile County School Board, various school officials, and the minor plaintiffs' three teachers as defendants. The complaint alleged that the appellees brought the action "seeking principally a declaratory judgment and an injunction restraining the Defendants and each of them from maintaining or allowing the maintenance of regular religious prayer services or other forms of religious observances in the Mobile County Public Schools in violation of the First Amendment as made applicable to states by the Fourteenth Amendment to the United States Constitution." The complaint further alleged that two of the children had been subjected to various acts of religious indoctrination "from the beginning of the school year in September, 1981"; that the defendant teachers had "on a daily basis" led their classes in saying certain prayers in unison; that the minor children were exposed to ostracism from their peer group class members if they did not participate; and that Ishmael Jaffree had repeatedly but unsuccessfully requested that the devotional services be stopped. The original complaint made no reference to any Alabama statute. . . .

Jaffree's complaint was later amended to challenge the revised "moment of silence" statute. The U.S. district court dismissed the challenge to the statute holding that "the Establishment Clause of the First Amendment to the U.S. Constitution does not prohibit the state from establishing a religion." The U.S. court of appeals reversed, finding the challenged law to be in violation of the First Amendment.

When the court has been called upon to construe the breadth of the Establishment Clause, it has examined the criteria developed over a period of many years. Thus, in *Lemon v. Kurtzman*, . . . we wrote:

> Every analysis in this area must begin with consideration of the cumulative criteria developed by the Court over many years. Three such tests may be gleaned from our cases. First, the statute must have a secular legislative purpose; second, its principal or primary effect must be one that neither advances nor inhibits religion, . . . finally, the statute must not foster "an excessive government entanglement with religion." . . .

It is the first of these three criteria that is most plainly implicated by this case. As the District Court correctly recognized, no consideration of the second or third criteria is necessary if a statute does not have a clearly secular purpose. For even though a statute that is motivated in part by a religious purpose may satisfy the first criterion, . . . the First Amendment requires that a statute must be invalidated if it is entirely motivated by a purpose to advance religion.

In applying the purpose test, it is appropriate to ask "whether government's actual purpose is to endorse or disapprove of religion." In this case, the answer to that question is dispositive. For the record not only provides us with an unambiguous affirmative answer, but it also reveals that the enactment of [the amended statute] was not motivated by any clearly secular purpose—indeed, the statute had *no* secular purpose.

The sponsor of the bill that became [the challenged law], Senator Donald Holmes, inserted into the legislative record—apparently without dissent—a statement indicating that the legislation was an "effort to return voluntary prayer" to the public schools. Later Senator Holmes confirmed this purpose before the District Court. In response to the question whether he had any purpose for the legislation other than returning voluntary prayer to public schools, he stated, "No, I did not have no other purpose in mind." The State did not present evidence of *any* secular purpose. . . .

The legislative intent to return prayer to the public schools is, of course, quite different from merely protecting every student's right to engage in voluntary prayer during an appropriate moment of silence during the school day. The 1978 statute already protected that right, containing nothing that prevented any student from engaging in voluntary prayer during a silent minute of meditation. Appellants have not identified any secular purpose that was not fully served by [the original statute] before the enactment of [the amendment]. Thus, only two conclusions are consistent with the text . . . (1) the statute was enacted to convey a message of State endorsement and promotion of prayer; or (2) the statute was enacted for no purpose. No one suggests that the statute was nothing but a meaningless or irrational act.

We must, therefore, conclude that the Alabama Legislature intended to change existing law and that it was motivated by the same purpose that the Governor's Answer to the Second Amended Complaint expressly admitted; that the statement inserted in the legislative history revealed; and that Senator Holmes' testimony frankly described. The Legislature enacted [the challenged statute] for the sole purpose of expressing the State's endorsement of prayer activities for one minute at the beginning of each school day. The addition of "or voluntary prayer" indicates that the State intended to characterize prayer as a favored practice. Such an endorsement is not consistent with the established principle that the Government must pursue a course of complete neutrality toward religion.

The importance of that principle does not permit us to treat this as an inconsequential case involving nothing more than a few words of symbolic speech on behalf of the political majority. For whenever the State itself speaks on a religious subject, one of the questions that we must ask is "whether the Government intends to convey a message of endorsement or disapproval of religion." The well-supported concurrent findings of the District Court and the Court of Appeals—that [the challenged law] was intended to convey a message of State-approval of prayer activities in the public schools—make it unnecessary, and indeed inappropriate, to evaluate the practical significance of the addition of the words "or voluntary prayer" to the statute. Keeping in mind, as we must, "both the fundamental place held by the Establishment Clause in our constitutional scheme and the myriad, subtle ways in which Establishment Clause values can be eroded," we conclude that [the challenged statute] violates the First Amendment.

The judgment of the Court of Appeals is affirmed.

Justice Powell, concurring. . . .

Justice O'Connor, concurring in the judgment.

Nothing in the United States Constitution as interpreted by this Court or in the laws of the State of Alabama prohibits public school students from voluntarily praying at any time before, during, or after the school day. Alabama has facilitated voluntary silent prayers of students who are so inclined by enacting [the 1978 law] which provides a moment of silence in appellees' schools each day. The parties to these proceedings concede the validity of this enactment. At issue in these appeals is the constitutional validity of an additional and subsequent Alabama statute, . . . which both the District Court and the Court of Appeals concluded was enacted solely to officially encourage prayer during the moment of silence. I agree with the judgment of the Court that, in light of the findings of the Courts below and the history of its enactment, [the challenged law] violates the Establishment Clause of the First Amendment. In my view, there can be little doubt that the purpose and likely effect of this subsequent enactment is to endorse and sponsor voluntary prayer in the public schools. I write separately to identify the peculiar features of the Alabama law that render it invalid, and to explain why moment of silence laws in other States do not necessarily manifest the same infirmity. I also write to explain why neither history nor the Free Exercise Clause of the First Amendment validate the Alabama law struck down by the Court today. . . .

After an extensive discussion of Supreme Court decisions interpreting the religion clauses of the First Amendment, Justice O'Connor concludes:

The Court does not hold that the Establishment Clause is so hostile to religion that it precludes the States from affording schoolchildren an opportunity for voluntary silent prayer. To the contrary, the moment of silence statutes of many States should satisfy the Establishment Clause standard we have here applied. The Court holds only that Alabama has intentionally crossed the line between creating a quiet moment during which those so inclined may pray, and affirmatively endorsing the particular religious practice of prayer. This line may be a fine one, but our precedents and the principles of religious lib-

erty require that we draw it. In my view, the judgment of the Court of Appeals must be affirmed.

Chief Justice Burger, dissenting. . . .

Justice White, dissenting. . . .

Justice Rehnquist, dissenting.

. . . The true meaning of the Establishment Clause can only be seen in its history. . . . As drafters of our Bill of Rights, the framers inscribed the principles that control today. Any deviation from their intentions frustrates the permanence of that Charter and will only lead to the type of unprincipled decisionmaking that has plagued our Establishment Clause cases since *Everson.*

The Framers intended the Establishment Clause to prohibit the designation of any church as a "national" one. The Clause was also designed to stop the Federal Government from asserting a preference for one religious denomination or sect over others. Given the "incorporation" of the Establishment Clause as against the States via the Fourteenth Amendment in *Everson,* States are prohibited as well from establishing a religion or discriminating between sects. As its history abundantly shows, however, nothing in the Establishment Clause requires government to be strictly neutral between religion and irreligion, nor does that Clause prohibit Congress or the States from pursuing legitimate secular ends through nondiscriminatory sectarian means.

The Court strikes down the Alabama statute . . . because the State wished to "endorse prayer as a favored practice." . . . It would come as much of a shock to those who drafted the Bill of Rights as it will to a large number of thoughtful Americans today to learn that the Constitution, as construed by the majority, prohibits the Alabama Legislature from "endorsing" prayer. George Washington himself, at the request of the very Congress which passed the Bill of Rights, proclaimed a day of "public thanksgiving and prayer, to be observed by acknowledging with grateful hearts the many and signal favors of Almighty God." History must judge whether it was the father of his country in 1789, or a majority of the Court today, which has strayed from the meaning of the Establishment Clause.

The State surely has a secular interest in regulating the manner in which public schools are conducted. Nothing in the Establishment Clause of the First Amendment, properly understood, prohibits any such generalized "endorsement" of prayer. I would therefore reverse the judgment of the Court of Appeals. . . .

Case

SANTA FE INDEPENDENT SCHOOL DISTRICT v. DOE

530 U.S. 290;, 120 S.Ct. 2266;, 147 L.Ed. 2d 295 (2000)
Vote: 6–3

In this case, the Supreme Court considers an Establishment Clause challenge to a practice at a public high school in Texas in which a student delivers prayers over the PA system before football games. The U.S. District Court upheld the practice on the condition that the school would permit only "nonsectarian, nonproselytizing prayer." However, the U.S. Court of Appeals held that the challenged practice was unconstitutional, even as modified by the district court.

Justice Stevens delivered the opinion of the Court.

. . . The Santa Fe Independent School District (District) is a political subdivision of the State of Texas, responsible for the education of more than 4,000 students in a small community in the southern part of the State. The District includes the Santa Fe High School, two primary schools, an intermediate school and the junior high school. Respondents are two sets of current or former students and their respective mothers. One family is Mormon and the other is Catholic. The District Court permitted respondents (Does) to litigate anonymously to protect them from intimidation or harassment.

Respondents commenced this action in April 1995 and moved for a temporary restraining order to prevent the District from violating the Establishment Clause at the imminent graduation exercises. In their complaint the Does alleged that the District had engaged in several proselytizing practices, such as promoting attendance at a Baptist revival meeting, encouraging membership in religious clubs, chastising children who held minority religious beliefs, and distributing Gideon Bibles on school premises. They also alleged that the District allowed students to read Christian invocations and benedictions from the stage at graduation ceremonies, and to deliver overtly Christian prayers over the public address system at home football games. . . .

We granted the District's petition for certiorari, limited to the following question: "Whether petitioner's policy permitting student-led, student-initiated prayer at football games violates the Establishment Clause." . . . We conclude, as did the Court of Appeals, that it does.

II

. . . In *Lee v. Weisman* . . . (1992), we held that a prayer delivered by a rabbi at a middle school graduation ceremony violated that Clause. Although this case involves student prayer at a different type of school function, our analysis is properly guided by the principles that we endorsed in *Lee*. . . .

These invocations are authorized by a government policy and take place on government property at government-sponsored school-related events. . . . The Santa Fe school officials simply do not "evince either 'by policy or by practice,' any intent to open the [pregame ceremony] to 'indiscriminate use,' . . . by the student body generally." Rather, the school allows only one student, the same student for the entire season, to give the invocation. The statement or invocation, moreover, is subject to particular regulations that confine the content and topic of the student's message. . . .

Granting only one student access to the stage at a time does not, of course, necessarily preclude a finding that a school has created a limited public forum. Here, however, Santa Fe's student election system ensures that only those messages deemed "appropriate" under the District's policy may be delivered. That is, the majoritarian process implemented by the District guarantees, by definition, that minority candidates will never prevail and that their views will be effectively silenced. . . .

. . . [W]hile Santa Fe's majoritarian election might ensure that most of the students are represented, it does nothing to protect the minority; indeed, it likely serves to intensify their offense.

Moreover, the District has failed to divorce itself from the religious content in the invocations. It has not succeeded in doing so, either by claiming that its policy is "one of neutrality rather than endorsement" or by characterizing the individual student as the "circuit-breaker" in the process. Contrary to the District's repeated assertions that it has adopted a "hands-off" approach to the pregame invocation, the realities of the situation plainly reveal that its policy involves both perceived and actual endorsement of religion. In this case . . . the "degree of school involvement" makes it clear that the pregame prayers bear "the imprint of the State and thus put school-age children who objected in an untenable position." . . .

The District has attempted to disentangle itself from the religious messages by developing the two-step student election process. . . . The elections take place at all only because the school "board *has chosen to permit* students to deliver a brief invocation and/or message." . . . The elections thus "shall" be conducted "by the high school student council" and "[u]pon advice and direction of the high school principal." . . . The decision whether to deliver a message is first made by majority vote of the entire student body, followed by a choice of the speaker in a separate, similar majority election. Even though the particular words used by the speaker are not determined by those votes, the policy mandates that the "statement or invocation" be "consistent with the goals and purposes of this policy," which are "to solemnize the event, to promote good sportsmanship and student safety, and to establish the appropriate environment for the competition." . . .

In addition to involving the school in the selection of the speaker, the policy, by its terms, invites and encourages religious messages. The policy itself states that the purpose of the message is "to solemnize the event." A religious message is the most obvious method of solemnizing an event. Moreover, the requirements that the message "promote good citizenship" and "establish the appropriate environment for competition" further narrow the types of message deemed appropriate, suggesting that a solemn, yet nonreligious, message, such as commentary on United States foreign policy, would be prohibited. Indeed, the only type of message that is expressly endorsed in the text is an "invocation"—a term that primarily describes an appeal for divine assistance. In fact, as used in the past at Santa Fe High School, an "invocation" has always entailed a focused religious message. Thus, the expressed purposes of the policy encourage the selection of a religious message, and that is precisely how the students understand the policy. The results of the elections described in the parties' stipulation make it clear that the students understood that the central question before them was whether prayer should be a part of the pregame ceremony. We recognize the important role that public worship plays in many communities, as well as the sincere desire to include public prayer as a part of various occasions so as to mark those occasions' significance. But such religious activity in public schools, as elsewhere, must comport with the First Amendment.

The actual or perceived endorsement of the message, moreover, is established by factors beyond just the text of the policy. Once the student speaker is selected and the message composed, the invocation is then delivered to a large audience assembled as part of a regularly scheduled, school-sponsored function conducted on school property. The message is broadcast over the school's public address system, which remains subject to the control of school officials. It is fair to assume that the pregame ceremony is clothed in the traditional indicia of school sporting events, which generally include not just the team, but also cheerleaders and band members dressed in uniforms sporting the school name and mascot. . . .

The text and history of this policy, moreover, reinforce our objective student's perception that the prayer is, in actuality, encouraged by the school. When a governmental entity professes a secular purpose for an arguably religious policy, the government's characterization is, of course, entitled to some deference. But it is nonetheless the duty of the courts to "distinguis[h] a sham secular purpose from a sincere one." . . .

According to the District, the secular purposes of the policy are to "foste[r] free expression of private persons . . . as well [as to] solemniz[e] sporting events, promot[e] good sportsmanship and student safety, and establis[h] an appropriate environment for competition." . . . We note, however, that the District's approval of only one specific kind of message, an "invocation," is not necessary to further any of these purposes. Additionally, the fact that only one student is permitted to give a content-limited message suggests that this policy does little to "foste[r] free expression." Furthermore, regardless of whether one considers a sporting event an appropriate occasion for solemnity, the use of an invocation to foster such solemnity is impermissible when, in actuality, it constitutes prayer sponsored by the school. And it is unclear what type of message would be both appropriately "solemnizing" under the District's policy and yet non-religious.

Most striking to us is the evolution of the current policy from the long-sanctioned office of "Student Chaplain" to the candidly titled "Prayer at Football Games" regulation. This history indicates that the District intended to preserve the practice of prayer before football games. . . .

School sponsorship of a religious message is impermissible because it sends the ancillary message to members of the audience who are nonadherants "that they are outsiders, not full members of the political community, and an accompanying message to adherants that they are insiders, favored members of the political community." . . . The delivery of such a message—over the school's public address system, by a speaker representing the student body, under the supervision of school faculty, and pursuant to a school policy that explicitly and implicitly encourages public prayer—is not properly characterized as "private" speech.

III

In this section the Court rejects the school district's contention that its football policy is distinguishable from the graduation prayer struck down in Lee v. Weisman *(1992).*

. . . Even if we regard every high school student's decision to attend a home football game as purely voluntary, we are nevertheless persuaded that the delivery of a pregame prayer has the improper effect of coercing those present to participate in an act of religious worship. For "the government may no more use social pressure to enforce orthodoxy than it may use more direct means." . . . As in *Lee*, "[w]hat to most believers may seem nothing more than a reasonable request that the nonbeliever respect their religious practices, in a school context may appear to the nonbeliever or dissenter to be an attempt to employ the machinery of the State to enforce a religious orthodoxy." . . . The constitutional command will not permit the District "to exact religious conformity from a student as the price" of joining her classmates at a varsity football game. . . .

IV

Finally, the District argues repeatedly that the Does have made a premature facial challenge . . . that necessarily must fail. The District emphasizes, quite correctly, that until a student actually delivers a solemnizing message under the latest version of the policy, there can be no certainty that any of the statements or invocations will be religious. . . .

The District . . . asks us to pretend that we do not recognize what every Santa Fe High School student understands clearly—that this policy is about prayer. The District further asks us to accept what is obviously untrue: that these messages are necessary to "solemnize" a football game and that this single-student, year-long position is essential to the protection of student speech. We refuse to turn a blind eye to the context in which this policy arose, and that context quells any doubt that this policy was implemented with the purpose of endorsing school prayer.

Therefore, the simple enactment of this policy, with the purpose and perception of school endorsement of student prayer, was a constitutional violation. We need not wait for the inevitable to confirm and magnify the constitutional injury. . . . Therefore, even if no Santa Fe High School student were ever to offer a religious message, the . . . policy fails a facial challenge because the attempt by the District to encourage prayer is also at issue. Government efforts to endorse religion cannot evade constitutional reproach based solely on the remote possibility that those attempts may fail.

This policy likewise does not survive a facial challenge because it impermissibly imposes upon the student body a majoritarian election on the issue of prayer. Through its election scheme, the District has established a governmental electoral mechanism that turns the school into a forum for religious debate. It further empowers the student body majority with the authority to subject students of minority views to constitutionally improper messages.

The award of that power alone, regardless of the students' ultimate use of it, is not acceptable. . . . Such a system encourages divisiveness along religious lines and threatens the imposition of coercion upon those students not desiring to participate in a religious exercise. . . .

To properly examine this policy on its face, we "must be deemed aware of the history and context of the community and forum." . . . Our examination of those circumstances above leads to the conclusion that this policy does not provide the District with the constitutional safe harbor it sought. The policy is invalid on its face because it establishes an improper majoritarian election on religion, and unquestionably has the purpose and creates the perception of encouraging the delivery of prayer at a series of important school events.

The judgment of the Court of Appeals is, accordingly, affirmed.

Chief Justice Rehnquist*,** with whom ***Justice Scalia and ***Justice Thomas*** join, dissenting.

The Court distorts existing precedent to conclude that the school district's student-message program is invalid on its face under the Establishment Clause. But even more disturbing than its holding is the tone of the Court's opinion; it bristles with hostility to all things religious in public life. Neither the holding nor the tone of the opinion is faithful to the meaning of the Establishment Clause, when it is recalled that George Washington himself, at the request of the very Congress which passed the Bill of Rights, proclaimed a day of "public thanksgiving and prayer, to be observed by acknowledging with grateful hearts the many and signal favors of Almighty God." . . .

The Court . . . applies the most rigid version of the oft-criticized test of *Lemon v. Kurtzman* . . . (1971). . . . *Lemon* has had a checkered career in the decisional law of this Court. . . . We have even gone so far as to state that it has never been binding on us. . . . Indeed, in *Lee v. Weisman* . . . (1992), an opinion upon which the Court relies heavily today, we mentioned but did not feel compelled to apply the *Lemon* test. . . .

Even if it were appropriate to apply the *Lemon* test here, the district's student-message policy should not be invalidated on its face. The Court applies *Lemon* and holds that the "policy is invalid on its face because it establishes an improper majoritarian election on religion, and unquestionably has the purpose and creates the perception of encouraging the delivery of prayer at a series of important school events." . . . The Court's reliance on each of these conclusions misses the mark.

First, the Court misconstrues the nature of the "majoritarian election" permitted by the policy as being an election on "prayer" and "religion." . . . To the contrary, the election permitted by the policy is a two-fold process whereby students vote first on whether to have a student speaker before football games at all, and second, if the students vote to have such a speaker, on who that speaker will be. . . . It is conceivable that the election could become one in which student candidates campaign on platforms that focus on whether or not they will pray if elected. It is also conceivable that the election could lead to a Christian prayer before 90 percent of the football games. If, upon implementation, the policy operated in this fashion, we would have a record before us to review whether the policy, as applied, violated the Establishment Clause or unduly suppressed minority viewpoints. But it is possible that the students might vote not to have a pregame speaker, in which case there would be no threat of a constitutional violation. It is also possible that the election would not focus on prayer, but on public speaking ability or social popularity. And if student campaigning did begin to focus on prayer, the school might decide to implement reasonable campaign restrictions.

. . . Support for the Court's holding cannot be found in any of our cases. And it essentially invalidates all student elections. A newly elected student body president, or even a newly elected prom king or queen, could use opportunities for public speaking to say prayers. Under the Court's view, the mere grant of power to the students to vote for such offices, in light of the fear that those elected might publicly pray, violates the Establishment Clause.

Second, with respect to the policy's purpose, the Court holds that "the simple enactment of this policy, with the purpose and perception of school endorsement of student prayer, was a constitutional violation." . . . But the policy itself has plausible secular purposes: "[T]o solemnize the event, to promote good sportsmanship and student safety, and to establish the appropriate environment for the competition." . . . Where a governmental body "expresses a plausible secular purpose" for an enactment, "courts should generally defer to that stated intent." . . . The Court grants no deference to—and appears openly hostile toward—the policy's stated purposes, and wastes no time in concluding that they are a sham. . . .

The Court bases its conclusion that the true purpose of the policy is to endorse student prayer on its view of the school district's history of Establishment Clause violations and the context in which the policy was written, that is, as "the latest step in developing litigation brought as a challenge to institutional practices that unquestionably violated the Establishment Clause." . . . But the context—attempted compliance with a District Court order—actually demonstrates that the school district was acting diligently to come within the governing constitutional law. The District Court ordered the school district to formulate a policy consistent with Fifth Circuit precedent, which permitted a school district to have a prayer-only policy.

. . . But the school district went further than required by the District Court order and eventually settled on a policy that gave the student speaker a choice to deliver either an invocation or a message. In so doing, the school district exhibited a willingness to comply with, and exceed, Establishment Clause restrictions. Thus, the policy cannot be viewed as having a sectarian purpose.

The Court also relies on our decision in *Lee v. Weisman* . . . to support its conclusion. In *Lee*, we concluded that the content of the speech at issue, a graduation prayer given by a rabbi, was "directed and controlled" by a school official. . . . In other words, at issue in *Lee* was *government* speech. Here, by contrast, the potential speech at issue, if the policy had been allowed to proceed, would be a message or invocation selected or created by a student. That is, if there were speech at issue here, it would be *private* speech. The "crucial difference between *government* speech endorsing religion, which the Establishment Clause forbids, and *private* speech endorsing religion, which the Free Speech and Free Exercise Clauses protect," applies with particular force to the question of endorsement. . . .

Had the policy been put into practice, the students may have chosen a speaker according to wholly secular criteria—like good public speaking skills or social popularity—and the student speaker may have chosen, on her own accord, to deliver a religious message. Such an application of the policy would likely pass constitutional muster. . . .

Finally, the Court seems to demand that a government policy be completely neutral as to content or be considered one that endorses religion. . . . This is undoubtedly a new requirement, as our Establishment Clause jurisprudence simply does not mandate "content neutrality." That concept is found in our First Amendment *speech* cases and is used as a guide for determining when we apply strict scrutiny. For example, we look to "content neutrality" in reviewing loudness restrictions imposed on speech in public forums, . . . and regulations against picketing. . . . The Court seems to think that the fact that the policy is not content neutral somehow controls the Establishment Clause inquiry. . . .

But even our speech jurisprudence would not require that all public school actions with respect to student speech be content neutral. . . . Schools do not violate the First Amendment every time they restrict student speech to certain categories. But under the Court's view, a school policy under which the student body president is to solemnize the graduation ceremony by giving a favorable introduction to the guest speaker would be facially unconstitutional. Solemnization "invites and encourages" prayer and the policy's content limitations prohibit the student body president from giving a solemn, yet non-religious, message like "commentary on United States foreign policy." . . .

The policy at issue here may be applied in an unconstitutional manner, but it will be time enough to invalidate it if that is found to be the case. I would reverse the judgment of the Court of Appeals.

Case

EDWARDS V. AGUILLARD

482 U.S. 578; 107 S.Ct. 2573; 96 L.Ed. 2d. 510 (1987)
Vote: 7–2

The teaching of evolution in the public schools has long been controversial. Indeed, some states have attempted to ban the teaching of evolution altogether. Such a prohibition was struck down in Epperson v. Arkansas *(1968). More recently, states have attempted to balance the teaching of evolution with the teaching of "creation science." Whether this is a legitimate secular requirement for public school curricula or an attempt to instruct public school students in the biblical account of creation is the issue before the Supreme Court in this case.*

Justice Brennan delivered the opinion of the Court.

The question for decision is whether Louisiana's "Balanced Treatment for Creation-Science and Evolution-Science in Public School Instruction" Act (Creationism Act) . . . is facially invalid as violative of the Establishment Clause of the First Amendment.

The Creationism Act forbids the teaching of the theory of evolution in public schools unless accompanied by instruction in "creation science." . . . No school is required to teach evolution or creation science. If either is taught, however, the other must also be taught. . . . The theories of evolution and creation science are statutorily defined as "the scientific evidences for [creation or evolution] and inferences from those scientific evidences." . . .

Appellees, who include parents of children attending Louisiana public schools, Louisiana teachers, and religious leaders, challenged the constitutionality of the Act in District Court, seeking an injunction and declaratory relief. Appellants, Louisiana officials charged with implementing the Act, defended on the ground that the purpose of the Act is to protect a legitimate secular interest, namely, academic freedom. Appellees attacked the Act as facially invalid because it violated the Establishment Clause and made a motion for summary judgment. The District Court granted the motion. . . . The court held that there can be no valid secular reason for prohibiting the teaching of evolution, a theory historically opposed by some religious denominations. The court further concluded that "the teaching of 'creation-science' and 'creationism,' as contemplated by the statute, involves teaching 'tailored to the

principles' of a particular religious sect or group of sects." . . . The District Court therefore held that the Creationism Act violated the Establishment Clause either because it prohibited the teaching of evolution or because it required the teaching of creation science with the purpose of advancing a particular religious doctrine.

The Court of Appeals affirmed. . . . The court observed that the statute's avowed purpose of protecting academic freedom was inconsistent with requiring, upon risk of sanction, the teaching of creation science whenever evolution is taught. . . . The court found that the Louisiana legislature's actual intent was "to discredit evolution by counterbalancing its teaching at every turn with the teaching of creationism, a religious belief." . . . Because the Creationism Act was thus a law furthering a particular religious belief, the Court of Appeals held that the Act violated the Establishment Clause. A suggestion for rehearing *en banc* was denied over a dissent. . . . We noted probable jurisdiction, . . . and now affirm.

The Establishment Clause forbids the enactment of any law "respecting an establishment of religion." The Court has applied a three-pronged test to determine whether legislation comports with the Establishment Clause. First, the legislature must have adopted the law with a secular purpose. Second, the statute's principal or primary effect must be one that neither advances nor inhibits religion. Third, the statute must not result in an excessive entanglement of government with religion. *Lemon v. Kurtzman* . . . (1971). State action violates the Establishment Clause if it fails to satisfy any of these prongs. . . .

Lemon's first prong focuses on the purpose that animated adoption of the Act. "The purpose prong of the *Lemon* test asks whether government's actual purpose is to endorse or disapprove of religion." . . . A governmental intention to promote religion is clear when the State enacts a law to serve a religious purpose. This intention may be evidenced by promotion of religion in general, . . . or by advancement of a particular religious belief. . . . If the law was enacted for the purpose of endorsing religion, "no consideration of the second or third criteria [of *Lemon*] is necessary." . . . In this case, the petitioners had identified no clear secular purpose for the Louisiana Act.

True, the Act's stated purpose is to protect academic freedom. . . . This phrase might, in common parlance, be understood as referring to enhancing the freedom of teachers to teach what they will. The Court of Appeals, however, correctly concluded that the Act was not designed to further that goal. We find no merit in the State's argument that the "legislature may not [have] use[d] the terms 'academic freedom' in the correct legal sense. They might have [had] in mind, instead, a basic concept of fairness: teaching all of the evidence." . . . Even if "academic freedom" is read to mean "teaching all of the evidence" with respect to the origin of human beings, the Act does not further this purpose. The goal of providing a more comprehensive science curriculum is not furthered either by outlawing the teaching of evolution or by requiring the teaching of creation science.

While the Court is normally deferential to a State's articulation of a secular purpose, it is required that the statement of such purpose be sincere and not a sham. . . .

It is clear from the legislative history that the purpose of the legislative sponsor, Senator Bill Keith, was to narrow the science curriculum. During the legislative hearings, Senator Keith stated: "My preference would be that neither [creationism nor evolution] be taught." . . . Such a ban on teaching does not promote—indeed, it undermines—the provision of a comprehensive scientific education.

It is equally clear that requiring schools to teach creation science with evolution does not advance academic freedom. The Act does not grant teachers a flexibility that they did not already possess to supplant the present science curriculum with the presentation of theories, besides evolution, about the origin of life. Indeed, the Court of Appeals found that no law prohibited Louisiana public schoolteachers from teaching any scientific theory. . . . As the president of the Louisiana Science Teachers Association testified, "[a]ny scientific concept that's based on established fact can be included in our curriculum already, and no legislation allowing this is necessary." . . . The Act provides Louisiana schoolteachers with no new authority. Thus the stated purpose is not furthered by it. . . .

Furthermore, the goal of basic "fairness" is hardly furthered by the Act's discriminatory preference for the teaching of creation science and against the teaching of evolution. While requiring that curriculum guides be developed for creation science, the Act says nothing of comparable guides for evolution. . . . Similarly, research services are supplied for creation science but not for evolution. . . . Only "creation scientists" can serve on the panel that supplies the resource services. . . . The Act forbids school boards to discriminate against anyone who "chooses to be a creation-scientist" or to teach "creationism," but fails to protect those who choose to teach evolution or any other noncreation science theory, or who refuse to teach creation science. . . .

If the Louisiana legislature's purpose was solely to maximize the comprehensiveness and effectiveness of science instruction, it would have encouraged the teaching of all scientific theories about the origins of humankind. But under the Act's requirements, teachers who were once free to teach any and all facets of this subject are now unable to do so. Moreover, the Act fails even to ensure that creation science will be taught, but instead requires the teaching of this theory only when the theory of evolution is taught. Thus we agree with the Court of Appeals' conclusion that the Act does not serve to protect academic freedom, but has the distinctly different purpose of discrediting "evolution by counterbalancing its teaching at every turn with the teaching of creation science." . . .

. . . [W]e need not be blind in this case to the legislature's preeminent religious purpose in enacting this statute. There is a historic and contemporaneous link between the teachings of certain religious denominations and the teaching of evolution. It was this link that concerned the Court in *Epperson v. Arkansas* [1968], . . . which also involved a facial challenge to a statute regulating the teaching of evolution. In that case, the Court reviewed an Arkansas statute that made it unlawful for an instructor to teach evolution or to use a textbook that referred to this scientific theory. Although the Arkansas antievolution law did not explicitly state its predominate religious purpose, the Court could not ignore that "[t]he statute was a product of the upsurge of 'fundamentalist' religious fervor" that has long viewed this particular scientific theory as contradicting the literal interpretation of the Bible. . . . After reviewing the history of antievolution statutes, the Court determined that "there can be no doubt that the motivation for the [Arkansas] law was the same [as other antievolution statutes]: to suppress the teaching of a theory which, it was thought, 'denied' the divine creation of man." . . . The Court found that there can be no legitimate state interest in protecting particular religions from scientific views "distasteful to them," . . . and concluded "that the First Amendment does not permit the State to require that teaching and learning must be tailored to the principles or prohibitions of any religious sect or dogma." . . .

These same historic and contemporaneous antagonisms between the teachings of certain religious denominations and the teaching of evolution are present in this case. The preeminent purpose of the Louisiana legislature was clearly to advance the religious viewpoint that a supernatural being created humankind. The term "creation science" was defined as embracing this particular religious doctrine by those responsible for the passage of the Creationism Act. Senator Keith's leading expert on creation science, Edward Boudreaux, testified at the legislative hearings that the theory of creation science included belief in the existence of a supernatural creator. . . . Senator Keith also cited testimony from other experts to support the creation-science view that "a creator [was] responsible for the universe and everything in it." . . . The legislative history therefore reveals that the term "creation science," as contemplated by the legislature that adopted this Act, embodies the religious belief that a supernatural creator was responsible for the creation of humankind.

Furthermore, it is not happenstance that the legislature required the teaching of a theory that coincided with this religious view. The legislative history documents that the Act's primary purpose was to change the science curriculum of public schools in order to provide persuasive advantage to a particular religious doctrine that rejects the factual basis of evolution in its entirety. The sponsor of the Creationism Act, Senator Keith, explained during the legislative hearings that his disdain for the theory of evolution resulted from the support that evolution supplied to views contrary to his own religious beliefs. According to Senator Keith, the theory of evolution was consonant with the "cardinal principle[s] of religious humanism, secular humanism, theological liberalism, aetheistism [sic]." . . . The state senator repeatedly stated that scientific evidence supporting his religious views should be included in the public school curriculum to redress the fact that the theory of evolution incidentally coincided with what he characterized as religious beliefs antithetical to his own. The legislation therefore sought to alter the science curriculum to reflect endorsement of a religious view that is antagonistic to the theory of evolution.

In this case, the purpose of the Creationism Act was to restructure the science curriculum to conform with a particular religious viewpoint. Out of many possible science subjects taught in the public schools, the legislature chose to affect the teaching of the one scientific theory that historically has been opposed by certain religious sects. As in *Epperson,* the legislature passed the Act to give preference to those religious groups which have as one of their tenets the creation of humankind by a divine creator. The "overriding fact" that confronted the Court in *Epperson* was "that Arkansas' law selects from the body of knowledge a particular segment which it proscribes for the sole reason that it is deemed to conflict with . . . a particular interpretation of the Book of Genesis by a particular religious group." . . . Similarly, the Creationism Act is designed either to promote the theory of creation science which embodies a particular religious tenet by requiring that creation science be taught whenever evolution is taught or to prohibit the teaching of a scientific theory disfavored by certain religious sects by forbidding the teaching of evolution when creation science is not also taught. The Establishment Clause, however, "forbids alike the preference of a religious doctrine or the prohibition of theory which is deemed antagonistic to a particular dogma." . . . Because the primary purpose of the Creationism Act is to advance a particular religious belief, the Act endorses religion in violation of the First Amendment.

We do not imply that a legislature could never require that scientific critiques of prevailing scientific theories be taught. Indeed, the Court acknowledged in *Stone* that its decision forbidding the posting of the Ten Commandments did not mean that no use could ever be made of the Ten Commandments, or that the Ten Commandments played an exclusively religious role in the history of Western civilization. . . . In a similar way, teaching a variety of scientific theories about the origins of humankind to schoolchildren might be validly done with the clear secular intent of enhancing the effectiveness of science instruction. But because the primary purpose of the Creationism Act is to endorse a particular religious doctrine, the Act furthers religion in violation of the Establishment Clause. . . .

Justice Powell, with whom **Justice O'Connor** joins, concurring. . . .

Justice White, concurring in the judgment. . . .

Justice Scalia, with whom the **Chief Justice** joins, dissenting.

Even if I agreed with the questionable premise that legislation can be invalidated under the Establishment Clause on the basis of its motivation alone, without regard to its effects, I would still find no justification for today's decision. The Louisiana legislators who passed the "Balanced Treatment for Creation-Science and Evolution-Science Act" (Balanced Treatment Act), . . . each of whom had sworn to support the Constitution, were well aware of the potential Establishment Clause problems and considered that aspect of the legislation with great care. After seven hearings and several months of study, resulting in substantial revision of the original proposal, they approved the Act overwhelmingly and specifically articulated the secular purpose they meant it to serve. Although the record contains abundant evidence of the sincerity of that purpose (the only issue pertinent to this case), the Court today holds, essentially on the basis of "its visceral knowledge regarding what must have motivated the legislators," . . . that the members of the Louisiana Legislature knowingly violated their oaths and then lied about it. I dissent. Had requirements of the Balanced Treatment Act that are not apparent on its face been clarified by an interpretation of the Louisiana Supreme Court, or by the manner of its implementation, the Act might well be found unconstitutional; but the question of its constitutionality cannot rightly be disposed of on the gallop, by impugning the motives of its supporters. . . .

Given the many hazards involved in assessing the subjective intent of governmental decisionmakers, the first prong of *Lemon [v. Kurtzman]* is defensible, I think, only if the text of the Establishment Clause demands it.

That is surely not the case. The Clause states that "Congress shall make no law respecting an establishment of religion." One could argue, I suppose, that any time Congress acts with the intent of advancing religion, it has enacted a "law respecting an establishment of religion"; but far from being an unavoidable reading, it is quite an unnatural one. I doubt, for example, that the Clayton Act . . . could reasonably be described as a "law respecting an establishment of religion" if bizarre new historical evidence revealed that it lacked a secular purpose, even though it has no discernible nonsecular effect. It is, in short, far from an inevitable reading of the Establishment Clause that it forbids all governmental action intended to advance religion; and if not inevitable, any reading with such untoward consequences must be wrong.

In the past we have attempted to justify our embarrassing Establishment Clause jurisprudence on the ground that it "sacrifices clarity and predictability for flexibility." . . . One commentator had aptly characterized this as "a euphemism . . . for . . . the absence of any principled rationale." . . . I think it time that we sacrifice some "flexibility" for "clarity and predictability." Abandoning *Lemon's* purpose test—a test which exacerbates the tension between the Free Exercise and Establishment Clause, has no basis in the language or history of the amendment, and, as today's decision shows, has wonderfully flexible consequences—would be a good place to start.

Case

AGOSTINI V. FELTON

521 U.S. 203;, 117 S.Ct. 1997;, 138 L.Ed. 2d. 391 (1997)
Vote: 5–4

Here the Court reconsiders its decision in Aguilar v. Felton *(1985), which held that the Establishment Clause prohibited a city from sending public school teachers into parochial schools to provide remedial education*

Justice O'Connor delivered the opinion of the Court.

. . . Petitioners maintain that *Aguilar* cannot be squared with our intervening Establishment Clause jurisprudence and ask that we explicitly recognize what our more recent cases already dictate: *Aguilar* is no longer good law. We agree with petitioners that *Aguilar* is not consistent with our subsequent Establishment Clause decisions. . . .

In order to evaluate whether *Aguilar* has been eroded by our subsequent Establishment Clause cases, it is necessary to understand the rationale upon which *Aguilar,* as well as its companion case, *School Dist. of Grand Rapids v. Ball,* . . . (1985), rested. . . .

Our more recent cases have undermined the assumptions upon which *Ball* and *Aguilar* relied. To be sure, the general principles we use to evaluate whether government aid violates the Establishment Clause have not changed since *Aguilar* was decided. For example, we continue to ask whether the government acted with the purpose of advancing or inhibiting religion, and the nature of that inquiry has remained largely unchanged. . . . Likewise, we continue to explore whether the aid has the "effect" of advancing or inhibiting religion. What has changed since we decided *Ball* and *Aguilar* is our understanding of the criteria used to assess whether aid to religion has an impermissible effect. . . .

. . . New York City's Title I program does not run afoul of any of three primary criteria we currently use to evaluate whether government aid has the effect of advancing religion: it does not result in governmental indoctrination; define its recipients by reference to religion; or create an excessive entanglement. We therefore hold that a federally funded program providing supplemental, remedial instruction to disadvantaged children on a neutral basis is not invalid under the Establishment Clause when such instruction is given on the premises of sectarian schools by government employees pursuant to a program containing safeguards such as those present here. The same considerations that justify this holding require us to conclude that this carefully constrained program also cannot reasonably be viewed as an endorsement of religion. . . . Accordingly, we must acknowledge that *Aguilar,* as well as the portion of *Ball* addressing Grand Rapids' Shared Time program, are no longer good law.

The doctrine of *stare decisis* does not preclude us from recognizing the change in our law and overruling *Aguilar* and those portions of *Ball* inconsistent with our more recent decisions. . . . That policy is at its weakest when we interpret the Constitution because our interpretation can be altered only by constitutional amendment or by overruling our prior decisions. . . . Thus, we have held in several cases that *stare decisis* does not prevent us from overruling a previous decision where there has been a significant change in or subsequent development of our constitutional law. . . . As discussed above, our Establishment Clause jurisprudence has changed significantly since we decided *Ball* and *Aguilar,* so our decision to overturn those cases rests on far more than "a present doctrinal disposition to come out differently from the Court of [1985]." . . . We therefore overrule *Ball* and *Aguilar* to the extent those decisions are inconsistent with our current understanding of the Establishment Clause. . . .

We . . . conclude that our Establishment Clause law has "significant[ly] change[d]" since we decided *Aguilar.* . . . We are only left to decide whether this change in law entitles petitioners to relief under Rule 60(b)(5). We conclude that it does. Our general practice is to apply the rule of law we announce in a case to the parties before us. . . . We adhere to this practice even when we overrule a case. . . .

We do not acknowledge, and we do not hold, that other courts should conclude our more recent cases have, by implication, overruled an earlier precedent. We reaffirm that "if a precedent of this Court has direct application in a case, yet appears to rest on reasons rejected in some other line of decisions, the Court of Appeals should follow the case which directly controls, leaving to this Court the prerogative of overruling its own decisions." . . . Adherence to this teaching by the District Court and Court of Appeals in this case does not insulate a legal principle on which they relied from our review to determine its continued vitality. The trial court acted within its discretion in entertaining the motion with supporting allegations, but it was also correct to recognize that the motion had to be denied unless and until this Court reinterpreted the binding precedent. . . .

. . . [O]ur decision today is intimately tied to the context in which it arose. This litigation involves a party's request under Rule 60(b)(5) to vacate a continuing injunction entered some years ago in light of a bona fide, significant change in subsequent law. The clause of Rule 60(b)(5) that petitioners invoke applies by its terms only to "judgment[s] hav[ing] prospective application." Intervening developments in the law by themselves rarely constitute the extraordinary circumstances required for relief under Rule 60(b)(6), the only remaining avenue for relief on this basis from judgments lacking any prospective component. . . . Our decision will have no effect outside the context of ordinary civil litigation where the propriety of continuing prospective relief is at issue. . . . Given that Rule 60(b)(5) specifically contemplates the grant of relief in the circumstances presented here, it can hardly be said that we have somehow warped the Rule into a means of "allowing an 'anytime' rehearing." . . .

Respondents further contend that "[p]etitioners' [p]roposed [u]se of Rule 60(b) [w]ill [e]rode the [i]nstitutional [i]ntegrity of the Court." . . . Respondents do not explain how a proper application of Rule 60(b)(5) undermines our legitimacy. Instead, respondents focus on the harm occasioned if we were to overrule *Aguilar.* But as discussed above, we do no violence to the doctrine of *stare decisis* when we recognize bona fide changes in our decisional law. And in those circumstances, we do no violence to the legitimacy we derive from reliance on that doctrine. . . .

As a final matter, we see no reason to wait for a "better vehicle" in which to evaluate the impact of subsequent cases on *Aguilar's* continued vitality. To evaluate the Rule 60(b)(5) motion properly before us today in no way undermines "integrity in the interpretation of procedural rules" or signals any departure from "the responsive, non agenda setting character of this Court." . . . Indeed, under these circumstances, it would be particularly inequitable for us to bide our time waiting for another case to arise while the city of New York labors under a continuing injunction forcing it to spend millions of dollars on mobile instructional units and leased sites when it could instead be spending that money to give economically disadvantaged children a better chance at success in life by means of a program that is perfectly consistent with the Establishment Clause.

For these reasons, we reverse the judgment of the Court of Appeals and remand to the District Court with instructions to vacate its September 26, 1985, order.

Justice Souter, with whom **Justice Stevens** and **Justice Ginsburg** join, and with whom **Justice Breyer** joins as to Part II, dissenting.

In this novel proceeding, petitioners seek relief from an injunction the District Court entered 12 years ago to implement our decision in *Aguilar v. Felton.* . . . [T]he Court's holding that petitioners are entitled to relief under Rule 60(b) is seriously mistaken. The Court's misapplication of the rule is tied to its equally erroneous reading of our more recent Establishment Clause cases, which the Court describes as having rejected the underpinnings of *Aguilar* and portions of *Aguilar's* companion case, *School Dist. of Grand Rapids v. Ball,* . . . (1985). The result is to repudiate the very reasonable line drawn in *Aguilar* and *Ball,* and to authorize direct state aid to religious institutions on an unparalleled scale, in violation of the Establishment Clause's central prohibition against religious subsidies by the government. . . .

. . . I believe *Aguilar* was a correct and sensible decision, and my only reservation about its opinion is that the emphasis on the excessive entanglement produced by monitoring religious instructional content obscured those facts that independently called for the application of two central tenets of Establishment Clause jurisprudence. The State is forbidden to subsidize religion directly and is just as surely forbidden to act in any way that could reasonably be viewed as religious endorsement. . . .

These principles were violated by the programs at issue in *Aguilar* and *Ball,* as a consequence of several significant features common to both Title I, as implemented in New York City before *Aguilar,* and the Grand Rapids Shared Time program: each provided classes on the premises of the religious schools, covering a wide range of subjects including some at the core of primary and secondary education, like reading and mathematics; while their services were termed "supplemental," the programs and their instructors necessarily assumed responsibility for teaching subjects that the religious schools would otherwise have been obligated to provide; the public employees carrying out the programs had broad responsibilities involving the exercise of considerable discretion; while the programs offered aid to nonpublic school students generally (and Title I went to public school students as well), participation by religious school students in each program was extensive; and, finally, aid under Title I and Shared Time flowed directly to the schools in the form of classes and programs, as distinct from indirect aid that reaches schools only as a result of independent private choice. . . .

What, therefore, was significant in *Aguilar* and *Ball* about the placement of state paid teachers into the physical and social settings of the religious schools was not only the consequent temptation of some of those teachers to reflect the schools' religious missions in the rhetoric of their instruction, with a resulting need for monitoring and the certainty of entanglement. . . . What was so remarkable was that the schemes in issue assumed a teaching responsibility indistinguishable from the responsibility of the schools themselves. The obligation of primary and secondary schools to teach reading necessarily extends to teaching those who are having a hard time at it, and the same is true of math. Calling some classes remedial does not distinguish their subjects from the schools' basic subjects, however inadequately the schools may have been addressing them.

What was true of the Title I scheme as struck down in *Aguilar* will be just as true when New York reverts to the old practices with the Court's approval after today. There is simply no line that can be drawn between the instruc-

tion paid for at taxpayers' expense and the instruction in any subject that is not identified as formally religious. While it would be an obvious sham, say, to channel cash to religious schools to be credited only against the expense of "secular" instruction, the line between "supplemental" and general education is likewise impossible to draw. If a State may constitutionally enter the schools to teach in the manner in question, it must in constitutional principle be free to assume, or assume payment for, the entire cost of instruction provided in any ostensibly secular subject in any religious school. . . .

. . . [T]he object of Title I is worthy without doubt, and the cost of compliance is high. In the short run there is much that is genuinely unfortunate about the administration of the scheme under *Aguilar*'s rule. But constitutional lines have to be drawn, and on one side of every one of them is an otherwise sympathetic case that provokes impatience with the Constitution and with the line. But constitutional lines are the price of constitutional government.

Justice Ginsburg, with whom **Justice Stevens, Justice Souter,** and **Justice Breyer** join, dissenting.

The Court today finds a way to rehear a legal question decided in respondents' favor in this very case some 12 years ago. . . . Subsequent decisions, the majority says, have undermined *Aguilar* and justify our immediate reconsideration. This Court's Rules do not countenance the rehearing here granted. For good reason, a proper application of those rules and the Federal Rules of Civil Procedure would lead us to defer reconsideration of *Aguilar* until we are presented with the issue in another case. . . .

Unlike the majority, I find just cause to await the arrival of . . . another case in which our review appropriately may be sought, before deciding whether *Aguilar* should remain the law of the land. That cause lies in the maintenance of integrity in the interpretation of procedural rules, preservation of the responsive, non agenda setting character of this Court, and avoidance of invitations to reconsider old cases based on "speculat[ions] on chances from changes in [the Court's membership]." . . .

Case

MARSH V. CHAMBERS

463 U.S. 783; 103 S.Ct. 3330; 77 L.Ed. 2d. 1019 (1983)
Vote: 6–3

Here the Court considers whether a state legislature's practice of opening each legislative day with a prayer by a chaplain paid from public funds violates the Establishment Clause.

Chief Justice Burger delivered the opinion of the Court.

. . . The Nebraska Legislature begins each of its sessions with a prayer offered by a chaplain who is chosen biennially by the Executive Board of the Legislative Council and paid out of public funds. Robert E. Palmer, a Presbyterian minister, has served as chaplain since 1965 at a salary of $319.75 per month for each month the legislature is in session.

Ernest Chambers is a member of the Nebraska Legislature and a taxpayer of Nebraska. Claiming that the Nebraska Legislature's chaplaincy practice violates the Establishment Clause of the First Amendment, he brought this action . . . seeking to enjoin enforcement of the practice. After denying a motion to dismiss on the ground of legislative immunity, the District Court held that the Establishment Clause was not breached by the prayers, but was violated by paying the chaplain from public funds. . . . It therefore enjoined the legislature from using public funds to pay the chaplain; it declined to enjoin the policy of beginning sessions with prayers. . . .

Applying the three-part test of *Lemon v. Kurtzman*, . . . the [Court of Appeals] held that the chaplaincy practice violated all three elements of the test: the purpose and primary effect of selecting the same minister for 16 years and publishing his prayers was to promote a particular religious expression; use of state money for compensation and publication led to entanglement. . . . Accordingly, the Court of Appeals modified the District Court's injunction and prohibited the State from engaging in any aspect of its established chaplaincy practice.

We granted certiorari limited to the challenge to the practice of opening sessions with prayers by a state-employed clergyman, . . . and we reverse.

The opening of sessions of legislative and other deliberative public bodies with prayer is deeply embedded in the history and tradition of this country. From colonial times through the founding of the Republic and ever since, the practice of legislative prayer has coexisted with the principles of disestablishment and religious freedom. In the very courtrooms in which the United States District Judge and later three Circuit Judges heard and decided this case, the proceedings opened with an announcement that concluded, "God save the United States and this Honorable Court." The same invocation occurs at all sessions of this Court.

The tradition in many of the colonies was, of course, linked to an established church, but the Continental Congress, beginning in 1774, adopted the traditional procedure of opening its sessions with a prayer offered by a paid chaplain. . . . Although prayers were not offered during the Constitutional Convention, the First Congress, as one of its early items of business, adopted the policy of selecting a chaplain to open each session with prayer. Thus on April 7, 1789, the Senate appointed a committee "to take under consideration the manner of electing Chaplains." . . . On April 9, 1789, a similar committee was appointed by the House of Representatives. On April 25, 1789, the Senate elected its first chaplain, . . . the House followed suit on May 1, 1789. . . . A statute providing for the payment of these chaplains was enacted into law on Sept. 22, 1789. . . .

On Sept. 25, 1789, three days after Congress authorized the appointment of paid chaplains, final agreement was reached on the language of the Bill of Rights. . . . Clearly the men who wrote the First Amendment Religion Clauses did not view paid legislative chaplains and opening prayers as a violation of that Amendment, for the practice of opening sessions with prayer has continued without interruption ever since that early session of Congress. It has also been followed consistently in most of the states, including Nebraska, where the institution of opening legislative sessions with prayer was adopted even before the State attained statehood. . . .

Standing alone, historical patterns cannot justify contemporary violations of constitutional guarantees, but there is far more here than simply historical patterns. In this context, historical evidence sheds light not only on what the draftsmen intended the Establishment Clause to mean, but also on how they thought that clause applied to the practice authorized by the First Congress—their actions reveal their intent. . . .

In *Walz v. Tax Comm'n.* [1970], . . . we considered the weight to be accorded to history:

> It is obviously correct that no one acquires a vested or protected right in violation of the Constitution by long use, even when that span of time covers our entire national existence and indeed predates it. Yet an unbroken practice . . . is not something to be lightly cast aside.

No more is Nebraska's practice of over a century, consistent with two centuries of national practice, to be cast aside. . . . In applying the First Amendment to the states through the Fourteenth Amendment, . . . it would be incongruous to interpret that clause as imposing more stringent First Amendment limits on the States than the draftsmen imposed on the Federal Government.

This unique history leads us to accept the interpretation of the First Amendment draftsmen who saw no real threat to the Establishment Clause arising from a practice of prayer similar to that now challenged. . . .

In light of the unambiguous and unbroken history of more than 200 years, there can be no doubt that the practice of opening legislative sessions with prayer has become part of the fabric of our society. To invoke Divine guidance on a public body entrusted with making the laws is not, in these circumstances, an "establishment" of religion or a step toward establishment; it is simply a tolerable acknowledgement of beliefs widely held among the people of this country. As Justice Douglas observed, "[w]e are a religious people whose institutions presuppose a Supreme Being." . . .

We turn then to the question of whether any features of the Nebraska practice violate the Establishment Clause. Beyond the bare fact that a prayer is offered, three points have been made: first, that a clergyman of only one denomination—Presbyterian—has been selected for 16 years; second, that the chaplain is paid at public expense; and third, that the prayers are in the Judeo-Christian tradition. Weighed against the historical background, these factors do not serve to invalidate Nebraska's practice.

The Court of Appeals was concerned that Palmer's long tenure has the effect of giving preference to his religious views. We, no more than Members of Congresses of this century, can perceive any suggestion that choosing a clergyman of one denomination advances the beliefs of a particular church. To the contrary, the evidence indicates that Palmer was reappointed because his performance and personal qualities were acceptable to the body appointing him. Palmer was not the only clergyman heard by the Legislature; guest chaplains have officiated at the request of various legislators and as substitutes during Palmer's absences. . . . Absent proof that the chaplain's reappointment stemmed from an impermissible motive, we conclude that his long tenure does not in itself conflict with the Establishment Clause.

Nor is the compensation of the chaplain from public funds a reason to invalidate the Nebraska Legislature's chaplaincy; remuneration is grounded in historic practice initiated . . . by the same Congress that adopted the Establishment Clause of the First Amendment. . . . The content of the prayer is not of concern to judges where, as here, there is no indication that the prayer opportunity has been exploited to proselytize or advance any one, or to disparage any other, faith or belief. That being so, it is not for us to embark on a sensitive evaluation or to parse the content of a particular prayer.

We do not doubt the sincerity of those, who like respondent, believe that to have prayer in this context risks the beginning of the establishment the Founding Fathers feared. But this concern is not well founded. . . . The unbroken practice for two centuries in the National Congress, for more than a century in Nebraska and in many other states, gives abundant assurance that there is no real threat "while this Court sits." . . .

The judgment of the Court of Appeals is reversed.

Justice Brennan, with whom *Justice Marshall* joins, dissenting.

. . . The Court makes no pretense of subjecting Nebraska's practice of legislative prayer to any of the formal "tests" that have traditionally structured our inquiry under the Establishment Clause. That it fails to do so is, in a sense, a good thing, for it simply confirms that the Court is carving out an exception to the Establishment Clause rather than reshaping Establishment Clause doctrine to accommodate legislative prayer. For my purposes, however, I must begin by demonstrating what should be obvious: that, if the Court were to judge legislative prayer through the unsentimental eye of our settled doctrine, it would have to strike it down as a clear violation of the Establishment Clause.

The most commonly cited formulation of prevailing Establishment Clause doctrine is found in *Lemon v. Kurtzman* [1971]: . . .

Every analysis in this area must begin with consideration of the cumulative criteria developed by the Court over many years. Three such tests may be gleaned from our cases. First, the statute [at issue] must have a secular legislative purpose; second, its principal or primary effect must be one that neither advances nor inhibits religion; finally, the statute must not foster "an excessive government entanglement with religion." . . .

That the "purpose" of legislative prayer is pre-eminently religious rather than secular seems to me to be self-evident. "To invoke Divine guidance on a public body entrusted with making the laws," . . . is nothing but a religious act. Moreover, whatever secular functions legislative prayer might play—formally opening the legislative session, getting the members of the body to quiet down, and imbuing them with a sense of seriousness and high purpose—could so plainly be performed in a purely nonreligious fashion that to claim a secular purpose for the prayer is an insult to the perfectly honorable individuals who instituted and continue the practice.

The "primary effect" of legislative prayer is also clearly religious. As we said in the context of officially sponsored prayers in the public schools, "prescribing a particular

form of religious worship," even if the individuals involved have the choice not to participate, places "indirect coercive pressure upon religious minorities to conform to the prevailing officially approved religion. . . ."
. . . More importantly, invocations in Nebraska's legislative halls explicitly link religious belief and the prestige of the State. "[T]he mere appearance of a joint exercise of legislative authority by Church and State provides a significant symbolic benefit to religion in the minds of some by reason of the power conferred." . . .

Finally, there can be no doubt that the practice of legislative prayer leads to excessive "entanglement" between the State and religion. *Lemon* pointed out that "entanglement" can take two forms: First, a state statute or program might involve the state impermissibly in monitoring and overseeing religious affairs. . . . In the case of legislative prayer, the process of choosing a "suitable" chaplain, whether on a permanent or rotating basis, and insuring that the chaplain limits himself to "suitable" prayers, involves precisely the sort of supervision that agencies of government should if at all possible avoid.

Second, excessive "entanglement" might arise out of "the divisive political potential" of a state statute or program. . . . In this case, this second aspect of entanglement is also clear. The controversy between Senator Chambers and his colleagues, which had reached the stage of difficulty and rancor long before this lawsuit was brought, has split the Nebraska Legislature precisely on issues of religion and religious conformity. . . . The record in this case also reports a series of instances, involving legislators other than Senator Chambers, in which invocations by Reverend Palmer and others led to controversy along religious lines. And in general, the history of legislative prayer has been far more eventful—and divisive—than a hasty reading of the Court's opinion might indicate.

In sum, I have no doubt that, if any group of law students were asked to apply the principles of *Lemon* to the question of legislative prayer, they would nearly unanimously find the practice to be unconstitutional. . . .

The argument is made occasionally that a strict separation of religion and state robs the nation of its spiritual identity. I believe quite the contrary. It may be true that individuals cannot be "neutral" on the question of religion. But the judgment of the Establishment Clause is that neutrality by the organs of government on questions of religion is both possible and imperative. . . .

Justice Stevens, dissenting.

In a democratically elected legislature, the religious beliefs of the chaplain tend to reflect the faith of the majority of the lawmakers' constituents. Prayers may be said by a Catholic priest in the Massachusetts Legislature and by a Presbyterian minister in the Nebraska Legislature, but I would not expect to find a Jehovah's Witness or a disciple of Mary Baker Eddy or the Reverend Moon serving as the official chaplain in any state legislature. Regardless of the motivation of the majority that exercises the power to appoint the chaplain, it seems plain to me that the designation of a member of one religious faith to serve as the sole official chaplain of a state legislature for a period of 16 years constitutes the preference of one faith over another in violation of the Establishment Clause of the First Amendment.

The Court declines to "embark on a sensitive evaluation or to parse the content of a particular prayer." . . . Perhaps it does so because it would be unable to explain away the clearly sectarian content of some of the prayers given by Nebraska's chaplain. Or perhaps the Court is unwilling to acknowledge that the tenure of the chaplain must inevitably be conditioned on the acceptability of that content to the silent majority.

I would affirm the judgment of the Court of Appeals.

Case

LYNCH V. DONNELLY

465 U.S. 668; 104 S.Ct. 1355; 79 L.Ed. 2d. 604 (1984)

Vote: 5–4

In this case the Court decides whether the Establishment Clause prohibits a city from including a nativity scene in its annual Christmas display.

The Chief Justice delivered the opinion of the Court.

. . . Each year, in cooperation with the downtown retail merchants' association, the City of Pawtucket, Rhode Island, erects a Christmas display as part of its observance of the Christmas holiday season. The display is situated in a park owned by a nonprofit organization and located in the heart of the shopping district. The display is essentially like those to be found in hundreds of towns or cities across the Nation—often on public grounds—during the Christmas season. The Pawtucket display comprises many of the figures and decorations traditionally associated with Christmas, including, among other things, a Santa Claus house, reindeer pulling Santa's sleigh, candy-striped poles, a Christmas tree, carolers, cutout figures representing such characters as a clown, an elephant, and a teddy bear, hundreds of colored lights, a large banner that reads "seasons greetings," and the crèche at issue here. All components of this display are owned by the city.

The crèche, which has been included in the display for 40 or more years, consists of the traditional figures, including the Infant Jesus, Mary and Joseph, angels, shepherds, kings, and animals, all ranging in height from 5" to 5'. In 1973, when the present crèche was acquired, it cost the City $1,365; it now is valued at $200. The erection and dismantling of the crèche costs the City about $20 per year; nominal expenses are incurred in lighting the crèche. No money has been expended on its maintenance for the past 10 years.

Respondents, Pawtucket residents and individual members of the Rhode Island affiliate of the American Civil Liberties Union, and the affiliate itself, brought this action in the United States District Court for Rhode Island, challenging the City's inclusion of the crèche in the annual display. The District Court held that the City's inclusion of the crèche in the display violates the Establishment Clause, . . . which is binding on the states through the Fourteenth Amendment. The District Court found that, by including the crèche in the Christmas display, the City has "tried to endorse and promulgate religious beliefs," . . . and that "erection of the crèche has the real and substantial effect of affiliating the City with the Christian beliefs that the crèche represents." . . . This "appearance of official sponsorship," it believed, "confers more than a remote and incidental benefit on Christianity." . . . Last, although the court acknowledged the absence of administrative entanglement, it found that excessive entanglement has been fostered as a result of the political divisiveness of including the crèche in the celebration. . . . The City was permanently enjoined from including the crèche in the display.

A divided panel of the Court of Appeals for the First Circuit affirmed. . . . We granted certiorari, . . . and we reverse.

. . . The Court has sometimes described the Religion Clause as erecting a "wall" between church and state. . . . The concept of a "wall" of separation is a useful figure of speech probably deriving from views of Thomas Jefferson. The metaphor has served as a reminder that the Establishment Clause forbids an established church or anything approaching it. But the metaphor itself is not a wholly accurate description of the practical aspects of the relationship that in fact exists between church and state.

No significant segment of our society and no institution within it can exist in a vacuum or in total or absolute isolation from all the other parts, much less from government. "It has never been thought either possible or desirable to enforce a regime of total separation. . . ." . . . Nor does the Constitution require complete separation of church and state; it affirmatively mandates accommodation, not merely tolerance, of all religions, and forbids hostility toward any. . . . Anything less would require the "callous indifference" we have said was never intended by the Establishment Clause. . . . Indeed, we have observed, such hostility would bring us into "war with our national tradition as embodied in the First Amendment's guaranty of the free exercise of religion." . . .

Our history is replete with official references to the value and invocation of Divine guidance in deliberations and pronouncements of the Founding Fathers and contemporary leaders. Beginning in the early colonial period long before Independence, a day of Thanksgiving was celebrated as a religious holiday to give thanks for the bounties of Nature as gifts from God. President Washington and his successors proclaimed Thanksgiving, with all its religious overtones, a day of national celebration and Congress made it a National Holiday more than a century ago. . . . That holiday has not lost its theme of expressing thanks for Divine aid any more than has Christmas lost its religious significance.

Executive Orders and other official announcements of Presidents and the Congress have proclaimed both Christmas and Thanksgiving National Holidays in religious terms. And, by Acts of Congress, it has long been the practice that federal employees are released from duties on these National Holidays, while being paid from the same public revenues that provide the compensation of the Chaplains of the Senate and the House and the military services. Thus, it is clear that Government has long recognized—indeed it has subsidized—holidays with religious significance.

Other examples of reference to our religious heritage are found in the statutorily prescribed national motto "In God We Trust," . . . which Congress and the President mandated for our currency, . . . and in the language "One nation under God," as part of the Pledge of Allegiance to the American flag. That pledge is recited by thousands of public school children—and adults—every year. . . .

. . . This history may help explain why the Court consistently has declined to take a rigid, absolutist view of the Establishment Clause. We have refused "to construe the Religion Clauses with a literalness that would undermine the ultimate constitutional objective as illuminated by history." . . . In our modern, complex society, whose traditions and constitutional underpinnings rest on and encourage diversity and pluralism in all areas, an absolutist approach in applying the Establishment Clause is simplistic and has been uniformly rejected by the Court. . . .

In each case, the inquiry calls for line drawing; no fixed, per se rule can be framed. The Establishment Clause like the Due Process Clauses is not a precise, detailed provision in a legal code capable of ready application. The purpose of the Establishment Clause "was to state an objective, not to write a statute." . . . The line between permissible relationships and those barred by the Clause can no more be straight and unwavering than due process can be defined in a single stroke or phrase or test. The Clause erects a "blurred, indistinct, and variable barrier depending on all the circumstances of a particular relationship." . . .

In the line-drawing process we have often found it useful to inquire whether the challenged law or conduct has a secular purpose, whether its principal or primary effect is to advance or inhibit religion, and whether it creates an excessive entanglement of government with religion. . . . But, we have repeatedly emphasized our unwillingness to be confined to any single test or criterion in this sensitive area. . . .

In this case, the focus of our inquiry must be on the crèche in the context of the Christmas season. . . . Focus exclusively on the religious component of any activity would inevitably lead to its invalidation under the Establishment Clause. . . .

The narrow question is whether there is a secular purpose for Pawtucket's display of the crèche. The display is sponsored by the City to celebrate the Holiday and to depict the origins of that Holiday. These are legitimate secular purposes. The District Court's inference, drawn from the religious nature of the crèche, that the City has no secular purpose was, on this record, clearly erroneous.

The District Court found that the primary effect of including the crèche is to confer a substantial and impermissible benefit on religion in general and on the Christian faith in particular. Comparisons of the relative benefits to religion of different forms of governmental support are elusive and difficult to make. But to conclude that the primary effect of including the crèche is to advance religion in violation of the Establishment Clause would require that we view it as more beneficial to and more an endorsement of religion, for example, than expenditure of large sums of public money for textbooks supplied throughout the country to students attending church-sponsored schools, . . . expenditure of public funds for transportation of students to church-sponsored schools, . . . federal grants for college buildings of church-sponsored institutions of higher education combining secular and religious education, . . . noncategorical grants to church-sponsored colleges and universities, . . . and tax exemptions for church properties. . . .

We are unable to discern a greater aid to religion deriving from inclusion of the crèche than from these benefits and endorsements previously held not violative of the Establishment Clause. . . .

Entanglement is a question of kind and degree. In this case, however, there is no reason to disturb the District Court's finding on the absence of administrative entanglement. There is no evidence of contact with church authorities concerning the content or design of the exhibit prior to or since Pawtucket's purchase of the crèche. No expenditures for maintenance of the crèche have been necessary; and since the City owns the crèche, now valued at $200, the tangible material it contributes is *de minimis*. In many respects the display requires far less ongoing, day-to-day interaction between church and state than religious paintings in public galleries. . . .

The Court of Appeals correctly observed that this Court has not held that political divisiveness alone can serve to invalidate otherwise permissible conduct. And we decline to so hold today. This case does not involve a direct subsidy to church-sponsored schools or colleges, or other religious institutions, and hence no inquiry into potential political divisiveness is even called for. . . . In any event, apart from this litigation there is no evidence of political friction or divisiveness over the crèche in the 40-year history of Pawtucket's Christmas celebration. The District Court stated that the inclusion of the crèche for the 40 years has been "marked by no apparent dissension" and that the display has had a "calm history." . . . Curiously, it went on to hold that the political divisiveness engendered by this lawsuit was evidence of excessive entanglement. A litigant cannot, by the very act of commencing a lawsuit, however, create the appearance of divisiveness and then exploit it as evidence of entanglement.

We are satisfied that the city has a secular purpose for including the crèche, that the city has not impermissibly advanced religion, and that including the crèche does not create excessive entanglement between religion and government. . . .

. . . Accordingly, the judgment of the Court of Appeals is reversed.

Justice O'Connor, concurring. . . .

Justice Brennan, with whom Justice Marshall, Justice Blackmun and Justice Stevens join, dissenting.

. . . As we have sought to meet new problems arising under the Establishment Clause, our decisions, with few exceptions, have demanded that a challenged governmental practice satisfy the following criteria:

First the [practice] must have a secular legislative purpose; second, its principal or primary effect must be one that neither advances nor inhibits religion; finally, [it] must not foster 'an excessive government entanglement with religion.' . . .

This well-defined three-part test expresses the essential concerns animating the Establishment Clause. Thus, the test is designed to ensure that the organs of government remain strictly separate and apart from religious affairs, for "a union of government and religion tends to destroy government and degrade religion." . . . And it seeks to guarantee that government maintains a position of neutrality with respect to religion and neither advances nor inhibits the promulgation and practice of religious beliefs. . . . In this regard, we must be alert in our examination of any challenged practice not only for an official establishment of religion, but also for those other evils at which the Clause was aimed—"sponsorship, financial support, and active involvement of the sovereign in religious activity." . . .

. . . Under our constitutional scheme, the role of safeguarding our "religious heritage" and of promoting religious beliefs is reserved as the exclusive prerogative of our nation's churches, religious institutions and spiritual leaders. Because the Framers of the Establishment Clause understood that "religion is too personal, too sacred, too holy to permit its 'unhallowed perversion' by civil [authorities]," . . . the Clause demands that government play no role in this effort. The Court today brushes aside these concerns by insisting that Pawtucket has done nothing more than include a "traditional" symbol of Christmas in its celebration of this national holiday, thereby muting the religious content of the crèche. . . . But the city's action should be recognized for what it is: a coercive, though perhaps small, step toward establishing the sectarian preferences of the majority at the expense of the minority, accomplished by placing public facilities and funds in support of the religious symbolism and theological tidings that the crèche conveys. As Justice Frankfurter, writing in *McGowan v. Maryland,* observed, the Establishment Clause "withdr[aws] from the sphere of legitimate legislative concern and competence a specific, but comprehensive area of human conduct: man's belief or disbelief in the verity of some transcendental idea and man's expression in action of that belief or disbelief." . . . That the Constitution sets this realm of thought and feeling apart from the pressures and antagonisms of government is one of its supreme achievements. Regrettably, the Court today tarnishes that achievement. . . .

Justice Blackmun, with whom ***Justice Stevens*** joins, dissenting.

. . . Not only does the Court's resolution of this controversy make light of our precedents, but also, ironically, the majority does an injustice to the crèche and the message it manifests. While certain persons, including the Mayor of Pawtucket, undertook a crusade to "keep 'Christ' in Christmas," . . . the Court today has declared that presence virtually irrelevant. The majority urges that the display, "with or without a crèche," "recall[s] the religious nature of the Holiday," and "engenders a friendly community spirit of goodwill in keeping with the season." . . . Before the District Court, an expert witness for the city made a similar, though perhaps more candid, point, stating that Pawtucket's display invites people "to participate in the Christmas spirit, brotherhood, peace, and let loose with their money." . . . The crèche has been relegated to the role of a neutral harbinger of the holiday season, useful for commercial purposes, but devoid of any inherent meaning and incapable of enhancing the religious tenor of a display of which it is an integral part. The city has its victory—but it is a Pyrrhic one indeed. . . .

Case

WALZ V. TAX COMMISSION

397 U.S. 664; 90 S.Ct. 1409; 25 L.Ed. 2d. 697 (1970)
Vote: 8–1

In this case the Court considers whether a property tax exemption for religious organizations constitutes a violation of the Establishment Clause.

Mr. Chief Justice Burger delivered the opinion of the Court.

. . . Appellant, owner of real estate in Richmond County, New York, sought an injunction in the New York courts to prevent the New York City Tax Commission from granting property tax exemptions to religious organizations for religious properties used solely for religious worship. The exemption from state taxes is authorized by Art. 16, Sec. 1, of the New York Constitution, which provides in relevant part:

Exemptions from taxation may be granted only by general laws. Exemptions may be altered or repealed except those exempting real or personal property used exclusively for religious, educational or charitable purposes as defined by law and owned by any corporation or association organized or conducted exclusively for one or more of such purposes and not operating for profit.

The essence of appellant's contention was that the New York City Tax Commission's grant of an exemption to church property indirectly requires the appellant to make a contribution to religious bodies and thereby violates provisions prohibiting establishment of religion under the First Amendment which under the Fourteenth Amendment is binding on the States.

Appellee's motion for summary judgment was granted and the Appellate Divisions of the New York Supreme Court, and the New York Court of Appeals affirmed. We noted probable jurisdiction . . . and affirm.

Prior opinions of this Court have discussed the development and historical background of the First Amendment in detail. . . . It would therefore serve no useful purpose to review in detail the background of the Establishment and Free Exercise Clauses of the First Amendment or to restate what the Court's opinions have reflected over the years. . . .

The course of constitutional neutrality in this area cannot be an absolutely straight line; rigidity could well defeat the basic purpose of these provisions, which is to insure that no religion be sponsored or favored, none commanded, and none inhibited. The general principle deducible from the First Amendment and all that has been said by the Court is this: that we will not tolerate either governmentally established religion or governmental interference with religion. Short of those expressly proscribed governmental acts there is room for play in the joints productive of a benevolent neutrality which will permit religious exercise to exist without sponsorship and without interference.

Each value judgment under the Religion Clauses must therefore turn on whether particular acts in question are intended to establish or interfere with religious beliefs and practices or have the effect of doing so. Adherence to the policy of neutrality that derives from an accommodation of the Establishment and Free Exercise Clauses has prevented the kind of involvement that would tip the balance toward government control of churches or governmental restraint on religious practice. Adherents of particular faiths and individual churches frequently take strong positions on public issues including . . . vigorous advocacy of legal or constitutional positions. Of course, churches as much as secular bodies and private citizens have that right. No perfect or absolute separation is really possible; the very existence of the Religion Clauses is an involvement of sorts—one that seeks to mark boundaries to avoid excessive entanglement. . . .

The legislative purpose of a property tax exemption is neither the advancement nor the inhibition of religion; it is neither sponsorship nor hostility. New York, in common with the other States, has determined that certain entities that exist in a harmonious relationship to the community at large, and that foster its "moral or mental improvement," should not be inhibited in their activities by property taxation or the hazard of loss of those properties for nonpayment of taxes. It has not singled out one particular church or religious group or even churches as such; rather, it has granted exemption to all houses of religious worship within a broad class of property owned by nonprofit, quasi-public corporations which include hospitals, libraries, playgrounds, scientific, professional, historical, and patriotic groups. The State has an affirmative policy that considers these groups as beneficial and stabilizing influences in community life and finds this classification useful, desirable, and in the public interest. Qualification for tax exemption is not perpetual or immutable; some tax-exempt groups lose that status when their activities take them outside the classification and new entities can come into being and qualify for exemption.

Governments have not always been tolerant of religious activity, and hostility toward religion has taken many shapes and forms—economic, political, and sometimes harshly oppressive. Grants of exemption historically reflect the concern of authors of constitutions and statutes as to the latent dangers inherent in the imposition of property taxes; exemption constitutes a reasonable and balanced attempt to guard against those dangers. The limits of permissible state accommodation to religion are by no means coextensive with the noninterference mandated by the Free Exercise Clause. To equate the two would be to deny a national heritage with roots in the Revolution itself. . . . We cannot read New York's statute as attempting to establish religion; it is simply sparing the exercise of religion from the burden of property taxation levied on private profit institutions. . . .

Granting tax exemptions to churches necessarily operates to afford an indirect economic benefit and also gives rise to some, but yet a lesser, involvement than taxing them. In analyzing either alternative the questions are whether the involvement is excessive, and whether it is a continuing one calling for official and continuing surveillance leading to an impermissible degree of entanglement. Obviously a direct money subsidy would be a relationship pregnant with involvement and, as with most governmental grant programs, could encompass sustained and detailed administrative relationships for enforcement of statutory or administrative standards, but that is not this case. The hazards of churches supporting government are hardly less in their potential than the hazards of government supporting churches, each relationship carries some involvement rather than the desired insulation and separation. We cannot ignore the instances in history when church support of government led to the kind of involvement we seek to avoid.

The grant of a tax exemption is not sponsorship since the government does not transfer part of its revenue to churches but simply abstains from demanding that the church support the state. No one has ever suggested that tax exemption has converted libraries, art galleries, or hospitals into arms of the state or put employees "on the public payroll." There is no genuine nexus between tax exemption and establishment of religion. As Mr. Justice Holmes commented in a related context "a page of history is worth a volume of logic." . . . The exemption creates only a minimal and remote involvement between church and state and far less than taxation of churches. It restricts the fiscal relationship between church and state, and tends to complement and reinforce the desired separation insulating each from the other.

Separation in this context cannot mean absence of all contact; the complexities of modern life inevitably produce some contact and the fire and police protection received by houses of religious worship are no more than incidental benefits accorded all persons or institutions within a State's boundaries, along with many other exempt organizations. The appellant has not established even an arguable quantitative correlation between the payment of an *ad valorem* property tax and the receipt of these municipal benefits.

All of the 50 States provide for tax exemption of places of worship, most of them doing so by constitutional guarantees. For so long as federal income taxes have had any potential impact on churches—over 75 years—religious organizations have been expressly exempt from the tax. Such treatment is an "aid" to churches no more and no less in principle than the real estate tax exemption granted by States. Few concepts are more deeply embedded in the fabric of our national life, beginning with pre-Revolutionary colonial times, than for the government to exercise at the very least this kind of benevolent neutrality toward churches and religious exercise generally so long as none was favored over others and none suffered interference. . . .

It is obviously correct that no one acquires a vested or protected right in violation of the Constitution by long use, even when that span of time covers our entire national existence and indeed predates it. Yet an unbroken practice of according the exemption to churches, openly and by affirmative state action, not covertly or by state inaction, is not something to be lightly cast aside. Nearly 50 years ago Mr. Justice Holmes stated:

"If a thing has been practiced for two hundred years by common consent, it will need a strong case for the Fourteenth Amendment to affect it. . . ." . . . Nothing in this national attitude toward religious tolerance and two centuries of uninterrupted freedom from taxation has given the remotest sign of leading to an established church or religion and on the contrary it has operated affirmatively to help guarantee the free exercise of all forms of religious belief. Thus, it is hardly useful to suggest that tax exemption is but the "foot in the door" or the "nose of the camel in the tent" leading to an established church. If tax exemption can be seen as this first step toward "establishment" of religion, as Mr. Justice Douglas fears, the second step has been long in coming. . . .

The argument that making "fine distinctions" between what is and what is not absolute under the Constitution is to render us a government of men, not laws, gives too little weight to the fact that it is an essential part of adjudication to draw distinctions, including fine ones, in the process of interpreting the Constitution. We must frequently decide, for example, what are "reasonable" searches and seizures under the Fourth Amendment. Determining what acts of government tend to establish or interfere with religion falls well within what courts have long been called upon to do in sensitive areas.

It is interesting to note that while the precise question we now decide has not been directly before the Court previously, the broad question was discussed by the Court in relation to real estate taxes assessed nearly a century ago on land owned by and adjacent to a church in Washington, D.C. At that time Congress granted real estate tax exemptions to buildings devoted to art, to institutions of public charity, libraries, cemeteries, and "church buildings, and grounds actually occupied by such buildings." In denying tax exemption as to land owned by but not used for the church, but rather to produce income, the Court concluded:

> In the exercise of this [taxing] power, Congress, like any State legislature unrestricted by constitutional provisions, may at its discretion wholly exempt certain classes of property from taxation, or may tax them at a lower rate than other property. . . .

It appears that at least up to 1885 this Court, reflecting more than a century of our history and uninterrupted practice, accepted without discussion the proposition that federal or state grants of tax exemption to churches were not a violation of the Religion Clauses of the First Amendment. As to the New York statute, we now confirm that view.

Affirmed.

Mr. Justice Brennan, concurring. . . .

. . . *Mr. Justice Harlan* [concurring]. . .

Mr. Justice Douglas, dissenting.

. . . [There] is a major difference between churches on the one hand and the rest of the nonprofit organizations on the other. Government could provide or finance operas, hospitals, historical societies, and all the rest because they represent social welfare programs within the reach of the police power. In contrast, government may not provide or finance worship because of the Establishment Clause any more than it may single out "atheistic" or "agnostic" centers or groups and create or finance them.

The Brookings Institution, writing in 1933, before the application of the Establishment Clause of the First Amendment to the States, said about tax exemptions of religious groups:

> Tax exemption, no matter what its form, is essentially a government grant or subsidy. Such grants would seem to be justified only if the purpose for which they are made is one for which the legislative body would be equally willing to make a direct appropriation from public funds equal to the amount of the exemption. This test would not be met except in the case where the exemption is granted to encourage certain activities of private interests, which, if not thus performed, would have to be assumed by the government at an expenditure at least as great as the value of the exemption. . . .

If believers are entitled to public financial support, so are nonbelievers. A believer and nonbeliever under the present law are treated differently because of the articles of their faith. Believers are doubtless comforted that the cause of religion is being fostered by this legislation. Yet one of the mandates of the First Amendment is to promote a viable, pluralistic society and to keep government neutral, not only between sects, but also between believers and nonbelievers. The present involvement of government in religion may seem *de minimis*. But it is, I fear, a long step down the Establishment path. Perhaps I have been misinformed. But as I have read the Constitution and its philosophy, I gathered that independence was the price of liberty.

I conclude that this tax exemption is unconstitutional.

10

THE CONSTITUTION AND CRIMINAL JUSTICE

"We could, of course, facilitate the process of administering justice to those who violate criminal laws by ignoring . . . the entire Bill of Rights—but it is the very purpose of the Bill of Rights to identify values that may not be sacrificed to expediency. In a just society those who govern, as well as those who are governed, must obey the law."

—JUSTICE JOHN PAUL STEVENS,

DISSENTING IN *UNITED STATES V. LEON* (1984)

John Paul Stevens: Associate Justice, 1975–

INTRODUCTION

Protecting citizens against crime is one of the fundamental obligations of any government. In the United States, of course, government must perform the function of crime control while respecting the constitutional rights of individuals. Balancing the public interest in crime control against the values of individual liberty and privacy is, without question, the most common problem facing trial and appellate courts today. Many of the nation's courts, especially in major metropolitan areas, are flooded with criminal cases, many of which raise vexing questions of constitutional law. This chapter examines the development of constitutional standards in this extremely important area of the law.

Relevant Constitutional Provisions

The most obvious source of constitutional protection for persons suspected, accused, or convicted of crimes is the Bill of Rights. Numerous provisions of the Bill of Rights bear directly on the administration of criminal justice in the United States. Several restrictions in the original Constitution, together with guarantees in the Fourth, Fifth, Sixth, and Eighth Amendments, were designed to prevent government from subjecting individuals to arbitrary arrest, prosecution, and punishment. Both the national government and the states are prohibited from enacting *ex post facto* laws and **bills of attainder** (Article I, Sections 9 and 10). By contrast, the **habeas corpus** guarantee (Article I, Section 9) applies only to the national government, leaving the preservation of this right in state jurisdictions up to the states themselves. Most provisions of the Bill of Rights, including those pertaining to criminal justice, have been incorporated into the Due Process Clause of the Fourteenth Amendment, thereby making them applicable to the states as well as the national government. (For a discussion of *ex post facto* laws, bills of attainder, habeas corpus, and "selective incorporation" of the Bill of Rights, see Chapter 6.)

SEARCH AND SEIZURE

The Fourth Amendment recognizes a right of personal privacy entitling the American people to protection against arbitrary intrusions by law enforcement officers. The framers of the Bill of Rights were acutely sensitive to the need to insulate people from unlimited governmental powers of **search and seizure.** One of the chief complaints of the American colonists was the power of police and customs officials to conduct "general" searches under the dreaded writs of assistance authorized by Parliament in 1662. In 1761, James Otis reviled the writs of assistance as "the worst instrument of arbitrary power, the most destructive of English liberty and the fundamental principles of law, that was ever found in an English law book" (quoted in *Boyd v. United States* [1886]).

When the 1st Congress considered the Bill of Rights, most state constitutions already contained limitations on government powers in this area. Thus, there was little objection in Congress to the search and seizure amendment contained in James Madison's proposal for a Bill of Rights. After minor changes in language, the Fourth Amendment was adopted:

> The right of the people to be secure in their persons, houses, papers, and effects, against unreasonable searches and seizures, shall not be violated, and no Warrants shall issue, but upon probable cause, supported by Oath or affirmation, and particularly describing the place to be searched, and the persons or things to be seized.

Like many of the broad provisions of the Constitution, the Fourth Amendment raises as many questions as it answers. It is clear that government cannot subject people to unreasonable searches and seizures, but what is meant by "unreasonable"? What exactly is a search? What is the precise meaning of "probable cause"? In our legal system, these are questions for the Supreme Court to answer. Unfortunately for the student, the police on the street, the criminal suspect, and the ordinary, law-abiding citizen, the answers to these questions can be very complicated and confusing.

Reasonable Expectations of Privacy

One of the most difficult problems in applying the eighteenth century language of the Fourth Amendment to modern conditions is determining the scope of the privacy to be protected. Obviously, the amendment prohibits unreasonable searches of one's dwelling. But what about the search of an individual's automobile, motor home, or boat? What about one's telephone conversations, fax transmissions, or e-mail? Are such communications protected by the Fourth Amendment?

In *Olmstead v. United States* (1928), the Supreme Court took a very strict view of the scope of the Fourth Amendment. Roy Olmstead, a suspected bootlegger, was charged with conspiracy to violate the National Prohibition Act. The government's evidence consisted of transcripts of Olmstead's telephone conversations obtained through a wiretap placed outside his property. The agents had obtained no warrant authorizing the wiretap. Although there was no search or seizure of his person or physical property, Olmstead maintained that the Fourth Amendment had been violated. The term *effects,* as used in the Fourth Amendment, could have been interpreted to include telephone conversations, but the Court opted for a narrower construction. Writing for the majority, Chief Justice William Howard Taft stated:

> The reasonable view is that one who installs in his house a telephone instrument with connecting wires intends to project his voice to those quite outside, and that the wires beyond his house, and messages passing over them, are not within the protection of the Fourth Amendment.

Justice Louis Brandeis, along with three of his colleagues, dissented. In one of his most forward-looking opinions, he asserted the need to keep the Constitution relevant to changing technological conditions:

> The progress of science in furnishing the government with means of espionage is not likely to stop with wiretapping. Ways may some day be developed by which the government, without removing papers from secret drawers, can reproduce them in court, and by which it will be enabled to expose to a jury the most intimate occurrences of the home. . . . Can it be that the Constitution affords no protection against such invasions of individual security?

In 1928, the telephone was in fairly wide use; today, it is virtually omnipresent. Perhaps it was this reality that motivated the Supreme Court in 1967 to overturn *Olmstead* in the landmark decision of *Katz v. United States*. Here, the Court reversed a conviction in which government agents, acting without a warrant, attached a "bug," or listening device, to the outside of a public telephone booth from which Charles Katz, a suspected bookie, often placed calls. Writing for the Court, Justice Potter Stewart stated that "the Fourth Amendment protects people—not places."

Adhering to Justice John M. Harlan's concurrence in *Katz*, the Supreme Court has since held that the Fourth Amendment extends to any place or any thing in which an individual has a **reasonable expectation of privacy**. The Court has demonstrated a willingness to consider hotel rooms, garages, offices, automobiles, sealed letters, suitcases, and other closed containers as protected by the Fourth Amendment. On the other hand, the Court has held that there is no Fourth Amendment protection for abandoned or discarded property or for the **open fields exception** that covers the "open fields" around a home, even if that area is private property (see *Oliver v. United States* [1984]).

Use of Thermal Imagers by Police   One of the more interesting problems in this area came to the Court during its 2000 term. In *Kyllo v. United States* (2001), the Court considered whether the use of a thermal imager by law enforcement agents constitutes a "search" within the meaning of the Fourth Amendment. In this case, police had used the device without first obtaining a warrant to scan a home they suspected to be housing an indoor marijuana growing operation. Having discerned the telltale infrared radiation associated with the use of indoor growing lights, and having obtained corroborating information, the police obtained a warrant to search the premises, where they found more than 100 cannabis plants.

The procedure used by police in the *Kyllo* case has been in wide use around the country as part of the national war on drugs. Police and prosecutors typically take the view that the thermal scan is not a search within the meaning of the Fourth Amendment, since it merely collects data on heat that is being released into the public space. In a 5-to-4 decision, the Supreme Court disagreed with this perspective. Writing for the Court, Justice Scalia opined that "[w]here, as here, the Government uses a device that is not in general public use, to explore details of the home that would previously have been unknowable without physical intrusion, the surveillance is a search and is presumptively unreasonable without a warrant." In dissent, Justice Stevens noted that "[a]ll that the infrared camera did . . . was passively measure heat emitted from the exterior surfaces of petitioners home; all that those measurements showed were relative differences in emission levels, vaguely indicating that some areas of the roof and outside walls were warmer than others." In Stevens's view, the police did not significantly intrude on the privacy of the occupants.

The *Kyllo* case is interesting because it shows how changing technology creates new and difficult Fourth Amendment problems. As technology in this area advances, courts will continue to confront such issues.

Probable Cause

The fundamental requirement imposed by the Fourth Amendment is that searches and seizures must be "reasonable." The amendment presupposes that searches will be authorized by warrants, and that warrants will not be issued without probable cause. The Supreme Court has recognized exceptions to the **warrant requirement**, but has for the most part viewed probable cause as an indispensable precondition of a valid search.

Probable cause is a term of art that does not have any precise meaning. The Supreme Court has observed that "probable cause is a fluid concept—turning on the assessment of probabilities in particular factual contexts—not readily, or even usefully, reduced to a neat set of legal rules" (*Illinois v. Gates* [1983]). As interpreted by the Court, probable cause means in effect that for a search to be valid, a police officer must have good reason to believe that the search will produce evidence of crime. According to the Court's decision in *Brinegar v. United States* (1949), officers have probable cause when "the facts and circumstances within their knowledge, and of which they had reasonably trustworthy information, [are] sufficient in themselves to warrant a man of reasonable caution in the belief that an offense has been or is being committed."

The Warrant Requirement

A **search warrant** is simply an order issued by a judge or magistrate that authorizes a search. To obtain a search warrant, a law enforcement officer must take an oath or sign an affidavit attesting to certain facts that, if true, constitute probable cause to support the issuance of a warrant.

In *Coolidge v. New Hampshire* (1971), the Supreme Court invalidated a warrant that was issued by the state's attorney general, rather than by a judge or magistrate. Thus, the Court places great importance on the role of the **neutral and detached officer** in maintaining the integrity of the Fourth Amendment. This amendment also requires that search warrants describe with particularity "the place to be searched, and the persons or things to be seized." This provision reflects the Framers' distaste for the **general warrants** used in colonial America. In *Stanford v. Texas* (1965), the Supreme Court reaffirmed this long-standing distaste for "dragnet" searches when it invalidated a five-hour search of a Communist Party headquarters resulting in the seizure of some 5,000 items, including books by Justice Hugo Black and Pope John XXIII.

Confidential and Anonymous Informants

One of the most controversial questions concerning the issuance of search warrants involves the use of **confidential or anonymous informants.** Police often use tips provided by confidential informants to obtain search warrants that lead to the discovery of incriminating evidence. In *Aguilar v. Texas* (1963), police obtained a warrant simply by swearing that they "had received reliable information from a credible person" that illegal drugs would be found at a certain location. The Supreme Court ultimately invalidated the warrant, holding that an affidavit must inform the magistrate of

> the underlying circumstances from which the informant concluded that the narcotics were where he claimed they were, and some of the underlying circumstances from which the officer concluded that the informant, whose identity need not be disclosed, . . . was "credible" or his information "reliable."

Five years later, the Court reaffirmed this two-pronged test in the case of *Spinelli v. United States* (1969). The so-called *Aguilar-Spinelli* test made it more difficult for police to obtain warrants based on tips from confidential informants. Accordingly, on this issue, as on several others, the Warren Court was much criticized for "handcuffing the police." In 1983, a more conservative Supreme Court under Chief Justice Warren E. Burger abandoned the rigorous *Aguilar-Spinelli* test in favor of a **totality of circumstances** approach that makes it easier for police to get search warrants. In *Illinois v. Gates,* Justice William Rehnquist asserted that the *Aguilar-Spinelli* test could not "avoid seriously impeding the task of law enforcement" because "anonymous tips seldom could survive a rigorous application of either of the *Spinelli* prongs."

Dissenting, Justice William Brennan argued that

> the Court [gave] virtually no consideration to the value of insuring that findings of probable cause are based on information that a magistrate can reasonably say has been obtained in a reliable way by an honest or credible person. I . . . fear that the Court's rejection of *Aguilar* and *Spinelli* . . . "may foretell an evisceration of the probable cause standard."

In 1984, the Court held that the totality of circumstances standard announced in the *Gates* decision was to be given a broad interpretation by lower courts (*Massachusetts v. Upton*). Subsequently, the Court moved beyond *Gates* and manifested an even greater level of permissiveness toward police reliance on anonymous tips (see, for example, *Alabama v. White* [1990]). Critics of these decisions argue that the Court's interest in facilitating law enforcement is eclipsing its traditional concern for the privacy of citizens subjected to police searches.

Execution of Search Warrants

Under federal law an officer is required to **knock and announce** upon arrival at the place to be searched. The purpose of this requirement is to reduce the potential for violence as well as to protect the occupants' right of privacy. In *Wilson v. Arkansas* (1995), the Court decided unanimously that the Fourth Amendment requires police, absent a threat of physical violence or other exigent circumstances, to knock and announce when serving a search warrant at a home. The most striking aspect of the Court's decision was that the opinion was authored by Justice Thomas, who generally takes a pro-law enforcement position in criminal cases. In keeping with his adherence to the doctrine of original intent, Thomas examined the state of the common law at the time the Fourth Amendment was adopted. He concluded that "[a]t the time of the framing, the common law of search and seizure recognized a law enforcement officer's authority to break open the doors of a dwelling, but generally indicated that he first ought to announce his presence and authority." Thomas concluded that the authors of the Bill of Rights intended for the common law knock and announce requirement to be part and parcel of the Fourth Amendment. *Wilson* resolved a conflict among lower courts as to whether the Constitution requires officers to knock and announce—a requirement that many states already observed under their respective constitutions, statutes, or judicial decisions.

One of the reasons police officers resist compliance with the knock and announce requirement is that by announcing their presence, officers risk losing evidence that is easily destroyed or disposed of. In *Wilson,* the Court said that officers facing exigent circumstances could dispense with the knock and announce requirement. But in *Richards v. Wisconsin* (1997), the Court ruled unanimously that states may not create a blanket "drug exception" to the requirement that police officers knock and announce prior to executing a search warrant.

Warrantless Searches

Although the Fourth Amendment clearly indicates a preference for search warrants, the Supreme Court has held that, under **exigent circumstances**, a **warrantless search** may nevertheless be "reasonable." One example of a legitimate warrantless search is the **search incidental to a lawful arrest.** In *Chimel v. California* (1969), Justice Potter Stewart's majority opinion stated:

> When an arrest is made, it is reasonable for the arresting officer to search the person arrested in order to remove any weapons that the latter might seek to use in order to resist arrest or effect his escape. . . . In addition, it is entirely reasonable for the arresting officer to search for and seize any evidence on the arrestee's person in order to prevent its concealment or destruction. And the area into which an arrestee might reach in order to grab a weapon or evidentiary items must, of course, be governed by a like rule.

Consent Searches   An obvious example of a legitimate warrantless search is one based on the consent of the individual whose privacy is to be invaded. It is an elementary principle of law that individuals may waive their constitutional rights; Fourth Amendment protections are no exception. In *Schneckloth v. Bustamonte* (1973), the Supreme Court upheld a **search based on consent** even though the police failed to advise the individual that he was not obligated to consent to the police request. In *Florida v. Bostick,* a highly publicized 1991 decision, the Court upheld the controversial police practice of boarding interstate buses in big-city terminals, approaching persons matching a **drug courier profile**, and asking them for permission to search their belongings. More recently, in *Ohio v. Robinette* (1996), the Court held that police are not required to inform motorists who are stopped for other reasons that they are "free to go" before asking them to consent to a search of their automobile. To determine whether consent was given voluntarily, and knowingly, the Court looks to the totality of circumstances surrounding the search.

Other Justifications for Warrantless Searches Other accepted justifications for warrantless searches include **plain view** (see *Coolidge v. New Hampshire* [1971]), **hot pursuit** (see *Warden v. Hayden* [1967]), **evanescent evidence** (see *Schmerber v. California* [1966]), and **emergency searches** (see *Michigan v. Tyler* [1978]). In each of these examples, compelling exigencies make the warrant requirement itself unreasonable, at least in the view of the nation's highest court.

Automobile Searches One of the most interesting—and most problematic—exceptions to the warrant requirement is the **automobile search.** In *Carroll v. United States* (1925), the Supreme Court upheld the warrantless search of an automobile believed to be carrying illegal liquor. The Court stressed, however, that probable cause was essential to justify a warrantless automobile search. Indiscriminately stopping and searching passing motorists in an effort to discover evidence of crime could never be constitutionally justified.

The case of *Arkansas v. Sanders* (1979) presented the Court with an interesting question. Can warrantless searches of automobiles extend to all the contents of said vehicles, or do police still need a warrant to search luggage taken from the trunk? In *Sanders,* the Court disallowed the search of the luggage, suggesting to some observers that the automobile exception was "in trouble." However, in *United States v. Ross* (1982), the Supreme Court demonstrated otherwise. In a 6-to-3 decision, the Court upheld a warrantless search of a paper bag and a leather pouch found in the locked trunk of a stopped automobile, a search that produced $3,200 in cash and a sizable quantity of heroin. Writing for the Court, Justice John Paul Stevens clarified the legitimate scope of a warrantless automobile search as that "no greater than a magistrate could have authorized by issuing a warrant based on the probable cause that justified the search." Dissenting vehemently in *Ross,* Justice Thurgood Marshall assailed the majority position as "flatly inconsistent . . . with established Fourth Amendment principles." In 1991, the Court went one step further and formally overruled *Arkansas v. Sanders* (see *California v. Acevedo*), removing any lingering doubts about judicial distinctions between searches of automobiles and closed containers found therein. Thus, under current interpretation of the Fourth Amendment, the legitimate scope of a warrantless search, whether of an automobile or any other place, is determined more by the nature of the object of the search than by the nature of the space being searched.

Investigatory Detention

One of the most controversial forms of police search is **investigatory detention.** This type of limited search involves the **stop and frisk** and occurs when police temporarily detain suspicious persons in an effort to prevent a crime from taking place. The seminal case in this area is *Terry v. Ohio* (1968). Here, an experienced plainclothes officer observed three men acting suspiciously. The officer concluded that they were preparing to rob a nearby store and approached them. He identified himself as a police officer and asked for their names. Unsatisfied with their mumbled responses, he then subjected one of the trio to a **pat-down search**, which produced a gun for which the individual had no permit. In this instance, the police officer had no warrant; indeed, he did not have probable cause in its traditional sense. The Court nevertheless allowed the pat-down search on the basis of **reasonable suspicion.** However, given that the "sole justification of the search . . . is the protection of the police officer and others nearby," the Court limited the frisk to "an intrusion reasonably designed to discover guns, knives, clubs or other hidden instruments for the assault of the police officer."

Of course, if police discover contraband or other evidence of crime in the process of performing the pat-down for weapons, such evidence is admissible under a theory analogous to the plain view doctrine. For example, if a pat-down reveals an object in a jacket pocket that the officer believes to be a knife, the officer may retrieve the object. If the object turns out to be a vial of cocaine, that contraband has been lawfully seized. But may an officer retrieve an object that does not appear to be a weapon but does have the characteristics of contraband or containers used to carry contraband? In *Minnesota v. Dickerson* (1993), the Supreme Court answered this question in the affirmative, saying that "the suspect's privacy interests are not advanced by a categorical rule barring the seizure of contraband plainly detected through the sense of touch."

The type of police encounter upheld in *Terry v. Ohio* and numerous subsequent court decisions has come to be known as the "*Terry* stop." Police may stop and question suspicious persons, pat them down for weapons, and even subject them to nonintrusive search procedures, such as the use of metal detectors and drug-sniffing dogs. While a suspect is being detained, a computer search can be performed to determine if the suspect is wanted for crimes in other jurisdictions. If so, then he or she may be arrested and a search conducted incident to that arrest.

Detention Based on "Profiling"   Investigatory detention has become extremely important in the highly publicized "war on drugs," as police officers have been given the power to detain, question, and investigate suspected drug couriers. In *United States v. Sokolow* (1989), the Supreme Court upheld a search and seizure that stemmed from a *Terry* stop conducted at an international airport. The defendant in the case aroused the suspicions of federal Drug Enforcement Administration (DEA) agents by conforming to a controversial drug courier profile developed by the DEA.

United States v. Sokolow is consistent with a host of judicial decisions affording law enforcement officers wide latitude to investigate and detain suspected drug smugglers at international airports. In one widely publicized case, such a suspect was held for sixteen hours while airport security officers obtained a court order permitting a rectal examination of the suspect. During the exam, officers retrieved a plastic balloon filled with cocaine and placed the suspect under arrest. Over the next few days, the suspect passed eighty-eight similar balloons! The Supreme Court upheld the long detention, even though security personnel lacked probable cause to make the initial stop. As in *Terry v. Ohio,* the Court found that there was reasonable suspicion to justify the original detention (*United States v. Montoya de Hernandez* [1985]).

Civil rights groups have long claimed that law enforcement officers target racial minorities in conducting investigatory detentions. They claim that police are much more likely to stop African-American motorists, especially if they are driving expensive cars. They claim that minority pedestrians are more likely be subjected to stop and frisk procedures. They claim that minority travelers are more likely to be searched extensively by customs agents and border patrol officers. A Gallup Poll released in December 1999 found that 56 percent of whites and 77 percent of African-Americans believed that racial profiling was "widespread." Four in ten African-Americans, and three-fourths of young African-American males, claimed to have been the victims of racial profiling.

In the wake of the terrorist attack of September 11, 2001, airport security measures were tightened considerably. Movement of people and automobiles in and around airports was restricted. Existing procedures for searching checked baggage as well as carry-on items, widely deemed to be inadequate after 9/11, were expanded and made more rigorous. Even automobiles entering airport parking lots were subjected to inspections. Americans generally applauded such precautions and few questioned their constitutionality. However, a more difficult problem arose in connection with the investigatory detention of passengers who fit a "terrorist profile" established by the FBI. Arab-American groups claimed that persons (including American citizens) of Middle Eastern descent were being singled out for close scrutiny, detention, and in some instances harassment by airport security personnel. While such practices do raise constitutional concern, one must remember that during times of war courts tolerate greater infringements of civil rights and liberties, as long as such infringements are related to the prosecution of the war or the maintenance of national security. Indeed, the *Korematsu* decision of 1944 (discussed and reprinted in Chapter 3) involved what may be the ultimate example of racial profiling—the relocation of Japanese-Americans on the West Coast after the outbreak of World War II.

Detention of an Automobile Based on an Anonymous Tip The Supreme Court has become increasingly permissive as to what constitutes reasonable suspicion for purposes of investigatory detention. For example, in *Alabama v. White* (1990), the Court upheld a *Terry* stop of an automobile based solely on an anonymous tip that described a certain car that would be at a specific location. Police went to the location, found the vehicle, and detained the driver, Vanessa White. The encounter led ultimately to the discovery of marijuana and cocaine in the automobile. Writing for the Court, Justice Byron White noted that "[a]lthough it is a close case, we conclude that under the totality of the circumstances, the anonymous tip, as corroborated, exhibited sufficient indicia of reliability to justify the investigatory stop of respondent's car." In a dissenting opinion joined by Justices Brennan and Marshall, Justice Stevens observed that under *Alabama v. White,* "every citizen is subject to being seized and questioned by any officer who is prepared to testify that the warrantless stop was based on an anonymous tip predicting whatever conduct the officer had just observed." Clearly, the Court's willingness to permit the detention in *Alabama v. White* stands in sharp contrast to the Warren Court's carefully drawn stop and frisk policy delineated in *Terry v. Ohio.*

Can Police Require People to Exit Their Car during an Automobile Stop? During automobile stops, police routinely request that drivers exit their cars. Sometimes they also request passengers to exit. These practices are justified by the police by the need to protect officers from weapons that might be concealed inside the passenger compartment of a stopped vehicle. In *Maryland v. Wilson* (1997), the Supreme Court noted that in 1994 eleven police officers were killed and more than 5,000 officers were assaulted during traffic stops. Of course, when drivers and passengers are required to exit their automobiles, police often discover contraband or observe behavior indicative of intoxication. Such was the case in *Maryland v. Wilson,* in which a passenger who had been ordered to exit a vehicle dropped a quantity of crack cocaine onto the ground. This evidence was used to secure a conviction for possession with intent to distribute and, ultimately, the conviction was sustained by the Supreme Court.

TO SUMMARIZE:

- The Fourth Amendment recognizes a right of personal privacy entitling the American people to protection against arbitrary intrusions by law enforcement officers.
- The Supreme Court has held that the Fourth Amendment extends to any place or any thing in which an individual has a reasonable expectation of privacy.
- The fundamental requirement imposed by the Fourth Amendment is that searches and seizures must be reasonable. The amendment presupposes that searches will be authorized by warrants, and that warrants will not be issued without probable cause.
- The Supreme Court has recognized exceptions to the warrant requirement, but has for the most part viewed the probable cause requirement as indispensable.
- Examples of legitimate warrantless searches include searches incidental to a lawful arrest, searches based on consent, seizures of evidence in plain view, searches for evanescent evidence, searches conducted during hot pursuit, and emergency searches.
- Police often use tips provided by confidential or anonymous informants to obtain search warrants that lead to the discovery of incriminating evidence. Such tips may or may not constitute probable cause, depending on the "totality of circumstances."
- The Supreme Court has said that, in the absence of exigent circumstances, police officers must "knock and announce" prior to executing a search warrant at a private residence.
- The Court has permitted police officers to subject persons to a "stop and frisk" as long as there is "reasonable suspicion" (a less demanding standard than probable cause) that criminal activity is afoot. This principle also applies to automobile stops and brief investigatory detentions of drivers and passengers.

THE EXCLUSIONARY RULE

In addition to the difficult questions involving police methods of obtaining incriminating evidence, we must also consider the controversial issue of how violations of the Fourth Amendment are to be remedied and deterred. As far back as 1886, in *Boyd v. United States,* the Supreme Court suggested that evidence obtained in violation of the Fourth Amendment should be excluded from trial. In *Weeks v. United States* (1914), the Court made this dictum a formal requirement of criminal procedure in federal courts. Writing for the Court in *Weeks,* Justice William R. Day suggested that the **exclusionary rule,** as it came to be known, was implicit in the requirements of the Fourth Amendment. Day also argued that to allow illegally obtained evidence to be used in a criminal trial would be an affront to the integrity of the judiciary.

In *Wolf v. Colorado* (1949), the Supreme Court held that the Fourth Amendment is incorporated within the Due Process Clause of the Fourteenth Amendment and is therefore applicable to state criminal justice systems. However, the Court refused to apply the exclusionary rule to the state courts, preferring instead to view the rule as a procedural device that the Supreme Court imposed on federal criminal cases by virtue of its **supervisory power** over the lower federal courts. According to Justice Felix Frankfurter's opinion for the Court, considerations of federalism and judicial restraint prohibited the Court from imposing the exclusionary rule on the states.

The Warren Court Expands the Exclusionary Rule

Under *Wolf v. Colorado,* states were free to adopt or ignore the *Weeks* exclusionary rule. Some adopted the rule; most did not. The discrepancy between the rules applicable to state and federal courts gave rise to the **silver platter doctrine.** Federal authorities could (and did) provide illegally obtained evidence to prosecutors in states that did not have the exclusionary rule. Moreover, because the *Weeks* decision applied only to illegal seizures by *federal* authorities, federal prosecutors could use evidence obtained illegally by state and local law enforcement agencies.

In *Mapp v. Ohio* (1961) the Court overturned *Wolf v. Colorado* and extended the exclusionary rule to state criminal prosecutions by way of the Fourteenth Amendment. Writing for the Court, Justice Tom Clark made clear that the exclusionary rule was "an essential ingredient of the Fourth Amendment," which was "vouchsafed against the states by the Due Process Clause" of the Fourteenth Amendment. In dissent, Justice Harlan accused the Court of forgetting its sense of judicial restraint and failing to show due regard for *stare decisis.*

The *Mapp* decision was certainly one of the Warren Court's major contributions to the law of criminal procedure and, accordingly, it remains a very controversial holding. Those who believe the exclusionary rule is merely a judicially created rule have criticized the Supreme Court for extending its supervisory power to the state courts. On the other hand, if the exclusionary rule is implicit in the Fourth Amendment and if the Fourth Amendment is made applicable to the states through the Fourteenth Amendment (see *Wolf v. Colorado* [1949]), then it follows that the exclusionary rule must be respected in state criminal prosecutions.

The Burger Court Curtails the Exclusionary Rule

The Supreme Court under Chief Justice Burger substantially curtailed the application of the exclusionary rule. In *United States v. Calandra* (1974), the Burger Court made its philosophy quite clear: "[T]he rule is a judicially created remedy designed to safeguard Fourth Amendment Rights generally through its deterrent effect, rather than a personal constitutional right of the party aggrieved."

The Court's current approach to cases involving the exclusionary rule is to weigh the perceived costs of its application against the potential benefits of deterring police misconduct. Using this approach, the Court has refused to extend the exclusionary rule to grand jury proceedings (*United States v. Calandra* [1974]) and to federal civil proceedings where evidence was obtained unlawfully by state agents (*United States v. Janis* [1976]). A majority on the current Supreme Court evidently agree with Chief Justice Burger's assessment (dissenting in *Bivens v. Six Unknown Named Federal Narcotics Agents* [1971]) of the social costs of suppressing otherwise valid evidence:

> Some clear demonstration of the benefits and effectiveness of the exclusionary rule is required to justify it in view of the high price it extracts from society—the release of countless guilty criminals. . . . But there is no empirical evidence to support the claim that the rule actually deters illegal conduct of law enforcement officials.

The Good-Faith Exception

Without question, the most important Burger Court decisions on the exclusionary rule were the companion cases of *United States v. Leon* and *Massachusetts v. Sheppard* (1984). In these cases, the Court adopted a limited **good-faith exception** to the exclusionary rule, allowing the use of evidence seized under a search warrant later held to be defective, if the officers were acting in good faith that the warrant was valid. In *Leon,* police officers obtained a search warrant acting on a tip from a confidential informant of unproven reliability. A subsequent search of a residence turned up a substantial amount of illegal drugs. At an evidentiary hearing prior to trial, a judge ruled that the warrant had been wrongly issued and that there was insufficient information to constitute probable cause. The Supreme Court ultimately held that the evidence could nevertheless be admitted against the defendants, because to exclude such evidence would have no deterrent effect on police misconduct. The error was made by the magistrate who issued the warrant, not by the police who were deemed to be acting in good faith. In like manner, in *Massachusetts v. Sheppard,* the Court held that use of the wrong warrant form as authorization for a search in a murder investigation did not render the seized evidence inadmissible. Dissenting in the *Leon* case, Justice Brennan exploded:

> The Court seeks to justify this result on the ground that the "costs" of adhering to the exclusionary rule . . . exceed the "benefits." But . . . it is clear that we have not been treated to an honest assessment of the merits of the exclusionary rule but have instead been drawn into a curious world where the "costs" of excluding illegally obtained evidence loom to exaggerated heights and where the "benefits" of such exclusion are made to disappear with a mere wave of the hand.

It is clear that the intense intra-Court conflict in *Leon* and *Sheppard* stemmed from basic differences of opinion as to the constitutional foundations of the exclusionary rule. If one agrees with Justice Brennan that suppression of illegally obtained evidence is a personal right under the Fourth Amendment, then clearly the exclusionary rule cannot be sacrificed on the altar of cost-benefit analysis. On the other hand, if the rule is nothing more than a judicially created rule of evidence or procedure designed to deter future police misconduct, then the Court is free to apply or dispense with the rule depending on its perceived utility.

The Rehnquist Court reaffirmed the good-faith exception in 1995. In *Arizona v. Evans* (1995) the Arizona Supreme Court had ruled that evidence seized by a police officer who acted in reliance on a police record indicating the existence of an outstanding arrest warrant—a record that was later determined to be erroneous—had to be suppressed regardless of the source of the error. In fact, the error had been committed by the court clerk's office. The U.S. Supreme Court reversed by a 7-to-2 vote. Chief Justice Rehnquist wrote for the Court, saying that the exclusionary rule need apply only where the error is attributable to the police. The *Evans* decision was based squarely on *Leon,* and did not represent a major innovation.

The controversy over the exclusionary rule is far from over. It remains to be seen whether the Rehnquist Court will extend the good-faith exception to warrantless searches involving unintended violations of constitutionally protected privacy. It is important to note, however, that a number of state supreme courts have refused to follow the good-faith exception with respect to interpretation of their own state constitutional protections against unlawful search and seizure.

Civil Suits to Enforce the Fourth Amendment

One alternative to the exclusionary rule is filing a civil suit for damages against the officers who performed the illegal search. This remedy is especially appealing to persons who are the victims of illegal searches or seizures but are not prosecuted for any crime. Such persons have no real alternative to filing a civil suit to obtain redress for the wrongs perpetrated against them. In *Malley v. Briggs* (1986), the Supreme Court allowed civil suits under 42 U.S. Code Section 1983 against police officers who "knowingly violate the law" or act in a fashion that "no reasonably competent officer" would consider to be legal in conducting arrests, searches, and seizures. In the *Malley* case, a Rhode Island state trooper obtained a warrant for the arrest of a prominent couple who were charged with "conspiring to possess marijuana." The warrant was based on a suggestion overheard by police wiretappers that the couple had hosted a marijuana party some three months earlier. The couple was taken into custody, but no physical evidence of any crime was discovered. Consequently, the grand jury refused to hand down an indictment. Not satisfied with this after-the-fact vindication, the couple filed a civil suit for damages against the police officer. The federal district court dismissed the case, holding that a police officer could not be held liable for actions based on a warrant issued by a magistrate. Ultimately, however, the Supreme Court disagreed, underscoring its previous recognition of civil suits as means of enforcing Fourth Amendment rights.

The civil remedy was advanced as an alternative to the exclusionary rule by Justice Felix Frankfurter in the 1949 case of *Wolf v. Colorado*. In a strongly worded dissenting opinion in *Wolf,* Justice Frank Murphy cast grave doubt on the viability of the civil remedy as a realistic alternative. The Warren Court, as reflected in its decisions on the exclusionary rule, apparently agreed with Murphy's assessment. But the civil liability approach was resurrected by Chief Justice Burger in his dissent in the *Bivens* case. Finally, in *Malley,* a majority of the Court found occasion to apply the civil remedy in the context of an outrageous Fourth Amendment violation.

TO SUMMARIZE:

- In *Weeks v. United States* (1914) the Court held that evidence obtained in violation of the Fourth Amendment may not be used in federal criminal trials. In *Mapp v. Ohio* (1961) the Court extended this Fourth Amendment exclusionary rule to state criminal prosecutions by way of the Fourteenth Amendment.
- The Supreme Court under Chief Justice Burger and Chief Justice Rehnquist has substantially curtailed the application of the exclusionary rule. The Court's current approach is to weigh the perceived costs of the rule's application against the potential benefits of deterring police misconduct.
- The Court has adopted a limited good-faith exception to the exclusionary rule, allowing the use of evidence seized under a search warrant later held to be defective, if the officers were acting in good faith that the warrant was valid.

ARREST

An **arrest** entails the deprivation of one's liberty by a law enforcement officer or other person with legal authority. Normally, an arrest occurs when someone suspected of having committed a crime is taken into custody by a police officer. Because an arrest is, in effect, a "seizure," it must conform to the probable cause and warrant requirements of the Fourth Amendment. In *Ker v. California* (1963), the Supreme Court held that the legality of arrests by state and local officers should be determined by the same standards applicable to federal law enforcement officials.

Use of Force by Police in Making Arrests

Since suspects often resist arrest, police on occasion must use force to take a person into custody. The courts have generally recognized that the Fourth Amendment permits police to use only such force as is "reasonable" and "necessary" in effectuating an arrest. In *Tennessee v. Garner* (1985), the Supreme Court held that police officers may use *deadly* force only when necessary to apprehend a fleeing felon and only when "the officer has probable cause to believe that the suspect poses a significant threat of death or physical injury to the officer or others." While most police officers take care to exercise force responsibly, police have committed acts of brutality in numerous instances. In such cases, police officers are subject not only to internal departmental sanctions but also to civil suit and even criminal prosecution under applicable state and federal statutes.

The Arrest Warrant

Arrests are often made pursuant to warrants based on preliminary investigations. An **arrest warrant**, like a search warrant, is issued by a judge or magistrate upon a showing of probable cause. Under some circumstances, however, warrantless arrests are permissible. The most common of these is where police observe someone committing a crime or have direct knowledge of criminal activity. Whether or not it is made pursuant to a warrant, an arrest must be based on probable cause.

The Probable Cause Hearing

As the warrant requirement of the Fourth Amendment implies, the legality of detention after arrest also depends on the existence of probable cause. It follows logically that a person arrested *without* a warrant must be brought *promptly* before a judicial officer for a **probable cause hearing**. This principle had in fact emerged in English common law by the late seventeenth century, long before ratification of the Fourth Amendment in 1791. It was not until 1975 that the Supreme Court, in *Gerstein v. Pugh,* explicitly recognized the probable cause hearing as a Fourth Amendment requirement in cases of **warrantless arrest.** This decision, however, did not specify the maximum time that a person could be held in custody prior to a probable cause determination. In *County of Riverside v. McLaughlin* (1991), the Rehnquist Court adopted a permissive interpretation of the probable cause hearing requirement. In this controversial 5-to-4 decision, the majority, speaking through Justice Sandra Day O'Connor, held that an individual could be detained for as long as forty-eight hours prior to a probable cause hearing without necessarily violating the Fourth Amendment.

In the *McLaughlin* case, the Court balanced Fourth Amendment rights against state interests in administrative convenience and local autonomy. In a sharply worded dissent, Justice Antonin Scalia, generally favorable to law enforcement claims, criticized the majority for going far beyond the Court's prevailing concern that criminals not go unpunished. He argued that the Court had improperly applied the *Gerstein* precedent, repudiating one of the "core applications" of the Fourth Amendment "so that the presumptively innocent may be left in jail." By definition, the failure to find probable cause points to the innocence of the arrestee. According to the many critics of the *McLaughlin* decision, the majority lost sight of this consideration in its apparent zeal to accommodate the practical demands of law enforcement.

TO SUMMARIZE:

- Because an arrest is, in effect, a "seizure," it must conform to the probable cause and warrant requirements of the Fourth Amendment.
- The courts have generally recognized that the Fourth Amendment permits police to use only such force as is "reasonable" and "necessary" in effectuating an arrest.

- Arrests are often made pursuant to warrants based on preliminary investigations. An arrest warrant, like a search warrant, is issued by a judge or magistrate upon a showing of probable cause. Under some circumstances warrantless arrests, like warrantless searches, are permissible assuming there is probable cause.
- A person arrested *without* a warrant must be brought *promptly* before a judicial officer for a probable cause hearing.

POLICE INTERROGATION AND CONFESSIONS OF GUILT

Another of the Warren Court's controversial contributions to the criminal process was its enlargement of protection for criminal suspects subjected to **custodial interrogation.** Clearly, police must have the authority to question suspects in order to solve crimes. But the Supreme Court held as far back as 1897 (*Bram v. United States*) that a coerced confession violates the Self-Incrimination Clause of the Fifth Amendment. Of course, the Self-Incrimination Clause was not incorporated into the Fourteenth Amendment until well into the 1960s. Prior to incorporation, the Court's scrutiny of police interrogation in the states was limited to a broad due process inquiry that examined the totality of circumstances in each case with one eye on the fairness of the defendant's trial and the other on methods of police interrogation.

The traditional test used by the Court was whether a challenged confession could reasonably be deemed to have been voluntary. Subjective voluntariness, however, is extremely difficult to discern, even through direct observation, let alone through appellate hindsight years later. Consequently, the Supreme Court's decisions in this area were often unclear and inconsistent. For example, in the 1944 case of *Ashcraft v. Tennessee,* the Court overturned a murder conviction on grounds that the defendant's alleged confession was coerced because it had been preceded by a thirty-six-hour period of continuous police interrogation. Writing for a six-member majority, Justice Black made no attempt to weigh the effect of this long and intense period of questioning on the suspect. Black simply concluded that thirty-six hours of questioning was "inherently coercive" and that use of the confession violated the Due Process Clause of the Fourteenth Amendment. Justice Robert H. Jackson dissented sharply, pointing out that coerciveness could not be measured simply by reference to the clock. Just over a month later, in *Lyons v. Oklahoma* (1944), the Court, dividing 5 to 4, held to be "voluntary" a confession repeated some twelve hours after the suspect, during incommunicado detention in the dead of night, had been forced to hold in his lap a pan containing the charred bones of his alleged murder victims.

By the 1960s, many believed that another approach to the law governing police interrogation was necessary. The Court's decision in *Malloy v. Hogan* (1964) to incorporate the Self-Incrimination Clause paved the way for a stricter attitude toward interrogation by state law enforcement personnel. A sharp break with the voluntariness approach came in 1964 when the Supreme Court decided *Escobedo v. Illinois*. Here, the Court held that once a police interrogation

> has begun to focus on a particular suspect, the suspect has been taken into custody, the police carry out a process of interrogations that lends itself to incriminating statements, the suspect has requested and been denied an opportunity to consult with his lawyer, and the police have not effectively warned him of his absolute constitutional right to remain silent . . . no statement elicited by the police during the interrogation may be used against him during the criminal trial.

In effect, *Escobedo* adopted an exclusionary rule similar to that of *Mapp v. Ohio* but applied to enforce Fifth and Sixth Amendment rights. Two years later, in *Miranda v.*

Arizona (1966), the Court elaborated on the need for constitutional safeguards to protect citizens from "inherently coercive" police interrogation.

It is obvious that such an interrogation environment is created for no purpose other than to subjugate the individual to the will of his examiner. This atmosphere carries its own badge of intimidation. To be sure this is not physical intimidation, but it is equally destructive to human dignity. The current practice of incommunicado interrogation is at odds with one of our nation's most cherished principles—that the individual may not be compelled to incriminate himself.

The *Miranda* Warnings

To safeguard the immunity against self-incrimination, the Court developed the well-known **Miranda warnings.** Unless police inform suspects of their rights to remain silent and have an attorney present during questioning and unless police obtain voluntary waivers of these rights, suspects' confessions and other statements are inadmissible at trial. When the *Miranda* decision came down in 1966, the Court was harshly criticized, especially by the law enforcement community, for "coddling criminals" and "hamstringing the police." However, the practice of "Mirandizing" suspects soon became standard operating procedure in law enforcement. Today, most people in law enforcement support the *Miranda* decision as a means of professionalizing police conduct and, perhaps more importantly, protecting legitimate confessions from later challenges. As long as the police provide suspects with the warning and avoid coercion, anything said by the suspect can be used against him or her in a court of law. Whereas, prior to *Miranda,* there was something of a presumption against the admissibility of a confession, today the presumption is clearly in favor of admitting confessions as evidence as long as the requirements of *Miranda* have been observed by the police.

The *Miranda* decision is firmly established in the Supreme Court's jurisprudence, as evidenced by the Court's recent decision in *Dickerson v. United States* (2000). In *Dickerson,* the Rehnquist Court was handed a good opportunity to overturn *Miranda* and some Court watchers expected the Court to do just that. Given the Rehnquist Court's generally conservative disposition, and given that *Miranda* is more than any other decision a symbol of the Warren Court's liberalism in the criminal justice area, there was some basis for thinking the Court might abandon this precedent. As it turns out, only two of the most conservative justices (Scalia and Thomas) voted to overturn *Miranda.* Writing for the majority, Chief Justice Rehnquist observed that "*Miranda* has become embedded in routine police practice to the point where the warnings have become part of our national culture."

Although the Supreme Court has reaffirmed the *Miranda* decision, most recently in the *Dickerson* case, it has over the years carved out a number of exceptions that have considerably softened *Miranda*'s impact on law enforcement. As Chief Justice Rehnquist recognized in *Dickerson,* the Court has "reduced the impact of the *Miranda* rule on legitimate law enforcement while reaffirming the decision's core ruling." For example, in *Harris v. New York* (1971), the Court ruled that confessions excluded from trial under *Miranda* could nevertheless be used to impeach the credibility of a defendant who takes the stand to testify in his or her own behalf. Writing for the Court, Chief Justice Burger pointed out that the privilege against compulsory self-incrimination "cannot be construed to include the right to commit perjury."

The Public Safety Exception to *Miranda* In 1984, the Supreme Court created the public safety exception to the requirement that *Miranda* warnings be given before any questioning of the suspect takes place. In *New York v. Quarles,* the Court examined an interesting factual situation. Two New York City police officers were approached by a woman who claimed she had just been raped and that her assailant had gone into a nearby grocery store. The police were informed that the assailant was carrying a gun. The officers proceeded to the store and immediately spotted Benjamin Quarles, who matched the description given by the victim. Upon seeing the police, Quarles turned and ran. One of the police officers drew his service revolver and ordered Quarles to freeze. Quarles complied with the officer's request. The officer frisked Quarles and discovered an empty shoulder holster. Before reading Quarles the *Miranda* warnings, the officer asked where the gun was. Quarles nodded in the direction of some empty boxes and said, "The gun is over there." He was then placed under arrest and given the *Miranda* warnings. Later, Quarles moved to have his statement suppressed from evidence since it was made prior to the *Miranda* warnings. He also moved for suppression of the gun under the **fruit of the poisonous tree doctrine**, which holds that evidence derived from illegally obtained evidence is itself tainted (see *Wong Sun v. United States* [1963]). The Supreme Court allowed both pieces of evidence to be used against Quarles, notwithstanding the delay in the *Miranda* warnings. Obviously, the Court felt that the officers were justified in locating a discarded weapon prior to Mirandizing Quarles. In so holding, the Court created the **public safety exception** to *Miranda*.

The Inevitable Discovery Exception Another exception to the *Miranda* exclusionary rule is based on inevitable discovery of physical evidence that is challenged as the fruit of the poisonous tree. In a macabre case decided in 1984 (*Nix v. Williams*), the Court allowed evidence to be admitted even though it was obtained through the statement of a suspect who had indicated his desire to remain silent until he could meet with his attorney. After one of the police officers involved made a speech emphasizing the need for a "Christian burial" for the victim, the suspect led police to the body of a young girl he had kidnapped and murdered. In allowing the body to be used as evidence, the Court reasoned that the body was not the fruit of a poisonous tree since a search under way in the area would eventually have located the body anyway. Hence, the Court created an **inevitable discovery exception** to the fruit of the poisonous tree doctrine.

Police Deception in Interrogations

The Court has refused to expand the scope of custodial interrogation beyond an actual arrest or significant "deprivation of freedom." In *Oregon v. Mathiason* (1977), the Court allowed the use of a confession obtained by police during voluntary interrogation of a suspect who was not at the time under arrest. An interesting fact in the *Mathiason* case is that the police officer who obtained the confession lied to the suspect about his fingerprints being found at the scene of the crime. Only after this deception did Mathiason confess. Nevertheless, he was not under formal arrest at the time and had even come to the station house unescorted to talk to police. In the Court's view, this was a "noncustodial" situation; hence, *Miranda* did not apply.

In another controversial decision involving **police deception** (*Moran v. Burbine* [1986]), the Court further delimited the scope of the *Miranda* rule. Police arrested Burbine for burglary and later obtained information that linked him to an unsolved murder. Burbine's sister, unaware of the possible murder charge, retained an attorney to represent her brother. The attorney telephoned the police, who assured her that Burbine was not to be questioned until the next day but failed to tell her of a possible murder charge against her client. Despite their assurances to the contrary, the police then interrogated Burbine, failing to tell him that an attorney had been obtained for him and had attempted to contact him. Burbine waived his rights to counsel and to remain silent and eventually confessed to the killing. The Supreme Court found no constitutional violation, holding that Burbine had knowingly, intelligently, and voluntarily waived his rights.

In one of the most significant decisions in this area, *Arizona v. Fulminante* (1991), the Supreme Court disallowed the use of a confession that was obtained by a prisoner who was also a confidential Federal Bureau of Investigation (FBI) informant. Oreste Fulminante, who was suspected of murdering his 11-year-old stepdaughter Jeneane, was incarcerated in federal prison on an unrelated charge. He was befriended by Anthony Sarivola, a former police officer serving time for extortion. Sarivola led Fulminante to believe that he had connections with organized crime organizations and could protect Fulminante from other prisoners who had heard that Fulminante was suspected of killing his stepdaughter. Sarivola insisted, however, that Fulminante tell him what really happened to his stepdaughter. Fulminante then confided in Sarivola that he had indeed taken his stepdaughter on his motorcycle into the desert where, in the words of Justice White, "he choked her, sexually assaulted her, and made her beg for her life, before shooting her twice in the head." Sarivola gave this information to the FBI, which, in turn, passed it along to Arizona authorities. After being released from prison, Fulminante was indicted for the murder of his stepdaughter. Denying his motion to suppress, the Arizona trial court allowed the confession to be introduced and subsequently found Fulminante guilty of first degree murder. In reviewing this conviction, the U.S. Supreme Court found that Fulminante's confession had been coerced. However, the most significant aspect of the Court's decision was its holding that a coerced confession is subject to **harmless error analysis**. Prior to this holding, a defendant was automatically entitled to reversal of his or her conviction if a coerced confession had been introduced into evidence at trial. Under the *Fulminante* decision, an appellate court is permitted to affirm a conviction if it determines that the defendant would have been convicted on other evidence even in the absence of the coerced confession. Note that the Supreme Court found that the use of Fulminante's confession was not harmless error and therefore reversed his conviction. Irrespective of this result, the *Fulminante* decision has been criticized as a further erosion of the constitutional protection against coerced confessions.

TO SUMMARIZE:

- The Supreme Court has long held that a coerced confession violates the Self-Incrimination Clause of the Fifth Amendment as well as the due process requirements of the Fifth and Fourteenth Amendments.
- The traditional test used by the Court was whether a challenged confession could reasonably be deemed to have been voluntary.
- To safeguard the immunity against self-incrimination, the Court developed the well-known *Miranda* warnings. Unless police inform suspects of their rights to remain silent and have an attorney present during questioning, and unless police obtain voluntary waivers of these rights, suspects' confessions and other statements are inadmissible at trial.
- Although the Supreme Court has reaffirmed the *Miranda* decision, it has substantially narrowed the scope of its application. The Court has refused to expand the scope of custodial interrogation beyond an actual arrest or significant "deprivation of freedom." The Court has also recognized a number of exceptions to *Miranda*, including the public safety and inevitable discovery exceptions.

THE RIGHT TO COUNSEL

Historically, the Sixth Amendment right to counsel in "all criminal prosecutions" had meant no more than that the government could not prevent a person accused of a crime from hiring a lawyer if he or she could afford to do so. The Supreme Court moved significantly away from this traditional view in the celebrated Scottsboro case of the 1930s. Here, the Court reversed the convictions of a group of young African-American men who had been sentenced to death in an Alabama court for allegedly raping two white women. During the rushed investigation and trial, conducted in an atmosphere of extreme racial animosity, the defendants were not represented by counsel in any meaningful sense. In *Powell v. Alabama* (1932), the Supreme Court found that the defendants had been denied due process of law in violation of the Fourteenth Amendment. Justice George Sutherland's majority opinion placed great importance on the failure of the trial judge to ensure effective representation and adequate time to prepare a defense.

The *Gideon* Decision

Under Chief Justice Earl Warren, the Supreme Court placed enormous stress on the need for professional representation of persons suspected or accused of crimes. In its *Escobedo* and *Miranda* decisions, for example, the Warren Court was obviously concerned about the absence of defense counsel during custodial police interrogation. In *Gideon v. Wainwright* (1963), the Court overruled precedent and held that the Sixth Amendment **right to counsel** as applied to the states via the Due Process Clause of the Fourteenth Amendment requires states to provide counsel to defendants who cannot afford to hire attorneys on their own. The *Gideon* Court recognized that "in our adversary system of criminal justice, any person haled into court, who is too poor to hire a lawyer, cannot be assured a fair trial unless counsel is provided for him."

In a related case decided the same day as *Gideon* (*Douglas v. California* [1963]), the Court held that a state must provide counsel to an indigent defendant who has a right under state law to appeal a conviction to a higher court. (However, in *Pennsylvania v. Finley* [1987], the Court made clear what had been only implicit in *Douglas v. California*—namely, that "the right to appointed counsel extends to the first appeal . . . and no further.")

Because *Gideon* was made retroactive, it had a tremendous impact on the criminal justice system. For example, in Florida, where the *Gideon* case originated, the state was required to retry hundreds of convicted felons who had not been represented by counsel at their first trials. In many cases, the key witnesses were no longer available, and the state was forced to drop its charges. In the wake of *Gideon,* many states decided it would be more economical in the long run to set up permanent offices to handle indigent defense rather than to have judges appoint counsel ad hoc. Most states now have public defenders to make good on the state's responsibility under the Due Process Clause of the Fourteenth Amendment. Although many state judges, legislators, governors, and law enforcement officers resented the Court's "meddling" in their affairs, the *Gideon* decision has come, like so many other Supreme Court rulings, to be accepted and even praised by state officials.

For the most part, the Burger Court maintained this commitment to providing counsel to indigent defendants. In *Argersinger v. Hamlin* (1972), the Court extended the *Gideon* ruling to cover misdemeanor trials (*Gideon* applied only to felonies). The *Argersinger* decision was ambiguous, however, on the issue of whether misdemeanor defendants were entitled to counsel if they faced possible jail terms or only if their convictions *actually resulted in* incarceration. In *Scott v. Illinois* (1979), the Supreme Court clarified the situation, holding that counsel had to be provided to indigent misdemeanants only if conviction would actually result in imprisonment. Writing for the Court, Justice Rehnquist thus opted for a narrow interpretation of *Argersinger,* arguing that "any extension would create confusion and impose unpredictable, but necessarily substantial costs on fifty quite diverse states."

Effectiveness of Appointed Counsel

One of the most elusive contemporary issues in the right to counsel area is that of **ineffective representation.** As the Court recognized in *Powell v. Alabama* (1932), the right to counsel is useless unless a defendant is competently represented. Until recently, most federal courts followed the **mockery of justice test** in determining the competency of appointed counsel. The question was whether the attorney was so ineffective as to constitute "a farce or mockery of justice" (see, for example, *Edwards v. United States* [1958]). This permissive standard was rapidly adopted by most of the state supreme courts. However, the federal circuit courts adopted different standards of varying strictness. In 1984, the Supreme Court finally standardized the test that courts must follow to comply with the Sixth Amendment. In *Strickland v. Washington,* the Court held that an indigent appellant must show (1) that his or her trial lawyer was less than reasonably effective and (2) that there is a reasonable probability that the outcome of the trial would have been different had counsel been more effective. Obviously, this is a difficult test to meet, allowing for reversal only in cases of egregious incompetence.

Self-Representation

Although decisions such as *Powell v. Alabama* and *Gideon v. Wainwright* stressed the importance of counsel in ensuring a fair trial, the Supreme Court has made it quite clear that a defendant has a constitutional right to refuse counsel, as long as the waiver is made "knowingly and intelligently." In *Faretta v. California* (1975), the Court decided a case in which Faretta, accused of grand theft, requested permission from the trial court to represent himself, arguing that the public defender's office was too busy to provide him with effective representation. The trial judge refused the request and appointed an assistant public defender to represent him. Faretta's conviction was ultimately vacated by the Supreme Court by a 6-to-3 vote. The majority asserted that "[t]he language and spirit of the Sixth Amendment contemplate that counsel, like the other defense tools guaranteed by the Amendment, shall be an aid to a willing defendant—not an organ of the state interposed between an unwilling defendant and his right to defend himself personally."

Although the *Faretta* decision did not produce a rash of **pro se defenses** (those in which the defendant conducts his or her own defense), occasionally a defendant will "go it alone" in the courtroom. One noteworthy example of **self-representation** occurred in the trial of serial killer Ted Bundy in Florida in the early 1980s. Bundy, a former law student, insisted on representing himself, although the trial judge appointed a lawyer to serve as standby counsel. Although most observers believed that Bundy did a reasonably effective job in representing himself, he still claimed on appeal that his conviction was invalid because he had ineffective representation at trial. Not surprisingly, the appellate court was unmoved by this attempt to have it both ways!

TO SUMMARIZE:

- Historically, the Sixth Amendment right to counsel in "all criminal prosecutions" had meant no more than that the government could not prevent a person accused of a crime from hiring a lawyer if he or she could afford to do so.

- In *Gideon v. Wainwright* (1963), the Court overruled precedent and held that the Sixth Amendment right to counsel as applied to the states via the Due Process Clause of the Fourteenth Amendment requires states to provide counsel to felony defendants who cannot afford to hire attorneys on their own.
- For the most part, the Burger and Rehnquist Courts have maintained this commitment to providing counsel to indigent defendants.
- The Court has made it quite clear that a defendant has a constitutional right to refuse to be represented by appointed counsel, as long as the waiver is made "knowingly and intelligently."

BAIL AND PRETRIAL DETENTION

Since persons accused of crime are presumed innocent until proven guilty, it is customary for defendants to be released from custody prior to **arraignment** and trial. Ordinarily, courts require defendants to post **bail** (a sum of money), which is forfeited if the defendant fails to appear in court or flees to escape prosecution. The Eighth Amendment prohibits "excessive bail." The Supreme Court has recognized that the purpose of bail is not to inflict punishment but to ensure that a defendant appears in court. In *Stack v. Boyle* (1951), the Court said that "[b]ail set at a figure higher than an amount reasonably calculated to fulfill this purpose is 'excessive' under the Eighth Amendment." However, the Court has never held that the Excessive Bail Clause is incorporated by the Fourteenth Amendment, leaving the issue of excessive bail in state criminal prosecutions to state constitutions, legislatures, and courts.

It has been a long-standing practice for courts to deny bail to defendants who are deemed especially dangerous or pose an unusual likelihood of fleeing to avoid prosecution. This raises the question of whether the Eighth Amendment implies a right to pretrial release. In *United States v. Salerno* (1987), the Supreme Court answered this question in the negative. Here, the Court upheld the Bail Reform Act of 1984, which permits **pretrial detention** in federal cases where a court determines that the release of a defendant would pose a serious threat to public safety. Writing for the Court, Chief Justice Rehnquist agreed that "a primary function of bail is to safeguard the courts' role in adjudicating the guilt or innocence of defendants" but rejected "the proposition that the Eighth Amendment categorically prohibits the government from pursuing other admittedly compelling interests through the regulation of pretrial release."

The Court's decision in *Salerno,* while applying formally only to federal criminal cases, suggests the validity of state laws denying bail to persons accused of violent felonies, especially where such persons have a record of violent crimes. It is doubtful that the Supreme Court would approve a policy of long-term pretrial detention for defendants accused of nonviolent crimes.

TO SUMMARIZE:

- Because persons accused of crime are presumed innocent until proven guilty, it is customary for defendants to be released from custody prior to arraignment and trial.
- The Supreme Court has upheld the common practice for courts to deny bail to defendants who are deemed especially dangerous or pose an unusual likelihood of fleeing to avoid prosecution.

PLEA BARGAINING

Most books dealing with the rights of the accused focus on problems associated with the criminal trial, such as jury selection, jury verdicts, the "public trial" controversy, and so on. It must be recognized, however, that only a small proportion of criminal cases ever get to trial. In a typical jurisdiction, only about 5 percent of felony arrests result in trials. Many cases are dropped by the prosecution after key evidence has been suppressed on Fourth, Fifth, or Sixth Amendment grounds. Other cases must be dropped because key witnesses cannot be located or made to testify. But the main reason that criminal cases do not often result in trials is the existence of the **plea bargain**, an agreement by the accused to plead guilty in exchange for some concession from the prosecution. This concession might be a reduction in the severity or number of the charges brought, or it might simply be a promise by the prosecutor not to seek the maximum sentence allowed by law.

Conventional wisdom holds that plea bargaining occurs because of the scarce resources allocated to the processing of criminal cases. The criminal trial can be a protracted process. There simply are not enough prosecutors, public defenders, and judges to try all the criminal cases coming into the system. Nor does the public or its elected representatives seem inclined to provide the necessary resources. But even if such resources were miraculously furnished, there is reason to believe plea bargaining would still exist; the evidence indicates that plea bargaining occurs in jurisdictions where scarce resources are really not a problem. In addition, an incentive to plea bargain may be built into the very nature of the criminal justice process. We know that organizations generally try to minimize uncertainties associated with their activities. The defense counsel group is probably no different. Lawyers especially dislike the uncertainty inherent in a trial governed by due process. The legal technicalities associated with proving guilt and the unpredictability of juries make the criminal trial a very uncertain enterprise. Many prosecutors and defense lawyers would rather settle on a plea bargain that is certain than to go into the courtroom and take their chances on losing the case. This suggests that plea bargaining is here to stay.

Nevertheless, plea bargaining has been and will continue to be an object of criticism. Some are offended by what they perceive to be insufficient penalties meted out to criminals through plea bargains. Others are concerned that our historic commitment to due process of law is being sacrificed on the altar of expediency.

The Supreme Court has addressed the issue of plea bargaining in several cases dating from the late 1960s (see, for example, *Jackson v. United States* [1968], *Boykin v. Alabama* [1969], *Brady v. United States* [1970], and *Santobello v. New York* [1971]). Basically, the Court has manifested concern over plea bargaining but nevertheless has recognized its practicality, if not its inevitability. However, the Court has stated emphatically that a trial judge must ascertain that the defendant has made a **knowing and intelligent waiver** of the right to a trial before accepting the defendant's plea of guilty. As the Court noted in *Boykin v. Alabama*:

> [A] plea of guilty is more than an admission of conduct, it is a conviction. Ignorance, incomprehension, coercion, terror, inducements, subtle or blatant threats might be a cover-up of unconstitutionality.

One of the more difficult cases decided by the Court in the area of plea bargaining was *Bordenkircher v. Hayes* (1978). Paul Hayes was indicted by a Kentucky grand jury for writing a bad check. It was not his first offense. The prosecutor informed Hayes that if he did not plead guilty, he (the prosecutor) would return to the grand jury to seek a tougher indictment based on the state's habitual offender statute. The defendant refused to "cop a plea," and the prosecutor carried out his threat. The grand jury handed down the more serious indictment. Hayes was tried, convicted, and sentenced to life imprisonment. Was this threat by the prosecutor constitutionally permissible? Dividing 5 to 4, the Supreme Court ruled that it was, since Hayes was "properly chargeable" under the recidivist statute from the start. Dissenting, Justice Harry Blackmun refused to approve what he perceived as "prosecutorial vindictiveness." In Blackmun's view, Hayes was being punished for the exercise of constitutional rights. The sharp division in *Bordenkircher* underscores the fact that reasonable people, including those trained in the law, can disagree on what offends the "fundamental fairness" required by due process.

TO SUMMARIZE:

- Plea bargaining refers to an agreement by the accused to plead guilty in exchange for some concession from the prosecution.
- The Supreme Court has approved the practice of plea bargaining but has stated emphatically that a trial judge must ascertain that the defendant has made a knowing and intelligent waiver of the right to a trial before accepting his or her plea of guilty.

TRIAL BY JURY

In spite of the pervasiveness of plea bargaining, the **jury trial** still plays a prominent role not only in American legal mythology but also in the day-to-day operation of the criminal justice process. Trial by jury is recognized as a federal constitutional right in criminal and civil cases. Reference to jury trial appears once in the original Constitution and twice in the Bill of Rights. Article III provides: "The Trial of all Crimes, except in Cases of Impeachment, shall be by Jury." The Seventh Amendment requires that "the right of trial by jury shall be preserved" in civil suits. Most pertinent to our concerns is the Sixth Amendment, which states: "In all criminal prosecutions, the accused shall enjoy the right to a speedy and public trial by an impartial jury." Of course, prior to the incorporation of this provision into the Fourteenth Amendment in 1968 (see *Duncan v. Louisiana*), "all criminal prosecutions" meant all *federal* criminal prosecutions. Ever since *Duncan,* however, defendants in both state and federal criminal cases have had a constitutional right to trial by jury. The only exception to the right to jury trial involves misdemeanor trials where defendants face incarceration for less than six months.

The Problem of Pretrial Publicity

Even before the Sixth Amendment right to trial by jury was incorporated into the Fourteenth Amendment, the Supreme Court had occasion to reverse jury verdicts in state criminal cases where the fairness of the trial was prejudiced by excessive publicity. In so doing, the Court used the **fair trial doctrine** under the Fourteenth Amendment, rather than the Sixth Amendment jury trial provision. *Sheppard v. Maxwell* (1966) is an excellent case in point. There, the Court reversed a murder conviction reached in a trial conducted against a backdrop of sensationalistic publicity. The circumstances surrounding the *Sheppard* case are almost comical in retrospect. Local officials allowed Dr. Sam Sheppard's murder trial to degenerate into a circus. The jurors in the case were constantly exposed to the intense media coverage of the case right up until the time at which they began their deliberations. Under these circumstances, the guilty verdict was virtually a foregone conclusion. Concluding that fundamental fairness had been denied, the Supreme Court reversed Sheppard's conviction.

Sheppard v. Maxwell leads one to wonder just what steps can be legitimately taken to insulate a jury from prejudicial **pretrial publicity** in a sensational case. One possibility is to take extreme care in the jury selection process, possibly by increasing the number of peremptory challenges available to the defense and the prosecution (such challenges, while limited in number, do not ordinarily require an explanation by counsel or a ruling by the trial judge). Another common step is to sequester the jury during the course of the trial. Another frequent measure is to postpone the trial until the publicity dies down. A less common approach is a **change of venue**—moving the trial to a locale less affected by the pretrial publicity. Although there is no question about the propriety of these measures, considerable doubt remains as to their efficacy.

Some judges have attempted more drastic means of protecting the defendant's right to a fair trial. One of these is to impose **gag orders** on the press, prohibiting the reportage of certain facts or incidents related to a sensational crime. In *Nebraska Press Association v. Stuart* (1976), the Supreme Court invalidated a gag order imposed by a trial judge to safeguard the rights of a man accused of a brutal mass murder. The Court viewed the order as a prior restraint in violation of the First Amendment's protection of the freedom of the press. The *Nebraska Press* case vividly illustrates the head-on conflict of two cherished constitutional principles: freedom of the press and the right to a fair trial. Although the Court was unanimous in striking down the gag order, Chief Justice Burger's majority opinion left open the possibility that such orders might be permissible under extreme circumstances.

Closure of Judicial Proceedings Another more drastic means of protecting the defendant's right to a fair trial is **closure of pretrial proceedings.** In *Gannet v. DePasquale* (1979), the Court allowed the closure of a pretrial hearing to determine the admissibility of evidence with the consent of both the prosecution and the defense. Writing for a divided Court, Justice Stewart stated that the right to a "public trial" guaranteed by the Sixth Amendment is personal to the defendant, not a general right of public access. Stewart went on to say that any First Amendment right of access by the press was outweighed by the right of the accused to receive a fair trial. In 1980, the Court appeared to alter its position somewhat. In *Richmond Newspapers v. Virginia,* the Court voted 7 to 1 to disallow the closure of a criminal trial. Although there was no majority opinion, the justices seemed to have agreed that the First Amendment prohibits trial closure. The very next year, in *Chandler v. Florida* (1981), the Court allowed television coverage of criminal trials, suggesting that *Richmond Newspapers* was no anomaly. The Court's decision in *Waller v. Georgia* (1984) also suggests a strong commitment to the value of a public trial. In *Waller,* the Court refused to allow closure of a pretrial suppression hearing that had been granted by the trial court over the objection of the accused. Although the Court in *Waller* suggested that extreme circumstances might allow the closure of a pretrial proceeding despite the objection of the defendant, the Court adopted a test that makes it very difficult to justify closure.

Jury Size

Historically, trial juries in the United States were composed of twelve persons, all of whom had to agree in order to convict a defendant. Although this is still the case in most states, some jurisdictions allow for six-person juries in noncapital cases. In *Williams v. Florida* (1970), the Supreme Court approved Florida's use of six-person juries in noncapital cases. Justice White's Opinion of the Court discussed the relationship between jury size and the Sixth Amendment:

> [T]he fact that the jury at common law was composed of precisely twelve is a historical accident, unnecessary to effect the purposes of the jury system and wholly without significance. . . . To read the Sixth Amendment as forever codifying a feature so incidental to the real purpose of the Amendment is to ascribe a blind formalism to the Framers.

Serious questions exist about the factual assertions made by the Court in the *Williams* case. Is it true, as the Court asserted, that "neither currently available evidence nor theory suggests that the twelve-member jury is necessarily more advantageous to the defendant"? Some experts on jury behavior have concluded otherwise. However, in *Ballew v. Georgia* (1978), the Court drew the line on jury size when it refused to permit the use of five-person juries. The Court cited studies to show that "the purpose and functioning of the jury . . . is seriously impaired . . . by a reduction in size to below six members." Thus, state legislatures are free to specify the number of persons to serve on juries in noncapital cases as long as they observe the constitutional minimum of six.

The Unanimity Principle

In *Johnson v. Louisiana* (1972) and its companion case *Apodaca v. Oregon* (1972), the Supreme Court surprised many observers by allowing state criminal trials to depart from the historic **unanimity rule**. In *Johnson,* the state of Louisiana passed a law allowing for convictions by nine votes on twelve-person juries in noncapital cases. Writing for a sharply divided Court, Justice White tried to reconcile nonunanimity with the **reasonable doubt standard** required by due process:

> Of course, the State's proof could be regarded as more certain if it had convinced all 12 jurors instead of only nine; it would have been even more compelling if it had . . . convinced 24 or 36 jurors. But the fact remains that nine jurors—a substantial majority of the jury—were convinced by the evidence. In our view disagreement of three jurors does not alone establish reasonable doubt.

One can argue, as Justice Marshall did in his dissent, that the refusal of three presumably reasonable jurors to sanction a guilty verdict might in and of itself indicate a reasonable doubt as to the guilt of the accused:

> The juror whose dissenting voice is unheard may be a spokesman, but simply for himself—and that, in my view, is enough. The doubts of a single juror are in my view evidence that the government has failed to carry its burden of proving guilt beyond a reasonable doubt.

The Court's decisions in *Williams v. Florida* and *Johnson v. Louisiana* left many observers wondering whether the Court would permit **nonunanimous verdicts** by six-member juries. In *Burch v. Louisiana* (1979), the Court allayed the fears of those who thought it was going too far to facilitate criminal convictions. Justice Rehnquist wrote the opinion for a unanimous Court:

> We agree . . . that the question presented is a "close" one. Nevertheless, we believe that conviction by a nonunanimous six-member jury in a state criminal trial for a nonpetty offense deprives an individual of his constitutional right to trial by jury.

Exclusion of Minorities from Juries

Another problem that has beset the courts with respect to trial juries is the exclusion of women, African-Americans, and other minority groups from juries, especially when the defendants are members of such groups. Although the Court has quite clearly stated that there is no constitutional right of a defendant to have on the jury individuals of his or her gender or ethnic identity, it has also held that the systematic exclusion of such groups is unconstitutional under the Fourteenth Amendment (see *Strauder v. West Virginia* [1879] and *Swain v. Alabama* [1965]). The Court has recognized that a jury should, at least ideally, represent a cross section of the community in order to be completely fair and just to the accused.

One of the more difficult issues in jury selection is the use of the **peremptory challenge** to eliminate prospective jurors on the grounds of race. In *Batson v. Kentucky* (1986), the Supreme Court held that a prosecutor's use of peremptory challenges to exclude African-Americans from a jury trying an African-American defendant constituted a basis for reversal on appeal. Consequently, today in the trial of an African-American defendant, the exclusion of a single African-American juror can be the basis for the trial court to deny the use of a peremptory challenge, if the judge is persuaded that the challenge is racially motivated. In 1991, the *Batson* rule was broadened so that a defendant need not be of the same race as the excluded juror to successfully challenge that juror's exclusion (*Powers v. Ohio*). In the same year, the Supreme Court extended the *Batson* rule to encompass civil trials as well (*Edmondson v. Leesville Concrete Company*).

In *Georgia v. McCollum* (1992), the Court revisited this area of the law and extended the *Batson* rule by holding that a defendant's exercise of peremptory challenges was state action, and that the Equal Protection Clause also prohibits defendants from engaging in purposeful discrimination on the ground of race. As a result of the pronouncements in *Batson, Powers,* and *McCollum,* federal and state courts have reevaluated their views on the exercise of peremptory challenges. In general, trial judges are still vested with broad discretion in reviewing **racially motivated peremptory challenges**, but many trial lawyers have expressed concern that peremptory challenges may become relics in our system of jurisprudence.

Gender-Based Peremptory Challenges   The view that peremptory challenges are on the way out was reinforced by a trend in the late 1980s and early 1990s to restrict **gender-based peremptory challenges**. By 1993 federal appellate courts had issued disparate rulings on the issue. Finally, in *J.E.B. v. Alabama ex rel. T. B.* (1994), the Supreme Court resolved that conflict and held that the Equal Protection Clause of the Fourteenth Amendment prohibits gender-based peremptory challenges. Writing for the majority, Justice Blackmun emphasized the relationship between racially based and gender-based peremptory challenges when he observed that "[f]ailing to provide jurors the same protection against gender discrimination as race discrimination could frustrate the purpose of *Batson* itself."

There may be reason to believe that the Court is retreating somewhat from the *Batson* decision. In *Purkett v. Elem* (1995), the Court held in effect that judges are not required to disallow a peremptory challenge, even if the lawyer making the challenge gives an implausible nonracial explanation for why the juror was excluded.

TO SUMMARIZE:

- Defendants in both state and federal criminal cases have a constitutional right to trial by jury, except in misdemeanor cases where defendants face incarceration for less than six months.

- Trial judges have at their disposal several means of protecting a defendant's right to a fair trial against potentially prejudicial media coverage. These include a change of venue, sequestration of the jury, and postponement of the trial.
- On rare occasions the Supreme Court has invoked the "fair trial doctrine" to limit media coverage of judicial proceedings. However, the Court tends to give the widest possible latitude to freedom of the press in this regard.
- Historically, trial juries have been composed of twelve persons, all of whom had to agree in order to convict a defendant. In recent decades, however, the Supreme Court has upheld state-level variations from the traditional size and unanimity requirements in noncapital cases.
- Although a defendant has no constitutional right to have on the jury individuals of his or her gender or ethnic identity, the Supreme Court has held that the systematic exclusion of such persons is unconstitutional. Since the mid-1980s, the Court has restricted the use of peremptory challenges in accordance with this principle.

THE PROTECTION AGAINST DOUBLE JEOPARDY

The Fifth Amendment provides that no person "shall . . . be subject for the same offence to be twice put in jeopardy of life or limb." This protection against **double jeopardy** has deep roots in the soil of the common law. To allow the government to continue to prosecute a defendant on the same charge, using the same evidence that had previously resulted in acquittal, would seem to violate "fundamental canons of decency and fairness." Yet, in *Palko v. Connecticut* (1937), the Supreme Court held otherwise in refusing to incorporate the Double Jeopardy Clause into the Fourteenth Amendment. This holding has since been overruled (see *Benton v. Maryland* [1969]), and the Double Jeopardy Clause has taken its place among those protections deemed "essential to a scheme of ordered liberty." However, the question of what exactly constitutes double jeopardy remains open. Essentially, the clause prevents the government from attempting to convict the accused of an illegal act after it has once failed to do so. However, there are a number of exceptions to this general rule.

Successive State and Federal Prosecutions

Given our system of federalism, it is possible for one set of actions to lead to separate criminal prosecutions in the state and federal courts. In *United States v. Lanza* (1922), the Supreme Court upheld successive state and federal prosecutions for the same offense, the Double Jeopardy Clause notwithstanding. Writing for the Court in Lanza, Chief Justice William Howard Taft observed:

> We have here two sovereignties, deriving power from different sources, capable of dealing with the same subject matter within the same territory. . . . Each government in determining what shall be an offense against its peace and dignity is exercising its own sovereignty, not that of the other.
>
> It follows that an act denounced as a crime by both national and state sovereignties is an offense against the peace and dignity of both and may be punished by each.

Of course, the *Lanza* decision was rendered prior to the incorporation of the Double Jeopardy Clause in *Benton v. Maryland* (1969). But the Court has held that application of the Clause to the states does not abrogate the dual sovereignty principle articulated in *Lanza*. Were it otherwise, the Court noted in *United States v. Wheeler* (1978), "[p]rosecution by one sovereign for a relatively minor offense might bar prosecution by the other for a much graver one, thus effectively depriving the latter of the right to enforce its own laws."

A good example of a successive prosecution by the federal government after an acquittal in state court is provided by the case of the Los Angeles police officers involved in the videotaped beating of African-American motorist Rodney King in 1992. The California Superior Court's verdict finding the police officers not guilty of criminal misconduct was followed by considerable outrage and large-scale destructive rioting in Los Angeles. Despite the officers' acquittal on state charges, the federal government brought new charges against them for violating King's civil rights. On appeal, the officers argued that the new federal charges were barred by the double jeopardy clause. In *United States v. Koon* (1994), the Ninth circuit rejected this claim, saying that "there is no evidence that the federal prosecution was a 'sham' or a 'cover' for the state prosecution." Ultimately, the defendants were convicted and served time in federal prison.

Mistrials

Another legitimate deviation from the double jeopardy principle occurs in the case of a **mistrial** granted on the request of the defense. Judges often declare a mistrial if some extraordinary event occurs, such as the death of a juror or attorney; if some prejudicial error cannot be corrected; or if a **hung jury** (that is, a jury unable to reach a verdict) results. The declaration of a mistrial, at least on the motion of the defendant, has the effect of "wiping the slate clean," of declaring that no trial took place. Thus, the state's renewal of its prosecution of the accused does not violate the Double Jeopardy Clause.

Confinement of Sexual Predators in Mental Institutions

In *Kansas v. Hendricks* (1997) the Court upheld the Kansas Sexually Violent Predator Act, which permits the state to continue to institutionalize certain sex offenders after they have completed their prison sentences. The Court concluded that the law, which provides for involuntary confinement in mental institutions, did not inflict "punishment" and was therefore beyond the pale of the Double Jeopardy Clause. Justice Thomas wrote the Opinion of the Court, joined by Chief Justice Rehnquist and Justices O'Connor, Kennedy, and Scalia. Dissenting, Justice Breyer (joined by Justices Stevens, Souter, and Ginsburg) argued that the confinement amounted to an unconstitutional *ex post facto* law. The Court, however, rejected this argument on the grounds that the confinement resulted from a civil commitment proceeding, not a criminal prosecution. Ever since *Calder v. Bull* (1798), the *Ex Post Facto* Clause has been limited to criminal punishments. Technically, civil confinement is not criminal punishment, although the result may be indistinguishable from the point of view of the person who loses his freedom. In *Kansas v. Crane* (2002), the Court held that substantive due process (see Chapter 6) prohibits civil commitment of sex offenders unless the state can show that the offender has at least some difficulty controlling his or her impulses. The Court was attempting to make states distinguish between sex offenders who pose real harm to others and those who do not pose such harm after their sentences are completed.

Civil Forfeitures, Double Jeopardy, and Excessive Fines

Federal law provides for the **forfeiture** of real estate and other property used in illegal drug trafficking. In *United States v. Ursery* (1996), the Court held that such forfeitures do not constitute "punishment" for purposes of the Double Jeopardy Clause. Two federal circuit courts had held that the Double Jeopardy Clause prohibits both punishing a defendant for a criminal offense and forfeiting his property for that same offense in a separate civil proceeding. The Supreme Court reversed, with Chief Justice

Rehnquist noting that "Congress long has authorized the Government to bring parallel criminal proceedings and civil forfeiture proceedings, and this Court consistently has found civil forfeitures not to constitute punishment under the Double Jeopardy Clause." In a lone dissent, Justice Stevens relied on the Court's prior decisions in *Austin v. United States* (1993) and *Department of Revenue of Montana v. Kurth Ranch* (1994). In *Austin,* the Court decided that a property forfeiture stemming from a drug crime is subject to limitation under the Eighth Amendment. In *Kurth Ranch,* the Court invoked the Double Jeopardy Clause in striking down a state tax imposed on a quantity of marijuana when the taxpayer had already been convicted of possessing the same contraband. In Stevens's view, these decisions dictated "a far different conclusion" from that reached by the Court.

TO SUMMARIZE:

- Essentially, the Double Jeopardy Clause prevents the government from attempting to convict the accused of an illegal act after it has once failed to do so. However, there are a number of exceptions to this general rule.
- Given our system of federalism, it is possible for one episode of criminal misconduct to lead to separate criminal prosecutions in the state and federal courts.
- The renewal of a prosecution after the declaration of a mistrial does not constitute double jeopardy.
- The Supreme Court has held that civil confinement of violent sexual predators after completion of their criminal sentences does not violate the double jeopardy prohibition.

INCARCERATION AND THE RIGHTS OF PRISONERS

The authors of the Bill of Rights were well aware of the sordid history of torture that characterized criminal punishment in pre-Revolutionary Europe. In *O'Neil v. Vermont* (1892), the Supreme Court said that the Eighth Amendment prohibition of **cruel and unusual punishments** was directed to "punishments which inflict torture, such as the rack, the thumb-screw, the iron boot, the stretching of limbs and the like, which are attended with acute pain and suffering." Yet the Court recognized that the Eighth Amendment also proscribed "punishments which by their excessive length or severity are greatly disproportionate to the offense charged."

Torture is no longer a significant legal issue in this country. Indeed, corporal punishment has been abolished as a penalty for criminal acts. Yet the question of proportionality of punishments and crimes remains a viable problem for contemporary courts of law. In *Robinson v. California* (1962), the Supreme Court held that state courts were bound by the Cruel and Unusual Punishments Clause. Since then, there have been numerous challenges to state sentencing policies as well as the conditions of state prisons.

Mandatory Life Imprisonment

Can imprisonment alone constitute cruel and unusual punishment? The answer to this general question depends on the circumstances of individual cases and the makeup of the Supreme Court at any given time. For example, in *Rummel v. Estelle* (1980), the Court upheld a mandatory life sentence imposed on a man who had committed three nonviolent felonies. In three separate cases over a period of years,

Rummel had been convicted of the fraudulent use of a credit card, forging a check, and obtaining money under false pretenses. Under Texas law, he was adjudged a **habitual offender** and sentenced to life in prison. In a similar case three years later, the Court struck down a South Dakota statute that authorized life imprisonment for habitual felons (see *Solem v. Helm* [1983]). Because the South Dakota law did not provide for release on parole, the Court distinguished this case from *Rummel v. Estelle*. In 1991, the Supreme Court, in *Harmelin v. Michigan,* upheld a life sentence without possibility of parole imposed on an individual for possessing 772 grams of cocaine. Michigan law required the automatic imposition of this sentence on anyone convicted of possessing 650 grams or more of any mixture containing cocaine. In all three of the aforementioned cases, the Court divided 5 to 4, indicating the absence of consensus in this area.

Prisoners' Rights

Because they have been convicted of serious crimes, the inmates in our nation's crowded prison system have lost many of the rights we take for granted. In *Price v. Johnson* (1948), the Supreme Court held that lawful incarceration necessarily requires suspension or limitation of rights. In *Hudson v. Palmer* (1984), the Court reiterated this position, stating: "The curtailment of certain rights is necessary as a practical matter, to accommodate a myriad of 'institutional needs and objectives' of prison facilities, . . . chief among which is internal security." The Court further observed that "these restrictions or retractions also serve, incidentally, as reminders that, under our system of justice, deterrence and retribution are factors in addition to correction."

By definition, prisoners have forfeited their right to live in civil society, to move about freely, to associate with whom they choose, and to make decisions about everyday matters such as eating, sleeping, recreation, and work. Under state and federal laws, many prisoners have also forfeited their right to vote or to hold public office. But they have not been stripped of all constitutional rights and protections. Just which of the many constitutional rights are retained by those confined to prison is still unclear. Judicial restraint dictates that such questions be left open until raised in specific controversies; the Court has yet to decide more than a handful of cases in this area.

Prior to the 1960s, courts appeared indifferent to **prisoners' rights.** The main reason for this was that so few cases were ever filed; for the most part, prisoners were denied access to counsel and the courts. As a result of favorable Supreme Court decisions of the 1950s and early 1960s, however, prisoners began to obtain access to the federal judiciary, using petitions for writs of habeas corpus. Then, in the 1970s, their cases began to reach the level of the Supreme Court. Today, several pronouncements from the High Court guide lower court judges, legislators, and prison officials in dealing with the legal aspects of prison confinement (see, for example, *Cruz v. Beto* [1972], *Procunier v. Martinez* [1974], and *Baxter v. Palmigiano* [1976]).

In *Hutto v. Finney* (1978), the Supreme Court upheld a federal court order imposing a thirty-day limit on the use of **punitive isolation** by a state prison. The case, which began in 1969 under the name *Holt v. Sarver,* involved an Eighth Amendment challenge to the conditions of confinement in the Arkansas prison system, particularly the notorious Cummins Farm. The challenged conditions included corporal punishment and torture; abysmal sanitation, diet, and health care; and an overall atmosphere of violence. The conditions that prevailed at Cummins Farm were not altogether atypical of conditions in maximum security state prisons at the time the litigation began. Today, as a result of increased judicial oversight, such conditions are rare exceptions.

In 1992, the Supreme Court demonstrated continuing solicitude toward prisoners subjected to inhumane treatment. In *Hudson v. McMillian,* the Court held that a prisoner who is beaten maliciously by guards may bring a civil suit to recover damages under a claim of cruel and unusual punishment, even if the injuries sustained are not serious. In one of his first dissenting opinions on the High Court, Justice Clarence Thomas (joined by Justice Scalia) expressed the view that nonserious injury to a prisoner does not rise to the level of cruel and unusual punishment.

Many people, especially prison officials, regard judicial oversight of prisons with disdain. Few observers—beyond prisoners themselves and groups representing their interests—are prepared to lavish praise on the federal courts for their involvement in this area. As a group, prisoners have very little political power and even less public support. Nevertheless, some argue that one of the most important functions of the judiciary is to protect **discrete and insular minorities** who have no effective means of representing themselves in the political process. Certainly prisoners are such a minority. And although they may well deserve harsh punishment, they are nevertheless persons and, as such, are entitled to the applicable protections of the Constitution.

TO SUMMARIZE:

- By definition, persons serving terms of imprisonment forfeit many of their civil and constitutional rights. The Supreme Court has recognized, however, that prisoners retain a few basic substantive and procedural rights. These include access to the courts and to legal counsel and protection against cruel and unusual punishment.
- In recent years the Supreme Court has shown less solicitude for the rights of prisoners and more concern for prison discipline and security.

THE DEATH PENALTY

Although already in decline, the **death penalty** was in widespread use when the Constitution was adopted—not only for murder but also for an array of lesser offenses. The Due Process Clauses of the Fifth and Fourteenth Amendments explicitly recognize, although they do not necessarily endorse, the death penalty, stating that no person shall "be deprived of *life,* liberty, or property, without due process of law" [emphasis added]. In *Trop v. Dulles* (1958), however, Chief Justice Warren indicated that the Cruel and Unusual Punishments Clause "must draw its meaning from the **evolving standards of decency** that mark the progress of a maturing society." By the 1960s, it was clear that public support for the death penalty had diminished substantially. By 1966, public opinion polls were finding that a majority of Americans opposed capital punishment. Reflecting this change in societal attitudes, only two persons were executed in the United States between 1967 and the Supreme Court's decision in *Furman v. Georgia* (1972), which struck down the Georgia death penalty law.

The *Furman* Case

In *Furman v. Georgia,* five justices voted to strike down Georgia's death penalty statute. There was, however, only a brief *per curiam* opinion announcing the judgment of the Court. For the majority's rationale, one had to look at five separate concurring opinions. Two of the five justices—Brennan and Marshall—held that the death penalty itself was cruel and unusual punishment, given the "evolving standards of decency." Throughout their subsequent tenure on the Court, Brennan and Marshall steadfastly maintained the position that the death penalty is inherently unconstitutional (Justice Brennan retired in 1990; Justice Marshall followed suit in 1991).

It should be pointed out that if "evolving standards of decency" have anything to do with public opinion, then the Brennan-Marshall position on the death penalty is difficult to defend. In the years after *Furman,* probably as a result of the increasing salience of the crime problem, the level of support for the death penalty rose steadily; in 2001 more than two-thirds of Americans supported capital punishment. It is therefore difficult to make the "evolving standards" argument unless one is talking about one's own standards! However, it is generally considered unacceptable for judges to impose their personal standards of morality on public policy under the aegis of the Constitution. Thus, Justice Marshall, dissenting in *Gregg v. Georgia* (1976), took the position that "the American people, fully informed as to the purposes of the death penalty and its liabilities, would in my view reject it as morally unacceptable." Justice Marshall's statement was regarded by many critics as arrogant, but it should be admitted that we simply do not know whether Marshall's assertion was correct. His hypothesis is possibly testable through empirical or experimental research; unfortunately, such research has yet to reach fruition.

Of the five justices who voted to invalidate the death penalty in the *Furman* case, Justice Stewart's opinion seems to have been the most influential. For Stewart, the problem with the death penalty was not the punishment itself but the manner in which it was being administered. Trial juries were being left with virtually unfettered discretion in deciding when to impose capital punishment. The result, according to Stewart, was that the death penalty was "wantonly and . . . freakishly imposed." Although Stewart explicitly linked his objection to the Cruel and Unusual Punishments Clause, it seems as though he was making a due process argument: The death penalty was invalid because it was being administered in an arbitrary and capricious fashion.

Gregg v. Georgia: The Court Reinstates the Death Penalty

In the wake of the *Furman* decision, some thirty-five state legislatures rewrote their death penalty laws. Georgia's revamped death penalty statute was before the Supreme Court in the *Gregg* case of 1976. The revised Georgia law required a bifurcated trial for capital crimes: In the first stage, guilt would be determined in the usual manner; the second stage would deal with the appropriate sentence. For the jury to impose the death penalty, it would have to find at least one of several statutorily prescribed **aggravating factors.** Automatic appeal to the state supreme court would also be provided. The appellate review would be required to consider not only the procedural regularity of the trial but also whether the evidence supports the finding of the aggravating factor and whether the death sentence is disproportionate to the penalty imposed in similar cases.

The Court had little difficulty upholding the new Georgia statute, with only Justices Brennan and Marshall dissenting. Thus, after a hiatus of four years, the death penalty was effectively reinstated. Although Justice Stewart's opinion in *Gregg* makes much of the procedural safeguards required by the Georgia law, one suspects that the marked increase in public support for the death penalty that occurred during the four years after *Furman* had at least some influence on the Court's decision to uphold Georgia's revised law. In this, as in other areas, the Court seldom strays far from a clear national consensus. Fortunately for the Court, the restraint demonstrated by several of the justices in *Furman* (by deciding the case on fairly narrow grounds) facilitated the reinstatement of the death penalty in *Gregg* four years later without the necessity of overruling a recent precedent.

Although the Burger Court effectively reinstated the death penalty, it refused to allow states to execute criminals convicted of lesser crimes than first degree murder. In *Coker v. Georgia* (1977), the Court invalidated an attempt to execute a man convicted of rape. Writing for a plurality, Justice White characterized the death sentence for rape as "disproportionate" and "excessive."

Later Burger Court Decisions on the Death Penalty Later decisions of the Burger Court indicated an increasingly permissive stance toward imposition of capital punishment. For the most part, the Burger Court was unsympathetic to challenges to the legal sufficiency of procedures used to impose the death penalty. For example, in *Lockhart v. McCree* (1986), the Court facilitated the use of capital punishment by ruling that potential jurors could be excluded before trial if their opposition to the death penalty was so intense that it would impair their ability to perform as impartial jurors.

One departure from this trend came in the summer of 1986. In *Ford v. Wainwright,* the Supreme Court held that the Eighth Amendment prohibits the execution of a prisoner who is insane. Invoking the "evolving standards of decency" test, the Court asserted that "the intuition that such an execution . . . offends humanity is shared across this Nation." Three years later, though, in *Penny v. Lynaugh* (1989), the Court held that mild mental retardation, in and of itself, is not a sufficient basis to bar the imposition of the death penalty.

The Death Penalty Jurisprudence of the Rehnquist Court

In terms of the death penalty, the Rehnquist Court picked up where the Burger Court left off. For example, In *McCleskey v. Kemp* (1987), the Court upheld the death sentence imposed on Warren McCleskey, an African-American defendant who relied on a thorough statistical study in contending that capital punishment in Georgia was infected by pervasive racial discrimination. The Court took the view that, even assuming the statistical validity of the study, McCleskey had not shown that his sentence was the result of racial discrimination.

The Court Rejects Vagueness Challenges to Capital Punishment Statutes In *Walton v. Arizona* (1990), the Court upheld a state law permitting the trial judge, rather than the jury, to determine the existence of aggravating and **mitigating circumstances.** In this case, the Court also concluded that Arizona's characterization of "heinous, cruel, or depraved" conduct as an aggravating factor was sufficiently specific to meet the requirements of the Eighth Amendment.

Similarly, in *Proctor v. California* (1994), the Court upheld California's death penalty statute against the challenge that it was excessively vague. The 8-to-1 decision, with only Justice Blackmun in dissent, came as a major disappointment to the 383 men awaiting execution on California's death row, many of whom would have been able to challenge their sentences had the Supreme Court decided differently. The challenge was brought by William Proctor, who was sentenced to death in 1982 for the murder of a woman whom he also robbed and raped. Proctor argued that California law failed to give juries adequate guidance in considering the factors that determine whether a given crime should merit a death sentence. In rejecting Proctor's challenge, the Court, speaking through Justice Kennedy, found that the law had a "common-sense core of meaning that criminal juries should be capable of understanding" (see *Tuilaepa v. California* [1994]).

Victim Impact Evidence In the late 1980s, growing concern for the rights of crime victims led some states to enact laws permitting the introduction of **victim impact statements**—statements related to personal characteristics of murder victims and the impact of their murders on family members—at the penalty phase of capital trials. In *Booth v. Maryland* (1987) and *South Carolina v. Gathers* (1989), the Supreme Court declared that the introduction of such victim impact evidence violated the Eighth Amendment. In a dramatic reversal of this position, a more conservative Court in 1991 held that "the Eighth Amendment erects no *per se* bar" to "the admission of victim impact evidence and prosecutorial argument on that subject" (*Payne v. Tennessee*). While victims' rights advocates praised this decision, civil libertarians and defense attorneys objected sharply to what they perceived as an invitation to infuse excessive emotion into the criminal process. In one of the last opinions he wrote before retiring, Justice Marshall, dissenting, delivered a broadside against the Rehnquist Court's disregard of precedent:

> In dispatching *Booth* and *Gathers* to their graves, today's majority ominously suggests that an even more extensive upheaval of this Court's precedents may be in store. . . . The majority today sends a clear signal that scores of established constitutional liberties are now ripe for reconsideration.

The Federal Death Penalty

In May 2001, Timothy McVeigh was put to death by lethal injection for his role in the bombing of the federal office building in Oklahoma City in 1995. In his federal trial, McVeigh was convicted of twenty-eight counts of murder of a federal law enforcement agent on active duty. Under federal law, executions are carried out in the state where the defendant was sentenced, unless that state has no death penalty, in which case the prisoner is transferred to another state for execution. Before the McVeigh execution, the federal government had not executed anyone since 1963.

The Federal Anti-Drug Abuse Act of 1988 allows the death penalty for so-called "drug kingpins" who control "continuing criminal enterprises" whose members intentionally kill or procure others to kill in furtherance of the enterprise. Moreover, the Violent Crime Control and Law Enforcement Act of 1994, better known as the Federal Crime Bill, dramatically increased the number of federal crimes eligible for the death penalty. Capital punishment is now authorized for dozens of federal crimes, including treason, murder of a federal law enforcement official, and kidnapping, carjacking, child abuse, and bank robbery that result in death. It remains to be seen whether the federal courts will permit the death penalty for nonhomicidal crimes. *Coker v. Georgia* (1977) would suggest otherwise.

TO SUMMARIZE:

- The Court has said that the Cruel and Unusual Punishments Clause "must draw its meaning from the evolving standards of decency that mark the progress of a maturing society." Consistent with this perspective, the Court in 1972 in effect invalidated capital punishment as it existed throughout the United States, but left the door open for states to revise their death penalty statutes. In 1976, the Court upheld several such revised statutes, thus effectively reinstating the death penalty.
- Since the late 1970s, the Court has found occasion to set aside particular death sentences, but in general has shown increasing deference to the states in the

implementation of capital punishment. An example of this trend is seen in the Court's willingness to allow the use of victim impact statements in the sentencing stage of capital trials.

APPEAL AND POSTCONVICTION RELIEF

The federal Constitution makes no mention of a defendant's right to appeal from a criminal conviction, although one could argue that such a right is implicit in the concept of procedural due process. In *McKane v. Durston* (1894), the Supreme Court held that there is no such constitutional right. Given the expansiveness of modern notions of due process, it is likely that the Supreme Court would reconsider *McKane v. Durston* but for the fact that Congress and all fifty state legislatures have created statutory rights of appeal. Indeed, a federal defendant's right of appeal is of fairly ancient vintage, having first been granted by the Judiciary Act of 1789. The so-called **appeal by right** granted by federal and state statutes applies to defendants who are convicted over their pleas of not guilty. The only situation in which a defendant who pleads guilty retains the right of appeal is where such a provision is made pursuant to a plea bargain. The prosecution is never permitted to appeal the acquittal of a defendant but may appeal certain pretrial rulings resulting in the dismissal of the case.

The appeal by right is an important means whereby defendants assert constitutional rights alleged to have been violated in their apprehension or in the investigation, prosecution, or trial of their case. The appeal by right thus permits appellate courts to perform the important function of **error correction.** Of course, not all errors constitute the basis for reversal on appeal. Only those errors deemed prejudicial to the accused necessitate reversal; other mistakes are referred to as **harmless errors** (see *Chapman v. California* [1967]).

In 1991, the Supreme Court made news when it decided that, under certain circumstances, the use of an involuntary confession as evidence at trial constitutes a harmless error (see *Arizona v. Fulminante,* discussed earlier). Previously, the use of an illegally obtained confession was considered a sufficient basis for reversal of a conviction, regardless of the strength of the other evidence against the accused.

Beyond the right to one appeal, defendants may petition higher courts to review their convictions, but such review is granted at the discretion of the higher court. In the U.S. Supreme Court and most state supreme courts, **discretionary review** involves the issuance of a writ of certiorari. In essence, the writ of certiorari is issued to the lower court, directing it to provide the record in a given case so that the higher court may conduct its review. The use of this type of discretionary review is usually limited to new and important issues of law, especially where the lower appellate courts are in conflict.

Federal Habeas Corpus Review of State Criminal Cases

A state prisoner who has exhausted his or her appeals in the state courts may petition a federal district court for a writ of habeas corpus. The power of federal courts to issue habeas corpus in state cases can be traced to an act of Congress adopted just after the Civil War (see *Ex parte McCardle* [1869], discussed and reprinted in Chapter 1). Rarely used prior to the 1950s, in the modern era this aspect of federal jurisdiction has played an important role in the development of constitutional law as it relates to the criminal process. In *Brown v. Allen* (1953), the Supreme Court held that state prisoners could readjudicate issues on federal habeas review that had already been addressed in state proceedings. Then in *Fay v. Noia* (1963), the Warren Court further expanded federal habeas corpus by deciding that state prisoners could raise issues in their federal habeas corpus petitions that they failed to raise in state appeals. Moreover, unless it was found that they deliberately abused the writ, there was no limit on the number of habeas corpus petitions state prisoners could file in federal district courts (see *Sanders v. United States* [1963]).

The Warren Court's decision to expand federal habeas corpus helped fuel the "criminal justice revolution" of the 1960s. Federal district courts could look at and correct the state courts' failures to implement the pronouncements of the High Court in such key areas as search and seizure, confessions, double jeopardy, and the right to counsel. Accordingly, one of the strategies of the Burger and Rehnquist Courts' "counterrevolution" in the criminal process area has been to restrict federal habeas corpus review of state criminal convictions.

Judicial Limitations on Federal Habeas Corpus Review   The first significant limitation on federal habeas corpus came in *Stone v. Powell* (1976). There, the Burger Court decided that state prisoners could not use federal habeas corpus petitions to raise Fourth Amendment issues where they had been provided "a full and fair opportunity" to litigate those issues in the state courts. Subsequently, in *Engle v. Isaac* (1982), the Court refused to allow a state prisoner to use federal habeas corpus to challenge a questionable jury instruction to which he failed to object during trial. Other decisions of the Burger Court chipped away at the Warren Court's expansive interpretations of federal habeas corpus relief (see, for example, *Kuhlmann v. Wilson* [1986] and *Straight v. Wainwright* [1986]).

The Rehnquist Court has continued the trend toward limiting access to federal habeas corpus. In *McCleskey v. Zant* (1991), the Court barred Warren McCleskey—whose 1987 appeal is discussed earlier in this chapter and who was still on Georgia's death row in 1991—from filing a second federal habeas corpus petition, holding that he had "abused the writ." In the second *McCleskey* case, the Court held that a state need not prove that a petitioner deliberately abandoned a constitutional claim in his or her first habeas corpus petition for the petitioner to be barred from raising the claim in a subsequent petition. The Court thus moved away from the "deliberate abandonment" standard the Warren Court had articulated in *Sanders v. United States* (1963). In another bitter dissent, Justice Marshall blasted the Court for departing from precedent, saying that "whatever 'abuse of the writ' today's decision is designed to avert pales in comparison with the majority's own abuse of the norms that inform the proper judicial function."

In *Keeney v. Tamayo-Reyes* (1992), the Court overturned *Townsend v. Sain* (1963), in which the Warren Court had held that state prisoners had the right to seek federal habeas corpus relief unless they had deliberately bypassed the state courts.

The Supreme Court's decisions in *McCleskey v. Zant* and *Keeney v. Tamayo-Reyes* came at a time when many in Congress were calling for legislative restrictions on federal habeas corpus. Both the Supreme Court and Congress were responding to a widespread perception that state prisoners were being afforded excessive opportunities to challenge their convictions in federal courts. Indeed, some conservative commentators questioned the need for federal postconviction review of state criminal cases altogether. While federal habeas corpus has been subject to abuse by state prisoners, eliminating this aspect of federal jurisdiction altogether would remove some of the pressure that has led to an increased awareness of and appreciation for defendants' rights in the state courts. Indeed, in the *McCleskey* case the Supreme Court expressed a commitment to the continued efficacy of habeas corpus to prevent miscarriages of justice in the state courts.

In 1993, the Supreme Court handed down two decisions restricting federal habeas corpus review of state criminal convictions. In *Herrera v. Collins,* the Court held that a belated claim of innocence does not entitle a state prisoner on death row to a federal district court hearing prior to his execution. In *Brecht v. Abrahamson,* the Court ruled that federal district courts may not overturn state criminal convictions unless the petitioner can show that he or she suffered "actual prejudice" from the errors cited in the habeas corpus petition. Previously, the state carried the burden of proving beyond a reasonable doubt that any constitutional error committed during or prior to trial was "harmless"—that is, not prejudicial to the defendant. *Brecht v. Abrahamson* had the effect of shifting the burden of proof from the state to the petitioner in a federal habeas corpus hearing.

Congress Modifies the Federal Habeas Corpus Procedure

On April 24, 1996, President Clinton signed into law the Antiterrorism and Effective Death Penalty Act of 1996. One of the provisions of this statute curtails second habeas corpus petitions by state prisoners who have already filed such petitions in federal court. Under the new statute, any second or subsequent habeas petition must meet a particularly high standard and must pass through a "gatekeeping" function exercised by the U.S. Courts of Appeals. A circuit court must grant a motion giving the inmate permission to file the petition in a district court; denial of this motion is not appealable to the Supreme Court. In *Felker v. Turpin* (1996), an inmate awaiting execution in Georgia challenged the constitutionality of this provision, posing two constitutional objections: (1) that the new law amounted to an unconstitutional "suspension" of the writ of habeas corpus and (2) that the prohibition against Supreme Court review of a circuit court's denial of permission to file a subsequent habeas petition is an unconstitutional interference with the Supreme Court's jurisdiction as defined in Article III of the Constitution.

In a unanimous decision rendered less than one month after the case was argued, the Supreme Court rejected these challenges and upheld the statute. In a "saving construction" of the statute, the Court interpreted the law in such a way as to preserve the right of state prisoners to file habeas petitions directly in the Supreme Court. The Court stated, however, that it would exercise this jurisdiction only in "exceptional circumstances." According to Chief Justice Rehnquist, who spoke for a unanimous bench, the fact that habeas corpus relief remains available by direct petition to the Supreme Court "obviates any claim by petitioner under the Exceptions Clause of Article III, Section 2, of the Constitution." Turning to the argument that Congress had, in effect, improperly suspended the writ of habeas corpus, Rehnquist observed that "[t]he new restrictions on successive petitions constitute a . . . restraint on what is called in habeas corpus practice 'abuse of the writ.'" Noting the evolving body of judicial decisions attempting to limit abuses of habeas corpus, the Chief Justice concluded that "[t]he added restrictions . . . on second habeas petitions are well within the compass of this evolutionary process."

Interestingly, in *Felker v. Turpin* the Court managed to sustain what Congress had done while at the same time reaffirming its own statutory and constitutional powers. Note, however, that the provision at issue in *Felker* was but one of several restrictions on habeas corpus petitions embodied in the Antiterrorism Act. Indeed, other challenges to various sections of the law are currently working their way through the lower federal courts. The Supreme Court will likely address these issues in the near future. The enactment of "habeas corpus reform," fully supported by the Clinton administration, and the Court's refusal to invalidate it, indicates the existence of a clear consensus in the national government that "abuse of the writ" of habeas corpus must be curtailed.

TO SUMMARIZE:

- Although there is no constitutional right of appeal in a criminal case, federal and state statutes provide this right to persons who are convicted after having pleaded not guilty.
- Federal law permits federal courts to grant writs of habeas corpus to review state court convictions after all state appellate remedies have been exhausted. The Warren Court expanded this form of postconviction relief, but in recent years Congress and the Court have significantly curtailed federal habeas corpus review.

JUVENILE JUSTICE

At the time of the founding of the United States, children were treated essentially as adults for the purposes of criminal justice. It was not uncommon for teenagers to be hanged, flogged, or placed in the public pillory as punishment for their crimes. Toward the end of the nineteenth century, public outcry against such treatment led to the establishment of a separate justice system for juveniles. Reformatories and specialized courts were created to deal with young offenders, not as hardened criminals but as misguided youth in need of special care. This special treatment was legally justified by the ***parens patriae*** concept: that the state is responsible for caring for those incapable of caring for themselves. The newly created juvenile courts were usually separate from the regular tribunals; often the judges or referees that presided over these courts did not have formal legal training. There was little procedural regularity or even opportunity for the juvenile offender to confront his or her accusers.

The abuses that came to be associated with **juvenile courts** were addressed by the Supreme Court in the landmark case *In re Gault* (1967). Along with *Mapp v. Ohio,* *Gideon v. Wainwright,* and *Miranda v. Arizona, Gault* is considered to be one of the "four horsemen" of the Warren Court's revolution in the criminal justice area. In *Gault,* the Court essentially made the juvenile courts adhere to standards of due process, applying most of the basic procedural safeguards enjoyed by adults accused of crimes. Moreover, *Gault* held that juvenile courts must respect the right of counsel, the freedom from compulsory self-incrimination, and the right to confront (cross-examine) hostile witnesses.

For the most part, the Supreme Court has reaffirmed the *Gault* decision (see, for example, *Breed v. Jones* [1975]). In *McKeiver v. Pennsylvania* (1971), however, the Court refused to extend the right to trial by jury to juvenile proceedings. Writing for a plurality, Justice Blackmun concluded that juries are not indispensable "to fair and equitable juvenile proceedings." Thirteen years later, in *Schall v. Martin* (1984), the Court upheld a pretrial detention program for juveniles that might well have been found violative of due process had it applied to adults. Writing for the Court, Justice Rehnquist stressed that "the Constitution does not mandate elimination of all differences in the treatment of juveniles." At this point, it appears likely that the Supreme Court will maintain the requirements imposed in *Gault* and a few subsequent cases. But further expansion of juvenile due process seems unlikely.

Capital Punishment of Juveniles

One of the most difficult issues facing the courts in the area of juvenile justice is whether, and under what circumstances, persons below the age of legal majority (but who are tried as adults in regular criminal courts) should face the death penalty when convicted of capital crimes. In *Eddings v. Oklahoma* (1982), the Supreme Court voted 5 to 4 to vacate the death sentence of a 16-year-old boy. In 1988, the Court divided 6 to 3 in ruling that the Constitution forbids execution of juveniles who are 15 or younger at the time they committed their capital crimes (*Thompson v. Oklahoma*). One year later, in *Stanford v. Kentucky* (1989), the Court split 5 to 4 in deciding that juveniles aged 16 and older at the time of their crimes may be sentenced to death.

According to Justice O'Connor's controlling opinion in *Stanford,* "it is sufficiently clear that no national consensus forbids the imposition of capital punishment on 16- or 17-year-old capital murderers." Thus, for the time being, the line appears to be drawn at 16 years; juveniles who were, at the time of their crimes, 16 or older may be subject to the death penalty without offending the current Court's interpretation of the Eighth Amendment. This line, of course, is subject to alteration as the membership of the Court and national opinion change.

TO SUMMARIZE:

- Persons under the age of legal majority who engage in criminal conduct are typically within the jurisdiction of specialized juvenile courts.
- Although juvenile courts need not conform to all of the procedural requirements that apply to adult criminal prosecutions (for example, trial by jury), the Supreme Court has held that they must respect the right of counsel, the freedom from compulsory self-incrimination, and the right to confront hostile witnesses.
- One of the most difficult issues in this area is whether juveniles who are tried as adults should face the death penalty when convicted of capital crimes. The Supreme Court has, in effect, permitted imposition of the death penalty on persons who were at least age 16 at the time they committed capital crimes.

CONCLUSION

This chapter has summarized the development of constitutional standards in the field of criminal justice. Here, as in much of its First Amendment jurisprudence, the Supreme Court has attempted to balance legitimate interests of public safety and public order with equally legitimate interests in individual liberty and privacy. In seeking to protect the constitutional rights of persons suspected, accused, or convicted of crimes, the Court has often challenged established law enforcement methods. This tendency began in the 1930s and was most pronounced in the areas of search and seizure and police interrogation. Sharp criticism resulted from Supreme Court efforts to "police the police" and to upgrade standards of criminal procedure in the courts. Such criticism was particularly strong near the end of the Earl Warren era in the late 1960s.

Reflecting strong currents of change in public opinion, as well as the impact of appointments by Presidents Nixon, Reagan, and Bush (the elder), the Supreme Court since the 1970s has been decidedly more sympathetic to law enforcement than was the Warren Court. By refusing to extend or in some cases by overturning Warren Court precedents, the Burger and Rehnquist Courts opened themselves to the charge of insensitivity to the rights of individuals. This criticism has been particularly strident with respect to decisions in the area of search and seizure.

The reason the authors of the Bill of Rights imposed constraints on law enforcement was not that they were opposed to law and order. Rather, they were deeply distrustful of power; they feared what well-meaning but overzealous officials might do if not constrained by the rule of law. Certainly there was ample historical evidence to support their fears. Consequently, they gave us a Bill of Rights that makes it more difficult for government to investigate, prosecute, and punish crime. But what we as a society lose in our ability to control crime, we gain in increased liberty and privacy. It is hard to have it both ways, but, of course, most of us would like to! The great challenge to courts, especially the Supreme Court, is to strike a delicate balance between society's need for crime control and our equally strong desires for individual privacy and freedom.

KEY TERMS

ex post facto laws
bills of attainder
habeas corpus
search and seizure
reasonable expectation of
    privacy
open fields exception
warrant requirement
probable cause
search warrant
neutral and detached officer
general warrants
confidential or anonymous
    informants
totality of circumstances
knock and announce
exigent circumstances
warrantless search
search incidental to a lawful
    arrest
search based on consent
drug courier profile
plain view

hot pursuit
evanescent evidence
emergency searches
automobile search
investigatory detention
stop and frisk
pat-down search
reasonable suspicion
exclusionary rule
supervisory power
silver platter doctrine
good-faith exception
arrest
arrest warrant
probable cause hearing
warrantless arrest
custodial interrogation
Miranda warnings
fruit of the poisonous tree
    doctrine
public safety exception
inevitable discovery exception
police deception

harmless error analysis
right to counsel
ineffective representation
mockery of justice test
pro se defenses
self-representation
arraignment
bail
pretrial detention
plea bargain
knowing and intelligent waiver
jury trial
fair trial doctrine
pretrial publicity
change of venue
gag orders
closure of pretrial proceedings
unanimity rule
reasonable doubt standard
nonunanimous verdicts
peremptory challenge
racially motivated peremptory
    challenges

gender-based peremptory
    challenges
double jeopardy
mistrial
hung jury
forfeiture
cruel and unusual punishments
habitual offender
prisoners' rights
punitive isolation
discrete and insular minorities
death penalty
evolving standards of decency
aggravating factors
mitigating circumstances
victim impact statements
appeal by right
error correction
harmless errors
discretionary review
parens patriae
juvenile courts

FOR FURTHER READING

Amar, Akhil Reed. *The Constitution and Criminal Procedure: First Principles*. New Haven, Conn.: Yale University Press, 1997.

Baker, Liva. Miranda: *Crime, Law, and Politics*. New York: Atheneum Press, 1983.

Bedau, Hugo Adam (ed.). *The Death Penalty in America: Current Controversies*. New York: Oxford University Press, 1997.

Berns, Walter. *For Capital Punishment*. New York: Basic Books, 1979.

Black, Charles, Jr. *Capital Punishment: The Inevitability of Caprice and Mistake*. New York: Norton, 1974.

Dershowitz, Alan M. *The Best Defense*. New York: Random House, 1982.

Eisenstein, James, Roy B. Fleming, and Peter F. Nardulli. *The Contours of Justice: Communities and Their Courts*. Boston: Little, Brown, 1988.

Heumann, Milton. *Plea Bargaining: The Experiences of Prosecutors, Judges, and Defense Attorneys*. Chicago: University of Chicago Press, 1978.

Jacob, Herbert. *Law and Politics in the United States*. Boston: Little, Brown, 1986.

Kalven, Harry, and Hans Zeisel. *The American Jury*. Chicago: University of Chicago Press, 1966.

Landynski, Jacob W. *Search and Seizure and the Supreme Court*. Baltimore: Johns Hopkins University Press, 1978.

Levy, Leonard W. *Against the Law: The Nixon Court and Criminal Justice*. New York: Harper and Row, 1974.

Lewis, Anthony. *Gideon's Trumpet*. New York: Vintage Books, 1964.

Miller, Leonard G. *Double Jeopardy and the Federal System*. Chicago: University of Chicago Press, 1968.

Packer, Herbert L. *The Limits of the Criminal Sanction*. Stanford, Calif.: Stanford University Press, 1968.

Scheb, John M., and John M. Scheb II. *Criminal Law and Procedure* (4th ed.). Belmont, Calif.: West/Wadsworth, 2002.

Scheingold, Stuart A. *The Politics of Law and Order: Street Crime and Public Policy*. New York: Longman, 1984.

Schlesinger, Stephen. *Exclusionary Injustice*. New York: Dekker, 1977.

Sigler, Jay. *Double Jeopardy: The Development of a Legal and Social Policy*. Ithaca, N.Y.: Cornell University Press, 1969.

Stephens, Otis H., Jr. *The Supreme Court and Confessions of Guilt*. Knoxville: University of Tennessee Press, 1973.

Way, H. Frank. *Criminal Justice and the American Constitution*. Belmont, Calif.: Duxbury Press, 1980.

White, Welsh. *The Death Penalty in the Eighties*. Ann Arbor: University of Michigan Press, 1988.

Zalman, Marvin, and Larry J. Siegel. *Criminal Procedure* (2nd ed.). Belmont, Calif.: West/Wadsworth, 1997.

INTERNET RESOURCES

Name of Resource	Description	URL
Bureau of Justice Statistics	Agency with the U.S. Department of Justice responsible for collecting and disseminating data dealing with crime and the justice system	http://www.ojp.usdoj.gov/bjs/
Federal Bureau of Investigation (FBI)	The premier federal law enforcement agency	http://www.fbi.gov/
Federal Bureau of Prisons (BOP)	Federal agency responsible for running the federal government's prison system	http://www.bop.gov/
U.S. Sentencing Commission	The federal agency responsible for promulgating federal sentencing guidelines	http://www.ussc.gov/
Court TV	Good source for news on crime, courts, and the legal system	http://www.courttv.com/

Case

OLMSTEAD V. UNITED STATES

277 U.S. 438; 48 S.Ct. 564; 72 L.Ed. 944 (1928)
Vote: 5–4

In this decision, which has since been overturned, the Court considers the admissibility of evidence obtained through wire-tapping conducted without prior judicial authorization.

Mr. Chief Justice Taft delivered the opinion of the Court.

These cases are here by certiorari from the Circuit Court of Appeals for the Ninth Circuit. They were granted with the distinct limitation that the hearing should be confined to the single question whether the use of evidence of private telephone conversations between the defendants and others, intercepted by means of wire tapping, amounted to a violation of the 4th and 5th Amendments.

The petitioners were convicted in the District Court for the Western District of Washington of a conspiracy to violate the National Prohibition Act by unlawfully possessing, transporting and importing intoxicating liquors and maintaining nuisances, and by selling intoxicating liquors. Seventy-two others in addition to the petitioners were indicted. Some were not apprehended, some were acquitted, and others pleaded guilty.

The evidence in the records discloses a conspiracy of amazing magnitude to import, possess and sell liquor unlawfully. It involved the employment of not less than fifty persons, of two seagoing vessels for the transportation of liquor to British Columbia, of smaller vessels for coastwise transportation to the state of Washington, the purchase and use of a ranch beyond the suburban limits of Seattle, with a large underground cache for storage and a number of smaller caches in that city, the maintenance of a central office manned with operators, the employment of executives, salesmen, deliverymen, dispatchers, scouts, bookkeepers, collectors and an attorney. In a bad month sales amounted to $176,000; the aggregate for a year must have exceeded two millions of dollars.

Olmstead was the leading conspirator and the general manager of the business. He made a contribution of $10,000 to the capital; eleven others contributed $1,000 each. The profits were divided one-half to Olmstead and the remainder to the other eleven. Of the several offices in Seattle the chief one was in a large office building. In this there were three telephones on three different lines. There were telephones in an office of the manager in his own home, at the homes of his associates, and at other places in the city. Communication was had frequently with Vancouver, British Columbia. Times were fixed for the deliveries of the "stuff," to places along Puget Sound near Seattle, and from there the liquor was removed and deposited in the caches already referred to. One of the chief men was always on duty at the main office to receive orders by the telephones and to direct their filing by a corps of men stationed in another room—the "bull pen." The call numbers of the telephones were given to those known to be likely customers. At times the sales amounted to 200 cases of liquor per day.

The information which led to the discovery of the conspiracy and its nature and extent was largely obtained by intercepting messages on the telephones of the conspirators by four Federal prohibition officers. Small wires were inserted along the ordinary telephone wires from the residences of four of the petitioners and those leading from the chief office. The insertions were made without trespass upon any property of the defendants. They were made in the basement of the large office building. The taps from house lines were made in the streets near the houses.

The gathering of evidence continued for many months. Conversations of the conspirators, of which refreshing stenographic notes were currently made, were testified to by the government witnesses. They revealed the large business transactions of the partners and their subordinates. Men at the wires heard the orders given for liquor by customers, and the acceptances; they became auditors of the conversations between the partners. All this disclosed the conspiracy charged in the indictment. Many of the intercepted conversations were not merely reports but parts of the criminal acts. The evidence also disclosed the difficulties to which the conspirators were subjected, the reported news of the capture of vessels, the arrest of their men and the seizure of cases of liquor in garages and other places. It showed the dealing by Olmstead, the chief conspirator, with members of the Seattle police, the messages to them which secured the release of arrested members of the conspiracy, and also direct promises to officers of payments as soon as opportunity offered. . . .

The well-known historical purpose of the 4th Amendment, directed against general warrants and writs of assistance, was to prevent the use of governmental force to search a man's house, his person, his papers, and his effects, and to prevent their seizure against his will. . . .

The Amendment itself shows that the search is to be of material things—the person, the house, his papers or his effects. The description of the warrant necessary to make the proceeding lawful is that it must specify the place to be searched and the person or things to be seized. . . .

. . . The 4th Amendment may have proper application to a sealed letter in the mail because of the constitutional provision for the Post Office Department and the relations between the government and those who pay to secure protection of their sealed letters. . . . It is plainly within the words of the Amendment to say that the unlawful rifling by a government agent of a sealed letter is a search and seizure of the sender's papers or effects. The letter is a paper, an effect, and in the custody of a government that forbids carriage except under its protection.

The United States takes no such care of telegraph or telephone messages as of mailed sealed letters. The Amendment does not forbid what was done here. There was no searching. There was no seizure. The evidence was secured by the use of the sense of hearing and that only. There was no entry of the house or offices of the defendants.

By the invention of the telephone fifty years ago, and its application for the purpose of extending communications, one can talk with another at a far distant place.

The language of the Amendment can not be extended and expanded to include telephone wires reaching to the whole world from the defendant's house or office. The intervening wires are not part of his house or office, any more than are the highways along which they are stretched. . . .

"The 4th Amendment is to be construed in the light of what was deemed an unreasonable search and seizure when it was adopted and in a manner which will conserve public interests as well as the interests and rights of individual citizens." . . .

Congress may, of course, protect the secrecy of telephone messages by making them, when intercepted, inadmissible in evidence in Federal criminal trials, by direct legislation, and thus depart from the common law of evidence. But the courts may not adopt such a policy by attributing an enlarged and unusual meaning to the 4th Amendment. The reasonable view is that one who installs in his house a telephone instrument with connecting wires intends to project his voice to those quite outside, and that the wires beyond his house and messages while passing over them are not within the protection of the 4th Amendment. Here those who intercepted the projected voices were not in the house of either party to the conversation. . . .

We think, therefore, that the wire tapping here disclosed did not amount to a search or seizure within the meaning of the 4th Amendment. . . .

Mr. Justice Holmes [dissenting]. . . .

Mr. Justice Brandeis, dissenting:

. . . The government makes no attempt to defend the methods employed by its officers. Indeed, it concedes that if wire-tapping can be deemed a search and seizure within the 4th Amendment, such wire-tapping as was practiced in the case at bar was an unreasonable search and seizure,

and that the evidence thus obtained was inadmissible. But it relies on the language of the Amendment; and it claims that the protection given thereby cannot properly be held to include a telephone conversation. . . .

Time and again, this court, in giving effect to the principle underlying the 4th Amendment, has refused to place an unduly literal construction upon it. . . .

The protection guaranteed by the Amendments is much broader in scope. The makers of our Constitution undertook to secure conditions favorable to the pursuit of happiness. They recognized the significance of man's spiritual nature, of his feelings and of his intellect. They knew that only a part of the pain, pleasure and satisfactions of life are to be found in material things. They sought to protect Americans in their beliefs, their thoughts, their emotions and their sensations. They conferred, as against the government, the right to be let alone—the most comprehensive of rights and the right most valued by civilized men. To protect that right, every unjustifiable intrusion by the government upon the privacy of the individual, whatever the means employed, must be deemed a violation of the 4th Amendment. . . .

. . . [T]he defendants' objections to the evidence obtained by a wiretapping must, in my opinion, be sustained. It is, of course, immaterial where the physical connection with the telephone wires leading into the defendants' premises was made. And it is also immaterial that the intrusion was in aid of law enforcement. Experience should teach us to be most on our guard to protect liberty when the government's purposes are beneficent. Men born to freedom are naturally alert to repel invasion of their liberty by evil-minded rulers. The greatest dangers to liberty lurk in insidious encroachment by men of zeal, well-meaning, but without understanding. . . .

Decency, security, and liberty alike demand that government officials shall be subjected to the same rules of conduct that are commands to the citizen. In a government of laws, existence of the government will be imperilled if it fails to observe the law scrupulously. Our government is the potent, the omnipresent, teacher. For good or for ill, it teaches the whole people by its example. Crime is contagious. If the government becomes a law-breaker, it breeds contempt for law; it invites every man to become a law unto himself; it invites anarchy. To declare that in the administration of the criminal law the end justifies the means—to declare that the government may commit crimes in order to secure the conviction of a private criminal—would bring terrible retribution. Against that pernicious doctrine this court should resolutely set its face.

Mr. Justice Butler, dissenting. . . .

Mr. Justice Stone, dissenting. . . .

Case

KATZ V. UNITED STATES

389 U.S. 347; 88 S.Ct. 507; 19 L.Ed. 2d 576 (1967)

Vote: 7–1

In this case the Court overturns its earlier ruling in Olmstead v. United States *and adopts a broad view of the scope of Fourth Amendment protection.*

Mr. Justice Stewart delivered the opinion of the Court.

The petitioner was convicted in the District Court for the Southern District of California under an eight-count indictment charging him with transmitting wagering information by telephone from Los Angeles to Miami and Boston in violation of a federal statute. At trial the Government was permitted, over the petitioner's objection, to introduce evidence of the petitioner's end of telephone conversations, overheard by FBI agents who had attached an electronic listening and recording device to the outside of the public telephone booth from which he had placed his calls. In affirming his conviction, the Court of Appeals rejected the contention that the recordings had been obtained in violation of the Fourth Amendment, because "[t]here was no physical entrance into the area occupied by [the petitioner]." We granted certiorari in order to consider the constitutional questions thus presented. . . .

. . . [T]he parties have attached great significance to the characterization of the telephone booth from which the petitioner placed his calls. The petitioner has strenuously argued that the booth was a "constitutionally protected area." The Government has maintained with equal vigor that it was not. But this effort to decide whether or not a given "area," viewed in the abstract, is "constitutionally protected" deflects attention from the problem presented by this case. For the Fourth Amendment protects people, not places. What a person knowingly exposes to the public, even in his own home or office, is not a subject of Fourth Amendment protection. But what he seeks to preserve as private, even in an area accessible to the public, may be constitutionally protected.

The Government stresses the fact that the telephone booth from which the petitioner made his calls was constructed partly of glass, so that he was as visible after he entered it as he would have been if he had remained outside. But what he sought to exclude when he entered the booth was not the intruding eye—it was the uninvited ear. He did not shed his right to do so simply because he made his calls from a place where he might be seen. No less than an individual in a business office, in a friend's apartment, or in a taxicab, a person in a telephone booth may rely upon the protection of the Fourth Amendment. One who occupies it, shuts the door behind him, and pays the toll that permits him to place a call is surely entitled to assume that the words he utters into the mouthpiece will not be broadcast to the world. To read the Constitution more narrowly is to ignore the vital role that the public telephone has come to play in private communication.

The Government contends, however, that the activities of its agents in this case should not be tested by Fourth Amendment requirements, for the surveillance technique they employed involved no physical penetration of the telephone booth from which the petitioner placed his calls. It is true that the absence of such penetration was at one time thought to foreclose further Fourth Amendment inquiry, . . . for that Amendment was thought to limit only searches and seizures of tangible property. But "[t]he premise that property interests control the right of the Government to search and seize has been discredited." Thus, although a closely divided Court supposed in *Olmstead* that surveillance without any trespass and without the seizure of any material object fell outside the ambit of the Constitution, we have since departed from the narrow view on which that decision rested. Indeed, we have expressly held that the Fourth Amendment governs not only the seizure of tangible items, but extends as well to the recording of oral statements overheard without any "technical trespass under . . . local property law." Once this much is acknowledged, and once it is recognized that the Fourth Amendment protects people—and not simply "areas"—against unreasonable searches and seizures it becomes clear that the reach of the Amendment cannot turn upon the presence or absence of a physical intrusion into any given enclosure.

We conclude that the underpinnings of . . . [*Olmstead v. United States*] . . . have been so eroded by our subsequent decisions that the "trespass" doctrine there enunciated can no longer be regarded as controlling. The Government's activities in electronically listening to and recording the petitioner's words violated the privacy upon which he justifiably relied while using the telephone booth and thus constituted a "search and seizure" within the meaning of the Fourth Amendment. The fact that the electronic device employed to achieve that end did not happen to penetrate the wall of the booth can have no constitutional significance.

The question remaining for decision, then, is whether the search and seizure conducted in this case complied with constitutional standards. In that regard, the Government's position is that its agents acted in an entirely defensible manner. They did not begin their electronic surveillance until investigation of the petitioner's activities had established a strong probability that he was using the telephone in question to transmit gambling information to persons in other States, in violation of federal law. Moreover, the surveillance was limited, both in scope and in duration, to the specific purpose of establishing the contents of the petitioner's unlawful telephone communications. The agents confined their surveillance to the brief periods during which he used the telephone booth, and they took great care to overhear only the conversations of the petitioner himself.

Accepting this account of the Government's actions as accurate, it is clear that this surveillance was so narrowly circumscribed that a duly authorized magistrate, properly notified of the need for such investigation, specifically informed of the basis on which it was to proceed, and clearly apprised of the precise intrusion it would entail, could constitutionally have authorized, with appropriate safeguards, the very limited search and seizure that the Government asserts in fact took place. . . .

. . . The government agents here ignored "the procedure of antecedent justification . . . that is central to the Fourth Amendment," . . . a procedure that we hold to be a constitutional precondition of the kind of electronic surveillance involved in this case. Because the surveillance here failed to meet that condition, and because it led to the petitioner's conviction, the judgment must be reversed. . . .

Mr. Justice Marshall took no part in the consideration or decision of this case.

Mr. Justice Douglas, with whom *Mr. Justice Brennan* joins, concurring. . . .

Mr. Justice Harlan, concurring.

. . . As the Court's opinion states, "the Fourth Amendment protects people, not places." The question, however, is what protection it affords to those people. Generally, as here, the answer to that question requires reference to a "place." My understanding of the rule that has emerged from prior decisions is that there is a twofold requirement, first that a person have exhibited an actual (subjective) expectation of privacy and, second, that the expectation be one that society is prepared to recognize as "reasonable." Thus a man's home is, for most purposes, a place where he expects privacy, but objects, activities, or statements that he exposes to the "plain view" of outsiders are not "protected" because no intention to keep them to himself has been exhibited. On the other hand, conversations in the open would not be protected against being overheard, for the expectation of privacy under the circumstances would be unreasonable.

The critical fact in this case is that "[o]ne who occupies it [a telephone booth], shuts the door behind him, and pays the toll that permits him to place a call is surely entitled to assume" that his conversation is not being intercepted. The point is not that the booth is "accessible to the public" at other times, but that it is a temporarily private place whose momentary occupants' expectations of freedom from intrusion are recognized as reasonable. . . .

Mr. Justice White, concurring. . . .

Mr. Justice Black, dissenting.

My basic objection is twofold: (1) I do not believe that the words of the Amendment will bear the meaning given them by today's decision, and (2) I do not believe that it is the proper role of this Court to rewrite the Amendment in order "to bring it into harmony with the times" and thus reach a result that many people believe to be desirable.

While I realize that an argument based on the meaning of words lacks the scope, and no doubt the appeal, of broad policy discussions and philosophical discourses on such nebulous subjects as privacy, for me the language of the Amendment is the crucial place to look in construing a written document such as our Constitution. . . .

The first clause [of the Fourth Amendment] protects "persons, houses, papers, and effects, against unreasonable searches and seizures. . . ." These words connote the idea of tangible things with size, form, and weight, things capable of being searched, seized, or both. The second clause of the Amendment still further established its Framers' purpose to limit its protection to tangible things by providing that no warrants shall issue but those "particularly describing the place to be searched, and the persons or things to be seized." A conversation overheard by eavesdropping, whether by plain snooping or wire-tapping, is not tangible and, under the normally accepted meanings of the words, can neither be searched nor seized. In addition the language of the second clause indicates that the Amendment refers not only to something tangible so it can be seized but to something already in existence so it can be described. Yet the Court's interpretation would have the Amendment apply to overhearing future conversations which by their very nature are nonexistent until they take place. How can one "describe" a future conversation, and, if one cannot, how can a magistrate issue a warrant to eavesdrop one in the future? It is argued that information showing what is expected to be said is sufficient to limit the boundaries of what later can be admitted into evidence; but does such general information really meet the specific language of the Amendment which says "particularly describing"? Rather than using language in a completely artificial way, I must conclude that the Fourth Amendment simply does not apply to eavesdropping. . . .

Since I see no way in which the words of the Fourth Amendment can be construed to apply to eavesdropping, that closes the matter for me. In interpreting the Bill of Rights, I willingly go as far as a liberal construction of the language takes me, but I simply cannot in good con-

science give a meaning to words which they have never before been thought to have and which they certainly do not have in common ordinary usage. I will not distort the words of the Amendment in order to "keep the Constitution up to date" or "to bring it into harmony with the time." It was never meant that this Court have such power, which in effect would make us a continuously functioning constitutional convention.

Case

KYLLO V. UNITED STATES

533 U.S. 27; 121 S.Ct. 2038; 150 L.Ed. 2d 94 (2001)
Vote: 5–4

In this case the Supreme Court considers whether the use of a thermal imager by law enforcement agents constitutes a "search" within the meaning of the Fourth Amendment. The facts are presented in Justice Scalia's majority opinion.

Justice Scalia delivered the opinion of the Court.

. . . In 1991 Agent William Elliott of the United States Department of the Interior came to suspect that marijuana was being grown in the home belonging to petitioner Danny Kyllo. . . . Indoor marijuana growth typically requires high-intensity lamps. In order to determine whether an amount of heat was emanating from petitioner's home consistent with the use of such lamps, at 3:20 A.M. on January 16, 1992, Agent Elliott and Dan Haas used an Agema Thermovision 210 thermal imager to scan the triplex. Thermal imagers detect infrared radiation, which virtually all objects emit but which is not visible to the naked eye. The imager converts radiation into images based on relative warmth. Black is cool, white is hot, shades of gray connote relative differences; in that respect, it operates somewhat like a video camera showing heat images. The scan of Kyllo's home took only a few minutes and was performed from the passenger seat of Agent Elliott's vehicle across the street from the front of the house and also from the street in back of the house. The scan showed that the roof over the garage and a side wall of petitioner's home were relatively hot compared to the rest of the home and substantially warmer than neighboring homes in the triplex. Agent Elliott concluded that petitioner was using halide lights to grow marijuana in his house, which indeed he was. Based on tips from informants, utility bills, and the thermal imaging, a Federal Magistrate Judge issued a warrant authorizing a search of petitioner's home, and the agents found an indoor grow-

ing operation involving more than 100 plants. Petitioner was indicted on one count of manufacturing marijuana. . . . He unsuccessfully moved to suppress the evidence seized from his home and then entered a conditional guilty plea.

The Court of Appeals for the Ninth Circuit remanded the case for an evidentiary hearing regarding the intrusiveness of thermal imaging. On remand the District Court found that the Agema 210 is a non-intrusive device which emits no rays or beams and shows a crude visual image of the heat being radiated from the outside of the house; it did not show any people or activity within the walls of the structure; [t]he device used cannot penetrate walls or windows to reveal conversations or human activities; and [n]o intimate details of the home were observed. . . . Based on these findings, the District Court upheld the validity of the warrant that relied in part upon the thermal imaging, and reaffirmed its denial of the motion to suppress. A divided Court of Appeals initially reversed, . . . but that opinion was withdrawn and the panel (after a change in composition) affirmed, . . . with Judge Noonan dissenting. The court held that petitioner had shown no subjective expectation of privacy because he had made no attempt to conceal the heat escaping from his home, . . . and even if he had, there was no objectively reasonable expectation of privacy because the imager did not expose any intimate details of Kyllo's life, only amorphous hot spots on the roof and exterior wall. . . . We granted certiorari. . . .

. . . At the very core of the Fourth Amendment stands the right of a man to retreat into his own home and there be free from unreasonable governmental intrusion. . . . With few exceptions, the question whether a warrantless search of a home is reasonable and hence constitutional must be answered no. . . .

On the other hand, the antecedent question of whether or not a Fourth Amendment search has occurred is not so simple under our precedent. The permissibility of ordinary visual surveillance of a home used to be clear because, well into the 20th century, our Fourth Amendment jurisprudence was tied to common-law trespass. . . . Visual surveillance was unquestionably lawful because the eye cannot by the laws of England be guilty of a trespass. . . . We have since decoupled violation of a person's Fourth Amendment rights from trespassory violation of his property, . . . but the lawfulness of warrantless visual surveillance of a home has still been preserved. As we observed in *California v. Ciraolo* . . . (1986), "[t]he Fourth Amendment protection of the home has never been extended to require law enforcement officers to shield their eyes when passing by a home on public thoroughfares."

One might think that the new validating rationale would be that examining the portion of a house that is in plain public view, while it is a search despite the absence of trespass, is not an unreasonable one under the Fourth Amendment. . . . But in fact we have held that visual observation is no search at all perhaps in order to preserve somewhat more intact our doctrine that warrantless searches are presumptively unconstitutional. . . . In assessing when a search is not a search, we have applied somewhat in reverse the principle first enunciated in *Katz v. United States* . . . (1967). . . . As Justice Harlan's oft-quoted concurrence described it, a Fourth Amendment search occurs when the government violates a subjective expectation of privacy that society recognizes as reasonable. . . . We have subsequently applied this principle to hold that a Fourth Amendment search does *not* occur—even when the explicitly protected location of a *house* is concerned—unless the individual manifested a subjective expectation of privacy in the object of the challenged search, and society [is] willing to recognize that expectation as reasonable. . . .

The present case involves officers on a public street engaged in more than naked-eye surveillance of a home. We have previously reserved judgment as to how much technological enhancement of ordinary perception from such a vantage point, if any, is too much. . . .

The *Katz* test—whether the individual has an expectation of privacy that society is prepared to recognize as reasonable—has often been criticized as circular, and hence subjective and unpredictable. . . . While it may be difficult to refine *Katz* when the search of areas such as telephone booths, automobiles, or even the curtilage and uncovered portions of residences are at issue, in the case of the search of the interior of homes the prototypical and hence most commonly litigated area of protected privacy there is a ready criterion, with roots deep in the common law, of the minimal expectation of privacy that *exists,* and that is acknowledged to be *reasonable.* To withdraw protection of this minimum expectation would be to permit police technology to erode the privacy guaranteed by the Fourth Amendment. We think that obtaining by sense-enhancing technology any information regarding the interior of the home that could not otherwise have been obtained without physical intrusion into a constitutionally protected area, . . . constitutes a search at least where (as here) the technology in question is not in general public use. This assures preservation of that degree of privacy against government that existed when the Fourth Amendment was adopted. On the basis of this criterion, the information obtained by the thermal imager in this case was the product of a search.

The Government maintains, however, that the thermal imaging must be upheld because it detected only heat radiating from the external surface of the house. . . . The dissent makes this its leading point, . . . contending that there is a fundamental difference between what it calls off-the-wall observations and through-the-wall surveillance. But just as a thermal imager captures only heat emanating from a house, so also a powerful directional microphone picks up only sound emanating from a house and a satellite capable of scanning from many miles away would pick up only visible light emanating from a house. We rejected such a mechanical interpretation of the Fourth Amendment in *Katz,* where the eavesdropping device picked up only sound waves that reached the exterior of the phone booth. Reversing that approach would leave the homeowner at the mercy of advancing technology including imaging technology that could discern all human activity in the home. While the technology used in the present case was relatively crude, the rule we adopt must take account of more sophisticated systems that are already in use or in development. The dissent's reliance on the distinction between off-the-wall and through-the-wall observation is entirely incompatible with the dissent's belief, which we discuss below, that thermal-imaging observations of the intimate details of a home are impermissible. The most sophisticated thermal imaging devices continue to measure heat off-the-wall rather than through-the-wall; the dissent's disapproval of those more sophisticated thermal-imaging devices, . . . is an acknowledgement that there is no substance to this distinction. As for the dissent's extraordinary assertion that anything learned through an inference cannot be a search, . . . that would validate even the through-the-wall technologies that the dissent purports to disapprove. Surely the dissent does not believe that the through-the-wall radar or ultrasound technology produces an 8-by-10 Kodak glossy that needs no analysis (i.e., the making of inferences). . . .

The Government also contends that the thermal imaging was constitutional because it did not detect private activities occurring in private areas. . . . The Fourth Amendment's protection of the home has never been tied to measurement of the quality or quantity of information obtained. In *Silverman,* for example, we made clear that any physical invasion of the structure of the home, by even a fraction of an inch, was too much, . . . and there is certainly no exception to the warrant requirement for the officer who barely cracks open the front door and sees nothing but the nonintimate rug on the vestibule floor. In the home, our cases show, *all* details are intimate details, because the entire area is held safe from prying government eyes. . . .

Limiting the prohibition of thermal imaging to intimate details would not only be wrong in principle; it would be impractical in application, failing to provide a workable accommodation between the needs of law enforcement and the interests protected by the Fourth Amendment. . . . To begin with, there is no necessary connection between the sophistication of the surveillance equipment and the intimacy of the details that it observes—which means that one cannot say (and the police cannot be assured) that use of the relatively crude equipment at issue here will always be lawful. The Agema Thermovision 210 might disclose, for example, at what hour each night the lady of the house takes her daily sauna and bath—a detail that many would consider intimate; and a much more sophisticated system might detect nothing more intimate than the fact that someone left a closet light on. We could not, in other words, develop a rule approving only that through-the-wall surveillance which identifies objects no smaller than 36 by 36 inches, but would have to develop a jurisprudence specifying which home activities are intimate and which are not. And even when (if ever) that jurisprudence were fully developed, no police officer would be able to know *in advance* whether his through-the-wall surveillance picks up intimate details—and thus would be unable to know in advance whether it is constitutional. . . .

We have said that the Fourth Amendment draws a firm line at the entrance to the house. . . . That line, we think, must be not only firm but also bright, which requires clear specification of those methods of surveillance that require a warrant. While it is certainly possible to conclude from the videotape of the thermal imaging that occurred in this case that no significant compromise of the homeowner's privacy has occurred, we must take the long view, from the original meaning of the Fourth Amendment forward. . . .

Where, as here, the Government uses a device that is not in general public use, to explore details of the home that would previously have been unknowable without physical intrusion, the surveillance is a search and is presumptively unreasonable without a warrant. . . .

Justice Stevens, with whom **The Chief Justice, Justice O'Connor,** and **Justice Kennedy** join, dissenting.

There is, in my judgment, a distinction of constitutional magnitude between through-the-wall surveillance that gives the observer or listener direct access to information in a private area, on the one hand, and the thought processes used to draw inferences from information in the public domain, on the other hand. The Court has crafted a rule that purports to deal with direct observations of the inside of the home, but the case before us merely involves indirect deductions from off-the-wall surveillance, that is, observations of the exterior of the home. Those observations were made with a fairly primitive thermal imager that gathered data exposed on the outside of petitioner's home but did not invade any constitutionally protected interest in privacy. Moreover, I believe that the supposedly bright-line rule the Court has created in response to its concerns about future technological developments is unnecessary, unwise, and inconsistent with the Fourth Amendment.

There is no need for the Court to craft a new rule to decide this case, as it is controlled by established principles from our Fourth Amendment jurisprudence. One of those core principles, of course, is that searches and seizures inside a home without a warrant are presumptively unreasonable. . . . But it is equally well settled that searches and seizures of property in plain view are presumptively reasonable. . . . Whether that property is residential or commercial, the basic principle is the same: What a person knowingly exposes to the public, even in his own home or office, is not a subject of Fourth Amendment protection. . . . That is the principle implicated here.

While the Court . . . decides this case based largely on the potential of yet-to-be-developed technology that might allow through-the-wall surveillance, . . . this case involves nothing more than off-the-wall surveillance by law enforcement officers to gather information exposed to the general public from the outside of petitioner's home. All that the infrared camera did in this case was passively measure heat emitted from the exterior surfaces of petitioner's home; all that those measurements showed were relative differences in emission levels, vaguely indicating that some areas of the roof and outside walls were warmer than others. As still images from the infrared scans show, . . . no details regarding the interior of petitioner's home were revealed. Unlike an x-ray scan, or other possible through-the-wall techniques, the detection of infrared radiation emanating from the home did not accomplish an unauthorized physical penetration into the premises, . . . nor did it obtain information that it could not have obtained by observation from outside the curtilage of the house. . . .

Indeed, the ordinary use of the senses might enable a neighbor or passerby to notice the heat emanating from a building, particularly if it is vented, as was the case here. Additionally, any member of the public might notice that one part of a house is warmer than another part or a nearby building if, for example, rainwater evaporates or snow melts at different rates across its surfaces. Such use of the senses would not convert into an unreasonable search if, instead, an adjoining neighbor allowed an officer onto her property to verify her perceptions with a sensitive thermometer. Nor, in my view, does such observation become an unreasonable search if made from a distance with the aid of a device that merely discloses that the exterior of one house, or one area of the house, is much warmer than another. Nothing more occurred in this case.

Thus, the notion that heat emissions from the outside of a dwelling is a private matter implicating the protections of the Fourth Amendment (the text of which guarantees the right of people to be secure *in* their houses against unreasonable searches and seizures [emphasis added]) is not only unprecedented but also quite difficult to take seriously. Heat waves, like aromas that are generated in a kitchen, or in a laboratory or opium den, enter the public domain if and when they leave a building. A subjective expectation that they would remain private is not only implausible but also surely not one that society is prepared to recognize as reasonable. . . .

To be sure, the homeowner has a reasonable expectation of privacy concerning what takes place within the home, and the Fourth Amendment's protection against physical invasions of the home should apply to their functional equivalent. But the equipment in this case did not penetrate the walls of petitioner's home, and while it did pick up details of the home that were exposed to the public, . . . it did not obtain any information regarding the *interior* of the home. . . . In the Court's own words, based on what the thermal imager showed regarding the outside of petitioner's home, the officers concluded that petitioner was engaging in illegal activity inside the home. . . . It would be quite absurd to characterize their thought processes as searches, regardless of whether they inferred (rightly) that petitioner was growing marijuana in his house, or (wrongly) that the lady of the house [was taking] her daily sauna and bath. . . . In either case, the only conclusions the officers reached concerning the interior of the home were at least as indirect as those that might have been inferred from the contents of discarded garbage, . . . or pen register data, . . . or, as in this case, subpoenaed utility records. . . . For the first time in its history, the Court assumes that an inference can amount to a Fourth Amendment violation. . . .

Since what was involved in this case was nothing more than drawing inferences from off-the-wall surveillance, rather than any through-the-wall surveillance, the officers' conduct did not amount to a search and was perfectly reasonable. . . .

Although the Court is properly and commendably concerned about the threats to privacy that may flow from advances in the technology available to the law enforcement profession, it has unfortunately failed to heed the tried and true counsel of judicial restraint. Instead of concentrating on the rather mundane issue that is actually presented by the case before it, the Court has endeavored to craft an all-encompassing rule for the future. It would be far wiser to give legislators an unimpeded opportunity to grapple with these emerging issues rather than to shackle them with prematurely devised constitutional constraints. . . .

Case

WEEKS V. UNITED STATES
232 U.S. 383; 34 S.Ct. 341; 58 L.Ed. 652 (1914)
Vote: 9–0

In this case the Court first establishes the Fourth Amendment exclusionary rule, although the ruling applies only to criminal trials in federal courts.

Mr. Justice Day delivered the opinion of the Court:

An indictment was returned against the plaintiff in error, defendant below, and herein so designated, in the District Court of the United States for the Western District of Missouri, containing nine counts. The seventh count, upon which a conviction was had, charged the use of the mails for the purpose of transporting certain coupons or tickets representing chances or shares in a lottery . . . in violation of the Criminal Code. Sentence of fine and imprisonment was imposed. This writ of error is to review that judgment.

The defendant was arrested by a police officer, so far as the record shows, without warrant, at the Union Station in Kansas City, Missouri, where he was employed by an express company. Other police officers had gone to the house of the defendant, and being told by a neighbor where the key was kept, found it and entered the house. They searched the defendant's room and took possession of various papers and articles found there, which were afterwards turned over to the United States marshal. Later in the same day police officers returned with the marshal, who thought he might find additional evidence, and, being admitted by someone in the house, probably a boarder, in response to a rap, the marshal searched the defendant's room and carried away certain letters and envelopes found in the drawer of a chiffonier. Neither the marshal nor the police officers had a search warrant.

The defendant filed in the cause before the time for trial . . . [a] . . . Petition to Return Private Papers, Books, and Other Property. . . .

Upon consideration of the petition the court entered an order directing the return of such property as was not pertinent to the charge against the defendant, but denied the petition as to pertinent matter, reserving the right to pass upon the pertinency at a later time. In obedience to the order the district attorney returned part of the property taken, and retained the remainder, concluding a list of the latter with the statement that, "all of which last above described property is to be used in evidence in the trial of the above-entitled cause, and pertains to the alleged sale of lottery tickets of the company above named."

After the jury had been sworn and before any evidence had been given, the defendant again urged his petition for the return of his property, which was denied by the court. Upon the introduction of such papers during the trial, the defendant objected on the ground that the papers had been obtained without a search warrant, and by breaking into his home, in violation of the 4th and 5th Amendments to the Constitution of the United States, which objection was overruled by the court. Among the papers retained and put in evidence were a number of lottery tickets and statements with reference to the lottery, taken at the first visit of the police to the defendant's room, and a number of letters written to the defendant in respect to the lottery, taken by the marshal upon his search of defendant's room.

The defendant assigns error, among other things, in the court's refusal to grant his petition for the return of his property, and in permitting the papers to be used at the trial.

It is thus apparent that the question presented involves the determination of the duty of the court with reference to the motion made by the defendant for the return of certain letters, as well as other papers, taken from his room by the United States marshal, who, without authority of process, if any such could have been illegally issued, visited the room of the defendant for the declared purpose of obtaining additional testimony to support the charge against the accused, and, having gained admission to the house, took from the drawer of a chiffonier there found certain letters

written to the defendant, tending to show his guilt. These letters were placed in the control of the district attorney, and were subsequently produced by him and offered in evidence against the accused at the trial. The defendant contends that such appropriation of his private correspondence was in violation of rights secured to him by the 4th and 5th Amendments to the Constitution of the United States. We shall deal with the 4th Amendment. . . .

The history of this Amendment is given with particularity in the opinion of Mr. Justice Bradley, speaking for the court in *Boyd v. United States* [1886]. . . . As was there shown, it took its origin in the determination of the framers of the Amendments to the Federal Constitution to provide for that instrument a Bill of Rights, securing to the American people, among other things, those safeguards which had grown up in England to protect the people from unreasonable searches and seizures, such as were permitted under the general warrants issued under authority of the government, by which there had been invasions of the home and privacy of the citizens, and the seizure of their private papers in support of charges, real or imaginary, made against them. Such practices had also received sanction under warrants and seizures under the so-called writs of assistance, issued in the American colonies. Resistance to these practices had established the principle which was enacted into the fundamental law in the 4th Amendment, that a man's house was his castle, and not to be invaded by any general authority to search and seize his goods and papers.

The effect of the 4th Amendment is to put the courts of the United States and Federal officials, in the exercise of their power and authority, under limitations and restraints as to the exercise of such power and authority, and to forever secure the people, their persons, houses, papers, and effects, against all unreasonable searches and seizures under the guise of law. This protection reaches all alike, whether accused of crime or not, and the duty of giving to it force and effect is obligatory upon all intrusted under our Federal system with the enforcement of the laws. The tendency of those who execute the criminal laws of the country to obtain conviction by means of unlawful seizures and enforced confessions, the latter often obtained after subjecting accused persons to unwarranted practices destructive of rights secured by the Federal Constitution, should find no sanction in the judgments of the courts, which are charged at all times with the support of the Constitution, and to which people of all conditions have a right to appeal for the maintenance of such fundamental rights.

What, then, is the present case? Before answering that inquiry specifically, it may be well by a process of exclusion to state what it is not. It is not an assertion of the right on the part of the government, always recognized under English and American law, to search the person of the accused when legally arrested, to discover and seize the fruits or evidences of crime. Nor is it the case of testimony offered at a trial where the court is asked to stop and consider the illegal means by which proofs, otherwise competent, were obtained—of which we shall have occasion to treat later in this opinion. Nor is it the case of burglar's tools or other proofs of guilt found upon his arrest within the control of the accused.

The case in the aspect in which we are dealing with it involves the right of the court in a criminal prosecution to retain for the purposes of evidence the letters and correspondence of the accused, seized in his house in his absence and without his authority, by a United States marshal holding no warrant for his arrest and none for the search of his premises. If letters and private documents can thus be seized and held and used in evidence against a citizen accused of an offense, the protection of the 4th Amendment, declaring his right to be secure against such searches and seizures, is of no value, and, so far as those thus placed are concerned, might as well be stricken from the Constitution. The efforts of the courts and their officials to bring the guilty to punishment, praise-worthy as they are, are not to be aided by the sacrifice of those great principles established by years of endeavor and suffering which have resulted in their embodiment in the fundamental law of the land. The United States marshal could only have invaded the house of the accused when armed with a warrant issued as required by the Constitution, upon sworn information, and describing with reasonable particularity the thing for which the search was to be made. Instead, he acted without sanction of law, doubtless prompted by the desire to bring further proof to the aid of the government, and under color of his office undertook to make a seizure of private papers in direct violation of the constitutional prohibition against such action. Under such circumstances, without sworn information and particular description, not even an order of court would have justified such procedure; much less was it within the authority of the United States marshal to thus invade the house and privacy of the accused.

We therefore reach the conclusion that the letters in question were taken from the house of the accused by an official of the United States, acting under color of his office, in direct violation of the constitutional rights of the defendant; that having made a seasonable application for their return, which was heard and passed upon by the court, there was involved in the order refusing the application of denial of the constitutional rights of the accused, and that the court should have restored these letters to the accused. In holding them and permitting their use upon the trial, we think prejudicial error was committed. . . .

It results that the judgment of the court below must be reversed, and the case remanded for further proceedings in accordance with this opinion. . . .

Case

MAPP V. OHIO

367 U.S. 643; 81 S.Ct. 1684; 6 L.Ed. 2d 1081 (1961)

Vote: 6–3

In this case the Court extends the Fourth Amendment exclusionary rule to state criminal prosecutions.

Mr. Justice Clark delivered the opinion of the Court.

Appellant stands convicted of knowingly having had in her possession and under her control certain lewd and lascivious books, pictures, and photographs in violation of . . . Ohio's Revised Code. . . . [T]he Supreme Court of Ohio found that her conviction was valid though "based primarily upon the introduction in evidence of lewd and lascivious books and pictures unlawfully seized during an unlawful search of defendant's home. . . ."

On May 23, 1957, three Cleveland police officers arrived at appellant's residence in that city pursuant to information that "a person [was] hiding out in the home, who was wanted for questioning in connection with a recent bombing, and that there was a large amount of policy [gambling] paraphernalia being hidden in the home." Miss Mapp and her daughter by a former marriage lived on the top floor of the two-family dwelling. Upon their arrival at that house, the officers knocked on the door and demanded entrance but appellant, after telephoning her attorney, refused to admit them without a search warrant. They advised their headquarters of the situation and undertook a surveillance of the house.

The officers again sought entrance some three hours later when four or more additional officers arrived on the scene. When Miss Mapp did not come to the door immediately at least one of the several doors to the house was forcibly opened and the policemen gained admittance.

Meanwhile Miss Mapp's attorney arrived, but the officers, having secured their own entry, and continuing in their defiance of the law, would permit him neither to see Miss Mapp nor to enter the house. It appears that Miss Mapp was halfway down the stairs from the upper floor to the front door when the officers, in this high-handed manner, broke into the hall. She demanded to see the search warrant. A paper, claimed to be a warrant, was held up by one of the officers. She grabbed the "warrant" and placed it in her bosom. A struggle ensued in which the officers recovered the piece of paper and as a result of which they handcuffed appellant because she had been "belligerent" in resisting their official rescue of the "warrant" from her person. Running roughshod over appellant, a policeman "grabbed" her, "twisted [her] hand," and she "yelled [and] pleaded with him" because "it was hurting." Appellant, in handcuffs, was then forcibly taken upstairs to her bedroom where the officers searched a dresser, a chest of drawers, a closet and some suitcases. They also looked into a photo album and through personal papers belonging to the appellant. The search spread to the rest of the second floor including the child's bedroom, the living room, the kitchen and a dinette. The basement of the building and a trunk found therein were also searched. The obscene materials for possession of which she was ultimately convicted were discovered in the course of that widespread search.

At the trial no search warrant was produced by the prosecution, nor was the failure to produce one explained or accounted for. At best, "There is, in the record, considerable doubt as to whether there ever was any warrant for the search of defendant's home." . . .

The State says that even if the search were made without authority, or otherwise unreasonably, it is not prevented from using the unconstitutionally seized evidence at trial, citing *Wolf v. Colorado* [1949], in which this Court did indeed hold "that in a prosecution in a State court for a State crime the Fourteenth Amendment does not forbid the admission of evidence obtained by an unreasonable search and seizure." . . . On this appeal, of which we have noted probable jurisdiction, . . . it is urged once again that we review that holding. . . .

[I]n the year 1914, in the *Weeks* Case, this Court "for the first time" held that, "in a federal prosecution the Fourth Amendment barred the use of evidence secured through an illegal search and seizure." . . . This Court has ever since required of federal law officers a strict adherence to that command which this Court has held to be a clear, specific, and constitutionally required—even if judicially implied—deterrent safeguard without insistence upon which the Fourth Amendment would have been reduced to "a form of words." . . . It meant, quite simply, that "con-

viction by means of unlawful seizures and enforced confessions . . . should find no sanction in the judgments of the courts. . . ." . . .

There are in the cases of this Court some passing references to the *Weeks* rule as being one of evidence. But the plain and unequivocal language of *Weeks*—and its later paraphrase in *Wolf*—to the effect that the *Weeks* rule is of constitutional origin, remains entirely undisturbed. In *Byars v. United States* . . . (1927), a unanimous Court declared that "the doctrine [cannot] . . . be tolerated under our constitutional system, that evidences of crime discovered by a federal officer in making a search without lawful warrant may be used against the victim of the unlawful search where a timely challenge has been interposed." . . .

In 1949, 35 years after *Weeks* was announced, this Court, in *Wolf v. Colorado* for the first time discussed the effect of the Fourth Amendment upon the States through the operation of the Due Process Clause of the Fourteenth Amendment. It said: "[W]e have no hesitation in saying that were a State affirmatively to sanction such police incursion into privacy it would run counter to the guaranty of the Fourteenth Amendment." . . . Nevertheless, after declaring that the "security of one's privacy against arbitrary intrusion by the police" is "implicit in 'the concept of ordered liberty' and as such enforceable against the States through the Due Process Clause," and announcing that it "stoutly adhere[d]" to the *Weeks* decision, the Court decided that the *Weeks* exclusionary rule would not then be imposed upon the States as "an essential ingredient of the right." . . . The Court's reasons for not considering essential to the right to privacy, as a curb imposed upon the States by the Due Process Clause, that which decades before had been posited as part and parcel of the Fourth Amendment's limitation upon federal encroachment of individual privacy, were bottomed on factual considerations.

While they are not basically relevant to a decision that the exclusionary rule is an essential ingredient of the Fourth Amendment as the right it embodies is vouchsafed against the States by the Due Process Clause, we will consider the current validity of the factual grounds upon which *Wolf* was based.

The Court in *Wolf* first stated that "[t]he contrariety of views of the States" on the adoption of the exclusionary rule of *Weeks* was "particularly impressive"; . . . and, in this connection that it could not "brush aside the experience of States which deem the incidence of such conduct by the police too slight to call for a deterrent remedy . . . by overriding the [States'] relevant rules of evidence." . . . While in 1949, prior to the *Wolf* Case, almost two-thirds of the States were opposed to the use of the exclusionary rule, now, despite the *Wolf* Case, more than half of those since passing upon it, by their own legislative or judicial decision, have wholly or partly adopted or adhered to the *Weeks* rule. . . . Significantly, among those now following the rule is California, which, according to its highest court, was "compelled to reach that conclusion because other remedies have completely failed to secure compliance with the constitutional provisions. . . ." . . . The experience of California that such other remedies have been worthless and futile is buttressed by the experience of other States. The obvious futility of relegating the Fourth Amendment to the protection of other remedies has, moreover, been recognized by this Court since *Wolf.* . . .

Likewise, time has set its face against what *Wolf* called the "weighty testimony" of *People v. Defore* . . . (1926). There Justice (then Judge) Cardozo, rejecting adoption of the *Weeks* exclusionary rule in New York, had said that "[t]he Federal rule as it stands is either too strict or too lax." . . . However, the force of that reasoning has been largely vitiated by later decisions of this Court. These include the recent discarding of the "silver platter" doctrine which allowed federal judicial use of evidence seized in violation of the Constitution by state agents; . . . the relaxation of the formerly strict requirements as to standing to challenge the use of evidence, thus seized, so that now the procedure of exclusion, "ultimately referable to constitutional safeguards," is available to anyone even "legitimately on [the] premises" unlawfully searched; . . . and, finally, the formulation of a method to prevent state use of evidence unconstitutionally seized by federal agents. . . . Because there can be no fixed formula, we are admittedly met with "recurring questions of the reasonableness of searches," but less is not to be expected when dealing with a Constitution, and, at any rate, "[r]easonableness is in the first instance for the [trial court] . . . to determine." . . .

It, therefore, plainly appears that the factual considerations supporting the failure of the *Wolf* Court to include the *Weeks* exclusionary rule when it recognized the enforceability of the right to privacy against the States in 1949, while not basically relevant to the constitutional consideration, could not, in any analysis, now be deemed controlling. . . .

Since the Fourth Amendment's right of privacy has been declared enforceable against the States through the Due Process Clause of the Fourteenth, it is enforceable against them by the same sanction of exclusion as is used against the Federal Government. Were it otherwise, then just as without the *Weeks* rule the assurance against unreasonable federal searches and seizures would be "a form of words," valueless and undeserving of mention in a perpetual charter of inestimable human liberties, so too, without that rule the freedom from state invasions of privacy would be so ephemeral and so neatly severed from its conceptual nexus with the freedom from all brutish means of coercing evidence as not to merit this Court's high regard as a freedom "implicit in the concept of ordered liberty." At the time that the Court held in *Wolf* that the Amendment was applicable to the States through the Due Process Clause, the cases of this Court, as we have seen, had steadfastly held that as to federal officers the Fourth Amendment included the exclusion of the evidence seized in violation of its provisions. Even *Wolf* "stoutly adhered" to that proposition. The right to privacy, when conceded operatively enforceable against the States, was not susceptible of destruction by avulsion of the sanction upon which its protection and enjoyment had always been deemed dependent under the *Boyd, Weeks* and *Silverthorne* cases. Therefore, in extending the substantive protections of due process to all constitutionally unreasonable searches—state or federal—it was logically and constitutionally necessary that the exclusion doctrine—an essential part of the right to privacy—be also insisted upon as an essential ingredient of the right newly recognized by the *Wolf* case. In short, the admission of the new constitutional right by *Wolf* could not consistently tolerate denial of its most important constitutional privilege, namely, the exclusion of the evidence which an accused had been forced to give by reason of the unlawful seizure. To hold otherwise is to grant the right but in reality to withhold its privilege and enjoyment. Only last year the Court itself recognized that the purpose of the exclusionary rule "is to deter—to compel respect for the constitutional guaranty in the only effectively available way—by removing the incentive to disregard it." . . .

Moreover, our holding that the exclusionary rule is an essential part of both the Fourth and Fourteenth Amendments is not only the logical dictate of prior cases, but it also makes very good sense. There is no war between the Constitution and common sense. Presently, a federal prosecutor may make no use of evidence illegally seized, but a State's attorney across the street may, although he supposedly is operating under the enforceable prohibitions of the same Amendment. Thus the State, by admitting evidence unlawfully seized, serves to encourage disobedience to the Federal Constitution which it is bound to uphold. Moreover, . . . "[t]he very essence of a healthy federalism depends upon the avoidance of needless conflict between state and federal courts." . . .

Federal-state cooperation in the solution of crime under constitutional standards will be promoted, if only by recognition of their now mutual obligation to respect the same fundamental criteria in their approaches. "However much in a particular case insistence upon such rules may appear as a technicality that inures to the benefit of a guilty person, the history of the criminal law proves that tolerance of shortcut methods in law enforcement impairs its enduring effectiveness." . . . Denying shortcuts to only one of two cooperating law enforcement agencies tends naturally to breed legitimate suspicion of "working arrangements" whose results are equally tainted. . . .

There are those who say, as did Justice (then Judge) Cardozo, that under our constitutional exclusionary doctrine "[t]he criminal is to go free because the constable has blundered." . . . In some cases this will undoubtedly be the result. But, . . . "there is another consideration—the imperative of judicial integrity." . . . The criminal goes free, if he must, but it is the law that sets him free. Nothing can destroy a government more quickly than its failure to observe its own laws, or worse, its disregard of the charter of its own existence. As Mr. Justice Brandeis, dissenting, said in *Olmstead v. United States:* "Our Government is the potent, the omnipresent teacher. For good or for ill, it teaches the whole people by its example. . . . If the Government becomes a lawbreaker, it breeds contempt for law; it invites every man to become a law unto himself; it invites anarchy." . . . Nor can it lightly be assumed that, as a practical matter, adoption of the exclusionary rule fetters law enforcement. Only last year this Court expressly considered that contention and found that "pragmatic evidence of a sort" to the contrary was not wanting. . . .

The ignoble shortcut to conviction left open to the State tends to destroy the entire system of constitutional restraints on which the liberties of the people rest. Having once recognized that the right to privacy embodied in the Fourth Amendment is enforceable against the States, and that the right to be secure against rude invasions of privacy by state officers is, therefore, constitutional in origin, we can no longer permit that right to remain an empty promise. Because it is enforceable in the same manner and to like effect as other basic rights secured by the Due Process Clause, we can no longer permit it to be revocable at the whim of any police officer who, in the name of law enforcement itself, chooses to suspend its enjoyment. Our decision, founded on reason and truth, gives to the individual no more than that which the Constitution guarantees him, to the police officer no less than that to which honest law enforcement is entitled, and, to the courts, that judicial integrity so necessary in the true administration of justice.

The judgment of the Supreme Court of Ohio is reversed and the case remanded for further proceedings not inconsistent with this opinion.

Reversed and remanded.

Mr. Justice Black, concurring.

I am still not persuaded that the Fourth Amendment, standing alone, would be enough to bar the introduction into evidence against an accused of papers and effects seized from him in violation of its commands. For the Fourth Amendment does not itself contain any provision expressly precluding the use of such evidence, and I am extremely doubtful that such a provision could properly be inferred from nothing more than the basic command against unreasonable searches and seizures. Reflection on the problem, however, in the light of cases coming before the Court since *Wolf,* has led me to conclude that when the Fourth Amendment's ban against unreasonable searches and seizures is considered together with the Fifth Amendment's ban against compelled self-incrimination, a constitutional basis emerges which not only justifies but actually requires the exclusionary rule. . . .

Mr. Justice Douglas, concurring. . . .

Mr. Justice Harlan, whom *Mr. Justice Frankfurter* and *Mr. Justice Whittaker* join, dissenting.

In overruling the *Wolf* case the Court, in my opinion, has forgotten the sense of judicial restraint which, with due regard for *stare decisis,* is one element that should enter into deciding whether a past decision of this Court should be overruled. Apart from that I also believe that the *Wolf* rule represents sounder Constitutional doctrine than the new rule which now replaces it.

From the Court's statement of the case one would gather that the central, if not controlling, issue on this appeal is whether illegally state-seized evidence is Constitutionally admissible in a state prosecution, an issue which would of course face us with the need for re-examining *Wolf.* However, such is not the situation. For, although that question was indeed raised here and below among appellant's subordinate points, the new and pivotal issue brought to the Court by this appeal is whether section 2905.34 of the Ohio Revised Code making criminal the mere knowing possession or control of obscene material, and under which appellant has been convicted, is consistent with the rights of free thought and expression assured against state action by the Fourteenth Amendment. That was the principal issue which was decided by the Ohio Supreme Court, which was tendered by appellant's Jurisdictional Statement, and which was briefed and argued in this Court.

In this posture of things, I think it fair to say that five members of this Court have simply "reached out" to overrule *Wolf.* With all respect for the views of the majority, and recognizing that *stare decisis* carries different weight in Constitutional adjudication than it does in nonconstitutional decision, I can perceive no justification for regarding this case as an appropriate occasion for re-examining *Wolf.* . . .

I would not impose upon the States this federal exclusionary remedy. The reasons given by the majority for now suddenly turning its back on *Wolf* seem to me notably unconvincing.

First, it is said that "the factual grounds upon which *Wolf* was based" have since changed, in that more States now follow the *Weeks* exclusionary rule than was so at the time *Wolf* was decided. While that is true, a recent survey indicates that at present one-half of the States still adhere to the common-law non-exclusionary rule, and one, Maryland, retains the rule as to felonies. . . . But in any case surely all this is beside the point, as the majority itself indeed seems to recognize. Our concern here, as it was in *Wolf,* is not with the desirability of that rule but only with the question whether the States are constitutionally free to follow it or not as they may themselves determine, and the relevance of the disparity of views among the States on this point lies simply in the fact that the judgment involved is a debatable one. Moreover, the very fact on which the majority relies, instead of lending support to what is now being done, points away from the need of replacing voluntary state action with federal compulsion.

The preservation of a proper balance between state and federal responsibility in the administration of criminal justice demands patience on the part of those who might like to see things move faster among the States in this respect. . . .

Memorandum of **Mr. Justice Stewart.**

Agreeing fully with Part I of Mr. Justice Harlan's dissenting opinion, I express no view as to the merits of the constitutional issue which the Court today decides. I would, however, reverse the judgment in this case, because I am persuaded that the provision . . . upon which the petitioner's conviction was based is, in the words of Mr. Justice Harlan, not "consistent with the rights of free thought and expression assured against state action by the Fourteenth Amendment."

Case

UNITED STATES V. LEON

468 U.S. 897; 104 S.Ct. 3405; 82 L.Ed. 2d 677 (1984)
Vote: 6–3

In this case the Court recognizes a limited good-faith exception to the Fourth Amendment exclusionary rule.

Justice White delivered the opinion of the Court.

This case presents the question whether the Fourth Amendment exclusionary rule should be modified so as not to bar the use in the prosecution's case-in-chief of evidence obtained by officers acting in reasonable reliance on a search warrant issued by a detached and neutral magistrate but ultimately found to be unsupported by probable cause. To resolve this question, we must consider once again the tension between the sometimes competing goals of, on the one hand, deterring official misconduct and removing inducements to unreasonable invasions of privacy and, on the other, establishing procedures under which criminal defendants are "acquitted or convicted on the basis of all the evidence which exposes the truth." . . .

In August 1981, a confidential informant of unproven reliability informed an officer of the Burbank Police Department that two persons known to him as "Armando" and "Patsy" were selling large quantities of cocaine and methaqualone from their residence at 620 Price Drive in Burbank, Cal. The informant also indicated that he had witnessed a sale of methaqualone by "Patsy" at the residence approximately five months earlier and had observed at that time a shoebox containing a large amount of cash that belonged to "Patsy." He further declared that "Armando" and "Patsy" generally kept only small quantities of drugs at their residence and stored the remainder at another location in Burbank.

On the basis of this information, the Burbank police initiated an extensive investigation focusing first on the Price Drive residence and later on two other residences as well. Cars parked at the Price Drive residence were determined to belong to respondents Armando Sanchez, who had previously been arrested for possession of marihuana, and Patsy Stewart, who had no criminal record. During the course of the investigation, officers observed an automobile belonging to respondent Ricardo Del Castillo, who had previously been arrested for possession of 50 pounds of marihuana, arrive at the Price residence. The driver of that car entered the house, exited shortly thereafter carrying a small paper sack, and drove away. A check of Del Castillo's probation records led the officers to respondent Alberto Leon, whose telephone number Del Castillo had listed as his employer's. Leon had been arrested in 1980 on drug charges, and a companion had informed the police at that time that Leon was heavily involved in the importation of drugs into this country. Before the current investigation began, the Burbank officers had learned that an informant had told a Glendale police officer that Leon stored a large quantity of methaqualone at his residence in Glendale. During the course of this investigation, the

Burbank officers learned that Leon was living at 716 South Sunset Canyon in Burbank.

Subsequently, the officers observed several persons, at least one of whom had prior drug involvement, arriving at the Price Drive residence and leaving with small packages; observed a variety of other material activity at the two residences as well as at a condominium at 7902 Via Magdalena; and witnessed a variety of relevant activity involving respondents' automobiles. The officers also observed respondents Sanchez and Stewart board separate flights for Miami. The pair later returned to Los Angeles together, consented to a search of their luggage that revealed only a small amount of marihuana, and left the airport. Based on these and other observations summarized in the affidavit, Officer Cyril Rombach of the Burbank Police Department, an experienced and well-trained narcotics investigator, prepared an application for a warrant to search 620 Price Drive, 716 South Sunset Canyon, 7902 Via Magdalena, and automobiles registered to each of the respondents for an extensive list of items believed to be related to respondent's drug-trafficking activities. Officer Rombach's extensive application was reviewed by several Deputy District Attorneys.

A facially valid search warrant was issued in September 1981 by a State Superior Court Judge. The ensuing searches produced large quantities of drugs at the Via Magdalena and Sunset Canyon addresses and a small quantity at the Price Drive residence. Other evidence was discovered at each of the residences and in Stewart's and Del Castillo's automobiles. . . .

The respondents then filed motions to suppress the evidence seized pursuant to the warrant. The District Court . . . concluded that the affidavit was insufficient to establish probable cause, but did not suppress all of the evidence as to all of the respondents because none of the respondents had standing to challenge all of the searches. In response to a request from the Government, the court made clear that Officer Rombach had acted in good faith, but it rejected the Government's suggestion that the Fourth Amendment exclusionary rule should not apply where evidence is seized in reasonable, good-faith reliance on a search warrant. . . .

The Fourth Amendment contains no provision expressly precluding the use of evidence obtained in violation of its commands, and an examination of its origin and purposes makes clear that the use of fruits of a past unlawful search or seizure "work[s] no new Fourth Amendment wrong." . . . The wrong condemned by the Amendment is "fully accomplished" by the unlawful search or seizure itself, . . . and the exclusionary rule is neither intended nor able to "cure the invasion of the defendant's rights which he has already suffered." . . . The rule thus operates as "a judicially created remedy designed to

safeguard Fourth Amendment rights generally through its deterrent effect, rather than a personal constitutional right of the person aggrieved." . . .

Whether the exclusionary sanction is appropriately imposed in a particular case, our decisions make clear, is "an issue separate from the question whether the Fourth Amendment rights of the party seeking to invoke the rule were violated by police conduct." . . . Only the former question is currently before us, and it must be resolved by weighing the costs and benefits of preventing the use in the prosecution's case-in-chief of inherently trustworthy tangible evidence obtained in reliance on a search warrant issued by a detached and neutral magistrate that ultimately is found to be defective.

The substantial social costs exacted by the exclusionary rule for the vindication of Fourth Amendment rights have long been a source of concern. "Our cases have consistently recognized that unbending application of the exclusionary sanction to enforce ideals of government rectitude would impede unacceptably the truth-finding functions of judge and jury." . . . An objectionable collateral consequence of this interference with the criminal justice system's truth-finding function is that some guilty defendants may go free or receive reduced sentences as a result of favorable plea bargains. Particularly when law enforcement officers have acted in objective good faith or their transgressions have been minor, the magnitude of the benefit conferred on such guilty defendants offends basic concepts of the criminal justice system. . . . Indiscriminate application of the exclusionary rule, therefore, may well "generat[e] disrespect for the law and the administration of justice." . . . Accordingly, "[a]s with any remedial device, the application of the rule has been restricted to those areas where its remedial objectives are thought most efficaciously served." . . .

. . . The Court has, to be sure, not seriously questioned, "in the absence of a more efficacious sanction, the continued application of the rule to suppress evidence from the [prosecution's] case where a Fourth Amendment violation has been substantial and deliberate. . . ." . . . Nevertheless, the balancing approach that has evolved in various contexts—including criminal trial—"forcefully suggest[s] that the exclusionary rule be more generally modified to permit the introduction of evidence obtained in the reasonable good-faith belief that a search or a seizure was in accord with the Fourth Amendment." . . .

As cases considering the use of unlawfully obtained evidence in criminal trials themselves make clear, it does not follow from the emphasis on the exclusionary rule's deterrent value that "anything which deters illegal searches is thereby commanded by the Fourth Amendment." . . . In determining whether persons aggrieved solely by the introduction of damaging evidence unlawfully obtained from their co-conspirators or co-defendants could seek suppression, for example, we found that the additional benefits of such an extension of the exclusionary rule would not outweigh its costs. . . . Standing to invoke the rule has thus been limited to cases in which the prosecution seeks to use the fruits of an illegal search or seizure against the victim of police misconduct. . . .

Because a search warrant "provides the detached scrutiny of a neutral magistrate, which is a more reliable safeguard against improper searches than the hurried judgment of a law enforcement officer 'engaged in the often competitive enterprise of ferreting out crime,' " . . . we have expressed a strong preference for warrants and declared that "in a doubtful or marginal case a search under a warrant may be sustainable where without one it would fall." . . . Reasonable minds frequently may differ on the question whether a particular affidavit establishes probable cause, and we have thus concluded that the preference for warrants is most appropriately effectuated by according "great deference" to a magistrate's determination. . . .

Deference to the magistrate, however, is not boundless. It is clear, first, that the deference accorded to a magistrate's finding of probable cause does not preclude inquiry into the knowing or reckless falsity of the affidavit on which that determination was based. . . . Second, the courts must also insist that the magistrate purport to "perform his 'neutral and detached' function and not serve merely as a rubber stamp for the police." . . .

Third, reviewing courts will not defer to a warrant based on an affidavit that does not "provide the magistrate with a substantial basis for determining the existence of probable cause." . . . Even if the warrant application was supported by more than a "bare bones" affidavit, a reviewing court may properly conclude that, notwithstanding the deference that magistrates deserve, the warrant was invalid because the magistrate's probable-cause determination reflected an improper analysis of the totality of the circumstances, . . . or because the form of the warrant was improper in some respect.

Only in the first of these three situations, however, has the Court set forth a rationale for suppressing evidence obtained pursuant to a search warrant; in the other areas, it has simply excluded such evidence without considering whether Fourth Amendment interests will be advanced. To the extent that proponents of exclusion rely on its behavioral effects on judges and magistrates in these areas, their reliance is misplaced. First, the exclusionary rule is designed to deter police misconduct rather than to punish the errors of judges and magistrates. Second, there exists no evidence suggesting that judges and magistrates are inclined to ignore or subvert the Fourth Amendment or that lawlessness among those actors requires application of the extreme sanction of exclusion.

Third, and most important, we discern no basis, and are offered none, for believing that exclusion of evidence seized pursuant to a warrant will have a significant deterrent effect on the issuing judge or magistrate. . . . Judges and magistrates are not adjuncts to the law enforcement team; as neutral judicial officers, they have no stake in the outcome of particular criminal prosecutions. The threat of exclusion thus cannot be expected significantly to deter them. Imposition of the exclusionary sanction is not necessary meaningfully to inform judicial officers of their errors, and we cannot conclude that admitting evidence obtained pursuant to a warrant while at the same time declaring that the warrant was somehow defective will in any way reduce judicial officers' professional incentives to comply with the Fourth Amendment, encourage them to repeat their mistakes, or lead to the granting of all colorable warrant requests.

If exclusion of evidence obtained pursuant to a subsequently invalidated warrant is to have any deterrent effect, therefore, it must alter the behavior of individual law enforcement officers or the policies of their departments. . . .

We have frequently questioned whether the exclusionary rule can have any deterrent effect when the offending officers acted in the objectively reasonable belief that their conduct did not violate the Fourth Amendment. "No empirical researcher, proponent or opponent of the rule, has yet been able to establish with any assurance whether the rule has a deterrent effect. . . ." . . . But even assuming that the rule effectively deters some police misconduct and provides incentives for the law enforcement profession as a whole to conduct itself in accord with the Fourth Amendment, it cannot be expected, and should not be applied, to deter objectively reasonable law enforcement activity. . . .

We conclude that the marginal or nonexistent benefits produced by suppressing evidence obtained in objectively reasonable reliance on a subsequently invalidated search warrant cannot justify the substantial costs of exclusion. . . .

When the principles we have enunciated today are applied to the facts of this case, it is apparent that the judgment of the Court of Appeals cannot stand. The Court of Appeals applied the prevailing legal standards to Officer Rombach's warrant application and concluded that the application could not support the magistrate's probable-cause determination. In so doing, the court clearly informed the magistrate that he had erred in issuing the challenged warrant. This aspect of the court's judgment is not under attack in this proceeding.

Having determined that the warrant should not have issued, the Court of Appeals understandably declined to adopt a modification of the Fourth Amendment exclusionary rule that this court had not previously sanctioned. Although the modification finds strong support in our previous cases, the Court of Appeals' commendable self-restraint is not to be criticized. We have now re-examined the purposes of the exclusionary rule and the propriety of its application in cases where officers have relied on a subsequently invalidated search warrant. Our conclusion is that the rule's purposes will only rarely be served by applying it in such circumstances. . . .

Accordingly, the judgment of the Court of Appeals is reversed.

Justice Blackmun, concurring. . . .

Justice Brennan, with whom *Justice Marshall* joins, dissenting.

Ten years ago in *United States v. Calandra* . . . (1974), I expressed the fear that the Court's decision "may signal that a majority of my colleagues have positioned themselves to reopen the door [to evidence secured by official lawlessness] still further and abandon altogether the exclusionary rule in search-and-seizure cases." . . . Since then, in case after case, I have witnessed the Court's gradual but determined strangulation of the rule. It now appears that the Court's victory over the Fourth Amendment is complete. . . .

The Court seeks to justify this result on the ground that the "costs" of adhering to the exclusionary rule in cases like those before us exceed the "benefits." But the language of deterrence and of cost/benefit analysis, if used indiscriminately, can have a narcotic effect. It creates an illusion of technical precision and ineluctability. It suggests that not only constitutional principle but also empirical data supports the majority's result. When the Court's analysis is examined carefully, however, it is clear that we have not been treated to an honest assessment of the merits of the exclusionary rule, but have instead been drawn into a curious world where the "costs" of excluding illegally obtained evidence loom to exaggerated heights and where the "benefits" of such exclusion are made to disappear with a mere wave of the hand.

The majority ignores the fundamental constitutional importance of what is at stake here. While the machinery of law enforcement and indeed the nature of crime itself have changed dramatically since the Fourth Amendment became part of the Nation's fundamental law in 1791, what the Framers understood then remains true today—that the task of combating crime and convicting the guilty will in every era seem of such critical and pressing concern that we may be lured by the temptations of expediency into forsaking our commitment to protecting individual liberty and privacy. It was for that very reason that the Framers of the Bill of Rights insisted that law enforcement efforts be permanently and unambiguously restricted in order to preserve personal freedoms. In the constitutional scheme they ordained, the sometimes unpopular task of ensuring that the government's enforcement efforts remain within the strict boundaries fixed by the Fourth Amendment was entrusted to the courts. . . . If those independent tribunals lose their resolve, however, as the Court has done today, and give way to the seductive call of expediency, the vital guarantees of the Fourth Amendment are reduced to nothing more than a "form of words." . . .

A proper understanding of the broad purposes sought to be served by the Fourth Amendment demonstrates that the principles embodied in the exclusionary rule rest upon a far firmer constitutional foundation than the shifting sands of the Court's deterrence rationale. But even if I were to accept the Court's chosen method of analyzing the question posed by these cases, I would still conclude that the Court's decision cannot be justified. . . .

At bottom, the Court's decision turns on the proposition that the exclusionary rule is merely a "judicially created remedy designed to safeguard Fourth Amendment rights generally through its deterrent effect, rather than a personal constitutional right." . . . The germ of that idea is found in *Wolf v. Colorado,* . . . and although I had thought that such a narrow conception of the rule had been forever put to rest by our decision in *Mapp v. Ohio,* . . . it has been revived by the present Court and reaches full flower with today's decision. The essence of this view, as expressed initially in the *Calandra* opinion and as reiterated today, is that the sole "purpose of the Fourth Amendment is to prevent unreasonable governmental intrusions into the privacy of one's person, house, papers, or effects. The wrong condemned is the unjustified governmental invasion of these areas of an individual's life. That wrong . . . is *fully* accomplished by the original search without probable cause." . . . This reading of the Amendment implies that its proscriptions are directed solely at those government agents, who may actually invade an individual's constitutionally protected privacy. The courts are not subject to any direct constitutional duty to exclude illegally obtained evidence, because the question of the admissibility of such evidence is not addressed by the Amendment. This view of the scope of the Amendment relegates the judiciary to the periphery. Because the only constitutionally cognizable injury has already been "fully accomplished" by the police by the time a case comes before the courts, the Constitution is not itself violated if the judge decides to admit the tainted evidence. Indeed, the most the judge *can* do is wring his hands and hope that perhaps by excluding such evidence he can deter future transgressions by the police.

Such a reading appears plausible, because, as critics of the exclusionary rule never tire of repeating, the Fourth Amendment makes no express provision of the exclusion of evidence secured in violation of its commands. A short answer to this claim, of course, is that many of the Constitution's most vital imperatives are stated in general terms and the task of giving meaning to these precepts is therefore left to subsequent judicial decisionmaking in the context of concrete cases. The nature of our Constitution, as Chief Justice Marshall long ago explained, "requires that only its great outlines should be marked, its important objects designated, and the minor ingredients which compose those objects be deduced from the nature of the objects themselves." . . .

A more direct answer may be supplied by recognizing that the Amendment, like other provisions of the Bill of Rights, restrains the power of the government as a whole; it does not specify only a particular agency and exempt all others. The judiciary is responsible, no less than the executive, for ensuring that constitutional rights are respected. . . .

. . . It is difficult to give any meaning at all to the limitations imposed by the Amendment if they are read to proscribe only certain conduct by the police but to allow other agents of the same government to take advantage of evidence secured by the police in violation of its requirements. The Amendment therefore must be read to condemn not only the initial unconstitutional invasion of privacy—which is done, after all, for the purpose of securing evidence—but also the subsequent use of any evidence so obtained.

The Court evades this principle by drawing an artificial line between the constitutional rights and responsibilities that are engaged by actions of the police and those that are engaged when a defendant appears before the courts. According to the Court, the substantive protections of the Fourth Amendment are wholly exhausted at the moment when police unlawfully invade an individual's privacy and thus no substantive force remains to those protections at the time of trial when the government seeks to use evidence obtained by the police.

I submit that such a crabbed reading of the Fourth Amendment casts aside the teaching of those Justices who first formulated the exclusionary rule, and rests ultimately on an impoverished understanding of judicial responsibility in our constitutional scheme. For my part, "[t]he right of the people to be secure in their persons, houses, papers and effects, against unreasonable searches and seizures" comprises a personal right to exclude all evidence secured by means of unreasonable searches and seizures. The right to be free from the initial invasion of privacy and the right of exclusion are coordinate components of the central embracing right to be free from unreasonable searches and seizures. . . .

Justice Stevens, dissenting. . . .

Case

MIRANDA V. ARIZONA

384 U.S. 436; 86 S.Ct. 1602; 16 L.Ed. 2d 694 (1966)
Vote: 5–4

In one of the most important criminal justice decisions of the Warren era, the Court imposes procedural safeguards on custodial police interrogations.

Mr. Chief Justice Warren delivered the opinion of the Court.

The cases before us raise questions which go to the roots of our concepts of American criminal jurisprudence: the restraints society must observe consistent with the Federal Constitution in prosecuting individuals for crime. More specifically, we deal with the admissibility of statements obtained from an individual who is subjected to custodial police interrogation and the necessity for procedures which assure that the individual is accorded his privilege under the Fifth Amendment to the Constitution not to be compelled to incriminate himself.

We dealt with certain phases of this problem recently in *Escobedo v. Illinois* . . . (1964). We start here, as we did in *Escobedo,* with the premise that our holding is not an innovation in our jurisprudence, but is an application of principles long recognized and applied in other settings. We have undertaken a thorough re-examination of the *Escobedo* decision and the principles it announced, and we reaffirm it. That case was but an explication of basic rights that are enshrined in our Constitution—that "No person . . . shall be compelled in any criminal case to be a witness against himself," and that "the accused shall . . . have the Assistance of Counsel"—rights which were put in jeopardy in that case through official overbearing. These precious rights were fixed in our Constitution only after centuries of persecution and struggle. And in the words of Chief Justice Marshall, they were secured "for ages to come, and . . . designed to approach immortality as nearly as human institutions can approach it." . . .

Our holding will be spelled out with some specificity in the pages which follow but briefly stated it is this: the prosecution may not use statements, whether exculpatory or inculpatory, stemming from custodial interrogation of the defendant unless it demonstrates the use of procedural safeguards effective to secure the privilege against self-incrimination. By custodial interrogation, we mean questioning initiated by law enforcement officers after a person has been taken into custody or otherwise deprived of his freedom of action in any significant way. As for the procedural safeguards to be employed, unless other fully effective means are devised to inform accused persons of their right of silence and to assure a continuous opportunity to exercise it, the following measures are required. Prior to any questioning, the person must be warned that he has a right to remain silent, that any statement he does make may be used as evidence against him, and that he has a right to the presence of an attorney, either retained or appointed. The defendant may waive effectuation of these rights, provided the waiver is made voluntarily, knowingly and intelligently. If, however, he indicates in any manner and at any stage of the process that he wishes to consult with an attorney before speaking there can be no questioning. Likewise, if the individual is alone and indicates in any manner that he does not wish to be interrogated, the police may not question him. The mere fact that he may have answered some questions or volunteered some statements on his own does not deprive him of the right to refrain from answering any further inquiries until he has consulted with an attorney and thereafter consents to be questioned.

The constitutional issue we decide . . . is the admissibility of statements obtained from a defendant questioned while in custody or otherwise deprived of his freedom of action in any significant way. In each, the defendant was questioned by police officers, detectives, or a prosecuting attorney in a room in which he was cut off from the outside world. In none of these cases was the defendant given a full and effective warning of his rights at the outset of the interrogation process. In all the cases, the questioning elicited oral admissions, and in three of them, signed statements as well which were admitted at their trials. They all thus share salient features—*incommunicado* interrogation of individuals in a police-dominated atmosphere, resulting in self-incriminating statements without full warnings of constitutional rights.

An understanding of the nature and setting of this in-custody interrogation is essential to our decisions today. The difficulty in depicting what transpires at such interrogations stems from the fact that in this country they have largely taken place *incommunicado*. From extensive factual studies undertaken in the early 1930's, including the famous Wickersham Report to Congress by a Presidential Commission, it is clear that police violence and the "third degree" flourished at that time. In a series of cases decided by this Court long after these studies, the police resorted to physical brutality—beating, hanging, whipping—and to sustained and protracted questioning *incommunicado* in order to extort confessions. The Commission on Civil Rights in 1961 found much evidence to indicate that "some policemen still resort to physical force to obtain confessions." The use of physical brutality and violence is not, unfortunately, relegated to the past or to any part of the country. Only recently in Kings County, New York, the police brutally beat, kicked and placed lighted cigarette butts on the back of a potential witness under interrogation for the purpose of securing a statement incriminating a third party. . . .

The examples given above are undoubtedly the exception now, but they are sufficiently widespread to be the object of concern. Unless a proper limitation upon custodial interrogation is achieved—such as these decisions will advance—there can be no assurance that practices of this nature will be eradicated in the foreseeable future.

Again we stress that the modern practice of in-custody interrogation is psychologically rather than physically oriented. Interrogation still takes place in privacy. Privacy results in secrecy and this in turn results in a gap in our knowledge as to what in fact goes on in the interrogation rooms. A valuable source of information about present police practices, however, may be found in various police manuals and texts which document procedures employed with success in the past, and which recommended various other effective tactics. These texts are used by law enforcement agencies themselves as guides. It should be noted that these texts professedly present the most enlightened and effective means presently used to obtain statements through custodial interrogation. By considering these texts and other data, it is possible to describe procedures observed and noted around the country.

Even without employing brutality, the "third degree" or the specific strategems described above, the very fact of custodial interrogation exacts a heavy toll on individual liberty and trades on the weakness of individuals.

In the cases before us today, given this background, we concern ourselves primarily with this interrogation atmosphere and the evils it can bring.

In these cases, we might not find the defendants' statements to have been involuntary in traditional terms. Our concern for adequate safeguards to protect precious Fifth Amendment rights is, of course, not lessened in the slightest. In each of the cases, the defendant was thrust into an unfamiliar atmosphere and run through menacing police interrogation procedures. The potentiality for compulsion is forcefully apparent, for example, in *Miranda,* where the indigent Mexican defendant was a seriously disturbed individual with pronounced sexual fantasies. . . .

It is obvious that such an interrogation environment is created for no purpose other than to subjugate the individual to the will of his examiner. This atmosphere carries its own badge of intimidation. . . . The current practice of *incommunicado* interrogation is at odds with one of our Nation's most cherished principles—that the individual may not be compelled to incriminate himself. Unless adequate protective devices are employed to dispel the compulsion inherent in custodial surroundings, no statement obtained from the defendant can truly be the product of his free choice.

From the foregoing, we can readily perceive an intimate connection between the privilege against self-incrimination and police custodial questioning. It is fitting to turn to history and precedent underlying the Self-Incrimination Clause to determine its applicability in this situation.

We sometimes forget how long it has taken to establish the privilege against self-incrimination, the sources from which it came and the fervor with which it was defended. Its roots go back into ancient times.

As a "noble principle often transcends its origins," the privilege has come rightfully to be recognized in part as an individual's substantive right, a "right to a private enclave where he may lead a private life. That right is the hallmark of our democracy." . . . We have recently noted that the privilege against self-incrimination—the essential mainstay of our adversary system—is founded on a complex of values. . . . All these policies point to one overriding thought: the constitutional foundation underlying the privilege is the respect a government—state or federal—must accord to the dignity and integrity of its citizens.

We are satisfied that all the principles embodied in the privilege apply to informal compulsion exerted by law-enforcement officers during in-custody questioning. An individual swept from familiar surroundings into police custody, surrounded by antagonistic forces, and subjected to the techniques of persuasion described above cannot be otherwise than under compulsion to speak. As a practical matter, the compulsion to speak in the isolated setting of the police station may well be greater than in courts or other official investigations, where there are often impartial observers to guard against intimidation or trickery.

The presence of counsel, in all the cases before us today, would be the adequate protective device necessary to make the process of police interrogation conform to the dictates of the privilege. His presence would insure that statements made in the government-established atmosphere are not the product of compulsion.

It is impossible for us to foresee the potential alternatives for protecting the privilege which might be devised by Congress or the States in the exercise of their creative rulemaking capacities. Therefore we cannot say that the Constitution necessarily requires adherence to any particular solution for the inherent compulsions of the interrogation process as it is presently conducted. Our decision in no way creates a constitutional straitjacket which will handicap sound efforts at reform, nor is it intended to have this effect. We encourage Congress and the States to continue their laudable search for increasingly effective ways of protecting the rights of the individual while promoting efficient enforcement of our criminal laws.

A recurrent argument made in these cases is that society's need for interrogation outweighs the privilege. This argument is not unfamiliar to this Court. . . .

In announcing these principles, we are not unmindful of the burdens which law enforcement officials must bear, often under trying circumstances. We also fully recognize the obligation of all citizens to aid in enforcing the criminal laws. This Court, while protecting individual rights, has always given ample latitude to law enforcement agencies in the legitimate exercise of their duties. The limit we have placed on the interrogation process should not constitute an undue interference with a proper system of law enforcement. As we have noted, our decision does not in any way preclude police from carrying out their traditional investigatory functions. Although confessions may play an important role in some convictions, the cases before us present graphic examples of the overstatement of the "need" for confessions.

Therefore, in accordance with the foregoing, the judgment of the Supreme Court of Arizona . . . [is] reversed. . . .

Mr. Justice Harlan, whom **Mr. Justice Stewart** and **Mr. Justice White** join, dissenting. . . .

Mr. Justice White, with whom **Mr. Justice Harlan** and **Mr. Justice Stewart** join, dissenting.

. . . The obvious underpinning of the Court's decision is a deep-seated distrust of all confessions. As the Court declares that the accused may not be interrogated without counsel present, absent a waiver of the right to counsel, and as the Court all but admonishes the lawyer to advise the accused to remain silent, the result adds up to a judicial judgment that evidence from the accused should not be used against him in any way, whether compelled or not. This is the not so subtle overtone of the opinion—that it is inherently wrong for the police to gather evidence from the accused himself. And this is precisely the nub of this dissent. I see nothing wrong or immoral, and certainly nothing unconstitutional, in the police's asking a suspect whom they have reasonable cause to arrest whether or not he killed his wife or in confronting him with the evidence on which the arrest was based, at least where he has been plainly advised that he may remain completely silent. . . .

The rule announced today will measurably weaken the ability of the criminal law to perform these tasks. It is a deliberate calculus to prevent interrogations, to reduce the incidence of confessions and pleas of guilty and to increase the number of trials. . . .

In some unknown number of cases the Court's rule will return a killer, a rapist or other criminal to the streets and to the environment which produced him, to repeat his crime whenever it pleases him. As a consequence, there will not be a gain, but a loss, in human dignity. The real concern is not the unfortunate consequences of this new decision on the criminal law as an abstract, disembodied series of authoritative proscriptions, but the impact on those who rely on the public authority for protection and who without it can only engage in violent self-help with guns, knives and the help of their neighbors similarly inclined. There is, of course, a saving factor: the next victims are uncertain, unnamed and unrepresented in this case.

Nor can this decision do other than have a corrosive effect on the criminal law as an effective device to prevent crime. A major component in its effectiveness in this regard is its swift and sure enforcement. The easier it is to get away with rape and murder, the less the deterrent effect on those who are inclined to attempt it. This is still good common sense. If it were not, we should posthaste liquidate the whole law enforcement establishment as a useless, misguided effort to control human conduct.

And what about the accused who has confessed or would confess in response to simple, noncoercive questioning and whose guilt could not otherwise be proved? Is it so clear that release is the best thing for him in every case? Has it so unquestionably been resolved that in each and every case it would be better for him not to confess and to return to his environment with no attempt whatsoever to help him? I think not. It may well be that in many cases it will be no less than a callous disregard for his own welfare as well as for the interests of his next victim.

Much of the trouble with the Court's new rule is that it will operate indiscriminately in all criminal cases, regardless of the severity of the crime or the circumstances involved. It applies to every defendant, whether the professional criminal or one committing a crime of momentary passion who is not part and parcel of organized crime. It will slow down the investigation and the apprehension of confederates in those cases where time is of the essence, such as kidnapping, those involving the national security, and some of those involving organized crime. In the latter context the lawyer who arrives may also be the lawyer for the defendant's colleagues and can be relied upon to insure that no breach of the organization's security takes place even though the accused may feel that the best thing he can do is to cooperate.

At the same time, the Court's *per se* approach may not be justified on the ground that it provides a "bright line" permitting the authorities to judge in advance whether interrogation may safely be pursued without jeopardizing the admissibility of any information obtained as a consequence. Nor can it be claimed that judicial time and effort, assuming that is a relevant consideration, will be conserved because of the ease of application of the new rule. Today's decision leaves open such questions as whether the accused was in custody, whether his statements were spontaneous or the product of interrogation, whether the accused has effectively waived his rights, and whether nontestimonial evidence introduced at trial is the fruit of statements made during a prohibited interrogation, all of which are certain to prove productive of uncertainty during investigation and litigation during prosecution. For all these reasons, if further restrictions on police interrogation are desirable at this time, a more flexible approach makes much more sense than the Court's constitutional straitjacket which forecloses more discriminating treatment by legislative or rule-making pronouncements. . . .

Mr. Justice Clark, dissenting. . . .

Case

DICKERSON V. UNITED STATES

520 U.S. 428; 120 S.Ct. 2326; 147 L.Ed. 2d 405 (2000)
Vote: 7–2

In this case the Supreme Court reconsiders its 1966 decision in Miranda v. Arizona.

Chief Justice Rehnquist delivered the opinion of the Court.

In *Miranda v. Arizona* . . . (1966), we held that certain warnings must be given before a suspect's statement made during custodial interrogation could be admitted in evidence. In the wake of that decision, Congress enacted 18 U.S.C. § 3501, which in essence laid down a rule that the admissibility of such statements should turn only on whether or not they were voluntarily made. We hold that *Miranda,* being a constitutional decision of this Court, may not be in effect overruled by an Act of Congress, and we decline to overrule *Miranda* ourselves. We therefore hold that *Miranda* and its progeny in this Court govern the admissibility of statements made during custodial interrogation in both state and federal courts.

Petitioner Dickerson was indicted for bank robbery, conspiracy to commit bank robbery, and using a firearm in the course of committing a crime of violence, all in violation of the applicable provisions of Title 18 of the United States Code. Before trial, Dickerson moved to suppress a statement he had made at a Federal Bureau of Investigation field office, on the grounds that he had not received "*Miranda* warnings" before being interrogated. The District Court granted his motion to suppress, and the Government took an interlocutory appeal to the United States Court of Appeals for the Fourth Circuit. That court, by a divided vote, reversed the District Court's suppression order. It agreed with the District Court's conclusion that petitioner had not received *Miranda* warnings before making his statement. But it went on to hold that § 3501, which in effect makes the admissibility of statements such as Dickerson's turn solely on whether they were made voluntarily, was satisfied in this case. It then concluded that our decision in *Miranda* was not a constitutional holding, and that therefore Congress could by statute have the final say on the question of admissibility. . . .

Because of the importance of the questions raised by the Court of Appeals' decision, we granted certiorari . . . and now reverse. . . .

Two years after *Miranda* was decided, Congress enacted § 3501. That section provides, in relevant part:

(a) In any criminal prosecution brought by the United States or by the District of Columbia, a confession . . . shall be admissible in evidence if it is voluntarily given. Before such confession is received in evidence, the trial judge shall, out of the presence of the jury, determine any issue as to voluntariness. If the trial judge determines that the confession was voluntarily made it shall be admitted in evidence and the trial judge shall permit the jury to hear relevant evidence on the issue of voluntariness and shall instruct the jury to give such weight to the confession as the jury feels it deserves under all the circumstances.

(b) The trial judge in determining the issue of voluntariness shall take into consideration all the circumstances surrounding the giving of the confession, including (1) the time elapsing between arrest and arraignment of the defendant making the confession, if it was made after arrest and before arraignment, (2) whether such defendant knew the nature of the offense with which he was charged or of which he was suspected at the time of making the confession, (3) whether or not such defendant was advised or knew that he was not required to make any statement and that any such statement could be used against him, (4) whether or not such defendant had been advised prior to questioning of his right to the assistance of counsel; and (5) whether or not such defendant was without the assistance of counsel when questioned and when giving such confession. . . .

Given § 3501's express designation of voluntariness as the touchstone of admissibility, its omission of any warning requirement, and the instruction for trial courts to consider a nonexclusive list of factors relevant to the circumstances of a confession, we agree with the Court of Appeals that Congress intended by its enactment to overrule *Miranda.* . . . Because of the obvious conflict between our decision in *Miranda* and § 3501, we must address whether Congress has constitutional authority to thus supersede *Miranda.* If Congress has such authority, § 3501's totality-of-the-circumstances approach must prevail over *Miranda*'s requirement of warnings; if not, that section must yield to *Miranda*'s more specific requirements.

The law in this area is clear. This Court has supervisory authority over the federal courts, and we may use that authority to prescribe rules of evidence and procedure that are binding in those tribunals. . . . However, the power to judicially create and enforce nonconstitutional "rules of procedure and evidence for the federal courts exists only in the absence of a relevant Act of Congress." . . . Congress retains the ultimate authority to modify or set aside any judicially created rules of evidence and procedure that are not required by the Constitution. . . .

But Congress may not legislatively supersede our decisions interpreting and applying the Constitution. . . . This case therefore turns on whether the *Miranda* Court announced a constitutional rule or merely exercised its supervisory authority to regulate evidence in the absence of congressional direction. Recognizing this point, the Court of Appeals surveyed *Miranda* and its progeny to determine the constitutional status of the *Miranda* decision. . . . Relying on the fact that we have created several exceptions to *Miranda*'s warnings requirement and that we have repeatedly referred to the *Miranda* warnings as "prophylactic," . . . the Court of Appeals concluded that the protections announced in *Miranda* are not constitutionally required. . . .

We disagree with the Court of Appeals' conclusion, although we concede that there is language in some of our opinions that supports the view taken by that court. But first and foremost of the factors on the other side—that *Miranda* is a constitutional decision—is that both *Miranda* and two of its companion cases applied the rule to proceedings in state courts—to wit, Arizona, California, and New York. . . . Since that time, we have consistently applied *Miranda*'s rule to prosecutions arising in state courts. . . . It is beyond dispute that we do not hold a supervisory power over the courts of the several States. . . . With respect to proceedings in state courts, our "authority is limited to enforcing the commands of the United States Constitution." . . .

The *Miranda* opinion itself begins by stating that the Court granted certiorari "to explore some facets of the problems . . . of applying the privilege against self-incrimination to in-custody interrogation, *and to give concrete constitutional guidelines for law enforcement agencies and courts to follow*" (emphasis added). In fact, the majority opinion is replete with statements indicating that the majority thought it was announcing a constitutional rule. Indeed, the Court's ultimate conclusion was that the unwarned confessions obtained in the four cases before the Court in *Miranda* "were obtained from the defendant under circumstances that did not meet constitutional standards for protection of the privilege." . . .

Additional support for our conclusion that *Miranda* is constitutionally based is found in the *Miranda* Court's invitation for legislative action to protect the constitutional right against coerced self-incrimination. After discussing the "compelling pressures" inherent in custodial police interrogation, the *Miranda* Court concluded that, "[i]n order to combat these pressures and to permit a full opportunity to exercise the privilege against self-incrimination, the accused must be adequately and effectively appraised of his rights and the exercise of those rights must be fully honored." . . . However, the Court emphasized that it could not foresee "the potential alternatives for protecting the privilege which might be devised by Congress or the States," and it accordingly opined that the Constitution would not preclude legislative solutions that differed from the prescribed *Miranda* warnings but which were "at least as effective in apprising accused persons of their right of silence and in assuring a continuous opportunity to exercise it." . . .

The Court of Appeals also relied on the fact that we have, after our *Miranda* decision, made exceptions from its rule in cases such as *New York v. Quarles* (1984), and *Harris v. New York* (1971). . . . But we have also broadened the application of the *Miranda* doctrine in cases such as *Doyle v. Ohio* (1976), and *Arizona v. Roberson* (1988). These decisions illustrate the principle—not that *Miranda* is not a constitutional rule—but that no constitutional rule is immutable. No court laying down a general rule can possibly foresee the various circumstances in which counsel will seek to apply it, and the sort of modifications represented by these cases are as much a normal part of constitutional law as the original decision. . . .

As an alternative argument for sustaining the Court of Appeals' decision, the court-invited *amicus curiae* contends that the section complies with the requirement that a legislative alternative to *Miranda* be equally as effective in preventing coerced confessions. . . . We agree with the *amicus'* contention that there are more remedies available for abusive police conduct than there were at the time *Miranda* was decided, . . . to hold that a suspect may bring a federal cause of action under the Due Process Clause for police misconduct during custodial interrogation. But we do not agree that these additional measures supplement § 3501's protections sufficiently to meet the constitutional minimum. *Miranda* requires procedures that will warn a suspect in custody of his right to remain silent and which will assure the suspect that the exercise of that right will be honored. . . . As discussed above, § 3501 explicitly eschews a requirement of pre-interrogation warnings in favor of an approach that looks to the administration of such warnings as only one factor in determining the voluntariness of a suspect's confession. The additional remedies cited by *amicus* do not, in our view, render them, together with § 3501 an adequate substitute for the warnings required by *Miranda*.

The dissent argues that it is judicial overreaching for this Court to hold § 3501 unconstitutional unless we hold that the *Miranda* warnings are required by the Constitution, in the sense that nothing else will suffice to satisfy constitutional requirements. . . . But we need not go farther than *Miranda* to decide this case. In *Miranda*, the Court noted that reliance on the traditional totality-of-the-circumstances test raised a risk of overlooking an involuntary custodial confession, . . . a risk that the Court found unacceptably great when the confession is offered in the case in chief to prove guilt. The Court therefore concluded that something more than the totality test was necessary. . . . As discussed above, § 3501 reinstates the totality test as sufficient. Section 3501 therefore cannot be sustained if *Miranda* is to remain the law.

Whether or not we would agree with *Miranda*'s reasoning and its resulting rule, were we addressing the issue in the first instance, the principles of *stare decisis* weigh heavily against overruling it now. . . .

. . . *Miranda* has become embedded in routine police practice to the point where the warnings have become part of our national culture. . . . While we have overruled our precedents when subsequent cases have undermined their doctrinal underpinnings, . . . we do not believe that this has happened to the *Miranda* decision. If anything, our subsequent cases have reduced the impact of the *Miranda* rule on legitimate law enforcement while reaffirming the decision's core ruling that unwarned statements may not be used as evidence in the prosecution's case in chief.

The disadvantage of the *Miranda* rule is that statements which may be by no means involuntary, made by a defendant who is aware of his "rights," may nonetheless be excluded and a guilty defendant go free as a result. But experience suggests that the totality-of-the-circumstances test which § 3501 seeks to revive is more difficult than *Miranda* for law enforcement officers to conform to, and for courts to apply in a consistent manner. . . . The requirement that *Miranda* warnings be given does not, of course, dispense with the voluntariness inquiry. But as we said in *Berkemer v. McCarty* (1984), "[c]ases in which a defendant can make a colorable argument that a self-incriminating statement was 'compelled' despite the fact that the law enforcement authorities adhered to the dictates of *Miranda* are rare." . . .

In sum, we conclude that *Miranda* announced a constitutional rule that Congress may not supersede legislatively. Following the rule of *stare decisis,* we decline to overrule *Miranda* ourselves. The judgment of the Court of Appeals is therefore *Reversed.*

Justice Scalia, with whom **Justice Thomas** joins, dissenting.

Those to whom judicial decisions are an unconnected series of judgments that produce either favored or disfavored results will doubtless greet today's decision as a paragon of moderation, since it declines to overrule *Miranda v. Arizona* (1966). Those who understand the judicial process will appreciate that today's decision is not a reaffirmation of *Miranda,* but a radical revision of the most significant element of *Miranda* (as of all cases): the rationale that gives it a permanent place in our jurisprudence.

Marbury v. Madison . . . held that an Act of Congress will not be enforced by the courts if what it prescribes violates the Constitution of the United States. That was the basis on which *Miranda* was decided. One will search today's opinion in vain, however, for a statement (surely simple enough to make) that what 18 U.S.C. § 3501 prescribes— the use at trial of a voluntary confession, even when a *Miranda* warning or its equivalent has failed to be given— violates the Constitution. The reason the statement does not appear is not only (and perhaps not so much) that it would be absurd, inasmuch as § 3501 excludes from trial precisely what the Constitution excludes from trial, viz., compelled confessions; but also that Justices whose votes are needed to compose today's majority are on record as believing that a violation of *Miranda* is *not* a violation of the Constitution. . . . And so, to justify today's agreed-upon result, the Court must adopt a significant *new,* if not entirely comprehensible, principle of constitutional law. As the Court chooses to describe that principle, statutes of Congress can be disregarded, not only when what they prescribe violates the Constitution, but when what they prescribe contradicts a decision of this Court that "announced a constitutional rule." . . . As I shall discuss in some detail, the only thing that can possibly mean in the context of this case is that this Court has the power, not merely to apply the Constitution but to expand it, imposing what it regards as useful "prophylactic" restrictions upon Congress and the States. That is an immense and frightening antidemocratic power, and it does not exist.

It takes only a small step to bring today's opinion out of the realm of power-judging and into the mainstream of legal reasoning: The Court need only go beyond its carefully couched iterations that "*Miranda* is a constitutional decision," . . . that "*Miranda* is constitutionally based," . . . that *Miranda* has "constitutional underpinnings," . . . and come out and say quite clearly: "We reaffirm today that custodial interrogation that is not preceded by *Miranda* warnings or their equivalent violates the Constitution of the United States." It cannot say that, because a majority of the Court does not believe it. The Court therefore acts in plain violation of the Constitution when it denies effect to this Act of Congress. . . .

. . . [W]hile I agree with the Court that § 3501 cannot be upheld without also concluding that *Miranda* represents an illegitimate exercise of our authority to review state-court judgments, I do not share the Court's hesitation in reaching that conclusion. For while the Court is also correct that the doctrine of *stare decisis* demands some "special justification" for a departure from longstanding precedent—even precedent of the constitutional variety— that criterion is more than met here.

Neither am I persuaded by the argument for retaining *Miranda* that touts its supposed workability as compared with the totality-of-the-circumstances test it purported to replace. *Miranda*'s proponents cite *ad nauseam* the fact that the Court was called upon to make difficult and subtle distinctions in applying the "voluntariness" test in some 30-odd due process "coerced confessions" cases in the 30 years between *Brown v. Mississippi* (1936), and *Miranda*. It is not immediately apparent, however, that the judicial burden has been eased by the "bright-line" rules adopted in *Miranda*. In fact, in the 34 years since *Miranda* was decided, this Court has been called upon to decide nearly 60 cases involving a host of *Miranda* issues, most of them predicted with remarkable prescience by Justice White in his *Miranda* dissent. . . .

Moreover, it is not clear why the Court thinks that the "totality-of-the-circumstances test . . . is more difficult than *Miranda* for law enforcement officers to conform to, and for courts to apply in a consistent manner." . . .

But even were I to agree that the old totality-of-the-circumstances test was more cumbersome, it is simply not true that *Miranda* has banished it from the law and replaced it with a new test. Under the current regime, which the Court today retains in its entirety, courts are frequently called upon to undertake *both* inquiries. That is because, as explained earlier, voluntariness remains the *constitutional* standard, and as such continues to govern the admissibility for impeachment purposes of statements taken in violation of *Miranda*, the admissibility of the "fruits" of such statements, and the admissibility of statements challenged as unconstitutionally obtained despite the interrogator's compliance with *Miranda*. . . .

Finally, I am not convinced by petitioner's argument that *Miranda* should be preserved because the decision occupies a special place in the "public's consciousness."

. . . As far as I am aware, the public is not under the illusion that we are infallible. I see little harm in admitting that we made a mistake in taking away from the people the ability to decide for themselves what protections (beyond those required by the Constitution) are reasonably affordable in the criminal investigatory process. And I see much to be gained by reaffirming for the people the wonderful reality that they govern themselves—which means that "[t]he powers not delegated to the United States by the Constitution" that the people adopted, "nor prohibited . . . to the States" by that Constitution, "are reserved to the States respectively, or to the people." . . .

Today's judgment converts *Miranda* from a milestone of judicial overreaching into the very Cheops' Pyramid (or perhaps the Sphinx would be a better analogue) of judicial arrogance. In imposing its Court-made code upon the States, the original opinion at least *asserted* that it was demanded by the Constitution. Today's decision does not pretend that it is—and yet *still* asserts the right to impose it against the will of the people's representatives in Congress. Far from believing that *stare decisis* compels this result, I believe we cannot allow to remain on the books even a celebrated decision—*especially* a celebrated decision—that has come to stand for the proposition that the Supreme Court has power to impose extra-constitutional constraints upon Congress and the States. This is not the system that was established by the Framers, or that would be established by any sane supporter of government by the people.

I dissent from today's decision, and, until § 3501 is repealed, will continue to apply it in all cases where there has been a sustainable finding that the defendant's confession was voluntary.

Case

POWELL V. ALABAMA

287 U.S. 45; 53 S.Ct. 55; 77 L.Ed. 158 (1932)
Vote: 7–2

Here, the Court reviews the convictions of eight young African-American men who had been sentenced to death by an Alabama court for allegedly raping two white women.

Mr. Justice Sutherland delivered the opinion of the Court.

. . . The record shows that on the day when the offense is said to have been committed, these defendants, together with a number of other negroes, were upon a freight train on its way through Alabama. On the

same train were seven white boys and two white girls. A fight took place between the negroes and the white boys, in the course of which the white boys, with the exception of one named Gilley, were thrown off the train. A message was sent ahead, reporting the fight and asking that every negro be gotten off the train. The participants in the fight, and the two girls, were in an open gondola car. The two girls testified that each of them was assaulted by six different negroes in turn, and they identified the seven defendants as having been among the number. None of the white boys was called to testify, with the exception of Gilley, who was called in rebuttal.

Before the train reached Scottsboro, Alabama, a sheriff's posse seized the defendants and two other negroes.

Both girls and the negroes then were taken to Scottsboro, the county seat. Word of their coming and of the alleged assault had preceded them, and they were met at Scottsboro by a large crowd. It does not sufficiently appear that the defendants were seriously threatened with, or that they were actually in danger of, mob violence; but it does appear that the attitude of the community was one of great hostility. The sheriff thought it necessary to call for the militia to assist in safeguarding the prisoners. Chief Justice Anderson pointed out in his opinion that every step taken from the arrest and arraignment to the sentence was accompanied by the military. Soldiers took the defendants to Gadsden for safekeeping, brought them back to Scottsboro for arraignment, returned them to Gadsden for safekeeping while awaiting trial, escorted them to Scottsboro for trial a few days later, and guarded the courthouse and grounds at every stage of the proceedings. It is perfectly apparent that the proceedings, from beginning to end, took place in an atmosphere of tense, hostile and excited public sentiment. During the entire time, the defendants were closely confined or were under military guard. The record does not disclose their ages, except that one of them was nineteen; but the record clearly indicates that most, if not all, of them were youthful, and they are constantly referred to as "the boys." They were ignorant and illiterate. All of them were residents of other states, where alone members of their families or friends resided.

However guilty defendants, upon due inquiry might prove to have been, they were, until convicted, presumed to be innocent. It was the duty of the court having their cases in charge to see that they were denied no necessary incident of a fair trial. With any error of the state court involving alleged contravention of the state statutes or constitution we, of course, have nothing to do. The sole inquiry which we are permitted to make is whether the federal Constitution was contravened . . . and as to that, we confine ourselves, as already suggested, to the inquiry whether the defendants were in substance denied the right to counsel, and if so, whether such denial infringes the Due Process Clause of the Fourteenth Amendment.

First. The record shows that immediately upon the return of the indictment defendants were arraigned and pleaded not guilty. Apparently they were not asked whether they had, or were able to employ, counsel, or wished to have counsel appointed; or whether they had friends or relatives who might assist in that regard if communicated with. . . .

It is hardly necessary to say that the right to counsel being conceded, a defendant should be afforded a fair opportunity to secure counsel of his own choice. Not only was that not done here, but such designation of counsel as was attempted was either so indefinite or so close upon the trial as to amount to a denial of effective and substantial aid in that regard. This will be amply demonstrated by a brief review of the record.

April 6, six days after indictment, the trial began. When the first case was called, the court inquired whether the parties were ready for trial. The state's attorney replied that he was ready to proceed. No one answered for the defendants or appeared to represent or defend them. Mr. Roddy, a Tennessee lawyer, not a member of the local bar, addressed the court, saying that he had not been employed, but that people who were interested had spoken to him about the case. He was asked by the court whether he intended to appear for the defendants, and answered that he would like to appear along with counsel that the court might appoint. The record then proceeds:

> THE COURT: If you appear for these defendants, then I will not appoint counsel: if local counsel are willing to appear and assist you under the circumstances all right, but I will not appoint them.

> MR. RODDY: Your Honor has appointed counsel, is that correct?

> THE COURT: I appointed all the members of the bar for the purpose of arraigning the defendants and then of course I anticipated them to continue to help them if no counsel appears.

> MR. RODDY: Then I don't appear then as counsel but I do want to stay in and not be ruled out in this case.

> THE COURT: Of course I would not do that—

> MR. RODDY: I just appear here through the courtesy of Your Honor.

> THE COURT: Of course I give you that right; . . .

. . . [T]his action of the trial judge in respect of appointment of counsel was little more than an expansive gesture, imposing no substantial or definite obligation upon any one . . . during perhaps the most critical period of the proceedings against these defendants, that is to say, from the time of their arraignment until the beginning of their trial, when consultation, thorough-going investigation and preparation were vitally important, the defendants did not have the aid of counsel in any real sense, although they were as much entitled to such aid during that period as at the trial itself. . . .

Nor do we think the situation was helped by what occurred on the morning of the trial. At that time, as appears from the colloquy printed above, Mr. Roddy stated to the court that he did not appear as counsel, but that he would like to appear along with counsel that the court might appoint; that he had not been given an opportunity to prepare the case; that he was not familiar with the procedure in Alabama, but merely came down as a friend of the people who were interested; that he thought the boys would be better off if he should step entirely out of the case. Mr. Moody, a member of the local bar, expressed a willingness to help Mr. Roddy in anything he would do under the circumstances. To this the court responded, "All right, all the lawyers that will; of course I would not require a lawyer to appear if—." And Mr. Moody continued, "I am willing to do that for him as a member of the bar; I will go ahead and help do anything I can do." With this dubious understanding, the trials immediately proceeded. The defendants, young, ignorant, illiterate, surrounded by hostile sentiment, haled back and forth under guard of soldiers, charged with an atrocious crime regarded with especial horror in the community where they were to be tried, were thus put in peril of their lives within a few moments after counsel for the first time charged with any degree of responsibility began to represent them.

It is not enough to assume that counsel thus precipitated into the case thought there was no defense, and exercised their best judgment in proceeding to trial without preparation. Neither they nor the court could say what a prompt and thorough-going investigation might disclose as to the facts. No attempt was made to investigate. No opportunity to do so was given. Defendants were immediately hurried to trial. Chief Justice Anderson, after disclaiming any intention to criticize harshly counsel who attempted to represent defendants at the trials, said: ". . . The record indicates that the appearance was rather *pro forma* than zealous and active. . . ." Under the circumstances disclosed, we hold that defendants were not accorded the right of counsel in any substantial sense. To decide otherwise, would simply be to ignore actualities. . . .

The prompt disposition of criminal cases is to be commended and encouraged. But in reaching that result a defendant, charged with a serious crime, must not be stripped of his right to have sufficient time to advise with counsel and prepare his defense. To do that is not to proceed promptly in the calm spirit of regulated justice but to go forward with the haste of the mob. . . .

Second. The Constitution of Alabama provides that in all criminal prosecutions the accused shall enjoy the right to have the assistance of counsel; and a state statute requires the court in a capital case, where the defendant is unable to employ counsel, to appoint counsel for him. The state supreme court held that these provisions had not been infringed. . . . The question, however, which it is our duty, and within our power, to decide, is whether the denial of the assistance of counsel contravenes the Due Process Clause of the Fourteenth Amendment to the federal Constitution.

If recognition of the right of a defendant charged with a felony to have the aid of counsel depended upon the existence of a similar right at common law as it existed in England when our Constitution was adopted, there would be great difficulty in maintaining it as necessary to due process. Originally, in England, a person charged with treason or felony was denied the aid of counsel, except in respect of legal questions which the accused himself might suggest. At the same time parties in civil cases and persons accused of misdemeanors were entitled to the full assistance of counsel. After the revolution of 1688, the rule was abolished as to treason, but was otherwise steadily adhered to until 1836, when by act of Parliament the full right was granted in respect of felonies generally. . . .

An affirmation of the right to the aid of counsel in petty offenses, and its denial in the case of crimes of the gravest character, where such aid is most needed, is so outrageous and so obviously a perversion of all sense of proportion that the rule was constantly, vigorously and sometimes passionately assailed by English statesmen and lawyers. As early as 1758, Blackstone, although recognizing that the rule was settled at common law, denounced it as not in keeping with the rest of the humane treatment of prisoners by the English law. "For upon what face of reason," he says, "can that assistance be denied to save the life of a man, which yet is allowed him in prosecutions for every petty trespass?" . . . One of the grounds upon which Lord Coke defended the rule was that in felonies the court itself was counsel for the prisoner. . . . But how can a judge, whose functions are purely judicial, effectively discharge the obligations of counsel for the accused? He can and should see to it that in the proceedings before the court the accused shall be dealt with justly and fairly. He cannot investigate the facts, advise and direct the defense, or participate in those necessary conferences between counsel and accused which sometimes partake of the inviolable character of the confessional. . . .

In light of the facts outlined in the forepart of this opinion—the ignorance and illiteracy of the defendants, their youth, the circumstances of public hostility, the imprisonment and the close surveillance of the defendants by the military forces, the fact that their friends and families were all in other states and communication with them necessarily difficult, and above all that they stood in deadly peril of their lives—we think the failure of the trial court to give them reasonable time and opportunity to secure counsel was a clear denial of due process.

But passing that, and assuming their inability, even if opportunity had been given, to employ counsel, as the trial court evidently did assume, we are of opinion that, under the circumstances just stated, the necessity of counsel was so vital and imperative that the failure of the trial court to make an effective appointment of counsel was likewise a denial of due process within the meaning of the Fourteenth Amendment. Whether this would be so in other criminal prosecutions, or under other circumstances, we need not determine. All that it is necessary now to decide, as we do decide, is that in a capital case, where the defendant is unable to employ counsel, and is incapable adequately of making his own defense because of ignorance, feeble-mindedness, illiteracy, or the like, it is the duty of the court, whether requested or not, to assign counsel for him as a necessary requisite of due process of law; and that duty is not discharged by an assignment at such a time or under such circumstances as to preclude the giving of effective aid in the preparation and trial of the case. To hold otherwise would be to ignore the fundamental postulate, already adverted to, "that there are certain immutable principles of justice which inhere in the very idea of free government which no member of the Union may disregard." . . . In a case such as this, whatever may be the rule in other cases, the right to have counsel appointed, when necessary, is a logical corollary from the constitutional right to be heard by counsel. . . .

The judgments must be reversed and the causes remanded for further proceedings not inconsistent with this opinion.

Mr. Justice Butler, dissenting.

If correct, the ruling that the failure of the trial court to give petitioners time and opportunity to secure counsel was denial of due process is enough, and with this the opinion should end. But the Court goes on to declare that "the failure of the trial court to make an effective appointment of counsel was likewise a denial of due process within the meaning of the Fourteenth Amendment." This is an extension of federal authority into a field hitherto occupied exclusively by the several States. Nothing before the Court calls for a consideration of the point. It was not suggested below and petitioners do not ask for its decision here. The Court, without being called upon to consider it, adjudges without a hearing an important constitutional question concerning criminal procedure in state courts.

It is a wise rule firmly established by a long course of decisions here that constitutional questions—even when properly raised and argued—are to be decided only when necessary for a determination of the rights of the parties in controversy before it. . . .

The record wholly fails to reveal that petitioners have been deprived of any right guaranteed by the Federal Constitution, and I am of opinion that the judgment should be affirmed.

Mr. Justice McReynolds concurs in this opinion.

Case

GIDEON V. WAINWRIGHT

372 U.S. 335; 83 S.Ct. 792; 9 L.Ed. 2d 799 (1963)
Vote: 9–0

Here the Court considers whether state courts must as a matter of course appoint counsel to represent indigent defendants accused of felonies.

Mr. Justice Black delivered the opinion of the Court.

Petitioner was charged in a Florida state court with having broken and entered a poolroom with intent to commit a misdemeanor. This offense is a felony under Florida law. Appearing in court without funds and without a lawyer, petitioner asked the court to appoint counsel for him, whereupon the following colloquy took place:

THE COURT: Mr. Gideon, I am sorry, but I cannot appoint Counsel to represent you in this case. Under the laws of the State of Florida, the only time the Court can appoint Counsel to represent a Defendant is when that person is charged with a capital offense. I am sorry, but I will have to deny your request to appoint Counsel to defend you in this case.

THE DEFENDANT: The United States Supreme Court says I am entitled to be represented by Counsel.

Put to trial before a jury, *Gideon* conducted his defense about as well as could be expected from a layman. He made an opening statement to the jury, cross-examined the State's witnesses, presented witnesses in his own defense, declined to testify himself, and made a short argument "emphasizing his innocence to the charge contained in the Information filed in this case." The jury returned a verdict of guilty, the petitioner was sentenced to serve five years in the state prison. Later, petitioner filed in the Florida Supreme Court this habeas corpus petition attacking his conviction and sentence on the ground that the trial court's refusal to appoint counsel for him denied him rights "guaranteed by the Constitution and the Bill of Rights by the United States Government." Treating the petition for habeas corpus as properly before it, the State Supreme Court, "upon consideration thereof" but without an opinion, denied all relief. Since 1942, when *Betts v. Brady* . . . was decided by a divided Court, the problem of a defendant's federal constitutional right to counsel in a state court has been a continuing source of controversy and litigation in both state and federal courts. To give this problem another review here, we granted certiorari. Since *Gideon* was proceeding *in forma pauperis,* we appointed counsel to represent him and requested both sides to discuss in their briefs and oral arguments the following: "Should this Court's holding in *Betts v. Brady* be reconsidered?"

Since the facts and circumstances of the two cases are so nearly indistinguishable, we think the *Betts v. Brady* holding if left standing would require us to reject Gideon's claim that the Constitution guarantees him the assistance of counsel. Upon full reconsideration we conclude that *Betts v. Brady* should be overruled.

The facts upon which Betts claimed that he had been unconstitutionally denied the right to have counsel appointed to assist him are strikingly like the facts upon which *Gideon* here bases his federal constitutional claim.

The Sixth Amendment provides, "In all criminal prosecutions, the accused shall enjoy the right . . . to have the Assistance of Counsel for his defense." We have construed this to mean that in federal courts counsel must be provided for defendants unable to employ counsel unless the right is competently and intelligently waived. Betts argued that this right is extended to indigent defendants in state courts by the Fourteenth Amendment. In response the Court stated that, while the Sixth Amendment laid down "no rule for the conduct of the states, the question recurs whether the constraint laid by Amendment upon the national courts expresses a rule so fundamental and essential to a fair trial, and so, to due process of law, that it is made obligatory upon the States by the Fourteenth Amendment." In order to decide whether the Sixth Amendment's guarantee of counsel is of this fundamental nature, the Court in *Betts* set out and considered "[r]elevant data on the subject . . . afforded by constitutional and statutory provisions subsisting in the colonies and the States prior to the inclusion of the Bill of Rights in the national Constitution, and in the constitutional, legislative, and judicial history of the States to the present date." . . . On the basis of this historical data the Court concluded that "appointment of counsel is not a fundamental right, essential to a fair trial." . . . It was for this reason the *Betts* Court refused to accept the contention that the Sixth Amendment's guarantee of counsel for indigent federal defendants was extended to or, in the words of that Court, "made obligatory upon the States by the Fourteenth Amendment." . . . Plainly, had the Court concluded that appointment of counsel for an indigent criminal defendant was "a fundamental right, essential to a fair trial," . . . it would have held that the Fourteenth Amendment requires appointment of counsel in a state court, just as the Sixth Amendment requires in a federal court.

We think the Court in *Betts* had ample precedent for acknowledging that those guarantees of the Bill of Rights which are fundamental safeguards of liberty immune from federal abridgment are equally protected against state invasion by the Due Process Clause of the Fourteenth Amendment. This same principle was recognized, explained, and applied in *Powell v. Alabama,* . . . a case upholding the right of counsel, where the Court held that despite sweeping language to the contrary in *Hurtado v. California,* . . . the Fourteenth Amendment "embraced" those "fundamental principles of liberty and justice which lie at the base of all our civil and political institutions," even though they had been "specifically dealt with in another part of the federal Constitution." . . . In many cases other than *Powell* and *Betts,* this Court has looked to the fundamental nature of original Bill of Rights guarantees to decide whether the Fourteenth Amendment makes them obligatory on the States.

In light of these and many other prior decisions of this Court, it is not surprising that the *Betts* Court, when faced with the contention that "one charged with crime, who is unable to obtain counsel, must be furnished counsel by the State," . . . conceded that "[e]xpressions in the opinions of this court lend color to the argument. . . ." . . . The fact is that in deciding as it did—that "appointment of counsel is not a fundamental right, essential to a fair trial" . . . —the Court in *Betts v. Brady* made an abrupt break with its own well-considered precedents. In returning to these old precedents, sounder we believe than the new, we but restore constitutional principles established to achieve a fair system of justice. Not only these precedents but also reason and reflection require us to recognize that in our adversary system of criminal justice, any person haled into court, who is too poor to hire a lawyer, cannot be assured a fair trial unless counsel is provided for him. This seems to us to be an obvious truth. Governments, both state and federal, quite properly spend vast sums of money to establish machinery to try defendants accused of crime. Lawyers to prosecute are everywhere deemed essential to protect the public's interest in an orderly society. Similarly, there are few defendants charged with crime, few indeed, who fail to hire the best lawyers they can get to prepare and present their defenses. That government hires lawyers to prosecute and defendants who have the money hire lawyers to defend are the strongest indications of the widespread belief that lawyers in criminal courts are necessities, not luxuries. The right of one charged with crime to counsel may not be deemed fundamental and essential to fair trials in some countries, but it is in ours. From the very beginning, our state and national constitutions and laws have laid great emphasis on procedural and substantive safeguards designed to assure fair trials before impartial tribunals in which every defendant stands equal before the law. This noble ideal cannot be realized if the poor man charged with crime has to face his accusers without a lawyer to assist him.

The Court in *Betts v. Brady* departed from the sound wisdom upon which the Court's holding in *Powell v. Alabama* rested. Florida, supported by two other States, has asked that *Betts v. Brady* be left intact. Twenty-two States, as friends of the Court, argue that *Betts* was "an anachronism when handed down" . . . and that it should now be overruled. We agree.

The judgment is reversed and the cause is remanded to the Supreme Court of Florida for further action not inconsistent with this opinion.

Mr. Justice Douglas, concurring. . . .

Mr. Justice Clark, concurring in the result. . . .

Mr. Justice Harlan, concurring. . . .

Case

BATSON V. KENTUCKY

476 U.S. 79; 106 S.Ct. 1712; 90 L.Ed. 2d 69 (1986)
Vote: 7–2

In this case the Court reexamines the practice of using peremptory challenges to exclude members of the defendant's race from the jury.

Justice Powell delivered the opinion of the Court.

. . . Petitioner, a black man, was indicted in Kentucky on charges of second-degree burglary and receipt of stolen goods. On the first day of trial in Jefferson Circuit Court, the judge conducted voir dire examination of the venire, excused certain jurors for cause, and permitted the parties to exercise peremptory challenges. The prosecutor used his peremptory challenges to strike all four black persons on the venire, and a jury composed only of white persons was selected. Defense counsel moved to discharge the jury before it was sworn on the ground that the prosecutor's removal of the black veniremen violated petitioner's rights under the Sixth and Fourteenth Amendments to a jury drawn from a cross-section of the community, and under the Fourteenth Amendment to equal protection of the laws. Counsel requested a hearing on his motion. Without expressly ruling on the request for a hearing, the trial judge observed that the parties were entitled to use their peremptory challenges to "strike anybody they want to." The judge then denied petitioner's motion, reasoning that the cross-section requirement applies only to selection of the venire and not to selection of the petit jury itself.

The jury convicted petitioner on both counts. . . .

The Supreme Court of Kentucky affirmed. . . . We granted certiorari . . . and now reverse.

In *Swain v. Alabama* [1965], this Court recognized that a "State's purposeful or deliberate denial to Negroes on account of race of participation as jurors in the adminis-

tration of justice violates the Equal Protection Clause." . . . This principle has been "consistently and repeatedly" reaffirmed, . . . in numerous decisions of this Court both preceding and following *Swain*. [For the Court's earliest interpretation of the Equal Protection Clause in this area, see *Strauder v. West Virginia* (1880).] We reaffirm the principle today. . . .

In holding that racial discrimination in jury selection offends the Equal Protection Clause, the Court in *Strauder* recognized . . . that a defendant has no right to a "petit jury composed in whole or in part of persons of his own race." . . . "The number of our races and nationalities stands in the way of evolution of such a conception" of the demand of equal protection. . . . But the defendant does have the right to be tried by a jury whose members are selected pursuant to nondiscriminatory criteria. . . . The Equal Protection Clause guarantees the defendant that the State will not exclude members of his race from the jury venire on account of race, . . . or on the false assumption that members of his race as a group are not qualified to serve as jurors. . . .

Purposeful racial discrimination in selection of the venire violates a defendant's right to equal protection because it denies him the protection that a trial by jury is intended to secure. "The very idea of a jury is a body . . . composed of the peers or equals of the person whose rights it is selected or summoned to determine; that is, of his neighbors, fellows, associates, persons having the same legal status in society as that which he holds." . . . The petit jury has occupied a central position in our system of justice by safeguarding a person accused of crime against the arbitrary exercise of power by prosecutor or judge. . . . Those on the venire must be "indifferently chosen" to secure the defendant's right under the Fourteenth Amendment to "protection of life and liberty against race or color prejudice." . . .

Racial discrimination in selection of jurors harms not only the accused whose life or liberty they are summoned to try. Competence to serve as a juror ultimately depends on an assessment of individual qualifications and ability impartially to consider evidence presented at a trial. . . . A person's race simply "is unrelated to his fitness as a juror." . . . As long ago as *Strauder,* therefore, the Court recognized that by denying a person participation in jury service on account of his race, the State unconstitutionally discriminated against the excluded juror. . . .

The harm from discriminatory jury selection extends beyond that inflicted on the defendant and the excluded juror to touch the entire community. Selection procedures that purposefully exclude black persons from juries undermine public confidence in the fairness of our system of justice. . . .

. . . The Constitution requires . . . that we look beyond the face of the statute defining juror qualifications and also consider challenged selection practices to afford "protection against action of the State through its administrative officers in effecting the prohibited discrimination." . . . Thus, the Court has found a denial of equal protection where the procedures implementing a neutral statute operated to exclude persons from the venire on racial grounds, and has made clear that the Constitution prohibits all forms of purposeful racial discrimination in selection of jurors. While decisions of this Court have been concerned largely with discrimination during selection of the venire, the principles announced there also forbid discrimination on account of race in selection of the petit jury. . . .

Accordingly, the component of the jury selection process at issue, here, the State's privilege to strike individual jurors through peremptory challenges, is subject to the commands of the Equal Protection Clause. Although a prosecutor ordinarily is entitled to exercise permitted peremptory challenges "for any reason at all, as long as that reason is related to his view concerning the outcome" of the case to be tried, . . . the Equal Protection Clause forbids the prosecutor to challenge potential jurors solely on account of their race or on the assumption that black jurors as a group will be unable impartially to consider the State's case against a black defendant.

. . . A recurring question in these cases, as in any case alleging a violation of the Equal Protection Clause, was whether the defendant had met his burden of proving purposeful discrimination on the part of the State. . . . That question also was at the heart of the portion of *Swain v. Alabama* we reexamine today.

Swain required the Court to decide, among other issues, whether a black defendant was denied equal protection by the State's exercise of peremptory challenges to exclude members of his race from the petit jury. . . . The record in *Swain* showed that the prosecutor had used the State's peremptory challenges to strike the six black persons included on the petit jury venire. . . . While rejecting the defendant's claim for failure to prove purposeful discrimination, the Court nonetheless indicated that the Equal Protection Clause placed some limits on the State's exercise of peremptory challenges. . . .

The Court sought to accommodate the prosecutor's historical privilege of peremptory challenge free of judicial control, . . . and the constitutional prohibition on exclusion of persons from jury service on account of race. . . . While the Constitution does not confer a right to peremptory challenges, . . . those challenges traditionally have been viewed as one means of assuring the selection of a qualified and unbiased jury. . . . To preserve the peremptory nature of the prosecutor's challenge, the Court in *Swain* declined to scrutinize his actions in a particular case by relying on a presumption that he properly exercised the State's challenges. . . .

The Court went on to observe, however, that a state may not exercise its challenges in contravention of the Equal Protection Clause. It was impermissible for a prosecutor to use his challenges to exclude blacks from the jury "for reasons wholly unrelated to the outcome of the particular case on trial" or to deny to blacks "the same right and opportunity to participate in the administration of justice enjoyed by the white population." . . . Accordingly, a black defendant could make out a prima facie case of purposeful discrimination on proof that the peremptory challenge system was "being perverted" in that manner. For example, an inference of purposeful discrimination would be raised on evidence that a prosecutor, "in case after case, whatever the circumstances, whatever the crime and whoever the defendant or the victim may be, is responsible for the removal of Negroes who have been selected as qualified jurors by the jury commissioners and who have survived challenges for cause, with the result that no Negroes ever serve on petit juries." . . . Evidence offered by the defendant in *Swain* did not meet that standard. While the defendant showed that prosecutors in the jurisdiction had exercised their strikes to exclude blacks from the jury, he offered no proof of the circumstances under which prosecutors were responsible for striking black jurors beyond the facts of his own case. . . .

A number of lower courts following the teaching of *Swain* reasoned that proof of repeated striking of blacks over a number of cases was necessary to establish a violation of the Equal Protection Clause. Since this interpretation of *Swain* has placed on defendants a crippling burden of proof, prosecutors' peremptory challenges are now largely immune from constitutional scrutiny. For reasons that follow, we reject this evidentiary formulation as inconsistent with standards that have been developed since *Swain* for assessing a prima facie case under the Equal Protection Clause. . . .

As in any equal protection case, the "burden is, of course," on the defendant who alleges discriminatory selection of the venire "to prove the existence of purposeful discrimination." . . . In deciding if the defendant has carried his burden of persuasion, a court must undertake "a sensitive inquiry into such circumstantial and direct evidence of intent as may be available." . . . Circumstantial evidence of invidious intent may include proof of disproportionate impact. . . . We have observed that under some circumstances proof of discriminatory impact "may for all practical purposes demonstrate unconstitutionality because in various circumstances the discrimination is very difficult to explain on nonracial grounds." . . . For example, "total or seriously disproportionate exclusion of Negroes from jury venires is itself such an 'unequal application of the law . . . as to show intentional discrimination.' " . . .

Moreover, since *Swain,* we have recognized that a black defendant alleging that members of his race have been impermissibly excluded from the venire may make out a prima facie case of purposeful discrimination by showing that the totality of the relevant facts gives rise to an inference of discriminatory purpose. . . . Once the defendant makes the requisite showing, the burden shifts to the State to explain adequately the racial exclusion. . . . The State cannot meet this burden on mere general assertions that its officials did not discriminate or that they properly performed their official duties. . . . Rather, the State must demonstrate that "permissible racially neutral selection criteria and procedures have produced the monochromatic result." . . .

The standards for assessing a prima facie case in the context of discriminatory selection of the venire have been fully articulated since *Swain.* . . . These principles support our conclusion that a defendant may establish a prima facie case of purposeful discrimination in selection of the petit jury solely on evidence concerning the prosecutor's exercise of peremptory challenges at the defendant's trial. To establish such a case, the defendant first must show that he is a member of a cognizable racial group, . . . and that the prosecutor has exercised peremptory challenges to remove from the venire members of the defendant's race. Second, the defendant is entitled to rely on the fact, as to which there can be no dispute, that peremptory challenges constitute a jury selection practice that permits "those to discriminate who are of a mind to discriminate." . . . Finally, the defendant must show that these facts and any other relevant circumstances raise an inference that the prosecutor used that practice to exclude the veniremen from the petit jury on account of their race.

This combination of factors in the empanelling of the petit jury, as in the selection of the venire, raises the necessary inference of purposeful discrimination.

In deciding whether the defendant has made the requisite showing, the trial court should consider all relevant circumstances. For example, a "pattern" of strikes against black jurors included in the particular venire might give rise to an inference of discrimination. Similarly, the prosecutor's questions and statements during voir dire examination and in exercising his challenges may support or refute an inference of discriminatory purpose. These examples are merely illustrative. We have confidence that trial judges, experienced in supervising voir dire, will be able to decide if the circumstances concerning the prosecutor's use of peremptory challenges creates a prima facie case of discrimination against black jurors.

Once the defendant makes a prima facie showing, the burden shifts to the State to come forward with a neutral explanation for challenging black jurors. Though this requirement imposes a limitation in some cases on the full peremptory character of the historic challenge, we emphasize that the prosecutor's explanation need not rise to the level justifying exercise of a challenge for cause. But the prosecutor may not rebut the defendant's prima facie case of discrimination by stating merely that he challenged jurors of the defendant's race on the assumption—or his intuitive judgment—that they would be partial to the defendant because of their shared race. . . . Just as the Equal Protection Clause forbids the States to exclude black persons from the venire on the assumption that blacks as a group are unqualified to serve as jurors, . . . so it forbids the States to strike black veniremen on the assumption that they will be biased in a particular case simply because the defendant is black. . . . Nor may the prosecutor rebut the defendant's case merely by denying that he had a discriminatory motive or "affirming his good faith in individual selections." . . . If these general assertions were accepted as rebutting a defendant's prima facie case, the Equal Protection Clause "would be but a vain and illusory requirement." . . . The prosecutor therefore must articulate a neutral explanation related to the particular case to be tried. The trial court then will have the duty to determine if the defendant has established purposeful discrimination.

The State contends that our holding will eviscerate the fair trial values served by the peremptory challenge. Conceding that the Constitution does not guarantee a right to peremptory challenges and that *Swain* did state that their use ultimately is subject to the strictures of equal protection, the State argues that the privilege of unfettered exercise of the challenge is of vital importance to the criminal justice system.

While we recognize, of course, that the peremptory challenge occupies an important position in our trial procedures, we do not agree that our decision today will undermine the contribution the challenge generally makes to the administration of justice. The reality of practice, amply reflected in many state and federal court opinions, shows that the challenge may be, and unfortunately at times has been, used to discriminate against black jurors. By requiring trial courts to be sensitive to the racially discriminatory use of peremptory challenges, our decision enforces the mandate of equal protection and furthers the ends of justice. In view of the heterogeneous population of our nation, public respect for our criminal justice system and the rule of law will be strengthened if we ensure that no citizen is disqualified from jury service because of his race.

Nor are we persuaded by the State's suggestion that our holding will create serious administrative difficulties. In those states applying a version of the evidentiary standard we recognize today, courts have not experienced serious administrative burdens, and the peremptory challenge system has survived. We decline, however, to formulate particular procedures to be followed upon a defendant's timely objection to a prosecutor's challenges.

In this case, petitioner made a timely objection to the prosecutor's removal of all black persons on the venire. Because the trial court flatly rejected the objection without requiring the prosecutor to give an explanation for his action, we remand this case for further proceedings. If the trial court decides that the facts establish, prima facie, purposeful discrimination and the prosecutor does not come forward with a neutral explanation for his action, our precedents require that petitioner's conviction be reversed. . . .

Justice White, concurring. . . .

Justice Marshall, concurring. . . .

Justice Stevens, with whom *Justice Brennan* joins, concurring. . . .

Justice Rehnquist, with whom the *Chief Justice* joins, dissenting.

. . . I cannot subscribe to the Court's unprecedented use of the Equal Protection Clause to restrict the historic scope of the peremptory challenge, which has been described as "a necessary part of trial by jury." . . . In my view, there is simply nothing "unequal" about the State using its peremptory challenges to strike blacks from the jury in cases involving black defendants, so long as such challenges are also used to exclude whites in cases involving white defendants, Hispanics in cases involving Hispanic defendants, Asians in cases involving Asian defendants, and so on. This case-specific use of peremptory challenges by the State does not single out blacks, or members of any other race for that matter, for discriminatory treatment. Such use of peremptories is at best based upon seat-of-the-pants instincts, which are undoubtedly crudely stereotypical and may in many cases be hopelessly mistaken. But as long as they are applied across the board to jurors of all races and nationalities, I do not see—and the Court most certainly has not explained—how their use violates the Equal Protection Clause.

Nor does such use of peremptory challenges by the State infringe upon any other constitutional interests. The Court does not suggest that exclusion of blacks from the jury through the State's use of peremptory challenges results in a violation of either the fair cross-section or impartiality component of the Sixth Amendment. . . . And because the case-specific use of peremptory challenges by the State does not deny blacks the right to serve as jurors in cases involving non-black defendants, it harms neither the excluded jurors nor the remainder of the community.

The use of group affiliations, such as age, race, or occupation, as a "proxy" for potential juror partiality, based on the assumption or belief that members of one group are more likely to favor defendants who belong to the same group, has long been accepted as a legitimate basis for the State's exercise of peremptory challenges. . . . Indeed, given the need for reasonable limitations on the time devoted to voir dire, the use of such "proxies" by both the State and the defendant may be extremely useful in eliminating from the jury persons who might be biased in one way or another. The Court today holds that the State may not use its peremptory challenges to strike black prospective jurors on this basis without violating the Constitution. But I do not believe there is anything in the Equal Protection Clause, or any other Constitutional provision, that justifies such a departure. . . . Petitioner in the instant case failed to make a sufficient showing to overcome the presumption announced in *Swain* that the State's use of peremptory challenges was related to the context of the case. I would therefore affirm the judgment of the court below.

Case

KANSAS V. HENDRICKS

521 U.S. 346; 117 S.Ct. 2072; 138 L.Ed. 2d 501 (1997)
Vote: 5–4

In this case the Court considers the constitutionality of state legislation that permits violent sexual predators to be confined even after their prison sentences are completed.

Justice Thomas delivered the opinion of the Court.

In 1994, Kansas enacted the Sexually Violent Predator Act, which establishes procedures for the civil commitment of persons who, due to a "mental abnormality" or a "personality disorder," are likely to engage in "predatory acts of sexual violence." . . . The State invoked the Act for the first time to commit Leroy Hendricks, an inmate who had a long history of sexually molesting children, and who was scheduled for release from prison shortly after the Act became law. Hendricks challenged his commitment on . . . "substantive" due process, double jeopardy, and ex post-facto grounds. The Kansas Supreme Court invalidated the Act, holding that its pre-commitment condition of a "mental abnormality" did not satisfy what the court perceived to be the "substantive" due process requirement that involuntary civil commitment must be predicated on a finding of "mental illness." . . . The State of Kansas petitioned for certiorari. Hendricks subsequently filed a cross petition in which he reasserted his federal double jeopardy and ex post-facto claims. We granted certiorari . . . and now reverse the judgment below. . . .

. . . Although freedom from physical restraint "has always been at the core of the liberty protected by the Due Process Clause from arbitrary governmental action," . . . that liberty interest is not absolute. The Court has recognized that an individual's constitutionally protected interest in avoiding physical restraint may be overridden even in the civil context. . . .

Accordingly, States have in certain narrow circumstances provided for the forcible civil detainment of people who are unable to control their behavior and who thereby pose a danger to the public health and safety. . . . We have consistently upheld such involuntary commitment statutes provided the confinement takes place pursuant to proper procedures and evidentiary standards. . . . It thus cannot be said that the involuntary civil confinement of a limited subclass of dangerous persons is contrary to our understanding of ordered liberty. . . .

The challenged Act unambiguously requires a finding of dangerousness either to one's self or to others as a pre-requisite to involuntary confinement. Commitment proceedings can be initiated only when a person "has been convicted of or charged with a sexually violent offense," and "suffers from a mental abnormality or personality disorder which makes the person likely to engage in the predatory acts of sexual violence." . . . The statute thus requires proof of more than a mere predisposition to violence; rather, it requires evidence of past sexually violent behavior and a present mental condition that creates a likelihood of such conduct in the future if the person is not incapacitated. As we have recognized, "[p]revious instances of violent behavior are an important indicator of future violent tendencies." . . . A finding of dangerousness, standing alone, is ordinarily not a sufficient ground upon which to justify indefinite involuntary commitment. We have sustained civil commitment statutes when they have coupled proof of dangerousness with the proof of some additional factor, such as a "mental illness" or "mental abnormality." . . . These added statutory requirements serve to limit involuntary civil confinement to those who suffer from a volitional impairment rendering them dangerous beyond their control. The Kansas Act is plainly of a kind with these other civil commitment statutes: It requires a finding of future dangerousness, and then links that finding to the existence of a "mental abnormality" or "personality disorder" that makes it difficult, if not impossible, for the person to control his dangerous behavior. . . . The precommitment requirement of a "mental abnormality" or "personality disorder" is consistent with the requirements of these other statutes that we have upheld in that it narrows the class of persons eligible for confinement to those who are unable to control their dangerousness.

Hendricks nonetheless argues that our earlier cases dictate a finding of "mental illness" as a prerequisite for civil commitment. . . . He then asserts that a "mental abnormality" is not equivalent to a "mental illness" because it is a term coined by the Kansas Legislature, rather than by the psychiatric community. Contrary to Hendricks' assertion, the term "mental illness" is devoid of any talismanic significance. Not only do "psychiatrists disagree widely and frequently on what constitutes mental illness," . . . but the Court itself has used a variety of expressions to describe the mental condition of those properly subject to civil confinement. . . .

Indeed, we have never required State legislatures to adopt any particular nomenclature in drafting civil commitment statutes. Rather, we have traditionally left to legislators the task of defining terms of a medical nature that have legal significance. . . . As a consequence, the

States have, over the years, developed numerous specialized terms to define mental health concepts. Often, those definitions do not fit precisely with the definitions employed by the medical community. The legal definitions of "insanity" and "competency," for example, vary substantially from their psychiatric counterparts. . . . Legal definitions, however, which must "take into account such issues as individual responsibility . . . and competency," need not mirror those advanced by the medical profession. . . .

To the extent that the civil commitment statutes we have considered set forth criteria relating to an individual's inability to control his dangerousness, the Kansas Act sets forth comparable criteria and Hendricks' condition doubtless satisfies those criteria. The mental health professionals who evaluated Hendricks diagnosed him as suffering from pedophilia, a condition the psychiatric profession itself classifies as a serious mental disorder. . . . Hendricks even conceded that, when he becomes "stressed out," he cannot "control the urge" to molest children. . . . This admitted lack of volitional control, coupled with a prediction of future dangerousness, adequately distinguishes Hendricks from other dangerous persons who are perhaps more properly dealt with exclusively through criminal proceedings. Hendricks' diagnosis as a pedophile, which qualifies as a "mental abnormality" under the Act, thus plainly suffices for due process purposes.

We granted Hendricks' cross petition to determine whether the Act violates the Constitution's double jeopardy prohibition or its ban on ex post-facto lawmaking. The thrust of Hendricks' argument is that the Act establishes criminal proceedings; hence confinement under it necessarily constitutes punishment. He contends that where, as here, newly enacted "punishment" is predicated upon past conduct for which he has already been convicted and forced to serve a prison sentence, the Constitution's Double Jeopardy and Ex Post-Facto Clauses are violated. We are unpersuaded by Hendricks' argument that Kansas has established criminal proceedings.

The categorization of a particular proceeding as civil or criminal "is first of all a question of statutory construction." . . . We must initially ascertain whether the legislature meant the statute to establish "civil" proceedings. If so, we ordinarily defer to the legislature's stated intent. Here, Kansas' objective to create a civil proceeding is evidenced by its placement of the Sexually Violent Predator Act within the Kansas probate code, instead of the criminal code, as well as its description of the Act as creating a "civil commitment procedure." . . . Nothing on the face of the statute suggests that the legislature sought to create anything other than a civil commitment scheme designed to protect the public from harm.

Although we recognize that a "civil label is not always dispositive," . . . we will reject the legislature's manifest intent only where a party challenging the statute provides "the clearest proof" that "the statutory scheme [is] so punitive either in purpose or effect as to negate [the State's] intention" to deem it "civil." . . . In those limited circumstances, we will consider the statute to have established criminal proceedings for constitutional purposes. Hendricks, however, has failed to satisfy this heavy burden.

As a threshold matter, commitment under the Act does not implicate either of the two primary objectives of criminal punishment: retribution or deterrence. The Act's purpose is not retributive because it does not affix culpability for prior criminal conduct. Instead, such conduct is used solely for evidentiary purposes, either to demonstrate that a "mental abnormality" exists or to support a finding of future dangerousness. We have previously concluded that an Illinois statute was nonpunitive even though it was triggered by the commission of a sexual assault, explaining that evidence of the prior criminal conduct was "received not to punish past misdeeds, but primarily to show the accused's mental condition and to predict future behavior." . . . In addition, the Kansas Act does not make a criminal conviction a prerequisite for commitment— persons absolved of criminal responsibility may nonetheless be subject to confinement under the Act. . . . An absence of the necessary criminal responsibility suggests that the State is not seeking retribution for a past misdeed. Thus, the fact that the Act may be "tied to criminal activity" is "insufficient to render the statut[e] punitive." . . .

Moreover, unlike a criminal statute, no finding of scienter is required to commit an individual who is found to be a sexually violent predator; instead, the commitment determination is made based on a "mental abnormality" or "personality disorder" rather than on one's criminal intent. The existence of a scienter requirement is customarily an important element in distinguishing criminal from civil statutes. . . . The absence of such a requirement here is evidence that confinement under the statute is not intended to be retributive.

Nor can it be said that the legislature intended the Act to function as a deterrent. Those persons committed under the Act are, by definition, suffering from a "mental abnormality" or a "personality disorder" that prevents them from exercising adequate control over their behavior. Such persons are therefore unlikely to be deterred by the threat of confinement. And the conditions surrounding that confinement do not suggest a punitive purpose on the State's part. The State has represented that an individual confined under the Act is not subject to the more restrictive conditions placed on state prisoners, but instead experiences essentially the same conditions as any involuntarily committed patient in the state mental institution. . . . Because none of the parties argues that people institutionalized under the Kansas general civil commitment statute are subject to punitive conditions, even though they may be involuntarily confined, it is difficult to conclude that persons confined under this Act are being "punished."

Although the civil commitment scheme at issue here does involve an affirmative restraint, "the mere fact that a person is detained does not inexorably lead to the conclusion that the government has imposed punishment." . . . The State may take measures to restrict the freedom of the dangerously mentally ill. This is a legitimate nonpunitive governmental objective and has been historically so regarded. . . . The Court has, in fact, cited the confinement of "mentally unstable individuals who present a danger to the public" as one classic example of nonpunitive detention. . . . If detention for the purpose of protecting the community from harm necessarily constituted punishment, then all involuntary civil commitments would have to be considered punishment. But we have never so held.

Hendricks focuses on his confinement's potentially indefinite duration as evidence of the State's punitive intent. That focus, however, is misplaced. Far from any punitive objective, the confinement's duration is instead linked to the stated purposes of the commitment, namely, to hold the person until his mental abnormality no longer causes him to be a threat to others. . . . If, at any time, the confined person is adjudged "safe to be at large," he is statutorily entitled to immediate release. . . .

Furthermore, commitment under the Act is only potentially indefinite. The maximum amount of time an individual can be incapacitated pursuant to a single judicial proceeding is one year. . . . If Kansas seeks to continue the detention beyond that year, a court must once again determine beyond a reasonable doubt that the detainee satisfies the same standards as required for the initial confinement. . . . This requirement again demonstrates that Kansas does not intend an individual committed pursuant to the Act to remain confined any longer than he suffers from a mental abnormality rendering him unable to control his dangerousness.

Hendricks next contends that the State's use of procedural safeguards traditionally found in criminal trials makes the proceedings here criminal rather than civil. . . . The numerous procedural and evidentiary protections afforded here demonstrate that the Kansas Legislature has taken great care to confine only a narrow class of particularly dangerous individuals, and then only after meeting the strictest procedural standards. That Kansas chose to afford such procedural protections does not transform a civil commitment proceeding into a criminal prosecution.

Finally, Hendricks argues that the Act is necessarily punitive because it fails to offer any legitimate "treat-ment." Without such treatment, Hendricks asserts, confinement under the Act amounts to little more than disguised punishment. Hendricks' argument assumes that treatment for his condition is available, but that the State has failed (or refused) to provide it. The Kansas Supreme Court, however, apparently rejected this assumption. . . .

Accepting the Kansas court's apparent determination that treatment is not possible for this category of individuals does not obligate us to adopt its legal conclusions. We have already observed that, under the appropriate circumstances and when accompanied by proper procedures, incapacitation may be a legitimate end of the civil law. . . . Accordingly, the Kansas court's determination that the Act's "overriding concern" was the continued "segregation of sexually violent offenders" is consistent with our conclusion that the Act establishes civil proceedings, . . . especially when that concern is coupled with the State's ancillary goal of providing treatment to those offenders, if such is possible. While we have upheld state civil commitment statutes that aim both to incapacitate and to treat, . . . we have never held that the Constitution prevents a State from civilly detaining those for whom no treatment is available, but who nevertheless pose a danger to others. A State could hardly be seen as furthering a "punitive" purpose by involuntarily confining persons afflicted with an untreatable, highly contagious disease. . . . Similarly, it would be of little value to require treatment as a precondition for civil confinement of the dangerously insane when no acceptable treatment existed. To conclude otherwise would obligate a State to release certain confined individuals who were both mentally ill and dangerous simply because they could not be successfully treated for their afflictions. . . .

Alternatively, the Kansas Supreme Court's opinion can be read to conclude that Hendricks' condition is treatable, but that treatment was not the State's "overriding concern," and that no treatment was being provided (at least at the time Hendricks was committed). . . . Even if we accept this determination that the provision of treatment was not the Kansas Legislature's "overriding" or "primary" purpose in passing the Act, this does not rule out the possibility that an ancillary purpose of the Act was to provide treatment, and it does not require us to conclude that the Act is punitive. Indeed, critical language in the Act itself demonstrates that the Secretary of Social and Rehabilitation Services, under whose custody sexually violent predators are committed, has an obligation to provide treatment to individuals like Hendricks. . . . Other of the Act's sections echo this obligation to provide treatment for committed persons. . . . Thus . . . "the State has a statutory obligation to provide 'care and treatment for [persons adjudged sexually dangerous] designed to effect recovery,' " . . . and we may therefore conclude that "the State has . . . provided for the treatment of those it commits."

Although the treatment program initially offered Hendricks may have seemed somewhat meager, it must be remembered that he was the first person committed under the Act. That the State did not have all of its treatment procedures in place is thus not surprising. What is significant, however, is that Hendricks was placed under the supervision of the Kansas Department of Health and Social and Rehabilitative Services, housed in a unit segregated from the general prison population and operated not by employees of the Department of Corrections, but by other trained individuals. And, before this Court, Kansas declared "[a]bsolutely" that persons committed under the Act are now receiving in the neighborhood of "31.5 hours of treatment per week." . . .

Where the State has "disavowed any punitive intent"; limited confinement to a small segment of particularly dangerous individuals; provided strict procedural safeguards; directed that confined persons be segregated from the general prison population and afforded the same status as others who have been civilly committed; recommended treatment if such is possible; and permitted immediate release upon a showing that the individual is no longer dangerous or mentally impaired, we cannot say that it acted with punitive intent. We therefore hold that the Act does not establish criminal proceedings and that involuntary confinement pursuant to the Act is not punitive. Our conclusion that the Act is nonpunitive thus removes an essential prerequisite for both Hendricks' double jeopardy and ex post-facto claims.

. . . Hendricks argues that, as applied to him, the Act violates double jeopardy principles because his confinement under the Act, imposed after a conviction and a term of incarceration, amounted to both a second prosecution and a second punishment for the same offense. We disagree.

Because we have determined that the Kansas Act is civil in nature, initiation of its commitment proceedings does not constitute a second prosecution. . . . Moreover, as commitment under the Act is not tantamount to "punishment," Hendricks' involuntary detention does not violate the Double Jeopardy Clause, even though that confinement may follow a prison term. . . . If an individual otherwise meets the requirements for involuntary civil commitment, the State is under no obligation to release that individual simply because the detention would follow a period of incarceration.

Hendricks also argues that even if the Act survives the "multiple punishments" test, it nevertheless fails the "same elements" test of *Blockburger v. United States* . . . (1932). Under *Blockburger*, "where the same act or transaction constitutes a violation of two distinct statutory provisions, the test to be applied to determine whether there are two offenses or only one, is whether each provision requires proof of a fact which the other does not." The *Blockburger* test, however, simply does not apply outside of the successive prosecution context. A proceeding under the Act does not define an "offense," the elements of which can be compared to the elements of an offense for which the person may previously have been convicted. Nor does the Act make the commission of a specified "offense" the basis for invoking the commitment proceedings. Instead, it uses a prior conviction (or previously charged conduct) for evidentiary purposes to determine whether a person suffers from a "mental abnormality" or "personality disorder" and also poses a threat to the public. Accordingly, we are unpersuaded by Hendricks' novel application of the *Blockburger* test and conclude that the Act does not violate the Double Jeopardy Clause.

Hendricks' ex post-facto claim is similarly flawed. The Ex Post-Facto Clause, which "forbids the application of any new punitive measure to a crime already consummated," has been interpreted to pertain exclusively to penal statutes. . . . As we have previously determined, the Act does not impose punishment; thus, its application does not raise ex post-facto concerns. Moreover, the Act clearly does not have retroactive effect. Rather, the Act permits involuntary confinement based upon a determination that the person currently both suffers from a "mental abnormality" or "personality disorder" and is likely to pose a future danger to the public. To the extent that past behavior is taken into account, it is used, as noted above, solely for evidentiary purposes. Because the Act does not criminalize conduct legal before its enactment, nor deprive Hendricks of any defense that was available to him at the time of his crimes, the Act does not violate the Ex Post-Facto Clause.

We hold that the Kansas Sexually Violent Predator Act comports with due process requirements and neither runs afoul of double jeopardy principles nor constitutes an exercise in impermissible ex post-facto lawmaking. Accordingly, the judgment of the Kansas Supreme Court is reversed.

Justice Kennedy, concurring. . . .

Justice Breyer, [joined by Justices Stevens, Souter and Ginsburg] dissenting.

I agree with the majority that the Kansas Act's "definition of 'mental abnormality'" satisfies the "substantive" requirements of the Due Process Clause. . . . Kansas, however, concedes that Hendricks' condition is treatable; yet the Act did not provide Hendricks (or others like him) with any treatment until after his release date from prison and only inadequate treatment thereafter. These, and certain other, special features of the Act convince me that it was not simply an effort to commit Hendricks civilly, but rather an effort to inflict further punishment upon him. The Ex Post-Facto Clause therefore prohibits the Act's application to Hendricks, who committed his crimes prior to its enactment. . . .

The statutory provisions before us do amount to punishment primarily because . . . the legislature did not tailor the statute to fit the nonpunitive civil aim of treatment, which it concedes exists in Hendricks' case. The Clause in these circumstances does not stand as an obstacle to achieving important protections for the public's safety; rather it provides an assurance that, where so significant a restriction of an individual's basic freedoms is at issue, a State cannot cut corners. Rather, the legislature must hew to the Constitution's liberty protecting line. . . .

Case

FURMAN V. GEORGIA

408 U.S. 238; 92 S.Ct. 2726; 33 L.Ed. 2d 346 (1972)
Vote: 5–4

In this landmark decision, the U.S. Supreme Court invalidates Georgia's death penalty statute. This decision represents three death penalty cases that were consolidated on appeal. All three defendants were African-American. One of them was convicted for murder; two were found guilty of rape. All three were sentenced to death by juries.

PER CURIAM. The Court holds that the imposition and carrying out of the death penalty in these cases constitutes cruel and unusual punishment in violation of the Eighth and Fourteenth Amendments. The judgment in each case is therefore reversed insofar as it leaves undisturbed the death sentence imposed, and the cases are remanded for further proceedings.

Mr. Justice Douglas, Mr. Justice Brennan, Mr. Justice Stewart, Mr. Justice White, and Mr. Justice Marshall have filed separate opinions in support of the judgments. The Chief Justice, Mr. Justice Blackmun, Mr. Justice Powell, and Mr. Justice Rehnquist have filed separate dissenting opinions.

Mr. Justice Douglas concurring.

. . . In each [of these cases] the determination of whether the penalty should be death or a lighter punishment was left by the State to the discretion of the judge or of the jury. . . . I vote to vacate each judgment, believing that the exaction of the death penalty does violate the Eighth and Fourteenth Amendments. . . .

The words "cruel and unusual" certainly include penalties that are barbaric. But the words, at least when read in light of the English proscription against selective and irregular use of penalties, suggest that it is "cruel and unusual" to apply the death penalty—or any other penalty—selectively to minorities whose numbers are few, who are outcasts of society, and who are unpopular, but whom society is willing to see suffer though it would not countenance general application of the same penalty across the board. . . .

. . . [W]e deal with a system of law and of justice that leaves to the uncontrolled discretion of judges or juries the determination whether defendants committing these crimes should die or be imprisoned. Under these laws no standards govern the selection of the penalty. People live or die, dependent on the whim of one man or of 12. In a Nation committed to equal protection of the laws there is no permissible "caste" aspect of law enforcement. Yet we know that the discretion of judges and juries in imposing the death penalty enables the penalty to be selectively applied, feeding prejudices against the accused if he is poor and despised, lacking political clout, or if he is a member of a suspect or unpopular minority, and saving those who by social position may be in a more protected position. . . .

The high service rendered by the "cruel and unusual" punishment clause of the Eighth Amendment is to require legislatures to write penal laws that are evenhanded, non-selective, and nonarbitrary, and to require judges to see to it that general laws are not applied sparsely, selectively, and spottily to unpopular groups.

. . . [T]hese discretionary statutes are unconstitutional in their operation. They are pregnant with discrimination and discrimination is an ingredient not compatible with the idea of equal protection of the laws that is implicit in the ban on "cruel and unusual" punishments.

Mr. Justice Brennan, concurring.

Ours would indeed be a simple task were we required merely to measure a challenged punishment against those that history has long condemned. That narrow and unwarranted view of the Clause, however, was left behind with the 19th century. Our task today is more complex. We know "that the words of the [Clause] are not precise and that their scope is not static." We know, therefore, that the Clause "must draw its meaning from the evolving standards of decency that mark the progress of a maturing society." That knowledge, of course, is but the beginning of the inquiry.

. . . [T]he question is whether [a] penalty subjects the individual to a fate forbidden by the principle of civilized treatment guaranteed by the [Clause]." It was also said that a challenged punishment must be examined "in light of the basic prohibition against inhuman treatment" embodied in the Clause.

. . . "The basic concept underlying the [Clause] is nothing less than the dignity of man. While the State has the power to punish, the [Clause] stands to assure that this power be exercised within the limits of civilized standards." At bottom, then, the Cruel and Unusual Punishment Clause prohibits the infliction of uncivilized and inhuman punishments. The State, even as it punishes, must treat its members with respect for their intrinsic worth as human beings. A punishment is "cruel and unusual," therefore, if it does not comport with human dignity. . . .

. . . [T]he punishment of death is inconsistent with . . . four principles: Death is an unusually severe and degrading punishment; there is a strong probability that it is inflicted arbitrarily; its rejection by contemporary society is virtually total; and there is no reason to believe that it serves any penal purpose more effectively than the less severe punishment of imprisonment. The function of these principles is to enable a court to determine whether a punishment comports with human dignity. Death, quite simply, does not. . . .

Mr. Justice Stewart, concurring.

. . . Legislatures—state and federal—have sometimes specified that the penalty of death shall be the mandatory punishment for every person convicted of engaging in certain designated criminal conduct.

If we were reviewing death sentences imposed under these or similar laws, we would be faced with the need to decide whether capital punishment is unconstitutional for all crimes and under all circumstances. We would need to decide whether a legislature—state or federal—could constitutionally determine that certain criminal conduct is so atrocious that society's interest in deterrence and retribution wholly outweighs any considerations of reform or rehabilitation of the perpetrator, and that, despite the inconclusive empirical evidence, only the automatic penalty of death will provide maximum deterrence.

On that score I would say only that I cannot agree that retribution is a constitutionally impermissible ingredient in the imposition of punishment. The instinct for retribu-

tion is part of the nature of man, and channeling that instinct in the administration of criminal justice serves an important purpose in promoting the stability of a society governed by law. When people begin to believe that organized society is unwilling or unable to impose upon criminal offenders the punishment they "deserve," then there are sown the seeds of anarchy—of self-help, vigilante justice and lynch law.

The constitutionality of capital punishment in the abstract is not, however, before us in these cases. For the Georgia and Texas Legislatures have not provided that the death penalty shall be imposed upon all those who are found guilty of forcible rape. And the Georgia Legislature has not ordained that death shall be the automatic punishment for murder.

Instead, the death sentences now before us are the product of a legal system that brings them, I believe, within the very core of the Eighth Amendment's guarantee against cruel and unusual punishments, a guarantee applicable against the States through the Fourteenth Amendment. In the first place, it is clear that these sentences are "cruel" in the sense that they excessively go beyond, not in degree but in kind, the punishments that the state legislatures have determined to be necessary. In the second place, it is equally clear that these sentences are "unusual" in the sense that the penalty of death is infrequently imposed for murder, and that its imposition for rape is extraordinarily rare. But I do not rest my conclusion upon these two propositions alone.

These death sentences are cruel and unusual in the same way that being struck by lightning is cruel and unusual. For, of all the people convicted of rapes and murders in 1967 and 1968, many just as reprehensible as these, the petitioners are among a capriciously selected random handful upon whom the sentence of death has in fact been imposed. My concurring Brothers have demonstrated that, if any basis can be discerned for the selection of these few to be sentenced to die, it is the constitutionally impermissible basis of race. But racial discrimination has not been proved, and I put it to one side. I simply conclude that the Eighth and Fourteenth Amendments cannot tolerate the infliction of a sentence of death under legal systems that permit this unique penalty to be so wantonly and so freakishly imposed.

Mr. Justice White, concurring.

. . . The narrow question to which I address myself concerns the constitutionality of capital punishment statutes under which (1) the legislature authorizes the imposition of the death penalty for murder or rape; (2) the legislature does not itself mandate the penalty in any particular class or kind of case (that is, legislative will is not frustrated if the penalty is never imposed), but delegates to judges or juries the decisions as to those cases, if any, in which the penalty will be utilized; and (3) judges and juries have ordered the death penalty with such infrequency that the odds are now very much against imposition and execution of the penalty with respect to any convicted murderer or rapist. It is in this context that we must consider whether the execution of these petitioners would violate the Eighth Amendment.

. . . [L]ike my Brethren, I must arrive at judgment; and I can do no more than state a conclusion based on 10 years of almost daily exposure to the facts and circumstances of hundreds and hundreds of federal and state criminal cases involving crimes for which death is the authorized penalty. That conclusion, as I have said, is that the death penalty is exacted with great infrequency even for the most atrocious crimes and that there is no meaningful basis for distinguishing the few cases in which it is imposed from the many cases in which it is not. The short of it is that the policy of vesting sentencing authority primarily in juries—a decision largely motivated by the desire to mitigate the harshness of the law and to bring community judgment to bear on the sentence as well as guilt or innocence—has so effectively achieved its aims that capital punishment within the confines of the statutes now before us has for all practical purposes run its course. . . .

Mr. Justice Marshall, concurring.

. . . Perhaps the most important principle in analyzing "cruel and unusual" punishment questions is one that is reiterated again and again in the prior opinions of the Court: i.e., the cruel and unusual language "must draw its meaning from the evolving standards of decency that mark the progress of a maturing society." Thus, a penalty that was permissible at one time in our Nation's history is not necessarily permissible today. . . .

In judging whether or not a given penalty is morally acceptable, most courts have said that the punishment is valid unless "it shocks the conscience and sense of justice of the people."

While a public opinion poll obviously is of some assistance in indicating public acceptance or rejection of a specific penalty, its utility cannot be very great. This is because whether or not a punishment is cruel and unusual depends, not on whether its mere mention "shocks the conscience and sense of justice of the people," but on whether people who were fully informed as to the purposes of the penalty and its liabilities would find the penalty shocking, unjust, and unacceptable.

In other words, the question with which we must deal is not whether a substantial proportion of American citizens would today, if polled, opine that capital punishment is barbarously cruel, but whether they would find it to be so in the light of all information presently available.

This information would almost surely convince the average citizen that the penalty was unwise, but a problem arises as to whether it would convince him that the penalty was morally reprehensible. This problem arises from the fact that the public's desire for retribution, even though this is a goal that the legislature cannot constitutionally pursue as its sole justification for capital punishment, might influence the citizenry's view of the morality of capital punishment. The solution to the problem lies in the fact that no one has ever seriously advanced retribution as a legitimate goal of our society. Defenses of capital punishment are always mounted on deterrent or other similar theories. This should not be surprising. It is the people of this country who have urged in the past that prisons rehabilitate as well as isolate offenders, and it is the people who have injected a sense of purpose into our penology. I cannot believe that at this stage in our history, the American people would ever knowingly support purposeless vengeance. Thus, I believe that the great mass of citizens would conclude on the basis of the material already considered that the death penalty is immoral therefore unconstitutional.

In striking down capital punishment, this Court does not malign our system of government. On the contrary, it pays homage to it. Only in a free society could right triumph in difficult times, and could civilization record its magnificent advancement. In recognizing the humanity of our fellow beings, we pay ourselves the highest tribute. We achieve "a major milestone in the long road up from barbarism" and join the approximately 70 other jurisdictions in the world which celebrate their regard for civilization and humanity by shunning capital punishment.

Mr. Chief Justice Burger, with whom *Mr. Justice Blackmun,* and *Mr. Justice Rehnquist,* join, dissenting.

. . . If we were possessed of legislative power, I would either join with Mr. Justice Brennan and Mr. Justice Marshall or, at the very least, restrict the use of capital punishment to a small category of the most heinous crimes. Our constitutional inquiry, however, must be divorced from personal feelings as to the morality and efficacy of the death penalty, and be confined to the meaning and applicability of the uncertain language of the Eighth Amendment. There is no novelty in being called upon to interpret a constitutional provision that is less than self-defining, but, of all our fundamental guarantees, the ban on "cruel and unusual punishments" is one of the most difficult to translate into judicially manageable terms. The widely divergent views of the Amendment expressed in today's opinions reveals the haze that surrounds this constitutional command. Yet it is essential to our role as a court that we not seize upon the enigmatic character of the guarantee as an invitation to enact our personal predilections into law.

Although the Eighth Amendment literally reads as prohibiting only those punishments that are both "cruel" and "unusual," history compels the conclusion that the Constitution prohibits all punishments of extreme and barbarous cruelty, regardless of how frequently or infrequently imposed.

But where, as here, we consider a punishment well known to history, and clearly authorized by legislative enactment, it disregards the history of the Eighth Amendment and all the judicial comment that has followed to rely on the term "unusual" as affecting the outcome of these cases. Instead, I view these cases as turning on the single question whether capital punishment is "cruel" in the constitutional sense. The term "unusual" cannot be read as limiting the ban on "cruel" punishments or as somehow expanding the meaning of the term "cruel." For this reason I am unpersuaded by the facile argument that since capital punishment has always been cruel in the everyday sense of the word, and has become unusual due to decreased use, it is, therefore, now "cruel and unusual." . . .

Mr. Justice Blackmun, dissenting.

. . . Cases such as these provide for me an excruciating agony of the spirit. I yield to no one in the depth of my distaste, antipathy, and, indeed, abhorrence, for the death penalty, with all its aspects of physical distress and fear and of moral judgment exercised by finite minds. That distaste is buttressed by a belief that capital punishment serves no useful purpose that can be demonstrated. For me, it violates childhood's training and life's experiences, and is not compatible with the philosophical convictions I have been able to develop. It is antagonistic to any sense of "reverence for life." Were I a legislator, I would vote against the death penalty for the policy reasons argued by counsel for the respective petitioners and expressed and adopted in the several opinions filed by the Justices who vote to reverse these convictions.

Although personally I may rejoice at the Court's result, I find it difficult to accept or to justify as a matter of history, of law, or of constitutional pronouncement. I fear the Court has overstepped. It has sought and has achieved an end.

Mr. Justice Powell, with whom the *Chief Justice, Mr. Justice Blackmun,* and *Mr. Justice Rehnquist* join, dissenting.

. . . The Court granted certiorari in these cases to consider whether the death penalty is any longer a permissible form of punishment. It is the judgment of five Justices that the death penalty, as customarily prescribed and implemented in this country today, offends the constitutional prohibition against cruel and unusual punishments. The reasons for that judgment are stated in five separate opinions, expressing as many separate rationales. In my view, none of these opinions provides a constitutionally adequate foundation for the Court's decision. . . .

Mr. Justice Rehnquist, with whom the *Chief Justice, Mr. Justice Blackmun,* and *Mr. Justice Powell* join, dissenting.

. . . Whatever its precise rationale, today's holding necessarily brings into sharp relief the fundamental question of the role of judicial review in a democratic society. How can government by the elected representatives of the people co-exist with the power of the federal judiciary, whose members are constitutionally insulated from responsiveness to the popular will, to declare invalid laws duly enacted by the popular branches of government?

Sovereignty resides ultimately in the people as a whole and, by adopting through their States a written Constitution for the Nation and subsequently adding amendments to that instrument, they have both granted certain powers to the National Government, and denied other powers to the National and the State Governments. Courts are exercising no more than the judicial function conferred upon them by Art. III of the Constitution when they assess, in a case before them, whether or not a particular legislative enactment is within the authority granted by the Constitution to the enacting body, and whether it runs afoul of some limitation placed by the Constitution on the authority of that body. For the theory is that the people themselves have spoken in the Constitution, and therefore its commands are superior to the commands of the legislature, which is merely an agent of the people.

The Founding Fathers thus wisely sought to have the best of both worlds, the undeniable benefits of both democratic self-government and individual rights protected against possible excesses of that form of government.

The very nature of judicial review, as pointed out by Justice Stone in his dissent in the Butler case, makes the courts the least subject to Madisonian check in the event that they shall, for the best of motives, expand judicial authority beyond the limits contemplated by the Framers. It is for this reason that judicial self-restraint is surely an implied, if not an expressed, condition of the grant of authority of judicial review. The Court's holding in these cases has been reached, I believe, in complete disregard of that implied condition.

Case

GREGG V. GEORGIA

428 U.S. 153; 96 S.Ct. 2909; 49 L.Ed. 2d 859 (1976)

Vote: 7–2

Here the Supreme Court effectively reinstates the death penalty by sustaining a revised Georgia death penalty law. The petitioner, Troy Gregg, was convicted of armed robbery and murder and was sentenced to death. In accordance with Georgia's death penalty law revised after Furman v. Georgia, the trial was conducted in two stages, a guilt stage and a sentencing stage.

Judgment of the Court, and opinion of **Mr. Justice Stewart, Mr. Justice Powell,** and **Mr. Justice Stevens,** announced by **Mr. Justice Stewart.**

. . . There is no question that death as a punishment is unique in its severity and irrevocability. When defendant's life is at stake, the Court has been particularly sensitive to insure that every safeguard is observed. But we are concerned here only with the imposition of capital punishment for the crime of murder, and when a life has been taken deliberately by the offender, we cannot say that the punishment is invariably disproportionate to the crime. It is an extreme sanction, suitable to the most extreme of crimes.

We hold that the death penalty is not a form of punishment that may never be imposed, regardless of the circumstances of the offense, regardless of the character of the offender, and regardless of the procedure followed in reaching the decision to impose it.

We now turn to consideration of the constitutionality of Georgia's capital-sentencing procedures. In the wake of *Furman,* Georgia amended its capital punishment statute, but chose not to narrow the scope of its murder provisions. Thus, now as before *Furman,* in Georgia "[a] person commits murder when he unlawfully and with malice aforethought, either express or implied, causes the death of another human being." All persons convicted of murder "shall be punished by death or by imprisonment for life."

Georgia did act, however, to narrow the class of murderers subject to capital punishment by specifying 10 statutory aggravating circumstances, one of which must be found by the jury to exist beyond a reasonable doubt before a death sentence can ever be imposed. In addition, the jury is authorized to consider any other appropriate aggravating or mitigating circumstances. The jury is not required to find any mitigating circumstance in order to make a recommendation of mercy that is binding on the trial court, but it must find a statutory aggravating circumstance before recommending a sentence of death.

These procedures require the jury to consider the circumstances of the crime and the criminal before it recommends sentence. No longer can a Georgia jury do as *Furman*'s jury did: reach a finding of the defendant's guilt and then, without guidance or direction, decide whether he should live or die. Instead, the jury's attention is directed to the specific circumstances of the crime: Was it committed in the course of another capital felony? Was it committed for money? Was it committed upon a peace officer or judicial officer? Was it committed in a particularly heinous way or in a manner that endangered the lives of many persons? In addition, the jury's attention is focused on the characteristics of the person who committed the crime: Does he have a record of prior convictions for capital offenses? Are there any special facts about this defendant that mitigate against imposing capital punishment (e.g., his youth, the extent of his cooperation with the police, his emotional state at the time of the crime). As a result, while some jury discretion still exists, "the discretion to be exercised is controlled by clear and objective standards so as to produce nondiscriminatory application."

As an important additional safeguard against arbitrariness and caprice, the Georgia statutory scheme provides for automatic appeal of all death sentences to the State's Supreme Court. That court is required by statute to review each sentence of death and determine whether it was imposed under the influence of passion or prejudice, whether the evidence supports the jury's finding of a statutory aggravating circumstance, and whether the sentence is disproportionate compared to those sentences imposed in similar cases.

In short, Georgia's new sentencing procedures require as a prerequisite to the imposition of the death penalty, specific jury findings as to the circumstances of the crime or the character of the defendant. Moreover to guard further against a situation comparable to that presented in *Furman,* the Supreme Court of Georgia compares each death sentence with the sentences imposed on similarly situated defendants to ensure that the sentence of death in a particular case is not disproportionate. On their face these procedures seem to satisfy the concerns of *Furman.* No longer should there be "no meaningful basis for distinguishing the few cases in which [the death penalty] is imposed from the many cases in which it is not."

The basic concern of *Furman* centered on those defendants who were being condemned to death capriciously and arbitrarily. Under the procedures before the Court in that case, sentencing authorities were not directed to give attention to the nature or circumstances of the crime committed or to the character or record of the defendant. Left unguided, juries imposed the death sentence in a way that could only be called freakish. The new Georgia sentencing procedures, by contrast, focus the jury's attention on the particularized nature of the crime and the particularized characteristics of the individual defendant. While the jury is permitted to consider any aggravating or mitigating circumstances, it must find and identify at least one statutory aggravating factor before it may impose a penalty of death. In this way the jury's discretion is channeled. No longer can a jury wantonly and freakishly impose the death sentence; it is always circumscribed by the legislative guidelines. In addition, the review function of the Supreme Court of Georgia affords additional assurance that the concerns that prompted our decision in *Furman* are not present to any significant degree in the Georgia procedure applied here.

Mr. Justice White, with whom the **Chief Justice** and **Mr. Justice Rehnquist** join, concurring in the judgment. . . .

Mr. Justice Blackmun, concurring in the judgment. . . .

Mr. Justice Marshall, dissenting.

In *Furman v. Georgia,* I set forth at some length my views on the basic issue presented to the Court in these cases. The death penalty, I concluded, is a cruel and unusual punishment prohibited by the Eighth and Fourteenth Amendments. That continues to be my view.

In *Furman* I concluded that the death penalty is constitutionally invalid for two reasons. First, the death penalty is excessive. And second, the American people, fully informed as to the purposes of the death penalty and its liabilities, would in my view reject it as morally unacceptable. . . .

The mere fact that the community demands the murderer's life in return for the evil he has done cannot sustain the death penalty, for as the plurality reminds us, "the Eighth Amendment demands more than that a challenged punishment be acceptable to contemporary society." To be sustained under the Eighth Amendment, the death penalty must "[comport] with the basic concept of human dignity at the core of the Amendment." . . . Under these standards, the taking of life "because the wrongdoer deserves it" surely must fall, for such a punishment has as its very basis the total denial of the wrongdoer's dignity and worth.

The death penalty, unnecessary to promote the goal of deterrence or to further any legitimate notion of retribution, is an excessive penalty forbidden by the Eighth and Fourteenth Amendments. I respectfully dissent from the Court's judgment upholding the sentences of death imposed upon the petitioners in these cases.

Mr. Justice Brennan, dissenting. . . .

Case

PAYNE V. TENNESSEE

501 U.S. 808; 111 S.Ct. 2597; 115 L.Ed. 2d 720 (1991)
Vote: 6–3

In this case the Supreme Court overturns its decisions in Booth v. Maryland *(1987) and* South Carolina v. Gathers *(1989), which had barred the admission of victim impact evidence during the sentencing phase of a capital trial.*

Chief Justice Rehnquist delivered the opinion of the Court.

. . . The petitioner, Pervis Tyrone Payne, was convicted by a jury on two counts of first-degree murder and one count of assault with intent to commit murder in the first degree. He was sentenced to death for each of the murders, and to 30 years in prison for the assault.

The victims of Payne's offenses were 28-year-old Charisse Christopher, her 2-year-old daughter Lacie, and her 3-year-old son Nicholas. The three lived together in an apartment in Millington, Tennessee, across the hall from Payne's girlfriend, Bobbie Thomas. On Saturday, June 27, 1987, Payne visited Thomas' apartment several times in expectation of her return from her mother's house in Arkansas, but found no one at home. On one visit, he left his overnight bag, containing clothes and other items for his weekend stay, in the hallway outside Thomas' apartment. With the bag were three cans of malt liquor.

Payne passed the morning and early afternoon injecting cocaine and drinking beer. Later, he drove around the town with a friend in the friend's car, each of them taking turns reading a pornographic magazine. Sometime around 3 P.M., Payne returned to the apartment complex, entered the Christophers' apartment, and began making sexual advances towards Charisse. Charisse resisted and Payne became violent. A neighbor who resided in the apartment directly beneath the Christophers, heard Charisse screaming, "'Get out, get out' as if she were telling the children to leave." The noise briefly subsided and then began "horribly loud." The neighbor called the police after she heard a "blood curdling scream" from the Christopher apartment. . . .

When the first police officer arrived at the scene, he immediately encountered Payne who was leaving the apartment building, so covered with blood that he appeared to be "sweating blood." The officer confronted Payne, who responded, "I'm the complainant." . . . When the officer asked, "What's going on up there?" Payne struck the officer with the overnight bag, dropped his tennis shoes, and fled.

Inside the apartment, the police encountered a horrifying scene. Blood covered the walls and floor throughout the unit. Charisse and her children were lying on the floor in the kitchen. Nicholas, despite several wounds inflicted by a butcher knife that completely penetrated through his body from front to back, was still breathing. Miraculously, he survived, but not until after undergoing seven hours of surgery and a transfusion of 1700 cc's of blood—400 to 500 cc's more than his estimated normal blood volume. Charisse and Lacie were dead.

Charisse's body was found on the kitchen floor on her back, her legs fully extended. She had sustained 42 direct knife wounds and 42 defensive wounds on her arms and hands. The wounds were caused by 41 separate thrusts of a butcher knife. None of the 84 wounds inflicted by Payne were individually fatal; rather, the cause of death was most likely bleeding from all of the wounds.

Lacie's body was on the kitchen floor near her mother. She had suffered stab wounds to the chest, abdomen, back, and head. The murder weapon, a butcher knife, was found at her feet. Payne's baseball cap was snapped on her arm near her elbow. Three cans of malt liquor bearing Payne's fingerprints were found on a table near her body, and a fourth empty one was on the landing outside the apartment door.

Payne was apprehended later that day hiding in the attic of the home of a former girlfriend. As he descended the stairs of the attic, he stated to the arresting officers, "Man, I ain't killed no woman." According to one of the officers, Payne had "a wild look about him. His pupils were contracted. He was foaming at the mouth, saliva. He appeared to be very nervous. He was breathing real rapid." He had blood on his body and clothes and several scratches across his chest. It was later determined that the blood stains matched the victims' blood types. A search of his pockets revealed a packet containing cocaine residue, a hypodermic syringe wrapper, and a cap from a hypodermic syringe. His overnight bag, containing a bloody white shirt, was found in a nearby dumpster.

At trial, Payne took the stand and, despite the overwhelming and relatively uncontroverted evidence against him, testified that he had not harmed any of the Christophers. Rather, he asserted that another man had raced by him as he was walking up the stairs to the floor where the Christophers lived. He stated that he had gotten blood on himself when, after hearing moans from the Christopher's apartment, he had tried to help the victims. According to his testimony, he panicked and fled when he heard police sirens and noticed the blood on his clothes. The jury returned guilty verdicts against Payne on all counts.

During the sentencing phase of the trial, Payne presented the testimony of four witnesses: his mother and father, Bobbie Thomas, and Dr. John T. Huston, a clinical psychologist specializing in criminal court evaluation work. Bobbie Thomas testified that she met Payne at church, during a time when she was being abused by her husband. She stated that Payne was a very caring person, and that he devoted much time and attention to her three children, who were being affected by her marital difficulties. She said that the children had come to love him very much and would miss him and that he "behaved just like a father that loved his kids." She asserted that he did not drink, nor did he use drugs, and that it was generally inconsistent with Payne's character to have committed these crimes.

Dr. Huston testified that based on Payne's low score on an IQ test, Payne was "mentally handicapped." Huston also said that Payne was neither psychotic nor schizophrenic, and that Payne was the most polite prisoner he had ever met. Payne's parents testified that their son had no prior criminal record and had never been arrested. They also stated that Payne had no history of alcohol or drug abuse, he worked with his father as a painter, he was good with children, and that he was a good son.

The State presented the testimony of Charisse's mother, Mary Zvolanek. When asked how Nicholas had been affected by the murders of his mother and sister, she responded:

> He cries for his mom. He doesn't seem to understand why she doesn't come home. And he cries for his sister Lacie. He comes to me many times during the week and asks me, Grandmama, do you miss my Lacie. And I tell him yes. He says, I'm worried about my Lacie. . . .

In arguing for the death penalty during closing argument, the prosecutor commented on the continuing effects of Nicholas' experience, stating:

> But we do know that Nicholas was alive. And Nicholas was in the same room. Nicholas was still conscious. His eyes were open. He responded to the paramedics. He was able to follow their directions. He was able to hold his

intestines in as he was carried to the ambulance. So he knew what happened to his mother and baby sister. . . .

There is nothing you can do to ease the pain of any of the families involved in this case. There is nothing you can do to ease the pain of Bernice or Carl Payne, and that's a tragedy. There is nothing you can do basically to ease the pain of Mr. and Mrs. Zvolanek, and that's a tragedy. They will have to live with it the rest of their lives. There is obviously nothing you can do for Charisse and Lacie Jo. But there is something that you can do for Nicholas.

Somewhere down the road Nicholas is going to grow up, hopefully. He's going to want to know what happened. And he is going to know what happened to his baby sister and his mother. He is going to want to know what type of justice was done. He is going to want to know what happened. With your verdict, you will provide the answer. . . .

In the rebuttal to Payne's closing argument, the prosecutor stated:

You saw the videotape this morning. You saw what Nicholas Christopher will carry in his mind forever. When you talk about cruel, when you talk about atrocious, and when you talk about heinous, that picture will always come into your mind, probably throughout the rest of your lives.

. . . No one will ever know about Lacie Jo because she never had the chance to grow up. Her life was taken from her at the age of two years old. So, no, there won't be a high school principal to talk about Lacie Jo Christopher, and there won't be anybody to take her to her high school prom. And there won't be anybody there—there won't be her mother there or Nicholas' mother there to kiss him at night. His mother will never kiss him good night or pat him as he goes off to bed, or hold him and sing him a lullaby.

[Petitioner's attorney] wants you to think about a good reputation, people who love the defendant and things about him. He doesn't want you to think about the people who love Charisse Christopher, her mother and daddy who loved her. The people who loved little Lacie Jo, the grandparents who are still here. The brother who mourns for her every single day and wants to know where his best little playmate is. He doesn't have anybody to watch cartoons with him, a little one. These are the things that go into why it is especially cruel, heinous, and atrocious, the burden that that child will carry forever. . . .

The jury sentenced Payne to death on each of the murder counts.

The Supreme Court of Tennessee affirmed the convictions and sentence. The court rejected Payne's contention that the admission of the grandmother's testimony and

the State's closing argument constituted prejudicial violations of his rights under the Eighth Amendment. . . .

We granted certiorari . . . to reconsider our holdings in *Booth* [*v. Maryland*] and [*South Carolina v.*] *Gathers*. . . .

We are now of the view that a State may properly conclude that for the jury to assess meaningfully the defendant's moral culpability and blameworthiness, it should have before it at the sentencing phase evidence of the specific harm caused by the defendant. "[T]he State has a legitimate interest in countering the mitigating evidence which the defendant is entitled to put in, by reminding the sentencer that just as the murderer should be considered as an individual, so too the victim is an individual whose death represents a unique loss to society and in particular to his family." . . . *Booth* deprives the State of the full moral force of its evidence and may prevent the jury from having before it all the information necessary to determine the proper punishment for a first-degree murder.

The present case is an example of the potential for such unfairness. The capital sentencing jury heard testimony from Payne's girlfriend that they met at church, that he was affectionate, caring, kind to her children, that he was not an abuser of drugs or alcohol, and that it was inconsistent with his character to have committed the murder. Payne's parents testified that he was a good son, and a clinical psychologist testified that Payne was an extremely polite prisoner and suffered from a low IQ. None of this testimony was related to the circumstances of Payne's brutal crimes. In contrast, the only evidence of the impact of Payne's offenses during the sentencing phase was Nicholas' grandmother's description—in response to a single question—that the child misses his mother and baby sister. Payne argues that the Eighth Amendment commands that the jury's death sentence must be set aside because the jury heard this testimony. But the testimony illustrated quite poignantly some of the harm that Payne's killing had caused; there is nothing unfair about allowing the jury to bear in mind that harm at the same time as it considers the mitigating evidence introduced by the defendant. The Supreme Court of Tennessee in this case obviously felt the unfairness of the rule pronounced by *Booth* when it said "[i]t is an affront to the civilized members of the human race to say that at sentencing in a capital case, a parade of witnesses may praise the background, character and good deeds of Defendant (as was done in this case) without limitation as to relevancy, but nothing may be said that bears upon the character of, or the harm imposed, upon the victims." . . .

We thus hold that if the State chooses to permit the admission of victim impact evidence and prosecutorial argument on that subject, the Eighth Amendment erects no *per se* bar. A State may legitimately conclude that evidence about the victim and about the impact of the murder on the victim's family is relevant to the jury's decision as to whether or not the death penalty should be imposed. There is no reason to treat such evidence differently than other relevant evidence is treated. . . . Reconsidering these decisions now, we conclude for the reasons heretofore stated, that they were wrongly decided and should be, and now are, overruled. We accordingly affirm the judgment of the Supreme Court of Tennessee.

Justice O'Connor, with whom *Justice White* and *Justice Kennedy* join, concurring. . . .

Justice Scalia, with whom *Justice O'Connor* and *Justice Kennedy* join [in part], concurring. . . .

Justice Souter, with whom *Justice Kennedy* joins, concurring. . . .

Justice Marshall, with whom *Justice Blackmun* joins, dissenting. . . .

Justice Stevens, with whom *Justice Blackmun* joins, dissenting.

. . . Until today our capital punishment jurisprudence has required that any decision to impose the death penalty be based solely on evidence that tends to inform the jury about the character of the offense and the character of the defendant. Evidence that serves no purpose other than to appeal to the sympathies or emotions of the jurors has never been considered admissible. Thus, if a defendant, who had murdered a convenience store clerk in cold blood in the course of an armed robbery, offered evidence unknown to him at the time of the crime about the immoral character of his victim, all would recognize immediately that the evidence was irrelevant and inadmissible. Even-handed justice requires that the same constraint be imposed on the advocate of the death penalty. . . .

11

PERSONAL AUTONOMY AND THE CONSTITUTIONAL RIGHT OF PRIVACY

"The makers of the Constitution . . . conferred, as against the Government, the right to be let alone—the most comprehensive of rights and the right most valued by civilized men."

—JUSTICE LOUIS D. BRANDEIS,

DISSENTING IN *OLMSTEAD V. UNITED STATES* (1928)

Louis D. Brandeis: Associate Justice, 1916–1939

INTRODUCTION

The **constitutional right of privacy** protects the individual from unwarranted government interference in intimate personal relationships or activities. As it has taken shape since the mid-1960s, the right of privacy includes the freedom of the individual to make fundamental choices involving sex, reproduction, family life, and other intimate personal relationships. Of the various constitutional rights addressed in this book, the right of privacy remains the most intensely disputed. The controversy stems in part from the absence of any specific reference to privacy in the Constitution. Some scholars and judges still adhere to Justice Hugo Black's view that a right of privacy cannot reasonably be inferred from the language of the original Constitution or any of its amendments. However, it is clear that this is a minority position today. Among recent Supreme Court nominees, only Judge Robert Bork has rejected the interpretive foundation of the right of privacy. For most Americans, the debate over privacy has less to do with competing theories of constitutional interpretation than with the profound implications of the privacy principle for divisive social and moral questions such as **abortion, gay rights**, and **euthanasia.**

In *Roe v. Wade* (1973), the Supreme Court held that the right of privacy "is broad enough to encompass a woman's decision whether or not to terminate her pregnancy." As the ongoing protest against legal abortion makes clear, abortion is hardly an ordinary issue of public policy. Nor was *Roe v. Wade* a run-of-the-mill Supreme Court decision. Unlike most constitutional decisions, *Roe* aroused deep philosophical conflict and even deeper political and emotional turmoil. *Roe v. Wade* drew the Supreme Court into a firestorm of political controversy that continues unabated after three decades. This controversy has dominated public discussion of the Court, often eclipsing other important issues and likewise influencing the debate surrounding nominations to the Supreme Court.

Although abortion is the focal point of the debate over the right of privacy, the viability of the right of privacy is not based solely on the continued vitality of *Roe v. Wade*. Even if *Roe* were to be overturned, the right of privacy would still exist as an independent constitutional right, albeit somewhat circumscribed. The right of privacy is now well established in both federal and state constitutional law and has application to numerous questions of public policy beyond abortion. This chapter examines some of the more salient ones.

Philosophical Foundations of the Right of Privacy

When the Supreme Court invoked the right of privacy to effectively legalize abortion within stated limits, it was giving expression to a sense of **moral individualism** that is deeply rooted in American culture. However, countervailing notions of traditional morality are also deeply ingrained in American society, as the relentless and widespread attacks on *Roe v. Wade* demonstrate. In no other area of constitutional law are individualism and traditional morality so sharply antagonistic as in the area of privacy rights.

The moral individualism underlying the constitutional right of privacy was conceived in the political liberalism of the Age of Enlightenment. In his influential essay *On Liberty* (1859), the English thinker John Stuart Mill argued that "there is a sphere of action in which society, as distinguished from the individual, has, if any, only an indirect interest; comprehending all that portion of a person's life and conduct which affects only himself, or if it also affects others, only with their free, voluntary and undeceived consent and participation."

In the modern era, this idea that each individual should be considered an autonomous actor with respect to personal matters, is associated with the philosophy of **libertarianism,** which holds that individual freedom is the highest good and that law should be interpreted to maximize the scope of liberty. During and after the 1960s, the libertarian perspective became increasingly widespread among Americans, especially younger people. In the late 1960s and throughout the 1970s, a large number of people began to question the authority of government to regulate the private lives of individuals in the name of traditional morality.

In the libertarian view, the legitimate role of government is protection of individuals from one another, not from their own vices. Thus, libertarians often object to laws regulating sexual conduct, living arrangements, and the private use of drugs—and even to laws mandating that motorcycle riders wear helmets. Perhaps the ultimate libertarian position is opposition to the criminal law against suicide. In the libertarian view, the individual has the right to make basic decisions regarding his or her own life—or death.

The countervailing position, which might be dubbed **classical conservatism,** holds that individuals must often be protected against their own vices. Classical conservatives not only defend traditional morality but the embodiment of that morality in the law. On the contemporary Supreme Court, Justice Antonin Scalia has endorsed the classical conservative view of law and morality. In *Barnes v. Glen Theatre, Inc.* (1991) (the "nude dancing" decision discussed and reprinted in Chapter 8), Scalia wrote:

> Our society prohibits, and all human societies have prohibited, certain activities not because they harm others but because they are considered . . . immoral. In American society, such prohibitions have included, for example, sadomasochism, cockfighting, bestiality, suicide, drug use, prostitution and sodomy. While there might be a great diversity of views on whether various of these prohibitions should exist, . . . there is no doubt that absent specific constitutional protection for the conduct involved, the Constitution does not prohibit them simply because they regulate "morality."

The debate over the constitutional right of privacy is ultimately a debate between two sharply divergent views of the law. In the libertarian view, the law exists to protect individuals from one another. In this view, morality is not in and of itself a legitimate basis for law. The classical conservative view, on the other hand, sees law and morality as inseparable and holds that the maintenance of societal morality is one of the essential functions of the legal system.

CONSTITUTIONAL FOUNDATIONS OF THE RIGHT OF PRIVACY

Although libertarianism has roots in the liberalism of the Enlightenment, it is doubtful that any of the Framers of the Constitution were libertarians in the modern sense of the term. Certainly the Framers believed in individual freedom, but most did not conceive of freedom as including the right to flout traditional principles of conduct embodied in the common law. Yet the right of privacy, in essence the constitutionalization of libertarianism, has been "found" by the Supreme Court to emanate from various provisions of the Bill of Rights (see *Griswold v. Connecticut* [1965]).

Several provisions of the Bill of Rights were adopted to protect individuals from unreasonable invasions of privacy. The Third Amendment explicitly protects the privacy of the home in peacetime from soldiers seeking quarters. The Fourth Amendment protects individuals from unreasonable searches and seizures where they have a "reasonable expectation of privacy" (*Katz v. United States* [1967], Harlan, J., concurring). The Fifth Amendment prohibits compulsory self-incrimination, thus protecting the privacy of an accused individual's thoughts. The First Amendment ensures freedom of conscience in both political and religious matters, again recognizing the autonomy of the individual. Finally, the First Amendment's implicit guarantee of freedom of association protects one's right to choose one's friends, one's spouse, one's business partners, and so on. In *Griswold v. Connecticut* (1965), the Supreme Court interpreted these protections as embodying a right to be free of those government intrusions into the realm of intimate personal decisions.

Proponents of a constitutional right of privacy often cite the Ninth Amendment, which guarantees rights "retained by the people" even though they are not enumerated in the Constitution. Indeed, historically, the courts have recognized a variety of unenumerated constitutional rights. The right to marry, to choose one's spouse, to select an occupation, to travel freely within the country, and to enter into contracts are all examples of long-standing rights retained by the people although they are not explicitly provided for in the Constitution. They have achieved constitutional status by virtue of the fact that they are elements of the "liberty" protected by the Due Process Clauses of the Fifth and Fourteenth Amendments.

Dissenting in *Olmstead v. United States* (1928), Justice Louis Brandeis wrote:

> The makers of our Constitution undertook to secure conditions favorable to the pursuit of happiness. They recognized the significance of man's spiritual nature, of his feelings and his intellect. They knew that only a part of his pain, pleasure, and satisfactions of life are to be found in material things. They sought to protect Americans in their beliefs, their thoughts, their emotions and their sensations. They conferred, as against the Government, the right to be let alone—the most comprehensive of rights and the right most valued by civilized men.

These words were written by way of dissent in a case dealing with the scope of the Fourth Amendment's protection against wiretapping (see Chapter 10). Yet they may be interpreted as foreshadowing the modern right of privacy, which is, in essence, the **right to be let alone.**

Substantive Due Process

To understand the emergence of the constitutional right of privacy, one must return to the era of economic due process (see Chapter 7). In a landmark decision in 1905, the Supreme Court broadly interpreted the Due Process Clause of the Fourteenth Amendment to impose a restriction on the power of state legislatures to engage in economic regulation. In *Lochner v. New York,* the Court held that the "liberty of contract" protected by the Fourteenth Amendment had been infringed when the state of New York adopted a law restricting the working hours of bakery employees. Although *Lochner* and related decisions were concerned exclusively with the protection of individual property rights (see Chapter 7), they paved the way for the creation of the right of privacy by giving a substantive (as distinct from a strictly procedural) interpretation to the Due Process Clause of the Fourteenth Amendment. Under the **substantive due process** formula, courts can "discover" in the Fourteenth Amendment rights that are "fundamental" or "implicit in a scheme of ordered liberty." Again, the Ninth Amendment's recognition of rights "retained by the people" provides additional justification for the substantive interpretation of the Fourteenth Amendment.

In the first two decades of the twentieth century, substantive due process was by and large confined to the protection of economic liberties from government regulation. Just two months before the Court handed down its controversial decision in *Lochner,* it refused to find in the Due Process Clause a prohibition against compulsory vaccination laws (*Jacobson v. Massachusetts* [1905]). Nevertheless, Justice John M. Harlan's majority opinion did recognize that "[t]here is, of course, a sphere within which the individual may assert the supremacy of his own will and rightfully dispute the authority of any human government, especially of any free government existing under a written constitution, to interfere with the exercise of that will."

For Justice Harlan and most of his brethren, the state's interest in promoting the public health through compulsory vaccination was superior to the individual "exercise of will." Nevertheless, in *Jacobson,* the Court suggested that the Fourteenth Amendment might protect certain noneconomic aspects of individual autonomy.

The expansion of substantive due process to include noneconomic rights took a quantum leap in 1923. In that year, the Court recognized that citizens have the right to study foreign languages in private schools, state statutes to the contrary notwithstanding (*Meyer v. Nebraska*). Two years later, the Court emphasized the right to a private education by striking down an Oregon law that required parents to send their children to public schools (*Pierce v. Society of Sisters* [1925]).

TO SUMMARIZE:

- The right of privacy, aptly defined by Justice Brandeis as "the right to be let alone," can be viewed as a constitutional expression of libertarianism, the doctrine that elevates individual freedom above all other values.
- Although nowhere mentioned explicitly in the Constitution, the right of privacy is generally viewed as implicit in the protections of the Bill of Rights or the broad guarantee of "liberty" found in the Due Process Clauses of the Fifth and Fourteenth Amendments.
- Proponents of the right of privacy often invoke the Ninth Amendment, which guarantees rights "retained by the people" even though they are not enumerated in the Constitution.
- To the extent that judicial recognition of the right of privacy relies on the Due Process Clauses of the Fifth and Fourteenth Amendments, it may be viewed as a modern application of the doctrine of substantive due process.

PROCREATION AND BIRTH CONTROL

The slowly emerging right of privacy experienced a temporary setback in *Buck v. Bell* (1927). There, the Court refused to find in the Fourteenth Amendment an immunity against **compulsory sterilization** for mentally retarded persons. Carrie Buck, a young woman crassly characterized by the Court as "feeble minded," was committed to a state institution, where her mother was also confined. Pursuant to state law, the director of the institution sought to have Carrie Buck sterilized after she had given birth to a mentally retarded child. Carrie Buck's attorneys immediately challenged the constitutionality of the statute, but the Supreme Court, in an 8-to-1 decision, upheld the sterilization law. Writing for the Court, Justice Oliver Wendell Holmes, Jr., declared that the principle announced in *Jacobson v. Massachusetts* was "broad enough to cover cutting the Fallopian tubes." In one of his more memorable (and most gratuitous) lines, Holmes went on to write that "[t]hree generations of imbeciles are enough."

Although *Buck v. Bell* has never been formally overruled, it is unlikely that it would command a majority today. In 1942, the Court struck down a state law providing for the compulsory sterilization of criminals (*Skinner v. Oklahoma*). Although the decision was based on the Equal Protection Clause of the Fourteenth Amendment, rather than on substantive due process, *Skinner* in effect recognized a constitutional right of procreation. The Court characterized the right to procreate as "one of the basic civil rights of man." The Court's decisions in *Meyer v. Nebraska, Pierce v. Society of Sisters,* and *Skinner v. Oklahoma* paved the way for the landmark 1965 decision in *Griswold v. Connecticut* recognizing an independent constitutional right of privacy.

The Connecticut Birth Control Controversy

The *Griswold* case involved a challenge to an 1879 Connecticut law that made the sale and possession of birth control devices a misdemeanor. The law also forbade anyone from assisting, abetting, or counseling another in the use of birth control devices.

In *Poe v. Ullman* (1961) the Supreme Court voted 5 to 4 to dismiss a challenge to the Connecticut law. The challenge stemmed not from a criminal prosecution but from a lawsuit brought by a married couple and their physician who complained of state interference in the doctor-patient relationship. Writing for a four-member plurality, Justice Felix Frankfurter said that there was no real "case or controversy" and that the issue was unripe for judicial review. Frankfurter alluded to a "tacit agreement" whereby the birth control law would no longer be enforced. In a forceful dissent, Justice William O. Douglas pointed out that an earlier criminal prosecution had effectively prevented birth control clinics from operating in the state. Douglas not only asserted that the case was properly before the Court but characterized the statute as "an invasion of the privacy implicit in a free society." Douglas's sharp dissent in *Poe v. Ullman* anticipated the Court's decision in *Griswold* four years later.

Estelle Griswold was the director of Planned Parenthood in Connecticut. Just three days after Planned Parenthood opened a clinic in New Haven, Griswold was arrested. Reportedly, she had given detectives a tour of the clinic, pointing out contraceptives that the clinic was dispensing. After a short trial, Griswold was convicted and fined $100. As expected, the Connecticut courts upheld her conviction, rejecting the contention that the state law was unconstitutional. Also as expected, Griswold's attorneys filed a petition for certiorari in the U.S. Supreme Court. When the Court agreed to take the case, it was clear that the justices were going to rule on the constitutionality of the Connecticut law.

Griswold's attorneys argued that the birth control law infringed a right of privacy implicit in the Bill of Rights, as embodied in the concept of personal liberty protected by the Fourteenth Amendment. Moreover, they maintained that the Connecticut statute lacked a reasonable relationship to a legitimate legislative purpose. The state of Connecticut responded by emphasizing its broad police powers, arguing that the birth control law was a rational means of promoting the welfare of Connecticut's people. Interestingly, however, Connecticut's brief failed to state the particular legislative purpose behind the birth control law. Rather, the brief was designed chiefly to persuade the justices that they should not second-guess the wisdom or desirability of social legislation.

On June 7, 1965, the Supreme Court announced its decision striking down the Connecticut birth control law. The vote was 7 to 2. Justice Douglas was given the task of writing the majority opinion. After a disclaimer that "[w]e do not sit as a super-legislature to determine the wisdom, need and propriety of laws," Douglas proceeded to explain why, in his view, the Connecticut law ran afoul of the Constitution. As an advocate of "total incorporation" (see Chapter 6), Justice Douglas sought to identify an implicit right of privacy in the Bill of Rights, rather than in the vague notions of "liberty" that the Court had in the past attached to the Due Process Clause of the Fourteenth Amendment.

In what has become frequently quoted language, Douglas asserted that "specific guarantees in the Bill of Rights have penumbras, formed by emanations from those guarantees that help give them life and substance." Douglas reasoned that the explicit language of the Bill of Rights, specifically the First, Third, Fourth, Fifth, and Ninth Amendments, when considered along with their "emanations" and "penumbras" as defined by previous decisions of the Court, add up to a general, independent right of privacy. In Douglas's view, this general right was infringed by the state of

Connecticut when it outlawed birth control. In the sharpest language of the majority opinion, Douglas wrote:

> Would we allow the police to search the sacred precincts of marital bedrooms for tell-tale signs of the use of contraceptives? The very idea is repulsive to the notions of privacy surrounding the marriage relationship.

While the prospect of the police searching one's bedroom for evidence of contraception is no doubt repulsive to many, the question is whether the law allowing such a search is constitutional. Obviously, Justices John Harlan (the younger) and Byron White, who voted to strike down the Connecticut law, were not altogether persuaded by Justice Douglas's discovery of a general right of privacy in the Bill of Rights. In their separate opinions concurring in the judgment, Harlan and White maintained that the Connecticut law infringed the "liberty" protected by the Fourteenth Amendment, a liberty that, in their view, transcends the particular protections of the Bill of Rights. In taking this course, Justices Harlan and White were not embarking on uncharted jurisprudential waters; they were merely using the substantive due process approach that had been employed in *Meyer v. Nebraska, Pierce v. Society of Sisters,* and the numerous cases in which the Court had used "liberty of contract" to invalidate economic legislation.

Dissenting sharply, Justice Black criticized what he perceived as a blatant attempt to amend the Constitution through loose interpretation. Justice Black never hesitated to urge invalidation of a legislative act if he believed it ran afoul of a specific provision of the Constitution. Consequently, he and Justice Douglas often found themselves voting together in civil liberties cases, thus earning the label "judicial activists." But, as one who preferred to adhere strictly to the text of the Constitution, Black refused in *Griswold* to go along with what he regarded as a discredited approach to constitutional interpretation:

> I cannot rely on the Due Process Clause or the Ninth Amendment or any mysterious and uncertain natural law concept as a reason for striking down this state law. . . . I had thought that we had laid that formula, as a means of striking down state legislation, to rest once and for all.

The debate over modes of constitutional interpretation is certainly a legitimate one. Cogent jurisprudential arguments can be made for and against the Court's decision in *Griswold.* However, it must be recognized that the Court's decision was not based on a radical departure from traditional jurisprudence, as a few extreme critics have claimed. Rather, there is ample precedent for the broad interpretation of the Constitution in general (for example, *Marbury v. Madison*), and the substantive due process formula in particular, in the rich history of the Court's constitutional decision making.

Although *Griswold* was sharply criticized by commentators who shared Justice Black's view of constitutional interpretation and by a few staunch social conservatives, the Court's decision was not subjected to the kind of public outcry occasioned by the desegregation decisions of the 1950s or the school prayer decisions of the early 1960s. Obviously, the average person is not particularly concerned with the legal aspects of a Supreme Court decision; he or she is much more likely to focus on the Court's substantive policy output. As a matter of public policy, *Griswold* was quite well received.

A Gallup Poll conducted in 1965 found that 81 percent of the American public agreed with the statement that "birth control information should be available to anyone who wants it." There can be little doubt that changing societal attitudes about sex, procreation, and contraception had more to do with the Court's decision in *Griswold* than did "emanations" from the Bill of Rights!

Beyond the Marital Bedroom

In the *Griswold* case, the Court was careful to invalidate the Connecticut law only insofar as it invaded marital privacy, thus leaving open the question of whether states could prohibit the use of birth control devices by unmarried persons. In *Eisenstadt v. Baird* (1972), the Court faced a challenge to a Massachusetts law that prohibited unmarried persons from obtaining and using contraceptives. William Baird, a former medical student, was arrested after he delivered a lecture on birth control at Boston University during which he provided some contraceptive foam to a female student. In reversing Baird's conviction and striking down the Massachusetts law, the Court established the right of privacy as an individual right, not a right enjoyed solely by married couples. As Justice William Brennan's opinion for the Court stated:

> [T]he marital couple is not an independent entity with a mind and heart of its own, but an association of two individuals each with separate intellectual and emotional makeup. If the right of privacy means anything, it is the right of the individual, married or single, to be free from unwarranted governmental intrusion into matters so fundamentally affecting a person as the decision whether or not to beget a child.

Having thus articulated an independent right of privacy protecting individual decisions in the area of sex and procreation, *Eisenstadt v. Baird* paved the way for the most controversial decision the Supreme Court was to make during the chiefjusticeship of Warren Burger: *Roe v. Wade*.

TO SUMMARIZE:

- The right of privacy was first invoked in the area of procreation and birth control. In *Griswold v. Connecticut* (1965), the Court struck down a state statute prohibiting the use of birth control devices insofar as the statute applied to married couples. Later, the Court made clear that because the right of privacy is an individual right, laws forbidding the use of contraceptives by unmarried adults are likewise invalid.
- Justice William O. Douglas's opinion for the Court in *Griswold* attempted to justify the right of privacy in terms of "emanations" from the Bill of Rights. Dissenting justices criticized the majority for loosely interpreting the Constitution.
- The *Griswold* case set the stage for the most controversial decision of the Court's modern era: *Roe v. Wade* (1973).

THE ABORTION CONTROVERSY

Norma McCorvey, also known as Jane Roe, was a 25-year-old unmarried Texas woman who was faced with an unwanted pregnancy resulting from an alleged gang rape that she later admitted never occurred. After her doctor informed her that abortion was illegal in Texas, she went to see an attorney. That attorney, Linda Coffee, introduced McCorvey to Sarah Weddington, a young woman just out of law school, who would ultimately argue the case before the U.S. Supreme Court. Weddington expressed her view that the Constitution allows a woman to control her own body, including the decision to terminate an unwanted pregnancy. Shortly thereafter, Coffee and Weddington filed suit in federal district court against Dallas District Attorney Henry Wade, seeking to enjoin him from enforcing what was claimed to be an unconstitutional law. The suit was filed as a class action—that is, not only on behalf of Jane Roe but on behalf of all women "similarly situated." The district court declared the Texas law unconstitutional but refused to issue the injunction, invoking the doctrine of abstention whereby federal courts refrain from interfering with state judicial processes (see Chapter 1). As permitted in cases of this kind, Jane Roe appealed directly to the U.S. Supreme Court.

The Supreme Court Decides *Roe v. Wade*

On January 22, 1973, the Supreme Court handed down a 7-to-2 decision striking down the Texas law. Justice Harry A. Blackmun wrote the majority opinion. After determining that the case was properly before the Court, Blackmun reviewed prior decisions on the right of privacy. In what is perhaps the best known statement from his opinion in *Roe,* Blackmun concluded that the right of privacy "is broad enough to encompass a woman's decision whether or not to terminate her pregnancy." Yet Blackmun's analysis did not end with this pronouncement, because the right of privacy, like all constitutional rights, may be limited if there is a sufficiently strong justification to do so by the state. Specifically, because the Court identified privacy as a **fundamental right,** the state of Texas had to demonstrate a **compelling interest** to justify regulating or prohibiting abortion. The Court recognized a compelling interest in protecting maternal health that justifies "reasonable" state regulations of abortions performed after the first trimester of pregnancy. However, the state of Texas sought not only to regulate but also to proscribe abortion altogether and claimed a compelling state interest in protecting unborn human life. The Court recognized this interest as legitimate but held that it does not become compelling until that point in pregnancy when the fetus becomes "viable"—that is, capable of "meaningful life outside the mother's womb." Beyond the point of **viability,** according to the Court, the state may prohibit abortion, except in cases where it is necessary to preserve the life or health of the mother.

The Court summarily rejected the argument that a fetus is a "person" as that term is used in the Constitution and thus possessed of a right to life, holding that the term "has application only postnatally." If a fetus is regarded as a person from the point of conception, then any abortion is certainly homicide. If that were the case, then states could not allow abortions even in cases of rape or where the pregnancy endangers the life of the mother (as the Texas law challenged in *Roe* allowed). Nor would intrauterine devices or "morning after" pills, both of which prevent implantation after conception, be permissible. Like abortion, these forms of birth control, which are regarded by most as morally acceptable, would be tantamount to murder. Clearly, the Court was not inclined to make such a pronouncement. Nor was it prepared to assert that the woman's right to obtain an abortion is absolute—"that she is entitled to terminate at whatever time, in whatever way and for whatever reason she alone chooses." The Court tried to steer a middle course, to accommodate what it regarded as legitimate interests on both sides of the issue.

Roe v. Wade was the product of sharp conflict, bargaining, and compromise within the Supreme Court. Although the Court's decision attempted to strike a reasonable balance between the state's interest in protecting unborn life and a woman's interest in controlling her own body, the abortion decision was not viewed by the pro-life forces as an acceptable compromise. The hostile reaction to *Roe v. Wade* was immediate and intense. Justices of the Supreme Court, especially Harry Blackmun, received hate mail and even death threats. The 1980s saw frequent public demonstrations, harassment of women entering abortion clinics, and even the occasional bombing of such facilities.

Since the *Roe* decision came down in 1973, public opinion has remained sharply divided on the abortion question. This sharp division was reflected in the U.S. Senate, which, in 1983, defeated by one vote a proposed constitutional amendment that would have provided that "[t]he right to an abortion is not secured by this Constitution." Although it is difficult to say with certainty which side of the issue is favored by public opinion, it was clear until recently that the antiabortion forces manifest greater intensity in their opposition to abortion than the pro-choice forces do in their support. In politics, intensity may count for as much as numbers. In constitutional law, neither is supposed to matter; but there is considerable evidence that both do!

Regulation of Abortion in the Wake of *Roe v. Wade*

In the wake of *Roe v. Wade,* many state and local governments enacted regulations governing the performance of abortions. As previously noted, the Court in *Roe* allowed for "reasonable" regulation of abortions to effectuate the state's legitimate interest in protecting maternal health. However, many state statutes and local ordinances affecting abortion were not intended to promote maternal health at all but rather to deter women from obtaining abortions.

In *Planned Parenthood of Central Missouri v. Danforth* (1976), the Court struck down a Missouri law that required minors to obtain the consent of their husbands or parents before obtaining an abortion. Three years later, in *Bellotti v. Baird* (1979), the Court struck down a similar law passed by the state of Massachusetts. This law required an unmarried pregnant minor to obtain parental consent for an abortion or, if parental consent was not given, to obtain authorization from a judge who was to determine whether the abortion was in the minor's best interest. Taken together, the decisions in *Bellotti* and *Danforth* emphasized the personal nature of the abortion decision. Other parties, whether one's spouse, parents, or the state, cannot be given a veto over the exercise of one's constitutional rights.

In 1983, the Court appeared to back away from the strong position taken in *Bellotti* and *Danforth.* In *Planned Parenthood v. Ashcroft,* the Court upheld a Missouri law that required parental consent for "unemancipated" minors but apparently only because the law provided a mechanism whereby exceptionally mature minors could obtain abortions by seeking judicial intervention.

The same day *Ashcroft* came down, the Court announced its decision in *Akron v. Akron Center for Reproductive Health* (1983). In this case, the Court struck down a city ordinance that, in addition to requiring parental consent for minors' abortions, required (1) that all abortions be performed in hospitals; (2) that there be a twenty-four-hour waiting period before abortions could be performed; (3) that physicians make certain specified statements to the woman seeking abortion to ensure that her decision is truly an informed one; and (4) that all fetal remains be disposed of in a manner that is both humane and sanitary. The Court found that these requirements imposed significant burdens on a woman's exercise of her constitutional rights without substantially furthering the state's legitimate interests. The "humane and sanitary" disposal requirement was invalidated as "impermissibly vague" in obliquely suggesting an intention on the part of the city to "mandate some sort of 'decent burial' of the embryo at the earliest stages of formation."

Restrictions on Public Funding of Abortions

One of the more successful legislative assaults on abortion involves the exemption of abortions not deemed to be medically necessary from medical welfare programs. As a matter of public policy, this exemption is highly questionable. For one thing, it creates a double standard for rich and poor. Moreover, it seems likely to increase the numbers of future dependents on food stamps, welfare, and Medicaid. However, as the Supreme Court has frequently observed, the wisdom of a particular public policy and the constitutionality thereof are separate questions. In *Maher v. Roe* (1977), the Court voted 6 to 3 to uphold a Connecticut welfare regulation that denied Medicaid benefits to indigent women seeking to have abortions, unless their attending physicians certified their abortions as "medically necessary." The Court's decision was based on the "new due process/equal protection" analysis developed by the Court during the last two decades (see Chapter 12). In a nutshell, the Court held that the denial of Medicaid benefits to poor women seeking elective abortions neither discriminated against a "suspect class" of persons nor unduly burdened the exercise of fundamental rights. Therefore, the Court judged the Connecticut regulation to be permissible under both the Equal Protection and Due Process Clauses of the Fourteenth Amendment.

Three years later, in *Harris v. McRae* (1980), the Court upheld a provision of federal law, commonly known as the **Hyde amendment**, forbidding the use of federal funds to support nontherapeutic abortions. Writing for a sharply divided Court, Justice Potter Stewart concluded that

> it simply does not follow that a woman's freedom of choice carries with it a constitutional entitlement to the financial resources to avail herself of the full range of protected choices. . . . Although government may not place obstacles in the path of a woman's exercise of her freedom of choice, it need not remove those not of its own creation. Indigency falls in the latter category.

The Hyde Amendment restricted federal funding of abortions, leaving states to decide whether to impose similar restrictions on the use of state funds. As noted, the U.S. Supreme Court upheld Connecticut's restriction on abortion funding in *Maher v. Roe* (1977). Yet several state supreme courts have invalidated similar restrictions under their state constitutions (see, for example, *Committee to Defend Reproductive Rights v. Myers* [Cal. S.Ct. 1981], *Moe v. Secretary of Administration* [Mass. S.Jud.Ct. 1981], and *Right to Choose v. Byrne* [N.J. S.Ct. 1982]).

Eroding Support for *Roe v. Wade* on the Supreme Court in the 1980s

By the early 1980s, the bloc of justices supportive of *Roe v. Wade* had begun to erode. In the *Akron Center* decision of 1983, the Court had explicitly reaffirmed *Roe* but by one less vote than the *Roe* majority of 1973. While Potter Stewart had voted with the majority in *Roe,* his successor on the Court, Sandra Day O'Connor, dissented in the *Akron* case. In one of her most significant early opinions, Justice O'Connor expressed considerable dissatisfaction with the **trimester framework** adopted by the Court in *Roe v. Wade.* O'Connor's *Akron* dissent went well beyond a critique of the particular formulation adopted by the Court in *Roe,* however. Her opinion suggested that a state has a sufficiently compelling interest in protecting potential life to allow it to ban abortion at any stage of pregnancy. O'Connor's apparent dissent from the *Roe* decision did not necessarily indicate that she opposed legalized abortion. It did suggest that O'Connor believed that the state legislature (not a court of law) is the proper forum for resolving the abortion issue. Again, quoting from her dissent in *Akron v. Akron Center:* "It is . . . difficult to believe that this Court, without the resources available to those bodies entrusted with making legislative choices, believes itself competent to make these inquiries."

Substantial support exists, even among those who favor some form of legalized abortion, for the position adopted by Justice O'Connor. Some would argue that the question of abortion is simply not one that courts should decide. These critics would call for judicial restraint, for deference to the legislative judgment. While many state legislators have criticized the Supreme Court for usurping the role of the legislature in deciding *Roe v. Wade,* others have expressed relief that the judiciary has "taken the heat" on the abortion issue. Few legislators relish the prospect of voting on the abortion question. On both sides of the issue are powerful interest groups, and a middle ground on abortion is difficult to locate, much less defend.

The Supreme Court reaffirmed *Roe v. Wade* again in *Thornburgh v. American College of Obstetricians and Gynecologists* (1986). However, in *Thornburgh,* the vote in favor of a constitutional right to abortion was 5 to 4, because Chief Justice Burger switched sides and joined the dissenters. Although Burger retired after the 1985 term, his departure did not strengthen the position of *Roe v. Wade.* President Ronald Reagan elevated Associate Justice William Rehnquist to the position of chief justice and appointed Antonin Scalia, a conservative, to fill the vacancy.

In 1987, it appeared that the opponents of legalized abortion were only one vote away from overturning *Roe v. Wade.* In that year, Justice Lewis Powell, a member of the *Roe* majority, retired from the Court. It looked as if the Court would be divided 4 to 4 on the abortion issue, possibly making the next appointee to the Court the swing vote on whether to overrule *Roe v. Wade.* To a great extent, this fact explains the furor surrounding President Reagan's nomination of conservative federal judge Robert Bork to fill the vacancy left by Justice Powell. A well-known critic of *Roe* and of the right of privacy generally, Bork entered a firestorm of political controversy when he appeared before the Senate Judiciary Committee. The Senate, controlled by the Democrats, ultimately rejected Bork, in no small measure due to his stand on the right of privacy. Eventually, the Senate confirmed Reagan's nomination of another federal judge, Anthony Kennedy. In his confirmation hearing, Kennedy was asked repeatedly about his views on abortion. He replied, "If I had a . . . fixed view . . . I might be obliged to disclose that to you. I don't have such a view." The nation would have to wait two years for Kennedy to register his opinion in the abortion debate.

The *Webster* Decision

Without question, the most significant abortion case of the 1980s was *Webster v. Reproductive Health Services* (1989). Many thought the *Webster* case would be the one in which the Supreme Court would overturn *Roe v. Wade.* Those who favored such an outcome were disappointed by the decision. Yet those who supported legalized abortion found cause for alarm in what they perceived as a significant departure from the philosophy of *Roe.*

The *Webster* case involved a challenge to a Missouri statute containing a number of restrictions on abortions. Most worrisome from the pro-choice perspective was the statement in the preamble of the law that "the life of each human being begins at conception." In its various provisions, the law forbade state employees from performing, assisting in, or counseling women to have abortions. It also prohibited the use of any state facilities for these purposes. Finally, it required all doctors who would perform abortions to conduct viability tests on fetuses at or beyond twenty weeks' gestation.

The Supreme Court, splitting 5 to 4, sustained the constitutionality of the Missouri statute. Yet in deciding the issues in *Webster,* the Supreme Court could not agree on a majority opinion. A plurality (Chief Justice Rehnquist and Associate Justices White, Kennedy, and O'Connor) expressed the view that the legislation could be sustained without overruling *Roe v. Wade.* In her separate concurrence, Justice O'Connor stressed the "fundamental rule of judicial restraint," which dictates that courts not decide major issues unless absolutely necessary. Only Justice Scalia, in a separate concurrence, called for the explicit overruling of *Roe* and chided his colleagues in the majority for not facing the issue squarely: "Of the four courses we might have chosen today—to reaffirm *Roe,* to overrule it explicitly, to overrule it *sub silentio,* or to avoid the question—the last is the least responsible." Justice Blackmun, the author of the Court's opinion in *Roe v. Wade,* accused the plurality of undermining *Roe:*

> With feigned restraint, the plurality announces that its analysis leaves *Roe* "undisturbed," albeit "modif[ied] and narrow[ed]." . . . But this disclaimer is totally meaning-

less. The plurality opinion is filled with winks, and nods, and knowing glances to those who would do away with *Roe* explicitly, but turns a stone face to anyone in search of what the plurality conceives as the scope of a woman's right under the Due Process Clause to terminate a pregnancy free from the coercive and brooding influence of the State.

Rust v. Sullivan: Restricting Information about Abortion

Supporters of legalized abortion were dealt another setback during the spring of 1991. In *Rust v. Sullivan,* the Supreme Court upheld a federal regulation that barred birth control clinics that received federal funds from providing information about abortion services to their clients. The regulation had been imposed in 1987 by the Department of Health and Human Services (HHS) at the direction of the Reagan administration, which opposed legalized abortion. The Supreme Court found the regulation to be a legitimate condition imposed on the receipt of financial assistance from the government. In the Court's view, the regulation was neither an invasion of privacy rights nor of freedom of speech, as plaintiffs in the lawsuit alleged. Congress, with broad public support, passed a measure designed to overturn the HHS regulation. However, this act was vetoed by President George Bush (the elder), and Congress was unable to muster the two-thirds vote necessary to override the veto.

The Court Reaffirms *Roe v. Wade*

In *Rust v. Sullivan,* as in the *Webster* decision two years earlier, the Court did not face squarely the question of whether *Roe v. Wade* should be maintained as the law of the land. Yet these decisions did send a strong signal that the Court was prepared to tolerate greater restrictions on legalized abortion. On January 21, 1992, on the eve of the nineteenth anniversary of its landmark decision in *Roe v. Wade,* the Supreme Court announced that it would hear a case challenging a Pennsylvania law that contained a series of restrictions on abortion (*Planned Parenthood of Southeastern Pennsylvania v. Casey* [1992]). Among other things, the law required spousal notification, parental consent in cases of minors, and a twenty-four-hour waiting period before an abortion could be performed. Identical requirements had been declared invalid by the Supreme Court in previous decisions, but the Third Circuit Court of Appeals in Philadelphia upheld most of the provisions of the Pennsylvania statute. The appellate court based its ruling largely on the Supreme Court's 1989 *Webster* decision, which it interpreted as a significant retreat from the "strict scrutiny" to which abortion regulations had been subjected.

On April 22, 1992, the Supreme Court heard oral arguments in *Planned Parenthood v. Casey.* Ernest Preate, Jr., attorney general of Pennsylvania, defended the constitutionality of the statute, contending, among other things, that "*Roe* did not establish an absolute right to abortion on demand, but rather a limited right subject to reasonable state regulations." Attacking the statute, Kathryn Kolbert, counsel for the American Civil Liberties Union, characterized Pennsylvania's regulations not only as unreasonable but as "cruel and oppressive." U.S. Solicitor General Kenneth W. Starr, speaking on behalf of the Bush administration, urged the Court to abandon the "compelling state interest" test and adopt a more lenient "rational basis test" for determining the constitutionality of statutes in this area. When asked by Justice White whether the adoption of such a test would lead to a conclusion that the Pennsylvania law should be upheld, Starr replied, "Exactly."

The Supreme Court handed down its much anticipated decision in *Planned Parenthood v. Casey* on June 29, 1992, the last day of the Court's 1991 term. To the surprise of many observers, the Court reaffirmed by a 5-to-4 vote the essential holding in *Roe v. Wade* that the constitutional right of privacy is broad enough to include a woman's decision to terminate her pregnancy. The Court was highly fragmented, however, producing five opinions. Two justices, Blackmun and Stevens, took the position that *Roe v. Wade* should be reaffirmed and that all of the challenged provisions of the Pennsylvania statute should be declared invalid. Four justices—Rehnquist, Scalia, White, and Thomas—took the view that *Roe* should be overruled and all of the Pennsylvania restrictions upheld. Adopting an extremely unusual method of presentation underscoring the gravity of the case, Justices O'Connor, Kennedy, and Souter jointly authored the controlling opinion of the Court. This lengthy joint opinion thoroughly reexamined *Roe v. Wade,* its underlying rationale and formulation, and the line of cases it spawned. While joining Justices Blackmun and Stevens in explicitly reaffirming *Roe,* the joint opinion abandoned the trimester framework and declared a new "undue burden" test for judging regulations of abortion. Applying this test, the joint opinion upheld the parental consent, waiting period, and record-keeping and reporting provisions but invalidated the spousal notification requirement.

The *Casey* decision was greeted with dismay and derision from both pro-life and pro-choice groups. Pro-choice groups expressed alarm that the Court was willing to overturn recent precedent (*Akron v. Akron Center for Reproductive Health* [1983] and *Thornburgh v. American College of Obstetricians and Gynecologists* [1986]) and uphold Pennsylvania's restrictions on abortion. Pro-life advocates were disappointed that two Reagan appointees (Kennedy and O'Connor) and one Bush appointee (Souter) voted to reaffirm *Roe v. Wade.*

In their separate opinions in *Casey,* Chief Justice Rehnquist and Justice Scalia, supported by Justices White and Thomas, made it clear that four members of the Court are fully prepared to overrule *Roe v. Wade.* However, with the replacement of Justice White by Justice Ruth Bader Ginsburg in 1993, the anti-*Roe* bloc on the Court was diminished. In 1994, Justice Blackmun, the author of the *Roe* opinion, resigned from the Court. His replacement by Justice Stephen G. Breyer, the second Clinton appointee to the Court, is not likely to weaken support of the *Roe* precedent.

The Partial-Birth Abortion Issue

During the 1990s, more than thirty states adopted statutes banning so-called "partial-birth abortions." Congress passed similar legislation but it was successfully vetoed by President Bill Clinton. Nebraska's statute defined partial-birth abortion as "an abortion procedure in which the person performing the abortion partially delivers vaginally a living unborn child before killing the unborn child and completing the delivery." The law provided an exception for procedures deemed necessary to protect a woman's life, but no exception for the purpose of protecting a woman's health. LeRoy Carhart, a Nebraska physician, brought suit to challenge the constitutionality of the statute. In a sharply divided decision, the Supreme Court invalidated the Nebraska law. Writing for the Court in *Stenberg v. Carhart* (2000), Justice Stephen Breyer found that the law went well beyond the prohibition of late-term abortions and could be invoked to prohibit certain early-term abortions as well. In Breyer's view, the law, if allowed to stand, could be interpreted to prohibit the "dilation and evacuation" procedure, "the most commonly used method for performing previability second trimester abortions." Breyer concluded:

> All those who perform abortion procedures using that method must fear prosecution, conviction, and imprisonment. The result is an undue burden upon a woman's right to make an abortion decision.

In dissent, Justice Anthony Kennedy, one of the architects of the compromise in *Planned Parenthood v. Casey,* objected that the Court had repudiated *Casey* "by invalidating a statute advancing critical state interests, even though the law denies no woman the right to choose an abortion and places no undue burden upon the right." Kennedy characterized partial-birth abortion as "a procedure many decent and civilized people find so abhorrent as to be among the most serious of crimes against human life." In his dissenting opinion, Justice Antonin Scalia stated, "Today's decision, that the Constitution of the United States prevents the prohibition of a horrible mode of abortion, will be greeted by a firestorm of criticism—as well it should."

Abortion Rights under State Constitutions

Even if the Supreme Court were to overrule *Roe v. Wade,* this would by no means result in the immediate recriminalization of abortion. If *Roe* were overruled, state legislatures would be permitted to determine their own policies in this area, subject to limits imposed by state courts under state constitutional provisions. Thus, state courts would have to determine the scope of abortion rights under their respective state constitutions. Indeed, some state supreme courts have moved in this direction. For example, Florida is one of four states whose constitutions contain explicit recognition of the right of privacy (the others are Alaska, California, and Montana). The Florida Supreme Court has said that "[s]ince the people of this state exercised their prerogative and enacted an amendment to the Florida Constitution which expressly and succinctly provides for a strong right of privacy . . . , it can only be concluded that the right is much broader in scope than that of the federal constitution" (*Winfield v. Division of PariMutuel Wagering* [Fla. S.Ct. 1985]). That court has also indicated quite clearly that a woman's right to choose abortion is protected by the privacy amendment to the state constitution (see *In re T.W.* [Fla. S.Ct. 1989]).

Even where state constitutions do not contain explicit rights of privacy, some state courts have recognized privacy as an implicit right and have even accorded it broader scope than the federal right as interpreted by the U.S. Supreme Court. For example, in *Planned Parenthood v. Sundquist* (2000), the Tennessee Supreme Court struck down several statutes restricting access to abortion in Tennessee. Speaking through Chief Justice Riley Anderson, the court asserted that

> a woman's right to terminate her pregnancy is a vital part of the right to privacy guaranteed by the Tennessee Constitution. As this right is inherent in the concept of ordered liberty embodied in the Tennessee Constitution, we conclude that the right to terminate one's pregnancy is fundamental. The standard we have traditionally applied to fundamental rights requires that statutes regulating fundamental rights be subjected to strict scrutiny analysis. Moreover, when reviewed under the strict scrutiny standard, we conclude that none of the statutory provisions at issue withstand such scrutiny.

In *Planned Parenthood v. Sundquist,* the Tennessee Supreme Court rejected the "undue burden" test of *Planned Parenthood v. Casey* and reaffirmed the fundamental rights/strict scrutiny approach of *Roe v. Wade.* Thus, even if the U.S. Supreme Court were to overturn *Roe,* it would not ipso facto return the abortion issue to the exclusive domain of the state legislatures. The right of privacy, including the right to abortion, is becoming well established as a matter of state constitutional law.

The abortion issue is *the* constitutional question of our time. But it is far more complex than most observers of American law and politics realize, going well beyond the domain of the U.S. Supreme Court and the fate of *Roe v. Wade.* It will be many years before this question is finally resolved.

TO SUMMARIZE:

- In *Roe v. Wade* (1973), the Court relied on the right of privacy in striking down a Texas statute criminalizing most abortions. In *Roe,* the Court held that the state's interest in protecting the fetus becomes compelling only at the point of fetal viability outside the womb. States may thus prohibit only those abortions that are performed after the point of viability.
- In the decades following *Roe,* the Court reviewed a number of cases in which state and local governments imposed various restrictions on abortion. During the 1970s, most of these restrictions were declared unconstitutional. In the 1980s, however, an increasingly conservative Supreme Court began to view such restrictions more favorably.
- By the late 1980s, it appeared that *Roe v. Wade* might be overturned. In *Planned Parenthood v. Casey* (1992), however, the Court reaffirmed its basic holding in *Roe*—but in so doing, gave states broader latitude in regulating access to abortion.
- In *Stenberg v. Carhart* (2000), the Court again reaffirmed *Roe* and manifested a renewed willingness to closely scrutinize state regulations on abortion.
- Even if the Court were to overturn *Roe v. Wade,* state courts would be free to determine whether their own states' restrictions on abortion violate relevant provisions of their state constitutions.

THE RIGHT OF PRIVACY AND LIVING ARRANGEMENTS

While Supreme Court decisions in the area of reproductive freedom receive most of the public attention, the Court's decisions applying the constitutional right of privacy are by no means confined to contraception and abortion. The right of privacy has also been applied in reviewing city ordinances governing residential occupancy. In *Belle Terre v. Boraas* (1974), the Supreme Court upheld a village ordinance that limited residential land use to one-family dwellings. A couple who had leased a house to six unrelated college students challenged the law on the ground that it "trenche[d] on the newcomers' rights of privacy." The Court, adopting the traditional rational basis test, found the ordinance to be a valid exercise of the police power. Justice Thurgood Marshall dissented, maintaining that fundamental rights of privacy and association were infringed and that the village failed to demonstrate a compelling justification for this infringement.

In *Moore v. City of East Cleveland* (1977), the Court struck down an ordinance that limited the occupancy of residences to members of single families. However, the East Cleveland ordinance defined "family" in such a way as to prohibit a grandmother from cohabiting with her two grandsons. Distinguishing the ordinance from the one upheld in *Belle Terre,* which primarily affected unrelated individuals, the Court stressed "freedom of choice in matters of marriage and family life":

> Our decisions teach that the Constitution protects the sanctity of the family precisely because the institution of the family is deeply rooted in our history and tradition. [Ours] is by no means a tradition limited to respect for [the] nuclear family. The tradition of uncles, aunts, cousins, and especially grandparents sharing a household along with parents and children has roots equally venerable and equally deserving of constitutional recognition.

In a rather caustic concurrence, Justice Brennan noted that "in today's America, the nuclear family is the pattern so often found in much of white suburbia" but that "the Constitution cannot tolerate the imposition by government upon the rest of us of white suburbia's preference in patterns of family living."

TO SUMMARIZE:

- While Supreme Court decisions in the area of reproductive freedom receive most of the public attention, the Court's decisions applying the constitutional right of privacy are by no means confined to contraception and abortion.
- Stressing "freedom of choice in matters of marriage and family life," the Court has used the right of privacy to scrutinize ordinances limiting residential living arrangements.

PRIVACY AND GAY RIGHTS

In *Eisenstadt v. Baird* (1972), the Supreme Court tacitly acknowledged the right of an unmarried adult to engage in heterosexual activity. If this right is based on the premise that one may decide what to do with his or her own body without interference by the state, how can laws that prohibit private, consensual homosexual conduct be justified? What is the compelling interest on the part of the state that could be advanced to justify such prohibitions? The question has been raised in federal court. In *Doe v. Commonwealth's Attorney* (1976), the Supreme Court summarily affirmed a federal district court decision that upheld Virginia's **sodomy** law. The district court, dividing 2 to 1, cited Justice Harlan's dissent in the 1961 case of *Poe v. Ullman*, which, although supportive of sexual privacy within marriage, suggested that homosexual conduct could be prosecuted even if practiced privately. The Supreme Court, in refusing to hear the appeal in *Doe v. Commonwealth's Attorney*, in effect endorsed Justice Harlan's position.

In *Bowers v. Hardwick* (1986), the Supreme Court reached the merits of a case challenging the application of Georgia's sodomy law to homosexual activity. Michael Hardwick, an admitted homosexual, was charged with committing sodomy with a consenting male adult in the privacy of his home. Although the state prosecutor decided not to take the case to the grand jury, Hardwick brought suit in federal court, seeking a declaration that the statute was unconstitutional. The district court dismissed the case, but the appeals court reversed, remanding the suit for trial. The U.S. Supreme Court granted the state's petition for certiorari and reversed the court of appeals.

In arguing his case before the Supreme Court, Hardwick relied on *Griswold v. Connecticut* and *Roe v. Wade*, as well as on the Court's 1969 decision in *Stanley v. Georgia*. In *Stanley,* the Court held that the First Amendment prohibits a state from punishing a person merely for the private possession of obscene materials. Although ostensibly a First Amendment case, the *Stanley* decision suggested that the home was a sanctuary from prosecution for acts that might well be criminal outside the home.

Dividing 5 to 4 in *Hardwick,* the Court upheld the Georgia law, refusing to recognize "a fundamental right to engage in homosexual sodomy." Writing for the Court, Justice White stressed the traditional legal and moral prohibitions against sodomy. Responding to the libertarian argument that the state has no right to legislate solely on the basis of morality, White wrote that "law . . . is constantly based on notions of morality, and if all laws representing essentially moral choices are to be invalidated . . . , the Courts will be very busy indeed."

Dissenting, Justice Blackmun disputed the Court's characterization of the issue. For Blackmun and three of his colleagues, the case was not about a "fundamental right to engage in homosexual sodomy" but the more general right of an adult, homosexual or heterosexual, to engage in consensual sexual acts with another adult. Striking a libertarian chord, Justice John Paul Stevens wrote that "the fact that the governing majority in a State has traditionally viewed a practice as immoral is not a sufficient reason for upholding a law prohibiting the practice."

Whether the Supreme Court would uphold a sodomy law as applied to heterosexual activity remains to be seen. If the Supreme Court were to strike down sodomy laws as applied to married couples, there would probably be little criticism of the Court. If, however, the Court were to invalidate sodomy laws as applied to unmarried persons, whether heterosexual or homosexual, then questions might be raised regarding the constitutionality of laws against prostitution, incest, and polygamy. In *Hardwick,* Justice White averred that the Court was "reluctant to start down that road."

Interestingly, retired Supreme Court Justice Lewis Powell, one of the members of the *Hardwick* majority, has expressed reservations about his vote in that case. In talking to a group of law students at New York University in October 1990, Justice Powell said, "I think I probably made a mistake in that one." In a subsequent interview, Powell said that the case was a "close call" and that his decision to support the majority was based in part on the fact that the sodomy law had been largely unenforced. Powell minimized the importance of the case, referring to it as "frivolous" and suggesting that it had been filed "just to see what the court would do" (*Washington Post,* October 26, 1990, p. A-3).

Is *Bowers v. Hardwick* Still Good Law?

The Court's decision in *Romer v. Evans* (1996) calls into question the precedential value of *Bowers v. Hardwick.* In what the American Civil Liberties Union hailed as a "transforming moment in the fight for equality for lesbians and gay men," the Court struck down a Colorado constitutional amendment that barred state and local government from providing various legal protections for gays and lesbians. In dissent, Justice Scalia argued that "if it is constitutionally permissible for a State to make homosexual conduct criminal, surely it is constitutionally permissible for a State to enact other laws merely disfavoring homosexual conduct." Although the Court did not reconsider *Bowers v. Hardwick* in *Romer v. Evans,* it is doubtful that *Hardwick* would command a majority if it came before the Court today. However, because people are rarely prosecuted for consensual sodomy, the Court may not have another occasion to reconsider *Hardwick.*

State Courts Overturn Sodomy Laws

As we have noted throughout this book, a state constitution may afford more protection to its citizens than does the federal constitution. A number of state courts, including appellate courts in Tennessee, New York, and Kentucky, have invalidated their states' sodomy laws on state constitutional grounds. Perhaps the most dramatic example of judicial federalism in this context came in 1998 when the Georgia Supreme Court struck down the same sodomy law upheld by the U.S. Supreme Court in *Bowers v. Hardwick.* Writing for the Georgia Supreme Court in *Powell v. State,* Chief Justice Robert Benham found that the sodomy statute, "insofar as it criminalizes the performance of private, non-commercial acts of sexual intimacy between persons legally able to consent, 'manifestly infringes upon a constitutional provision' . . . which guarantees to the citizens of Georgia the right of privacy."

TO SUMMARIZE:

- Gay rights activists and most libertarians generally argue that laws prohibiting homosexual conduct violate the right of privacy, and that traditional morality is an insufficient basis for upholding such legislation.

- In *Bowers v. Hardwick* (1986), the Supreme Court narrowly upheld a Georgia anti-sodomy law as applied to homosexual conduct. It is doubtful whether this position would command a majority if the issue were revisited by the current Court.
- A number of state courts have struck down their state sodomy statutes on the basis of protections found in their respective state constitutions. This illustrates the viability of judicial federalism in the area of civil liberties.

OTHER APPLICATIONS OF THE RIGHT OF PRIVACY

Controversy has long surrounded the so-called **victimless crimes** of gambling, use of "recreational" drugs, prostitution, and so forth. Libertarians argue that the state has no business criminalizing conduct where no individual claims to have been injured. Individuals charged with such offenses have sometimes invoked the right of privacy by way of defense.

The Private Use of "Recreational" Drugs

Unlike the U.S. Constitution and the constitutions of most states, the Alaska constitution contains an explicit right of privacy. In a widely publicized decision in 1975, *Ravin v. State,* the Alaska Supreme Court held that the right of privacy under the Alaska Constitution was broad enough to encompass the right to possess marijuana for personal use. In its opinion, the court noted the strong libertarian orientation of Alaskans. A state supreme court is the final authority on matters of constitutional interpretation unless and until the state constitution is amended. Even if the U.S. Supreme Court were to rule that the right of privacy under the U.S. Constitution did not protect the private use of marijuana, the Alaska Supreme Court's decision would still be valid on independent state constitutional grounds. To date, however, the Alaska Supreme Court decision has not been emulated by the federal courts or by the courts of other states.

Helmet and Seat Belt Laws

Another application of the right of privacy is in the area of safety laws, as exemplified by laws requiring motorcyclists to wear protective helmets and drivers to wear seat belts. Again, the libertarian thesis would be that the government has no right to protect the individual from him- or herself. In *State v. Albertson* (1970), the Idaho Supreme Court rejected a privacy-based challenge to that state's motorcycle helmet law, citing an important public safety interest. In all likelihood, most state courts would find sufficient public safety interests to uphold helmet laws, as well as mandatory seat belt laws.

TO SUMMARIZE:

- The right of privacy has been used with limited success at the state court level in attacking the constitutionality of laws prohibiting the recreational use of drugs and other victimless crimes. The U.S. Supreme Court has shown little interest in this area.

A RIGHT TO DIE?

Since the mid-1970s, the right of privacy has been successfully asserted as a basis for refusing medical treatment. For example, in *Superintendent of Belchertown State School v. Saikewicz* (Mass. 1977), the Massachusetts Supreme Judicial Court permitted the guardian of an elderly, retarded man to assert his ward's right of privacy and refuse chemotherapy treatment for the elderly man's leukemia. Under the right of privacy, courts have also authorized the discontinuation of artificial means of life support, even if it results in the immediate death of the patient. For example, in the case of *Guardianship of Andrew Barry* (1984), a Florida appellate court allowed the removal of a respirator that was maintaining the life of a comatose infant. Andrew Barry was one of twins, the other of whom died at birth. Andrew had a serious brain defect that kept him comatose and unable to breathe without mechanical assistance. After it became clear that Andrew would never achieve a "sapient existence" and would spend his life on the ventilator, his parents asked the hospital to remove the machine. Not surprisingly, the hospital refused to do so without a court order.

The Karen Quinlan Case

In both *Saikewicz* and *Barry,* courts relied on the doctrine of "substituted judgment" whereby legal guardians are permitted to exercise the rights of persons under their authority. The best known case involving the doctrine of substituted judgment in relation to the so-called right to die is *In re Quinlan* (N.J. 1976). Karen Quinlan was a healthy young woman who became permanently comatose after she ingested large quantities of drugs and alcohol. In this condition, she was unable to maintain normal breathing without a ventilator. After it became clear that Karen Quinlan would not regain consciousness, her parents asked her physicians to remove the respirator. The physicians refused, no doubt concerned about possible criminal prosecution or civil liability. The Quinlans went to court and obtained an order allowing removal of the life-support machine. According to the New Jersey Supreme Court, the right of privacy was "broad enough to encompass [Karen Quinlan's] decision to decline medical treatment under certain circumstances, in much the same way as it is broad enough to encompass a woman's decision to terminate pregnancy." Of course, Karen Quinlan, lying comatose in the hospital, was unable to communicate her intentions to exercise this aspect of the right of privacy. According to the Court's opinion, the "only practical way to prevent destruction of [Karen Quinlan's] right is to permit the guardian and family . . . to render their best judgment as to whether she would exercise [the right to decline treatment] in these circumstances."

After Karen Quinlan was taken off the breathing machine, she lived for nine years in a coma, taking food and water through a nasogastric tube. Her parents never asked that this feeding be discontinued, but therein lies another troubling question. Does the right of privacy empower a terminally ill patient to refuse food and water provided through a nasogastric tube? In *Bouvia v. Superior Court* (Cal. 1986), the California Supreme Court answered this question in the affirmative in a case involving a young woman who, although competent, was suffering the terrible effects of an advanced degenerative illness.

A Right to Commit Suicide?

Court decisions such as *Quinlan* and *Bouvia* have led to a national debate over the **right to die.** In what circumstances and by what means does a person have a right to bring about his or her own demise? Critics of the right to die argue that it is a "slippery slope" leading inexorably to the legal recognition of "mercy killing" and suicide. If the right of privacy allows an individual to make "fundamental life choices" and to decide what happens to his or her body, then how can laws that forbid suicide (or aiding and abetting suicide) be constitutional? During the 1990s, the public debate over the right to die took an eerie turn when it was revealed that a doctor named Jack Kevorkian was assisting terminally ill people in committing suicide. After several unsuccessful attempts to pros-ecute Kevorkian, in 1999 a Michigan jury found him guilty of second-degree murder in the death of a man suffering from Lou Gehrig's disease. The court sentenced him to serve 10 to 25 years in prison. The case of Dr. Kevorkian raised a troubling question: If suicide is a constitutional right, as the California Supreme Court suggested in the *Bouvia* case, how can it be a crime to assist someone in committing suicide?

The Nancy Cruzan Case

The U.S. Supreme Court's only significant decision to date involving the right to die is the 1990 case of *Cruzan v. Missouri Health Department.* When the case reached the Supreme Court, Nancy Cruzan had for six years been confined to a hospital bed in a state of unconsciousness. Her condition was the result of extreme brain damage that occurred in an automobile accident. When it became apparent that Cruzan's condi-tion was irreversible, her parents asked the hospital to remove the nasogastric tube that was keeping her alive. The hospital refused absent a court order. The trial court issued the order, but the Missouri Supreme Court reversed, citing the state's "policy strongly favoring the preservation of life." The Missouri Supreme Court said that since Nancy Cruzan was unable to communicate, there would have to be clear and con-vincing evidence of her desire to have the feeding tube removed. Dividing 5 to 4, the U.S. Supreme Court upheld the Missouri Supreme Court's decision. Writing for the Court, Chief Justice Rehnquist held that, although Nancy Cruzan had a right to ter-minate life-prolonging treatment, it was reasonable for the state to impose the clear and convincing evidence standard as a means of guarding against potential abuse of the "substituted judgment" doctrine.

Critics of the right to die, many of whom also oppose legalized abortion, hailed the *Cruzan* decision as a victory for the pro-life movement. It remains to be seen, how-ever, whether the *Cruzan* decision represented a turnaround in the development of the right to die or merely the fine-tuning of a right that is now well established in American jurisprudence. It is likely that state, rather than federal, courts will continue to take the lead in developing this important new area of the law.

Doctor-Assisted Suicide

The courts have recognized a sharp distinction between termination of life-support systems and the active administration of means designed to end a person's life. But recently this distinction between passive and active euthanasia has been called into question. There are those in the medical community who believe that physicians should be able to provide active assistance to terminally ill patients who wish to has-ten their own deaths. There are those who argue that **doctor-assisted suicide** is well within the scope of privacy protected by the Constitution. But such views have yet to be accepted by the mainstream of the medical and legal communities.

To prevent assisted suicide in the state of Washington, the legislature enacted a law providing that "[a] person is guilty of promoting a suicide attempt when he knowingly causes or aids another person to attempt suicide." Promoting a suicide attempt is a felony punishable by up to five years' imprisonment and up to a $10,000 fine. In 1994, a federal judge ruled that Washington's statute banning assisted suicide was unconstitutional. Hearing the case en banc, the Ninth Circuit concluded that the State's assisted suicide ban was unconstitutional as applied to "terminally ill competent adults who wish to hasten their deaths with medication prescribed by their physicians."

In *Washington v. Glucksberg* (1997), the Supreme Court reversed the Ninth Circuit's decision. Writing for a unanimous Court, Chief Justice Rehnquist discussed the historical and cultural background of laws prohibiting assisted suicide. He pointed out that in almost every state it is a crime to assist in a suicide, and that the statutes banning assisted suicide are long-standing expressions of the states' commitment to the protection and preservation of all human life. Rehnquist analyzed the interests that come into play in determining whether a statute banning assisted suicide passes constitutional muster. He rejected any parallel between a person's right to terminate medical treatment and the "right" to have assistance in committing suicide. The Court's decision in *Glucksberg* recognized that a serious debate was taking place throughout the nation about the morality and legality of assisted suicide—a debate that the Court's decision permitted to continue. It is likely, though, that the Court will revisit this issue in the not too distant future.

TO SUMMARIZE:

- Since the mid-1970s, the right of privacy has been successfully asserted in state courts as a basis for competent adults to refuse medical treatment. It has been extended to allow the termination of artificial life-support systems in cases where patients are found to be in a persistent vegetative state resulting from injury or illness.
- The courts have generally rejected a thoroughgoing "right to die" that would allow any competent adult to commit suicide under any conditions.
- In 1990 the Supreme Court recognized that terminally ill patients have the right to order removal of life-support systems, but permitted states to impose a requirement that there be clear and convincing evidence of patients' desire that such systems be removed.
- In 1997 the Court entered the debate over physician-assisted suicide, holding that there is no constitutional right to engage in such conduct. This decision effectively permits states to regulate in this area, although state courts can play a significant role under the relevant provisions of state constitutions.

CONCLUSION

The modern Supreme Court has fashioned a general, independent constitutional right of privacy by drawing on the Fourteenth Amendment and on various provisions of the Bill of Rights. While the legal logic underlying the right of privacy is debatable, the right is now firmly established in American constitutional law. The right of privacy has been recognized by the courts of most states, and several state constitutions now even contain explicit protections of the right of privacy.

It is unclear whether, and how far, the courts will further extend the right of privacy. In 1965, when the Supreme Court decided *Griswold v. Connecticut,* public sentiment had become decidedly more liberal in the area of sex and reproduction. The 1973 abortion decision did not meet with the same extent of popular approbation, and the opposition to abortion has been much more intense than the opposition to the use of devices that prevent conception. The so-called right to die, if it is limited to the withholding of extraordinary means of life prolongation, seems to be socially acceptable. But there would be considerable opposition to the legalization of active euthanasia or suicide. At this time, prevailing social norms do not condone homosexual conduct or the private use of "recreational" drugs. For courts to assert constitutional protections for such activities would be a bold move indeed, possibly leading to political retaliation. One certainly would not expect the U.S. Supreme Court, which has become steadily more conservative in recent years, to adopt such libertarian positions in the near future. The evolution of the right of privacy thus illustrates the give and take of American constitutional law. It also dramatizes the fact that constitutional rights do not exist in a social, political, or moral vacuum.

KEY TERMS

constitutional right of privacy	libertarianism	fundamental right	sodomy
abortion	classical conservatism	compelling interest	victimless crimes
gay rights	right to be let alone	viability	right to die
euthanasia	substantive due process	Hyde amendment	doctor-assisted suicide
moral individualism	compulsory sterilization	trimester framework	

FOR FURTHER READING

Barnett, Randy (ed.). *The Rights Retained by the People: The History and Meaning of the Ninth Amendment.* Fairfax, Va.: George Mason University Press, 1989.

DeRosa, Marshall. *The Ninth Amendment and the Politics of Creative Jurisprudence: Disparaging the Fundamental Right of Popular Control.* Somerset, N.J.: Transaction Publishers, 1996.

Glick, Henry R. *The Right to Die.* New York: Columbia University Press, 1994.

Hull, N. E. H, and Peter Charles Hoffer. *Roe v. Wade: The Abortion Rights Controversy in American History* (Lawrence: University Press of Kansas, 2001).

Luker, Kristin. *Abortion and the Politics of Motherhood.* Berkeley: University of California Press, 1980.

McClellan, Grant S. (ed.). *The Right to Privacy.* New York: H. W. Wilson, 1976.

Miller, Arthur R. *The Assault on Privacy.* Ann Arbor: University of Michigan Press, 1971.

Murphy, Paul L. *The Right to Privacy and the Ninth Amendment.* New York: Garland, 1990.

Neeley, G. Steven. *The Constitutional Right to Suicide: A Legal and Philosophical Examination.* New York: Peter Lang Publishing, 1994.

O'Brien, David M. *Privacy, Law, and Public Policy.* New York: Praeger, 1979.

O'Connor, Karen. *No Neutral Ground? Abortion Politics in an Age of Absolutes.* Boulder, Colo.: Westview Press, 1996.

Rubin, Eva R. *Abortion, Politics, and the Courts: Roe v. Wade and Its Aftermath.* New York: Greenwood Press, 1987.

Shattuck, John H. F. *Rights of Privacy.* Skokie, Ill.: National Textbook Company, 1977.

Steiner, Gilbert Y. (ed.). *The Abortion Dispute and the American System.* Washington, D.C.: Brookings Institution, 1983.

Tribe, Laurence. *Abortion: The Clash of Absolutes.* New York: Norton, 1990.

Westin, Alan F. *Privacy and Freedom.* New York: Atheneum Press, 1970.

INTERNET RESOURCES

Name of Resource	Description	URL
National Abortion Rights Action League	An interest group dedicated to maintaining legalized abortion	http://www.naral.org/
Operation Save America	An antiabortion interest group	http://www.operationsaveamerica.org
Lambda Legal Defense and Education Fund	An interest group promoting the cause of gay rights	http://www.lambdalegal.org/
The Hemlock Society	An Organization supporting the right to die and legalization of physician-assisted suicide	http://www.hemlock.org/default.asp
Compassion in Dying Federation	Another organization supporting the right to die	http://www.compassionindying.org/

Case

JACOBSON V. MASSACHUSETTS

197 U.S. 11; 25 S.Ct. 358; 49 L.Ed. 643 (1905)
Vote: 7–2

Acting under authority of state law, the board of health of Cambridge, Massachusetts, adopted a regulation requiring that, with certain exceptions, inhabitants of the city be vaccinated against smallpox. State law imposed a $5 fine for violation of the vaccination requirement. Henning Jacobson, a resident of Cambridge, refused to comply with the regulation. As a result, charges were filed against him: He was convicted, and the fine was imposed. Jacobson appealed his conviction, contending that the compulsory vaccination law and implementing regulation violated his rights under the Fourteenth Amendment. The state, in response, argued that the statute was a legitimate exercise of its police power. The Massachusetts Supreme Judicial Court sustained the constitutionality of the law, and Jacobson obtained review by the U.S. Supreme Court.

Mr. Justice Harlan delivered the opinion of the Court:

This case involves the validity, under the Constitution of the United States, of certain provisions in the statutes of Massachusetts relating to vaccination. . . .

Is the statute . . . inconsistent with the liberty which the Constitution of the United States secures to every person against deprivation by the state?

The authority of the state to enact this statute is to be referred to what is commonly called the police power—a power which the state did not surrender when becoming a member of the Union under the Constitution. Although this court has refrained from any attempt to define the limits of that power, yet it has "health laws of every description"; indeed, all laws that relate to matters completely within its territory and which do not by their necessary operation affect the people of other states. According to settled principles, the police power of a state must be held to embrace, at least, such reasonable regulations established directly by legislative enactment as will protect the public health and the public safety. . . .

We come, then, to inquire whether any right given or secured by the Constitution is invaded by the statute as interpreted by the state court. The defendant insists that his liberty is invaded when the state subjects him to fine or imprisonment for neglecting or refusing to submit to vaccination; that a compulsory vaccination law is unreasonable, arbitrary, and oppressive, and, therefore, hostile to the inherent right of every freeman to care for his own body and health in such a way as to him seems best; and that the execution of such a law against one who objects

to vaccination, no matter for what reason, is nothing short of an assault upon his person. But the liberty secured by the Constitution of the United States to every person within its jurisdiction does not import an absolute right in each person to be, at all times and in all circumstances, wholly freed from restraint. There are manifold restraints to which every person is necessarily subject for the common good. On any other basis organized society could not exist with safety to its members. Society based on the rule that each one is a law unto himself would soon be confronted with disorder and anarchy. Real liberty for all could not exist under the operation of a principle which recognizes the right of each individual person to use his own, whether in respect of his person or his property, regardless of the injury that may be done to others. . . .

Applying these principles to the present case, it is to be observed that the legislature of Massachusetts required the inhabitants of a city or town to be vaccinated only when, in the opinion of the board of health, that was necessary for the public health or the public safety. The authority to determine for all what ought to be done in such an emergency must have been lodged somewhere or in some body; and surely it was appropriate for the legislature to refer that question, in the first instance, to a board of health composed of persons residing in the locality affected, and appointed, presumably, because of their fitness to determine such questions. To invest such a body with authority over such matters was not an unusual, nor an unreasonable or arbitrary, requirement. Upon the principle of self-defense, of paramount necessity, a community has the right to protect itself against an epidemic of disease which threatens the safety of its members. . . .

There is, of course, a sphere within which the individual may assert the supremacy of his own will, and rightfully dispute the authority of any human government, especially of any free government existing under a written constitution, to interfere with the exercise of that will. But it is equally true that in every well-ordered society charged with the duty of conserving the safety of its members the rights of the individual in respect of his liberty may at times, under the pressure of great dangers, be subjected to such restraint, to be enforced by reasonable regulations, as the safety of the general public may demand. . . .

Whatever may be thought of the expediency of this statute, it cannot be affirmed to be, beyond question, in palpable conflict with the Constitution. Nor, in view of the methods employed to stamp out the disease of smallpox, can anyone confidently assert that the means prescribed by the state to that end has no real or substantial relation to the protection of the public health and the public safety? Such an assertion would not be consistent with the experience of this and other countries whose authorities have dealt with the disease of smallpox. And the principle of vaccination as a means to prevent the spread of smallpox has been enforced in many states by statutes making the vaccination of children a condition of their right to enter or remain in public school. . . .

We are not prepared to hold that a minority, residing or remaining in any city or town where smallpox is prevalent, and enjoying the general protection afforded by an organized local government, may thus defy the will of its constituted authorities, acting in good faith for all, under the legislative sanction of the state. If such be the privilege of a minority, then a like privilege would belong to each individual of the community, and the spectacle would be presented of the welfare and safety of an entire population being subordinated to the notions of a single individual who chooses to remain a part of that population. We are unwilling to hold it to be an element in the liberty secured by the Constitution of the United States that one person, or a minority of persons, residing in any community and enjoying the benefits of

its local government, should have the power thus to dominate the majority when supported in their action by the authority of the state. While this court should guard with firmness every right appertaining to life, liberty, or property as secured to the individual by the supreme law of the land, it is of the last importance that it should not invade the domain of local authority except when it is plainly necessary to do so in order to enforce that law. The safety and the health of the people of Massachusetts are, in the first instance, for that commonwealth to guard and protect. They are matters that do not ordinarily concern the national government. So far as they can be reached by any government, they depend, primarily, upon such action as the state, in its wisdom, may take; and we do not perceive that this legislation has invaded any right secured by the Federal Constitution. . . .

We now decide only that the statute covers the present case, and that nothing clearly appears that would justify this Court in holding it to be unconstitutional and inoperative in its application to the plaintiff in error.

The judgment of the court below must be affirmed.

Mr. Justice Brewer and *Mr. Justice Peckham* dissent.

Case

MEYER V. NEBRASKA

262 U.S. 390; 43 S.Ct. 625; 67 L.Ed. 1042 (1923)
Vote: 7–2

Here the Court reviews a state law that forbids teaching foreign languages to children.

Mr. Justice McReynolds delivered the opinion of the Court.

Plaintiff in error was tried and convicted in the District Court for Hamilton County, Nebraska, under an information which charged that on May 25, 1920, while an instructor in Zion Parochial School, he unlawfully taught the subject of reading in the German language to Raymond Parpart, a child of ten years, who had not attained and successfully passed the eighth grade. The information is based upon "An act relating to the teaching of foreign languages in the State of Nebraska," approved April 9, 1919. . . .

The following excerpts from the opinion [of the Supreme Court of Nebraska] sufficiently indicate the reasons advanced to support [its] conclusion.

The salutary purpose of the statute is clear. The legislature had seen the baneful effects of permitting foreigners, who

had taken residence in this country, to rear and educate their children in the language of their native land. The result of that condition was found to be inimical to our own safety. To allow the children of foreigners, who had emigrated here, to be taught from early childhood the language of the country of their parents was to rear them with that language as their mother tongue. It was to educate them so that they must always think in that language, and, as a consequence, naturally inculcate in them the ideas and sentiments foreign to the best interests of this country. The statute, therefore, was intended not only to require that the education of all children be conducted in the English language, but that, until they had grown into that language and until it had become a part of them, they should not in the schools be taught any other language. The obvious purpose of this statute was that the English language should become the mother tongue of all children reared in this state. The enactment of such a statute comes reasonably within the police power of the state. . . .

While this Court has not attempted to define with exactness the liberty [guaranteed by the Fourteenth Amendment], the term has received much consideration and some of the included things have been definitely stated. Without doubt, it denotes not merely freedom from bodily restraint but also the right of the individual to contract, to engage in any of the common occupations of life, to acquire useful knowledge, to marry, establish a home and bring up children, to worship God according to the dictates of his own conscience, and generally to enjoy those privileges long recognized at common law as essential to the orderly pursuit of happiness by free men. . . . The established doctrine is that this liberty may not be interfered with, under the guise of protecting the public interest, by legislative action which is arbitrary or without reasonable relation to some purpose within the competency of the State to effect. Determination by the legislature of what constitutes proper exercise of police power is not final or conclusive but is subject to supervision by the courts. . . .

Corresponding to the right of control, it is the natural duty of the parent to give his children education suitable to their station in life; and nearly all the States, including Nebraska, enforce this obligation by compulsory laws.

Practically, education of the young is only possible in schools conducted by especially qualified persons who devote themselves thereto. The calling always has been regarded as useful and honorable, essential, indeed, to the public welfare. Mere knowledge of the German language cannot reasonably be regarded as harmful. Heretofore it has been commonly looked upon as helpful and desirable. Plaintiff in error taught this language in school as part of his occupation. His right thus to teach and the right of parents to engage him so to instruct their children, we think, are within the liberty of the Amendment.

The challenged statute forbids the teaching in school of any subject except in English; also the teaching of any other language until the pupil has attained and successfully passed the eighth grade, which is not usually accomplished before the age of twelve. The Supreme Court of the State has held that "the so-called ancient or dead languages" are not "within the spirit or the purpose of the act." . . . Latin, Greek, Hebrew are not proscribed; but German, French, Spanish, Italian and every other alien speech are within the ban. Evidently the legislature has attempted materially to interfere with the calling of modern language teachers, with the opportunities of pupils to acquire knowledge, and with the power of parents to control the education of their own. . . .

Mr. Justice Holmes [with whom *Justice Sutherland* concurred], dissenting.

We all agree, I take it, that it is desirable that all the citizens of the United States should speak a common tongue, and therefore that the end aimed at by the statute is a lawful and proper one. The only question is whether the means adopted deprive teachers of the liberty secured to them by the Fourteenth Amendment. It is with hesitation and unwillingness that I differ from my brethren with regard to a law like this but I cannot bring my mind to believe that in some circumstances, and circumstances existing it is said in Nebraska, the statute might not be regarded as a reasonable or even necessary method of reaching the desired result. The part of the act with which we are concerned deals with the teaching of young children. Youth is the time when familiarity with a language is established and if there are sections in the State where a child would hear only Polish or French or German spoken at home I am not prepared to say that it is unreasonable to provide that in his early years he shall hear and speak only English at school. But if it is reasonable it is not an undue restriction of the liberty either of teacher or scholar. No one would doubt that a teacher might be forbidden to teach many things, and the only criterion of his liberty under the Constitution that I can think of is "whether, considering the end in view, the statute passes the bounds of reason and assumes the character of a merely arbitrary fiat." . . . I think I appreciate the objection to the law but it appears to me to present a question upon which men reasonably might differ and therefore I am unable to say that the Constitution of the United States prevents the experiment being tried. . . .

Case

BUCK V. BELL

274 U.S. 200; 47 S.Ct. 584; 71 L.Ed. 1000 (1927)
Vote: 8–1

In this notorious case, the Court considers whether the Constitution permits a state to order the sterilization of a "mentally defective" person who is in state custody.

Mr. Justice Holmes delivered the opinion of the Court.

This is a writ of error to review a judgment of the Supreme Court of Appeals of the State of Virginia, affirming a judgment of the Circuit Court of Amherst County, by which the defendant in error [Dr. J. H. Bell], the superintendent of the State Colony for Epileptics and Feeble Minded, was ordered to perform the operation of salpingectomy upon Carrie Buck, the plaintiff in error, for the purpose of making her sterile. . . . The case comes here upon the contention that the statute authorizing the judgment is void under the Fourteenth Amendment as denying to the plaintiff in error due process of law and the equal protection of the laws.

Carrie Buck is a feeble minded white woman who was committed to the State Colony above mentioned in due form. She is the daughter of a feeble-minded mother in the same institution, and the mother of an illegitimate feeble-minded child. She was eighteen years old at the time of the trial of her case in the Circuit Court, in the latter part of 1924. An Act of Virginia, approved March 20, 1924, recites that the health of the patient and the welfare of society may be promoted in certain cases by the sterilization of mental defectives, under careful safeguard. . . .

The attack is not upon the procedure but upon the substantive law. . . . In view of the general declarations of the legislature and the specific findings of the Court, obviously we cannot say as matter of law that the grounds do not exist, and if they exist they justify the result. . . . It is better for all the world, if instead of waiting to execute degenerate offspring for crime, or to let them starve for their imbecil-

ity, society can prevent those who are manifestly unfit from continuing their kind. The principle that sustains compulsory vaccination is broad enough to cover cutting the Fallopian tubes. Three generations of imbeciles are enough.

But, it is said, however it might be if this reasoning were applied generally, it fails when it is confined to the small number who are in the institutions named and is not applied to the multitudes outside. It is the usual last resort of constitutional arguments to point out shortcomings of this sort. But the answer is that the law does all that is needed when it does all that it can, indicates a policy, applies it to all within the lines, and seeks to bring within the lines all similarly situated so far and so fast as its means allow. Of course so far as the operations enable those who otherwise must be kept confined to be returned to the world, and thus open the asylum to others, the equality aimed at will be more nearly reached.

Judgment affirmed.

Mr. Justice Butler dissents.

Case

GRISWOLD V. CONNECTICUT

381 U.S. 479; 85 S.Ct. 1678; 14 L.Ed. 2d 510 (1965)

Vote: 7–2

In this landmark case the Court considers the constitutionality of a state statute criminalizing the use of birth control devices.

Mr. Justice Douglas delivered the opinion of the Court.

Appellant Griswold is Executive Director of the Planned Parenthood League of Connecticut. Appellant Buxton is a licensed physician and a professor at the Yale Medical School who served as Medical Director for the League at its Center in New Haven—a center open and operating from November 1 to November 10, 1961, when appellants were arrested.

They gave information, instruction and medical advice to *married* persons as to the means of preventing conception. They examined the wife and prescribed the best contraceptive device or material for her use. Fees were usually charged, although some couples were serviced free.

The statutes whose constitutionality is involved in this appeal [provide]:

Any person who uses any drug, medicinal article or instrument for the purpose of preventing conception shall be fined not less than fifty dollars or imprisoned not less than

sixty days nor more than one year or be both fined and imprisoned.

Any person who assists, abets, counsels, causes, hires or commands another to commit any offense may be prosecuted and punished as if he were the principal offender.

The appellants were found guilty as accessories and fined $100 each, against the claim that the accessory statute as so applied violated the Fourteenth Amendment. The Appellate Division of the Circuit Court affirmed. The Supreme Court of Errors affirmed that judgment. . . .

We think that appellants have standing to raise the constitutional rights of the married people with whom they had a professional relationship. . . . Certainly the accessory should have standing to assert that the offense which he is charged with assisting is not, or cannot constitutionally be, a crime. . . .

Coming to the merits, we are met with a wide range of questions that implicate the Due Process Clause of the Fourteenth Amendment. Overtones of some arguments suggest that *Lochner v. New York* . . . should be our guide. But we decline that invitation. . . . We do not sit as a superlegislature to determine the wisdom, need, and propriety of laws that touch economic problems, business affairs, or social conditions. This law, however, operates directly on an intimate relation of husband and wife and their physician's role in one aspect of that relation.

The association of people is not mentioned in the Constitution nor in the Bill of Rights. The right to educate a child in a school of the parents' choice—whether public or private or parochial—is also not mentioned. Nor is the right to study any particular subject or any foreign language. Yet the First Amendment has been construed to include certain of those rights.

By *Pierce v. Society of Sisters,* the right to educate one's children as one chooses is made applicable to the States by the force of the First and Fourteenth Amendments. By *Meyer v. Nebraska,* the same dignity is given the right to study the German language in a private school. In other words, the State may not, consistently with the spirit of the First Amendment, contract the spectrum of available knowledge. The right of freedom of speech and press includes not only the right to utter or to print, but the right to distribute, the right to receive, the right to read . . . and freedom of inquiry, freedom of thought, and freedom to teach . . . indeed the freedom of the entire university community. . . . Without those peripheral rights the specific rights would be less secure. And so we reaffirm the principle of the *Pierce* and the *Meyer* cases.

In *NAACP v. Alabama* . . . we protected the "freedom to associate and privacy in one's associations," noting that freedom of association was a peripheral First Amendment right. Disclosure of membership lists of a constitutionally valid association, we held, was invalid "as entailing the likelihood of a substantial restraint upon the exercise by petitioner's members of their right to freedom of association." In other words, the First Amendment has a penumbra where privacy is protected from governmental intrusion. In like context, we have protected forms of "association" that are not political in the customary sense but pertain to the social, legal, and economic benefit of the members. . . .

[Previous] . . . cases suggest that specific guarantees in the Bill of Rights have penumbras, formed by emanations from those guarantees that help give them life and substance. Various guarantees create zones of privacy. The right of association contained in the penumbra of the First Amendment is one, as we have seen. The Third Amendment in its prohibition against the quartering of soldiers "in any house" in time of peace without the consent of the owner is another facet of that privacy. The Fourth Amendment explicitly affirms the "right of the people to be secure in their persons, houses, papers, and effects, against unreasonable searches and seizures." The Fifth Amendment in its Self-Incrimination Clause enables the citizen to create a zone of privacy which government may not force him to surrender to his detriment. The Ninth Amendment provides: "The enumeration in the Constitution, of certain rights, shall not be construed to deny or disparage others retained by the people."

The Fourth and Fifth Amendments were described in *Boyd v. United States* . . . as protection against all governmental invasions "of the sanctity of a man's home and the privacies of life." We recently referred in *Mapp v. Ohio* . . . to the Fourth Amendment as creating a "right to privacy, no less important than any other right carefully and particularly reserved to the people." . . .

We have had many controversies over these penumbral rights of "privacy and repose." . . . These cases bear witness that the right of privacy which presses for recognition here is a legitimate one.

The present case, then, concerns a relationship lying within the zone of privacy created by several fundamental constitutional guarantees. And it concerns a law which, in forbidding the *use* of contraceptives rather than regulating their manufacture or sale, seeks to achieve its goals by means having a maximum destructive impact upon that relationship. Such a law cannot stand in light of the familiar principle, so often applied by this Court, that a "governmental purpose to control or prevent activities constitutionally subject to state regulation may not be achieved by means which sweep unnecessarily broadly and thereby invade the area of protected freedoms." . . . Would we allow the police to search the sacred precincts of marital bedrooms for telltale signs of the use of contraceptives? The very idea is repulsive to the notions of privacy surrounding the marriage relationship. . . .

Mr. Justice Goldberg, whom the **Chief Justice** and **Mr. Justice Brennan** join, concurring.

I agree with the Court that Connecticut's birth-control law unconstitutionally intrudes upon the right of marital privacy, and I join in its opinion and judgment. Although I have not accepted the view that "due process" as used in the Fourteenth Amendment incorporates all of the first eight Amendments, . . . I do agree that the concept of liberty protects those personal rights that are fundamental, and is not confined to the specific terms of the Bill of Rights. My conclusion that the concept of liberty is not so restricted and that it embraces the right of marital privacy though that right is not mentioned explicitly in the Constitution is supported both by numerous decisions of this Court, referred to in the Court's opinion, and by the language and history of the Ninth Amendment. . . . In reaching the conclusion that the right of marital privacy is protected, as being within the protected penumbra of specific guarantees of the Bill of Rights, the Court refers to the Ninth Amendment. . . . I add these words to emphasize the relevance of that Amendment to the Court's holding. . . .

The Ninth Amendment reads, "The enumeration in the Constitution, of certain rights, shall not be construed to deny or disparage others retained by the people." The Amendment is almost entirely the work of James

Madison. It was introduced in Congress by him and passed the House and Senate with little or no debate and virtually no change in language. It was proffered to quiet expressed fears that a bill of specifically enumerated rights could not be sufficiently broad to cover all essential rights and that the specific mention of certain rights would be interpreted as a denial that others were protected. . . .

. . . The Ninth Amendment to the Constitution may be regarded by some as a recent discovery and may be forgotten by others, but since 1791 it has been a basic part of the Constitution which we are sworn to uphold. To hold that a right so basic and fundamental and so deep-rooted in our society as the right of privacy in marriage may be infringed because that right is not guaranteed in so many words by the first eight amendments to the Constitution is to ignore the Ninth Amendment and to give it no effect whatsoever. Moreover, a judicial construction that this fundamental right is not protected by the Constitution because it is not mentioned in explicit terms by one of the first eight amendments or elsewhere in the Constitution would violate the Ninth Amendment. . . .

A dissenting opinion suggests that my interpretation of the Ninth Amendment somehow "broaden[s] the powers of this Court." . . . With all due respect, I believe that it misses the import of what I am saying. I do not take the position of my Brother Black in his dissent in *Adamson v. California* . . . that the entire Bill of Rights is incorporated in the Fourteenth Amendment, and I do not mean to imply that the Ninth Amendment is applied against the States by the Fourteenth. Nor do I mean to state that the Ninth Amendment constitutes an independent source of rights protected from infringement by either the States or the Federal Government. Rather, the Ninth Amendment shows a belief of the Constitution's authors that fundamental rights exist that are not expressly enumerated in the first eight amendments and an intent that the list of rights included there not be deemed exhaustive. As any student of this Court's opinions knows, this Court has held, often unanimously, that the Fifth and Fourteenth Amendments protect certain fundamental personal liberties from abridgment by the Federal Government or the States. . . . The Ninth Amendment simply shows the intent of the Constitution's authors that other fundamental personal rights should not be denied such protection or disparaged in any other way simply because they are not specifically listed in the first eight constitutional amendments. I do not see how this broadens the authority of the Court; rather it serves to support what this Court has been doing in protecting fundamental rights.

Nor am I turning somersaults with history in arguing that the Ninth Amendment is relevant in a case dealing with a *State's* infringement of a fundamental right. While the Ninth Amendment—and indeed the entire Bill of Rights—originally concerned restrictions upon *federal* power, the subsequently enacted Fourteenth Amendment prohibits the States as well from abridging fundamental personal liberties. And, the Ninth Amendment, in indicating that not all such liberties are specifically mentioned in the first eight amendments, is surely relevant in showing the existence of other fundamental personal rights, now protected from state, as well as federal, infringement. In sum, the Ninth Amendment simply lends strong support to the view that the "liberty" protected by the Fifth and Fourteenth Amendments from infringement by the Federal Government or the States is not restricted to rights specifically mentioned in the first eight amendments. . . .

In determining which rights are fundamental, judges are not left at large to decide cases in light of their personal and private notions. Rather, they must look to the "traditions and [collective] conscience of our people" to determine whether a principle is "so rooted [there] . . . as to be ranked as fundamental." . . . The inquiry is whether a right involved "is of such a character that it cannot be denied without violating those 'fundamental principles of liberty and justice which lie at the base of all our civil and political institutions.'" . . .

The entire fabric of the Constitution and the purposes that clearly underlie its specific guarantees demonstrate that the rights to marital privacy and to marry and raise a family are of similar order and magnitude as the fundamental rights specifically protected.

Although the Constitution does not speak in so many words of the right of privacy in marriage, I cannot believe that it offers these fundamental rights no protection. The fact that no particular provision of the Constitution explicitly forbids the State from disrupting the traditional relation of the family—a relation as old and as fundamental as our entire civilization—surely does not show that the Government was meant to have the power to do so. Rather, as the Ninth Amendment expressly recognizes, there are fundamental personal rights such as this one, which are protected from abridgment by the Government though not specifically mentioned in the Constitution. . . .

The logic of the dissents would sanction federal or state legislation that seems to me even more plainly unconstitutional than the statute before us. Surely the Government, absent a showing of a compelling subordinating state interest, could not decree that all husbands and wives must be sterilized after two children have been born to them. Yet by their reasoning such an invasion of marital privacy would not be subject to constitutional challenge because, while it might be "silly," no provision of the Constitution specifically prevents the Government from curtailing the marital right to bear children and raise a family. While it may shock some of my Brethren that the Court today holds that the Constitution protects the right of marital privacy, in my view it is far more shocking to believe that the personal liberty guaranteed by the Constitution does not include protection against such totalitarian limitation of family size, which is at complete variance with our constitutional concepts. Yet, if upon a showing of a slender basis of rationality, a law outlawing voluntary birth control by married persons is valid, then, by the same reasoning, a law requiring compulsory birth control also would seem to be valid. In my view, however, both types of law would unjustifiably intrude upon rights of marital privacy which are constitutionally protected.

In a long series of cases this Court has held that where fundamental personal liberties are involved, they may not be abridged by the States simply on a showing that a regulatory statute has some rational relationship to the effectuation of a proper state purpose. . . .

Although the Connecticut birth-control law obviously encroaches upon a fundamental personal liberty, the State does not show that the law serves any "subordinating [state] interest which is compelling" or that it is "necessary . . . to the accomplishment of a permissible state policy." The State, at most, argues that there is some rational relation between this statute and what is admittedly a legitimate subject of state concern—the discouraging of extramarital relations. It says that preventing the use of birth-control devices by married persons helps prevent the indulgence by some in such extra-marital relations. The rationality of this justification is dubious, particularly in light of the admitted widespread availability to all persons in the State of Connecticut, unmarried as well as married, of birth-control devices for the prevention of disease, as distinguished from the prevention of conception. . . . But, in any event, it is clear that the state interest in safeguarding marital fidelity can be served by a more discriminately tailored statute, which does not, like the present one, sweep unnecessarily broadly, reaching far beyond the evil sought to be dealt with and intruding upon the privacy of all married couples. . . .

Finally, it should be said of the Court's holding today that it in no way interferes with a State's proper regulation of sexual promiscuity or misconduct. . . .

In sum, I believe that the right of privacy in the marital relation is fundamental and basic—a personal right "retained by the people" within the meaning of the Ninth Amendment. Connecticut cannot constitutionally abridge this fundamental right, which is protected by the Fourteenth Amendment from infringement by the States. I agree with the Court that petitioners' convictions must therefore be reversed.

Mr. Justice Harlan, concurring in the judgment.

I fully agree with the judgment of reversal, but find myself unable to join the Court's opinion. The reason is that it seems to me to evince an approach to this case very much like that taken by my Brothers Black and Stewart in dissent, namely: the Due Process Clause of the Fourteenth Amendment does not touch this Connecticut statute unless the enactment is found to violate some right assured by the letter or penumbra of the Bill of Rights.

In other words, what I find implicit in the Court's opinion is that the "incorporation" doctrine may be used to *restrict* the reach of Fourteenth Amendment Due Process. For me this is just as unacceptable constitutional doctrine as is the use of the "incorporation" approach to *impose* upon the States all the requirements of the Bill of Rights as found in the provisions of the first eight amendments and in the decisions of this court interpreting them. . . .

In my view, the proper constitutional inquiry in this case is whether this Connecticut statute infringes the Due Process Clause of the Fourteenth Amendment because the enactment violates basic values "implicit in the concept of ordered liberty." . . . For reasons stated at length in my dissenting opinion in *Poe v. Ullman,* I believe that it does. While the relevant inquiry may be aided by resort to one or more of the provisions of the Bill of Rights, it is not dependent on them or any of their radiations. The Due Process Clause of the Fourteenth Amendment stands, in my opinion, on its own bottom. . . .

While I could not more heartily agree that judicial "self restraint" is an indispensable ingredient of sound constitutional adjudication, I do submit that the formula suggested for achieving it is more hollow than real. "Specific" provisions of the Constitution, no less than "due process," lend themselves as readily to "personal" interpretations by judges whose constitutional outlook is simply to keep the Constitution in supposed "tune with the times." . . .

Judicial self-restraint will not, I suggest, be brought about in the "due process" area by the historically unfounded incorporation formula long advanced by my Brother Black, and now in part espoused by my Brother Stewart. It will be achieved in this area, as in other constitutional areas, only by continual insistence upon respect for the teachings of history, solid recognition of the basic values that underlie our society, and wise appreciation of the great roles that the doctrines of federalism and separation of powers have played in establishing and preserving American freedoms. . . . Adherence to these principles will not, of course, obviate all constitutional differences of opinion among judges, nor should it. Their continued recognition will, however, go farther toward keeping most judges from roaming at large in the constitutional field than will the interpolation into the Constitution of an artificial and largely illusory restriction on the content of the Due Process Clause.

Mr. Justice White, concurring in the judgment.

In my view this Connecticut law as applied to married couples deprives them of "liberty" without due process of law, as that concept is used in the Fourteenth Amendment. I therefore concur in the judgment of the Court reversing these convictions under the Connecticut aiding and abetting statute. . . .

Mr. Justice Black, with whom *Mr. Justice Stewart* joins, dissenting.

I agree with my Brother Stewart's dissenting opinion. And like him I do not to any extent whatever base my view that this Connecticut law is constitutional on a belief that the law is wise or that its policy is a good one. In order that there may be no room at all to doubt why I vote as I do, I feel constrained to add that the law is every bit as offensive to me as it is to my Brethren of the majority and my Brothers Harlan, White and Goldberg who, reciting reasons why it is offensive to them, hold it unconstitutional. There is no single one of the graphic and eloquent strictures and criticisms fired at the policy of this Connecticut law either by the Court's opinion or by those of my concurring brethren to which I cannot subscribe— except their conclusion that the evil qualities they see in the law make it unconstitutional.

. . . I get nowhere in this case by talk about a constitutional "right of privacy" as an emanation from one or more constitutional provisions. I like my privacy as well as the next one, but I am nevertheless compelled to admit that government has a right to invade it unless prohibited by some specific constitutional provision. For these reasons I cannot agree with the Court's judgment and the reasons it gives for holding this Connecticut law unconstitutional. . . .

I realize that many good and able men have eloquently spoken and written, sometimes in rhapsodical strains, about the duty of this Court to keep the Constitution in tune with the times. The idea is that the Constitution must be changed from time to time and that this Court is charged with a duty to make those changes. For myself, I must with all deference reject that philosophy. The Constitution makers knew the need for change and provided for it. Amendments suggested by the people's elected representatives can be submitted to the people or their selected agents for ratification. That method of change was good enough for our Fathers, and being somewhat old-fashioned I must add it is good enough for me. And so, I cannot rely on the Due Process Clause or the Ninth Amendment or any mysterious and uncertain natural law concept as a reason for striking down this state law. The Due Process Clause with an "arbitrary and capricious" or "shocking to the conscience" formula was liberally used by this Court to strike down economic legislation in the early decades of this century, threatening, many people thought, the tranquility and stability of the Nation. . . . That formula, based on subjective considerations of "natural justice," is no less dangerous when used to enforce this Court's views about personal rights than those about economic rights. I had thought that we had laid that formula, as a means for striking down state legislation, to rest once and for all. . . .

Mr. Justice Stewart, whom *Mr. Justice Black* joins, dissenting.

Since 1879 Connecticut has had on its books a law which forbids the use of contraceptives by anyone. I think this is an uncommonly silly law. As a practical matter, the law is obviously unenforceable, except in the oblique context of the present case. As a philosophical matter, I believe the use of contraceptives in the relationship of marriage should be left to personal and private choice, based upon the individual's moral, ethical, and religious beliefs. As a matter of social policy, I think professional counsel about methods of birth control should be available to all, so that each individual's choice can be meaningfully made. But we are not asked in this case to say whether we think this law is unwise, or even asinine. We are asked to hold that it violates the United States Constitution. And that I cannot do.

In the course of its opinion the Court refers to no less than six Amendments to the Constitution: the First, the Third, the Fourth, the Fifth, the Ninth, and the Fourteenth. But the Court does not say which of these Amendments, if any, it thinks is infringed by this Connecticut law.

We are told that the Due Process Clause of the Fourteenth Amendment is not, as such, the "guide" in this case. With that much I agree. There is no claim that this law, duly enacted by the Connecticut Legislature, is unconstitutionally vague. There is no claim that the appellants were denied any of the elements of procedural due process at their trial, so as to make their convictions constitutionally invalid. And, as the Court says, the day has long passed since the Due Process Clause was regarded as a proper instrument for determining "the wisdom, need, and propriety" of state laws. . . . My Brothers Harlan and White to the contrary, "[w]e have returned to the original constitutional proposition that courts do not substitute their social and economic beliefs for the judgment of legislative bodies, who are elected to pass laws." . . .

As to the First, Third, Fourth, and Fifth Amendments, I can find nothing in any of them to invalidate this Connecticut law, even assuming that all those Amendments are fully applicable against the States. It has not even been argued that this is a law "respecting an establishment of religion, or prohibiting the free exercise thereof." And surely, unless the solemn process of constitutional adjudication is to descend to the level of a play on words, there is not involved here any abridgment of "the freedom of speech, or of the press; or the right of the people peaceably to assemble, and to petition the Government for a redress of grievances." No soldier has been quartered in any house. There has been no search, and no seizure. Nobody has been compelled to be a witness against himself.

The Court also quotes the Ninth Amendment, and my Brother Goldberg's concurring opinion relies heavily upon it. But to say that the Ninth Amendment has anything to do with this case is to turn somersaults with history. The Ninth Amendment, like its companion the Tenth, which this Court held "states but a truism that all is retained which has not been surrendered," . . . was framed by James Madison and adopted by the States simply to make clear that the adoption of the Bill of Rights did not alter the plan that the Federal Government was to be a government of express and limited powers, and that all rights and powers not delegated to it were retained by the people and the individual States. Until today no member of this Court has ever suggested that the Ninth Amendment meant anything else, and the idea that a federal court could ever use the Ninth Amendment to annul a law passed by the elected representatives of the people of the State of Connecticut would have caused James Madison no little wonder.

What provision of the Constitution, then, does make this state law invalid? The Court says it is the right of privacy "created by several fundamental constitutional guarantees." With all deference, I can find no such general right of privacy in the Bill of Rights, in any other part of the Constitution, or in any case ever before decided by this Court.

At the oral argument in this case we were told that the Connecticut law does not "conform to current community standards." But it is not the function of this Court to decide cases on the basis of community standards. We are here to decide cases "agreeably to the Constitution and laws of the United States." It is the essence of judicial duty to subordinate our own personal views, our own ideas of what legislation is wise and what is not. If, as I should surely hope, the law before us does not reflect the standards of the people of Connecticut, the people of Connecticut can freely exercise their true Ninth and Tenth Amendment rights to persuade their elected representative to repeal it. That is the constitutional way to take this law off the books.

Case

ROE V. WADE

410 U.S. 113; 93 S.Ct. 705; 35 L.Ed. 2d 147 (1973)

Vote: 7–2

In what is perhaps the most controversial judicial decision of the modern era, the Supreme Court reviews a Texas law criminalizing abortion.

Mr. Justice Blackmun delivered the opinion of the Court.

. . . The Texas statutes that concern us here . . . make it a crime to "procure an abortion," as therein defined, or to attempt one, except with respect to "an abortion procured or attempted by medical advice for the purpose of saving the life of the mother." Similar statutes are in existence in a majority of the States.

Texas first enacted a criminal abortion statute in 1854. . . . This was soon modified into language that has remained substantially unchanged to the present time. . . .

Jane Roe, a single woman who was residing in Dallas County, Texas, instituted this federal action in March 1970 against the District Attorney of the county. She sought a declaratory judgment that the Texas criminal abortion statutes were unconstitutional on their face, and an injunction restraining the defendant from enforcing the statutes.

Roe alleged that she was unmarried and pregnant; that she wished to terminate her pregnancy by an abortion "performed by a competent, licensed physician, under safe, clinical conditions"; that she was unable to get a "legal" abortion in Texas because her life did not appear to be threatened by the continuation of her pregnancy; and that she could not afford to travel to another jurisdiction in order to secure a legal abortion under safe conditions. She claimed that the Texas statutes were unconstitutionally vague and that they abridged her right of personal privacy, protected by the First, Fourth, Fifth, Ninth, and Fourteenth Amendments. By an amendment to her complaint Roe purported to sue "on behalf of herself and all other women" similarly situated. . . .

The principal thrust of appellant's attack on the Texas statutes is that they improperly invade a right, said to be possessed by the pregnant woman, to choose to terminate her pregnancy. Appellant would discover this right in the concept of personal "liberty" embodied in the Fourteenth Amendment's Due Process Clause; or in personal, marital, familial, and sexual privacy said to be protected by the Bill of Rights or its penumbras, . . . or among those rights reserved to the people by the Ninth Amendment. . . . Before addressing this claim, we feel it desirable briefly to survey, in several aspects, the history of abortion, for such insight as that history may afford us, and then to examine the state purposes and interests behind the criminal abortion laws. . . .

Three reasons have been advanced to explain historically the enactment of criminal abortion laws in the 19th century and to justify their continued existence.

It has been argued occasionally that these laws were the product of a Victorian social concern to discourage illicit sexual conduct. Texas, however, does not advance this justification in the present case, and it appears that no court or commentator has taken the argument seriously. . . .

A second reason is concerned with abortion as a medical procedure. When most criminal abortion laws were first enacted, the procedure was a hazardous one for the woman. This was particularly true prior to the development of antisepsis. Antiseptic techniques, of course, were based on discoveries by Lister, Pasteur, and others first announced in 1867, but were not generally accepted and employed until about the turn of the century. Abortion mortality was high. Even after 1900, and perhaps until as late as the development of antibiotics in the 1940s, standard modern techniques such as dilation and curettage were not nearly so safe as they are today. Thus, it has been argued that a State's real concern in enacting a criminal abortion law was to protect the pregnant woman, that is, to restrain her from submitting to a procedure that placed her life in serious jeopardy.

Modern medical techniques have altered this situation. Mortality rates for women undergoing early abortions, where the procedure is legal, appear to be as low as or lower than the rates for normal childbirth. Consequently, any interest of the State in protecting the woman from an inherently hazardous procedure, except when it would be equally dangerous for her to forgo it, has largely disappeared. Of course, important state interests in the area of health and medical standards do remain. . . .

The third reason is the State's interest—some phrase it in terms of duty—in protecting prenatal life. Some of the argument for this justification rests on the theory that a new human life is present from the moment of conception. The State's interest and general obligation to protect life then extends, it is argued, to prenatal life. Only when the life of the pregnant mother herself is at stake, balanced against the life she carries within her, should the interest of the embryo or fetus not prevail. Logically, of course, a legitimate state interest in this area need not stand or fall on acceptance of the belief that life begins at conception or at some other point prior to live birth. In assessing the State's interest, recognition may be given to the less rigid claim that as long as at least potential life is involved, the State may assert interests beyond the protection of the pregnant woman alone. . . .

The Constitution does not explicitly mention any right of privacy. In a line of decisions, . . . the Court has recognized that a right of personal privacy or a guarantee of certain areas or zones of privacy, does exist under the Constitution. . . .

This right of privacy, whether it be founded in the Fourteenth Amendment's concept of personal liberty and restrictions upon state action, as we feel it is, or, as the District Court determined, in the Ninth Amendment's reservation of rights to the people, is broad enough to encompass a woman's decision whether or not to terminate her pregnancy. The detriment that the State would impose upon the pregnant woman by denying this choice altogether is apparent. Specific and direct harm medically diagnosable even in early pregnancy may be involved. Maternity, or additional offspring, may force upon the woman a distressful life and future. Psychological harm may be imminent. Mental and physical health may be taxed by child care. There is also the distress, for all concerned, associated with the unwanted child, and there is the problem of bringing a child into a family already unable, psychologically and otherwise, to care for it. In other cases, as in this one, the additional difficulties and continuing stigma of unwed motherhood may be involved. All these are factors the woman and her responsible physician necessarily will consider in consultation.

On the basis of elements such as these, appellant and some *amici* argue that the woman's right is absolute and that she is entitled to terminate her pregnancy at whatever time, in whatever way, and for whatever reason she alone chooses. With this we do not agree. Appellant's arguments that Texas either has no valid interest at all in regulating the abortion decision, or no interest strong enough to support any limitation upon the woman's sole determination, is unpersuasive. The Court's decisions recognizing a right of privacy also acknowledge that some state regulation in areas protected by the right is appropriate. As noted above, a State may properly assert important interests in safeguarding health, in maintaining medical standards, and in protecting potential life. At some point in pregnancy, these respective interests become sufficiently compelling to sustain regulation of the factors that govern the abortion decision. The privacy right involved, therefore, cannot be said to be absolute. . . .

We, therefore, conclude that the right of personal privacy includes the abortion decision, but that this right is not unqualified and must be considered against important state interests in regulation.

We note that those federal and state courts that have recently considered abortion law challenges have reached the same conclusion. A majority, in addition to the District Court in the present case, have held state laws unconstitutional, at least in part, because of vagueness or because of overbreadth and abridgment of rights. . . .

Although the results are divided, most of these courts have agreed that the right of privacy, however based, is broad enough to cover the abortion decision; that the right, nonetheless, is not absolute and is subject to some limitations; and that at some point the state interests as to protection of health, medical standards, and prenatal life, become dominant. We agree with this approach.

Where certain "fundamental rights" are involved, the Court has held that regulation limiting these rights may be justified only by a "compelling state interest," . . . and that legislative enactments must be narrowly drawn to express only the legitimate state interests at stake. . . .

The District Court held that the appellee failed to meet his burden of demonstrating that the Texas statute's infringement upon Roe's rights was necessary to support a compelling state interest, and that, although the appellee presented "several compelling justifications for state presence in the area of abortions," the statutes outstripped these justifications and swept "far beyond any areas of compelling state interest." Appellant and appellee both contest that holding. Appellant, as has been indicated, claims an absolute right that bars any state imposition of criminal penalties in the area. Appellee argues that the State's determination to recognize and protect prenatal life from and after conception constitutes a compelling state interest. As noted above, we do not agree fully with either formulation.

The appellee and certain *amici* argue that the fetus is a "person" within the language and meaning of the Fourteenth Amendment. In support of this, they outline at length and in detail the well-known facts of fetal development. If this suggestion of personhood is established, the appellant's case, of course, collapses, for the fetus' right to life is then guaranteed specifically by the Amendment. The appellant conceded as much on reargument. On the other hand, the appellee conceded on reargument that no case could be cited that holds that a fetus is a person within the meaning of the Fourteenth Amendment.

The Constitution does not define "person" in so many words. Section 1 of the Fourteenth Amendment contains three references to "person." The first, in defining "citizens," speaks of "persons born or naturalized in the United States." The word also appears both in the Due Process Clause and in the Equal Protection Clause. "Person" is used in other places in the Constitution. . . . But in nearly all these instances, the use of the word is such that it has application only postnatally. None indicates, with any assurance, that it has any possible prenatal application.

All this, together with our observation, that throughout the major portion of the 19th century prevailing legal abortion practices were far freer than they are today, persuades us that the word "person," as used in the Fourteenth Amendment, does not include the unborn.

This conclusion, however, does not of itself fully answer the contentions raised by Texas, and we pass on to other considerations.

The pregnant woman cannot be isolated in her privacy. She carries an embryo and, later, a fetus, if one accepts the medical definitions of the developing young in the human uterus. The situation there is inherently different from marital intimacy, or bedroom possession of obscene material, or marriage, or procreation, or education. . . . As we have intimated above, it is reasonable and appropriate for a State to decide that at some point in time another interest, that of the health of the mother or that of potential human life, becomes significantly involved. The woman's privacy is no longer sole and any right of privacy she possesses must be measured accordingly.

Texas urges that, apart from the Fourteenth Amendment, life begins at conception and is present throughout pregnancy, and that, therefore, the State has a compelling interest in protecting that life from and after conception. We need not resolve the difficult question of when life begins. When those trained in the respective disciplines of medicine, philosophy, and theology are unable to arrive at any consensus, the judiciary, at this point in the development of man's knowledge, is not in a position to speculate as to the answer.

It should be sufficient to note briefly the wide divergence of thinking on this most sensitive and difficult question. There has always been strong support for the view that life does not begin until live birth. This was the belief of the Stoics. It appears to be the predominant, though not the unanimous, attitude of the Jewish faith. It may be taken to represent also the position of a large segment of the Protestant community, insofar as that can be ascertained; organized groups that have taken a formal position on the abortion issue have generally regarded abortion as a matter for the conscience of the individual and her family. As we have noted, the common law found greater significance in quickening. Physicians and their scientific colleagues have regarded that event with less interest and have tended to focus either upon conception, upon live birth, or upon the interim point at which the fetus becomes "viable," that is, potentially able to live outside the mother's womb, albeit with artificial aid. Viability is usually placed at about seven months (28 weeks) but may occur earlier, even at 24 weeks. The Aristotelian theory of "mediate animation," that held sway throughout the Middle Ages and the Renaissance in Europe, continued to be official Roman Catholic dogma until the 19th century, despite opposition to this "ensoulment" theory from those in the Church who would recognize the existence of life from the moment of conception. The latter is now, of course, the official belief of the Catholic Church. As one of the briefs *amicus* discloses, this is a view strongly held by many non-Catholics as well, and by many physicians. Substantial problems for precise definition of this view are posed, however, by new embryological data that purport to indicate that conception is a "process" over time, rather than an event, and by new medical techniques such as menstrual extraction, the "morning-after" pill, implantation of embryos, artificial insemination, even artificial wombs.

In areas other than criminal abortion, the law has been reluctant to endorse any theory that life, as we recognize it, begins before live birth or to accord legal rights to the unborn except in narrowly defined situations and except when the rights are contingent upon live birth. For example, the traditional rule of tort law denied recovery for prenatal injuries even though the child was born alive. That rule has been changed in almost every jurisdiction. In most States, recovery is said to be permitted only if the fetus was viable, or at least quick, when the injuries were sustained, though few courts have squarely so held. In a recent development, generally opposed by the commentators, some States permit the parents of a stillborn child to maintain an action for wrongful death because of prenatal injuries. Such an action, however, would appear to be one to vindicate the parents' interest and is thus consistent with the view that the fetus, at most, represents only the potentiality of life. Similarly, unborn children have been recognized as acquiring rights or interests by way of inheritance or other devolution of property, and have been represented by guardians *ad litem*. Perfection of the interests involved, again, has generally been contingent upon live birth. In short, the unborn have never been recognized in the law as persons in the whole sense.

In view of all this, we do not agree that, by adopting one theory of life, Texas may override the rights of the pregnant woman that are at stake. We repeat, however, that the State does have an important and legitimate interest in preserving and protecting the health of the pregnant woman, whether she be a resident of the State or a nonresident who seeks medical consultation and treatment there, and that it has still another important and legiti-

mate interest in protecting the potentiality of human life. These interests are separate and distinct. Each grows in substantiality as the woman approaches term and, at a point during pregnancy, each becomes "compelling."

With respect to the State's important and legitimate interest in the health of the mother, the "compelling" point, in the light of present medical knowledge, is at approximately the end of the first trimester. This is so because of the now-established medical fact that until the end of the first trimester mortality in abortion may be less than mortality in normal childbirth. It follows that, from and after this point, a State may regulate the abortion procedure to the extent that the regulation reasonably relates to the preservation and protection of maternal health. Examples of permissible state regulation in this area are requirements as to the qualifications of the person who is to perform the abortion; as to the licensure of that person; as to the facility in which the procedure is to be performed, that is, whether it must be a hospital or may be a clinic or some other place of less-than-hospital status; as to the licensing of the facility; and the like.

This means, on the other hand, that for the period of pregnancy prior to this "compelling" point, the attending physician, in consultation with his patient, is free to determine, without regulation by the State, that, in his medical judgment, the patient's pregnancy should be terminated. If that decision is reached, the judgment may be effectuated by an abortion free of interference by the State.

With respect to the State's important and legitimate interest in potential life, the "compelling" point is at viability. This is so because the fetus then presumably has the capability of meaningful life outside the mother's womb. State regulation protective of fetal life after viability thus has both logical and biological justifications. If the State is interested in protecting fetal life after viability, it may go so far as to proscribe abortion during that period, except when it is necessary to preserve the life or health of the mother.

Measured against these standards, the Texas Penal Code, in restricting legal abortions to those "procured or attempted by medical advice for the purpose of saving the life of the mother," sweeps too broadly. The statute makes no distinction between abortions performed early in pregnancy and those performed later, and it limits to a single reason, "saving" the mother's life, the legal justification for the procedure. The statute, therefore, cannot survive the constitutional attack made upon it here.

To summarize and to repeat:

1. A state criminal abortion statute of the current Texas type, that excepts from criminality only a life-saving procedure on behalf of the mother, without regard to

pregnancy stage and without recognition of the other interests involved, is violative of the Due Process Clause of the Fourteenth Amendment.

(a) For the stage prior to approximately the end of the first trimester, the abortion decision and its effectuation must be left to the medical judgment of the pregnant woman's attending physician.

(b) For the stage subsequent to approximately the end of the first trimester, the State, in promoting its interest in the health of the mother, may, if it chooses, regulate the abortion procedure in ways that are reasonably related to maternal health.

(c) For the stage subsequent to viability, the State in promoting its interest in the potentiality of human life may, if it chooses, regulate, and even proscribe, abortion except where it is necessary, in appropriate medical judgment, for the preservation of the life or health of the mother.

This holding, we feel, is consistent with the relative weights of the respective interests involved, with the lessons and examples of medical and legal history, with the lenity of the common law, and with the demands of the profound problems of the present day. The decision leaves the State free to place increasing restrictions on abortion as the period of pregnancy lengthens, so long as those restrictions are tailored to the recognized state interests. The decision vindicates the right of the physician to administer medical treatment according to his professional judgment up to the points where important state interests provide compelling justifications for intervention. Up to those points, the abortion decision in all its aspects is inherently, and primarily, a medical decision, and basic responsibility for it must rest with the physician. If an individual practitioner abuses the privilege of exercising proper medical judgment, the usual remedies, judicial and intraprofessional, are available. . . .

Mr. Chief Justice Burger, concurring.

. . . I do not read the Court's holdings today as having the sweeping consequences attributed to them by dissenting Justices; the dissenting views discount the reality that the vast majority of physicians observe the standards of their profession, and act only on the basis of carefully deliberated medical judgments relating to life and health. Plainly, the Court today rejects any claim that the Constitution requires abortion on demand.

Mr. Justice Douglas, concurring. . . .

Mr. Justice Stewart, concurring. . . .

Mr. Justice White, with whom **Mr. Justice Rehnquist** joins, dissenting.

At the heart of the controversy in these cases are those recurring pregnancies that pose no danger whatsoever to the life or health of the mother but are, nevertheless, unwanted for any one or more of a variety of reasons—convenience, family planning, economics, dislike of children, the embarrassment of illegitimacy, etc. The common claim before us is that for any one of such reasons, or for no reason at all, and without asserting or claiming any threat to life or health, any woman is entitled to an abortion at her request if she is able to find a medical advisor willing to undertake the procedure.

The Court for the most part sustains this position: During the period prior to the time the fetus becomes viable, the Constitution of the United States values the convenience, whim, or caprice of the putative mother more than the life or potential life of the fetus; the Constitution, therefore, guarantees the right to an abortion as against any state law or policy seeking to protect the fetus from an abortion not prompted by more compelling reasons of the mother.

With all due respect, I dissent. I find nothing in the language or history of the Constitution to support the Court's judgment. The Court simply fashions and announces a new constitutional right for pregnant mothers and, with scarcely any reason or authority for its action, invests that right with sufficient substance to override most existing state abortion statutes. The upshot is that the people and the legislatures of the 50 States are constitutionally disentitled to weigh the relative importance of the continued existence and development of the fetus, on the one hand, against a spectrum of possible impacts on the mother, on the other hand. As an exercise of raw judicial power, the Court perhaps has authority to do what it does today; but in my view its judgment is an improvident and extravagant exercise of the power of judicial review that the Constitution extends to this Court. . . .

Mr. Justice Rehnquist, dissenting.

. . . The Due Process Clause of the Fourteenth Amendment undoubtedly does place a limit, albeit a broad one, on legislative power to enact laws such as this. If the Texas statute were to prohibit an abortion even where the mother's life is in jeopardy, I have little doubt that such a statute would lack a rational relation to a valid state objective. . . . But the Court's sweeping invalidation of any restrictions on abortion during the first trimester is impossible to justify under that standard, and the conscious weighing of competing factors that the Court's opinion apparently substitutes for the established test is far more appropriate to a legislative judgment than to a judicial one.

The Court eschews the history of the Fourteenth Amendment in its reliance on the "compelling state interest" test. But the Court adds a new wrinkle to this test by transposing it from the legal considerations associated with the Equal Protection Clause of the Fourteenth Amendment to this case arising under the Due Process Clause of the Fourteenth Amendment. Unless I misapprehend the consequences of this transplanting of the "compelling state interest test," the Court's opinion will accomplish the seemingly impossible feat of leaving this area of the law more confused than it found it.

. . . While the Court's opinion quotes from the dissent of Mr. Justice Holmes in *Lochner v. New York,* the result it reaches is more closely attuned to the majority opinion of Mr. Justice Peckham in that case. As in *Lochner* and similar cases applying substantive due process standards to economic and social welfare legislation, the adoption of the compelling state interest standard will inevitably require this Court to examine the legislative policies and pass on the wisdom of these policies in the very process of deciding whether a particular state interest put forward may or may not be "compelling." The decision here to break pregnancy into three distinct terms and to outline the permissible restrictions the State may impose in each one, for example, partakes more of judicial legislation than it does of a determination of the intent of the drafters of the Fourteenth Amendment.

The fact that a majority of the States reflecting, after all, the majority sentiment in those States, have had restrictions on abortions for at least a century is a strong indication, it seems to me, that the asserted right to an abortion is not "so rooted in the traditions and conscience of our people as to be ranked as fundamental. . . ." Even today, when society's views on abortion are changing, the very existence of the debate is evidence that the "right" to an abortion is not so universally accepted as the appellants would have us believe. . . .

Case

Planned Parenthood of Southeastern Pennsylvania v. Casey

505 U.S. 833; 112 S.Ct. 2791; 120 L.Ed. 2d 674 (1992)
Vote: 5–4 / 7–2

In this case, Planned Parenthood of Southeastern Pennsylvania brought suit against Pennsylvania Governor Robert Casey to challenge the constitutionality of a series of provisions of the Pennsylvania Abortion Control Act of 1982, as amended in 1988 and 1989. The act required a woman seeking an abortion to give her informed consent prior to the abortion procedure, and specified that she be provided with certain information at least twenty-four hours before the abortion is performed. For a minor to obtain an abortion, the act required the informed consent of one of her parents, but provided for a "judicial bypass" option if the minor did not wish to or could not obtain a parent's consent. Another provision of the act required that, with some exceptions, a married woman seeking an abortion must sign a statement indicating that she has notified her husband of her intended abortion. The act exempted compliance with these three requirements in the event of a medical emergency. Finally, the act imposed certain reporting requirements on facilities that provide abortion services.

After a trial, the federal district court declared all of these provisions unconstitutional. The Court of Appeals for the Third Circuit reversed in part, upholding all of the requirements with the exception of the spousal notification provision.

A fragmented Supreme Court upheld all of the statutory provisions with the exception of the spousal notification requirement. The Court produced five opinions. Two justices, Blackmun and Stevens, took the position (in separate opinions concurring in part and dissenting in part) that Roe v. Wade should be reaffirmed and that all of the statutory provisions should be declared invalid. Four justices—Rehnquist, Scalia, White, and Thomas—took the view that Roe should be overruled and that all of the Pennsylvania restrictions should be upheld. The controlling opinion, coauthored by Justices O'Connor, Kennedy, and Souter, joined Justices Blackmun and Stevens in explicitly reaffirming Roe v. Wade. However, the "joint opinion" abandoned the Roe trimester framework and declared a new "unduly burdensome" test for judging regulations of abortion. Applying this test, the joint opinion upheld the parental consent and informed consent provisions but invalidated the spousal notification requirement. Thus, the vote on the Court was 5 to 4 to reaffirm Roe v. Wade and invalidate the spousal notification requirement and 7 to 2 to uphold the other statutory provisions.

Justice O'Connor, Justice Kennedy, and **Justice Souter** . . . delivered the opinion of the Court. . . .

. . . Liberty finds no refuge in a jurisprudence of doubt. Yet 19 years after our holding that the Constitution protects a woman's right to terminate her pregnancy in its early stages, *Roe v. Wade* . . . (1973), that definition of liberty is still questioned. Joining the respondents as *amicus curiae,* the United States, as it has done in five other cases in the last decade, again asks us to overrule *Roe.* . . .

After considering the fundamental constitutional questions resolved by *Roe,* principles of institutional integrity, and the rule of *stare decisis,* we are led to conclude this: the essential holding of *Roe v. Wade* should be retained and once again reaffirmed. . . .

. . . Men and women of good conscience can disagree, and we suppose some always shall disagree, about the profound moral and spiritual implications of terminating a pregnancy, even in its earliest stage. Some of us as individuals find abortion offensive to our most basic principles of morality, but that cannot control our decision. Our obligation is to define the liberty of all, not to mandate our own moral code. The underlying constitutional issue is whether the state can resolve these philosophic questions in such a definitive way that a woman lacks all choice in the matter, except perhaps in those rare circumstances in which the pregnancy is itself a danger to her own life or health, or is the result of rape or incest.

It is conventional constitutional doctrine that where reasonable people disagree the Government can adopt one position or the other. . . . That theorem, however, assumes a state of affairs in which the choice does not intrude upon a protected liberty. Thus, while some people might disagree about whether or not the flag should be saluted, or disagree about the proposition that it may not be defiled, we have ruled that a state may not compel or enforce one view or the other. . . .

. . . Our cases recognize "the right of the individual, married or single, to be free from unwarranted governmental intrusion into matters so fundamentally affecting a person as the decision whether to bear or beget a child." . . . Our precedents "have respected the private realm of family life which the state cannot enter." . . . These matters, involving the most intimate and personal choices a person may make in a lifetime, choices central to personal dignity and autonomy, are central to the liberty protected by the Fourteenth Amendment. At the heart of liberty is the right to define one's own concept of existence, of meaning, of the universe, and of the mystery of human life. Beliefs about these matters could not define the attributes of personhood were they formed under compulsion of the State.

These considerations begin our analysis of the woman's interest in terminating her pregnancy but cannot end it, for this reason: though the abortion decision may originate within the zone of conscience and belief, it is more than a philosophic exercise. Abortion is a unique act. It is an act fraught with consequences for others: for the woman who must live with the implications of her deci-

sion; for the persons who perform and assist in the procedure; for the spouse, family, and society which must confront the knowledge that these procedures exist, procedures some deem nothing short of an act of violence against innocent human life; and, depending on one's beliefs, for the life or potential life that is aborted. Though abortion is conduct, it does not follow that the State is entitled to proscribe it in all instances. That is because the liberty of the woman is at stake in a sense unique to the human condition and so unique to the law. . . .

. . . [W]hen this Court reexamines a prior holding, its judgment is customarily informed by a series of prudential and pragmatic considerations designed to test the consistency of overruling a prior decision with the ideal of the rule of law, and to gauge the respective costs of reaffirming and overruling a prior case. Thus, for example, we may ask whether the rule has proved to be intolerable simply in defying practical workability, . . . whether the rule is subject to a kind of reliance that would lend a special hardship to the consequences of overruling and add inequity to the cost of repudiation, . . . whether related principles of law have so far developed as to have left the old rule no more than a remnant of abandoned doctrine, . . . or whether facts have so changed or come to be seen so differently, as to have robbed the old rule of significant application or justification. . . .

Although *Roe* has engendered opposition, it has in no sense proven "unworkable," . . . representing as it does a simple limitation beyond which a state law is unenforceable. While *Roe* has, of course, required judicial assessment of state laws affecting the exercise of the choice guaranteed against government infringement, and although the need for such review will remain as a consequence of today's decision, the required determinations fall within judicial competence.

. . . [F]or two decades of economic and social developments, people have organized intimate relationships and made choices that define their views of themselves and their places in society, in reliance on the availability of abortion in the event that contraception should fail. The ability of women to participate equally in the economic and social life of the nation has been facilitated by their ability to control their reproductive lives. . . . The Constitution serves human values, and while the effect of reliance on *Roe* cannot be exactly measured, neither can the certain cost of overruling *Roe* for people who have ordered their thinking and living around that case be dismissed.

No evolution of legal principle has left *Roe's* doctrinal footings weaker than they were in 1973. No development of constitutional law since the case was decided has implicitly or explicitly left *Roe* behind as a mere survivor of obsolete constitutional thinking. . . .

We have seen how time has overtaken some of *Roe's* factual assumptions: advances in maternal health care allow for abortions safe to the mother later in pregnancy than was true in 1973, . . . and advances in neonatal care have advanced viability to a point somewhat earlier. . . . But these facts go only to the scheme of time limits on the realization of competing interests, and the divergences from the factual premises of 1973 have no bearing on the validity of *Roe's* central holding, that viability marks the earliest point at which the state's interest in fetal life is constitutionally adequate to justify a legislative ban on nontherapeutic abortions.

The soundness or unsoundness of that constitutional judgment in no sense turns on whether viability occurs at approximately 28 weeks, as was usual at the time of *Roe,* at 23 to 24 weeks, as it sometimes does today, or at some moment even slightly earlier in pregnancy, as it may if fetal respiratory capacity can somehow be enhanced in the future. Whenever it may occur, the attainment of viability may continue to serve as the critical fact, just as it has done since *Roe* was decided; which is to say that no change in *Roe's* factual underpinning has left its central holding obsolete, and none supports an argument for overruling it.

The sum of the precedential inquiry to this point shows *Roe's* underpinnings unweakened in any way affecting its central holding. While it has engendered disapproval, it has not been unworkable. An entire generation has come of age free to assume *Roe's* concept of liberty in defining the capacity of women to act in society, and to make reproductive decisions; no erosion of principle going to liberty or personal autonomy has left *Roe's* central holding a doctrinal remnant; *Roe* portends no developments at odds with other precedent for the analysis of personal liberty; and no changes of fact have rendered viability more or less appropriate as the point at which the balance of interests tips. Within the bounds of normal *stare decisis* analysis, then, and subject to the considerations on which it customarily turns, the stronger argument is for affirming *Roe's* central holding, with whatever degree of personal reluctance any of us may have, not for overruling it. . . .

The Court's duty in the present case is clear. In 1973, it confronted the already-divisive issue of governmental power to limit personal choice to undergo abortion, for which it provided a new resolution based on the due process guaranteed by the Fourteenth Amendment. Whether or not a new social consensus is developing on that issue, its divisiveness is no less today than in 1973, and pressure to overrule the decision, like pressure to retain it, has grown only more intense. A decision to overrule *Roe's* essential holding under the existing circum-stances would address error, if error there was, at the cost of both profound and unnecessary damage to the Court's legitimacy, and to the Nation's commitment to the rule of law. It is therefore imperative to adhere to the essence of *Roe's* original decision, and we do so today.

From what we have said so far it follows that it is a constitutional liberty of the woman to have some freedom to terminate her pregnancy. We conclude that the basic decision in *Roe* was based on a constitutional analysis which we cannot now repudiate. The woman's liberty is not so unlimited, however, that from the outset the State cannot show its concern for the life of the unborn, and at a later point in fetal development the state's interest in life has sufficient force so that the right of the woman to terminate the pregnancy can be restricted. . . .

Yet it must be remembered that *Roe v. Wade* speaks with clarity in establishing not only the woman's liberty but also the state's "important and legitimate interest in potential life." . . . That portion of the decision in *Roe* has been given too little acknowledgement and implementation by the Court in its subsequent cases. Those cases decided that any regulation touching upon the abortion decision must survive strict scrutiny, to be sustained only if drawn in narrow terms to further a compelling state interest. . . . Not all of the cases decided under that formulation can be reconciled with the holding in *Roe* itself that the state has legitimate interests in the health of the woman and in protecting the potential life within her. In resolving this tension, we choose to rely upon *Roe,* as against the later cases.

. . . Regulations which do no more than create structural mechanisms by which the state, or the parent or guardian of a minor, may express profound respect for the life of the unborn are permitted, if they are not a substantial obstacle to the woman's exercise of the right to choose. . . . Unless it has that effect on her right of choice, a state measure designed to persuade her to choose childbirth over abortion will be upheld if reasonably related to that goal. Regulations designed to foster the health of a woman seeking an abortion are valid if they do not constitute an undue burden.

Even when jurists reason from shared premises, some disagreement is inevitable. . . . That is to be expected in the application of any legal standard which must accommodate life's complexity. We do not expect it to be otherwise with respect to the undue burden standard. We give this summary:

   (a) To protect the central right recognized by *Roe v. Wade* while at the same time accommodating the state's profound interest in potential life, we will employ the undue burden analysis. . . . An undue burden exists, and therefore a provision of law is invalid, if its purpose or effect is to place a substantial obstacle in the path of a woman seeking an abortion before the fetus attains viability.

(b) We reject the rigid trimester framework of *Roe v. Wade.* To promote the state's profound interest in potential life, throughout pregnancy the state may take measures to ensure that the woman's choice is informed, and measures designed to advance this interest will not be invalidated as long as their purpose is to persuade the woman to choose childbirth over abortion. The measures must not be an undue burden on the right.

(c) As with any medical procedure, the state may enact regulations to further the health or safety of a woman seeking an abortion. Unnecessary health regulations that have the purpose or effect of presenting a substantial obstacle seeking an abortion impose an undue burden on the right.

(d) Our adoption of the undue burden analysis does not disturb the central holding of *Roe v. Wade,* and we reaffirm that holding. Regardless of whether exceptions are made for particular circumstances, a State may not prohibit any woman from making the ultimate decision to terminate her pregnancy before viability.

(e) We also reaffirm *Roe's* holding that "subsequent to viability, the State in promoting its interest in the potentiality of human life may, if it chooses, regulate, and even proscribe, abortion except where it is necessary, in appropriate medical judgment, for the preservation of the life or health of the mother." . . .

The Court of Appeals applied what it believed to be the undue burden standard and upheld each of the provisions [of the Pennsylvania law] except for the husband notification requirement. We agree generally with this conclusion, but refine the undue burden analysis in accordance with the principles articulated above. We now consider the separate statutory sections at issue.

Because it is central to the operation of other requirements, we begin with the statute's definition of medical emergency. Under the statute, a medical emergency is "[t]hat condition which, on the basis of the physician's good faith clinical judgment, so complicates the medical condition of a pregnant woman as to necessitate the immediate abortion of her pregnancy to avert her death or for which a delay will create serious risk of substantial and irreversible impairment of a major bodily function." . . .

. . . [T]he Court of Appeals . . . stated: "we read the medical emergency exception as intended by the Pennsylvania legislature to assure that compliance with its abortion reg-

ulations would not in any way pose a significant threat to the life or health of a woman." . . . Normally . . . we defer to the construction of a state statute given it by the lower federal courts. Indeed, we have said that we will defer to lower court interpretations of state law unless they amount to "plain" error. . . . We adhere to that course today, and conclude that, as construed by the Court of Appeals, the medical emergency definition imposes no undue burden on a woman's abortion right.

We next consider the informed consent requirement. . . . Except in a medical emergency, the statute requires that at least 24 hours before performing an abortion a physician inform the woman of the nature of the procedure, the health risks of the abortion and of childbirth, and the "probable gestational age of the unborn child." . . . The physician or a qualified nonphysician must inform the woman of the availability of printed materials published by the State describing the fetus and providing information about medical assistance for childbirth, information about child support from the father, and a list of agencies which provide adoption and other services as alternatives to abortion. An abortion may not be performed unless the woman certifies in writing that she has been informed of the availability of these printed materials and has been provided them if she chooses to view them.

. . . Petitioners challenge the statute's definition of informed consent because it includes the provision of specific information by the doctor and the mandatory 24-hour waiting period. The conclusions reached by a majority of the Justices in the separate opinions filed today and the undue burden standard adopted in this opinion require us to overrule in part some of the Court's past decisions, decisions driven by the trimester framework's prohibition of all pre-viability regulations designed to further the State's interest in fetal life.

[*The Court then proceeds to overrule portions of* Akron v. Akron Center for Reproductive Health (1983), *Thornburgh v. American College of Obstetricians and Gynecologists* (1986), *and* Planned Parenthood of Central Missouri v. Danforth (1976).]

. . . [O]n the record before us, and in the context of this facial challenge, we are not convinced that the 24-hour waiting period constitutes an undue burden.

We are left with the argument that the various aspects of the informed consent required are unconstitutional because they place barriers in the way of abortion on demand. Even the broadest reading of *Roe,* however, has not suggested that there is a constitutional right to abortion on demand. . . . Rather, the right protected by *Roe* is a right to decide to terminate a pregnancy free of undue interference by the State. Because the informed consent requirement facilitates the wise exercise of that right it cannot be classified as an interference with the right *Roe* protects. The informed consent requirement is not an undue burden on that right.

. . . Pennsylvania's abortion law provides, except in cases of medical emergency, that no physician shall perform an abortion on a married woman without receiving a signed statement from the woman that she has notified her spouse that she is about to undergo an abortion. The woman has the option of providing an alternative signed statement certifying that her husband is not the man who impregnated her; that her husband could not be located; that the pregnancy is the result of spousal sexual assault which she has reported; or that the woman believes that notifying her husband will cause him or someone else to inflict bodily injury upon her. A physician who performs an abortion on a married woman without receiving the appropriate signed statement will have his or her license revoked, and is liable to the husband for damages. . . .

. . . In well-functioning marriages, spouses discuss important intimate decisions such as whether to bear a child. But there are millions of women in this country who are the victims of regular physical and psychological abuse at the hands of their husbands. Should these women become pregnant, they may have very good reasons for not wishing to inform their husbands of their decision to obtain an abortion. . . .

The spousal notification requirement is thus likely to prevent a significant number of women from obtaining an abortion. It does not merely make abortions a little more difficult or expensive to obtain; for many women, it will impose a substantial obstacle. We must not blind ourselves to the fact that the significant number of women who fear for their safety and the safety of their children are likely to be deterred from procuring an abortion as surely as if the Commonwealth had outlawed abortion in all cases. . . . It is an undue burden, and therefore invalid.

This conclusion is in no way inconsistent with our decisions upholding parental notification or consent requirements. . . . Those enactments, and our judgment that they are constitutional, are based on the quite reasonable assumption that minors will benefit from consultation with their parents and that children will often not realize that their parents have their best interests at heart. We cannot adopt a parallel assumption about adult women. . . .

We next consider the parental consent provision. Except in a medical emergency, an unemancipated young woman under 18 may not obtain an abortion unless she and one of her parents (or guardian) provides informed consent. . . . If neither a parent nor a guardian provides consent, a court may authorize the performance of an abortion upon a determination that the young woman is mature and capable of giving informed consent and has in

fact given her informed consent, or that an abortion would be in her best interests.

We have been over most of this ground before. Our cases establish, and we reaffirm today, that a State may require a minor seeking an abortion to obtain the consent of a parent or guardian, provided that there is an adequate judicial bypass procedure. . . . Under these precedents, in our view, the one-parent consent requirement and judicial bypass procedure are constitutional. . . .

Under the record keeping and reporting requirements of the statute, every facility which performs abortions is required to file a report stating its name and address as well as the name and address of any related entity, such as controlling or subsidiary organization. In the case of state-funded institutions, the information becomes public.

For each abortion performed, a report must be filed identifying: the physician (and the second physician where required); the facility; the referring physician or agency; the woman's age; the number of prior pregnancies and prior abortions she has had; gestational age; the type of abortion procedure; the date of the abortion; whether there were any pre-existing medical conditions which would complicate pregnancy; medical complications with the abortion; where applicable, the basis for the determination that the abortion was medically necessary; the weight of the aborted fetus; and whether the woman was married, and if so, whether notice was provided or the basis for the failure to give notice. Every abortion facility must also file quarterly reports showing the number of abortions performed broken down by trimester. . . . In all events, the identity of each woman who has had an abortion remains confidential.

In [*Planned Parenthood v.*] *Danforth,* . . . we held that record keeping and reporting provisions "that are reasonably directed to the preservation of maternal health and that properly respect a patient's confidentiality and privacy are permissible." We think that under this standard all the provisions at issue here except that relating to spousal notice are constitutional. Although they do not relate to the State's interest in informing the woman's choice, they do relate to health. The collection of information with respect to actual patients is a vital element of medical research, and so it cannot be said that the requirements serve no purpose other than to make abortions more difficult. Nor do we find that the requirements impose a substantial obstacle to a woman's choice. At most they might increase the cost of some abortions by a slight amount. While at some point increased cost could become a substantial obstacle, there is no such showing on the record before us.

Subsection (12) of the reporting provision requires the reporting of, among other things, a married woman's "reason for failure to provide notice" to her husband. . . . This provision in effect requires women, as a condition of obtaining an abortion, to provide the Commonwealth with the precise information we have already recognized that many women have pressing reasons not to reveal. Like the spousal notice requirement itself, this provision places an undue burden on a woman's choice, and must be invalidated for that reason. . . .

Justice Stevens, concurring in part and dissenting in part.

. . . The Court is unquestionably correct in concluding that the doctrine of *stare decisis* has controlling significance in a case of this kind, notwithstanding an individual justice's concerns about the merits. The central holding of *Roe v. Wade* . . . has been a "part of our law" for almost two decades. It was a natural sequel to the protection of individual liberty established in *Griswold v. Connecticut.* . . . The societal costs of overruling *Roe* at this late date would be enormous. *Roe* is an integral part of a correct understanding of both the concept of liberty and the basic equality of men and women. . . .

In my opinion, the principles established in [the] long line of cases [since *Roe v. Wade*] . . . should govern our decision today. Under these principles, [the informed consent provisions] of the Pennsylvania statute are unconstitutional. Those sections require a physician or counselor to provide the woman with a range of materials clearly designed to persuade her to choose not to undergo the abortion. . . .

The 24-hour waiting period raises even more serious concerns. . . . Part of the constitutional liberty to choose is the equal dignity to which each of us is entitled. A woman who decides to terminate her pregnancy is entitled to the same respect as a woman who decides to carry the fetus to term. The mandatory waiting period denies women that equal respect. . . .

Justice Blackmun, concurring in part and dissenting in part.

Three years ago, in *Webster v. Reproductive Health Services,* . . . four members of this Court appeared poised to "cas(t) into darkness the hopes and visions of every woman in this country" who had come to believe that the Constitution guaranteed her the right to reproductive choice. . . . All that remained between the promise of *Roe* and the darkness of the plurality was a single, flickering flame. Decisions since *Webster* gave little reason to hope that this flame would cast much light. But now, just when so many expected the darkness to fall, the flame has grown bright.

I do not underestimate the significance of today's joint opinion. Yet I remain steadfast in my belief that the right

to reproductive choice is entitled to the full protection afforded by the Court before *Webster*. And I fear for the darkness as four Justices anxiously await the single vote necessary to extinguish the light. . . .

Make no mistake, the joint opinion of Justices O'Connor, Kennedy, and Souter is an act of personal courage and constitutional principle. In contrast to previous decisions in which Justices O'Connor and Kennedy postponed reconsideration of *Roe v. Wade,* . . . the authors of the joint opinion today join Justice Stevens and me in concluding that "the essential holding of *Roe* should be retained and once again reaffirmed." . . . In brief, five members of this Court today recognize that "the Constitution protects a woman's right to terminate her pregnancy in its early stages." . . .

A fervent view of individual liberty and the force of *stare decisis* have led the Court to this conclusion. . . .

In one sense, the Court's approach is worlds apart from that of the Chief Justice and Justice Scalia. And yet, in another sense, the distance between the two approaches is short—the distance is but a single vote. I am 83 years old. I cannot remain on this Court forever, and when I do step down, the confirmation process for my successor well may focus on the issue before us today. That, I regret, may be exactly where the choice between the two worlds will be made.

Chief Justice Rehnquist, with whom **Justice White, Justice Scalia,** and **Justice Thomas** join, concurring in part and dissenting in part.

The joint opinion, following its newly-minted variation on *stare decisis,* retains the outer shell of *Roe v. Wade,* but beats a wholesale retreat from the substance of that case. We believe that *Roe* was wrongly decided, and that it can and should be overruled consistently with our traditional approach to *stare decisis* in constitutional cases. We would adopt the approach of the plurality in *Webster v. Reproductive Health Services* . . . and uphold the challenged provisions of the Pennsylvania statute in their entirety. . . .

The joint opinion of Justices O'Connor, Kennedy, and Souter cannot bring itself to say that *Roe* was correct as an original matter, but the authors are of the view that "the immediate question is not the soundness of *Roe's* resolution of the issue, but the precedential force that must be accorded to its holding." . . .

Instead of claiming that *Roe* was correct as a matter of original constitutional interpretation, the opinion therefore contains an elaborate discussion of *stare decisis.* . . .

In our view, authentic principles of *stare decisis* do not require that any portion of the reasoning in *Roe* be kept intact. "*Stare decisis* is not . . . a universal, inexorable command," . . . especially in cases involving the interpretation of the Federal Constitution. Erroneous decisions in such constitutional cases are uniquely durable, because correction through legislation action, save for constitutional amendment, is impossible. It is therefore our duty to reconsider constitutional interpretations that "depar(t) from a proper understanding" of the Constitution. . . .

The Judicial Branch derives its legitimacy, not from following public opinion, but from deciding by its best lights whether legislative enactments of the popular branches of Government comport with the Constitution. The doctrine of *stare decisis* is an adjunct of this duty, and should be no more subject to the vagaries of public opinion than is the basic judicial task. . . .

The decision in *Roe* has engendered large demonstrations, including repeated marches on this Court and on Congress, both in opposition to and in support of that opinion. A decision either way on *Roe* can therefore be perceived as favoring one group or the other. But this perceived dilemma arises only if one assumes, as the joint opinion does, that the Court should make its decisions with a view toward speculative public perceptions. . . .

The sum of the joint opinion's labors in the name of *stare decisis* and "legitimacy" is this: *Roe v. Wade* stands as a sort of judicial Potemkin Village, which may be pointed out to passers by as a monument to the importance of adhering to precedent. But behind the facade, an entirely new method of analysis, without any roots in constitutional law, is imported to decide the constitutionality of state laws regulating abortion. Neither *stare decisis* nor "legitimacy" are truly served by such an effort. . . .

Justice Scalia, with whom the **Chief Justice, Justice White,** and **Justice Thomas** join, concurring in part and dissenting in part.

My views on this matter are unchanged. . . . The states may, if they wish, permit abortion-on-demand, but the Constitution does not require them to do so.

The permissibility of abortion, and the limitations upon it, are to be resolved like most important questions in our democracy: by citizens trying to persuade one another and then voting. As the Court acknowledges, "where reasonable people disagree the government can adopt one position or the other." . . .

The Court is correct in adding the qualification that this "assumes a state of affairs in which the choice does not intrude upon a protected liberty," . . . but the crucial part of that qualification is the penultimate word. A State's choice between two positions on which reasonable people can disagree is constitutional even when (as is often the case) it intrudes upon a "liberty" in the absolute sense.

Laws against bigamy, for example—which entire societies of reasonable people disagree with—intrude upon men and women's liberty to marry and live with one another. But bigamy happens not to be a liberty specially "protected" by the Constitution.

That is, quite simply, the issue in this case: not whether the power of a woman to abort her unborn child is a "liberty" in the absolute sense; or even whether it is a liberty of great importance to many women. Of course it is both. The issue is whether it is a liberty protected by the Constitution of the United States. I am sure it is not.

I reach that conclusion not because of anything so exalted as my views concerning the "concept of existence, of meaning, of the universe, and of the mystery of life." . . . Rather, I reach it for the same reason that bigamy is not constitutionally protected—because of two simple facts: (1) the Constitution says absolutely nothing about it, and (2) the longstanding traditions of American society have permitted it to be legally proscribed. . . .

The Court's description of the place of *Roe* in the social history of the United States is unrecognizable. Not only did *Roe* not, as the Court suggests, resolve the deeply divisive issue of abortion; it did more than anything else to nourish it, by elevating it to the national level where it is infinitely more difficult to resolve.

National politics were not plagued by abortion protests, national abortion lobbying, or abortion marches on Congress, before *Roe v. Wade* was decided. Profound disagreement existed among our citizens over the issue—as it does over other issues, such as the death penalty—but that disagreement was being worked out at the state level. As with many other issues, the division of sentiment within each State was not as closely balanced as it was among the population of the Nation as a whole, meaning not only that more people would be satisfied with the results of state-by-state resolution, but also that those results would be more stable. Pre-*Roe,* moreover, political compromise was possible.

Roe's mandate for abortion-on-demand destroyed the compromises of the past, rendered compromises impossible for the future, and required the entire issue to be resolved, uniformly, at the national level. At the same time, *Roe* created a vast new class of abortion consumers and abortion proponents by eliminating the moral opprobrium that had attached to the act ("If the Constitution guarantees abortion, how can it be bad?"—not an accurate line of thought, but a natural one).

Many favor all of those developments, and it is not for me to say that they are wrong. But to portray *Roe* as the statesmanlike "settlement" of a divisive issue, a jurisprudential Peace of Westphalia that is worth preserving, is nothing less than Orwellian. . . .

Case

STENBERG V. CARHART

530 U.S. 914; 120 S.Ct. 2597; 147 L.Ed. 2d 743 (2000)
Vote: 5–4

In this case the Supreme Court considers a constitutional challenge to a Nebraska law that prohibits any partial-birth abortion unless that procedure is necessary to save the life of the mother. The statute defines partial-birth abortion as a procedure in which the doctor "partially delivers vaginally a living unborn child before killing the . . . child." In a suit brought by Leroy Carhart, a Nebraska doctor who performs abortions, a federal district court held the statute unconstitutional. The Court of Appeals affirmed.

Justice Breyer delivered the opinion of the Court.

. . . Three established principles determine the issue before us. We shall set them forth in the language of the joint opinion in [*Planned Parenthood v.*] *Casey* [1992]. First, before "viability . . . the woman has a right to choose to terminate her pregnancy." . . . Second, "a law designed to further the State's interest in fetal life which imposes an undue burden on the woman's decision before fetal viability" is unconstitutional. . . . An "undue burden is . . . shorthand for the conclusion that a state regulation has the purpose or effect of placing a substantial obstacle in the path of a woman seeking an abortion of a nonviable fetus." . . . Third, "subsequent to viability, the State in promoting its interest in the potentiality of human life may, if it chooses, regulate, and even proscribe, abortion except where it is necessary, in appropriate medical judgment, for the preservation of the life or health of the mother." . . .

We apply these principles to a Nebraska law banning "partial birth abortion." . . . We hold that this statute violates the Constitution. . . .

Because Nebraska law seeks to ban one method of aborting a pregnancy, we must describe and then discuss several different abortion procedures. Considering the fact that those procedures seek to terminate a potential human life, our discussion may seem clinically cold or callous to some, perhaps horrifying to others. There is no alternative way, however, to acquaint the reader with the technical distinctions among different abortion methods and related factual matters, upon which the outcome of this case depends. For that reason, drawing upon the findings of the trial court, underlying testimony, and related medical texts, we shall describe the relevant methods of performing abortions in technical detail.

The evidence before the trial court, as supported or supplemented in the literature, indicates the following:

1. About 90% of all abortions performed in the United States take place during the first trimester of pregnancy, before 12 weeks of gestational age. . . . During the first trimester, the predominant abortion method is "vacuum aspiration," which involves insertion of a vacuum tube (cannula) into the uterus to evacuate the contents. Such an abortion is typically performed on an outpatient basis under local anesthesia. . . . Vacuum aspiration is considered particularly safe. The procedure's mortality rates for first trimester abortion are, for example, 5 to 10 times lower than those associated with carrying the fetus to term. Complication rates are also low. . . . As the fetus grows in size, however, the vacuum aspiration method becomes increasingly difficult to use. . . .

2. Approximately 10% of all abortions are performed during the second trimester of pregnancy (12 to 24 weeks). . . . In the early 1970's, inducing labor through the injection of saline into the uterus was the predominant method of second trimester abortion. . . . Today, however, the medical profession has switched from medical induction of labor to surgical procedures for most second trimester abortions. The most commonly used procedure is called "dilation and evacuation" (D&E). That procedure (together with a modified form of vacuum aspiration used in the early second trimester) accounts for about 95% of all abortions performed from 12 to 20 weeks of gestational age. . . .

3. D&E "refers generically to transcervical procedures performed at 13 weeks gestation or later." . . . "D&E is similar to vacuum aspiration except that the cervix must be dilated more widely because surgical instruments are used to remove larger pieces of tissue. Osmotic dilators are usually used. Intravenous fluids and an analgesic or sedative may be administered. A local anesthetic such as a paracervical block may be administered, dilating agents, if used, are removed and instruments are inserted through the cervix into the uterus to removal fetal and placental tissue. Because fetal tissue is fragile and easily broken, the fetus may not be removed intact. The walls of the uterus are scraped with a curette to ensure that no tissue remains." . . . After 15 weeks: "Because the fetus is larger at this stage of gestation (particularly the head), and because bones are more rigid, dismemberment or other destructive procedures are more likely to be required than at earlier gestational ages to remove fetal and placental tissue." After 20 weeks: "Some physicians use intrafetal potassium chloride

or digoxin to induce fetal demise prior to a late D&E (after 20 weeks), to facilitate evacuation." . . . There are variations in D&E operative strategy. However, the common points are that D&E involves (1) dilation of the cervix; (2) removal of at least some fetal tissue using nonvacuum instruments; and (3) (after the 15th week) the potential need for instrumental disarticulation or dismemberment of the fetus or the collapse of fetal parts to facilitate evacuation from the uterus.

4. When instrumental disarticulation incident to D&E is necessary, it typically occurs as the doctor pulls a portion of the fetus through the cervix into the birth canal. . . .

5. The D&E procedure carries certain risks. The use of instruments within the uterus creates a danger of accidental perforation and damage to neighboring organs. Sharp fetal bone fragments create similar dangers. And fetal tissue accidentally left behind can cause infection and various other complications. . . . Nonetheless studies show that the risks of mortality and complication that accompany the D&E procedure between the 12th and 20th weeks of gestation are significantly lower than those accompanying induced labor procedures (the next safest midsecond trimester procedures). . . .

6. At trial, Dr. Carhart and Dr. Stubblefield described a variation of the D&E procedure, which they referred to as an "intact D&E." . . . Like other versions of the D technique, it begins with induced dilation of the cervix. The procedure then involves removing the fetus from the uterus through the cervix "intact," i.e., in one pass, rather than in several passes. . . . It is used after 16 weeks at the earliest, as vacuum aspiration becomes ineffective and the fetal skull becomes too large to pass through the cervix. . . . The intact D proceeds in one of two ways, depending on the presentation of the fetus. If the fetus presents head first (a vertex presentation), the doctor collapses the skull; and the doctor then extracts the entire fetus through the cervix. If the fetus presents feet first (a breech presentation), the doctor pulls the fetal body through the cervix, collapses the skull, and extracts the fetus through the cervix. . . . The breech extraction version of the intact D is also known commonly as "dilation and extraction," or D&X. . . . In the late second trimester, vertex, breech, and traverse/compound (sideways) presentations occur in roughly similar proportions. . . .

7. The intact D&E procedure can also be found described in certain obstetric and abortion clinical textbooks, where two variations are recognized. The first, as just described, calls for the physician to adapt his method for extracting the intact fetus depending on fetal presentation. . . . This is the method used by Dr. Carhart. . . . A slightly different version of the intact D procedure . . . calls for conversion to a breech presentation in all cases. . . .

8. The American College of Obstetricians and Gynecologists describes the D&X procedure in a manner corresponding to a breech-conversion intact D&E, including the following steps:

1. deliberate dilatation of the cervix, usually over a sequence of days; 2. instrumental conversion of the fetus to a footling breech; 3. breech extraction of the body excepting the head; and 4. partial evacuation of the intracranial contents of a living fetus to effect vaginal delivery of a dead but otherwise intact fetus. . . .

Despite the technical differences we have just described, intact D&E and D&X are sufficiently similar for us to use the terms interchangeably.

9. Dr. Carhart testified he attempts to use the intact D&E procedure during weeks 16 to 20 because (1) it reduces the dangers from sharp bone fragments passing through the cervix, (2) minimizes the number of instrument passes needed for extraction and lessens the likelihood of uterine perforations caused by those instruments, (3) reduces the likelihood of leaving infection-causing fetal and placental tissue in the uterus, and (4) could help to prevent potentially fatal absorption of fetal tissue into the maternal circulation. . . . The District Court made no findings about the D&X procedure's overall safety. . . . The District Court concluded, however, that "the evidence is both clear and convincing that Carhart's D&X procedure is superior to, and safer than, the . . . other abortion procedures used during the relevant gestational period in the 10 to 20 cases a year that present to Dr. Carhart." . . .

10. The materials presented at trial referred to the potential benefits of the D&X procedure in circumstances involving nonviable fetuses, such as fetuses with abnormal fluid accumulation in the brain (hydrocephaly). . . . Others have emphasized its potential for women with prior uterine scars, or for women for whom induction of labor would be particularly dangerous. . . .

11. There are no reliable data on the number of D&X abortions performed annually. Estimates have ranged between 640 and 5,000 per year. . . .

The question before us is whether Nebraska's statute, making criminal the performance of a "partial birth abortion," violates the Federal Constitution, as interpreted in *Planned Parenthood of Southeastern Pa. v. Casey* (1992), and *Roe v. Wade* (1973). We conclude that it does for at least two independent reasons. First, the law lacks any exception "for the preservation of the . . . health of the mother." . . . Second, it "imposes an undue burden on a woman's ability" to choose a D&E abortion, thereby unduly burdening the right to choose abortion itself. . . .

The fact that Nebraska's law applies both pre- and postviability aggravates the constitutional problem presented. The State's interest in regulating abortion previability is considerably weaker than postviability. . . . Since the law requires a health exception in order to validate even a postviability abortion regulation, it at a minimum requires the same in respect to previability regulation. . . .

The quoted standard also depends on the state regulations "promoting [the State's] interest in the potentiality of human life." The Nebraska law, of course, does not directly further an interest "in the potentiality of human life" by saving the fetus in question from destruction, as it regulates only a *method* of performing abortion. Nebraska describes its interests differently. It says the law "show[s] concern for the life of the unborn," "prevent[s] cruelty to partially born children," and "preserve[s] the integrity of the medical profession." . . . But we cannot see how the interest-related differences could make any difference to the question at hand, namely, the application of the "health" requirement.

Consequently, the governing standard requires an exception "where it is necessary, in appropriate medical judgment for the preservation of the life or health of the mother," . . . for this Court has made clear that a State may promote but not endanger a woman's health when it regulates the methods of abortion. . . .

. . . Nebraska has not convinced us that a health exception is "never necessary to preserve the health of women." . . . Rather, a statute that altogether forbids D&X creates a significant health risk. The statute consequently must contain a health exception. . . . By no means must a State grant physicians "unfettered discretion" in their selection of abortion methods. . . . But where substantial medical authority supports the proposition that banning a particular abortion procedure could endanger women's health, *Casey* requires the statute to include a health exception when the procedure is "necessary, in appropriate medical judgment, for the preservation of the life or health of the mother." . . . Requiring such an exception in this case is no departure from *Casey,* but simply a straightforward application of its holding.

The Eighth Circuit found the Nebraska statute unconstitutional because, in *Casey*'s words, it has the "effect of placing a substantial obstacle in the path of a woman seeking an abortion of a nonviable fetus." . . . It thereby places an "undue burden" upon a woman's right to terminate her pregnancy before viability. . . . Nebraska does not deny that the statute imposes an "undue burden" *if* it applies to the more commonly used D&E procedure as well as to D&X. And we agree with the Eighth Circuit that it does so apply.

Even if the statute's basic aim is to ban D&X, its language makes clear that it also covers a much broader category of procedures.

The Nebraska State Attorney General argues that the statute does differentiate between the two procedures [D&X and D&E]. . . .

We cannot accept the Attorney General's narrowing interpretation of the Nebraska statute. This Court's case law makes clear that we are not to give the Attorney General's interpretative views controlling weight. For one thing, this Court normally follows lower federal-court interpretations of state law. . . . It "rarely reviews a construction of state law agreed upon by the two lower federal courts." . . . In this case, the two lower courts have both rejected the Attorney General's narrowing interpretation. . . .

We are aware that adopting the Attorney General's interpretation might avoid the constitutional problem discussed in this section. But we are "without power to adopt a narrowing construction of a state statute unless such a construction is reasonable and readily apparent." . . .

In sum, using this law some present prosecutors and future Attorneys General may choose to pursue physicians who use D&E procedures, the most commonly used method for performing previability second trimester abortions. All those who perform abortion procedures using that method must fear prosecution, conviction, and imprisonment. The result is an undue burden upon a woman's right to make an abortion decision. We must consequently find the statute unconstitutional.

Justice Stevens, with whom *Justice Ginsburg* joins, concurring.

Although much ink is spilled today describing the gruesome nature of late-term abortion procedures, that rhetoric does not provide me a *reason* to believe that the procedure Nebraska here claims it seeks to ban is more brutal, more gruesome, or less respectful of "potential life" than the equally gruesome procedure Nebraska claims it still allows. . . . The rhetoric is almost, but not quite, loud enough to obscure the quiet fact that during the past 27 years, the central holding of *Roe v. Wade* . . . has been endorsed by all but 4 of the 17 Justices who have addressed the issue. That holding—that the word "liberty" in the Fourteenth Amendment includes a woman's right to make this difficult and extremely personal decision—makes it impossible for me to understand how a State has any legitimate interest in requiring a doctor to follow any procedure other than the one that he or she reasonably believes will best protect the woman in her exercise of this constitutional liberty. But one need not even approach this view today to conclude that Nebraska's law must fall. For the notion that either of these two equally gruesome procedures performed at this late stage of gestation is more akin to infanticide than the other, or that the State furthers any legitimate interest by banning one but not the other, is simply irrational. . . .

Justice O'Connor, concurring.

. . . For the reasons stated in the Court's opinion, I agree that Nebraska's statute cannot be reconciled with our decision in *Planned Parenthood v. Casey* (1992), and is therefore unconstitutional. I write separately to emphasize the following points.

First, the Nebraska statute is inconsistent with *Casey* because it lacks an exception for those instances when the banned procedure is necessary to preserve the health of the mother. . . . The statute at issue here, however, only excepts those procedures "necessary to save the life of the mother whose life is endangered by a physical disorder, physical illness, or physical injury." . . . This lack of a health exception necessarily renders the statute unconstitutional. . . .

Second, Nebraska's statute is unconstitutional on the alternative and independent ground that it imposes an undue burden on a woman's right to choose to terminate her pregnancy before viability. Nebraska's ban covers not just the dilation and extraction procedure [D&X], but also the dilation and evacuation procedure [D&E], "the most commonly used method for performing previability second trimester abortions." . . .

If Nebraska's statute limited its application to the D&X procedure and included an exception for the life and health of the mother, the question presented would be quite different than the one we face today. . . . If there were adequate alternative methods for a woman safely to obtain an abortion before viability, it is unlikely that prohibiting the D&X procedure alone would "amount in practical terms to a substantial obstacle to a woman seeking an abortion." . . . Thus, a ban on partial-birth abortion that only proscribed the D&X method of abortion and that included an exception to preserve the life and health of the mother would be constitutional in my view.

Nebraska's statute, however, does not meet these criteria. It contains no exception for when the procedure, in appropriate medical judgment, is necessary to preserve the health of the mother; and it proscribes not only the D&X procedure but also the D&E procedure, the most commonly used method for previability second trimester abortions, thus making it an undue burden on a woman's right to terminate her pregnancy. For these reasons, I agree with the Court that Nebraska's law is unconstitutional.

Justice Ginsburg, with whom Justice Stevens joins, concurring. . . .

Chief Justice Rehnquist, dissenting. . . .

Justice Scalia, dissenting.

I am optimistic enough to believe that, one day, *Stenberg v. Carhart* will be assigned its rightful place in the history of this Court's jurisprudence beside *Korematsu* and *Dred Scott*. The method of killing a human child—one cannot even accurately say an entirely unborn human child—proscribed by this statute is so horrible that the most clinical description of it evokes a shudder of revulsion. And the Court must know (as most state legislatures banning this procedure have concluded) that demanding a "health exception"—which requires the abortionist to assure himself that, in his expert medical judgment, this method is, in the case at hand, marginally safer than others (how can one prove the contrary beyond a reasonable doubt?)—is to give live-birth abortion free rein. The notion that the Constitution of the United States, designed, among other things, "to establish Justice, insure domestic Tranquility, . . . and secure the Blessings of Liberty to ourselves and our Posterity," prohibits the States from simply banning this visibly brutal means of eliminating our half-born posterity is quite simply absurd. . . .

Justice Kennedy, with whom The Chief Justice joins, dissenting.

For close to two decades after *Roe v. Wade* . . . the Court gave but slight weight to the interests of the separate States when their legislatures sought to address persisting concerns raised by the existence of a woman's right to elect an abortion in defined circumstances. When the Court reaffirmed the essential holding of *Roe,* a central premise was that the States retain a critical and legitimate role in legislating on the subject of abortion . . . *Planned Parenthood of Southeastern Pa. v. Casey* (1992). The political processes of the State are not to be foreclosed from enacting laws to promote the life of the unborn and to ensure respect for all human life and its potential. . . . The State's constitutional authority is a vital means for citizens to address these grave and serious issues, as they must if we are to progress in knowledge and understanding and in the attainment of some degree of consensus.

The Court's decision today, in my submission, repudiates this understanding by invalidating a statute advancing critical state interests, even though the law denies no woman the right to choose an abortion and places no undue burden upon the right. The legislation is well within the State's competence to enact. Having concluded Nebraska's law survives the scrutiny dictated by a proper understanding of *Casey*, I dissent from the judgment invalidating it. . . .

Ignoring substantial medical and ethical opinion, the Court substitutes its own judgment for the judgment of

Nebraska and some 30 other States and sweeps the law away. The Court's holding stems from misunderstanding the record, misinterpretation of *Casey,* outright refusal to respect the law of a State, and statutory construction in conflict with settled rules. The decision nullifies a law expressing the will of the people of Nebraska that medical procedures must be governed by moral principles having their foundation in the intrinsic value of human life, including life of the unborn. Through their law the people of Nebraska were forthright in confronting an issue of immense moral consequence. The State chose to forbid a procedure many decent and civilized people find so abhorrent as to be among the most serious of crimes against human life, while the State still protected the woman's autonomous right of choice as reaffirmed in *Casey.* The Court closes its eyes to these profound concerns. . . .

Justice Thomas, with whom **The Chief Justice** and **Justice Scalia** join, dissenting.

. . . In the years following *Roe,* this Court applied, and, worse, extended, that decision to strike down numerous state statutes that purportedly threatened a woman's ability to obtain an abortion. . . .

It appeared that this era of Court-mandated abortion on demand had come to an end . . . in our decision in *Planned Parenthood v. Casey* (1992). Although in *Casey* the separate opinions of The Chief Justice and Justice Scalia urging the Court to overrule *Roe* did not command a majority, seven Members of that Court, including six Members sitting today, acknowledged that States have a legitimate role in regulating abortion and recognized the States' interest in respecting fetal life at all stages of development. . . . The joint opinion authored by Justices O'Connor, Kennedy, and Souter concluded that prior case law "went too far" in "undervalu[ing] the State's interest in potential life" and in "striking down . . . some abortion regulations which in no real sense deprived women of the ultimate decision." . . .

My views on the merits of the *Casey* joint opinion have been fully articulated by others. . . . I will not restate those views here, except to note that the *Casey* joint opinion was constructed by its authors out of whole cloth. The standard set forth in the *Casey* joint opinion has no historical or doctrinal pedigree. The standard is a product of its authors' own philosophical views about abortion, and it should go without saying that it has no origins in or relationship to the Constitution and is, consequently, as illegitimate as the standard it purported to replace. Even assuming, however, as I will for the remainder of this dissent, that *Casey*'s fabricated undue-burden standard merits adherence (which it does not), today's decision is extraordinary. Today, the Court inexplicably holds that the States cannot constitutionally prohibit a method of abor-

tion that millions find hard to distinguish from infanticide and that the Court hesitates even to describe. . . . This holding cannot be reconciled with *Casey*'s undue-burden standard, as that standard was explained to us by the authors of the joint opinion, and the majority hardly pretends otherwise. In striking down this statute—which expresses a profound and legitimate respect for fetal life and which leaves unimpeded several other safe forms of abortion—the majority opinion gives the lie to the promise of *Casey* that regulations that do no more than "express profound respect for the life of the unborn are permitted, if they are not a substantial obstacle to the woman's exercise of the right to choose" whether or not to have an abortion. . . . Today's decision is so obviously irreconcilable with *Casey*'s explication of what its undue-burden standard requires, let alone the Constitution, that it should be seen for what it is, a reinstitution of the pre-*Webster* abortion-on-demand era in which the mere invocation of "abortion rights" trumps any contrary societal interest. If this statute is unconstitutional under *Casey,* then *Casey* meant nothing at all, and the Court should candidly admit it.

To reach its decision, the majority must take a series of indefensible steps. The majority must first disregard the principles that this Court follows in every context but abortion: We interpret statutes according to their plain meaning and we do not strike down statutes susceptible of a narrowing construction. The majority also must disregard the very constitutional standard it purports to employ, and then displace the considered judgment of the people of Nebraska and 29 other States. The majority's decision is lamentable, because of the result the majority reaches, the illogical steps the majority takes to reach it, and because it portends a return to an era I had thought we had at last abandoned. . . .

In the almost 30 years since *Roe,* this Court has never described the various methods of aborting a second- or third-trimester fetus. From reading the majority's sanitized description, one would think that this case involves state regulation of a widely accepted routine medical procedure. Nothing could be further from the truth. The most widely used method of abortion during this stage of pregnancy is so gruesome that its use can be traumatic even for the physicians and medical staff who perform it. . . . And the particular procedure at issue in this case, "partial birth abortion," so closely borders on infanticide that 30 States have attempted to ban it. . . .

"Partial birth abortion" is a term that has been used by a majority of state legislatures, the United States Congress, medical journals, physicians, reporters, even judges, and has never, as far as I am aware, been used to refer to the D&E procedure. The number of instances in which "partial birth abortion" has been equated with the breech extraction form of intact D&E (otherwise known as "D&X") and explicitly contrasted with D&E, are numerous. . . .

Were there any doubt remaining whether the statute could apply to a D&E procedure, that doubt is no ground for invalidating the statute. Rather, we are bound to first consider whether a construction of the statute is fairly possible that would avoid the constitutional question. . . .

The majority contends that application of the Nebraska statute to D&E would pose constitutional difficulties because it would eliminate the most common form of second-trimester abortions. To the extent that the majority's contention is true, there is no doubt that the Nebraska statute is susceptible of a narrowing construction by Nebraska courts that would preserve a physicians' ability to perform D&E. . . . The term "substantial portion" is susceptible to a narrowing construction that would exclude the D&E procedure. . . . If nothing else, a court could construe the statute to require that the fetus be "largely, but not wholly," delivered out of the uterus before the physician performs a procedure that he knows will kill the unborn child. . . .

The next question, therefore, is whether the Nebraska statute is unconstitutional because it does not contain an exception that would allow use of the procedure whenever "necessary in appropriate medical judgment, for the preservation of the . . . health of the mother." . . . It is clear that the Court's understanding of when a health exception is required is not mandated by our prior cases. In fact, we have, post-*Casey,* approved regulations of methods of conducting abortion despite the lack of a health exception. . . .

As if this state of affairs were not bad enough, the majority expands the health exception rule articulated in *Casey* in one additional and equally pernicious way. Although *Roe* and *Casey* mandated a health exception for cases in which abortion is "necessary" for a woman's health, the majority concludes that a procedure is "necessary" if it has any comparative health benefits. . . . In other words, according to the majority, so long as a doctor can point to support in the profession for his (or the woman's) preferred procedure, it is "necessary" and the physician is entitled to perform it. . . . But such a health exception requirement eviscerates *Casey's* undue burden standard and imposes unfettered abortion-on-demand. The exception entirely swallows the rule. In effect, no regulation of abortion procedures is permitted because there will always be *some* support for a procedure and there will always be some doctors who conclude that the procedure is preferable. If Nebraska reenacts its partial birth abortion ban with a health exception, the State will not be able to prevent physicians like Dr. Carhart from using partial birth abortion as a routine abortion procedure. This Court has now expressed its own conclusion that there is "highly plausible" support for the view that partial birth abortion is safer, which, in the majority's view, means that the procedure is therefore "necessary." . . . Any doctor who wishes to perform such a procedure under the new statute will be able to do so with impunity. . . . The majority's insistence on a health exception is a fig leaf barely covering its hostility to any abortion regulation by the States—a hostility that *Casey* purported to reject. . . .

Case

BOWERS V. HARDWICK
478 U.S. 186; 106 S.Ct. 2841; 92 L.Ed. 2d 140 (1986)
Vote: 5–4

In this case the Court considers the constitutionality of a state sodomy statute as applied to homosexual conduct.

Justice White delivered the opinion of the Court.

In August 1982, respondent was charged with violating the Georgia statute criminalizing sodomy by committing that act with another adult male in the bedroom of respondent's home. After a preliminary hearing, the District Attorney decided not to present the matter to grand jury unless further evidence developed.

Respondent then brought suit in the Federal District Court, challenging the constitutionality of the statute insofar as it criminalized consensual sodomy. He asserted that he was a practicing homosexual, that the Georgia sodomy statute, as administered by the defendants, placed him in imminent danger of arrest, and that the statute for several reasons violates the Federal Constitution. The District Court granted the defendants' motion to dismiss [relying on *Doe v. Commonwealth's Attorney* (1976)]. . . .

A divided panel of the Court of Appeals for the Eleventh Circuit reversed. . . . Relying on our decisions in *Griswold v. Connecticut,* . . . *Eisenstadt v. Baird,* . . . *Stanley v. Georgia,* . . . and *Roe v. Wade,* . . . the court went on to hold that the Georgia statute violated respondent's fundamental rights because his homosexual activity is a private and intimate association that is beyond the reach of the state regulation by reason of the Ninth Amendment and the Due Process Clause of the Fourteenth Amendment. The case was remanded for trial, at which, to prevail, the State would have to prove that the statute is supported by a compelling interest and is the most narrowly drawn means of achieving that end.

Because other Courts of Appeals have arrived at judgments contrary to that of the Eleventh Circuit in this case, we granted the State's petition for certiorari. . . .

This case does not require a judgment on whether laws against sodomy between consenting adults in general, or between homosexuals in particular, are wise or desirable. It raises no question about the right or propriety of state legislative decisions to repeal their laws that criminalize homosexual sodomy, or of state court decisions invalidating those laws on state constitutional grounds. The issue presented is whether the Federal Constitution confers a fundamental right upon homosexuals to engage in sodomy and hence invalidates the laws of the many States that still make such conduct illegal and have done so for a very long time. The case also calls for some judgment about the limits of the Court's role in carrying out its constitutional mandate.

We first register our disagreement with the Court of Appeals and with respondent that the Court's prior cases have construed the Constitution to confer a right of privacy that contends to homosexual sodomy and for all intents and purposes have decided this case. . . .

Accepting the decisions in these cases and the above description of them, we think it evident that none of the rights announced in those cases bears any resemblance to the claimed constitutional right of homosexuals to engage in acts of sodomy, that is asserted in this case. No connection between family, marriage, or procreation on the one hand and homosexual activity on the other has been demonstrated, either by the Court of Appeals or by respondent. Moreover, any claim that these cases nevertheless stand for the proposition that any kind of private sexual conduct between consenting adults is constitutionally insulated from state proscription is unsupportable. Indeed, the Court's opinion in *Carey* [*v. Population Services*] twice asserted that the privacy right, which the *Griswold* line of cases found to be one of the protections provided by the Due Process Clause, did not reach so far. . . .

Precedent aside, however, respondent would have us announce, as the Court of Appeals did, a fundamental right to engage in homosexual sodomy. This we are quite unwilling to do. It is true that despite the language of the Due Process Clauses of the Fifth and Fourteenth Amendments, which appears to focus only on the processes by which life, liberty, or property is taken, the cases are legion in which Clauses have been interpreted to have substantive content, subsuming rights that to a great extent are immune from federal or state regulation or proscription. Among such cases are those recognizing rights that have little or no textual support in the constitutional language. . . .

Striving to assure itself and the public that announcing rights not readily identifiable in the constitution's text involves much more than the imposition of the Justices' own choice of values on the States and the Federal Government, the Court has sought to identify the nature of the rights qualifying for heightened judicial protection. In *Palko v. Connecticut* . . . (1937), it was said that this category includes those fundamental liberties that are "implicit in the concept of the record liberty," such that "neither liberty nor justice would exist if [they] were sacrificed." A different description of fundamental liberties appeared in *Moore v. East Cleveland* . . . where they are characterized [by Justice Powell] as those liberties that are "deeply rooted in this Nation's history and tradition."

It is obvious to us that neither of these formulations would extend a fundamental right to homosexuals to engage in acts of consensual sodomy. Proscriptions against that conduct have ancient roots. . . . Sodomy was a criminal offense at common law and was forbidden by the laws of the original thirteen States when they ratified the Bill of Rights. In 1868, when the Fourteenth Amendment was ratified, all but 5 of the 37 States in the Union had criminal sodomy laws. In fact, until 1961, all States outlawed sodomy, and today, 24 States and the District of Columbia continue to provide criminal penalties for sodomy performed in private and between consenting adults. . . . Against this background, to claim that a right to engage in such conduct is "deeply rooted in this Nation's history and tradition" or "implicit in the concept of ordered liberty" is, at best, facetious. . . .

Nor are we inclined to take a more expansive view of our authority to discover new fundamental rights imbedded in the Due Process Clause. The Court is most vulnerable and comes nearest to illegitimacy when it deals with judge-made constitutional law having little or no cognizable roots in the language or design of the Constitution. That this is so was painfully demonstrated by the face-off between the Executive and the Court in the 1930's, which resulted in the repudiation of much of the substantive gloss that the Court had placed on the Due Process Clause of the Fifth and Fourteenth Amendments. There should be therefore, great resistance to expand the substantive reach of those Clauses, particularly if it requires redefining the category of rights deemed to be fundamental. Otherwise, the Judiciary necessarily takes to itself further authority to govern the country without express constitutional authority. The claimed right pressed on us today falls far short of overcoming this resistance.

Respondent, however, asserts that the result should be different where the homosexual conduct occurs in the privacy of the home. He relies on *Stanley v. Georgia* . . . (1969), where the Court held that the First Amendment prevents conviction for possessing and reading obscene material in the privacy of his home: "If the First Amendment means anything, it means that a State has no business telling a man, sitting alone in his house, what books he may read or what films he may watch." . . .

Stanley did protect conduct that would not have been protected outside the home, and it partially prevented the enforcement of state obscenity laws; but the decision was firmly grounded in the First Amendment. The right pressed upon us here has no similar support in the text of the Constitution, and it does not qualify for recognition under the prevailing principles for construing the Fourteenth Amendment. Its limits are also difficult to discern. Plainly enough, otherwise illegal conduct is not always immunized whenever it occurs in the home. Victimless crimes, such as the possession and use of illegal drugs, do not escape the law where they are committed at home. *Stanley* itself recognized that its holding offered no protection for the possession in the home of drugs, firearms, or stolen goods. . . . And if respondent's submission is limited to the voluntary sexual conduct between consenting adults, it would be difficult, except by fiat, to limit the claimed right to homosexual conduct while leaving exposed to prosecution adultery, incest, and other sexual crimes even though they are committed in the home. We are unwilling to start down that road.

Even if the conduct at issue here is not a fundamental right, respondent asserts that there must be a rational basis for the law and that there is none in this case other than the presumed belief of a majority of the electorate in Georgia that homosexual sodomy is immoral and unacceptable. This is said to be an inadequate rationale to support the law. The law, however, is constantly based on notions of morality, and if all laws representing essentially moral choices are to be invalidated under the Due Process Clause, the courts will be very busy indeed. Even respondent makes no such claim, but insists that majority sentiments about the morality of homosexuality should be declared inadequate. We do not agree, and are unpersuaded that the sodomy laws of some 25 States should be invalidated on this basis. . . .

Accordingly, the judgment of the Court of Appeals is reversed.

Chief Justice Burger, concurring.

I join the Court's opinion, but I write separately to underscore my view that in constitutional terms there is no such thing as a fundamental right to commit homosexual sodomy.

As the Court notes, . . . the proscriptions against sodomy have very "ancient roots." Decisions of individuals relating to homosexual conduct have been subject to state intervention throughout the history of Western Civilization. Condemnation of those practices is firmly rooted in Judeo-Christian moral and ethical standards. Homosexual sodomy was a capital crime under Roman law. . . . During the English Reformation when powers of the ecclesiastical courts were transferred to the King's Courts, the first English statute criminalizing sodomy was passed. . . . Blackstone described "the infamous crime against nature" as an offense of "deeper malignity" than rape, an heinous act "the very mention of which is a disgrace to human nature," and "a crime not fit to be named." . . . The common law of England, including its prohibition of sodomy, became the received law of Georgia and the other Colonies. In 1816 the Georgia Legislature passed the statute at issue here, and that statute has been continuously in force in one form or another since that time. To hold that the act of homosexual sodomy is somehow protected as a fundamental right would be to cast aside millennia of moral teaching.

This is essentially not a question of personal "preferences" but rather that of the legislative authority of the State. I find nothing in the Constitution depriving a State of the power to enact the statute challenged here.

Justice Powell, concurring. . . .

Justice Blackmun, with whom Justice Brennan, Justice Marshall, and Justice Stevens join, dissenting.

This case . . . is about "the most comprehensive of rights and the right most valued by civilized men," namely, "the right to be let alone." . . .

The statute at issue denies individuals the right to decide for themselves whether to engage in particular forms of private, consensual sexual activity. The Court concludes that [it] is valid essentially because "the laws of . . . many States . . . still make such conduct illegal and have done so for a very long time." . . . But the fact that the moral judgments expressed by statutes like [such] may be "natural and familiar . . . ought not to conclude our judgment upon the question whether statutes embodying them conflict with the Constitution of the United States." . . .

I believe that "[i]t is revolting to have not better reason for a rule of law than that so it was laid down in the time of Henry IV. It is still more revolting if the grounds upon which it was laid down have vanished long since, and the rule simply persists from blind imitation of the past." . . . I believe we must analyze respondent's claim in the light of the values that underlie the constitutional right to privacy. If that right means anything, it means that, before Georgia can prosecute its citizens for making choices about the most intimate aspects of their lives, it must do more than assert that the choice they have made is an "abominable crime not fit to be named among Christians." . . .

In its haste to reverse the Court of Appeals and hold that the Constitution does not "confe[r] a fundamental right upon homosexuals to engage in sodomy," the Court relegates the actual statute being challenged to a footnote and ignores the procedural posture of the case before it. A fair reading of the statute and of the complaint clearly reveals that the majority has distorted the question this case presents.

First, the Court's almost obsessive focus on homosexual activity is particularly hard to justify in light of the broad language Georgia has used. Unlike the Court, the Georgia Legislature has not proceeded on the assumption that homosexuals are so different from other citizens that their lives may be controlled in a way that would not be tolerated if it limited the choices of those other citizens. . . . Rather, Georgia has provided that "[a] person commits the offense of sodomy when he performs or submits to any sexual act involving the sex organs of one person and the mouth or anus of another." . . . The sex or status of the persons who engage in the act is irrelevant as a matter of state law. In fact, to the extent I can discern a legislative purpose for Georgia's 1968 enactment . . . that purpose seems to have been to broaden the coverage of the law to reach heterosexual as well as homosexual activity. I therefore see no basis for the Court's decision to treat this case as an "as applied" challenge to Sec. 16-6-2, . . . or for Georgia's attempt, both in its brief and at oral argument, to defend Sec. 16-6-2 solely on the grounds that it prohibits homosexual activity. Michael Hardwick's standing may rest in significant part on Georgia's apparent willingness to enforce against homosexuals a law it seems not to have any desire to enforce against heterosexuals. . . . But his claim that Sec. 16-6-2 involves an unconstitutional intrusion into his privacy and his right of intimate association does not depend . . . on his sexual orientation.

Until 1968, Georgia defined sodomy as "the carnal knowledge and connection against the order of nature, by man with man, or in the same unnatural manner with woman." . . . In *Thompson v. Aldredge* . . . (1939), the Georgia Supreme Court held that [the law] did not prohibit lesbian activity. And in *Riley v. Garrett* . . . (1963), the Georgia Supreme Court held that [the law] did not prohibit heterosexual cunnilingus. Georgia passed the act-specific statute currently in force "perhaps in response to the restrictive court decisions such as *Riley*." . . .

Second, I disagree with the Court's refusal to consider whether [the sodomy law] runs afoul of the Eighth or Ninth Amendments or the Equal Protection Clause of the Fourteenth Amendment. . . . Respondent's complaint expressly invoked the Ninth Amendment, . . . and he relied heavily before this Court on *Griswold v. Connecticut* . . . (1965), which identifies that Amendment as one of the specific constitutional provisions giving "life and substance" to our understanding of privacy. . . . More impor-

tantly, the procedural posture of the case requires that we affirm the Court of Appeals' judgment if there is any ground on which respondent may be entitled to relief. . . .

Despite historical views of homosexuality, it is no longer viewed by mental health professionals as a "disease" or disorder. . . . But, obviously, neither is it simply a matter of deliberate personal election. Homosexual orientation may well form part of the very fiber of an individual's personality. Consequently, . . . the Eighth Amendment may pose a constitutional barrier to sending an individual to prison for acting on that attraction regardless of the circumstances. An individual's ability to make constitutionally protected "decisions concerning sexual relations," . . . is rendered empty indeed if he or she is given no real choice but a life without any physical intimacy.

With respect to the Equal Protection Clause's applicability to [the challenged law], I note that Georgia's exclusive stress before this Court on its interest in prosecuting homosexual activity despite the gender-neutral terms of the statute may arise serious questions of discriminatory enforcement, questions that cannot be disposed of before the Court on a motion to dismiss. . . . The legislature having decided that the sex of the participants is irrelevant to the legality of the acts, I do not see why the State can defend [the law] on the ground that individuals singled out for prosecution are of the same sex as their partners. Thus, under the circumstances of this case, a claim under the Equal Protection Clause may well be available without having to reach the more controversial question whether homosexuals are a suspect class. . . .

The Court concludes today that none of our prior cases dealing with various decisions that individuals are entitled to make free of governmental interference "bears any resemblance to the claimed constitutional right of homosexuals to engage in acts of sodomy that is asserted in this case." . . . While it is true that these cases may be characterized by their connection to protection of the family, . . . the Court's conclusion that they extend no further than this boundary ignores the warning in *Moore v. East Cleveland,* . . . against "clos[ing] our eyes to the basic reasons why certain rights associated with the family have been accorded shelter under the Fourteenth Amendment's Due Process Clause." We protect those rights not because they contribute, in some direct and material way, to the general public welfare, but because they form so central a part of an individual's life. "[T]he concept of privacy embodies the 'moral fact that a person belongs to himself and not others nor to society as a whole.' " . . .

. . . The Court claims that its decision today merely refuses to recognize a fundamental right to engage in homosexual sodomy; what the Court really has refused to recognize is the fundamental interest all individuals have in controlling the nature of their intimate associations with others.

The behavior for which Hardwick faces prosecution occurred in his own home, a place to which the Fourth Amendment attaches special significance. The Court's treatment of this aspect of the case is symptomatic of its overall refusal to consider the broad principles that have informed our treatment of privacy in specific cases. Just as the right to privacy is more than the mere aggregation of a number of entitlements to engage in specific behavior,

so too, protecting the physical integrity of the home is more than merely a means of protecting specific activities that often take place there. . . .

Indeed, the right of an individual to conduct intimate relationships in the intimacy of his or her own home seems to me to be the heart of the Constitution's protection of privacy. . . .

Justice Stevens, with whom *Justice Brennan* and *Justice Marshall* join, dissenting. . . .

Case

POWELL V. STATE
GEORGIA SUPREME COURT

510 S.E. 2d 18 (1998)

Powell was charged with rape and aggravated sodomy by the state of Georgia stemming from an episode of sexual activity involving his wife's 17-year-old niece. At trial, the niece testified that Powell had sexual intercourse with her and engaged in an act of oral sex without her consent and against her will. Powell testified that he performed the acts with the consent of the complainant. In charging the jury, the trial judge included an instruction on the law of sodomy. Powell was acquitted of rape and aggravated sodomy but found guilty of sodomy. Powell appealed to the Georgia Supreme Court, challenging the constitutionality of Georgia's sodomy statute, the same law that had been upheld by the United States Supreme Court in Bowers v. Hardwick *(1986).*

Benham, Chief Justice.

The right of privacy has a long and distinguished history in Georgia. In 1905, the Court expressly recognized that Georgia citizens have a "liberty of privacy" guaranteed by the Georgia constitutional provision which declares that no person shall be deprived of liberty except by due process of law. *Pavesich v. New England Life Ins.* . . . The *Pavesich* decision constituted the first time any court of last resort in this country recognized the right of privacy. . . . Since that time, the Georgia courts have developed a rich appellate jurisprudence in the right of privacy which recognizes the right of privacy as a fundamental constitutional right, "having a value so essential to individual liberty in our society that [its] infringement merits careful scrutiny by the courts." . . .

In *Pavesich,* the Court found the right of privacy to be "ancient law," with "its foundation in the instincts of

nature[.]" derived from "the Roman conception of justice" and natural law, making it immutable and absolute. . . . The Court described the liberty interest derived from natural law as "embrac[ing] the right of man to be free in the enjoyment of the faculties with which he has been endowed by his Creator, subject only to such restraints as are necessary for the common good." . . . "Liberty" includes "the right to live as one will, so long as that will does not interfere with the rights of another or of the public" . . . and the individual is "entitled to a liberty of choice as to his manner of live, and neither an individual nor the public has the right to arbitrarily take away from him his liberty." . . . The *Pavesich* Court further recognized that the "right of personal liberty" also embraces "[t]he right of personal liberty" also embraces "[t]he right to withdraw from the public gaze at such times as a person may see fit, when his presence in public is not demanded by any rule of law. . . ." Stated succinctly, the Court ringingly endorsed the "right 'to be let alone' so long as [one] was not interfering with the rights of other individuals or of the public." . . .

Today, we are faced with whether the constitutional right of privacy screens from governmental interference a non-commercial sexual act that occurs without force in a private home between persons legally capable of consenting to the act. While *Pavesich* and its progeny do not set out the full scope of the right of privacy in connection with sexual behavior, it is clear that unforced sexual behavior conducted in private between adults is covered by the principles espoused in *Pavesich* since such behavior between adults in private is recognized as a private matter by "[a]ny person whose intellect is in a normal condition. . . ." Who "withdraw from the public gaze" to engage in private unforced sexual behavior are exercising a right "embraced within the right of personal liberty.". . . We cannot think of any other activity that reasonable persons would rank as more private and deserving of protection from governmental interference than unforced, private, adult sexual activity. . . . We conclude that such activity is at the heart of the Georgia Constitution's protection of the right of privacy.

Having determined that appellant's behavior falls within the area protected by the right of privacy, we next examine whether the government's infringement upon that right is constitutionally sanctioned. As judicial consideration of the right to privacy has developed, this Court has concluded that the right of privacy is a fundamental right. . . . And that a government-imposed limitation on the right to privacy will pass constitutional muster if the limitation is shown to serve a compelling state interest and to be narrowly tailored to effectuate only that compelling interest. . . . Implicit in our decisions curtailing the assertion of a right to privacy in sexual assault cases involving sexual activity taking place in public, performed with those legally incapable of giving consent, performed in exchange for money, or performed with force and against the will of a participant, is the determination that the State has a role in shielding the public from inadvertent exposure to the intimacies of others, in protecting minors and others legally incapable of consent from sexual abuse, and in preventing people from being forced to submit to sex acts against their will. The State fulfills its role in preventing sexual assaults and shielding and protecting the public from sexual acts by the enactment of criminal statutes prohibiting such conduct. . . . And by the vigorous enforcement of those laws through the arrest of prosecution of offenders. In light of the existence of these statutes, the sodomy statute's *raison d'etre* can only be to regulate the private sexual conduct of consenting adults, which Georgians' right of privacy puts beyond the bounds of government regulation.

The State also maintains that the furtherance of "social morality," giving "due regard to the collective will of the citizens of Georgia," is a constitutional basis for legislative control of the non-commercial, unforced, private sexual activity of those legally capable of consenting to such activity. It is well within the power of the legislative branch to establish public policy through legislative enactment. It is also without dispute that oftentimes the public policy so established and the laws so enacted reflect the will of the majority of Georgians as well as the majority's notion of morality. However, "it does not follow . . . that simply because the legislature has enacted as law what may be a moral choice of the majority, the courts are, thereafter, bound to simply acquiesce." . . . "Social morality legislation," like any legislative enactment, is subject to the scrutiny of the judicial branch under our tripartite system of "checks and balances."

In undertaking the judiciary's constitutional duty, it is not the prerogative of members of the judiciary to base decisions on their personal notions of morality. Indeed, if we were called upon to pass upon the propriety of the conduct herein involved, we would not condone it. Rather, the judiciary is charged with the task of examining a legislative enactment when it is alleged to impinge upon the freedoms and guarantees contained in the Georgia Bill of Rights and the U.S. Constitution, and scrutinizing the law, the interests it promotes, and the means by which it seeks to achieve those interests, to ensure that the law meets constitutional standards. While many believe that acts of sodomy, even those involving consenting adults, are morally reprehensible, this repugnance alone does not create a compelling justification for state regulation of the activity. . . .

We conclude that OCGA § 16-6-2, insofar as it criminalizes the performance of private, unforced, noncommercial acts of sexual intimacy between persons legally able to consent, "manifestly infringes upon a constitutional provision" . . . which guarantees to the citizens of Georgia the right of privacy. Appellant was convicted for performing an unforced act of sexual intimacy with one legally capable of consenting thereto in the privacy of his home. Accordingly, appellant's conviction for such behavior must be reversed.

Judgment reversed.

Sears, Justice, concurring. . . .

Carley, Justice, dissenting.

"The responsibility of this Court . . . is to construe and enforce the Constitution and laws of the [State] as they are and not to legislate social policy on the basis of our own personal inclinations." . . . The issue in this case is not whether private and consensual acts of sodomy should be legal or illegal in Georgia, because that question has already been resolved by the General Assembly. Under the unambiguous provisions of OCGA § 16-62(a), commission of an act of sodomy is against the criminal law of this state, and performance of such an act in private between consenting adults is not exempted from that statutory prohibition. Therefore, the only issue presented for decision is whether the General Assembly has the constitutional authority to prohibit such conduct. This Court is not authorized to impede the State's unrestricted enforcement of OCGA § 16-6-2(a) unless that statute manifestly impinges upon a constitutional right of adults to perform consensual sodomy in private. . . . Powell has no right under the federal constitution to engage in the act proscribed by OCGA § 16-6-2(a), since there is no fundamental right under the Constitution of the United States to engage in consensual sodomy. . . . Today, however, a majority of this Court concludes that our state constitution does confer upon the citizens of Georgia a fundamental right to engage in a consensual act which the majority itself concedes, as it must, that many Georgians find "morally reprehensible." I believe that, in so holding, the majority not only misconstrues the Constitution of Georgia, but that it also violates the fundamental constitutional principle of separation of powers. It is my opinion that there is no state constitutional impediment to the General Assembly's enactment of OCGA § 16-6-2(a) and that, by holding otherwise, the Court has exceeded the limits of its judicial authority and usurped the legislative power "to enact laws to promote the public health, safety, morals, and welfare of its citizens. . . . Therefore, the only perceptible unconstitutionality in this case is that which is evidenced by the majority's determination, acting as social engineers rather than as jurists, to elevate their notion of individual "liberty" over the collective wisdom of the people's elective representatives that a proscription on sodomy, consensual or otherwise, is "in furtherance of the moral welfare of the public." Therefore, I respectfully, but vigorously, dissent to the holding that OCGA § 16-6-2(a) is unconstitutional.

The premise of the majority is that the right of privacy guaranteed by the Georgia Constitution grants to the citizens of this state the right to engage in private consensual sodomy. Unlike the constitutions of some other states, the Georgia Constitution contains no express recognition of a right to privacy . . . . That right stems entirely from this Court's holding in *Pavesich v. New England Life In. Co.* (1905). *Pavesich* does not hold that the citizens of this state have an immutable constitutional right to engage in a private consensual act of sodomy or in any other conduct which constitutes a crime pursuant to an enactment of the General Assembly. It merely defines the right of privacy generally, as an implicit element of the "liberty" guaranteed to Georgia citizens under the Due Process Clause of the state constitution. . . . In accordance with *Pavesich,* an individual's liberty and, hence, his privacy is not completely unrestricted, but is subject to "such restraints as are necessary for the common welfare." Thus, a citizen of Georgia does not have the right "to violate the valid regulations of the organized government under which he lives." . . . At the time *Pavesich* was decided, one such valid regulation was a criminal statute of this state which prohibited a citizen's commission of an act of sodomy, without regard to whether that act was consensual or not. . . . Indeed, the original statutory law of Georgia made it a crime to engage in an act of sodomy, and the punishment upon conviction was "imprisonment at laboring the penitentiary for and during the natural life of the person con-

victed of this de[te]stable crime." . . . Moreover, sodomy "was a felony by the ancient common law." . . . Thus, even assuming that the general constitutional right to privacy recognized by *Pavesich* was broad enough to encompass participation in certain private consensual sexual acts, it nevertheless is undeniable that sodomy could not have been included among those protected acts, since that sexual practice was expressly made criminal by that statutory law of this state.

Although, as the majority notes, the right of privacy has a long history in Georgia dating from *Pavesich* until today this Court has never cited that right as authority for the incongruous proposition that a citizen is at liberty to commit an act which has constituted criminal conduct throughout the even longer history of Georgia as a state and, indeed, throughout the entire history of English common law. In its haste to confer upon Powell a constitutionally protected right to engage in private consensual acts of sodomy, the majority simply seizes upon *Pavesich*'s general recognition of the guarantee of "liberty" afforded to Georgia citizens under the state constitution, while choosing to ignore completely *Pavesich*'s equally important recognition of the principle that Georgia citizens also have the responsibility to comply with this state's criminal law. Thus, unlike the majority, I believe that *Pavesich* is clear-cut authority for the proposition that a violation of the criminal law of this state can never be justified as an element of the "liberty" guaranteed by the Due Process Clause of this state's constitution. In my opinion, freedom to violate the criminal law is simply anarchy and, thus, the antithesis of an ordered constitutional system. . . .

Until the majority's advancement of its overly expansive notion of the state constitutional guarantee of "liberty," there has never been any doubt that the General Assembly, in the exercise of the police power, has the authority to define as crimes the commission of acts which, without regard to the infliction of any other injury, are considered to be immoral. Simply put, commission of what the legislature has determined to be an immoral act, even if consensual and private, is an injury against society itself. "[T] protection of 'societal order and morality' [is] a 'substantial government interest.'" . . . The law is "constantly based on notions of morality, and if all laws representing essentially moral choices are to be invalidated under the Due Process Clause, the courts will be very busy indeed.". . . The only justification given by the majority for concluding that OCGA § 16-6-2(a) cannot be upheld as a constitutional exercise of the State's police power to proscribe immoral conduct is that, in Georgia, the right to engage in consensual and private sodomy, although legislatively determined to be morally reprehensible, is guaranteed under our constitution. As previously demonstrated, however, this constitutional "right" has been manufactured out of whole cloth by the majority's misconstruction of *Pavesich*. A constitutional right to privacy obviously cannot include the right to engage in private conduct which was condemned as criminal at the very time that the constitution was ratified. No reasonable Georgian would consider that the effect of voting to ratify a general constitutional guarantee of "liberty" would be to divest his or her elected legislators of the right to continue the specific statutory proscription against sodomy or any other criminal act. To the contrary, any reasonable citizen of this state would consider that he or she thereby was retaining the liberty to make such determinations for themselves through their elected legislators. The majority, having simply invented the constitutional right to engage in sodomy in the first instance, then relies upon that fictional right as support for its ultimate conclusion that the General Assembly has no constitutional authority to pro-scribe that conduct. A reviewing court should strive "to assure itself and the public that announcing rights not readily identifiable in a [c]onstitution's text involves much more than the imposition of the Justice's own choice of values." . . . Given the utter lack of support for the purported constitutional right to engage in sodomy, I can only conclude that the majority has chosen to substitute its own public policy determination for that of the General Assembly.

The majority promotes itself as a judicial defender of constitutional rights against the imposition by the General Assembly of those "norms" of "societal normality" held by most Georgia citizens. . . . Because the majority's discovery of a constitutional right to engage in sodomy notwithstanding this legislative ban is based upon a serious misinterpretation of the Constitution of Georgia and is completely contrary to the constitutional principle of separation of powers, I dissent.

Case

WASHINGTON V. GLUCKSBERG

521 U.S. 702; 117 S.Ct. 2258; 138 L.Ed. 2d 772 (1997)
Vote: 9–0

In this case the Court reviews a state statute prohibiting doctor-assisted suicide.

Chief Justice Rehnquist delivered the opinion of the Court.

The question presented in this case is whether Washington's prohibition against "caus[ing]" or "aid[ing]" a suicide offends the Fourteenth Amendment to the United States Constitution. We hold that it does not.

It has always been a crime to assist a suicide in the State of Washington. In 1854, Washington's first Territorial Legislature outlawed "assisting another in the commission of self murder." Today, Washington law provides: "A person is guilty of promoting a suicide attempt when he knowingly causes or aids another person to attempt suicide." . . . "Promoting a suicide attempt" is a felony, punishable by up to five years' imprisonment and up to a $10,000 fine. . . . At the same time, Washington's Natural Death Act, enacted in 1979, states that the "withholding or withdrawal of life sustaining treatment" at a patient's direction "shall not, for any purpose, constitute a suicide." . . .

Petitioners in this case are the State of Washington and its Attorney General. Respondents Harold Glucksberg, M.D., Abigail Halperin, M.D., Thomas A. Preston, M.D., and Peter Shalit, M.D., are physicians who practice in Washington. These doctors occasionally treat terminally ill, suffering patients, and declare that they would assist these patients in ending their lives if not for Washington's assisted suicide ban. In January 1994, respondents, along with three gravely ill, pseudonymous plaintiffs who have since died and Compassion in Dying, a nonprofit organization that counsels people considering physician assisted suicide, sued in the United States District Court, seeking a declaration that [the statute] is, on its face, unconstitutional. . . .

The plaintiffs asserted "the existence of a liberty interest protected by the Fourteenth Amendment which extends to a personal choice by a mentally competent, terminally ill adult to commit physician assisted suicide." . . . Relying primarily on *Planned Parenthood v. Casey* . . . (1992), and *Cruzan v. Director, Missouri Dept. of Health* . . . (1990), the District Court agreed, . . . and concluded that Washington's assisted suicide ban is unconstitutional because it "places an undue burden on the exercise of [that] constitutionally protected liberty interest." . . . The District Court also decided that the Washington statute violated the Equal Protection Clause's requirement that "all persons similarly situated . . . be treated alike." . . .

A panel of the Court of Appeals for the Ninth Circuit reversed, emphasizing that "[i]n the two hundred and five years of our existence no constitutional right to aid in killing oneself has ever been asserted and upheld by a court of final jurisdiction." . . . The Ninth Circuit reheard the case *en banc,* reversed the panel's decision, and affirmed the District Court. . . . Like the District Court, the *en banc* Court of Appeals emphasized our *Casey* and *Cruzan* decisions. . . . The court also discussed what it described as "historical" and "current societal attitudes" toward suicide and assisted suicide, . . . and concluded that "the Constitution encompasses a due process liberty interest in controlling the time and manner of one's death— that there is, in short, a constitutionally recognized 'right to die.' " . . . After "[w]eighing and then balancing" this interest against Washington's various interests, the court held that the State's assisted suicide ban was unconstitutional "as applied to terminally ill competent adults who wish to hasten their deaths with medication prescribed by their physicians." . . . The court did not reach the District Court's equal protection holding. . . . We granted certiorari. . . . and now reverse.

We begin, as we do in all due process cases, by examining our Nation's history, legal traditions, and practices. . . . In almost every State—indeed, in almost every western democracy—it is a crime to assist a suicide. The States' assisted suicide bans are not innovations. Rather, they are longstanding expressions of the States' commitment to the protection and preservation of all human life. . . . Indeed, opposition to and condemnation of suicide—and, therefore, of assisting suicide—are consistent and enduring themes of our philosophical, legal, and cultural heritages. . . .

More specifically, for over 700 years, the Anglo American common law tradition has punished or otherwise disapproved of both suicide and assisting suicide. . . .

. . . [C]olonial and early state legislatures and courts did not retreat from prohibiting assisting suicide. . . . And the prohibitions against assisting suicide never contained exceptions for those who were near death. . . .

The earliest American statute explicitly to outlaw assisting suicide was enacted in New York in 1828 . . . and many of the new States and Territories followed New York's example. . . . In this century, the Model Penal Code also prohibited "aiding" suicide, prompting many States to enact or revise their assisted suicide bans. The Code's drafters observed that "the interests in the sanctity of life that are represented by the criminal homicide laws are threatened by one who expresses a willingness to participate in taking the life of another, even though the act may be accomplished with the consent, or at the request, of the suicide victim." . . .

Though deeply rooted, the States' assisted suicide bans have in recent years been reexamined and, generally, reaffirmed. Because of advances in medicine and technology, Americans today are increasingly likely to die in institutions, from chronic illnesses. . . . Public concern and democratic action are therefore sharply focused on how best to protect dignity and independence at the end of life, with the result that there have been many significant changes in state laws and in the attitudes these laws reflect. Many States, for example, now permit "living wills," surrogate health care decision making, and the withdrawal or refusal of life sustaining medical treatment. . . . At the same time, however, voters and legislators continue for the most part to reaffirm their States' prohibitions on assisting suicide.

The Washington statute at issue in this case . . . was enacted in 1975 as part of a revision of that State's criminal code. Four years later, Washington passed its Natural Death Act, which specifically stated that the "withholding or withdrawal of life sustaining treatment . . . shall not, for any purpose, constitute a suicide" and that "[n]othing in this chapter shall be construed to condone, authorize, or approve mercy killing. . . ." . . . In 1991, Washington voters rejected a ballot initiative which, had it passed, would have permitted a form of physician assisted suicide. Washington then added a provision to the Natural Death Act expressly excluding physician assisted suicide. . . .

California voters rejected an assisted suicide initiative similar to Washington's in 1993. On the other hand, in 1994, voters in Oregon enacted, also through ballot initiative, that State's "Death With Dignity Act," which legalized physician assisted suicide for competent, terminally ill adults. Since the Oregon vote, many proposals to legalize assisted suicide have been and continue to be introduced in the States' legislatures, but none has been enacted. And just last year, Iowa and Rhode Island joined the overwhelming majority of States explicitly prohibiting assisted suicide. . . .

Thus, the States are currently engaged in serious, thoughtful examinations of physician assisted suicide and other similar issues. For example, New York State's Task Force on Life and the Law—an ongoing, blue ribbon commission composed of doctors, ethicists, lawyers, religious leaders, and interested laymen—was convened in 1984 and commissioned with "a broad mandate to recommend public policy on issues raised by medical advances." . . . Over the past decade, the Task Force has recommended laws relating to end of life decisions, surrogate pregnancy, and organ donation. . . . After studying physician assisted suicide, however, the Task Force unanimously concluded that "[l]egalizing assisted suicide and euthanasia would pose profound risks to many individuals who are ill and vulnerable. . . . [T]he potential dangers of this dramatic change in public policy would outweigh any benefit that might be achieved." . . .

Attitudes toward suicide itself have changed . . . but our laws have consistently condemned, and continue to prohibit, assisting suicide. Despite changes in medical technology and notwithstanding an increased emphasis on the importance of end of life decision making, we have not retreated from this prohibition. Against this backdrop of history, tradition, and practice, we now turn to respondents' constitutional claim. . . .

The Due Process Clause guarantees more than fair process, and the "liberty" it protects includes more than the absence of physical restraint. . . . The Clause also provides heightened protection against government interference with certain fundamental rights and liberty interests. . . . In a long line of cases, we have held that, in addition to the specific freedoms protected by the Bill of Rights, the "liberty" specially protected by the Due Process Clause includes the rights to marry, . . . to have children, . . . to direct the education and upbringing of one's children, . . . to marital privacy, . . . to use contraception, . . . to bodily integrity, . . . and to abortion. . . . We have also assumed, and strongly suggested, that the Due Process Clause protects the traditional right to refuse unwanted lifesaving medical treatment. . . .

But we "ha[ve] always been reluctant to expand the concept of substantive due process because guideposts for responsible decision making in this uncharted area are scarce and open ended." . . . By extending constitutional protection to an asserted right or liberty interest, we, to a great extent, place the matter outside the arena of public debate and legislative action. We must therefore "exercise the utmost care whenever we are asked to break new ground in this field," . . . lest the liberty protected by the Due Process Clause be subtly transformed into the policy preferences of the members of this Court. . . .

Our established method of substantive due process analysis has two primary features: First, we have regularly observed that the Due Process Clause specially protects those fundamental rights and liberties which are, objectively, "deeply rooted in this Nation's history and tradition," . . . and "implicit in the concept of ordered liberty," such that "neither liberty nor justice would exist if they were sacrificed." . . . Second, we have required in substantive due process cases a "careful description" of the asserted fundamental liberty interest. . . . Our Nation's history, legal traditions, and practices thus provide the crucial "guideposts for responsible decision making," . . . that direct and restrain our exposition of the Due Process Clause. As we stated recently . . . , the Fourteenth Amendment "forbids the government to infringe . . . 'fundamental' liberty interests at all, no matter what process is provided, unless the infringement is narrowly tailored to serve a compelling state interest." . . .

. . . The Washington statute at issue in this case prohibits "aid[ing] another person to attempt suicide," . . . and, thus, the question before us is whether the "liberty" specially protected by the Due Process Clause includes a right to commit suicide which itself includes a right to assistance in doing so.

. . . [W]e are confronted with a consistent and almost universal tradition that has long rejected the asserted right, and continues explicitly to reject it today, even for terminally ill, mentally competent adults. To hold for respondents, we would have to reverse centuries of legal doctrine and practice, and strike down the considered policy choice of almost every State. . . .

Respondents contend, however, that the liberty interest they assert is consistent with this Court's substantive due process line of cases, if not with this Nation's history and practice. Pointing to *Casey* and *Cruzan,* respondents read our jurisprudence in this area as reflecting a general tradition of "self sovereignty," . . . and as teaching that the "liberty" protected by the Due Process Clause includes "basic and intimate exercises of personal autonomy." . . . According to respondents, our liberty jurisprudence, and the broad, individualistic principles it reflects, protects the "liberty of competent, terminally ill adults to make end of life decisions free of undue government interference." . . . The question presented in this case, however, is whether the protections of the Due Process Clause include a right to commit suicide with another's assistance. . . .

The history of the law's treatment of assisted suicide in this country has been and continues to be one of the rejection of nearly all efforts to permit it. That being the case, our decisions lead us to conclude that the asserted "right" to assistance in committing suicide is not a fundamental liberty interest protected by the Due Process Clause. The Constitution also requires, however, that Washington's assisted suicide ban be rationally related to legitimate government interests. . . . This requirement is unquestionably met here. As the court below recognized, . . . Washington's assisted suicide ban implicates a number of state interests. . . .

First, Washington has an "unqualified interest in the preservation of human life." . . . The State's prohibition on assisted suicide, like all homicide laws, both reflects and advances its commitment to this interest. . . .

Respondents admit that "[t]he State has a real interest in preserving the lives of those who can still contribute to society and enjoy life." . . .

Relatedly, all admit that suicide is a serious public health problem, especially among persons in otherwise vulnerable groups. . . .

Those who attempt suicide—terminally ill or not—often suffer from depression or other mental disorders. . . . Research indicates, however, that many people who request physician assisted suicide withdraw that request if their depression and pain are treated. . . . [B]ecause depression is difficult to diagnose, physicians and medical professionals often fail to respond adequately to seriously ill patients' needs. . . . Thus, legal physician assisted suicide could make it more difficult for the State to protect depressed or mentally ill persons, or those who are suffering from untreated pain, from suicidal impulses.

The State also has an interest in protecting the integrity and ethics of the medical profession. . . . [T]he American Medical Association, like many other medical and physicians' groups, has concluded that "[p]hysician assisted suicide is fundamentally incompatible with the physician's role as healer." . . .

Next, the State has an interest in protecting vulnerable groups—including the poor, the elderly, and disabled persons—from abuse, neglect, and mistakes. . . . If physician assisted suicide were permitted, many might resort to it to spare their families the substantial financial burden of end of life health care costs.

The State's interest here goes beyond protecting the vulnerable from coercion; it extends to protecting disabled and terminally ill people from prejudice, negative and inaccurate stereotypes, and "societal indifference." . . . The State's assisted suicide ban reflects and reinforces its policy that the lives of terminally ill, disabled, and elderly people must be no less valued than the lives of the young and healthy, and that a seriously disabled person's suicidal impulses should be interpreted and treated the same way as anyone else's. . . .

Finally, the State may fear that permitting assisted suicide will start it down the path to voluntary and perhaps even involuntary euthanasia. . . . [W]hat is couched as a limited right to "physician assisted suicide" is likely, in effect, a much broader license, which could prove extremely difficult to police and contain. Washington's ban on assisting suicide prevents such erosion.

This concern is further supported by evidence about the practice of euthanasia in the Netherlands. The Dutch government's own study revealed that in 1990, there were 2,300 cases of voluntary euthanasia (defined as "the deliberate termination of another's life at his request"), 400 cases of assisted suicide, and more than 1,000 cases of euthanasia without an explicit request. In addition to these latter 1,000 cases, the study found an additional 4,941 cases where physicians administered lethal morphine overdoses without the patients' explicit consent. . . . This study suggests that, despite the existence of various reporting procedures, euthanasia in the Netherlands has not been limited to competent, terminally ill adults who are enduring physical suffering, and that regulation of the practice may not have prevented abuses in cases involving vulnerable persons, including severely disabled neonates and elderly persons suffering from dementia. . . .

We need not weigh exactly the relative strengths of these various interests. They are unquestionably important and legitimate, and Washington's ban on assisted suicide is at least reasonably related to their promotion and protection. We therefore hold that [the challenged statute] does not violate the Fourteenth Amendment, either on its face or "as applied to competent, terminally ill adults who wish to hasten their deaths by obtaining medication prescribed by their doctors." . . .

Throughout the Nation, Americans are engaged in an earnest and profound debate about the morality, legality, and practicality of physician assisted suicide. Our holding permits this debate to continue, as it should in a democratic society. The decision of the *en banc* Court of Appeals is reversed, and the case is remanded for further proceedings consistent with this opinion.

Justice O'Connor, concurring. . . .

Justice Stevens, concurring in the judgments.

The Court ends its opinion with the important observation that our holding today is fully consistent with a continuation of the vigorous debate about the "morality, legality, and practicality of physician assisted suicide" in a democratic society. . . . I write separately to make it clear that there is also room for further debate about the limits that the Constitution places on the power of the States to punish the practice.

The morality, legality, and practicality of capital punishment have been the subject of debate for many years. In 1976, this Court upheld the constitutionality of the practice in cases coming to us from Georgia, Florida, and Texas. In those cases we concluded that a State does have the power to place a lesser value on some lives than on others; there is no absolute requirement that a State treat all human life as having an equal right to preservation. Because the state legislatures had sufficiently narrowed the category of lives that the State could terminate, and had enacted special procedures to ensure that the defendant belonged in that limited category, we concluded that the statutes were not unconstitutional on their face. In later cases coming to us from each of those States, however, we found that some applications of the statutes were unconstitutional.

Today, the Court decides that Washington's statute prohibiting assisted suicide is not invalid "on its face," that is to say, in all or most cases in which it might be applied. That holding, however, does not foreclose the possibility that some applications of the statute might well be invalid. . . .

. . . [J]ust as our conclusion that capital punishment is not always unconstitutional did not preclude later decisions holding that it is sometimes impermissibly cruel, so is it equally clear that a decision upholding a general statutory prohibition of assisted suicide does not mean that every possible application of the statute would be valid. A State, like Washington, that has authorized the death penalty and thereby has concluded that the sanctity of human life does not require that it always be preserved, must acknowledge that there are situations in which an interest in hastening death is legitimate. Indeed, not only is that interest sometimes legitimate, I am also convinced that there are times when it is entitled to constitutional protection. . . .

There remains room for vigorous debate about the outcome of particular cases that are not necessarily resolved by the opinions announced today. How such cases may be decided will depend on their specific facts. In my judgment, however, it is clear that the so called "unqualified interest in the preservation of human life," . . . is not itself sufficient to outweigh the interest in liberty that may justify the only possible means of preserving a dying patient's dignity and alleviating her intolerable suffering.

Justice Souter, concurring in the judgment.

. . . Legislatures [in contrast to courts] have superior opportunities to obtain the facts necessary for a judgment about the present controversy. Not only do they have more flexible mechanisms for fact finding than the Judiciary, but their mechanisms include the power to experiment, moving forward and pulling back as facts emerge within their own jurisdictions. There is, indeed, good reason to suppose that in the absence of a judgment for respondents here, just such experimentation will be attempted in some of the States. . . .

. . . Sometimes a court may be bound to act regardless of the institutional preferability of the political branches as forums for addressing constitutional claims. . . . Now, it is enough to say that our examination of legislative reasonableness should consider the fact that the Legislature of the State of Washington is no more obviously at fault than this Court is in being uncertain about what would happen if respondents prevailed today. We therefore have a clear question about which institution, a legislature or a court, is relatively more competent to deal with an emerging issue as to which facts currently unknown could be dispositive. The answer has to be, for the reasons already stated, that the legislative process is to be preferred. There is a closely related further reason as well.

One must bear in mind that the nature of the right claimed, if recognized as one constitutionally required, would differ in no essential way from other constitutional rights guaranteed by enumeration or derived from some more definite textual source than "due process." An unenumerated right should not therefore be recognized, with the effect of displacing the legislative ordering of things, without the assurance that its recognition would prove as durable as the recognition of those other rights differently derived. To recognize a right of lesser promise would simply create a constitutional regime too uncertain to bring with it the expectation of finality that is one of this Court's central obligations in making constitutional decisions. . . .

Legislatures, however, are not so constrained. The experimentation that should be out of the question in constitutional adjudication displacing legislative judgments is entirely proper, as well as highly desirable, when the legislative power addresses an emerging issue like assisted suicide. The Court should accordingly stay its hand to allow reasonable legislative consideration. While I do not decide for all time that respondents' claim should not be recognized, I acknowledge the legislative institutional competence as the better one to deal with that claim at this time

Justice Ginsburg, concurring in the judgments. . . .

Justice Breyer, concurring in the judgments.

. . . I agree with the Court . . . that the articulated state interests justify the distinction drawn between physician assisted suicide and withdrawal of life support. I also agree with the Court that the critical question in both of the cases before us is whether "the 'liberty' specially protected by the Due Process Clause includes a right" of the sort that the respondents assert. . . . I do not agree, however, with the Court's formulation of that claimed "liberty" interest. The Court describes it as a "right to commit suicide with another's assistance." . . . But I would not reject the respondents' claim without considering a different formulation, for which our legal tradition may provide greater support. That formulation would use words roughly like a "right to die with dignity." But irrespective of the exact words used, at its core would lie personal control over the manner of death, professional medical assistance, and the avoidance of unnecessary and severe physical suffering . . .

I do not believe . . . that this Court need or now should decide whether or a not such a right is "fundamental." That is because, in my view, the avoidance of severe physical pain (connected with death) would have to comprise an essential part of any successful claim and because, as Justice O'Connor points out, the laws before us do not force a dying person to undergo that kind of pain. . . . Rather, the laws of New York and of Washington do not prohibit doctors from providing patients with drugs sufficient to control pain despite the risk that those drugs themselves will kill. . . . And under these circumstances the laws of New York and Washington would overcome any remaining significant interests and would be justified, regardless.

Medical technology, we are repeatedly told, makes the administration of pain relieving drugs sufficient, except for a very few individuals for whom the ineffectiveness of pain control medicines can mean, not pain, but the need for sedation which can end in a coma. . . . We are also told that there are many instances in which patients do not receive the palliative care that, in principle, is available, . . . but that is so for institutional reasons or inadequacies or obstacles, which would seem possible to overcome, and which do not include a prohibitive set of laws. . . .

This legal circumstance means that the state laws before us do not infringe directly upon the (assumed) central interest (what I have called the core of the interest in dying with dignity) as, by way of contrast, the state anticontraceptive laws . . . did interfere with the central interest there at stake—by bringing the State's police powers to bear upon the marital bedroom.

Were the legal circumstances different—for example, were state law to prevent the provision of palliative care, including the administration of drugs as needed to avoid pain at the end of life—then the law's impact upon serious and otherwise unavoidable physical pain (accompanying death) would be more directly at issue. And as Justice O'Connor suggests, the Court might have to revisit its conclusions in these cases.

12

EQUAL PROTECTION AND THE ANTIDISCRIMINATION PRINCIPLE

"Our constitution is color-blind, and neither knows nor tolerates classes among citizens. In respect of civil rights all are equal before the law."

—JUSTICE JOHN M. HARLAN (THE ELDER),

  DISSENTING IN *PLESSY V. FERGUSON* (1896)

John M. Harlan (the elder): Associate Justice,
1877–1911

INTRODUCTION

One of the philosophical foundations of American democracy is the idea that all individuals are equal before the law. This ideal is expressed both in the Declaration of Independence and in the **Equal Protection Clause** of the Fourteenth Amendment, which provides that no state shall "deny to any person within its jurisdiction the equal protection of the laws." The Equal Protection Clause prohibits states from denying any person or class of persons the same protection and rights that the law extends to other similarly situated persons or classes of persons.

Like other rights guaranteed by the post-Civil War amendments, the Equal Protection Clause was motivated in large part by a desire to protect the civil rights of African-Americans recently freed from slavery. However, the text of the clause makes no mention of race; rather, it refers to "any person" within the jurisdiction of a state. Although the Supreme Court attempted initially to limit the scope of the Equal Protection Clause to discrimination claims brought by African-Americans (see *The Slaughter-House Cases* [1873] and *Strauder v. West Virginia* [1880]), it has developed into a broad prohibition against unreasonable governmental discrimination directed at any identifiable group.

In the late nineteenth century, the Supreme Court declared that the word "person" in the Equal Protection Clause included corporations (see *Santa Clara County v. Southern Pacific Railroad Company* [1886]). Occasionally, the clause was employed as a basis for invalidating discriminatory business regulation (see *Yick Wo v. Hopkins* [1886]). In the modern era, the Equal Protection Clause has been invoked successfully to challenge discrimination against racial and ethnic minorities, as well as discrimination against women, the poor, illegitimate children, the mentally retarded, illegal aliens, and, most recently, gay men and lesbians. Under the **New Equal Protection**, the Supreme Court has used the Equal Protection Clause to scrutinize closely any state law or practice that discriminates among groups in their enjoyment of **fundamental rights.** Without question, the scope of the Equal Protection Clause has been expanded far beyond the expectations of its authors. Along with the Due Process Clause of the Fourteenth Amendment, the Equal Protection Clause has become the principal basis for challenging the constitutionality of a broad range of state laws, actions, and policies.

The "Equal Protection Component" of the Fifth Amendment

Because the Fourteenth Amendment applies only to the states, and because the Bill of Rights contains no explicit equal protection provision, does it follow that the national government is under no constitutional obligation to provide equal protection of the laws? The Supreme Court has answered this question emphatically in the negative, "finding" an "equal protection component" in the Due Process Clause of the Fifth Amendment. The Court has concluded that the values underlying the equal protection guarantee are embraced within the broad definition of due process of law (see *Bolling v. Sharpe* [1954]). Since the Fourteenth Amendment contains a Due Process Clause virtually identical to that found in the Fifth Amendment, one might conclude that the Equal Protection Clause of the Fourteenth Amendment is superfluous. Although this may be true in a formal, logical sense, the Equal Protection Clause was the historic basis for judicial scrutiny of governmental policies challenged as discriminatory. In the absence of the Equal Protection Clause, such scrutiny would have been more difficult to justify.

LEVELS OF JUDICIAL SCRUTINY IN EQUAL PROTECTION CASES

Although the adoption and early development of the Equal Protection Clause must be understood in the context of the historic struggle for racial equality in this country, courts have over the years entertained a variety of equal protection claims going well beyond issues of racial discrimination. The Supreme Court has developed a set of standards for judging the constitutionality of policies that are challenged on equal protection grounds.

The Rational Basis Test

State and federal laws are replete with discriminations, or "classifications," of various kinds. Yet very few of these classifications are considered constitutionally offensive. For example, a state law that requires a person to possess a license to practice psychiatry discriminates against those persons who are unable to meet the qualifications necessary to obtain a license. Yet few would question the reasonableness of such discrimination. Similarly, when the state limits the driving privilege to persons aged 16 and older, it is engaging in age discrimination. But, again, few would challenge the reasonableness of such discrimination.

The traditional test employed by courts in judging challenged legislative classifications is the **rational basis test** (first articulated by the Supreme Court in *Gulf, Colorado, & Santa Fe Railway Company v. Ellis* [1897]). Under this deferential approach, the burden is on the party challenging the statute to show that (1) the purpose of the challenged discrimination is an illegitimate state objective and (2) the means employed by the state are not rationally related to the achievement of its objective. Thus, for example, the state law requiring psychiatrists to be licensed reflects a legitimate state interest in protecting the public health and safety and is rationally related to that end. The rational basis test remains the primary test for determining the constitutionality of classifications that impinge on economic interests.

As noted in previous chapters, during the age of conservative activism (1890–1937), the Supreme Court emphasized the protection of private property against government regulation and redistribution. The Equal Protection Clause played a limited role in this protection, as the Court relied more heavily on the Due Process Clauses of the Fifth and Fourteenth Amendments. During the laissez-faire period, Justice Oliver Wendell Holmes, Jr., trivialized the significance of the Equal Protection Clause by characterizing it as "the usual last resort of constitutional arguments" (*Buck v. Bell* [1927]).

In the wake of the constitutional revolution of 1937, the locus of Supreme Court activism moved away from the protection of economic individualism. Instead, the post-New Deal Court focused its attention on civil rights and liberties, especially the rights of traditionally disadvantaged minorities. In a famous footnote to his opinion in *United States v. Carolene Products Company* (1938), Justice Harlan Fiske Stone stated that "prejudice against discrete and insular minorities may be a special condition, which tends seriously to curtail the operation of those political processes ordinarily to be relied upon to protect minorities and . . . may call for a more searching judicial scrutiny."

The Court's desire to protect **discrete and insular minorities** who lack political clout in Congress and/or the state legislatures resulted in numerous controversial decisions concerning the rights of the accused, prisoners, aliens (legal and illegal), persons with disabilities, and unorthodox religious sects. The Equal Protection Clause figured prominently in this process. In expanding the scope of the Equal Protection Clause, the Court developed a style of analysis that to a great extent superseded the traditional rational basis test.

The Suspect Classification Doctrine

Korematsu v. United States (1944) provided the first real indication that the Court was embarking on a new approach to the Equal Protection Clause. In *Korematsu,* the Court upheld the constitutionality of the "relocation" of Japanese-Americans living on the West Coast during the Second World War (for further discussion and excerpts from the opinions, see Chapter 3). In his majority opinion, Justice Hugo Black stated that

> all legal restrictions which curtail the civil rights of a single group are immediately suspect. That is not to say that all such restrictions are unconstitutional. It is to say that courts must subject them to the most rigid scrutiny. Pressing public necessity may sometimes justify the existence of such restrictions; racial antagonism never can.

It is now widely recognized that no compelling justification supported the relocation order. However, the majority in *Korematsu* apparently did not have full access to information, later made public, clearly indicating that the relocation order stemmed more from racial prejudice than from military necessity.

Although on its face the *Korematsu* decision was hardly a victory for civil rights, it marked the inception of the **suspect classification doctrine**, which holds that certain kinds of discrimination are inherently suspect and therefore must be subjected to **strict judicial scrutiny.** Included among those laws that are inherently suspect are those that classify persons based on race, religion, or ethnicity, as well as those that impinge on fundamental rights.

Operationally speaking, strict judicial scrutiny means that the ordinary **presumption of constitutionality** is reversed; the government carries the **burden of proof** that its challenged policy is constitutional. To carry that burden, government must show that its policy is necessary to the achievement of a **compelling interest** and that it is "narrowly tailored" to further that interest.

Although judicial tests are far from precise, in that courts seldom define the terms that comprise these tests, the compelling interest test is generally understood to be far more stringent than the traditional rational basis test. Using the suspect classification doctrine, the Court has invalidated, explicitly or implicitly, virtually all public policies that overtly discriminate among persons on the basis of their race (see, for example, *Loving v. Virginia* [1967]). In the Court's view, it is virtually impossible for government to have a compelling interest that would require or justify racial or ethnic discrimination.

Judging the Disparate Impact of Facially Neutral Policies

The suspect classification doctrine applies only to policies that overtly discriminate on the basis of race, religion, or ethnicity. What standard should be applied to judge policies that are neutral on their face but have disparate impacts on people of different races? In *Washington v. Davis* (1976), the Supreme Court considered a challenge to the practice of requiring applicants to the District of Columbia police department to pass a verbal skills test that was used widely in the federal civil service. African-American applicants were approximately four times as likely to fail this test as were white applicants. The Court rejected the argument that the testing requirement should be subjected to strict scrutiny under the suspect classification doctrine. Writing for the Court, Justice Byron White said:

> A rule that a statute designed to serve neutral ends is nevertheless invalid, absent compelling justification, if in practice it benefits or burdens one race more than another would be far-reaching and would raise serious questions about, and perhaps invalidate, a whole range of tax, welfare, public service, regulatory and licensing statutes.

Under *Washington v. Davis* and similar decisions, a policy that is racially neutral on its face but has a **disparate impact** on people of different races will be upheld unless plaintiffs can show that it was adopted to serve a racially discriminatory purpose.

Heightened Scrutiny

To complicate matters further, the Supreme Court has developed still another level of equal protection review, falling somewhere between the rational basis test and the suspect classification doctrine. This approach, often described as **heightened scrutiny**, has been applied most prominently, but not exclusively, to gender discrimination claims. Under this approach, government must show that a challenged policy bears a "substantial" relationship to an "important" government interest. How exactly this test differs from either the less stringent rational basis test or the more stringent compelling interest test is difficult to articulate.

Thus, there are currently three tiers of review for judging equal protection claims. Shortly before his retirement in 1991, Justice Thurgood Marshall suggested that the Court adopt a "sliding scale" that would embrace a "spectrum of standards" of review. Others on the Court have been put off by what they regard as needless doctrinal complexity. Justice John Paul Stevens, for example, has argued for a return to the rational basis standard, which he believes to be adequate to invalidate all invidious forms of discrimination. Others on the Court, most notably Chief Justice Rehnquist, are dissatisfied with the modern Court's special solicitude for the claims of discrete and insular minorities. Given the conservative character of the contemporary Supreme Court, we can anticipate significant doctrinal changes in the Court's equal protection jurisprudence.

TO SUMMARIZE:

- The Supreme Court has developed three tiers of review for determining whether challenged policies violate the Equal Protection Clause.
- The most lenient approach is the *rational basis test*. In this test, the burden is on the party challenging the policy to show that its purpose is illegitimate and/or that the means employed are not rationally related to the achievement of the government's objective.
- The Court employs *strict scrutiny* in judging policies that discriminate on the basis of race, religion, or national origin, classifications that are deemed to be "inherently suspect." In such cases the burden is on the government to show that its challenged policy is narrowly tailored to the achievement of a compelling governmental interest.
- In cases involving claims of gender discrimination and in certain other areas, the Court employs *heightened scrutiny* in which government must show that a challenged policy bears a "substantial" relationship to an "important" government interest.

THE STRUGGLE FOR RACIAL EQUALITY

Although the Equal Protection Clause is now recognized as a broad shield against arbitrary government action, little doubt exists that the Fourteenth Amendment was adopted primarily to protect the rights of the newly freed former slaves. Specifically, the Fourteenth Amendment was designed to provide constitutional authority for newly enacted federal civil rights legislation aimed at ending discrimination against

Federal Civil Rights Statutes Enacted during Reconstruction

During the Reconstruction Era, Congress passed four major civil rights acts. Some provisions of these statutes remain important components of contemporary civil rights law.

THE CIVIL RIGHTS ACT OF 1866. This act provided that citizens of all races have the same rights to make and enforce contracts, to sue and give evidence in the courts, and to own, purchase, sell, rent, and inherit real and personal property. For modern counterparts, see 42 U.S. Code, Sections 1981 and 1982.

THE CIVIL RIGHTS ACT OF 1870. Also known as the Ku Klux Klan Act, this statute made it a federal crime to conspire to "injure, oppress, threaten or intimidate any citizen in the free exercise of any right or privilege secured to him by the Constitution or laws of the United States." For modern counterpart, see 18 U.S. Code, Section, 241. The statute also criminalized any act under color of state law

that subjects persons to deprivations of constitutional rights. See 18 U.S. Code, Section 242.

THE CIVIL RIGHTS ACT OF 1871. This statute made individuals acting under color of state law personally liable for acts violating the constitutional rights of others. Civil actions under this statute are commonly referred to as "Section 1983 actions" because the act is codified at 42 U.S. Code, Section 1983. The 1871 act also permitted civil suits against those conspiring to violate the civil rights of others (codified at 42 U.S. Code, Section 1985).

THE CIVIL RIGHTS ACT OF 1875. This statute forbade denial of equal rights and privileges by places of public accommodation. It was declared invalid as applied to privately owned public accommodations in *The Civil Rights Cases* (1883). Access to public accommodations was ultimately achieved under Title II of the Civil Rights Act of 1964.

African-Americans. Section 5 of the Fourteenth Amendment gives Congress the power to enforce, "by appropriate legislation," the abstract promises of the Equal Protection Clause and other provisions of the amendment.

Early Interpretations of the Equal Protection Clause

Shortly before the Fourteenth Amendment was ratified, Congress passed the **Civil Rights Act of 1866**, which, among other things, protected the right of African-Americans to inherit, own, and convey property. In the wake of the Civil War, many of the southern states had adopted **Black Codes,** which denied such basic economic rights to former slaves. Under the new Civil Rights Act, violation of these rights was made a federal offense where it could be shown that the violator was acting "under color of state law." Apparently having some reservations about the constitutionality of this law, Congress rushed to adopt the Fourteenth Amendment, believing that the Equal Protection Clause of Section 1 together with the enforcement provision of Section 5 would provide an adequate constitutional basis for far-ranging civil rights legislation.

***The Civil Rights Cases* (1883)**   While the modern Supreme Court recognizes broad congressional power under the Fourteenth Amendment, the Supreme Court's early view of congressional authority in the field of civil rights was much more restrictive. In adopting the **Civil Rights Act of 1875**, Congress made a serious attempt to eradicate racial discrimination in **places of public accommodation**, including hotels, taverns, restaurants, theaters, and "public conveyances." In *The Civil Rights Cases* (1883), however, the Supreme Court struck down the key provisions of this act, ruling that the Fourteenth Amendment limited congressional action to the prohibition of official, state-sponsored discrimination as distinct from discrimination practiced by privately owned places of public accommodation. The Supreme Court's decision in *The Civil Rights Cases* may have been motivated by a desire to promote reconciliation between North and South and between the federal and state governments. Unfortunately, any such reconciliation was achieved at the expense of African-Americans.

Adoption of Jim Crow Laws

Not only did the Court's decision in *The Civil Rights Cases* preserve widespread practices of racial discrimination in restaurants, hotels, and the like, but it was also regarded as a green light for the passage of legislation mandating strict racial segregation. The so-called **Jim Crow laws** adopted in the aftermath of *The Civil Rights Cases* required segregation in virtually every area of public life. They required blacks and whites to attend separate schools, to use separate parks, to ride in separate railroad cars, and even to be buried in separate cemeteries. Perhaps the most ludicrous of the many Jim Crow laws required white and black witnesses in court to take their oaths on separate Bibles!

The Separate but Equal Doctrine

In *Plessy v. Ferguson* (1896), the Supreme Court upheld racial segregation in the context of public transportation. The Court's ruling provided a rationale for government-mandated segregation on a broad scale. At issue in *Plessy* was an 1890 Louisiana law requiring passenger trains operating within the state to provide "equal but separate" accommodations for the "white and colored races." Homer Plessy, who was considered "colored" under Louisiana law because one of his great-grandparents was black, was ordered to leave a railroad car reserved for whites. Plessy, who intended to challenge the constitutionality of the law, refused to vacate his seat and was arrested. Dividing 7 to 1 (Justice David Brewer not participating), the Court sustained the Louisiana statute. Writing for the majority, Justice Henry Billings Brown asserted that "in the nature of things, [the Fourteenth Amendment] could not have been intended to abolish distinctions based upon color, or to enforce social, as distinguished from political, equality, or a commingling of the two races upon terms unsatisfactory to either."

In one of the most widely quoted opinions in American constitutional law, Justice John M. Harlan (the elder) dissented vehemently. For Justice Harlan, ironically a former Kentucky slave owner, the "arbitrary separation of citizens on the basis of race" was tantamount to imposing a "badge of servitude" on the Negro race. He asserted that "our Constitution is color-blind, and neither knows nor tolerates classes among citizens."

The **separate but equal doctrine** approved in *Plessy* remained the authoritative interpretation of the Equal Protection Clause for fifty-eight years. Ultimately, of course, it was repudiated by the Supreme Court in *Brown v. Board of Education of Topeka* (1954). The **state action doctrine** announced in *The Civil Rights Cases* remains authoritative to this day—and in fact not until the 1960s was Congress willing or able to prohibit discrimination in places of public accommodation. When Congress did finally act in passing the **Civil Rights Act of 1964**, it chose to rely primarily on its broad powers under the Commerce Clause, rather than on Section 5 of the Fourteenth Amendment (see Chapter 2).

The net effect of *The Civil Rights Cases* and *Plessy v. Ferguson* was to defer the dream of legal and political equality for African-Americans for nearly a century after ratification of the Fourteenth Amendment. During this period, racial discrimination was simply a way of life for many Americans, both black and white. Even today, although considerable progress toward racial equality has been achieved, racial discrimination and hatred have by no means disappeared from American society.

The Decline of de Jure Racial Segregation

The Court's decision in *Plessy v. Ferguson* rested on two obvious fictions: (1) that racial segregation conveyed no negative statement about the status of African-Americans and (2) that separate accommodations and facilities for blacks were in fact equal to those reserved for whites. Blacks, and no doubt whites as well, knew better. As time went by, it became increasingly obvious to the Supreme Court that the separate but equal doctrine was a mere rationalization for relegating African-Americans to second-class citizenship.

In a series of cases decided between 1938 and 1950, the Supreme Court chipped away at the separate but equal doctrine, as applied to higher education, without repudiating the doctrine altogether. In *Missouri ex rel. Gaines v. Canada* (1938), the Court mandated the admission of a qualified African-American resident of Missouri to the state university law school. The Court held that a state could not escape its obligation by making provisions for its African-American students to attend out-of-state law schools. The Supreme Court reaffirmed its holding in *Gaines* a decade later in *Sipuel v. Oklahoma Board of Regents* (1948). Two years later, in *McLaurin v. Oklahoma State Regents* (1950), the Court disallowed an attempt by the University of Oklahoma to segregate a black graduate student from his white colleagues after he was admitted pursuant to a court order. In class, the student, McLaurin, was required to sit in a row of desks restricted to blacks. In the cafeteria, he was required to eat alone at a particular table. He was restricted to a designated table in the library. He was even prohibited from visiting his professors during their regular office hours in order to minimize his interactions with white students. In the Court's view, this isolation significantly detracted from McLaurin's educational experience and thus could not be justified under the separate but equal doctrine.

In *Sweatt v. Painter* (1950), the Court considered an attempt by the state of Texas to provide a separate law school for African-Americans. The Court found that the newly created law school at the Texas College for Negroes was substantially inferior, in terms of both measurable and intangible factors, to the white-only law school at the University of Texas.

Desegregation

By the early 1950s, it was clear that the Supreme Court would no longer tolerate the provision of demonstrably inferior educational services or facilities to African-Americans under the aegis of the separate but equal doctrine. But considerable uncertainty remained, both within and outside the Court, as to whether the justices would, or should, abandon the *Plessy* doctrine altogether. The NAACP mounted a major challenge to segregated public schools, instituting lawsuits in four states and the District of Columbia. These cases were first argued before the Supreme Court in 1952, but because of the political magnitude of the issue presented, the Court directed that the cases be reargued in 1953. Before the second round of oral argument, Chief Justice Fred M. Vinson died and was succeeded by Earl Warren.

The *Brown* Decision

Finally, on May 17, 1954, the uncertainty regarding segregated public schools came to an end when the Court handed down its landmark decision in *Brown v. Board of*

Education. In one of the most important decisions in its history, the Court unanimously struck down racial segregation in the public schools of Kansas, South Carolina, Delaware, and Virginia. Speaking for the Court in *Brown,* Chief Justice Warren declared that "in the field of public education, the doctrine of 'separate but equal' has no place. Separate educational facilities are inherently unequal." Thus, in a concise and forceful opinion, the Warren Court abandoned a long-standing constitutional precedent and precipitated a revolution in public education.

In a companion case, *Bolling v. Sharpe,* the Court held that the operation of segregated schools by the District of Columbia violated the Due Process Clause of the Fifth Amendment. Here, as noted at the beginning of this chapter, the Court recognized an "equal protection component" in the Fifth Amendment due process requirement, indicating that uniform antidiscrimination mandates were to be applied to the federal government as well as the states.

Implementation of *Brown*

The *Brown* decision of 1954 left open the question of how and when desegregation would have to be achieved. In a follow-up decision in 1955 (referred to as *Brown II*), the Court blunted the revolutionary potential of the original decision by adopting a formula calling for implementation of **desegregation** with "all deliberate speed." Recognizing that compliance would be more difficult to achieve in the South than in other sections of the country, the Court left it up to federal district judges to apply this formula, taking into account the particular circumstances characterizing race relations within their respective jurisdictions. This approach ensured great diversity in the implementation of *Brown I* and invited the use of delaying tactics by state and local officials. Despite its concern for the difficulties public officials would face in bringing about desegregation, the Court was reviled in many quarters for "meddling" in state and local affairs. Some of the Court's harsher critics went so far as to call for the impeachment of Chief Justice Warren.

Some of the more extreme critics of school desegregation called for militant noncompliance with the Court's directive. John Kasper, a well-known white supremacist and self-styled protégé of the fascist poet Ezra Pound, went around the country preaching the use of violence and intimidation to prevent black students from entering formerly all-white public schools. In the late summer of 1956, Kasper went to Clinton, Tennessee, where he succeeded in fomenting violent resistance to court-ordered integration of Clinton High School. In late August, Kasper was ordered by federal judge Robert Taylor "to cease hindering, obstructing, or in any wise interfering" with court-ordered integration. Kasper persisted in his efforts, and Clinton experienced a turbulent fall replete with riots, beatings, death threats directed at various school officials, and harassment of African-American students. After the National Guard was called in to restore order, Kasper was arrested and convicted for violating the federal court injunction. Ultimately, peace returned to Clinton, and desegregation proceeded apace.

The Little Rock Crisis In one of the best known and most dramatic efforts to resist the Supreme Court's desegregation decisions, Arkansas Governor Orval Faubus called out the National Guard in 1957 to prevent nine African-American students from entering Little Rock Central High School. The Guard was soon withdrawn, but an angry mob of whites continued to harass the black students. President Dwight D. Eisenhower, who had expressed serious reservations about the *Brown* decision, nevertheless intervened with federal troops to quell the violence and enforce the court-ordered integration. In *Cooper v. Aaron* (1958), the Court delivered a sharp rebuke to Arkansas officials who had attempted to frustrate the Court's mandate (see Chapter 1). One wonders, however, if the Court's language in *Cooper v. Aaron* would have been so strong in the absence of Eisenhower's intervention in Little Rock.

The Court Repudiates "All Deliberate Speed" In efforts less dramatic than what transpired in Little Rock, state and local governments intent on avoiding desegregation adopted a strategy of "legislate and litigate" that delayed universal compliance with *Brown* for well over a decade. But in *Alexander v. Holmes County* (1969), after many years of delay, the Supreme Court finally abandoned the permissive "all deliberate speed" policy and ordered desegregation "at once." This set the stage for the busing controversy of the 1970s.

The Busing Controversy

As previously noted, the Supreme Court's *Brown II* decision left the implementation of school desegregation largely to the discretion of federal district judges. Of the various measures that these judges employed in dismantling dual school systems, "forced busing" was by far the most controversial. In *Swann v. Charlotte-Mecklenburg Board of Education* (1971), the Supreme Court unanimously approved the use of **court-ordered busing** to achieve the goal of desegregation. In 1973, the Court turned its attention to school desegregation outside the South. In *Keyes v. Denver School District,* the Court, with only Justice Rehnquist dissenting, found **de jure discrimination** where a series of administrative decisions in the 1960s had helped to maintain racially segregated public schools in the city of Denver. Thus, in *Keyes,* as in *Swann,* the Supreme Court upheld a busing plan imposed by a federal district court.

As court-ordered busing became more pervasive, it erupted into a major political issue. In the 1972 presidential campaign, candidate George Wallace exploited the busing issue quite successfully, goading incumbent Richard Nixon into taking a stronger antibusing posture than he had previously maintained. Perhaps as a reaction to widespread criticism of *Swann* and *Keyes,* as well as antibusing rumblings in Congress, the Supreme Court backed away from busing in the case of *Milliken v. Bradley* (1974). *Milliken* involved a challenge to a court-ordered desegregation plan for greater Detroit that involved busing students across school district lines within the metropolitan area. Although *Milliken* by no means overturned *Swann* and *Keyes,* a 5-to-4 majority of the justices held that court-ordered busing of students across school district lines is permissible only if all affected districts had been guilty of past discriminatory practices. By thus limiting interdistrict busing plans, the Supreme Court placed substantial limits on this approach to school desegregation in metropolitan areas.

To the proponents of racial busing, the decision in *Milliken* was an unfortunate retreat from the Court's long-standing commitment to integration. For others, *Milliken* was a welcome concession to public opinion, which was generally negative toward busing. Clearly, the effect of the *Milliken* decision was to defuse much of the harsh criticism that had previously been directed at the Court over the busing issue. Nevertheless, interdistrict busing schemes continued to be ordered by federal judges where interdistrict violations were uncovered. In the unfortunate case of Boston, interdistrict busing in 1974 produced intense hostility and violence.

The use of busing to achieve desegregation continues to this day, although it is not as pervasive as it was in the early 1970s. Indeed, African-American intellectuals and educators no longer uniformly support busing. Some reject what they regard as a racist implication that black children cannot improve themselves without exposure to white children. Clearly, the political and intellectual impetus behind racial busing has diminished dramatically. Consequently, busing is no longer a salient political issue. The Supreme Court continues to hear cases in this area, but the major thrust of current litigation is toward the termination, rather than the continued implementation, of busing and related desegregation plans. In a significant 1991 decision, *Board of Education v. Dowell,* the Court granted federal district courts clear authority to terminate desegregation orders provided that two conditions are met: (1) that the local school board in question has complied in good faith with the desegregation decree, and (2) that all vestiges of prior discrimination have been effectively removed. The *Dowell* decision left many questions unanswered, but the Court made it clear that judicial supervision of school desegregation is, after all, temporary in nature.

In *Freeman v. Pitts* (1992) the Supreme Court amplified its decision in *Dowell* by permitting a federal district court that for many years had supervised desegregation of the DeKalb County, Georgia, schools to relinquish supervision over certain aspects of school administration. The Court held that district judges have discretion to relinquish supervision of school systems where racial imbalances stemming from de jure segregation have disappeared, even if schools remain "racially identifiable" due to demographic factors. Under the approach taken in *Dowell* and *Freeman,* local school districts that show good-faith efforts to comply with court-mandated desegregation plans will eventually regain full control of their school systems.

The Kansas City Desegregation Case In *Missouri v. Jenkins* (1995), the Supreme Court reviewed a federal district judge's efforts to desegregate the Kansas City school system. The plan would redistribute the students within the system, and also included magnet schools to attract nonminority students from outside the Kansas City Metropolitan School District. Splitting 5 to 4, the Supreme Court invalidated the judge's order, finding interdistrict reassignment to be excessive and abusive of the district court's remedial powers. The Court also instructed the lower court to review the rest of its remedial orders under the stricter level of scrutiny articulated in *Freeman v. Pitts* (1992). Writing for the Court, Chief Justice Rehnquist reminded the district court "that its end purpose is not only 'to remedy the violation' to the extent practicable, but also 'to restore state and local authorities to the control of a school system that is operating in compliance with the Constitution.'"

In her concurring opinion in *Jenkins,* Justice O'Connor emphasized the narrowness of the Court's holding. In contrast, Justice Thomas's twenty-seven-page concurring opinion launched a broadside against desegregation jurisprudence: "Given that desegregation has not produced the predicted leaps forward in black educational achievement, there is no reason to think that black students cannot learn as well when surrounded by members of their own race as when they are in an integrated environment." Thomas also attacked the "virtually unlimited" power of federal district judges to craft desegregation remedies: "Federal courts simply cannot gather sufficient information to render an effective decree, have limited resources to induce compliance, and cannot seek political and public support for their remedies. When we presume to have the institutional ability to set effective educational, budgetary, or administrative policy, we transform the least dangerous branch into the most dangerous one."

Dissenting in *Jenkins,* Justice Souter noted that state and local officials "intentionally created this segregated system of education, and subsequently failed to correct it." Clearly, in Souter's view, officials "defaulted in their obligation to uphold the Constitution." In remedying the violation, the district court must be accorded broad latitude. It must be "authorized to remedy all conditions flowing directly from the constitutional violations committed by state or local officials, including the educational deficits that result from a segregated school system." Justice Souter was joined in this view by Justices Ginsburg, Breyer, and Stevens. In her separate dissent, Justice Ginsburg sounded a cautionary note: "Given the deep, inglorious history of segregation in Missouri, to curtail desegregation at this time and in this manner is an action at once too swift and too soon."

TO SUMMARIZE:

- Although the Equal Protection Clause is now recognized as a broad shield against arbitrary governmental action, little doubt exists that the Fourteenth Amendment was adopted primarily to protect the rights of the newly freed former slaves.
- The Supreme Court was slow to take up the cause of civil rights, and in early cases refused to use the Fourteenth Amendment to invalidate racial discrimination and segregation. The Warren Court, most notably in *Brown v. Board of Education* (1954), made civil rights a major priority and in so doing wrought major changes in American politics and society.
- Section 5 of the Fourteenth Amendment gives Congress the power to enforce, "by appropriate legislation," the abstract promises of the Equal Protection Clause and other provisions of the amendment. In the wake of the Civil War, Congress adopted a number of important civil rights statutes. In the modern era, Congress has continued to rely on Section 5 of the Fourteenth Amendment in legislating in the civil rights field.
- *Brown v. Board of Education* was the beginning of a process of desegregating public schools, a process that involved considerable resistance from supporters of segregation and numerous legal controversies over busing of students and federal judicial supervision of many public school systems.

THE AFFIRMATIVE ACTION CONTROVERSY

The furor over court-ordered busing that occurred during the 1970s had largely subsided by the late 1980s. But as usually happens in American politics, a new ongoing controversy emerged to take its place. The controversy involves **affirmative action**, a broad term referring to a variety of efforts designed to assist members of traditionally disfavored minority groups. The affirmative action concept is manifested in three major areas of distributive policy: employment, government contracts, and higher education. Affirmative action actually emerged through executive orders handed down during the Kennedy, Johnson, and Nixon administrations of the 1960s and early 1970s. Initially, it was limited to the requirement that federal government contractors make increased efforts to recruit minority employees. Thereafter, state higher education programs were subjected to affirmative action guidelines as a condition of accepting federal subsidies. Soon federal and state courts were adopting **race-conscious remedies** (for example, racial busing) in resolving desegregation lawsuits. Eventually, what began as little more than a public exhortation became a series of goals, quotas, and timetables designed to integrate African-Americans, Hispanics, Native Americans, and other traditionally disfavored minorities into the economic and educational mainstream.

Although the ultimate objective of affirmative action was, and is, universally applauded, the means of achieving it—quotas, formulas, and ratios based on immutable racial characteristics—are distasteful to many and appear downright unjust to others. To many critics, affirmative action represents an unfortunate degeneration of the noble ideal of equality of opportunity into "statistical parity." For some legal critics, affirmative action is a violation of the color-blind Constitution idealized by Justice Harlan's dissent in *Plessy v. Ferguson*. Still others, some of them members of nonpreferred ethnic minorities, object to affirmative action not on principle but because they have not been given preferred status. Yet, the many defenders of affirmative action characterize it as the only practicable means of realizing the American dream for those who have been traditionally locked out.

Competing Models of Justice

Affirmative action is problematic legally because it involves two competing models of racial justice. One theory views race discrimination and its appropriate remedies in terms of identifiable groups. Under this theory, all individuals properly belonging to a traditionally disfavored minority are entitled to partake of a remedy. The competing individualistic theory holds that remedies are to be provided only to those individuals who can show that they have been the targets of invidious discrimination. The conflict can also be viewed as one between contemporary politics and traditional principles of law. In the contemporary pluralistic political process, we are accustomed to thinking in terms of group interests. However, our system of law rests on a foundation of individualism and does not easily accommodate the concept of **group rights.**

Naturally, people on all sides of the affirmative action controversy looked to the Supreme Court for a settlement of the issue. The Supreme Court initially avoided the constitutionality of affirmative action when it decided *DeFunis v. Odegaard* (1974), holding that the question presented in this case was moot.

The *Bakke* and *Fullilove* Cases

Eventually, however, the Supreme Court did hand down a ruling on affirmative action, but *Regents of the University of California v. Bakke* (1978) could hardly be regarded as a definitive resolution of the issue. Alan Bakke, a 37-year-old white male engineer, brought suit to challenge the affirmative action policy of the medical school at the University of California-Davis (Cal-Davis). Bakke had been denied admission to the medical school, although his objective indicators (that is, Medical College Admission Test score and grade point average) were better than those of several of the sixteen minority students admitted under a **set-aside** policy. The California Supreme Court found this to be a violation of equal protection and ordered Bakke to be admitted to the medical school. Seeking a more authoritative resolution of the issue, the university appealed. Bakke ultimately won the appeal, completed his medical school program, and is now a practicing anesthesiologist.

In a fragmented decision, the Court voted 5 to 4 to invalidate the Cal-Davis quota system and admit Alan Bakke to medical school. However, also by a 5-to-4 margin, the Court endorsed affirmative action in the abstract, by recognizing race as a legitimate criterion of admission to medical school. According to Justice Lewis Powell's controlling opinion in *Bakke,* the state has a compelling interest in achieving diversity in its medical school, and this interest justifies the use of race as one of several criteria of admission. However, the use of a rigid quota system

> tells applicants who are not Negro, Asian or Chicano that they are totally excluded from a specific percentage of the seats in an entering class. No matter how strong their qualifications, quantitative and extracurricular, including their own potential for contribution to educational diversity, they are never afforded the chance to compete with applicants from the preferred groups for the special admissions seats.

For Justice Powell, this was the fatal flaw in the Cal-Davis affirmative action plan. Powell's brethren were less equivocal. Four members of the Court—Burger, Stewart, Rehnquist, and Stevens—would have declared the entire policy to be in violation of the Civil Rights Act, which, in their judgment, requires government to observe a standard of color-blindness. On the other hand, Justices Brennan, Marshall, White, and Blackmun found no statutory or constitutional violation in the minority "set-aside" policy. According to Justice William Brennan, "[g]overnment may take race into account when it acts not to demean or insult any racial group, but to remedy disadvantages cast on minorities by past racial prejudice."

An equally equivocal endorsement of affirmative action was provided by the Supreme Court in *Fullilove v. Klutznick* (1980). In *Fullilove,* the Court upheld a federal public works program that provided a 10 percent set-aside of federal funds for "minority business enterprises." Because this case involved an act of Congress, rather than state action, the set-aside policy was challenged as a violation of the equal protection component of the Fifth Amendment Due Process Clause. The Supreme Court upheld the minority set-aside by a vote of 6 to 3. Unfortunately, as in *Bakke,* the Court was unable to produce a majority opinion. Chief Justice Warren Burger's plurality opinion stressed Congress's broad powers under Section 5 of the Fourteenth Amendment but stopped far short of providing a wholesale endorsement of affirmative action. In a concurring opinion, Justice Brennan echoed the strong pro-affirmative action position he had taken in *Bakke:*

> [The] principles outlawing the irrelevant or pernicious use of race [are] inapposite to racial classifications that provide benefits to minorities for the purpose of remedying the present effects of past racial discrimination. Such classifications may disadvantage some whites, but whites as a class lack the "traditional indicia of suspectness: the class is not saddled with such disabilities, or subjected to such a history of purposeful unequal treatment, or relegated to such a position of political powerlessness as to command extraordinary protection from the majoritarian political process."

Justice Stewart, joined by Justice Rehnquist, cited Justice Harlan's *Plessy* dissent as a barrier to any sort of race preferences, while Justice Stevens's dissenting opinion focused on Congress's failure to demonstrate that remedial preferences were being bestowed on a truly disadvantaged class. The Court's failure to produce majority opinions in *Bakke* and *Fullilove* compounded the uncertainties surrounding the myriad affirmative action policies in effect by the early 1980s.

The Rehnquist Court Curtails Affirmative Action

In the wake of *Bakke* and *Fullilove,* the Supreme Court continued to grapple with the affirmative action issue, most notably through a series of decisions interpreting the federal civil rights statutes. In general, the Court continued to support various affirmative action programs (see, for example, *Steelworkers v. Weber* [1979], *Sheet Metal Workers v. Equal Employment Opportunity Commission* [1986], *Firefighters v. Cleveland* [1986], and *Johnson v. Transportation Agency of Santa Clara* [1987]).

Despite its apparent acceptance of affirmative action, the Court placed limits on the scope of affirmative action policies—for example, by refusing to allow affirmative action objectives to override seniority in determining layoffs (see *Memphis Firefighters v. Stotts* [1984]). The Court also held that, if their interests are adversely affected, white employees may challenge the legality of affirmative action plans that are established under **consent decrees,** even if they were not parties to the original litigation (*Martin v. Wilks* [1989]).

The biggest change in the perspective of the Court in this area came in *City of Richmond v. J. A. Croson Company* (1989), when the Rehnquist Court dealt a serious blow to affirmative action. In 1983, the Richmond City Council passed an ordinance requiring that construction companies awarded city contracts in turn award at least 30 percent of their subcontracts to minority-owned business enterprises. A plumbing contractor, the J. A. Croson Company, sued the city in federal court, arguing that the set-aside was unconstitutional. The federal district court upheld the ordinance, relying heavily on the Supreme Court's earlier decision in *Fullilove v. Klutznick.* The Court of Appeals reversed, however, and the city of Richmond asked the Supreme Court to review the case.

The personnel on the High Court in 1989 had changed significantly since *Fullilove,* of course. Justice Stewart had been replaced by Justice Sandra Day O'Connor in 1981.

Justice Antonin Scalia had joined the Court after Chief Justice Burger retired, and Justice Rehnquist became chief justice in 1986. Justice Anthony Kennedy joined the Court in 1988 after the retirement of Justice Powell. These personnel changes produced a shift in the ideological character of the Court, moving it substantially to the right. It was no surprise, therefore, that the Court, voting 6 to 3, struck down the Richmond set-aside plan. Writing for the Court, Justice O'Connor noted that "[t]he Richmond Plan denies certain citizens the opportunity to compete for a fixed percentage of public contracts based solely upon their race." After reviewing the relevant history and facts, Justice O'Connor concluded that

> the city has failed to demonstrate a compelling interest in apportioning public contracting opportunities on the basis of race. To accept Richmond's claim that past societal discrimination alone can serve as the basis for rigid racial preferences would be to open the door to competing claims for "remedial relief" for every disadvantaged group. The dream of a Nation of equal citizens in a society where race is irrelevant to personal opportunity and achievement would be lost in a mosaic of shifting preferences based on inherently unmeasurable claims of past wrongs.

In a bitter dissent, Justice Marshall (joined by Justices Brennan and Blackmun) characterized the decision as a "deliberate and giant step backward" and "a full-scale retreat from the Court's long-standing solicitude to race-conscious remedial efforts." Marshall predicted that the decision would "inevitably discourage or prevent governmental entities, particularly States and localities, from acting to rectify the scourge of past discrimination."

In her *Croson* opinion, Justice O'Connor attempted to distinguish the Richmond set-aside plan from the congressional program that the Court had approved in *Fullilove v. Klutznick.* O'Connor emphasized the broad powers of Congress under Section 5 of the Fourteenth Amendment, indicating that municipalities lack equally broad powers. Many critics of the *Croson* decision found this distinction unpersuasive. Students reading *Croson* and *Fullilove* should consider whether the two cases can in fact be distinguished from one another.

It is interesting to speculate as to how the Supreme Court would have decided *Fullilove* if that case had come to the Court in 1989, instead of 1980. As the Court became even more conservative with the departures of Justices Marshall and Brennan and the arrival of Justices Souter and Thomas, many commentators thought that the *Croson* case was the beginning of a process of dismantling affirmative action policies.

Those who believed that affirmative action was on the way out were surprised when the Supreme Court decided *Metro Broadcasting v. Federal Communications Commission* (FCC) in 1990. In *Metro Broadcasting* the Court upheld an FCC affirmative action policy designed to foster increased minority participation in the broadcasting industry. From a jurisprudential point of view, the significance of *Metro Broadcasting* was the distinction the Court drew between state and local affirmative action programs on the one hand and federal affirmative action programs on the other. Relying on *Fullilove v. Klutznick,* the Court said in effect that federal affirmative action programs were entitled to a greater presumption of validity. The Court said that federal affirmative action programs are "constitutionally permissible to the extent that they serve important governmental objectives within the power of Congress and are substantially related to achievement of those objectives." Obviously, this was a more lenient approach than the Court took in the *Croson* case.

Five years later the Court repudiated *Metro Broadcasting* and the approach it embodied. In *Adarand Constructors, Inc. v. Peña* (1995), the Court held that one standard of review should govern all affirmative action programs, whether local, state, or federal.

The *Adarand* case dealt with federal highway contracts. Under a policy of the U.S. Department of Transportation, general contractors were given a financial incentive to hire subcontractors controlled by "socially and economically disadvantaged individuals." Even though it submitted a lower bid, Adarand Constructors was passed over as a subcontractor on a federal highway project in favor of a company that received preferred status under the affirmative action policy. Adarand unsuccessfully argued in the lower courts that federal affirmative action programs should be subjected to the same standard applied to state and local programs.

In a 5-to-4 decision, the Supreme Court sent the case back to the trial court for reconsideration. Writing for the Court, Justice O'Connor held that "all racial classifications, imposed by whatever federal, state, or local governmental actor, must be analyzed by a reviewing court under strict scrutiny. In other words, such classifications are constitutional only if they are narrowly tailored measures that further compelling governmental interests." But O'Connor also recognized that, given sufficient justification, a racial preference might be sustained: "The unhappy persistence of both the practice and the lingering effects of racial discrimination against minority groups in this country is an unfortunate reality, and government is not disqualified from acting in response to it." Dissenting, Justice Stevens argued that "[i]nvidious discrimination is an engine of oppression, subjugating a disfavored group to enhance or maintain the power of the majority. Remedial race-based preferences reflect the opposite impulse: a desire to foster equality in society. No sensible conception of the Government's constitutional obligation to 'govern impartially,' should ignore this distinction."

In their separate concurring opinions, Justices Scalia and Thomas stated their unequivocal opposition to affirmative action. Their position did not prevail in *Adarand,* but it could command a majority in some future case. Although the *Adarand* decision did not sound the death knell for affirmative action, it increased the likelihood that federal affirmative action programs will be challenged and invalidated.

The *Hopwood* Case In *Hopwood v. Texas* (1995), the Fifth U.S. Circuit Court of Appeals struck down an affirmative action program at the University of Texas law school. In an effort to obtain an entering class consisting of at least 10 percent Mexican-Americans and 5 percent blacks, the law school established lower test-score standards and created a separate admissions process for black and Mexican-American applicants. The court of appeals ruled that this system violated the rights of four unsuccessful white applicants. In a move that startled many observers, the court went further and held that the Supreme Court's landmark 1978 *Bakke* decision was no longer good law. In *Hopwood,* the Fifth Circuit court flatly stated that "the law school may not use race as a factor in law school admissions." This decision created a firestorm of controversy among civil rights groups and within higher education. Many commentators hoped and expected that the Supreme Court would grant certiorari. The Clinton administration, the District of Columbia, and nine states filed *amicus curiae* briefs in support of Texas's cert petition. But the Supreme Court was unmoved, denying cert on the closing day of the 1995 term. Two of the Court's more liberal members, Justices Ginsburg and Souter, produced a brief opinion stating that although affirmative action "is an issue of great national importance," the case presented no live controversy because the program that motivated the lawsuit to begin with had been discontinued. The denial of cert left the *Hopwood* decision intact, but *Hopwood* applies only within the three states (Texas, Louisiana, and Mississippi) that comprise the Fifth Circuit. This created an unusual legal situation in that while institutions of higher education in the Fifth Circuit are barred from using race as a criterion in their admissions, other colleges and universities across the country are under court order to do exactly that! Eventually, the Supreme Court will be compelled to take up this matter in order to standardize the law on this controversial issue.

Proposition 209   Buoyed by recent federal judicial decisions, opponents of affirmative action in California in 1996 succeeded in passing an amendment to the state constitution banning race and gender preferences in hiring and educational admissions. Proposition 209 provides that state and local government agencies in California may not discriminate against or grant preferential treatment to any individual or group on the basis of race, sex, color, ethnicity, or national origin. Within days after Proposition 209 was adopted by popular referendum, opponents went to federal court and obtained an injunction against its enforcement. But the federal district court eventually upheld the measure, as did the Ninth Circuit Court of Appeals. The Coalition for Economic Equity, which brought the suit, backed by civil rights groups across the country, asked the Supreme Court to grant review. But, as in the *Hopwood* case, the Court denied cert, at least in part because the controversy remained abstract (see *Coalition for Economic Equity v. Wilson* [1997]).

The Piscataway Case   In 1989, Sharon Taxman, a white teacher in Piscataway, New Jersey, was laid off so that the school board could retain a black teacher in the same department. The two teachers had been hired on the same date and were judged by supervisors to be equally qualified. Thus race was the only factor accounting for the school board's decision to lay off Taxman while retaining her black colleague. Taxman sued in federal court, claiming "reverse discrimination." The board defended its action by asserting that race-based personnel decisions could be justified in order to promote faculty diversity. In ruling in Taxman's favor, the 3rd Circuit Court of Appeals held that the only justification for race-based affirmative action was to remedy documented past discrimination. The school board petitioned the Supreme Court for certiorari and the Court granted review. At this point civil rights groups became concerned that the Court would use the case to review and possibly reverse its 1978 *Bakke* decision. After civil rights groups agreed to contribute more than two-thirds of the $433,500 needed to pay Taxman's back salary and legal bills, the school board voted to settle the case and Taxman agreed. The Supreme Court then dismissed the case.

The Court's failure to review the *Hopwood,* Prop 209, and Piscataway cases frustrated those who wished to see a definitive resolution of the affirmative action question. But the Court was merely exercising self-restraint in not deciding an issue before it was necessary to do so. Eventually, however, the Court will have to confront these issues squarely. When it does, the outcome will depend, as always, on who is on the Court at the time.

TO SUMMARIZE:

- Affirmative action is a broad term referring to a variety of efforts designed to assist members of traditionally disfavored minority groups. It is manifested in three major areas of distributive policy: employment, government contracts, and higher education.
- The affirmative action concept emerged in the 1960s, and by the 1970s it was a major topic of litigation chiefly initiated by those who challenged it as "reverse discrimination."
- The Burger Court sought middle ground in the affirmative action area, approving the basic concept but rejecting its more rigid applications.
- The Rehnquist Court has taken a more negative view of affirmative action but has not repudiated the concept altogether.

GENDER-BASED DISCRIMINATION

Women are hardly a "discrete and insular minority." In fact, they comprise a majority of the adult population. Nevertheless, women have been historically subjected to considerable legal discrimination. Some of this discrimination was ostensibly benign, reflecting the paternalism of a patriarchal society. Not only were women once thought unfit to vote or hold public office, they were also regarded as in need of special protection from a cruel world. Thus, some **gender-based classifications** actually benefited females and burdened males. For example, a number of states, and the federal government for a time, maintained minimum-wage requirements for women but not for men. Most graphically, women have traditionally been exempted from compulsory military service.

Until very recently, the Supreme Court refused to recognize even the most blatant forms of sex discrimination as constitutionally offensive. In *Bradwell v. Illinois* (1873), the Court upheld an Illinois law that prohibited women from practicing law. Similarly, in *Minor v. Happersett* (1875), the Court held that women had no constitutional right to vote. Even as late as 1948, the Court upheld a Michigan law that prohibited women from serving as bartenders (see *Goesaert v. Cleary*). These decisions reflected broader societal attitudes that relegated women, much like African-Americans, to a position of social inferiority and second-class citizenship.

The Second World War did much to change the social status of women. Women in great numbers left the home and entered the industrial workplace, often assuming jobs many thought they were incapable of handling. By the 1970s, women had begun to compete with men for managerial and professional positions. Although women are still on average paid less than men, even for equal work, society has come to accept women in the workplace. Society is also learning to accept women in political roles: in Congress, in state legislatures, as mayors, governors, presidential candidates, and as justices of the Supreme Court. Naturally, the changing role of women is accompanied by demands for legal equality.

Congressional Responses to Demands for Sexual Equality

Congress responded to growing demands for legal equality between the sexes by passing the Equal Pay Act of 1963, the 1972 Amendments to Title VII of the Civil Rights Act of 1964, and Title IX of the Federal Education Act of 1972. The first and second of these statutes were aimed at eliminating sex discrimination in the workplace. The third authorized the withholding of federal funds from educational institutions that engaged in sex discrimination. These statutes have been an important source of civil rights for women and have given rise to a number of significant Supreme Court decisions. For example, in *Meritor Savings Bank v. Vinson* (1986), the Court held that Title VII of the Civil Rights Act of 1964 bars **sexual harassment** on the job.

The Equal Rights Amendment   In 1972, Congress attempted to broaden legal protection of women's rights by adopting a constitutional amendment that read as follows:

Section 1. Equality of rights under the law shall not be denied or abridged by the United States or by any State on account of sex.

Section 2. The Congress shall have the power to enforce, by appropriate legislation, the provisions of this article.

Section 3. This amendment shall take effect two years after the date of ratification.

Like all constitutional amendments, the **Equal Rights Amendment** (ERA) had to be ratified by at least three-fourths of the states to become part of the Constitution. Initially, the ERA met with much enthusiasm and little controversy in the state legislatures. By 1976, it had been ratified by thirty-five of the necessary thirty-eight states. However, in the late 1970s, opposition to the ERA crystallized in those states that had yet to ratify. Although Congress extended the period for ratification until 1982, the amendment ultimately failed to win approval by the requisite number of states.

Judicial Scrutiny of Gender-Based Discrimination

The demise of the Equal Rights Amendment left constitutional interpretation in the field of sex discrimination largely in the domain of the Fourteenth Amendment. In the early 1970s, it appeared that the Supreme Court was going to add sex to the list of "suspect classifications" under the Fourteenth Amendment. In *Reed v. Reed* (1971), the Court struck down a provision of the Idaho Probate Code that required probate judges to prefer males to females in appointing administrators of estates. Writing for the majority in *Reed,* Chief Justice Burger noted that "to give a mandatory preference to members of either sex over members of the other . . . is to make the very kind of arbitrary legislative choice forbidden by the Equal Protection Clause."

In *Frontiero v. Richardson* (1973), the Supreme Court divided 8 to 1 (Justice Rehnquist dissenting) in upholding Lt. Sharron Frontiero's claim that the Air Force violated the equal protection component of the Fifth Amendment in requiring women, but not men, to demonstrate that their spouses were in fact dependents for the purpose of receiving medical and dental benefits. While the Court was receptive to the equal protection claim, it was unable to achieve majority support for the proposition that sex is a suspect classification. Expressing the views of four members of the Court, Justice Brennan's plurality opinion was unequivocal in declaring gender-based discrimination to be inherently suspect and thus presumptively unconstitutional:

> [S]ince sex, like race and national origin, is an immutable characteristic determined solely by the accident of birth, the imposition of special disabilities upon the members of a particular sex because of their sex would seem to violate "the basic concept of our system that legal burdens should bear some relationship to individual responsibility."

The remaining four members of the majority were not prepared to go so far. In an opinion concurring in the judgment only, Justice Powell wrote that "[i]t is unnecessary for the Court in this case to characterize sex as a suspect classification, with all of the far-reaching implications of such a holding."

Heightened Scrutiny   As yet, the Supreme Court has not recognized sex discrimination as inherently suspect. It should be noted, however, that some state courts have applied strict scrutiny analysis to gender-based classifications (see, for example, the California Supreme Court's decision in *Hardy v. Stumpf* [1978]). While it has not adopted strict scrutiny for gender discrimination cases, the U.S. Supreme Court has invalidated a number of gender-based policies under a "heightened scrutiny" or "intermediate scrutiny" approach. For example, in *Weinberger v. Wiesenfeld* (1975), the Court unanimously voided a provision of the Social Security Act that authorized survivors' benefits for the widows of deceased workers but withheld them for men in the same situation. Similarly, in *Califano v. Goldfarb* (1977), a sharply divided Court struck down another Social Security requirement that widowers, but not widows, had to demonstrate their financial dependence on their deceased spouses as a condition for obtaining survivors' benefits.

In *Craig v. Boren* (1976), the Court articulated a test for judging gender-based policies under the intermediate standard of review. According to this test, a gender-based policy must be substantially related to an important government objective. Presumably, this test is stricter than the rational basis test but less strict than the compelling state interest test.

In *Craig v. Boren*, the Court struck down an Oklahoma law that forbade the sale of "3.2" beer to females under the age of 18 and males under 21. Oklahoma attempted to justify the statute as a means of promoting its interest in traffic safety, citing data that were purported to show that men in the 18–21 age bracket were more likely to be arrested for drunk driving than were women in the same age bracket. Unpersuaded by the statistical evidence, the Court held that the state had failed to demonstrate a substantial relationship between its sexually discriminatory policy and its admittedly important interest in traffic safety. In a sharp dissent, Justice Rehnquist challenged the new intermediate standard of equal protection review. In Rehnquist's view, the terms "important objective" and "substantial relation" were so "elastic as to invite subjective judicial preferences or prejudices." Despite this criticism, the Court has maintained the intermediate standard of review for gender-based policies.

In *Orr v. Orr* (1979), the Court considered the question of differential alimony requirements for men and women. The Alabama law in question required divorced men, under certain circumstances, to make alimony payments to their ex-wives but exempted women in the same circumstances from paying alimony to their ex-husbands. Somewhat disingenuously, the state argued that its gender-based alimony policy was designed to compensate women for economic discrimination produced by the institution of marriage. The Court accepted the state's asserted interest as both legitimate and important but rejected the argument that its alimony policy was substantially related to the achievement of this objective. Writing for the Court, Justice Brennan asserted that

> Alabama's alleged compensatory purpose may be effectuated without placing burdens solely on husbands. Progress toward fulfillment of such a purpose would not be hampered, and it would cost the state nothing more, if it were to treat men and women equally by making alimony burdens independent of sex. . . . Thus, "[t]he [wives] who benefit from the disparate treatment are those who were . . . nondependent on their husbands. . . ." They are precisely those who are not "needy spouses" and who are the "least likely to have been victims of discrimination" by the institution of marriage.

The preceding sample of cases is not meant to suggest that the Supreme Court's sex-discrimination decisions have uniformly cut in one direction. On the contrary, the flexible approach to sex discrimination employed by the Court has resulted in a number of decisions upholding challenged gender-based policies. For example, in *Kahn v. Shevin* (1974), the Court let stand a Florida statute that gave property tax exemptions to widows but not widowers. According to Justice William O. Douglas's majority opinion, the distinction was

> reasonably designed to further the state policy of cushioning the financial impact of spousal loss upon the sex for which that loss imposes a disproportionately heavy burden. . . . The financial difficulties confronting the lone woman in Florida or any other state exceed those facing the man.

The same year, in *Geduldig v. Aiello* (1974), the Court upheld a state health insurance policy that excluded pregnancy from the list of disabilities for which a state employee could be compensated. In approving the policy, the Court concluded that it did not discriminate

> against any definable group or class in terms of the aggregate risk protection derived by the group or class from the program. There is no risk from which men are protected and women are not. Likewise, there is no risk from which women are protected and men are not.

Not surprisingly, a number of observers took issue with the Court's assumption that a state's refusal to extend its disability policy to include pregnancy was **gender-neutral.**

One of the most controversial issues in the area of sex discrimination is the role that women should play in military service. Opponents of the Equal Rights Amendment argued that adoption of the amendment would result in women being drafted into combat, a prospect that many people still find unacceptable. In *Rostker v. Goldberg* (1981), the Supreme Court considered the constitutionality of the male-only draft registration law. Emphasizing its traditional deference to Congress in the area of military affairs, the Court upheld the challenged policy by a vote of 6 to 3. Writing for the majority, Justice Rehnquist asserted that exclusion of women from the draft "was not an 'accidental by-product of a traditional way of thinking about women.'" According to Justice Rehnquist, men and women "are simply not similarly situated for purposes of a draft or registration for a draft." No doubt many women and men would challenge Rehnquist's assumption, especially in light of the expanded role women played in the war against Iraq in early 1991.

It is difficult to say with any precision what principles have guided the Court's treatment of sex discrimination cases under the intermediate scrutiny approach. Perhaps each decision rests on each justice's intuitive sense of whether the challenged discrimination is "benign" or "invidious." As Justice Oliver Wendell Holmes, Jr., pointed out in his dissent in *Lochner v. New York* (1905), judicial decisions often "depend on a judgment or intuition more subtle than any articulate major premise." What Holmes was suggesting was that judicial decision making is preeminently political behavior: that any exercise in legal methodology is subordinate to the assertion of judicial values. While this position can be overstated, one cannot examine the history of American constitutional decision making and deny the essential validity of Holmes's observation.

Sex Discrimination by Educational Institutions

In perhaps the most significant of its sex discrimination decisions, the Burger Court voted 5 to 4 to require the Mississippi University for Women (MUW) to admit a male student to its nursing school (*Mississippi University for Women v. Hogan* [1982]). Joe Hogan was a registered nurse working in Columbus, the city where MUW is located. Lacking a bachelor's degree, he applied for admission to the MUW nursing program and was denied solely on account of sex, although the school did inform him that he could register on a noncredit basis. Rather than quit his job to enroll in another state institution, Hogan filed suit. The state of Mississippi argued that operating a school solely for women compensated for sex discrimination in the past. Additionally, the state argued that the presence of men would detract from the performance of female students. Writing for the Supreme Court, Justice O'Connor gave both of the state's arguments short shrift. Justice O'Connor rejected the "compensation" argument as contrived since the state had made no showing that women had historically lacked opportunities in the field of nursing. O'Connor then pointed out that the state's argument that male students would adversely affect the performance of females was undermined by the university's willingness to accept male students as auditors. In O'Connor's view, the principal effect of the female-only nursing program was to "perpetuate the stereotyped view of nursing as an exclusively women's job."

In a strongly worded dissent, Justice Powell asserted that the Court's decision adversely affected the opportunities of women by forbidding the "States from providing women with an opportunity to choose the type of university they prefer." Powell further suggested that the Court's decision "bows deeply to conformity."

The *Hogan* decision addressed the question of whether state-operated professional schools could limit enrollment to one sex. It did not address the broader question of whether publicly operated or supported educational institutions generally may constitutionally impose such restrictions. Of course, the only two state-supported institutions of higher education that limited enrollment to members of one sex were military schools: the Citadel in Charleston, South Carolina, and Virginia Military Institute (VMI) in Lexington. In the wake of the *Hogan* decision, young women seeking admission to these institutions brought suit in federal court. Ultimately, they prevailed.

The VMI Case   In one of the most widely anticipated decisions of the 1990s, *United States v. Virginia* (1996), the Supreme Court struck down VMI's male-only admissions policy. In so doing, the Court closed the book on a case that had been in litigation for nearly six years. The suit had been brought by the Justice Department, after a complaint was filed by a female high school student who wanted to go to VMI but was barred from doing so by the Institute's prohibition against admitting women.

In a 7-to-1 decision, the Supreme Court, speaking through Justice Ginsburg, ruled that the state of Virginia had "fallen far short of establishing the 'exceedingly persuasive justification,' that must be the solid base for any gender-defined classification." Although the Court rejected the argument advanced by the Clinton administration that sex discrimination should be subjected to the same "strict scrutiny" the courts apply to race discrimination, Justice Ginsburg's opinion suggested that the current Court has increased the level of scrutiny applied to policies that treat men and women differently. According to Ginsburg, the Court should apply a "skeptical scrutiny" under which government must demonstrate an "exceedingly persuasive justification" for any gender discrimination. "The justification must be genuine, not hypothesized or invented *post hoc* in response to litigation," said Ginsburg. Moreover, it must not rely on "overbroad generalizations about the different talents, capacities, or preferences of males and females."

Although technically applicable only to the VMI case, the decision in *United States v. Virginia* affected the resolution of a similar widely publicized case involving the Citadel in South Carolina. In fact, within days after the VMI decision was announced, the Citadel's governing board voted unanimously to eliminate sex as a criterion for admission, ending a 154-year tradition of admitting only men.

The sweeping character of the Court's opinion seemed to imply that it would be extremely difficult for any state to defend any single-sex educational institution. Chief Justice Rehnquist, who concurred in the judgment only, adopted a more restrained position. For Rehnquist, the state had failed in its obligation to provide equal protection because it had not demonstrated any serious effort to provide comparable opportunities to women who were interested in the kind of "citizen-soldier" training that men receive at VMI. According to Rehnquist, it was "not the 'exclusion of women' that violate[d] the Equal Protection Clause, but the maintenance of an all-men school without providing any—much less a comparable—institution for women." Rehnquist's opinion left open the possibility that single-sex public higher education might, under certain circumstances, pass constitutional muster. Of course, Rehnquist's concurrence is just one person's opinion. Six justices representing the Court's liberal and moderate blocs clearly wanted to make a stronger and a more definitive statement.

In another of his scathing dissents, Justice Scalia asserted that the majority's "amorphous 'exceedingly persuasive justification' phrase" was an unwarranted departure from the "heightened scrutiny" test used by the Court in gender-discrimination cases. Scalia concluded by lamenting the fact that, in his view, "single-sex public education is functionally dead." Scalia expressed his regret that the Court had, in his view, "shut down an institution that has served the people of the commonwealth of Virginia with pride and distinction for over a century and a half." He ended by observing that "I do not think any of us, women included, will be better off for its destruction."

Not surprisingly, Justice Scalia's sentiments were shared by students, faculty, and administrators at VMI. Major General Josiah Bunting III, the superintendent of VMI, described the Court's decision as a "savage disappointment." Of course, women's rights groups hailed the decision as a major victory.

Gender Equity in Collegiate Athletics

Intercollegiate athletics, once the sole province of men, has witnessed considerable change in recent years. Under the rubric of **gender equity**, state colleges and universities have been putting more resources into women's athletic programs. Still, there are some who believe that forbidding women to participate in male-only athletic programs at state institutions constitutes invidious discrimination. Is the separate but equal doctrine appropriate when considering collegiate athletics? Suppose a female student wants to play football at a state university. Since the university does not have a women's football program, does the Equal Protection Clause require the university to let the woman try out for the men's team? While some may feel that such issues trivialize the Constitution, these matters tend to be far from trivial in the minds of plaintiffs.

TO SUMMARIZE:

- Since the 1970s, the Supreme Court has recognized that the Equal Protection Clause imposes significant restrictions on official discrimination on the basis of gender.
- The failure to ratify the Equal Rights Amendment left the issue of gender discrimination solely within the province of the Equal Protection Clause as interpreted by the courts.
- The Court has applied an intermediate standard of review in judging classifications based on gender, often finding that such classifications merely perpetuate sex-based stereotypes.
- The Court's most important decisions in this area have focused on discrimination against women in the military and in public institutions of higher education.

OTHER FORMS OF DISCRIMINATION

Today, the only suspect classifications that have been identified by the Supreme Court are those based on race, national origin, and religious affiliation. As previously noted, gender-based classifications, which are the subject of much current controversy, have not been added to the inventory of suspect classifications. Rather, sex discrimination, along with illegitimacy and alienage, occupies a middle tier in what has become a complex, multitiered approach to judging challenged classifications. The Court has addressed other bases of discrimination, notably age and disability, using the traditional rational basis test. The Court's decisions in the areas of age and disability have focused largely on the power of Congress under Section 5 of the Fourteenth Amendment to combat discrimination.

Age Discrimination

The Supreme Court first dealt with age discrimination as a constitutional matter in the 1976 case of *Massachusetts Board of Retirement v. Murgia*. The case involved a state law requiring uniformed police officers to retire at age 50. In upholding the statute, the Court explicitly recognized the rational basis test as the appropriate one for judging claims of age discrimination. The Court reasoned that physical fitness requirements for police officers could reasonably be linked to a mandatory retirement age. The Court held 8-0 (Justice Stevens not participating) that mandatory retirement was rationally related to the State's legitimate objective of protecting the public by assuring that police officers are physically fit.

In 2000, the Court returned to the age discrimination problem in the context of its recent emphasis on issues of federalism. *Kimel v. Board of Regents* involved the application of the Age Discrimination in Employment Act of 1967 to state employers. The specific question was whether Congress could abrogate states' sovereign immunity by authorizing state employees to sue their state employers for damages stemming from allegations of age discrimination. In a sharply divided 5-to-4 decision, the Court answered this question in the negative. In her majority opinion, Justice O'Connor concluded:

> A review of the ADEA's legislative record as a whole, then, reveals that Congress had virtually no reason to believe that state and local governments were unconstitutionally discriminating against their employees on the basis of age. Although that lack of support is not determinative of the § 5 inquiry, . . . Congress' failure to uncover any significant pattern of unconstitutional discrimination here confirms that Congress had no reason to believe that broad prophylactic legislation was necessary in this field. In light of the indiscriminate scope of the Act's substantive requirements, and the lack of evidence of widespread and unconstitutional age discrimination by the States, we hold that the ADEA is not a valid exercise of Congress' power under § 5 of the Fourteenth Amendment. The ADEA's purported abrogation of the States' sovereign immunity is accordingly invalid.

In dissent, Justice Stevens (joined by Justices Souter, Ginsburg, and Breyer) objected to the Court's narrow view of Congress's enforcement powers under Section 5 of the Fourteenth Amendment:

> Congress' power to regulate the American economy includes the power to regulate both the public and the private sectors of the labor market. Federal rules outlawing discrimination in the workplace, like the regulation of wages and hours or health and safety standards, may be enforced against public as well as private employers. In my opinion, Congress' power to authorize federal remedies against state agencies that violate federal statutory obligations is coextensive with its power to impose those obligations on the States in the first place.

Persons with Disabilities

Although persons with disabilities can be viewed as constituting a "discrete and insular minority," policies and practices that discriminate against such persons have not been recognized as "inherently suspect" under the Fourteenth Amendment. Nor has the Supreme Court yet held that the Constitution imposes an obligation on government to equalize physical access for persons with disabilities to government buildings or other physical facilities. Arguably, a government's failure to provide a wheelchair ramp at a place where votes are cast could be viewed as an unreasonable burden on the exercise of a "fundamental right." Congress has attempted to increase access to the polls for persons with disabilities through passage of the Voting Accessibility Act of 1984. For the most part Congress, not the Supreme Court, has taken the lead in recognizing the rights of persons with disabilities. With the passage of Title V of the Rehabilitation Act of 1973, the Education for All Handicapped Children Act of 1975, and especially the **Americans with Disabilities Act** of 1990, Congress has attempted to remove barriers confronting persons with disabilities in such areas as employment, education, and public transportation. Some commentators have criticized the Supreme Court for narrowly interpreting legislation in this field, thus constraining the rights of persons with disabilities. Others believe Congress and the courts have gone too far in this area, creating difficult problems for local governments, school systems, and businesses.

Certainly the Supreme Court has not been completely insensitive to the rights of individuals with disabilities. For example, in *Cleburne v. Cleburne Living Center* (1985), the Court struck down a zoning law that had been applied to prohibit a home for persons with mental retardation from operating in a residential neighborhood. Justice White's majority opinion not only rejected the argument that retardation is a suspect classification but also rejected the lower court's characterization of retardation as "quasi-suspect." Opting for the traditional standard of review, Justice White nevertheless found no rational basis for the city's decision. The *Cleburne* case demonstrates that the rational basis standard is not necessarily synonymous with judicial tolerance of discrimination.

The Court's most important recent disability rights decision is *Board of Trustees of the University of Alabama v. Garrett* (2001). As in the previously discussed case of *Kimel v. Board of Regents* (2000), the Court addressed the problem of discrimination on the basis of disability within the larger constitutional context of federalism. Again dividing 5 to 4, the justices ruled that Congress lacked the power to authorize suits for damages brought against the states by their employees on the basis of allegations of disability discrimination. In this highly controversial decision, the Court pointed out that other avenues of legal relief remained open to state employees who experience discrimination based on disability. These include the possibility of obtaining injunctions against state officials in federal court as well suits for damages brought under state laws.

Illegitimacy

Although laws discriminating against persons based on **illegitimacy** have not been declared to be inherently suspect, blatant instances of this type of discrimination have been invalidated. For example, in *Weber v. Aetna Casualty and Surety Company* (1972), the Supreme Court struck down a Louisiana law barring illegitimate offspring from collecting death benefits under workers' compensation. And in *Jimenez v. Weinberger* (1974), the Court invalidated a federal provision that denied welfare benefits to the illegitimate dependent children of disabled persons. However, in a case reminiscent of the landmark sex discrimination case *Reed v. Reed* (1971), the Court upheld a law subordinating illegitimate offspring to other relatives in determining intestate succession (*Labine v. Vincent* [1971]). And in *Lalli v. Lalli* (1978), the Court upheld a law allowing illegitimate children to inherit from their intestate fathers only if paternity had been judicially determined during the lifetime of the deceased.

More recently, in *Michael H. v. Gerald D.* (1989), the Court upheld a California statute that created a legal presumption that a child born to a married woman living with her husband is the product of that marriage, thus making it more difficult for natural fathers of children who are the product of extramarital affairs to establish paternity. While clear principles are difficult to discern in this area, the Court has not hesitated to invalidate laws it perceives to be based solely on prejudice against illegitimate children. At the same time, however, it has recognized the primacy of the nuclear family and the social undesirability of producing children outside of wedlock.

Residency and Alienage

The Fifth and Fourteenth Amendments do not protect citizens alone from arbitrary or unjust government actions. Rather, the amendments use the broader term "persons." The Supreme Court has stressed the text of the Fourteenth Amendment in striking down a number of state laws that differentiate between residents and nonresidents or between citizens and aliens. For example, in *Shapiro v. Thompson* (1969), the Supreme Court struck down a series of laws that imposed one-year waiting periods on new state residents seeking welfare benefits. Then, in *Sugarman v. McDougall* (1973), the Court struck down a New York law that denied civil service jobs to aliens. In 1976, the Court extended this ruling to invalidate similar federal civil service restrictions (*Hampton v. Mow Sun Wong*).

In a controversial 1982 decision, the Supreme Court went so far as to invalidate discrimination against the children of illegal aliens. In *Plyler v. Doe,* the Court voted 5 to 4 to strike down a Texas law that denied free public education to the children of illegal immigrants. Using heightened scrutiny, Justice Brennan found no "substantial interest" of the state to justify the denial of educational benefits to the children of illegal aliens. Dissenting sharply, Chief Justice Burger complained that "if ever a court was guilty of an unabashedly result-oriented approach, this case is a prime example." The Court's decisions in *Shapiro v. Thompson* and *Plyler v. Doe* involved not merely the distinction between residents and nonresidents or between legal residents and illegal aliens, they also implicated the underlying issue of poverty.

Wealth, Poverty, and Equal Protection

Discrimination based on wealth has never been held to be inherently suspect, although some justices on the Supreme Court have indicated a desire to do so. However, the Court has often invalidated forms of economic discrimination that prevent individuals from exercising their constitutional rights. Wealth-based discriminations that burden fundamental rights have been subjected to strict judicial scrutiny; those that do not involve fundamental rights have been judged by the traditional rational basis test. For example, in the case of *Shapiro v. Thompson,* described above, the Court found that the state residency requirement infringed the fundamental right of interstate travel. Similarly, in *Harper v. Virginia State Board of Elections* (1966), the Supreme Court invalidated a state's poll tax as a denial of equal protection. Certainly the imposition of a tax on voting can be seen as a burden on the exercise of a fundamental right (see Chapter 13).

In *Gideon v. Wainwright* (1963), the Court, relying on the Sixth Amendment right to counsel, required states to appoint counsel for indigent defendants accused of felonies. On the same day, in *Douglas v. California,* the Court required states to provide counsel to indigent defendants seeking appellate review in state courts. These wealth discrimination rulings of the Warren Court were closely related to the maintenance of procedural due process in the context of criminal prosecutions (see Chapter 10).

To what extent does the Equal Protection Clause require the equalization of services or benefits provided by state and local governments? Can a city's provision of public goods, such as roads, sewage systems, parks, and recreational facilities, vary according to neighborhood property tax revenues? The answer depends on whether such discriminations involve fundamental rights or "interests." But which interests are "fundamental"? Is education a fundamental right?

The Controversy over Public School Funding   In *San Antonio Independent School District v. Rodriguez* (1973), the Court considered a challenge to the Texas system of financing public schools primarily through local property taxes. The Texas system, which is similar to that employed in most states, resulted in dramatically different amounts of money being spent among the state's school districts. In reviewing the Texas system of school funding, a sharply divided Court employed the traditional rational basis test, refusing to recognize wealth as a suspect classification. Using this approach, the Court found no constitutional violation. According to Justice Powell's majority opinion, the school finance system

> allegedly discriminates against a large, diverse, and amorphous class, unified only by the common factor of residence in districts which happen to have less taxable wealth than other districts. The system of alleged discrimination and the class it defines have none of the traditional indicia of suspectness; the class is not saddled with such disabilities, or subjected to such history of purposeful unequal treatment, or relegated to such a position of political powerlessness as to command extraordinary protection from the majoritarian political process.

Justice Marshall protested vehemently in *Rodriguez,* arguing that education was a "fundamental interest" and that "poverty" was indeed a "suspect classification." According to Justice Marshall:

> [The] Court has never suggested that because some "adequate" level of benefits is provided to all, discrimination in the provision of services is therefore constitutionally excusable. The Equal Protection Clause is not addressed to the minimal sufficiency but to the unjustifiable inequalities of state action.

The Supreme Court's interpretation of the Fourteenth Amendment in *Rodriguez* in no way prevents state courts from adopting a contrary view of the relevant provisions of their state constitutions. Indeed, the California Supreme Court did so in *Serrano v. Priest* (1971). Since then, numerous state supreme courts have followed suit in holding that disparities in funding among school districts violate state constitutional equal protection requirements or state constitutional provisions guaranteeing a right to public education. A dramatic example is *Rose v. Council for Better Education, Inc.* (1989), where the Kentucky Supreme Court declared unconstitutional the entire system of public schools in that state. This forced the state legislature to overhaul the system. School funding was increased significantly and the discrepancies between wealthy and poor districts were alleviated.

The decision of the Kentucky Supreme Court is yet another illustration of the principle of **judicial federalism**, under which state courts are free to interpret their state laws in a way that provides additional rights beyond those secured by federal law. At a time in which the U.S. Supreme Court is dominated by conservatives, advocates of civil rights and liberties may find state tribunals receptive to claims that would be rejected by the federal courts.

Restriction of Abortion Funding for Indigent Women   Another controversial issue reaching the Burger Court under the aegis of the New Equal Protection was the dispute over legislative efforts to cut off government funds to support abortions. In *Maher v. Roe* (1977), the Court upheld the constitutionality of a Connecticut policy withholding Medicaid payments for nonessential abortions. Writing for a majority of six justices, Justice Powell opined that

> [a]n indigent woman desiring an abortion does not come within the limited category of disadvantaged classes so recognized by our cases. Nor does the fact that the impact of the regulation falls upon those who cannot pay lead to a different conclusion. In a sense, every denial of welfare to an indigent creates a wealth classification as compared to nonindigents who are able to pay for the desired goods or services. But this Court has never held that financial need alone identifies a suspect class for purposes of Equal Protection analysis.

Subsequently, in *Harris v. McRae* (1980), the Court upheld the **Hyde amendment**, a federal law that severely limited the use of federal funds to support abortions for indigent women. Writing for the sharply divided bench, Justice Stewart observed that

> [t]he Hyde Amendment, like the Connecticut welfare regulation at issue in *Maher*, places no governmental obstacle in the path of a woman who chooses to terminate her pregnancy, but rather, by means of unequal subsidization of abortion and other medical services, encourages alternative activity deemed in the public interest. The present case does differ factually from *Maher* insofar as that case involved a failure to fund nontherapeutic abortions, whereas the Hyde Amendment withholds funding of certain medically necessary abortions.

Nevertheless, Justice Stewart concluded that

> [h]ere as in *Maher*, the principal impact of the Hyde Amendment falls on the indigent. But that fact does not itself render the funding restriction constitutionally invalid, for this Court has held repeatedly that poverty, standing alone, is not a suspect classification.

Dissenting, Justice Marshall chastised the majority for its insensitivity to the plight of the poor, saying that "[t]here is another world 'out there,' the existence of which the Court . . . either chooses to ignore or refuses to recognize." In Marshall's view, "it is only by blinding itself to that other world" that the Court could uphold the Hyde amendment. (This issue is also addressed in Chapter 11.)

Possible Interpretations of Economic Equal Protection Although most commentators have associated an expansion of the Equal Protection Clause to protect economic interests with liberal, redistributive policy objectives, such a broadening of equal protection might well turn out to be a double-edged sword. If a more conservative Supreme Court were to make "wealth," as distinct from "poverty," a suspect classification, then government presumably would have to show a compelling interest to justify progressive taxation, subsidies, and a host of redistributive policies. Just as the Due Process Clause was once used to frustrate progressivism, populism, and the New Deal, so the Equal Protection Clause could conceivably be employed by a more conservative Supreme Court to attack the welfare state.

As we have pointed out repeatedly in this book, constitutional language, such as "due process" and "equal protection," is sufficiently broad to embrace various potential applications. Indeed, socialists could "find" in the Equal Protection Clause a requirement that government equalize material conditions in society. Similarly, the Takings Clause of the Fifth Amendment could be cited to provide a constitutional justification for the nationalization of private industries. This is not to say that the Constitution has no plain or obvious meanings, which it surely does. It is only to say that certain language in the Constitution, such as the Equal Protection Clause, is written broadly enough to allow for various, even opposing, interpretations. The constitutional values that are actualized through decision making depend greatly on the political ideologies of the justices who happen to be on the Court and on the broader political culture within which the Court functions.

Discrimination on the Basis of Sexual Orientation

While some states and cities have enacted laws protecting homosexuals against discrimination in housing, employment, and the like, there is no such protection under federal civil rights laws. Moreover, the federal courts have had little to say about gay rights in terms of the equal protection requirements of the U.S. Constitution.

One question of gay rights that came to the fore during the 1980s was the military's policy of discharging persons who admitted to being homosexual. In *Watkins v. U.S. Army* (1988), the U.S. Court of Appeals for the Ninth Circuit invalidated this policy. Writing for the court, Judge Norris concluded that "the Army's regulations violate the constitutional guarantee of equal protection of the laws because they discriminate against persons of homosexual orientation, a suspect class, and because the regulations are not necessary to promote a legitimate compelling governmental interest." On en banc rehearing the Court of Appeals affirmed the judgment but did so on nonconstitutional grounds, finding it "unnecessary to reach the constitutional issues." The Supreme Court denied certiorari, thus leaving open the constitutional question as to whether the military's ban on homosexuals violates constitutional equal protection standards. Shortly after his election to the presidency in November 1992, Bill Clinton announced that he intended to issue an executive order abolishing the military's ban on homosexuals. But a firestorm of controversy caused Clinton to back down. Instead, Clinton issued an order instituting a "don't ask, don't tell" policy in the military. Although this approach has alleviated some of the conflict over gays in the military, gay rights activists have continued to press the issue in the courts. As yet, the Supreme Court has not addressed the question.

In 1996, however, the Court did take up the issue of gay rights in a case involving an unusual legal measure. In what may turn out to be a pivotal decision in this area, the Court in *Romer v. Evans* struck down Colorado's controversial Amendment 2, which banned state and local government from providing various legal protections for gays and lesbians. Writing for a majority of six, Justice Kennedy concluded that "Amendment 2 . . . in making a general announcement that gays and lesbians shall not have any particular protections from the law, inflicts on them immediate, continuing, and real injuries that outrun and belie any legitimate justifications that may be claimed for it." In dissent, Justice Scalia argued that Amendment 2 "is not the manifestation of a 'bare . . . desire to harm' homosexuals, but is rather a modest attempt by seemingly tolerant Coloradans to preserve traditional sexual mores against the efforts of a politically powerful minority to revise those mores through use of the laws." Scalia attacked the reasoning of the majority, saying that the Court's opinion "has no foundation in American constitutional law, and barely pretends to." But the Court concluded that "it is not within our constitutional tradition to enact laws of this sort." Justice Kennedy opined that "a law declaring that in general it shall be more difficult for one group of citizens than for all others to seek aid from the government is itself a denial of equal protection of the laws in the most literal sense."

The *Romer* decision halts a movement in which communities around the country sought to copy the Colorado amendment. Law professor Susan Bloch of Georgetown University has observed that the Colorado amendment was "the most vulnerable to constitutional challenge" because it represented "the essence of what it is to deny people equal protection of the law." Justice Kennedy seemed to make the same point in the majority opinion, asserting that Amendment 2 was unconstitutional because "it identifies persons by a single trait and then denies them equal protection across the board." This suggests that Kennedy, as well as the other moderate members of the Court, might have been more sympathetic to a measure that merely outlawed preferential treatment for gays and lesbians. It may be that the Court will be called upon to rule on other, perhaps narrower, versions of Amendment 2 in the future. Of course, other gay rights issues remain on the Supreme Court's horizon, including same-sex marriage and the controversy surrounding gays in the military. Intense partisans on both sides of the gay rights debate will be watching closely as the Supreme Court navigates its way through this cultural minefield.

Same-Sex Marriage, Civil Unions, and Judicial Federalism In 1996 the Hawaii Supreme Court ruled that the state law restricting marriage licenses to heterosexual couples violates the equal protection requirements of the Hawaii constitution. Not surprisingly, the decision produced a tremendous controversy in that state. In 1999, Hawaii voters amended the state constitution to authorize the legislature to limit marriage to heterosexual couples, thus effectively nullifying the state supreme court's decision. In Vermont, however, a similar court decision led to a very different outcome. In *Baker v. State* (1999), the Vermont Supreme Court ruled that same-sex couples are entitled to "the same benefits and protections afforded by Vermont law to married opposite-sex couples." The decision was based on the Common Benefits Clause of the Vermont Constitution, which is that state's counterpart to the Equal Protection Clause of the Fourteenth Amendment. Although there was some negative reaction from the public, the state legislature complied with the court's mandate and adopted a law permitting same-sex couples to enter into "civil unions" having all of the legal rights and duties of marriage. As yet, no other state has followed Vermont's lead, but most observers believe that this approach will eventually be widely emulated. For now, the salient federal constitutional question is whether the Full Faith and Credit Clause of Article IV, Section 2, requires states to recognize same-sex marriages granted in other states. (For more discussion of this issue, including the enactment of the Defense of Marriage Act, see Chapter 5.) However, the civil union approach taken by Vermont may circumvent this problem, as civil unions are not technically marriages. One might argue that as long as a state does not permit civil unions between its own residents, it would not be required to recognize civil unions granted by other states. In any event, it is clear that state courts and state legislatures will continue to confront a number of issues associated with the cause of gay rights.

TO SUMMARIZE:

- The Supreme Court has recognized constitutional issues of discrimination in a number of areas, including classifications based on wealth, residency, alienage, illegitimacy, age, and disability. To the extent that discriminatory practices in these areas impinge on fundamental rights, the Court has subjected them to strict scrutiny. Otherwise, the court has employed the rational basis test or, in some instances, heightened scrutiny.
- The Court has taken a decidedly conservative approach in dealing with the issue of discrimination against the poor. The Court has, for example, refused to invalidate local systems of public school finance alleged to disadvantage poor students and

has upheld restrictions on public funding of nontherapeutic abortions for indigent women.
- One of the most controversial issues in the equal protection area involves discrimination against gays and lesbians. The Supreme Court has indicated its willingness to scrutinize public policies in this area and it is likely that the Court will act further in this area in the future.

THE ONGOING PROBLEM OF PRIVATE DISCRIMINATION

The repudiation of the separate but equal doctrine in *Brown* and subsequent decisions led to the virtual disappearance of de jure racial segregation—that is, segregation required or created by law or public policy. Yet, **de facto segregation** in housing, employment, and education still exists to a great extent, as a function of both social norms and economic disparities. As the Supreme Court held as far back as 1883 (see *The Civil Rights Cases*), segregation that is purely de facto is beyond the purview of the Equal Protection Clause per se. Many forms of de facto segregation, however, may be within the remedial power of both state and federal statutes. For example, under the Fair Housing Act of 1968, Congress prohibited racial discrimination in the rental or sale of homes where the transaction is handled by a licensed agent. The questions surrounding such attempts at eradicating de facto discrimination are by no means closed.

As we previously noted, the Supreme Court in 1883 drew a sharp distinction between racial discrimination that is purely private in character and that which is supported by state action. Without formally overruling *The Civil Rights Cases,* the Court has blurred this distinction as applied to racial discrimination. Nevertheless, the Court has shown no inclination to abandon the state action doctrine. For example, in the case of a racially restrictive private club's refusal to serve the African-American guest of a white member, the Court determined that the mere grant of a liquor license did not convert the club's discriminatory policy into state action under the Fourteenth Amendment (*Moose Lodge v. Irvis* [1972]). A decade earlier, in *Burton v. Wilmington Parking Authority* (1961), the Court had found state action when a state agency leased property to a restaurant that refused to serve African-Americans. Legalistically, whether there is state action in support of discrimination depends on whether there is a "close nexus" between the functions of the state and the private discrimination. More realistically, it probably depends on whether circumstances foster a perception that the state approves of the discrimination at issue.

Restrictive Covenants

A classic form of private discrimination was the **restrictive covenant** in which a group of homeowners agreed not to sell or rent their homes to African-Americans, Jews, and other disfavored minorities. Under the decision in *The Civil Rights Cases,* this purely private form of racial discrimination was deemed to be beyond the purview of the Equal Protection Clause. However, in *Shelley v. Kraemer* (1948), the Supreme Court held such covenants to be unenforceable in state courts, because any such enforcement would amount to state action in contravention of the Fourteenth Amendment. Arguably, for a state court to enforce such an agreement would foster a public perception that the state approves of racially restrictive covenants. On the other hand, it would be a mistake to conclude that the mere judicial enforcement of every private agreement necessarily constitutes state action for purposes of the Fourteenth Amendment. In fact, ordinary contracts and other private transactions are generally not brought within the limitations of the Fourteenth Amendment merely because they are enforced in court. *Shelley v. Kraemer* seems to stand for the proposition that questions of private racial discrimination constitute a unique category.

Although restrictive covenants are no longer judicially enforceable, racial restrictions are still written into many deeds, a fact that aroused considerable public attention during the 1986 Senate confirmation hearings on the elevation of William Rehnquist to be chief justice. In the course of these hearings, it was revealed that the deed to a piece of property owned by Rehnquist himself contained a restrictive covenant.

Finally, it should be noted that although the decision in *The Civil Rights Cases* has not been overruled, Congress has employed its broad powers, chiefly under the Commerce Clause (Article I, Section 8) to prohibit racial discrimination by places of public accommodation whose operations affect interstate commerce (see Chapter 2). In *Heart of Atlanta Motel v. United States* (1964), the Supreme Court upheld Title II of the 1964 Civil Rights Act, thus allowing Congress to accomplish under its commerce power what the Court in 1883 prevented it from doing under the Fourteenth Amendment.

State Powers to Prohibit Private Discrimination

Historically, the state governments were anything but leaders in the struggle for civil rights. Yet today, many states have civil rights or **human rights statutes.** An emerging constitutional issue is the extent to which states can act affirmatively to foster integration. Can a state adopt legislation that outlaws racial discrimination in the places of public accommodation perceived as not currently subject to federal civil rights laws? Can the states require quasi-public organizations, such as the Rotary Club, the Kiwanis, or the Jaycees, to admit women? What about private social clubs? Can the states require racially or religiously exclusive country clubs to admit those whom their membership policies currently exclude? Here, we have a classic confrontation between the state's legitimate interest in eradicating invidious discrimination and the freedom of association protected by the First and Fourteenth Amendments. In the landmark decision *Roberts v. United States Jaycees* (1984) (see Chapter 8), the Court upheld a Minnesota human rights law requiring a civic organization to accept women as full members, despite the organization's reliance on the First Amendment. For Justice Brennan, the state's interest in eradicating discrimination was more compelling than the Jaycees' claim to free association. However, Justice O'Connor was careful to point out that the Jaycees behaved more like a commercial enterprise than a political organization or a private club. Justice O'Connor's concurrence left open the question of whether "less public" entities are subject to state intervention.

The principle articulated in the *Jaycees* decision has been followed fairly consistently by the Supreme Court. For example, in 1987, the Court unanimously extended this principle to encompass the Rotary Club as well (*Rotary International v. Rotary Club of Duarte*). Likewise, in 1988, a unanimous Court relied on *Roberts v. Jaycees* in upholding a New York City ordinance that required certain all-male social clubs to admit women (*New York Club Association v. City of New York*).

On the other hand, the Court has shown that it is not willing to eviscerate the First Amendment right of free association to achieve the goal of ending discrimination. In *Hurley v. Irish-American Gay, Lesbian, and Bisexual Group of Boston* (1995), the Court held that the state of Massachusetts could not prohibit a private organization from excluding a gay rights group from its annual St. Patrick's Day parade (see Chapter 8).

A state court had ruled that gay groups could not be excluded under Massachusetts's **public accommodations statute.** The Supreme Court reversed, holding that the state could not compel the parade's organizers to promote a message of which they disapproved. Some commentators suggested that the Court's decision might reflect animus toward gays and lesbians and wondered whether the decision would have been the same had the parade's organizers sought to exclude women or African-Americans. Others argued that the Court had struck a blow for freedom from state coercion.

In 2000, the Court considered a more difficult case of private discrimination on the basis of sexual orientation. In *Boy Scouts of America v. Dale* (discussed and reprinted in Chapter 8), the Court held that the Boy Scouts could not be required by state courts to accept gay Scout leaders under a state public accommodations law. In the Court's view, this requirement would be a "severe intrusion on the Boy Scouts' rights to freedom of expressive association." In a stinging dissent, Justice Stevens quoted Justice Louis Brandeis, who once wrote that "we must be ever on our guard, lest we erect our prejudices into legal principles."

TO SUMMARIZE:

- The Supreme Court held long ago that the prohibitions of the Fourteenth Amendment extend only to discrimination fostered by government. Thus, to challenge a particular discriminatory practice under the Equal Protection Clause, a plaintiff must demonstrate that there is "state action" in support of the challenged practice.
- The existence of state action in support of discrimination depends on whether there is a "close nexus" between the functions of the state and the challenged discriminatory practice.
- Discrimination that is purely de facto or private in nature is beyond the reach of the Fourteenth Amendment. However, such discrimination may violate federal, state, and local laws, such as the laws prohibiting discrimination by places of public accommodation.
- In some instances, courts may find that the application of civil rights laws to private organizations violates the First Amendment's implicit freedom of association.

CONCLUSION

In a brief introductory essay such as this, it is impossible to discuss all the important issues of equal protection, both actual and potential. After nearly three decades of the New Equal Protection, it is clear that any government policy that differentiates among identifiable groups poses a potential equal protection problem. For example, as longevity of the American population increases and more people stay on the job beyond the traditional age of retirement, discrimination against the elderly is becoming a more prominent equal protection issue. Another issue on the horizon is whether laws forbidding same-sex marriage unreasonably discriminate against homosexuals.

In spite of recent changes in the ideological makeup of the Supreme Court, there exists an elaborate framework of statutes and judicial decisions reflecting a strong national commitment to the antidiscrimination principle. Some observers may view recent limitations on affirmative action programs and disengagement of the federal courts from supervision of public school desegregation as departures from this commitment. The antidiscrimination principle, however, is far broader than specific remedial measures adopted to address immediate problems. The fundamental commitment to this principle is likely to outlast ephemeral changes in the political landscape.

Politically, one of the most important applications of the Equal Protection Clause has been to the historic problem of legislative malapportionment. This problem, along with other issues related to the themes of representation and political participation, is examined in Chapter 13.

KEY TERMS

Equal Protection Clause	disparate impact	desegregation	gender-neutral
New Equal Protection	heightened scrutiny	court-ordered busing	gender equity
fundamental rights	Civil Rights Act of 1866	de jure discrimination	Americans with Disabilities Act
rational basis test	Black Codes	affirmative action	illegitimacy
discrete and insular minorities	Civil Rights Act of 1875	race-conscious remedies	judicial federalism
suspect classification doctrine	places of public	group rights	Hyde amendment
strict judicial scrutiny	accommodation	set-aside	de facto segregation
presumption of	Jim Crow laws	consent decrees	restrictive covenant
constitutionality	separate but equal doctrine	gender-based classifications	human rights statutes
burden of proof	state action doctrine	sexual harassment	public accommodations statute
compelling interest	Civil Rights Act of 1964	Equal Rights Amendment	

FOR FURTHER READING

Balkin, J. M., and Bruce Ackerman (eds.). *What Brown v. Board of Education Should Have Said: The Nation's Top Legal Experts Rewrite America's Landmark Civil Rights Decision.* New York: New York University Press, 2001.

Baer, Judith. *Equality under the Constitution: Reclaiming the Fourteenth Amendment.* Ithaca, N.Y.: Cornell University Press, 1983.

Berger, Raoul. *Government by Judiciary: The Transformation of the Fourteenth Amendment.* Cambridge, Mass.: Harvard University Press, 1977.

Finch, Minnie. *The NAACP: Its Fight for Justice.* Metuchen, N.J.: Scarecrow Press, 1981.

Franklin, John Hope. *From Slavery to Freedom: A History of Negro Americans.* New York: Knopf, 1980.

Gerstmann, Evan. *The Constitutional Underclass : Gays, Lesbians, and the Failure of Class-Based Equal Protection.* Chicago: University of Chicago Press, 1999.

Ginsberg, Ruth. *Constitutional Aspects of Sex-Based Discrimination.* St. Paul, Minn.: West, 1974.

Glazer, Nathan. *Affirmative Discrimination: Ethnic Inequality and Public Policy.* New York: Basic Books, 1975.

Graham, Hugh Davis. *The Civil Rights Era: Origins and Development of a National Policy.* New York: Oxford University Press, 1990.

Kennedy, Randall. *Race, Crime, and the Law.* New York: Pantheon Books, 1997.

Kluger, Richard. *Simple Justice.* New York: Vintage Books, 1975.

O'Connor, Karen. *Women's Organizations' Use of the Courts.* Lexington, Mass.: Lexington Books, 1980.

Peltason, Jack W. *58 Lonely Men: Southern Federal Judges and School Desegregation.* Urbana: University of Illinois Press, 1961.

Rhode, Deborah. *Justice and Gender.* Cambridge, Mass.: Harvard University Press, 1989.

Rossum, Ralph. *Reverse Discrimination: The Constitutional Debate.* New York: Dekker, 1980.

Schwartz, Bernard (ed.). *The Fourteenth Amendment.* New York: New York University Press, 1970.

Sindler, Allan P. *Bakke, DeFunis, and Minority Admissions.* New York: Longman, 1978.

Wasby, Stephen L., Anthony A. D'Amato, and Rosemary Metrailer. *Desegregation from Brown to Alexander: An Exploration of Supreme Court Strategies.* Carbondale: Southern Illinois University Press, 1977.

Wilkinson, J. Harvie III. *From Brown to Bakke: The Supreme Court and School Integration: 1954-1978.* New York: Oxford University Press, 1981.

Wolters, Raymond. *The Burden of Brown: Thirty Years of School Desegregation.* Knoxville: University of Tennessee Press, 1984.

Woodward, C. Vann. *The Strange Career of Jim Crow.* New York: Oxford University Press, 1968.

INTERNET RESOURCES

Name of Resource	Description	URL
Civil Rights Division, U.S. Department of Justice	Division of the Justice Department responsible for enforcing civil rights laws	http://www.usdoj.gov/crt/
NAACP	The oldest and best known organization devoted to promoting civil rights for African-Americans	http://www.naacp.org/
National Organization for Women	The leading interest group in the movement for women's rights	http://www.now.org/
The National Gay and Lesbian Task Force (NGLTF)	A leading gay rights organization	http://www.ngltf.org/
Eagle Forum	Phyllis Shlafly's organization—a conservative alternative to feminism	http://www.eagleforum.org/
The Southern Poverty Law Center	A prominent civil rights organization with a particular emphasis on combating hate groups and hate crimes	http://www.splcenter.org/

Case

THE CIVIL RIGHTS CASES

109 U.S. 3; 3 S.Ct. 18; 27 L.Ed. 835 (1883)
Vote: 8–1

In this landmark opinion, the Court holds that private discrimination is, in and of itself, beyond the purview of the Fourteenth Amendment.

Mr. Justice Bradley delivered the opinion of the Court:

These cases are all founded on the . . . "Civil Rights Act," passed March 1, 1875. . . . Two of the cases . . . are indictments for denying to persons of color the accommodations and privileges of an inn or hotel; two of them, . . . for denying to individuals the privileges and accommodations of a theater. . . . The case of Robinson and wife against the Memphis & Charleston Railroad Company was an action . . . to recover the penalty of $500 given by the second section of the act; and the gravamen was the refusal by the conductor of the railroad company to allow the wife to ride in the ladies' car, [because] she was a person of African descent.

The sections of the law referred to provide as follows:

Sec. 1. That all persons within . . . United States shall be entitled to the full and equal enjoyment of the accommodations, advantages, facilities, and privileges of inns, public conveyances on land or water, theaters, and other places of public amusement; subject only to the conditions and limitations established by law, and applicable alike to citizens of every race and color, regardless of any previous condition of servitude.

Sec. 2. That any person who shall violate the foregoing section . . . shall, for every such offense, forfeit and pay the sum of $500 to the person aggrieved [and] be deemed guilty of a misdemeanor, and upon conviction thereof shall be fined not less than $500 nor more than $1,000, or shall be imprisoned not less than 30 days nor more than one year. . . .

The first section of the Fourteenth Amendment . . . declares that "no state shall make or enforce any law which shall abridge the privileges or immunities of citizens of the United States; nor shall any state deprive any person of life, liberty, or property without due process of law; nor deny to any person within its jurisdiction, the equal protection of the laws." It is state action of a particular character that is prohibited. Individual invasion of individual rights is not the subject-matter of the amendment. . . . It nullifies and makes void all state legislation, and state action of every kind, which impairs the privileges and immunities of citizens of the United States, or which injures them in life, liberty, or property without due process of law, or which denies to any of them the equal protection of the laws. . . . [T]he last section of the amendment invests Congress with power to enforce it by appropriate legislation. To enforce what? To enforce the prohibition. To adopt appropriate legislation for correcting the effects of such prohibited state law and state acts, and thus to render them effectually null, void, and innocuous. . . . It does not invest Congress with power to legislate upon subjects which are within the domain of state legislation. . . . It does not authorize Congress to create a code of municipal law for the regulation of private rights; but to provide modes of redress against the operation of state laws, and the action of state officers, executive or judicial, when these are subversive of the fundamental rights specified in the amendment. . . .

An inspection of the law shows that it makes no reference whatever to any supposed or apprehended violation of the Fourteenth Amendment on the part of the states. . . . It proceeds ex directo to declare that certain acts committed by individuals shall be deemed offenses, and shall be prosecuted and punished by proceedings in the courts of the United States. It does not profess to be corrective of any constitutional wrong committed by the states. . . . [I]t steps into the domain of local jurisprudence, and lays down rules for the conduct of individuals in society towards each other . . . without referring in any manner to any supposed action of the state or its authorities.

If this legislation is appropriate for enforcing the prohibitions of the amendment, it is difficult to see where it is to stop. Why may not Congress, with equal show of authority, enact a code of laws for the enforcement and vindication of all rights of life, liberty, and property? If it is supposable that the states may deprive persons of life, liberty, and property without due process of law (and the amendment itself does suppose this), why should not Congress proceed at once to prescribe due process of law for the protection of every one of these fundamental rights, in every possible case, as well as to prescribe equal privileges in inns, public conveyances, and theaters. The truth is that the implication of a power to legislate in this manner is based upon the assumption that if the states are forbidden to legislate or act in a particular way on a particular subject, and power is conferred upon Congress to enforce the prohibition, this gives Congress power to legislate generally upon that subject, and not merely power to provide modes of redress against such state legislation or action. The assumption is certainly unsound. It is repugnant to the Tenth Amendment. . . .

. . . [C]ivil rights, such as are guarantied by the Constitution against state aggression, cannot be impaired by the wrongful acts of individuals, unsupported by state authority in the shape of laws, customs, or judicial or executive proceedings. The wrongful act of an individual, unsupported by any such authority, is simply a private wrong, or a crime of that individual. . . . An individual cannot deprive a man of his right to vote, to hold property, to buy and to sell, to sue in the courts, or to be a witness or a juror; he may, by force or fraud, interfere with the enjoyment of the right in a particular case; . . . but unless protected in these wrongful acts by some shield of state law or state authority, he cannot destroy or injure the right; he will only render himself amenable to satisfaction or punishment; and amenable therefore to the laws of the state where the wrongful acts are committed. Hence, in all those cases where the Constitution seeks to protect the rights of the citizen against discriminative and unjust laws of the state by prohibiting such laws, it is not individual offenses, but abrogation and denial of rights, which it denounces, and for which it clothes the Congress with power to provide a remedy. This abrogation and denial of rights, for which the states alone were or could be responsible, was the great seminal and fundamental wrong which was intended to be remedied. . . .

Of course, these remarks do not apply to those cases in which Congress is clothed with direct and plenary powers of legislation over the whole subject, accompanied with an express or implied denial of such power to the states, as in the regulation of commerce with foreign nations, among the several states, and with the Indian tribes, the coining of money, the establishment of post-offices and post-roads, the declaring of war, etc. In these cases Congress has power to pass laws for regulating the subjects specified, in every detail, and the conduct and transactions of individuals in respect thereof. . . .

But the power of Congress to adopt direct and primary, as distinguished from corrective, legislation on the subject in hand, is sought, in the second place, from the Thirteenth Amendment, which . . . declares "that neither slavery, nor involuntary servitude, except as a punishment for crime, whereof the party shall have been duly convicted, shall exist within the United States, or any place subject to their jurisdiction;" and it gives Congress power to enforce the amendment by appropriate legislation. . . .

. . . [I]t is assumed that the power vested in Congress to enforce the article by appropriate legislation, clothes Congress with power to pass all laws necessary and proper for abolishing all badges and incidents of slavery

in the United States; and upon this assumption it is claimed that this is sufficient authority for declaring by law that all persons shall have equal accommodations and privileges in all inns, public conveyances, and places of public amusement; the argument being that the denial of such equal accommodations and privileges is in itself a subjection to a species of servitude within the meaning of the amendment. . . .

. . . [T]he civil rights bill of 1866, passed in view of the Thirteenth Amendment, before the Fourteenth was adopted, understood to wipe out these burdens and disabilities, the necessary incidents of slavery, constituting its substance and visible form; and to secure to all citizens of every race and color, and without regard to previous servitude, those fundamental rights which are the essence of civil freedom, namely, the same right to make and enforce contracts, to sue, be parties, give evidence, and to inherit, purchase, lease, sell, and convey property, as is enjoyed by white citizens. Whether this legislation was fully authorized by the Thirteenth Amendment alone, without the support which it afterwards received from the Fourteenth Amendment, after the adoption of which it was re-enacted with some additions, it is not necessary to inquire. It is referred to for the purpose of showing that at that time (in 1866) Congress did not assume, under the authority given by the Thirteenth Amendment, to adjust what may be called the social rights of men and races in the community; but only to declare and vindicate those fundamental rights which appertain to the essence of citizenship, and the enjoyment or deprivation of which constitutes the essential distinction between freedom and slavery.

. . . Many wrongs may be obnoxious to the prohibitions of the Fourteenth Amendment which are not, in any just sense, incidents or elements of slavery. Such, for example, would be the taking of private property without due process of law; or allowing persons who have committed certain crimes (horse-stealing, for example) to be seized and hung by the posse comitatus without regular trial; or denying to any person, or class of persons, the right to pursue any peaceful avocations allowed to others. What is called class legislation would belong to this category, and would be obnoxious to the prohibitions of the Fourteenth Amendment, but would not necessarily be so to the Thirteenth, when not involving the idea of any subjection of one man to another. . . . Can the act of a mere individual, the owner of the inn, the public conveyance, or place of amusement, refusing the accommodation, be justly regarded as imposing any badge of slavery or servitude upon the applicant, or only as inflicting an ordinary civil injury . . . ? [S]uch an act of refusal has nothing to do with slavery or involuntary servitude, . . . if it is violative of any right of the party, his redress is to be sought under the laws of the state; or, if those laws are adverse to his rights and do not protect him, his remedy will be found in the corrective legislation which Congress has adopted, or may adopt, for counter-acting the effect of state laws, or state action, prohibited by the Fourteenth Amendment. It would be running the slavery argument into the ground to make it apply to every act of discrimination which a person may see fit to make as to the guests he will entertain, or as to the people he will take into his coach or cab or car, or admit to his concert or theater, or deal with in other matters of intercourse or business. Innkeepers and public carriers, by the laws of all the states, so far as we are aware, are bound, to the extent of their facilities, to furnish proper accommodation to all unobjectionable persons who in good faith apply for them. If the laws themselves make any unjust discrimination, amenable to the prohibitions of the Fourteenth Amendment, Congress has full power to afford a remedy under that amendment and in accordance with it.

. . . There were thousands of free colored people in this country before the abolition of slavery, enjoying all the essential rights of life, liberty, and property the same as white citizens; yet no one, at that time, thought that it was any invasion of their personal status as freemen because they were not admitted to all the privileges enjoyed by white citizens, or because they were subjected to discriminations in the enjoyment of accommodations in inns, public conveyances, and places of amusement. Mere discriminations on account of race or color were not regarded as badges of slavery. . . .

On the whole, we are of the opinion that no countenance of authority for the passage of the law in question can be found in either the Thirteenth or Fourteenth Amendment of the Constitution; and no other ground of authority for its passage being suggested, it must necessarily be declared void. . . .

Mr. Justice Harlan, dissenting.

The opinion in these cases proceeds, as it seems to me, upon grounds entirely too narrow and artificial. The substance and spirit of the recent amendments of the Constitution have been sacrificed by a subtle and ingenious verbal criticism. . . .

The Thirteenth Amendment, my brethren concede, did something more than to prohibit slavery as an institution, resting upon distinctions of race, and upheld by positive law. They admit that it established and decreed universal civil freedom throughout the United States. But did the freedom thus established involve nothing more . . . than to forbid one man from owning another as property? . . . I do not contend that the Thirteenth Amendment invests Congress with authority, by legislation, to regulate the entire body of the civil rights which citizens enjoy, or may enjoy, in the several states. But I do hold that since slavery . . . was the moving or principal cause of the adoption of

that amendment, and since that institution rested wholly upon the inferiority, as a race, of those held in bondage, their freedom necessarily involved immunity from, and protection against, all discrimination against them, because of their race, in respect of such civil rights as belong to freemen of other races. Congress, therefore, under its express power to enforce that amendment, by appropriate legislation, may enact laws to protect that people against the deprivation, on account of their race, of any civil rights enjoyed by other freemen in the same state; and such legislation may be of a direct and primary character, operating upon states, their officers and agents, and also upon, at least, such individuals and corporations as exercise public functions and wield power and authority under the State. . . .

I am of the opinion that . . . discrimination practised by corporations and individuals in the exercise of their public or quasi-public functions is a badge of servitude, the imposition of which Congress may prevent under its power through appropriate legislation, to enforce the Thirteenth Amendment. . . .

It remains now to consider these cases with reference to the power Congress has possessed since the adoption of the Fourteenth Amendment. . . .

The first clause of the first section—"all persons born or naturalized in the United States, and subject to the jurisdiction thereof, are citizens of the United States, and of the state wherein they reside"—is of a distinctly affirmative character. In its application to the colored race, previously liberated, it created and granted, as well citizenship of the United States, as citizenship of the state in which they respectively resided. . . . Further, they were brought, by this supreme act of the nation, within the direct operation of the provision of the Constitution which declares that "the citizens of each state shall be entitled to all privileges and immunities of citizens in the several states." . . .

The citizenship thus acquired by that race, in virtue of an affirmative grant by the nation, may be protected, not alone by the judicial branch of the government, but by congressional legislation of a primary direct character; this, because the power of Congress is not restricted to the enforcement of prohibitions upon state laws or state action. It is, in terms distinct and positive, to enforce "the provisions of this article" of amendment; not simply those of a prohibitive character, but the provisions—all of the provisions—affirmative and prohibitive, of the amendment. . . .

But what was secured to colored citizens of the United States—as between them and their respective states—by the grant to them of state citizenship? With what rights, privileges, or immunities did this grant from the nation invest them? There is one, if there be no others—exemption from race discrimination in respect of any civil right belonging to citizens of the white race in the same state. . . . It is fundamental in American citizenship that, in respect of such rights, there shall be no discrimination by the state, or its officers, or by individuals, or corporations exercising public functions or authority, against any citizen because of his race or previous condition of servitude.

. . . [T]o hold that the amendment remits that right to the states for their protection, primarily, and stays the hands of the nation, until it is assailed by state laws or state proceedings, is to adjudge that the amendment, so far from enlarging the powers of Congress—as we have heretofore said it did—not only curtails them, but reverses the policy which the general government has pursued from its very organization. Such an interpretation of the amendment is a denial to Congress of the power, by appropriate legislation, to enforce one of its provisions. In view of the circumstances under which the recent amendments were incorporated into the Constitution, and especially in view of the peculiar character of the new rights they created and secured, it ought not to be presumed that the general government has abdicated its authority, by national legislation, direct and primary in its character, to guard and protect privileges and immunities secured by that instrument. . . . It was perfectly well known that the great danger to the equal enjoyment by citizens of their rights, as citizens, was to be apprehended, not altogether from unfriendly state legislation, but from the hostile action of corporations and individuals in the states. And it is to be presumed that it was intended, by [the Fourteenth Amendment] to clothe Congress with power and authority to meet that danger. . . .

It is said that any interpretation of the Fourteenth Amendment different from that adopted by the court, would authorize Congress to enact a municipal code for all the states, covering every matter affecting the life, liberty, and property of the citizens of the several states. Not so. Prior to the adoption of that amendment the constitutions of the several states, without, perhaps, an exception, secured all persons against deprivation of life, liberty, or property, otherwise than by due process of law, and, in some form, recognized the right of all persons to the equal protection of the laws. These rights, therefore, existed before that amendment was proposed or adopted. . . .

Case

PLESSY V. FERGUSON

163 U.S. 537; 16 S.Ct. 1138; 41 L.Ed. 256 (1896)
Vote: 7–1

A Louisiana law passed in 1890 required all passenger trains in the state to have "equal but separate accommodations for the white, and colored races." Homer Plessy, claiming that he "was seven-eighths Caucasian and one-eighth African blood; that the mixture of colored blood was not discernible in him; and that he was entitled to every right . . . of the white race," was arrested after refusing to vacate a seat in a car that was reserved for white passengers. Plessy's attack on the statute's constitutionality was unsuccessful in the Louisiana courts. He appealed.

Mr. Justice Brown . . . delivered the opinion of the Court.

. . . That [the statute] does not conflict with the Thirteenth Amendment, which abolished slavery and involuntary servitude, except as a punishment for crime, is too clear for argument. Slavery implies involuntary servitude,—a state of bondage; the ownership of mankind as a chattel, or, at least, the control of the labor and services of one man for the benefit of another, and the absence of a legal right to the disposal of his own person, property, and services. This amendment . . . was regarded by the states-men of that day as insufficient to protect the colored race from certain laws which had been enacted in the Southern states, imposing upon the colored race onerous disabilities and burdens, and curtailing their rights in the pursuit of life, liberty, and property to such an extent that their freedom was of little value; and . . . the Fourteenth Amendment was devised to meet this exigency. . . .

The object of the amendment was undoubtedly to enforce the absolute equality of the two races before the law, but, in the nature of things, it could not have been intended to abolish distinctions based upon color, or to enforce social, as distinguished from political, equality, or a commingling of the two races upon terms unsatisfactory to either. Laws permitting, and even requiring, their separation, in places where they are liable to be brought into contact . . . have been generally, if not universally, recognized as within the competency of the state legislatures in the exercise of their police power. The most common instance of this is connected with the establishment of separate schools for white and colored children, which have been [upheld] even by courts of states where the political rights of the colored race have been longest and most earnestly enforced.

One of the earliest of these cases is that of *Roberts v. City of Boston* . . . (1849). "The great principle," said Chief Justice Shaw, "advanced by the learned and eloquent advocate for the plaintiff (Mr. Charles Sumner), is that, by the constitution and laws of Massachusetts, all persons, without distinction of age or sex, birth, or color, origin or condition, are equal before the law. . . . But, when this great principle comes to be applied to the actual and various conditions of persons in society, it will not warrant the assertion that men and women are legally clothed with the same civil and political powers, and that children and adults are legally to have the same functions and be subject to the same treatment; but only that the rights of all, as they are settled and regulated by law, are equally entitled to the paternal consideration and protection of the law for their maintenance and security." Similar laws have been enacted by Congress under its general power of legislation over the District of Columbia, as well as by the legislatures of many of the states, and have been generally, if not uniformly, sustained by the courts. . . .

Laws forbidding the intermarriage of the two races may be said in a technical sense to interfere with the freedom of contract, and yet have been universally recognized as within the police power of the state. . . .

The distinction between laws interfering with the political equality of the negro and those requiring the separation of the two races in schools, theaters, and railway carriages has been frequently drawn by this court.

[It is suggested] that the same argument that will justify the state legislature in requiring railways to provide separate accommodations for the two races will also authorize them to require separate cars to be provided for people whose hair is of a certain color, or who are aliens, or who belong to certain nationalities, or to enact laws requiring colored people to walk upon one side of the street, and white people upon the other, or requiring white men's houses to be painted white, and colored men's black, or their vehicles or business signs to be of different colors, upon the theory that one side of the street is as good as the other, or that a house or vehicle of one color is as good as one of another color. The reply to all this is that every exercise of the police power must be reasonable, and extend only to such laws as are enacted in good faith for the promotion of the public good, and not for the annoyance or oppression of a particular class. . . .

So far, then, as a conflict with the Fourteenth Amendment is concerned, the case reduces itself to the question whether the statute of Louisiana is a reasonable regulation, and with respect to this there must necessarily be a large discretion on the part of the legislature. In determining the question of reasonableness, it is at liberty to act with reference to the established usages, customs, and traditions of the people, and with a view to the promotion of their comfort, and the preservation of the public peace and good order. Gauged by this standard, we cannot say [that this law] is unreasonable, or more obnoxious to the Fourteenth Amendment than the acts of Congress requiring separate schools for colored children in the District of Columbia, the constitutionality of which does not seem to have been questioned, or the corresponding acts of state legislatures.

We consider the underlying fallacy of the plaintiff's argument to consist in the assumption that the enforced separation of the two races stamps the colored race with a badge of inferiority. If this be so, it is not by reason of anything found in the act, but solely because the colored race chooses to put that construction upon it. The argument necessarily assumes that if, as has been more than once the case, and is not unlikely to be so again, the colored race should become the dominant power in the state legislature, and should enact a law in precisely similar terms, it would thereby relegate the white race to an inferior position. We imagine that the white race, at least, would not acquiesce in this assumption. The argument also assumes that social prejudices may be overcome by legislation, and that equal rights cannot be secured to the negro except by an enforced commingling of the two races. We cannot accept this proposition. If the two races are to meet upon terms of social equality, it must be the result of natural affinities, a mutual appreciation of each other's merits, and a voluntary consent of individuals. . . . Legislation is powerless to eradicate racial instincts, or to abolish distinctions based upon physical differences, and the attempt to do so can only result in accentuating the difficulties of the present situation. If the civil and political rights of both races be equal, one cannot be inferior to the other civilly or politically. If one race be inferior to the other socially, the Constitution of the United States cannot put them upon the same plane. . . .

Mr. Justice Brewer did not . . . participate in the decision of this case.

Mr. Justice Harlan dissenting.

. . . In respect of civil rights, common to all citizens, the Constitution of the United States does not, I think, permit any public authority to know the race of those entitled to be protected in the enjoyment of such rights. Every true man has pride of race, and under appropriate circumstances, when the rights of others, his equals before the law, are not to be affected, it is his privilege to express such pride and to take such action based upon it as to him seems proper. But I deny that any legislative body or judicial tribunal may have regard to the race of citizens when the civil rights of those citizens are involved. Indeed, such legislation as that here in question is inconsistent not only with that equality of rights which pertains to citizenship, national and state, but with the personal liberty enjoyed by every one within the United States.

The Thirteenth Amendment does not permit the withholding or the deprivation of any right necessarily inhering in freedom. It not only struck down the institution of slavery as previously existing in the United States, but it prevents the imposition of any burdens or disabilities that constitute badges of slavery or servitude. . . . It was followed by the Fourteenth [and Fifteenth] amendment[s], which added greatly to the dignity and glory of American citizenship, and to the security of personal liberty. . . .

It was said in argument that the statute of Louisiana does not discriminate against either race, but prescribes a rule applicable alike to white and colored citizens. But this argument does not meet the difficulty. Everyone knows that the statute in question had its origin in the purpose, not so much to exclude white persons from railroad cars occupied by blacks, as to exclude colored people from coaches occupied by or assigned to white persons. . . . No one would be so wanting in candor as to assert the contrary. The fundamental objection, therefore, to the statute, is that it interferes with the personal freedom of citizens. "Personal liberty," it has been well said, "consists in the power of locomotion, of changing situation, or removing one's person to whatsoever places one's own inclination may direct, without imprisonment or restraint, unless by due course of law." . . . If a white man and a black man choose to occupy the same public conveyance on a public highway, it is their right to do so; and no government, proceeding alone on grounds of race, can prevent it without infringing the personal liberty of each.

. . . If a state can prescribe, as a rule of civil conduct, that whites and blacks shall not travel as passengers in the same railroad coach, why . . . may it not require sheriffs to assign whites to one side of a court room, and blacks to the other? And why may it not also prohibit the commingling of the two races in the galleries of legislative halls or in public assemblages convened for the consideration of the political questions of the day? [W]hy may not the state require the separation in railroad coaches of native and naturalized citizens of the United States, or of Protestants and Roman Catholics? . . .

The white race deems itself to be the dominant race in this country. And so it is, in prestige, in achievements, in education, in wealth, and in power. So, I doubt not, it will continue to be for all time, if it remains true to its great heritage, and holds fast to the principles of constitutional liberty. But in view of the Constitution, in the eye of the law, there is in this country no superior, dominant, ruling class of citizens. There is no caste here. Our Constitution is color-blind, and neither knows nor tolerates classes among citizens. . . .

In my opinion, the judgment this day rendered will, in time, prove to be quite as pernicious as the decision made by this tribunal in the *Dred Scott* Case . . . that the descendants of Africans who were imported into this country, and sold as slaves, were not included nor intended to be included under the word "citizens" in the Constitution; . . . that, at the time of the adoption of the Constitution, they were "considered as a subordinate and inferior class of beings, who had been subjugated by the dominant race, and, whether emancipated or not, yet remained subject to their authority, and had not rights or privileges but such as those who held the power and the government might choose to grant them." . . . The recent amendments of the Constitution, it was supposed, has eradicated these principles from our institutions. But it seems that we have yet, in some of the states, a dominant race—a superior class of citizens—which assumes to regulate the enjoyment of civil rights, common to all citizens, upon the basis of race. The present decision . . . will encourage the belief that it is possible by means of state enactments, to defeat the beneficent purposes which the people of the United States had in view when they adopted the recent amendments of the Constitution. . . . What can more certainly arouse race hate, what more certainly create and perpetuate a feeling of distrust between these races, than state enactments which, in fact, proceed on the ground that colored citizens are so inferior and degraded that they cannot be allowed to sit in public coaches occupied by white citizens? . . . This question is not met by the suggestion that social equality cannot exist between the white and black races in this country . . . for social equality no more exists between two races when traveling in a passenger coach or a public highway than when members of the same races sit by each other in a street car or in the jury box, or stand or sit with each other in a political assembly. . . .

If evils will result from the comminglings of the two races upon public highways established for the benefit of all, they will be infinitely less than those that will surely come from state legislation regulating the enjoyment of civil rights upon the basis of race. We boast of the freedom enjoyed by our people above all other peoples. But it is difficult to reconcile that boast with a state of the law which, practically, puts the brand of servitude and degradation upon a large class of our fellow citizens—our equals before the law. The thin disguise of "equal" accommodations for passengers in railroad coaches will not mislead any one, nor atone for the wrong this day done. . . .

I do not deem it necessary to review the decisions of state courts to which reference was made in argument. Some, and the most important, of them, are wholly inapplicable, because rendered prior to the adoption of the last amendments of the Constitution. . . . Others were made at a time when public opinion, in many localities, was dominated by the institution of slavery; when it would not have been safe to do justice to the black man; and when, so far as the rights of blacks were concerned, race prejudice was, practically, the supreme law of the land. Those decisions cannot be guides in the era introduced by the recent amendments of the supreme law, which established universal civil freedom. . . .

Case

BROWN V. BOARD OF EDUCATION OF TOPEKA I

347 U.S. 483; 74 S.Ct. 686; 98 L.Ed. 873 (1954)
Vote: 9–0

In what has been dubbed "the case of the century," the Supreme Court invalidates compulsory racial segregation in the public schools.

Mr. Chief Justice Warren delivered the opinion of the Court:

These cases come to us from the States of Kansas, South Carolina, Virginia, and Delaware. They are premised on different facts and different local conditions, but a common legal question justifies their consideration in this consolidated opinion.

In each of the cases, minors of the Negro race, through their legal representatives, seek the aid of the courts in obtaining admission to the public schools of their community on a nonsegregated basis. In each instance, they had been denied admission to schools attended by white children under laws requiring or permitting segregation according to race. This segregation was alleged to deprive the plaintiffs of the equal protection of the laws under the Fourteenth Amendment. In each of the cases other than the Delaware case, a three-judge federal district court denied relief to the plaintiffs on the so-called "separate but equal" doctrine announced by this Court in *Plessy v. Ferguson*. . . . Under that doctrine, equality of treatment is accorded when the races are provided substantially equal facilities, even though these facilities be separate. In the Delaware case, the Supreme Court of Delaware adhered to that doctrine, but ordered that the plaintiffs be admitted to the white schools because of their superiority to the Negro schools. . . .

Because of the obvious importance of the question presented, the Court took jurisdiction. Argument was heard in the 1952 Term, and reargument was heard this Term on certain questions propounded by the Court.

Reargument was largely devoted to the circumstances surrounding the adoption of the Fourteenth Amendment in 1868. It covered exhaustively consideration of the Amendment in Congress, ratification by the states, then existing practices in racial segregation, and the views of proponents and opponents of the Amendment. This discussion and our own investigation convince us that, although these sources cast some light, it is not enough to resolve the problem with which we are faced. At best, they are inconclusive. The most avid proponents of the post-War Amendments undoubtedly intended them to remove all legal distinctions among "all persons born or naturalized in the United States." Their opponents, just as certainly, were antagonistic to both the letter and the spirit of the Amendments and wished them to have the most limited effect. What others in Congress and the state legislatures had in mind cannot be determined with any degree of certainty.

An additional reason for the inconclusive nature of the Amendment's history, with respect to segregated schools, is the status of public education at that time. In the South, the movement toward free common schools, supported by general taxation, had not yet taken hold. Education of white children was largely in the hands of private groups. Education of Negroes was almost nonexistent, and practically all of the race were illiterate. In fact, any education of Negroes was forbidden by law in some states. Today, in contrast, many Negroes have achieved outstanding success in the arts and sciences as well as in the business and professional world. It is true that public education had already advanced further in the North, but the effect of the Amendment on Northern States was generally ignored in the congressional debates. Even in the North, the conditions of public education did not approximate those existing today. The curriculum was rudimentary; ungraded schools were common in rural areas; the school term was but three months a year in many states; and compulsory school attendance was virtually unknown. As a consequence, it is not surprising that there should be so little in the history of the Fourteenth Amendment relating to its intended effect on public education.

In the first cases in this Court construing the Fourteenth Amendment, decided shortly after its adoption, the Court interpreted it as proscribing all state-imposed discriminations against the Negro race. The doctrine of "separate but equal" did not make its appearance in this Court until 1896 in the case of *Plessy v. Ferguson*, . . . involving not education but transportation. American courts have since labored with the doctrine for over half a century. In this Court, there have been six cases involving the "separate but equal" doctrine in the field of public education. In *Cumming v. County Board of Education* . . . and *Gong Lum v. Rice,* . . . the validity of the doctrine itself was not challenged. In more recent cases, all on the graduate school level, inequality was found in that specific benefits enjoyed by white students were denied to Negro students of the same educational qualifications. . . . In none of these cases was it necessary to reexamine the doctrine to grant relief to the Negro plaintiff. And in *Sweatt v. Painter,* . . . the Court expressly reserved decision on the question whether *Plessy v. Ferguson* should be held inapplicable to public education.

In the instant cases, that question is directly presented. Here, unlike *Sweatt v. Painter,* there are findings below that the Negro and white schools involved have been equalized, or are being equalized, with respect to buildings, curricula, qualifications and salaries of teachers, and other "tangible" factors. Our decision, therefore, cannot turn on merely a comparison of these tangible factors in the Negro and white schools involved in each of the cases. We must look instead to the effect of segregation itself on public education.

In approaching this problem, we cannot turn the clock back to 1868 when the Amendment was adopted, or even to 1896 when *Plessy v. Ferguson* was written. We must consider public education in the light of its full development and its present place in American life throughout the Nation. Only in this way can it be determined if segregation in public schools deprives these plaintiffs of the equal protection of the laws.

Today, education is perhaps the most important function of state and local governments. Compulsory school attendance laws and the great expenditures for education both demonstrate our recognition of the importance of education to our democratic society. It is required in the performance of our most basic public responsibilities, even service in the armed forces. It is the very foundation of good citizenship. Today it is a principal instrument in awakening the child to cultural values, in preparing him for later professional training, and in helping him to adjust normally to his environment. In these days, it is doubtful that any child may reasonably be expected to succeed in life if he is denied the opportunity of an education. Such an opportunity, where the state has undertaken to provide it, is a right which must be made available to all on equal terms.

We come then to the question presented: Does segregation of children in public schools solely on the basis of race, even though the physical facilities and other "tangible" factors may be equal, deprive the children of the minority group of equal educational opportunities? We believe that it does.

In *Sweatt v. Painter,* in finding that a segregated law school for Negroes could not provide them equal educational opportunities, this Court relied in large part on "those qualities which are incapable of objective measurement but which make for greatness in a law school." In *McLaurin v. Oklahoma State Regents,* . . . the Court, in requiring that a Negro admitted to a white graduate school be treated like all other students, again resorted to intangible considerations: ". . . his ability to study, to engage in discussions and exchange views with other students, and, in general, to learn his profession." Such considerations apply with added force to children in grade and high schools. To separate them from others of similar age and qualifications solely because of their race generates a feeling of inferiority as to their status in the community that may affect their hearts and minds in a way unlikely ever to be undone. The effect of this separation on their educational opportunities was well stated by a finding in the Kansas case by a court which nevertheless felt compelled to rule against the Negro plaintiffs.

Segregation of white and colored children in public schools has a detrimental effect upon the colored children. The impact is greater when it has the sanction of the law; for the policy of separating the races is usually interpreted as denoting the inferiority of the Negro group. A sense of inferiority affects the motivation of a child to learn. Segregation with the sanction of law, therefore, has a tendency to retard the educational and mental development of Negro children and to deprive them of some of the benefits they would receive in a racially integrated school system.

Whatever may have been the extent of psychological knowledge at the time of *Plessy v. Ferguson,* this finding is amply supported by modern authority. Any language in *Plessy v. Ferguson* contrary to this finding is rejected.

We conclude that in the field of public education the doctrine of "separate but equal" has no place. Separate educational facilities are inherently unequal. Therefore, we hold that the plaintiffs and others similarly situated for whom the actions have been brought are, by reason of the segregation complained of, deprived of the equal protection of the laws guaranteed by the Fourteenth Amendment. This disposition makes unnecessary any discussion whether such segregation also violates the Due Process Clause of the Fourteenth Amendment.

Because these are class actions, because of the wide applicability of this decision, and because of the great variety of local conditions, the formulation of decrees in these cases presents problems of considerable complexity. On reargument, the consideration of appropriate relief was necessarily subordinated to the primary question—the constitutionality of segregation in public education. We have now announced that such segregation is a denial of the equal protection of the laws. In order that we may have the full assistance of the parties in formulating decrees, the cases will be restored to the docket, and the parties are requested to present further argument. . . .

Case

BROWN V. BOARD OF EDUCATION OF TOPEKA II

349 U.S. 294; 75 S.Ct. 753; 99 L.Ed. 1083 (1955)
Vote: 9–0

Here the Court considers how its holding in Brown I should be implemented by the lower federal courts.

Mr. Chief Justice Warren delivered the opinion of the Court.

These cases were decided on May 17, 1954. The opinions of that date, declaring the fundamental principle that racial discrimination in public education is unconstitutional, are incorporated herein by reference. All provisions of federal, state, or local law requiring or permitting such discrimination must yield to this principle. There remains for consideration the manner in which relief is to be accorded.

Because these cases arose under different local conditions and their disposition will involve a variety of local problems, we requested further argument on the question of relief. In view of the nationwide importance of the decision, we invited the Attorney General of the United States and the Attorneys General of all states requiring or permitting racial discrimination in public education to present their views on that question. The parties, the United States, and the States of Florida, North Carolina, Arkansas, Oklahoma, Maryland, and Texas filed briefs and participated in the oral argument.

These presentations were informative and helpful to the Court in its consideration of the complexities arising from the transition to a system of public education freed of racial discrimination. The presentations also demonstrated that substantial steps to eliminate racial discrimination in public schools have already been taken, not only in some of the communities in which these cases arose, but in some of the states appearing as *amici curiae,* and in other states as well. Substantial progress has been made in the District of Columbia and in the communities in Kansas and Delaware involved in this litigation. The defendants in the cases coming to us from South Carolina and Virginia are awaiting the decision of this Court concerning relief.

Full implementation of these constitutional principles may require solution of varied local school problems. School authorities have the primary responsibility for elucidating, assessing, and solving these problems; courts will have to consider whether the action of school authorities constitutes good faith implementation of the governing constitutional principles. Because of their proximity to local conditions and the possible need for further hearings, the courts which originally heard these cases can best perform this judicial appraisal. Accordingly, we believe it appropriate to remand the cases to those courts.

In fashioning and effectuating the decrees, the courts will be guided by equitable principles. Traditionally, equity has been characterized by a practical flexibility in shaping its remedies and by a facility for adjusting and reconciling public and private needs. These cases call for the exercise of these traditional attributes of equity power. At stake is the personal interest of the plaintiffs in admission to public schools as soon as practicable on a nondiscriminatory basis. To effectuate this interest may call for elimination of a variety of obstacles in making the transition to school systems operated in accordance with the constitutional principles set forth in our May 17, 1954, decision. Courts of equity may properly take into account the public interest in the elimination of such obstacles in a systematic and effective manner. But it should go without saying that the vitality of these constitutional principles cannot be allowed to yield simply because of disagreement with them.

While giving weight to these public and private considerations, the courts will require that the defendants make a prompt and reasonable start toward full compliance with our May 17, 1954, ruling. Once such a start has been made, the courts may find that additional time is necessary to carry out the ruling in an effective manner. The burden rests upon the defendants to establish that such time is necessary in the public interest and is consistent with good faith compliance at the earliest practicable date. To that end, the courts may consider problems related to administration, arising from the physical condition of the school plant, the school transportation system, personnel, revision of school districts and attendance areas into compact units to achieve a system of determining admission to the public schools on a nonracial basis, and revision of local laws and regulations which may be necessary in solving the foregoing problems. They will also consider the adequacy of any plans the defendants may propose to meet these problems and to effectuate a transition to a racially nondiscriminatory school system. During this period of transition, the courts will retain jurisdiction of these cases.

The judgments below, except that in the Delaware case, are accordingly reversed and remanded to the District courts to take such proceedings and enter such orders and decrees consistent with this opinion as are necessary and proper to admit to public schools on a racially nondiscriminatory basis with all deliberate speed the parties to these cases. The judgment in the Delaware case—ordering the immediate admission of the plaintiffs to schools previously attended only by white children—is affirmed on the basis of the principles stated in our May 17, 1954, opinion, but the case is remanded to the Supreme Court of Delaware for such further proceedings as that court may deem necessary in light of this opinion. . . .

Case

LOVING V. VIRGINIA

388 U.S. 1; 87 S.Ct. 1817; 18 L.Ed. 2d 1010 (1967)
Vote: 9–0

Here the Court reviews a Virginia law prohibiting interracial marriage.

Mr. Chief Justice Warren delivered the opinion of the Court.

This case presents a constitutional question never addressed by this Court: whether a statutory scheme adopted by the State of Virginia to prevent marriages between persons solely on the basis of racial classifications violates the . . . Fourteenth Amendment. For reasons which seem to us to reflect the central meaning of those constitutional commands, we conclude that these statutes cannot stand consistently with the Fourteenth Amendment.

In June 1958, two residents of Virginia, Mildred Jeter, a Negro woman, and Richard Loving, a white man, were married in the District of Columbia pursuant to its laws. Shortly after their marriage, the Lovings returned to Virginia and established their marital abode in Caroline County. At the October Term, 1958, of the Circuit Court of Caroline County, a grand jury issued an indictment charging the Lovings and violating Virginia's ban on interracial marriages. On January 6, 1959, the Lovings pleaded guilty to the charge and were sentenced to one year in jail; however the trial judge suspended the sentence for a period of 25 years on the condition that the Lovings leave the State and not return to Virginia together for 25 years, stating that:

Almighty God created the races white, black, yellow, malay, and red, and he placed them on separate conti-nents. And but for the interference with his arrangements there would be no cause for such marriages. The fact that he separated the races shows that he did not intend for the races to mix.

After their convictions the Lovings took up residence in the District of Columbia. On November 6, 1963, they filed a motion in the state trial court to vacate the judgment and set aside the sentence on the ground that the statutes which they had violated were repugnant to the Fourteenth Amendment. The motion not having been decided by October 28, 1964, the Lovings instituted a class action in the United States District Court for the Eastern District of Virginia requesting that a three-judge court be convened to declare the Virginia antimiscegenation statutes unconstitutional and to enjoin state officials from enforcing their convictions. On January 22, 1965, the state trial judge denied the motion to vacate the sentences, and the Lovings perfected an appeal to the Supreme Court of Appeals of Virginia. On February 11, 1965, the three-judge District Court continued the case to allow the Lovings to present their constitutional claims to the highest state court.

The [Virginia] Supreme Court of Appeals upheld the constitutionality of the antimiscegenation statutes and, after modifying the sentence, affirmed the convictions. The Lovings appealed this decision, and we noted probable jurisdiction on December 12, 1966. The two statutes under which appellants were convicted and sentenced are part of a comprehensive statutory scheme aimed at prohibiting and punishing interracial marriages. The Lovings were convicted of violating Sec. 20-58 of the Virginia Code:

Leaving State to Evade Law. If any white person and colored person shall go out of this State, for the purpose of being married, and with the intention of returning, and be married out of it, and afterwards return to and reside in it, cohabiting as man and wife, they shall be punished as provided in Section 20-59, and the marriage shall be governed by the same law as if it had been solemnized in this State. The fact of their cohabitation here as man and wife shall be evidence of their marriage.

Section 20-59, which defines the penalty for miscegenation, provides:

Punishment for Marriage. If any white person intermarry with a colored person, or any colored person intermarry with a white person, he shall be guilty of a felony and shall be punished by confinement in the penitentiary for not less than one nor more than five years.

Other central provisions in the Virginia statutory scheme are Section 20-57, which automatically voids all marriages between "a white person and a colored person" without any judicial proceeding, and Sections 20-54 and 1-14 which, respectively, define "white persons" and "colored persons and Indians" for purposes of the statutory prohibitions. The Lovings have never disputed in course of this litigation that Mrs. Loving is a "colored person" or that Mr. Loving is a "white person" within the meanings given those terms by the Virginia statutes.

Virginia is now one of 16 States which prohibit and punish marriages on the basis of racial classifications. Penalties for miscegenation arose as an incident to slavery and have been common in Virginia since the colonial period. The present statutory scheme dates from the adoption of the Racial Integrity Act of 1924, passed during the period of extreme nativism which followed the end of the First World War. The central features of this Act, and current Virginia law, are the absolute prohibition of a "white person" marrying other than another "white person," a prohibition against issuing marriage licenses until the issuing official is satisfied that the applicants' statements as to their race are correct, certificates of "racial composition" to be kept by both local and state registrars, and the carrying forward of earlier prohibitions against racial intermarriage. . . .

In upholding the constitutionality of these provisions in the decision below, the Supreme Court of Appeals of Virginia referred to its 1955 decision in *Naim v. Naim*, . . . as stating the reasons supporting the validity of these laws. In *Naim*, the state court concluded that the State's legitimate purposes were "to preserve the racial integrity of its citizens," and to prevent "the corruption of blood," "a mongrel breed of citizens," and "the obliteration of racial pride," obviously an endorsement of the doctrine of White Supremacy. The court also reasoned that marriage has traditionally been subject to state regulation without federal intervention, and, consequently, the regulation of

marriage should be left to exclusive state control by the Tenth Amendment.

While the state court is no doubt correct in asserting that marriage is a social relation subject to the State's police power, . . . the State does not contend in its argument before this Court that its powers to regulate marriage are unlimited notwithstanding the commands of the Fourteenth Amendment. Nor could it do so in light of *Meyer v. State of Nebraska* . . . (1923) and *Skinner v. State of Oklahoma* . . . (1942). Instead, the State argues that the meaning of the Equal Protection Clause, as illuminated by the statements of the Framers, is only that state penal laws containing an interracial element as part of the definition of the offense must apply equally to whites and Negroes in the sense that members of each race are punished to the same degree. Thus, the State contends that, because its miscegenation statutes punish equally both the white and the Negro participants in an interracial marriage, these statutes, despite their reliance on racial classifications do not constitute an invidious discrimination based upon race. The second argument advanced by the State assumes the validity of its equal application theory. The argument is that, if the Equal Protection Clause does not outlaw miscegenation statutes because of their reliance on racial classifications, the question of constitutionality would thus become whether there was any rational basis for a State to treat interracial marriages differently from other marriages. On this question, the State argues, the scientific evidence is substantially in doubt and, consequently, this Court should defer to the wisdom of the state legislature in adopting its policy of discouraging interracial marriages.

Because we reject the notion that the mere "equal application" of a statute containing racial classification is enough to remove the classifications from the Fourteenth Amendment's proscription of all invidious racial discriminations, we do not accept the State's contention that these statutes should be upheld if there is any possible basis for concluding that they serve a rational purpose. The mere fact of equal application does not mean that our analysis of this statute should follow the approach we have taken in cases involving no racial discrimination where the Equal Protection Clause has been arrayed against a statute discriminating between the kinds of advertising which may be displayed on trucks in New York City, . . . or an exemption in Ohio's ad valorem tax for merchandise owned by a non-resident in a storage warehouse. . . . In these cases, involving distinctions not drawn according to race, the Court has merely asked whether there is any rational foundation for the discriminations, and has deferred to the wisdom of the state legislatures. In the case at bar, however, we deal with statutes containing racial classifications, and the fact of equal application does not immunize the statute from the very heavy burden of justification which the Fourteenth Amendment has traditionally required of state statutes drawn according to race.

The State argues that statements in the Thirty-ninth Congress about the time of the passage of the Fourteenth Amendment indicate that the Framers did not intend the Amendment to make unconstitutional state miscegenation laws. Many of the statements alluded to by the State concern the debates over the Freemen's Bureau Bill, which President Johnson vetoed, and the Civil Rights Act of 1966, enacted over his veto. While these statements have some relevance to the intention of Congress in submitting the Fourteenth Amendment, it must be understood that they pertained to the passage of specific statutes and not to the broader, organic purpose of a constitutional amendment. As for the various statements directly concerning the Fourteenth Amendment, we have said in connection with a related problem, that although these historical sources "cast some light" they are not sufficient to resolve the problem; "[a]t best, they are inconclusive. The most avid proponents of the post-War Amendments undoubtedly intended them to remove all legal distinctions among 'all persons born or naturalized in the United States.' Their opponents, just as certainly, were antagonistic to both the letter and the spirit of the Amendments and wished them to have the most limited effect." . . . We have rejected the proposition that the debates in the Thirty-ninth Congress or in the state legislatures which ratified the Fourteenth Amendment supported the theory advanced by the State, that the requirement of equal protection of the laws is satisfied by penal laws defining offenses based on racial classifications so long as white and Negro participants in the offense were similarly punished. . . .

The State finds support for its "equal application" theory in the decision of the Court in *Pace v. Alabama* . . . (1882). In that case, the Court upheld a conviction under an Alabama statute forbidding adultery or fornication between a white person and a Negro which imposed a greater penalty than that of a statute proscribing similar conduct by members of the same race. The Court reasoned that the statute could not be said to discriminate against Negroes because the punishment for each participant in the offense was the same. However, as recently as the 1964 Term, in rejecting the reasoning of that case, we stated "Pace represents a limited view of the Equal Protection Clause which has not withstood analysis in the subsequent decisions of this Court." . . . As we there demonstrated, the Equal Protection Clause requires the consideration of whether the classifications drawn by any statute constitute an arbitrary and invidious discrimination. The clear and central purpose of the Fourteenth Amendment was to eliminate all official state sources of invidious racial discrimination in the States. . . .

There can be no question but that Virginia's miscegenation statutes rest solely upon distinctions drawn according to race. The statutes proscribe generally accepted conduct if engaged in by members of different races. Over the years, this Court has consistently repudiated "[d]istinctions between citizens solely because of their ancestry" as being "odious to a free people whose institutions are founded upon the doctrine of equality." . . . At the very least, the Equal Protection Clause demands that racial classifications, especially suspect in criminal statutes, be subjected to the "most rigid scrutiny," . . . and, if they are ever to be upheld, they must be shown to be necessary to the accomplishment of some permissible state objective, independent of the racial discrimination which it was the object of the Fourteenth Amendment to eliminate. Indeed, two members of this Court have already stated that they "cannot conceive of a valid legislative purpose . . . which makes the color of a person's skin the test of whether his conduct is a criminal offense." . . .

There is patently no legitimate overriding purpose independent of invidious racial discrimination which justifies this classification. The fact that Virginia only prohibits interracial marriages involving white persons demonstrates that the racial classifications must stand on their own justification, as measures designed to maintain White Supremacy. We have consistently denied the constitutionality of measures which restrict the rights of citizens on account of race. There can be no doubt that restricting the freedom to marry solely because of racial classification violates the central meaning of the Equal Protection Clause. . . .

These convictions must be reversed. It is so ordered.

Mr. Justice Stewart, concurring. . . .

Case

SWANN V. CHARLOTTE-MECKLENBURG BOARD OF EDUCATION

402 U.S. 1; 91 S.Ct. 1267; 28 L.Ed. 2d 554 (1971)
Vote: 9–0

In Charlotte-Mecklenburg, North Carolina, the nation's forty-third largest school district, the board of education devised a desegregation plan in order to comply with the Supreme Court's ruling in the Brown case. The U.S. district court, however, rejected the board's plan as not producing sufficient racial integration at the elementary level. Instead, the district court accepted a plan prepared by an outside expert that called for, among other things, racial quotas, alteration of attendance zones, and busing of students. In this case, the Supreme Court considers the permissibility of such measures.

Mr. Chief Justice Burger delivered the opinion of the Court.

. . . The central issue in this case is that of student assignment, and there are essentially four problem areas: (1) to what extent racial balance or racial quotas may be used as an implement in a remedial order to correct a previously segregated system; (2) whether every all-Negro and all-white school must be eliminated as an indispensable part of a remedial process of desegregation; (3) what are the limits, if any, on the rearrangement of school districts and attendance zones, as a remedial measure; and (4) what are the limits, if any, on the use of transportation facilities to correct state-enforced racial school segregation.

(1) Racial Balance or Racial Quotas.

The constant theme and thrust of every holding from *Brown I* (1954) to date is that state-enforced separation of races in public schools is discrimination that violates the Equal Protection clause. The remedy commanded was to dismantle dual school systems.

We are concerned in these cases with the elimination of the discrimination inherent in the dual school systems, not with myriad factors of human existence which can cause discrimination in a multitude of ways on racial, religious, or ethnic grounds. The target of the cases from *Brown I* to the present was the dual school system. The elimination of racial discrimination in public schools is a large task and one that should not be retarded by efforts to achieve broader purposes lying beyond the jurisdiction of school authorities. One vehicle can carry only a limited amount of baggage. . . .

Our objective in dealing with the issues presented by these cases is to see that school authorities exclude no pupil or a racial minority from any school, directly or indirectly, on account of race; it does not and cannot embrace all the problems of racial prejudice, even when those problems contribute to disproportionate racial concentrations in some schools.

In this case it is urged that the District Court has imposed a racial balance requirement of 71%–29% on individual schools. . . . If we were to read the holding of the District Court to require, as a matter of substantive constitutional right, any particular degree of racial balance or mixing, that approach would be disapproved and we would be obliged to reverse. The constitutional command to desegregate schools does not mean that every school in every community must always reflect the racial composition of the school system as a whole. . . .

. . . The use made of mathematical ratios was no more than a starting point in the process of shaping a remedy, rather than an inflexible requirement. From that starting point the District Court proceeded to frame a decree that was within its discretionary powers, an equitable remedy for the particular circumstances. As we said in *Green* [*v. County School Board*] a school authority's remedial plan or a district court's remedial decree is to be judged by its effectiveness. Awareness of the racial composition of the whole school system is likely to be a useful starting point in shaping a remedy to correct past constitutional violations. In sum, the very limited use made of mathematical ratios was within the equitable remedial discretion of the District Court.

(2) One-Race Schools.

The record in this case reveals the familiar phenomenon that in metropolitan areas minority groups are often found concentrated in one part of the city. In some circumstances certain schools may remain all or largely of one race until new schools can be provided or neighborhood patterns change. Schools all or predominately of one race in a district of mixed population will require close scrutiny to determine that school assignments are not part of state-enforced segregation.

In light of the above, it should be clear that the existence of some small number of one-race, or virtually one-race, schools within a district is not in and of itself the mark of a system which still practices segregation by law. . . . Where the school authority's proposed plan for conversion from a dual to a unitary system contemplates the continued existence of some schools that are all or predominately of one race, they have the burden of showing that such school assignments are genuinely nondiscriminatory. The court should scrutinize such schools, and the burden upon the school authorities will be to satisfy the court that their racial composition is not the result of present or past discriminatory action on their part.

An optional minority-to-minority transfer provision has long been recognized as a useful part of every desegregation plan. Provision for optional transfer of those in the majority racial group of a particular school to other schools where they will be in the minority is an indispensable remedy for those students willing to transfer to other schools in order to lessen the impact on them of the state-imposed stigma of segregation. In order to be effective, such a transfer arrangement must grant the transferring student free transportation and space must be made available in the school to which he desires to move. . . . The court orders in this and the companion Davis case now provide such an option.

(3) Remedial Altering of Attendance Zones.

The maps submitted in these cases graphically demonstrate that one of the principal tools employed by school planners and by courts to break up the dual school system has been a frank—and sometimes drastic—gerrymandering of school districts and attendance zones. An additional step was pairing, "clustering," or "grouping" of schools with attendance assignments made deliberately to accomplish the transfer of Negro students out of formerly segregated Negro schools and transfer of white students to formerly all-Negro schools. More often than not, these zones are neither compact nor contiguous; indeed they may be on opposite ends of the city. As in interim corrective measure, this cannot be said to be beyond the broad remedial powers of a court.

Absent a constitutional violation there would be no basis for judicially ordering assignment of students on a racial basis. All things being equal, with no history of discrimination, it might well be desirable to assign pupils to schools nearest their homes. But all things are not equal in a system that has been deliberately constructed and maintained to enforce racial segregation. . . .

No fixed or even substantially fixed guidelines can be established as to how far a court can go, but it must be recognized that there are limits. The objective is to dismantle the dual school system. "Racially neutral" assignment plans proposed by school authorities to a district court may be inadequate; such plans may fail to counteract the continuing effects of past school segregation resulting from discriminatory location of school sites or distortion of school size in order to achieve or maintain an artificial racial separation. When school authorities present a district court with a "loaded game board," affirmative action in the form of remedial altering of attendance zones is proper to achieve truly nondiscriminatory assignments.

In short, an assignment plan is not acceptable simply because it appears to be neutral. . . .

We hold that the pairing and grouping of non-contiguous school zones is a permissible tool and such action is to be considered in light of the objectives sought. . . .

(4) Transportation of Students.

The scope of permissible transportation of students as an implement of a remedial decree has never been defined by this Court and by the very nature of the problem it cannot be defined with precision. . . .

The importance of bus transportation as a normal and accepted tool of educational policy is readily discernible in this and the companion case. The Charlotte school authorities did not purport to assign students on the basis of geographically drawn zones until 1965 and then they allowed almost unlimited transfer privileges. The District Court's conclusion that assignment of children to the school nearest their home serving their grade would not produce an effective dismantling of the dual system is supported by the record.

Thus the remedial techniques used in the District Court's order were within that court's power to provide equitable relief; implementation of the decree is well within the capacity of the school authority.

The decree provided that the buses used to implement the plan would operate on direct routes. Students would be picked up at schools near their homes and transported to the schools they were to attend. The trips for elementary school pupils average about seven miles and the District Court found that they would take "not over 35 minutes at the most." This system compares favorably with the transportation plan previously operated in Charlotte under which each day 23,600 students on all grade levels were transported an average of 15 miles one way for an average trip requiring over an hour. In these circumstances, we find no basis for holding that the local school authorities may not be required to employ bus transportation as one tool of school desegregation. Desegregation plans cannot be limited to the walk-in school. . . .

. . . At some point, these school authorities and others like them should have achieved full compliance with this Court's decision in *Brown I*. The systems will then be "unitary" in the sense required by our decisions in *Green* [v. *County School Board*] and *Alexander* [v. *Holmes County Board of Education*].

It does not follow that the communities served by such systems will remain demographically stable, for in a growing, mobile society, few will do so. Neither school authorities nor district courts are constitutionally required to make year-by-year adjustments of the racial composition of student bodies once the affirmative duty to desegregate has been accomplished and racial discrimination through official action is eliminated from the system. This does not mean that federal courts are without power to deal with future problems; but in the absence of a showing that either the school authorities or some other agency of the State has deliberately attempted to fix or alter demographic patterns to affect the racial composition of the schools, further intervention by a district court should not be necessary. . . .

Case

MISSOURI V. JENKINS

515 U.S. 70; 115 S.Ct. 2038; 132 L.Ed. 2d 63 (1995)
Vote: 5–4

As of 1995, this case involving the Kansas City Metropolitan School District (KCMSD) had been in litigation for more than seventeen years. In 1977, a federal district court found that "prior to 1954 'Missouri mandated segregated schools for black and white children'" and that, since then, Kansas City school authorities "had failed in their affirmative obligations to eliminate the vestiges of the State's dual school system." The court then issued a series of remedial orders that necessitated dramatic funding increases in order to establish "magnet schools" to attract whites from the suburbs. The court also ordered salary increases for approximately 5,000 school employees at a cost of more than $200 million since 1987. Here the Supreme Court reviews the permissibility of the district court's mandates.

Chief Justice Rehnquist delivered the opinion of the Court.

. . . Almost 25 years ago, in *Swann v. Charlotte-Mecklenburg Bd. of Ed.* . . . (1971), we dealt with the authority of a district court to fashion remedies for a school district that had been segregated in law in violation of the Equal Protection Clause of the Fourteenth Amendment. Although recognizing the discretion that must necessarily adhere in a district court in fashioning a remedy, we also recognized the limits on such remedial power. . . .

Three years later, in *Milliken v. Bradley I* . . . (1974), we held that a District Court had exceeded its authority in fashioning interdistrict relief where the surrounding school districts had not themselves been guilty of any constitutional violation. . . . We said that a desegregation remedy "is necessarily designed, as all remedies are, to restore the victims of discriminatory conduct to the position they would have occupied in the absence of such conduct." . . . "[W]ithout an interdistrict violation and interdistrict effect, there is no constitutional wrong calling for an interdistrict remedy." . . . We also rejected "[t]he suggestion . . . that schools which have a majority of Negro students are not 'desegregated,' whatever the makeup of the school

district's population and however neutrally the district lines have been drawn and administered." . . .

Three years later, in *Milliken II* [1977], we articulated a three part framework derived from our prior cases to guide district courts in the exercise of their remedial authority. "In the first place, like other equitable remedies, the nature of the desegregation remedy is to be determined by the nature and scope of the constitutional violation. . . . Second, the decree must indeed be remedial in nature, that is, it must be designed as nearly as possible 'to restore the victims of discriminatory conduct to the position they would have occupied in the absence of such conduct.' . . . Third, the federal courts in devising a remedy must take into account the interests of state and local authorities in managing their own affairs, consistent with the Constitution." . . .

We added that the "principle that the nature and scope of the remedy are to be determined by the violation means simply that federal court decrees must directly address and relate to the constitutional violation itself." . . . In applying these principles, we have identified "student assignments, . . . 'faculty, staff, transportation, extracurricular activities and facilities,'" as the most important indicia of a racially segregated school system. . . .

Because "federal supervision of local school systems was intended as a temporary measure to remedy past discrimination," . . . we also have considered the showing that must be made by a school district operating under a desegregation order for complete or partial relief from that order.

. . . The ultimate inquiry is "whether the [constitutional violator] ha[s] complied in good faith with the desegregation decree since it was entered, and whether the vestiges of past discrimination ha[ve] been eliminated to the extent practicable." . . .

Proper analysis of the District Court's orders challenged here, then, must rest upon their serving as proper means to the end of restoring the victims of discriminatory conduct to the position they would have occupied in the absence of that conduct and their eventual restoration of "state and local authorities to the control of a school system that is operating in compliance with the Constitution." . . . We turn to that analysis.

The State argues that the order approving salary increases is beyond the District Court's authority because it was crafted to serve an "interdistrict goal," in spite of the fact that the constitutional violation in this case is "intradistrict" in nature. . . . The proper response to an intradistrict violation is an intradistrict remedy, . . . that serves to eliminate the racial identity of the schools within the effected school district by eliminating, as far as practicable, the vestiges of *de jure* segregation in all facets of their operations. . . .

Here, the District Court has found, and the Court of Appeals has affirmed, that this case involved no interdistrict constitutional violation that would support interdistrict relief. . . . Thus, the proper response by the District Court should have been to eliminate to the extent practicable the vestiges of prior *de jure* segregation within the KCMSD: a system wide reduction in student achievement and the existence of 25 racially identifiable schools with a population of over 90% black students. . . .

The District Court and Court of Appeals, however, have felt that because the KCMSD's enrollment remained 68.3% black, a purely intradistrict remedy would be insufficient. . . . But, as noted in *Milliken I,* . . . we have rejected the suggestion "that schools which have a majority of Negro students are not 'desegregated' whatever the racial makeup of the school district's population and however neutrally the district lines have been drawn and administered." . . .

Instead of seeking to remove the racial identity of the various schools within the KCMSD, the District Court has set out on a program to create a school district that was equal to or superior to the surrounding SSD's. Its remedy has focused on "desegregative attractiveness," coupled with "suburban comparability." Examination of the District Court's reliance on "desegregative attractiveness" and "suburban comparability" is instructive for our ultimate resolution of the salary order issue.

The purpose of desegregative attractiveness has been not only to remedy the system wide reduction in student achievement, but also to attract nonminority students not presently enrolled in the KCMSD. This remedy has included an elaborate program of capital improvements, course enrichment, and extracurricular enhancement not simply in the formerly identifiable black schools, but in schools throughout the district. The District Court's remedial orders have converted every senior high school, every middle school, and one half of the elementary schools in the KCMSD into "magnet" schools. The District Court's remedial order has all but made the KCMSD itself into a magnet district.

We previously have approved of intradistrict desegregation remedies involving magnet schools. . . . Magnet schools have the advantage of encouraging voluntary movement of students within a school district in a pattern that aids desegregation on a voluntary basis, without requiring extensive busing and redrawing of district boundary lines. . . . As a component in an intradistrict remedy, magnet schools also are attractive because they promote desegregation while limiting the withdrawal of white student enrollment that may result from mandatory student reassignment. . . .

The District Court's remedial plan in this case, however, is not designed solely to redistribute the students within the KCMSD in order to eliminate racially identifiable schools within the KCMSD. Instead, its purpose is to attract nonminority students from outside the KCMSD schools. But this interdistrict goal is beyond the scope of the intradistrict violation identified by the District Court. In effect, the District Court has devised a remedy to accomplish indirectly what it admittedly lacks the remedial authority to mandate directly: the interdistrict transfer of students. . . .

In *Milliken I* we determined that a desegregation remedy that would require mandatory interdistrict reassignment of students throughout the Detroit metropolitan area was an impermissible interdistrict response to the intradistrict violation identified. . . . In that case, the lower courts had ordered an interdistrict remedy because "any less comprehensive a solution than a metropolitan area plan would result in an all black school system immediately surrounded by practically all white suburban school systems, with an overwhelmingly white majority population in the total metropolitan area." . . . We held that before a district court could order an interdistrict remedy, there must be a showing that "racially discriminatory acts of the state or local school districts, or of a single school district have been a substantial cause of interdistrict segregation." . . . Because the record "contain[ed] evidence of *de jure* segregated conditions only in the Detroit Schools" and there had been "no showing of significant violation by the 53 outlying school districts and no evidence of interdistrict violation or effect," we reversed the District Court's grant of interdistrict relief. . . .

What we meant in *Milliken I* by an interdistrict violation was a violation that caused segregation between adjoining districts. Nothing in *Milliken I* suggests that the District Court in that case could have circumvented the limits on its remedial authority by requiring the State of Michigan, a constitutional violator, to implement a magnet program designed to achieve the same interdistrict transfer of students that we held was beyond its remedial authority. Here, the District Court has done just that: created a magnet district of the KCMSD in order to serve the interdistrict goal of attracting nonminority students from the surrounding SSD's and redistributing them within the KCMSD. The District Court's pursuit of "desegregative attractiveness" is beyond the scope of its broad remedial authority. . . .

. . . A district court seeking to remedy an intradistrict violation that has not "directly caused" significant interdistrict effects . . . exceeds its remedial authority if it orders a remedy with an interdistrict purpose. This conclusion follows directly from . . . the bedrock principle that "federal court decrees exceed appropriate limits if they are aimed at eliminating a condition that does not violate the Constitution or does not flow from such a violation." . . . In *Milliken II,* we also emphasized that "federal courts in devising a remedy must take into account the interests of state and local authorities in managing their own affairs, consistent with the Constitution." . . .

The District Court's pursuit of "desegregative attractiveness" cannot be reconciled with our cases placing limitations on a district court's remedial authority. It is certainly theoretically possible that the greater the expenditure per pupil within the KCMSD, the more likely it is that some unknowable number of nonminority students not presently attending schools in the KCMSD will choose to enroll in those schools. Under this reasoning, however, every increased expenditure, whether it be for teachers, noninstructional employees, books, or buildings, will make the KCMSD in some way more attractive, and thereby perhaps induce nonminority students to enroll in its schools. But this rationale is not susceptible to any objective limitation. . . . This case provides numerous examples demonstrating the limitless authority of the District Court operating under this rationale. . . . In short, desegregative attractiveness has been used "as the hook on which to hang numerous policy choices about improving the quality of education in general within the KCMSD." . . .

Nor are there limits to the duration of the District Court's involvement. The expenditures per pupil in the KCMSD currently far exceed those in the neighboring SSD's. . . . Sixteen years after this litigation began, the District Court recognized that the KCMSD has yet to offer a viable method of financing the "wonderful school system being built." . . . Each additional program ordered by the District Court—and financed by the State—to increase the "desegregative attractiveness" of the school district makes the KCMSD more and more dependent on additional funding from the State; in turn, the greater the KCMSD's dependence on state funding, the greater its reliance on continued supervision by the District Court. But our cases recognize that local autonomy of school districts is a vital national tradition, . . . and that a district court must strive to restore state and local authorities to the control of a school system operating in compliance with the Constitution. . . .

The District Court's pursuit of the goal of "desegregative attractiveness" results in so many imponderables and

is so far removed from the task of eliminating the racial identifiability of the schools within the KCMSD that we believe it is beyond the admittedly broad discretion of the District Court. In this posture, we conclude that the District Court's order of salary increases, which was "grounded in remedying the vestiges of segregation by improving the desegregative attractiveness of the KCMSD," . . . is simply too far removed from an acceptable implementation of a permissible means to remedy previous legally mandated segregation. . . .

Similar considerations lead us to conclude that the District Court's order requiring the State to continue to fund the quality education programs because student achievement levels were still "at or below national norms at many grade levels" cannot be sustained. The State does not seek from this Court a declaration of partial unitary status with respect to the quality education programs. . . . It challenges the requirement of indefinite funding of a quality education program until national norms are met, based on the assumption that while a mandate for significant educational improvement, both in teaching and in facilities, may have been justified originally, its indefinite extension is not. . . .

In reconsidering this order, the District Court should apply our three part test from [1992] *Freeman v. Pitts.* . . . The District Court should consider that the State's role with respect to the quality education programs has been limited to the funding, not the implementation, of those programs. As all the parties agree that improved achievement on test scores is not necessarily required for the State to achieve partial unitary status as to the quality education programs, the District Court should sharply limit, if not dispense with, its reliance on this factor. . . . Just as demographic changes independent of *de jure* segregation will affect the racial composition of student assignments, . . . so too will numerous external factors beyond the control of the KCMSD and the State affect minority student achievement. So long as these external factors are not the result of segregation, they do not figure in the remedial calculus. . . . Insistence upon academic goals unrelated to the effects of legal segregation unwarrantably postpones the day when the KCMSD will be able to operate on its own.

The District Court also should consider that many goals of its quality education plan already have been attained: the KCMSD now is equipped with "facilities and opportunities not available anywhere else in the country." . . . It may be that in education, just as it may be in economics, a "rising tide lifts all boats," but the remedial quality education program should be tailored to remedy the injuries suffered by the victims of prior *de jure* segregation. . . . Minority students in kindergarten through grade 7 in the KCMSD always have attended AAA rated schools;

minority students in the KCMSD that previously attended schools rated below AAA have since received remedial education programs for a period of up to seven years.

On remand, the District Court must bear in mind that its end purpose is not only "to remedy the violation" to the extent practicable, but also "to restore state and local authorities to the control of a school system that is operating in compliance with the Constitution." . . .

The judgment of the Court of Appeals is reversed.

Justice O'Connor, concurring. . . .

Justice Thomas, concurring.

. . . The mere fact that a school is black does not mean that it is the product of a constitutional violation. A "racial imbalance does not itself establish a violation of the Constitution." . . . Instead, in order to find unconstitutional segregation, we require that plaintiffs "prove all of the essential elements of *de jure* segregation—that is, stated simply, a current condition of segregation resulting from intentional state action directed specifically to the [allegedly segregated] schools." . . .

In the present case, the District Court inferred a continuing constitutional violation from two primary facts: the existence of *de jure* segregation in the KCMSD prior to 1954, and the existence of *de facto* segregation today. The District Court found that in 1954, the KCMSD operated 16 segregated schools for black students, and that in 1974 39 schools in the district were more than 90% black. Desegregation efforts reduced this figure somewhat, but the District Court stressed that 24 schools remained "racially isolated," that is, more than 90% black, in 1983–1984. . . . For the District Court, it followed that the KCMSD had not dismantled the dual system entirely. . . . The District Court also concluded that because of the KCMSD's failure to "become integrated on a system wide basis," the dual system still exerted "lingering effects" upon KCMSD black students, whose "general attitude of inferiority" produced "low achievement . . . which ultimately limits employment opportunities and causes poverty." . . .

Without more, the District Court's findings could not have supported a finding of liability against the state. It should by now be clear that the existence of one race schools is not by itself an indication that the State is practicing segregation. . . . The continuing "racial isolation" of schools after *de jure* segregation has ended may well reflect voluntary housing choices or other private decisions. Here, for instance, the demography of the entire KCMSD has changed considerably since 1954. Though blacks accounted for only 18.9% of KCMSD's enrollment in 1954, by 1983–1984 the school district was 67.7% black. . . . That certain schools are overwhelmingly black in a district that is now more than two thirds black is hardly a sure sign of intentional state action. . . .

Even if segregation were present, we must remember that a deserving end does not justify all possible means. The desire to reform a school district, or any other institution, cannot so captivate the Judiciary that it forgets its constitutionally mandated role. Usurpation of the traditionally local control over education not only takes the judiciary beyond its proper sphere, it also deprives the States and their elected officials of their constitutional powers. At some point, we must recognize that the judiciary is not omniscient, and that all problems do not require a remedy of constitutional proportions.

Justice Souter, with whom *Justice Stevens, Justice Ginsburg,* and *Justice Breyer* join, dissenting.

. . . On its face, the Court's opinion projects an appealing pragmatism in seeming to cut through the details of many facts by applying a rule of law that can claim both precedential support and intuitive sense, that there is error in imposing an interdistrict remedy to cure a merely intradistrict violation. Since the District Court has consistently described the violation here as solely intradistrict, and since the object of the magnet schools under its plan includes attracting students into the district from other districts, the Court's result seems to follow with the necessity of logic, against which arguments about detail or calls for fair warning may not carry great weight.

The attractiveness of the Court's analysis disappears, however, as soon as we recognize two things. First, the District Court did not mean by an "intradistrict violation" what the Court apparently means by it today. The District Court meant that the violation within the KCMSD had not led to segregation outside of it, and that no other school districts had played a part in the violation. It did not mean that the violation had not produced effects of any sort beyond the district. Indeed, the record that we have indicates that the District Court understood that the violation here did produce effects spanning district borders and leading to greater segregation within the KCMSD, the reversal of which the District Court sought to accomplish by establishing magnet schools. Insofar as the Court assumes that this was not so in fact, there is at least enough in the record to cast serious doubt on its assumption. Second, the Court violates existing case law even on its own apparent view of the facts, that the segregation violation within the KCMSD produced no proven effects, segregative or otherwise, outside it. Assuming this to be true, the Court's decision that the rule against interdistrict remedies for intradistrict violations applies to this case, solely because the remedy here is meant to produce effects outside the district in which the violation occurred, is flatly contrary to established precedent. . . .

Justice Ginsburg, dissenting. . . .

Case

ADARAND CONSTRUCTORS, INC. V. PEÑA

515 U.S. 200; 115 S.Ct. 2097; 132 L.Ed. 2d 158 (1995)
Vote: 5–4

In this case the Court reexamines the controversial issue of affirmative action in the context of the federal government's practice of providing financial incentives to contractors to hire minority subcontractors.

Justice O'Connor announced the judgment of the Court. . . .

Petitioner Adarand Constructors, Inc., claims that the Federal Government's practice of giving general contractors on government projects a financial incentive to hire subcontractors controlled by "socially and economically disadvantaged individuals," and in particular, the Government's use of race-based presumptions in identifying such individuals, violates the equal protection component of the Fifth Amendment's Due Process Clause. The Court of Appeals rejected Adarand's claim. We conclude, however, that courts should analyze cases of this kind under a different standard of review than the one the Court of Appeals applied. We therefore vacate the Court of Appeals' judgment and remand the case for further proceedings. . . .

In 1989, the Central Federal Lands Highway Division (CFLHD), which is part of the United States Department of Transportation (DOT), awarded the prime contract for a highway construction project in Colorado to Mountain Gravel & Construction Company. Mountain Gravel then solicited bids from subcontractors for the guardrail portion of the contract. Adarand, a Colorado-based highway construction company specializing in guardrail work, submitted the low bid. . . . Gonzales Construction Company also submitted a bid.

The prime contract's terms provide that Mountain Gravel would receive additional compensation if it hired subcontractors certified as small businesses controlled by "socially and economically disadvantaged individuals," . . . Gonzales is certified as such a business; Adarand is not. Mountain Gravel awarded the subcontract to Gonzales, despite Adarand's low bid, and Mountain Gravel's Chief Estimator has submitted an affidavit stating that Mountain Gravel would have accepted Adarand's bid, had it not been for the additional payment it received by hiring Gonzales instead. . . . Federal law requires that a subcontracting clause similar to the one used here must appear in most federal agency contracts, and it also requires the clause to state that "[t]he contractor shall pre-

sume that socially and economically disadvantaged individuals include Black Americans, Hispanic Americans, Native Americans, Asian Pacific Americans, and other minorities, or any other individual found to be disadvantaged by the [Small Business] Administration pursuant to section 8(a) of the Small Business Act." . . . Adarand claims that the presumption set forth in that statute discriminates on the basis of race in violation of the Federal Government's Fifth Amendment obligation not to deny anyone equal protection of the laws. . . .

The Government urges that "[t]he Subcontracting Compensation Clause program is . . . a program based on disadvantage, not on race," and thus that it is subject only to "the most relaxed judicial scrutiny." . . . To the extent that the statutes and regulations involved in this case are race neutral, we agree. The Government concedes, however, that "the race-based rebuttable presumption used in some certification determinations under the Subcontracting Compensation Clause" is subject to some heightened level of scrutiny. . . . The parties disagree as to what that level should be. . . .

. . . [T]he Court's cases through [*Richmond v. J. A. Croson Co.*] had established three general propositions with respect to governmental racial classifications. First, skepticism: "[a]ny preference based on racial or ethnic criteria must necessarily receive a most searching examination." . . . Second, consistency: "the standard of review under the Equal Protection Clause is not dependent on the race of those burdened or benefited by a particular classification." . . . And third, congruence: "[e]qual protection analysis in the Fifth Amendment area is the same as that under the Fourteenth Amendment." . . . Taken together, these three propositions lead to the conclusion that any person, of whatever race, has the right to demand that any governmental actor subject to the Constitution justify any racial classification subjecting that person to unequal treatment under the strictest judicial scrutiny. . . .

A year later, however, the Court took a surprising turn. *Metro Broadcasting, Inc. v. FCC* . . . (1990) involved a Fifth Amendment challenge to two race-based policies of the Federal Communications Commission. In *Metro Broadcasting,* the Court repudiated the long-held notion that "it would be unthinkable that the same Constitution would impose a lesser duty on the Federal Government" than it does on a State to afford equal protection of the laws. . . . It did so by holding that "benign" federal racial classifications need only satisfy intermediate scrutiny, even though *Croson* had recently concluded that such classifications enacted by a State must satisfy strict scrutiny. "[B]enign" federal racial classifications, the Court said, "even if those measures are not 'remedial' in the sense of being designed to compensate victims of past governmental or societal discrimination are constitutionally permissible to the extent that they serve important governmental objectives within the power of Congress and are substantially related to achievement of those objectives." . . . The Court did not explain how to tell whether a racial classification should be deemed "benign," other than to express "confiden[ce] that an 'examination of the legislative scheme and its history' will separate benign measures from other types of racial classifications." . . .

Applying this test, the Court first noted that the FCC policies at issue did not serve as a remedy for past discrimination. . . . Proceeding on the assumption that the policies were nonetheless "benign," it concluded that they served the "important governmental objective" of "enhancing broadcast diversity," . . . and that they were "substantially related" to that objective. . . . It therefore upheld the policies.

By adopting intermediate scrutiny as the standard of review for congressionally mandated "benign" racial classifications, *Metro Broadcasting* departed from prior cases in two significant respects. First, it turned its back on *Croson*'s explanation of why strict scrutiny of all governmental racial classifications is essential. . . .

Second, *Metro Broadcasting* squarely rejected one of the three propositions established by the Court's earlier equal protection cases, namely, congruence between the standards applicable to federal and state racial classifications, and in so doing also undermined the other two—skepticism of all racial classifications, and consistency of treatment irrespective of the race of the burdened or benefited group. . . . Under *Metro Broadcasting,* certain racial classifications ("benign" ones enacted by the Federal Government) should be treated less skeptically than others; and the race of the benefited group is critical to the determination of which standard of review to apply. *Metro Broadcasting* was thus a significant departure from much of what had come before it.

The three propositions undermined by *Metro Broadcasting* all derive from the basic principle that the Fifth and Fourteenth Amendments to the Constitution protect persons, not groups. It follows from that principle that all governmental action based on race—a group classification long recognized as "in most circumstances irrelevant and therefore prohibited," . . . should be subjected to detailed judicial inquiry to ensure that the personal right to equal protection of the laws has not been infringed. These ideas have long been central to this Court's understanding of equal protection, and holding "benign" state and federal racial classifications to different standards does not square with them. "[A] free people whose institutions are founded upon the doctrine of equality," . . . should tolerate no retreat from the principle that government may treat people differently because of their race only for the most compelling reasons. Accordingly, we hold today that all racial classifications, imposed by whatever federal, state, or local governmental actor, must be analyzed by a reviewing court under strict scrutiny. In other words, such classifications are constitutional only if they are narrowly tailored measures that further compelling governmental interests. To the extent that *Metro Broadcasting* is inconsistent with that holding, it is overruled. . . .

"Although adherence to precedent is not rigidly required in constitutional cases, any departure from the doctrine of *stare decisis* demands special justification." . . . In deciding whether this case presents such justification, we recall Justice Frankfurter's admonition that "*stare decisis* is a principle of policy and not a mechanical formula of adherence to the latest decision, however recent and questionable, when such adherence involves collision with a prior doctrine more embracing in its scope, intrinsically sounder, and verified by experience." . . . Remaining true to an "intrinsically sounder" doctrine established in prior cases better serves the values of *stare decisis* than would following a more recently decided case inconsistent with the decisions that came before it; the latter course would simply compound the recent error and would likely make the unjustified break from previously established doctrine complete. In such a situation, "special justification" exists to depart from the recently decided case.

As we have explained, *Metro Broadcasting* undermined important principles of this Court's equal protection jurisprudence, established in a line of cases stretching back over fifty years. . . . Those principles together stood for an "embracing" and "intrinsically soun[d]" understanding of equal protection "verified by experience," namely, that the Constitution imposes upon federal, state, and local governmental actors the same obligation to respect the personal right to equal protection of the laws. . . .

Some have questioned the importance of debating the proper standard of review of race-based legislation. . . . But we agree . . . that, "[b]ecause racial characteristics so seldom provide a relevant basis for disparate treatment, and because classifications based on race are potentially so harmful to the entire body politic, it is especially important that the reasons for any such classification be clearly identified and unquestionably legitimate," and that "[r]acial classifications are simply too pernicious to permit any but the most exact connection between justification and classification." . . . We think that requiring strict scrutiny is the best way to ensure that courts will consistently give racial classifications that kind of detailed examination, both as to ends and as to means.

. . . Any retreat from the most searching judicial inquiry can only increase the risk of another such error occurring in the future.

Finally, we wish to dispel the notion that strict scrutiny is "strict in theory, but fatal in fact." . . . The unhappy persistence of both the practice and the lingering effects of racial discrimination against minority groups in this country is an unfortunate reality, and government is not disqualified from acting in response to it. As recently as 1987, for example, every Justice of this Court agreed that the Alabama Department of Public Safety's "pervasive, systematic, and obstinate discriminatory conduct" justified a narrowly tailored race-based remedy. . . . When race-based action is necessary to further a compelling interest, such action is within constitutional constraints if it satisfies the "narrow tailoring" test this Court has set out in previous cases. . . .

Because our decision today alters the playing field in some important respects, we think it best to remand the case to the lower courts for further consideration in light of the principles we have announced. The Court of Appeals, following *Metro Broadcasting* and *Fullilove*, analyzed the case in terms of intermediate scrutiny. It upheld the challenged statutes and regulations because it found them to be "narrowly tailored to achieve [their] significant governmental purpose of providing subcontracting opportunities for small disadvantaged business enterprises." . . . The Court of Appeals did not decide the question whether the interests served by the use of subcontractor compensation clauses are properly described as "compelling." It also did not address the question of narrow tailoring in terms of our strict scrutiny cases, by asking, for example, whether there was "any consideration of the use of race-neutral means to increase minority business participation" in government contracting, . . . whether the program was appropriately limited such that it "will not last longer than the discriminatory effects it is designed to eliminate." . . .

Moreover, unresolved questions remain concerning the details of the complex regulatory regimes implicated by the use of subcontractor compensation clauses. . . . The question whether any of the ways in which the Government uses subcontractor compensation clauses can survive strict scrutiny, and any relevance distinctions such as these may have to that question, should be addressed in the first instance by the lower courts.

Accordingly, the judgment of the Court of Appeals is vacated, and the case is remanded for further proceedings consistent with this opinion. . . .

Justice Scalia, concurring in part and concurring in the judgment.

I join the opinion of the Court, except . . . insofar as it may be inconsistent with the following: In my view, government can never have a "compelling interest" in discriminating on the basis of race in order to "make up" for past racial discrimination in the opposite direction. . . . Individuals who have been wronged by unlawful racial discrimination should be made whole; but under our Constitution there can be no such thing as either a creditor or a debtor race. That concept is alien to the Constitution's focus upon the individual . . . and its rejection of dispositions based on race. . . . To pursue the concept of racial entitlement—even for the most admirable and benign of purposes—is to reinforce and preserve for future mischief the way of thinking that produced race slavery, race privilege and race hatred. In the eyes of government, we are just one race here. It is American.

It is unlikely, if not impossible, that the challenged program would survive under this understanding of strict scrutiny, but I am content to leave that to be decided on remand.

Justice Thomas, concurring in part and concurring in the judgment.

I agree with the majority's conclusion that strict scrutiny applies to all government classifications based on race. I write separately, however, to express my disagreement with the premise underlying Justice Stevens' and Justice Ginsburg's dissents: that there is a racial paternalism exception to the principle of equal protection. I believe that there is a "moral [and] constitutional equivalence" . . . between laws designed to subjugate a race and those that distribute benefits on the basis of race in order to foster some current notion of equality. Government cannot make us equal; it can only recognize, respect, and protect us as equal before the law.

That these programs may have been motivated, in part, by good intentions cannot provide refuge from the principle that under our Constitution, the government may not make distinctions on the basis of race. As far as the Constitution is concerned, it is irrelevant whether a government's racial classifications are drawn by those who wish to oppress a race or by those who have a sincere desire to help those thought to be disadvantaged. There can be no doubt that the paternalism that appears to lie at the heart of this program is at war with the principle of inherent equality that underlies and infuses our Constitution. . . .

These programs not only raise grave constitutional questions, they also undermine the moral basis of the equal protection principle. Purchased at the price of immeasurable human suffering, the equal protection principle reflects our Nation's understanding that such classifications ultimately have a destructive impact on the individual and our society. Unquestionably, "[i]nvidious [racial] discrimination is an engine of oppression." . . . It is also true that "[r]emedial" racial preferences may reflect "a desire to foster equality in society." . . . But there can be no doubt that racial paternalism and its unintended consequences can be as poisonous and pernicious as any other form of discrimination. So-called "benign" discrimination teaches many that because of chronic and apparently immutable handicaps, minorities cannot compete with them without their patronizing indulgence. Inevitably, such programs engender attitudes of superiority or, alternatively, provoke resentment among those who believe that they have been wronged by the government's use of race. These programs stamp minorities with a badge of inferiority and may cause them to develop dependencies or to adopt an attitude that they are "entitled" to preferences. . . .

In my mind, government-sponsored racial discrimination based on benign prejudice is just as noxious as discrimination inspired by malicious prejudice. In each instance, it is racial discrimination, plain and simple. . . .

Justice Stevens, with whom **Justice Ginsburg** joins, dissenting.

. . . This is the third time in the Court's entire history that it has considered the constitutionality of a federal affirmative-action program. On each of the two prior occasions, the first in 1980, . . . and the second in 1990, . . . the Court upheld the program. Today the Court explicitly overrules *Metro Broadcasting* . . . and undermines *Fullilove* [v. *Klutznick* (1980)] by recasting the standard on which it rested and by calling even its holding into question. . . . By way of explanation, Justice O'Connor advises the federal agencies and private parties that have made countless decisions in reliance on those cases that "we do not depart from the fabric of the law; we restore it." A skeptical observer might ask whether this pronouncement is a faithful application of the doctrine of *stare decisis.* . . .

The Court's holding in *Fullilove* surely governs the result in this case. The Public Works Employment Act of 1977 . . . which this Court upheld in *Fullilove,* is different in several critical respects from the portions of the Small Business Act (SBA) . . . and the Surface Transportation and Uniform Relocation Assistance Act of 1987 (STURAA) . . . challenged in this case. Each of those differences makes the current program designed to provide assistance to disadvantaged business enterprises (DBE's) significantly less objectionable than the 1977 categorical grant of $400 million in exchange for a 10% set-aside in public contracts to "a class of investors defined solely by racial characteristics." . . . In no meaningful respect is the current scheme

more objectionable than the 1977 Act. Thus, if the 1977 Act was constitutional, then so must be the SBA and STURAA. Indeed, even if my dissenting views in *Fullilove* had prevailed, this program would be valid.

Unlike the 1977 Act, the present statutory scheme does not make race the sole criterion of eligibility for participation in the program. Race does give rise to a rebuttable presumption of social disadvantage which, at least under STURAA, gives rise to a second rebuttable presumption of economic disadvantage. . . . But a small business may qualify as a DBE, by showing that it is both socially and economically disadvantaged, even if it receives neither of these presumptions. . . . Thus, the current preference is more inclusive than the 1977 Act because it does not make race a necessary qualification.

More importantly, race is not a sufficient qualification. Whereas a millionaire with a long history of financial successes, who was a member of numerous social clubs and trade associations, would have qualified for a preference under the 1977 Act merely because he was an Asian American or an African American, . . . neither the SBA nor STURAA creates any such anomaly. The DBE program excludes members of minority races who are not, in fact, socially or economically disadvantaged. . . . The presumption of social disadvantage reflects the unfortunate fact that irrational racial prejudice—along with its lingering effects—still survives. The presumption of economic disadvantage embodies a recognition that success in the private sector of the economy is often attributable, in part, to social skills and relationships. Unlike the 1977 set-asides, the current preference is designed to overcome the social and economic disadvantages that are often associated with racial characteristics. If, in a particular case, these disadvantages are not present, the presumptions can be rebutted. . . . The program is thus designed to allow race to play a part in the decisional process only when there is a meaningful basis for assuming its relevance. . . .

The current program contains another forward-looking component that the 1977 set-asides did not share. Section 8(a) of the SBA provides for periodic review of the status of DBE's, . . . and DBE status can be challenged by a competitor at any time under any of the routes to certification. . . . Such review prevents ineligible firms from taking part in the program solely because of their minority ownership, even when those firms were once disadvantaged but have since become successful. The emphasis on review also indicates the Administration's anticipation that after their presumed disadvantages have been overcome, firms will "graduate" into a status in which they will be able to compete for business, including prime contracts, on an equal basis. . . . As with other phases of the statutory policy of encouraging the formation and growth of small business enterprises, this program is intended to facilitate entry and increase competition in the free market.

Significantly, the current program, unlike the 1977 set-aside, does not establish any requirement—numerical or otherwise—that a general contractor must hire DBE subcontractors. The program we upheld in *Fullilove* required that 10% of the federal grant for every federally funded project be expended on minority business enterprises. In contrast, the current program contains no quota. Although it provides monetary incentives to general contractors to hire DBE subcontractors, it does not require them to hire DBE's, and they do not lose their contracts if they fail to do so. The importance of this incentive to general contractors (who always seek to offer the lowest bid) should not be underestimated; but the preference here is far less rigid, and thus more narrowly tailored, than the 1977 Act. . . .

Finally, the record shows a dramatic contrast between the sparse deliberations that preceded the 1977 Act, . . . and the extensive hearings conducted in several Congresses before the current program was developed. However we might evaluate the benefits and costs—both fiscal and social—of this or any other affirmative-action program, our obligation to give deference to Congress' policy choices is much more demanding in this case than it was in *Fullilove*. If the 1977 program of race-based set-asides satisfied the strict scrutiny dictated by Justice Powell's vision of the Constitution—a vision the Court expressly endorses today—it must follow as night follows the day that the Court of Appeals' judgment upholding this more carefully crafted program should be affirmed. . . .

My skeptical scrutiny of the Court's opinion leaves me in dissent. The majority's concept of "consistency" ignores a difference, fundamental to the idea of equal protection, between oppression and assistance. The majority's concept of "congruence" ignores a difference, fundamental to our constitutional system, between the Federal Government and the States. And the majority's concept of *stare decisis* ignores the force of binding precedent. I would affirm the judgment of the Court of Appeals.

Justice Souter, with whom **Justice Ginsburg** and **Justice Breyer** join, dissenting. . . .

Justice Ginsburg, with whom **Justice Breyer** joins, dissenting.

Case

Frontiero v. Richardson

411 U.S. 677; 93 S.Ct. 1764; 36 L.Ed. 2d 583 (1973)
Vote: 8–1

In this landmark case, the Court considers the appropriate standard of equal protection review in cases alleging gender discrimination by the government.

Mr. Justice Brennan announced the judgment of the Court and an opinion in which **Mr. Justice Douglas, Mr. Justice White,** and **Mr. Justice Marshall** join.

The question before us concerns the right of a female member of the uniformed services to claim her spouse as a "dependent" for the purposes of obtaining increased quarters allowances and medical and dental benefits . . . on an equal footing with male members. Under [the statutes at issue], a serviceman may claim his wife as a "dependent" without regard to whether she is in fact dependent upon him for any part of her support. A servicewoman, on the other hand, may not claim her husband as a "dependent" under these programs unless he is in fact dependent upon her for over one-half of his support. . . . Thus, the question for decision is whether this difference in treatment constitutes an unconstitutional discrimination against servicewomen in violation of the [equal protection component] of the Fifth Amendment. A three-judge District Court for the Middle District of Alabama, one judge dissenting, rejected this contention and sustained the constitutionality of the provisions of the statutes making this distinction. . . . We noted probable jurisdiction. . . . We reverse. . . .

In an effort to attract career personnel through reenlistment, Congress established . . . a scheme for the provision of fringe benefits to members of the uniformed services on a competitive basis with business and industry. . . . [A] member of the uniformed services with dependents is entitled to an increased "basic allowance for quarters" and . . . a member's dependents are provided comprehensive medical and dental care.

Appellant Sharron Frontiero, a lieutenant in the United States Air Force, sought increased quarters allowance, and housing and medical benefits for her husband, appellant Joseph Frontiero, on the ground that he was her "dependent." Although such benefits would automatically have been granted with respect to the wife of a male member of the uniformed services, appellant's application was denied because she failed to demonstrate that her husband was dependent on her for more than one-half of his support. Appellants then commenced this suit, contending that, by making this distinction, the statutes unreasonably discriminate on the basis of sex in violation of the Due Process Clause of the Fifth Amendment. In essence, appellants asserted that the discriminatory impact of the statutes is two-fold: first, as a procedural matter, a female member is required to demonstrate her spouse's dependency, while no such burden is imposed upon male members; and second, as a substantive matter, a male member who does not provide more than one-half of his wife's support receives benefits, while a similarly situated female member is denied such benefits. Appellants therefore sought a permanent injunction against the continued enforcement of these statutes and an order directing the appellees to provide Lieutenant Frontiero with the same housing and medical benefits that a similarly situated male member would receive.

Although the legislative history of these statutes sheds virtually no light on the purposes underlying the differential treatment accorded male and female members, a majority of the three-judge District Court surmised that Congress might reasonably have concluded that, since the husband in our society is generally the "breadwinner" in the family—and the wife typically the "dependent" partner—"it would be more economical to require married female members claiming husbands to prove actual dependency than to extend the presumption of dependency to such members." . . . Indeed, given the fact that approximately 99% of all members of the uniformed services are male, the District Court speculated that such differential treatment might conceivably lead to a "considerable saving of administrative expense and manpower." . . .

At the outset, appellants contend that classifications based upon sex, like classifications based upon race, alienage, and national origin, are inherently suspect and must therefore be subjected to close judicial scrutiny. We agree and, indeed, find at least implicit support for such an approach in our unanimous decision only last Term in *Reed v. Reed.* . . .

In *Reed,* the Court considered the constitutionality of an Idaho statute providing that, when two individuals are otherwise equally entitled to appointment as administrator of an estate, the male applicant must be preferred to the female. Appellant, the mother of the deceased, and appellee, the father, filed competing petitions for appointment as administrator of their son's estate. Since the parties, as parents of the deceased, were members of the same entitlement class, the statutory preference was invoked and the father's petition was therefore granted. Appellant claimed that this statute, by giving a mandatory preference to males over females without regard to their individual qualifications, violated the Equal Protection Clause of the Fourteenth Amendment.

The Court noted that the Idaho statute "provides that different treatment be accorded to the applicants on the basis of their sex; it thus establishes a classification subject to scrutiny under the Equal Protection Clause." . . . Under "traditional" equal protection analysis, a legislative classification must be sustained unless it is "patently arbitrary" and bears no rational relationship to a legitimate governmental interest. . . .

In an effort to meet this standard, appellee contended that the statutory scheme was a reasonable measure designed to reduce the workload on probate courts by eliminating one class of contests. Moreover, appellee argued that the mandatory preference for male applicants was in itself reasonable since "men [are] as a rule more conversant with business affairs than . . . women." Indeed, appellee maintained that "it is a matter of common knowledge, that women still are not engaged in politics, the professions, business or industry to the extent that men are." And the Idaho Supreme Court, in upholding the constitutionality of this statute, suggested that the Idaho Legislature might reasonably have "concluded that in general men are better qualified to act as an administrator than are women."

Despite these contentions, however, the Court held the statutory preference for male applicants unconstitutional. In reaching this result, the Court implicitly rejected appellee's apparently rational explanation of the statutory scheme, and concluded that, by ignoring the individual qualifications of particular applicants, the challenged statute provided "dissimilar treatment for men and women who are . . . similarly situated." . . . The Court therefore held that, even though the State's interest in achieving administrative efficiency "is not without some legitimacy," . . . "[t]o give a mandatory preference to members of either sex over members of the other, merely to accomplish the elimination of hearings on the merits, is to make the very kind of arbitrary legislative choice forbidden by the [Constitution]. . . ." . . . This departure from "traditional" rational basis analysis with respect to sex-based classifications is clearly justified.

There can be no doubt that our Nation has had a long and unfortunate history of sex discrimination. Traditionally, such discrimination was rationalized by an attitude of "romantic paternalism" which, in practical effect, put women not on a pedestal, but in a cage. Indeed, this paternalistic attitude became so firmly rooted in our national consciousness that, exactly 100 years ago, a distinguished member of this Court was about to proclaim:

> Man is, or should be, woman's protector and defender. The natural and proper timidity and delicacy which

belongs to the female sex evidently unfits it for many of the occupations of civil life. The constitution of the family organizations, which is founded in the divine ordinance, as well as in the nature of things, indicates the domestic sphere as that which properly belongs to the domain and functions of womanhood. The harmony, not to say identity, of interests and views which belong, or should belong, to the family institution is repugnant to the ideas of a woman adopting a distinct and independent career from that of her husband. . . . The paramount destiny and mission of woman are to fulfill the noble and benign offices of wife and mother. This is the law of the Creator. . . .

As a result of notions such as these, our statute books gradually became laden with gross, stereotypical distinctions between the sexes and, indeed, throughout much of the 19th century the position of women in our society was, in many respects, comparable to that of blacks under the pre-Civil War slave codes. Neither slaves nor women could hold office, serve on juries, or bring suit in their own names, and married women traditionally were denied the legal capacity to hold or convey property or to serve as legal guardians of their own children. . . . And although blacks were guaranteed the right to vote in 1870, women were denied even that right—which is itself "preservative of other basic civil and political rights"—until adoption of the Nineteenth Amendment half a century later.

It is true, of course, that the position of women in America has improved markedly in recent decades. Nevertheless, it can hardly be doubted that, in part because of the high visibility of the sex characteristic, women still face pervasive, although at times more subtle, discrimination in our educational institutions, on the job market and, perhaps most conspicuously, in the political arena. . . .

Moreover, since sex, like race and national origin, is an immutable characteristic determined solely by the accident of birth, the imposition of special disabilities upon the members of a particular sex because of their sex would seem to violate "the basic concept of our system that legal burdens should bear some relationship to individual responsibility. . . ." . . . And what differentiates sex from such nonsuspect statuses as intelligence or physical disability, and aligns it with the recognized suspect criteria, is that the sex characteristic frequently bears no relation to ability to perform or contribute to society. As a result, statutory distinctions between the sexes often have the effect of invidiously relegating the entire class of females to inferior legal status without regard to the actual capabilities of its individual members.

We might also note that, over the past decade, Congress has itself manifested an increasing sensitivity to sex-based classifications. In Title VII of the Civil Rights Act of 1964,

for example, Congress expressly declared that no employer, labor union, or other organization subject to the provisions of the Act shall discriminate against any individual on the basis of "race, color, religion, sex, or national origin." Similarly, the Equal Pay Act of 1963 provides that no employer covered by the Act "shall discriminate . . . between employees on the basis of sex." And Section 1 of the Equal Rights Amendment, passed by Congress on March 22, 1972, and submitted to the legislatures of the States for ratification, declares that "[e]quality of rights under the law shall not be denied or abridged by the United States or by any State on account of sex." Thus, Congress has itself concluded that classifications based upon sex are inherently invidious, and this conclusion of a coequal branch of government is not without significance to the question presently under consideration. . . .

With these considerations in mind, we can only conclude that classifications based upon sex, like classifications based upon race, alienage, or national origin, are inherently suspect, and must therefore be subjected to strict judicial scrutiny. Applying the analysis mandated by that stricter standard of review, it is clear that the statutory scheme now before us is constitutionally invalid.

The sole basis of the classification established in the challenged statutes is the sex of the individuals involved. Thus . . . a female member of the uniformed services seeking to obtain housing and medical benefits for her spouse must prove his dependency in fact, whereas no such burden is imposed upon male members. In addition, the statutes operate so as to deny benefits to a female member, such as appellant Sharron Frontiero, who provides less than one-half of her spouse's support, while at the same time granting such benefits to a male member who likewise provides less than one-half of his spouse's support. Thus to this extent at least, it may fairly be said that these statutes command "dissimilar treatment for men and women who are . . . similarly situated." . . .

Moreover, the Government concedes that the differential treatment accorded men and women under these statutes serves no purpose other than mere "administrative convenience." In essence, the Government maintains that, as an empirical matter, wives in our society frequently are dependent upon their husbands, while husbands rarely are dependent upon their wives. Thus, the Government argues that Congress might reasonably have concluded that it would be both cheaper and easier simply conclusively to presume that wives of male members are financially dependent upon their husbands, while burdening female members with the task of establishing dependency in fact.

The Government offers no concrete evidence, however, tending to support its view that such differential treatment in fact saves the Government any money. In order to satisfy the demands of strict judicial scrutiny, the Government must demonstrate, for example, that it is actually cheaper to grant increased benefits with respect to all male members, than it is to determine which male members are in fact entitled to such benefits and to grant increased benefits only to those members whose wives actually meet the dependency requirement. Here, however, there is substantial evidence that, if put to the test, many of the wives of male members would fail to qualify for benefits. And in light of the fact that the dependency determination with respect to the husbands of female members is presently made solely on the basis of affidavits, rather than through the more costly hearing process, the Government's explanation of the statutory scheme is, to say the least, questionable.

In any case, our prior decisions make clear that, although efficacious administration of governmental programs is not without some importance, "the Constitution recognizes higher values than speed and efficiency." . . . And when we enter the realm of "strict judicial scrutiny," there can be no doubt that "administrative convenience" is not a shibboleth, the mere recitation of which dictates constitutionality. . . . On the contrary, any statutory scheme which draws a sharp line between the sexes, solely for the purpose of achieving administrative convenience, necessarily commands "dissimilar treatment for men and women who are . . . similarly situated," and therefore involves the "very kind of arbitrary legislative choice forbidden by the [Constitution]. . . ." . . . We therefore conclude that, by according differential treatment to male and female members of the uniformed services for the sole purpose of achieving administrative convenience, the challenged statutes violate the Due Process Clause of the Fifth Amendment insofar as they require a female member to prove the dependency of her husband. . . .

Mr. Justice Powell, with whom the *Chief Justice* and **Mr. Justice Blackmun** join, concurring in the judgment.

I agree that the challenged statutes constitute an unconstitutional discrimination against service women in violation of the Due Process Clause of the Fifth Amendment, but I cannot join the opinion of Mr. Justice Brennan, which would hold that all classifications based upon sex, "like classifications based upon race, alienage, and national origin," are "inherently suspect and must therefore be subjected to close judicial scrutiny." . . . It is unnecessary for the Court in this case to characterize sex as a suspect classification, with all of the far-reaching implications of such a holding. . . . In my view, we can and should decide this case on the authority of *Reed* and reserve for the future any expansion of its rationale.

There is another, and I find compelling, reason for deferring a general categorizing of sex classifications as invoking the strictest test of judicial scrutiny. The Equal Rights Amendment, which if adopted will resolve the substance of this precise question, has been approved by the Congress and submitted for ratification by the States. If this Amendment is duly adopted, it will represent the will of the people accomplished in the manner prescribed by the Constitution. By acting prematurely and unnecessarily, as I view it, the Court has assumed a decisional responsibility at the very time when state legislatures, functioning within the traditional democratic process, are debating the proposed Amendment. It seems to me that this reaching out to pre-empt by judicial action a major political decision which is currently in process of resolution does not reflect appropriate respect for duly prescribed legislative processes.

There are times when this Court, under our system, cannot avoid a constitutional decision on issues which normally should be resolved by the elected representatives of the people. But democratic institutions are weakened, and confidence in the restraint of the Court is impaired, when we appear unnecessarily to decide sensitive issues of broad social and political importance at the very time they are under consideration within the prescribed constitutional processes.

Mr. Justice Stewart concurs in the judgment, agreeing that the statutes before us work an invidious discrimination in violation of the Constitution. . . .

Mr. Justice Rehnquist dissents.

Case

UNITED STATES V. VIRGINIA

518 U.S. 515; 116 S.Ct. 2264; 135 L.Ed. 2d 735 (1996)
Vote: 7–1

In this case the Court considers the male-only admissions policy of Virginia Military Institute. Justice Ruth Ginsburg, who as an attorney argued a number of important gender discrimination cases before the High Court, authors the majority opinion.

Justice Ginsburg delivered the opinion of the Court.

Virginia's public institutions of higher learning include an incomparable military college, Virginia Military Institute (VMI). The United States maintains that the Constitution's equal protection guarantee precludes Virginia from reserving exclusively to men the unique educational opportunities VMI affords. We agree.

Founded in 1839, VMI is today the sole single-sex school among Virginia's 15 public institutions of higher learning. VMI's distinctive mission is to produce "citizen-soldiers," men prepared for leadership in civilian life and in military service. VMI pursues this mission through pervasive training of a kind not available anywhere else in Virginia. Assigning prime place to character development, VMI uses an "adversative method" modeled on English public schools and once characteristic of military instruction. VMI constantly endeavors to instill physical and mental discipline in its cadets and impart to them a strong moral code. The school's graduates leave VMI with heightened comprehension of their capacity to deal with duress and stress, and a large sense of accomplishment for completing the hazardous course.

VMI has notably succeeded in its mission to produce leaders; among its alumni are military generals, Members of Congress, and business executives. The school's alumni overwhelmingly perceive that their VMI training helped them to realize their personal goals. VMI's endowment reflects the loyalty of its graduates; VMI has the largest per-student endowment of all undergraduate institutions in the Nation.

Neither the goal of producing citizen-soldiers nor VMI's implementing methodology is inherently unsuitable to women. And the school's impressive record in producing leaders has made admission desirable to some women. Nevertheless, Virginia has elected to preserve exclusively for men the advantages and opportunities a VMI education affords.

From its establishment in 1839 as one of the Nation's first state military colleges, . . . VMI has remained finan-cially supported by Virginia and "subject to the control of the [Virginia] General Assembly." . . .

VMI today enrolls about 1,300 men as cadets. Its academic offerings in the liberal arts, sciences, and engineering are also available at other public colleges and universities in Virginia. But VMI's mission is special. It is the mission of the school "to produce educated and honorable men, prepared for the varied work of civil life, imbued with love of learning, confident in the functions and attitudes of leadership, possessing a high sense of public service, advocates of the American democracy and free enterprise system, and ready as citizen-soldiers to defend their country in time of national peril." . . .

VMI produces its "citizen-soldiers" through "an adversative, or doubting, model of education" which features "[p]hysical rigor, mental stress, absolute equality of treatment, absence of privacy, minute regulation of behavior, and indoctrination in desirable values." . . .

VMI cadets live in spartan barracks where surveillance is constant and privacy nonexistent; they wear uniforms, eat together in the mess hall, and regularly participate in drills. . . . Entering students are incessantly exposed to the rat line, "an extreme form of the adversative model," comparable in intensity to Marine Corps boot camp. . . . Tormenting and punishing, the rat line bonds new cadets to their fellow sufferers and, when they have completed the 7-month experience, to their former tormentors. . . .

VMI's "adversative model" is further characterized by a hierarchical "class system" of privileges and responsibilities, a "dyke system" for assigning a senior class mentor to each entering class "rat," and a stringently enforced "honor code," which prescribes that a cadet "does not lie, cheat, steal nor tolerate those who do." . . .

VMI attracts some applicants because of its reputation as an extraordinarily challenging military school, and "because its alumni are exceptionally close to the school." . . . "[W]omen have no opportunity anywhere to gain the benefits of [the system of education at VMI]." . . .

In 1990, prompted by a complaint filed with the Attorney General by a female high-school student seeking admission to VMI, the United States sued the Commonwealth of Virginia and VMI, alleging that VMI's exclusively male admission policy violated the Equal Protection Clause of the Fourteenth Amendment. . . .

. . . Parties who seek to defend gender-based government action must demonstrate an "exceedingly persuasive justification" for that action. . . .

Measuring the record in this case against the review standard just described, we conclude that Virginia has shown no "exceedingly persuasive justification" for excluding all women from the citizen-soldier training afforded by VMI. . . .

Single-sex education affords pedagogical benefits to at least some students, Virginia emphasizes, and that reality is uncontested in this litigation. Similarly, it is not disputed that diversity among public educational institutions can serve the public good. But Virginia has not shown that VMI was established, or has been maintained, with a view to diversifying, by its categorical exclusion of women, educational opportunities within the State. In cases of this genre, our precedent instructs that "benign" justifications proffered in defense of categorical exclusions will not be accepted automatically; a tenable justification must describe actual state purposes, not rationalizations for actions in fact differently grounded. . . .

Neither recent nor distant history bears out Virginia's alleged pursuit of diversity through single-sex educational options. In 1839, when the State established VMI, a range of educational opportunities for men and women was scarcely contemplated. Higher education at the time was considered dangerous for women; reflecting widely held views about women's proper place, the Nation's first universities and colleges—for example, Harvard in Massachusetts, William and Mary in Virginia—admitted only men. . . . VMI was not at all novel in this respect: In admitting no women, VMI followed the lead of the State's flagship school, the University of Virginia, founded in 1819.

"[N]o struggle for the admission of women to a state university," a historian has recounted, "was longer drawn out, or developed more bitterness, than that at the University of Virginia." . . . In 1879, the State Senate resolved to look into the possibility of higher education for women, recognizing that Virginia "has never, at any period of her history," provided for the higher education of her daughters, though she "has liberally provided for the higher education of her sons.". . . Despite this recognition, no new opportunities were instantly open to women.

Virginia eventually provided for several women's seminaries and colleges. Farmville Female Seminary became a public institution in 1884. . . . Two women's schools, Mary Washington College and James Madison University, were founded in 1908; another, Radford University, was founded in 1910. . . . By the mid-1970's, all four schools had become coeducational. . . .

Debate concerning women's admission as undergraduates at the main university continued well past the century's midpoint. Familiar arguments were rehearsed. If women were admitted, it was feared, they "would encroach on the rights of men; there would be new problems of government, perhaps scandals; the old honor system would have to be changed; standards would be low-

ered to those of other coeducational schools; and the glorious reputation of the university, as a school for men, would be trailed in the dust." . . .

Ultimately, in 1970, "the most prestigious institution of higher education in Virginia," the University of Virginia, introduced coeducation and, in 1972, began to admit women on an equal basis with men. . . . A three-judge Federal District Court confirmed: "Virginia may not now deny to women, on the basis of sex, educational opportunities at the Charlottesville campus that are not afforded in other institutions operated by the [S]tate." . . .

Virginia describes the current absence of public single-sex higher education for women as "an historical anomaly." . . . But the historical record indicates action more deliberate than anomalous: First, protection of women against higher education; next, schools for women far from equal in resources and stature to schools for men; finally, conversion of the separate schools to coeducation. The state legislature, prior to the advent of this controversy, had repealed "[a]ll Virginia statutes requiring individual institutions to admit only men or women." . . . And in 1990, an official commission, "legislatively established to chart the future goals of higher education in Virginia," reaffirmed the policy "of affording broad access" while maintaining "autonomy and diversity." . . . Significantly, the Commission reported: "Because colleges and universities provide opportunities for students to develop values and learn from role models, it is extremely important that they deal with faculty, staff, and students without regard to sex, race, or ethnic origin." . . .

This statement, the Court of Appeals observed, "is the only explicit one that we have found in the record in which the Commonwealth has expressed itself with respect to gender distinctions." . . .

In sum, we find no persuasive evidence in this record that VMI's male-only admission policy "is in furtherance of a state policy of 'diversity.'" . . . No such policy, the Fourth Circuit observed, can be discerned from the movement of all other public colleges and universities in Virginia away from single-sex education. . . . That court also questioned "how one institution with autonomy, but with no authority over any other state institution, can give effect to a state policy of diversity among institutions." . . . A purpose genuinely to advance an array of educational options, as the Court of Appeals recognized, is not served by VMI's historic and constant plan—a plan to "affor[d] a unique educational benefit only to males." . . . However "liberally" this plan serves the State's sons, it makes no provision whatever for her daughters. That is not equal protection. . . .

VMI . . . offers an educational opportunity no other Virginia institution provides, and the school's "prestige"—

associated with its success in developing "citizen-soldiers"—is unequaled. . . . Women seeking and fit for a VMI-quality education cannot be offered anything less, under the State's obligation to afford them genuinely equal protection. . . .

Justice Thomas took no part in the consideration or decision of this case.

Chief Justice Rehnquist, concurring in the judgment. . . .

Justice Scalia, dissenting.

Today the Court shuts down an institution that has served the people of the Commonwealth of Virginia with pride and distinction for over a century and a half. To achieve that desired result, it rejects (contrary to our established practice) the factual findings of two courts below, sweeps aside the precedents of this Court, and ignores the history of our people. As to facts: it explicitly rejects the finding that there exist "gender-based developmental differences" supporting Virginia's restriction of the "adversative" method to only a men's institution, and the finding that the all-male composition of the Virginia Military Institute (VMI) is essential to that institution's character. As to precedent: it drastically revises our established standards for reviewing sex-based classifications. And as to history: it counts for nothing the long tradition, enduring down to the present, of men's military colleges supported by both States and the Federal Government. . . .

Much of the Court's opinion is devoted to deprecating the closed-mindedness of our forebears with regard to women's education, and even with regard to the treatment of women in areas that have nothing to do with education. Closed-minded they were—as every age is, including our own, with regard to matters it cannot guess, because it simply does not consider them debatable. The virtue of a democratic system with a First Amendment is that it readily enables the people, over time, to be persuaded that what they took for granted is not so, and to change their laws accordingly. That system is destroyed if the smug assurances of each age are removed from the democratic process and written into the Constitution. So to counterbalance the Court's criticism of our ancestors, let me say a word in their praise: they left us free to change. The same cannot be said of this most illiberal Court, which has embarked on a course of inscribing one after another of the current preferences of the society (and in some cases only the counter-majoritarian preferences of the society's law-trained elite) into our Basic Law. Today it enshrines the notion that no substantial educational value is to be served by an all-men's military academy—so that the decision by the people of Virginia to maintain such an institution denies equal protection to women who cannot attend that institution but can attend others. Since it is entirely clear that the Constitution of the United States—the old one—takes no sides in this educational debate, I dissent. . . .

Case

BOARD OF TRUSTEES OF THE UNIVERSITY OF ALABAMA V. GARRETT

531 U.S. 356; 121 S.Ct. 955; 148 L.Ed. 2d 866 (2001)
Vote: 5–4

In this case the Court considers whether Section 5 of the Fourteenth Amendment empowers Congress to enforce the Equal Protection Clause by authorizing state employees to seek monetary damages from their state employers for alleged violations of the Americans with Disabilities Act (ADA).

Chief Justice Rehnquist delivered the opinion of the Court.

. . . The ADA prohibits certain employers, including the States, from "discriminat[ing] against a qualified individual with a disability because of the disability of such individual in regard to job application procedures, the hiring, advancement, or discharge of employees, employee compensation, job training, and other terms, conditions, and privileges of employment." . . . To this end, the Act requires employers to "mak[e] reasonable accommodations to the known physical or mental limitations of an otherwise qualified individual with a disability who is an applicant or employee, unless [the employer] can demonstrate that the accommodation would impose an undue hardship on the operation of the [employer's] business." . . .

The Act also prohibits employers from "utilizing standards, criteria, or methods of administration . . . that have the effect of discrimination on the basis of disability." . . .

The Act defines "disability" to include "(A) a physical or mental impairment that substantially limits one or more of the major life activities of such individual; (B) a record of such an impairment; or (C) being regarded as having such an impairment." . . . A disabled individual is otherwise "qualified" if he or she, "with or without reasonable accommodation, can perform the essential functions of the employment position that such individual holds or desires." . . .

Respondent Patricia Garrett, a registered nurse, was employed as the Director of Nursing, OB/Gyn/Neonatal Services, for the University of Alabama in Birmingham Hospital. . . . In 1994, Garrett was diagnosed with breast cancer and subsequently underwent a lumpectomy, radiation treatment, and chemotherapy. . . . Garrett's treatments required her to take substantial leave from work. Upon returning to work in July 1995, Garrett's supervisor informed Garrett that she would have to give up her Director position. . . . Garrett then applied for and received a transfer to another, lower paying position as a nurse manager. . . .

Garrett . . . [sued] in the District Court, . . . seeking money damages under the ADA.

Petitioners moved for summary judgment, claiming that the ADA exceeds Congress' authority to abrogate the State's Eleventh Amendment immunity. The District Court agreed with petitioners' position and granted their motions for summary judgment. . . . The Court of Appeals reversed. . . .

We granted certiorari . . . to resolve a split among the Courts of Appeals on the question whether an individual may sue a State for money damages in federal court under the ADA.

I

The Eleventh Amendment provides:

> The Judicial power of the United States shall not be construed to extend to any suit in law or equity, commenced or prosecuted against one of the United States by Citizens of another State, or by Citizens or Subjects of any Foreign State.

Although by its terms the Amendment applies only to suits against a State by citizens of another State, our cases have extended the Amendment's applicability to suits by citizens against their own States. . . .The ultimate guarantee of the Eleventh Amendment is that nonconsenting States may not be sued by private individuals in federal court. . . .

We have recognized, however, that Congress may abrogate the States' Eleventh Amendment immunity when it both unequivocally intends to do so and "act[s] pursuant to a valid grant of constitutional authority." . . . The first of these requirements is not in dispute here. . . . The question, then, is whether Congress acted within its constitutional authority by subjecting the States to suits in federal court for money damages under the ADA.

Congress may not, of course, base its abrogation of the States' Eleventh Amendment immunity upon the powers enumerated in Article I. . . . Congress may subject nonconsenting States to suit in federal court when it does so

pursuant to a valid exercise of its § 5 power. Accordingly, the ADA can apply to the States only to the extent that the statute is appropriate § 5 legislation.

Section 1 of the Fourteenth Amendment provides, in relevant part:

> No State shall make or enforce any law which shall abridge the privileges or immunities of citizens of the United States; nor shall any State deprive any person of life, liberty, or property, without due process of law; nor deny to any person within its jurisdiction the equal protection of the laws.

Section 5 of the Fourteenth Amendment grants Congress the power to enforce the substantive guarantees contained in § 1 by enacting "appropriate legislation." . . . Congress is not limited to mere legislative repetition of this Court's constitutional jurisprudence. "Rather, Congress' power 'to enforce' the Amendment includes the authority both to remedy and to deter violation of rights guaranteed thereunder by prohibiting a somewhat broader swath of conduct, including that which is not itself forbidden by the Amendment's text." . . .

. . . [I]t is the responsibility of this Court, not Congress, to define the substance of constitutional guarantees. . . . Accordingly, § 5 legislation reaching beyond the scope of § 1's actual guarantees must exhibit "congruence and proportionality between the injury to be prevented or remedied and the means adopted to that end." . . .

II

The first step in applying these now familiar principles is to identify with some precision the scope of the constitutional right at issue. Here, that inquiry requires us to examine the limitations § 1 of the Fourteenth Amendment places upon States' treatment of the disabled. . . .

In *Cleburne v. Cleburne Living Center, Inc.* (1985), we considered an equal protection challenge to a city ordinance requiring a special use permit for the operation of a group home for the mentally retarded. The specific question before us was whether the Court of Appeals had erred by holding that mental retardation qualified as a "quasi-suspect" classification under our equal protection jurisprudence. . . . We answered that question in the affirmative, concluding instead that such legislation incurs only the minimum "rational-basis" review applicable to general social and economic legislation. . . .

Under rational-basis review, where a group possesses "distinguishing characteristics relevant to interests the State has the authority to implement," a State's decision to act on the basis of those differences does not give rise to a constitutional violation. . . . "Such a classification cannot run afoul of the Equal Protection Clause if there is a rational relationship between the disparity of treatment and some legitimate governmental purpose." . . . Moreover, the State need not articulate its reasoning at the moment a particular decision is made. Rather, the burden is upon the challenging party to negative "any reasonably conceivable state of facts that could provide a rational basis for the classification." . . .

[T]he result of *Cleburne* is that States are not required by the Fourteenth Amendment to make special accommodations for the disabled, so long as their actions towards such individuals are rational. They could quite hard headedly—and perhaps hardheartedly—hold to job-qualification requirements which do not make allowance for the disabled. If special accommodations for the disabled are to be required, they have to come from positive law and not through the Equal Protection Clause.

III

Once we have determined the metes and bounds of the constitutional right in question, we examine whether Congress identified a history and pattern of unconstitutional employment discrimination by the States against the disabled. Just as § 1 of the Fourteenth Amendment applies only to actions committed "under color of state law," Congress' § 5 authority is appropriately exercised only in response to state transgressions. . . . The legislative record of the ADA, however, simply fails to show that Congress did in fact identify a pattern of irrational state discrimination in employment against the disabled.

Respondents contend that the inquiry as to unconstitutional discrimination should extend not only to States themselves, but to units of local governments, such as cities and counties. All of these, they say, are "state actors" for purposes of the Fourteenth Amendment. . . . This is quite true, but the Eleventh Amendment does not extend its immunity to units of local government. . . . These entities are subject to private claims for damages under the ADA without Congress' ever having to rely on § 5 of the Fourteenth Amendment to render them so. It would make no sense to consider constitutional violations on their part, as well as by the States themselves, when only the States are the beneficiaries of the Eleventh Amendment.

Congress made a general finding in the ADA that "historically, society has tended to isolate and segregate individuals with disabilities, and, despite some improvements, such forms of discrimination against individuals with disabilities continue to be a serious and pervasive social problem." . . . The record assembled by Congress includes many instances to support such a finding. But the great majority of these incidents do not deal with the activities of States. . . .

Even were it possible to squeeze out of these examples a pattern of unconstitutional discrimination by the States, the rights and remedies created by the ADA against the States would raise the same sort of concerns as to congruence and proportionality. . . . For example, whereas it would be entirely rational (and therefore constitutional) for a state employer to conserve scarce financial resources by hiring employees who are able to use existing facilities, the ADA requires employers to "mak[e] existing facilities used by employees readily accessible to and usable by individuals with disabilities." . . . The ADA does except employers from the "reasonable accommodatio[n]" requirement where the employer "can demonstrate that the accommodation would impose an undue hardship on the operation of the business of such covered entity." . . . However, even with this exception, the accommodation duty far exceeds what is constitutionally required in that it makes unlawful a range of alternate responses that would be reasonable but would fall short of imposing an "undue burden" upon the employer. The Act also makes it the employer's duty to prove that it would suffer such a burden, instead of requiring (as the Constitution does) that the complaining party negate reasonable bases for the employer's decision. . . .

The ADA also forbids "utilizing standards, criteria, or methods of administration" that disparately impact the disabled, without regard to whether such conduct has a rational basis. . . . Although disparate impact may be relevant evidence of racial discrimination, . . . such evidence alone is insufficient even where the Fourteenth Amendment subjects state action to strict scrutiny. . . .

The ADA's constitutional shortcomings are apparent when the Act is compared to Congress' efforts in the Voting Rights Act of 1965 to respond to a serious pattern of constitutional violations. . . .

In that Act, Congress documented a marked pattern of unconstitutional action by the States. State officials, Congress found, routinely applied voting tests in order to exclude African-American citizens from registering to vote. . . . Congress also determined that litigation had proved ineffective and that there persisted an otherwise inexplicable 50-percentage-point gap in the registration of white and African-American voters in some States. . . . Congress' response was to promulgate in the Voting Rights Act a detailed but limited remedial scheme designed to guarantee meaningful enforcement of the Fifteenth Amendment in those areas of the Nation where abundant evidence of States' systematic denial of those rights was identified.

The contrast between this kind of evidence, and the evidence that Congress considered in the present case, is stark. Congressional enactment of the ADA represents its judgment that there should be a "comprehensive national mandate for the elimination of discrimination against individuals with disabilities." . . . Congress is the final authority as to desirable public policy, but in order to authorize private individuals to recover money damages against the States, there must be a pattern of discrimination by the States which violates the Fourteenth Amendment, and the remedy imposed by Congress must be congruent and proportional to the targeted violation. Those requirements are not met here, and to uphold the Act's application to the States would allow Congress to rewrite the Fourteenth Amendment law laid down by this Court in *Cleburne*. Section 5 does not so broadly enlarge congressional authority. The judgment of the Court of Appeals is therefore . . . Reversed.

Justice Kennedy, with whom **Justice O'Connor** joins, concurring. . . .

Justice Breyer, with whom **Justice Stevens, Justice Souter,** and **Justice Ginsburg** join, dissenting.

Reviewing the congressional record as if it were an administrative agency record, the Court holds the statutory provision before us . . . unconstitutional. The Court concludes that Congress assembled insufficient evidence of unconstitutional discrimination, . . . that Congress improperly attempted to "re-write" the law we established in *Cleburne v. Cleburne Living Center, Inc.,* . . . and that the law is not sufficiently tailored to address unconstitutional discrimination. . . .

Section 5, however, grants Congress the "power to enforce, by appropriate legislation" the Fourteenth Amendment's equal protection guarantee. . . . As the Court recognizes, state discrimination in employment against persons with disabilities might "'run afoul of the Equal Protection Clause'" where there is no "rational relationship between the disparity of treatment and some legitimate governmental purpose." . . . In my view, Congress reasonably could have concluded that the remedy before us constitutes an "appropriate" way to enforce this basic equal protection requirement. And that is all the Constitution requires.

I

The Court says that its primary problem with this statutory provision is one of legislative evidence. It says that "Congress assembled only . . . minimal evidence of unconstitutional state discrimination in employment." . . . In fact, Congress compiled a vast legislative record documenting "massive, society-wide discrimination" against persons with disabilities. . . . In addition to the information presented at 13 congressional hearings, and its own prior experience gathered over 40 years during which it contemplated and enacted considerable similar legislation. Congress created a special task force to assess the need for comprehensive legislation. That task force held hearings in every State, attended by more than 30,000 people, including thousands who had experienced discrimination first hand. . . . The task force hearings, Congress' own hearings, and an analysis of "census data, national polls, and other studies" led Congress to conclude that "people with disabilities, as a group, occupy an inferior status in our society, and are severely disadvantaged socially, vocationally, economically, and educationally." . . . As to employment, Congress found that "[t]wo-thirds of all disabled Americans between the age of 16 and 64 [were] not working at all," even though a large majority wanted to, and were able to, work productively. . . . And Congress found that this discrimination flowed in significant part from "stereotypic assumptions" as well as "purposeful unequal treatment." . . .

The powerful evidence of discriminatory treatment throughout society in general, including discrimination by private persons and local governments, implicates state governments as well, for state agencies form part of that same larger society. There is no particular reason to believe that they are immune from the "stereotypic assumptions" and pattern of "purposeful unequal treatment" that Congress found prevalent. The Court claims that it "make[s] no sense" to take into consideration constitutional violations committed by local governments. . . . But the substantive obligation that the Equal Protection Clause creates applies to state and local governmental entities alike. . . . Local governments often work closely with, and under the supervision of, state officials, and in general, state and local government employers are similarly situated. Nor is determining whether an apparently "local" entity is entitled to Eleventh Amendment immunity as simple as the majority suggests—it often requires a "detailed examination of the relevant provisions of [state] law." . . .

In any event, there is no need to rest solely upon evidence of discrimination by local governments or general societal discrimination. There are roughly 300 examples of discrimination by state governments themselves in the legislative record. . . . I fail to see how this evidence "fall[s] far short of even suggesting the pattern of unconstitutional discrimination on which § 5 legislation must be based." . . .

II

The Court's failure to find sufficient evidentiary support may well rest upon its decision to hold Congress to a strict, judicially created evidentiary standard, particularly in respect to lack of justification. . . .

The problem with the Court's approach is that neither the "burden of proof" that favors States nor any other rule of restraint applicable to *judges* applies to *Congress* when it exercises its § 5 power. "Limitations stemming from the nature of the judicial process . . . have no application to Congress." . . . Rational-basis review—with its presumptions favoring constitutionality—is "a paradigm of *judicial* restraint." . . . And the Congress of the United States is not a lower court.

Indeed, the Court in *Cleburne* drew this very institutional distinction. We emphasized that "courts have been very reluctant, as they should be in our federal system and with our respect for the separation of powers, to closely scrutinize legislative choices." . . . Our invocation of judicial deference and respect for Congress was based on the fact that "[§] 5 of the [Fourteenth] Amendment empowers *Congress* to enforce [the equal protection] mandate." . . . Indeed, we made clear that the absence of a contrary congressional finding was critical to our decision to apply mere rational-basis review to disability discrimination claims—a "congressional direction" to apply a more stringent standard would have been "controlling." . . . In short, the Court's claim that "to uphold the Act's application to the States would allow Congress to rewrite the Fourteenth Amendment law laid down by this Court in *Cleburne*" . . . is repudiated by *Cleburne* itself.

There is simply no reason to require Congress, seeking to determine facts relevant to the exercise of its § 5 authority, to adopt rules or presumptions that reflect a court's institutional limitations. Unlike courts, Congress can readily gather facts from across the Nation, assess the magnitude of a problem, and more easily find an appropriate remedy. . . . Unlike courts, Congress directly reflects public attitudes and beliefs, enabling Congress better to understand where, and to what extent, refusals to accommodate a disability amount to behavior that is callous or unreasonable to the point of lacking constitutional justification. Unlike judges, Members of Congress can directly obtain information from constituents who have first-hand experience with discrimination and related issues.

Moreover, unlike judges, Members of Congress are elected. When the Court has applied the majority's burden of proof rule, it has explained that we, *i.e.,* the courts, do not "sit as a superlegislature to judge the wisdom or desirability of legislative policy determinations." . . . To apply a rule designed to restrict courts as if it restricted Congress' legislative power is to stand the underlying principle—a principle of judicial restraint—on its head. But without the use of this burden of proof rule or some other unusually stringent standard of review, it is difficult to see how the Court can find the legislative record here inadequate. Read with a reasonably favorable eye, the record indicates that state governments subjected those with disabilities to seriously adverse, disparate treatment. And Congress could have found, in a significant number of instances, that this treatment violated the substantive principles of justification—shorn of their judicial-restraint-related presumptions—that this Court recognized in *Cleburne.*

III

The Court argues in the alternative that the statute's damage remedy is not "congruent" with and "proportional" to the equal protection problem that Congress found. . . . The Court suggests that the Act's "reasonable accommodation" requirement, . . ."far excee[d] what is constitutionally required." . . . But we have upheld disparate impact standards in contexts where they were not "constitutionally required." . . .

And what is wrong with a remedy that, in response to unreasonable employer behavior, requires an employer to make accommodations that are reasonable? Of course, what is "reasonable" in the statutory sense and what is "unreasonable" in the constitutional sense might differ. In other words, the requirement may exceed what is necessary to avoid a constitutional violation. But it is just that power—the power to require more than the minimum— that § 5 grants to Congress, as this Court has repeatedly confirmed. . . .

In keeping with these principles, the Court has said that "[i]t is not for us to review the congressional resolution of "the various conflicting considerations—the risk or pervasiveness of the discrimination in governmental services . . . , the adequacy or availability of alternative remedies, and the nature and significance of the state interests that would be affected." . . . Nothing in the words "reasonable accommodation" suggests that the requirement has no "tend[ency] to enforce" the Equal Protection Clause, . . . that it is an irrational way to achieve the objective, . . . that it would fall outside the scope of the Necessary and Proper Clause, . . . or that it somehow otherwise exceeds the bounds of the "appropriate." . . .

The Court's more recent cases have professed to follow the longstanding principle of deference to Congress. . . . And even today, the Court purports to apply, not to depart from, these standards. . . . But the Court's analysis and ultimate conclusion deprive its declarations of practical significance. The Court "sounds the word of promise to the ear but breaks it to the hope."

IV

The Court's harsh review of Congress' use of its § 5 power is reminiscent of the similar (now-discredited) limitation that it once imposed upon Congress' Commerce Clause power. . . . I could understand the legal basis for such review were we judging a statute that discriminated against those of a particular race or gender, . . . or a statute that threatened a basic constitutionally protected liberty such as free speech. . . . The legislation before us, however, does not discriminate against anyone, nor does it pose any threat to basic liberty. And it is difficult to understand why the Court, which applies "minimum 'rational-basis' review" to statutes that *burden* persons with disabilities . . . subjects to far stricter scrutiny a statute that seeks to *help* those same individuals.

I recognize nonetheless that this statute imposes a burden upon States in that it removes their Eleventh Amendment protection from suit, thereby subjecting them to potential monetary liability. Rules for interpreting § 5 that would provide States with special protection, however, run counter to the very object of the Fourteenth Amendment. By its terms, that Amendment prohibits *States* from denying their citizens equal protection of the laws. . . . Hence "principles of federalism that might otherwise be an obstacle to congressional authority are necessarily overridden by the power to enforce the Civil War Amendments 'by appropriate legislation.' Those Amendments were specifically designed as an expansion of federal power and an intrusion on state sov-

ereignty." . . . And, ironically, the greater the obstacle the Eleventh Amendment poses to the creation by Congress of the kind of remedy at issue here—the decentralized remedy of private damage actions—the more Congress, seeking to cure important national problems, such as the problem of disability discrimination before us, will have to rely on more uniform remedies, such as federal standards and court injunctions, . . . which are sometimes draconian and typically more intrusive. . . . For these reasons, I doubt that today's decision serves any constitutionally based federalism interest.

The Court, through its evidentiary demands, its nondeferential review, and its failure to distinguish between judicial and legislative constitutional competencies, improperly invades a power that the Constitution assigns to Congress. . . . Its decision saps § 5 of independent force, effectively "confin[ing] the legislative power . . . to the insignificant role of abrogating only those state laws that the judicial branch [is] prepared to adjudge unconstitutional." . . . Whether the Commerce Clause does or does not enable Congress to enact this provision . . . § 5 gives Congress the necessary authority.

For the reasons stated, I respectfully dissent.

Case

ROMER V. EVANS

517 U.S. 620; 116 S.Ct. 1620; 134 L.Ed. 2d 855 (1996)

Vote: 6–3

Here the Court addresses the issue of gay rights in the context of a state constitutional amendment disallowing minority status, preferred treatment, or claims of discrimination on the basis of homosexual or lesbian orientation.

Justice Kennedy delivered the opinion of the Court.

. . . The enactment challenged in this case is an amendment to the Constitution of the State of Colorado, adopted in a 1992 statewide referendum. The parties and the state courts refer to it as "Amendment 2," its designation when submitted to the voters. The impetus for the amendment and the contentious campaign that preceded its adoption came in large part from ordinances that had been passed in various Colorado municipalities. For example, the cities of Aspen and Boulder and the City and County of Denver each had enacted ordinances which banned discrimination in many transactions and activities, including housing, employment, education, public accommodations, and health and welfare services.

. . . What gave rise to the statewide controversy was the protection the ordinances afforded to persons discriminated against by reason of their sexual orientation. . . . Amendment 2 repeals these ordinances to the extent they prohibit discrimination on the basis of "homosexual, lesbian or bisexual orientation, conduct, practices or relationships." . . .

Yet Amendment 2, in explicit terms, does more than repeal or rescind these provisions. It prohibits all legislative, executive or judicial action at any level of state or local government designed to protect the named class, a class we shall refer to as homosexual persons or gays and lesbians. The amendment reads:

No Protected Status Based on Homosexual, Lesbian, or Bisexual Orientation. Neither the State of Colorado, through any of its branches or departments, nor any of its agencies, political subdivisions, municipalities or school districts, shall enact, adopt or enforce any statute, regulation, ordinance or policy whereby homosexual, lesbian or bisexual orientation, conduct, practices or relationships shall constitute or otherwise be the basis of or entitle any person or class of persons to have or claim any minority status, quota preferences, protected status or claim of discrimination. This Section of the Constitution shall be in all respects self-executing. . . .

Soon after Amendment 2 was adopted, this litigation to declare its invalidity and enjoin its enforcement was commenced in the District Court for the City and County of Denver. . . .

The trial court granted a preliminary injunction to stay enforcement of Amendment 2, and an appeal was taken to the Supreme Court of Colorado. Sustaining the interim injunction and remanding the case for further proceedings, the State Supreme Court held that Amendment 2 was subject to strict scrutiny under the Fourteenth Amendment because it infringed the fundamental right of gays and lesbians to participate in the political process. . . . To reach this conclusion, the state court relied on our voting rights cases . . . and on our precedents involving discriminatory restructuring of governmental decision making. . . . On remand, the State advanced various arguments in an effort to show that Amendment 2 was narrowly tailored to serve compelling interests, but the trial court found none sufficient. It enjoined enforcement of Amendment 2, and the Supreme Court of Colorado, in a second opinion, affirmed the ruling. . . . We granted certiorari and now affirm the judgment, but on a rationale different from that adopted by the State Supreme Court.

The State's principal argument in defense of Amendment 2 is that it puts gays and lesbians in the same position as all other persons. So, the State says, the measure does no more than deny homosexuals special rights. This reading of the amendment's language is implausible. We rely not upon our own interpretation of the amendment but upon the authoritative construction of Colorado's Supreme Court. The state court, deeming it unnecessary to determine the full extent of the amendment's reach, found it invalid even on a modest reading of its implications. . . .

Sweeping and comprehensive is the change in legal status effected by this law. So much is evident from the ordinances that the Colorado Supreme Court declared would be void by operation of Amendment 2. Homosexuals, by state decree, are put in a solitary class with respect to transactions and relations in both the private and governmental spheres. The amendment withdraws from homosexuals, but no others, specific legal protection from the injuries caused by discrimination, and it forbids reinstatement of these laws and policies.

The change that Amendment 2 works in the legal status of gays and lesbians in the private sphere is far-reaching, both on its own terms and when considered in light of the structure and operation of modern antidiscrimination laws. That structure is well illustrated by contemporary statutes and ordinances prohibiting discrimination by providers of public accommodations. "At common law, innkeepers, smiths, and others who 'made profession of a public employment,' were prohibited from refusing, without good reason, to serve a customer." . . . The duty was a general one and did not specify protection for particular groups. The common law rules, however, proved insufficient in many instances, and it was settled early that the Fourteenth Amendment did not give Congress a general power to prohibit discrimination in public accommodations. . . . In consequence, most States have chosen to counter discrimination by enacting detailed statutory schemes. . . .

Colorado's state and municipal laws typify this emerging tradition of statutory protection and follow a consistent pattern. The laws first enumerate the persons or entities subject to a duty not to discriminate. The list goes well beyond the entities covered by the common law. The Boulder ordinance, for example, has a comprehensive definition of entities deemed places of "public accommodation." They include "any place of business engaged in any sales to the general public and any place that offers services, facilities, privileges, or advantages to the general public or that receives financial support through solicitation of the general public or through governmental subsidy of any kind." . . . The Denver ordinance is of similar breadth, applying, for example, to hotels, restaurants, hospitals, dental clinics, theaters, banks, common carriers, travel and insurance agencies, and "shops and stores dealing with goods or services of any kind." . . .

These statutes and ordinances also depart from the common law by enumerating the groups or persons within their ambit of protection. Enumeration is the essential device used to make the duty not to discriminate concrete and to provide guidance for those who must comply. In following this approach, Colorado's state and local governments have not limited antidiscrimination laws to groups that have so far been given the protection of heightened equal protection scrutiny under our cases. . . . Rather, they set forth an extensive catalogue of traits which cannot be the basis for discrimination, including age, military status, marital status, pregnancy, parenthood, custody of a minor child, political affiliation, physical or mental disability of an individual or of his or her associates—and, in recent times, sexual orientation. . . .

Amendment 2 bars homosexuals from securing protection against the injuries that these public-accommodations laws address. That in itself is a severe consequence, but there is more. Amendment 2, in addition, nullifies specific legal protections for this targeted class in all transactions in housing, sale of real estate, insurance, health and welfare services, private education, and employment. . . .

Not confined to the private sphere, Amendment 2 also operates to repeal and forbid all laws or policies providing specific protection for gays or lesbians from discrimination by every level of Colorado government. The State Supreme Court cited two examples of protections in the governmental sphere that are now rescinded and may not be reintroduced. The first is Colorado Executive Order D0035 (1990), which forbids employment discrimination against "'all state employees, classified and exempt' on the basis of sexual orientation." . . . Also repealed, and now forbidden, are "various provisions prohibiting discrimination based on sexual orientation at state colleges." . . . The repeal of these measures and the prohibition against their future reenactment demonstrates that Amendment 2 has the same force and effect in Colorado's governmental sector as it does elsewhere and that it applies to policies as well as ordinary legislation.

Amendment 2's reach may not be limited to specific laws passed for the benefit of gays and lesbians. It is a fair, if not necessary, inference from the broad language of the amendment that it deprives gays and lesbians even of the protection of general laws and policies that prohibit arbitrary discrimination in governmental and private settings. . . . At some point in the systematic administration of these laws, an official must determine whether homosexuality is an arbitrary and thus forbidden basis for decision. Yet a decision to that effect would itself amount to a policy prohibiting discrimination on the basis of homosexuality, and so would appear to be no more valid under Amendment 2 than the specific prohibitions against discrimination the state court held invalid.

If this consequence follows from Amendment 2, as its broad language suggests, it would compound the constitutional difficulties the law creates. The state court did not decide whether the amendment has this effect, however, and neither need we. In the course of rejecting the argument that Amendment 2 is intended to conserve resources to fight discrimination against suspect classes, the Colorado Supreme Court made the limited observation that the amendment is not intended to affect many antidiscrimination laws protecting non-suspect classes. . . . In our view that does not resolve the issue. In any event, even if, as we doubt, homosexuals could find some safe harbor in laws of general application, we cannot accept the view that Amendment 2's prohibition on specific legal protections does no more than deprive homosexuals of special rights. To the contrary, the amendment imposes a special disability upon those persons alone. Homosexuals are forbidden the safeguards that others enjoy or may seek without constraint. They can obtain specific protection against discrimination only by enlisting the citizenry of Colorado to amend the state constitution or perhaps, on the State's view, by trying to pass helpful laws of general applicabil-

ity. This is so no matter how local or discrete the harm, no matter how public and widespread the injury. We find nothing special in the protections Amendment 2 withholds. These are protections taken for granted by most people either because they already have them or do not need them; these are protections against exclusion from an almost limitless number of transactions and endeavors that constitute ordinary civic life in a free society.

The Fourteenth Amendment's promise that no person shall be denied the equal protection of the laws must coexist with the practical necessity that most legislation classifies for one purpose or another, with resulting disadvantage to various groups or persons. . . . We have attempted to reconcile the principle with the reality by stating that, if a law neither burdens a fundamental right nor targets a suspect class, we will uphold the legislative classification so long as it bears a rational relation to some legitimate end. . . .

Amendment 2 fails, indeed defies, even this conventional inquiry. First, the amendment has the peculiar property of imposing a broad and undifferentiated disability on a single named group, an exceptional and, as we shall explain, invalid form of legislation. Second, its sheer breadth is so discontinuous with the reasons offered for it that the amendment seems inexplicable by anything but animus toward the class that it affects; it lacks a rational relationship to legitimate state interests.

Taking the first point, even in the ordinary equal protection case calling for the most deferential of standards, we insist on knowing the relation between the classification adopted and the object to be attained. The search for the link between classification and objective gives substance to the Equal Protection Clause; it provides guidance and discipline for the legislature, which is entitled to know what sorts of laws it can pass; and it marks the limits of our own authority. In the ordinary case, a law will be sustained if it can be said to advance a legitimate government interest, even if the law seems unwise or works to the disadvantage of a particular group, or if the rationale for it seems tenuous. . . . The laws challenged in the cases just cited were narrow enough in scope and grounded in a sufficient factual context for us to ascertain that there existed some relation between the classification and the purpose it served. By requiring that the classification bear a rational relationship to an independent and legitimate legislative end, we ensure that classifications are not drawn for the purpose of disadvantaging the group burdened by the law. . . .

Amendment 2 confounds this normal process of judicial review. It is at once too narrow and too broad. It identifies persons by a single trait and then denies them protection across the board. The resulting disqualification of a class of persons from the right to seek specific protection from the law is unprecedented in our jurisprudence. The absence of precedent for Amendment 2 is itself instructive; "[d]iscriminations of an unusual character especially suggest careful consideration to determine whether they are obnoxious to the constitutional provision." . . .

It is not within our constitutional tradition to enact laws of this sort. Central both to the idea of the rule of law and to our own Constitution's guarantee of equal protection is the principle that government and each of its parts remain open on impartial terms to all who seek its assistance. "Equal protection of the laws is not achieved through indiscriminate imposition of inequalities." . . . Respect for this principle explains why laws singling out a certain class of citizens for disfavored legal status or general hardships are rare. A law declaring that in general it shall be more difficult for one group of citizens than for all others to seek aid from the government is itself a denial of equal protection of the laws in the most literal sense. "The guaranty of 'equal protection of the laws is a pledge of the protection of equal laws.' " . . .

. . . A second and related point is that laws of the kind now before us raise the inevitable inference that the disadvantage imposed is born of animosity toward the class of persons affected. "[I]f the constitutional conception of 'equal protection of the laws' means anything, it must at the very least mean that a bare . . . desire to harm a politically unpopular group cannot constitute a legitimate governmental interest." . . . Even laws enacted for broad and ambitious purposes often can be explained by reference to legitimate public policies which justify the incidental disadvantages they impose on certain persons. Amendment 2, however, in making a general announcement that gays and lesbians shall not have any particular protections from the law, inflicts on them immediate, continuing, and real injuries that outrun and belie any legitimate justifications that may be claimed for it. We conclude that, in addition to the far-reaching deficiencies of Amendment 2 that we have noted, the principles it offends, in another sense, are conventional and venerable; a law must bear a rational relationship to a legitimate governmental purpose, . . . and Amendment 2 does not.

The primary rationale the State offers for Amendment 2 is respect for other citizens' freedom of association, and in particular the liberties of landlords or employers who have personal or religious objections to homosexuality. Colorado also cites its interest in conserving resources to fight discrimination against other groups. The breadth of the Amendment is so far removed from these particular justifications that we find it impossible to credit them. We cannot say that Amendment 2 is directed to any identifiable legitimate purpose or discrete objective. It is a status-based enactment divorced from any factual context from which we could discern a relationship to legitimate state interests; it is a classification of persons undertaken for its own sake, something the Equal Protection Clause does not permit. "[C]lass legislation . . . [is] obnoxious to the prohibitions of the Fourteenth Amendment. . . ." . . .

We must conclude that Amendment 2 classifies homosexuals not to further a proper legislative end but to make them unequal to everyone else. This Colorado cannot do. A State cannot so deem a class of persons a stranger to its laws. Amendment 2 violates the Equal Protection Clause, and the judgment of the Supreme Court of Colorado is affirmed. . . .

Justice Scalia, with whom the *Chief Justice* and *Justice Thomas* join, dissenting.

The Court has mistaken a Kulturkampf for a fit of spite. The constitutional amendment before us here is not the manifestation of a "bare . . . desire to harm" homosexuals, . . . but is rather a modest attempt by seemingly tolerant Coloradans to preserve traditional sexual mores against the efforts of a politically powerful minority to revise those mores through use of the laws. That objective, and the means chosen to achieve it, are not only unimpeachable under any constitutional doctrine hitherto pronounced (hence the opinion's heavy reliance upon principles of righteousness rather than judicial holdings); they have been specifically approved by the Congress of the United States and by this Court.

In holding that homosexuality cannot be singled out for disfavorable treatment, the Court contradicts a decision, unchallenged here, pronounced only 10 years ago, see *Bowers v. Hardwick* . . . (1986), and places the prestige of this institution behind the proposition that opposition to homosexuality is as reprehensible as racial or religious bias. Whether it is or not is precisely the cultural debate that gave rise to the Colorado constitutional amendment (and to the preferential laws against which the amendment was directed). Since the Constitution of the United States says nothing about this subject, it is left to be resolved by normal democratic means, including the democratic adoption of provisions in state constitutions. This Court has no business imposing upon all Americans the resolution favored by the elite class from which the Members of this institution are selected, pronouncing that "animosity" toward homosexuality . . . is evil. I vigorously dissent. . . .

. . . The Court's opinion contains grim, disapproving hints that Coloradans have been guilty of "animus" or "animosity" toward homosexuality, as though that has been established as Unamerican. Of course it is our moral heritage that one should not hate any human being or class of human beings. But I had thought that one could consider certain conduct reprehensible—murder, for example, or polygamy, or cruelty to animals—and could exhibit even "animus" toward such conduct. Surely that is the only sort of "animus" at issue here: moral disapproval of homosexual conduct, the same sort of moral disapproval that produced the centuries-old criminal laws that we held constitutional in *Bowers*. The Colorado amendment does not, to speak entirely precisely, prohibit giving favored status to people who are homosexuals; they can be favored for many reasons—for example, because they are senior citizens or members of racial minorities. But it prohibits giving them favored status because of their homosexual conduct—that is, it prohibits favored status for homosexuality.

But though Coloradans are, as I say, entitled to be hostile toward homosexual conduct, the fact is that the degree of hostility reflected by Amendment 2 is the smallest conceivable. The Court's portrayal of Coloradans as a society fallen victim to pointless, hate-filled "gay-bashing" is so false as to be comical. Colorado not only is one of the 25 States that have repealed their antisodomy laws, but was among the first to do so. . . . But the society that eliminates criminal punishment for homosexual acts does not necessarily abandon the view that homosexuality is morally wrong and socially harmful; often, abolition simply reflects the view that enforcement of such criminal laws involves unseemly intrusion into the intimate lives of citizens. . . .

There is a problem, however, which arises when criminal sanction of homosexuality is eliminated but moral and social disapprobation of homosexuality is meant to be retained. The Court cannot be unaware of that problem; it is evident in many cities of the country, and occasionally bubbles to the surface of the news, in heated political disputes over such matters as the introduction into local schools of books teaching that homosexuality is an optional and fully acceptable "alternate life style." The problem (a problem, that is, for those who wish to retain social disapprobation of homosexuality) is that, because those who engage in homosexual conduct tend to reside in disproportionate numbers in certain communities, . . . and of course care about homosexual-rights issues much more ardently than the public at large, they possess political power much greater than their numbers, both locally and statewide. Quite understandably, they devote this political power to achieving not merely a grudging social toleration, but full social acceptance, of homosexuality. . . .

By the time Coloradans were asked to vote on Amendment 2, their exposure to homosexuals' quest for social endorsement was not limited to newspaper accounts of happenings in places such as New York, Los Angeles, San Francisco, and Key West. Three Colorado cities—Aspen, Boulder, and Denver—had enacted ordinances that listed "sexual orientation" as an impermissible ground for discrimination, equating the moral disapproval of homosex-

ual conduct with racial and religious bigotry. . . . The phenomenon had even appeared statewide: the Governor of Colorado had signed an executive order pronouncing that "in the State of Colorado we recognize the diversity in our pluralistic society and strive to bring an end to discrimination in any form," and directing state agency-heads to "ensure non-discrimination" in hiring and promotion based on, among other things, "sexual orientation." . . . I do not mean to be critical of these legislative successes; homosexuals are as entitled to use the legal system for reinforcement of their moral sentiments as are the rest of society. But they are subject to being countered by lawful, democratic countermeasures as well.

That is where Amendment 2 came in. It sought to counter both the geographic concentration and the disproportionate political power of homosexuals by (1) resolving the controversy at the statewide level, and (2) making the election a single-issue contest for both sides. It put directly, to all the citizens of the State, the question: Should homosexuality be given special protection? They answered no. The Court today asserts that this most democratic of procedures is unconstitutional. Lacking any cases to establish that facially absurd proposition, it simply asserts that it must be unconstitutional, because it has never happened before. . . .

I would not myself indulge in . . . official praise for heterosexual monogamy, because I think it no business of the courts (as opposed to the political branches) to take sides in this culture war. But the Court today has done so, not only by inventing a novel and extravagant constitutional doctrine to take the victory away from traditional forces, but even by verbally disparaging as bigotry adherence to traditional attitudes. To suggest, for example, that this constitutional amendment springs from nothing more than "a bare . . . desire to harm a politically unpopular group," . . . is nothing short of insulting. (It is also nothing short of preposterous to call "politically unpopular" a group which enjoys enormous influence in American media and politics, and which, as the trial court here noted, though composing no more than 4% of the population had the support of 46% of the voters on Amendment 2. . . .)

When the Court takes sides in the culture wars, it tends to be with the knights rather than the villains—and more specifically with the Templars, reflecting the views and values of the lawyer class from which the Court's Members are drawn. How that class feels about homosexuality will be evident to anyone who wishes to interview job applicants at virtually any of the Nation's law schools. The interviewer may refuse to offer a job because the applicant is a Republican; because he is an adulterer; because he went to the wrong prep school or belongs to the wrong country club; because he eats snails; because he is a womanizer;

because she wears real-animal fur; or even because he hates the Chicago Cubs. But if the interviewer should wish not to be an associate or partner of an applicant because he disapproves of the applicant's homosexuality, then he will have violated the pledge which the Association of American Law Schools requires all its member-schools to exact from job interviewers: "assurance of the employer's willingness" to hire homosexuals. . . . This law-school view of what "prejudices" must be stamped out may be contrasted with the more plebeian attitudes that apparently still prevail in the United States Congress, which has been unresponsive to repeated attempts to extend to homosexuals the protections of federal civil rights laws . . . and which took the pains

to exclude them specifically from the Americans With Disabilities Act of 1990. . . .

Today's opinion has no foundation in American constitutional law, and barely pretends to. The people of Colorado have adopted an entirely reasonable provision which does not even disfavor homosexuals in any substantive sense, but merely denies them preferential treatment. Amendment 2 is designed to prevent piecemeal deterioration of the sexual morality favored by a majority of Coloradans, and is not only an appropriate means to that legitimate end, but a means that Americans have employed before. Striking it down is an act, not of judicial judgment, but of political will. I dissent.

Case

BAKER V. STATE OF VERMONT

744 A. 2d 864 (1999)

In this path-breaking case the Vermont Supreme Court considers whether same-sex couples can be excluded from the benefits and protections that state laws provide to heterosexual married couples.

Amestoy, C.J.

. . . Plaintiffs are three same-sex couples who have lived together in committed relationships for periods ranging from four to twenty-five years. Two of the couples have raised children together. Each couple applied for a marriage license from their respective town clerk, and each was refused a license as ineligible under the applicable state marriage laws. Plaintiffs thereupon filed this lawsuit against defendants—the State of Vermont, the Towns of Milton and Shelburne, and the City of South Burlington—seeking a declaratory judgment that the refusal to issue them a license violated the marriage statutes and the Vermont Constitution. . . .

Assuming that the marriage statutes preclude their eligibility for a marriage license, plaintiffs contend that the exclusion violates their right to the common benefit and protection of the law guaranteed by Chapter I, Article 7 of the Vermont Constitution. They note that in denying them access to a civil marriage license, the law effectively excludes them from a broad array of legal benefits and protections incident to the marital relation, including access to a spouse's medical, life, and disability insurance, hospital visitation and other medical decision-making privileges, spousal support, intestate succession, homestead protections, and many other statutory protections. They claim the trial court erred in upholding the law on

the basis that it reasonably served the State's interest in promoting the "link between procreation and child rearing." They argue that the large number of married couples without children, and the increasing incidence of same-sex couples with children, undermines the State's rationale. They note that Vermont law affirmatively guarantees the right to adopt and raise children regardless of the sex of the parents, . . . and challenge the logic of a legislative scheme that recognizes the rights of same-sex partners as parents, yet denies them—and their children—the same security as spouses.

In considering this issue, it is important to emphasize at the outset that it is the Common Benefits Clause of the Vermont Constitution we are construing, rather than its counterpart, the Equal Protection Clause of the Fourteenth Amendment to the United States Constitution. . . .

As we explain in the discussion that follows, the Common Benefits Clause of the Vermont Constitution differs markedly from the federal Equal Protection Clause in its language, historical origins, purpose, and development. While the federal amendment may thus supplement the protections afforded by the Common Benefits Clause, it does not supplant it as the first and primary safeguard of the rights and liberties of all Vermonters. . . .

. . . Vermont case law has consistently demanded in practice that statutory exclusions from publicly-conferred benefits and protections must be "premised on an appropriate and overriding public interest." . . . The rigid categories utilized by the federal courts under the Fourteenth Amendment find no support in our early case law and, while routinely cited, are often effectively ignored in our more recent decisions. . . . [T]hese decisions are consistent with the text and history of the Common Benefits Clause which, similarly, yield no rigid categories or formulas of analysis. The balancing approach . . . implicit in our recent decisions reflects the language, history, and values at the core of the Common Benefits Clause. We turn, accordingly, to a brief examination of constitutional language and history. . . .

We first focus on the words of the Constitution themselves. . . . One of the fundamental rights included in Chapter I of the Vermont Constitution of 1777, entitled "A Declaration of Rights of the Inhabitants of the State of Vermont," the Common Benefits Clause as originally written provided:

> That government is, or ought to be, instituted for the common benefit, protection, and security of the people, nation or community; and not for the particular emolument or advantage of any single man, family or set of men, who are a part only of that community; and that the community hath an indubitable, unalienable and indefeasible right, to reform, alter or abolish government, in such manner as shall be, by that community, judged most conducive to the public weal.

. . . Article 7 is intended to ensure that the benefits and protections conferred by the State are for the common benefit of the community and are not for the advantage of persons "who are a part only of that community." When a statute is challenged under Article 7, we first define that "part of the community" disadvantaged by the law. We examine the statutory basis that distinguishes those protected by the law from those excluded from the State's protection. Our concern here is with delineating, not with labelling the excluded class as "suspect," "quasi-suspect," or "non-suspect" for purposes of determining different levels of judicial scrutiny.

We look next to the government's purpose in drawing a classification that includes some members of the community within the scope of the challenged law but excludes others. Consistent with Article 7's guiding principle of affording the protection and benefit of the law to all members of the Vermont community, we examine the nature of the classification to determine whether it is reasonably necessary to accomplish the State's claimed objectives.

We must ultimately ascertain whether the omission of a part of the community from the benefit, protection and security of the challenged law bears a reasonable and just relation to the governmental purpose. Consistent with the core presumption of inclusion, factors to be considered in this determination may include: (1) the significance of the benefits and protections of the challenged law; (2) whether the omission of members of the community from the benefits and protections of the challenged law promotes the government's stated goals; and (3) whether the classification is significantly underinclusive or overinclusive. . . .

Ultimately, the answers to these questions, however useful, cannot substitute for "[t]he inescapable fact . . . that

adjudication of . . . claims may call upon the Court in interpreting the Constitution to exercise that same capacity which by tradition courts always have exercised: reasoned judgment." . . . The balance between individual liberty and organized society which courts are continually called upon to weigh does not lend itself to the precision of a scale. It is, indeed, a recognition of the imprecision of "reasoned judgment" that compels both judicial restraint and respect for tradition in constitutional interpretation. . . .

With these general precepts in mind, we turn to the question of whether the exclusion of same-sex couples from the benefits and protections incident to marriage under Vermont law contravenes Article 7. The first step in our analysis is to identify the nature of the statutory classification. As noted, the marriage statutes apply expressly to opposite-sex couples. Thus, the statutes exclude anyone who wishes to marry someone of the same sex.

Next, we must identify the governmental purpose or purposes to be served by the statutory classification. The principal purpose the State advances in support of the excluding same-sex couples from the legal benefits of marriage is the government's interest in "furthering the link between procreation and child rearing." The State has a strong interest, it argues, in promoting a permanent commitment between couples who have children to ensure that their offspring are considered legitimate and receive ongoing parental support. The State contends, further, that the Legislature could reasonably believe that sanctioning same-sex unions "would diminish society's perception of the link between procreation and child rearing . . . [and] advance the notion that fathers or mothers . . . are mere surplusage to the functions of procreation and child rearing." The State argues that since same-sex couples cannot conceive a child on their own, state-sanctioned same-sex unions "could be seen by the Legislature to separate further the connection between procreation and parental responsibilities for raising children." Hence, the Legislature is justified, the State concludes, "in using the marriage statutes to send a public message that procreation and child rearing are intertwined."

Do these concerns represent valid public interests that are reasonably furthered by the exclusion of same-sex couples from the benefits and protections that flow from the marital relation? It is beyond dispute that the State has a legitimate and long-standing interest in promoting a permanent commitment between couples for the security of their children. It is equally undeniable that the State's interest has been advanced by extending formal public sanction and protection to the union, or marriage, of those couples considered capable of having children, i.e., men and women. And there is no doubt that the overwhelming majority of births today continue to result from natural conception between one man and one woman. . . .

It is equally undisputed that many opposite-sex couples marry for reasons unrelated to procreation, that some of these couples never intend to have children, and that others are incapable of having children. Therefore, if the purpose of the statutory exclusion of same-sex couples is to "further the link between procreation and child rearing," it is significantly under-inclusive. The law extends the benefits and protections of marriage to many persons with no logical connection to the stated governmental goal.

Furthermore, while accurate statistics are difficult to obtain, there is no dispute that a significant number of children today are actually being raised by same-sex parents, and that increasing numbers of children are being conceived by such parents through a variety of assisted-reproductive techniques. . . .

Thus, with or without the marriage sanction, the reality today is that increasing numbers of same-sex couples are employing increasingly efficient assisted-reproductive techniques to conceive and raise children. . . . The Vermont Legislature has not only recognized this reality, but has acted affirmatively to remove legal barriers so that same-sex couples may legally adopt and rear the children conceived through such efforts. . . . The State has also acted to expand the domestic relations laws to safeguard the interests of same-sex parents and their children when such couples terminate their domestic relationship. . . .

Therefore, to the extent that the State's purpose in licensing civil marriage was, and is, to legitimize children and provide for their security, the statutes plainly exclude many same-sex couples who are no different from opposite-sex couples with respect to these objectives. If anything, the exclusion of same-sex couples from the legal protections incident to marriage exposes their children to the precise risks that the State argues the marriage laws are designed to secure against. In short, the marital exclusion treats persons who are similarly situated for purposes of the law, differently.

The State also argues that because same-sex couples cannot conceive a child on their own, their exclusion promotes a "perception of the link between procreation and child rearing," and that to discard it would "advance the notion that mothers and fathers . . . are mere surplusage to the functions of procreation and child rearing." Apart from the bare assertion, the State offers no persuasive reasoning to support these claims. Indeed, it is undisputed that most of those who utilize non-traditional means of conception are infertile married couples, . . . and that many assisted-reproductive techniques involve only one of the married partner's genetic material, the other being supplied by a third party through sperm, egg, or embryo donation. . . . The State does not suggest that the use of these technologies undermines a married couple's sense of parental responsibility, or fosters the perception that they are "mere surplusage" to the conception and parenting of the child so conceived. Nor does it even remotely suggest that access to such techniques ought to be restricted as a matter of public policy to "send a public message that procreation and child rearing are intertwined." Accordingly, there is no reasonable basis to conclude that a same-sex couple's use of the same technologies would undermine the bonds of parenthood, or society's perception of parenthood.

The question thus becomes whether the exclusion of a relatively small but significant number of otherwise qualified same-sex couples from the same legal benefits and protections afforded their opposite-sex counterparts contravenes the mandates of Article 7. It is, of course, well settled that statutes are not necessarily unconstitutional because they fail to extend legal protection to all who are similarly situated. . . . Courts have upheld underinclusive statutes out of a recognition that, for reasons of pragmatism or administrative convenience, the legislature may choose to address problems incrementally. . . . The State does not contend, however, that the same-sex exclusion is necessary as a matter of pragmatism or administrative convenience. We turn, accordingly, from the principal justifications advanced by the State to the interests asserted by plaintiffs.

As noted, in determining whether a statutory exclusion reasonably relates to the governmental purpose it is appropriate to consider the history and significance of the benefits denied. . . .

While the laws relating to marriage have undergone many changes during the last century, largely toward the goal of equalizing the status of husbands and wives, the benefits of marriage have not diminished in value. On the contrary, the benefits and protections incident to a marriage license under Vermont law have never been greater. They include, for example, the right to receive a portion of the estate of a spouse who dies intestate and protection against disinheritance through elective share provisions; preference in being appointed as the personal representative of a spouse who dies intestate; the right to bring a lawsuit for the wrongful death of a spouse; the right to bring an action for loss of consortium; the right to workers' compensation survivor benefits; the right to spousal benefits statutorily guaranteed to public employees, including health, life, disability, and accident insurance; the opportunity to be covered as a spouse under group life insurance policies issued to an employee; the opportunity to be covered as the insured's spouse under an individual health insurance policy; the right to claim an evidentiary privilege for marital communications; homestead rights and protections; the presumption of joint ownership of property and the concomitant right of survivorship; hospital visitation and other rights incident to the medical treatment of a family member; and the right to receive, and the obligation to provide, spousal support, maintenance, and property division in the event of separation or divorce. . . .

. . . The legal benefits and protections flowing from a marriage license are of such significance that any statutory exclusion must necessarily be grounded on public concerns of sufficient weight, cogency, and authority that the justice of the deprivation cannot seriously be questioned. Considered in light of the extreme logical disjunction between the classification and the stated purposes of the law—protecting children and "furthering the link between procreation and child rearing"—the exclusion falls substantially short of this standard. The laudable governmental goal of promoting a commitment between married couples to promote the security of their children and the community as a whole provides no reasonable basis for denying the legal benefits and protections of marriage to same-sex couples, who are no differently situated with respect to this goal than their opposite-sex counterparts. Promoting a link between procreation and child-rearing similarly fails to support the exclusion. We turn, accordingly, to the remaining interests identified by the State in support of the statutory exclusion.

The State asserts that a number of additional rationales could support a legislative decision to exclude same-sex partners from the statutory benefits and protections of marriage. Among these are the State's purported interests in "promoting child rearing in a setting that provides both male and female role models," minimizing the legal complications of surrogacy contracts and sperm donors, "bridging differences" between the sexes, discouraging marriages of convenience for tax, housing or other benefits, maintaining uniformity with marriage laws in other states, and generally protecting marriage from "destabilizing changes." The most substantive of the State's remaining claims relates to the issue of childrearing. It is conceivable that the Legislature could conclude that opposite-sex partners offer advantages in this area, although we note that child-development experts disagree and the answer is decidedly uncertain. The argument, however, contains a more fundamental flaw, and that is the Legislature's endorsement of a policy diametrically at odds with the State's claim. In 1996, the Vermont General Assembly enacted, and the Governor signed, a law removing all prior legal barriers to the adoption of children by same-sex couples. . . . At the same time, the Legislature provided additional legal protections in the form of court-ordered child support and parent-child contact in the event that same-sex parents dissolved their "domestic relationship." . . . In light of these express policy choices, the State's arguments that Vermont public policy favors opposite-sex over same-sex parents or disfavors the use of artificial reproductive technologies, are patently without substance.

Similarly, the State's argument that Vermont's marriage laws serve a substantial governmental interest in maintaining uniformity with other jurisdictions cannot be reconciled with Vermont's recognition of unions, such as first-cousin marriages, not uniformly sanctioned in other states. . . . In an analogous context, Vermont has sanctioned adoptions by same-sex partners, . . . notwithstanding the fact that many states have not. . . . Thus, the State's claim that Vermont's marriage laws were adopted because the Legislature sought to conform to those of the other forty-nine states is not only speculative, but refuted by two relevant legislative choices which demonstrate that uniformity with other jurisdictions has not been a governmental purpose.

The State's remaining claims (e.g., recognition of same-sex unions might foster marriages of convenience or otherwise affect the institution in "unpredictable" ways) may be plausible forecasts as to what the future may hold, but cannot reasonably be construed to provide a reasonable and just basis for the statutory exclusion. The State's conjectures are not, in any event, susceptible to empirical proof before they occur.

Finally, it is suggested that the long history of official intolerance of intimate same-sex relationships cannot be reconciled with an interpretation of Article 7 that would give state-sanctioned benefits and protection to individuals of the same sex who commit to a permanent domestic relationship. We find the argument to be unpersuasive for several reasons. First, to the extent that state action historically has been motivated by an animus against a class, that history cannot provide a legitimate basis for continued unequal application of the law. . . . Furthermore, as noted earlier, recent enactments of the General Assembly have removed barriers to adoption by same-sex couples, and have extended legal rights and protections to such couples who dissolve their "domestic relationship." . . .

Thus, viewed in the light of history, logic, and experience, we conclude that none of the interests asserted by the State provides a reasonable and just basis for the continued exclusion of same-sex couples from the benefits incident to a civil marriage license under Vermont law. Accordingly, in the faith that a case beyond the imagining of the framers of our Constitution may, nevertheless, be safely anchored in the values that infused it, we find a constitutional obligation to extend to plaintiffs the common benefit, protection, and security that Vermont law provides opposite-sex married couples. . . .

We hold . . . that plaintiffs are entitled under Chapter I, Article 7, of the Vermont Constitution to obtain the same benefits and protections afforded by Vermont law to married opposite-sex couples. We do not purport to infringe upon the prerogatives of the Legislature to craft an appropriate means of addressing this constitutional mandate, other than to note that the record here refers to a number of potentially constitutional statutory schemes from other jurisdictions. These include what are typically referred to as "domestic partnership" or "registered partnership" acts, which generally establish an alternative legal status to marriage for same-sex couples, impose similar formal requirements and limitations, create a parallel licensing or registration scheme, and extend all or most of the same rights and obligations provided by the law to married partners. . . .

While many have noted the symbolic or spiritual significance of the marital relation, it is plaintiffs' claim to the secular benefits and protections of a singularly human relationship that, in our view, characterizes this case. The State's interest in extending official recognition and legal protection to the professed commitment of two individuals to a lasting relationship of mutual affection is predicated on the belief that legal support of a couple's commitment provides stability for the individuals, their family, and the broader community. Although plaintiffs' interest in seeking state recognition and protection of their mutual commitment may—in view of divorce statistics—represent "the triumph of hope over experience," the essential aspect of their claim is simply and fundamentally for inclusion in the family of State-sanctioned human relations.

The past provides many instances where the law refused to see a human being when it should have.

. . .The future may provide instances where the law will be asked to see a human when it should not. . . . The challenge for future generations will be to define what is most essentially human. The extension of the Common Benefits Clause to acknowledge plaintiffs as Vermonters who seek nothing more, nor less, than legal protection and security for their avowed commitment to an intimate and lasting human relationship is simply, when all is said and done, a recognition of our common humanity. . . .

Johnson, J., concurring in part and dissenting in part.

. . . Although I concur with the majority's conclusion that Vermont law unconstitutionally excludes same-sex couples from the benefits of marriage, I write separately to state my belief that this is a straightforward case of sex discrimination.

As I argue below, the marriage statutes establish a classification based on sex. Whether such classification is legally justifiable should be analyzed under our common-benefits jurisprudence, which until today, has been closely akin to the federal equal-protection analysis under the Fourteenth Amendment. Therefore, the State must show that the classification is narrowly tailored to further important, if not compelling, interests. Not only do the rationalizations advanced by the State fail to pass constitutional muster under this or any other form of heightened scrutiny, they fail to satisfy the rational-basis test as articulated under the Common Benefits Clause. . . .

13

ELECTIONS, REPRESENTATION, AND VOTING RIGHTS

"Undoubtedly, the right of suffrage is a fundamental matter in a free and democratic society. Especially since the right to exercise the franchise in a free and unimpaired manner is preservative of other basic civil and political rights, any alleged infringement of the right of citizens to vote must be carefully and meticulously scrutinized."

—CHIEF JUSTICE EARL WARREN, WRITING FOR

THE COURT IN *REYNOLDS V. SIMS* (1964)

Earl Warren: Chief Justice, 1953–1969

INTRODUCTION

The right to vote is essential to **representative democracy**, that form of government in which policy decisions are made by representatives chosen in periodic competitive elections. Because democracy is based on the principle of political equality, a genuine democracy entails **universal suffrage**, the right of all law-abiding adult citizens to vote. Of course, the right to vote is meaningless if elections are rigged or susceptible to fraud. Nor is the right to vote as meaningful if one is compelled to vote, as is the case in some countries. Ideally, then, the right to vote involves voluntary participation in free and fair elections.

From a constitutional standpoint, voting is among the most important rights that citizens possess. As the Supreme Court recognized in *Yick Wo v. Hopkins* (1886), voting is "a fundamental political right, because [it is] preservative of all rights." Like free speech, voting has important instrumental value as a means of ensuring the continuing viability of constitutional democracy in this country. Of course, voting is by no means a sufficient guarantee of liberty. Indeed, it may foster the **tyranny of the majority**, which is precisely what the Framers of the Constitution wanted to prevent.

Although the United States today is a democratic country, the term "democracy" was an anathema to many of the Framers. They accepted the notion of **popular sovereignty** in the abstract, but they certainly did not believe that every question of policy was to be subjected to majority rule. Many of the delegates to the Constitutional Convention of 1787 shared Alexander Hamilton's view that democracy was little more than legitimized mob rule, an ever-present danger to personal security, liberty, and property. The Framers thus sought to establish a **constitutional republic**, in which public policy would be made by elected representatives within limits delineated in the Constitution. As we have noted in previous chapters, the Constitution was adopted to place certain values above the political fray, in order to protect individual rights from the tyranny of transient majorities. With its several elitist elements and many limitations on majority rule, the Framers' Constitution can be seen as rather undemocratic. But two centuries of history have witnessed the democratization of the U.S. Constitution. What was conceived as a constitutional *republic* has become a constitutional *democracy*.

The Democratization of America

It should be remembered that property qualifications for voting still existed in 1787 and that the franchise was granted originally only to white males. With the advent of Jacksonian democracy in the 1830s, property qualifications rapidly diminished and were virtually nonexistent by the time of the Civil War. The Fifteenth Amendment, adopted in 1870, theoretically extended the franchise to African-Americans, although another century of struggle was necessary to realize the promise of the amendment. The Nineteenth Amendment, ratified in 1920, removed sex as a qualification for voting. In addition to women's suffrage, another accomplishment of the progressive movement was passage of the Seventeenth Amendment in 1913, providing for the direct election of U.S. senators. The Twenty-fourth Amendment, ratified in 1964, abolished **poll taxes** as prerequisites for voting in federal elections. Finally, the minimum voting age was lowered to 18 with the adoption of the Twenty-sixth Amendment in 1971. Thus, through two centuries of political change highlighted by historic amendments, the U.S. Constitution has undergone a democratic transformation.

Despite theories of the "ruling class" and the "power elite," which portray power as concentrated in a few hands, most observers would agree that political influence is more widely dispersed in the United States than in most other countries. Through mass media, political parties, interest group activity, and public demonstrations, the

American people have numerous opportunities to make their demands and preferences known to their political leaders. And, of course, many of these leaders are accountable to the public through regular, competitive elections. The American people elect an astonishing array of public officials from the president all the way down to local school board members. Unfortunately, however, election practices, and even the laws governing elections, have not always reflected a serious commitment to the ideal of political equality.

Policing the Democratic Process

What happens when the majority decides to strip the minority of certain rights, even to exclude it from political participation? In a political system based solely on majority rule, there would be no remedy for the minority group. The problem is far from hypothetical. History resounds with instances of majorities oppressing minorities. Even in the United States, the "people's representatives" have passed laws isolating minority groups, diluting their right to vote, and even excluding them from the political process altogether. Such sordid conduct underscores the need for limitations on legislative power, especially in the area of voting rights. Those constitutional amendments safeguarding the right to vote and to organize politically are essential to a minority group's ability to protect itself from a hostile majority. Equally important, however, is the role that courts have played in ensuring that minorities are not locked out of the political process. Indeed, one of the paradoxes of American democracy is that the U.S. Supreme Court, a fundamentally elitist institution, has played a major part in the progressive democratization of the country. Through its exercise of judicial review, the Court, especially during the first half of the twentieth century, struck down a number of laws restricting the right to vote. More recently, it has upheld and thus reinforced the constitutional legitimacy of statutes, such as the Voting Rights Act of 1965, designed to safeguard and expand the franchise.

Justice Harlan Fiske Stone's famous footnote in *United States v. Carolene Products* (1938) recognized potential problems that could result from efforts to limit political participation, including "restrictions upon the right to vote," "restraints upon the dissemination of information," "interferences with political organizations," and "prohibition[s] of peaceable assembly." Stone asserted that "prejudice against discrete and insular minorities may be a special condition, which tends seriously to curtail the operation of those political processes ordinarily to be relied upon to protect minorities. . . ." Accordingly, claims brought by groups that have been locked out of the political process call for a "more searching judicial inquiry."

RACIAL DISCRIMINATION IN VOTING RIGHTS

As previously noted, the ratification of the Fifteenth Amendment in 1870 did not result in the immediate enfranchisement of most African-Americans. In some areas, public officials blatantly refused to honor the mandates of the Fifteenth Amendment. In other areas, groups such as the Ku Klux Klan resorted to terrorism to prevent African-Americans from exercising their newly won right to vote. The Supreme Court initially aided such resistance by limiting congressional power to enforce the Fifteenth Amendment. In *United States v. Reese* (1876), the Court struck down the Enforcement Act of 1870, by which Congress attempted to protect the right of blacks to vote in state elections. By 1884, the Court changed course and recognized Congress's power to enforce the Fifteenth Amendment (see *Ex parte Yarbrough*). By this time, however, Congress was not particularly concerned with the rights of African-Americans. Nevertheless, once it became clear that the Court would permit the federal government to secure blacks' voting rights, states bent on maintaining African-Americans in a position of second-class citizenship resorted to disingenuous methods designed to exclude them from the political process.

Grandfather Clauses

Perhaps the most blatant official means of preventing black Americans from exercising their newly granted constitutional right to vote was the **grandfather clause.** First enacted by Mississippi in 1890, this device soon spread throughout southern and border states. Oklahoma's version, adopted as an amendment to the state constitution in 1910, was typical in that it required literacy tests for all voters whose ancestors had not been entitled to vote prior to 1866. The overall effect of grandfather clauses was to subject almost all potential black voters to literacy tests arbitrarily administered by white officials, while exempting numerous illiterate whites from this requirement.

Largely in response to invidious discrimination of this kind, the National Association for the Advancement of Colored People (NAACP) was formed in the early twentieth century. The first of many legal victories won by the NAACP came in 1915 when the Supreme Court struck down the Oklahoma grandfather clause (*Guinn v. United States*). Undaunted, the Oklahoma legislature in 1916 adopted a new law aimed at keeping African-Americans from the polls. This statute granted permanent voting registration to all persons who had voted in 1914, when the grandfather clause was still in effect. All other persons were required to register to vote during a twelve-day period or be permanently disqualified from voting. The Supreme Court ultimately invalidated this blatant subterfuge as well (see *Lane v. Wilson* [1939]).

The White Primary

After the demise of the grandfather clause, southern states resorted to the equally infamous **white primary.** This device was an extremely effective means of keeping African-Americans from exercising their right to vote in any meaningful sense. Until the 1960s, the "solid South" maintained a virtual one-party political system. Thus, in all but a few areas, nomination by the Democratic Party was tantamount to election. In fact, Republicans seldom bothered to run in the general elections. In order to keep African-Americans out of the political process, the Democratic Party in many states adopted a rule excluding them from party membership. Concomitantly, state legislatures closed the primaries to everyone except party members. The Supreme Court had previously ruled that political parties were private organizations, not part of the government election apparatus (see *Newberry v. United States* [1921]). Consequently, through the white primary device, blacks were effectively disenfranchised but, arguably, not by official state action.

In a series of cases from the late 1920s through the early 1950s, the Supreme Court grappled with the white primary issue. In two early decisions, it effectively barred formal state endorsement of the white primary (see *Nixon v. Herndon* [1927] and *Nixon v. Condon* [1932]). However, in *Grovey v. Townsend* (1935), the Supreme Court upheld a Texas white primary based not on legislative enactment but exclusively on a resolution adopted by the state Democratic Party. The Court's decision in *Grovey* thus reinforced the prevailing legal view that political parties were merely private organizations beyond the purview of the Constitution. In *United States v. Classic* (1941), however, the Court moved away from this highly artificial view of party primaries. The *Classic* case involved the question of whether the federal government could regulate party primaries in order to prevent election fraud. In upholding this exercise of congressional power, the Court overruled *Newberry* and undercut the logic of *Grovey v. Townsend*. In *Smith v. Allwright* (1944), the Court struck down the white primary as violative of the Fifteenth Amendment, thus overruling the *Grovey* decision. Writing for the Court, Justice Stanley Reed expressed a pragmatic view of the concept of state action:

> This grant to the people of the opportunity for choice is not to be nullified by a State through casting its electoral process in a form which permits a private organization to practice racial discrimination in the election. Constitutional rights would be of little value if they could be thus indirectly denied.

In an attempt to circumvent the Supreme Court's ruling in *Smith v. Allwright,* Texas Democrats established the "Jaybird Democratic Association," from which African-Americans were excluded. The Jaybirds held "preprimary" elections in which candidates for the Democratic primaries were selected. This shabby attempt at further evasion of constitutional requirements was invalidated by the Supreme Court (*Terry v. Adams* [1953]). In *Terry,* the Court observed that under the preprimary scheme, both the primary and the general election were little more than "perfunctory ratifiers" of the Jaybirds' choices for elected officials.

Literacy Tests

The eradication of grandfather clauses and white primaries was insufficient to integrate African-Americans into the political process, because die-hard racism manifested itself in alternative exclusionary tactics. For example, many states relied on **literacy tests** that, despite superficial neutrality, were administered in a highly discriminatory manner. Quite frequently, white people were not required to take the tests, even if their literacy was questionable. However, since the Constitution had left the determination of voting qualifications to the states and since these tests were on their face racially neutral, the Supreme Court refused to strike them down. In *Lassiter v. Northampton County Board of Education* (1959), the Court explicitly upheld the use of literacy tests. Writing for the Court, Justice William O. Douglas reasoned that "in our society where newspapers, periodicals, books and other printed matter canvass and debate campaign issues, a State might conclude that only those who are literate should exercise the franchise." Ultimately, literacy tests as devices of racial discrimination were done away with, not by the Supreme Court but by Congress through the landmark Voting Rights Act of 1965.

Poll Taxes

Another less common but equally effective means of keeping African-Americans from voting was the poll tax. At the time the Constitution was adopted, poll taxes were widely used as a legitimate means of raising revenue. During the 1780s, however, poll taxes did not significantly hamper voting because only white property owners were entitled to vote anyway! By the mid-nineteenth century, poll taxes had virtually disappeared. Around 1900, a number of states resurrected the poll tax for the obvious purpose of preventing African-Americans from voting. The tax generally amounted to $2 per election—quite sufficient to deter many blacks, as well as poor whites, from exercising the franchise. On its face, however, the poll tax was racially neutral, and the Supreme Court initially refused to strike it down (see *Breedlove v. Suttles* [1937]). Eventually, however, the poll tax was thoroughly repudiated. In 1964, the poll tax was abolished in federal elections through adoption of the Twenty-fourth Amendment. Three years later, in *Harper v. Virginia Board of Elections* (1966), the Supreme Court held that poll taxes in state elections violated the Fourteenth Amendment. Writing for the Court, Justice Douglas emphasized the arbitrariness of the tax:

To introduce wealth, or payment of a fee as a measure of a voter's qualifications is to introduce a capricious or irrelevant factor. . . . Wealth, like race, creed, or color, is not germane to one's ability to participate intelligently in the electoral process.

Racial Gerrymandering

Perhaps the most outrageous attempt to disenfranchise African-American voters occurred in Tuskegee, Alabama, in 1957. At the city's behest, the all-white Alabama legislature dramatically altered the boundaries of Tuskegee from a square to a twenty-eight-sided figure. The purpose of the **gerrymander** was obvious in that all but five of the city's 400 black voters were placed outside the city limits, while no white voters were displaced. A number of the "former residents" of Tuskegee brought suit in federal court, seeking a declaratory judgment that the **racial gerrymandering** measure was unconstitutional and an injunction to prohibit its enforcement. The U.S. District Court for the Middle District of Alabama dismissed the case for lack of jurisdiction, stating that it had "no control over, no supervision over, and no power to change any boundaries of a municipal corporation fixed by a duly convened legislative body." The Court of Appeals for the Fifth Circuit agreed. But the Supreme Court reversed the lower courts and reinstated the complaint, saying that the "petitioners are entitled to prove their allegations at trial." Speaking for a unanimous bench, Justice Felix Frankfurter stated that if the plaintiffs' allegations were proven, it would be "difficult to appreciate what stands in the way of adjudging [the redistricting measure] invalid" (*Gomillion v. Lightfoot* [1960]). Indeed, plaintiffs prevailed at trial, and the gerrymander was invalidated.

The Voting Rights Act of 1965

A 1961 report of the U.S. Commission on Civil Rights documented the pervasiveness of voting discrimination in the South. According to the report, fewer than 10 percent of eligible African-Americans were registered to vote in at least 129 counties in ten southern states. In counties where blacks comprised a majority of the population, the average level of black registration was only 3 percent. As the Civil Rights movement of the early 1960s galvanized the nation's conscience, the demand for federal action grew. The federal government responded with the Civil Rights Act of 1964 and the **Voting Rights Act of 1965,** both of which were pushed through Congress under the skillful leadership of President Lyndon B. Johnson.

The Voting Rights Act employed a rough index of discrimination to apply the scrutiny of the federal government to those states that had historically been most recalcitrant in refusing to allow African-Americans to vote: Alabama, Georgia, Louisiana, Mississippi, South Carolina, and Virginia. Specifically, the act waived accumulated poll taxes and abolished literacy tests and similar devices in those areas to which the statute applied. The act also required the aforementioned states to obtain preclearance from the U.S. Department of Justice before making changes in their electoral systems. Not surprisingly, this historic and far-reaching act was challenged on the ground that Congress had exceeded its power to enforce the Fifteenth Amendment. The Supreme Court, although recognizing the Voting Rights Act as "inventive," upheld the law (see *South Carolina v. Katzenbach* [1966]). Writing for a nearly unanimous Court (only Justice Hugo Black partially dissented), Chief Justice Earl Warren expressed optimism about the Voting Rights Act:

Hopefully, millions of non-white Americans will now be able to participate for the first time on an equal basis in the government under which they live. We may finally look forward to the day when truly "the right of citizens of the United States to vote shall not be denied or abridged by the United States or by any State on account of race, color or previous condition of servitude."

Despite its strong endorsement by the Warren Court and subsequent extension by Congress, the Voting Rights Act remained controversial. Of particular concern to many were the strict preclearance requirements of Section 5, under which designated states are required to submit proposed changes in election laws to the Justice Department for approval. Equally controversial is Section 2, which allows plaintiffs in any jurisdiction to challenge electoral schemes that impermissibly dilute the voting strength of minority groups. These provisions led many conservatives to oppose renewal of the Voting Rights Act in 1982.

The Reagan administration, more conservative than its Democratic and Republican predecessors in the field of civil rights, initially opposed the extension of the act without major changes in these controversial provisions. However, bipartisan support in Congress for extending the act forced the administration to back down. The act was renewed and strengthened in 1982. Although some civil rights activists argue that the Voting Rights Act has not been enforced vigorously enough, one must recognize the very real impact it has had on minority political participation. Enforcement of the Voting Rights Act has resulted in substantially higher levels of voter registration among African-Americans, particularly in the Deep South. Accordingly, many politicians who formerly made overt appeals to white supremacy tempered their racist rhetoric in order to draw support from new black voters. Perhaps the best example of this metamorphosis was Alabama Governor George Wallace who, in the face of the Civil Rights movement of the 1960s, maintained a strong segregationist stance. In the late 1970s and early 1980s, Wallace dropped the racist rhetoric in order to appeal to newly enfranchised African-Americans who might be tempted to vote Republican. Another excellent example of this political realism is seen in the long career of Republican Senator Strom Thurmond of South Carolina. In 1948, when he was the Democratic governor of the state, Thurmond ran for president on the strongly segregationist Dixiecrat ticket. With the enfranchisement of African-Americans, however, Thurmond began actively soliciting (and often receiving) their support in his U.S. Senate races.

At-Large Elections

As African-Americans began to register and vote in greater numbers, black politicians made substantial gains, especially at the local level. Seeking to thwart the growing influence of black voters, a number of white-dominated cities and counties adopted basic structural changes in their systems of representation. Because the overt racial gerrymander had been declared unconstitutional in *Gomillion v. Lightfoot* (1960), these communities converted to **at-large elections** in which local candidates ran for office on a citywide or countywide basis. This election method was by no means novel in the United States, but its use as a deliberate means of limiting the political clout of African-American voters raised new constitutional issues. At-large systems of voting were often coupled with the annexation of predominantly white suburban areas, thereby further diluting black voting power. Since the 1970s, many of these at-large and annexation schemes have been challenged in court as unlawful attempts to undermine the voting strength of minority groups.

The Supreme Court Rules on At-Large Elections In 1980, the Supreme Court handed down a ruling on the constitutionality of at-large elections (*Mobile v. Bolden*). Since

1911, the city of Mobile, Alabama, had used at-large elections to choose its three-member city commission. At the time the lawsuit was filed, more than 35 percent of the residents of Mobile were African-American. Despite several attempts, however, no African-American had ever been elected to the city commission. Plaintiffs argued that the at-large system was unconstitutional because it had the effect of unfairly diluting the voting strength of racial minorities. The U.S. District Court for the Southern District of Alabama agreed, as did the Fifth Circuit Court of Appeals. The Supreme Court reversed, holding that there must be a showing of a discriminatory intent on the part of public officials in order to warrant a finding that the Constitution has been violated. Dissenting vehemently, Justice Thurgood Marshall asserted that "[s]uch judicial deference to official decision making has no place under the Fifteenth Amendment." Marshall went on to accuse the Court of being "an accessory to the perpetuation of racial discrimination."

In spite of, or perhaps in response to Justice Marshall's accusatory rhetoric in *Mobile v. Bolden,* the Supreme Court in 1982 demonstrated that the "intentional discrimination" standard can in fact be met. In *Rogers v. Lodge,* the Court, voting 6 to 3, struck down an at-large election scheme in Burke County, Georgia, on the basis of the standard handed down in the *Mobile* case. In this case, the Court reasserted a commitment to the Fifteenth Amendment that some critics found lacking in *Mobile v. Bolden.*

The Effects Test under the 1982 Voting Rights Act Amendments   In its 1982 extension of the Voting Rights Act, Congress amended Section 2 to allow plaintiffs to prevail in voting dilution cases on the basis of an effects test, rather than on the intent standard of *Mobile v. Bolden.* In other words, Congress accomplished through statute what the Supreme Court refused to do under the Fifteenth Amendment. Thus, *Mobile v. Bolden* is essentially irrelevant to a group of minority plaintiffs seeking to challenge an election scheme. It matters not to plaintiffs whether they prevail under a provision of the federal Constitution or under Section 2 of the Voting Rights Act. Here is an important lesson for students of the American legal system: Civil rights law is by no means the exclusive province of courts and constitutions. Legislatures may act to enhance civil rights through their power to adopt ordinary legislation.

The Problem of Racially Proportionate Representation

The voting dilution cases raise the serious question of proportionate representation (not to be confused with *proportional* representation existing under some parliamentary systems). A scheme of proportionate representation would require citizens to be represented by individuals possessing specific racial, sexual, religious, occupational, or other characteristics in proportion to their occurrence in the population. Thus, under a scheme of racial proportionate representation, African-Americans in Mobile (see *Mobile v. Bolden,* discussed earlier) would be "entitled" to one seat on the city commission. Indeed, ostensibly because of its opposition to racially proportionate representation, the Reagan administration consistently opposed the effects standard in voting rights litigation, whether brought under the Fifteenth Amendment or Section 2 of the Voting Rights Act.

The Supreme Court has said repeatedly that the Constitution does not require or permit proportionate representation. Few would disagree with the Court on this point of theory. The problem is of a more practical nature. Suppose a federal district judge finds that a city's system of at-large elections was established for the single purpose of diluting the voting strength of African-Americans. Clearly, the court may order the city to set up a system of single-member districts, but how should those districts be drawn? Should the court impose a scheme that virtually ensures proportionate representation of African-Americans on the city council? Would such a **race-conscious remedy** be constitutionally acceptable? In fact, what usually happens in voting rights cases is that both the plaintiff and the defendant submit remedial plans and the court attempts to fashion an equitable compromise. The final remedy that emerges will almost certainly enhance the electoral prospects for African-American candidates but may not ensure proportionate representation.

Challenges to Judicial Election Systems

When Congress extended the Voting Rights Act in 1982, it changed the statutory language in a way that eventually proved to be highly significant. Instead of applying only to elections of "legislators," the act now refers to "representatives." This suggests the applicability of Voting Rights Act challenges to nonlegislative elections, but which elections? In a controversial 6-to-3 decision, the Supreme Court held in 1991 that plaintiffs may challenge judicial election systems under Section 2 of the Voting Rights Act. In *Chisom v. Roemer,* the Court decided that the statutory term "representatives" includes elected judges. The *Chisom* case is one of myriad examples of important civil rights policies being determined through statutory, as opposed to constitutional, interpretation. Students of constitutional law must realize that much of the important law of civil rights stems not from judicial interpretation of the Fourteenth and Fifteenth Amendments but from the broad-gauged statutes passed under Congress's power to enforce the guarantees of those amendments.

Chisom v. Roemer involved a challenge to Louisiana's system for electing judges to the state supreme court. Under that system, five of the seven state supreme court judges were elected from single-member districts; the remaining two jurists were elected at large from a sixth district that included predominantly black Orleans Parish and several other parishes where African-Americans were in the minority. Plaintiffs in the case argued that this scheme had the effect of diluting the voting strength of blacks in New Orleans. Had Orleans Parish been set up as a separate single-member district, an African-American candidate would have had a greater chance of being elected to the state supreme court. Under the existing system, no black had ever been elected to Louisiana's highest tribunal, despite a number of attempts. After a bench trial, the U.S. district court concluded that there had been no violation of the Voting Rights Act under the standard set forth in the landmark case of *Thornburgh v. Gingles* (1986). On appeal, the Fifth Circuit Court of Appeals concluded that the Voting Rights Act did not apply to judicial elections, holding that the district court should have dismissed the complaint altogether. On certiorari, the U.S. Supreme Court reversed, declaring that "[w]hen each of several members of a court must be a resident of a different district, and must be elected by the voters of that district, it seems both reasonable and realistic to characterize the winners as representatives of that district." The Supreme Court expressed no opinion on the merits of the plaintiffs' case. It merely remanded the case to the Fifth Circuit Court of Appeals for further consideration.

In a related case, the Supreme Court decided that Section 2 of the Voting Rights Act applies also to the election of state trial judges. In *Houston Lawyers' Association v. Attorney General of Texas* (1991), the Court said that "[i]f a State decides to elect its trial judges, . . . those elections must be conducted in compliance with the Voting Rights Act." Since at least half the states still use elections to select some or all of their judges, the Court's decisions in *Chisom v. Roemer* and *Houston Lawyers' Association* have plowed a fertile field for litigation. It remains to be seen whether plaintiffs will be successful in mounting challenges to judicial elections. However, one can be sure that the Supreme Court will be revisiting this area of voting rights law.

The Rehnquist Court Restricts Race-Conscious Redistricting

In a decision carrying great potential to affect litigation under the Voting Rights Act of 1965, the Court ruled that strangely shaped legislative districts designed to produce African-American electoral majorities are subject to challenge under the Equal Protection Clause of the Fourteenth Amendment. In *Shaw v. Reno* (1993), white voters had sued to challenge the "racial gerrymandering" that led to the creation of the unusually shaped 12th Congressional District of North Carolina. A three-judge panel in the federal district court dismissed the suit for failure to state a cause of action for which relief is available under the Fourteenth Amendment. On appeal, the Supreme Court reversed by a vote of 5 to 4. Writing for the Court, Justice O'Connor observed that "[w]hen a district is created solely to effectuate the perceived common interests of one racial group, elected officials are more likely to believe that their primary obligation is to represent only the members of that group, rather than their constituency as a whole." In O'Connor's view, such an effect would be "altogether antithetical to our system of representative democracy." In dissent, Justice White argued that "the notion that North Carolina's plan, under which whites remain a voting majority in a disproportionate number of congressional districts, and pursuant to which the State has sent its first black representatives since Reconstruction to the United States Congress, might have violated appellants' constitutional rights is both a fiction and a departure from settled equal protection principles."

In *Shaw v. Reno*, the Supreme Court stopped short of invalidating the North Carolina plan, leaving that determination to the lower federal courts. On remand, the district court in North Carolina upheld the redistricting plan on the ground that the plan was narrowly tailored to further the state's compelling interests in complying with the Voting Rights Act of 1965. Not surprisingly, the Supreme Court granted cert and the case returned to the High Bench.

In *Shaw v. Hunt* (1996), the Supreme Court struck down the North Carolina plan. Writing for the majority of five, Chief Justice Rehnquist took issue with the district court's conclusion that the plan was justified as a means of meeting the state's responsibilities under the Voting Rights Act. Among other things, this statute protects minorities from **vote dilution.** In Rehnquist's view, vote dilution suffered by African-American voting in congressional elections throughout North Carolina is "not remedied by creating a safe majority-black district somewhere else in the State."

The real thrust of the Court's opinion appears to have been a repudiation of the Justice Department's policy of maximizing the number of majority-black districts. Rehnquist asserted that "this maximization policy is not properly grounded in Section 5 [of the Voting Rights Act] and the Department's authority thereunder." In a stinging dissent, Justice Stevens observed that "[t]here is no small irony in the fact that the Court's decision to intrude into the State's districting process comes in response to a lawsuit brought on behalf of white voters who have suffered no history of exclusion from North Carolina's political process, and whose only claims of harm are at best rooted in speculative and stereotypical assumptions about the kind of representation they are likely to receive from the candidates that their neighbors have chosen."

In a similar case, *Bush v. Vera* (1996), the Court invalidated a Texas redistricting plan that created three minority-majority districts. Writing for a plurality, Justice O'Connor observed that the "districts' shapes are bizarre, and their utter disregard of city limits, local election precincts, and voter tabulation district lines has caused a severe disruption of traditional forms of political activity and created administrative headaches for local election officials." O'Connor noted that the "appellants adduced evidence that incumbency protection played a role in determining the bizarre district lines" but concluded, as had the district court, that "the districts' shapes are unexplainable on grounds other than race and, as such, are the product of presumptively unconstitutional racial gerrymandering is inescapably corroborated by the evidence." Justices Stevens, Souter, Ginsburg, and Breyer dissented, as they did in *Shaw v. Hunt.*

The Supreme Court Revisits the North Carolina Redistricting Plan   After the Supreme Court's decision in *Shaw v. Hunt,* the North Carolina legislature redrew the boundaries of the disputed congressional district. Again, litigation ensued. A three-judge panel of the federal district court invalidated the plan, finding that race had again been the dominant consideration. In *Hunt v. Cromartie* (2001), the Supreme Court reversed the district court and upheld the revised plan. Noting the high correlation between race and party identification, the Court concluded that the plaintiffs had failed to show that race was the predominant consideration in the legislature's redistricting plan and that the district court's contrary conclusion was "clearly erroneous." In dissent, Justice Clarence Thomas (joined by Chief Justice Rehnquist and Justices Scalia and Kennedy) observed that "racial gerrymandering offends the Constitution whether the motivation is malicious or benign." Thomas argued that it "is not a defense that the legislature merely may have drawn the district based on the stereotype that blacks are reliable Democratic voters." *Hunt v. Cromartie* did not overturn *Shaw v. Hunt,* but it arguably makes it more difficult for plaintiffs to challenge race-conscious redistricting plans. The litigation over the use of race in redrawing the North Carolina congressional districts lasted nearly ten years and went before the Supreme Court four times. When, in 2001, the Court terminated the litigation, the 2000 census had been completed and it was time for the state legislature to begin redistricting anew. On the issue of "reverse racial gerrymandering," is litigation inevitable and interminable?

TO SUMMARIZE:

- In spite of the ratification of the Fifteenth Amendment in 1870, African-Americans did not achieve full voting rights until implementation of the Voting Rights Act of 1965.
- States intent on inhibiting electoral participation by blacks developed a variety of mechanisms, including grandfather clauses, white primaries, literacy tests, racial gerrymanders, and poll taxes. All of these efforts to frustrate political participation by African-Americans were eventually invalidated either by Supreme Court decisions, federal statutes, or amendments to the U.S. Constitution.
- Federal courts have continued to scrutinize changes in state and local electoral systems, using both the Voting Rights Act of 1965, as amended, and the Fourteenth and Fifteenth Amendments to the U.S. Constitution. Many such changes have been challenged by minority groups on the ground that they impermissibly dilute minority influence.
- During the 1990s, the Rehnquist Court shifted the focus of judicial scrutiny away from efforts to dilute the voting power of minorities and toward efforts to increase the political influence of African-Americans through the race-conscious redrawing of district lines.

THE REAPPORTIONMENT DECISIONS

Questions of inequality with respect to voting rights are by no means limited to the issue of racial discrimination. For many years, one of the most intractable and pervasive forms of inequality was that of legislative **malapportionment.**

Representation in the U.S. House of Representatives, in all fifty state legislatures, and in most local governments is apportioned on the basis of population. Representatives in state legislatures and in the U.S. House are elected from single-member districts (although a few states are allotted only one representative who of course is elected statewide). Malapportionment exists to the extent that the number of voters comprising such districts is unequal. Malapportionment can come about in two ways. It has generally occurred as a function of natural population shifts due to urbanization and interstate migration. It has also come about through gerrymandering, where district lines are intentionally drawn to create inequalities for political purposes.

Historically, malapportionment of the state legislatures and the U.S. House favored rural over urban interests. In many states, it was not uncommon for urban districts to be ten times as populous as rural districts, thus diluting the value of urban votes by a factor of ten. A particularly egregious example of malapportionment was provided by Georgia's "county unit system" (declared unconstitutional by the Supreme Court in *Gray v. Sanders* [1963]). Under that scheme, Fulton County (comprising much of metropolitan Atlanta) with a population of more than half a million was entitled to three seats in the state House of Representatives. Echols County in rural South Georgia, with a 1960 population of only 1,876, was entitled to one representative. Thus, the discrepancy in representation was more than 100 to 1 in favor of Echols County!

Even though apportionment discrepancies throughout the United States were great and growing, it was unrealistic to expect elected officials (many of whom benefited from the status quo) to address the problem. Yet most Americans seemed to assume that this problem, like so many others, had a legal solution. Accordingly, voters from grossly underrepresented urban areas turned for relief to the federal courts, citing, among other things, the Equal Protection Clause of the Fourteenth Amendment. In *Colegrove v. Green* (1946), the Supreme Court invoked the political questions doctrine to foreclose judicial relief, at least from the federal bench. Writing for a plurality of the Court, Justice Frankfurter warned of the dangers of entering the "political thicket" of malapportionment:

> It is hostile to a democratic system to involve the judiciary in the politics of the people. . . . The remedy for unfairness in districting is to secure state legislatures that will apportion properly, or to invoke the ample powers of Congress.

The Reapportionment Revolution

Between 1946 and 1962, groups representing urban interests tried, without much success, to secure **reapportionment** through the state legislatures and through the ballot box. Beginning in 1962, however, the Supreme Court produced a series of decisions on reapportionment that would permanently alter the American political landscape and draw the Court into a firestorm of criticism.

In *Baker v. Carr* (1962), the Supreme Court opened the doors of the federal courthouse to plaintiffs pressing reapportionment claims. The Court reversed its previous position and declared malapportionment to be justiciable (see Chapter 1). Shortly thereafter, the Court declared malapportionment in its various contexts unconstitutional (see Table 13.1). Reapportionment, wrote Chief Justice Warren in *Reynolds v. Sims* (1964), would have to follow the principle of "one person, one vote." In *Reynolds,* the Court held that "the Equal Protection Clause requires that a State make an honest and good faith effort to construct districts, in both houses of its legislature, as nearly of equal population as is practicable."

Not surprisingly, many observers soon began to wonder just how strict the Court would be in requiring population equality among legislative districts. In *Reynolds,* Chief Justice Warren had observed that "it is a practical impossibility to arrange

TABLE 13.1   Major Supreme Court Decisions Extending Reapportionment

Case	Year	Target of Reapportionment
Gray v. Sanders	1963	Georgia "county unit" system of apportioning state legislature
Wesberry v. Sanders	1964	Congressional districts
Reynolds v. Sims	1964	All state legislatures
Lucas v. Colorado 44th General Assembly	1964	State legislative apportionment based on constitutional provisions
Avery v. Midland County	1968	Local governing bodies
Hadley v. Junior College District	1970	School boards

legislative districts so that each one has an identical number of residents, or citizens, or voters. Mathematical exactness is hardly a workable constitutional requirement."

In 1969, the Court provided an indication of just how strict it intended to be when it struck down an apportionment scheme for congressional districts in Missouri. The plan invalidated by the Court in *Kirkpatrick v. Preisler* involved a 6 percent population deviation between the smallest and the largest districts and only a 1.8 percent average deviation from the ideal district population. Many praised the Court for its rigorous application of the one-person, one-vote principle. Others decried the Court's meddling in the technicalities of legislative apportionment. Regardless of the position one takes on this issue, the importance of the Court's reapportionment decisions can hardly be overstated. Indeed, on a number of occasions, Chief Justice Warren himself pointed without hesitation to the reapportionment decisions as his principal contribution to constitutional law.

Reapportionment under the Burger Court

For the most part, the Supreme Court under Chief Justice Warren Burger maintained the Warren Court's strong commitment to the one-person, one-vote principle. The counterrevolution many critics feared from a more conservative Court did not materialize, at least not in the realm of apportionment cases. The Burger Court, however, did allow state legislatures more leeway in determining state legislative boundaries than in drawing congressional district lines. The Court made it clear that, in scrutinizing state districts, it was willing to entertain "legitimate considerations incident to the effectuation of a rational state policy." Thus, in *Brown v. Thomson* (1983), the Court upheld an apportionment scheme for the Wyoming legislature based on county lines, even though the scheme had a population deviation of nearly 90 percent between the largest and the smallest districts. On the very same day, in *Karcher v. Daggett*, the Court invalidated a New Jersey scheme for congressional districts where the maximum deviation was less than 1 percent! The majority agreed with the federal district court that the plan was "not a good-faith effort to achieve population equality using the best available census data."

The 1990 Census and Congressional Reapportionment

Although state legislatures are responsible for drawing the boundaries of congressional districts, the Constitution empowers Congress to determine the number of representatives that each state shall have. Every ten years, after completion of the census, Congress reallocates congressional seats among the states. Article I, Section

2, of the Constitution imposes three restrictions on the exercise of Congress's discretion in this area: (1) every state is guaranteed at least one congressional seat; (2) district lines may not cross state borders; and (3) no district shall include fewer than 30,000 persons.

In 1941, Congress enacted a law specifying that "the method of equal proportions" would be used to ascertain the number of congressional seats to which each state would be entitled. Applying this method to the results of the 1990 census, Congress determined that Montana would lose one of its two congressional seats. After reapportionment, the average population of congressional districts was 572,466, while Montana's population was 803,655. Montana's single district was thus 231,189 persons larger than the average district. Had Montana retained two districts, each would have been 170,638 persons smaller than the average district. Because the loss of a congressional seat means the decline of influence in Congress and the Electoral College, Montana promptly filed suit to challenge the allocation. Relying on *Wesberry v. Sanders* (1964) and *Kirkpatrick v. Preisler* (1969), the state argued that the greater discrepancy between actual and ideal district size by its loss of a seat violated the principle of one person, one vote. A three-judge district court issued a summary judgment upholding Montana's claim and declaring the 1941 statute unconstitutional. On direct appeal, the Supreme Court unanimously reversed (see *Department of Commerce v. Montana* [1992]). Writing for the Court, Justice John Paul Stevens concluded that Congress had ample power to adopt the method of least proportions or any other reasonable method as long as it is applied consistently after each census. The *Montana* decision suggests that the contemporary Supreme Court is willing to accord far more latitude to Congress than to state legislatures in the field of reapportionment.

Assessing the Reapportionment Decisions

The Supreme Court's reapportionment decisions have been sharply criticized by conservative scholars and by some politicians. In the mid-1960s, a widely publicized effort to overrule the reapportionment decisions through constitutional amendment was spearheaded by Senate Minority Leader Everett Dirksen (R-Ill.). Despite auspicious beginnings, the Dirksen amendment proved to be a flash in the pan. It soon became clear that the American people fundamentally approved of the reapportionment decisions, irrespective of the strident attacks by many elected officials. A Gallup Poll conducted shortly after *Reynolds v. Sims* was decided found that 47 percent approved of the decision, 30 percent disapproved, and 23 percent expressed no opinion. Apparently the one-person, one-vote principle appealed to the American people's sense of fair play.

While many observers believe that the Supreme Court's school prayer and desegregation decisions were somewhat damaging to its prestige and credibility, the reapportionment decisions seem to have had the opposite effect. Thus, while the continuing debate over the proper role of the Court is important, the Court's legitimacy does not depend so much on fastidious adherence to legal principles, procedures, and traditions as it does on public support for the substance of the Court's decisions. One of the great ironies of American democracy (and perhaps its greatest strength) is that the judicial elite must from time to time interfere with the people's elected representatives for the purpose of maintaining the norm of political equality.

For some jurisprudential thinkers, such as John Hart Ely, the primary utility of and justification for judicial review is to maintain the integrity of the democratic process. Certainly the reapportionment decisions make sense from this perspective. It is noteworthy that the reapportionment decisions, although much reviled by incumbent politicians, were met with a far greater degree of compliance than, for example, the school prayer decisions. The strong public support for reapportionment as a policy was undoubtedly a critical factor promoting legislative compliance. The clarity of the Supreme Court's one-person, one-vote mandate likewise facilitated implementation of reapportionment. Finally, the obvious nature of noncompliance probably had a substantial effect on legislative willingness to abide by the Court's decisions.

TO SUMMARIZE:

- By the mid-twentieth century, malapportionment of legislative bodies at all levels of government had become a serious problem, one that state legislatures were unwilling to address. After refusing an invitation to enter this political thicket in the mid-1940s, the Supreme Court in *Baker v. Carr* (1962) precipitated a revolution in American politics by determining that malapportionment was a justiciable issue under the Equal Protection Clause of the Fourteenth Amendment.
- In *Reynolds v. Sims* (1964) and related cases, the Court applied the principle of "one person, one vote" to legislative districts at all levels of government. As a result, reapportionment today is a regularly recurring feature of American politics.

POLITICAL PARTIES AND ELECTORAL FAIRNESS

Although the Framers of the Constitution neither desired nor anticipated the development of political parties, by 1800 a two-party system had taken root in the young republic. While particular political parties have come and gone since then, the two-party system remains an established feature of the political order. Most political scientists regard the two-party system as a source of desirable political stability.

The merits of the two-party system aside, there is surely a constitutional right for disaffected voters to form new parties or support independent candidates who challenge the established order. Despite ideological disagreements, the two established parties tend to collaborate in suppressing competition by rival third parties and independent candidates. State legislatures frequently adopt laws making it difficult, if not impossible, for third parties to get candidates on the ballot. Unrealistic filing deadlines and petition requirements are often employed to frustrate the electoral ambitions of third-party and independent candidates.

In 1980, independent presidential candidate John Anderson filed suit in federal court to challenge Ohio's March filing deadline for the November general elections. In *Anderson v. Celebrezze* (1983), Anderson received a favorable ruling from the Supreme Court, which declared the Ohio regulation to be excessively burdensome on the efforts of independent candidates. Anderson's belated legal victory, however, did not altogether eliminate problems that third-party and independent candidates encounter when attempting to get their names on the ballot, as Ralph Nader and Pat Buchanan discovered in their 2000 presidential campaigns.

Partisan Gerrymandering

Historically, one of the weapons of interparty competition has been the gerrymander, the intentional manipulation of district lines for political purposes. Although legislative apportionment must proceed on the principle of one person, one vote and must not be based on race discrimination, there remains the prospect that the party in power in the state legislature will redraw district lines so as to minimize the likelihood that the opposing party will gain seats in the next election. The process of reapportionment, which occurs after each decennial census, thus provides an opportunity for the party holding the majority of seats in the legislature to further strengthen its position. Until recently, this **partisan gerrymandering** was thought to be constitutionally unassailable.

In a significant 1986 decision, however, the Supreme Court upheld the justiciability of cases challenging partisan gerrymandering. In *Davis v. Bandemer* (1986), the Court ruled that Indiana Democrats could challenge a 1981 reapportionment plan adopted by the Republican-controlled state legislature. A plurality of four justices maintained, however, that to prevail in such cases, plaintiffs would have to make "a threshold showing of discriminatory vote dilution." In a concurring opinion reminiscent of Justice Frankfurter's plea for judicial restraint in *Colegrove v. Green*, Justice Sandra Day O'Connor lamented the Court's "far-reaching step into the 'political thicket'" and predicted dire consequences. According to Justice O'Connor, a former state legislator:

> To turn these matters over to the federal judiciary is to inject the courts into the most heated partisan issues. It is predictable that the courts will respond by moving away from the nebulous standard a plurality of the Court fashions today and toward some form of proportional representation.

The consequences of federal court involvement in partisan gerrymandering will certainly be closely examined by lawyers, scholars, and politicians. Whether *Davis v. Bandemer* represents a permanent entry into the field remains to be seen. As yet, few significant developments have taken place in this area.

The Supreme Court and the 2000 Presidential Election

Without question, the most salient and controversial decision of the Supreme Court in recent years is *Bush v. Gore* (2000), in which the Court effectively decided the outcome of the 2000 presidential election. The case arose from a dispute over the procedures to be used and timetable to be followed in a recount of the popular vote in the state of Florida, where the margin separating candidates George W. Bush and Al Gore was razor thin. Due to the closeness of the election nationally, Florida's electoral votes would be decisive in determining the next president, but deciding who should receive Florida's electoral votes proved to be anything but simple. Although Bush ostensibly won the popular vote in Florida as recorded by the voting machines, Democrats claimed that a manual recount would prove Gore to be the winner. Litigation in the Florida courts led to decisions by that state's supreme court extending the period for a manual recount and limiting the recount to selected counties that used different procedures for conducting their recounts.

At the request of candidate Bush, the U.S. Supreme Court became involved in the dispute. In *Bush v. Gore,* the Court ruled 7 to 2 that the selective manual recount was unconstitutional, a violation of the Equal Protection Clause. According to the *per curiam* opinion issued by the Court, "[t]he recount mechanisms implemented in response to the decisions of the Florida Supreme Court do not satisfy the minimum requirement for non-arbitrary treatment of voters necessary to secure the fundamental right [to vote]." Justice David Souter, who concurred in this aspect of the decision, could "conceive of no legitimate state interest served by these differing treatments of the expressions of voters' fundamental rights." In Souter's view, the different procedures for conducting the manual recount appeared "wholly arbitrary." Under normal circumstances, the remedy for this constitutional violation would be to order a statewide manual recount under judicial supervision using standardized procedures. Of course, the circumstances surrounding this case were anything but normal. By a bare majority, the Court decided to halt the recount and effectively declare Bush the winner. Exacerbating the controversy was the fact that the five justices who voted to halt the recount were the court's five conservatives: Rehnquist, Scalia, Thomas,

Kennedy, and O'Connor. All five had been appointed by Republican presidents, making the decision appear to many observers, including the four dissenters, to be a case of partisan loyalty trumping judicial self-restraint.

In his dissenting opinion, Justice Stevens expressed worry that the decision would undermine "the Nation's confidence in the judge as an impartial guardian of the rule of law." Needless to say, Democrats around the country were outraged and looked for ways to circumvent the Court's decision. Some even called for impeachment of the five Republican appointees who constituted the Court's majority. Few scholars came to the Court's defense. Alan M. Dershowitz went so far as to accuse the Court of "hijacking" the election. Bruce Ackerman characterized *Bush v. Gore* as a "constitutional coup" and suggested that "when sitting justices retire or die, the Senate should refuse to confirm any nominations offered up by President Bush." Laurence Tribe, who took part in the oral argument of the case in support of candidate Gore, suggested that the Court had displayed its "disdain for the messy processes of democracy."

What will be the impact of *Bush v. Gore* on public confidence in the Supreme Court and on the constitutional law of equal protection and voting rights? At least one scholar has predicted that the decision will send a "substantial jolt of justice into the voting arena." Writing in the *New York Times* on December 14, 2000, two days after the fateful decision, Columbia Law School professor Samuel Issacharoff opined:

> The lasting significance of *Bush v. Gore* is likely to be the reinvigoration of the line of cases from the 1960s that deemed voting a fundamental right. The Court's language has now opened the door for constitutional challenges of flawed election methods. The spotlight on Florida revealed just how infirm the operations of elections are.

Only time will tell if Professor Issacharoff's prediction will come true, but in looking at the decision a year later, it seems obvious that *Bush v. Gore* did not result in a dramatic loss of public confidence in the Supreme Court. Certainly, *Bush v. Gore* was not a self-inflicted wound of the magnitude of the *Dred Scott* case, as some observers had suggested in the immediate aftermath of the decision.

TO SUMMARIZE:

- Although the Supreme Court has on occasion invalidated restrictions on candidates' access to the ballot, such restrictions still pose a formidable obstacle to independent or third-party candidates.
- The Court has held that partisan gerrymandering is a justiciable issue, but has provided little guidance to lower federal courts in this area.
- *Bush v. Gore* (2000) shows the potential impact of judicial involvement in the electoral process. It remains to be seen what impact this decision will have on constitutional law in the equal protection and voting rights areas.

THE PROBLEM OF CAMPAIGN FINANCE

Reformers have long advocated measures designed to remove what they see as the corrupting influence of money in the political process. In particular, reformers have proposed limitations on campaign spending, restrictions on campaign contributions, and various degrees of public financing of campaigns. The most extreme proposals call for eliminating private funding altogether and providing all candidates equal amounts of public money with which to conduct their campaigns.

In the midst of the Watergate scandal, Congress attempted to tackle the thorny problem of campaign finance. Among other things, the Federal Election Campaign Act Amendments of 1974 limited campaign spending by candidates in federal elections and limited individual contributions to such candidates. In *Buckley v. Valeo* (1976), both of these limitations were challenged as infringements of political expression as protected by the First Amendment. In a convoluted and fragmented set of opinions, the Supreme Court struck down the spending limits but upheld the limits on individual contributions. The Court also upheld provisions providing for public funding of campaigns and the limits on expenditures that accompanied the acceptance of public funds. Subsequently, in *Federal Election Commission v. National Conservative Political Action Committee* (1985), the Court said that such limits cannot be applied to persons or parties who spend money in support of a candidate who accepts public funds.

The Court reinforced this position in *Colorado Republican Federal Campaign Committee v. Federal Election Commission* (1996), where it struck down spending limits set by the Federal Election Campaign Act as applied to the Colorado Republican Party's "independent expenditures." Writing for a plurality in that decision, Justice Breyer concluded that: "We do not see how a Constitution that grants to individuals, candidates, and ordinary political committees the right to make unlimited independent expenditures could deny the same right to political parties." However, upon later review of the case, the Court held, per Justice Souter, that "a party's coordinated expenditures, unlike expenditures truly independent, may be restricted to minimize circumvention of contribution limits" (*Federal Election Commission v. Colorado Republican Federal Campaign Committee* [2001]).

Independent or "soft money" expenditures continue to play an important and controversial role in presidential and congressional campaigns. However, unless and until the Supreme Court abandons the position that spending money in a political campaign is a form of political expression protected by the First Amendment, there is little that can be done to control such expenditures. Of course, not all reformers—and certainly not all political scientists—agree that limiting spending and contributions has a salutary effect on the system. Many would argue that such limits tend to benefit incumbents, who already enjoy a number of advantages. However, most would agree that current laws requiring full disclosure of contributions and expenditures are both necessary and proper. Certainly, the Supreme Court has never held or implied that such laws violate the First Amendment or any other constitutional provision.

In March 2002, Congress enacted sweeping campaign finance reform legislation. The centerpiece of the McCain-Feingold bill was a ban on unlimited soft money contributions to political parties. The most controversial provision of the legislation prohibited the use of soft money to purchase "issue ads" within sixty days of a general election or thirty days of a primary. Critics of the bill—and there were many—questioned the constitutionality of these limitations on political activity. Some vowed to challenge the new law in court. Anticipating a legal challenge, the bill contained a provision calling for judicial review by a three-judge panel of the federal district court followed by expedited direct appeal to the Supreme Court. Many observers expected the High Court to strike at least some of the more extreme provisions of the bill on First Amendment grounds.

TO SUMMARIZE:

- Congress has attempted to regulate campaign finance, most notably through the Federal Election Campaign Act Amendments of 1974. In *Buckley v. Valeo* (1976), the

Supreme Court struck down spending limits imposed on candidates but upheld the limits imposed on individual contributions. The Court recognized that campaign spending is a form of political expression protected by the First Amendment.

CONCLUSION

The fundamental question of whether courts of law ought to have the power to invalidate legislative and executive acts has long since been put to rest. Yet there remains substantial controversy over the appropriate role of courts in applying the tenets of the Constitution to challenged legislation. Many are troubled by substantive due process decisions in which the Supreme Court has invalidated legislative policies on the basis of arguably dubious principles, such as liberty of contract and the right of privacy, nowhere mentioned in the Constitution. While the appropriate role of the Supreme Court in addressing substantive issues of policy is debatable, there is little disagreement about the legitimacy of the Court's role in maintaining the integrity of the democratic process.

Applying a standard of strict scrutiny, the Supreme Court since *Baker v. Carr* (1962) and *Reynolds v. Sims* (1964) has had a significant impact with respect to representation and voting rights. The Court's major decisions in this area reflect three fundamental principles: First, suffrage must be universally available; second, all votes must count equally; and third, elections must offer the voter a choice among candidates and parties. Although politicians may resent the Court's "meddling" with the political process, the principles underlying the Court's decisions are essential to the realization of constitutional democracy.

Attempts by legislative majorities to close the channels of political participation to disfavored groups of citizens, whether they are city dwellers, ethnic minorities, or rival political parties, are antithetical to the ideals underlying our system of representative government. Guarding the ideal of political equality is thus without question one of the most important obligations of the Supreme Court. Like its concern for separation of powers, checks and balances, and freedom of expression, the Court's protection of voting rights is critical to the preservation of constitutional democracy in the United States.

KEY TERMS

representative democracy	poll taxes	racial gerrymandering	malapportionment
universal suffrage	grandfather clause	Voting Rights Act of 1965	reapportionment
tyranny of the majority	white primary	at-large elections	partisan gerrymandering
popular sovereignty	literacy tests	race-conscious remedy	
constitutional republic	gerrymander	vote dilution	

FOR FURTHER READING

Ackerman, Bruce A. (ed.). *Bush v. Gore: The Question of Legitimacy* (New Haven, Conn.: Yale University Press, 2002).

Ackerman, Bruce A. (ed.). *Voting with Dollars: A New Paradigm for Campaign Finance* (New Haven, Conn.: Yale University Press, 2002).

Baker, Gordon E. *The Reapportionment Revolution.* New York: Random House, 1966.

Ball, Howard. *The Warren Court's Conceptions of Democracy: An Evaluation of the Supreme Court's Apportionment Cases.* Rutherford, N.J.: Fairleigh Dickinson University Press, 1971.

Berger, Raoul. *Government by Judiciary: The Transformation of the Fourteenth Amendment.* Cambridge, Mass.: Harvard University Press, 1977.

Bullock, Charles S., and Kathryn S. Butler. "Voting Rights." In Tinsley E. Yarbrough (ed.), *The Reagan Administration and Human Rights.* New York: Praeger, 1985.

Cortner, Richard C. *The Reapportionment Cases.* Knoxville: University of Tennessee Press, 1970.

Davidson, Chandler, and Bernard Grofman (eds.). *Quiet Revolution in the South: The Impact of the Voting Rights Act 1965–1990.* Princeton, N.J.: Princeton University Press, 1994.

Dershowitz, Alan M. *Supreme Injustice: How the High Court Hijacked Election 2000.* New York: Oxford University Press, 2001.

Dixon, Robert G., Jr. *Democratic Representation: Reapportionment in Law and Politics.* New York: Oxford University Press, 1968.

Ely, John Hart. *Democracy and Distrust.* Cambridge, Mass.: Harvard University Press, 1980.

Grofman, Bernard. *Political Gerrymandering and the Courts.* New York: Agathon Press, 1990.

Hamilton, Howard D. (ed.). *Legislative Reapportionment: Key to Power.* New York: Harper and Row, 1964.

Hanson, Royce. *The Political Thicket: Reapportionment and Constitutional Democracy.* Englewood Cliffs, N.J.: Prentice-Hall, 1966.

Issacharoff, Samuel, Pamela Karlin, and Richard Pildes. *When Elections Go Bad: The Law of Democracy and the Presidential Election of 2000.* New York: Foundation Press, 2001.

Mendelson, Wallace. *Discrimination.* Englewood Cliffs, N.J.: Prentice-Hall, 1962.

Norrell, Robert J. *Reaping the Whirlwind: The Civil Rights Movement in Tuskegee* (rev. ed.). Chapel Hill: University of North Carolina Press, 1998.

Polsby, Nelson W. (ed.). *Reapportionment in the 1970s.* Berkeley: University of California Press, 1971.

Taper, Bernard. *Gomillion v. Lightfoot: Apartheid in Alabama.* New York: McGraw-Hill, 1967.

United States *Commission on Civil Rights. 1961 Report.* Washington, D.C.: U.S. Government Printing Office, 1961.

INTERNET RESOURCES

Name of Resource	Description	URL
Center for Voting and Democracy	Organization interested in the impact of different voting systems on voter turnout, representation, accountability, and the influence of money on elections	http://www.fairvote.org/
Ballot Access News	A nonpartisan online newsletter reporting on the problems associated with ballot access for independent and third-party candidates	http://www.ballot-access.org/
Voting Rights HelpNet	Web site maintained by the Southern Regional Council, a civil rights organization based in Atlanta	http://www.src.w1.com/helpnet/index.html
ACLU Voting Rights Project	Effort by the ACLU to promote its vision of voting rights and political equality	http://www.aclu.org/issues/voting/hmvr.html

Case

SMITH V. ALLWRIGHT

321 U.S. 649; 64 S.Ct. 757; 88 L.Ed. 987 (1944)
Vote: 8–1

In 1927, the Texas legislature passed a law that authorized political parties to set qualifications for party membership. Pursuant to this law, the state Democratic Party, at its convention in May 1932, adopted the following resolution: "Be it resolved that all white citizens of the State of Texas who are qualified to vote under the Constitution and laws of the State shall be eligible to membership in the Democratic Party and, as such, entitled to participate in its deliberations." Lonnie Smith, a black resident of Texas, sued S. E. Allwright, an election judge, for refusing to allow him to vote in a Democratic primary at which candidates for state and national office were to be nominated. Through the efforts of the National Association for the Advancement of Colored People, this case ultimately reached the U.S. Supreme Court. Thurgood Marshall, as counsel for the NAACP, participated in the argument of the case on behalf of Smith.

Mr. Justice Reed delivered the opinion of the Court.

. . . Texas is free to conduct her elections and limit her electorate as she may deem wise, save only as her action may be affected by the prohibitions of the United States Constitution or in conflict with powers delegated to and exercised by the National Government. The Fourteenth Amendment forbids a State from making or enforcing any law which abridges the privileges or immunities of citizens of the United States and the Fifteenth Amendment specifically interdicts any denial or abridgement by a State of the right of citizens to vote on account of color. Respondents appeared in the District Court and the Circuit Court of Appeals and defended on the ground that the Democratic Party of Texas is a voluntary organization with members banded together for the purpose of selecting individuals of the group representing the common political beliefs as candidates in the general election. As such a voluntary organization, it was claimed, the Democratic Party is free to select its own membership and limit to whites participation in the party primary. Such action, the answer asserted, does not violate the Fourteenth, Fifteenth or Seventeenth Amendments as officers of government cannot be chosen at primaries and the Amendments are applicable only to general elections where governmental officers are actually elected. . . .

Since *Grovey v. Townsend* and prior to the present suit, no case from Texas involving primary elections has been before this Court. We did decide, however, *United States v. Classic.* . . . We there held that Section 4 of Article I of the Constitution authorized Congress to regulate primary as well as general elections, "where the primary is by law made an integral part of the election machinery." . . . Consequently, in the *Classic* case, we upheld the applicability to frauds in a Louisiana primary of Sections 19 and 20 of the Criminal Code. . . . *Classic* bears upon *Grovey v. Townsend* not because exclusion of Negroes from primaries is any more or less state action by reason of the unitary character of the electoral process but because the recognition of the place of the primary in the electoral scheme makes clear that state delegation to a party of the power to fix the qualifications of primary elections is delegation of a state function that may make the party's action the action of the State. When *Grovey v. Townsend* was written, the Court looked upon the denial of a vote in a primary as a mere refusal by a party of party membership. . . . As the Louisiana statutes for holding primaries are similar to those of Texas, our ruling in *Classic* as to the unitary character of the electoral process calls for a reexamination as to whether or not the exclusion of Negroes from a Texas party primary was state action. . . .

It may now be taken as a postulate that the right to vote in such a primary for the nomination of candidates without discrimination by the State, like the right to vote in a general election, is a right secured by the Constitution. . . . By the terms of the Fifteenth Amendment that right may not be abridged by any State on account of race. Under our Constitution the great privilege of the ballot may not be denied a man by the State because of his color.

We are thus brought to an examination of the qualifications for Democratic primary electors in Texas, to determine whether state action or private action has excluded Negroes from participation. Despite Texas' decision that the exclusion is produced by private or party action . . . federal courts must for themselves appraise the facts leading to that conclusion. It is only by the performance of this obligation that a final and uniform interpretation can be given to the Constitution, the "supreme Law of the Land." . . .

Primary elections are conducted by the party under state statutory authority. The county executive committee selects precinct election officials and the county, district or state executive committees, respectively, canvass the returns. These party committees or the state convention certify the party's candidates to the appropriate officers for inclusion on the official ballot for the general election. No name which has not been so certified may appear upon the ballot for the general election as a candidate of a political party. No other name may be printed on the ballot which has not been placed in nomination by qualified voters who must take oath that they did not participate in a primary for the selection of a candidate for the office for which the nomination is made.

The state courts are given exclusive original jurisdiction of contested elections and of *mandamus* proceedings to compel party officers to perform their statutory duties.

We think that this statutory system for the selection of party nominees for inclusion on the general election ballot makes the party which is required to follow these legislative directions an agency of the State in so far as it determines the participants in a primary election. The party takes its character as a state agency from the duties imposed upon it by state statutes; the duties do not become matters of private law because they are performed by a political party. The plan of the Texas primary follows substantially that of Louisiana, with the exception that in Louisiana the State pays the cost of the primary while Texas assesses the cost against candidates. In numerous instances, the Texas statutes fix or limit the fees to be charged. Whether paid directly by the State or through state requirements, it is state action which compels. When primaries become a part of the machinery for choosing officials, state and national, as they have here, the same tests to determine the character of discrimination or abridgement should be applied to the primary as are applied to the general election. If the State requires a certain electoral procedure, prescribes a general election ballot made up of party nominees so chosen and limits the choice of the electorate in general elections for state offices, practically speaking, to those whose names appear on such a ballot, it endorses, adopts and enforces the discrimination against Negroes, practiced by a party entrusted by Texas law with the determination of the qualifications of participants in the primary. This is state action within the meaning of the Fifteenth Amendment. . . .

The United States is a constitutional democracy. Its organic law grants to all citizens a right to participate in the choice of elected officials without restriction by any State because of race. This grant to the people of the opportunity for choice is not to be nullified by a State through casting its electoral process in a form which permits a private organization to practice racial discrimination in the election. Constitutional rights would be of little value if they could be thus indirectly denied. . . .

. . . In reaching this conclusion we are not unmindful of the desirability of continuity of decision in constitutional questions. However, when convinced of former error, this Court has never felt constrained to follow precedent. In constitutional questions, where correction depends upon amendment and not upon legislative action this Court throughout its history has freely exer-

cised its power to reexamine the basis of its constitutional decisions. This has long been accepted practice, and this practice has continued to this day. This is particularly true when the decision believed erroneous is the application of a constitutional principle rather than an interpretation of the Constitution to extract the principle itself. Here we are applying, contrary to the recent decision in *Grovey v. Townsend,* the well-established principle of the Fifteenth Amendment, forbidding the abridgement by a State of a citizen's right to vote. *Grovey v. Townsend* is overruled.

Mr. Justice Frankfurter concurs in the result.

Mr. Justice Roberts [dissenting]:

. . . I have expressed my views with respect to the present policy of the court freely to disregard and to overrule considered decisions and the rules of law announced in them. This tendency, it seems to me, indicates an intolerance for what those who have composed this court in the past have conscientiously and deliberately concluded, and involves an assumption that knowledge and wisdom reside in us which was denied to our predecessors. I shall not repeat what I there said for I consider it fully applicable to the instant decision, which but points the moral anew. . . .

The reason for my concern is that the instant decision, overruling that announced about nine years ago, tends to bring adjudications of this tribunal into the same class as a restricted railroad ticket, good for this day and train only. I have no assurance, in view of current decisions, that the opinion announced today may not shortly be repudiated and overruled by justices who deem they have new light on the subject. In the present term the court has overruled three cases.

In the present case, . . . the court below relied, as it was bound to, upon our previous decision. As that court points out, the statutes of Texas have not been altered since *Grovey v. Townsend* was decided. The same resolution is involved as was drawn in question in *Grovey v. Townsend.* Not a fact differentiates that case from this except the names of the parties.

It is suggested that *Grovey v. Townsend* was overruled *sub silentio* in *United States v. Classic.* . . . If so, the situation is even worse than that exhibited by the outright repudiation of an earlier decision, for it is the fact that, in the *Classic* case, *Grovey v. Townsend* was distinguished in brief and argument by the Government without suggestion that it was wrongly decided, and was relied on by the appellee, not as a controlling decision, but by way of analogy. The case is not mentioned in either of the opinions in the *Classic* case. Again and again it is said in the opinion of the court in that case that the voter who was denied the right to vote was a fully qualified voter. In other words, there was no question of his being a person entitled under state law to vote in the primary. The offense charged was the fraudulent denial of his conceded right by an election officer because of his race. Here the question is altogether different. It is whether, in a Democratic primary, he who tendered his vote was a member of the Democratic Party. . . .

It is regrettable that in an era marked by doubt and confusion, an era whose greater need is steadfastness of thought and purpose, this court, which has been looked to as exhibiting consistency in adjudication, and a steadiness which would hold the balance even in the face of temporary ebbs and flows of opinion, should now itself become the breeder of fresh doubt and confusion in the public mind as to the stability of our institutions.

Case

GOMILLION V. LIGHTFOOT

364 U.S. 339; 81 S.Ct. 125; 5 L.Ed. 2d 110 (1960)
Vote: 9–0

Here the Court confronts a blatant attempt to disenfranchise minority voters by gerrymandering the boundaries of a city.

Mr. Justice Frankfurter delivered the opinion of the Court.

This litigation challenges the validity, under the United States Constitution, of Local Act No. 140, passed by the Legislature of Alabama in 1957, redefining the boundaries of the City of Tuskegee. Petitioners, Negro citizens of Alabama who were, at the time of this redistricting measure, residents of the City of Tuskegee, brought an action in the United States District Court for the Middle District of Alabama for a declaratory judgment that Act 140 is unconstitutional, and for an injunction to restrain the Mayor and officers of Tuskegee and the officials of Macon County, Alabama, from enforcing the Act against them and other Negroes similarly situated. Petitioners' claim is that enforcement of the statute, which alters the shape of Tuskegee from a square to an uncouth twenty-eight-sided figure, will constitute a discrimination against them in violation of the Due Process and Equal Protection Clauses of the Fourteenth Amendment to the Constitution and will deny them the right to vote in defiance of the Fifteenth Amendment.

The respondents moved for dismissal of the action for failure to state a claim upon which relief could be granted and for lack of jurisdiction of the District Court. The court granted the motion, stating, "This court has no control over, no supervision over, and no power to change any boundaries of municipal corporations fixed by a duly convened and elected legislative body, acting for the people for the State of Alabama." . . . On appeal, the Court of Appeals for the Fifth Circuit affirmed the judgment, one judge dissenting. . . . We brought the case here since serious questions were raised concerning the power of a State over its municipalities in relation to the Fourteenth and Fifteenth Amendments. . . . The essential inevitable effect of this redefinition of Tuskegee's boundaries is to remove from the city all save only four or five of its 400 Negro voters while not removing a single white voter or resident. The result of the Act is to deprive the Negro petitioners discriminatorily of the benefits of residence in Tuskegee, including, *inter alia,* the right to vote in municipal elections.

These allegations, if proven, would abundantly establish that Act 140 was not an ordinary geographic redistricting measure even within familiar abuses of gerrymandering. If these allegations upon a trial remained uncontradicted or unqualified, the conclusion would be irresistible, tantamount for all practical purposes to a mathematical demonstration, that the legislation is solely concerned with segregating white and colored voters by fencing Negro citizens out of town so as to deprive them of their preexisting municipal vote.

It is difficult to appreciate what stands in the way of adjudging a statute having this inevitable effect invalid in light of the principles by which this Court must judge, and uniformly has judged, statutes that, howsoever speciously defined, obviously discriminate against colored citizens. "The [Fifteenth] Amendment nullified sophisticated as well as simple-minded modes of discrimination." . . .

The complaint amply alleges a claim of racial discrimination. Against this claim the respondents have never suggested, either in their brief or in oral argument, any countervailing municipal function which Act 140 is designed to serve. The respondents invoke generalities expressing the State's unrestricted power—unlimited, that is, by the United States Constitution—to establish, destroy, or reorganize by contraction or expansion its political subdivisions, to wit, cities, counties, and other local units. We freely recognize the breadth and importance of this aspect of the State's political power. To exalt this power into an absolute is to misconceive the reach and rule of this Court's decisions. . . .

. . . The Court has never acknowledged that the States have power to do as they will with municipal corporations regardless of consequences. Legislative control of municipalities, no less than other state power, lies within the scope of relevant limitations imposed by the United States Constitution. . . .

. . . Such power, extensive though it is, is met and overcome by the Fifteenth Amendment to the Constitution of the United States, which forbids a State from passing any law which deprives a citizen of his vote because of his race. The opposite conclusion, urged upon us by respondents, would sanction the achievement by a State of any impairment of voting rights whatever so long as it was cloaked in the garb of the realignment of political subdivisions. "It is inconceivable that guaranties embedded in the Constitution of the United States may thus be manipulated out of existence." . . .

When a State exercises power wholly within the domain of state interest, it is insulated from federal judicial review. But such insulation is not carried over when state power is used as an instrument for circumventing a federally protected right. This principle has had many applications. It has long been recognized in cases which have prohibited a State from exploiting a power acknowledged to be absolute in an isolated context to justify the imposition of an "unconstitutional condition." What the Court has said in those cases is equally applicable here, viz., that "Act generally lawful may become unlawful when done to accomplish an unlawful end, . . . and a constitutional power cannot be used by way of condition to attain an unconstitutional result." The petitioners are entitled to prove their allegations at trial.

For these reasons, the principal conclusions of the District Court and the Court of Appeals are clearly erroneous . . . .

Mr. Justice Douglas, [concurring]. . . .

Mr. Justice Whittaker, concurring.

I concur in the Court's judgment, but not in the whole of its opinion. It seems to me that the decision should be rested not on the Fifteenth Amendment, but rather on the equal Protection Clause of the Fourteenth Amendment to the Constitution. I am doubtful that the averments of the complaint, taken for present purposes to be true, show a purpose by Act No. 140 to abridge petitioners' "right . . . to vote," in the Fifteenth Amendment sense. It seems to me that the "right . . . to vote" that is guaranteed by the Fifteenth Amendment is but the same right to vote as is enjoyed by all others within the same election precinct, ward or other political division. And, inasmuch as no one has the right to vote in a political division, or in a local election concerning only an area in which he does not reside, it would seem to follow that one's right to vote in Division A is not abridged by a redistricting that places his residence in Division B if he there enjoys the same voting privileges as all others in that Division, even though the redistricting was done by the State for the purposes of placing a racial group of citizens in Division B rather than A.

But it does seem clear to me that accomplishment of a State's purpose—to use the Court's phrase—of "fencing Negro citizens out of" Division A and into Division B is an unlawful segregation of races of citizens, in violation of the Equal Protection Clause of the Fourteenth Amendment, . . . and, as stated, I would think the decision should be rested on that ground. . . .

Case

MOBILE V. BOLDEN

446 U.S. 55; 100 S.Ct. 1490; 64 L.Ed. 2d 47 (1980)
Vote: 6–3

In this case, the Supreme Court considers a challenge to at-large local elections based on the Voting Rights Act of 1965 and the Fifteenth Amendment.

Mr. Justice Stewart announced the judgment of the court and delivered an opinion, in which the **Chief Justice, Mr. Justice Powell,** and **Mr. Justice Rehnquist** joined.

The City of Mobile, Ala., has since 1911 been governed by a City Commission consisting of three members

elected by the voters of the city at large. The question in this case is whether this at-large system of municipal elections violates the rights of Mobile's Negro voters in contravention of federal statutory or constitutional law.

The appellees brought this suit in the Federal District Court for the Southern District of Alabama as a class action on behalf of all Negro citizens of Mobile. Named as defendants were the city and its three incumbent Commissioners, who are the appellants before this Court. The complaint alleged that the practice of electing the City Commissioners at large unfairly diluted the voting strength of Negroes in violation of [Section] 2 of the Voting Rights Act of 1965, of the Fourteenth Amendment, and of the Fifteenth Amendment. Following a bench trial, the District Court found that the constitutional rights of the appellees had been violated, entered a judgment in their favor, and ordered that the City Commission be disestablished and replaced by a municipal government consisting of a Mayor and a City Council with members elected from single-member districts. . . . The Court of Appeals affirmed the judgment in its entirety. . . .

In Alabama, the form of municipal government a city may adopt is governed by state law. Until 1911, cities not covered by specific legislation were limited to governing themselves through a mayor and city council. In that year, the Alabama Legislature authorized every large municipality to adopt a commission form of government. Mobile established its City Commission in the same year, and has maintained that basic system of municipal government ever since.

Three Commissioners jointly exercise all legislative, executive, and administrative power in the municipality. They are required after election to designate one of their number as Mayor, a largely ceremonial office, but no formal provision is made for allocating specific executive or administrative duties among the three. As required by the state law enacted in 1911, each candidate for the Mobile City Commission runs for election in the city at large for a term of four years in one of three numbered posts, and may be elected only by a majority of the total vote. This is the same basic electoral system that is followed by literally thousands of municipalities and other local governmental units throughout the Nation.

Although required by general principles of judicial administration to do so, . . . neither the District Court nor the Court of Appeals addressed the complaint's statutory claim—that the Mobile electoral system violates [Section] 2 of the Voting Rights Act of 1965. Even a cursory examination of that claim, however, clearly discloses that it adds nothing to the appellees' complaint.

Section 2 of the Voting Rights Act provides:

> No voting qualification or prerequisite to voting, or standard, practice, or procedure shall be imposed or applied by any State or political subdivision to deny or abridge the right of any citizen of the United States to vote on account of race or color. . . .

Assuming, for present purposes, that there exists a private right of action to enforce this statutory provision, it is apparent that the language of [Section] 2 no more than elaborates upon that of the Fifteenth Amendment, and the sparse legislative history of [Section] 2 makes clear that it was intended to have an effect no different from that of the Fifteenth Amendment itself.

Section 2 was an uncontroversial provision in proposed legislation whose other provisions engendered protracted dispute. The House Report on the bill simply recited that [Section] 2 "grants . . . a right to be free from enactment or enforcement of voting qualifications . . . or practices which deny or abridge the right to vote on account of race or color." . . . The view that this section simply restated the prohibitions already contained in the Fifteenth Amendment was expressed without contradiction during the Senate hearings. Senator Dirksen indicated at one point that all States, whether or not covered by the preclearance provisions of [Section] 5 of the proposed legislation, were prohibited from discriminating against Negro voters by [Section] 2, which he termed "almost a rephrasing of the 15th [A]mendment." Attorney General Katzenbach agreed. . . .

In view of the section's language and its sparse but clear legislative history, it is evident that this statutory provision adds nothing to the appellees' Fifteenth Amendment claim. We turn, therefore, to a consideration of the validity of the judgment of the Court of Appeals with respect to the Fifteenth Amendment.

The Court's early decision under the Fifteenth Amendment established that it imposes but one limitation on the powers of the States. It forbids them to discriminate against Negroes in matters having to do with voting. . . . The Amendment's command and effect are wholly negative. "The Fifteenth Amendment does not confer the right of suffrage upon any one," but has "invested the citizens of the United States with a new constitutional right which is within the protecting power of Congress. That right is exemption from discrimination in the exercise of the elective franchise on account of race, color, or previous condition of servitude." . . .

Our decisions, moreover, have made clear that action by a State that is racially neutral on its face violates the Fifteenth Amendment only if motivated by a discriminatory purpose. . . .

The Court's more recent decisions confirm the principle that racially discriminatory motivation is a necessary ingredient of a Fifteenth Amendment violation. . . .

While other of the Court's Fifteenth Amendment decisions have dealt with different issues, none has questioned the necessity of showing purposeful discrimination in order to show a Fifteenth Amendment violation. The cases of *Smith v. Allwright* . . . [1944] and *Terry v. Adams* . . . [1953] for example, dealt with the question whether a State was so involved with racially discriminatory voting practices as to invoke the Amendment's protection. . . .

The answer to the appellees' argument is that, as the District Court expressly found, their freedom to vote has not been denied or abridged by anyone. The Fifteenth Amendment does not entail the right to have Negro candidates elected, and neither *Smith v. Allwright* nor *Terry v. Adams* contains any implication to the contrary. That

Amendment prohibits only purposefully discriminatory denial or abridgment by government of the freedom to vote "on account of race, color, or previous condition of servitude." Having found that Negroes in Mobile "register and vote without hindrance," . . . the District Court and Court of Appeals were in error in believing that the appellants invaded the protection of that Amendment in the present case.

The Court of Appeals also agreed with the District Court that Mobile's at-large electoral system violates the Equal Protection Clause of the Fourteenth Amendment. There remains for consideration, therefore, the validity of its judgment on that score.

The claim that at-large electoral schemes unconstitutionally deny to some persons the equal protection of the laws has been advanced in numerous cases before this Court. That contention has been raised most often with regard to multimember constituencies within a state legislative apportionment system. The constitutional objection to multimember districts is not and cannot be that, as such, they depart from apportionment on a population basis in violation of *Reynolds v. Sims* [1964] and its progeny. Rather the focus in such cases has been on the lack of representation multimember districts afford various elements of the voting population in a system of representative legislative democracy. "Criticism [of multimember districts] is rooted in their winner-take-all aspects, their tendency to submerge minorities . . . , a general preference for legislatures reflecting community interests as closely as possible and disenchantment with political parties and elections as devices to settle policy differences between contending interests." . . .

Despite repeated constitutional attacks upon multimember legislative districts, the Court has consistently held that they are not unconstitutional *per se*. . . . We have recognized, however, that such legislative apportionments could violate the Fourteenth Amendment if their purpose were invidiously to minimize or cancel out the voting potential of racial or ethnic minorities. . . . To prove such a purpose it is not enough to show that the group allegedly discriminated against has not elected representatives in proportion to its numbers. . . .

The judgment is reversed, and the case is remanded to the Court of Appeals for further proceedings.

Mr. Justice Blackmun, concurring in the result.

Assuming that proof of intent is a prerequisite to appellees' prevailing on their constitutional claim of vote dilution, I am inclined to agree with Mr. Justice White that, in this case, "the findings of the District Court amply support an inference of purposeful discrimination." . . . I concur in the Court's judgment of reversal, however, because I believe that the relief afforded appellees by the

District Court was not commensurate with the sound exercise of judicial discretion.

It seems to me that the city of Mobile, and its citizenry, have a substantial interest in maintaining the commission form of government that has been in effect there for nearly 70 years. The District Court recognized that its remedial order, changing the form of the city's government to a mayor-council system, "raised serious constitutional issues." . . . Nonetheless, the court was "unable to see how the impermissibly unconstitutional dilution can be effectively corrected by any other approach." . . .

Contrary to the District Court, I do not believe that, in order to remedy the unconstitutional vote dilution it found, it was necessary to convert Mobile's city government to a mayor-council system. In my view, the District Court should have at least considered alternative remedial orders that would have maintained some of the basic elements of the commission system Mobile long ago had selected. . . .

Mr. Justice Stevens, concurring in the judgment. . . .

Mr. Justice Brennan, dissenting. . . .

Mr. Justice White, dissenting. . . .

Mr. Justice Marshall, dissenting.

. . . The plurality concludes that our prior decisions establish the principle that proof of discriminatory intent is a necessary element of a Fifteenth Amendment claim. In contrast, I continue to adhere to my conclusion . . . that "[t]he Court's decisions relating to the relevance of purpose-and/or-effect analysis in testing the constitutionality of legislative enactments are somewhat less than a seamless web." . . . [A]t various times the Court's decisions have seemed to adopt three inconsistent approaches: (1) that purpose alone is the test for unconstitutionality; (2) that effect alone is the test; and (3) that purpose or effect, either alone or in combination, is sufficient to show unconstitutionality. . . . In my view, our Fifteenth Amendment jurisprudence on the necessity of proof of discriminatory purpose is no less unsettled than was our approach to the importance of such proof in Fourteenth Amendment racial discrimination cases prior to *Washington v. Davis* . . . (1976). What is called for in the present cases is a fresh consideration—similar to our inquiry in *Washington v. Davis* with regard to Fourteenth Amendment discrimination claims—of whether proof of discriminatory purpose is necessary to establish a claim under the Fifteenth Amendment. . . .

. . . [I]t is beyond dispute that a standard based solely upon the motives of official decision makers creates significant problems of proof for plaintiffs and forces the inquiring court to undertake an unguided, tortuous look into the minds of officials in the hope of guessing why certain policies were adopted and others rejected. . . . An approach based on motivation creates the risk that officials will be able to adopt policies that are the products of discriminatory intent so long as they sufficiently mask their motives through the use of subtlety and illusion. . . .

I continue to believe, then, that under the Fifteenth Amendment an "[e]valuation of the purpose of a legislative enactment is just too ambiguous a task to be the sole tool of constitutional analysis. . . . [A] demonstration of effect ordinarily should suffice. If, of course, purpose may conclusively be shown, it too should be sufficient to demonstrate a statute's unconstitutionality." . . . The plurality's refusal in this case even to consider this approach bespeaks an indifference to the plight of minorities who, through no fault of their own, have suffered diminution of the right preservative of all other rights.

The American approach to government is premised on the theory that, when citizens have the unfettered right to vote, public officials will make decisions by the democratic accommodation of competing beliefs, not by deference to the mandates of the powerful. The Ameri-

can approach to civil rights is premised on the complementary theory that the unfettered right to vote is preservative of all other rights. The theoretical foundations for these approaches are shattered where, as in the present cases, the right to vote is granted in form, but denied in substance.

It is time to realize that manipulating doctrines and drawing improper distinctions under the Fourteenth and Fifteenth Amendments, as well as under Congress' remedial legislation enforcing those Amendments, make this Court an accessory to the perpetuation of racial discrimination. The plurality's requirement of proof of intentional discrimination, so inappropriate in today's cases, may represent an attempt to bury the legitimate concerns of the minority beneath the soil of a doctrine almost as impermeable as it is spacious. If so, the superficial tranquility created by such measures can be but short-lived. If this Court refuses to honor our long-recognized principle that the Constitution "nullifies sophisticated as well as simpleminded modes of discrimination," . . . it cannot expect the victims of discrimination to respect political channels of seeking redress. I dissent.

Case

ROGERS V. LODGE

458 U.S. 613; 102 S.Ct. 3272; 73 L.Ed. 2d 1012 (1982)
Vote: 6–3

Here the Court considers whether an at-large voting system in Burke County, Georgia, violates the constitutional rights of African-American voters there.

Justice White delivered the opinion of the Court.

. . . Burke County is a large, predominately rural county located in eastern Georgia. Eight hundred and thirty-one square miles in area, it is approximately two-thirds the size of the State of Rhode Island. According to the 1980 census, Burke County had a total population of 19,349, of whom 10,385, or 53.6%, were black. The average age of blacks living there is lower than the average age of whites and therefore whites constitute a slight majority of the voting age population. As of 1978, 6,373 persons were registered to vote in Burke County, of whom 38% were black.

The Burke County Board of Commissioners governs the county. It was created in 1911 . . . and consists of five members elected at large to concurrent 4-year terms by all qualified voters in the county. The county has never been divided into districts, either for the purpose of imposing a

residency requirement on candidates or for the purpose of requiring candidates to be elected by voters residing in a district. In order to be nominated or elected, a candidate must receive a majority of the votes cast in the primary or general election, and a runoff must be held if no candidate receives a majority in the first primary or general election. . . . Each candidate must run for a specific seat on the Board, and a voter may vote only once for any candidate. No Negro has been elected to the Burke County Board of Commissioners.

Appellees, eight black citizens of Burke County, filed this suit in 1976 in the United States District Court for the Southern District of Georgia. The suit was brought on behalf of all black citizens in Burke County. The class was certified in 1977. The complaint alleged that the county's system of at-large elections violates appellees' First, Thirteenth, Fourteenth and Fifteenth Amendment rights . . . by diluting the voting power of black citizens. Following a bench trial at which both sides introduced extensive evidence, the court issued an order on September 29, 1978, stating that appellees were entitled to prevail and ordering that Burke County be divided into five districts for purposes of electing County Commissioners. . . .

The Court of Appeals affirmed. . . . It stated that while the proceedings in the District Court took place prior to the decision in *Mobile v. Bolden,* . . . the District Court correctly anticipated *Mobile* and required appellees to prove that the at-large voting system was maintained for a discriminatory purpose. . . . The Court of Appeals also held that the District Court's findings were not clearly erroneous, and that its conclusion that the at-large system was maintained for invidious purpose was "virtually mandated by the overwhelming proof." . . . We noted probable jurisdiction, and now affirm. . . .

At-large voting schemes and multimember districts tend to minimize the voting strength of minority groups by permitting the political majority to elect all representatives of the district. A distinct minority, whether it be a racial, ethnic, economic, or political group, may be unable to elect any representatives if the political unit is divided into single-member districts. The minority's voting power in a multimember district is particularly diluted when bloc voting occurs and ballots are cast along strict majority-minority lines. While multimember districts have been challenged for "their winner-take-all aspects, their tendency to submerge minorities and to over-represent the winning party," . . . this Court has repeatedly held that they are not unconstitutional *per se*. . . . The Court has recognized, however, that multimember districts violate the Fourteenth Amendment if "conceived or operated as purposeful devices to further racial discrimination" by minimizing, canceling out or diluting the voting strength of racial elements in the voting population. . . . Cases charging that multimember districts unconstitutionally dilute the voting strength of racial minorities are thus subject to the standard of proof generally applicable to Equal Protection Clause cases. . . . In order for the Equal Protection Clause to be violated, "the invidious quality of a law claimed to be racially discriminatory must ultimately be traced to a racially discriminatory purpose."

Arlington Heights [*v. Metropolitan Housing Development Corp.*] . . . and *Washington v. Davis* . . . both rejected the notion that a law is invalid under the Equal Protection Clause simply because it may affect a greater proportion of one race than another. However, both cases recognized that discriminatory intent need not be proved by direct evidence. "Necessarily, an invidious discriminatory purpose may often be inferred from the totality of the relevant facts, including the fact, if it is true, that the law bears more heavily on one race than another." . . . Thus determining the existence of a discriminatory purpose "demands a sensitive inquiry into such circumstantial and direct evidence of intent as may be available." . . .

In *Mobile v. Bolden,* the Court was called upon to apply these principles to the at-large election system in Mobile, Ala. Mobile is governed by three commissioners who exercise all legislative, executive, and administrative power in the municipality. . . . Each candidate for the City Commission runs for one of three numbered posts in an at-large election and can only be elected by a majority vote. . . . Plaintiffs brought a class action on behalf of all Negro citizens of Mobile alleging that the at-large scheme diluted their voting strength in violation of several statutory and constitutional provisions. The District Court concluded that the at-large system "violates the constitutional rights of the plaintiffs by improperly restricting their access to the political process," . . . and ordered that the commission form of government be replaced by a mayor and a nine-member City Council elected from single-member districts. . . . The Court of Appeals affirmed. . . . This Court reversed.

Justice Stewart, writing for himself and three other Justices, noted that to prevail in their contention that the at-large voting system violates the Equal Protection Clause of the Fourteenth Amendment, plaintiffs had to prove the system was "conceived or operated as [a] purposeful devic[e] to further racial . . . discrimination." . . . Such a requirement "is simply one aspect of the basic principle that only if there is purposeful discrimination can there be a violation of the Equal Protection Clause of the Fourteenth Amendment." . . .

The plurality went on to conclude that the District Court had failed to comply with this standard. The District Court had analyzed plaintiffs' claims in light of the standard which had been set forth in *Zimmer v. McKeithen.* . . . *Zimmer* set out a list of factors . . . that a court should consider in assessing the constitutionality of at-large and multimember district voting schemes. Under *Zimmer,* voting dilution is established "upon proof of the existence of an aggregate of these factors." . . .

The plurality in *Mobile* was of the view that *Zimmer* was "decided upon the misunderstanding that it is not necessary to show a discriminatory purpose in order to prove a violation of the Equal Protection Clause—that proof of a discriminatory effect is sufficient." . . . The plurality observed that while "the presence of the indicia relied on in *Zimmer* may afford some evidence or a discriminatory purpose," the mere existence of those criteria is not a substitute for a finding of discriminatory purpose. . . . The District Court's standard in *Mobile* was likewise flawed. Finally, the plurality concluded that the evidence on which the lower courts had relied was "insufficient to prove an unconstitutionally discriminatory purpose in the present case." . . . Justice Stevens rejected the intentional discrimination standard but concluded that the proof failed to satisfy the legal standard that in his view was the applicable rule. He therefore concurred in the judgment of reversal. . . .

Because the District Court in the present case employed the evidentiary factors outlined in *Zimmer,* it is urged that its judgment is infirm for the same reasons that led to the reversal in *Mobile.* We do not agree. First, and fundamentally, we are unconvinced that the District Court in this case applied the wrong legal standard.

The District Court . . . demonstrated its understanding by observing that a determination of discriminatory intent is "a requisite to a finding of unconstitutional vote dilution" under the Fourteenth and Fifteenth Amendments. . . . Furthermore, while recognizing that the evidentiary factors identified in *Zimmer* were to be considered, the District Court was aware that it was "not limited in its determination only to the *Zimmer* factors" but could consider other relevant factors as well. . . . The District Court then proceeded to deal with what it considered to be the relevant proof and concluded that the at-large scheme of electing commissioners, "although racially neutral when adopted, is being maintained for invidious purposes." . . . That system "while neutral in origin . . . has been subverted to invidious purposes." . . .

. . . The District court found that blacks have always made up a substantial majority of the population in Burke County, . . . but that they are a distinct minority of the registered voters. . . . There was also overwhelming evidence of bloc voting along racial lines. Hence, although there had been black candidates, no black had ever been elected to the Burke County Commission. These facts bear heavily on the issue of purposeful discrimination. Voting along racial lines allows those elected to ignore black interests without fear of political consequences, and without bloc voting the minority candidates would not lose elections solely because of their race. Because it is sensible to expect that at least some blacks would have been elected in Burke County, the fact that none have ever been elected is important evidence of purposeful exclusion. . . .

Under our cases, however, such facts are insufficient in themselves to prove purposeful discrimination absent other evidence such as proof that blacks have less opportunity to participate in the political processes and to elect candidates of their choice. . . . Both the District Court and the Court of Appeals thought the supporting proof in this case was sufficient to support an inference of intentional discrimination. . . .

The District Court began by determining the impact of past discrimination on the ability of blacks to participate effectively in the political process. Past discrimination was found to contribute to low black voter registration because prior to the Voting Rights Act of 1965, blacks had been denied access to the political process by means such as literacy tests, poll taxes, and white primaries. The result was that "Black suffrage in Burke County was virtually nonexistent." . . . Black voter registration in Burke County has increased following the Voting Rights Act to the point that some 38% of blacks eligible to vote are registered to do so. . . . On that basis the District Court inferred that "past discrimination has had an adverse effect on black voter reg-

istration which lingers to this date." . . . Past discrimination against blacks in education also had the same effect. Not only did Burke County schools discriminate against blacks as recently as 1969, but also some schools still remain essentially segregated and blacks as a group have completed less formal education than whites. . . .

The District Court found further evidence of exclusion from the political process. Past discrimination had prevented blacks from effectively participating in Democratic Party affairs and in primary elections. Until this lawsuit was filed, there had never been a black member of the County Executive Committee of the Democratic Party. There were also property ownership requirements that made it difficult for blacks to serve as chief registrar in the county. There had been discrimination in the selection of grand jurors, the hiring of county employees, and in the appointments to boards and committees which oversee the county government. . . . The District Court thus concluded that historical discrimination had restricted the present opportunity of blacks effectively to participate in the political process. Evidence of historical discrimination is relevant to drawing an inference of purposeful discrimination, particularly in cases such as this one where the evidence shows that discriminatory practices were commonly utilized, that they were abandoned when enjoined by courts or made illegal by civil rights legislation, and that they were replaced by laws and practices which, though neutral on their face, serve to maintain the status quo.

Extensive evidence was cited by the District Court to support its finding that elected officials of Burke County have been unresponsive and insensitive to the needs of the black community, which increases the likelihood that the political process was not equally open to blacks. This evidence ranged from the effects of past discrimination which still haunt the county courthouse to the infrequent appointment of blacks to county boards and committees; the overtly discriminatory pattern of paving county roads; the reluctance of the county to remedy black complaints, which forced blacks to take legal action to obtain school and grand jury desegregation; and the role played by the County Commissioners in the incorporation of an all-white private school to which they donated public funds for the purchase of band uniforms. . . .

The District Court also considered the depressed socioeconomic status of Burke County blacks. It found that proportionately more blacks than whites have incomes below the poverty level. . . . Nearly 53% of all black families living in Burke County had incomes equal to or less than three-fourths of a poverty-level income. . . . Not only have blacks completed less formal education than whites, but also the education they have received "was qualitatively inferior to a marked degree." . . . Blacks tend to receive less pay than whites, even for similar work, and they tend to be employed in menial jobs more often than whites. . . . Seventy-three percent of houses occupied by blacks lacked all or some plumbing facilities; only 16% of white-occupied houses suffered the same deficiency. . . . The District Court concluded that the depressed socio-economic status of blacks results in part from "the lingering effects of past discrimination. . . ."

Although finding that the state policy behind the at-large electoral system in Burke County was "neutral in origin," the District Court concluded that the policy "has been subverted to invidious purposes." . . . As a practical matter, maintenance of the state statute providing for at-large elections in Burke County is determined by Burke County's state representatives, for the legislature defers to their wishes on matters of purely local application. The court found that Burke County's state representatives "have retained a system which has minimized the ability of Burke County blacks to participate in the political system." . . .

The trial court considered, in addition, several factors which this Court has indicated enhance the tendency of multimember districts to minimize the voting strength of racial minorities. . . . It found that the sheer geographic size of the county, which is nearly two-thirds the size of Rhode Island, "has made it more difficult for blacks to get to polling places or to campaign for office." The court concluded, as a matter of law, that the size of the county tends to impair the access of blacks to the political process. The majority vote requirement was found "to submerge the will of the minority" and thus "deny the minority's access to the system." . . . The court also found the requirements that candidates run for specific seats, enhances appellees' lack of access because it prevents a cohesive political group from concentrating on a single candidate. Because Burke County has no residency requirement, "[a]ll candidates could reside in Waynesboro, or in '[lily]-white' neighborhoods. To that extent, the denial of access becomes enhanced." . . .

None of the District Court's findings underlying its ultimate finding of intentional discrimination appears to us to be clearly erroneous; and as we have said, we decline to overturn the essential finding of the District Court, agreed to by the Court of Appeals, that the at-large system in Burke County has been maintained for the purpose of denying blacks equal access to the political processes in the county. As in *White v. Regester,* . . . the District Court's findings were "sufficient to sustain [its] judgment . . . and, on this record, we have no reason to disturb them."

We also find no reason to overturn the relief ordered by the District Court. Neither the District Court nor the Court of Appeals discerned any special circumstances that would militate against utilizing single-member districts.

Where "a constitutional violation has been found, the remedy is tailored to cure the 'condition that offends the Constitution.'" . . .

The judgment of the Court of Appeals is affirmed.

Justice Powell, with whom *Justice Rehnquist* joins, dissenting.

. . . *Mobile v. Bolden* . . . establishes that an at-large voting system must be upheld against constitutional attack unless maintained for a discriminatory purpose. In *Mobile* we reversed a finding of unconstitutional vote dilution because the lower courts had relied on factors insufficient as a matter of law to establish discriminatory intent. . . . The District Court and Court of Appeals in this case based their findings of unconstitutional discrimination on the same factors held insufficient in *Mobile.* Yet the Court now finds their conclusion unexceptionable. The *Mobile* plurality also affirmed that the concept of "intent" was no mere fiction, and held that the District Court had erred in "its failure to identify the state officials whose intent it considered relevant." . . . Although the courts below did not answer that question in this case, the Court today affirms their decision.

Whatever the wisdom of *Mobile,* the Court's opinion cannot be reconciled persuasively with that case. There are some variances in the largely sociological evidence presented in the two cases. But *Mobile* held that this kind of evidence was not enough. Such evidence, we found in *Mobile,* did not merely fall short, but "fell far short[,] of showing that [an at-large electoral scheme was] 'conceived or operated [as a] purposeful devic[e] to further racial . . . discrimination.'" . . . Because I believe that *Mobile* controls this case, I dissent. . . .

Justice Stevens, dissenting.

Our legacy of racial discrimination has left its scars on Burke County, Georgia. The record in this case amply supports the conclusion that the governing officials of Burke County have repeatedly denied black citizens rights guaranteed by the Fourteenth and Fifteenth Amendments to the Federal Constitution. No one could legitimately question the validity of remedial measures, whether legislative or judicial, designed to prohibit discriminatory conduct by public officials and to guarantee that black citizens are effectively afforded the rights to register and to vote. Public roads may not be paved only in areas in which white citizens live; black citizens may not be denied employment opportunities in county government; segregated schools may not be maintained.

Nor, in my opinion, could there be any doubt about the constitutionality of an amendment to the Voting Rights Act that would require Burke County and other covered jurisdictions to abandon specific kinds of at-large voting schemes that perpetuate the effects of past discrimination. . . .

The Court's decision today, however, is not based on either its own conception of sound policy or any statutory command. The decision rests entirely on the Court's interpretation of the requirements of the Federal Constitution. Despite my sympathetic appraisal of the Court's laudable goals, I am unable to agree with its approach to the constitutional issue that is presented. In my opinion, this case raises questions that encompass more than the immediate plight of disadvantaged black citizens. I believe the Court errs by holding the structure of the local governmental unit unconstitutional without identifying an acceptable, judicially manageable standard for adjudicating cases of this kind. . . .

Ever since I joined the Court, I have been concerned about the Court's emphasis on subjective intent as a criterion for constitutional adjudication. Although that criterion is often regarded as a restraint on the exercise of judicial power, it may in fact provide judges with a tool for exercising power that otherwise would be confined to the legislature. My principal concern with the subjective-intent standard, however, is unrelated to the quantum of power it confers upon the judiciary. It is based on the quality of that power. For in the long run constitutional adjudication that is premised on a case-by-case appraisal of the subjective intent of local decision-makers cannot possibly satisfy the requirement of impartial administration of the law that is embodied in the Equal Protection Clause of the Fourteenth Amendment.

The facts of this case illustrate the ephemeral character of a constitutional standard that focuses on subjective intent. When the suit was filed in 1976, approximately 58 percent of the population of Burke County was black and approximately 42 percent was white. Because black citizens had been denied access to the political process—through means that have since been outlawed by the Voting Rights Act of 1965—and because there had been insufficient time to enable the registration of black voters to overcome the history of past injustice, the majority of registered voters in the county were white. The at-large electoral system therefore served, as a result of the presence of bloc voting, to maintain white control of the local government. Whether it would have continued to do so would have depended on a mix of at least three different factors—the continuing increase in voter registration among blacks, the continuing exodus of black residents from the county, and the extent to which racial block voting continued to dominate local politics.

If those elected officials in control of the political machinery had formed the judgment that these factors created a likelihood that a bloc of black voters was about to achieve sufficient strength to elect an entirely new administration, they might have decided to abandon the at-large system and substitute five single-member districts with the boundary lines drawn to provide a white majority in three districts and a black majority in only two. Under the Court's intent standard, such a change presumably would violate the Fourteenth Amendment. It is ironic that the remedy ordered by the District fits that pattern precisely. . . .

Case

REYNOLDS V. SIMS

377 U.S. 533; 84 S.Ct. 1362; 12 L.Ed. 2d 506 (1964)
Vote: 8–1

Prior to this lawsuit, the apportionment scheme for the Alabama legislature created a thirty-five-member senate elected from districts whose population varied from 15,417 to 634,864 and a house of representatives with 106 members elected from districts whose populations varied from 6,731 to 104,767. Registered voters from two urban counties brought this lawsuit challenging the constitutionality of the existing apportionment. The U.S. district court ruled for the plaintiffs and ordered a temporary reapportionment plan. On appeal, the Supreme Court affirmed the lower court's decision.

Mr. Chief Justice Warren delivered the opinion of the Court.

. . . A predominant consideration in determining whether a State's legislative apportionment scheme constitutes an invidious discrimination violative of rights asserted under the Equal Protection Clause is that the rights allegedly impaired are individual and personal in nature. . . . [T]he judicial focus must be concentrated upon ascertaining whether there has been any discrimination against certain of the State's citizens which constitutes an impermissible impairment of their constitutionally protected right to vote. . . . Undoubtedly, the right of suffrage is a fundamental matter in a free and democratic society. Especially since the right to exercise the franchise in a free and unimpaired manner is preservative of other basic civil and political rights, any alleged infringement of the right of citizens to vote must be carefully and meticulously scrutinized. . . .

Legislators represent people, not trees or acres. Legislators are elected by voters, not farms or cities or economic interests. As long as ours is a representative form of government, and our legislatures are those instruments of government elected directly by and directly representative of the people, the right to elect legislators in a free and unimpaired fashion is a bedrock of our political system. It could hardly be gainsaid that a constitutional claim had been asserted by an allegation that certain otherwise qualified voters had been entirely prohibited from voting for members of their state legislature. And, if a State should provide that the votes of citizens in one part of the State should be given two times, or five times, or 10 times the weight of votes of citizens in another part of the State, it could hardly be contended that the right to vote of those residing in the disfavored area had not been effectively diluted. It would appear extraordinary to suggest that a State could be constitutionally permitted to enact a law providing that certain of the State's voters could vote two, five, or 10 times for their legislative representatives, while voters living elsewhere could vote only once. And it is inconceivable that a state law to the effect that, in counting votes for legislators, the votes of citizens in one part of the State would be multiplied by two, five, or 10, while the votes of persons in another area would be counted only at face value, could be constitutionally sustainable. Of course, the effect of state legislative districting schemes which give the same number of representatives to unequal numbers of constituents is identical. Overweighting and overvaluation of the votes of those living here has the certain effect of dilution and under valuation of the votes of those living there. The resulting discrimination against those individual voters living in disfavored areas is easily demonstrable mathematically. Their right to vote is simply not the same right to vote as that of those living in a favored part of the State. Two, five, or 10 of them must vote before the effect of their voting is equivalent to that of their favored neighbor. Weighting the votes of citizens differently, by any method or means, merely because of where they happen to reside, hardly seems justifiable. . . .

State legislatures are, historically, the fountainhead of representative government in this country. . . . Most citizens can achieve [full and effective] participation only as qualified voters through the election of legislators to represent them. Full and effective participation by all citizens in state government requires, therefore, that each citizen have an equally effective voice in the election of members of his state legislature. Modern and viable state government needs, and the Constitution demands, no less.

Logically, in a society ostensibly grounded on representative government, it would seem reasonable that a majority of the people of a State could elect a majority of that State's legislators. To conclude differently, and to sanction minority control of state legislature bodies, would appear to deny majority rights in a way that far surpasses any possible denial of minority rights that might otherwise be thought to result. Since legislatures are responsible for enacting laws by which all citizens are to be governed, they should be bodies which are collectively responsive to the popular will. And the concept of equal protection has been traditionally viewed as requiring the uniform treatment of persons standing in the same relation to the governmental action questioned or challenged. With respect to the allocation of legislative representation, all voters, as citizens of a State, stand in the same relation regardless of where they live. Any suggested criteria for the differentiation of citizens are insufficient to justify any discrimination, as to the weight of their votes, unless relevant to the permissible purposes of legislative apportionment. Since the achieving of fair and effective representation for all citizens is concededly the basic aim of legislative apportionment, we conclude that the Equal Protection Clause guarantees the opportunity for equal participation by all voters in the election of state legislators. Diluting the weight of votes because of place of residence impairs basic constitutional rights under the Fourteenth Amendment just as much as invidious discriminations based upon factors such as race . . . or economic status. . . . Our constitutional system amply provides for the protection of minorities by means other than giving them majority control of state legislatures. And the democratic ideals of equality and majority rule, which have served this Nation so well in the past, are hardly of any less significance for the present and the future.

We are told that the matter of apportioning representation in a state legislature is a complex and many-faceted one. We are advised that States can rationally consider factors other than population in apportioning legislative representation. We are admonished not to restrict the power of the States to impose differing views as to political philosophy on their citizens. We are cautioned about the dangers of entering into political thickets and mathematical quagmires. Our answer is this: a denial of constitutionally protected rights demands judicial protection; our oath and our office require no less of us.

To the extent that a citizen's right to vote is debased, he is that much less a citizen. The fact that an individual lives here or there is not a legitimate reason for overweighting or diluting the efficacy of his vote. The complexions of societies and civilizations change, often with amazing rapidity. A nation once primarily rural in character becomes predominantly urban. Representation schemes once fair and equitable become archaic and outdated. But the basic principle of representative government remains, and must remain, unchanged—the weight of a citizen's vote cannot be made to depend on where he lives. Population is, of necessity, the starting point for consideration and the controlling criterion for judgment in legislative apportionment controversies. A citizen, a qualified voter, is no more nor no less so because he lives in the city or on the farm. This is the clear and strong command of our Constitution's Equal Protection Clause. This is an essential part of the concept of a government of laws and not men. This is at the heart of Lincoln's vision of "government of the people, by the people, [and] for the people." The Equal Protection Clause demands no less than substantially equal state legislative representation for all citizens, of all places as well as of all races. . . .

By holding that as a federal constitutional requisite both houses of a state legislature must be apportioned on a population basis, we mean that the Equal Protection Clause requires that a State make an honest and good faith effort to construct districts, in both houses of its legislature, as nearly of equal population as is practicable. We realize that it is a practical impossibility to arrange legislative districts so that each one has an identical number of residents, or citizens, or voters. Mathematical exactness or precision is hardly a workable constitutional requirement. . . .

. . . So long as the divergences from a strict population standard are based on legitimate considerations incident to the effectuation of a rational state policy, some deviations from the equal-population principle are constitutionally permissible with respect to the apportionment of seats in either or both of the two houses of a bicameral state legislature. But neither history alone, nor economic or other sorts of group interests, are permissible factors in attempting to justify disparities from population-based representation. Citizens, not history or economic interests, cast votes. Considerations of area alone provide an insufficient justification for deviations from the equal-population principle. Again, people, not land or trees or pastures, vote. Modern developments and improvements in transportation and communications make rather hollow, in the mid-1960's, most claims that deviations from population-based representation can validly be based solely on geographical considerations. Arguments for allowing such deviations in order to insure effective representation for sparsely settled areas and to prevent legislative districts from becoming so large that the availability of access of citizens to their representatives is impaired are today, for the most part, unconvincing.

A consideration that appears to be of more substance in justifying some deviations from population-based representation in state legislatures is that of insuring some voice to political subdivisions, as political subdivisions. . . . In many States much of the legislature's activity involves the enactment of so-called local legislation, directed only to the concerns of particular political subdivisions. And a State may legitimately desire to construct districts along political

subdivision lines to deter the possibilities of gerrymandering. But if, even as a result of a clearly rational state policy of according some legislative representation to political subdivisions, population is submerged as the controlling consideration in the apportionment of seats in the particular legislative body, then the right of all of the State's citizens to cast an effective and adequately weighted vote would be unconstitutionally impaired. . . .

Mr. Justice Clark, concurring. . . .

Mr. Justice Stewart, concurring. . . .

Mr. Justice Harlan, dissenting:

. . . The Court's constitutional discussion . . . is remarkable . . . for its failure to address itself at all to the Fourteenth Amendment as a whole or to the legislative history of the Amendment pertinent to the matter at hand. Stripped of aphorisms, the Court's argument boils down to the assertion that appellee's right to vote has been invidiously "debased" or "diluted" by systems of apportionment which entitle them to vote for fewer legislators than other voters, an assertion which is tied to the Equal Protection Clause only by the constitutionally frail tautology that "equal" means "equal."

Had the Court paused to probe more deeply into the matter, it would have found that the Equal Protection Clause was never intended to inhibit the States in choosing any democratic method they pleased for the apportionment of their legislatures. . . .

The history of the adoption of the Fourteenth Amendment provides conclusive evidence that neither those who proposed nor those who ratified the Amendment believed that the Equal Protection Clause limited the power of the States to apportion their legislatures as they saw fit. Moreover, the history demonstrates that the intention to leave this power undisturbed was deliberate and was widely believed to be essential to the adoption of the Amendment. . . .

Although the Court—necessarily, as I believe—provides only generalities in elaboration of its main thesis, its opinion nevertheless fully demonstrates how far removed these problems are from fields of judicial competence. Recognizing that "indiscriminate districting" is an invitation to "partisan gerrymandering," . . . the Court nevertheless excludes virtually every basis for the formation of electoral districts other than "indiscriminate districting." In one or another of today's opinions, the Court declares it unconstitutional for a State to give effective consideration to any of the following in establishing legislative districts:

1. history;
2. "economic or other sorts of group interests";
3. area;

4. geographical considerations;
5. a desire "to insure effective representation for sparsely settled areas";
6. "availability of access of citizens to their representatives";
7. theories of bicameralism (except those approved by the Court);
8. occupation;
9. "an attempt to balance urban and rural power";
10. the preference of a majority of voters in the State.

So far as presently appears, the only factor which a State may consider, apart from numbers, is political subdivisions. But even "a clearly rational state policy" recognizing this factor is unconstitutional if "population is submerged as the controlling consideration. . . ."

I know of no principle of logic or practical or theoretical politics, still less any constitutional principle, which establishes all or any of these exclusions. Certain it is that the Court's opinion does not establish them. So far as the Court says anything at all on this score, it says only that "legislators represent people, not trees or acres," . . . that "citizens, not history or economic interests, cast votes," . . . that "people, not land or trees or pastures, vote." . . . All this may be conceded. But it is surely equally obvious, and, in the context of elections, more meaningful to note that people are not ciphers and that legislators can represent their electors only by speaking for their interests—economic, social, political—many of which do reflect the place where the electors live. The Court does not establish, or indeed even attempt to make a case for the proposition that conflicting interests within a State can only be adjusted by disregarding them when voters are grouped for purposes of representation. . . .

Case

KARCHER V. DAGGETT

462 U.S. 725; 103 S.Ct. 2653; 77 L.Ed. 2d 133 (1983)
Vote: 5–4

The guiding principle is "one person, one vote," but as a practical matter it is impossible to make legislative districts exactly equal in population. How much deviation from absolute equality is permissible? Here the Court addresses this question in the context of a 1982 reapportionment plan for New Jersey's congressional districts.

Justice Brennan delivered the opinion of the Court.

. . . A three-judge District Court declared New Jersey's 1982 reapportionment plan unconstitutional on the authority of *Kirkpatrick v. Preisler* . . . (1969) and *White v. Weiser* (1973), . . . because the population deviations among districts, although small, were not the result of a good-faith effort to achieve population equality. . . .

After the results of the 1980 decennial census had been tabulated, the Clerk of the United States House of Representatives notified the governor of New Jersey that the number of Representatives to which the State was entitled had decreased from 15 to 14. Accordingly, the New Jersey Legislature was required to reapportion the State's congressional districts. The State's 199th Legislature passed two reapportionment bills. One was vetoed by the Governor, and the second, although signed into law, occasioned significant dissatisfaction among those who felt it

diluted minority voting strength in the city of Newark. . . . In response, the 200th Legislature returned to the problem of apportioning congressional districts when it convened in January 1982, and it swiftly passed a bill (S-711) introduced by Senator Feldman, President pro tem of the State Senate, which created the apportionment plan at issue in this case. The bill was signed by the Governor on January 19, 1982. . . .

Like every plan considered by the legislature, the Feldman Plan contained 14 districts, with an average population per district (as determined by the 1980 census) of 526,059. Each district did not have the same population. On the average, each district differed from the "ideal" figure by 0.1384%, or about 726 people. The largest district, the Fourth District, which includes Trenton, had a population of 527,472, and the smallest, the Sixth District, embracing most of Middlesex County, a population of 523,798. The difference between them was 3,674 people, or 0.6984% of the average district. The populations of the other districts also varied. The Ninth District, including most of Bergen County, in the northeastern corner of the State, had a population of 527,349, while the population of the Third District, along the Atlantic shore, was only 524,825. . . .

The legislature had before it other plans with appreciably smaller population deviations between the largest and smallest districts. The one receiving the most attention in the District Court was designed by Dr. Ernest Reock, a political science professor at Rutgers University and

Director of the Bureau of Government Research. A version of the Reock Plan introduced in the 200th Legislature by Assemblyman Hardwick had a maximum population difference of 2,375, or 0.4514% of the average figure. . . .

Almost immediately after the Feldman Plan became law, a group of individuals with varying interests, including all incumbent Republican Members of Congress from New Jersey, sought a declaration that the apportionment plan violated Article I, Section 2, of the Constitution and an injunction against proceeding with the primary election for United States Representatives under the plan. . . .

Shortly thereafter, the District Court issued an opinion and order declaring the Feldman Plan unconstitutional. Denying the motions for summary judgment and resolving the case on the record as a whole, the District Court held that the population variances in the Feldman Plan were not "unavoidable despite a good-faith effort to achieve absolute equality." . . . The court rejected appellants' argument that a deviation lower than the statistical imprecision of the decennial census was "the functional equivalent of mathematical equality." . . . It also held that appellants had failed to show that the population variances were justified by the legislature's purported goals of preserving minority voting strength and anticipating shifts in population. . . . The District Court enjoined appellants from conducting primary or general elections under the Feldman Plan, but that order was stayed pending appeal to this Court. . . .

Article I, Section 2, establishes a "high standard of justice and common sense" for the apportionment of congressional districts: "equal representation for equal numbers of people." . . . Precise mathematical equality, however, may be impossible to achieve in an imperfect world; therefore the "equal representation" standard is enforced only to the extent of requiring that districts be apportioned to achieve population equality "as nearly as is practicable." . . . As we explained further in *Kirkpatrick v. Preisler:*

> [T]he "as nearly as practicable" standard requires that the State make a good-faith effort to achieve precise mathematical equality. . . . Unless population variances among congressional districts are shown to have resulted despite such effort, the State must justify each variance, no matter how small. . . .

Article I, Section 2, therefore, "permits only the limited population variances which are unavoidable despite a good-faith effort to achieve absolute equality, or for which justification is shown." . . .

Thus two basic questions shape litigation over population deviations in state legislation apportioning congressional districts. First, the court must consider whether the population differences among districts could have been reduced or eliminated altogether by a good-faith effort to draw districts of equal population. Parties challenging apportionment legislation must bear the burden of proof on this issue, and if they fail to show that the differences could have been avoided the apportionment scheme must be upheld. If, however, the plaintiffs can establish that the population differences were not the result of a good-faith effort to achieve equality, the State must bear the burden of proving that each significant variance between districts was necessary to achieve some legitimate goal. . . .

Appellants' principal argument in this case is addressed to the first question described above. They contend that the Feldman Plan should be regarded per se as the product of a good-faith effort to achieve population equality because the maximum population deviation among districts is smaller than the predictable undercount in available census data. . . .

Kirkpatrick squarely rejected a nearly identical argument. "The whole thrust of the 'as nearly as practicable' approach is inconsistent with adoption of fixed numerical standards which excuse population variances without regard to the circumstances of each particular case." . . . Adopting any standard other than population equality, using the best census data available, . . . would subtly erode the Constitution's ideal of equal representation. If state legislators knew that a certain *de minimis* level of population differences was acceptable, they would doubtless strive to achieve that level rather than equality. . . .

Furthermore, choosing a different standard would import a high degree of arbitrariness into the process of reviewing apportionment plans. . . . In this case, appellants argue that a maximum deviation of approximately 0.7% should be considered *de minimis.* If we accept that argument, how are we to regard deviations of 0.8%, 0.9%, 1%, or 1.1%?

Any standard, including absolute equality, involves a certain artificiality. As appellants point out, even the census data are not perfect, and the well-known restlessness of the American people means that population counts for particular localities are outdated long before they are completed. Yet problems with the data at hand apply equally to any population-based standard we could choose. As between two standards—equality or something less than equality—only the former reflects the aspirations of Article I, Section 2. [Accepting the] population deviations in this case would mean to reject the basic premise of *Kirkpatrick* and *Wesberry* [*v. Sanders*]. We decline appellants' invitation to go that far. The unusual rigor of their standard has been noted several times. Because of that rigor, we have required that absolute population equality be the paramount objective of apportionment only in the case of congressional districts, for which the command of Article I, Section 2 as regards the National Legislature outweighs the local interests that a State may deem relevant in apportioning districts for representatives to state and local legislatures. . . . The principle of population equality for congressional districts has not proved unjust or socially or economically harmful in experience. . . . If anything, this standard should cause less difficulty now for state legislatures than it did when we adopted it in *Wesberry*. The rapid advances in computer technology and education during the last two decades make it relatively simple to draw contiguous districts of equal population and at the same time to further whatever secondary goals the State has. Finally, to abandon unnecessarily a clear and oft-confirmed constitutional interpretation would impair our authority in other cases, . . . would implicitly open the door to a plethora of requests that we reexamine other rules that some may consider burdensome, and would prejudice those who have relied upon the rule of law in seeking an equipopulous congressional apportionment in New Jersey. . . . We thus reaffirm that there are no *de minimis* population variations, which could practically be avoided, but which nonetheless meet the standard of Article I, Section 2, without justification.

The sole difference between appellants' theory and the argument we rejected in *Kirkpatrick* is that appellants have proposed a *de minimis* line that gives the illusion of rationality and predictability: the "inevitable statistical imprecision of the census." They argue: "Where, as here, the deviation from ideal district size is less than the known imprecision of the census figures, that variation is the functional equivalent of zero." . . . There are two problems with this approach. First, appellants concentrate on the extent to which the census systematically undercounts actual population—a figure which is not known precisely and which, even if it were known, would not be relevant to this case. Second, the mere existence of statistical imprecisions does not make small deviations among districts the functional equivalent of equality. . . .

The census may systematically undercount population, and the rate of undercounting may vary from place to place. Those facts, however, do not render meaningless the differences in population between congressional districts, as determined by uncorrected census counts. To the contrary, the census data provide the only reliable—albeit less than perfect—indication of the districts' "real" relative population levels. Even if one cannot say with certainty that one district is larger than another merely because it has a higher census count, one can say with certainty that the district with a larger census count is more likely to be larger than the other district than it is to be smaller or the same size. That certainty is sufficient for

decision-making. . . . Furthermore, because the census count represents the "best population data available," . . . it is the only basis for good-faith attempts to achieve population equality. Attempts to explain population deviations on the basis of flaws in census data must be supported with a precision not achieved here. . . .

Given that the census-based population deviations in the Feldman Plan reflect real differences among the districts, it is clear that they could have been avoided or significantly reduced with a good-faith effort to achieve population equality. For that reason alone, it would be inappropriate to accept the Feldman Plan as "functionally equivalent" to a plan with districts of equal population.

The District Court found that several other plans introduced in the 200th Legislature had smaller maximum deviations than the Feldman Plan. . . . Appellants object that the alternative plans considered by the District Court were not comparable to the Feldman Plan because their political characters differed profoundly. . . . We have never denied that apportionment is a political process, or that state legislatures could pursue legitimate secondary objectives as long as those objectives were consistent with a good-faith effort to achieve population equality at the same time. Nevertheless, the claim that political considerations require population differences among congressional districts belongs more properly to the second level of judicial inquiry in these cases, . . . in which the State bears the burden of justifying the differences with particularity.

In any event, it was unnecessary for the District Court to rest its finding on the existence of alternative plans with radically different political effects. As in *Kirkpatrick*, "resort to the simple device of transferring entire political subdivisions of known population between contiguous districts would have produced districts much closer to numerical equality." . . . Starting with the Feldman Plan itself and the census data available to the legislature at the time it was enacted, . . . one can reduce the maximum population deviation of the plan merely by shifting a handful of municipalities from one district to another. . . .

Thus the District Court did not err in finding that the plaintiffs had met their burden of showing that the Feldman Plan did not come as nearly as practicable to population equality. . . .

By itself, the foregoing discussion does not establish that the Feldman Plan is unconstitutional. Rather, appellees' success in proving that the Feldman Plan was not the product of a good-faith effort to achieve population equality means only that the burden shifted to the State to prove that the population deviations in its plan were necessary to achieve some legitimate state objective. *White v. Weiser* demonstrates that we are willing to defer to state legislative policies, so long as they are consistent with constitutional norms, even if they require small differences in the population of congressional districts. . . . Any number of consistently applied legislative policies might justify some variance, including, for instance, making districts compact, respecting municipal boundaries, preserving the cores of prior districts, and avoiding contests between incumbent Representatives. As long as the criteria are nondiscriminatory, . . . these are all legitimate objectives that on a proper showing could justify minor population deviations. . . .

The State must, however, show with some specificity that a particular objective required the specific deviations in its plan, rather than simply relying on general assertions. The showing required to justify population deviations is flexible, depending on the size of the deviations, the importance of the State's interests, the consistency with which the plan as a whole reflects those interests, and the availability of alternatives that might substantially vindicate those interests yet approximate population equality more closely. By necessity, whether deviations are justified requires case-by-case attention to these factors. . . .

The District Court properly applied the two-part test of *Kirkpatrick v. Preisler* to New Jersey's 1982 apportionment of districts for the United States House of Representatives. It correctly held that the population deviations in the plan were not functionally equal as a matter of law, and it found that the plan was not a good-faith effort to achieve population equality using the best available census data. It also correctly rejected appellants' attempt to justify the population deviations as not supported by the evidence. The judgment of the District Court, therefore, is affirmed.

Justice Stevens, concurring. . . .

Justice White, with whom the *Chief Justice, Justice Powell,* and *Justice Rehnquist* join, dissenting.

. . . "[T]he achieving of fair and effective representation for all citizens is concededly the basic aim of legislative apportionment." . . . One must suspend credulity to believe that the Court's draconian response to a trifling 0.6984% maximum deviation promotes "fair and effective representation" for the people of New Jersey. . . .

There can be little question but that the variances in the New Jersey plan are "statistically insignificant." Although the Government strives to make the decennial census as accurate as humanly possible, the Census Bureau has never intimated that the results are a perfect count of the American population. The Bureau itself estimates the inexactitude in the taking of the 1970 census at 2.3%, a figure which is considerably larger than the 0.6984% maximum variance in the New Jersey plan, and which dwarfs the 0.2470% differ-

ence between the maximum deviations of the selected plan and the leading alternative plan. . . . Because the amount of undercounting differs from district to district, there is no point for a court of law to act under an unproved assumption that such tiny differences between redistricting plans reflect actual differences in population. . . .

Even if the 0.6984% deviation here is not encompassed within the scope of the statistical imprecision of the census, it is minuscule when compared with the variations among the districts inherent in translating census numbers into citizens' votes. First, the census "is more of an event than a process." . . . "It measures population at only a single instant in time. District populations are constantly changing, often at different rates in either direction, up or down." As the Court admits, "the well-known restlessness of the American people means that population counts for particular localities are outdated long before they are completed." . . . Second, far larger differences among districts are introduced because a substantial percentage of the total population is too young to register or is disqualified by alienage. Third, census figures cannot account for the proportion of all those otherwise eligible individuals who fail to register. The differences in the number of eligible voters per district for these reasons overwhelm the minimal variations attributable to the districting plan itself.

Accepting that the census, and the districting plans which are based upon it, cannot be perfect represents no backsliding in our commitment to assuring fair and equal representation in the election of Congress. I agree with the views of Judge Gibbons, who dissented in the District Court, that Kirkpatrick should not be read as a "prohibition against toleration of *de minimis* population variances which have no statistically relevant effect on relative representation." A plus-minus deviation of 0.6984% surely falls within this category.

If today's decision simply produced an unjustified standard with little practical import, it would be bad enough. Unfortunately, I fear that the Court's insistence that "there are no *de minimis* population variations, which could practicably be avoided, but which nonetheless meet the standard of Article I, Section 2, without justification," . . . invites further litigation of virtually every congressional redistricting plan in the Nation. At least 12 States which have completed redistricting on the basis of the 1980 census have adopted plans with a higher deviation than that presented here, and 4 others have deviations quite similar to New Jersey's. Of course, under the Court's rationale, even Rhode Island's plan—whose two districts have a deviation of 0.02% or about 95 people—would be subject to constitutional attack.

In all such cases, state legislatures will be hard pressed to justify their preference for the selected plan. A good-faith effort to achieve population equality is not enough if the population variances are not "unavoidable." The court must consider whether the population differences could have been further "reduced or eliminated altogether." . . . With the assistance of computers, there will generally be a plan with an even more minimal deviation from the mathematical ideal. Then, "the State must bear the burden of proving that each significant variance between districts was necessary to achieve some legitimate goal." . . . As this case illustrates, literally any variance between districts will be considered "significant." . . .

Yet no one can seriously contend that such an inflexible insistence upon mathematical exactness will serve to promote "fair and effective representation." The more likely result of today's extension of *Kirkpatrick* is to move closer to fulfilling Justice Fortas' prophecy that "a legislature might have to ignore the boundaries of common sense, running the congressional district line down the middle of the corridor of an apartment house or even dividing the residents of a single-family house between two districts." . . . Such sterile and mechanistic application only brings the principle of "one man, one vote" into disrepute. . . .

Justice Powell, dissenting. . . .

Case

BUSH V. GORE

531 U.S. 98; 121 S.Ct. 525; 148 L.Ed. 2d 388 (2000)
Vote: 5–4

In what may be the most controversial use of judicial power since Roe v. Wade (1973), the Supreme Court here involves itself in the 2000 presidential election process. In this highly unusual case, in which the opposing parties are rival presidential candidates, the Court reviews the Florida Supreme Court's decision upholding manual recounts of ballots cast in three counties.

PER CURIAM.

I

On December 8, 2000, the Supreme Court of Florida ordered that the Circuit Court of Leon County tabulate by hand 9,000 ballots in Miami-Dade County. It also ordered the inclusion in the certified vote totals of 215 votes identified in Palm Beach County and 168 votes identified in Miami-Dade County for Vice President Albert Gore, Jr., and Senator Joseph Lieberman, Democratic Candidates for President and Vice President. The Supreme Court noted that petitioner, Governor George W. Bush asserted that the net gain for Vice President Gore in Palm Beach County was 176 votes, and directed the Circuit Court to resolve that dispute on remand. . . . The court further held that relief would require manual recounts in all Florida counties where so-called "undervotes" had not been subject to manual tabulation. The court ordered all manual recounts to begin at once. Governor Bush and Richard Cheney, Republican Candidates for the Presidency and Vice Presidency, filed an emergency application for a stay of this mandate. On December 9, we granted the applica-tion, treated the application as a petition for a writ of certiorari, and granted certiorari. . . .

The proceedings leading to the present controversy are discussed in some detail in our opinion in *Bush v. Palm Beach County Canvassing Bd.* . . . (per curiam) (*Bush I*). On November 8, 2000, the day following the Presidential election, the Florida Division of Elections reported that petitioner, Governor Bush, had received 2,909,135 votes, and respondent, Vice President Gore, had received 2,907,351 votes, a margin of 1,784 for Governor Bush. Because Governor Bush's margin of victory was less than "one-half of a percent . . . of the votes cast," an automatic machine recount was conducted under § 102.141(4) of the election code, the results of which showed Governor Bush still winning the race but by a diminished margin. Vice President Gore then sought manual recounts in Volusia, Palm Beach, Broward, and Miami-Dade Counties, pursuant to Florida's election protest provisions. Fla. Stat. § 102.166 (2000). A dispute arose concerning the deadline for local county canvassing boards to submit their returns to the Secretary of State (Secretary). The Secretary declined to waive the November 14 deadline imposed by statute. §§ 102.111, 102.112. The Florida Supreme Court, however, set the deadline at November 26. We granted certiorari and vacated the Florida Supreme Court's decision, finding considerable uncertainty as to the grounds on which it was based. . . . On December 11, the Florida Supreme Court issued a decision on remand reinstating that date. . . .

On November 26, the Florida Elections Canvassing Commission certified the results of the election and declared Governor Bush the winner of Florida's 25 electoral votes. On November 27, Vice President Gore, pursuant to Florida's contest provisions, filed a complaint in Leon County Circuit Court contesting the certification.

Fla. Stat. § 102.168 (2000). He sought relief pursuant to § 102.168(3)(c), which provides that "[r]eceipt of a number of illegal votes or rejection of a number of legal votes sufficient to change or place in doubt the result of the election" shall be grounds for a contest. The Circuit Court denied relief, stating that Vice President Gore failed to meet his burden of proof. He appealed to the First District Court of Appeal, which certified the matter to the Florida Supreme Court.

Accepting jurisdiction, the Florida Supreme Court affirmed in part and reversed in part. . . . The court held that the Circuit Court had been correct to reject Vice President Gore's challenge to the results certified in Nassau County and his challenge to the Palm Beach County Canvassing Board's determination that 3,300 ballots cast in that county were not, in the statutory phrase, "legal votes."

The Supreme Court held that Vice President Gore had satisfied his burden of proof under § 102.168(3)(c) with respect to his challenge to Miami-Dade County's failure to tabulate, by manual count, 9,000 ballots on which the machines had failed to detect a vote for President ("undervotes"). . . . Noting the closeness of the election, the Court explained that "[o]n this record, there can be no question that there are legal votes within the 9,000 uncounted votes sufficient to place the results of this election in doubt." . . . A "legal vote," as determined by the Supreme Court, is "one in which there is a 'clear indication of the intent of the voter.'" . . . The court therefore ordered a hand recount of the 9,000 ballots in Miami-Dade County. Observing that the contest provisions vest broad discretion in the circuit judge to "provide any relief appropriate under such circumstances," . . . the Supreme Court further held that the Circuit Court could order "the Supervisor of Elections and the Canvassing Boards, as well as the necessary public officials, in all counties that have not conducted a manual recount or tabulation of the undervotes . . . to do so forthwith, said tabulation to take place in the individual counties where the ballots are located." . . .

The Supreme Court also determined that both Palm Beach County and Miami-Dade County, in their earlier manual recounts, had identified a net gain of 215 and 168 legal votes for Vice President Gore. . . . Rejecting the Circuit Court's conclusion that Palm Beach County lacked the authority to include the 215 net votes submitted past the November 26 deadline, the Supreme Court explained that the deadline was not intended to exclude votes identified after that date through ongoing manual recounts. As to Miami-Dade County, the Court concluded that although the 168 votes identified were the result of a partial recount, they were "legal votes [that] could change the outcome of the election." . . . The Supreme Court therefore directed the Circuit Court to include those totals in the certified results, subject to resolution of the actual vote total from the Miami-Dade partial recount.

The petition presents the following questions: whether the Florida Supreme Court established new standards for resolving Presidential election contests, thereby violating Art. II, § 1, cl. 2, of the United States Constitution and failing to comply with 3 U.S.C. § 5, and whether the use of standardless manual recounts violates the Equal Protection and Due Process Clauses. With respect to the equal protection question, we find a violation of the Equal Protection Clause.

II

A

The closeness of this election, and the multitude of legal challenges which have followed in its wake, have brought into sharp focus a common, if heretofore unnoticed, phenomenon. Nationwide statistics reveal that an estimated 2% of ballots cast do not register a vote for President for whatever reason, including deliberately choosing no candidate at all or some voter error, such as voting for two candidates or insufficiently marking a ballot. . . . In certifying election results, the votes eligible for inclusion in the certification are the votes meeting the properly established legal requirements.

This case has shown that punch card balloting machines can produce an unfortunate number of ballots which are not punched in a clean, complete way by the voter. After the current counting, it is likely legislative bodies nationwide will examine ways to improve the mechanisms and machinery for voting.

B

The individual citizen has no federal constitutional right to vote for electors for the President of the United States unless and until the state legislature chooses a statewide election as the means to implement its power to appoint members of the Electoral College. U.S. Const., Art. II, § 1. This is the source for the statement in *McPherson v. Blacker* (1892), that the State legislature's power to select the manner for appointing electors is plenary; it may, if it so chooses, select the electors itself, which indeed was the manner used by State legislatures in several States for many years after the Framing of our Constitution. . . . History has now favored the voter, and in each of the several States the citizens themselves vote for Presidential electors. When the state legislature vests the right to vote for President in its people, the right to vote as the legislature has prescribed is fundamental; and one source of its fundamental nature lies in the equal weight accorded to each vote and the equal dignity owed to each voter. The State, of course, after granting the franchise in the special context of Article II, can take back the power to appoint electors. . . .

The right to vote is protected in more than the initial allocation of the franchise. Equal protection applies as well to the manner of its exercise. Having once granted the right to vote on equal terms, the State may not, by later arbitrary and disparate treatment, value one person's vote over that of another. . . . It must be remembered that "the right of suffrage can be denied by a debasement or dilution of the weight of a citizen's vote just as effectively as by wholly prohibiting the free exercise of the franchise." . . .

There is no difference between the two sides of the present controversy on these basic propositions. Respondents say that the very purpose of vindicating the right to vote justifies the recount procedures now at issue. The question before us, however, is whether the recount procedures the Florida Supreme Court has adopted are consistent with its obligation to avoid arbitrary and disparate treatment of the members of its electorate.

Much of the controversy seems to revolve around ballot cards designed to be perforated by a stylus but which, either through error or deliberate omission, have not been perforated with sufficient precision for a machine to count them. In some cases a piece of the card—a chad—is hanging, say by two corners. In other cases there is no separation at all, just an indentation.

The Florida Supreme Court has ordered that the intent of the voter be discerned from such ballots. For purposes of resolving the equal protection challenge, it is not necessary to decide whether the Florida Supreme Court had the authority under the legislative scheme for resolving election disputes to define what a legal vote is and to mandate a manual recount implementing that definition. The recount mechanisms implemented in response to the decisions of the Florida Supreme Court do not satisfy the minimum requirement for non-arbitrary treatment of voters necessary to secure the fundamental right. Florida's basic command for the count of legally cast votes is to consider the "intent of the voter." . . . This is unobjectionable as an abstract proposition and a starting principle. The problem inheres in the absence of specific standards to ensure its equal application. The formulation of uniform rules to determine intent based on these recurring circumstances is practicable and, we conclude, necessary.

The law does not refrain from searching for the intent of the actor in a multitude of circumstances; and in some cases the general command to ascertain intent is not susceptible to much further refinement. In this instance, however, the question is not whether to believe a witness but how to interpret the marks or holes or scratches on an inanimate object, a piece of cardboard or paper which, it is said, might not have registered as a vote during the machine count. The factfinder confronts a thing, not a person. The search for intent can be confined by specific rules designed to ensure uniform treatment.

The want of those rules here has led to unequal evaluation of ballots in various respects. . . . As seems to have been acknowledged at oral argument, the standards for accepting or rejecting contested ballots might vary not only from county to county but indeed within a single county from one recount team to another.

The record provides some examples. A monitor in Miami-Dade County testified at trial that he observed that three members of the county canvassing board applied different standards in defining a legal vote. . . . And testimony at trial also revealed that at least one county changed its evaluative standards during the counting process. Palm Beach County, for example, began the process with a 1990 guideline which precluded counting completely attached chads, switched to a rule that considered a vote to be legal if any light could be seen through a chad, changed back to the 1990 rule, and then abandoned any pretense of a per se rule, only to have a court order that the county consider dimpled chads legal. This is not a process with sufficient guarantees of equal treatment. . . .

The State Supreme Court ratified this uneven treatment. It mandated that the recount totals from two counties, Miami-Dade and Palm Beach, be included in the certified total. The court also appeared to hold *sub silentio* that the recount totals from Broward County, which were not completed until after the original November 14 certification by the Secretary of State, were to be considered part of the new certified vote totals even though the county certification was not contested by Vice President Gore. Yet each of the counties used varying standards to determine what was a legal vote. Broward County used a more forgiving standard than Palm Beach County, and uncovered almost three times as many new votes, a result markedly disproportionate to the difference in population between the counties.

In addition, the recounts in these three counties were not limited to so-called undervotes but extended to all of the ballots. The distinction has real consequences. A manual recount of all ballots identifies not only those ballots which show no vote but also those which contain more than one, the so-called overvotes. Neither category will be counted by the machine. This is not a trivial concern. At oral argument, respondents estimated there are as many as 110,000 overvotes statewide. As a result, the citizen whose ballot was not read by a machine because he failed to vote for a candidate in a way readable by a machine may still have his vote counted in a manual recount; on the other hand, the citizen who marks two candidates in a way discernable by the machine will not have the same opportunity to have his vote count, even if a manual examination of the ballot would reveal the requisite indicia of intent. Furthermore, the citizen who marks two candidates, only one of which is discernable by the machine, will have his vote counted even though it should have been read as an invalid ballot. The State Supreme Court's inclusion of vote counts based on these variant standards exemplifies concerns with the remedial processes that were under way.

That brings the analysis to yet a further equal protection problem. The votes certified by the court included a partial total from one county, Miami-Dade. The Florida Supreme Court's decision thus gives no assurance that the recounts included in a final certification must be complete. Indeed, it is respondent's submission that it would be consistent with the rules of the recount procedures to include whatever partial counts are done by the time of final certification, and we interpret the Florida Supreme Court's decision to permit this. . . . This accommodation no doubt results from the truncated contest period established by the Florida Supreme Court in *Bush I*, at respondents' own urging. The press of time does not diminish the constitutional concern. A desire for speed is not a general excuse for ignoring equal protection guarantees.

In addition to these difficulties the actual process by which the votes were to be counted under the Florida Supreme Court's decision raises further concerns. That order did not specify who would recount the ballots. The county canvassing boards were forced to pull together ad hoc teams comprised of judges from various Circuits who had no previous training in handling and interpreting ballots. Furthermore, while others were permitted to observe, they were prohibited from objecting during the recount.

The recount process, in its features here described, is inconsistent with the minimum procedures necessary to protect the fundamental right of each voter in the special instance of a statewide recount under the authority of a single state judicial officer. Our consideration is limited to the present circumstances, for the problem of equal protection in election processes generally presents many complexities.

The question before the Court is not whether local entities, in the exercise of their expertise, may develop different systems for implementing elections. Instead, we are presented with a situation where a state court with the power to assure uniformity has ordered a statewide recount with minimal procedural safeguards. When a court orders a statewide remedy, there must be at least some assurance that the rudimentary requirements of equal treatment and fundamental fairness are satisfied.

Given the Court's assessment that the recount process underway was probably being conducted in an unconstitutional manner, the Court stayed the order directing the recount so it could hear this case and render an expedited decision. The contest provision, as it was mandated by the State Supreme Court, is not well calculated to sustain the confidence that all citizens must have in the outcome of elections. The State has not shown that its procedures include the necessary safeguards. The problem, for instance, of the estimated 110,000 overvotes has not been addressed, although Chief Justice Wells called attention to the concern in his dissenting opinion. . . .

Upon due consideration of the difficulties identified to this point, it is obvious that the recount cannot be conducted in compliance with the requirements of equal protection and due process without substantial additional work. It would require not only the adoption (after opportunity for argument) of adequate statewide standards for determining what is a legal vote, and practicable procedures to implement them, but also orderly judicial review of any disputed matters that might arise. In addition, the Secretary of State has advised that the recount of only a portion of the ballots requires that the vote tabulation equipment be used to screen out undervotes, a function for which the machines were not designed. If a recount of overvotes were also required, perhaps even a second screening would be necessary. Use of the equipment for this purpose, and any new software developed for it, would have to be evaluated for accuracy by the Secretary of State. . . .

The Supreme Court of Florida has said that the legislature intended the State's electors to "participat[e] fully in the federal electoral process," as provided in 3 U.S.C. § 5. . . . That statute, in turn, requires that any controversy or contest that is designed to lead to a conclusive selection of electors be completed by December 12. That date is upon us, and there is no recount procedure in place under the State Supreme Court's order that comports with minimal constitutional standards. Because it is evident that any recount seeking to meet the December 12 date will be unconstitutional for the reasons we have discussed, we reverse the judgment of the Supreme Court of Florida ordering a recount to proceed.

Seven Justices of the Court agree that there are constitutional problems with the recount ordered by the Florida Supreme Court that demand a remedy. . . . The only disagreement is as to the remedy. Because the Florida Supreme Court has said that the Florida Legislature intended to obtain the safe-harbor benefits of 3 U.S.C. § 5, . . . remanding to the Florida Supreme Court for its ordering of a constitutionally proper contest until December 18 . . . contemplates action in violation of the

Florida election code, and hence could not be part of an "appropriate" order. . . .

None are more conscious of the vital limits on judicial authority than are the members of this Court, and none stand more in admiration of the Constitution's design to leave the selection of the President to the people, through their legislatures, and to the political sphere. When contending parties invoke the process of the courts, however, it becomes our unsought responsibility to resolve the federal and constitutional issues the judicial system has been forced to confront.

The judgment of the Supreme Court of Florida is reversed, and the case is remanded for further proceedings not inconsistent with this opinion. . . .

Chief Justice Rehnquist, with whom **Justice Scalia** and **Justice Thomas** join, concurring.

We join the per curiam opinion. We write separately because we believe there are additional grounds that require us to reverse the Florida Supreme Court's decision.

. . . In most cases, comity and respect for federalism compel us to defer to the decisions of state courts on issues of state law. That practice reflects our understanding that the decisions of state courts are definitive pronouncements of the will of the States as sovereigns. . . . Of course, in ordinary cases, the distribution of powers among the branches of a State's government raises no questions of federal constitutional law, subject to the requirement that the government be republican in character. . . . But there are a few exceptional cases in which the Constitution imposes a duty or confers a power on a particular branch of a State's government. This is one of them. Article II, § 1, cl. 2, provides that "[e]ach State shall appoint, in such Manner as the Legislature thereof may direct," electors for President and Vice President. . . . Thus, the text of the election law itself, and not just its interpretation by the courts of the States, takes on independent significance.

In *McPherson v. Blacker* (1892), we explained that Art. II, § 1, cl. 2, "convey[s] the broadest power of determination" and "leaves it to the legislature exclusively to define the method" of appointment. . . . A significant departure from the legislative scheme for appointing Presidential electors presents a federal constitutional question.

3 U.S.C. § 5 informs our application of Art. II, § 1, cl. 2, to the Florida statutory scheme, which, as the Florida Supreme Court acknowledged, took that statute into account. Section 5 provides that the State's selection of electors "shall be conclusive, and shall govern in the counting of the electoral votes" if the electors are chosen under laws enacted prior to election day, and if the selection process is completed six days prior to the meeting of the electoral college. . . .

If we are to respect the legislature's Article II powers, therefore, we must ensure that postelection state-court actions do not frustrate the legislative desire to attain the "safe harbor" provided by § 5.

In Florida, the legislature has chosen to hold statewide elections to appoint the State's 25 electors. Importantly, the legislature has delegated the authority to run the elections and to oversee election disputes to the Secretary of State (Secretary). . . . Isolated sections of the code may well admit of more than one interpretation, but the general coherence of the legislative scheme may not be altered by judicial interpretation so as to wholly change the statutorily provided apportionment of responsibility among these various bodies. In any election but a Presidential election, the Florida Supreme Court can give as little or as much deference to Florida's executives as it chooses, so far as Article II is concerned, and this Court will have no cause to question the court's actions. But, with respect to a Presidential election, the court must be both mindful of the legislature's role under Article II in choosing the manner of appointing electors and deferential to those bodies expressly empowered by the legislature to carry out its constitutional mandate.

In order to determine whether a state court has infringed upon the legislature's authority, we necessarily must examine the law of the State as it existed prior to the action of the court. Though we generally defer to state courts on the interpretation of state law . . . there are of course areas in which the Constitution requires this Court to undertake an independent, if still deferential, analysis of state law. . . .

This inquiry does not imply a disrespect for state courts but rather a respect for the constitutionally prescribed role of state legislatures. To attach definitive weight to the pronouncement of a state court, when the very question at issue is whether the court has actually departed from the statutory meaning, would be to abdicate our responsibility to enforce the explicit requirements of Article II.

II

Acting pursuant to its constitutional grant of authority, the Florida Legislature has created a detailed, if not perfectly crafted, statutory scheme that provides for appointment of Presidential electors by direct election. . . . Under the statute, "[v]otes cast for the actual candidates for President and Vice President shall be counted as votes cast for the presidential electors supporting such candidates." . . . The legislature has designated the Secretary of State as the "chief election officer," with the responsibility to "[o]btain and maintain uniformity in the application, operation, and interpretation of the election laws." . . . The state legislature has delegated to county canvassing boards the duties of administering elections. . . . Those boards are responsible for providing results to the state Elections Canvassing Commission, comprising the Governor, the Secretary of State, and the Director of the Division of Elections. . . .

After the election has taken place, the canvassing boards receive returns from precincts, count the votes, and in the event that a candidate was defeated by .5% or less, conduct a mandatory recount. . . . The county canvassing boards must file certified election returns with the Department of State by 5 P.M. on the seventh day following the election. . . . The Elections Canvassing Commission must then certify the results of the election. . . .

The state legislature has also provided mechanisms both for protesting election returns and for contesting certified election results. Section 102.166 governs protests. Any protest must be filed prior to the certification of election results by the county canvassing board. . . . Once a protest has been filed, "the county canvassing board may authorize a manual recount." . . . If a sample recount conducted pursuant to § 102.166(5) "indicates an error in the vote tabulation which could affect the outcome of the election," the county canvassing board is instructed to: "(a) Correct the error and recount the remaining precincts with the vote tabulation system; (b) Request the Department of State to verify the tabulation software; or (c) Manually recount all ballots," . . . In the event a canvassing board chooses to conduct a manual recount of all ballots, [Florida law] prescribes procedures for such a recount.

[Under Florida law] . . . [t]he grounds for contesting an election include "[r]eceipt of a number of illegal votes or rejection of a number of legal votes sufficient to change or place in doubt the result of the election." . . . Any contest must be filed in the appropriate Florida circuit court, . . . and the canvassing board or election board is the proper party defendant. . . . . Section 102.168(8) provides that "[t]he circuit judge to whom the contest is presented may fashion such orders as he or she deems necessary to ensure that each allegation in the complaint is investigated, examined, or checked, to prevent or correct any alleged wrong, and to provide any relief appropriate under such circumstances." In Presidential elections, the contest period necessarily terminates on the date set by 3 U.S.C. § 5 for concluding the State's "final determination" of election controversies."

In its first decision, *Palm Beach Canvassing Bd. v. Harris* . . . (*Harris I*), the Florida Supreme Court extended the 7-day statutory certification deadline established by the legislature. This modification of the code, by lengthening the protest period, necessarily shortened the contest period for Presidential elections. Underlying the extension of the certification deadline and the shortchanging of the con-

test period was, presumably, the clear implication that certification was a matter of significance: The certified winner would enjoy presumptive validity, making a contest proceeding by the losing candidate an uphill battle. In its latest opinion, however, the court empties certification of virtually all legal consequence during the contest, and in doing so departs from the provisions enacted by the Florida Legislature.

The court determined that canvassing boards' decisions regarding whether to recount ballots past the certification deadline (even the certification deadline established by *Harris I*) are to be reviewed de novo, although the election code clearly vests discretion whether to recount in the boards, and sets strict deadlines subject to the Secretary's rejection of late tallies and monetary fines for tardiness. . . . Moreover, the Florida court held that all late vote tallies arriving during the contest period should be automatically included in the certification regardless of the certification deadline (even the certification deadline established by *Harris I*), thus virtually eliminating both the deadline and the Secretary's discretion to disregard recounts that violate it.

Moreover, the court's interpretation of "legal vote," and hence its decision to order a contest-period recount, plainly departed from the legislative scheme. Florida statutory law cannot reasonably be thought to require the counting of improperly marked ballots. Each Florida precinct before election day provides instructions on how properly to cast a vote; each polling place on election day contains a working model of the voting machine it uses; and each voting booth contains a sample ballot. In precincts using punch-card ballots, voters are instructed to punch out the ballot cleanly:

> AFTER VOTING, CHECK YOUR BALLOT CARD TO BE SURE YOUR VOTING SELECTIONS ARE CLEARLY AND CLEANLY PUNCHED AND THERE ARE NO CHIPS LEFT HANGING ON THE BACK OF THE CARD.

. . . No reasonable person would call it "an error in the vote tabulation," . . . when electronic or electromechanical equipment performs precisely in the manner designed, and fails to count those ballots that are not marked in the manner that these voting instructions explicitly and prominently specify. The scheme that the Florida Supreme Court's opinion attributes to the legislature is one in which machines are required to be "capable of correctly counting votes," . . . but which nonetheless regularly produces elections in which legal votes are predictably not tabulated, so that in close elections manual recounts are regularly required. This is of course absurd. The Secretary of State, who is authorized by law to issue binding interpretations of the election code, . . . rejected this peculiar reading of the statutes. . . . The Florida Supreme Court, although it must defer to the Secretary's interpretations, . . . rejected her reasonable interpretation and embraced the peculiar one. . . .

But as we indicated in our remand of the earlier case, in a Presidential election the clearly expressed intent of the legislature must prevail. And there is no basis for reading the Florida statutes as requiring the counting of improperly marked ballots, as an examination of the Florida Supreme Court's textual analysis shows. We will not parse that analysis here, except to note that the principal provision of the election code on which it relied . . . was entirely irrelevant. . . . The State's Attorney General (who was supporting the Gore challenge) confirmed in oral argument here that never before the present election had a manual recount been conducted on the basis of the contention that "undervotes" should have been examined to determine voter intent. . . . For the court to step away from this established practice, prescribed by the Secretary of State, the state official charged by the legislature with "responsibility to . . . [o]btain and maintain uniformity in the application, operation, and interpretation of the election laws," . . . was to depart from the legislative scheme.

III

The scope and nature of the remedy ordered by the Florida Supreme Court jeopardizes the "legislative wish" to take advantage of the safe harbor provided by 3 U.S.C. § 5. . . . December 12, 2000, is the last date for a final determination of the Florida electors that will satisfy § 5. Yet in the late afternoon of December 8th—four days before this deadline—the Supreme Court of Florida ordered recounts of tens of thousands of so-called "undervotes" spread through 64 of the State's 67 counties. This was done in a search for elusive—perhaps delusive—certainty as to the exact count of 6 million votes. But no one claims that these ballots have not previously been tabulated; they were initially read by voting machines at the time of the election, and thereafter reread by virtue of Florida's automatic recount provision. No one claims there was any fraud in the election. The Supreme Court of Florida ordered this additional recount under the provision of the election code giving the circuit judge the authority to provide relief that is "appropriate under such circumstances." . . .

Surely when the Florida Legislature empowered the courts of the State to grant "appropriate" relief, it must have meant relief that would have become final by the cutoff date of 3 U.S.C. § 5. In light of the inevitable legal challenges and ensuing appeals to the Supreme Court of Florida and petitions for certiorari to this Court, the entire recounting process could not possibly be completed by that date. Whereas the majority in the Supreme Court of Florida stated its confidence that "the remaining undervotes in these counties can be [counted] within the required time frame," . . . it made no assertion that the seemingly inevitable appeals could be disposed of in that time. Although the Florida Supreme Court has on occasion taken over a year to resolve disputes over local elections, . . . it has heard and decided the appeals in the present case with great promptness. But the federal deadlines for the Presidential election simply do not permit even such a shortened process. . . .

Given all these factors, and in light of the legislative intent identified by the Florida Supreme Court to bring Florida within the "safe harbor" provision of 3 U.S.C. § 5, the remedy prescribed by the Supreme Court of Florida cannot be deemed an "appropriate" one as of December 8. It significantly departed from the statutory framework in place on November 7, and authorized open-ended further proceedings which could not be completed by December 12, thereby preventing a final determination by that date.

For these reasons, in addition to those given in the per curiam, we would reverse.

Justice Stevens, with whom *Justice Ginsburg* and *Justice Breyer* join, dissenting.

. . . What must underlie petitioners' entire federal assault on the Florida election procedures is an unstated lack of confidence in the impartiality and capacity of the state judges who would make the critical decisions if the vote count were to proceed. Otherwise, their position is wholly without merit. The endorsement of that position by the majority of this Court can only lend credence to the most cynical appraisal of the work of judges throughout the land. It is confidence in the men and women who administer the judicial system that is the true backbone of the rule of law. Time will one day heal the wound to that confidence that will be inflicted by today's decision. One thing, however, is certain. Although we may never know with complete certainty the identity of the winner of this year's Presidential election, the identity of the loser is perfectly clear. It is the Nation's confidence in the judge as an impartial guardian of the rule of law. . . .

Justice Souter, with whom *Justice Breyer* joins and with whom *Justice Stevens* and *Justice Ginsburg* join . . . , dissenting.

The Court should not have reviewed either *Bush v. Palm Beach County Canvassing Bd.* or this case, and should not have stopped Florida's attempt to recount all undervote ballots, . . . by issuing a stay of the Florida Supreme Court's orders during the period of this review. . . . If this Court had allowed the State to follow the course indicated by the opinions of its own Supreme Court, it is entirely possible that there would ultimately have been no issue requiring our review, and political tension could have worked itself out in the Congress following the procedure provided in 3 U.S. C. § 15. The case being before us, however, its resolution by the majority is another erroneous decision. . . .

There are three issues: whether the State Supreme Court's interpretation of the statute providing for a contest of the state election results somehow violates 3 U.S.C. § 5; whether that court's construction of the state statutory provisions governing contests impermissibly changes a state law from what the State's legislature has provided, in violation of Article II, § 1, cl. 2, of the national Constitution; and whether the manner of interpreting markings on disputed ballots failing to cause machines to register votes for President (the undervote ballots) violates the equal protection or due process guaranteed by the Fourteenth Amendment. None of these issues is difficult to describe or to resolve. . . .

The 3 U.S.C. § 5 issue is not serious. That provision sets certain conditions for treating a State's certification of Presidential electors as conclusive in the event that a dispute over recognizing those electors must be resolved in the Congress under 3 U.S.C. § 15. Conclusiveness requires selection under a legal scheme in place before the election, with results determined at least six days before the date set for casting electoral votes. But no State is required to conform to § 5 if it cannot do that (for whatever reason); the sanction for failing to satisfy the conditions of § 5 is simply loss of what has been called its "safe harbor." And even that determination is to be made, if made anywhere, in the Congress. . . .

The second matter here goes to the State Supreme Court's interpretation of certain terms in the state statute governing election "contests," Fla. Stat. § 102.168 (2000); there is no question here about the state court's interpretation of the related provisions dealing with the antecedent process of "protesting" particular vote counts, § 102.166, which was involved in the previous case, *Bush v. Palm Beach County Canvassing Board*. The issue is whether the judgment of the state supreme court has displaced the state legislature's provisions for election contests: is the law as declared by the court different from the provisions made by the legislature, to which the national Constitution commits responsibility for determining how each State's Presidential electors are chosen? . . . Bush does not, of course, claim that any judicial act interpreting a statute of uncertain meaning is enough to displace the legislative provision and violate Article II; statutes require interpretation, which does not without more affect the legislative character of a statute within the meaning of the Constitution. . . . What Bush does argue, as I understand the contention, is that the interpretation of § 102.168 was

so unreasonable as to transcend the accepted bounds of statutory interpretation, to the point of being a nonjudicial act and producing new law untethered to the legislative act in question.

The starting point for evaluating the claim that the Florida Supreme Court's interpretation effectively rewrote § 102.168 must be the language of the provision on which Gore relies to show his right to raise this contest: that the previously certified result in Bush's favor was produced by "rejection of a number of legal votes sufficient to change or place in doubt the result of the election." . . . None of the state court's interpretations is unreasonable to the point of displacing the legislative enactment quoted. . . .

In sum, the interpretations by the Florida court raise no substantial question under Article II. That court engaged in permissible construction in determining that Gore had instituted a contest authorized by the state statute, and it proceeded to direct the trial judge to deal with that contest in the exercise of the discretionary powers generously conferred by Fla. Stat. § 102.168(8) (2000), to "fashion such orders as he or she deems necessary to ensure that each allegation in the complaint is investigated, examined, or checked, to prevent or correct any alleged wrong, and to provide any relief appropriate under such circumstances." . . .

It is only on the third issue before us that there is a meritorious argument for relief, as this Court's Per Curiam opinion recognizes. It is an issue that might well have been dealt with adequately by the Florida courts if the state proceedings had not been interrupted, and if not disposed of at the state level it could have been considered by the Congress in any electoral vote dispute. But because the course of state proceedings has been interrupted, time is short, and the issue is before us, I think it sensible for the Court to address it.

Petitioners have raised an equal protection claim . . . in the charge that unjustifiably disparate standards are applied in different electoral jurisdictions to otherwise identical facts. It is true that the Equal Protection Clause does not forbid the use of a variety of voting mechanisms within a jurisdiction, even though different mechanisms will have different levels of effectiveness in recording voters' intentions; local variety can be justified by concerns about cost, the potential value of innovation, and so on. But evidence in the record here suggests that a different order of disparity obtains under rules for determining a voter's intent that have been applied (and could continue to be applied) to identical types of ballots used in identical brands of machines and exhibiting identical physical characteristics (such as "hanging" or "dimpled" chads). . . . I can conceive of no legitimate state interest served by these differing treatments of the expressions of voters' fundamental rights. The differences appear wholly arbitrary.

In deciding what to do about this, we should take account of the fact that electoral votes are due to be cast in six days. I would therefore remand the case to the courts of Florida with instructions to establish uniform standards for evaluating the several types of ballots that have prompted differing treatments, to be applied within and among counties when passing on such identical ballots in any further recounting (or successive recounting) that the courts might order.

Unlike the majority, I see no warrant for this Court to assume that Florida could not possibly comply with this requirement before the date set for the meeting of electors, December 18. Although one of the dissenting justices of the State Supreme Court estimated that disparate standards potentially affected 170,000 votes, . . . the number at issue is significantly smaller. The 170,000 figure apparently represents all uncounted votes, both undervotes (those for which no Presidential choice was recorded by a machine) and overvotes (those rejected because of votes for more than one candidate). . . . But . . . no showing has been made of legal overvotes uncounted, and counsel for Gore made an uncontradicted representation to the Court that the statewide total of undervotes is about 60,000. . . . To recount these manually would be a tall order, but before this Court stayed the effort to do that the courts of Florida were ready to do their best to get that job done. There is no justification for denying the State the opportunity to try to count all disputed ballots now. . . .

Justice Ginsburg, with whom *Justice Stevens* joins, and with whom *Justice Souter* and *Justice Breyer* join as to Part I, dissenting.

. . . The extraordinary setting of this case has obscured the ordinary principle that dictates its proper resolution: Federal courts defer to state high courts' interpretations of their state's own law. This principle reflects the core of federalism, on which all agree. "The Framers split the atom of sovereignty. It was the genius of their idea that our citizens would have two political capacities, one state and one federal, each protected from incursion by the other. . . . Were the other members of this Court as mindful as they generally are of our system of dual sovereignty, they would affirm the judgment of the Florida Supreme Court. . . .

. . . The Court assumes that time will not permit "orderly judicial review of any disputed matters that might arise." . . . But no one has doubted the good faith and diligence with which Florida election officials, attorneys for all sides of this controversy, and the courts of law

have performed their duties. Notably, the Florida Supreme Court has produced two substantial opinions within 29 hours of oral argument. In sum, the Court's conclusion that a constitutionally adequate recount is impractical is a prophecy the Court's own judgment will not allow to be tested. Such an untested prophecy should not decide the Presidency of the United States. . . .

Justice Breyer, with whom *Justice Stevens* and *Justice Ginsburg* join except as to Part I-A-1, and with whom *Justice Souter* joins as to Part I, dissenting.

The Court was wrong to take this case. It was wrong to grant a stay. It should now vacate that stay and permit the Florida Supreme Court to decide whether the recount should resume. . . .

The political implications of this case for the country are momentous. But the federal legal questions presented, with one exception, are insubstantial. . . .

. . . The majority concludes that the Equal Protection Clause requires that a manual recount be governed not only by the uniform general standard of the "clear intent of the voter," but also by uniform subsidiary standards (for example, a uniform determination whether indented, but not perforated, "undervotes" should count). The opinion points out that the Florida Supreme Court ordered the inclusion of Broward County's undercounted "legal votes" even though those votes included ballots that were not perforated but simply "dimpled," while newly recounted ballots from other counties will likely include only votes determined to be "legal" on the basis of a stricter standard. In light of our previous remand, the Florida Supreme Court may have been reluctant to adopt a more specific standard than that provided for by the legislature for fear of exceeding its authority under Article II. However, since the use of different standards could favor one or the other of the candidates, since time was, and is, too short to permit the lower courts to iron out significant differences through ordinary judicial review, and since the relevant distinction was embodied in the order of the State's highest court, I agree that, in these very special circumstances, basic principles of fairness may well have counseled the adoption of a uniform standard to address the problem. . . .

Nonetheless, there is no justification for the majority's remedy, which is simply to reverse the lower court and halt the recount entirely. An appropriate remedy would be, instead, to remand this case with instructions that, even at this late date, would permit the Florida Supreme Court to require recounting all undercounted votes in Florida, including those from Broward, Volusia, Palm Beach, and Miami-Dade Counties, whether or not previously recounted prior to the end of the protest period, and to do so in accordance with a single-uniform substandard. . . .

By halting the manual recount, and thus ensuring that the uncounted legal votes will not be counted under any standard, this Court crafts a remedy out of proportion to the asserted harm. And that remedy harms the very fairness interests the Court is attempting to protect.

. . . [I]n a system that allows counties to use different types of voting systems, voters already arrive at the polls with an unequal chance that their votes will be counted. I do not see how the fact that this results from counties' selection of different voting machines rather than a court order makes the outcome any more fair. Nor do I understand why the Florida Supreme Court's recount order, which helps to redress this inequity, must be entirely prohibited based on a deficiency that could easily be remedied. . . .

Despite the reminder that this case involves "an election for the President of the United States," . . . no preeminent legal concern, or practical concern related to legal questions, required this Court to hear this case, let alone to issue a stay that stopped Florida's recount process in its tracks. With one exception, petitioners' claims do not ask us to vindicate a constitutional provision designed to protect a basic human right. . . . Petitioners invoke fundamental fairness, namely, the need for procedural fairness, including finality. But with the one "equal protection" exception, they rely upon law that focuses, not upon that basic need, but upon the constitutional allocation of power. Respondents invoke a competing fundamental consideration—the need to determine the voter's true intent. But they look to state law, not to federal constitutional law, to protect that interest. Neither side claims electoral fraud, dishonesty, or the like. And the more fundamental equal protection claim might have been left to the state court to resolve if and when it was discovered to have mattered. It could still be resolved through a remand conditioned upon issuance of a uniform standard; it does not require reversing the Florida Supreme Court.

Of course, the selection of the President is of fundamental national importance. But that importance is political, not legal. And this Court should resist the temptation unnecessarily to resolve tangential legal disputes, where doing so threatens to determine the outcome of the election.

The Constitution and federal statutes themselves make clear that restraint is appropriate. They set forth a road map of how to resolve disputes about electors, even after an election as close as this one. That road map foresees resolution of electoral disputes by state courts. . . . But it nowhere provides for involvement by the United States Supreme Court. . . .

THE CONSTITUTION OF THE UNITED STATES OF AMERICA

We the People of the United States, in Order to form a more perfect Union, establish Justice, insure domestic Tranquility, provide for the common defence, promote the general Welfare, and secure the Blessings of Liberty to ourselves and our Posterity, do ordain and establish this Constitution for the United States of America.

Article I

Section 1

All legislative Powers herein granted shall be vested in a Congress of the United States, which shall consist of a Senate and House of Representatives.

Section 2

(1) The House of Representatives shall be composed of Members chosen every second Year by the People of the several States, and the Electors in each State shall have the Qualifications requisite for Electors of the most numerous Branch of the State Legislature.

(2) No Person shall be a Representative who shall not have attained to the Age of twenty-five Years, and been seven Years a Citizen of the United States, and who shall not, when elected, be an Inhabitant of that State in which he shall be chosen.

(3) Representatives and direct Taxes shall be apportioned among the several States which may be included within this Union, according to their respective Numbers, which shall be determined by adding to the whole Number of free Persons, including those bound to Service for a Term of Years, and excluding Indians not taxed, three fifths of all other Persons. The actual Enumeration shall be made within three Years after the first Meeting of the Congress of the United States, and within every subsequent Term of ten Years, in such Manner as they shall by Law direct. The Number of Representatives shall not exceed one for every thirty Thousand, but each State shall have at Least one Representative; and until such enumeration shall be made, the State of New Hampshire shall be entitled to chuse three, Massachusetts eight, Rhode Island and Providence Plantations one, Connecticut five, New York six, New Jersey four, Pennsylvania eight, Delaware one, Maryland six, Virginia ten, North Carolina five, South Carolina five, and Georgia three.

(4) When vacancies happen in the Representation from any State, the Executive Authority thereof shall issue Writs of Election to fill such Vacancies.

(5) The House of Representatives shall chuse their Speaker and other Officers; and shall have the sole Power of Impeachment.

Section 3

(1) The Senate of the United States shall be composed of two Senators from each State, chosen by the Legislature thereof, for six Years; and each Senator shall have one Vote.

(2) Immediately after they shall be assembled in Consequence of the first Election, they shall be divided as equally as may be into three Classes. The Seats of the Senators of the first Class shall be vacated at the Expiration of the second Year, of the second Class at the Expiration of the fourth Year, and of the third Class at the Expiration of the sixth Year, so that one third may be chosen every second Year; and if Vacancies happen by Resignation, or otherwise, during the Recess of the Legislature of any State, the Executive thereof may make temporary Appointments until the next Meeting of the Legislature, which shall then fill such Vacancies.

(3) No Person shall be a Senator who shall not have attained to the Age of thirty Years, and been nine Years a Citizen of the United States, and who shall not, when elected, be an Inhabitant of that State for which he shall be chosen.

(4) The Vice President of the United States shall be President of the Senate, but shall have no Vote, unless they be equally divided.

(5) The Senate shall chuse their other Officers, and also a President pro tempore, in the Absence of the Vice President, or when he shall exercise the Office of the President of the United States.

(6) The Senate shall have the sole Power to try all Impeachments. When sitting for that Purpose, they shall be on Oath or Affirmation. When the President of the United States is tried, the Chief Justice shall preside: And no Person shall be convicted without the Concurrence of two thirds of the Members present.

(7) Judgment in Cases of Impeachment shall not extend further than to removal from Office, and disqualification to hold and enjoy any Office of honor, Trust or Profit under the United States: but the Party convicted shall nevertheless be liable and subject to Indictment, Trial, Judgment and Punishment, according to Law.

Section 4

(1) The Times, Places and Manner of holding Elections for Senators and Representatives, shall be prescribed in each State

by the Legislature thereof; but the Congress may at any time by Law make or alter such Regulations, except as to the Places of chusing Senators.

(2) The Congress shall assemble at least once in every Year, and such Meeting shall be on the first Monday in December, unless they shall by Law appoint a different Day.

Section 5

(1) Each House shall be the Judge of the Elections, Returns and Qualifications of its own Members, and a Majority of each shall constitute a Quorum to do Business; but a smaller Number may adjourn from day to day, and may be authorized to compel the Attendance of absent Members, in such Manner, and under such Penalties as each House may provide.

(2) Each House may determine the Rules of its Proceedings, punish its Members for disorderly Behaviour, and, with the Concurrence of two thirds, expel a Member.

(3) Each House shall keep a Journal of its Proceedings, and from time to time publish the same, excepting such Parts as may in their Judgment require Secrecy; and the Yeas and Nays of the Members of either House on any question shall, at the Desire of one fifth of those Present, be entered on the Journal.

(4) Neither House, during the Session of Congress, shall, without the Consent of the other, adjourn for more than three days, nor to any other Place than that in which the two Houses shall be sitting.

Section 6

(1) The Senators and Representatives shall receive a Compensation for their Services, to be ascertained by Law, and paid out of the Treasury of the United States. They shall in all Cases, except Treason, Felony and Breach of the Peace, be privileged from Arrest during their Attendance at the Session of their respective Houses, and in going to and returning from the same; and for any Speech or Debate in either House, they shall not be questioned in any other Place.

(2) No Senator or Representative shall, during the Time for which he was elected, be appointed to any civil Office under the Authority of the United States, which shall have been created, or the Emoluments whereof shall have been increased during such time; and no Person holding any Office under the United States, shall be a Member of either House during his Continuance in Office.

Section 7

(1) All Bills for raising Revenue shall originate in the House of Representatives; but the Senate may propose or concur with Amendments as on other Bills.

(2) Every Bill which shall have passed the House of Representatives and the Senate, shall, before it become a Law, be presented to the President of the United States; If he approve he shall sign it, but if not he shall return it, with his Objections to that House in which it shall have originated, who shall enter the Objections at large on their Journal, and proceed to reconsider it. If after such Reconsideration two thirds of that House shall agree to pass the Bill, it shall be sent, together with the Objections, to the other House, by which it shall likewise be reconsidered, and if approved by two thirds of that House, it shall become a Law. But in all such Cases the Votes of both Houses shall be determined by Yeas and Nays, and the Names of the Persons voting for and against the Bill shall be entered on the Journal of each House respectively. If any Bill shall not be returned by the President within ten Days (Sunday excepted) after it shall have been presented to him, the Same shall be a Law, in like Manner as if he had signed it, unless the Congress by their Adjournment prevent its Return, in which Case it shall not be a Law.

(3) Every Order, Resolution, or Vote to which the Concurrence of the Senate and House of Representatives may be necessary (except on a question of Adjournment) shall be presented to the President of the United States; and before the Same shall take Effect, shall be approved by him, or being disapproved by him, shall be repassed by two thirds of the Senate and House of Representatives, according to the Rules and Limitations prescribed in the Case of a Bill.

Section 8

(1) The Congress shall have Power To lay and collect Taxes, Duties, Imposts and Excises, to pay the Debts and provide for the common Defence and general Welfare of the United States; but all Duties, Imposts and Excises shall be uniform throughout the United States;

(2) To borrow Money on the credit of the United States;

(3) To regulate Commerce with foreign Nations, and among the several States, and with the Indian Tribes;

(4) To establish an uniform Rule of Naturalization, and uniform Laws on the subject of Bankruptcies throughout the United States;

(5) To coin Money, regulate the Value thereof, and of foreign Coin, and to fix the Standard of Weights and Measures;

(6) To provide for the Punishment of counterfeiting the Securities and current Coin of the United States;

(7) To establish Post Offices and post Roads;

(8) To promote the Progress of Science and useful Arts, by securing for limited Times to Authors and Inventors the exclusive Right to their respective Writings and Discoveries;

(9) To constitute Tribunals inferior to the supreme Court;

(10) To define and punish Piracies and Felonies committed on the high Seas, and Offenses against the Law of Nations;

(11) To declare War, grant Letters of Marque and Reprisal, and make Rules concerning Captures on Land and Water;

(12) To raise and support Armies, but no Appropriation of Money to that Use shall be for a longer Term than two Years;

(13) To provide and maintain a Navy;

(14) To make Rules for the Government and Regulation of the land and naval Forces;

(15) To provide for calling forth the Militia to execute the Laws of the Union, suppress Insurrections and repel Invasions;

(16) To provide for organizing, arming, and disciplining the Militia, and for governing such Part of them as may be employed in the Service of the United States, reserving to the States respectively, the Appointment of the Officers, and the Authority of training the Militia according to the discipline prescribed by Congress;

(17) To exercise exclusive Legislation in all Cases whatsoever, over such District (not exceeding ten Miles square) as may, by Cession of particular States, and the Acceptance of Congress, become the Seat of the Government of the United States, and to exercise like Authority over all Places purchased by the Consent of the Legislature of the State in which the Same shall be, for the Erection of Forts, Magazines, Arsenals, dock-Yards, and other needful Buildings;—And

(18) To make all Laws which shall be necessary and proper for carrying into Execution the foregoing Powers, and all other Powers vested by this Constitution in the Government of the United States, or in any Department or Officer thereof.

Section 9

(1) The Migration or Importation of such Persons as any of the States now existing shall think proper to admit, shall not be prohibited by the Congress prior to the Year one thousand eight hundred and eight, but a Tax or Duty may be imposed on such Importation, not exceeding ten dollars for each Person.

(2) The Privilege of the Writ of Habeas Corpus shall not be suspended unless when in Cases of Rebellion or Invasion the public Safety may require it.

(3) No Bill of Attainder or ex post facto Law shall be passed.

(4) No Capitation, or other direct, Tax shall be laid, unless in Proportion to the Census or Enumeration herein before directed to be taken.

(5) No Tax or Duty shall be laid on Articles exported from any State.

(6) No Preference shall be given by any Regulation of Commerce or Revenue to the Ports of one State over those of another; nor shall Vessels bound to, or from, one State, be obliged to enter, clear or pay Duties in another.

(7) No Money shall be drawn from the Treasury, but in Consequence of Appropriations made by Law; and a regular Statement and Account of the Receipts and Expenditures of all public Money shall be published from time to time.

(8) No Title of Nobility shall be granted by the United States: And no Person holding any Office of Profit or Trust under them, shall, without the Consent of the Congress, accept of any present, Emolument, Office, or Title, of any kind whatever, from any King, Prince or foreign State.

Section 10

(1) No State shall enter into any Treaty, Alliance, or Confederation; grant Letters of Marque and Reprisal; coin Money; emit Bills of Credit; make any Thing but gold and silver Coin a Tender in Payment of Debts; pass any Bill of Attainder, ex post facto Law, or Law impairing the Obligation of Contracts, or grant any Title of Nobility.

(2) No State shall, without the Consent of Congress, lay any Imposts or Duties on Imports or Exports, except what may be absolutely necessary for executing its inspection Laws: and the net Produce of all Duties and Imposts, laid by any State on Imports or Exports, shall be for the Use of the Treasury of the United States; and all such Laws shall be subject to the Revision and Control of the Congress.

(3) No State shall, without the Consent of Congress, lay any Duty of Tonnage, keep Troops, or Ships of War in time of Peace, enter into any Agreement or Compact with another State, or with a foreign Power, or engage in War, unless actually invaded, or in such imminent Danger as will not admit of delay.

Article II

Section 1

(1) The executive Power shall be vested in a President of the United States of America. He shall hold his Office during the Term of four Years, and, together with the Vice President, chosen for the same Term, be elected, as follows:

(2) Each State shall appoint, in such Manner as the Legislature thereof may direct, a Number of Electors, equal to the whole Number of Senators and Representatives to which the State may be entitled in the Congress: but no Senator or Representative, or Person holding an Office of Trust or Profit under the United States, shall be appointed an Elector.

(3) The Electors shall meet in their respective States, and vote by Ballot for two Persons, of whom one at least shall not be an Inhabitant of the same State with themselves. And they shall make a List of all the Persons voted for, and of the Number of Votes for each; which List they shall sign and certify, and transmit sealed to the Seat of the Government of the United States, directed to the President of the Senate. The President of the Senate shall, in the presence of the Senate and House of Representatives, open all the Certificates, and the Votes shall then be counted. The Person having the greatest Number of Votes shall be the President, if such Number be a Majority of the whole Number of Electors appointed; and if there be more than one who have such Majority, and have an equal Number of Votes, then the House of Representatives shall immediately chuse by Ballot one of them for President; and if no Person have a Majority, then from the five highest on the List the said House shall in like Manner chuse the President. But in chusing the President, the Votes shall be taken by States, the Representation from each State having one Vote; a quorum for this Purpose shall consist of a Member or Members from two thirds of the States, and a Majority of all the States shall be necessary to a Choice. In every Case, after the Choice of the President, the Person having the greatest Number of Votes of the Electors shall be the Vice President. But if there should remain two or more who have equal Votes, the Senate shall chuse from them by Ballot the Vice President.

(4) The Congress may determine the Time of chusing the Electors, and the Day on which they shall give their Votes; which Day shall be the same throughout the United States.

(5) No Person except a natural born Citizen, or a Citizen of the United States, at the time of the Adoption of this Constitution, shall be eligible to the Office of President; neither shall any Person be eligible to that Office who shall not have attained to the Age of thirty five Years, and been fourteen Years a Resident within the United States.

(6) In Case of the Removal of the President from Office, or of his Death, Resignation, or Inability to discharge the Powers and Duties of the said Office, the Same shall devolve on the Vice President, and the Congress may by Law provide for the Case of Removal, Death, Resignation or Inability, both of the President and Vice President, declaring what Officer shall then act as President, and such Officer shall act accordingly, until the Disability be removed, or a President shall be elected.

(7) The President shall, at stated Times, receive for his Services, a Compensation, which shall neither be increased nor diminished during the Period for which he shall have been elected, and he shall not receive within that Period any other Emolument from the United States, or any of them.

(8) Before he enter on the Execution of his Office, he shall take the following Oath or Affirmation:—"I do solemnly swear (or affirm) that I will faithfully execute the Office of President of the United States, and will to the best of my Ability, preserve, protect and defend the Constitution of the United States."

Section 2

(1) The President shall be Commander in Chief of the Army and Navy of the United States, and of the Militia of the several States, when called into the actual Service of the United States; he may require the Opinion, in writing, of the principal Officer in each of the executive Departments, upon any Subject relating to the Duties of their respective Offices, and he shall have Power to grant Reprieves and Pardons for Offenses against the United States, except in Cases of Impeachment.

(2) He shall have Power, by and with the Advice and Consent of the Senate, to make Treaties, provided two thirds of the Senators present concur; and he shall nominate, and by and with the Advice and Consent of the Senate, shall appoint Ambassadors, other public Ministers and Consuls, Judges of the supreme Court, and all other Officers of the United States, whose Appointments are not herein otherwise provided for, and which shall be established by Law: but the Congress may by Law vest the Appointment of such inferior Officers, as they think proper, in the President alone, in the Courts of Law, or in the Heads of Departments.

(3) The President shall have Power to fill up all Vacancies that may happen during the Recess of the Senate, by granting Commissions which shall expire at the End of their next Session.

Section 3

He shall from time to time give to the Congress Information of the State of the Union, and recommend to their Consideration such Measures as he shall judge necessary and expedient; he may, on extraordinary Occasions, convene both Houses, or either of them, and in Case of Disagreement between them, with Respect to the Time of Adjournment, he may adjourn them to such Time as he shall think proper; he shall receive Ambassadors and other public Ministers; he shall take Care that the Laws be faithfully executed, and shall Commission all the Officers of the United States.

Section 4

The President, Vice President and all Civil Officers of the United States, shall be removed from Office on Impeachment for, and Conviction of, Treason, Bribery, or other high Crimes and Misdemeanors.

Article III

Section 1

The judicial Power of the United States, shall be vested in one supreme Court, and in such inferior Courts as the Congress may from time to time ordain and establish. The Judges, both of the supreme and inferior Courts, shall hold their Offices during good Behaviour, and shall, at stated Times, receive for their Services, a Compensation, which shall not be diminished during their Continuance in Office.

Section 2

(1) The judicial Power shall extend to all Cases, in Law and Equity, arising under this Constitution, the Laws of the United States, and Treaties made, or which shall be made, under their Authority;—to all Cases affecting Ambassadors, other public Ministers and Consuls;—to all Cases of admiralty and maritime Jurisdiction;—to Controversies to which the United States shall be a Party;—to Controversies between two or more States;—between a State and Citizens of another State;—between Citizens of different States;—between Citizens of the same State claiming Lands under Grants of different States, and between a State, or the Citizens thereof, and foreign States, Citizens or Subjects.

(2) In all Cases affecting Ambassadors, other public Ministers and Consuls, and those in which a State shall be Party, the supreme Court shall have original Jurisdiction. In all the other Cases before mentioned, the supreme Court shall have appellate Jurisdiction, both as to Law and Fact, with such Exceptions, and under such Regulations as the Congress shall make.

(3) The Trial of all Crimes, except in Cases of Impeachment, shall be by Jury; and such Trial shall be held in the State where the said Crimes shall have been committed; but when not committed within any State, the Trial shall be at such Place or Places as the Congress may by Law have directed.

Section 3

(1) Treason against the United States, shall consist only in levying War against them, or in adhering to their Enemies, giving them Aid and Comfort. No Person shall be convicted of Treason unless on the Testimony of two Witnesses to the same overt Act, or on Confession in open Court.

(2) The Congress shall have Power to declare the Punishment of Treason, but no Attainder of Treason shall work Corruption of Blood, or Forfeiture except during the Life of the Person attainted.

Article IV

Section 1

Full Faith and Credit shall be given in each State to the public Acts, Records, and judicial Proceedings of every other State. And the Congress may by general Laws prescribe the Manner in which such Acts, Records and Proceedings shall be proved, and the Effect thereof.

Section 2

(1) The Citizens of each State shall be entitled to all privileges and Immunities of Citizens in the several States.

(2) A Person charged in any State with Treason, Felony, or other Crime, who shall flee from Justice, and be found in another State, shall on Demand of the executive Authority of the State from which he fled, be delivered up, to be removed to the State having Jurisdiction of the Crime.

(3) No Person held to Service of Labour in one State, under the Laws thereof, escaping into another, shall, in Consequence of any Law or Regulation therein, be discharged from such Service or Labour, but shall be delivered up on Claim of the Party to whom such Service or Labour may be due.

Section 3

(1) New States may be admitted by the Congress into this Union; but no new State shall be formed or erected within the Jurisdiction of any other State; nor any State be formed by the Junction of two or more States, or Parts of States, without the Consent of the Legislatures of the States concerned as well as of the Congress.

(2) The Congress shall have power to dispose of and make all needful Rules and Regulations respecting the Territory or other Property belonging to the United States; and nothing in this Constitution shall be so construed as to Prejudice any Claims of the United States, or of any particular State.

Section 4

The United States shall guarantee to every State in this Union a Republican Form of Government, and shall protect each of them against Invasion; and on Application of the Legislature, or of the Executive (when the Legislature cannot be convened) against domestic Violence.

Article V

The Congress, whenever two thirds of both Houses shall deem it necessary, shall propose Amendments to this Constitution, or, on the Application of the Legislatures of two thirds of the several States, shall call a Convention for proposing Amendments, which, in either Case, shall be valid to all Intents and Purposes, as Part of this Constitution, when ratified by the Legislatures of three fourths of the several States, or by Conventions in three fourths thereof, as the one or the other Mode of Ratification may be proposed by the Congress; Provided that no Amendment which may be made prior to the Year One thousand eight hundred and eight shall in any Manner affect the first and fourth Clauses in the Ninth Section of the first Article; and that no State, without its Consent, shall be deprived of its equal Suffrage in the Senate.

Article VI

(1) All Debts contracted and Engagements entered into, before the Adoption of this Constitution, shall be as valid against the United States under this Constitution, as under the Confederation.

(2) This Constitution, and the Laws of the United States which shall be made in Pursuance thereof; and all Treaties made, or which shall be made, under the Authority of the United States, shall be the supreme Law of the Land; and the Judges in every State shall be bound thereby, any Thing in the Constitution or Laws of any State to the Contrary notwithstanding.

(3) The Senators and Representatives before mentioned, and the Members of the several State Legislatures, and all executive and judicial Officers, both of the United States and of the several States, shall be bound by Oath or Affirmation, to support this Constitution; but no religious Test shall ever be required as a Qualification to any Office or public Trust under the United States.

Article VII

The Ratification of the Conventions of nine States, shall be sufficient for the Establishment of this Constitution between the States so ratifying the Same.

Articles in Addition to, and Amendment of, the Constitution of the United States of America, Proposed by Congress, and Ratified by the Several States, Pursuant to the Fifth Article of the Original Constitution

Amendment I (1791)

Congress shall make no law respecting an establishment of religion, or prohibiting the free exercise thereof; or abridging the freedom of speech, or of the press; or the right of the people peaceably to assemble, and to petition the Government for a redress of grievances.

Amendment II (1791)

A well regulated Militia, being necessary to the security of a free State, the right of the people to keep and bear Arms, shall not be infringed.

Amendment III (1791)

No Soldier shall, in time of peace be quartered in any house, without the consent of the Owner, nor in time of war, but in a manner to be prescribed by law.

Amendment IV (1791)

The right of the people to be secure in their persons, houses, papers, and effects, against unreasonable searches and seizures, shall not be violated, and no Warrants shall issue, but upon probable cause, supported by Oath or affirmation, and particularly describing the place to be searched, and the persons or things to be seized.

Amendment V (1791)

No person shall be held to answer for a capital, or otherwise infamous crime, unless on a presentment or indictment of a Grand Jury, except in cases arising in the land or naval forces, or in the Militia, when in actual service in time of War or public danger; nor shall any person be subject for the same offence to be twice put in jeopardy of life or limb; nor shall be compelled in any criminal case to be a witness against himself, nor be deprived of life, liberty, or property, without due process of law; nor shall private property be taken for public use, without just compensation.

Amendment VI (1791)

In all criminal prosecutions, the accused shall enjoy the right to a speedy and public trial, by an impartial jury of the State and district wherein the crime shall have been committed, which district shall have been previously ascertained by law, and to be informed of the nature and cause of the accusation; to be confronted with the witnesses against him; to have compulsory process for obtaining witnesses in his favor, and to have the Assistance of Counsel for his defence.

Amendment VII (1791)

In Suits at common law, where the value in controversy shall exceed twenty dollars, the right of trial by jury shall be preserved, and no fact tried by a jury, shall be otherwise reexamined in any Court of the United States, than according to the rules of the common law.

Amendment VIII (1791)

Excessive bail shall not be required, nor excessive fines imposed, nor cruel and unusual punishments inflicted.

Amendment IX (1791)

The enumeration in the Constitution, of certain rights, shall not be construed to deny or disparage others retained by the people.

Amendment X (1791)

The powers not delegated to the United States by the Constitution, nor prohibited by it to the States, are reserved to the States respectively, or to the people.

Amendment XI (1798)

The Judicial power of the United States shall not be construed to extend to any suit in law or equity, commenced or prosecuted against one of the United States by Citizens of another State, or by Citizens or Subjects of any Foreign State.

Amendment XII (1804)

The Electors shall meet in their respective states and vote by ballot for President and Vice-President, one of whom, at least, shall not be an inhabitant of the same state with themselves; they shall name in their ballots the person voted for as President, and in distinct ballots the person voted for as Vice-President, and they shall make distinct lists of all persons voted for as President, and of all persons voted for as Vice-President, and of the number of votes for each, which lists they shall sign and certify, and transmit sealed to the seat of the government of the United States, directed to the President of the Senate;—The President of the Senate shall, in the presence of the Senate and House of Representatives, open all the certificates and the votes shall then be counted;—The person having the greatest number of votes for President, shall be the President, if such number be a majority of the whole number of Electors appointed; and if no person have such majority, then from the persons having the highest numbers not exceeding three on the list of those voted for as President, the House of Representatives shall choose immediately, by ballot, the President. But in choosing the President, the votes shall be taken by states, the representation from each state having one vote; a quorum for this purpose shall consist of a member or members from two-thirds of the states, and a majority of all the states shall be necessary to a choice. And if the House of Representatives shall not choose a President whenever the right of choice shall devolve upon them, before the fourth day of March next following, then the Vice-President shall act as President, as in the case of the death or other constitutional disability of the President—The person having the greatest number of votes as Vice-President, shall be the Vice-President, if such number be a majority of the whole number of Electors appointed, and if no person have a majority, then from the two highest numbers on the list, the Senate shall choose the Vice-President; a quorum for the purpose shall consist of two-thirds of the whole number of Senators, and a majority of the whole number shall be necessary to a choice. But no person constitutionally ineligible to the office of President shall be eligible to that of Vice-President of the United States.

Amendment XIII (1865)

Section 1

Neither slavery nor involuntary servitude, except as a punishment for crime whereof the party shall have been duly convicted, shall exist within the United States, or any place subject to their jurisdiction.

Section 2

Congress shall have power to enforce this article by appropriate legislation.

Amendment XIV (1868)

Section 1

All persons born or naturalized in the United States and subject to the jurisdiction thereof, are citizens of the United States and of the State wherein they reside. No State shall make or enforce any law which shall abridge the privileges or immunities of citizens of the United States; nor shall any State deprive any person of life, liberty, or property, without due process of law; nor deny to any person within its jurisdiction the equal protection of the laws.

Section 2

Representatives shall be apportioned among the several States according to their respective numbers, counting the whole number of persons in each State, excluding Indians not taxed. But when the right to vote at any election for the choice of electors for President and Vice-President of the United States, Representatives in Congress, the Executive and Judicial officers of a State, or the members of the Legislature thereof, is denied to any of the male inhabitants of such State, being twenty-one years of age, and citizens of the United States, or in any way abridged, except for participation in rebellion, or other crime, the basis of representation therein shall be reduced in the proportion which the number of such male citizens shall bear to the whole number of male citizens twenty-one years of age in such State.

Section 3

No person shall be a Senator or Representative in Congress, or elector of President and Vice-President, or hold any office, civil or military, under the United States, or under any State, who, having previously taken an oath, as a member of Congress, or as an officer of the United States, or as a member of any State legislature, or as an executive or judicial officer of any State, to support the Constitution of the United States, shall have engaged in insurrection or rebellion against the same, or given aid or comfort to the enemies thereof. But Congress may by a vote of two-thirds of each House, remove such disability.

Section 4

The validity of the public debt of the United States, authorized by law, including debts incurred for payment of pensions and bounties for services in suppressing insurrection or rebellion, shall not be questioned. But neither the United States nor any State shall assume or pay any debt or obligation incurred in aid of insurrection or rebellion against the United States, or any claim for the loss or emancipation of any slave; but all such debts, obligations and claims shall be held illegal and void.

Section 5

The Congress shall have power to enforce, by appropriate legislation, the provisions of this article.

Amendment XV (1870)

Section 1

The right of citizens of the United States to vote shall not be denied or abridged by the United States or by any State on account of race, color, or previous condition of servitude.

Section 2

The Congress shall have power to enforce this article by appropriate legislation.

Amendment XVI (1913)

The Congress shall have power to lay and collect taxes on incomes, from whatever source derived, without apportionment among the several States, and without regard to any census or enumeration.

Amendment XVII (1913)

The Senate of the United States shall be composed of two Senators from each State, elected by the people thereof, for six years; and each Senator shall have one vote. The electors in each State shall have the qualifications requisite for electors of the most numerous branch of the State legislatures.

When vacancies happen in the representation of any State in the Senate, the executive authority of such State shall issue writs of election to fill such vacancies: *Provided,* That the legislature of any State may empower the executive thereof to make temporary appointments until the people fill the vacancies by election as the legislature may direct.

This amendment shall not be so construed as to affect the election or term of any Senator chosen before it becomes valid as part of the Constitution.

Amendment XVIII (1919)

Section 1

After one year from the ratification of this article the manufacture, sale, or transportation of intoxicating liquors within, the importation thereof into, or the exportation thereof from the United States and all territory subject to the jurisdiction thereof for beverage purposes is hereby prohibited.

Section 2

The Congress and the several States shall have concurrent power to enforce this article by appropriate legislation.

Section 3

This article shall be inoperative unless it shall have been ratified as an amendment to the Constitution by the legislatures of the several States, as provided in the Constitution, within seven years from the date of the submission hereof to the States by the Congress.

Amendment XIX (1920)

The right of citizens of the United States to vote shall not be denied or abridged by the United States or by any State on account of sex.

Congress shall have power to enforce this article by appropriate legislation.

Amendment XX (1933)

Section 1

The terms of the President and Vice President shall end at noon on the 20th day of January, and the terms of Senators and Representatives at noon on the 3d day of January, of the years in which such terms would have ended if this article had not been ratified; and the terms of their successors shall then begin.

Section 2

The Congress shall assemble at least once in every year, and such meeting shall begin at noon on the 3d day of January, unless they shall by law appoint a different day.

Section 3

If, at the time fixed for the beginning of the term of the President, the President elect shall have died, the Vice President elect shall become President. If a President shall not have been chosen before the time fixed for the beginning of his term, or if the President elect shall have failed to qualify, then the Vice President elect shall act as President until a President shall have qualified; and the Congress may by law provide for the case wherein neither a President elect nor a Vice President elect shall have qualified, declaring who shall then act as President, or the manner in which one who is to act shall be selected, and such person shall act accordingly until a President or Vice President shall have qualified.

Section 4

The Congress may by law provide for the case of the death of any of the persons from whom the House of Representatives may choose a President whenever the right of choice shall have devolved upon them, and for the case of the death of any of the persons from whom the Senate may choose a Vice President whenever the right of choice shall have devolved upon them.

Section 5

Sections 1 and 2 shall take effect on the 15th day of October following the ratification of this article.

Section 6

This article shall be inoperative unless it shall have been ratified as an amendment to the Constitution by the legislatures of three-fourths of the several States within seven years from the date of its submission.

Amendment XXI (1933)

Section 1

The eighteenth article of amendment to the Constitution of the United States is hereby repealed.

Section 2

The transportation or importation into any State, Territory or possession of the United States for delivery or use therein of intoxicating liquors, in violation of the laws thereof, is hereby prohibited.

Section 3

This article shall be inoperative unless it shall have been ratified as an amendment to the Constitution by conventions in the several States, as provided in the Constitution, within seven years from the date of the submission hereof to the States by the Congress.

Amendment XXII (1951)

Section 1

No person shall be elected to the office of the President more than twice, and no person who has held the office of President, or acted as President, for more than two years of a term to which some other person was elected President shall be elected to the office of the President more than once. But this Article shall not apply to any person holding the office of President when this Article was proposed by the Congress, and shall not prevent any person who may be holding the office of President, or acting as

President, during the term within which this Article becomes operative from holding the office of President or acting as President during the remainder of such term.

Section 2

This Article shall be inoperative unless it shall have been ratified as an amendment to the Constitution by the legislatures of three-fourths of the several States within seven years from the date of its submission to the States by the Congress.

Amendment XXIII (1961)

Section 1

The District constituting the seat of Government of the United States shall appoint in such manner as the Congress may direct:

A number of electors of President and Vice President equal to the whole number of Senators and Representatives in Congress to which the District would be entitled if it were a State, but in no event more than the least populous State; they shall be in addition to those appointed by the States, but they shall be considered, for the purposes of the election of President and Vice President, to be electors appointed by a State; and they shall meet in the District and perform such duties as provided by the twelfth article of amendment.

Section 2

The Congress shall have power to enforce this article by appropriate legislation.

Amendment XXIV (1964)

Section 1

The right of citizens of the United States to vote in any primary or other election for President or Vice President, for electors for President or Vice President, or for Senator or Representative in Congress, shall not be denied or abridged by the United States or any State by reason of failure to pay any poll tax or other tax.

Section 2

The Congress shall have power to enforce this article by appropriate legislation.

Amendment XXV (1967)

Section 1

In case of the removal of the President from office or of his death or resignation, the Vice President shall become President.

Section 2

Whenever there is a vacancy in the office of the Vice President, the President shall nominate a Vice President who shall take office upon confirmation by a majority vote of both Houses of Congress.

Section 3

Whenever the President transmits to the President pro tempore of the Senate and the Speaker of the House of Representatives his written declaration that he is unable to discharge the powers and duties of his office, and until he transmits to them a written declaration to the contrary, such powers and duties shall be discharged by the Vice President as Acting President.

Section 4

Whenever the Vice President and a majority of either the principal officers of the executive departments or of such other body as Congress may by law provide, transmit to the President pro tempore of the Senate and the Speaker of the House of Representatives their written declaration that the President is unable to discharge the powers and duties of his office, the Vice President shall immediately assume the powers and duties of the office as Acting President.

Thereafter, when the President transmits to the President pro tempore of the Senate and the Speaker of the House of Representatives his written declaration that no inability exists, he shall resume the powers and duties of his office unless the Vice President and a majority of either the principal officers of the executive department or of such other body as Congress may by law provide, transmit within four days to the President pro tempore of the Senate and the Speaker of the House of Representatives their written declaration that the President is unable to discharge the powers and duties of his office. Thereupon Congress shall decide the issue, assembling within forty-eight hours for that purpose if not in session. If the Congress, within twenty-one days after receipt of the latter written declaration, or, if Congress is not in session, within twenty-one days after Congress is required to assemble, determines by two-thirds vote of both Houses that the President is unable to discharge the powers and duties of his office, the Vice President shall continue to discharge the same as Acting President; otherwise, the President shall resume the powers and duties of his office.

Amendment XXVI (1971)

Section 1

The right of citizens of the United States, who are eighteen years of age or older, to vote shall not be denied or abridged by the United States or by any State on account of age.

Section 2

The Congress shall have power to enforce this article by appropriate legislation.

Amendment XXVII (1992)

No law, varying the compensation for the services of the Senators and Representatives, shall take effect, until an election of Representatives shall have intervened.

Chronology of Justices of the United States Supreme Court

Year of Court as Constituted	Chief Justice	Associate Justices							
1789	Jay	Rutledge, J.	Cushing	Wilson	Blair				
1790–91	Jay	Rutledge, J.	Cushing	Wilson	Blair	Iredell			
1792	Jay	Johnson, T.	Cushing	Wilson	Blair	Iredell			
1793–94	Jay	Paterson	Cushing	Wilson	Blair	Iredell			
1795	Rutledge, J.	Paterson	Cushing	Wilson	Blair	Iredell			
1796–97	Ellsworth	Paterson	Cushing	Wilson	Chase, S.	Iredell			
1798–99	Ellsworth	Paterson	Cushing	Washington	Chase, S.	Iredell			
1800	Ellsworth	Paterson	Cushing	Washington	Chase, S.	Moore			
1801–03	Marshall, J.	Paterson	Cushing	Washington	Chase, S.	Moore			
1804–05	Marshall, J.	Paterson	Cushing	Washington	Chase, S.	Johnson, W.			
1806	Marshall, J.	Livingston	Cushing	Washington	Chase, S.	Johnson, W.			
1807–10	Marshall, J.	Livingston	Cushing	Washington	Chase, S.	Johnson, W.	Todd		
1811–12	Marshall, J.	Livingston	Story	Washington	Duvall	Johnson, W.	Todd		
1813–25	Marshall, J.	Thompson	Story	Washington	Duvall	Johnson, W.	Todd		
1826–28	Marshall, J.	Thompson	Story	Washington	Duvall	Johnson, W.	Trimble		
1829	Marshall, J.	Thompson	Story	Washington	Duvall	Johnson, W.	McLean		
1830–34	Marshall, J.	Thompson	Story	Baldwin	Duvall	Johnson, W.	McLean		
1835	Marshall, J.	Thompson	Story	Baldwin	Duvall	Wayne	McLean		
1836	Taney	Thompson	Story	Baldwin	Barbour	Wayne	McLean		
1837–40	Taney	Thompson	Story	Baldwin	Barbour	Wayne	McLean	Catron	McKinley
1841–44	Taney	Thompson	Story	Baldwin	Daniel	Wayne	McLean	Catron	McKinley
1845	Taney	Nelson	Woodbury	(vacant)	Daniel	Wayne	McLean	Catron	McKinley
1846–50	Taney	Nelson	Woodbury	Grier	Daniel	Wayne	McLean	Catron	McKinley
1851–52	Taney	Nelson	Curtis	Grier	Daniel	Wayne	McLean	Catron	McKinley
1853–57	Taney	Nelson	Curtis	Grier	Daniel	Wayne	McLean	Catron	Campbell
1858–60	Taney	Nelson	Clifford	Grier	Daniel	Wayne	McLean	Catron	Campbell

Year of Court as Constituted	Chief Justice	Associate Justices								
1861	Taney	Nelson	Clifford	Grier	(vacant)	Wayne	McLean	Catron	Campbell	
1862	Taney	Nelson	Clifford	Grier	Miller	Wayne	Swayne	Catron	Davis	
1863	Taney	Nelson	Clifford	Grier	Miller	Wayne	Swayne	Catron	Davis	Field
1864–65	Chase, S. P.	Nelson	Clifford	Grier	Miller	Wayne	Swayne	Catron	Davis	Field
1866–67	Chase, S. P.	Nelson	Clifford	Grier	Miller	Wayne	Swayne	(ended)*	Davis	Field
1868–69	Chase, S. P.	Nelson	Clifford	Grier	Miller	(vacant)	Swayne		Davis	Field
1870–71	Chase, S. P.	Nelson	Clifford	Strong	Miller	Bradley	Swayne		Davis	Field
1872–73	Chase, S. P.	Hunt	Clifford	Strong	Miller	Bradley	Swayne		Davis	Field
1874–76	Waite	Hunt	Clifford	Strong	Miller	Bradley	Swayne		Davis	Field
1877–79	Waite	Hunt	Clifford	Strong	Miller	Bradley	Swayne		Harlan	Field
1880	Waite	Hunt	Clifford	Woods	Miller	Bradley	Swayne		Harlan	Field
1881	Waite	Hunt	Gray	Woods	Miller	Bradley	Matthews		Harlan	Field
1882–87	Waite	Blatchford	Gray	Woods	Miller	Bradley	Matthews		Harlan	Field
1888	Fuller	Blatchford	Gray	Lamar, L.	Miller	Bradley	Matthews		Harlan	Field
1889	Fuller	Blatchford	Gray	Lamar, L.	Miller	Bradley	Brewer		Harlan	Field
1890–91	Fuller	Blatchford	Gray	Lamar, L.	Brown	Bradley	Brewer		Harlan	Field
1892	Fuller	Blatchford	Gray	Lamar, L.	Brown	Shiras	Brewer		Harlan	Field
1893	Fuller	Blatchford	Gray	Jackson, H.	Brown	Shiras	Brewer		Harlan	Field
1894	Fuller	White	Gray	Jackson, H.	Brown	Shiras	Brewer		Harlan	Field
1895–97	Fuller	White	Gray	Peckham	Brown	Shiras	Brewer		Harlan	Field
1898–1901	Fuller	White	Gray	Peckham	Brown	Shiras	Brewer		Harlan	McKenna
1902	Fuller	White	Holmes	Peckham	Brown	Shiras	Brewer		Harlan	McKenna
1903–05	Fuller	White	Holmes	Peckham	Brown	Day	Brewer		Harlan	McKenna
1906–08	Fuller	White	Holmes	Peckham	Moody	Day	Brewer		Harlan	McKenna
1909	Fuller	White	Holmes	Lurton	Moody	Day	Brewer		Harlan	McKenna
1910–11	White, E.	Van Devanter	Holmes	Lurton	Lamar, J.	Day	Hughes		Harlan	McKenna
1912–13	White, E.	Van Devanter	Holmes	Lurton	Lamar, J.	Day	Hughes		Pitney	McKenna
1914–15	White, E.	Van Devanter	Holmes	McReynolds	Lamar, J.	Day	Hughes		Pitney	McKenna
1916–20	White, E.	Van Devanter	Holmes	McReynolds	Brandeis	Day	Clarke		Pitney	McKenna
1921	Taft	Van Devanter	Holmes	McReynolds	Brandeis	Day	Clarke		Pitney	McKenna
1922	Taft	VanDevanter	Holmes	McReynolds	Brandeis	Butler	Sutherland		Pitney	McKenna
1923–24	Taft	Van Devanter	Holmes	McReynolds	Brandeis	Butler	Sutherland		Sanford	McKenna

*Congress ended the use of a ten-person Court in this year.

Year of Court as Constituted	Chief Justice	Associate Justices							
1925–29	Taft	Van Devanter	Holmes	McReynolds	Brandeis	Butler	Sutherland	Sanford	Stone
1930–31	Hughes	Van Devanter	Holmes	McReynolds	Brandeis	Butler	Sutherland	Roberts	Stone
1932–36	Hughes	Van Devanter	Cardozo	McReynolds	Brandeis	Butler	Sutherland	Roberts	Stone
1937	Hughes	Black	Cardozo	McReynolds	Brandeis	Butler	Sutherland	Roberts	Stone
1938	Hughes	Black	Cardozo	McReynolds	Brandeis	Butler	Reed	Roberts	Stone
1939	Hughes	Black	Frankfurter	McReynolds	Douglas	Butler	Reed	Roberts	Stone
1940	Hughes	Black	Frankfurter	McReynolds	Douglas	Murphy	Reed	Roberts	Stone
1941–42	Stone	Black	Frankfurter	Byrnes	Douglas	Murphy	Reed	Roberts	Jackson, R.
1943–44	Stone	Black	Frankfurter	Rutledge, W.	Douglas	Murphy	Reed	Roberts	Jackson, R.
1945	Stone	Black	Frankfurter	Rutledge, W.	Douglas	Murphy	Reed	Burton	Jackson, R.
1946–48	Vinson	Black	Frankfurter	Rutledge, W.	Douglas	Murphy	Reed	Burton	Jackson, R.
1949–52	Vinson	Black	Frankfurter	Minton	Douglas	Clark	Reed	Burton	Jackson, R.
1953–54	Warren	Black	Frankfurter	Minton	Douglas	Clark	Reed	Burton	Jackson, R.
1955	Warren	Black	Frankfurter	Minton	Douglas	Clark	Reed	Burton	Harlan
1956	Warren	Black	Frankfurter	Brennan	Douglas	Clark	Reed	Burton	Harlan
1957	Warren	Black	Frankfurter	Brennan	Douglas	Clark	Whittaker	Burton	Harlan
1958–61	Warren	Black	Frankfurter	Brennan	Douglas	Clark	Whittaker	Stewart	Harlan
1962–65	Warren	Black	Goldberg	Brennan	Douglas	Clark	White, B.	Stewart	Harlan
1965–67	Warren	Black	Fortas	Brennan	Douglas	Clark	White, B.	Stewart	Harlan
1967–69	Warren	Black	Fortas	Brennan	Douglas	Marshall, T.	White, B.	Stewart	Harlan
1969	Burger	Black	Fortas	Brennan	Douglas	Marshall, T.	White, B.	Stewart	Harlan
1969–70	Burger	Black	(vacant)	Brennan	Douglas	Marshall, T.	White, B.	Stewart	Harlan
1970–71	Burger	Black	Blackmun	Brennan	Douglas	Marshall, T.	White, B.	Stewart	Harlan
1972–75	Burger	Powell	Blackmun	Brennan	Douglas	Marshall, T.	White, B.	Stewart	Rehnquist
1975–81	Burger	Powell	Blackmun	Brennan	Stevens	Marshall, T.	White, B.	Stewart	Rehnquist
1981–86	Burger	Powell	Blackmun	Brennan	Stevens	Marshall, T.	White, B.	O'Connor	Rehnquist
1986–87	Rehnquist	Powell	Blackmun	Brennan	Stevens	Marshall, T.	White, B.	O'Connor	Scalia
1987–90	Rehnquist	Kennedy	Blackmun	Brennan	Stevens	Marshall, T.	White, B.	O'Connor	Scalia
1990–91	Rehnquist	Kennedy	Blackmun	Souter	Stevens	Marshall, T.	White, B.	O'Connor	Scalia
1991–93	Rehnquist	Kennedy	Blackmun	Souter	Stevens	Thomas	White, B.	O'Connor	Scalia
1993–94	Rehnquist	Kennedy	Blackmun	Souter	Stevens	Thomas	Ginsburg	O'Connor	Scalia
1994–	Rehnquist	Kennedy	Breyer	Souter	Stevens	Thomas	Ginsburg	O'Connor	Scalia

SUPREME COURT JUSTICES

by Appointing President, State Appointed from, and Political Party

President/Justices Appointed	State Appointed from	Political Party
Washington		
John Jay (1745–1829)*	N.Y.	Federalist
John Rutledge (1739–1800)	S.C.	Federalist
William Cushing (1732–1810)	Mass.	Federalist
James Wilson (1724–1798)	Pa.	Federalist
John Blair (1732–1800)	Va.	Federalist
James Iredell (1751–1799)	N.C.	Federalist
Thomas Johnson (1732–1819)	Md.	Federalist
William Paterson (1745–1806)	N.J.	Federalist
Samuel Chase (1741–1811)	Md.	Federalist
Oliver Ellsworth (1745–1807)	Conn.	Federalist
Adams, J.		
Bushrod Washington (1762–1829)	Va.	Federalist
Alfred Moore (1755–1810)	N.C.	Federalist
John Marshall (1755–1835)	Va.	Federalist
Jefferson		
William Johnson (1771–1834)	S.C.	Dem.—Rep.
Henry Livingston (1757–1823)	N.Y.	Dem.—Rep.
Thomas Todd (1765–1826)	Va.	Dem.—Rep.
Madison		
Gabriel Duvall (1752–1844)	Md.	Dem.—Rep.
Joseph Story (1779–1845)	Mass.	Dem.—Rep.

President/Justices Appointed	State Appointed from	Political Party
Monroe		
Smith Thompson (1768–1843)	N.Y.	Dem.—Rep.
Adams, J. Q.		
Robert Trimble (1776–1828)	Ky.	Dem.—Rep.
Jackson		
John McLean (1785–1861)	Ohio	Dem. (later Rep.)
Henry Baldwin (1780–1844)	Penn.	Democrat
James M. Wayne (1790–1867)	Ga.	Democrat
Roger B. Taney (1777–1864)	Va.	Democrat
Philip P. Barbour (1783–1841)	Va.	Democrat
Van Buren		
John Catron (1778–1865)	Tenn.	Democrat
John McKinley (1780–1852)	Ala.	Democrat
Peter V. Daniel (1784–1860)	Va.	Democrat
Tyler		
Samuel Nelson (1792–1873)	N.Y.	Democrat
Polk		
Levi Woodbury (1789–1851)	N.H.	Democrat
Robert C. Grier (1794–1870)	Pa.	Democrat
Fillmore		
Benjamin R. Curtis (1809–1874)	Mass.	Whig

*Dates in parentheses indicate birth and death dates.

President/Justices Appointed	State Appointed from	Political Party	President/Justices Appointed	State Appointed from	Political Party
Pierce			**McKinley**		
John A. Campbell (1811–1889)	Ala.	Democrat	Joseph McKenna (1843–1926)	Calif.	Republican
Buchanan			**Roosevelt, T.**		
Nathan Clifford (1803–1881)	Maine	Democrat	Oliver W. Holmes (1841–1935)	Mass.	Republican
			William R. Day (1849–1923)	Ohio	Republican
Lincoln			William H. Moody (1853–1917)	Mass.	Republican
Noah H. Swayne (1804–1884)	Ohio	Republican			
Samuel F. Miller (1816–1890)	Iowa	Republican	**Taft**		
David Davis (1815–1886)	Ill.	Republican (later Dem.)	Horace H. Lurton (1844–1914)	Tenn.	Democrat
			Charles E. Hughes (1862–1948)	N.Y.	Republican
Stephen J. Field (1816–1899)	Calif.	Democrat	Willis Van Devanter (1859–1941)	Wyo.	Republican
Salmon P. Chase (1808–1873)	Ohio	Republican	Joseph R. Lamar (1857–1916)	Ga.	Democrat
			Mahlon Pitney (1858–1924)	N.J.	Republican
Grant					
William Strong (1808–1895)	Pa.	Republican	**Wilson**		
Joseph P. Bradley (1813–1892)	N.J.	Republican	James C. McReynolds (1862–1946)	Tenn.	Democrat
Ward Hunt (1810–1886)	N.Y.	Republican	Louis D. Brandeis (1856–1941)	Mass.	Independent
Morrison Waite (1816–1888)	Ohio	Republican	John H. Clarke (1857–1945)	Ohio	Democrat
Hayes			**Harding**		
John M. Harlan (1833–1911)	Ky.	Republican	William H. Taft (1857–1930)	Conn.	Republican
William B. Woods (1824–1887)	Ga.	Republican	George Sutherland (1862–1942)	Utah	Republican
			Pierce Butler (1866–1939)	Minn.	Democrat
Garfield			Edward T. Sanford (1865–1930)	Tenn.	Republican
Stanley Matthews (1824–1889)	Ohio	Republican			
			Coolidge		
Arthur			Harlan F. Stone (1872–1946)	N.Y.	Republican
Horace Gray (1828–1902)	Mass.	Republican			
Samuel Blatchford (1820–1893)	N.Y.	Republican	**Hoover**		
			Owen J. Roberts (1875–1955)	Pa.	Republican
Cleveland			Benjamin N. Cardozo (1870–1938)	N.Y.	Democrat
Lucius Q. C. Lamar (1825–1893)	Miss.	Democrat			
Melville W. Fuller (1833–1910)	Ill.	Democrat	**Roosevelt, F. D.**		
			Hugo L. Black (1886–1971)	Ala.	Democrat
Harrison			Stanley F. Reed (1884–1980)	Ky.	Democrat
David J. Brewer (1837–1910)	Kans.	Republican	Felix Frankfurter (1882–1965)	Mass.	Independent
Henry B. Brown (1836–1913)	Mich.	Republican	William O. Douglas (1898–1980)	Conn.	Democrat
George Shiras, Jr. (1832–1924)	Pa.	Republican	Frank Murphy (1890–1949)	Mich.	Democrat
Howell E. Jackson (1832–1895)	Tenn.	Democrat	James F. Byrnes (1879–1972)	S.C.	Democrat
			Robert H. Jackson (1892–1954)	N.Y.	Democrat
Cleveland			Wiley B. Rutledge (1894–1949)	Iowa	Democrat
Edward D. White (1845–1921)	La.	Democrat			
Rufus W. Peckham (1838–1909)	N.Y.	Democrat			

President/Justices Appointed	State Appointed from	Political Party	President/Justices Appointed	State Appointed from	Political Party
Truman			**Nixon**		
Harold H. Burton (1888–1964)	Ohio	Republican	Warren E. Burger (b. 1907–1995)	Minn.	Republican
Fred M. Vinson (1890–1953)	Ky.	Democrat	Harry R. Blackmun (b. 1908–1999)	Minn.	Republican
Tom C. Clark (1899–1977)	Texas	Democrat	Lewis F. Powell, Jr. (b. 1907–1998)	Va.	Democrat
Sherman Minton (1890–1965)	Ind.	Democrat	William H. Rehnquist (b. 1924)	Ariz.	Republican
Eisenhower			**Ford**		
Earl Warren (1891–1974)	Calif.	Republican	John Paul Stevens (b. 1920)	Ill.	Republican
John M. Harlan (1899–1971)	N.Y.	Republican	**Reagan**		
William J. Brennan (b. 1906)	N.J.	Democrat	Sandra Day O'Connor (b. 1930)	Ariz.	Republican
Charles E. Whittaker (1901–1973)	Mo.	Republican	Antonin Scalia (b. 1936)	N.J.	Republican
Potter Stewart (1915–1986)	Ohio	Republican	Anthony M. Kennedy (b. 1936)	Calif.	Republican
Kennedy			**Bush**		
Byron R. White (b. 1917–2002)	Colo.	Democrat	David Souter (b. 1939)	N.H.	Republican
Arthur J. Goldberg (b. 1908–1990)	Ill.	Democrat	Clarence Thomas (b. 1948)	Va.	Republican
Johnson, L. B.			**Clinton**		
Abe Fortas (1910–1982)	Tenn.	Democrat	Ruth Bader Ginsburg (b. 1933)	Wa., D.C.	Democrat
Thurgood Marshall (b. 1908–1993)	N.Y.	Democrat	Stephen G. Breyer (b. 1938)	Mass.	Democrat

GLOSSARY

abate To do away with or lessen the impact of, as in abatement of a nuisance.

abortion The intentional termination of a pregnancy through destruction of the fetus.

abrogate To annul, destroy, or cancel.

abstention The doctrine under which the U.S. Supreme Court and other federal courts do not decide on, or interfere with, state cases even when empowered to do so. This doctrine is typically invoked when a case can be decided on the basis of state law.

accessory A person who aids in the commission of a crime.

accessory after the fact A person who with knowledge that a crime has been committed conceals or protects the offender.

accessory before the fact A person who aids or assists another in commission of an offense.

accommodation An approach to interpreting the Establishment Clause of the First Amendment that holds that government can and should accommodate religion whenever possible, while at the same time being officially neutral.

accomplice A person who voluntarily unites with another in commission of an offense.

accusatorial system A system of criminal justice in which the prosecution bears the burden of proving the defendant's guilt.

acquittal A judicial finding that a defendant is not guilty of a crime with which he or she has been charged.

act of omission The failure to perform an act required by law.

actual damages Money awarded to a plaintiff in a civil suit to compensate for injuries to that party's rights.

actual imprisonment standard The standard governing the applicability of the federal constitutional right of an indigent person to have counsel appointed in a misdemeanor case. In order for the right to be violated, the indigent defendant must actually be sentenced to jail time after having been tried without appointed counsel.

actual malice The deliberate intention to cause harm or injury.

actual possession Possession of something with the possessor having immediate control.

actus reus A "wrongful act" that, combined with other necessary elements of crime, constitutes criminal liability.

ad hoc "For this." For a special purpose.

ad hoc balancing An effort by a court to balance competing interests in the context of the unique facts of a given case. In constitutional law, this term is used most frequently in connection with the adjudication of First Amendment issues.

adjudication The formal process by which courts decide cases.

adjudicatory hearing A proceeding in juvenile court to determine whether a juvenile has committed an act of delinquency.

ad litem "For the lawsuit"; pending the lawsuit, as in "guardian ad litem."

administrative law The body of law dealing with the structure, authority, policies, and procedures of administrative and regulatory agencies.

Administrative Procedure Act The 1946 act of Congress specifying rule making and adjudicatory procedures for federal agencies.

administrative searches Searches of premises by a government official to determine compliance with health and safety regulations.

adultery Voluntary sexual intercourse where at least one of the parties is married to someone other than the sexual partner.

ad valorem "According to the value." Referring to a tax or duty guaranteed according to the assessed value of the matter taxed.

adversary proceeding A legal action involving parties with adverse or opposing interests. A basic aspect of the American legal system, the adversary proceeding provides the framework within which most constitutional cases are decided. For an exception to this generalization, *see*: ex parte.

adversary system A system of justice involving conflicting parties where the role of the judge is to remain neutral.

advisory opinion A judicial opinion, not involving adverse parties in a "case or controversy," that is given at the request of the legislature or the executive. It has been a long-standing policy of the U.S. Supreme Court not to render advisory opinions.

affiant A person who makes an affidavit.

affidavit   A person's voluntary sworn declaration attesting to a set of facts.

affirm   To uphold, ratify, or approve.

affirmative action   A program under which women and/or persons of particular minority groups are granted special consideration in employment, government contracts, and/or admission to programs of higher education.

a fortiori   "With greater force of reason."

aggravating circumstances   Factors attending the commission of a crime that make the crime or its consequences worse.

aggravating factors   *See*: aggravating circumstances.

aiding and abetting   Assisting in or otherwise facilitating the commission of a crime.

alibi   Defense to a criminal charge that places the defendant at some place other than the scene of the crime at the time the crime occurred.

allegation   Assertion or claim made by a party to a legal action.

amendment   A modification, addition, or deletion.

Americans with Disabilities Act   The 1990 federal statute forbidding discrimination on grounds of disability and guaranteeing access for the handicapped to public buildings.

amici   "Friends," usually in reference to "friends of the Court." *See*: amicus curiae.

amicus curiae   "Friend of the court." An individual or organization allowed to take part in a judicial proceeding, not as one of the adversaries, but as a party interested in the outcome. Usually an *amicus curiae* files a brief in support of one side or the other but occasionally takes a more active part in the argument of the case.

amnesty   A blanket pardon issued to a large group of lawbreakers.

anonymous informant   An informant whose identity is unknown to the police. *See also*: confidential informant.

anonymous tip   Information from an unknown source concerning alleged criminal activity.

answer brief   The appellee's written response to the appellant's law brief filed in an appellate court.

anticipatory search warrant   A search warrant issued based on an affidavit that at a future time evidence of a crime will be at a specific place.

appeal   Review by a higher court of a lower court decision.

appeal by right   An appeal brought to a higher court as a matter of right under federal or state law.

appellant   A person who takes an appeal to a higher court.

appellate courts   Judicial tribunals that review decisions from lower tribunals.

appellate jurisdiction   The legal authority of a court of law to hear an appeal from or otherwise review a decision by a lower court.

appellee   The party against whom a case is appealed to a higher court.

appointment power   The power of the president to appoint, with the consent of the Senate, judges, ambassadors, and high-level executive officials.

apportionment   The allocation of representatives among a set of legislative districts.

arguendo   "For the sake of argument."

arraignment   An appearance before a court of law for the purpose of pleading to a criminal charge.

arrest   To take someone into custody or otherwise deprive that person of freedom of movement.

arrest warrant   A document issued by a magistrate or judge directing that a named person be taken into custody for allegedly having committed an offense.

arrestee   A person who is arrested.

Article I, Section 8   Key section of the Constitution outlining the powers of Congress.

Articles of Confederation   The constitution under which the United States was governed between 1781 and 1789.

assault   The attempt or threat to inflict bodily injury upon another person.

assign   To transfer or grant a legal right.

assignee   One to whom a legal right is transferred.

assignments of error   A written presentation to an appellate court identifying the points the appellant claims constitute errors made by the lower tribunal.

asylum   Sanctuary; a place of refuge.

at bar   Before the court, as in "the case at bar."

at-large election   An election in which a number of officials are chosen to represent the entire district, as opposed to an arrangement under which each of the officials would represent one smaller district or ward.

attempt   An intent to commit a crime coupled with an act taken toward committing the offense.

attorney general   The highest legal officer of a state or of the United States.

attorney–client privilege   The right of a person (client) not to testify about matters discussed in confidence with an attorney in the course of the attorney's representation.

automobile exception   An exception to the Fourth Amendment search warrant requirement that allows the warrantless search of a vehicle by police who have probable cause to search, but for which it is impracticable to secure a warrant because of exigent circumstances.

automobile search   The search of an automobile by police, usually performed without a warrant.

bad tendency test   A restrictive interpretation of the First Amendment under which government may prohibit expression having a tendency to cause people to break the law.

bail   The conditional release from custody of a person charged with a crime pending adjudication of the case.

battery   The unlawful use of force against another person, entailing some injury or offensive touching.

bench trial   A trial before a judge rather than a jury.

bench warrant   An arrest warrant issued by a judge.

benevolent neutrality   An approach to interpreting the Establishment Clause of the First Amendment that holds that government can and should take a benevolent posture toward religion while at the same time being officially neutral on such matters.

beyond a reasonable doubt   The standard of proof that is constitutionally required to be introduced before a defendant can be found guilty of a crime or before a juvenile can be adjudicated a delinquent.

bicameralism   The characteristic of having two houses or chambers. The U.S. Congress is a bicameral body in that it has a Senate and a House of Representatives.

bifurcated trial   A capital trial with separate phases for determining guilt and punishment.

bigamy   The crime of being married to more than one person at the same time.

bill of attainder   A legislative act imposing punishment on a party without the benefit of a judicial proceeding.

Bill of Rights   The first ten amendments to the Constitution, ratified in 1791, concerned primarily with individual rights and liberties.

Black Codes   Statutes enacted in southern states after the Civil War denying African-Americans a number of basic rights.

bloc   A group of decision makers in a collegial body who usually vote the same way. In judicial politics, the term refers to groups of judges or justices on appellate courts who usually vote together.

bona fide   "In good faith"; without the attempt to defraud or deceive.

border search   A search of persons entering the borders of the United States.

bounty hunter   A person paid a fee or commission to capture a defendant who had fled a jurisdiction to escape punishment.

Brady Bill   Legislation passed by Congress in 1993 requiring a five-day waiting period before the purchase of a handgun during which time a background check is conducted on the buyer.

Brandeis brief   Pioneered by attorney Louis D. Brandeis in 1908, a type of appellate brief that emphasizes empirical evidence of the social or economic impact of law, as distinguished from a conventional brief that focuses solely on legal analysis.

breach of contract   The violation of a provision in a legally enforceable agreement that gives the damaged party the right to recourse in a court of law.

breach of the peace   The crime of disturbing the public tranquility and order. A generic term encompassing disorderly conduct, riot, and similar behaviors.

brief   (1) In the judicial process, a document submitted by counsel setting forth legal arguments germane to a particular case. (2) In the study of constitutional law, a summary of a given case, reviewing the essential facts, issues, holdings, and reasoning of the court.

burden of persuasion   The legal responsibility of a party to convince a court of the correctness of a position asserted.

burden of production of evidence   The obligation of a party to produce some evidence in support of a proposition asserted.

burden of proof   The requirement to introduce evidence to prove an alleged fact or set of facts.

bureaucracy   Any large, complex, hierarchical organization staffed by appointed officials.

business affected with a public interest   A nineteenth century doctrine holding that certain businesses are more closely associated with the public interest and are therefore more subject to government regulation.

cabinet   The collective term for the heads of the executive departments of the federal government, such as the secretary of state, the attorney general, and the secretary of defense.

capias   "That you take." A general term for various court orders requiring that some named person be taken into custody.

capitalist economy   An economy based on private ownership and free enterprise.

capital offense   A crime punishable by death.

capital punishment   The death penalty.

carnal knowledge   Sexual intercourse.

case   A legal dispute between adverse parties to be resolved by a court of law.

case law   Law derived from judicial decisions, also known as decisional law.

case or controversy requirement   The requirement, under Article III of the Constitution, that the federal judicial power shall be extended to actual cases or controversies, not to hypothetical or abstract questions of law.

case reporters   A series of books reprinting the decisions of a given court or set of courts. For example, the decisions of the U.S. Courts of Appeals are reported in the *Federal Reporter*, published by West Publishing Company.

castle doctrine   The doctrine that "a man's home is his castle." At common law, the right to use whatever force is necessary to protect one's dwelling and its inhabitants from an unlawful entry or attack.

causation   An act that produces an event or an effect.

cause   A synonym for case; a reason or justification. *See also*: probable cause; show cause.

caveat emptor   "Let the buyer beware." Common law maxim requiring the consumer to judge the quality of a product before making a purchase.

censorship   Broadly defined, any restriction imposed by the government on speech, publication, or other form of expression.

certification   A procedure under which a lower court requests a decision by a higher court on specified questions in a case, pending a final decision by the lower court.

certiorari   "To be informed." A petition similar to an appeal, but it may be granted or refused at the discretion of the appellate court.

certiorari, writ of   An order from a higher court to a lower court directing that the record of a particular case be sent up for review. *See also*: certiorari.

challenge for cause   Objection to a prospective juror on some specified ground (for example, a close relationship to a party to the case).

change of venue   The removal of a legal proceeding, usually a trial, to a new location.

checks and balances   The constitutional powers granted each branch of government to prevent one branch from dominating the others.

child benefit theory   The doctrine that government assistance to religious schools can be justified if the effect is to benefit the child rather than to promote religion.

chilling effect   The effect of discouraging persons from exercising their rights.

circumstantial evidence   Indirect evidence from which the existence of certain facts may be inferred.

citation   (1) A summons to appear in court, often used in traffic violations. (2) A reference to a statute or court decision, often designating a publication where the law or decision appears.

civil action   A lawsuit brought to enforce private rights and to remedy violations thereof.

civil case   *See*: civil action.

civil infractions   Noncriminal violation of a law, often referring to minor traffic violations.

civil law   (1) The law relating to rights and obligations of parties. (2) The body of law, based essentially on Roman law, that exists in most non-English-speaking nations.

civil liberties   The freedoms protected by the Constitution and statutes—for example, freedom of speech, religion, and assembly.

civil rights   Legal protection against invidious discrimination in citizens' exercise of the rights of life, liberty, and property. The right to equality before the law and equal treatment by government.

Civil Rights Act of 1866   Federal civil rights law passed after the Civil War, aimed at eliminating the discriminatory Black Codes enacted by southern states.

Civil Rights Act of 1875   Federal civil rights law aimed at ending racial discrimination by places of public accommodation. Declared unconstitutional in 1883.

Civil Rights Act of 1964   Landmark civil rights statute aimed at ending racial discrimination in employment and by places of public accommodation.

Civil Rights movement   The social movement beginning in the 1950s aimed at securing civil rights for African-Americans.

civil service   The system under which government employees are selected and retained based on merit, rather than political patronage.

civil suit   *See*: civil action.

Civil War Amendments   Reference to the Thirteenth, Fourteenth, and Fifteenth Amendments to the Constitution, designed primarily to protect the civil rights of former slaves.

claim of right   A contention that an item was taken in a good-faith belief that it belonged to the taker; sometimes asserted as a defense to a charge of larceny or theft.

class action   A lawsuit brought by one or more parties on behalf of themselves and others similarly situated.

classical conservatism   Traditional conservatism stressing preservation of order and maintenance of traditional values.

clear and convincing evidence standard   An evidentiary standard that is higher than the standard of "preponderance of the evidence" applied in civil cases, but lower than the standard of "beyond a reasonable doubt" applied in criminal cases. For example, under the new federal standard for the affirmative defense of insanity, the defendant must establish the defense of insanity by "clear and convincing evidence."

clear and present danger test   The First Amendment test that protects expression up to the point that it poses a clear and present danger of bringing about some substantive evil that government has a right to prevent.

clear and probable danger test   A somewhat more restrictive First Amendment test than clear and present danger. The test is "whether the gravity of the 'evil,' discounted by its improbability, justifies such invasion of speech as is necessary to avoid the danger."

clemency   A grant of mercy by an executive official commuting a sentence or pardoning a criminal.

closing arguments   Arguments presented at trial by counsel at the conclusion of the presentation of evidence.

closure of pretrial proceedings   Decision by a judge to close proceedings prior to trial of a criminal case in order to protect the defendant's right to a fair trial.

code   A systematic collection of laws.

coercive federalism   Term used to describe the fact that the federal government often uses federal grants to coerce states into adopting policies that it cannot directly mandate.

collateral attack   The attempt to defeat the outcome of a judicial proceeding by challenging it in another court.

collateral estoppel   A rule barring the making of a claim in one judicial proceeding that has been adjudicated in another, earlier proceeding.

comity   Courtesy, respect, civility. A matter of good will and tradition, rather than of right; particularly important in a federal system where one jurisdiction is bound to respect the judgments of another.

commander in chief   Term describing the president's authority to command the armed forces of the country.

commercial speech   Commercial advertising, now viewed as entitled to some protection under the First Amendment.

common law   A body of law that develops primarily through judicial decisions, rather than legislative enactments. The common law is not a fixed system but an ever-changing body of rules and principles articulated by judges and applied to changing needs and circumstances. *See also*: English Common law.

community control   A sentence imposed on a person found guilty of a crime that requires the offender to be placed in an individualized program of noninstitutional confinement.

community service A sentence requiring that the criminal perform some specific service to the community for some specified period of time.

community standards Standards of decency, which may vary from community to community.

commutation A form of clemency that lessens the punishment for a person convicted of a crime.

comparative proportionality review A judicial examination to determine whether the sentence imposed in a given criminal case is proportionate to sentences imposed in similar cases.

compelling government interest A government interest sufficiently strong that it overrides the fundamental rights of persons adversely affected by government action or policy.

compelling interest An interest or justification of the highest order.

competency The state of being legally fit to give testimony or stand trial.

complicity A person's voluntary participation with another person in commission of a crime or wrongful act.

comprehensive planning A guide for the orderly development of a community, usually implemented by enactment of zoning ordinances.

compulsory process The requirement that witnesses appear and testify in court or before a legislative committee. *See also*: subpoena.

compulsory self-incrimination The requirement that an individual give testimony leading to his or her own criminal conviction; forbidden by the Fifth Amendment.

compulsory sterilization The requirement that an individual undergo procedures that render him or her unable to conceive children.

concurrent jurisdiction Jurisdiction that is shared by different courts of law.

concurrent powers Powers exercised jointly by the state and federal governments.

concurrent resolution An act expressing the will of both houses of the legislature but lacking a mechanism through which to enforce that will on parties outside the legislature.

concurrent sentencing The practice in which a trial court imposes separate sentences that may be served at the same time.

concurring in the judgment An agreement by a judge or justice in the judgment of an appellate court without necessarily agreeing to the court's reasoning processes.

concurring opinion An opinion by a judge or justice agreeing with the decision of the court. A concurring opinion may or may not agree with the rationale adopted by the court in reaching its decision. *See also*: Opinion of the Court.

conditions of probation A set of rules that must be observed by a person placed on probation.

conference As applied to the appellate courts, a private meeting of judges to decide a case or to determine whether to grant review in a case.

confidential informant An informant known to the police but whose identity is held in confidence. *See also*: anonymous informant.

conscientious objector One who opposes military service on religious or moral grounds.

consecutive sentencing The practice in which a trial court imposes a sentence or sentences to be served following completion of a prior sentence or sentences.

consent Voluntarily yielding to the will or desire of another person.

consent decree A court-enforced agreement reached by mutual consent of parties in a civil case or administrative proceeding.

conspiracy The crime of two or more persons planning to commit a specific criminal act.

constitutional case A judicial proceeding involving an issue of constitutional law.

Constitutional Convention of 1787 Convention of state delegates held in Philadelphia during the summer of 1787, ostensibly for the purpose of revising the Articles of Confederation. The convention resulted in a new Constitution, which was ratified in 1788.

constitutional democracy A democratic system of government in which majority rule is limited by constitutional principles such as limited government and individual rights.

constitutional law The fundamental and supreme law of the land defining the structure and powers of government and the rights of individuals vis-à-vis government.

constitutional republic A republican form of government based on a written constitution. The Framers of the U.S. Constitution avoided the term *democracy*, which they equated with unrestrained majoritarianism. They preferred the term *republican form of government*, which connoted representative institutions constrained by the rule of law.

constitutional right of privacy The right to make choices in matters of intimate personal concern without interference by government.

constitutional supremacy The doctrine that the Constitution is the supreme law of the land and that all actions and policies of government must be consistent with it.

constitutional theory (1) Broad term referring to theories about the Constitution generally, or particular theories about particular provisions of the Constitution. (2) In the area of the presidency, the theory that the president can exercise only those powers specifically granted by Article II.

construction Interpretation.

contemnor A person found to be in contempt of court.

contempt An action that embarrasses, hinders, obstructs, or is calculated to lessen the dignity of a judicial or legislative body.

contempt of Congress Any action that embarrasses, hinders, obstructs, or is calculated to lessen the dignity of Congress.

contempt of court Any action that embarrasses, hinders, obstructs, or is calculated to lessen the dignity of a court of law.

content-neutral   Term referring to a time, place, or manner regulation that is enforced without regard to the content of expression.

continuance   Delay of a judicial proceeding on the motion of one of the parties.

contraband   Any property that is inherently illegal to produce or possess.

contracts   Legally binding agreements between or among specific parties.

Contracts Clause   Provision of Article I, Section 10, forbidding states from impairing the obligations of contracts.

contractual immunity   A grant by a prosecutor with approval of the court that makes a witness immune from prosecution for the witness's testimony.

controlled substance   A drug designated by law as contraband.

convening authorities   The military authorities with jurisdiction to convene a court-martial for trial of persons subject to the Uniform Code of Military Justice.

conversion   The unlawful assumption of the rights of ownership to someone else's property.

cooperative federalism   A modern approach to American federalism in which powers and functions are shared among national, state, and local authorities.

corporal punishment   Punishment that inflicts pain or injury on a person's body.

corpus delicti   "The body of the crime." The material thing upon which a crime has been committed (for example, a burned-out building in a case of arson).

corrections system   The system of prisons, jails, and other penal and correctional institutions.

corroboration   Evidence that strengthens or validates evidence already given.

counsel   A lawyer who represents a party.

court-martial   A military tribunal convened by a commander of a military unit to try a person subject to the Uniform Code of Military Justice who is accused of violating a provision of that code.

Court of Appeals for the Armed Forces   A court consisting of five civilian judges that reviews sentences affecting a general or flag officer or imposing the death penalty as well as cases certified for review by the judge advocate general of a branch of service. May grant review of convictions and sentences on petitions by service members.

court of general jurisdiction   A court that conducts trials in felony and major misdemeanor cases. Also refers to a trial court with broad authority to hear and decide a wide range of civil and criminal cases.

court of last resort   The highest court in a judicial system; the last resort for deciding appeals.

court of limited jurisdiction   A trial court with narrow authority to hear and decide cases, typically pretrial matters, misdemeanors, and/or small claims.

court-ordered busing   The transportation of public school students to schools outside their area, under court orders to alleviate racial segregation.

court system   A set of trial and appellate courts established to resolve legal disputes in a particular jurisdiction.

creation science   The idea that there are scientific reasons to believe in creationism as opposed to evolution.

criminal   Pertaining to crime; a person convicted of a crime.

criminal action   A judicial proceeding initiated by government against a person charged with the commission of a crime.

criminal case   A judicial proceeding in which a person is accused of a crime.

criminal conspiracy   *See*: conspiracy.

criminal contempt   Punishment imposed by a judge against a person who violates a court order or otherwise intentionally interferes with the administration of the court.

criminal intent   A necessary element of a crime; the evil intent associated with the criminal act.

criminal law   The law defining crimes and punishments.

criminal negligence   A failure to exercise the degree of caution or care necessary to avoid being charged with a crime.

criminal procedure   The rules of law governing the procedures by which crimes are investigated, prosecuted, adjudicated, and punished.

criminal prosecution   Legal action brought against a person accused of a crime.

criminal responsibility   Term referring to the set of doctrines under which individuals are held accountable for criminal conduct.

criminal syndicalism   The crime of advocating violence as a means to accomplish political change (archaic).

criminology   The study of the nature of, causes of, and means of dealing with crime.

critical pretrial stages   Significant procedural steps that occur preliminary to a criminal trial. A defendant has the right to counsel at these critical stages.

cross-examination   The process of interrogating a witness who has testified on direct examination by asking the witness questions concerning testimony given. Cross-examination is designed to bring out any bias or inconsistencies in the witness's testimony.

cruel and unusual punishments   Degrading punishments that shock the moral standards of the community, such as torturing or physically beating a prisoner.

culpability   Guilt.

curtilage   At common law, the enclosed space surrounding a dwelling house; in modern codes this space has been extended to encompass other buildings.

custodial interrogation   Questioning by the police of a suspect in custody.

damages   Monetary compensation awarded by a court to a person who has suffered injuries or losses to person or property as a result of someone else's conduct.

deadlocked jury   A jury where the jurors cannot agree on a verdict. *See also*: hung jury.

deadly force   The degree of force that may result in the death of the person against whom the force is applied.

death penalty   Capital punishment; a sentence to death for the commission of a crime.

death-qualified jury   A trial jury composed of persons who do not entertain scruples against imposing a death sentence.

decision on the merits   A judicial decision that reaches the subject matter of a case.

decisional law   Law declared by appellate courts in their written decisions and opinions.

declaratory judgment   A judicial ruling conclusively declaring the rights, duties, or status of the parties but imposing no additional order, restriction, or requirement on them.

de facto   "In fact"; as a matter of fact.

de facto segregation   Racial segregation that exists in fact, even though it is not required by law

defamation   A tort involving the injury to one's reputation by the malicious or reckless dissemination of a falsehood.

defendant   A person charged with a crime or against whom a civil action is brought.

defense   A defendant's stated reasons of law or fact as to why the prosecution or plaintiff should not prevail.

defense attorneys   Lawyers who represent defendants in criminal cases.

definite sentencing   Legislatively determined sentencing with no discretion given to judges or corrections officials to individualize punishment.

de jure   "In law"; as a matter of law.

de jure discrimination   Discrimination that results from law, whether on its face or as applied.

delegation of legislative power   A legislative act authorizing an administrative or regulatory agency to promulgate rules and regulations having the force of law.

delinquency petition   A written document alleging that a juvenile has committed an offense and asking the court to hold an adjudicatory hearing to determine the merits of the petition.

de minimis   Minimal, trifling, trivial.

demurrer   An action of a defendant admitting to a set of alleged facts but nevertheless challenging the legal sufficiency of a complaint or criminal charge.

de novo   Anew; for a second time.

Department of Justice   The department of the federal government that is headed by the attorney general and staffed by U.S. attorneys.

deposition   The recorded sworn testimony of a witness; not given in open court.

derivative evidence   Evidence that is derived from or obtained only as a result of other evidence.

desegregation   Efforts to eliminate de jure or de facto racial segregation.

detention   Holding someone in custody.

detention hearing   A proceeding held to determine whether a juvenile charged with an offense should be detained pending an adjudicatory hearing.

determinate sentence   Variation on definite sentencing whereby a judge fixes the term of incarceration within statutory limits.

deterrence   Prevention of criminal activity by punishing criminals so that others will not engage in such activity.

dicta   *See: obiter dicta.*

diplomatic immunity   A privilege to be free from arrest and prosecution, granted under international law to diplomats, their staffs, and household members.

direct contempt   An obstructive or insulting act committed by a person in the immediate presence of the court.

directed verdict   A verdict rendered by a jury upon direction of the presiding judge.

direct evidence   Evidence that applies directly to proof of a fact or proposition. For example, a witness who testifies to having seen an act performed or having heard a statement made is giving direct evidence.

direct filing   The filing an information by a prosecutor charging a juvenile with an offense, rather than filing a petition in juvenile court to declare the juvenile delinquent for having committed the offense.

direct–indirect test   A test once used by the Supreme Court in its Commerce Clause jurisprudence. Under this test, a statute was valid only if the targeted activity had a direct impact on interstate commerce.

discrete and insular minorities   Minority groups that are locked out of the political process.

discretion   The power of public officials to act in certain situations according to their own judgment rather than relying on set rules or procedures.

discretionary review   Form of appellate court review of lower court decisions that is not mandatory but occurs at the discretion of the appellate court. *See also:* certiorari.

discuss list   The list of petitions for certiorari that are deemed worthy of discussion in conference.

dismissal   A judicial order terminating a case.

disorderly conduct   Illegal behavior that disturbs the public peace or order.

disparate impact   Differential, often discriminatory effect of a facially neutral law or policy on members of different races or genders.

disposition   The final settlement of a case.

dissent   An appellate judge's formal vote against the judgment of the court in a given case.

dissenting opinion   A written opinion by a judge or justice setting forth reasons for disagreeing with a particular decision of the court.

distinction between manufacturing and commerce   An important element of the Supreme Court's Commerce Clause jurisprudence in the late nineteenth and early twentieth centuries. The distinction between manufacturing, or production, on the one hand, and commerce, or distribution, on the other hand, served to limit the reach of Congress's power under the Commerce Clause.

distributive articles   Articles I, II, and III of the U.S. Constitution, delineating the powers and functions of the legislative, executive, and judicial branches, respectively, of the national government.

diversity jurisdiction   The authority of a federal court to entertain a civil suit in which the parties are citizens of different states and the amount in controversy exceeds $50,000.

diversity of citizenship action   A federal civil suit in which the parties are citizens of different states and the amount in controversy exceeds seventy-five thousand dollars.

diversity of citizenship jurisdiction   The authority of federal courts to hear lawsuits in which the parties are citizens of different states and the amount in controversy exceeds $75,000.

docket   The set of cases pending before a court of law.

doctor-assisted suicide   Administration by a physician of lethal drugs or gas to a terminally ill patient in order to produce death.

doctrine   A legal principle or rule developed through judicial decisions.

doctrine of abstention   The doctrine that federal courts should refrain from interfering with state judicial processes.

doctrine of incorporation   The doctrine under which provisions of the Bill of Rights are held to be incorporated within the Due Process Clause of the Fourteenth Amendment and are thereby made applicable to actions of the state and local governments.

doctrine of original intent   The doctrine that the Constitution is to be understood in terms of the intentions of the Framers.

doctrine of overbreadth   The doctrine under which a person makes a facial challenge to a law on the ground that the law might be applied in the future against activities protected by the First Amendment.

doctrine of saving construction   The doctrine under which courts adopt an interpretation of a statute that saves the statute from being declared unconstitutional.

doctrine of strict necessity   The doctrine under which courts engage in judicial review only when strictly necessary to the settlement of a case.

double jeopardy   The condition of being prosecuted a second time for the same offense.

drug courier profile   A controversial law enforcement practice of identifying possible drug smugglers by relying on a set of characteristics and patterns of behavior believed to typify persons who smuggle drugs.

drug paraphernalia   Items closely associated with the use of illegal drugs.

drug testing   The practice of subjecting employees to urine tests to determine whether they are using illegal substances.

dual federalism   A concept of federalism in which the national and state governments exercise authority within separate, self-contained areas of public policy and public administration.

Due Process Clause   The clause found in both the Fifth and Fourteenth Amendments that prohibits government from taking a person's life, liberty, or property without due process of law.

Due Process Clause of the Fourteenth Amendment   The provision of the Fourteenth Amendment that prohibits states from taking a person's life, liberty, or property without due process of law.

due process of law   Procedural and substantive rights of citizens against government actions that threaten the denial of life, liberty, or property.

duress   The use of illegal confinement or threats of harm to coerce someone to do something he or she would not do otherwise.

duty   An obligation that a person has by law or contract.

easement   A right of use over the property of another; frequently refers to a right-of-way across privately owned land.

ecclesiastical   Pertaining to religious laws or institutions.

economic due process   The doctrine under which the Supreme Court in the late nineteenth and early twentieth centuries used the Due Process Clauses of the Fifth and Fourteenth Amendments to protect free enterprise from government intervention.

economic freedom   Another term for free enterprise—that is, the ability to conduct one's business without interference by government.

economic protectionism   An attempt by one state to protect its domestic economy from outside competition.

Eighth Amendment   Amendment included in the Bill of Rights prohibiting excessive bail, excessive fines, and cruel and unusual punishments.

Electoral College   The body of electors chosen by the voters of each state and the District of Columbia for the purpose of formally electing the president and vice president of the United States. The number of electors (538) is equivalent to the total number of representatives and senators to which each state is entitled, plus three electors from the District of Columbia.

electronic eavesdropping   Covert listening to or recording of a person's conversations by electronic means.

electronic media   Electronic means of mass communication, including television, radio, and the Internet.

Eleventh Amendment   Amendment to the Constitution prohibiting federal courts from hearing suits brought by a citizen of one state against the government of another state.

emergency search   A warrantless search performed during an emergency, such as a fire or potential explosion.

eminent domain   The power of government, or of individuals and corporations authorized to perform public functions, to take private property for public use.

enabling legislation   As applied to public law, a statute authorizing the creation of a government program or agency and defining the functions and powers thereof.

en banc   "In the bench."

en banc rehearing   A rehearing in an appellate court in which all or a majority of the judges participate.

enforcement power under the Fourteenth Amendment   Congress's authority, recognized by Section 5 of the Fourteenth Amendment, to legislate in furtherance of the substantive provisions of the amendment.

English common law   A system of legal rules and principles recognized and developed by English judges prior to the colonization of America and accepted as a basic aspect of the American legal system.

entrapment   The act of government agents in inducing someone to commit a crime that the person otherwise would not be disposed to commit.

enumerated powers   Powers specified in the text of the federal and state constitutions.

equal access   Policies that permit religious and secular groups the same access to public buildings for purposes of meetings.

equality   A condition in which persons hold the same status with respect to a particular criterion such as wealth, standing, or power.

Equal Protection Clause   Clause in Section 1 of the Fourteenth Amendment that prohibits states from denying equal protection of the laws to persons within their jurisdictions.

equal protection of the laws   Constitutional requirement that the government not engage in prohibited forms of discrimination against persons under its jurisdiction.

Equal Rights Amendment   Failed attempt to amend the Constitution to guarantee equal rights for women.

equity   Historically, a system of rules, remedies, customs, and principles developed in England to supplement the harsh common law by emphasizing the concept of fairness. In addition, because the common law served only to recompense after injury, equity was devised to prevent injuries that could not be repaired or recompensed after the fact. While American judges continue to distinguish between law and equity, these systems of rights and remedies are, for the most part, administered by the same courts.

error correction   The function of appellate courts in correcting more or less routine errors committed by lower courts.

error, writ of   An order issued by an appellate court for the purpose of correcting an error revealed in the record of a lower court proceeding.

escape   Unlawfully fleeing to avoid arrest or confinement.

Establishment Clause   Clause in the First Amendment prohibiting Congress from enacting laws "respecting an establishment of religion."

establishment of religion   Official government support of religion or religious institutions. Prohibited by the First Amendment. *See also*: separation of church and state.

et al.   "And others."

euthanasia   Mercy killing.

evanescent evidence   Evidence that will likely disappear if not immediately seized.

evidence   Testimony, writings, or material objects offered in proof of an alleged fact or proposition.

evidentiary   Pertaining to the rules of evidence or the evidence in a particular case.

evidentiary hearing   A hearing on the admissibility of evidence into a civil or criminal trial.

evidentiary presumption   A situation in which the establishment of one fact allows inference of another fact or circumstance.

evolving standards of decency   Doctrine that holds that what constitutes cruel and unusual punishment must be determined in light of changing social standards of acceptable government conduct.

excessive bail   An unreasonably large dollar amount or unreasonable conditions imposed by a court as a prerequisite for a defendant to be released before trial; prohibited by the Eighth Amendment.

excessive fines   Fines that are deemed to be greater than is appropriate for the punishment of a particular crime.

exclusionary rule   Judicial doctrine forbidding the use of evidence in a criminal trial where the evidence was obtained in violation of the defendant's constitutional rights.

exculpatory   That which tends to exonerate a person of allegations of wrongdoing.

excusable homicide   A death caused by accident or misfortune.

executive agreement   An agreement between the United States and one or more foreign countries entered into by the president without ratification by the Senate.

executive order   An order by a president or governor directing some particular action to be taken.

executive privilege   The right of the president to withhold certain information from Congress or a court of law.

exhaustion of remedies   The requirement that a party seeking review by a court first exhaust all legal options for resolution of the issue by nonjudicial authorities or lower courts.

exigent circumstances   Situations that demand unusual or immediate action.

ex officio   "By virtue of the office."

ex parte   Term for a proceeding in which only one party is involved or represented.

expert witness   A witness with specialized knowledge or training called to testify in his or her field of expertise.

ex post facto   "After the fact."

***ex post facto* law**   A retroactive law that criminalizes actions that were innocent at the time they were taken or that increases punishment for a criminal act after it was committed.

expressive conduct   Conduct undertaken to express a message.

expressive religious conduct   Conduct undertaken to express a religious message.

ex proprio vigore   "By its own force."

***ex rel*.**   "On the relation or information of." A term usually designating the name of a person on whose behalf the government is bringing legal action against another party.

extradition   The surrender of a person by one jurisdiction to another for the purpose of criminal prosecution.

ex vi termini   "By definition"; from the very meaning of the term or expression used.

facial attack   A legal attack on the constitutionality of a law as it is written, as opposed to how it is applied in practice.

facial neutrality   Condition existing when a law, on its face, does not discriminate between or among classes of persons.

facial validity   The quality of being legitimate or permissible on its face. A law may nevertheless be invalid as applied in a given case.

fair hearing   A hearing in a court of law that conforms to standards of procedural justice.

fair notice   The requirement stemming from due process that government provide adequate notice to a person before it deprives that person of life, liberty, or property.

fair trial doctrine   The doctrine whereby, under the Fourteenth Amendment, states are required to provide fair trials to persons accused of crimes.

federal bureaucracy   The collective term for the myriad departments, agencies, and bureaus of the federal government.

Federal Bureau of Investigation   The primary agency charged with investigating violations of federal criminal laws.

federal courts   The courts operated by the U.S. government.

federal habeas corpus review   Review of a state criminal trial by a federal district court on a writ of habeas corpus after the defendant has been convicted, incarcerated, and has exhausted appellate remedies in the state courts.

federalism   The constitutional distribution of government power and responsibility between the national government and the states.

The Federalist Papers   The collection of essays written in 1788 by James Madison, Alexander Hamilton, and John Jay in support of ratification of the Constitution.

federal preemption   The doctrine that federal law preempts states from enforcing regulations in areas necessarily occupied solely by the federal government.

federal question   An issue arising under the U.S. Constitution or a federal statute, executive order, regulation, or treaty.

federal question jurisdiction   The authority of federal courts to decide issues of national law.

Federal Register   The publication containing all regulations proposed and promulgated by federal agencies.

Federal Rules of Appellate Procedure   Rules governing the practice of law in the U.S. Courts of Appeals.

federal system   A political system in which sovereignty is shared by national and regional governments.

fee simple   Ownership of real property; the highest interest in real estate the law will permit.

felony   A serious crime for which a person may be incarcerated for more than one year.

felony murder   A homicide committed during the course of committing another felony other than murder (for example, armed robbery). The felonious act substitutes for malice aforethought ordinarily required in murder.

field sobriety test   A test administered by police to persons suspected of driving while intoxicated. Usually consists of requiring the suspect to demonstrate the ability to perform such physical acts as touching one's finger to nose or walking backwards.

Fifteenth Amendment   Amendment to the Constitution, ratified in 1870, that prohibits states from denying the right to vote on account of race.

Fifth Amendment   Amendment included in the Bill of Rights providing for due process of law and prohibiting compulsory self-incrimination.

Fifth Amendment Due Process Clause   The clause of the Fifth Amendment that forbids the federal government from depriving persons of life, liberty, or property without due process of law.

fighting words   Utterances that are inherently likely to provoke a violent response from the audience.

fighting words doctrine   The First Amendment doctrine that holds that certain utterances are not constitutionally protected as free speech if they are inherently likely to provoke a violent response from the audience.

First Amendment   Amendment included in the Bill of Rights that protects freedom of religion and freedom of expression.

First Amendment absolutism   The idea that the First Amendment prohibits any and all attempts by government to regulate the content of expression.

first appearance   An initial judicial proceeding at which the defendant is informed of the charges, and the right to counsel, and a determination is made as to bail.

first degree murder   The highest degree of unlawful homicide usually defined as "an unlawful act committed with the premeditated intent to take the life of a human being."

force   The element of compulsion in such crimes against persons as rape and robbery.

forcible rape   Rape, as defined by common law; that is, sexual intercourse with a female, other than the offender's wife, by force and against the will of the victim.

forensic experts   Persons qualified in the application of scientific knowledge to legal principles, usually applied to those who participate in discourse or who testify in court.

forensic methods   Investigatory procedures that apply scientific knowledge to legal principles.

foreperson   The person selected by fellow jurors to chair deliberations and report the jury's verdict.

forfeiture   Sacrifice of ownership or some right (usually property) as a penalty.

forgery   The crime of making a false written instrument or materially altering a written instrument (such as a check, promissory note, or college transcript) with the intent to defraud.

fornication   Sexual intercourse between unmarried persons; an offense in some jurisdictions.

Fourteenth Amendment   Amendment to the Constitution, ratified in 1868, prohibiting states from depriving persons in their jurisdiction of due process of law.

Fourth Amendment   Amendment within the Bill of Rights prohibiting unreasonable searches and seizures.

fraud   Intentional deception or distortion in order to gain something of value.

freedom of assembly   The right of people to peaceably assemble in a public place.

freedom of association   The right of people to associate freely without unwarranted interference by government; implicitly protected by the First Amendment.

freedom of expression   A summary term embracing freedom of speech and freedom of the press as well as symbolic speech and expressive conduct.

Freedom of Information Act   Federal statute providing citizens a broad right of access to government information.

freedom of religion   The First Amendment right to free exercise of one's religion.

freedom of speech   The right to speak or express oneself freely without unreasonable interference by government.

freedom of the press   The right to publish newspapers, magazines, and other print media free from prior restraint or sanctions by the government.

Free Exercise Clause   Clause in the First Amendment prohibiting Congress from abridging the free exercise of religion.

free exercise of religion   The constitutional right to be free from government coercion or restraint with respect to religious beliefs and practices; guaranteed by the First Amendment.

free marketplace of ideas   The notion that expression should be unrestricted so that ideas can be traded freely in society, much as goods are freely exchanged in the marketplace.

frivolous appeals   An appeal wholly lacking in legal merit.

fruit of the poisonous tree doctrine   The doctrine that evidence derived from illegally obtained and thus inadmissible evidence is itself tainted and therefore likewise inadmissible.

Full Faith and Credit Clause   The constitutional requirement (Article IV, Section 1) that states recognize and give effect to the records and legal proceedings of other states.

full opinion decision   An appellate judicial decision rendered with one or more written opinions expressing the views of the judges in the case.

fundamental constitutional rights   Those constitutional rights that have been declared to be fundamental by the courts. Includes First Amendment freedoms, the right to vote, and the right to privacy.

fundamental error   An error in a judicial proceeding that adversely affects the substantial rights of the accused.

fundamental rights   Those rights, whether or not explicitly stated in the Constitution, deemed to be basic and essential to a person's liberty and dignity.

gag order   An order by a judge prohibiting certain parties from speaking publicly or privately about a particular case.

gambling   Operating or playing a game for money in the expectation of gaining more than the amount played.

gay rights   Summary term referring to the idea that persons should be permitted to engage in private homosexual conduct and be free from discrimination based on their sexual orientation.

gender-based classifications   Laws that discriminate on the basis of gender.

gender-based peremptory challenges   A challenge to a prospective juror's competency to serve based solely on the prospective juror's gender.

gender equity   The idea that women should receive equal benefits conferred by government.

gender-neutral   Term for a law or practice that applies equally to males and females—that is, one that is nondiscriminatory. For example, rape laws traditionally proscribed acts by a male against a female, whereas newer sexual battery laws proscribe acts by or against a person of either gender and thus are gender-neutral.

general court-martial   A court-martial composed of three or more military members and a military judge or a military judge alone with jurisdiction to try the most serious offenses under the Uniform Code of Military Justice.

general objection   An objection raised against a witness's testimony or introduction of evidence when the objecting party does not recite a specific ground for the objection.

general warrant   A search or arrest warrant that is not particular as to the person to be arrested or the property to be seized.

gerrymander   To intentionally manipulate legislative district boundaries for political purposes.

good-faith exception   An exception to the exclusionary rule. Whereas the exclusionary rule bars the use of evidence obtained by a search warrant later found to be defective, the exception allows use of such evidence if the police acted in good faith that the warrant was valid.

good-time credit   Credit toward early release from prison based on good behavior during confinement (often referred to as "gain time").

grandfather clause   (1) In its modern, general sense, any legal provision protecting someone from losing a right or benefit as a result of a change in policy. (2) In its historic sense, a legal provision limiting the right to vote to persons whose ancestors held the right to vote prior to passage of the Fifteenth Amendment in 1870.

grand jury   A group of twelve to twenty-three citizens convened to hear evidence in criminal cases to determine whether indictment is warranted.

group rights   Rights that people have by virtue of membership in a group, as distinct from purely individual rights.

habeas corpus   "You have the body." *See*: habeas corpus, writ of.

habeas corpus, writ of   A judicial order issued to an official holding someone in custody, requiring the official to bring the prisoner to court for the purpose of allowing the court to determine whether that person is being held legally. *See also*: habeas corpus.

habitual offender   One who has been repeatedly convicted of crimes.

habitual offender statute   A law that imposes an additional punishment on a criminal who has previously been convicted of crimes.

handwriting exemplar   A sample of a suspect's handwriting.

hard-core pornography   Pornography that is extremely graphic in its depiction of sexual conduct.

harmless error   A procedural or substantive error that does not affect the outcome of a judicial proceeding.

harmless error analysis   Judicial determination as to whether a particular procedural error requires reversal of a lower court's judgment.

harmless error doctrine   The doctrine by which minor or harmless errors during a trial do not require reversal of the lower court's judgment by an appellate court. To be considered harmless, an error of constitutional magnitude must be found by the appellate court to be "harmless beyond any reasonable doubt."

hate crimes   Crimes in which the victim is selected on the basis of race, religion, or ethnicity.

hate speech   Offensive speech directed at members of racial, religious, or ethnic minorities.

hearing   A public proceeding in a court of law, legislature, or administrative body for the purpose of ascertaining facts and deciding matters of law or policy.

hearsay evidence   Statements made by someone other than a witness offered in evidence at a trial or hearing to prove the truth of the matter asserted.

heightened scrutiny   The requirement that government justify a challenged policy by showing that it is substantially necessary to the achievement of an important objective.

high crimes and misdemeanors   Offenses for which an official of the federal government may be impeached and removed from office by Congress.

holding   The legal principle drawn from a judicial decision.

homicide   The killing of a human being.

hot pursuit   (1) The right of police to cross jurisdictional lines to apprehend a suspect or criminal. (2) The Fourth Amendment doctrine allowing warrantless searches and arrests where police pursue a fleeing suspect into a protected area.

house arrest   A sentencing alternative to incarceration where the offender is allowed to leave home only for employment and approved community service activities.

human rights statutes   State laws protecting people from discrimination in a variety of forms.

hung jury   A trial jury unable to reach a verdict.

Hyde amendment   A federal law that prohibits the use of federal welfare funds to pay for nontherapeutic abortions.

hypothetical question   A question based on an assumed set of facts. Hypothetical questions may be asked of expert witnesses in criminal trials.

illegitimacy   The condition of being born out of wedlock.

imminent lawless action   Unlawful conduct that is about to take place and which is inevitable unless there is intervention by the authorities.

imminently dangerous or outrageous conduct   The type of action that, when resulting in someone's death, usually characterizes second-degree murder.

immunity   Exemption from civil suit or prosecution. *See also:* transactional immunity; use immunity.

impeachment   (1) A legislative act bringing a charge against a public official that, if proven in a legislative trial, will cause his or her removal from public office. (2) Impugning the credibility of a witness by introducing contradictory evidence or proving his or her bad character.

implied consent   An agreement or acquiescence manifested by a person's actions or inaction.

implied consent statute   A law providing that by accepting a license a driver arrested for a traffic offense consents to urine, blood, and breath tests to determine blood alcohol content.

implied powers   Governmental powers not stated in but implied by the Constitution.

implied powers, doctrine of   A basic doctrine of American constitutional law derived from the Necessary and Proper Clause of Article I, Section 8. Under this doctrine, Congress is not limited to exercising those powers specifically enumerated in Article I but rather may exercise powers reasonably related to the fulfillment of its broad constitutional powers and responsibilities.

Imports-Exports Clause   Article I, Section 10, clause 2 of the Constitution, restricting state power to tax imports and exports.

impoundment   (1) Action by a president in refusing to allow expenditures approved by Congress. (2) In criminal law, the seizure and holding of a vehicle or other property by the police.

in camera   "In a chamber." In private; term referring to a judicial proceeding or conference from which the public is excluded.

incapacitation   The process of making it impossible for someone to do something.

incapacity   An inability, legal or actual, to act.

incarceration   Imprisonment.

incest   Sexual intercourse with a close blood relative or, in some cases, a person related by affinity.

inchoate offenses   Offenses preparatory to committing other crimes. Inchoate offenses include attempt, conspiracy, and solicitation.

incite   To provoke or set in motion.

inciting a riot   The crime of instigating or provoking a riot.

incorporation   The process by which most provisions of the Bill of Rights have been extended to limit state action by way of the Due Process Clause of the Fourteenth Amendment. Specific protections of the Bill of Rights are said to be incorporated within the Fourteenth Amendment's broad restrictions on the states.

inculpatory   That which tends to incriminate.

indefinite sentence   Form of criminal sentencing whereby a judge imposes a term of incarceration within statutory parameters, and corrections officials determine actual time served through parole or other means.

independent agencies   Federal agencies located outside the major cabinet-level departments.

independent counsel   A special prosecutor appointed to investigate and, if warranted, prosecute official misconduct.

independent source doctrine   The doctrine that permits evidence to be admitted at trial as long as it was obtained independently from illegally obtained evidence.

independent state grounds   The doctrine that an individual's claim to a right or benefit not supported by federal law will nevertheless be recognized by a federal court if a state court has found that the claimed right or benefit rests on a valid provision of state law.

indeterminate sentence   A prison sentence for an indefinite time, but within stipulated parameters, that allows correction officials to determine the prisoner's release date.

indictment   A formal document handed down by a grand jury accusing one or more persons of the commission of a crime or crimes.

indigency   Poverty; inability to afford legal representation.

indigent defendants   Defendants who cannot afford to retain private legal counsel and are therefore entitled to be represented by a public defender or a court-appointed lawyer.

indirect contempt   An act committed outside the presence of the court that insults the court or obstructs a judicial proceeding.

individual rights   In the traditional constitutional law sense, the legal protections for individuals against government actions that threaten life, liberty, or property.

ineffective representation   Representation by an attorney who is incompetent or less than reasonably effective.

inevitable discovery exception   An exception to the *Miranda* requirements and the fruit of the poisonous tree doctrine; allows the admission of evidence that was derived from inadmissible evidence if it inevitably would have been discovered independently by lawful means.

inflammatory remarks   Remarks by counsel during a trial designed to excite the passions of the jury.

in forma pauperis   "In the manner of a pauper." Waiver of filing costs and other fees associated with judicial proceedings to allow an indigent person to proceed.

information   A document filed by a prosecutor charging one or more persons with commission of crime.

infra   "Below."

inherent executive power   The powers of the president that flow from the nature of the office rather than from specific provisions of Article II.

inherent power   The power existing in an agency, institution, or individual by definition of the office.

inherently suspect   A law, policy, or classification that is, from a constitutional standpoint, questionable on its face.

initial appearance   After arrest, the first appearance of the accused before a judge or magistrate.

injunction   A judicial order requiring a person to do, or to refrain from doing, a designated thing.

in loco parentis   "In the place of the parent(s)."

inmate   One who is confined in a jail or prison.

in personam   Term referring to legal actions brought against a person, as distinct from actions against property. *See also: in rem.*

in propria persona   "In one's proper person." Term referring to the proper person to bring a legal action or make a motion before a court of law.

in re   "In the matter of."

in rem   Term referring to legal actions brought against things rather than persons. *See also: in personam.*

insanity   A degree of mental illness that negates the legal capacity or responsibility of the affected person.

insanity defense   A defense that seeks to exonerate the accused by showing that he or she was insane at the time of the crime and thus not legally responsible.

insufficient evidence   Evidence that falls short of establishing that required by law; usually referring to evidence that does not legally establish an offense or a defense.

intelligible principle standard   The doctrine whereby, in delegating power to the executive branch, Congress must provide a clear statement of policy to guide executive discretion.

intent   A state of mind in which a person seeks to accomplish a given result through a course of action.

inter alia   "Among other things."

intergovernmental tax immunity   The doctrine that federal and state governments may not levy taxes on one another.

intermediate appellate courts   Appellate courts positioned below the supreme or highest appellate court, whose primary function is to decide routine appeals not deserving review by the Supreme Court.

intermediate scrutiny   *See*: heightened scrutiny.

interposition   The archaic doctrine holding that when the federal government attempts to act unlawfully on an object within the domain of the state governments, a state may interpose itself between the federal government and the object of the federal government's action.

interpretation   The process of assigning meaning to a text.

interpretivism   The theory of constitutional interpretation holding that judges should confine themselves to the plain meaning of the text, the intentions of the Framers, and/or the historical meaning of the document.

interrogation   Questioning of a suspect by police or questioning of a witness by counsel.

interrogatories   Written questions put to a witness.

interstate agreements   Formal agreements or compacts between or among states.

interstate commerce   Commercial activity potentially extending beyond the boundaries of a state.

Interstate Commerce Act of 1887   Landmark act of Congress establishing the Interstate Commerce Commission.

interstate compacts   Agreements between or among state governments, somewhat analogous to treaties.

intoxication   A state of drunkenness resulting from the use of alcoholic beverages or drugs.

invalidate   Annul, negate, set aside.

invasion of privacy   A tort involving the unreasonable or unwarranted intrusion on the privacy of an individual.

inventory search   An exception to the warrant requirement that allows police who legally impound a vehicle to conduct a routine inventory of the contents of the vehicle.

investigatory detention   Brief detention of suspects by a police officer who has reasonable suspicion that criminal activity is afoot. *See also*: stop and frisk.

invidious   Arousing animosity, envy, or resentment.

ipse dixit   "He himself said it." An assertion resting on the authority of an individual.

ipso facto   "By the mere fact"; by the fact itself.

irreparable injury   An injury for which the award of money may not be adequate compensation and that may require the issuance of an injunction to fulfill the requirements of justice.

irresistible impulse   A desire that cannot be resisted due to impairment of the will by mental disease.

Jim Crow laws   Laws originating in the nineteenth century requiring various forms of racial segregation.

joinder   The coupling of two or more criminal prosecutions.

joinder and severance of parties   The uniting or severing of two or more parties charged with a crime or crimes.

joinder of offenses   The uniting for trial in one case of different charges or counts alleged in an information or indictment.

joint resolution   An act expressing the will of both houses of Congress in attempting to impose duties or limitations on parties outside the Congress; must be presented to the president for signature or veto.

judgment   A judicial determination as to the claims made by parties to a lawsuit. In a criminal case, the court's formal declaration to the accused regarding the legal consequences of a determination of guilt.

judgment of acquittal   (1) In a nonjury trial, a judge's order exonerating a defendant based on a finding that the defendant is not guilty. (2) In a case heard by a jury that finds a defendant guilty, a judge's order exonerating the defendant on the ground that the evidence was not legally sufficient to support the jury's finding of guilt.

judicial activism   Approach to jurisprudence whose underlying philosophy is that judges should exercise power vigorously, as opposed to exercising judicial restraint.

judicial behavior   The way judges make decisions; the academic study thereof.

judicial conference   A meeting of judges to deliberate on the disposition of a case.

judicial federalism   The constitutional relationship between federal and state courts of law.

judicial notice   The act of a court recognizing, without proof, the existence of certain facts that are commonly known. Such facts are often brought to the court's attention through the use of a calendar or almanac.

judicial restraint   Approach to jurisprudence whose underlying philosophy is that judges should exercise power cautiously and show deference to precedent and to the decisions of other branches of government, as opposed to exercising judicial activism.

judicial review   Generally, the review of any issue by a court of law. In American constitutional law, the authority of a court to invalidate acts of government on constitutional grounds.

Judiciary Act of 1789   Landmark statute establishing the federal courts system.

juris privati   "The private law," including such areas as torts, contracts, and property.

jurisdiction   "To speak the law." The geographical area within which, the subject matter with respect to which, and the persons over whom a court can properly exercise its power.

jurist   A person who is skilled or well versed in the law; often applied to lawyers and judges.

jury   A group of citizens convened for the purpose of deciding factual questions relevant to a civil or criminal case.

jury instructions   A judge's explanation of the law applicable to a case being heard by a jury.

jury nullification   The act of a jury disregarding the court's instructions and rendering a verdict based on the consciences of the jurors.

jury pardon   An action taken by a jury, despite the quality of the evidence, acquitting a defendant or convicting the defendant of a lesser crime than charged.

jury selection   The process of selecting prospective jurors at random from lists of persons representative of the community.

jury trial   A judicial proceeding to determine a defendant's guilt or innocence, conducted before a body of persons sworn to render a verdict based on the law and the evidence presented.

just compensation   The constitutional requirement that a party whose property is taken by government under the power of eminent domain be justly compensated for the loss.

Just Compensation Clause   Clause found in the Fifth Amendment requiring the federal government to provide owners reasonable and fair compensation when taking their property for a public use.

justiciability   Appropriateness for judicial decision. A justiciable dispute is one that can be effectively decided by a court of law.

justifiable homicide   Killing another in self-defense or defense of others when there is serious danger of death or great bodily harm to self or others, or when authorized by law.

justifiable use of force   The necessary and reasonable use of force by a person in self-defense, defense of another, or defense of property.

justification   A valid reason for one's actions.

juvenile   A person who has not yet attained the age of legal majority.

juvenile court   A judicial tribunal having jurisdiction over minors defined as juveniles who are alleged to be status offenders or to have committed acts of delinquency.

juvenile delinquency   Actions of a juvenile in violation of the criminal law.

juvenile delinquency hearing   Hearing in which a juvenile court determines whether a juvenile should be found to be delinquent. Analogous to a criminal trial in the adult justice system.

knock and announce   The provision under federal and most state laws that requires a law enforcement officer to first knock and announce his or her presence and purpose before entering a person's home to serve a search warrant.

knowing and intelligent waiver   A waiver of rights that is made with an awareness of the consequences.

laissez-faire capitalism   The theory holding that a capitalist economy functions best when government refrains from interfering with the marketplace.

law clerk   A judge's staff attorney.

lawmaking function   One of the principal functions of an appellate court, often referred to as the law development function.

leading question   A question that suggests an answer; permitted at a criminal trial on cross-examination of witnesses and in other limited instances.

least restrictive means test   A judicial inquiry as to whether a particular policy that is being challenged as an infringement of some fundamental right is the least burdensome means of achieving the government's objective.

legislation   Law enacted by a lawmaking body.

legislative veto   A statutory provision under which a legislative body is permitted to overrule a decision of an executive agency.

legislature   An elected lawmaking body such as the Congress of the United States or a state assembly.

Lemon test   Three-part test set forth in *Lemon v. Kurtzman* (1971). To pass muster under the Establishment Clause, a law must have a secular purpose, must not have the principal effect of advancing or inhibiting religion, and must avoid excessive entanglement between government and religious institutions.

lex non scripta   "The unwritten law" or common law.

liability   A broad legal term connoting debt, responsibility, or obligation; the condition of being bound to pay a debt, obligation, or judgment. This responsibility can be either civil or criminal.

libel   The tort of defamation through published material. *See*: defamation.

libertarianism   A philosophy that stresses individual freedom as the highest good.

liberty   The absence of restraint.

liberty of contract   The freedom to enter into contracts without undue interference from government.

limited government   An idea central to republican constitutionalism in which the power of government is limited by constitutional provisions specifically defining the nature and scope of governmental powers and prohibiting government from acting in detriment to individual rights and liberties.

limiting doctrines   Doctrines by which courts may refuse to render a decision on the merits in a case. *See*: abstention; exhaustion of remedies; political questions doctrine; mootness; standing.

line-item veto   Executive act nullifying certain portions of a bill.

lineup   A police identification procedure in which a suspect is included in a lineup with other persons who are exhibited to a victim or witness.

literacy test   A test of reading and/or writing skills, often given as a prerequisite to employment. At one time, literacy tests were required by many states as preconditions for voting in elections.

litigant   A party to, or participant in, a legal action.

local aspects of interstate commerce   Regulations of interstate commerce imposed by local governments in response to unique local conditions such as the shape of a harbor.

loitering   Standing around idly; "hanging around."

loss of civil rights   Forfeiture of certain rights, such as voting, as a result of a criminal conviction.

lottery   A drawing in which prizes are distributed to winners selected by lot from among those who have participated by paying a consideration.

magistrate   A judge with minor or limited authority.

Magna Carta   The "Great Charter" signed by King John in 1215 guaranteeing the legal rights of English subjects. Generally considered the foundation of Anglo-American constitutionalism.

majority opinion   An appellate court opinion joined in by a majority of the judges who heard the appeal.

mala in se   "Evil in itself." Term referring to crimes like murder that are universally condemned.

malapportionment   A condition that exists when legislative districts in a state or subdivisions of a county or municipality contain substantially unequal numbers of voters; may result naturally as a function of population shifts or through deliberate gerrymandering.

mala prohibita   "Prohibited evil." Term referring to crimes that are wrong primarily because the law declares them to be wrong.

malfeasance   Misconduct that adversely affects the performance of official duties.

malice aforethought   The mental predetermination to commit an illegal act.

mandamus, writ of   "We command." A judicial order commanding a public official or an organization to perform a specified duty.

mandate   A command or order.

manifest necessity   That is which clearly or obviously necessary or essential.

market participant exception   The doctrine where-by states may impose regulations to inhibit competition by out-of-state competitors where the state is itself a participant in the market.

material   Important, relevant, necessary.

memorandum decision   A judicial decision rendered without a supporting Opinion of the Court.

mens rea   "Guilty mind"; criminal intent.

militia   Historically, a military force composed of all able-bodied citizens, in service only during time of war, rebellion, or emergency.

minimal scrutiny   The most lenient form of judicial review of policies challenged as violations of civil rights and liberties.

Miranda warning   The warning given by police to individuals who are taken into custody before they are interrogated. Based on the Supreme Court's decision in *Miranda v. Arizona* (1966), the warning informs persons in custody that they have the right to remain silent and to have a lawyer present during questioning, and that anything they say can and will be used against them in a court of law.

misappropriation   Wrongful taking or diversion of funds or other property.

miscarriage of justice   Decision of a court that is inconsistent with the substantial rights of a party to the case.

misdemeanor   A minor crime usually punishable by a fine or confinement for less than one year.

misrepresentation   An untrue statement of fact made to deceive or mislead.

mistake of fact   Unconscious ignorance of a fact or belief in the existence of something that does not exist.

mistake of law   An erroneous opinion of legal principles applied to a set of facts.

mistrial   A trial that is terminated due to misconduct, procedural error, or a hung jury (one that is unable to reach a verdict).

mitigating circumstances   Circumstances or factors that tend to lessen culpability.

mitigating factors   *See*: mitigating circumstances.

mitigation   Reduction or alleviation, usually of punishment.

mockery of justice test   Judicial test for determining whether a defendant was provided adequate representation. The question is whether performance by counsel constituted a mockery of justice.

modern administrative state   Term for the highly bureaucratized federal government that emerged in the twentieth century.

moment of silence   Policy under which public school students are required to observe a minute of silence at the beginning of the school day.

monetary fines   Sums of money offenders are required to pay as punishment for the commission of crimes.

monogamy   The practice of having only one spouse, as distinct from bigamy or polygamy.

moot   A point that no longer has any practical significance; academic.

mootness   Term referring to a question that does not involve rights currently at issue in, or pertinent to, the outcome of a case.

moral individualism   The doctrine that individuals, not society or government, should make moral choices.

motion   An application to a court to obtain a particular ruling or order.

motion for a new trial   A formal request made to a trial court to hold a new trial in a particular case that has already been adjudicated.

motion for rehearing   A formal request made to a court of law to convene another hearing in a case in which the court has already ruled.

motion to dismiss   A formal request to a trial court to dismiss the criminal charges against the defendant.

motive   A person's conscious reason for acting.

myth of legality   The belief that judicial decisions are a function of legal rules, procedures, and principles rather than the ideological leanings or policy preferences of judges.

narrowly tailored   Term used to describe a policy that is carefully designed to achieve its intended goal with a minimal negative impact on civil liberties.

narrowness doctrine   The doctrine that judicial decisions should be framed in the narrowest possible terms or based on the narrowest possible grounds.

national supremacy   The doctrine that holds that when state and federal authority collide, the federal authority must prevail.

natural law   Principles of human conduct believed to be ordained by God or nature, existing prior to and superseding human law.

natural rights   Rights believed to be inherent in human beings, the existence of which is not dependent on their recognition by government. In classical liberalism, natural rights are "life, liberty, and property." As recognized by the Declaration of Independence, they are "life, liberty, and the pursuit of happiness."

negligence   The failure to exercise ordinary care or caution.

neutral and detached officer   A judge or magistrate who is without an interest in the outcome of a case.

New Equal Protection   A modern interpretation of the Equal Protection Clause of the Fourteenth Amendment under which policies that impinge on fundamental rights or discriminate on the basis of suspect classifications are presumed invalid by the courts.

new federalism   Term for the variety of efforts in recent decades aimed at revitalizing the role of the states in the federal system or returning power to them.

New Jersey Plan   A plan introduced by the New Jersey delegation at the Constitutional Convention of 1787. It called for a unicameral legislature in which all states would be equally represented.

new property   Term referring to a person's interest in government benefits or entitlements.

Nineteenth Amendment   Amendment to the Constitution, adopted in 1920, which prohibits the denial of voting rights on account of gender.

Ninth Amendment   Amendment contained within the Bill of Rights that recognizes rights retained by the people even though they are not specifically enumerated in the Constitution.

no contest plea   A plea to a criminal charge that, although it is not an admission of guilt, generally has the same effect as a plea of guilty. *See also: nolo contendere*.

nolo contendere   "I will not contest it." Alternate term for a plea of no contest in a criminal case.

nondeadly force   Force that does not result in death.

nondelegation doctrine   The doctrine that Congress may not delegate its legislative authority to the executive branch.

noninterpretivism   A term referring to a variety of theories of constitutional interpretation, the common element of which is the rejection of interpretivism. *See also*: interpretivism.

nonunanimous verdicts   Jury verdicts rendered by a less-than-unanimous vote of the jurors.

notary public   A person empowered by law to administer oaths, to certify things as true, and to perform various minor official acts.

notice of appeal   Document filed with an appellate court notifying the court of an appeal from a judgment of a lower court.

nuisance   An unlawful or unreasonable use of a person's property that results in an injury to another or to the public.

nullification   The act of rendering something invalid; the process by which something may be invalidated. Historically, a doctrine under which states claimed the right to nullify actions of the national government.

obiter dicta   "Something said in passing." Incidental statements in a judicial opinion that are not binding and are unnecessary to support the decision.

objective test   A legal test based on external circumstances rather than the perceptions or intentions of an individual actor.

obscenity   Explicit sexual material that is patently offensive, appeals to a prurient or unnatural interest in sex, and lacks serious scientific, artistic, or literary content.

obstruction of justice   The crime of impeding or preventing law enforcement or the administration of justice.

open fields exception   An exception to the Fourth Amendment search warrant requirement, holding that Fourth Amendment protection does not apply to the open fields around a home, even if these open fields are private property.

open public trial   A trial that is held in public and is open to spectators.

opening statement   A prosecutor's or defense lawyer's initial statement to the judge or jury in a trial.

opinion   A written statement accompanying a judicial decision, authored by one or more judges, supporting or dissenting from that decision.

opinion concurring in the judgment   A judicial opinion in which the author agrees with the decision of the court, but for reasons other than those stated in the court's principal opinion.

opinion evidence   Testimony in which the witness expresses an opinion, as distinct from knowledge of specific facts.

Opinion of the Court   An opinion announcing both the decision of the court and its supporting rationale. The opinion can either be a majority opinion or a unanimous opinion.

oral argument   A hearing before an appellate court in which counsel for the parties appear for the purpose of making statements and answering questions from the bench.

ordinance   An enactment of a local governing body such as a city council or commission.

organized crime   Syndicates involved in racketeering and other criminal activities.

original intent, doctrine of   The doctrine holding that the Constitution should be interpreted and applied according to the intentions of the Framers, insofar as those intentions can be determined.

originalism   The doctrine that courts must preserve the original meaning of the Constitution.

original jurisdiction   The authority of a court of law to hear a case in the first instance.

original package doctrine   Archaic doctrine under which states were prohibited from imposing taxes on imported goods that, although no longer in the stream of commerce, remained in their original packages.

overbreadth doctrine   First Amendment doctrine that holds that a law is invalid if it can be applied to punish people for engaging in constitutionally protected expression.

overrule   To reverse or annul by subsequent action.

oversight   The responsibility of a legislative body to monitor the activities of government agencies it created.

oversight hearings   Formal hearings conducted for the purpose of monitoring actions by government agencies.

panel   A set of jurors or judges assigned to hear a case.

pardon   An executive action that mitigates or sets aside punishment for a crime.

parens patriae   "The parent of the country." Term referring to the role of the state as guardian of minors or other legally disabled persons.

parliamentary system   A democratic system of government in which there is no formal separation of the legislative and executive offices. The leader of the majority party in the parliament is the prime minister, or chief executive.

parochial legislation   Legislation that favors narrow, localized interests.

parole   The conditional early release from prison.

parole revocation hearing   An administrative hearing held for the purpose of determining whether an offender's parole should be revoked.

partisan gerrymandering   The intentional manipulation of legislative district lines in order to provide one political party a competitive advantage over another.

party   (1) A person taking part in a legal transaction; includes plaintiffs and defendants in lawsuits but also has a far broader legal connotation. (2) In politics, an organization established for the principal purpose of recruiting and nominating candidates for public office.

pat-down search   A manual search of the exterior of a suspect's outer garments.

patently offensive   Plainly or obviously offensive; disgusting.

penal   Of or pertaining to punishment.

pendency of the appeal   The period after an appeal is filed but before the appeal is adjudicated.

penitentiary   A prison.

penology   The study or practice of prison management.

penumbra   An implied right or power emanating from an enumerated right or power.

per curiam   "By the court." Term referring to an opinion attributed to a court collectively, usually not identified with the name of any particular member of the court.

peremptory challenge   An objection to the selection of a prospective juror in which the attorney making the challenge is not required to state the reason for the objection.

per se   "By itself"; in itself.

petition   A written request, usually addressed to a court, asking for a specified action. Sometimes the term indicates written requests in an *ex parte* proceeding, where there is no adverse party. In some jurisdictions, the term refers to the first pleading in a lawsuit.

petitioner   A person who brings a petition before a court of law.

petit jury   A trial jury, usually composed of either six or twelve persons.

petty (petit) offenses   Minor crimes for which fines or short jail terms are the only prescribed modes of punishment.

picketing   Carrying signs of protest in the public forum.

places of public accommodation   Businesses that open their doors to the general public.

plaintiff   The party initiating legal action; the complaining party.

plain view   Readily visible to the naked eye. *See also:* plain view doctrine.

plain view doctrine   The Fourth Amendment doctrine under which a police officer may seize evidence of crime that is readily visible to the officer's naked eye as long as the officer is legally in the place where the evidence becomes visible.

plea bargain   An agreement between a defendant and a prosecutor whereby the defendant agrees to plead guilty in exchange for some concession (for example, a reduction in the severity or number of charges brought).

plea of guilty   A formal answer to a criminal charge in which the accused acknowledges guilt and waives the right to trial.

plea of not guilty   A formal answer to a criminal charge in which the accused denies guilt and thus exercises the right to a trial.

plenary   Full, complete; often used with reference to the nature and extent of governmental powers enumerated in the federal Constitution.

plenary review   Full, complete review by an appellate court.

pluralism   A social or political system in which diverse groups compete for status or power; the theory that the role of government is to serve as broker among competing interest groups.

plurality opinion   An opinion that states the judgment of the Court but that does not have the endorsement of a majority of justices.

pocket veto   The power of a chief executive to effectively veto legislation by not acting on a bill passed within ten days prior to adjournment of a legislative session.

police deception   Intentional deception by police in order to elicit incriminating statements from a suspect.

police interrogation   Questioning by the police of a suspect in custody.

police power   The power of government to legislate to protect public health, safety, welfare, and morality.

police powers of the states   The powers of state governments to enact laws to further the public health, safety, welfare, and morality.

political dissent   Organized or public opposition to the government.

political question   A question that a court believes to be appropriate for decision by the legislative or the executive branch of government and thus improper for judicial decision making.

political questions doctrine   The doctrine that holds that courts should avoid ruling on political questions.

poll tax   A tax that must be paid before a person is permitted to vote in an election.

polling the jury   Practice in which trial judge asks each member of the jury to affirm that he or she supports the jury's verdict.

polygamy   Plural marriage; having more than one spouse.

polygraph evidence   Results of lie detector tests (generally inadmissible into evidence).

popular sovereignty   The idea that political authority is vested ultimately not in the rulers but in the people they rule.

pornography   Material that appeals to the sexual impulse or appetite.

postconviction relief   Term applied to various mechanisms a defendant may use to challenge a conviction after other routes of appeal have been exhausted.

power of contempt   The authority of a court of law to punish someone who insults the court or flouts its authority.

power to investigate   The power of a legislative body to conduct hearings and subpoena witnesses in order to investigate an issue or area over which it has legislative authority.

power to regulate interstate commerce   The power of Congress, and to a lesser extent the powers of state and local governments, to enact laws and regulations affecting commerce involving more than one state.

precedent   A judicial decision cited as authority controlling or influencing the outcome of a similar case.

preemption   In constitutional law, the doctrine under which a field of public policy, previously open to action by the states, is brought by the U.S. Congress within the primary or exclusive control of the national government.

preferred freedoms   Certain freedoms, in particular the First Amendment freedom of speech, that are accorded greater protection than other activities. When a legislative measure that restricts preferred freedoms is challenged, the ordinary presumption that the restriction is constitutional is reversed in favor of the presumptive protection of free expression.

prejudicial error   An error at trial that substantially affects the interests of the accused.

preliminary hearing   A hearing held to determine whether there is sufficient evidence to hold an accused for trial.

preliminary injunction   An injunction issued pending a trial on the merits of the case.

preparatory conduct   Actions taken in order to prepare to commit a crime.

preponderance of evidence   Evidence that has greater weight than countervailing evidence.

presentment   A synonym for indictment.

presentment requirement   As outlined in the Presentment Clause (Article I, Section 7) of the Constitution, the requirement that a bill that has passed both houses of Congress be "presented" to the president for signature or veto.

presidential immunity   The barrier against bringing a civil suit against the president for any of his official actions.

presidential pardon   Action by the president pardoning one or more persons for the commission of a crime.

presidential power to make foreign policy   The president's broad authority to set policy as it relates to international relations and foreign affairs.

presidential war powers   Term referring to the president's authority as commander in chief.

presumption   (1) An inference drawn by reasoning. (2) A rule of law subject to rebuttal.

presumption of constitutionality   The doctrine of constitutional law holding that laws are presumed to be constitutional with the burden of proof resting on the plaintiff to demonstrate otherwise.

presumption of innocence   The notion that the accused in a criminal trial is presumed innocent until proven guilty.

presumption of validity   See: presumption of constitutionality.

preterm conference   The Supreme Court's conference held prior to the beginning of its annual term in which the Court disposes of numerous petitions for certiorari.

pretextual stop   An incident in which police stop a suspicious vehicle on the pretext of a motor vehicle infraction.

pretrial detention   The holding of a defendant in custody prior to trial.

pretrial discovery   The process by which the defense and prosecution interrogate witnesses for the opposing party and gain access to the evidence possessed by the opposing party prior to trial.

pretrial diversion program   A program in which a first-time offender is afforded the opportunity to avoid a criminal conviction by participating in some specified treatment, counseling, or community service.

pretrial motion   Any of a variety of motions made by counsel prior to the inception of a trial.

pretrial publicity   Media coverage of a case that has the potential to deprive a defendant of the right to a fair trial by an impartial jury.

pretrial release   The release of a defendant pending trial.

preventive detention   Holding a suspect in custody before trial to prevent escape or other wrongdoing.

prima facie   "On the face of it"; at first glance. Term referring to a point that will be considered true unless contested or refuted.

principals   Persons whose conduct involves direct participation in a crime.

prior restraint   An official act preventing publication of a particular work.

prisoners' rights   The set of rights that prisoners retain or attempt to assert through litigation.

private property   Property held by individuals or corporations, not by the public generally.

privilege   In general, an activity in which a person may engage without interference. The term is often used interchangeably with "right" in American constitutional law, with reference to the Privileges and Immunities Clauses of Article IV and the Fourteenth Amendment of the Constitution.

privileges   Rights extended to persons by virtue of law.

Privileges and Immunities Clause   (1) Article IV, Section 2, clause 1, of the Constitution, providing that "Citizens of each State shall be entitled to all Privileges and Immunities of Citizens in the several States." (2) Similar provision contained in Section 1 of the Fourteenth Amendment.

probable cause   Knowledge of specific facts providing reasonable grounds for believing that criminal activity is afoot.

probable cause hearing   A hearing held in a court to make a formal determination on an issue of probable cause.

probation   Conditional release of a convicted criminal in lieu of incarceration.

probative   Tending to prove the truth or falsehood of a proposition.

pro bono   "For the good." Performing service without compensation.

procedural criminal law   The branch of the criminal law that deals with the processes by which crimes are investigated, prosecuted, and punished.

procedural due process   Set of procedures designed to ensure fairness in a judicial or administrative proceeding.

procedural law   The law regulating governmental procedure (for example, rules of criminal procedure).

profanity   Vulgar, coarse, or filthy language; irreverence toward sacred things.

pro forma   Merely for the sake of form.

prohibition, writ of   An appellate court order preventing a lower court from exercising its jurisdiction in a particular case.

promissory estoppel   The doctrine of contract law under which a promise that induces action on the part of the promisee may be legally enforceable.

pronouncement of sentence   Formal announcement of a criminal punishment by a trial judge.

proof beyond a reasonable doubt   The standard of proof in a criminal trial or a juvenile delinquency hearing.

proper forum   The correct court or other institution in which to press a particular claim.

property rights   The bundle of rights that exist relative to private ownership and control of property.

proportionality   The degree to which a particular punishment matches the seriousness of a crime or matches the penalty other offenders have received for the same crime.

proportional representation   An electoral system in which the percentage of votes received by a given political party entitles that party to the same percentage of seats in the legislature.

proportionate representation   The idea that certain groups should be represented by ensuring that the legislature is composed according to the proportion of such groups in society.

proscribe   To forbid; prohibit.

pro se   "On one's own behalf." *See also*: pro se defense.

prosecution   Initiation and conduct of a criminal case.

prosecutor   A public official empowered to initiate criminal charges and conduct prosecutions.

prosecutorial discretion   The leeway afforded prosecutors in deciding whether or not to bring charges and to engage in plea bargaining.

prosecutorial immunity   A prosecutor's legal shield against civil suits stemming from his or her official actions.

pro se defense   Representing oneself in a criminal case.

protective tariffs   Taxes on products imported from other nations, which increase their cost and thus make domestic products more appealing to consumers. Opposed by supporters of free trade.

provocation   An action or behavior that prompts another person to react through criminal conduct.

proximate cause   The cause that is nearest a given effect in a causal relationship.

prurient interest   An excessive or unnatural interest in sex.

public accommodations statute   A law prohibiting various forms of discrimination by businesses that open their doors to the general public.

public defender   An attorney responsible for defending indigent persons charged with crimes.

public drunkenness   The offense of appearing in public while intoxicated.

public figures   Public officials or persons who are in the public eye.

public forum   A public space generally acknowledged as appropriate for public assemblies or expressions of views.

public law   General classification of law consisting of constitutional law, administrative law, international law, and criminal law.

public safety exception   Exception to the *Miranda* requirement that police officers promptly inform suspects taken into custody of their rights to remain silent and have an attorney present during questioning. Under the public safety exception, police may ask suspects questions motivated by a desire to protect public safety without jeopardizing the admissibility of suspects' answers to those questions or subsequent statements.

punitive damages   A sum of money awarded to the plaintiff in a civil case as a means of punishing the defendant for wrongful conduct.

punitive isolation   Solitary confinement of a person who is incarcerated.

pure speech   Communication that is purely spoken.

putting witnesses under the rule   Placing witnesses under the rule that requires them to remain outside the courtroom except when testifying.

qua   As; in the character or capacity of.

quash   To vacate or annul.

quasi-judicial authority   The authority of certain regulatory or administrative agencies to make determinations with respect to the rights of private parties under their jurisdiction.

race-conscious remedies   Remedies to racial injustices that specifically take race into account.

racial gerrymandering   The intentional manipulation of legislative district boundaries in order to diminish or enlarge the political influence of African-American or other minority voters.

racially motivated peremptory challenges   Peremptory challenges to prospective jurors, based solely on racial animus or racial stereotypes.

rational basis test   The test of the validity of a statute inquiring whether it is rationally related to a legitimate government objective.

real property   Land and buildings permanently attached thereto.

reapportionment   The redrawing of legislative district lines so as to remedy malapportionment.

reasonable doubt standard   The standard of proof in a criminal trial under which a defendant must not be convicted of a crime if, after hearing all the evidence, a reasonable person would have doubt as to the defendant's guilt. Sometimes the term "reasonable doubt" is equated to lack of moral certainty.

reasonable expectation of privacy   A person's reasonable expectation that his or her activities in a certain place are private; society's expectations with regard to whether activities in certain places are private.

reasonable force   The maximum degree of force that is necessary to accomplish a lawful purpose.

reasonable suspicion   A reasonable person's suspicion that criminal activity is afoot.

reasoning   The logic of a legal argument or judicial opinion.

rebuttal witnesses   Witnesses called to dispute the testimony of the opposing party's witnesses.

reciprocal immunity   *See*: intergovernmental tax immunity.

recognizance   An obligation to appear in a court of law at a given time.

recusal   A decision of a judge to withdraw from a case, usually due to bias or personal interest in the outcome.

recuse   To disqualify oneself from participating in a court case.

redeeming social importance   Value to society that redeems an otherwise worthless instance of expression.

referendum   An election in which voters decide a question of public policy.

regulation   A legally binding rule or order prescribed by a controlling authority; generally used with respect to the rules promulgated by administrative and regulatory agencies.

rehabilitation   The process of restoring someone or something to its former status; a justification for punishment emphasizing reform rather than retribution.

release on personal recognizance   Pretrial release of a defendant based solely on the defendant's promise to appear for future court dates.

released time programs   Public school programs in which students are permitted to leave school grounds to attend religious exercises.

relevant evidence   Evidence tending to prove or disprove an alleged fact.

Religion Clauses of the First Amendment   The Establishment Clause and Free Exercise Clause of the First Amendment.

Religious Freedom Restoration Act (RFRA)   Act of Congress designed to enhance religious freedom vis-à-vis government; declared unconstitutional by the Supreme Court in 1997.

religious speech   Expression of a religious nature.

religious tests   Tests to determine whether individuals hold "appropriate" religious convictions.

remand   To send back, as from a higher court to a lower court, for the latter to take specified action in a case or to follow proceedings designated by the higher court.

remedy   The means by which a right is enforced or a wrong is redressed.

removal power   The power of the president to remove officials in executive departments and agencies.

rendition   The act of one state in surrendering a fugitive to another state.

Rendition Clause   Clause of Article IV, Section 2 of the Constitution, requiring states to surrender fugitives to other states upon proper request.

repeal   A legislative act removing a law from the statute books.

reply brief   A brief submitted in response to an appellee's answer brief.

reporters   Books containing judicial decisions and accompanying opinions. *See*: case reporters.

representative democracy   A form of government in which policy decisions are made by representatives chosen in periodic competitive elections. *See*: representative government.

representative government   Form of government in which officials responsible for making policy are elected by the people in periodic free elections. *See*: representative democracy.

reprimands   Minor punitive actions taken by military commanders for various infractions committed by military servicepersons.

resentencing   A new sentencing hearing ordered by an appellate court.

reserved powers   Powers reserved to the states or the people under the Tenth Amendment.

res judicata   "A thing decided." A matter decided by a judgment, connoting the firmness and finality of the judgment as it affects the parties to the lawsuit; has the general effect of bringing litigation on a contested point to an end.

res nova   "New thing." A new issue or case.

resolution   A legislative act expressing the will of one or both houses of the legislature. Unlike a statute, a resolution has no enforcement clause. *See also:* concurrent resolution; joint resolution.

respondent   A person asked to respond to a lawsuit or writ.

restitution   The act of compensating someone for losses suffered.

restrictive covenant   An agreement among property holders restricting the use of property or prohibiting the rental or sale of it to certain parties.

retribution   Something demanded in payment for a debt; in criminal law, the demand that a criminal pay his or her debt to society.

retroactive   Changing the legal status or character of past events or transactions.

reverse   To set aside a decision on appeal.

review   An examination by an appellate court of a lower court's decision.

revocation   The withdrawal of some right or power (for example, the revocation of parole).

RICO Act   The Racketeer Influenced and Corrupt Organizations Act, passed in 1970, which essentially prohibits infiltration of organized crime into organizations or enterprises engaged in interstate commerce.

rider   A small provision attached to a contract, document, or bill.

right   Anything to which a person has a just and valid claim.

right of confrontation   The right to cross-examine witnesses for the opposing party in a criminal case.

right of cross-examination   *See*: right of confrontation.

right of privacy   Constitutional right to engage in intimate personal conduct or make fundamental life decisions without interference by the state.

right to appeal   Statutory right to appeal decisions of lower courts in certain circumstances.

right to a speedy trial   Constitutional right to have an open public trial conducted without unreasonable delay.

right to be let alone   Another term for the right of privacy.

right to counsel   (1) The right to retain an attorney to represent oneself in court. (2) The right of an indigent person to have an attorney provided at public expense.

right to die   Controversial "right" to terminate one's own life under certain circumstances.

right to keep and bear arms   Right to possess certain weapons, protected against federal infringement by the Second Amendment to the Constitution.

right to refuse medical treatment   The right of a patient or patient's surrogate in some instances to refuse to allow doctors to perform medical treatment.

right to vote   The right of an individual to cast a vote in an election.

riot   A public disturbance involving acts of violence, usually by three or more persons.

ripeness   Readiness for review by a court of law. An issue is "ripe for review" in the Supreme Court when a case presents adverse parties who have exhausted all other avenues of appeal.

ripeness doctrine   The doctrine under which courts consider only those questions that are deemed to be "ripe for review."

roadblocks   Barriers set up by police to stop motorists.

robbery   The crime of taking money or property from a person against that person's will by means of force.

rule making   The power of a court or agency to promulgate rules; the process through which rules are promulgated.

rule of four   U.S. Supreme Court rule whereby the Court grants certiorari only on the agreement of at least four justices.

rule of law   The idea that law, not the discretion of officials, should govern public affairs.

rules of procedure   Rules promulgated by courts governing civil, criminal, and appellate procedure.

sanction Penalty or other mechanism of enforcement.

saving construction, doctrine of   The doctrine that, given two plausible interpretations of a statute, a court will adopt the interpretation that prevents the statute from being declared unconstitutional.

scarcity theory   Theory holding that government can and should regulate access to the public airwaves, as these are scarce commodities.

school prayer   Various activities of a religious nature in the public schools.

school prayer decisions   Collective term for the Supreme Court's decisions of the 1960s prohibiting various activities of a religious nature in the public schools.

scientific evidence   Evidence obtained through scientific and technological innovations.

Scopes trial   Sensational criminal trial held in 1925 in Dayton, Tennessee, in which John Scopes, a high school biology teacher, was convicted under a state law (now defunct) prohibiting the teaching of evolution.

search and seizure   Term referring to the police search for and/or seizure of contraband or other evidence of crime.

search based on consent   A search of person or property conducted after a person voluntarily permits police to do so.

search incident to a lawful arrest   Search of a person placed under arrest and the area within the arrestee's grasp and control.

search warrant   A court order authorizing a search of a specified area for a specified purpose.

secession   Action by a state formally withdrawing from the Union.

Second Amendment   Amendment contained within the Bill of Rights guaranteeing the "right to keep and bear arms."

Section 1983 action   A federal lawsuit brought under 42 U.S. Code Section 1983 to redress violations of civil and/or constitutional rights.

secular government   Government that is not affiliated with or controlled by religious authorities.

secular humanism   The philosophy that man, not God, is the source of standards of right and wrong.

sedition   The crime of inciting insurrection or attempting to overthrow the government.

seditious speech   Expression aimed at inciting insurrection or overthrow of the government.

seduction   The common law crime of inducing a woman of previously chaste character to have sexual intercourse outside of wedlock on the promise of marriage.

seizure   Action of police in taking possession or control of property or persons.

selective incorporation   Doctrine under which selected provisions comprising most of the Bill of Rights are deemed applicable to the states by way of the Fourteenth Amendment.

selective prosecution   Singling out defendants for prosecution on the basis of race, religion, or other impermissible classifications.

self-representation   *See*: pro se defense.

sentence   The official pronouncement of punishment in a criminal case.

sentencing guidelines   Legislative guidelines mandating that sentencing conform to guidelines absent a compelling reason for departing from them.

sentencing hearing   A hearing held by a trial court prior to the pronouncement of sentence.

separate but equal doctrine   A now defunct doctrine that permitted racial segregation as long as equal facilities or accommodations were provided.

separation of church and state   First Amendment doctrine that holds that there must be a "wall of separation" between religion and government.

separation of powers   Constitutional assignment of legislative, executive, and judicial powers to different branches of government.

sequestration   Holding jurors incommunicado during trial.

seriatim   Serially, individually.

set-aside   Term for the affirmative action policies that reserve a certain proportion of government contracts for minority businesses.

Seventh Amendment   Amendment contained within the Bill of Rights guaranteeing the right to a jury trial in federal civil suits.

severability   The doctrine under which courts will declare invalid only the offending provision of a statute and allow the other provisions to remain in effect.

severability clause   A clause found in a statute indicating that if any particular provision of the law is invalidated, the other provisions remain in effect.

sexual harassment   Offensive interaction of a sexual nature in the workplace.

Shays's rebellion   A 1786 uprising of farmers in Massachusetts led by Daniel Shays, a former Revolutionary Army captain. The rebellion was spawned by economic conditions that the rebels believed to be grossly unfair to farmers and working people. It was put down in January 1787. Shays and thirteen other leaders of the rebellion were tried for treason and sentenced to death. Two were executed. Shays and the other leaders were eventually pardoned by Massachusetts governor John Hancock.

Sherman Antitrust Act of 1890 A federal statute prohibiting any contract, combination, or conspiracy in restraint of trade. The act is designed to protect and preserve a system of free and open competition. Its scope is broad and reaches individuals and entities in profit and nonprofit activities as well as local governments and educational institutions.

show cause A court order requiring a party to appear and present a legal justification for a particular act.

showup An event in which a crime victim is taken to see a suspect to make an identification.

silver platter doctrine Doctrine under which federal and state authorities could share illegally obtained evidence before the exclusionary rule was made applicable to all jurisdictions.

similar fact evidence Evidence of facts similar to the facts in the crime charged. The test of admissibility is whether such evidence is relevant and has a probative value in establishing a material issue. Under some limited circumstances, evidence of other crimes or conduct similar to that charged against the defendant may be admitted in evidence in a criminal prosecution.

sine qua non "Without which not." A necessary or indispensable condition or prerequisite.

Sixth Amendment Amendment contained within the Bill of Rights guaranteeing the right to counsel and the right to trial by jury in criminal cases.

slander The tort of defaming someone's character through verbal statements.

small claims Minor civil suits.

sobriety checkpoints Roadblocks set up for the purpose of administering field sobriety tests to motorists who appear to be intoxicated.

social contract The theory that government is the product of agreement among rational individuals who subordinate themselves to collective authority in exchange for security of life, liberty, and property.

social Darwinism The theory that society improves through unrestricted competition and the "survival of the fittest."

sodomy Oral or anal sex between persons, or sex between a person and an animal (the latter is often referred to as bestiality).

solicitation (1) The crime of offering someone money or other thing of value in order to persuade that person to commit a crime. (2) An active effort on the part of an attorney or other professional to obtain business.

sovereign immunity A common law doctrine under which the sovereign may be sued only with its consent.

special prosecutor A prosecutor appointed specifically to investigate a particular episode and, if criminal activity is found, to prosecute those involved. Also referred to as an independent counsel.

specific performance A court-imposed requirement that a party perform obligations incurred under a contract.

Speech or Debate Clause Provision of Article I, Section 6, protecting members of Congress from arrest or interference with their official duties.

speedy and public trial An open and public criminal trial held without unreasonable delay; guaranteed by the Sixth Amendment to the Constitution.

spending power The power of the legislature to spend public money for public purposes.

standby counsel An attorney appointed to assist an indigent defendant who elects to represent himself or herself at trial.

standing The right to initiate a legal action or challenge based on the fact that one has suffered or is likely to suffer a real and substantial injury.

stare decisis "To stand by decided matters." The principle that past decisions should stand as precedents for future decisions. This principle, which supports the proposition that precedents are binding on later decisions, is said to be followed less rigorously in constitutional law than in other branches of the law.

state action doctrine The doctrine that limits constitutional prohibitions to official government or government-sponsored action, as opposed to action that is merely private in character.

state power to regulate interstate commerce The limited power of a state government to make and enforce rules affecting commerce that transcends the state.

state's attorney A state prosecutor.

states' rights The constitutional rights and powers reserved to state governments under the Tenth Amendment. Historically, the philosophy that states should be accorded broad latitude within the American federal system.

status offenses Noncriminal conduct on the part of juveniles that may subject them to the jurisdiction of the court.

statute A generally applicable law enacted by a legislature.

statute of limitations A law proscribing prosecutions for specific crimes after specified periods of time.

statutory construction The official interpretation of a statute rendered by a court of law.

statutory rape The strict-liability offense of having sexual intercourse with a minor.

stay To postpone, hold off, or stop the execution of a judgment.

stay of execution An order suspending the enforcement of a judgment of a court.

stewardship theory The theory that the president, being steward of the country, may exercise any and all powers he deems necessary to that end, unless they are specifically prohibited by the Constitution.

stop and frisk An encounter between a police officer and a suspect during which the latter is temporarily detained and subjected to a pat-down search for weapons.

stream of commerce doctrine The doctrine, first articulated by Justice Holmes in 1905, permitting federal regulation of commerce that is no longer of an interstate nature.

strict judicial scrutiny Judicial review of government action or policy in which the ordinary presumption of constitutionality is reversed.

strict liability offenses Offenses that do not require proof of the defendant's intent.

strict necessity, doctrine of The doctrine that a court should consider a constitutional question only when strictly necessary to resolve the case at bar.

strict neutrality   The doctrine that government must be strictly neutral on matters of religion.

strict scrutiny   The most demanding level of judicial review in cases involving alleged infringements of civil rights or liberties.

strip searches   Searches of suspects' or prisoners' private parts.

sua sponte   "Of its own will." Voluntarily, without coercion or suggestion.

subjective test   A legal test based on the perceptions or intentions of an individual actor, rather than external circumstances.

subpoena   "Under penalty." A judicial order requiring a person to appear in court in connection with a designated proceeding.

subpoena duces tecum   "Under penalty you shall bring with you." A judicial order requiring a party to bring certain described records, papers, books, or documents to court.

substantial federal question   A significant legal question pertaining to the U.S. Constitution, a federal statute, treaty, regulation, or judicial interpretation of any of the foregoing.

substantial step   A significant step toward completion of an intended result.

substantive criminal law   That branch of the criminal law that defines criminal offenses and defenses and specifies criminal punishments.

substantive due process   Doctrine that the Due Process Clauses of the Fifth and Fourteenth Amendments require legislation to be fair and reasonable in content as well as application.

substantive law   That part of the law that creates rights and proscribes wrongs.

sui juris   "Under law"; having full legal rights.

summary decisions   Decisions made by appellate courts without the submission of briefs or oral arguments.

summary judgment   A decision rendered without extended argument where no material legal question is presented in a case.

summary justice   Trial held by court of limited jurisdiction without benefit of a jury.

summary trial   A bench trial of a minor misdemeanor.

summons   A court order requiring a person to appear in court to answer a criminal charge.

Sunday closing laws   Laws, now largely defunct, prohibiting business from opening on Sundays.

supervisory power   The power of the Supreme Court to supervise the lower federal courts.

suppression doctrine   *See*: exclusionary rule.

supra   "Above."

Supremacy Clause   Provision of Article VI of the Constitution making that document, and all federal legislation consistent with it, the "supreme Law of the Land."

suspect classification doctrine   The doctrine that laws classifying people according to race, ethnicity, and religion are inherently suspect and should be subjected to strict judicial scrutiny.

suspended sentence   A trial court's decision to place a defendant on probation or under community control instead of imposing an announced sentence, on the condition that the original sentence may be imposed if the defendant violates the conditions of the suspended sentence.

sustain   To uphold.

symbolic speech   An activity that expresses a point of view or message symbolically, rather than through pure speech.

taking   Government action taking private property or depriving owner the use and control thereof.

tax exemptions   Rules under which certain organizations or individuals are not required to pay certain taxes.

taxing power   The power of government to levy taxes.

taxpayer suits   Suits brought by taxpayers to challenge certain government actions. Taxpayer suits as such are prohibited in the federal courts in that one does not acquire standing merely by virtue of paying taxes to support policies of which one does not approve.

Tenth Amendment   Amendment to the Constitution reserving to the states powers not delegated to the federal government.

Terry **stop**   *See*: stop-and-frisk.

testimony   Evidence given by a witness who has sworn to tell the truth.

Third Amendment   Amendment found in the Bill of Rights prohibiting the military from quartering soldiers in citizens' homes without their consent.

third party   A person not directly connected with a legal proceeding but potentially affected by its outcome.

third party consent   Consent, usually to a search, given by a person on behalf of another. For example, a college roommate who allows the police to search his or her roommate's effects.

Thirteenth Amendment   Amendment to the Constitution, ratified in 1865, formally abolishing slavery.

time, place, and manner doctrine   First Amendment doctrine holding that government may impose reasonable limitations on the time, place, and manner of expressive activities.

time, place, and manner regulations   Reasonable government regulations as to the time, place, and manner of expressive activities protected by the Constitution.

tolling   Ceasing. For example, someone who conceals himself or herself from the authorities generally causes a tolling of the statutes of limitation on prosecution of a crime.

tort   A wrong or injury other than a breach of contract for which the remedy is a civil suit for damages.

totality of circumstances   The entire collection of relevant facts in a particular case.

transactional immunity   A grant of immunity applying to offenses to which a witness's testimony relates.

transcript   A written record of a trial or hearing.

treason   The crime of attempting by overt acts to overthrow the government, or of betraying the government to a foreign power.

treaty   A legally binding agreement between one or more countries. In the United States, treaties are negotiated by the president but must be ratified by the Senate.

trespass   An unlawful interference with one's person or property.

trial   A judicial proceeding held for the purpose of making factual and legal determinations.

trial by jury   A trial in which the verdict is determined not by the court but by a jury of the defendant's peers.

trial courts   Courts whose primary function is the conduct of civil and/or criminal trials.

trial de novo   "A new trial." Refers to trial court review of convictions for minor offenses by courts of limited jurisdiction by conducting a new trial instead of merely reviewing the record of the initial trial.

trial jury   A fixed number of citizens, usually six or twelve, selected according to law and sworn to hear the evidence presented at a trial and to render a verdict based on the law and the evidence.

tribunal   A court of law.

trimester framework   The framework established in *Roe v. Wade* (1973) governing the validity of laws regulating abortion in the three stages of pregnancy.

true bill   An indictment handed down by a grand jury.

trustee   A person entrusted to handle the affairs of another.

trusty   A prisoner entrusted with authority to supervise other prisoners in exchange for certain privileges and status.

tuition tax credits   Vouchers that taxpayers may "spend" at schools of their choice, be they public or private.

Twenty-fifth Amendment   Amendment ratified in 1967 dealing with issues of presidential disability and removal.

Twenty-first Amendment   Amendment ratified in 1933 repealing the unpopular Eighteenth Amendment (1919) that had established Prohibition.

Twenty-second Amendment   Amendment ratified in 1951 limiting presidents to two terms in office.

Twenty-sixth Amendment   Amendment ratified in 1971 lowering the voting age in federal and state elections to 18.

two-party system   A political system, such as that of the United States, organized around two major competing political parties.

two-witness rule   A requirement that to prove a defendant guilty of perjury the prosecution must prove the falsity of the defendant's statements either by two witnesses or by one witness and corroborating documents or circumstances.

tyranny of the majority   A political system in which the rights of the individual or minority group are not protected against the will of the majority.

ultra vires   "Beyond the power"; beyond the scope of a prescribed authority.

umpire of the federal system   Term that describes the Supreme Court's role in refereeing disputes between the national government and the states.

unalienable rights   Rights that are vested in individuals by birth, not granted by government.

unanimity rule   A decision rule requiring a unanimous vote.

unconstitutional as applied   Declaration by a court of law that a statute is invalid insofar as it is enforced in some particular context.

unconstitutional per se   A statute that is unconstitutional under any given circumstances.

unconventional religious practices   Practices outside the religious mainstream.

unicameral legislature   A one-house legislative body.

Uniform Code of Military Justice (UCMJ)   A code of laws enacted by Congress that govern military servicepersons and define the procedural and evidentiary requirements in military law and the substantive criminal offenses and punishments.

unitary system   A political system in which all power is vested in one central government.

universal suffrage   The requirement that all citizens (at least all competent adults not guilty of serious crimes) be eligible to vote in elections.

unlawful assembly   A group of individuals, usually five or more, assembled to commit an unlawful act or to commit a lawful act in an unlawful manner.

unreasonable searches and seizures   Searches that violate the Fourth Amendment to the Constitution.

U.S. attorneys   Attorneys appointed by the president with consent of the U.S. Senate to prosecute federal crimes in a specific geographical area of the United States.

U.S. Court of Appeals for the Armed Forces   *See*: Court of Appeals for the Armed Forces.

U.S. Courts of Appeals   The intermediate appellate courts of appeals in the federal system that sit in geographical areas of the United States and in which panels of appellate judges hear appeals in civil and criminal cases primarily from the U.S. District Courts.

U.S. District Courts   The principal trial courts in the federal system that sit in ninety-four districts where usually one judge hears proceedings and trials in both civil and criminal cases.

use immunity   A grant of immunity that forbids prosecutors from using immunized testimony as evidence in criminal prosecutions.

U.S. Sentencing Commission   A federal body that proposes guideline sentences for defendants convicted of federal crimes.

U.S. Supreme Court   The highest court in the United States, consisting of nine justices, with jurisdiction to review, by appeal or writ of certiorari, the decisions of lower federal courts and many decisions of the highest courts of each state.

vacate   To annul, set aside, or rescind.

vagrancy   The crime of going about without visible means of support (virtually archaic).

vagueness doctrine   Doctrine of constitutional law holding unconstitutional (as a violation of due process) legislation that fails to clearly inform the person what is required or proscribed.

venire   The set of persons summoned for jury duty. The actual jury is selected from the venire. *See*: voir dire.

venue   The location of a trial or hearing.

verdict   The formal decision rendered by a jury in a civil or criminal trial.

vested rights   Rights acquired by the passage of time.

veto   The power of a chief executive to block adoption of a law by refusing to sign the legislation.

viability   That point in pregnancy where the fetus is able to survive outside the womb.

victim impact statements   Statements during the sentencing phase of a criminal trial in which evidence is introduced relating to the physical, economic, and psychological impact that the crime had on the victim or victim's family.

victimless crimes   Crimes in which no particular person appears or claims to be injured, such as prostitution or gambling.

Virginia Plan   A plan introduced by James Madison, a member of the Virginia delegation to the Constitutional Convention of 1787. It called for a bicameral Congress, in which members of the House of Representatives would be elected by the people and members of the Senate would be elected by the state legislatures. State representation in both bodies would be based on population.

voice exemplar   A sample of a person's voice; usually taken by police for the purpose of identifying a suspect.

void-for-vagueness doctrine   *See*: vagueness doctrine.

voir dire   "To speak the truth." The process by which prospective jurors are questioned by counsel and/or the court before being selected to serve on a jury.

voluntariness of confessions   The quality of a confession having been freely given.

vote dilution   The reduction or diminution of the voting power of individuals or minorities as a result of malapportionment, gerrymandering, or some other discriminatory practice.

voting blocs   Groups of individuals who usually vote together.

Voting Rights Act of 1965   Landmark federal legislation protecting voters from racial discrimination.

waiver   The intentional and voluntary relinquishment of a right, or conduct from which such relinquishment may be inferred.

waiver of juvenile court jurisdiction   A relinquishment by a juvenile court to allow prosecution of a juvenile in an adult court.

waiver of *Miranda* rights   A known relinquishment of the right against self-incrimination provided by the Fifth Amendment to the Constitution.

War Powers Resolution   The 1973 act of Congress purporting to limit a president's authority to commit troops to a combat situation abroad.

warrant   A court order authorizing a search, seizure, or arrest.

warrant requirement   The Fourth Amendment's "preference" that searches be based on warrants issued by judges or magistrates.

warrantless arrest   An arrest made by police who do not possess an arrest warrant.

warrantless search   A search made by police who do not possess a search warrant.

weight of the evidence   The balance or preponderance of the evidence. Weight of the evidence is to be distinguished from "legal sufficiency of the evidence," which is the concern of an appellate court.

well-regulated militia   Body of citizens organized for military service but subject to government regulation.

white primary   Historically, a primary election in which participation was limited to whites.

wiretap order   A court order permitting electronic surveillance for a limited period.

wiretapping   The use of highly sensitive electronic devices designed to intercept electronic communications.

writ   An order issued by a court of law requiring the performance of some specific act.

writ of certiorari   *See*: certiorari, writ of.

writ of error   *See*: error, writ of.

writ of habeas corpus   *See*: habeas corpus, writ of.

writ of mandamus   *See*: mandamus, writ of.

writ of prohibition   *See*: prohibition, writ of.

writs of assistance   Ancient writs issuing from the Court of Exchequer in England granting sheriffs broad powers of search and seizure for the purpose of assisting in the collection of debts owed to the Crown.

yellow dog contracts   Contracts, generally illegal, making the right to work conditioned upon the employee's agreement not to join a labor union.

zoning   Laws regulating the use of land.

TABLE OF CASES

Principal cases are in bold type. Non-principal cases are in roman type. References are to pages.

INDEX